Chris Lewis

INTRODUCTORY CORPORATE FINANCE

INTRODUCTORY CORPORATE FINANCE

ROBERT S. HARRIS
THE UNIVERSITY OF NORTH CAROLINA, CHAPEL HILL

JOHN J. PRINGLE
THE UNIVERSITY OF NORTH CAROLINA, CHAPEL HILL

SCOTT, FORESMAN AND COMPANY
GLENVIEW, ILLINOIS
LONDON, ENGLAND

Photo credits:

Cover Photo: Bullaty-Lomeo/The Image Bank
Pages 2–3, Hedrich-Blessing
Pages 58–59, Hedrich-Blessing
Page 164, Hedrich-Blessing
Page 274, Peter Aaron/Esto
Page 410, Peter Aaron/Esto
Page 610, Courtesy Murphy/Jahn Architects
Pages 696–697, Peter Aaron/Esto

Acknowledgments are listed at the back of the
book on page 763, which constitutes a legal
extension of the copyright page.

Library of Congress Cataloging-in-Publication Data

Harris, Robert S., 1949–
     Introductory corporate finance / Robert S. Harris, John J.
 Pringle.
         p.   cm.
     Includes bibliographies and index.
     ISBN 0-673-38115-3
     1. Corporations — Finance.   I. Pringle, John J.   II. Title.
 HG4026.H343   1989
 658.1′5 — dc 19   88-39543
                                                                         CIP

1 2 3 4 5 6-RRC-94 93 92 91 90 89

Preface

Introductory Corporate Finance is intended for beginning students in financial management, primarily for use in the first finance course for undergraduates. Because of its managerial focus, however, the book also appeals to a wider audience, including practicing managers who want an overview of corporate finance and students who require supplementary reading in a case course.

The text does not assume any prior background in finance. While most users will have some accounting background, we include a section on financial statements in Chapter 6 to make the book accessible even to students without it.

We focus on corporate financial decisions about the best uses and sources of funds. Wise uses of funds through investment decisions are the ultimate determinants of a firm's long-run success or failure. For example, the key to Apple Computer's success was realizing the tremendous potential of a niche in the computer market. At the same time, prudent decisions about raising funds (sources) are necessary both to fund investment and to compensate corporate owners. Throughout the text, valuation is the underlying theme. In every instance we look to value creation as the operational objective guiding financial-management decisions.

Throughout the book, financial management is viewed as part of a broader management process linking the firm with external markets in which it must raise funds, purchase inputs, and sell products. We emphasize developing a sound conceptual framework and presenting it clearly. We also tie concepts to practical skills and techniques that aid managers in making difficult financial decisions.

This focus on managerial decision making occurs within the context of the contributions of modern finance theory and a constantly changing financial environment. We weave key developments and insights of finance theory throughout the text. For example, we use the capital-asset-pricing model as a framework to discuss the trade-off between required returns and risk, and we note the conflicts that may arise because of managers' role as agents for shareholders. We also provide simplified treatments of options and futures in a separate chapter and arbitrage pricing theory in a separate appendix to a chapter for readers who are interested in these more advanced topics. In all cases, however, we focus on simplified exposition and important insights rather than detailed mathematical developments of theory.

Given the dynamic developments in financial markets, we integrate real-world financial settings throughout the book. We present entire chapters on leasing and takeovers. We also note changes in tax laws and the impact of these changes on financial managers. A separate chapter on international finance discusses exchange rates and other topics.

Organization of the Text

There are many ways to teach financial management. The topics in the book are more numerous than a single course can usually cover. The text is organized into seven parts — twenty-five chapters in all. Instructors may select and sequence chapters according to their course objectives and their students' backgrounds.

Part One introduces the scope and objectives of financial management and the environment in which financial-management decisions must be made. Part Two deals with two factors that are part of practically all financial decisions — time and risk. It is here that finance makes its distinctive contribution to the management process; Part Two concentrates on the concepts of finance and their distinction from business financial management. For instance, Chapter 3 develops the concepts of the time value of money and discounted cash flow. Chapter 4 applies the concepts of discounted cash flow to values determined in financial markets, with specific attention to valuation of bonds and common stocks. Chapter 5 focuses on risk, introduces a simplified treatment of portfolios and the capital-asset-pricing model, and includes a short appendix on arbitrage pricing theory.

Part Three presents the basic accounting information and financial analysis and planning techniques that will be used throughout the book. Chapter 6 focuses on measuring profits and cash flows and sources and uses of funds. Chapter 7 discusses methods of analyzing financial performance, including ratio analysis, while Chapter 8 covers cost/volume/profit relationships and Chapter 9 planning and pro-forma analysis. These chapters emphasize useful techniques and provide a great many straightforward examples.

Parts Two and Three provide the background for analyzing investment decisions, the topic of Part Four. We believe successful firms put commercial strategy first, then tailor the financial structure to fit. Hence, treatment of capital budgeting precedes discussion of financing decisions. The four chapters of Part Four provide a thorough introduction to the topic — decision criteria in Chapter 10, cash-flow estimation in Chapter 11, return targets and the cost of capital in Chapter 12, and techniques for dealing with risk in Chapter 13.

Having discussed ways to analyze uses of funds in Part Four, we then turn in Part Five to the matter of sources. The seven chapters of Part Five cover sources of long-term funds (Chapter 14); the effects of financial leverage (Chapter 15); choosing a debt level (Chapter 16); dividend policy (Chapter 17); options, futures and specialized forms of financing such as convertibles (Chapter 18); and leases (Chapter 19). Chapter 20 discusses more applied problems of issuing new securities and managing outstanding issues.

Part Six treats working-capital management by discussing sources of short-term financing, cash management, and accounts receivable and inventories. Finally, Part Seven concentrates on two special areas, international finance and mergers and acquisitions, which play an increasingly important role in financial-management decisions.

Pedagogical Features of the Text

Introductory Corporate Finance has the following features:

- Each chapter begins with learning objectives.
- Important terms are in boldface in the text, defined in color in the margins (where space permits), and listed in the glossary.
- Key ideas are set off in color in the margins.
- Finance in Practice sections in each chapter discuss important real-life financial situations ranging from the stock-market crash of October 1987 to building a tunnel beneath the English channel to trading in stock-index futures.
- International Focus sections throughout the book highlight the global nature of corporate finance decisions.
- Sample problems with solutions are integrated into text discussions.
- End-of-chapter material includes summary, questions, problems, and references.
- Extensive problem sections contain two types of problems — those that reinforce the concepts and techniques presented and those that enrich the discussions. Solutions to odd-numbered questions and problems are presented in appendixes at the end of the text.
- The comprehensive, end-of-text glossary contains chapter references for each entry.
- The *Financial Tool Kit* software packaged with the text transforms the text into a dynamic learning tool. It helps students understand financial concepts and solve problems. It also provides conceptual review with such features as the ratio quiz, the financial calculator, cash budget, and

many more. Students can run "what if" scenarios by changing variables to see how results change. Graphics are included in some modules.

The Instructional Package

Introductory Corporate Finance is supplemented with a complete instructional package. The *Instructor's Manual/Test Bank,* prepared by David R. Durst at the University of Akron, is composed of alternative course outlines, chapter commentaries, teaching tips, supplemental class handouts, and solutions to all questions and problems in the text. The *Test Bank* contains more than 1,000 challenging items.

The *Study Guide,* also prepared by David R. Durst, includes extensive chapter outlines, key term usage, sample test questions, and numerous analytical problem sets referenced to the *Financial Tool Kit.* Each *Tool Kit* module is explained in the appropriate *Study Guide* chapter. The *Transparency Masters* supplement contains more than 50 figures from the text.

The *Microcomputer Problem Sets Disk* is a computer-assisted instruction program that emphasizes step-by-step solutions. Problems for each chapter are written to use a core of numbers and names, and a random number generator makes each problem unique. A separate *Microcomputer Problem Sets Disk for Use with LOTUS 1-2-3* is also available.

Comparison with *Essentials of Financial Management*

Introductory Corporate Finance shares the same managerial philosophy as our earlier book, *Essentials of Financial Management, Second Edition.* There are, however, a number of important differences. *Introductory* is designed primarily for an undergraduate audience with emphasis on simplicity of exposition. For a somewhat more technical treatment of topics as well as more complex applications and examples, *Essentials* is designed for use at both the MBA and rigorous undergraduate level. In addition, *Introductory* contains important new material based on financial market developments in the few years since *Essentials* was revised.

ACKNOWLEDGMENTS

We deeply appreciate the assistance of many able reviewers who gave us the benefit of their thinking, especially:

David R. Durst, University of Akron
Manak C. Gupta, Temple University
Val Hinton, Tennessee Technological University
Roger P. Hill, University of North Carolina at Wilmington
Linda Johnson, Appalachian State University
Gary Noreiko, University of Southern Colorado

Like all writers of finance textbooks, we owe an intellectual debt to those who have contributed to the development of the field of finance. Given the objectives of this book, however, we have kept footnotes to a minimum and have provided only limited references. We are grateful to colleagues at the University of North Carolina at Chapel Hill and elsewhere who have influenced our thinking on the subject of finance and who have contributed specific suggestions for the book. Special thanks go to Jennifer Conrad, Bob Conroy, Mustafa Gultekin, and Dick Rendleman. We are grateful also to our students, who have stimulated our interest in teaching over the years.

We especially thank David Durst for his key role in this effort. In addition to making invaluable comments as a reviewer of the text, David has taken prime responsibility for preparing end-of-chapter materials, the *Instructor's Manual,* the *Test Bank,* the *Study Guide,* and the *Financial Tool Kit.* By sharing his ideas and efforts with us, David has greatly enhanced the quality of the book.

Finally, we wish to thank those who contributed directly to the preparation of the manuscript. Leonne Harris edited the manuscript, provided quality control, and managed the entire project. Her contribution was immense, and we are deeply grateful. Joe

Bryson and Vivat Vichitboonyaseth supplied valuable assistance in gathering data.

At Scott, Foresman, George Lobell provided his usual enthusiasm as well as sound advice and guidance for the project. Bruce Kaplan and Kathy Richmond gave excellent editorial assistance and made many substantive contributions to the manuscript.

Regardless of the amount of effort that goes into a project, there are always opportunities for improvement. Suggestions from users of previous books have been most helpful to us in subsequent revisions. We invite users to continue to send us their feedback.

Robert S. Harris
John J. Pringle

Contents

Comparing Net Present Value and Internal Rate of Return   289

Capital Budgeting in Practice   298

Chapter 11   Estimating Cash Flows   306

Cash Flows: Basic Concepts   308

Incremental Cash Flows   309

Separating Operating Flows and Financing Flows   317

Allocated Overhead and Use of Existing Facilities   320

Tax Laws   321
Depreciation   322
Working Capital   324

Changes in Prices   328

Cash-Flow Estimation in Practice   330

Chapter 25   Mergers and Acquisitions   728

INTRODUCTORY CORPORATE FINANCE

Part **1**/**Introduction**

1 **An Overview of Financial Management**

2 **The Environment of Financial Decision Making**

This book is about *financial management,* financial decision making in business firms and other organizations. Financial management involves two basic kinds of activities: (1) obtaining funds and (2) using funds. Business firms *obtain* funds by borrowing from banks, or by issuing shares of stock to the public, or in numerous other ways. The discipline of financial management deals with decisions of this sort. Firms *use* funds in many ways, including building manufacturing plants and other

facilities and expanding inventories. Financial management can provide guidance for these types of decisions as well.

In Part One of the book, we discuss the basic problems facing financial managers in making such decisions, the objectives that managers pursue, and the financial environment in which managers operate. Chapter 1 provides an overview of the finance function in a firm and the scope and objectives of financial management. There we see that, as shareholders' representatives, financial managers should make decisions that increase the *value* of the firm to those shareholders. Such value, established in financial markets, reflects both the timing and riskiness of benefits the corporation can provide to shareholders. As a result, we see that dealing with time and risk is important for financial managers. In addition,

Chapter 1 outlines the rest of the book.

Chapter 2 details the environment in which financial managers operate. It describes forms of business organization, types of financial markets, participants in financial markets, government regulation, taxes, and inflation. This chapter examines the institutional and financial surroundings in which financial managers find themselves.

The two chapters of Part One provide background on the goals and environment of financial managers so that we can better appreciate the decisions they face. These decisions are analyzed in subsequent parts of this book.

Chapter 1

An Overview of Financial Management

- Over an 8-year period ending in 1987, General Motors spends $460 billion redesigning its cars and factories.
- In 1987, Citicorp announces plans to issue 20 million new shares of stock.
- IBM announces plans to purchase $1 billion of its own shares. Ford announces that it will spend $2 billion of its $9.4 billion doing the same thing—buying its own shares.
- Major corporations such as Exxon, Goodyear Tire and Rubber, and United Technologies make extensive use of leasing as a means of financing facilities and equipment.

What do these statements have in common? They each describe the result of a basic management decision about how either to *use* money (the case of General Motors) or to *raise* money (the case of Citicorp). This book will talk about how to explain and analyze such financial decisions. Why were the decisions made? Do the decisions make sense? Do the decisions make more sense than other attractive decisions? We will get to investment decisions such as those of General Motors in Chapters 10 and 11, financing decisions such as that of Citicorp in Chapters 14 through 16, repurchase of shares (IBM and Ford) in Chapter 20, and leasing of equipment in Chapter 19. In the meantime there is a wealth of descriptive and analytical material to explore.

We will set the stage for what follows by discussing the role of financial managers, their environment, and their decisions.

The Finance Function

In most business organizations, there is no single individual who is designated as the "financial manager" and who has all the responsibilities of financial management. Firms have controllers and corporate treasurers, vice-presidents of finance, and heads of finance committees, and sometimes all four titles are found within a single enterprise. On the other hand, we may find only one and some-times none of these titles in the organizational structure of a firm. Yet the financial-management function is always performed in some fashion, regardless of whether anyone has a job with the title of financial manager. Each firm must decide how to raise and invest money. A simplified, but useful, characterization of the financial manager's job is to think of a financial manager as making decisions that tie a firm to financial markets. Figure 1–1 displays the situation.

On the one hand, a financial manager must understand the operations and prob-lems of the firm—the products produced, the technological capabilities, and the personalities of individuals. On the other hand, a financial manager must know a great deal about **financial markets**, the markets in which the firm can raise funds (for example, by borrowing money) and in which the firm itself may be valued. For example, **stocks**—shareholder ownership claims—of many large U.S. cor-porations are traded each day on the New York Stock Exchange, and the prices of these stocks fluctuate daily. Such prices represent the financial-market assessments of the value of the firm.

Being in such a position, financial managers operate in financial markets when they must decide on the best way to raise money. For example, should the firm raise money by borrowing from a bank in New York for a year, by borrowing from a bank in London for six months, or by selling new shares of stock? The possibilities are almost endless in a complex economy. Of course, the money be-ing raised is to be used (invested); thus, the financial manager must make deci-sions about how to allocate the funds to be spent inside the corporation. Should a new plant be built, or should an old one be refurbished? Is an oil heating system

Financial markets—markets where firms can raise funds and where their securities are valued, if they are publicly owned.

Stock—a legal claim to ownership in a corporation; it is usually divided into shares and represented by transferable certificates.

Figure 1—1
The Role of Financial Management

1. Cash raised from financial markets
2. Cash invested in the firm
3. Cash from the firm's operation (and/or disposal of assets)
4. Cash returned to investors
5. Cash reinvested in the firm

better than a coal-burning system? At what rate should the firm expand (if at all)? If all goes well, the financial manager will also have to decide what to do with funds earned from profitable investments. Should they be paid to the corporation's owners, or reinvested in hopes of even greater profits? To complicate the manager's life, all the decisions about using and raising money are interdependent and must be coordinated over time.

Although most of our discussion will concern financial management in business firms, business firms are not the only organizations that face financial decisions about how to invest and raise money. Other important organizations must make these same decisions, including federal, state, and local governments and government-owned enterprises; nonprofit organizations, such as churches, educational institutions, and hospitals; and mutual associations owned by their customers, such as farm cooperatives and mutual insurance companies, savings banks, and savings-and-loan associations. Businesses owned by single individuals (for example, independent lawyers, doctors, and accountants) face financial decisions. All of these entities must make economic choices about how to raise and spend money.

This book is designed to help financial managers learn how to make better decisions. Some of the material in the book is descriptive — explaining the nature of financial markets — and can (and should!) be usefully supplemented by a regular reading of financial news, such as the *Wall Street Journal*. Other sections in the book explain the analytical tools a manager can use.

Before we jump ahead of the story, we first need to establish what objectives a manager has or should have in making decisions. After all, a "good" decision is one that in some sense furthers the manager's and firm's objectives. In finance, we typically assume that a manager's objective is to maximize the value of the firm to existing *shareholders,* or owners. This important concept requires a bit of background explanation about the economic role of corporations.

> A financial manager's objective is to maximize the value of the firm to existing shareholders.

Profits and Value

In practically any business endeavor, one common goal is to bring in more money than is paid out; that is, to make a **profit. Profit maximization** — making such profits as large as possible — seems to be a fairly reasonable goal for an entrepreneur who owns a firm because increases in such profits generally increase the entrepreneur's well-being.

In most economic studies of the way a **market economy** (economy in which goods are bought and sold at prices determined in markets) operates, profit maximization is viewed as the goal of corporate activity. Managers of firms have been found to direct their efforts toward areas of attractive profit potential, using prices as their signals.

Goods and services valued highly by consumers command higher prices, which in turn result in higher profits for producers. Other producers are attracted by profit opportunities, and supplies of the valued goods and services increase. In principle, a point of equilibrium is reached at which price and profit opportunities are just sufficient to bring forth the quantity demanded by consumers at that price.

> **Profit maximization** — the goal of making a firm's profits as large as possible.

> **Market economy** — an economic system in which resources are allocated and prices are determined through the interaction of buyers and sellers in markets.

In the jargon of the economist, the **equilibrium price** is the price that *clears the market,* or equates quantity supplied and quantity demanded.

In the case of goods and services not highly valued or for other reasons in abundant supply, the process works in reverse. Prices and profits fall, producers drop out to search for better opportunities, and supply decreases. As a case in point, have you seen many new manual typewriters recently?

Thus, in a market economy, decisions to produce and consume are guided by prices set in markets by the actions of producers and consumers themselves. That is, the **price system** guides economic activity.

This important role for prices—signaling what consumers want and bringing forth quantity supplied—has not gone unnoticed even in centrally planned economies. In recent years, some parts of the economy in mainland China have been freed to allow prices to act as signals for production and investment. The planners recognize the useful role of prices in at least some areas of economic activity.

A central feature of a market economy is the decentralization of decision making. Decisions with respect to production and consumption are made by millions of economic units acting independently. As a member of one of these independent economic units, a financial manager would desire to maximize profits. Unfortunately, profit maximization, in its simplest form, cannot be used as the basic criterion for decisions made by the financial managers of privately owned and controlled firms because of two main problems: *time* and *risk.*

Time

A major shortcoming of the simple profit-maximization criterion is that it does not take into account the fact that the timing of benefits expected from investments varies widely. For example, suppose your company is introducing a new product, and you anticipate a total of $100 profit (add as many zeros as you require) over the next two years. If you speed up production now (using production policy "Fast"), you expect to realize the entire $100 in the first year and none in the second. If you continue with your present schedule (production policy "Slow"), however, you expect to realize no profits in the first year and $100 in the second. Table 1–1 summarizes the situation. Which strategy should you, as a financial manager, select?

Table 1–1
Timing of Anticipated Profit

Production Policy	Anticipated Profit (dollars)	
	Year 1	Year 2
"Fast"	100	0
"Slow"	0	100

Simply adding the profits over time and picking the alternative with the highest total profit does not answer the question because both alternatives provide $100. However, one of the strategies — the "Fast" policy of speeding up production — is clearly better because it supplies the money earlier. To see why this policy is clearly better, consider that if you increased the speed of production and received $100 in year one, this $100 could be invested elsewhere between years one and two. For example, an available (if unexciting) possibility would be to put the $100 in a bank account and earn interest. Even at an interest rate of 6 percent a year, investing this $100 for one year would produce $100 + 0.06($100) = $106 in year two, an amount $6 larger than the $100 available in year two from the "Slow" policy.

Money can be put to work to earn a return, so savers and investors are not in-different to the timing of cash receipts. As a result, cash flows in early years are valued more highly than equivalent cash flows in later years. For this reason, the "Fast" policy in Table 1–1 is superior to the "Slow" policy, even though both pro-vide the same $100 profit. The profit-maximization criterion, therefore, must be modified to take into account differences in timing of cash flows and the time value of money.

In practice, most investment and financing decisions involve much more com-plex patterns of cash flows over many periods, but the same message applies: a dollar today is worth more than a dollar tomorrow.

Risk

The second problem with assuming that financial managers are motivated simply by profit maximization is the problem of *uncertainty,* or *risk*. In this book, when discussing future events, we will use these two terms interchangeably. *Uncertainty* is present when we are not certain about what will happen in the future, and in most decisions (both personal and business) uncertainty is the rule, not the exception.

Consider two investment opportunities, A and B, whose profits depend on the state of the economy, as indicated in Table 1–2. If a normal economy is the most likely prospect, then the most likely profit from alternatives A and B is the same, $100. However, profit from A will lie between $90 and $110, whereas that from B

Table 1–2
Uncertainty About Outcomes

	Outcome of Investment (dollars)	
State of Economy	*Investment A*	*Investment B*
Recession	$ 90	$ 0
Normal	$100	$100
Boom	$110	$200

can vary from 0 to $200, a much wider range. The most likely outcome is the same, but B is far more *risky*.

A decision criterion that considers only the most likely outcomes (the $100 in Table 1–2) provides no basis for choosing between alternatives A and B, whereas few investors would be indifferent between the two. As we will see later, nearly all investors who provide capital funds to firms are *risk-averse*, meaning that, other things being equal, they prefer less uncertainty to more. A risk-averse investor would prefer A to B in Table 1–2. Risk preferences of investors are reflected in the financial markets and must be taken into account by firms when they make decisions.

As a decision criterion for practical use, profit maximization thus has two main shortcomings. It does not take into account either the time value of money or risk. For these reasons, **value maximization** has advantages over profit maximization as the operational criterion for financial-management decisions.

Measuring Value

The **value** of certain assets is relatively easy to see and define. For example, the value of a $100 bill is that it can be exchanged for other assets given the prices of those assets (admittedly prices that are higher now than they once were). In a sense, the value of a dollar derives from its command over purchasing power. The value of a college education is a bit harder to explain; surely, it brings both monetary and psychic rewards. In discussing financial assets or decisions in this book, we will talk of value in terms of cash benefits. Specifically, we will define the value of an asset as the dollar amount that persons would need to have today to be just as well off as they would be owning the asset. For example, suppose your favorite banker gave you a piece of paper that allowed you to receive $120 from her at any time. As long as the banker's credit is good, that piece of paper has a value of $120, since you can exchange it for $120 today if you desire. If, however, you were not sure that the banker could pay upon demand, you might decide that you would be just as well off having $115 in your hand (for certain) as having the piece of paper. If this were the case, the value of the paper would be $115. In the language of finance, because you are *risk-averse*, you have imposed a $120 − $115 = $5 penalty because of your uncertainty about the banker's ability to pay.

Fortunately, in the United States, the federal government guarantees many promises made by banks; however, most bank promises involve time delays. Returning to our example, suppose the banker promised to pay you $120 one year from today. Even if you were certain that the banker would pay up, it would take less than $120 today to make you just as happy as you would be if you received $120 in one year—because of the time value of money, which we discussed earlier. Suppose, for example, you knew that you could earn 20 percent interest per year; having just $100 today would allow you to accumulate $120 at the end of one year. That is, your $100 plus the $20 interest would give you $120. In this instance, the $100 today is the value of the banker's promise because it will make you just as well off as the banker's promise (assuming you can earn interest of 20 percent per year). In the language of finance, time has a value, and you have imposed

Generally investors dislike risk: they are risk-averse.

Value maximization has advantages over profit maximization as a decision criterion because it considers risk and the time value of money.

Value maximization—the goal of making a firm's value as large as possible; can be used as a criterion for making financial-management decisions.

Value—the dollar amount a person would have to receive today to be just as well off as he or she would be owning the asset.

a $120 $-$ $100 = $20 penalty for having to wait a year. Chapter 3 will discuss the time value of money in more detail.

In general, values will reflect both time and risk, and the value of an asset is best viewed not in terms of its costs but in terms of the *future benefits* it can produce. The longer one has to wait for a benefit and the more uncertain the benefit, the lower the **present value** of that benefit will be.

The value-maximization decision criterion involves a comparison of value to cost. An action with a present value, reflecting both time and risk, that exceeds its cost can be said to create value. Such actions increase the value of the firm and should be undertaken. Conversely, actions with value less than cost reduce the value of the firm and should be avoided. In the case of mutually exclusive alternatives, when only one is to be chosen, the alternative with the greatest net present value (excess of value over cost) should be selected. The objective of financial management is to maximize the value of the firm to existing shareholders.

Note that value maximization is simply the extension of profit maximization to a world where time and uncertainty are important. Where the time period is short and the degree of uncertainty is not great, value maximization and profit maximization amount to essentially the same thing.

Value and Markets

Making an estimate of the value of an asset is often a difficult task. One useful guide, however, is the fact that many assets are traded in financial markets. For example, on May 21, 1982, the Bank of Virginia (see Figure 1–2) advertised a promise (similar to our earlier example of a banker's promise) in the *Wall Street Journal*. The bank promised to pay the owner of a piece of paper the lump sum (**principal** payment) of $1,000 on February 1, 1993. The price of obtaining such a piece of paper was $250. That is, if you had bought the paper in May 1982, you could get back $4 for every dollar invested ($1,000/$250 = 4). Why was there a $4-to-$1 ratio and a $750 difference between the promise to pay $1,000 and the price of obtaining the promise? The answer again is the importance of time and risk. Suppose that the Bank of Virginia had priced its promises well and that $250 was the maximum price that people would pay for the promise. In financial markets, the $750 penalty reflects the fact that $250 in May 1982 was as good as this particular promise of $1,000 to be received more than 10 years later. In other words, in May 1982, $250 was one estimate of the present value of the $1,000 to be received in 1993.

Although we'll spend more time in Chapters 3 through 5 developing specific techniques to derive present values of future cash amounts, the important point now is that financial markets place values on assets, often values we can observe. The interaction of buyers and sellers determines a market price for an asset — in this case, the asset is a promise of $1,000 in the future, and the market price is $250 today. This price is one measure of value because it tells us what present dollar amount we would need in order to obtain the $1,000 in the future. Because of their role in establishing or reflecting value, financial markets will be extremely important to financial managers attempting to maximize value.

Value depends on the future benefits an asset can produce: value reflects both time and risk.

Present value — the value today of a future payment or stream of payments.

Principal — a dollar amount borrowed, loaned, or deposited upon which interest is owed or earned.

The value of assets is determined in financial markets.

Figure 1–2
An Advertisement for a Certificate of Deposit

This announcement is not an offer to sell or a solicitation of an offer to buy any of these securities.
The offering is made only by the Offering Circular.

NEW ISSUE   May 21, 1982

$60,000,000
Bank of Virginia

CERTIFICATES OF DEPOSIT*
(Zero Coupon)

	Price to the Public	Principal Amount at Maturity
Certificate of Deposit Maturing September 18, 1987 Totaling $20,000,000	$500	$1,000
Certificate of Deposit Maturing February 1, 1993 Totaling $40,000,000	$250	$1,000

*The Certificates of Deposit are insured by the Federal Deposit Insurance
Corporation to a maximum amount of $100,000 for each depositor.

*Copies of the Offering Circular may be obtained in any State in
which this announcement is circulated only from such of the Underwriters as are qualified to act as dealers in securities in such State.*

Wheat, First Securities, Inc.

Alex. Brown & Sons   A.G. Edwards & Sons, Inc.

J.C. Bradford & Co.   Butcher & Singer, Inc.   Craigie Incorporated

Davenport & Co. of Virginia, Inc.   Interstate Securities Corporation

Investment Corporation of Virginia   Johnston, Lemon & Co.   Legg Mason Wood Walker
                                              Incorporated   Incorporated

Scott & Stringfellow, Inc. Cecil, Waller & Sterling, Inc. Ferris & Company Strader & Company
                                                            Incorporated   Incorporated

Source: Bank of Virginia.

**Certificate of deposit
(CD)** — a bank's promise to
make certain future cash
payments to the person who
buys the CD for a stated
price.

The Bank of Virginia's promise is called a zero-coupon **certificate of deposit
(CD).** A CD is a promise by the bank to make certain future cash payments to the
owner of the CD. Typically, the payments consist of a series of interest payments
and a larger final lump-sum payment. The interest payments (sometimes called
coupon payments) on this particular CD are zero (because it is a *zero-coupon* CD),
so only the lump-sum payment of $1,000 has been promised.

Is the value of a firm to its shareholders equal to the market price of its stock
quoted in the financial pages of the daily newspaper? For example, on December 24,
1987, one share of IBM stock sold for $120. During the preceding 12 months,
however, a share of IBM had sold for as much as $176 and as little as $102. The
extent to which market prices fairly reflect true value is a complex and difficult issue about which we will have much to say later.

In the short run, stock-market prices are influenced by many factors beyond the
control of management, such as general economic conditions, government actions,

In the long run, market prices reflect the wisdom or folly of managerial decisions.

and the emotions of investors. Over the long run, market prices are a function of underlying economic variables: earning power and cash flows. Using valuation as a conceptual framework does not require that we consider every change in stock price as an indicator of the wisdom of our policies. Even though external factors may cause short-run fluctuations, our valuation criterion assumes that, eventually, wise managerial decisions will be recognized and reflected in market prices. In other words, in the long run, "true value will out."

Value and Managers: Theory Versus Practice

So far we have established that financial managers should have the objective of increasing their firm's value to shareholders. In a small firm with a single shareholder, this view of a manager's job is clear-cut. The owner of a corner drugstore would have every right to expect the store manager to work on the owner's behalf—especially if the owner and manager happen to be the same person. The modern corporation (which we will discuss further in the next chapter) is, however, much more complex than the corner store. As an example, in the early 1980s, IBM had more than 20 divisions and subsidiaries, operations in more than 100 countries, more than 350,000 employees, and more than 700,000 stockholders.

In the complex modern corporation, managers serve as agents for thousands of shareholders.

In such a complex organization, there is typically no single shareholder who can control corporate decisions. Instead share ownership is spread over thousands of individuals. Shareholders take on the role of suppliers of funding, while managers specialize in evaluating and making the firm's decisions. Managers are directly responsible to the board of directors elected by shareholders. This compact in forming a corporation gives managers the role of agents. But instead of representing a handful of professional athletes, corporate managers may be agents working on behalf of thousands of shareholders. Such a set of agreements has real benefits. It allows knowledgeable managers to use their specialized information and talents to make good business decisions. It allows shareholders to invest their money without having to learn about and keep track of the day-to-day operations of the firm. On the other hand, as with any set of agreements, the legal details can fast become complex. Managers are empowered to exercise their authority subject to the approval of the board of directors. If shareholders do not agree with managers' or directors' decisions, they have the right to vote for new members of the board of directors, which is empowered to change management.

If a manager's compensation were directly tied to whether or not he or she furthered shareholder interests, we probably would not have to worry about managers deviating from the pursuit of the shareholders' best interests—maximizing the value of the firm to existing shareholders. However, in a world where measurement of performance is difficult and information is costly, the interests of managers do not always coincide with those of shareholders. For example, managers might be tempted to support the decision to acquire another company if they viewed their income and prestige as being based on the size of their corporation, even if the purchase provided no benefits (or perhaps even losses) to existing shareholders. As another example, a manager might focus on achieving a short-term profit (even

International Focus

The Global Economy in the 1990s

The world economy is becoming more and more intertwined. Young Americans, Europeans, and Japanese wear similar clothes, listen to similar compact-disc players, go to McDonald's for hamburgers, and hang out in similar places. Someone recently described this phenomenon as the "Californianization" of the world.

The world economic outlook reflects this integration. In a study done for *Fortune* magazine, Data Resources, Inc., an economic consulting firm, made the following forecasts of growth in real (i.e., adjusted for inflation) gross national product:

Expected Annual Growth in Real GNP, 1987–2000

United States	2.6%
Western Europe	2.6
Japan	3.5
China	7.1
South Korea	6.2
Brazil	5.9
Taiwan	5.8
Mexico	4.7

As this growth occurs, national boundaries will become increasingly irrelevant for consumers and business alike. Joint ventures and other alliances will become common between firms in different countries as they cooperate to pool their talents in production and marketing. The Japanese are leading the way in locating manufacturing facilities in foreign countries and by the mid-1990s are expected to own some $400 billion of American factories, up from $195 billion in 1987. The expectation is that continued globalization of trade and commerce will contribute to a steady improvement in the standard of living of the world's citizens.

Source: Richard I. Kirkland, Jr., "We're All in This Together," *Fortune*, February 2, 1987. The data on growth rates are from a study by Data Resources, Inc., quoted in the *Fortune* article.

at the expense of overall shareholder value) if management compensation were based on that profit figure. In practice, situations arise in which the interests of owners and managers may diverge, and it is undoubtedly true that managers do not always act in the interests of owners.

When managers fail to act in behalf of those whose interests they represent (normally the shareholders of the firm), we would expect those managers ultimately to be replaced. Just how well the system of managerial selection works in practice is an important question, but it is beyond the scope of this book. We will assume in our discussion that a manager's job is to act in the interests of those for whom he or she is trustee, recognizing the interests of other parties as well. We will discuss analytical techniques, concepts, and policies that are useful to managers in discharging this responsibility.

Even if managers adopt value maximization as their goal, their job is difficult. In most corporate decisions, obtaining and interpreting information is a large problem. How does one measure the future benefits of the decision to enter the business of making personal computers? For that matter, how can we measure benefits even after they have occurred? As a result, some of our discussion in this book will focus on the use of accounting tools as a means of gathering useful information. Even the best of accounting techniques, however, will not solve all the problems of dealing with time and risk.

In a world of costly and imperfect information it is not possible to analyze quantitatively the effects of every corporate decision. In fact, given the costs involved in gathering information on possible decisions, firms frequently state their goals (what they intend to accomplish) in qualitative, mission-oriented terms.

A firm might see itself as a builder of commercial aircraft, a provider of financial services, or a provider of equipment and technology for processing information. Around such a basic statement of purpose is built the firm's commercial strategy, which defines its markets, products, and production technology. From these follow supporting policies in operations, marketing, accounting, personnel, financial management, and so on.

That firms operate in such a mission-oriented fashion is not inconsistent with our notion of value maximization. Firms decide that they do a certain set of activities best and that the way to create value is to concentrate on these activities.

Another real-world factor complicating financial management is that there typically is no single financial manager. The functions of financial management may be diffused throughout the organization. Operating managers frequently have a considerable say in proposing and analyzing investment opportunities that lead to the commitment of corporate funds in plant, equipment, inventory, or acquisition of other firms. Central staff groups — sometimes under the treasurer, but just as frequently under the controller or an executive in charge of planning — play a large role in analyzing investment and financing ideas. Investment and financing decisions often involve committees of senior officers of the firm and, in the case of most major decisions, the board of directors as well.

Not only are financial-management functions frequently diffused among many individuals, but the functions are also diverse in character. Some of these functions — such as the receipt, disbursement, and custody of funds and **securities** (claims to ownership, such as stocks and bonds); the preparation of confidential payrolls; the supervision of how securities are registered or transferred; the payment of various taxes; the negotiation and placement of insurance policies — are better classified as administrative functions incidental to finance, rather than as financial management proper. Other functions are more central to financial management: the preparation and review of cash budgets; the investment of temporarily idle funds; the hedging of foreign-exchange risks; the arrangement of bank credit; the supervision of the company's pension funds; the decision to change the company's dividend rate or to issue new securities; the task of explaining the company's performance and prospects to groups of financial analysts.

The criterion for financial-management decisions in nonprofit organizations requires careful consideration. Benefits often are difficult or even impossible to measure. Dollar values cannot be attached to the output of churches or schools, for example. Where both benefits and costs of a course of action can be quanti-

The manager's job is to act in the interests of owners, recognizing the interests of other parties as well.

Securities — claims to ownership, such as stocks and bonds.

Cost minimization — the goal of making a firm's costs as low as possible; can be used as a criterion for making financial-management decisions.

fied, value maximization can still be used to guide decisions. Where only costs can be quantified, a cost/benefit approach still is useful, with cost estimates compared to benefits in qualitative terms. Where mutually exclusive alternatives are under consideration — that is, where two or more alternatives exist but only one can be chosen — **cost minimization** is the appropriate criterion. Where cash flows occur over long periods, techniques for dealing with the time value of money are as useful to a university or a church as to a business firm.

Plan of the Book

To discuss the essentials of financial management, we have divided this book into seven parts.

Part One: Introduction

The present chapter and Chapter 2 are designed both to give an overview of financial management and to examine the legal, tax, and financial environments of a financial manager.

Part Two: Time and Risk

As already discussed, time and risk are two fundamental problems for a manager attempting to make decisions that will maximize the value of the firm. Chapter 3 develops the *discounted-cash-flow* method of valuing cash that comes in or goes out at different points in time. Chapter 4 shows how the concepts of discounted cash flow can be applied to values placed on securities in financial markets. One of the major difficulties in applying valuation techniques, such as discounted cash flow, is accounting for risk. Chapter 5 examines methods that can be used in dealing with risk. By the end of Part Two, we will have thus developed some key tools and ways of thinking in finance.

Part Three: Financial Analysis and Planning

To apply any technique, one needs to have some sort of information or data. Part Three examines some of the standard ways in which information about a firm's performance (both past and prospective) is developed, reported, and analyzed. Chapters 6, 7, 8, and 9 discuss basic accounting statements and tools of financial analysis and planning using these statements.

Part Four: Analyzing Investment Decisions

Having developed tools for dealing with time and risk (Part Two) and for analyzing information (Part Three), we turn in Part Four to an examination of how to make the basic decision of financial management — how to use funds. Chapters 10 through 13 look at ways to decide which (if any) of the investment opportunities

Finance in Practice 1–1

The Performance of the *Fortune* 500

Each year in the spring, *Fortune* magazine publishes an extensive analysis of the 500 largest corporations in the United States, a listing that has come to be known as the "*Fortune* 500." The "500" had their best year ever in 1987, posting record sales and earnings. Sales increased 9 percent over 1986 to $1.88 trillion (a big number). Profits rose an impressive 41 percent to $91 billion. Many observers pointed to restructuring and redirection of corporate resources during 1985–87 as one reason for the good performance. Strong exports,

due in part to the decline in the dollar (see Finance in Practice 24–1), also were a factor.

General Motors retained the top rank in terms of sales at $101.8 billion. General Motors had unseated Exxon for the top spot in 1985, having lost the title to Exxon in 1979. In fact, GM and Exxon are the only two companies to have held the top ranking since the listing was established in 1954. GM held it undisputed until 1974, when Exxon first took the lead. GM regained the title in 1977, then lost it again in 1979. In 1987, GM's sales were $101.8 billion, well above Exxon's $76.4 billion but still below Exxon's 1981 record of $108 billion. The accompanying Table A gives the top ten companies in the 1987 *Fortune* 500 rankings by sales revenue.

Sales is not the only measure of success. If total profits had been the criterion, a different company would have won: IBM Corporation. For the fourth year in a row, IBM led all firms in profits. In 1987, IBM generated profits of $5.3 billion on sales of $54 billion versus GM's $3.5 billion profit on sales of $101.8 billion. Ford, number three in sales behind GM and Exxon, also beat GM in profits. In terms of

Table A

The *Fortune* 500: Largest U.S. Industrial Corporations

| Rank | | | Sales | | Profits | | | Assets | |
1987	1986	Company	Millions of Dollars	% change from 1986	Millions of Dollars	Rank	% change from 1986	Millions of Dollars	Rank
1	1	General Motors	101,781.9	(1.0)	3,550.9	4	20.6	87,421.9	1
2	2	Exxon	76,416.0	9.3	4,840.0	2	(9.7)	74,042.0	2
3	3	Ford Motor	71,643.4	14.2	4,625.2	3	40.8	44,955.7	4
4	4	International Business Machines	54,217.0	5.8	5,258.0	1	9.8	63,688.0	3
5	5	Mobil	51,223.0	14.2	1,258.0	11	(10.6)	41,140.0	5
6	6	General Electric	39,315.0	11.7	2,915.0	5	17.0	38,920.0	6
7	8	Texaco	34,372.0	8.7	(4,407.0)	480	—	33,962.0	9
8	7	American Tel. & Tel.	33,598.0	(1.4)	2,044.0	6	1,370.5	38,426.0	7
9	9	E.I. Du Pont de Nemours	30,468.0	12.2	1,786.0	8	16.1	28,209.0	10
10	11	Chrysler	26,257.7	16.6	1,289.7	10	(8.1)	19,944.6	15

profitability, or profits *per dollar* of sales, IBM was the clear winner among the top ten, although there were many smaller companies with higher profitability. In fact, IBM has been a consistent leader in profitability (profits in relation to sales) over a period of many years.

But dollar profits are not the whole story, either. Another important measure of performance is *return on investment,* which measures profits per dollar of assets, or (alternatively) profits per dollar of shareholder investment. Using return on investment, Ford took top honors in 1987 among the larger firms, although there were many smaller firms that did better on this measure (see Table B).

Another important measure of performance is *return to shareholders,* which measures not company profits but the return actually received by shareholders. Shareholders receive part of their return through dividends paid by the corporation and part through an increase in the value of their shares of stock. Looking now at *industries* rather than individual companies, the 1987 winner in total return to shareholders was a surprise — not electronics, not computers, not

aerospace, but metals. The metals industry chalked up a total return to shareholders of 50.5 percent for the year, the best among 25 industry groups measured by *Fortune* and far above the all-industry average of 6.8 percent. Metals may be a flash in the pan, however; metals came in last among the 25 industries over the period 1977–87, delivering an average return to shareholders of 10.0 percent per year versus an all-industry average of 17.2 percent. The winner over the longer period was tobacco at 23.4 percent. Table C (on p. 18) gives the average annual return to shareholders for the 10-year period for the 25 industry groups.

There are many ways to measure performance. Looking at sales, profits, return on investment, and return to shareholders are just some of the possibilities. This book will examine these and other measures of performance but will also explore how to achieve excellence over the long run.

Source: Adapted from "The Good Times Finally Roll — The 500 Largest U.S. Industrial Corporations," *Fortune,* April 25, 1988.

Table B

The *Fortune* 500: Largest U.S. Industrial Corporations

| Rank | | | Profits as Percent of | | | | | |
| 1987 | 1986 | Company | Sales | | Assets | | Stockholders' Equity | |
			%	Rank	%	Rank	%	Rank
1	1	General Motors	3.5	307	4.1	336	10.7	314
2	2	Exxon	6.3	165	6.5	217	14.4	213
3	3	Ford Motor	6.5	161	10.3	75	25.0	50
4	4	International Business Machines	9.7	66	8.3	144	13.7	227
5	5	Mobil	2.5	369	3.1	360	7.5	366
6	6	General Electric	7.4	127	7.5	181	17.7	148
7	8	Texaco	—		—		—	
8	7	American Tel. & Tel.	6.1	172	5.3	278	14.1	221
9	9	E.I. Du Pont de Nemours	5.9	181	6.3	229	12.5	261
10	11	Chrysler	4.9	224	6.5	219	19.8	102

Table C

Industry Medians: Total Return to Investors — 1977–87 Annual Average

Tobacco	23.4%
Publishing, Printing	22.8
Rubber products	21.9
Metal products	21.3
Apparel	21.2
Furniture	21.1
Computers (includes office equipment)	20.9
Food	20.7
Textiles	19.6
Beverages	18.9
Pharmaceuticals	18.6
Transportation equipment	18.3
Forest products	17.8
Building materials	17.1
Aerospace	16.8
Chemicals	16.4
Electronics	16.0
Motor vehicles and parts	13.8
Scientific and photographic equipment	13.2
Mining, Crude-oil production	12.2
Soaps, Cosmetics	12.0
Petroleum refining	12.0
Industrial and farm equipment	10.2
Metals	10.0
The 500 Median	**17.2**

facing a firm should be undertaken. Making such investments involves allocating scarce funds among competing uses and requires an understanding that investment opportunities are typically risky and involve benefits and costs that are spread over time.

Part Five: Financing the Firm's Assets

Having discussed ways to analyze the *uses* of funds in Part Four, we turn in Part Five to an analysis of *sources* of funds. Chapters 14 through 20 examine what forms of financing are available to the firm. What are the differences between the various sources? Which sources are best for the corporation to use?

Chapter 14 describes the types of long-term financing available in financial markets and discusses the efficiency of those markets in valuing securities (such as common stock) issued by corporations. Chapter 15 focuses on basic differences between debt (borrowing) and equity (stock) financing, leading to our discussion in Chapter 16 of the appropriate amount of borrowing for a firm. Chapter 17 examines the basic decision of whether to pay out money to shareholders or reinvest in the firm — the dividend decision. Chapters 18 and 19 are devoted to the specialized topics of options, futures, and leasing, and Chapter 20 to the practical side of actually issuing and managing the long-term securities, such as bonds, that the corporation may issue.

Part Six: Managing Working Capital

Since our discussion in Parts Four and Five focuses on the long-term investment and financing decisions of the firm, Part Six is devoted to a discussion of making decisions about certain shorter-term investments, such as inventory. Chapter 21 examines the different types of short-term financing; Chapter 22 looks at the management of cash; Chapter 23 analyzes the management of accounts receivable and inventory.

Part Seven: Special Topics

Having concluded our discussion of the major types of corporate decisions about investing and obtaining funds, we turn to a discussion of two specialized topics in Part Seven: international financial management (Chapter 24) and mergers and acquisitions (Chapter 25).

Guide to the Reader

In moving from chapter to chapter in a textbook, it is often easy to lose track of how the individual parts contribute to the whole process. As you read through this text, a useful reference point is Figure 1–1. Everything in this book is directed at developing an understanding of how financial managers can best make decisions about the *uses* and *sources* of money. To that end, we provide some background on the environment of the manager (Part One), basic tools of dealing with time, risk, and information (Parts Two and Three), and application of these tools to specific corporate decisions (Parts Four through Seven).

KEY CONCEPTS

1. Financial managers make decisions about the *sources* (financing decisions) and *uses* (investment decisions) of funds. In both situations, financial management ties the firm to financial markets.

2. Financial managers use value maximization as the basic decision rule to help them make good decisions. Value maximization is an extension of profit maximization.

3. Value is based on future benefits and reflects both time and risk.

4. Money has a time value: a dollar today is worth more than a dollar in the future. Generally, participants in financial markets are risk-averse.

5. The discipline of financial management encourages a long-range view in dealing with the fundamental issue of efficient use of capital funds.

SUMMARY

Financial management deals with the efficient acquisition and use of capital funds by firms and other organizations. Financial-management decisions link the firm to financial markets and establish both *sources* and *uses* of funds. Financial decisions are interdependent and must be coordinated over time as part of the process of financial planning.

Value maximization has replaced profit maximization as the operational criterion for financial-management decisions. Values reflect the facts that (1) money has a time value: dollars received today are more valuable than dollars received in the future; and (2) financial-market participants typically are risk-averse.

Although the theory and practice of financial management have developed around business firms, many of the concepts are applicable to the decisions of nonprofit organizations and individuals as well.

QUESTIONS

1. What is the role of business firms in a market economy? Contrast profit maximization and value maximization as criteria for financial-management decisions in practice.
2. List the activities and duties of a financial manager. How does each of these activities relate to value maximization? Suggestion: review the table of contents of this text.
3. How does risk affect value?
4. Explain why money has *time value*.
5. What is the difference between a goal and a decision criterion? Use an example in your answer.
6. A large manufacturing firm offered executive bonuses tied to the level of net profit and earnings per share. Over a period of years total earnings increased, but the price of the stock declined in the market. Why? What decisions may increase earnings, but cause stock prices to fall?

Chapter 2

The Financial Environment

In this chapter we will discuss the environment in which financial managers have to operate. We will examine various types of financial markets, government regulations, and taxes. Additionally, we will see how inflation affects this environment.

In Chapter 1 we discussed the scope and objectives of financial management and the conceptual framework within which financial-management decisions are made. We found that modern financial management focuses on making decisions in a world that is uncertain and changing over time. The environment in which financial managers actually must operate is complex. It is a world of laws, regulations, taxes, institutions, and highly competitive financial markets. This chapter discusses some of the important factors that shape the environment in which financial-management decisions are made in practice.

As a guide to that discussion, Figure 2–1 is an expansion of Figure 1–1, which showed the role of a financial manager. Figure 2–1 diagrams a specific corporate decision: borrowing money from a bank (a source of funds) and investing the funds in a new piece of equipment (a use of funds).

In exchange for signing a loan agreement, the financial manager obtains funds. The colored arrows in Figure 2–1 show the deal struck between the financial manager as the corporation's representative and the bank. The funds (usually along with funds from other sources) are then invested in the firm in hopes of future cash benefits. The financial manager realizes, however, that part of the future benefits will go to the government in the form of taxes. Looking at the right side of Figure 2–1, we see that the bank actually obtained its money from individual savers as a result of savings-account deposits (dashed arrows). Both the bank and the savers also know they will owe taxes to the government.

Actually, Figure 2–1 is much too simplified. Financial managers can work for all sorts of business organizations, not just corporations. Financial managers have numerous ways to obtain money from other **financial institutions** (besides banks) and in **financial markets** (for example, by selling shares of stock). Banks can also obtain funds in a variety of ways in these markets. For example, recall the Bank

Financial institution — an institution, such as an insurance company, a leasing company, a mutual fund, a savings-and-loan association, or a commercial bank, that channels funds from savers to borrowers.

Financial market — a market where firms can raise funds and where firms may be valued; it is a vast network linking institutions, instruments, and submarkets; it brings together millions of buyers and sellers of financial instruments.

Figure 2–1
The Environment of the Financial Manager

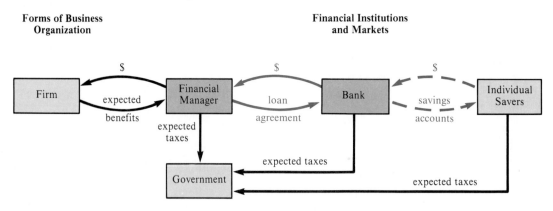

Government Taxes and Laws

of Virginia zero-coupon certificate of deposit (CD) discussed in Chapter 1. A CD is one way banks can obtain funds. Finally, the government's regulation of business activity and its tax laws are quite complicated. In fact, some have claimed that the U.S. tax code is the most complex document in the history of civilization.

Before we can discuss whether a financial manager's decisions about sources and uses of funds are good ones, we need to get some idea of the environment in which the manager operates. In this chapter we will discuss various business organizations, financial institutions, financial markets, government regulations, and taxes.

Forms of Business Organization

Sole proprietorship—a business owned and operated by a single individual that is not incorporated.

Corporation—an entity created by law that owns assets, incurs liabilities, enters into contracts, and engages in ongoing activities.

Partnership—an unincorporated business owned by two or more persons.

There are three major forms of business organization: the sole proprietorship, the partnership, and the corporation.

More than 16 million firms operate in the United States. In terms of the number of firms, the **sole proprietorship** is the most prevalent organizational form, representing about three fourths of all firms. A sole proprietorship is a business owned and operated by a single individual. On the other hand, the **corporation** is by far the dominant form in terms of income, output, and assets. For example, corporations account for about 90 percent of all business (as measured by dollar value of business receipts) in the United States.

The form of business organization varies widely by the line of business. In agriculture, for example, proprietorships account for the majority in terms of both number and sales. In manufacturing and transportation, however, corporations account for more than 90 percent of sales. In retail trade and services, proprietorships account for more in number of firms, and corporations account for more in sales. In many of these fields, the **partnership** is found less often than is either the proprietorship or the corporation, but partnerships do find wide use in professions such as law and architecture.

Even among corporations, small firms outnumber large ones, but the large firms dominate in sales and output. In the 1980s, the 500 largest industrial corporations in the United States represented only a small fraction of the active manufacturing corporations in the United States but generated sales that accounted for almost half of the gross national product.

Sole Proprietorship

In a sole proprietorship, one individual owns all the assets of the firm and is responsible for all its liabilities. The proprietor is entitled to all profits and must stand all losses. He or she is responsible for all actions of the firm and is personally liable in the event of civil damage suits against the firm. With respect to such suits and debts of the firm, the proprietor's liability is *unlimited;* that is, it is not limited to his or her investment in the firm. Creditors or plaintiffs can proceed in legal actions against the personal assets of the proprietor.

The principal virtue of the proprietorship is its simplicity; in most cases, it is necessary only to set up shop and begin operations. The principal disadvantages of the proprietorship are unlimited liability and limitations on size. Generally, a proprietorship can raise funds only to the extent that the individual proprietor can do so. Often, this keeps the firm from raising large amounts of money.

A proprietorship itself is not subject to taxation of income. Rather, the income or loss derived from the proprietorship is included and taxed in the personal tax return of the proprietor.

> The principal disadvantages of proprietorships: unlimited liability and limitation on size.

Partnership

Partnerships are similar to proprietorships in all essential aspects except one: partnerships involve two or more owners. In a **general partnership,** all partners have unlimited liability for the debts and acts of the firm. Normally, a partnership agreement is made that specifies the capital contribution of the partners, the share of each partner both in the assets and in the profits of the firm, and provisions for the withdrawal or death of a partner. Aside from the need for an agreement, partnerships are about as easy to form as proprietorships. As in the case of a proprietorship, the income of a partnership is included in the personal tax returns of the partners.

> **General partnership**—a partnership in which all partners have unlimited liability for the debts and actions of the firm.

Some states permit the formation of a **limited partnership,** which consists of at least one general partner and one or more limited partners. The general partner (or partners) manages the firm and has the responsibilities of a partner described above, including unlimited liability. The limited partners' main function is to contribute capital; they share in the profits but have no voice in directing the operations of the firm; their liability is limited to their investment.

> **Limited partnership**—a partnership in which there is at least one general partner and one or more limited partners. Limited partners contribute capital, share in the profits, have limited liability for debts, and have no voice in directing the firm.

Relative to proprietorships, a partnership has the advantages of allowing a number of individuals to share expenses and work but to remain as owners. In addition, often a combination of partners will be able to raise more money than can a single individual. On the other hand, partners, like proprietors, often have unlimited liability and may face limitations in obtaining funds.

Corporation

By far the dominant form of business organization in the United States is the corporation. Although only about one in six firms is a corporation, corporations account for more than 80 percent of business sales. Large U.S. companies, such as IBM, General Motors, and Exxon, are corporations. As defined more than a century and a half ago by John Marshall, Chief Justice of the United States, "A corporation is an artificial being, invisible, intangible, and existing only in contemplation of the law." A corporation is, thus, an entity created by law that is empowered to own assets, to incur liabilities, and to engage in certain specified activities.

> *First* (and probably most important), liability of owners is limited to their investment.

> *Second,* ownership is easily transferable.

> *Third,* it is easier for a corporation to raise funds.

The corporation differs from the proprietorship and the partnership in several important respects. First, and probably most important, the liability of owners for debts and actions of the corporation is limited to their investment in the firm. Creditors and plaintiffs in damage suits can proceed against the assets of the cor-

Stock — the legal claim to ownership of a business corporation, divided into shares and represented by certificates that can be transferred from one owner to another.

poration but not against the personal assets of the owners. Second, ownership in a corporation is easily transferable, which is not true for a partnership. The corporation is a perpetual entity. Shares of **stock** give the shareowner certain claims of ownership in the corporation, such as receiving dividend payments and voting on the election of directors who monitor the activity of corporate managers. Generally, owners may sell their shares without affecting the operation of the firm. Third, because the corporation itself may incur liabilities, the corporate form provides better access to external sources of capital. As noted earlier, the corporation is the dominant form of business organization in the United States in terms of total output of goods and services. This dominance is due to the advantages of limited liability, transferability of ownership, continuous long-term existence, and access to capital.

A disadvantage of corporations: as legal entities, they pay taxes.

A disadvantage of the corporate form is that, because it is a legal entity, the corporation itself pays taxes on its income — and, as we will discuss later, corporate tax rates are different from personal tax rates. In addition, choosing the corporate form of organization may subject owners' income to a form of double taxation. Income is taxed once at the corporate level and once more as part of personal income when income is distributed to shareholders as dividends.

Corporations are formed under the laws of the various states. A charter is issued by the state, establishing the corporation as a legal entity and setting forth its purpose and its relationship to the state. Corporate bylaws, governing the internal management of the firm, are then established. A board of directors is elected by the owners to set policy and oversee the firm in the owners' behalf. The directors appoint the executive officers of the firm, often referred to as the management, who normally are full-time employees of the firm. Managers are charged with executing the policies established by the directors and administering the operations of the firm. Selecting the firm's top management personnel and evaluating their performance are major functions of the board of directors.

Subchapter S Corporations

Subchapter S corporation — a small corporation that may legally be treated as if it were a partnership for income-tax purposes.

Under a provision of the tax law known as "Subchapter S," certain small business corporations may elect to be treated in a manner similar to partnerships for income-tax purposes. Although such a corporation enjoys limited liability, the corporation's income is taxed directly at the shareholder level and not at the corporate and personal levels. This form of organization is widely used in the professional-service sector of the economy. In 1982, the Subchapter Revision Act redefined rules for **subchapter S corporations** and expanded the maximum number of shareholders allowed under the subchapter S rule to 35.

The Financial Environment: Financial Markets

No matter what form of business organization is chosen, a firm's managers will be making decisions that affect the firm's relationship to the financial market — decisions about raising and using money. Recall our diagram of a simplified deci-

A firm's financial managers make decisions about raising and using money that relate the firm to the financial markets.

The ultimate determination of the success or failure of a firm's policies is made in the financial market.

sion of a financial manager in Figure 2–1. In a fundamental sense, financial management is a continuing two-way interaction between the firm and its financial environment.

In the financial market, the firm raises the funds required for its current operations and for its capital expenditures. Here also the firm temporarily invests its surplus funds, pending their more long-term disposition. Finally, and most importantly, it is the financial market that ultimately determines whether the firm's policies are a success or a failure.

The financial market is not a single, physical place. It comprises millions of participants spread across the world, along with offices linked by an extensive telecommunications network that brings buyers and sellers together and sets prices in the process of doing so. In order to understand the complex institutions, instruments, and submarkets that collectively make up the financial market, it is useful to break down the financial market into smaller components. There are many ways of doing this; one way is to address the following questions:

1. What functions does the financial market perform?
2. What major types of financial claims or instruments are traded in the financial market?
3. Who are the principal participants?
4. What are the major submarkets with which the financial manager deals?

The Functions of the Financial Market

Financial claims — promises to pay money in the future, exchanged in financial markets for money. Examples are stocks, bonds, and loans.

Surplus spending units — individuals, companies, or government bodies that have excess funds.

Deficit spending units— individuals, companies, or government bodies that need funds.

Like most markets, the financial market is where buyers and sellers meet in order to exchange things for money and vice versa. The things exchanged in financial markets are **financial claims,** or promises to pay money in the future. Individuals, companies, or government bodies who have excess funds exchange these funds in return for claims to future sums of money. Traders with excess funds are also known as **surplus spending units.** On the other side of the equation, individuals, companies, or government bodies who need funds sell claims that promise to pay money in the future in exchange for present funds. Traders who need funds are also known as **deficit spending units.** For example, as we saw in Chapter 1, an individual could pay $250 to the Bank of Virginia in exchange for the bank's promise to pay back $1,000 in the future. This specific type of financial claim is a certificate of deposit. Many other types of financial claims exist.

Figure 2–1 depicts a corporation's decision to borrow money from a bank, which in turn has received deposits from individual savers. The individual savers had excess funds that were ultimately channeled to a corporation that needed money. Organized financial markets make this process seem rather routine, but it does involve two sets of trades in which claims to *future* sums of money are exchanged for money today. In the first trade (dashed arrows), the bank promises to pay savers their money back (plus interest) in the future in exchange for the savers' making a deposit. The financial claim here might be a savings-account passbook showing the right of the saver to withdraw money from the bank. Alternatively, the bank could have used a certificate of deposit, as did the Bank of Vir-

Financial intermediary — a financial go-between, such as a bank, that makes possible the easy transfer of funds from savers to spenders. Financial intermediaries gather funds, analyze credit possibilities, evaluate risk, and handle administrative and legal details for borrowers and lenders.

Financial markets provide convenient ways for deferring or accelerating consumption.

Capital formation — investment in real assets, such as new buildings, machinery, or technology; it is facilitated by financial markets.

ginia. In the second trade (colored arrows), the company promises to pay back the loan from the bank at some future date (also paying interest on the loan) in exchange for receiving the money today. The bank serves an important role as the financial go-between, or **financial intermediary,** that enables funds from surplus spending units (individual savers in Figure 2–1) to be channeled easily to deficit spending units (the corporation).

Of course, financial-market transactions can become much more complicated than those outlined in Figure 2–1, and there are all sorts of other financial claims traded and other financial intermediaries. Basically, however, the financial market performs several functions essential to a society.

1. The financial market allows those who wish to defer consumption (that is, to save) a convenient way of doing so.
2. The financial market allows those who wish to accelerate consumption (that is, to dissave) to do so conveniently. Consumer credit, credit cards, and mortgage loans enable millions of individuals to enjoy cars, appliances, and homes now, rather than later.
3. The financial market provides a channel through which new savings can flow into productive investment. If a firm needs money to build a new plant or develop a new technology, it may raise those funds by borrowing money from a bank, by selling new stock, or in numerous other ways. The financial market provides a ready source of funds and, thus, makes it possible for some organizations, mainly firms, to specialize in investing in real assets. Such investment is called **capital formation.** In order for living standards to rise, an economy must add to its stock of tangible capital; that is, it must create additional residences, roads, plants, equipment, and inventory. The resources required for these purposes must come from **current saving** — that part of current output (gross national product) not immediately consumed. A major purpose of the financial market is to gather the current saving of millions of surplus spending units and put this saving to productive use.
4. The financial market provides a **secondary market** where existing financial claims can be bought and sold so that decisions to save and dissave are not irrevocable. For example, if a person saves money and buys a share of IBM stock, that person would want to be able to sell that stock at some future date in case the money became needed for consumption. On the other hand, IBM would not want to sell off its plant and equipment to satisfy the desires of shareholders who want to cash in on their stock. The secondary market solves this problem by allowing shareholders to sell their IBM stock to other individuals without requiring IBM to take any action at all. The better the secondary market, the more likely it is that people will be willing to save and transfer their current saving to those who can use it.

People are more likely to save and transfer their savings if a good secondary market exists which ensures that decisions to save or dissave are not irrevocable.

The financial market can be divided functionally into two connected parts. One is the **new-issues market,** or **primary market,** through which society's annual saving eventually flows from the surplus spending units in society to the deficit spending units in exchange for newly issued claims. The other is the secondary market in which units that hold previously issued claims can exchange

The new-issues market is much smaller than the secondary market which includes *all* past issues still outstanding.

Financial markets set prices (values).

Corporate bond — a long-term debt claim representing a corporation's promise to repay with interest money borrowed from a bondholder.

them for money. For example, IBM's sale of new stock in exchange for money would be an exchange in the new-issues market. The purchase of old IBM stock from another individual would be a secondary-market transaction. As might be expected, the size of the new-issues market is small relative to the size of the secondary market because the latter includes all past issues still outstanding.

5. In the process of facilitating saving and investment, financial markets also set prices, or values. For example, when people buy and sell shares of stock in IBM, the natural forces of supply and demand determine a market price, or *market value,* for a share of stock. On July 6, 1988, for instance, the market value of a share of IBM stock was $126⅞ per share. Similarly, the financial market also determines how much money a person can receive one year hence if he or she is willing to give up a dollar today. In this case, the market value is an interest rate. At an interest rate of 6 percent per year, a person can obtain $1.06 in one year for each dollar saved today. As mentioned in Chapter 1, value plays a critical role in financial-management decisions when the objective is to maximize the value of the firm to existing shareholders. We will return to valuation in detail in Chapters 3 through 5.

Major Types of Financial Claims

Table 2–1 shows the major types of financial claims outstanding as of the end of 1987. The last column shows the net new issues of each type of claim during 1987.

Corporate stocks represent shareholder claims to the ownership of a corporation. A **corporate bond** is a debt claim representing a corporation's promise to pay interest plus principal to the bond owner. At the time of the original issue of a bond, the corporation receives money (borrows) in return for its promise to make future

Table 2–1
Major Financial Claims (billions of dollars)

	Outstanding 12/31/87	New Issues During 1987
Corporate stocks	3,019.9	(52.1)
Corporate bonds	1,101.6	110.2
U.S. government securities (bonds, notes, bills)	1,682.4	107.5
U.S. government-agency securities	945.1	163.5
State and local government securities	776.3	22.2
Residential mortgages	2,113.0	214.6
Business and farm mortgages	735.5	55.9
Commercial bank loans	1,692.9	112.3

Note: The figures are estimations. Corporate bonds are domestic corporate and foreign bonds sold in the United States.

Source: Salomon Brothers, *1987 Prospects for Financial Markets* (New York: Salomon Brothers, 1987). Copyright © 1987 Salomon Brothers, Inc. Reprinted by permission.

cash payments. Bondholders have a legal right to receive their interest and principal payments, but they are not legal owners of the corporation. The U.S. government also borrows money by issuing bonds. In addition, it issues shorter-term debt claims in the form of notes and bills. U.S. government agencies and state and local governments raise funds by issuing debt claims such as bonds. Both individual homeowners (residents) and business firms take out **mortgages**, which supply them with the money they need now to buy property or buildings in return for promised interest payments and repayment of the borrowed amount. Finally, commercial banks make large numbers of **commercial loans** to business concerns. While Table 2–1 shows the major types of financial claims — stocks and forms of borrowing (bonds, notes, bills, mortgages, and loans) — there are many other sorts of specialized claims that are traded in the financial market. Chapters 12 and 18 will discuss the details of the ways corporations can raise money and will describe some of these additional claims.

Principal Participants in the Financial Market

Who are the participants in the financial market? The answer is almost everybody. But it is convenient to distinguish among three categories of participants: operating sectors, financial intermediaries, and specialized institutions.

Operating Sectors. This first category consists of the ultimate providers and users of society's flow of savings — namely, households (or individuals), businesses (including corporations), and government. The "rest of the world" is our fourth operating sector, which lumps together our transactions with parties outside the United States. The household sector, collecting the largest part of income generated by economic activity, is generally a net saver and, hence, a net provider to the other three sectors. These other sectors, however, also participate as providers of funds to the market. For example, a corporation might lend its temporary excess of funds rather than use them to reduce debt. Likewise, individual households may become users as well as providers of funds by borrowing from the market to buy homes and cars.

Financial Intermediaries. The transfer of funds from surplus units (mainly households) to deficit units (mainly business, government, and some households) can take place directly, but **direct finance** is inconvenient for both the ultimate provider and the ultimate user of funds. Imagine a firm attempting to borrow millions of dollars under conditions of direct finance. Given that individual households typically save a few hundred or a few thousand dollars a year, the financial officer would be extremely busy knocking on thousands of doors to obtain the total amount needed. The cost to the firm for search and acquisition would be quite high, thus increasing the cost of borrowing. This cost of obtaining funds in turn restricts the number of investment opportunities that can be undertaken and reduces the firm's level of investment. The saver also faces problems with direct finance. Lending to just one borrower is risky; to ensure reasonable diversification, the saver should lend to a number of firms. The costs to the saver in time and ef-

Mortgage — a loan in which designated property is pledged as security.

Commercial loan — the transfer of funds from a bank to a business firm in exchange for the firm's promise to repay the funds with interest according to a specified schedule.

Operating sectors are composed of the ultimate providers and users of savings: households, businesses, governments, and "the rest of the world."

Direct finance — the direct transfer of funds from savers to investors without going through a financial intermediary.

Compared to direct finance, financial intermediaries provide higher returns to lenders and lower costs to borrowers.

Direct finance between savers and investors requires considerable costs for search, acquisition, analysis, and diversification.

Financial friction — the costs for search, acquisition, analysis, and sale involved with financial transactions.

fort required to analyze credit, evaluate risk, and make a contract with each firm would be large in relation to the interest earned. Also, the claims by the saver would be highly *illiquid,* meaning they could not be turned back into cash quickly at low cost.

Direct finance between savers and investors thus involves significant costs of search, acquisition, analysis, and diversification. The net return to savers would be so small (perhaps negative) that lending would not be worth the effort. Borrowing costs to firms would be so high that investment would be low. In short, losses due to **financial friction** would be so great that little saving and investment would take place. Thus, financial intermediaries came on the scene to collect funds from savers and to transfer them to ultimate users. Today the largest part of saving goes into investment through financial intermediaries such as commercial banks, mutual saving banks, savings-and-loan associations, and life-insurance companies. Figure 2–2 shows the role of the financial intermediary, and Table 2–2 shows the importance of some of the types of intermediaries.

Specialized Institutions. The financial intermediaries just discussed channel the flow of saving from surplus to deficit units. Another tier of specialized institution in the financial market facilitates the flow of funds among the intermediaries themselves as well as to and from the ultimate operating sectors. These include institutions such as investment bankers, securities dealers and brokers, the organized

Figure 2–2
Direct Finance Versus Intermediation

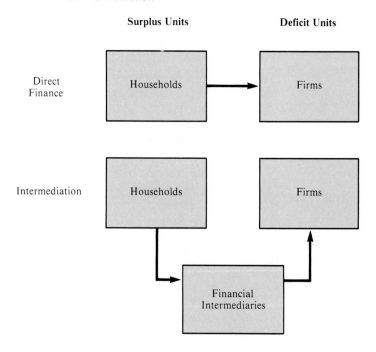

Table 2–2

Total Assets of Selected Financial Intermediaries, for Year-End 1965, 1985, and 1986

	Total Assets, 1965		Total Assets, 1985		Total Assets, 1986	
	Billions of Dollars	*Percent*	*Billions of Dollars*	*Percent*	*Billions of Dollars*	*Percent*
Depository types						
Commercial banks	340.7	38.2	2328.4	35.9	2580.6	35.1
Savings-and-loan associations	127.4	14.3	1072.1	16.6	1158.3	15.8
Mutual savings banks	59.1	6.6	218.8	3.4	239.2	3.3
Credit unions	11.0	1.2	137.2	2.1	166.1	2.3
Contractual types						
Life-insurance companies	154.2	17.3	796.1	12.3	905.1	12.3
Pension and retirement funds[a][b]	108.5	12.2	1011.0	15.6	1104.5	15.0
Other						
Mutual funds[b][c]	35.2	4.0	484.0	7.5	705.6	9.6
Finance companies	44.7	5.2	354.4	5.5	412.1	5.6
Security brokers and dealers	10.3	1.2	75.8	1.2	77.9	1.1
Total	**891.1**	**100.0**	**6477.8**	**100.0**[d]	**7349.4**	**100.0**[d]

[a]Excludes Social Security and other federal retirement funds.
[b]Influenced by the level of stock prices.
[c]Includes money-market funds.
[d]Subtotals do not add to 100 due to rounding.

Source: Board of Governors, Federal Reserve System, *Flow of Funds Accounts Financial Assets and Liabilities,* Year-End 1963–86.

securities exchanges, and mortgage bankers, to name just a few of the many types of highly specialized financial institutions within the market.

Investment banker—a financial intermediary that underwrites and distributes new securities offerings and helps a business obtain financing.

When a corporation or a municipality issues a new security, it generally sells that issue through a syndicate of **investment bankers.** In effect, the bankers buy the issue and then wholesale and retail it to financial intermediaries and individuals. Investment bankers often provide advice to their customers on a wide range of financial issues, ranging from how to set a price on a newly issued share of stock to how to go about acquiring another company. Most of the largest investment-banking firms are based in New York, although there are many regional firms as well.

Securities brokers and dealers—financial intermediaries that buy and sell stocks, bonds, and other financial claims in return for a commission fee.

The major investment-banking houses (referred to in England as merchant banks) resell new issues through their own branches or through the branch network of hundreds of **securities brokers and dealers.** This same group of brokers and dealers provides the marketplace in which individuals and institutions can sell or buy stocks and bonds.

Government-bond dealers—financial intermediaries that buy and sell government bonds.

The federal government does not use investment bankers, but rather sells directly to **government-bond dealers** through the Federal Reserve system. The government-bond dealers buy the bulk of each new government issue and eventually retail it to institutions and individuals.

Exchanges—actual organizations with physical locations where financial claims are bought and sold.

Organized **exchanges** are actual organizations that have physical locations where financial claims are bought and sold. Exchanges such as the New York Stock Exchange (NYSE) and the American Stock Exchange (AMEX), both located in New York City, provide the means through which the public can buy and sell existing stocks and bonds listed on those exchanges. In addition to the NYSE and AMEX, there are other regional exchanges, each having its own rules and operating in a different location.

To be listed on an exchange, a firm must satisfy certain financial requirements. For example, for listing purposes, the NYSE requires firms to have at least 2,000 stockholders (owning 100 shares or more each), a minimum of 1 million shares of stock outstanding that is publicly held, a total market value of its publicly traded shares of at least $16 million, and certain standards of demonstrated earning power. In addition, certain governmental requirements imposed by the Securities and Exchange Commission (SEC) must be met. Other exchanges, including the AMEX and other regional exchanges, have less stringent requirements. Most larger corporations are listed by the NYSE or AMEX.

Over-the-counter (OTC) market—the network of buyers, sellers, and brokers who interact by means of telecommunication and deal in securities not listed on an organized exchange.

Bonds (corporate and government) and all stocks not listed on the major exchanges are bought and resold on the **over-the-counter (OTC) market.** The OTC market is not an actual organization with a physical location. It is a way of trading securities. The participants here are many of the same brokers, dealers, and investment-banking houses mentioned earlier. Rather than trading at a physical location, as is done on an organized exchange, the participants are linked by a telecommunications network. The National Association of Securities Dealers Automated Quotation (NASDAQ) System is an automated system that provides up-to-date prices on thousands of securities and is an important link between participants in the OTC markets.

Mortgage banker — a financial intermediary who transfers funds from institutions that want to invest in mortgages to institutions or individuals who wish to borrow mortgage funds.

The mortgage market is large and complex, with its own set of specialized institutions. Among them is the **mortgage banker** who serves as an intermediary between institutions that want to place some of their funds in mortgages rather than in securities and individuals and institutions who wish to borrow mortgage funds.

Finally, there are several groups of specialized dealers in the financial market — such as dealers in commercial paper, in federal funds, or in foreign exchange. Virtually every function and subfunction that can be specialized has been specialized.

Major Submarkets: The Money Market and the Capital Market

Money market — the market for transactions in short-term loans.

Capital market — the market for transactions in longer-term debt issues and stock.

One widely used classification divides the financial market as a whole into the **money market** and the **capital market.** The money market makes possible open-market transactions in highly marketable short-term debt instruments, while the capital market is reserved for transactions in longer-term debt issues and stocks. The dividing line between short-term and long-term is necessarily arbitrary. By convention, short-term claims are those financial claims with maturities of less than one year. By this definition, a 60-day certificate of deposit (CD), with payment promised in 60 days, issued by a commercial bank would be a short-term security traded in the money market, while a 20-year government bond would be traded in the capital market. There is, however, no physical distinction between money and capital markets. In addition, a bond maturing in 1.5 years, which is by standard convention part of the capital market, is in many ways more like a 60-day CD than it is like a 20-year bond. Recognizing these difficulties, this book will adopt the standard convention of a maturity of one year as the dividing line between the money and capital markets.

Principal money-market participants are commercial banks, the U.S. government, and nonfinancial corporations.

The Money Market. The principal participants in the money market are commercial banks (especially the large money-center banks located in New York, Chicago, and San Francisco), the U.S. government, and nonfinancial corporations.

Commercial bank — a depository financial institution that offers checking-account services, accepts savings and other types of deposits, and makes loans.

In recent years, **commercial banks** have also become major borrowers in the money market through the sale of short-term negotiable certificates of deposit (CDs). The CDs issued by the larger banks are now actively traded and have emerged as a major money-market instrument. It should be noted that banks also issue long-term CDs, such as the Bank of Virginia zero-coupon CD (mentioned in Chapter 1), which at issuance had a maturity of over ten years.

Federal-funds market — the market in which excess bank reserves are borrowed and lent by federal banks.

Banks are also the principal participants in a highly specialized submarket known as the **federal-funds market.** Member banks of the Federal Reserve system are required by law to hold legal reserves — that is, deposits at the Federal Reserve Bank. Given the large ebb and flow of payments into and out of each bank, an active market has developed through which banks with excess reserves on a given day lend these funds to banks with deficient reserves. Such day-to-day transactions among banks are known as federal-funds transactions.

The U.S. government is a major demander of funds in the money market. A large part of the federal debt has been financed by the issuance of short-term marketable securities. For example, at the end of 1987, there were more than $390 billion worth of short-term (maturities of less than one year) U.S. Treasury bills outstanding. A large volume of this government short-term debt matures every week and has to be refinanced, which the Treasury does through its weekly auction of new short-term bills or certificates. The interest rates set in these auctions, especially the 3-month Treasury-bill rate, are key rates in the money market and are followed closely both by government economists and by participants in financial markets.

Business corporations are important participants in the money market, as both borrowers and lenders. Two types of commercial borrowers use the open market as a continuing source of short-term funds. Well-known nonfinancial firms issue short-term notes known as **commercial paper,** typically of less than 6 months' maturity, to finance short-term fund needs. Large finance companies, such as General Motors Acceptance Corporation, issue commercial paper (known as *finance paper* when issued by a financial firm) either directly or through dealers. We will discuss commercial paper in more depth in Chapter 21.

In addition to the major money-market participants discussed above, there are several other sectors that use the market regularly. Securities brokers and dealers, who have to hold inventories of securities in the course of their businesses, finance themselves through money-market borrowing. Brokers also need funds to lend to customers who desire to purchase securities on margin (that is, with a cash down payment less than the market value of the purchase). Exporters and importers require short-term funds to finance goods in transit or in warehouses. State and local governments borrow in the money market when they need current funds for brief periods pending the expected arrival of large, periodic tax receipts.

The Capital Market. The capital market makes possible the flow of long-term financing required for such purposes as long-term investment in business plant and equipment, residential construction, municipal building projects, and financing portions of the debt of the U.S. government. It also provides a place where investors who hold long-term instruments can sell them expeditiously to other groups; thus, the capital market gives long-term instruments a degree of liquidity.

The major borrowers in the capital market are: business corporations, who issue various forms of debt and stock; federal, state, and local governments (or their agencies), who issue bonds and notes; and apartment and home buyers, who borrow money by taking out mortgages. Most of the supply of long-term funds is channeled to the capital market through financial intermediaries such as insurance companies, pension funds, savings institutions, and commercial banks. The instruments themselves will be discussed more fully in Chapter 14, which deals with long-term financing instruments.

International Financial Markets. Our discussion to this point has focused on U.S. financial markets. Today, however, an increasing amount of financial activity is taking place in international financial markets. These markets bring together different economies and have flourished with the explosive growth in international

Commercial paper — short-term borrowing, typically notes of less than 6 months' maturity.

Capital markets facilitate long-term financing for long-term projects.

A growing amount of financial activity is occurring in international financial markets.

International Focus

The Global Stock Market

As late as the mid 1970s the U.S. stock markets represented close to 60 percent of all the stock value traded in the world. By 1987, however, that figure had shrunk to about 34 percent, and at prevailing exchange rates the Tokyo stock market actually had a higher dollar market value than New York's.

These figures illustrate the increasing importance of global equity markets. Accompanying these developments, better computer technology has allowed efficient trading around the world and deregulation of financial markets internationally has made for increased ease of dealing in many markets.

Large U.S. pension funds now routinely think of buying foreign securities to diversify their portfolios, and foreign investors spend large amounts on U.S. equities.

These developments have made for an exciting but often weary 24-hour day for financial market traders. At 5 A.M. New York time it's 10 A.M. in London and the London stock market is in business. And at 7 P.M. New York time it's 9 A.M. in Tokyo and the Tokyo exchange is just opening for the day. It is now routine for traders in New York to start their day early with reports of trading in London on some of the same stocks that will trade later in the day in New York. In fact, the major investment firms have traders in London, Tokyo, and New York who inherit the firm's position from another exchange as the day moves on. Fascinating work, but it can make for a long day!

Source: Adapted from "How Merrill Lynch Moves Its Stock Deals All Around the World," *Wall Street Journal,* November 9, 1987.

---

trade and investment. For example, many large U.S. corporations now borrow some of their funds not from U.S. banks but from banks in other countries. Sometimes these borrowings may be denominated in dollars, other times in other currencies such as French francs or German marks. Chapter 24 will discuss in more detail international capital markets and their impact on financial managers.

Government Regulation

The actions of a large number of federal and state regulatory agencies affect business firms.

We have examined the role of financial markets and intermediaries as part of the environment facing managers. Another important feature of this environment is the set of government rules and regulations.

Business firms are affected by the actions of a wide range of federal and state regulatory agencies. For many top managers, especially of larger companies, dealing with governmental regulation has become the single most attention-consuming function.

In fact, perhaps the largest financial-management challenge in U.S. history was a direct result of the interaction of corporate activity and government regulation.

Finance in Practice 2–1

Medium-Term Notes in International Markets

Financial markets expand beyond national boundaries. For example, a company like General Motors has its own finance subsidiary that raises funds, often to be used to provide car loans to prospective buyers. This subsidiary, General Motors Acceptance Corporation (GMAC), borrows money not only in the United States but also in Europe in the so-called Euromarket. The Euromarket allows GMAC to borrow in U.S. dollars and repay in U.S. dollars, but the transactions are outside the United States. Consider the case of the market for medium-term notes. We tell the story as of mid-1988 as reported by *The Economist*.

From zero in 1978, America's medium-term note (MTN) market has grown to $65 billion; in Europe, borrowers have issued only $4.3 billion of MTNs but the market is still double the size it was a year ago — and growing fast. By the end of next year, outstanding Euro-MTNs could total $10 billion–15 billion.

MTNs are a bit like commercial paper and are sold in much the same way. A would-be borrower approaches a half-dozen dealing banks (called simply dealers) with details of the amounts and maturities it would like to borrow; the banks, normally acting only as agents, seek out potential investors. The borrower pays the dealing banks a fixed commission for acting as a broker. Unlike commercial paper, which typically matures in less than a year, MTNs are repaid between 18 and 36 months.

Countries, as well as corporations, issue MTNs. In Europe there has been a recent rash of MTN issues by sovereign states, including Spain and Belgium, but the largest issuer of Euro-MTNs and one of the most active users of the market is General Motors Acceptance Corporation. GMAC often has more than $1 billion of these notes outstanding.

For borrowers like GMAC, the appeal of MTNs over Eurobonds is their flexibility. A Eurobond issue always consists of one large block of debt, all of which carries the same maturity. An MTN programme, by contrast, can have its repayments tailored to suit the requirements of the borrower.

For example, a finance company which wants to match liabilities and assets could need, at a particular moment, $10m of 13-month money, $18.2m of 17-month money and $79m of 23-month money. While the Eurobond market could not supply such small or precise amounts of debt, a company with an MTN programme could post appealing rates at those maturities to create the demand for its notes.

That is precisely what GMAC does. It treats its European programme as part of a "global" one. Through MTNs it shifts its borrowings between Europe and America, depending on which market is cheapest. Like many MTN borrowers with a voracious appetite for debt, GMAC publishes rates daily — that is, it advertises the interest rates at which it will issue notes over the full range of the MTN maturity spectrum. Investors are free to approach GMAC, through its dealers, to buy MTNs. Depending on its own particular requirements, GMAC will shift the rates it advertises to encourage investors to lend at the maturities it most needs.

In the early days of the market, MTN enthusiasts expected that the principal source of demand would come from investors used to buying money-market instruments (such as commercial paper and certificates of deposit). But traditional Eurobond investors — investment institutions, Europe's central banks and the Japanese — are the keenest investors. They take about three quarters of MTNs.

MTNs had been slow to take off in Europe because investors were worried about an illiquid secondary market. Unlike Eurobonds, in which dozens of firms make markets, only the dealing agents buy MTN paper back from investors. Now investors' perceptions have changed. Last year's crisis in the Eurobond market showed that many issues were less liquid than had been thought; at the same time investors in MTNs have discovered that their dealing agents do provide liquidity.

Source: From *The Economist,* August 13, 1988, p. 65.

On January 1, 1984, the U.S. telecommunications industry was transformed by the breakup of the Bell System. For generations, most local telephone service had been provided by one giant corporation, American Telephone and Telegraph (AT&T), which was the parent company of local telephone companies throughout the country as well as of manufacturing and research subsidiaries. AT&T also dominated the market for long-distance phone service and telephone equipment. Due to its monopoly position in many markets and the importance of telephone service, this Bell System of companies was subject to government regulation. In 1984, however, AT&T was divided into eight new companies: seven operating companies that provide phone service on a regional basis and a new AT&T, which retains the long-distance services as well as manufacturing and research facilities. This corporate divestiture resulted when AT&T agreed to participate in a corporate restructuring rather than continue to fight legal action taken against AT&T by the U.S. government on the grounds that AT&T was in violation of antitrust laws (discussed later in this chapter). The corporate reorganization involved more than $100 billion worth of assets and fundamentally changed the telecommunications market in the United States. Critics of the breakup argued "if it ain't broke, don't fix it" and pointed to the high standards of phone service provided in the United States up to that time. On the other hand, proponents of divestiture pointed to the likely benefits of increased competition in telecommunications markets. Needless to say, financial managers in the telephone business have new challenges in the new telecommunications environment.

We cannot begin to cover in this textbook all the numerous and complex effects of government regulation on the business environment. We will, therefore, briefly review those aspects of current regulation that have direct implications for financial decisions.

Financial Institutions

All major types of financial institutions are subject to close controls by a large number of regulatory agencies. Commercial banks are regulated by state banking

A large number of regulatory agencies provide control over major types of financial institutions.

commissions, the Federal Reserve Board, the Comptroller of the Currency in the case of national banks, and the Federal Deposit Insurance Corporation. Federal savings-and-loan associations are regulated by the Federal Home Loan Bank Board, and mutual savings banks and insurance companies are regulated by state authorities. In the case of most of these institutions, regulation extends to capital positions that must be maintained, activities in which the institutions may engage, and credit standards. As a result, these regulations affect the financial environment in which financial managers must raise funds. Regulatory agencies in many cases act also as the lender of last resort in the event of serious difficulties.

The financial environment is in the process of major change. Congress passed the Depository Institutions Deregulation and Monetary Control Act of 1980 (DIDMCA) which, in effect, changed many of the traditional boundaries between financial institutions. For many years commercial banks were prohibited by law from paying interest on checking accounts, and there were major restrictions on the types of services specific financial institutions could provide. Prior to the enactment of DIDMCA, commercial banks were effectively isolated from competition; they were the only type of federally charted depository institution able to accept demand deposits from consumers or businesses. They also had the unique authority to issue commercial loans.

Thrift institution — a financial intermediary that accepts savings deposits and makes certain types of loans.

DIDMCA represented an important step in relaxing many of these restrictions. It permitted **thrift institutions** the same range of consumer services as commercial banks, including consumer demand deposits, and granted them limited commercial loan power. It also allowed interest-bearing checking accounts, called **negotiable-order-of-withdrawal (NOW) accounts,** to be established nationwide. Finally, it provided for the phasing out of interest-rate ceilings and imposed uniform reserve requirements on all depository institutions.

Negotiable-order-of-withdrawal (NOW) account — a type of checking account at a depository institution that pays interest.

The Garn/St. Germain Depository Institutions Act of 1982 (DIA) altered further the traditional boundaries between financial institutions. It granted commercial demand-deposit authority to savings-and-loan associations and augmented their commercial- and consumer-loan power. It also allowed commercial banks and savings-and-loan institutions to issue **money-market deposit accounts (MMDA).** These accounts, designed to compete with money-market mutual funds, offer money-market rates but restrict check writing. Super NOW accounts, authorized in January 1983, allow unrestricted check writing but offer returns somewhat below those offered on MMDAs.

Money-market deposit account (MMDA) — a deposit account offered by a bank or depository institution that offers money-market interest rates but restricts check writing.

The Securities and Exchange Commission

Securities and Exchange Commission (SEC) — regulates (1) the markets where stocks and bonds are traded, (2) the issuance of new securities, and (3) the merger of firms.

The business-regulating agency that most frequently affects the financial manager of publicly owned firms is the **Securities and Exchange Commission (SEC).** The commission directly regulates (1) all the securities markets in which corporate stocks and bonds are traded, (2) all major new issues of securities, and (3) mergers between existing firms (or acquisitions of one firm by another). In addition, it indirectly regulates communications between a firm and its bondholders and shareholders, including financial and other statements released to the public. In recent years, the SEC has been active in influencing accounting practices underlying financial statements as well as practices related to the internal control of a company's financial flows, including the composition and function of the audit committees of a firm's board of directors.

Although the SEC has the power to set accounting standards, it has thus far delegated this task to self-regulation by the private sector. Private bodies such as the American Institute of Certified Public Accountants (AICPA), the Financial Accounting Standards Board (FASB), and the New York Stock Exchange (NYSE) now share responsibility for seeing that disclosure of a firm's financial affairs is as full and complete as the SEC deems sufficient. Nonetheless, almost nothing a financial officer says or does that might be related to the value placed on a company's securities is outside the potential purview of the commission.

Regulation and Deregulation

The competitive behavior and financial performance of specific businesses and industries have for many years been under the watchful eyes of state and federal agencies and commissions. The Department of Justice and the Federal Trade Commission, for example, oversee one of the oldest forms of economic regulation in the United States—antitrust policy. Enforcement of antitrust law is designed to promote competitive behavior and to prevent the development of monopolies. In other areas, however, there are companies which have monopoly power with government's blessing. In return for these monopolies, these companies are regulated by agencies as to the prices they can charge, their accounting practices, and their dividend and financing policies. These regulated monopolies are the public utilities such as electric and gas utilities, telephone and telegraph companies, and pipelines transporting natural gas. Where interstate commerce is involved, these monopolies are also regulated by the Federal Energy Regulatory Commission and the Federal Communications Commission.

Social regulatory agencies differ from older agencies: the latter usually have jurisdiction over specific industries, while the newer social regulatory agencies have jurisdiction over many businesses and industries.

The late 1960s and 1970s saw a widening of the scope of regulation with the passage of far-reaching social legislation. Agencies created by this legislation, such as the Equal Employment Opportunity Commission (**EEOC**), the Environmental Protection Agency (**EPA**), and the Occupational Safety and Health Administration (**OSHA**), possess major powers of control over many areas of a corporation's activities. For example, some corporations must make investments to modify plant and equipment or production techniques to meet standards set by the EPA and/or by the OSHA. Additionally, the Employment Retirement-Income Security Act, which became law in 1974, strengthened the legal obligation of employers to make annual contributions to pension funds designed to pay pension benefits to employees.

While all of this regulation has a profound impact on corporate investment and financing needs for the modern manager, the picture has changed somewhat in the last decade. Government has deregulated both the trucking and airline industries, opening these industries to increased competition. The AT&T divestiture in 1984 has been accompanied by a loosening of many regulatory restrictions on companies providing telecommunication services. Such shifts have dramatically affected the business decisions of managers who must now respond to market forces rather than to decisions made by regulators.

Regulation and the Changing Financial Environment

It is almost certain that the relationship between government regulation and the financial environment will change over time. In recent years we have seen significant changes in the roles of some specific financial institutions, at least in part due to changes in regulations. For example, for most of U.S. history commercial banks were the only institutions providing checking accounts, and most Americans who saved relatively small amounts of money placed their deposits in savings accounts at either banks or savings-and-loan associations. In the 1980s, things have changed. Sears, a retail chain, provides checking services and bill paying by telephone, sells you insurance, and has one of the largest credit-card operations in the country. American Express, of credit-card renown, has acquired a stock-brokerage house and owns a Boston bank. As a result, American Express can do just about everything a commercial bank can do, plus more. Banking firms, once confined to specific geographic locations for some of their operations, have diversified by acquiring banks in other states.

In such a dynamic financial environment, financial managers face the continuing challenge of keeping abreast of new developments.

Taxes

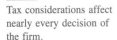

Tax considerations affect nearly every decision of the firm.

A cynical observer of life in the United States once observed, "Only two things in life are certain—death and taxes." In fact, tax considerations affect nearly every decision a firm makes and are especially important in financial-management decisions. Tax considerations also affect many decisions of individuals. Most nonprofit organizations, on the other hand, are exempt from many of the taxes to which firms and individuals are subject.

Different chapters in this book will be dealing with many aspects of taxation; here we will mention only some general considerations. The tax laws are so complex and their impact so important that nearly all firms and many individuals require expert tax advice that goes far beyond the discussion in this book.

Taxes have been much in the news in the 1980s. The Tax Reform Act of 1986 instituted sweeping changes in the structure of tax rates and other features of the tax code such as deductions and exemptions. These changes affect almost all Americans who pay taxes, individuals and firms alike. The changes brought about by the new law took effect in 1987 and 1988. Before getting into the specifics of the tax law, let us first go into a bit of background on tax reform in the United States.

Tax Reform in the United States

The U.S. tax code has been in a continuous state of evolution throughout this century. Tax rates reached a peak in the 1940s and 1950s (the top rate for individuals reached a peak of 94 percent during World War II!) and then began a slow and irregular decline over the next two decades. Maximum rates during the 1970s were

48 percent for corporations and, for individuals, 50 percent on "earned" income (wages and salary) and 70 percent on "unearned" income (interest, dividends, and the like).

During the late 1970s some economists and political leaders began to argue that high marginal tax rates distorted economic decisions and reduced efficiency. In 1981 the Reagan Administration proposed and Congress passed a major tax bill that lowered tax rates and also significantly reduced the total tax burden of both individuals and business. The resulting reduction in tax revenue to the government was a major factor in the very large deficits run by the federal government during the 1980s.

Some economists and politicians felt that rates should be reduced even further, and the tax code simplified and made more equitable. The Reagan Administration made tax reform its most important domestic priority at the beginning of its second term in 1984, and in late 1984 sent a bill to the Congress proposing a major overhaul of the entire tax code. The principal objectives of the overhaul were to lower marginal tax rates, while holding total tax revenue constant, and to simplify the code and reduce inequities.

The Congress debated tax reform throughout 1985 and into 1986. The House passed a bill in December 1985 that embodied the broad outlines of the Reagan proposal, and the Senate passed a similar bill in June 1986. The differences between the two were resolved in a joint conference committee during the summer of 1986, and the bill was signed into law by President Reagan in the fall.

Personal Taxes

In the United States, as in most other countries, the income of individuals is subject to taxes. Both the federal government and many states levy personal taxes. The amount of tax due normally is based on (1) taxable income, and (2) a schedule of tax rates. Tax rates under the 1986 Act (for years 1988 and beyond) are given in Table 2–3 on page 42.

A look at the Internal Revenue Service (IRS) Form 1040 (the personal income-tax form individuals must file with the U.S. government) will quickly reveal that tax calculations can be very complicated. The figure for taxable income is the result of subtracting **tax-deductible expenses** from one's taxable sources of income. Such expenses range from medical bills to interest costs on a loan taken to buy a home. Taxable sources of income include salaries and wages as well as "unearned" income, such as dividends received from owning stock or interest received from owning a corporate bond or a bank certificate of deposit.

Once taxable income is computed, Table 2–3 can be used to compute the tax due. For example, assume that a couple is filing jointly and has a taxable income of $60,000. Using Table 2–3, we can see that the tax would be $4,463 plus 28% of all income above $29,750 and the tax computation would be:

$$\text{Tax} = \$4,463 + 0.28(\$60,000 - \$29,750)$$

$$= \$4,463 + \$8,470$$

$$= \$12,933$$

Tax-deductible expenses— expenses that can legally be subtracted from total income to determine taxable income.

Table 2—3

Personal Federal Income Tax Schedule, 1988 and Subsequent Years

Individuals

Taxable Income	Tax
Up to $17,850	$0 + 15%
$17,851 to $43,150	$2,678 + 28% of all amounts over $17,850
$43,151 to $100,048*	$9,759 + 33% of all amounts over $43,150
$100,481 and up	$28,678 + 28% of all amounts over $100,480

Married Couples Filing Jointly

Taxable Income	Tax
Up to $29,750	$0 + 15%
$29,751 to $71,900	$4,463 + 28% of all amounts over $29,750
$71,901 to $171,090*	$16,265 + 33% of all amounts over $71,900
$171,091 and over	$48,998 + 28% of all amounts over $171,090

*The top of the 33% bracket is extended by $10,920 for each dependent claimed.

Marginal tax rate—the tax rate on the last dollar of income, or the change in a taxpayer's tax payment divided by the change in taxable income.

Average tax rate—a taxpayer's tax payment divided by taxable income.

Progressive tax rates—tax rates where the higher the amount of taxable income, the higher the percentage payable as taxes.

For this couple, the tax paid on each additional dollar of income, or the **marginal tax rate,** equals 28 percent. The **average tax rate** for this couple is $12,933/$60,000 = 21.6 percent. The average tax rate is lower than the marginal rate because some of the income, the first $29,750, is taxed at 15 percent. As the table shows, the highest marginal tax rate for personal taxes is 33%. State or local income tax would be in addition to this federal tax.

The U.S. tax code has generally provided for taxing personal income at **progressive tax rates**—that is, the higher the amount of one's taxable income, the higher the percentage payable as taxes. The law now in effect has three different rates, 15 percent, 33 percent, and 28 percent. It seems strange to have the top rate, 33 percent, kick in for "middle range" incomes, and then to drop back to 28 percent for higher incomes. This was necessary for technical reasons in order to make the rules work smoothly in conjunction with other rules on exemptions. While this may seem complicated, it is much simpler than the rates in effect in 1986 and earlier. Then there were no fewer than sixteen different tax rates for individuals, ranging from zero to 50 percent.

Sample Problem 2—1

Figuring Taxes for an Individual Under the 1986 Tax Act

Blaze Pascal, a computer programmer by trade, has just received a salary increase of $10,000. Her taxable income now is $50,000 versus $40,000 before the raise. Calculate Ms. Pascal's total tax, and her marginal and average tax rates before and after the raise.

Solution

Using Table 2–3, before the raise, Ms. Pascal's marginal tax rate was 28%. Her tax was $2,678 + 0.28 × ($40,000 − $17,850), or $8,880, and her average tax rate was $8,880/$40,000 = 0.222 = 22.2%.

After the raise, her marginal tax rate (from the table) will be 33% and her tax will be $9,759 + 0.33 × ($50,000 − $43,150) = $12,020. Her average tax rate will be $12,020/$50,000 = 0.24 = 24%.

	Taxable Income	Marginal Tax Rate	Tax	Average Tax Rate
Before raise	$40,000	28.0%	$ 8,880	22.2%
After raise	50,000	33.0%	12,020	24.0%

Business Taxes

The federal government and most state governments tax the income of all business firms.

The income of all firms is also taxed by the federal government and by most state governments. The income of proprietorships and partnerships is taxed as part of the owners' personal income. Corporations, on the other hand, pay specific corporate taxes on their income. The rate at which the income of proprietorships and partnerships is taxed depends on the personal-tax status of the owners. Corporate income is taxed by the federal government at specified rates.

Table 2–4 presents the revised federal income-tax schedule for corporations for 1988 and beyond. Rates for 1986 and earlier are also shown for comparison. As for individuals, corporate income is subject to many adjustments in figuring taxable income. Some of the most important of these are the adjustments for interest expenses and for depreciation. Under the old tax law, the highest marginal tax rate

Table 2–4
Federal Tax Rates for Corporations

Taxable Income	1986 and earlier	1988 and later
0–$25,000	15%	15%
$25,000–$50,000	18	15
$50,000–$75,000	30	25
$75,000–$100,000	40	34
$100,000–$335,000	46	39
Over $335,000	46	34

Notes: The old tax law imposed an additional tax of 5% on all income between $100,000 and $1,405,000. The 39% rate for income between $100,000–$335,000 under the 1986 law is caused by special rules for larger firms. Special rates were in effect for the transition year 1987 and are not shown above.

was 46%, but with the new law the highest rate will be 39%. For large corporations, the effective marginal tax rate will be 34%.

Table 2–4 compares the corporate tax rates currently in effect with rates for earlier periods. Based on the 1988 rates, the first $50,000 of income would be taxed at a 15 percent rate, the next $25,000 at a 25 percent rate, and so on. Thus, a firm with $100,000 of taxable income would figure its taxes as follows: 0.15($50,000) + 0.25($25,000) + 0.34($25,000) = $22,250. While the firm's marginal rate on the last dollar of income is 34 percent, its average rate is only $22,250/$100,000 = 22 percent. For large firms with incomes above $335,000, the marginal rate now is 34 percent, versus 46 percent prior to 1987. As the preceding calculations show, there can be quite a difference between marginal and average tax rates for small corporations.

Table 2–5 reports both marginal and average tax rates for different levels of taxable income using the 1988 tax rates. The marginal and average tax rates can vary greatly for corporations with smaller amounts of taxable income. On extra income the government collects tax dollars at the marginal rate; the average tax rate simply reflects the total tax bill as a fraction of taxable income.

Taxes are a key issue in business decisions, and the tax rate has a significant effect on net income after taxes. Where the applicable marginal tax rate is T, of each $1 of revenue, the government gets T and the firm keeps $1 (1 − T)$. To illustrate, if $T = 0.34$ (34 percent), then out of $100 of revenue, the government gets $34 and the owners keep $66. Likewise, $1 of expense costs the firm only $1 (1 − T)$. A $100 expense item reduces taxes by $34, so the net outlay by the owners is only $66. If IBM hires a new financial manager at a salary of $50,000 a year, the salary costs IBM only $50,000 (1 − 0.34) = $33,000 on an after-tax basis since salaries are tax-deductible (assuming that IBM is paying taxes at a 34 percent marginal rate). On the other hand, 34 percent of any new taxable income earned as a result of the new manager's efforts will go to the government as tax payments. Ultimately, cash flow after taxes is of greater concern to owners than before-tax cash flow. As the tax rates in Tables 2–4 and 2–5 suggest, tax considerations loom large in investment and financing decisions, but not so large as before. At 1986 rates, $100 in revenue yielded only $54 after taxes, versus $66

Table 2–5

1988 Marginal and Average Federal Tax Rates for Corporations

Taxable Income	Marginal Tax Rate	Average Tax Rate
$ 20,000	15%	15%
$140,000	15	15
$160,000	25	17
$180,000	34	19
$100,000	34	23
$200,000	39	31
$500,000	34	34

now; and a $100 expense cost only $54, versus $66 now. An important and very desirable effect of the lower tax rates is to reward effort more highly, and to penalize waste and inefficiency.

Sample Problem 2–2
Figuring Taxes for a Corporation

Advanced Personal Systems, Inc. (APS), a firm specializing in designing automated accounting systems for personal computers, is figuring its taxes for tax-year 1988. The firm's president, Ellen Cee, wants to know also what the firm's taxes would have been under the tax code in effect prior to 1987. The firm earned $400,000 before taxes in 1988, and $200,000 in 1986.

Compute taxes and average tax rates under both the 1986 Tax Act and the older code for both income levels, $400,000 and $200,000.

Solution

Using Table 2–4, in 1986 the firm's marginal rate was 46% under the prior tax code. The following calculations show what the firm's taxes were under the old and new codes at an income level of $200,000, and what they would have been if the firm had earned $400,000 in 1986:

Old Tax Code

| Tax Rate | $200,000 Income | | | $400,000 Income | | |
	Income Level	Tax		Income Level	Tax
15%	$ 25,000	$ 3,750		$ 25,000	$ 3,750
18	25,000	4,500		25,000	4,500
30	25,000	7,500		25,000	7,500
40	25,000	10,000		25,000	10,000
46	100,000	46,000		300,000	138,000
Total tax		$ 71,750			$163,750
Taxable income		$200,000			$400,000
Average tax rate		35.9%			40.9%

1986 Tax Act

| Tax Rate | $200,000 Income | | | $400,000 Income | | |
	Income Level	Tax		Income Level	Tax
15%	$ 50,000	$ 7,500		$ 50,000	$ 7,500
25	25,000	6,250		25,000	6,250
34	25,000	8,500		25,000	8,500
39	100,000	39,000		235,000	91,650
34	—	—		65,000	22,100
Total tax		$ 61,250			$136,000
Taxable income		$200,000			$400,000
Average tax rate		30.6%			34.0%

Note that, at an income level of $400,000, the average rate for APS under the 1986 Act is 34%, the same as its marginal rate. At lower income levels (say $200,000), and under the old tax code, the average rate was always lower than the marginal rate. We now can see what Congress had in mind in designing the rate structure under the 1986 Tax Act. It appears strange for the marginal rate to go up to 39% and then back down to 34%. The effect is to cause larger firms—those with pre-tax net incomes of $335,000 or greater—to pay taxes at an average rate of 34%. Hence such firms get no benefit from the lower marginal rates on income less than $335,000. ▪

Interest and Dividends

Interest and dividends deserve special mention. Interest paid on the debt obligations of a firm is deductible as an expense item to the firm for income-tax purposes, whereas dividends paid on common and preferred stock are not. Because this differential tax treatment has very important implications for the financing decisions of firms, we will discuss these matters in more depth later in this book.

With respect to dividend income, the current federal tax law exempts from taxation 80 percent of dividends received by a corporation on its holdings of preferred or common stock of other firms (versus 85 percent prior to 1987). This 80 percent exclusion is intended to reduce the effect of multiple taxation of the same income, since it already has been taxed once when earned by the corporation before the dividend was determined. Interest is fully taxable to the recipient.

Depreciation

Depreciation—the allocation of the cost of a long-lived asset to different time periods over the life of the asset.

The 1986 Act changed **depreciation** in three fundamental ways, but maintained the basic framework of the Accelerated Cost Recovery System (ACRS) in effect in 1986 and earlier. The first major change was the reclassification of **asset lives,** the length of time over which depreciation is calculated. Heavy trucks, for example, must be depreciated over a five-year period. In general asset lives were lengthened for depreciation purposes. This is usually costly to businesses because it postpones the tax savings due to the depreciation tax shield. The second major change in depreciation was allowing a faster percentage depreciation rate, and the third change was the adoption of an assumption about when assets are placed in service. Details of the current depreciation rules are given in an appendix to Chapter 11 (placed there because that is the chapter most concerned with depreciation), along with examples of depreciation calculations.

Other Factors

Prior to the 1986 law, *capital gains* were treated differently from ordinary income. In the case of firms, capital gains are gains on the sale of assets that are not used in the ordinary course of the firm's business. For individuals, capital gains or losses were gains or losses on assets such as stocks. Prior to 1987, capital gains were taxed at a lower rate than ordinary income, such as salary. Since 1987, capital gains and ordinary income have been treated identically under the federal tax code.

Investment tax credit (ITC)—a specified percentage of capital expenditures a firm is permitted to subtract from its tax liability; eliminated by the 1986 Tax Act.

Tax liability—the amount of tax a taxpayer must pay in a given period.

Prior to 1987, the **investment tax credit (ITC)** was a special provision in the tax laws that permitted a firm to subtract from its **tax liability** (the amount it owes in taxes, not its taxable income) a specified percentage of the purchase price of new capital assets of certain types. The investment tax credit was first instituted in 1962, eliminated in 1966, reinstituted in 1971, significantly liberalized in 1978, modified further in 1981, and eliminated again in 1986. Who knows? We may see it again in some future year.

Tax laws can affect dramatically the cash that a corporation or individual will receive as a result of any business decision. As a result, financial managers must be careful to incorporate the effects of taxes in analyzing corporate investment and financing decisions. The general thrust of the 1986 law was to eliminate many tax preferences (deductions and exemptions) and at the same time to lower marginal tax rates. The 1986 Act included a number of simplifying features that tend to raise taxes for both corporations and individuals. For corporations, the Act eliminated the investment tax credit, tightened depreciation, and reduced the deductibility of some expenses. For individuals, the new law reduced interest deductions for consumer purchases. In return for these factors tending to increase taxes, both individuals and corporations are now taxed at lower rates.

Interest Rates

Interest rate—the price of borrowing funds over time, usually a percentage of the amount borrowed.

There is no single interest rate, but rather a multitude of interest rates in financial markets.

In effect, interest rates are the prices at which one can borrow or lend. Major differences in interest rates on securities result from differences in the tax status, risk, and maturity of securities.

One item of major interest to individual investors and corporate financial managers is the rate at which they can lend or borrow money—that is, the **interest rate.** Actually, there is no single interest rate, but rather a multitude of interest rates in financial markets. For example, in early 1988 the *Wall Street Journal* reported the prime bank-loan rate (the rate charged by commercial banks to their prime customers) to be 8¾ percent (by tradition in financial circles, an interest rate will always refer to a one-year period unless explicitly stated otherwise). At the same time, commercial paper maturing in 30 to 59 days placed directly by companies such as General Motors Acceptance Corporation (a financial arm of General Motors) carried an interest rate of 6.9 percent, and high-quality long-term bonds issued by public utilities, such as power companies, had interest rates of around 9.9 percent. Figure 2–3 displays the interest rates on a number of different financial instruments.

Natural questions are: Why do the rates differ over time? Why is the rate on one sort of security different from that on another? Why, for example, in early 1988 could state and local governments issue municipal bonds and as a result borrow money at 7.7 percent while creditworthy corporations had to pay over 10 percent interest on their bonds?

In an ideal world, all securities should have about the same interest rate because of the natural pressures of buying and selling. If one security had a higher interest rate than all other securities, it would be in high demand by investors. Facing such high demand, the issuer of the security would be able to sell it at a lower interest rate, eventually driving down the interest rate on this security until it was equal to interest rates on other securities. In one sense, an interest rate is nothing more than the price of borrowing; in an ideal financial market, we would expect there to be only one price—that is, one interest rate. This ideal world,

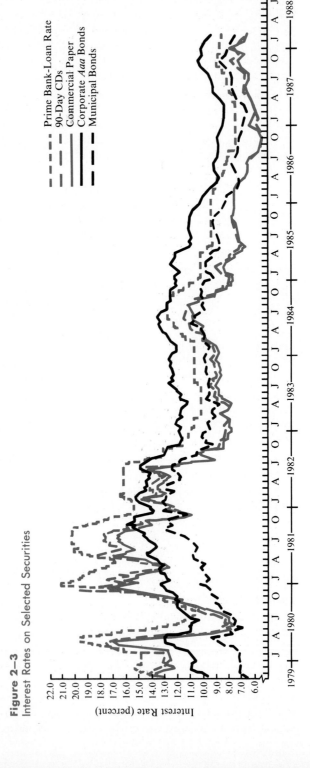

Figure 2–3
Interest Rates on Selected Securities

Prime Bank-Loan Rate
90-Day CDs
Commercial Paper
Corporate *Aaa* Bonds
Municipal Bonds

however, assumes away most of what makes a financial manager's job interesting and difficult. Major differences in interest rates on securities can be understood by examining such factors as the tax status, risk, and maturity of a security.

For example, the income received from owning a municipal bond is generally tax-free, while income from corporate bonds is taxable. As a result, a lower before-tax interest return on a municipal bond may be just as good to a taxed investor as a higher before-tax interest rate on a corporate bond. Given this differential tax treatment, municipal bonds typically carry lower interest rates than U.S. government bonds.

Maturity — the time period over which interest and principal payments are to be made on a loan or bond.

A subtler difference between interest rates depends on the **maturity** of the security. A 90-day certificate of deposit promises a given interest rate for only a 90-day period (even though it might be stated in annual terms, a rate of 12 percent per year is equivalent to 12 percent/4 = 3 percent for the next 90 days, or 1/4 of a year). A long-term corporate bond, on the other hand, promises a given annual interest rate over a 20-year period. If a buyer were comparing investment in a 90-day CD to investment in a 20-year corporate bond, he or she would have to compare two very different time horizons, and in the resultant comparison there is no assurance that the same stated interest rate on the two securities would make the buyer equally happy. For example, if I thought interest rates would go up 90 days from now, I might take a lower current interest rate on a 90-day CD (relative to a 20-year bond) in order to take best advantage of the ability to have money to invest at the higher rate 3 months hence. In practice, interest rates on different securities differ for a variety of reasons, including taxes, risk, and maturity.

At numerous points in our discussion of a financial manager's job, we will again have reason to discuss interest rates. After all, one of a financial manager's primary decisions is how best to raise money; interest rates reflect the cost of raising funds by borrowing.

In addition, rates of return required by individuals on their investments in shares of stock will be affected by interest rates, since individuals have the ability to shift funds between stocks and bonds depending on the opportunities for return available in each.

The financial market plays a critical role in determining the interest rates that affect managers' decisions.

Impact of Inflation on Financial Markets

Inflation—the general rate of increase in the level of prices of goods and services in the economy.

One factor that has had a tremendous impact on financial managers in recent years is **inflation** — the general rate of increase in the level of prices of goods and services in the economy. During most of the 1950s and 1960s, inflation was not a problem for financial managers, or for nearly anyone else for that matter. For the period 1926–1980, inflation averaged only about 3 percent per year, but in recent U.S. financial history, things have changed. Consider the data in Table 2–6 and compare inflation rates in the 1970s and 1980s with those of earlier years. Not only was the rate of general price increase higher in the later period, but it was

Table 2–6

Inflation Rates

Year	Inflation Rate (percent per year)
1955	0.4
1960	1.5
1965	1.9
1970	5.5
1971	3.4
1972	3.4
1973	8.8
1974	12.2
1975	7.0
1976	4.8
1977	6.8
1978	9.4
1979	13.4
1980	12.4
1981	8.9
1982	3.9
1983	3.8
1984	4.0
1985	3.7
1986	1.3
1987	4.4

Source: Federal Reserve Bank of St. Louis.

Inflation has led to a much more uncertain environment in which financial managers have to operate.

also much more variable. As a result, financial managers have faced an increasingly uncertain environment in which to operate. Predicting the course of future inflation has become a significantly more difficult task in recent years, adding to the complexity of a financial manager's job.

Inflation has a pervasive impact on individuals, firms, and other organizations. It affects everything from the revenues, costs, and profits of large corporations to the price of hot dogs at a ball game. Let us consider the problem of inflation from the viewpoint of the financial manager. Inflation has a number of important effects on financial markets, on interest rates, on returns to investors, on capital investment by firms, on corporate projects, and on debt and dividend policies.

Impact of Inflation on the Financial Market

For the financial manager, inflation has a very profound effect on interest rates.

Figure 2–4 displays the rate of change in consumer prices (inflation) and the level of short-term interest rates, as represented by the rates paid on commercial paper (a type of short-term borrowing) issued by large creditworthy corporations. Note how interest rates fell during the 1980s as inflation declined. Let us explore the relationship between inflation and interest rates.

Consider a lender and a borrower about to make a deal for a $1,000 loan. The lender asks the borrower to pay 3 percent interest in addition to the $1,000 princi-

Figure 2–4
Inflation and Short-Term Interest Rates

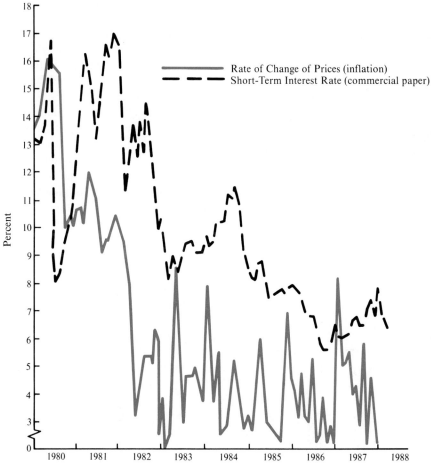

Source: National Economic Trends, U.S. Financial Data, Federal Reserve Bank of St. Louis, various
dates. Inflation is measured as the rate of change in the Consumer Price Index. The short-term interest rate is measured as the rate for 4-month commercial paper; beginning Jan. 1, 1983, the rate is for
1-month commercial paper.

pal when the borrower repays the loan in one year, and the borrower agrees. Both
expect zero inflation. But suppose that inflation unexpectedly occurs, and prices
rise by 2 percent over the ensuing year. The borrower repays the lender a total of
$1,030, as agreed. The lender discovers that this $1,030 is worth in real terms, after inflation, only $1,030/1.02 = $1,009.80. The lender's real return, adjusted
for inflation, is only about 1 percent.[1]

[1]We can determine the real return approximately, and fairly accurately, by subtracting the inflation rate
from the nominal return: 3 percent − 2 percent = 1 percent. The exact method involves division:
1.03/1.02 = 1.00980, so the investor has a rate of return of 1.0098 − 1 = 0.0098 = 0.98 percent.

Inflation premium — an additional charge for anticipated or expected inflation that investors add to the real rate of return they are requiring.

The lender expected 3 percent but received only 1 percent. What does he or she do next time? The answer is, the lender includes an **inflation premium** in the contract rate. If the lender expects 2 percent inflation over the next year, he or she asks 5 percent. If inflation does turn out to be 2 percent, the lender will receive a real return of $5 - 2 = 3$ percent, which is the required rate.

Is the borrower willing to pay the extra 2 percent? If he or she can invest the funds in something that itself generates a return that includes the inflation premium, or in assets (such as inventories) whose price is rising with inflation, the answer is yes. The borrower's real cost, adjusted for inflation, is $5 - 2 = 3$ percent.

Nominal interest rate — the interest rate observed in financial markets.

Imagine this sort of reasoning and negotiating process being repeated in thousands of individual transactions throughout the economy. The result is that expectations regarding inflation gradually work themselves into the entire structure of market interest rates, affecting the relationship between **nominal interest rates** and **real interest rates.** The *nominal* interest rate is the rate we observe in the financial markets, the actual contract rate on the loan, bond, or savings account. The *real* interest rate is the nominal rate minus the inflation rate.

Real interest rate — the rate of increase in the ability to purchase goods and services, or the nominal interest rate minus the expected rate of inflation.

When inflation is widely anticipated in the future, all nominal rates move up to include an inflation premium. In the absence of inflation, the rate on long-term U.S. government bonds would undoubtedly be rather low, as would the rate on corporate bonds with the best credit ratings, such as IBM bonds. Where were these rates in the 1980s? Table 2–7 provides some interest-rate figures.

Rates are higher in the 1980s than they were in the 1950s for one main reason: inflation. At certain times in the 1980s, lenders expected inflation on the order of 5 to 10 percent per year. To protect themselves, they included an inflation premium in the rate they demanded. Borrowers, anticipating the receipt of an inflation premium themselves, were willing to pay it.

Expectations about inflation are incorporated in market interest rates.

The result is that all market rates include an inflation premium reflecting the market's consensus judgment regarding future inflation rates. This premium is best seen in long-term rates, because short-term rates are more subject to supply and demand pressures induced by the monetary policy of the Federal Reserve. The course of future inflation is unknown, and we hope that in the future we will be able to discuss high levels of inflation totally in the past tense. Inflation remains an ever-present prospect, however, and a critical consideration for financial managers.

Table 2–7

Interest Rates and Inflation (percent per year)

	1955	1981	1982	1983	1984	1985	1986	1987
Interest rate on 90-day Treasury bill	2.4	11.4	8.0	8.9	7.7	7.0	6.0	5.8
Interest rate on long-term Treasury bond	3.0	13.7	10.5	11.78	11.4	9.5	7.3	9.1
Interest rate on *Aaa* corporate bond	3.2	14.5	11.8	12.5	12.2	10.0	9.0	9.3
Inflation rate	0.4	8.9	3.9	3.8	4.0	3.7	1.3	4.4

Note: Interest rates are year-end. Inflation rate is for prior 12 months.

Source: Federal Reserve Bank of St. Louis.

Finance in Practice 2—2

The Real Rate of Interest

The real rate of return actually earned on financial assets depends on two things: (1) payments received by investors (interest and principal on bonds, dividends and price appreciation on stocks), and (2) the rate of inflation. If the rate of inflation turns out to be high, realized real returns will be low, assuming no change in payments received.

Looking ahead, no one knows what the real return on financial assets is going to be, in part because no one knows what the inflation rate will turn out to be. In the case of risky assets,

such as common stocks and real estate, the payments themselves are uncertain. Some uncertainty is also attached to corporate bonds because companies sometimes do default. There is no uncertainty, we all fervently hope, in the payments to be made on U.S. government securities. Nevertheless, the real return to be earned in the future on government securities is uncertain because future inflation is uncertain.

Since future inflation is so important to the real returns to be earned looking ahead, investors are constantly attempting to estimate what the inflation rate will turn out to be. Investors' estimates of future inflation are reflected in market (stated) interest rates. If investors expect inflation to be low, they will add a small inflation premium to the required real rate, and stated rates will be only slightly above real rates. This situation prevailed in the mid-1950s, as shown in Table 2–7. When inflation increased rapidly during the 1970s, investors consistently underestimated it, and nominal rates rose less

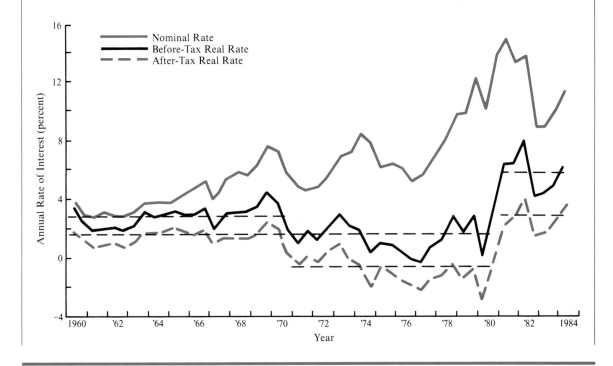

rapidly than inflation. During some periods in the late 1970s, the realized real rate was actually negative! By 1981, investors had learned a lot, estimates of inflation had caught up, and market rates reflected a substantial inflation premium, as indicated in Table 2–7.

Thus, realized real interest rates are affected by actual inflation rates, while nominal market interest rates are affected by anticipated inflation, looking ahead. Many years ago, a well-known economist, Irving Fisher, suggested that the nominal rate of interest would always equal the real rate plus the expected rate of inflation.

Nominal rates can be determined by looking them up in the newspaper. The real rate, however, like the inflation rate, we can only estimate by looking ahead. If we can estimate one of the two, we can use Fisher's relationship to estimate the third. If we knew the real rate,

we could infer the inflation rate the markets appear to expect. If we knew what inflation the market expected, we could calculate the real rate of interest. Fisher's relationship is used in both of these ways.

In one recent study, opinions of a large group of economists regarding expected inflation were collected, averaged, and used as the estimate of future inflation in Fisher's equation. The study yielded the estimates of real interest rates in the accompanying figure. (The horizontal dashed lines represent average levels of before- and after-tax real interest rates over selected time periods.)

Source: Irving Fisher, *The Theory of Interest* (New York: Macmillan, 1930); A. S. Holland, "Real Interest Rates—What Accounts for Their Recent Rise?" *Review,* Federal Reserve Bank of St. Louis, December 1984, 18–29. The data for the figure comes from the Federal Reserve Bank of St. Louis.

KEY CONCEPTS

1. Financial managers must operate in a complex world of laws, regulations, taxes, institutions, and highly competitive financial markets.

2. The main forms of business organization are the sole proprietorship, the partnership, and the corporation. Corporations are by far the dominant form in terms of income, output, and assets.

3. A major function of financial markets is to allow surplus spending units to provide funds to deficit spending units.

4. Financial intermediaries facilitate the flow of funds from surplus to deficit units. There are many types of financial intermediaries, including banks, insurance companies, mutual funds, and investment bankers.

5. The financial market is divided into the money market (for trades of securities of less than one year's maturity) and the capital market (for trades of longer-term securities).

6. An increasing amount of financial activity is taking place in international financial markets.

7. Government regulation and taxes play an important role in many business decisions.

8. Interest rates in financial markets differ for a variety of reasons, including taxes, risk, and maturity.

9. Inflation has a major impact on financial markets.

SUMMARY

Business firms may be organized as sole proprietorships, partnerships, or corporations. Proprietorships are the simplest and most prevalent in terms of the number of firms. Corporations, though fewer in number, are much larger, on the average, and produce by far the largest part of the nation's output of goods and services. The major distinctions among the three forms of organization concern taxes and the liability of owners for debts of the firm. Proprietorships and partnerships pay no taxes themselves; taxes on income earned by such firms are paid by the owners personally. Corporations pay taxes on income earned, and, under present law, any profits distributed as dividends are taxed again as income to owners. Proprietors and general partners have unlimited liability for the debts and acts of the firm. The liability of shareholders or corporations, on the other hand, is limited to their investment in the firm. The corporate form provides other advantages in terms of transferability of ownership and access to capital markets.

An appreciation of the financial environment in which the firm operates is important to the financial manager. The financial system transmits the savings of surplus spending units (mainly households) to investing units (mainly firms and government). Financial markets provide the meeting place for suppliers and users of funds to make their transactions. Suppliers of funds receive claims against the assets and future income of borrowers. The participants in the financial markets include the operating sectors, the financial intermediaries, and the specialized institutions. The operating sectors comprise the ultimate suppliers and users of funds. Financial intermediaries act as conduits to channel funds from suppliers to users. Financial intermediaries also play a key role in the economy by reducing the costs to lenders and borrowers of search, acquisition, analysis, and diversification. By their actions, financial intermediaries provide higher interest returns to lenders and lower interest costs to borrowers. Specialized institutions, the third category of participants, act to facilitate the flow of funds. Some, though not all, financial claims are publicly traded in markets that can be classified under two general headings, the money market and the capital market. The money market makes possible transactions involving short-term, highly marketable debt instruments. The capital market involves transactions in longer-term debt issues and stocks.

Government regulation is another important factor in the financial-management decisions of certain specialized types of firms, such as public utilities and financial institutions. All firms whose securities are publicly owned are subject to regulation by the Securities and Exchange Commission.

Taxes on income and capital gains are an important factor in business decisions. Ultimately, owners are concerned about after-tax cash flow. Tax laws are so complex that tax implications constitute an important aspect of financial analysis.

One important responsibility of the financial manager is to be familiar with the levels and movement of interest rates, because interest rates reflect the cost of borrowing funds.

Inflation has profound effects on financial markets, on the level of interest rates, on returns to investors, on returns to capital investment by firms, and on financial planning. The ability to cope with inflation is an important skill for financial managers.

QUESTIONS

1. What are the three basic forms of business organization in the United States? In what essential respects do they differ and how does each affect the risk assumed by the investor?

2. Why are our largest businesses organized as corporations?

3. Why is it said that income earned by corporations is subject to double taxation? Name a situation where triple taxation exists.

4. In terms of the number of firms, sole proprietorships represent the dominant form of business organization in the United States. Can you explain why this is so?

5. Economists sometimes argue that a reduction in the marginal tax rate on income leads to more efficient decisions by individuals and firms. Disregarding the impact on government revenues, why might this be so?

6. Discuss the tax implications of a dollar of dividends received and paid by a corporation. How is interest paid and interest income treated for tax purposes for the corporation and an individual?

7. Explain marginal versus average tax rates. Which is usually used in financial decision making?

8. What is the difference between a tax deduction and a tax credit?

9. What economic units are, in the aggregate, the net providers of funds in the U.S. economy? Which are the net users of funds?

10. What are the principal functions of the financial markets? What is traded in these markets? Name several financial markets. Where are they located?

11. Why does government often regulate financial markets and intermediaries? What are the economic trade-offs (costs vs. benefits) for the market participants with regulation, and recently, deregulation?

12. What is the function of financial intermediaries in the financial system?

13. What are the major types of financial intermediaries in the financial system?

14. Differentiate nominal interest rates from real interest rates. Which are listed in the financial press?

15. How does inflation affect interest rates?

16. If actual inflation exceeds expectations, who is better off — lenders or borrowers?

Problems

1. Using the recent corporate tax rates in the text, calculate the amount of taxes on $100,000 of taxable income. On $1,000,000 of taxable income.

2. What are the marginal and average tax rates for the two amounts in problem (1) above?

3. DRD Corp. has an average tax rate of 30 percent and a marginal tax rate of 34 percent. Management is considering a decision that is expected to add $44,000 in taxable income. What is their after-tax estimate of additional income?

4. Records of Sam's Pizza are listed in the table. Calculate Sam's taxes for 1989 and the after-tax income of the company. Use the current corporate tax rate in the text after determining the taxable income. (Hint: Prepare an income statement and calculate taxable income.)

Sam's Pizza Inc.

Sales	$96,000
Interest expense	4,500
Common dividends paid	4,000
Cost of goods sold	42,000
Salaries	27,000
Interest income	2,600
Advertising expense	3,500
Dividend income	1,200
Preferred dividends paid	2,000

5. If an investor wanted a real after-tax return of 4 percent, expected inflation to be 4 percent, and was in the 28 percent marginal tax bracket, what interest rate would he or she charge the U.S. Treasury for a one-year loan? (Hint: The investor will pay taxes on interest received.)

REFERENCES

For an overview of financial markets and institutions see R. O. Edmister, *Financial Institutions: Markets and Management* (2nd ed.), New York: McGraw-Hill Book Company, 1986.

2/Time and Risk

3 Time: Fundamentals of Discounted Cash Flow

4 Value in Markets

5 Risk

The next three chapters will lay some important groundwork for much of this book. Part Two focuses on two main topics: *time* and *risk*.

As we saw in Chapter 1, the value of any asset is affected by both the time you have to wait to receive the benefits of owning that asset and the risk that those benefits will not be received at all. For example, suppose I promise to pay you $100. How much is that promise worth? Among other things, that depends on how long you have to wait to get

the money and how likely you think it is that I will honor my promise in full. That is, the value of the promise depends on time and risk.

Since time and risk affect value, they are especially important to financial managers because, as we discussed in Chapter 1, the objective of financial managers is to maximize the value of the firm to existing shareholders. Financial-management decisions about how to invest money or raise money will affect the value of the firm. Since these decisions involve both time and risk, we must understand the effects of time and risk on value.

Consider an automobile company that is analyzing a proposal to redesign its cars to increase gas mileage. Such a project will require huge dollar outlays now. The benefits will come in future years *if* the redesigning effort works and *if* the company's automobile sales improve as a result of the effort. Should the company

adopt the proposal? The answer is yes if the proposal will increase the value of the firm. The financial manager's job is to estimate the likelihood of an increase in value. This estimate requires trading off dollar costs today against risky dollar benefits in future time periods.

Chapter 3 will develop the concepts of discounted cash flow, our basic technology for dealing with time. Chapter 4 then can use this tool to develop *valuation* as the basic

conceptual framework of financial management. Chapter 4 also discusses how *risk* and *risk aversion* affect values. Chapter 5 provides a more thorough discussion of risk.

The tools and concepts developed in these three chapters will give us an ability to deal with time and risk. Developing this ability will set the stage for analyzing corporate decisions and their effects on the value of the firm.

3

Time: Fundamentals of Discounted Cash Flow

In this chapter we examine the time value of money. The chapter begins with the basic concepts of compound interest and uses these concepts to develop the notions of future value and present value. We then outline the steps for calculating the future and present values of both single sums of money and streams of payments over time. We pay special attention to the cases of level streams of equal payments (annuities) and level streams that continue forever (perpetuities). Finally, this chapter shows how these basic techniques of discounted cash flow can be applied to practical problems in finance.

Most financial decisions involve risky benefits and costs that are spread out over time. When people buy stocks, they pay money today (the price of the stock) and expect benefits in the future (dividends plus a rising stock price). When financial managers consider purchasing a new piece of equipment, money is spent today and benefits (for example, cost savings) are expected in the future. Facing such decisions, we need to have some way of gauging whether the decisions are good ones. In terms of financial management, does the decision create value? Restated, does the positive value of the benefits exceed the negative value of the costs?

Getting estimates of value is a difficult task. In finance, one of the essential methods of obtaining such estimates is **discounted cash flow (DCF).** DCF assumes that the value of an asset depends not on its cost or its past usefulness, but on its *future* usefulness. For example, suppose you own a share of stock in IBM. Its value today depends on what dividend payments IBM may make in the future and on the price for which you can sell the stock — *not* on what you paid for the stock when you bought it. This value is obtained by taking the *cash* flows associated with the assets and penalizing them, or *discounting* them, if you have to wait for the cash or if you are uncertain about whether the cash will actually be there even if you wait. Thus, discounted cash flow is a way of evaluating future benefits in terms of time and risk.

Discounted cash flow (DCF) — a method of estimating the value of an asset by taking the cash flows associated with the asset and discounting them for time and risk.

Time Value of Money

Money has time value: a dollar today is worth more than a dollar in the future.

This chapter will focus on the way discounted cash flow handles time. The key point to understanding the time value of money is that a dollar today is worth more than a dollar in the future because waiting for future dollars involves forgoing the opportunity to earn a rate of return. If, for example, I gave you $1 today and you could put it in the bank and earn 6 percent interest per year, at the end of a year you would have $1.06. As a result, a dollar today is able to become more than a dollar in one year because of the interest rate. In this case, the interest rate of 6 percent per year is the **opportunity cost** of waiting for future dollars — it is a return that you would have to forgo if you choose to receive money in the future rather than to receive money today.

Opportunity cost — the return on the best alternative investment forgone by making the chosen investment.

Interest rate — the rate at which individuals or firms will be compensated for exchanging money now for money to be received later.

Compound Interest

The **interest rate** is simply the rate at which an individual or firm will be compensated for exchanging money it has now for money it will receive later. The original amount is known as the **principal**. At the end of the first time period, a dollar amount of interest is calculated and added to the principal amount. This dollar amount of interest is calculated as the interest rate times the principal. **Compound interest** is interest that is earned in the next period on the prior period's interest as well as on the principal.

Principal — the initial amount of money loaned or borrowed.

To illustrate, suppose you deposited $100.00 (the principal amount) in a bank account that promised to pay 6 percent per year compounded annually; that is, the account promises to pay 6 percent interest on the principal balance and on any ac-

Compound interest—
interest figured on both the
initial principal and the
interest earned in prior
periods. Interest on interest
is the key feature of
compound interest.

cumulated interest at the end of each year. At the end of the first year, you would
have $100.00 principal plus $6.00 interest (6 percent of $100.00), or $106.00 total.

The bank has simply paid you interest of 6 percent (or 0.06 in decimal notation)
of the principal amount (0.06 × $100 = $6.00). In total, the bank owes you
$106.00—your original balance plus interest. This $106.00 balance can also be
calculated as $100(1 + 0.06) = $106.00 where the 1 in parentheses represents
the repayment of principal and the 0.06 figure represents the addition of interest at
6 percent per year.

The distinguishing feature of compound interest can be seen by looking at how
much money you would have in the bank at the end of two years. At the end of
the second year, the bank would calculate your balance as $106.00 (the balance at
the beginning of the second year) plus $6.36 interest (6 percent of $106.00), or
$112.36 total.

Note that the bank compounds your account at the end of the first year, calculating
a balance of $106.00. You then earn interest during the second year on this entire
$106.00, not just on the original deposit of $100.00. As a result, at the end of two
years you have a balance of $112.36. This amount is $0.36 more than the $112
you would get if you earned only the same interest in year two as you did in year
one ($100 + $6 + $6 = $112). The $0.36 difference is precisely the interest
earned during the second year on the interest paid in the first year ($0.36 =
0.06 × $6). Of course, you have to leave this $6 in the bank account to earn the
$0.36. While this $0.36 doesn't seem like much, we'll soon see that the power of
compounding, or earning interest on interest, can be quite amazing. Table 3–1, for
example, shows our bank account extended over a 10-year period. As can be seen
in column (3) of Table 3–1, interest in year 10 is $10.14, or $4.14 greater than the
$6.00 interest in year one. The $4.14 difference is interest on the interest paid in
the first 9 years.

Table 3–1
Illustration of Compound Interest Calculations

Year (1)	Beginning Value (dollars) (2)	Interest Earned at 6 Percent (dollars) (3) = (2) × 0.06	Ending Value (dollars) (4) = (2) + (3)
1	100.00	6.00	106.00
2	106.00	6.36	112.36
3	112.36	6.74	119.10
4	119.10	7.15	126.25
5	126.25	7.57	133.82
6	133.82	8.03	141.85
7	141.85	8.51	150.36
8	150.36	9.02	159.38
9	159.38	9.56	168.94
10	168.94	10.14	179.08

Figure 3–1
Time Line of Compound-Interest Calculations at 6 Percent Annual Interest

Panel A: One Period

Panel B: Two Periods

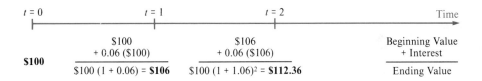

A useful way to look at the process of compound interest is to use a time line that shows cash amounts at different points in time. Figure 3–1 shows the bank-account example on a time line. Moving to the right on the time line means moving forward in time. For convenience, we have chosen to divide time into one-year periods (time 0 = now, time 1 = 1 year from now, and so on), although we could have chosen any other time interval (day, month, quarter) that suited our purposes. A year is convenient because in this case compounding occurs at the end of each year. Panel A in Figure 3–1 shows the status of the bank account after one year, while Panel B carries the account through two years.

Figure 3–1 simply restates our earlier calculations and shows that at the end of one year the bank balance will be $106.00 (Panel A) and that at the end of two years the bank-account balance will be $112.36 (Panel B).

Future Value

The notation in Figure 3–1 shows some specific relationships between the initial deposit ($100) and the bank-account balance at any future time. Specifically, the balance at the end of the second year can be calculated as $112.36 = $100(1 + 0.06)^2$. In general terms, we can express the relationships which are shown in Figure 3–1 as shown in Equation (1).

The future value (FV) of a certain present dollar amount that earns interest at rate i compounded periodically for n periods can be calculated as

$$FV = \text{present dollar amount} \times (1 + i)^n$$

$$= \text{present dollar amount} \times FVF(i, n) \qquad (1)$$

where $FVF(i, n)$ stands for future-value factor at an interest rate of i for n periods. $FVF(i, n)$ is calculated as $FVF = (1 + i)^n$ and is just a name we give to the mathematical result of calculating $(1 + i)^n$.

In terms of our example in Figure 3–1, the present dollar amount is \$100. The future-value factor $FVF(i, n) = (1 + i)^n = (1 + 0.06)^2 = 1.1236$, since the interest rate $i = 0.06$ (note that we put the interest rate in decimal form) and $n = 2$ years since we are going two years in the future. Applying Equation (1), we can solve for the future amount accumulated in 2 periods.

$$FV = \text{present dollar amount} \times (1 + i)^n$$

$$FV = \text{present dollar amount} \times FVF(i, n)$$

$$= \$100 \times FVF(0.06, 2)$$

$$= \$100 \times 1.1236$$

$$= \$112.36$$

Future value (FV) — the value of a certain current dollar amount compounded forward through time at an appropriate interest rate. It is the amount to which a payment or series of payments will grow by a given future date.

Future-value factor — for a single cash flow, the number by which a given present value is multiplied to determine the amount into which that present value will grow in the future (future value). A future-value factor $FVF(i, n)$ is calculated as $(1 + i)^n$.

Equation (1) allows us to calculate directly the **future value** (**FV**) that we can accumulate if we have a certain present dollar amount and can earn interest at rate i for n periods. To apply Equation (1), we need to be able to calculate future-value factors ($FVF(i, n)$). Fortunately, computers and many hand calculators can perform such a calculation almost instantly. Additionally, Appendix Table III at the end of this book provides **future-value factors** — the calculated values of $(1 + i)^n$ for different interest rates and periods. Table 3–2 reproduces part of Appendix Table III and shows that $FVF(0.06, 10) = 1.791$. We find this by looking at the intersection of the 6% column and 10 period row. In 10 years, we would have accumulated 1.791 dollars for each dollar deposited in year 0. In our example, we deposited \$100 in year 0, so we would have \$100(1.791) = \$179.10 in year 10. Except for rounding, this \$179.10 is precisely the same figure shown in year 10 of Table 3–1.[1]

The Power of Compound Interest

Over long periods, compound interest is very powerful. Adding 6 percent each year does not sound like much, but a look at Table 3–2 shows that it can be quite impressive. After 15 years, $FVF(0.06, 15) = 2.397$, which means that a dollar will have more than doubled. After 25 years, $FVF(0.06, 25) = 4.292$, showing your money will have grown by a factor of more than four. If you were lucky enough to earn 10% for 25 years, you would see your money increase more than ten times, $FVF(0.10, 25) = 10.835$. As these calculations show, the higher the interest rate and the longer the length of the investment, the more money an investor can obtain for each dollar invested.

Figure 3–2 shows that over longer periods, the power of interest can be impressive. For example, if you could earn 6 percent compound interest per

[1]The figures in Table 3–2 are rounded to three decimals and are, thus, less accurate than the calculations done by most calculators. The reader should be aware that such rounding differences are not important when small amounts of money are involved but may represent huge sums of money when millions of dollars are involved.

Table 3–2

Excerpts from Appendix Table III: Future Value $FVF(i, n)$ (at interest rate of i per period) at the End of n Periods of One Dollar Received Today

n	$i = 1\%$	2%	3%	4%	5%	6%	7%	8%	9%	10%
1	1.010	1.020	1.030	1.040	1.050	1.060	1.070	1.080	1.090	1.100
2	1.020	1.040	1.061	1.082	1.103	1.124	1.145	1.166	1.188	1.210
3	1.030	1.061	1.093	1.125	1.158	1.191	1.225	1.260	1.295	1.331
4	1.041	1.082	1.126	1.170	1.216	1.263	1.311	1.361	1.417	1.464
5	1.051	1.104	1.159	1.217	1.276	1.338	1.403	1.469	1.539	1.611
6	1.062	1.126	1.194	1.265	1.340	1.419	1.501	1.587	1.677	1.772
7	1.072	1.149	1.230	1.316	1.407	1.504	1.606	1.714	1.828	1.949
8	1.083	1.172	1.267	1.369	1.478	1.594	1.718	1.851	1.993	2.144
9	1.094	1.195	1.305	1.423	1.551	1.690	1.839	1.999	2.172	2.358
10	1.105	1.219	1.344	1.480	1.629	**1.791**	1.967	2.159	2.367	2.594
11	1.116	1.243	1.384	1.540	1.710	1.898	2.105	2.332	2.580	2.853
12	1.127	1.268	1.426	1.602	1.796	2.012	2.252	2.518	2.813	3.138
13	1.138	1.294	1.469	1.665	1.886	2.133	2.410	2.720	3.066	3.452
14	1.150	1.320	1.513	1.732	1.980	2.261	2.579	2.937	3.342	3.798
15	1.161	1.346	1.558	1.801	2.079	2.397	2.759	3.172	3.643	4.177
16	1.173	1.373	1.605	1.873	2.183	2.540	2.952	3.426	3.970	4.595
17	1.184	1.400	1.653	1.948	2.292	2.693	3.159	3.700	4.328	5.054
18	1.196	1.428	1.702	2.026	2.407	2.854	3.380	3.996	4.717	5.560
19	1.208	1.457	1.754	2.107	2.527	3.026	3.617	4.316	5.142	6.116
20	1.220	1.486	1.806	2.191	2.653	3.207	3.870	4.661	5.604	6.728
21	1.232	1.516	1.860	2.279	2.786	3.400	4.141	5.034	6.109	7.400
22	1.245	1.546	1.916	2.370	2.925	3.604	4.430	5.437	6.659	8.140
23	1.257	1.577	1.974	2.465	3.072	3.820	4.741	5.871	7.258	8.954
24	1.270	1.608	2.033	2.563	3.225	4.049	5.072	6.341	7.911	9.850
25	1.282	1.641	2.094	2.666	3.386	4.292	5.427	6.849	8.623	10.835

Note: Future value $FVF(i, n)$ is calculated as $(1 + i)^n$.

year for 70 years you would earn over $59 for each dollar initially invested: $FVF(0.06, 70) = 59.076$. Such a powerful effect of compounding is certainly a great incentive to save! Of course we must be careful in interpreting the real benefits of compound interest in an inflationary world. To illustrate, suppose there were inflation at a 7 percent rate for 25 years: $FVF(0.07, 25) = 5.427$ shows that something that costs a dollar today would cost 5.427 dollars in 25 years. Thus if we had earned 10% for 25 years and hence accumulated $10.835 for every dollar invested, we would only have approximately doubled our ability to purchase real goods — if there had been 7 percent inflation. This is because $10.835 divided by $5.427 = 1.996$.

Length of Time to Double

Suppose I offer you a contract that promises to pay you double your money back in 20 years. Am I being generous? The answer can be found by knowing what interest rate I am offering. In this and other situations it is sometimes useful to know

Figure 3–2
Compound Growth of $1 at 6 Percent Annual Interest, $FVF(0.06, n) = (1 + 0.06)^n$

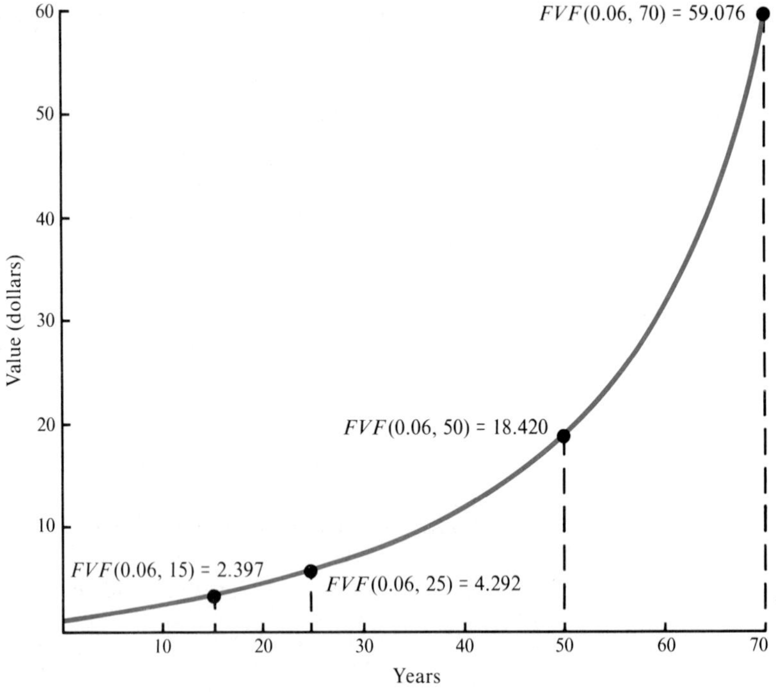

how long it will take something to double in value. Table 3–3 shows selected interest rates and how long it takes money to double at those rates. A rough rule of thumb for calculating the time to double is to divide the interest rate into 70. We get 70 years at 1 percent, 35 years at 2 percent, 17.5 years at 4 percent, and so on. We can see from Table 3–3 that the approximation is fairly close at low interest rates but not so close at rates above 10 percent.

Now let us return to the question of whether a promise to double your money in 20 years is generous. Using our rule of thumb, if money doubles in 20 years, the interest rate being offered is approximately 3.5 percent per year—70 divided by 20 = 3.5. If you can earn higher interest rates than 3.5 percent by investing elsewhere, the promise of doubling your money in 20 years is not so generous. For example, if you can earn 5 percent per year, Table 3–2 (or Appendix Table III at the end of the book) shows that you could accumulate $2.653 in year 20 for every dollar invested today—clearly better than just doubling your funds.

Frequency of Compounding

In Equation (1) above, we carefully defined n as the number of periods and i as the rate per period. In many financial contracts, the period is a year. However, the

Table 3–3

Time for Money to Double

Interest Rate (percent)	Time Required to Double (years)
1	69.7
2	35.0
4	17.7
6	11.9
8	9.0
10	7.3
15	5.0
20	3.8

period can be defined anyway we wish: as a year, a quarter, a month, or even a day. Sometimes we will find situations in which interest is compounded over a period shorter than one year.

In practice, interest rates are expressed in terms of percent per year. For example, a savings-and-loan association might offer interest at the rate of 8 percent per year but might offer to compound interest *semiannually*. If we deposit $100 in such an account, how much will we have at the end of a year (2 six-month periods)? To use Equation (1), we need to make sure that n corresponds to the number of time periods in the future and that i corresponds to the interest rate relevant for each of those time periods. Since we are looking 2 six-month periods into the future, $n = 2$ and the interest rate is 4 percent per six-month period ($i = 0.08/2 = 0.04$). We can apply Equation (1) to determine that the future value in one year of $100 invested today will be $108.16, as is shown below.

$$FV = \$100(1 + 0.04)^2$$

$$FV = \$100 \times FVF(i = 0.04, n = 2)$$

$$= \$100 \times 1.0816$$

$$= \$108.16$$

Note that the interest rate per period is 8 percent divided by 2, or 4 percent, and that the number of periods is 2. Also note that we get $108.16 and not the $108.00 we would get if we used 8 percent per year and did not worry about semiannual compounding. Let's explore the issue of compounding in more detail.

In general, in developing Equation (1) we assumed that the interest rate was named over the same time period as it was compounded—for example, 8 percent per *year* compounded *annually*. When we encounter a situation like 8 percent interest per year compounded semiannually, we need to distinguish between the **interest period,** or the calendar period over which the interest rate is named, and the **compounding period,** or the calendar period over which compounding occurs.

Interest period—the calendar period over which an interest rate is named.

Compounding period—the calendar period over which compounding occurs.

To calculate future value when the compounding period is not the same as the interest period, as a rule we (1) convert the named interest rate to the rate per compounding period and then (2) use Equation (1), letting *n* be the number of compounding periods that have elapsed and letting *i* be the interest rate per compounding period.

For example, suppose we deposited $100 in a bank account paying 8 percent per year compounded quarterly. Since a quarter (3 months) is a compounding period, the bank would give us one fourth of the annual interest rate (0.08/4 = 0.02 = 2 percent) for the first quarter and then compound our account; the bank would pay us (2 percent) for the second quarter and then compound our account; and so on. As Figure 3–3 displays, at the end of a year (four quarters), the bank would owe us an amount we could calculate from Equation (1) as

$$FV = \$100(1 + 0.02)^4$$

$$FV = \$100 \; FVF(0.02, 4)$$

$$= \$100 \times 1.0824 = \$108.24$$

In our example, $n = 4$ quarters in a year and $i = 0.08/4 = 0.02 =$ the interest rate per quarter. In fact, Figure 3–3 is like Figure 3–1, except in Figure 3–3 we divide time into three-month periods rather than into years. Thus, Equation (1) can handle all sorts of compounding situations as long as we are careful to think of dividing time into compounding periods.

Effective Interest Rates

One thing that is clear from the example above is that 8 percent per year can mean different things depending on the compounding period assumed.

Consider the results for annual, semiannual, and quarterly compounding shown in Table 3–4. When interest is compounded semiannually on a $100 deposit at an annual rate of 8 percent, the depositor has accumulated $108.16 by the end of one year. The annual **effective interest rate** is 8.16 percent per year: $100(1 + 0.0816) = $108.16. In other words, 8 percent per year compounded semiannually

Effective interest rate — the rate compounded *once* per interest period that provides the same dollar payoff as a financial contract (such as a bank account).

Figure 3–3
Quarterly Compounding

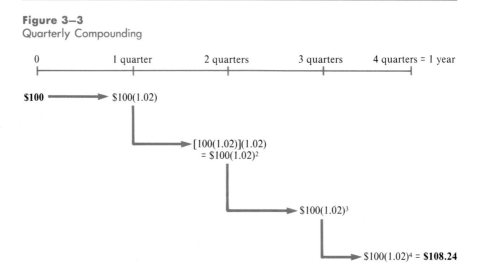

Table 3–4

Comparison of Results for Different Compounding Periods

Initial Investment (dollars)	Interest Rate per Year (percent)	Frequency of Compounding	Interest Rate per Compounding Period	Money at the End of One Year (dollars)	Effective Annual Interest Rate (percent)
100	8	Annually	8	$100(1 + 0.08) = 108.00$	8.00
100	8	Semiannually	4	$100(1 + 0.04)^2 = 108.16$	8.16
100	8	Quarterly	2	$100(1 + 0.02)^4 = 108.24$	8.24

is the equivalent of 8.16 percent per year compounded annually. For any form of financial contract (such as a bank account), the effective interest rate of the contract is the rate compounded *once* per interest period that provides the same dollar payoff as the financial contract. In our example, the interest period is one year, and 8.16 percent is the effective annual rate (compounded once per year).

Similarly, 8 percent per year compounded quarterly has an annual effective interest rate of 8.24 percent. Obviously, the more frequent the compounding, the more interest is earned on interest, and the higher the effective interest rate.

Frequency of compounding is discussed in more depth in Appendix 3A at the end of this chapter. In the case of savings accounts in banks or savings-and-loan associations, the frequency of compounding is an important consideration. In many other cases, it is not so important. Unless otherwise noted, this book will express interest rates in terms of percent per year and assume annual compounding. This convention of assuming annual compounding will simplify matters. In many decisions facing financial managers—for example, a decision to purchase a new machine—the difficulties in picking an appropriate interest rate are so great that concern for frequency of compounding is a misplaced emphasis.

Sample Problem 3–1

The Future Value of Savings for a Rainy Day

A. Suppose you invested $1,000 savings for a rainy day, and it earned interest of 10 percent per year compounded annually for the next 5 years. How much money would you have at the end of the 5-year period?

Solution

Using Equation (1) and Appendix Table III,

$$FV = \$1,000(1 + 0.10)^5$$

$$= \$1,000 \, FVF(0.10, 5)$$

$$= \$1,000(1.611)$$

$$= \$1,611.00 \text{ at the end of 5 years}.$$

B. How much money would you have at the end of the 5 years if interest were compounded semiannually rather than annually?

Solution

The interest rate is $(0.10/2) = 0.05$ per six-month period, and there are 10 six-month periods in 5 years. Again using Equation (1) and Appendix Table III,

$$FV = \$1,000(1.05)^{10}$$

$$FV = \$1,000 \times FVF(0.05, 10)$$

$$= \$1,000(1.629)$$

$$= \$1,629.00 \text{ at the end of 5 years}.$$

Note that in part (B) the answer is $18.00 higher than in part (A). This $18.00 is the extra interest earned on interest when compounding occurs semiannually instead of annually. ▮▮▮

Sample Problem 3–2

Effective Interest Rates on Two Bank Accounts

Suppose you are trying to decide between two bank accounts. Bank A offers 12 percent per year compounded quarterly on all your deposits, while Bank B offers 12.1 percent per year compounded annually. You plan to deposit $100 in one of the two accounts and to leave it there for the next year. Which account should you choose?

Solution

To solve this problem, we need to determine which account accumulates more money by the end of the year. Alternatively, we can find out which account has the higher effective annual interest rate and choose that account. Because compounding occurs quarterly at Bank A, we must divide time into 3-month (quarterly) periods; hence, $i = (0.12/4) = 0.03$, and $n = 4$ (quarters). Using Equation (1) and Appendix Table III, the future value at the end of one year of the $100 deposited at Bank A can be calculated as

$$FV = \$100 \times FVF(0.03, 4) = FV = \$100(1 + 0.03)^4$$
$$= \$100(1.126) = \$112.60.$$

Because the compounding period at Bank B is the same as the interest period (one year), we can use Equation (1) and assume that $i = 0.121$ and that $n = 1$. The future value at the end of one year of the $100 deposited at Bank B can then be calculated as

$$FV = \$100 \times FVF(0.121, 1)$$

$$FV = \$100(1 + 0.121)^1$$

$$= \$100(1.121)^1 = \$112.10.$$

Thus, Bank A offers the better deal because $112.60 is larger than $112.10. Note also that Bank A provides an effective annual interest rate of 12.6 percent (that is, a $100 deposit accumulates interest of $12.60 in a year's time), which is higher than Bank B's effective annual interest rate of 12.1 percent. ▮▮▮

Finance in Practice 3–1

Saving for College — "Baccalaureate Bonds"

Many families face a challenging financial problem — saving for college. A number of state governments have responded with a helpful alternative, the "baccalaureate bond." These are tax-exempt municipal bonds designed to help parents save for their children's college education.

Baccalaureate bonds are "zero-coupon" issues, which means they do not pay interest or principal until maturity. But they are also sold at a big discount to their face value, making them accessible to many financially strapped parents. For example, in 1988 the state of Washington was offering a $5,000 bond due in 20 years for $1,070. (Purchases are limited to five bonds.) In buying these bonds, a purchaser has to invest $1,070 now in order to receive $5,000 twenty years later. Using time-value concepts, we can calculate the annual rate of return as follows:

$$\$1,070(1 + i)^{20} = \$5,000$$

$$\$1,070 \times FVF(i, 20) = \$5,000.$$

By rearranging this equation we see that FVF must be equal to about 4.67:

$$FVF(i, 20) = \frac{\$5,000}{\$1,070} = 4.673.$$

Using Appendix Table III, we find that at 8 percent for 20 years, $FVF(0.08, 20) = 4.66$. As a result, the bond offers a tax-free annual return of about 8 percent.

In addition to yielding tax-free return, baccalaureate bonds are an attractive investment for many families because of their relative safety. The bonds are often backed by a promise that the state will raise taxes if necessary to pay investors; most municipal bonds don't have such backing. As a result, the baccalaureate bonds' payments are very safe if investors can keep their money tied up until the bonds mature. The major risk is that an investor may have to sell before maturity. Because all of the payoff is at maturity (zero-coupon), the bond's market value fluctuates more than that of conventional bonds as interest rates rise and fall. (This will be discussed in Chapter 4.)

Some states provide yet another incentive to purchase baccalaureate bonds. They pay a cash bonus at the bond's maturity if the proceeds are used to finance education at a state college. For example, holders of Illinois baccalaureate bonds due in 2008 will get a $400 bonus if the funds are used for education at a state school.

Source: Adapted from the *Wall Street Journal*, August 23, 1988, p. 29.

Present Value

Time value of money — the opportunity to earn interest on money one receives now rather than later. Because of the time value of money, a dollar today is worth more than a dollar in the future.

Our discussion to this point has shown how a dollar today will grow into more than a dollar in the future because of the **time value of money** — that is, there is an opportunity to earn interest if money is received now rather than later. Equation (1) provided the necessary mechanics to determine the future value of today's dollars.

If we reverse our thought process, we can pose the question: How much money is needed today in order to get a certain dollar amount in the future? For example, in Table 3–1 we showed that if you had $100.00 today and could earn 6 percent

Present value (*PV*)—the value today of a future payment or stream of payments, discounted at the appropriate discount rate.

Present-value factor—the number by which a given future value is multiplied to determine that future value's present value; it is calculated as $1/(1 + i)^n$.

annual interest compounded annually for 10 years, you would have \$179.10 at the end of 10 years. (If you did not round off your calculations, you would get \$179.08, but the difference is not important for present purposes.) In other words, at a 6 percent annual interest rate, \$100.00 today is just as good as \$179.10 to be received 10 years from now. Having \$100.00 today would allow us to have \$179.10 in 10 years if we can earn 6 percent annual interest. As a result, \$100 is the **present value (*PV*)** of \$179.10 to be received in 10 years if the interest rate is 6 percent per year. The present value of a future sum of money is the amount of money today (at present) that has the same value as the future sum.

The mechanics of calculating present value are simply the inverse of the mechanics of calculating future value. In general, the future-value factor we used in Equation (1) is calculated as $FVF(i, n) = (1 + i)^n$. Similarly we can develop **present-value factors,** *PVF*, as shown in Equation (2).

The present value (*PV*) of a certain future dollar amount to be received n periods in the future when the interest rate is i can be calculated as

$$PV = \text{future dollar amount} \times (1)/(1 + i)^n$$

$$PV = \text{future dollar amount} \times PVF(i, n)\,. \tag{2}$$

$PVF(i, n)$ is a present-value factor at an interest rate of i for n periods. This *PVF* is calculated as $PVF = 1/(1 + i)^n$ where n is the number of interest periods.

Note that the present-value factor is just 1 divided by the future-value factor. This is because we are *reversing* the process by bringing future dollars back to their present dollar equivalents:[2]

$$PVF(i, n) = 1/(FVF)(i, n)$$

$$FVF(i, n) = 1/(PVF)(i, n)\,.$$

Instead of having to calculate present-value factors (*PVF*s), Appendix Table I at the end of the book gives these factors for different interest rates (i) and time periods (n). Table 3–5 reproduces part of Appendix Table I.

Let us consider an example. Suppose we have an opportunity to receive \$100 a year from now. What is its value today if the interest rate is 6 percent? Applying Equation (2) and using Appendix Table I, the present value of \$100 to be received a year from now is

$$PV = \$100 \times PVF(0.06, 1)$$

$$= \$100 \times 0.943 = \$94.30\,.$$

[2]From algebra theory, recall that negative exponents denote division. As a result, another way to write $1/(1 + i)^n$ is $(1 + i)^{-n}$. To get from Equation (1) to Equation (2), divide both sides of Equation (1) by $(1 + i)^n$.

Table 3–5
Present Value* (at i per period) of $1 Received at the End of n Periods, $PVF(i, n)$

n	$i = 1\%$	2%	3%	4%	5%	6%	7%	8%	9%	10%
1	0.990	0.980	0.970	0.962	0.952	0.943	0.935	0.926	0.917	0.909
2	0.980	0.961	0.943	0.925	0.907	0.890	0.873	0.857	0.842	0.826
3	0.971	0.942	0.915	0.889	0.864	0.840	0.816	0.794	0.772	0.751
4	0.961	0.924	0.888	0.855	0.823	0.792	0.763	0.735	0.708	0.683
5	0.951	0.906	0.863	0.822	0.784	0.747	0.713	0.681	0.650	0.621
6	0.942	0.888	0.837	0.790	0.746	0.705	0.666	0.630	0.596	0.564
7	0.933	0.871	0.813	0.760	0.711	0.665	0.623	0.583	0.547	0.513
8	0.923	0.853	0.789	0.731	0.677	0.627	0.582	0.540	0.502	0.467
9	0.914	0.837	0.766	0.703	0.645	0.592	0.544	0.500	0.460	0.424
10	0.905	0.820	0.744	0.676	0.614	0.558	0.508	0.463	0.422	0.386
11	0.896	0.804	0.722	0.650	0.585	0.527	0.475	0.429	0.388	0.350
12	0.887	0.788	0.701	0.625	0.557	0.497	0.444	0.397	0.356	0.319
13	0.879	0.773	0.681	0.601	0.530	0.469	0.415	0.368	0.326	0.290
14	0.870	0.758	0.661	0.577	0.505	0.442	0.388	0.340	0.299	0.263
15	0.861	0.743	0.642	0.555	0.481	0.417	0.362	0.315	0.275	0.239
16	0.853	0.728	0.623	0.534	0.458	0.394	0.339	0.299	0.252	0.218
17	0.844	0.714	0.605	0.513	0.436	0.371	0.317	0.270	0.231	0.198
18	0.836	0.700	0.587	0.494	0.416	0.350	0.296	0.250	0.212	0.180
19	0.828	0.686	0.570	0.475	0.396	0.331	0.277	0.232	0.194	0.164
20	0.820	0.673	0.554	0.456	0.377	0.312	0.258	0.215	0.178	0.149
21	0.811	0.660	0.538	0.439	0.359	0.294	0.242	0.199	0.164	0.135
22	0.803	0.647	0.522	0.422	0.342	0.278	0.226	0.184	0.150	0.123
23	0.795	0.634	0.507	0.406	0.326	0.262	0.211	0.170	0.138	0.112
24	0.788	0.622	0.492	0.390	0.310	0.247	0.197	0.158	0.126	0.102
25	0.780	0.610	0.478	0.375	0.295	0.233	0.184	0.146	0.116	0.092
30	0.742	0.552	0.412	0.308	0.231	0.174	0.131	0.099	0.075	0.057
35	0.706	0.500	0.355	0.253	0.181	0.130	0.094	0.068	0.049	0.036
40	0.672	0.453	0.307	0.208	0.142	0.097	0.067	0.046	0.032	0.022
45	0.639	0.410	0.264	0.171	0.111	0.073	0.048	0.031	0.021	0.014
50	0.608	0.372	0.228	0.141	0.087	0.054	0.034	0.021	0.013	0.009

*$PVF(i, n)$ is calculated as $\dfrac{1}{(1 + i)^n}$.

What is the present value of the same amount if it is to be received 2 years from today? Applying Equation (2), the present value of $100 to be received 2 years from now is

$$PV = \$100 \times PVF(0.06, 2)$$
$$= \$100 \times 0.890 = \$89.00.$$

The above examples demonstrated how to calculate the present value of a future sum. If 6 percent represents the rate that we can earn on savings, then we would pay no more than $94.30 for an opportunity to receive $100 a year from now, and we would pay no more than $89.00 to receive the $100 in 2 years. In other words, $100 a year from now is equivalent to $94.30 today; we would be indifferent between the two sums. The same can be said of $89.00 now versus $100.00 in 2 years; we would be as happy with one sum as the other. Note that we are assuming that 6 percent correctly expresses our time preference—that is, the rate at which we are willing to exchange present for future sums and vice versa. Note also that as the interest rate increases, the present-value factor will decrease. For example, the present value at 6 percent of $100 to be received in 1 year is $94.30, as we calculated above. At 10 percent, however, the present value is only $100 \times PVF(0.10, 1) = $100(909) = 90.90—more than $3 less than the figure calculated at 6 percent. Common sense tells us that an inverse relationship should exist between interest rates and present value. The higher the interest rate you can earn, the less money you need today to accumulate a given amount of money in the future.

Whereas we spoke of **compounding** cash flows forward in time earlier in the chapter, we speak of **discounting** cash flows backward in time. In calculating a present value, the interest rate usually is referred to as the **discount rate.**

Sample Problem 3–3
Present Value and the Frequency of Compounding

Calculate the present value of $2,000 to be received 2 years from now, assuming
A. a 5 percent discount rate, compounded annually and
B. an 8 percent discount rate, compounded semiannually.

Solution
A. The present value of $2,000 to be received in 2 years when the discount rate is 5 percent and interest is compounded annually can be calculated, using Equation (2) and Appendix Table I, as

$$PV = \$2,000/(1 + 0.05)^2$$

$$PV = \$2,000 \times PVF(0.05, 2)$$

$$= \$2,000(0.907)$$

$$= \$1,814.00.$$

Thus, if today we deposited $1,814.00 in a bank account and earned 5 percent annual interest (compounded annually), our bank balance would be $2,000 in 2 years.

B. When interest is compounded semiannually, the interest rate per period becomes $0.08/2 = 0.04$, and there are 4 six-month periods in 2 years. Using Equation (2) and Appendix Table I, where $i = 0.04$ and $n = 4$, the present value of $2,000 to be received in 2 years when the discount rate is 8 percent and interest is compounded semiannually can be calculated as

To calculate the *future* value of a present cash flow, we *compound* the cash flow forward in time. To calculate the *present* value of a future cash flow, we *discount* the cash flow back in time.

Compounding—the evaluation of how a certain interest rate will cause a certain present dollar amount to grow in the future.

Discounting—the evaluation of how a certain discount rate will decrease the value of a certain future dollar amount to convert it to its present value.

Discount rate—the rate of exchange between the future and the present time period, or the interest rate used in the discounting process.

$$PV = \$2,000/(1 + 0.04)^4$$

$$PV = \$2,000 \times PVF(0.04, 4)$$

$$= \$2,000(0.855)$$

$$= \$1,710.00 .$$

Thus, if we have \$1,710.00 today and could earn 8 percent per year (compounded semiannually), we could accumulate \$2,000.00 at the end of 2 years. ▩

Streams of Cash Flows

In our preceding examples we have worked with a single cash flow to be received in the future. In practice, however, there are many situations in which we need to deal with a whole stream of cash flows. For example, if you buy a U.S. government bond, the government promises to give you interest payments (cash) each year for a number of years.

Present Value of a Stream of Cash Flows

How do we calculate the present value of a stream of payments to be received at different dates in the future? The answer is that we simply calculate the present value of each payment separately and add the results. Thus, the present value of \$100 to be received at the end of 1 year and \$200 to be received at the end of 2 years, at a discount rate of 6 percent, is

$$PV = \$100 \times PVF(0.06, 1) + \$200 \times PVF(0.06, 2)$$

$$= \$100(0.943) + \$200(0.890)$$

$$= \$94.30 + \$178.00$$

$$= \$272.30 .$$

▩
To calculate the present value of a stream of payments occurring at different times, calculate the present value of each payment separately and then add these present values.

The present value (PV) of a stream of future payments can be calculated as the sum of the present values of each of the payments. We can express this in equation form as

$$PV = \sum_{t=1}^{n} \frac{C_t}{(1 + i)^t} \tag{3}$$

where t = the period in which a payment is received, C_t = the amount to be received in period t, n = the number of periods, and i = the discount rate. Figure 3–4 illustrates what is going on in Equation (3).

The Σ notation simply indicates that t should take on different values from 1 (note that $t = 1$ at the bottom of the Σ) to n (note the n at the top of the Σ) and that these values should then be added up. For example, suppose you were promised payments of \$100 a year for each of the next two years and \$200 in

Figure 3—4
Present Value of a Stream of Cash Payments

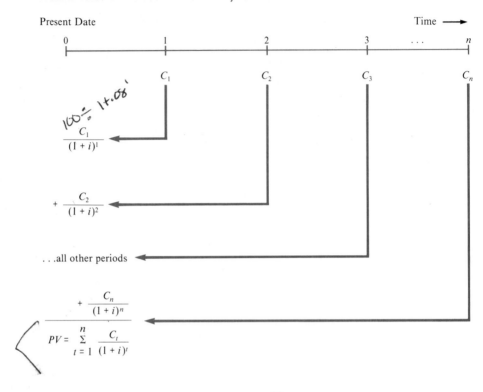

year 3 and that the interest rate was $i = 8$ percent per year. The present value of this stream of payments could be calculated, with the help of Appendix Table I, as

$$PV = \$100/(1 + 0.08)^1 + \$100/(1 + 0.08)^2 + \$200/(1 + 0.08)^3$$

$$= 100 \ PVF(0.08, 1) + \$100 \ PVF(0.08, 2) + \$200 \ PVF(0.08, 3)$$

$$= \$92.60 + \$85.70 + \$158.80$$

$$= \$337.10 .$$

The sigma notation of Equation (3) is simply a shorthand way of expressing this kind of calculation. In period 1, the amount to be received is $100, and it is to be discounted at 8 percent for one period. In period 2, the amount to be received is $100, and it is to be discounted at 8 percent for 2 periods. In period 3, the amount to be received is $200, and it is to be discounted at 8 percent for 3 periods. The sigma notation of Equation (3) says we should add up the present values of the separate cash flows, which is exactly what we did to get the $337.10 amount as the present value of the three cash flows.

Future Value of a Stream of Cash Flows

The future value (FV) of a stream of cash payments can be calculated as the sum of the future values of each payment.

Just as we can calculate the present value of a stream of payments, we can also calculate the *future value* of a series of cash flows occurring at different times. The process is simply to add up the cash amounts plus any interest that is earned on the amounts — as of the future date. For example, suppose you put $5,000 in the bank today and $3,000 in the bank one year from today. How much money would you have in the bank at the end of four years if you made no further deposits or withdrawals and if the bank paid interest of 10 percent per year compounded annually?

In this case we can calculate two future values, using Equation (1) above, and then add them up. The $5,000 will earn interest for four years (from now to the end of year 4), and the $3,000 will earn interest for three years (from the end of year 1 to the end of year 4). The total amount in the bank, or future value (FV), can be calculated with the help of Appendix Table III as

$$FV = \$5,000 \times FVF(0.10, 4) + \$3,000 \times FVF(0.10, 3)$$
$$= \$5,000 \,(1.464) + \$3,000 \,(1.331)$$
$$= \$7,320 + \$3,993$$
$$= \$11,313.00.$$

Sample Problem 3–4
Present and Future Values of a Stream of Education Payments

Suppose you needed to spend $2,000 next year, $3,000 two years from now, and $3,500 three years from now in order to finish your current education. Also suppose that you could invest your money in a bank account earning 6 percent annual interest compounded annually.

A. How much money would you have to put in the bank account today in order to be able to make all three payments out of that account?

B. If, instead of spending these three dollar amounts on education, you placed them in the bank account, what would your balance be at the end of three years (right after depositing the $3,500)?

Solution

A. The present value of this stream of cash flows is the amount needed in the bank today. For this problem, $i = 0.06$. Using Appendix Table I, we can calculate the present value as

$$PV = \$2,000 \times PVF(0.06, 1) + \$3,000 \times PVF(0.06, 2)$$
$$+ \$3,500 \times PVF(0.06, 3)$$
$$= \$2,000(0.943) + \$3,000(0.890) + \$3,500(0.840)$$
$$= \$1,886 + \$2,670 + \$2,940$$
$$= \$7,496.$$

Thus, depositing $7,496 in the bank today will make it possible to accumulate the money for the three future payments. Note that we must be sure to calculate the number of years (n) for each payment in terms of years from today.

B. The future value of the stream of payments would be the bank balance in three years if the three payments were deposited in a bank account at the three specified times. Using Appendix Table III, this future value can be calculated as

$$FV = \$2,000(1.06)^2 + \$3,000(1.06)^1 + \$3,500(1.06)^0$$
$$= \$2,000 \, FVF(0.06, 2) + \$3,000 \, FVF(0.06, 1) + \$3,500$$
$$= \$2,000(1.124) + \$3,000(1.06) + \$3,500$$
$$= \$2,248 + \$3,180 + \$3,500$$
$$= \$8,928 \, .$$

This future value of $8,928 is the amount that would have accumulated in the bank account in three years. In calculating the future values of each payment, note that we must be sure to calculate the number of years (n) that each payment will earn interest. For example, the $2,000 deposit next year will earn interest for 2 years by the end of year 3. As a result, we multiply the $2,000 by $FVF(i = 0.06, n = 2)$. The $3,000 deposit will, however, only earn interest for one year, so we use $FVF(i = 0.06, n = 1)$. The $3,500 will earn no interest at all. Note that this future value, $8,928, is also equal to the present value, calculated in part (A), plus interest for three years at 6 percent. That is,

$$FV(\text{year } 3) = PV \times FVF(0.06, 3)$$
$$\$8,928 = \$7,496(1.191) \, .   \quad \blacksquare$$

Annuities: Streams of Level Payments

The approach adopted above will always allow us to calculate present or future values of any stream of payments given an interest rate. Unfortunately, when there are many payments, the adding-up process can be quite tedious. For some special cases of cash flows we can develop shortcuts. The most common of such patterns is an annuity. An **annuity** is a stream of equal payments at regular time intervals. For example, many commonly encountered payments, such as apartment rent, mortgage payments, and life-insurance premiums, take the form of an annuity when equal payments are evenly spaced out over time.

Annuity—a stream of equal payments at regular time intervals.

Present Value of an Annuity

We can calculate the present value of an annuity as shown in Equation (4).

The present value (PV_A) of an annuity, where the amount to be received at each period in the future is a constant value (A), can be calculated as

$$PV_A = A \times PVAF(i, n) \tag{4}$$

where A = the annuity payment per period, i = the discount rate, t = the time period, n = the number of payments, and $PVAF(i, n)$ is a present-value annuity factor.

In Equation (4), we see that we can get the present value of an annuity by multiplying the annuity payment, A, by a present-value annuity factor, $PVAF(i, n)$. This factor is just the sum of the present-value factors (PVF) for each payment period. To illustrate, using the long approach, the present value of $1 per year for 3 years at a discount rate of 6 percent can be calculated using Equation (3) with the help of Appendix Table I as

$$PV = \$1 \times PVF(0.06, 1) + \$1 \times PVF(0.06, 2) + \$1 \times PVF(0.06, 3)$$

$$= \$1(0.943) + \$1(0.890) + \$1(0.840)$$

$$= \$1(0.943 + 0.890 + 0.840)$$

$$= \$1(2.673)$$

$$= \$2.673$$

The benefit of working the problem this way is that special tables can be constructed that allow us to skip the adding up we did above. Thus, Appendix Table II at the end of this book gives present-value factors for annuities ($PVAF$s). In Appendix Table II, we see 2.673 in the 6 percent column in the row for 3 periods—precisely the totaled term we needed for the above calculation. The remaining factors in Appendix Table II were calculated in exactly the same way, by adding up the present-value factors (from Appendix Table I) for various interest rates (i) and periods (n). The values assume compounding once per period, with the $1 payment received at the end of each period.

To illustrate the use of Appendix Table II, suppose we want to find the present value of $15,000 received each year for the next 4 years at a discount rate of 10 percent. In the 10 percent column in the row for 4 years, we find $PVAF = 3.170$. Therefore, using Equation (4), we have

$$PV_A = \$15,000 \times PVAF(0.10, 4)$$

$$= \$15,000 \times 3.170$$

$$= \$47,550.$$

In Appendix Table II, as in Appendix Table I, we assume that payments are made or received at the end of the period in question.

Sample Problem 3–5
The Present Value of a Lifetime Annuity

Suppose David Brown, aged 70, wanted to buy an insurance contract that would assure him of an annual income of $10,000 for the rest of his life. Life-insurance companies sell annuity contracts, a special form of which is called a *lifetime annuity*. Insurance companies estimate average life expectancy for persons of all ages. Persons 70 years old might have a life expectancy of, say, 15 more years. Some will live longer, and some will live not as long, but the average 70-year-old person will live 15 more years.

Solution

An insurance company would base the annuity contract's purchase price on a 15-year life expectancy and a particular rate of interest based on what it would expect to earn over the following 15 years. Let us assume that this rate is 6 percent. Ignoring commissions and other expenses, the purchase price of the annuity contract would be the present value of $10,000 per year for 15 years at a discount rate of 6 percent. Using Equation (4) and Appendix Table II, the purchase price of the annuity would be calculated as

$$PV_A = \$10,000 \times PVAF(0.06, 15)$$

$$= \$10,000(9.712)$$

$$= \$97,120.$$

Suppose David Brown does not have $97,120 but has saved $50,000. How large an annual annuity could he purchase? Rearranging Equation (4), the amount of the annuity payment Mr. Brown would receive each year could be calculated as

$$\text{Annuity payment} = \text{present value} \div PVAF(0.06, 15)$$

$$= \$50,000/9.712$$

$$= \$5,148.27.$$

Mr. Brown's $50,000 would buy him a lifetime annuity of $5,148.27 per year. ▨

Future Value of an Annuity

Just as we develop present-value factors for annuities, we can develop future-value factors for annuities. Equation (5) shows how to calculate the future value of an annuity.

The future value FV of an annuity, where the amount being paid each period is a constant value (A), can be calculated as

$$FV_A = A \times FVAF(i, n) \tag{5}$$

where A = the payment amount per period, i = the interest rate, n = the number of payments, and $FVAF(i, n)$ is a future-value annuity factor.

The $FVAF$ is the sum of the future-value factors $((FVF)$ for each of the individual payments. Appendix Table IV provides the calculated values of $FVAF$s.

To illustrate the use of Equation (5), suppose you plan to work hard over the next 4 years and anticipate saving $1,000 each year. You plan to put your savings in the bank at 6 percent interest. If your plan is to deposit $1,000 at the end of each of the next 4 years, how much would you have accumulated by the end of the fourth year? We can calculate the final sum by applying Equation (5) as

$$FV_A = \$1,000 \times FVAF(0.06, 4)$$

$$= \$1,000 \times 4.375$$

$$= \$4,375.00.$$

Appendix Table IV shows the 4.375 figure for $FVAF(0.06, 4)$ at the intersection of the interest-rate column for 6 percent and the time-period row for 4 periods. The 4.375 is calculated as the addition of the appropriate FVF figures in Appendix Table III.

Sample Problem 3–6
The Future Value of a Savings Annuity

What would be the future value of $500 deposited at the end of each year for 5 years in a savings account offering 5 percent interest compounded annually?

Solution
We can use Appendix Table IV and Equation (5). Note that $i = 0.05$ and $n = 5$.

$$FV_A = \$500 \times FVAF(0.05, 5) = \$500(5.526) = \$2,763.00.$$ ▓▓▓

Perpetuities

Perpetuity—an annuity that continues forever.

An annuity that goes on forever is called a **perpetuity**. The present value of a perpetuity of A dollars per year can be calculated as shown in Equation (6).

The present value (PV_P) of a perpetuity, or a stream of equal $\$A$ payments that is to continue for an infinite number of time periods, can be calculated as

$$PV_P = (A)/(i) \tag{6}$$

where i denotes the discount rate.

To illustrate, the present value of $5 per year to be received each year forever at a 6 percent discount rate can be calculated, using Equation (6), as

$$PV_P = \$5/0.06 = \$83.33.$$

We will find later that the valuation equation for a perpetuity—Equation (6)—is very useful in valuing certain kinds of income streams. It also has a common-sense interpretation. Consider a bank account that promised to pay 10 percent interest per year compounded annually. How much money would you have to put in the bank if you would like to withdraw $8.00 per year without ever cutting into your original deposit? A bit of thinking suggests that you would have to deposit enough money so that the interest would be $8.00; that way you could withdraw all the interest, leaving the original deposit intact. Clearly, an $80 deposit is necessary to get $8 interest a year at 10 percent interest. Note that Equation (6) produces exactly this $80 figure as the present value of $8 a year to be received forever at an annual 10 percent discount rate:

$$PV_P = \$8/0.10 = \$80.$$

This initial $80 could generate $8 of annual interest forever (as long as the interest rate is 10 percent and you withdraw only $8 per year). It is, thus, equivalent to a perpetuity of $8 per year.

Since a perpetuity, by definition, continues indefinitely, there is no well-defined future value of a perpetuity. Since it doesn't stop, there is no date at which we can calculate a future value that includes all of the perpetuity payments.

The Discount Rate: Moving Money Through Time

The discount rate is the rate of exchange between time periods.

In our discussion of the time value of money, the *discount rate* plays a central role. The discount rate is the rate of exchange between time periods. If we know the rate of exchange over time, we can use it to discount a stream of payments to a single present value that is exactly equivalent in value, or to compound the stream forward to a single terminal value that also is equivalent in value. The discount rate, thus, is the rate at which we can shift cash flows between time periods without changing their present value.

Assume a hypothetical depositor will deposit in a bank account $200 in period 1, $350 in period 2, and $250 in period 3. Assuming, for example, that 6 percent represents the rate of exchange over time, we can apply Equation (3) to shift the three flows back to period 0 and thereby determine the present value of the stream, which we find to be $710.

$$PV = \$200 \times PVF(0.06, 1) + \$350 \times PVF(0.06, 2)$$
$$+ \ \$250 \times PVF(0.06, 3)$$
$$= \$200(0.943) + \$350(0.890) + \$250(0.840)$$
$$= \$710 .$$

Receipt of $710 at period 0 is equivalent to receiving the three amounts at the dates indicated. Likewise, we can shift the three flows forward in time, finding them equivalent to $846 received at the end of period 3.

$$FV = \$200 \times FVF(0.06, 2) + \$350 \times FVF(0.06, 1) + \$250$$
$$= \$200(1.124) + \$350(1.06) + \$250$$
$$= \$846 .$$

The three alternative but equivalent cash-flow patterns are shown in Table 3–6. Provided that we have correctly chosen the discount rate, the three cash-flow patterns—A, B, and C in Table 3–6—are exactly equivalent; we would be just as

Table 3–6
Equivalent Cash Flows

Investment	Cash Flows (dollars)			
	Period 0	Period 1	Period 2	Period 3
A	710	0	0	0
B	0	200	350	250
C	0	0	0	846

happy to receive one as another. This example demonstrates the real utility of discounted cash flow. With proper choice of the discount rate, we can shift cash flows through time while maintaining value equivalence. Complex patterns of cash flows can be reduced to an equivalent single figure, and decisions about those cash flows are made far easier. If, for example, we can obtain pattern B in Table 3–6 for a current outlay less than $710, we know that we have a good investment. In addition, by calculating present values (and future values) for a number of different possible investments, we can compare alternative investments.

Solving for an Unknown Interest Rate

Rate of return — the percentage benefit earned per dollar invested.

So far we have solved problems in which the interest rate is known, and we calculated either the present value or the future value of payments. In many cases, however, you may be interested in what **rate of return,** or interest rate, you either have earned or expect to earn. Suppose you are buying a share of stock today for $100 and expect its price to be $115 at the end of 2 years (assume, for simplicity, that the stock pays no dividends). What annual rate of return are you expecting on the investment? Equation (1) can be used to determine what interest rate would give a present amount of $100 a future value of $115:

$$FV = \$100 \; FVF(i, n)$$
$$\$115 = \$100 \; FVF(i, 2).$$

Rearranging,

$$FVF(i, 2) = \$115/\$100 = 1.15$$

From the above we know that $FVF(i, 2) = 1.15$. Looking in Appendix Table III in the row for 2 years, we see that at 7 percent the FV factor is 1.145 and that at 8 percent it is 1.166. Therefore, the interest rate corresponding to a future-value factor of 1.15 must be slightly above 7 percent. Specially designed calculators or computer programs can give us a more precise answer, but this is sufficiently close for most purposes. Note also that $FVF(i, 2) = (1 + i)^2$, so that we could solve the equation $(1 + i)^2 = 1.15$ for the value of i.

We can perform the same sort of calculation with an annuity. Suppose an annuity of $1,000 per year for 3 years costs $2,500 today. What is the implied rate of return? From Equation (4), we know that the present value of an annuity can be calculated, with the help of Appendix Table II, as

$$PV_A = \text{annuity payment} \times PVAF(i, n)$$

Therefore,

$$\$2,500 = \$1,000 \times PVAF(i, 3)$$
$$PVAF(i, 3) = \$2,500/\$1,000$$
$$= 2.500.$$

In Appendix Table II, in the row for 3 years, we find $PVAF = 2.531$ when the discount rate is 9 percent and $PVAF = 2.487$ when the discount rate is 10 percent. Therefore, the discount rate corresponding to $PVAF = 2.500$ must lie somewhere between 9 percent and 10 percent.

To calculate the rate of return earned, find the rate that makes the present value of the dollars received equal to the present value of the dollars paid.

In practice, cash flows can be complicated so that solving for an unknown rate requires trial and error. The principle, however, is the same: Find the rate of return that makes the present value of the dollars received equal to the present value of the dollars paid. Appendix 3B provides an example.

Using Discounted Cash Flow in Practice

We have developed the mechanics of discounted cash flow (DCF), and we have discussed the details of calculating both future values and present values. Finance in Practice 3–2 and 3–3 show the power of these techniques when they are applied to corporate-investment and bond-market decisions.

In each of the Finance in Practice examples, discounted-cash-flow techniques were used to make a decision. Such techniques will be important throughout this book because they provide a specific way to place a value on cash flows. DCF techniques assume that the value of an asset is the sum of all the payments the asset will generate in the future, discounted back to their present value. The DCF valuation model is quite general in its applicability and can be used in any situation in which value is a function of future cash payments. For example, the value of a bond is simply the present value of all interest and principal payments that the holder of the bond expects to receive. The value of a share of stock is the present value of all payments that its holder expects to receive—namely, dividends and the proceeds from sale at some future date. The value of an entire company may be thought of as the present value of all future cash flows that the company will generate. Again and again throughout this book, we will find applications for the DCF valuation model. Chapter 1 noted that the general criterion for financial-management decisions is value maximization; that is, financial managers do things that increase value and avoid things that decrease it. The DCF valuation model provides the basic conceptual framework for the valuation criterion.

Finance in Practice 3–2 and 3–3 make discounted cash flow look like pretty powerful medicine. Indeed, it is useful, but it is not the answer to every manager's prayer. It has its limitations, especially in situations involving uncertainty. The bond examples involved cash flows that were fixed in amount by contract. The corporate-investment example treated the cash savings as if they were known with certainty. In practice, DCF techniques often must be applied in cases where the cash flows are subject to a great deal of uncertainty.

Suppose you are the top managers of Apple Computer, contemplating introducing a new computer designed for executives in medium and large companies. It is a market quite different from the markets for computers for small business, home, and education use—Apple's main markets to that time. The market for computers for executives is potentially huge, but it will put Apple into competition with Xerox, Digital Equipment Corporation, and, alas, mighty IBM. Development

Finance in Practice 3–2

Using DCF Techniques to Evaluate a Corporate Investment

A firm is planning to purchase and install some new equipment at a cost of $500,000. It is expected that the equipment will have an economic life of 5 years, after which it will be sold in the secondhand market, bringing in an expected $60,000 in year 5. During the next 5 years, the firm has a fixed-price 5-year contract to manufacture a definite number of artillery shells for the U.S. Army. The new equipment is expected to save the firm material, energy, and labor costs each year. The engineering and accounting departments estimate that the total after-tax cash savings will be $80,000 in year 1, $100,000 in year 2, $125,000 in year 3, $150,000 in year 4, and $200,000 in year 5. The annual benefits rise over time because material costs, energy costs, and labor costs are all expected to rise rapidly.

The firm has set a 15 percent per annum after-tax rate as a required rate of return on cost-saving investment. What is the present value of the benefits expected from the equipment?

To answer this question, we need to find the present value, at 15 percent per year, of the stream of cost savings as estimated. In addition, we must remember that the used equipment is to be sold for an estimated $60,000 at the end of year 5.

The calculation is shown in the accompanying table. Column (1) shows the stream of expected benefits (including the sale value of the used equipment in year 5). Column (2), drawn from Appendix Table I at the end of this book, shows the present-value factor at a 15 percent discount rate. Assuming for computational simplicity that the benefits accrue at the end of each year, column (3) shows the present value of each year's total benefit. The sum of those benefits is shown at the foot of column (3). The present value of all the benefits is $442,470. This is lower than the cost of the equipment ($500,000), so the proposed investment should be rejected. The value of the dollars going out more than offsets the cost savings anticipated. Chapters 10 and 11 will discuss such corporate-investment decisions and related tax issues in more detail.

Year	Expected Benefit (dollars) (1)	Present-Value Factor at Interest Rate of 15 Percent a Year (percent) (2)	Present Value of Benefits (dollars) (3) = (1) × (2)
1	80,000	0.870	69,600
2	100,000	0.756	75,600
3	125,000	0.658	82,250
4	150,000	0.572	85,800
5	260,000	0.497	129,220
Total (1–5)			442,470

Finance in Practice 3–3

Using DCF Techniques to Evaluate a U.S. Government Bond

When the U.S. Treasury borrows money, it may sell a bond, which is a promise to repay a certain *face value* to the owner at the end of a certain number of years — when the bond reaches its *maturity*. In addition, the bond's owner receives annual interest payments (sometimes called *coupon payments*). (In practice, half of the annual interest payment is made every six months, but we will ignore this complication.) Consider a U.S. government bond with a face value of $1,000 and a maturity of 20 years issued in 1977 and maturing in 1997 that carries a coupon rate of 8 percent [that is, there are annual interest payments of 8 percent of the face value, or 0.08($1,000) = $80]. Suppose that at the end of year 1986, the bond is selling for $840, and you are considering purchasing it. You feel you can earn 10 percent per year on investments that are similar in risk to the bond. Is the bond a good buy?

We can use the present-value formulas to see what the present value of the bond is at 10 percent per year. In essence, this figure is the amount of money we would need today to duplicate the cash flows on the bond (if we can earn 10 percent per year).

As of 1986, the bond promises an annuity of $80 a year for 11 years (1987–1997) and a repayment of $1,000 at 11 years in the future. Using Equation (4) and Appendix Table II, we can calculate the present value of the annuity of $80 coupon payments as

$$PV = \$80 \times PVAF(0.10, 11)$$

$$= \$80(6.495) = \$519.60.$$

Using Equation (2) and Appendix Table I, we can calculate the present value of the $1,000 repayment of face value as

$$PV = \$1,000 \times PVF(0.10, 11)$$

$$= \$1,000(0.350) = \$350.00.$$

Adding the two present-value amounts together, the total present value of the bond is

$$PV = \$519.60 + \$350.00 = \$869.60.$$

This means that if we had $869.60 in 1986 and put it in a bank account paying 10 percent interest, we could withdraw $80 a year for each of the next 11 years, and in year 11 (1997) we would still have $1,000 left in our account to withdraw from the bank. That is, at an interest rate of 10 percent, $869.60 can duplicate the cash flows from the bond.

Since you can purchase the bond for $840, the bond is a good buy. Buying the bond, in effect, puts you ahead of the game by $29.60 — the difference between $869.60 and $840.00. In the absence of the bond, we would have had to put up $869.60 in our alternative investments earning 10 percent to get the same cash flows as those the bond promises. In a real sense, the bond has a positive *net present value* (value in excess of cost) of $29.60 and is, thus, a wise purchase, given our assumptions.

Note that one of these assumptions was that our required rate of return on the bond was 10 percent. At a 10 percent required return the bond has a positive net present value. Suppose other people also required 10 percent on the bond. They would also see the bond as a good buy. If many such buyers saw the bond as a good buy at its current price, we would expect them to try to buy the bond. This increased demand for the bond would drive up the bond's price until, at the new higher price, the bond is likely to have a net present value of zero — value equal to costs. This process is precisely what happens in well-developed financial markets. Chapter 4 will elaborate more on using DCF techniques to evaluate bonds.

costs will be very high and subject to great uncertainty. The commercial success of the venture and, hence, the sales and profits it will generate, are subject to even more uncertainty.

Will the use of DCF techniques to evaluate the decision guarantee that Apple will do the right thing? It most certainly will not. If Apple's managers make mistakes in estimating the cash flows of the project, they can easily make the wrong decision. Even if they make good cash-flow estimates, there remains a second problem — what discount rate to apply. A mistake here could also lead to the wrong decision. If managers use an inappropriate discount rate, a project that was initially considered worthwhile may, in fact, decrease value rather than increase it.

DCF is a useful tool, but it is no substitute for careful analysis and sound judgment. The numbers that go into a DCF analysis must be based on reasonable assumptions and a full assessment of the facts; otherwise, the numbers that come out will be unreliable.

DCF is a useful tool, but it is no substitute for careful analysis and judgment.

KEY CONCEPTS

1. Current value depends on future benefits.

2. Money has time value. A dollar now is more valuable than a dollar in the future.

3. The interest rate represents the rate of exchange over time — that is, the rate of exchange between money now and money later.

4. Present value is future value discounted back to the present.

5. The present value of a stream of payments equals the sum of the present values of the individual elements.

6. The interest rate that equates a present sum with a future sum can be viewed as the rate of return on the present sum if the present sum were invested.

7. The notion of present value provides the basic valuation framework on which the theory of financial management rests. The general DCF valuation model is fundamental in its importance.

8. The discount rate in a present-value calculation represents the rate of exchange between time periods. Using discounted-cash-flow techniques, cash flows can be moved forward or backward in time.

SUMMARY

The notion that money has time value is a basic concept of finance. The sooner funds are received, the sooner they can be put to work in other new investments. If funds are received later rather than sooner, the recipient forgoes the interest that could have been earned in the meantime. Therefore, to analyze the economic worth of investment opportunities, managers must take into account the *timing* of cash flows as well as their amounts.

The rate of interest represents the rate at which present funds can be exchanged for future funds,

and vice versa. The interest rate is the rate of exchange over time and is the tool for adjusting cash flows to account for differences in timing. Time affects cash flows through the mechanism of compound interest.

The future value of a sum of money equals its present value compounded forward through time at the appropriate interest rate. Similarly, the present value of a future sum is its future value discounted back to the present. The present value of a stream of payments is the sum of the present values of its separate elements. In the case of level streams (annuities), the computation of present value can be simplified using present-value tables especially designed for annuities.

The general discounted-cash-flow (DCF) valuation model expresses the value of an asset as the sum of all payments the asset will generate, discounted to their present value. Using DCF techniques, a complex pattern of cash flows extending over many time periods can be reduced to a single figure that is equivalent in value. The present value of a stream of cash inflows can be compared to the outlay required to generate it. Similarly, two or more alternative investments (each of which generates a complex cash-flow stream) can be reduced to present values and compared directly. DCF techniques greatly simplify the evaluation of complex cash-flow patterns.

QUESTIONS

1. Why does money have a time value?

2. What does the rate of interest represent in time-value analysis?

3. What happens to the effective rate of interest as the frequency of compounding is increased? Explain with an example.

4. Increasing the interest rate and lengthening the time has what effect on the present value and the future value? Is the relationship direct or inverse?

5. If you have a choice between a savings account that pays 5 percent compounded quarterly and one that pays 5 percent compounded daily, which would you prefer? Why? Show an example.

6. What is an annuity? A perpetuity? Make up a problem and solution for each.

7. If you had a choice between $1,000 today, with interest rates at 8 percent, and $1,500 five years from today, which would you take? What are your assumptions?

FINANCIAL TOOL KIT ASSIGNMENT

Work the time-value example problems discussed in this chapter using the Financial Tool Kit software. Prove the answer shown in the text example. The formula on the screen represents the calculation of the interest factors found in each of the four interest-rate tables. If your PC has a printer capability, print the screens for each problem. See the *Study Guide* that accompanies the text for more details related to using the *Financial Tool Kit*.

Problems

Unless otherwise stated, assume annual interest rates compounded once per year. Problems preceded by an asterisk (*) assume knowledge of Appendixes 3A and 3B.

1. $100 today is equivalent in value to how much at the end of 3 years,
   a. assuming an interest rate of 10 percent?
   b. assuming an interest rate of 30 percent?
   c. assuming an interest rate of 0 percent?

2. $100 at the end of 3 years is equivalent in value to how much today,
   a. assuming an interest rate of 10 percent?
   b. assuming an interest rate of 30 percent?
   c. assuming an interest rate of 0 percent?

3. $500 received at the end of each of the next 3 years is equivalent in value to how much today,

a. assuming an interest rate of 4 percent?

b. assuming an interest rate of 25 percent?

4. $500 received at the end of the next 3 years is equivalent in value to how much at the end of the third year,

a. assuming an interest rate of 4 percent?

b. assuming an interest rate of 25 percent?

5. $100 is to be received at the end of 1 year, $400 at the end of 2 years, and $800 at the end of 3 years. These receipts are equivalent in value to how much today,

a. assuming an interest rate of 6 percent?

b. assuming an interest rate of 20 percent?

6. $800 is to be received at the end of 1 year, $400 at the end of 2 years, and $100 at the end of 3 years. These receipts are equivalent in value to how much today,

a. assuming an interest rate of 6 percent?

b. assuming an interest rate of 20 percent?

c. Contrast the results with those of Problem (5). Why are the results different?

7. Find the effective annual rate of interest for:

a. 8 percent compounded semiannually.

b. 8 percent compounded quarterly.

c. 8 percent compounded monthly.

8. Calculate (without using tables) the future value of:

a. $1,000 invested for 2 years at 4 percent per year compounded annually.

b. $1,000 invested for 1 year at 4 percent per year compounded semiannually.

c. $4,000 invested for 6 months at 8 percent per year compounded quarterly.

d. $2,000 invested for 10 months at 6 percent per year compounded monthly.

9. Calculate (without using tables) the present value of:

a. $1,000 to be received at the end of 2 years at 6 percent compounded annually.

b. $4,000 to be received at the end of 1 year at 4 percent compounded quarterly.

c. $1,000 to be received at the end of 6 months at 12 percent compounded monthly.

d. $3,000 to be received at the end of 2 years at 8 percent compounded semiannually.

10. Rework Problem (9) using the present-value tables.

11. Calculate the present value of the stream of payments given in Table A below, assuming discount rates of 4 percent, 8 percent, and 12 percent.

Table A

Period	Cash Flow (dollars)
1	300
2	400
3	600
4	100

12. Calculate the present value of the following annuities if the annual discount rate is 8 percent:

a. $1,000 per year for 5 years.

b. $3,000 per year for 7 years.

*c. $1,000 every 6 months for 2 years. (Assume semiannual compounding.)

*d. $500 per quarter for 3 years. (Assume quarterly compounding.)

13. Find the present value of the cash flows given in Table B using a discount rate of 8 percent.

Table B

Year	Cash Flow (dollars per year)
1–4	100
5	200
6	300
7–15	100
16	400

14. Calculate the price of a 10-year bond paying a 6 percent annual coupon (half of the 6 percent semiannually) on a face value of $1,000 if investors can earn 8 percent per year on alternative investments. That is, suppose investors require an 8 percent return on the bond in setting the market price. Assume semiannual compounding.

15. Consider cash flows of $100 at the end of year 1, $300 at the end of year 2, and $200 at

the end of year 3. Assuming an interest rate of 10 percent, calculate the single amount that is equivalent in value

a. if received today.
b. if received at the end of year 1.
c. if received at the end of year 2.
d. if received at the end of year 3.

16. Consider cash flows of $200 at the end of year 1, $100 at the end of year 2, $100 at the end of year 3, and $300 at the end of year 4. Calculate the present value of these cash flows

   a. at an interest rate of 5 percent.
   b. at an interest rate of 20 percent.

17. What is the present value of $600 received now plus $600 at the end of each of the next three years at 10 percent? Note the variation in cash flows compared to an ordinary annuity.

18. What is the present value of cash flows of $80 per year forever (in perpetuity),

   a. assuming an interest rate of 8 percent?
   b. assuming an interest rate of 10 percent?

19. Pam deposited her most recent paycheck in Akron National Bank's Big A account that pays interest at a rate of 6 percent compounded quarterly. What is the effective annual rate of interest on the Big A account?

20. According to a local department store, the store charges customers 1 percent per month on the outstanding balance. Is this equivalent to 12 percent per year? What is the effective annual rate on such consumer credit? Assume the store recalculates your account balance at the end of each month.

21. Suppose you are 16 years old and plan to start college exactly 2 years hence. You now have $2,000 in the bank earning 10 percent per year. Your first college tuition payment (due in 2 years) will be $2,500. Do you presently have enough saved to finance that payment?

22. P & H, Inc., has just obtained a $10 million loan from a local insurance company. The terms of the loan require repayment in five annual payments of $2,773,925 each. The first payment is to be paid one year after receipt of the $10 million.

a. What is the effective annual interest rate of the loan?
b. Suppose that P & H, Inc., has just made the second of the five payments. What is the smallest amount of money that P & H would have to put into a bank account on the date of this payment in order for this bank account to contain a large enough balance to be the only source of funds to make the last three payments? Assume that the bank pays 10 percent per year compounded annually.

23. You have purchased a new $8,000 sailboat and have the option of paying the entire $8,000 now or making equal, annual payments for the next 4 years, with the first payment due one year from now. If your time value of money is 7 percent, what would be the largest amount for the annual payments that you would be willing to undertake?

24. You have just borrowed some money from Hank the friendly loan maker. To pay off the debt, you will make three annual payments of $3,000 (the first payment made one year from today) and you will make a "balloon" payment of $20,000 four years from now. If Hank charged you 8 percent per year compounded annually, how much money must you have borrowed?

25. Your bank has offered you a $15,000 loan. The terms of the loan require you to pay back the loan in five equal annual installments of $4,161.00. The first payment will be made a year from today. What is the effective rate of interest on this loan?

26. Suppose you plan to purchase a new stereo system. Noise, a local sound shop, has offered the following terms. The cash price (including all taxes plus free home delivery) is $600. Alternatively, you can make 12 monthly payments (the first coming one month from the date of purchase) of $56.76 each. What is the effective annual interest rate on this financing?

27. The Canadian Pacific Railroad has an issue of 4 percent perpetual bonds outstanding—that is, bonds that have no maturity and promise to pay $20 semiannually forever. If the market rate of interest is 9 percent per year (compounded semi-

annually) for bonds of this risk class, at what price should the Canadian Pacific "Perpetual 4s" sell?

28. As a graduation present, a wealthy relative has given you $5,000 to be put into one of three investment opportunities. The cash flows generated by each investment are given in Table C. If you must invest the entire $5,000 in only one of these alternatives and if all three have the same risk, which alternative offers the highest rate of return? (Assume you cannot sell your rights to these opportunities and that you will hold any investment to its maturity in year 5. Hint: In Investment B you can think of the last payment as receiving back your $5,000 investment plus income of $650.)

Table C

	Cash Flows Received, Year End (dollars)				
Investment	Year 1	Year 2	Year 3	Year 4	Year 5
A	1500	1500	1500	1500	1500
B	650	650	650	650	5650
C	0	0	0	0	9000

29. V. B. Smith paid $1,000 for 10 shares of stock 12 years ago ($100 per share). He received dividends of $6 a share at the end of each of the first 7 years and $3 a share at the end of each of the next 5 years. He just sold the stock for $860 (immediately after he received the last dividend). What rate of return did he make on his investment? Set up a formula to solve.

30. The Fair Finance Company offers you a $5,000 loan. After a bit of fast talking, Fair's chief loan officer tells you that the repayment schedule will be four annual payments of $1,416.00. The first payment will be deducted from the loan amount, the second payment is due one year from now, etc. What is the approximate effective annual rate of interest on this loan?

31. You have a checking account at Lobell National Bank that you established two years ago when you entered college. You have found it necessary to keep an average balance of $450 in the account to cover your checks. Now you learn that if you are willing to leave an additional $500 in a savings account at Lobell you can establish a NOW account; that is, you will receive interest on both checking and savings balances at the rate of 5.5 percent per year compounded on a daily basis. Presently, you have the additional $500 in a six-month certificate, which pays 10 percent, compounded semi-annually, and is about to mature. You can buy another identical certificate. Will you make the switch to the NOW account? (Assume the bank uses a 365-day year in all its daily compounding calculations.)

32. Litka Publishing Company is trying to decide whether to revise its popular textbook *Law for Simpletons*. It has estimated that the revisions will cost $40,000 initially, but after-tax cash flow from increased sales will be $10,000 the first year and will increase by 8 percent per year for two years and then remain stable for two more years, at which time the book will go out of print. If the company requires a 10 percent return for such an investment, should it undertake the revision?

33. When 35 years old, you wish to plan for your old age. Suppose you invest $1,000 per year at an effective rate of 5 percent per year for the next 25 years, with the first deposit beginning one year hence. Beginning at age 60 you start withdrawing $X per year for the next 20 years. How large will X be in order to use up all of your funds?

34. You have agreed to pay a creditor $5,000 one year hence, $4,000 two years hence, $3,000 three years hence, $2,000 four years hence, and a final payment of $1,000 five years from now. Because of budget considerations, you would like to make five equal annual payments ($X) to satisfy your contract. If the agreed-upon interest rate is 5 percent effective per year, what will X be?

35. Suppose you have decided to start saving money to take a long-awaited world cruise, which you estimate will cost you $6,000. You want to take your cruise 5 years from today. The savings ac-

count you established for your trip offers 6 percent interest, compounded annually.

a. How much will you have to deposit each year (at year end) to have your $6,000 if your first deposit is made one year from today and the final deposit is made on the day the cruise departs?

b. How much will you have to deposit each year if the final deposit is made one year before the cruise departs?

c. Suppose the cost of living (or cruising) increases 4 percent per year over the next 5 years. What would be the effective purchasing power in year 5 of your deposits calculated in part (a)?

36. A U.S. government bond, maturing exactly 5 years from now, pays annual interest of 7 percent payable once a year. The first interest payment is due exactly one year hence. The face value of the bond is $1,000. Suppose you can earn an effective annual rate of 8 percent for 5 years in what you consider to be an investment of the same risk class as the government bond. How much would you be willing to pay for the 7 percent bond? What if you could earn only 5 percent on your money in alternative investments?

37. M. Grow, a 60-year-old penniless freelance gardener, quite unexpectedly found himself named the beneficiary in the estate proceedings of a woman whose roses he used to prune. After all pertinent fees had been extracted from M. Grow's largesse, he found he had netted $87,500. M. Grow immediately retired and placed $80,500 of his inheritance in a savings account on which he would earn 6 percent per year compounded annually. He planned to extract $7,000 from the account at yearly intervals commencing one year from the date of his deposit, to satisfy the modest needs of his retirement years. Given that he lives long enough, about how old will he be when his money runs out?

38. Susan Potter put $5,000 into a savings account that paid 8 percent annual interest. She then let the money grow (no deposits or withdrawals) for 10 years. At that point, she decided to reap some of the rewards of her thrift and planned to begin systematic annual withdrawals from the account. Each withdrawal would be the same dollar amount. The first withdrawal would be in one year (on the 11th anniversary of her initial deposit) and Sue planned to make 12 of these withdrawals, the last of which would clean out her account. How large a withdrawal (Y) could Sue make in each of the 12 years?

*39. Suppose you decide to purchase a $3,500 car, pay $1,500 in cash, and assume a 13.5 percent add-on installment contract for the remaining $2,000. Your installment contract runs for one year and requires you to pay [$2,000 + 0.135($2,000)]/12 = $189.17 per month for one year. What is the effective monthly rate you pay on the outstanding balance? The effective yearly rate?

40. At a New Year's party, a friend approaches you for some financial advice. Your friend is celebrating his 30th birthday and wants to start saving for his anticipated retirement at age 65. He wants to be able to withdraw $10,000 from his savings account at the end of each year for 10 years following his retirement (the first withdrawal will be at the end of his 65th year). Your friend is very risk-averse and will invest his money only in the local savings bank, which offers 8 percent interest compounded annually. He wants to make equal, annual deposits at the end of each year in a new savings account he will establish for his retirement fund.

a. If he starts making these deposits at the end of this year and continues to make deposits until he is 65 (the last deposit will be at the end of his 64th year), what amount must he deposit annually to be able to make the desired withdrawals upon retirement?

b. Suppose your friend has just inherited a large sum of money and has decided to make one lump-sum payment at the end of this year to cover his retirement needs rather than make equal annual payments. What amount would he have to deposit?

Appendix 3A

Compounding

Equation (1) from Chapter 3 gave the general formula for calculating future value and is reproduced here as this appendix's Equation (A–1).

The future value FV of a certain present dollar amount that earns interest at rate i compounded periodically for n can be calculated as

$$FV = \text{present dollar amount}(1 + i)^n \qquad \text{(A–1)}$$

where FV = the amount accumulated n periods later, n = the number of interest periods, and i = the interest rate per period.

Chapter 3 considered the cases of semiannual and quarterly compounding. In principle, we can compound as often as we wish: monthly, weekly, daily, hourly, or by the second! To explore the effects of increasing the frequency of compounding, we can assume a present dollar amount of $1 and modify Equation (A–1) as shown in Equation (A–2).

$$FV = \$1\left(1 + \frac{i}{x}\right)^{xn} \qquad \text{(A–2)}$$

where FV = the amount accumulated n interest periods later, n = the number of *interest* periods, i = the interest rate, x = the number of compoundings per interest period, i/x = the interest rate per compounding period, and xn = the number of *compounding periods*.

For example, with an interest period of a year and semiannual compounding, x will be 2 in Equation (A–2). How much money would you have after 3 years if you invested $1 today at 10 percent per year compounded semiannually? In Equation (A–2), n would be 3, x would be 2, xn would be 2 times 3, or 6, and i would be 0.10. Therefore, the future value can be calculated, with the help of Appendix Table III, as

$$FV = \$1(1 + 0.05)^6$$

$$= \$1(1.34)$$

$$= \$1.34 .$$

Note that Equation (A–2) simply converts the interest rate to the interest rate per compounding period (i/x) and then raises this to a power equal to the number of compounding periods (xn).

3B

Estimating Realized Returns on Stocks

In the text we solved for an unknown rate of return. Let us apply the same principle to a more complicated pattern of cash flow related to purchase and sale of a share of stock. Here we focus on the actual return earned on a past transaction.

Suppose we have data on TMI stock that are listed in Table 3B–1. If someone bought a share of TMI stock for $6.50 at the end of 1983 and sold it for for $11.50 at the end of 1988, what actual rate of return (R) did he or she receive? Assume that the investor did not receive the $0.50 dividend paid in 1983 since the stock was bought at year end.

To solve for the unknown rate, R, we need to find the discount rate that makes the present value of the dollars received (five dividends plus the final price) equal the purchase price. This means that we are viewing 1983 as time 0. The equation below sets up the problem.

$$\$6.50 = \$0.50/(1 + R) + \$0.75/(1 + R)^2 + \$0.75/(1 + R)^3$$
$$+ \ \$0.75/(1 + R)^4 + (\$0.90 + \$11.50)/(1 + R)^5$$
$$= \$0.50 \ PVF(R, 1) + \$0.75 \ PVF(R, 2) + \$0.75 \ PVF(R, 3)$$
$$+ \ \$0.75 \ PVF(R, 4) + \$12.40(R, 5)$$

The only way to use the Appendix Tables (Appendix Table I in this case) to find R is by trial and error. For example, let us try $R = 20$ percent and calculate the present value of the dollars received.

$$PV = 0.50 \ PVF(0.20, 1) + 0.75 \ PVF(0.20, 2) + 0.75 \ PVF(0.20, 3)$$
$$+ \ 0.75 \ PVF(0.20, 4) + 12.40 \ PVF(0.20, 5)$$

Table 3B–1
TMI Stock Prices and Dividends Paid — 1983 through 1988, Year End (dollars)

	Stock Price	Dividend Paid
1983	6.50	0.50
1984	9.00	0.50
1985	9.75	0.75
1986	11.25	0.75
1987	10.00	0.75
1988	11.50	0.90

$$PV = 0.50(0.833) + 0.75(0.694) + 0.75(0.579)$$
$$+ 0.75(0.482) + 12.40(0.402)$$

$$PV = \$6.72 .$$

Our answer of $6.72 is higher than the $6.50 figure we desired, so we know that 20 percent is too low a rate for R. It has not penalized the cash flows enough. If we repeat the calculation using $R = 21$ percent, we find a present value of $6.48. While this is not exactly equal to $6.50, it is very close. We then can say that R is approximately 21 percent. Many calculators can be used to calculate the actual return more precisely: in this example, R turns out to be 20.9 percent.

Chapter 4

Value in Markets

In Chapter 3 we developed discounted-cash-flow (DCF) techniques as a way to estimate the value of a stream of cash flows. DCF techniques are one of the most important tools financial managers can use since they allow us to collapse a whole series of cash flows into one *present value* — the value in today's dollars. To apply the DCF model, we need estimates of cash flows and some interest rate, or discount rate. In practice, estimating cash flows and choosing discount rates are complex and difficult tasks. Nevertheless, the effort often leads to handsome rewards in terms of improved decisions.

This chapter shows how values observed in financial markets can be explained in terms of DCF techniques. In Chapter 1, we settled on value maximization as the objective of financial management.

Values are determined in financial markets by thousands of investors making decisions about whether to buy or sell assets. DCF techniques allow us to explain and estimate values and, thus, make operable our objective of value maximization. Extending the DCF model to market values provides us with a number of very useful insights. First, it gives financial managers a better understanding of the financial environment in which they operate. Second, it forces us to confront a second important dimension of financial problems — risk. Looking at market values in a DCF context helps us find ways to deal with risk, as we will see later in this chapter. Specifically, we will discuss how rates of return available on financial securities vary with the risk of the securities.

The Discounted-Cash-Flow Model and Market Value

The last chapter developed the basic DCF model to determine the present value of a stream of payments. The basis for the discounted-cash-flow model is: present value equals the sum of all of the cash flows at various times, each discounted back to the present. The "discounting" reduces the value of future cash flows since present-value factors are less than one, due to the time value of money.

In all the problems considered so far, we have glossed over the fact that cash flows are typically only estimates — we often (in fact, usually) don't know what the cash flow will be. For now, let us call the cash flow the expected cash flow. For example, suppose I offered you the following bet. I'll toss a coin. If it comes up heads I'll pay you $10; if it comes up tails I'll pay you $0. What is your expected cash flow? If you believe that the coin is fair and that there is an equal chance for either heads or tails, you could say the expected (average) cash flow is the average outcome of $5; that is, $0.5(\$10) + 0.5(\$0) = \$5$. Later we'll have more to say about expected values. If there is no uncertainty about payment at all, the expected cash flow is just the cash flow promised.

The value for the discount rate has also been assumed in the discussions thus far, but the discount rate can vary from situation to situation. For example, the discount rate for risky cash flows should be higher than for safe cash flows.

Let us see how we can apply the DCF model to cash flows and discount rates that actually occur in markets. First we will consider a simple case with only one future cash flow. Then we will turn to more complicated examples.

Turn back to the Bank of Virginia's zero-coupon certificate of deposit (CD) discussed in Chapter 1. In 1982, the Bank of Virginia asked a price of $250 for a certificate of deposit that promised to make a single payment — $1,000 — in 1993.

Our DCF model allows us to interpret what the market is saying about a security like this CD. To illustrate, assume you found a CD that promised to pay $1,000 exactly 5 years after you purchased it. Furthermore, assume the CD could be purchased today for $621. Figure 4–1 displays the situation.

What is the present value of the $1,000 payment according to our DCF model? That depends on the discount rate, i, we use in the DCF model. For example, if we use a 10 percent required rate of return ($i = 0.10$), we can use Equation (2) from Chapter 3 to find the present value:

> It is important to recognize that future cash flows are typically only estimates.

Figure 4–1
Present Value of Zero-Coupon Certificate of Deposit

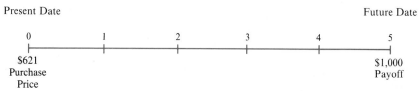

Present Date   Future Date

| 0 | 1 | 2 | 3 | 4 | 5 |

$621
Purchase
Price

$1,000
Payoff

$$PV = \text{future dollar amount}/(1.10)^5$$

$$PV = \text{future dollar amount} \times PVF(i, n)$$

$$= \$1,000 \times PVF(0.10, 5)$$

$$= \$1,000 \times 0.621$$

$$= \$621.$$

The present-value factor of 0.621 (from Appendix Table I) shows us that $1,000 receivable in 5 years is worth only $621 today if we want to earn at a 10 percent rate of return.

Now realize that you can purchase this CD today for $621. This is exactly equal to the present value of the $1,000 at a 10 percent interest rate as we calculated above. In fact, in constructing this example we chose the 10 percent rate carefully to make sure we obtained a present value of $621. We did this so we could use what we know about the DCF model to interpret the price of the CD. Because $621 is the present value of $1,000 at 10 percent, we know from our DCF model that if we can buy the promise of $1,000 for $621 (today), we can earn 10 percent per year. Paying such a $621 price today, you would earn 10 percent per year if you hold the CD for five years and then receive the $1,000. The key point is that at a current price of $621 the CD promises a 10 percent annual rate of return. This rate of return can be compared to other investments available in financial markets. If another CD offered an 11 percent return, you might prefer to buy it rather than this one offering only 10 percent.

Let's review what our DCF model has allowed us to do. If we observe a current market price (in our example $621 today) and a future dollar return for the investment (in our example $1,000 receivable in five years), we can translate this financial investment into its effective rate of return (10%). That rate of return is the rate that makes the present value of the dollars received equal to the dollars paid.

Capitalization rate or discount rate—the rate of exchange betweeen various time periods.

The discount rate, such as the 10 percent we calculated above, also goes by other names. Frequently this rate is called the **capitalization rate** because it allows us to transform a stream of expected cash flows into a single number called *present value,* **capital value,** or simply *value.* In the DCF valuation framework, the capitalization rate is simply another term for the discount rate.

Capital value—the present value of a stream of expected cash flows.

The 10 percent rate of return on this CD can also be thought of as the market's **required rate of return** on this type of investment. The interaction of buyers and sellers in financial markets established a price of $621. In trading at this price, investors in the CD are revealing what rate of return they require on such an investment—the minimum return the investor will accept on the investment. As a result, this book will use the term *required rate of return,* or *required return,* to refer to the discount rate applied to future cash flows. When market prices are used to estimate this rate, the rate is the *market's required return.*

Required rate of return—the *minimum* return prospective investors should accept in evaluating an investment.

To illustrate how useful this application of DCF can be, suppose the CD's price dropped from $621 to $519. What rate of return would the CD offer if you could purchase at $519? We proceed by making the present value of the dollars to be received equal to the price paid today.

$$\text{Price} = \text{future dollar amount}/(1 + i)^5$$

$$\$519 = \$1,000 \times PVF(i, 5).$$

Now we solve this equation for the unknown *PVF*.

$$PVF(i, 5) = \$519/\$1,000 = 0.519$$

Using Appendix Table I, we find that $i = 0.14$ gives a *PVF* of 0.519 for 5 periods. As a result, we can say that at a price of $519 the CD offers a 14 percent annual rate of return. Note that as the market price drops the prospective buyer receives a higher rate of return. This makes sense since the buyer pays less money to get the same $1,000.

We can use the DCF model to understand how major corporations interact with the financial markets. Figure 4–2 shows how General Mills could in July 1982 advertise to pay back $100 million in November 1987 in order to borrow $50 million in 1982.[1] In General Mills's case, it promised to pay back double the money it received. As noted in Figure 4–2, this doubling of money in a little more than 5 years represents about a 13.50 percent annual return (compounded semiannually) to someone lending money to General Mills. The relevant calculations are just like those we did for the CD in the text.

General Mills's borrowing scheme is called a *zero-coupon money-multiplier note,* which makes no payment except for the lump-sum payment at maturity. Such an investment may be especially desirable for people trying to accumulate money at a future date through retirement plans, such as an *individual retirement account (IRA).* IRAs are retirement-savings plans with special tax-savings provisions. IRAs allow individuals to defer paying taxes on portions of income that are placed in these special accounts.

Valuation of Bonds

Disc. Cash Flow

In the last chapter we used a simplified example to illustrate the valuation of U.S. government bonds. We can learn more about how financial markets work by examining a few additional details of valuation in terms of DCF analysis.

Figure 4–3, taken from the *Wall Street Journal,* shows the prices of a number of U.S. government bonds and notes. Like bonds, notes pay interest and principal but when issued are of shorter maturity than bonds. Since a note is essentially the same as a bond, notes are often referred to as bonds. The prices given in the figure are for transactions of at least $1 million (a bit expensive for most private individuals!), reflecting trades made by large institutions, such as insurance companies, pension funds, and brokerage houses. An individual could also participate in the

---

[1]Later, in the summer of 1982, when General Mills actually issued the notes, the maturity was set at January 4, 1988. Since the payment was later than November, General Mills was able to pay a lower interest rate than the 13.5 percent figure indicated in Figure 4–2. General Mills paid 13.30 percent because interest rates had dropped from the higher levels of earlier months.

Figure 4—2
Request for Funds to Borrow, Issued by General Mills

A registration statement relating to debt securities of which these securities are a part has been filed with the Securities and Exchange Commission and has become effective, but a final prospectus supplement with respect to the offering of these securities has not yet been filed. These securities may not be sold nor may offers to buy be accepted prior to the time a final prospectus supplement is delivered. This advertisement shall not constitute an offer to sell or the solicitation of an offer to buy nor shall there be any sale of these securities in any State in which such offer, solicitation or sale would be unlawful prior to registration or qualification under the securities laws of such State.

$100,000,000

General Mills, Inc.

Money Multiplier Notes*
(Zero Coupon)

Price to the Public per Note	Amount Payable at Maturity per Note	Approximate Maturity
$500	$1,000	November 1987

In lieu of interest payments, a purchaser of Money Multiplier Notes will receive double the original investment if the Notes are held to maturity. Money Multiplier Notes will be offered at $500 per Note and will be payable at maturity at $1,000 per Note. The actual maturity of the Notes will be established on the offering date expected to be in late July 1982. Based on current market conditions, the anticipated yield to maturity for the Notes, computed on a semiannual basis, would be approximately 13.50% per annum. The final selection of the maturity will reflect the then current market conditions and demand for the Notes, and the actual resultant yield for the Notes may vary significantly from that given above.

This proposed new issue of securities is designed primarily for purchase by IRA's, Keogh plans, IRA rollovers, pension plans and other investors not subject to federal income taxes.

General Mills, Inc. is a diversified consumer products company with operations in consumer foods, restaurants, toys, fashion and specialty retailing.

A Preliminary Prospectus Supplement, which gives details of the offering and includes a prospectus dated July 16, 1982, is available. To obtain a copy, please contact your broker, dealer or investment advisor.

Copies of the Preliminary Prospectus Supplement may be obtained in any State from securities dealers who may legally offer these securities in compliance with the securities laws of such State.

Salomon Brothers, Inc.
Dillon, Read & Co. Inc.
Merrill Lynch White Weld Capital Markets Group
Merrill Lynch, Pierce, Fenner & Smith Incorporated

*Trademark of Salomon Brothers Inc.

Source: General Mills Money-multiplier notes. Reproduced by courtesy of General Mills, Inc.
Money-multiplier notes is a trademark of Salomon Brothers, Inc.

market by purchasing shares (for much less than $1 million) in mutual funds specializing in bonds. Such funds pool money from individual investors.

A few details of the way figures are reported need to be discussed in order to understand the pricing of bonds. For example, look at the entry marked with a colored screen in Figure 4–3.

Figure 4–3
Treasury Issues as of January 15, 1988: Bonds, Notes, and Bills

TREASURY BONDS, NOTES & BILLS

Friday, January 15, 1988

Representative Over-the-Counter quotations based on transactions of $1 million or more as of 4 p.m. Eastern time.

Decimals in bid-and-asked and bid changes represent 32nds; 101.1 means 101 1/32. a-Plus 1/64. b-Yield to call date. d-Minus 1/64. k-Nonresident aliens exempt from withholding taxes. n-Treasury notes. p-Treasury note; nonresident aliens exempt from withholding taxes.

Source: Bloomberg Financial Markets

Treasury Bonds and Notes

Rate	Mat. Date		Bid	Asked	Bid Chg.	Yld.
$8\frac{1}{8}$s,	1988	Jan p	99.31	100.2	.....	5.98
$10\frac{1}{8}$s,	1988	Feb n	100.6	100.9	− .1	6.01
$10\frac{3}{8}$s,	1988	Feb p	100.6	100.9	.....	6.25
8s,	1988	Feb p	100.3	100.6	− .1	6.13
12s,	1988	Mar n	100.31	101.2	− .2	6.30
$7\frac{1}{8}$s,	1988	Mar p	100.2	100.5	.....	6.19
$6\frac{5}{8}$s,	1988	Apr p	99.30	100.1	+ .1	6.42
$13\frac{1}{4}$s,	1988	Apr n	101.16	101.20	− .1	6.10
$8\frac{1}{4}$s,	1988	May n	100.14	100.17	.....	6.47
$7\frac{1}{8}$s,	1988	May p	100.3	100.6	.....	6.53
$9\frac{7}{8}$s,	1988	May n	100.30	101.1	.....	6.49
10s,	1988	May p	100.31	101.2	.....	6.51
7s,	1988	Jun p	100.3	100.6	+ .1	6.55
$13\frac{5}{8}$s,	1988	Jun n	103	103.3	− .1	6.47
$6\frac{5}{8}$s,	1988	Jul p	99.26	99.29	+ .1	6.80
14s,	1988	Jul n	103.15	103.18	− .2	6.47
$6\frac{1}{8}$s,	1988	Aug p	99.14	99.18	+ .2	6.85
$9\frac{1}{2}$s,	1988	Aug p	101.11	101.15	.....	6.83
$10\frac{1}{2}$s,	1988	Aug n	101.28	102	.....	6.86
$6\frac{3}{8}$s,	1988	Sep p	99.16	99.20	+ .2	6.92
$11\frac{3}{8}$s,	1988	Sep p	102.26	102.30	+ .1	6.95
$15\frac{3}{8}$s,	1988	Oct n	106.2	106.6	− .1	6.60
$6\frac{3}{8}$s,	1988	Oct p	99.12	99.16	+ .2	7.03
$6\frac{1}{4}$s,	1988	Nov p	99.6	99.10	+ .3	7.07
$8\frac{3}{4}$s,	1988	Nov n	101.6	101.10	+ .1	7.06
$8\frac{5}{8}$s,	1988	Nov p	101.3	101.7	+ .2	7.05

• • •

Rate	Mat. Date		Bid	Asked	Bid Chg.	Yld.
$10\frac{1}{2}$s,	1992	Nov n	109.2	109.6	+ .27	8.15
$8\frac{3}{4}$s,	1993	Jan p	102.2	102.6	+ .25	8.21
4s,	1988-93	Feb	92.24	93.10	− .3	5.53
$6\frac{3}{4}$s,	1993	Feb	94.4	94.22	+ .26	8.04
$7\frac{7}{8}$s,	1993	Feb	98.21	98.25	+ .27	8.17
$8\frac{1}{4}$s,	1993	Feb p	100.11	100.15	+ .27	8.12
$10\frac{7}{8}$s,	1993	Feb n	110.16	110.20	+ .24	8.27
$7\frac{3}{8}$s,	1993	Apr p	96.8	96.12	+ .29	8.24
$10\frac{1}{8}$s,	1993	May n	107.18	107.22	+ .28	8.30
$7\frac{1}{4}$s,	1993	Jul p	95.8	95.12	+ .24	8.32
$7\frac{1}{2}$s,	1988-93	Aug	96.8	96.14	+ .28	8.31
$8\frac{5}{8}$s,	1993	Aug	101.19	101.27	+ .31	8.20
$11\frac{7}{8}$s,	1993	Aug n	115.12	115.16	+ .31	8.34
$7\frac{1}{8}$s,	1993	Oct p	94.16	94.20	+ .27	8.32
$8\frac{5}{8}$s,	1993	Nov	102.2	102.8	+1.10	8.13
$11\frac{3}{4}$s,	1993	Nov	115.11	115.15	+1.2	8.34
7s,	1994	Jan	93.26	93.30	+1.5	8.30
9s,	1994	Feb	103.7	103.11	+1.5	8.29
7s,	1994	Apr p	93.13	93.17	+1.5	8.35
$4\frac{1}{8}$s,	1989-94	May	93.2	93.20	+ .8	5.32
$13\frac{1}{8}$s,	1994	May p	122.28	123	+1.6	8.36
8s,	1994	Jul n	98	98.4	+1.5	8.38
$8\frac{3}{4}$s,	1994	Aug	102.13	102.17	+1.11	8.24
$12\frac{5}{8}$s,	1994	Aug p	120.23	120.27	+1.6	8.43
$9\frac{1}{2}$s,	1994	Oct k	105.6	105.10	+2.2	8.45
$10\frac{1}{8}$s,	1994	Nov	108.18	108.22	+1.7	8.42
$11\frac{5}{8}$s,	1994	Nov	116.3	116.7	+1.10	8.44
$8\frac{5}{8}$s,	1995	Jan p	100.30	101.2	+1.3	8.42
3s,	1995	Feb	92.25	93.11	− .1	4.09
$10\frac{1}{2}$s,	1995	Feb	110.14	110.18	+1.3	8.48
$11\frac{1}{4}$s,	1995	Feb p	114.8	114.12	+1.8	8.50
$10\frac{3}{8}$s,	1995	May	109.29	110.1	+1.3	8.50
$11\frac{1}{4}$s,	1995	May p	114.16	114.20	+1.10	8.52
$12\frac{5}{8}$s,	1995	May	122.7	122.11	+1.6	8.46
$10\frac{1}{2}$s,	1995	Aug p	110.18	110.22	+1.4	8.55
$9\frac{1}{2}$s,	1995	Nov p	105.4	105.8	+1.8	8.56
$11\frac{1}{2}$s,	1995	Nov	116.19	116.23	+1.4	8.52
$8\frac{7}{8}$s,	1996	Feb p	101.21	101.25	+1.9	8.56
$7\frac{3}{8}$s,	1996	May p	92.16	92.20	+1.6	8.63
$8\frac{5}{8}$s,	1997	Aug k	99.21	99.25	+1.22	8.66
$7\frac{1}{4}$s,	1996	Nov p	91.13	91.17	+1.9	8.64
$8\frac{1}{2}$s,	1997	May k	98.30	99.2	+1.14	8.65
$8\frac{7}{8}$s,	1997	Nov	101.21	101.25	+1.15	8.60
7s,	1993-98	May	89.5	89.9	+1.15	8.58
$3\frac{1}{2}$s,	1998	Nov	94.15	95.1	+1.15	4.07
$8\frac{1}{2}$s,	1994-99	May	98.16	98.20	+1.16	8.69
$7\frac{7}{8}$s,	1995-00	Feb	93.21	93.25	+1.23	8.72
$8\frac{3}{8}$s,	1995-00	Aug	97.21	97.25	+2.10	8.67
$11\frac{3}{4}$s,	2001	Feb	123.2	123.8	+2.21	8.73
$13\frac{1}{8}$s,	2001	May	133.26	134	+2.23	8.75
8s,	1996-01	Aug	94.16	94.22	+3.2	8.67
$13\frac{3}{8}$s,	2001	Aug	135.30	136.4	+2.21	8.77
$15\frac{3}{4}$s,	2001	Nov	154.26	155	+2.23	8.79
$14\frac{1}{4}$s,	2002	Feb	143.6	143.12	+2.23	8.81
$11\frac{5}{8}$s,	2002	Nov	122.14	122.20	+2.25	8.85
$10\frac{3}{4}$s,	2003	Feb	115.14	115.20	+2.23	8.85

• • •

Source: Wall Street Journal, January 18, 1988.

Coupon rate—the stated percentage of the face value of a bond or note paid in interest each period.

The rate of "7S," called the **coupon rate,** means that this Treasury obligation pays 7 percent of its face value in interest each year. Treasury obligations pay half of these coupon payments every six months. For example, if the face value of the bond is $1,000, the bond will pay annual interest of $0.07 \times \$1,000 = \$70$. Half of this amount, $\$70/2 = \$35$, would be paid every six months. Most bonds, both corporate and government, make semiannual payments of interest.

The maturity date of "1994 Jan" means that the last interest payment will be made in January 1994 along with repayment of the face value.

Figure 4–4
Cash Flows from a U.S. Government Note

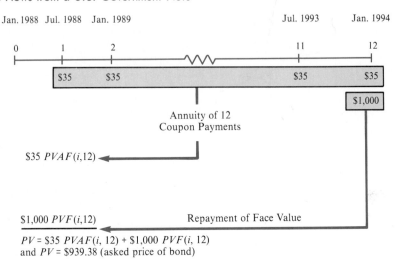

$$PV = \$35 \; PVAF(i, 12) + \$1{,}000 \; PVF(i, 12)$$
and $PV = \$939.38$ (asked price of bond)

Figure 4–4 displays the cash flows the purchaser of the bond would receive on a bond with a face value of $1,000 if it were bought in January 1988 and held until maturity in 1994 (assuming, of course, the U.S. government makes all the promised payments). Note that Figure 4–4 divides time into six-month periods, because for this Treasury security, interest is paid every six months (in January and July of each year).

The next figures in the highlighted row of Figure 4–3, "93.26 (Bid)" and "93.30 (Asked)," require some explanation. They are quotes by government-bond dealers in the over-the-counter market (see Chapter 2) and indicate the price at which the dealers would buy this bond (the *bid price*) or sell this bond (the *asked price*). Both prices are quoted in terms of the percentage of face value of the bond and use a special convention for decimals. As stated at the top of Figure 4–3, decimals represent 32nds—not tenths; thus, 93.26 for a bid price means that dealers have bid, or offered to pay, 93 26/32 percent of the face value of the bond to buy the bond.[2] In the case of a $1,000-face-value bond, this amount is 93.813 percent of $1,000, or $938.13. The bid change, "1.5," is the change in the bid price since the previous day.

Note that the bid price of 93.26 is less than the asked price of 93.30. This means that dealers are asking 93 30/32 percent of face value to sell you the note, but they are willing to pay only 93 26/32 percent of face value to buy the same note from you. The difference between the bid and asked price of 4/32 percent = 0.125 percent (or $1.25 per $1,000 face value) is called the *spread* and represents one of the

---

[2]This convention can lead to what are, at first, confusing results. For example, as this convention is used, 99.22 is greater than 99.9 because 99.22 = 99 22/32 and 99.9 = 99 9/32. Also, 99.20 is not equal to 99.2.

ways a government-bond dealer would make money by buying securities at a slightly lower price (bid price) and selling them at a higher (asked) price.[3]

At what price could you buy this bond? While a large, powerful buyer, such as a major investment bank, might be able to negotiate and buy the bond at less than the asked price, a good assumption is that most buyers would have to pay the full amount of the asked price—that is, 93 30/32 percent of face value, or $939.38 for a note with a $1,000 face value. In the market, $939.38 is the value in today's dollars of this note maturing in January 1994.

We can now put the cash flows from this bond into the DCF model as shown in Figure 4–4 by using the following equation:

$$PV = \sum_{t=1}^{12} \frac{\$35}{(1 + i)^t} + \frac{\$1,000}{(1 + i)^{12}}$$

$$\$939.38 = \$35 \, PVAF(i, 12) + \$1,000 \, PVF(i, 12).$$

Note that in applying the DCF model, we have broken the cash flow in pe-riod 12 into two parts—the coupon payment of $35 and the principal repayment of $1,000. Note also that there are a total of 12 periods from January 1988 to January 1994. The one unknown in the equation above is the discount rate, i. What discount rate is the market using to value the cash flows from this bond? Observe that because our time line in Figure 4–4 is divided into six-month peri-ods, the rate i for this problem is defined for only a six-month period compounded once per six months.

Finding the value of i to satisfy the above equation is mechanical but not very interesting. Some calculators will solve the problem, and there are even bond tables that give interest rates that will equate price to the present value of interest and principal payments.

In general, the problem is to find the value of i in Appendix Tables I and II at the end of the book that will work. For example, at a discount rate of 5 percent, Appendix Table II gives $PVAF(0.05, 12) = 8.863$ and Appendix Table I gives $PVF(0.05, 12) = 0.557$. Thus, at 5 percent,

$$PV = \$35(8.863) + \$1,000(0.557) = \$867.10.$$

At a discount rate of 3 percent, the appropriate present value factor from Appendix Table II is 9.954 and from Appendix Table I is 0.701. Thus, at 3 percent,

$$PV = \$35(9.954) + \$1,000(0.701) = \$1,049.80.$$

We can see from this that the correct value of i must lie somewhere between 5 percent and 3 percent, because $939.38, the actual present value of the note in the market, lies between $867.10 (the PV at 5 percent) and $1,049.80 (the PV at 3 percent). In fact, with precise tables, i could be calculated as 4.15 percent. Re-member, however, that this value for i is per six months. On an annual basis the

---

[3]Bid prices will never be greater than asked prices unless the dealer wants to lose money continuously. If the bid price were greater than the asked price, a buyer could buy at the asked price and turn right around and sell at the bid price, making an instant and riskless profit.

rate is double that, or $2 \times 4.15 = 8.30$ percent.[4] Note also that the compounding period would be six months because Figure 4–4 is divided into six-month periods. Thus, we can finally state that the market's discount rate on this note is 8.30 percent per year compounded semiannually. In the government-bond market, this rate is called the **yield to maturity.** The yield to maturity is the rate a bondholder could earn on the bond (or note) if he or she bought it at the current price, held the bond to maturity, and received all the cash flows promised by the bond. This yield to maturity, sometimes shortened to *yield,* is understood to be compounded semiannually, so the January 1994 bond would be said to have a yield of 8.30 percent. Note this yield figure of 8.30 percent is precisely the last number in the *Wall Street Journal* entry for the January 1994 bond.

Yield to maturity — the rate that could be earned on a bond or note if the investor bought it at the current price, held it to maturity, and received all the cash flows promised.

An initial reaction might be, why go to all the trouble of calculating the yield when it is right there in the newspaper? In fact, the benefit of seeing a yield calculation (at least once) is in understanding exactly what that number does and does not mean. The yield is a rate of return you can earn on this Treasury bond *if you hold it to maturity.*

Valuation of Stocks

In the case of the U.S. government bond analyzed above, the cash flows (at least if you held the bond to maturity) are fairly easy to predict — the payment of interest and face value. The same is the case for most bonds issued by corporations that have stated coupon rates, maturities, and face amounts.

We now move one step further to see how the same DCF model provides a basis for valuing the stream of benefits associated with owning a firm or a share in that firm. Shareholders purchase a share of a firm when they acquire common stock. Shareholders are also referred to as *equity owners* of the corporation because stock is sometimes called *equity.* The stream of cash flows associated with stock is much more uncertain than that associated with bonds (unlike a bond, common stock offers no contractual payment), and common stock offers no specified date for repayment of principal.

Common stocks offer an uncertain stream of cash flows (dividends) with no repayment of principal, while bonds offer a contractually fixed stream of cash flows (interest) with a specified repayment date for principal.

Does the same general DCF valuation formula apply? It does. The formula allows us to convert a *stream* of expected benefits (or cash flows), whether finite or infinite, whether riskless or risky, whether equal or unequal, into a *single* present value. The big difference in using the valuation formula for equity securities (common stock) is that the future stream of benefits expected on equities is much harder to predict than the cash flows we have analyzed so far. Although it may be a difficult task, predicting future benefits is important for managers in making de-

---

[4]Many hand-held calculators now have the capability to solve for the precise yield to maturity. With tables, the process simply involves trial and error until you find an interest rate that makes the present value of the coupon payments and face value equal to the asked price. This text follows the convention used in the market for U.S. government securities that yields to maturity are quoted assuming semiannual compounding. As a result, we refer to an annual rate of 8.30 percent, which is double 4.15 percent. A rate of 8.30 percent per year compounded semiannually has an *effective* annual rate of $(1.0415)^2 - 1$, or about 8.47 percent. The difference between 8.47 and 8.30 reflects the semiannual compounding.

cisions that will increase the value of their firm's stock and, hence, the well-being of the firm's shareholders.

Dividend-Valuation Model

The general DCF model tells us that value is a function of the future cash flows to be received. The cash flows that the owner of shares in a firm actually stands to receive are dividends plus the proceeds from the sale of the shares at some future date. The dividend is the only cash payment made by the firm to the shareholder. In most cases, firms pay out part of their earnings in the form of dividends and retain a part for reinvestment. The value of a share of stock at time period 0 (the present) can be calculated as shown in Equation (1).

$$P_0 = \frac{D_1}{1 + K_e} + \frac{D_2}{(1 + K_e)^2} + \cdots + \frac{D_n + P_n}{(1 + K_e)^n}$$

$$= \sum_{t=1}^{n} \frac{D_t}{(1 + K_e)^t} + \frac{P_n}{(1 + K_e)^n} \tag{1}$$

where D_t = the dividend expected in period t, P_n = the price at which the share is expected to be sold at the end of the final period, and K_e = the rate of return required by the market on the firm's stock.

The required rate of return is simply the discount rate that shareholders in the market are applying to the stock. The subscript e refers to the fact that stocks are also called equities. Note that the value of the shares depends only on *cash payments that the holder expects to receive*. Equation (1) is a straightforward application of the DCF model to the valuation of equity securities and has come to be known as the **dividend-valuation model.**

Dividend-valuation model — the discounted-cash-flow model applied to the valuation of stock, or equity.

Sample Problem 4–1
Applying the Dividend-Valuation Model to TMI Stock

Triangle Microsystems Inc. (TMI), producer of both business and home computers, is expected to pay a dividend of $1 per share in 1990. In addition, shareholders expect this dividend to grow steadily at 7 percent per year for the next 3 years. At the end of the 3-year period, financial experts expect TMI stock to be selling for between $12 and $16 per share; let's assume an average expectation of $14 per share. If the market's required rate of return (discount rate) on TMI stock is 15 percent, what would be the market price of TMI stock at the end of 1989?

Solution
First, let's summarize the relevant cash flows to the nearest penny. In year 1— 1990—the expected dividend is $1.00; in year 2—1991—the expected dividend is $1(1 + 0.07) = $1.07; in year 3—1992—the expected dividend is $1(1 + 0.07)^2 = $1.14 and the expected proceeds from the sale of stock are $14.00.

Applying Equation (1), the current (1989) price (P_0) for a share of TMI stock can be calculated as follows:

$$P_0 = \$1.00 \, PVF(0.15, 1) + \$1.07 \, PVF(0.15, 2) + \$1.14 \, PVF(0.15, 3)$$
$$+ \$14.00 \, PVF(0.15, 3)$$
$$= \$1.00(0.870) + \$1.07(0.756) + \$1.14(0.658) + \$14.00(0.658)$$
$$= \$0.87 + \$0.81 + \$0.75 + \$9.21 = \$2.43 + \$9.21$$
$$= \$11.64 \,.$$

From these calculations, we see that TMI's market price must be \$11.64 if shareholders require a 15 percent annual return on the expected cash flows. This \$11.64 is the sum of the present value of dividends for the next three years (a present value of \$2.43) plus the present value of the proceeds of selling the stock for \$14.00 in 1989 (a present value of \$9.21).

Companies often pay dividends on a quarterly basis, so we have simplified the problem by using annual figures. Further, the cash flows are only guesses about what might occur. In practice, obtaining such cash-flow estimates is a major difficulty. Anyone who buys TMI at \$11.64 will likely get either more or less than the cash flows (dividends and stock price) projected. The cash flows are, however, the best guesses presently available. ▣

Constant-Growth Dividend-Valuation Model

Looking at Equation (1), a natural question is: On what does the share price, P_n, in period n depend? This price depends on dividends to be received from that point further into the future and on the proceeds from a sale at an even further point. Value at that further point in turn depends on dividends from that point on. So we can say that the value of a share of stock is simply the present value of *all* future dividends expected on the share.

Estimating future dividends for a two- or three-year period is difficult enough. How would one estimate dividends forever? A pragmatic way of providing such estimates is to assume that the dividend is going to grow steadily at the constant rate, g. If we make this assumption, it turns out that we get a usable way to calculate share price.

The present value, P_0, of a share of stock, when calculated as simply the present value of all future dividends expected and assuming that the dividend will grow steadily at the constant rate, g, is

$$P_0 = \frac{D_1}{K_e - g} \tag{2}$$

where D_1 = the dividend expected in the first year, K_e = the rate of return required by the market, and g = the expected rate of growth in dividends.

---

[5]Except for the growth rate, g, Equation (2) is just like the perpetuity formula in Equation (6) of Chapter 3. Stated another way, a perpetuity has a growth rate of zero—it is a payment that is the same each period. Chapter 3's Equation (6) indicated that for a perpetuity, present value was just the payment amount divided by the discount rate, which is equivalent to this chapter's Equation (2) because $g = 0$ for a perpetuity. With growth, the denominator in Equation (2) becomes smaller than without growth. The lower denominator with growth implies a higher present value. This makes common sense—all other things equal, a stock with growth in dividends is worth more than one without growth. Equation (2) reflects this fact. Technically speaking, Equation (2) holds only when K_e exceeds g. If g exceeds K_e forever, the present value, P_0, becomes infinitely large. In financial markets, we don't find stocks with infinite prices, which means that in practice g does not exceed K_e.

Equation (2) is known as the **constant-growth dividend-valuation model.**

Constant-growth dividend-valuation model — a method for valuing stock that assumes the dividend will grow at a constant rate.

Sample Problem 4–2
Applying the Constant-Growth Dividend-Valuation Model to TMI Stock

Let's return to Triangle Microsystems Inc. and make some different assumptions about its future. Suppose that TMI is expected to pay a dividend of $1 per share in 1990 and that future dividends are expected to grow steadily at 7 percent per year. The market's required rate of return (the discount rate) on TMI stock is 15 percent. Assume that this growth in dividends is expected to continue indefinitely. Apply the constant-growth dividend-valuation model from Equation (2) to determine the market price of TMI stock at the end of 1989.

Solution
The market price of the stock can be calculated as

$$P_0 = \$1.00/(0.15 - 0.07) = \$1.00/0.08 = \$12.50 \text{ per share.}$$

This price differs from the answer to Sample Problem 4–1 of $11.64 because we made different assumptions about cash flows.

Equation (2) allows us to estimate the value of a share of stock assuming we can make assumptions about future dividend growth and shareholders' required return. We can use the same relationships to look at shareholders' required return by rearranging Equation (2) as shown in Equation (3).

The capitalization rate, or discount rate, that equates the present value of a share of stock and the stream of all future dividends expected, assuming that the dividends will grow at a steady rate, can be calculated as

$$K_e - g = \frac{D_1}{P_0}$$

$$K_e = \frac{D_1}{P_0} + g \qquad (3)$$

where D_1 = expected dividend per share at time 1, P_0 = current market price per share, g = expected growth rate in dividends, and K_e = the discount rate, or capitalization rate.

Using the constant-growth dividend model, the discount or capitalization rate applied to a stock can be estimated as the sum of the growth rate and the dividend rate. The dividend rate, also called the dividend "yield," is the dividend divided by the price of the stock.

That is, the capitalization rate implied by a given dividend rate, D_1/P_0, and a given growth rate, g, is simply the sum of the two. Equation (3) shows that the shareholders' required return will be equated to the sum of next period's dividend yield (D_1/P_0 = dividends as a percentage of share price) and the expected growth (g) in dividends.

In interpreting Equation (3) we must realize that it is the stock price, P_0, that adjusts in financial markets so that the relationship shown in Equation (3) will hold. If little growth is expected in dividends (if g is low), share price (P_0) will be low, and hence dividend yield (D_1/P_0) will be high. The result will be that the shareholder's required return will be satisfied largely by dividend yield. In contrast, if dividend growth is expected to be high, the share price will (all other things being constant) be higher, and as a result the dividend yield will be lower.

In the higher-growth case, the shareholder's required return may be satisfied largely by expected growth even if current dividend yield is low.

Sample Problem 4–3

The Capitalization Rate Applicable to TMI Stock

Given the information supplied about TMI stock in Sample Problem 4–2, what capitalization rate is applicable to the relationship between stock price and expected future benefits?

Solution

Equation (3) can be used to interpret the data in Sample Problem 4–2. Note that TMI's current dividend yield is the \$1 dividend divided by the stock price of \$12.50, or 8 percent. Adding this figure to the expected growth rate of 7 percent gives us 15 percent, which is the market's required rate of return (K_e) on TMI stock. In other words, investors expect to receive a total return on TMI stock of 15 percent—8 percent in current yield plus an additional 7 percent through capital gain achieved through a growing stock price as dividends grow.

Variable-Growth Dividend-Valuation Models

The constant-growth dividend-valuation model is an oversimplified depiction of a complex world. The insights that these models provide are useful, and, in fact, they are widely used to estimate the rate of return required by the marketplace on equity securities. Nonetheless, no simple model can give us the ultimate truth. There will always be situations in which the assumptions of the model do not hold.

The weakness of the constant-growth dividend-valuation model is its assumption that a single growth rate will persist into the future indefinitely. This assumption can be especially misleading when it is applied to companies that have grown very rapidly.

As an extreme example, consider Teledyne, a company in the business of industrial electronics, specialty metals, and consumer products. According to the 1985 *Fortune 500* directory, the company's earnings per share grew at a rate of more than 52 percent per year between 1974 and 1984.

Common sense tells us that we cannot project an observed 52 percent growth rate very far into the future and certainly not to infinity. At 52 percent growth a year, the company's sales (which were \$3.494 billion in 1984) will grow past the \$15 trillion mark in 20 years, a figure more than four times the 1984 gross national product of the United States!

Variable-growth dividend-valuation model—a method for valuing stock that assumes that a rapid growth in the dividend can continue for only a short period and will then decline to a more normal growth level.

One way to resolve the issue is to use a **variable-growth dividend-valuation model.** Such a model would assume that rapid growth can continue for only a short period into the future, beyond which growth declines to a more normal level close to the growth of the economy as a whole. One problem with this approach is that there are few objective methods for estimating how long above-normal growth will continue.

How Portfolio Managers Use the Dividend-Valuation Model

"**T**his is a very hysterical business," remarked an executive with a major investment-counseling firm in describing his industry. "Emotion rides high, and things tend to get exaggerated, and that creates opportunities."

To help identify the opportunities that emotion creates, a number of major investment-management firms since the late 1970s have been making heavy use of the dividend-valuation model, or *dividend-discount model (DDM),* as many practitioners call it. The success of those using the dividend-valuation model has spawned a boom in what one observer called "born-again value players," who have brought the model into wider popularity. "The user universe for our dividend-discount model has gone straight up," commented a vice-president of one of several Wall Street firms offering the models to outside users. An analyst at one firm making heavy use of the dividend-valuation model stated that the top 20 percent of stocks ranked by the model from 1970 through 1983 would have outperformed the Standard & Poor's (S&P) 500 stock index by 7 to 8 percentage points. The S&P 500 index is a widely followed average of 500 stocks.

Advocates of the dividend-valuation model differ in the ways they use it and in the extent to which they rely on it. For some firms, it is the core of their approach. One firm uses the model to rank a universe of about 500 stocks from highest expected returns to lowest. The top 100 stocks become buy candidates. Stocks become candidates for sale once they drop out of the top 20 percent and are automatic sells when they drop below the top 40 percent. Performance in 1984 for this firm was an average return of 11 percent versus 6.3 percent for the Standard & Poor's 500 index; for the five years ending in 1983, performance for this firm was 26 percent per year versus 17.3 for the S&P index.

A larger group of firms, estimated by some to be between 50 and 100 in number, use the dividend-valuation model as one tool among several upon which they rely heavily. One firm uses the model as one of five equally weighted screens, along with measures of momentum, current and historical price/earnings ratios, and normalized measures of earnings (that is, measures adjusted for the effects of the business cycle). Finally, there is an even larger group of firms that use the model as a cross-check, or an indicator to be heeded or ignored at will. One analyst commented that "two out of three institutional money managers are casual DDM practitioners."

Users of the dividend-valuation model are quick to point out that the model has its limitations. The model tends to underperform in comparison to some other techniques at times when emotion rules the stock market. That means that users of the model will not always lead the pack. Also, the model is only as good as the data that go into it. One early user of the dividend-valuation model pointed to a case in which his firm was badly burned in energy stocks in spite of use of the model because of one analyst's euphoric predictions for the industry. "It is impossible to stress too strongly the importance of consistent inputs and the political integration of the process," commented an executive of one firm.

In summing up use of the dividend-valuation model in investment management over the past six to eight years, an analyst stated that the model has gone from "a hard (thing to) sell in 1979 to part of the landscape today." Some users expect it ultimately to become the standard way of doing investment analysis.

Source: Material for this section was adapted from the article by B. Donnelly, "The Dividend Discount Model Comes Into Its Own," *Institutional Investor,* March 1985, pp. 77–82.

Using the DCF Model to Value Securities

The DCF model relates three critical variables: cash flows, the discount rate, and the value of the security.

In previous examples, we have applied the basic DCF model to place a value on a number of different types of securities—CDs, bonds, and stocks. In the process we saw that the DCF formula relates three critical sets of variables—the projected *cash flows,* the *discount rate,* and the *value* of the security. Given an estimate of cash flows and given a discount rate, we can determine the value of an asset. Alternatively, given a value and a set of projected cash flows, we can infer what the market's discount rate must have been.

These relationships are especially important to financial managers. Most investment decisions facing a manager involve paying out cash in hopes of receiving future cash. These cash trade-offs will directly affect the value of the firm, as our DCF formula suggests. If a financial manager wants to increase the value of the firm, he or she must understand how values are determined.

Risk Characteristics

Risk—the degree of uncertainty about an outcome.

So far so good. The main problem with valuation arises when we remember that the assets we were valuing (and will value in the future) are characterized by very different sorts of **risk**—or the degree of uncertainty about an outcome. A U.S. government bond is almost certain to pay off the promised interest and face value if we hold it to maturity. A bond issued by a corporation is typically very safe, but occasionally some corporations are not able to meet their promised payments and, thus, *default* on their promise.

Default risk—the risk that the issuer of a bond will not meet promised payments.

Even ownership of a bond that has for practical purposes no **default risk** (such as a U.S. government bond) is not without its uncertainties. Suppose you buy a 20-year bond and must sell it one year later. Your actual return will depend on the price of the bond in one year—and that price will depend on next year's market required rate of return on government bonds, a rate that you can now only guess at. Such uncertainty about future interest rates is called **interest-rate risk.**

Interest-rate risk—uncertainty about future interest rates as they affect future value.

Sample Problem 4–4
Interest-Rate Risk on a U.S. Government Bond

Suppose that in January 1988 you bought the January 1994 U.S. government bond highlighted in Figure 4–3 for the asked price of $939.38 (the dollar equivalent of 93 30/32 percent of the $1,000 face value of the bond). We already know that the bond has a yield of 8.30 percent, so 8.30 percent will be your annual return if you hold it until it matures in January 1994. Suppose, however, that you have to sell the bond in July 1988, at which time yields on such bonds have risen to 12 percent per year. What would be the price, P, of the bond in July 1988? What would be your annualized rate of return over the six months that you owned the bond? (The 12 percent rate is hypothetical.)

Solution
As of July 1988 (right after the July coupon payment), the note will have 11 more semiannual coupon payments of $35 each to make as well as repayment of the

$1,000 face value in January 1994. Using the DCF model, the present value of the stream of payments associated with the bond can be calculated, with the help of Appendix Tables II and I at the end of this book, as

$$P = \$35 \ PVAF(0.06, 11) + \$1,000 \ PVF(0.06, 11)$$

$$= \$35(7.887) + \$1,000(0.527)$$

$$= \$830. \text{ or } 803$$

Note that $i = 0.12/2 = 0.06$ because we are dealing with six-month periods rather than years. We use the 12 percent rate (6 percent every six months) because the market now requires 12 percent interest on bonds such as this: 12 percent is the opportunity cost of money for this security.

Since we paid $939.38 for the note, received one coupon payment of $35, and then sold the bond for $P_1 = \$803$, our return, R, must satisfy the equation

$$\$939.38 = \$35/(1 + R) + \$830/(1 + R)$$

$$1 + R = (\$35 + \$830)/\$939.38$$

$$R = -0.108 .$$

We find that R is approximately equal to -0.108 per six months, or -0.216 per year. The price of the note dropped as interest rates went up from 8.30 percent to 12 percent. As a result, the actual return, R, earned on the bond from January to July 1988 would be negative if interest rates changed so dramatically. Even though the bond had no default risk, its return from January to July 1988 would be substantially lower than the yield to maturity because of *interest-rate risk.* Fortunately for bondholders, such a dramatic change in interest rates did not occur in early 1988.

Purchasing-power risk — the risk that money received in the future will not purchase the same goods and services it can today, or the risk that inflation will decrease the value of future cash flows.

Even if you know what dollar amounts you will receive, you can't be sure of what goods and services those dollars will be able to purchase, because purchasing power depends on future prices — that is, it depends on the rate of inflation. Thus, there is some **purchasing-power risk** associated with the uncertainties of inflation.

Financial risk — the additional risk to shareholders, over and above operating risk, that results from the use of debt (or debt-like) financing.

Operating risk or *business risk* — the risk to shareholders that arises from uncertainty about a firm's product markets or operations.

The true returns to stocks can be even more difficult to predict than those to bonds. Future dividends depend on many variables: corporate earnings, economic conditions, and management decisions. Stock prices can fluctuate dramatically. The investment risk borne by shareholders is the sum of a company's **financial risk** and its **operating risk.** Operating risk, sometimes referred to as *business risk,* is the uncertainty associated with a firm's product markets and operations. For example, a firm planning to enter the fast-food business faces unknowns about trends in the fast-food market. Will health-conscious consumers start to avoid hamburgers? A new firm might also face uncertainty about how its products will fare against competition from market giants like McDonald's or Burger King. Financial risk is the additional risk, over and above operating risk, to which shareholders are exposed when a company uses debt (or debt-like) financing. As the portion of future earnings committed to such fixed-cost obligations increases, so do risks to shareholders.

For example, suppose a project required an outlay of $100 now, and the financial manager expects that at the end of one year the project will end and earn either 20 percent ($120 for $100 invested) in a good outcome or 5 percent ($105 for $100 invested) in a bad outcome. Each of the outcomes is equally likely. While real-world operating risk is more complex, the uncertainty about the good or bad outcomes for the project is the underlying operating risk in this example. Given this operating risk, a firm has a number of options about how to finance the project. Table 4–1 describes two of these options. One option is to raise all money from shareholders (all-equity financing). The All-Equity Plan in Table 4–1 shows the returns to shareholders if the firm follows this strategy and uses no debt. The shareholders' returns exactly mirror those of the project. Another alternative is to use **financial leverage** — to finance part of the project with borrowing. Plan B in Table 4–1 traces through the shareholder returns if shareholders put up $10 for the project, with the remaining $90 being borrowed at a market interest rate of 10 percent per year. At time 1, the shareholders' return comes after repayment of the loan ($90 principal plus $9 interest). Table 4–1 shows that if the project turns out well (the good outcome is achieved) using Plan B, shareholders earn a whopping 110 percent, more than doubling their $10 investment. Financial leverage has magnified a 20 percent return on the project into more than a 100 percent return to shareholders — quite a profitable prospect that often provides a powerful incentive for borrowing when you expect the underlying investment will earn a rate of return higher than the interest rate charged on borrowing.

A further look at the results of using Plan B shows, however, that financial leverage is a two-edged sword. If the project turns sour (the bad outcome results),

Financial leverage — the use of debt, or borrowing, to finance investment.

Table 4–1

Financial Leverage and Financial Risk

Financing Plan (1)	Shareholder Investment (dollars) at $t = 0$ (2)	Outcome	Dollars to Shareholder at $t = 1$ (3)	Percent Return to Shareholder at $t = 1$ (4) $= [(3) - (2)]/(2)$
A. All-Equity Plan (entire $100 investment financed by shareholders)	$100	Good	$120	20
		Bad	$105	5
B. Financial-Leverage Plan ($10 financed by shareholders; $90 borrowed at 10 percent annual interest)	$ 10	Good	$120 − $99 (loan) = $21	110
		Bad	$105 − $99 (loan) = $6	−40

shareholders will experience a 40 percent loss because they end up borrowing money at 10 percent to invest it in a project that earns 5 percent—clearly a raw deal for shareholders. What should the firm do? If it knows the project outcome is going to be good, it should borrow. Because of operating risk, however, the project's future is uncertain. (We'll return to the firm's choice of financing in Part Four of this book.) What is clear is that a firm's use of debt increases risks to shareholders. This extra risk over and above operating risk is the financial risk to shareholders. As a result, even if two companies have basically the same operating risk, the stock of one may be more risky if that firm uses more debt financing than its counterpart. Also, individuals do not have to rely on firms to supply financial leverage. They can borrow for themselves (for example, from the bank) to increase the potential rewards and risks of investments. As Table 4–1 shows, the use of financial leverage adds financial risk to the operating risk already inherent in a firm's activities.

Required Return and Value

How can our discounted-cash-flow valuation model take into account these different types of uncertainties?

Some help in answering this question can be found by returning to some basic elements of value outlined in Chapter 1 — time and risk. There we defined the *value* of an asset as "the dollar amount that people would have to have today to make them just as well off as they would be owning the asset."

As we developed our DCF model in Chapter 3, the discount rate reduced the value of future cash dollars relative to present dollars. That is, future dollars were discounted back to their present value to reflect the forgone opportunity to earn a rate of return on money while we wait. We must remember that to fit our definition of *value* there must also be a penalty imposed for any uncertainty we have to bear as a result of holding the asset. Fortunately, the DCF model can also incorporate this penalty for risk by applying a higher discount rate. In effect, investors require higher returns (a higher discount rate) to compensate them for additional risks — and as the discount rate goes up, value goes down in the DCF model.

Suppose you expect the price of a certain share of stock in one year to be $50 and *require* a 19 percent annual return; that is, 19 percent is the minimum return you will accept. The stock is not expected to pay a dividend in the next year. What is the maximum price you would pay today for the stock? This price can be calculated as

$$P_0 = \$50 \ PVF(0.19, 1) = \$50(0.840) = \$42 \ .$$

Suppose, however, that you become more uncertain about the company's prospects. (For example, foreign competition increases.) While you still expect a price of $50 in one year, you now require a 25 percent return (an additional 6 percent over the previous 19 percent to compensate you for the new uncertainty). The maximum price you would now pay today for the stock can also be calculated as

$$P_0 = \$50 \; PVF(0.25, 1) = \$50(0.800) = \$40 \,.$$

■

The DCF model can be used to incorporate the effects of both time and risk on value.

■

Risk/expected-return trade-off— the greater the risk of an investment opportunity, the greater the return required by an investor.

■

The required rate of return is the minimum expected return the investor will accept on the investment. The required return compensates investors for the passage of time and for risk and is higher the higher the risk of the investment.

The higher required return (25 percent versus 19 percent) lowered the value of the stock from $42 to $40 per share—that is, there was a penalty for the new uncertainty associated with the company.

The DCF model can thus be used to capture the effects of both time and risk on value. The discount rate, or the *required rate of return* on an investment, becomes larger to compensate investors for greater risk.

Figure 4–5 illustrates the **risk/expected-return trade-off** explained by the DCF model. The greater the risk of the investment opportunity, the greater the return required by the investor. The line in Figure 4–5 symbolizes the terms of the risk/expected-return trade-off.[6] At point *B*, a higher return is required than at point *A* because there is extra return required for bearing extra risk. To economize on words, we will sometimes refer to this trade-off as simply the *risk/return trade-off*.

Note that the risk/return trade-off depicted in Figure 4–5 assumes that investors do not like risk. Because they are risk-averse, they require compensation for bearing risk. The fact that an investment has zero risk, however, does not mean it will have a required return of zero.[7] As shown in Figure 4–5, even at zero

---

[6] In Figure 4–5, the risk/return trade-off is drawn as a positively sloped straight line. While the trade-off need not be a straight line, there must be a positive relationship between risk and required return—the higher the risk, the higher the required return.

[7] In reality, there is no such thing as a riskless investment. U.S. government bonds are widely used as the risk-free benchmark. While such bonds are relatively free of default risk, they are not free of the risk of price fluctuations as the level of interest rates rises and falls. The term *risk-free* is used in this chapter to be consistent with common usage in the finance literature. When referring to investment alternatives that actually exist in practice, "risk-free" should be interpreted to mean "least-risk."

Figure 4–5
The Risk/Expected-Return Trade-Off

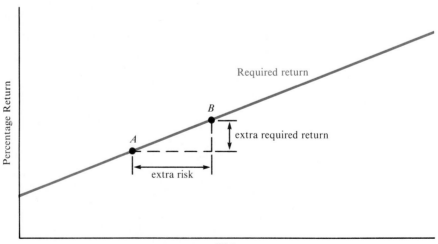

risk there is a positive required return; investors still require compensation for the passage of time. Thus, the required return compensates the investor for both the passage of time and risk. In symbolic terms, the required return can be represented as shown in Equation (4), where the **risk premium (*rp*)** is the extra return required as compensation for risk.

Risk premium (*rp*)—the extra return required as compensation for risk.

The required rate of return can be represented symbolically as

$$(4) \qquad\qquad K = R_f + rp \qquad\qquad (4)$$

where K = the required rate of return, R_f = the risk-free rate of return, and rp = the risk premium.

Risk and Risk Aversion

To explain adequately how risky benefits are valued in the financial markets, we must draw a clear distinction between the *risk* of investments and the *attitude toward risk* of investors. Since investors will buy and sell the firm's stock and thereby determine the stock's value in financial markets, it is important for financial managers to consider investors' attitudes toward risk.

Risk

As mentioned earlier in the chapter, *risk* is the degree of uncertainty about an outcome. Consider two investments, A and B, that have the possible payoffs listed in Table 4–2, depending on the state of the economy. Assuming that the three states of the economy are equally likely, the average expected return from both investments is $100. But the return from investment A will range between $90 and $110, whereas that from B may vary between $0 and $200. Thus, there is considerably more uncertainty about the return from B. As a result, we say that B is riskier than A.

Risk Aversion

Now let us consider the effect of investor attitudes toward risk. Suppose you were offered an opportunity to choose one of the two investments, A or B, in Table 4–2.

Table 4–2
Estimating Outcomes for Investments Based on States of the Economy

State of Economy	Outcome (dollars)	
	Investment A	Investment B
Recession	90	0
Normal	100	100
Boom	110	200

Expected value—the weighted average of possible outcomes where each weight is the probability associated with the outcome.

Both investments are expected to have a $100 payoff. If your choice is A, you are *risk-averse* with respect to this decision—you dislike risk. If your choice is B, you are *risk-preferent* —you like risk. If you are indifferent between A and B, you are *risk-neutral* with respect to this decision.

Consider another illustration. Suppose you are offered an opportunity to undertake investment B in return for a cash payment. The **expected value** of investment B is $100, as calculated in Table 4–3. This $100 figure comes from adding up each possible payoff multiplied by the probability that the payoff will occur, as shown in the last column of Table 4–3.

What is the maximum you would be willing to pay for an opportunity to invest in B? If your maximum were less than $100, you would be exhibiting risk-averse behavior with respect to this investment opportunity. If your maximum were more than $100, you would be exhibiting risk preference. If your maximum were exactly $100, you would be exhibiting risk neutrality. In general, an unwillingness to pay an amount as great as the expected value of an uncertain investment opportunity indicates risk-averse behavior; a willingness to pay exactly the expected value indicates risk neutrality; a willingness to pay more indicates risk preference.

Any given individual may exhibit risk-averse behavior toward some decisions and risk-preferent behavior toward others. An individual who plays roulette in Las Vegas, an example of risk-preferent behavior, also may own fire insurance on a house, an example of risk-averse behavior. The size of the gamble also may be a factor. The same individual may be risk-preferent toward small gambles, such as flipping coins for nickels, and risk-averse toward large gambles, such as flipping coins for $1,000 a flip.

There is nothing inconsistent or irrational about the behavior of an individual who exhibits risk aversion toward some gambles and risk preference toward others. In the case of an individual who is risk-averse toward most financial decisions but who also occasionally exhibits risk-preferent behavior, it is likely that the risk-preferent behavior contains elements of entertainment—for example, gambling in Las Vegas.

Where matters of income and wealth are concerned, as distinct from entertainment, we can safely assume risk aversion to be characteristic of nearly all individuals. An individual making an investment decision affecting only himself or

Table 4–3

Calculating the Expected Value of an Investment

Payoff (dollars) (1)	Probability (2)	Weighted Outcome (dollars) (3) = (1) × (2)
0	0.333	0
100	0.333	33.33
200	0.333	66.67
Expected Value of Payoff		100.00

When the DCF method is used, the discount rate used must vary with the riskiness of the investment.

Risk aversion, risk neutrality, and risk preference are three types of investor attitudes toward risk. A risk-averse investor requires compensation for bearing risk. A risk-preferent investor will pay for the opportunity to gamble. A risk-neutral investor is indifferent toward risk; that is, he or she requires no compensation for bearing risk.

herself can determine his or her own attitude toward risk. With respect to investors in general, studies of the securities markets provide convincing evidence that the majority of investors in stocks and bonds are risk-averse. This suggests that they are unwilling to pay an amount equal to the expected value of an investment opportunity; that is, they demand a premium for bearing risk.[8] The greater the perceived risk, the lower the value placed on uncertain benefits.

Risk aversion does not imply complete avoidance of risk; it merely implies that compensation is required. The greater the risk, the greater the compensation must be. A risk-averse person will undertake a risky investment, even an investment of very high risk, provided the compensation is sufficiently high.

The concept of risk aversion has very important implications for investment decisions. A higher expected return is required to motivate individual investors to take on greater risk. Similarly, if shareholders of a professionally managed firm are risk-averse (and, in general, they are), and if management is to act as agent of those shareholders, then investments of differing risk must be evaluated using different required rates of return. In applying the DCF method, the discount rate used must vary with the riskiness of the investment opportunity, which is determined by the degree of uncertainty surrounding the stream of cash flows that the investment generates.

[8]For evidence of risk aversion, see I. Friend and M. Blume, "The Demand for Risky Assets," *American Economic Review* 55 (December 1975): 900–22.

Finance in Practice 4–2

The Crash of '87

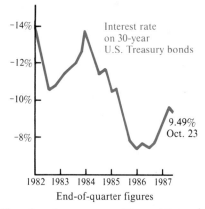

End-of-quarter figures

From August 1982 until the end of 1986, the stock market more than doubled, making many people happy. Much of the gain appears to have come because of the decline in interest rates that took place over that period. As inflation declined beginning in 1981, long-term interest rates fell from 14 percent in mid-1982 to under 8 percent by late 1986 (see interest-rate chart). The market benefited from the lower "capitalization rate" in the valuation equation.

In early 1987, articles began to appear questioning whether the market was "fully

priced" and perhaps even getting a bit too high. But it kept on going up. The Dow Jones Index of 30 industrial stocks closed above 2,000 for the first time on January 8, 1987. From that point until its peak on August 25, it went up another 36 percent. But this time, interest rates were going *up,* not down. Starting from 7.6 percent in March 1987, rates on long-term Treasurys rose to 10.2 percent in October (the chart on p. 117 shows end-of-quarter figures and doesn't show the actual peak). Rising interest rates are usually bad for the stock market, not good, yet the market kept on going up.

On August 10, two weeks before what we now know was the 1987 peak, the *Wall Street Journal* ran a major feature story asking "How Much Power Is Left in the Bull?", i.e., the "bull market." Some of the experts interviewed for the article expressed caution, while others said the bull market would continue. "Are Stocks Too High?" asked *Fortune* in the cover story of its September 28 issue. The answer: "By the old gauges of value, no doubt about it. But while merger mania lasts, the new math of takeovers and buyouts could keep pushing prices skyward." *Fortune's* timing was exquisite, for hindsight now tells us that the market had already peaked in August, and was in decline as the article was being prepared. The dividend-discount model, one of the "old gauges" of value, was flashing red warning signals, indicating that stocks were selling for 149 percent of their fair value (see chart below). The

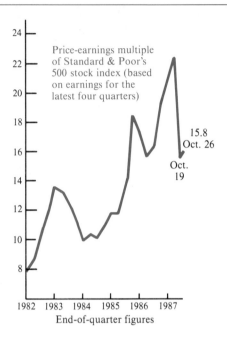

Price-earnings multiple of Standard & Poor's 500 stock index (based on earnings for the latest four quarters)

15.8
Oct. 26

Oct.
19

1982 1983 1984 1985 1986 1987
End-of-quarter figures

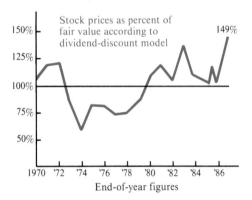

Stock prices as percent of fair value according to dividend-discount model

149%

1970 '72 '74 '76 '78 '80 '82 '84 '86
End-of-year figures

price/earnings ratio of the Standard & Poor's 500 stock index was above 22, higher than at any point since the mid-1960s (see chart in next column). "Things are different this time," said those who wished to ignore the warnings.

It turned out that the old gauges were right and the new math wrong. The market declined about 4 percent during September, then went down another 5 percent during the first 12 days of October. The week of October 12 was very bad. The Dow Jones 30 Industrials went down slightly on Monday the 12th, up a bit on Tuesday, then down sharply on each of the next three days. On Friday, October 16, it dropped 108 points, the first 100-point decline ever, and it was down 230 points for the week. All professional money managers and many amateurs pondered these events over the weekend, and by Monday morning a large number were of one mind: get out before everyone else does. On Monday, October 19, 1987, everyone headed for the exits at the same time. As the charts on p. 119 show, the market, measured by the DJI 30 index, on that one day made a sickening plunge of over 500 points, exceeding even the most dire predictions of those who had issued warnings earlier.

On "Black Monday," tens of thousands of individual investors called their brokers during the day to issue sell orders; thousands of others dialed in to their mutual funds with sell orders and forced the funds to sell to raise cash. Large institutional portfolio managers entered sell

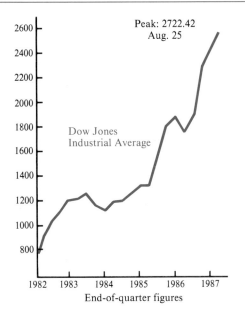

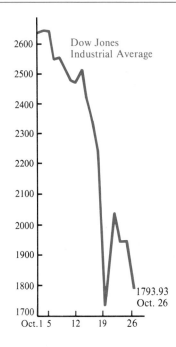

orders totaling billions of dollars. In the post mortem, the finger of blame has been pointed at two innovations of recent years, "portfolio insurance," and "program trading."

Portfolio insurance is a hedging approach whose objective is to limit losses. Executing the approach involves buying a complex mix of stocks and stock index "futures," which are contracts to buy stocks for future delivery at a price agreed upon today (see Chapter 20 for a discussion of financial futures). Cutting through the complexity, portfolio insurance results in buying when the market is rising and selling when it is falling. The more the market falls, the more selling is required in an "insured" portfolio. On October 19, 1987, about $60 billion in institutional portfolios were insured, and they all began the day selling in large quantities. As the market went into free fall, their insurance strategies required more and more selling, further depressing the market.

"Program trading" is another highly sophisticated and complex strategy that involves using computers to execute large volumes of transactions quickly to exploit differences between current prices and prices of futures

contracts. Leaving aside all the technical detail, the important thing about program trading for understanding the events of October 19, 1987, is that it involves massive volumes of transactions. On "Black Monday," program trading interacted with portfolio insurance to make things happen very fast.

Many experts now agree that the market was "overvalued" during the summer of 1987 (where were they before the fact?). What was frightening about "Black Monday" was the speed of the decline. Before the days of computers, high-speed data transmission, portfolio insurance, and program trading, the same decline might have taken place. But one might guess that it would have been spread over more than just a few days. One thing all market participants learned from this experience is that it isn't possible for all to exit simultaneously.

Sources: Adapted from Beatrice E. Garcia, "How Much Power Is Left in the Bull?" *The Wall Street Journal*, August 10, 1987; John J. Curran, "Are Stocks Too High?" *Fortune*, September 28, 1987; Wilton Woods, "Charting An Avalanche," *Fortune*, November 23, 1987.

International Focus

Stock-Market Fallout — Japanese Style

In October 1987, the long bull stock market of the 1980s came to a grinding halt with a drop of over 20 percent in the Dow Jones Industrial Average on a single day, October 19. The equity market drop wasn't restricted to the United States, either; it hit stock markets around the world, including the major exchanges in London and Japan.

But bull markets are not necessarily restricted to share prices, and in Japan the golf market was also affected. Between 1982 and early 1987 the Tokyo stock market nearly tripled — only to fall by 15 percent on a single October day. In the same 1982–1987 span, golf-club memberships in the Tokyo area increased tenfold — certainly a bull market for golf. What happened to memberships in October? Hard data are hard to come by, but some expensive clubs saw the value of a membership drop by half. Some brokers reported their clients had even been selling golf-club memberships to cover losses in the stock market.

Source: Adapted from "Into the Bunker," *The Economist,* November 21, 1987, p. 78.

The Discount Rate, Risk, and Financial Markets

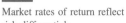

Market rates of return reflect risk differentials.

Increasing discount rates to provide compensation for risk is not just a mechanical device to use in DCF calculations: rates of return in markets reflect these risk differentials. Consider the data in Figure 4–6, which show that in mid-1987 the yield (required return) on long-term U.S. government obligations averaged about one percentage point less than yields on long-term bonds issued by public utilities (for example, power companies). At least part of the reason is that U.S. government bonds are safer than those issued by individual corporations. U.S. Treasury bonds are backed by the full taxing authority and financial power of the U.S. government. While public utilities are typically not small companies, they certainly don't have the financial resources of the federal government. The yield on municipal bonds was fully one percentage point below that on long-term U.S. government obligations, largely due to the tax advantages on these securities. As discussed in Chapter 2, such advantages motivate investors to require a lower before-tax rate of return on municipal bonds.

Such risk-related return differences are also reflected in past returns that investors have earned. Table 4–4 shows some average rates of return earned by investors in different sorts of securities over a long period of U.S. financial history — 1926–1986. As one would expect, common stocks have, on average, provided higher returns (12.1 percent) than corporate bonds (5.3 percent), which in turn have provided higher returns than long-term government bonds (4.7 percent). These results are consistent with the notion of higher returns for higher risks.

There is, however, a critical difference between *required return* and *actual return.* Our reasoning suggests that required returns ought to be higher as the risks

Figure 4–6
Differences in Bond Yields

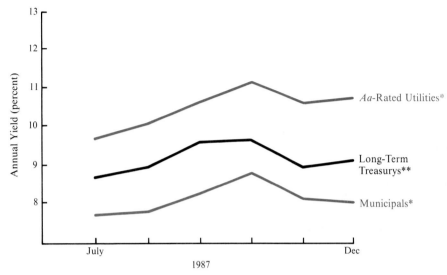

Source: *From Domestic Financial Statistics, January 1988. **From Federal Reserve Bank of St. Louis, February 18, 1988.

Table 4–4
Average Annual Returns for Various Types of Investments, 1926–1986

Type of Investment	Percentage Annual Return (arithmetic average)
Long-Term U.S. Government Bonds	4.7
Long-Term Corporate Bonds	5.3
Common Stocks	12.1

Source: Ibbotson Associates — Chicago

The required return of an investment may differ from the actual return investors receive after they make an investment; for example, stocks may perform better or worse than expected.

perceived by investors become greater. That does not mean, however, that investors will always receive their required return. For example, Table 4–4 shows that shareholders averaged 12.1 percent per year over the period 1926–1986. Figure 4–7 shows the numbers that went into that average. As Figure 4–7 shows, anyone owning stocks takes risks. The average of 12.1 percent does not capture fully the nature of what happened to someone who happened to invest in stocks during a year like 1974, when the return was −26.5 percent, or in 1985, when the return was 32.2 percent. After all, risk implies that the outcome may not be as good as you expect it to be.

Figure 4—7
Year-by-Year Returns on Common Stocks, 1926—1986

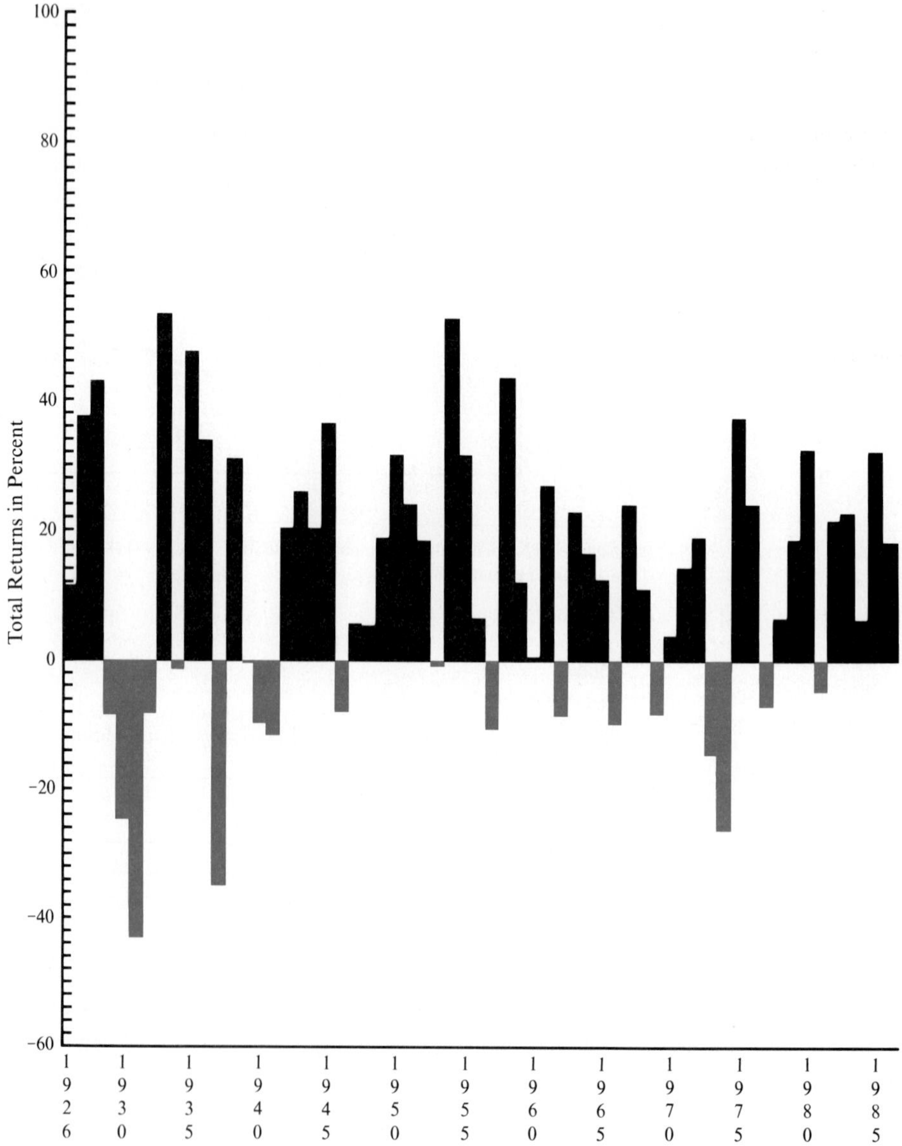

Source: Ibbotson Associates.

The Role of Markets

It is no accident that returns in financial markets reflect differences in risk. A major function of financial markets is to establish prices for financial assets; as a result, markets determine returns on those assets.

In a market for goods or services, trading occurs until a price is established that clears the market (equates quantity supplied with quantity demanded).

Equilibrium price, or **market-clearing price**—the price at which the quantity demanded of a good or service equals the quantity supplied.

Demand curve—shows the amounts of a good or service buyers are prepared to purchase at different prices during a specified time period.

Supply curve—shows the amounts of a good or service suppliers are willing to offer for sale at different prices during a specified time period.

In a market for goods and services, trading takes place until an **equilibrium price,** or **market-clearing price,** is established; that is, the price equates quantity demanded by buyers with quantity supplied by sellers. Figure 4–8 illustrates the typical supply and demand curves of microeconomic theory. The **demand curve** shows the amounts of a given item buyers are prepared to purchase at different prices during a specified time period. The **supply curve** shows the amounts of the item offered for sale at different prices during a specified time period.

As a result of buying and selling decisions by market participants, an equilibrium price of P^* is established. At a price of P^*, exactly Q^* units are both demanded and supplied. If the price falls below the equilibrium level, some demand is left unsatisfied, so the price is bid back up. If the price rises above the equilibrium level, excess supply results, causing the price to fall. Thus, the equilibrium price of P^* equates quantity supplied and quantity demanded.

For financial assets such as stocks and bonds, demand and supply curves like those in Figure 4–8 depend on the expectations of market participants about future rewards from owning those assets. All investors will be hoping to earn superior returns—after all, that is most of the potential fun in picking stocks. One strategy to earn such returns would be to buy stocks currently "underpriced" by the market. If an investor believes a certain stock is underpriced, he or she believes that the current price is below the equilibrium level—perhaps because of unwarranted market pessimism about the company's prospects. Buying at the low price, the smart investor could reap a capital gain when the market realizes the error of its ways and the stock price goes up. Sounds like a great strategy, but is it possible to pick underpriced stocks consistently? The answer to that question is the subject of considerable controversy. Clearly, many brokers feel they can pick winners—doing so is part of their business, and many fortunes have been made in the stock

Figure 4–8
The Equilibrium Price in a Market

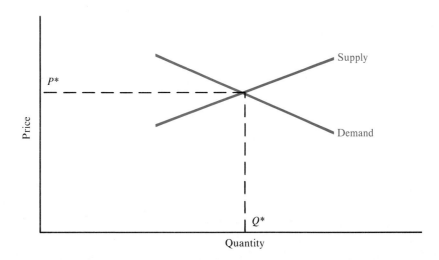

Efficient market — a market in which current market prices impound all available information and are a fair reflection of the true value of a financial asset.

market. On the other hand, there is substantial evidence that many financial markets (such as the well-organized stock and bond markets in the United States) are relatively efficient. An **efficient market** is one in which current market prices impound all available information and are, as a result, a fair reflection of the true value of a financial asset. Facing such prices, an investor is unlikely to consistently pick assets that turn out to be underpriced. After the fact, some prices will turn out to have been too high, and some too low; the difficulty lies in determining in advance which ones are which. Similarly, in an efficient market, a financial manager of a firm need not worry that his or her company's stock is underpriced when considering raising funds through the sale of new shares unless, of course, that manager has some unannounced information not yet available to the market. In short, the manager relies on an efficient market to price the firm's shares fairly.

We'll return to a more detailed discussion of market efficiency (and possible inefficiencies) in Part Four. For present purposes, it is important to remember that in well-organized financial markets information is readily available, and literally thousands of investors compete in the buying and selling of assets to establish prices. As a result of that competition, prices reflect a wealth of information. This does not mean that financial markets have perfect forecasting ability. In the future, some stocks will provide high financial returns and others will produce losses — the question is which one to buy now. No one wants to buy a stock to lose money. The basic uncertainty associated with securities is that the future is unknown. The key is that if markets are efficient, current prices will appropriately reflect this uncertainty.

The Market Required Rate of Return

A major function of financial markets is to establish prices. In principle, the market establishes a different required rate of return for each degree of risk.

This chapter has discussed the relationship between prices and returns on financial assets. A higher current price, other factors equal, implies a lower return, and vice versa. In establishing prices of financial assets, the market simultaneously is establishing expected returns. Given that investors are risk-averse, different rates of return are established for different degrees of risk. In effect, investments of differing risk are different commodities, each having a different price — that is, a different required rate of return. In principle, a different rate is established by the market for each degree of risk, thus resulting in a **market risk/return schedule,** as illustrated in Figure 4–9. Figure 4–9 shows that as the risk of an asset increases, the risk premium (rp) on that asset will increase. This increased risk premium is necessary to compensate risk-averse individuals for investing in risky securities. As the risk and risk premium increase, the required return (K) also increases. Chapter 5 will examine more carefully the measurement of risk and the nature of the risk/return trade-off.

Market risk/return schedule — shows the return required by investors at different levels of risk.

Opportunities to invest exist for all assets for which there are organized and public markets. Such markets exist for a wide variety of financial and real (physical) assets. Financial assets at the low end of the risk spectrum (left portion of Figure 4–9) include savings accounts and, for those with sufficient funds, U.S. government securities. Of slightly greater, but still low, risk are bonds issued by corporations. Then come common stocks, varying widely as to risk. Next there are

Figure 4–9
The Market Risk/Return Schedule

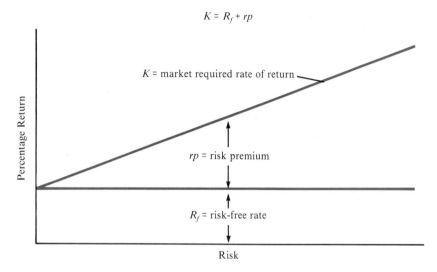

$$K = R_f + rp$$

K = market required rate of return

Percentage Return

rp = risk premium

R_f = risk-free rate

Risk

investments such as *commodity futures* (agreements about purchasing and selling commodities such as wheat at future dates), *financial futures* (agreements to purchase or sell financial assets at future dates), and *options* to purchase or sell financial assets at future dates. These latter investments usually are considered to be of high risk. (We will return in a later chapter to a discussion of financial futures and options.) The point we need to focus on here is that markets for all these assets are public and highly organized; information is readily available to participants, and costs of entering and transacting are relatively low. Other markets for investment assets, such as real estate, present additional opportunities for some investors but are less highly organized.

Returns in organized and public markets, which are available at low cost and little effort, represent the minimum an investor should accept on any investment opportunity. Hence, organized markets establish, for every degree of risk, the required rate of return. Since everyone faces essentially the same set of opportunities in the markets, the opportunity cost for any given degree of risk is the same for every investor.

Since everyone faces essentially the same set of opportunities in the markets, the opportunity cost for any given degree of risk is the same for every investor.

Applying the DCF Model

The DCF model provides a conceptual framework for handling both time and risk. The difficulty in practice is getting more specific. How do we estimate cash flows? How do we measure risk? How do we translate risk into appropriate required rates of return?

There are no easy answers to these questions. Useful tools for the analysis, however, can be borrowed from the field of statistics, as Chapter 5 will show. Using such tools, we can be more precise about dealing with risk.

KEY CONCEPTS

1. To make decisions that will increase the value of the firm, financial managers need to understand how values are determined in financial markets.

2. Discounted-cash-flow techniques provide a method for analyzing the value of assets.

3. The value of any asset depends on the future benefits of owning or using the asset. Present value, discussed in Chapter 3, provides the basic analytical framework for valuation of financial assets, the benefits of which are future cash flows.

4. The value of a future cash-flow stream depends on its size, its timing, and its risk. The greater the risk, the higher the discount rate used to calculate its present value.

5. Risk is uncertainty about an outcome and is characteristic of investment opportunities.

6. Shareholder returns are subject to operating risk, which is uncertainty related strictly to the firm's operations. This risk is magnified by financial risk, which is the additional uncertainty caused by the use of financial leverage.

7. Risk aversion, risk neutrality, and risk preference are three types of investor attitudes toward risk.

8. In general, suppliers of capital are risk-averse and demand a risk premium for bearing risk. The greater the risk, the higher the rate of return required by the investor.

9. Required rates of return are established in the financial markets.

SUMMARY

Chapter 1 established value maximization as the objective of financial managers. To make decisions that will increase value, financial managers need to understand how values are determined in financial markets.

The DCF model can be used to value assets, such as stocks and bonds. To estimate value, we need a set of estimated cash flows and a discount rate that reflects the risks associated with those cash-flow estimates. The higher the risk, the higher the discount rate, which is also called the required rate of return.

Financial markets can give financial managers guidance on appropriate discount rates because a wide array of alternative investment opportunities are available in such markets.

QUESTIONS

1. What determines the value of a business asset?

2. In the DCF valuation model, discounting the expected cash flows by the minimally acceptable return or discount rate generates a maximum present value or price. Explain by example.

3. Explain the differences between risk aversion, risk neutrality, and risk preference.

4. How does risk-averse behavior by investors affect returns in the financial markets?

5. What is the dividend-valuation model? How can it be used? Make up an example.

6. Who determines the value of business firms? Explain.

7. Which characteristics of financial markets ensure that financial asset prices are a fair reflection of their true value?

8. From a recent *Wall Street Journal* or *Barron's,* find the current price of the U.S. Treasury bond discussed in this chapter. Look for a table labeled U.S. Treasury Securities. Using the current price, calculate the yield to maturity. Have interest rates increased or decreased since the book was published?

9. Support or refute this statement: Where there is risk, there is return.

10. Note the likely impact upon the required rate of return and stock- and bond-market prices in the following situations:

   A. Standard & Poor's, because of increasing debt levels, lowers the debt rating of XYZ Corp. from *A* to *BB*.

   B. ABC Oil Corp. announces the discovery of a large new oil field in the Gulf of Mexico.

   C. The Federal Reserve Board announces a new forecast for increased inflation over the next few years.

   D. Many corporations are expected to sell new bond issues in the next month.

   E. Domestic manufacturing firms have been surprised at the decline in the value of the dollar in foreign-exchange markets.

11. Name and discuss several factors which affect the general level of interest rates in the economy.

FINANCIAL TOOL KIT ASSIGNMENT

Work the valuation problems discussed in the text using the Tool Kit, Chapter Four. The Tool Kit also has several models related to studying the impact of inflation. Review these inflation adjustment models. See the *Study Guide* for details.

Problems

1. How much would you pay for a $1,000-face-value zero-coupon bond maturing in five years if the annual market rate of interest is 10 percent? (Assume semiannual compounding.)

2. What would you pay for the government bond in Sample Problem 4–4 in this chapter if market interest rates were to increase to 12 percent because of increased inflation expectations? What is happening to the bond price? Why?

3. In Sample Problem 4–4, if inflation subsides and market rates fall to 8 percent, at what price will the bond trade? Why did the price increase? Why would anyone pay more than face value? What has apparently happened to inflation expectations since the time of Problem 2 above?

4. If Milan Edison Utility's common stock will always pay a $3.00 annual dividend and if investors now desire a 15 percent rate of return, what is the current market price of Milan Edison's common?

5. Sarah has been considering buying the common stock of Wesig Tree Inc. Sarah estimates the stock will pay dividends of $4.00 per share per year and could probably be sold for $60.00 four years from now. Her minimum rate of return is 18 percent, and Wesig common is now selling for $36.00 per share. Should she buy the stock now?

6. In Sample Problem 4–2, calculate the price of the stock assuming a required rate of return of 17 percent.

7. Suppose that the dividends per share of common stock of Ron's Marine Supply, Inc., are expected to grow indefinitely at a rate of 4 percent per year. The company's current price/earnings ratio — defined here as this year's ($t = 0$) price per share divided by next year's ($t = 1$) earnings per share (EPS) — has been and will continue to be 10. Furthermore, Ron's dividend payout ratio (dividend/share) is expected to remain at 0.75 EPS. What rate of return is required by rational investors on an investment in this stock?

8. Suppose you read in the *Wall Street Journal* that a U.S. government bond is selling at par (price = face value), matures in 5 years, and carries a coupon rate of 14 percent.

a. What is the present yield to maturity on that bond?

b. What would the bond sell for if its yield to maturity were 8 percent? (Assume a face value of $1,000.)

Suppose the lower yield to maturity was due to lower required returns as people expected the inflation rate to decrease.

c. What would the bond sell for if its yield to maturity increased to 20 percent?

d. What would be your rate of return (one year) if you bought the bond today at face value and sold the bond next year? Assume that next year the yield to maturity on the bond (then maturing in four years) will have dropped to 8 percent.

e. Repeat part (d) assuming the yield to maturity next year is 20 percent.

9. Suppose Apple Computer Core Incorporated (ACC, Inc.) sold its new 10-year bonds at face value ($1,000) to provide a yield to maturity of 12 percent. Suppose, at the same time, 10-year U.S. government bonds were yielding 9 percent. In terms of dollars per bond, for how much less is an ACC bond trading because it is more risky than government debt? (To simplify matters, assume annual interest payments and yields compounded only once per year. In addition, assume that ACC bonds are in all respects except risk similar to U.S. government bonds. At the date of issuance the coupon rate and the YTM are the same.)

10. Last year Wolfpack Whistles Corporation had earnings per share of $4. WWC pays out half of its earnings in dividends. The firm's earnings and dividends are expected to grow at 7 percent per year for the foreseeable future.

a. Suppose you bought the stock at the end of last year for $35 and expect to hold it for 4 years and then sell it. You believe the stock will then sell at a P/E ratio (price per share divided by earnings per share) of 10 times. What is your expected rate of return?

b. Suppose you do not know what the P/E ratio will be. Use the constant-growth dividend-valuation model to calculate the expected rate of return on the stock. Why does this differ from your answer in part (a)?

c. Suppose the earnings and dividends are expected to grow at 7 percent for 3 years, 10 percent for the following 2 years, and 8 percent indefinitely after that. If your required return is 14 percent, how much will you pay for the stock?

11. Please refer to Table 4–1 in this chapter to respond to the following questions.

a. What is the expected return to shareholders if Plan A (all-equity financing) is used?

b. What is the expected return to shareholders if Plan B (financial-leverage strategy) is used?

c. Which is a better strategy? Why?

(Hint: The expected return is calculated as an expected value, which will be discussed in detail in the following chapter. The expected value is defined by multiplying the payoff of each outcome by the probability of that outcome and then summing these products over all possible outcomes.)

REFERENCES

Friend, I., and M. Blume, "The Demand for Risky Assets." *American Economic Review* 55 (December 1975): 900–22.

For a more complete treatment of security valuation see

Kolb, R. W., *Investments*. 2nd ed. Glenview, Ill.: Scott, Foresman and Company, 1989.

or

Sharpe, W. F., *Investments*. 3rd ed. Englewood Cliffs, N.J.: Prentice-Hall, Inc., 1985.

Chapter 5

Risk

This chapter investigates the measurement of risk and how risk affects required returns and the value of assets. After developing some statistical tools to deal with risk, we then examine the effects of diversification when a number of assets are combined in a portfolio. The chapter also examines the capital-asset-pricing model, which attempts to explain how risk affects expected returns.

Chapters 3 and 4 developed one way to estimate value, taking time and risk into account. In this discounted-cash-flow method, the discount rate is used to reflect both time and risk. We saw how such a method is useful in explaining the way in which various assets, such as stocks and bonds, are valued in financial markets. Thus, we have come a long way in providing one of the tools necessary for financial management — a way to place *values* on sets of cash flows.

This chapter analyzes risk more carefully. In the process, we can obtain a better appreciation of exactly how we might define and measure risk.

What Is Risk?

Before we start a detailed analysis of risk, let's take a moment to get an overview. In finance we can think of risk as the lack of certainty about a future outcome, much like the risk involved with a bet on a horse race or a football game. We can make reasonable predictions, but we can't be sure of what will actually happen. In this sense, we can view risk as the variability of possible outcomes.

Fortunately, in finance we often have a way to control at least some of the variability because we make a number of investment decisions, not just one. For example, by dividing their money, investors can buy a number of different stocks rather than just one. If we spread our money around through *diversification*, some risks will offset one another. This is true because some of the stock picks will do well while others will do poorly; it is just as if you placed bets on a number of horses in the same race — you've increased your chances of not losing your entire wager.

As a result, the risk that ultimately affects financial investors is the risk they cannot eliminate by diversification. This remaining risk is often referred to as non-diversifiable risk. Such nondiversifiable risk is a key risk factor that an investor or financial manager must be concerned with. If a decision will expose you to a high level of risk, you must be compensated for that uncertainty. A way to receive such compensation is to require a higher rate of return. As a result, if you are going to buy a risky stock, you will require a higher return than you would on a safer stock. As with horse racing, you expect a better payoff on a longshot.

Since investors impose such penalties for risk, the market values of traded assets will also reflect such risks. All other things equal, the higher the asset's risk, the lower its market value because of the penalty of risk. This effect of risk on value is especially important for financial managers to keep in mind since they are expected to manage the firm to increase value for shareholders. If a manager plans to take on extra risks, he or she must require a higher return in order to avoid a drop in shareholder value.

Suppose a company planned to spend billions to build a tunnel under the English channel to provide lower-cost rail and automotive connections between England and France. As we will discuss later in Chapter 11, that tunnel is a real, not hypothetical, financial-management problem. Is the plan a good investment? The answer depends on weighing the costs and benefits of the tunnel. Both these costs and benefits are, however, unknown. Managers can at best make educated guesses about the magnitude of cash flows associated with the tunnel. One thing is certain: risk (and its analysis) plays a large role in the decision.

In this chapter we will cover risk in detail. Let's begin with the basic risk/return trade-off.

The Risk/Return Trade-Off

Figure 5–1 reproduces the risk/return trade-off line discussed in the last chapter. We have already explained the reasoning behind the trade-off. People generally dislike risk; because they are risk-averse, they require higher returns to compen-

Figure 5–1
The Risk/Return Trade-Off

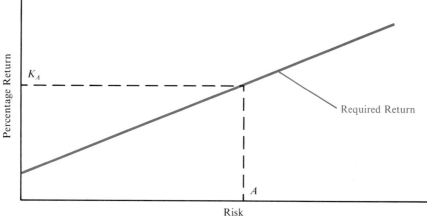

sate them for bearing risk. If a set of cash flows is characterized by *A* units of risk, as measured along the horizontal axis in Figure 5–1, the appropriate required return is K_A, as measured along the vertical axis.

The problems with using the concepts depicted in Figure 5–1 are (1) providing some way to measure risk (how do we measure the risk associated with a point like *A*?) and (2) establishing how such risk translates into a required return (what does the risk/return trade-off look like?).

Using Statistics to Measure Return and Risk

The field of statistics assumes that we can describe the nature of our uncertainty about a future event—say, a set of cash flows—in measurable terms. In this section, we will discuss these terms. Let's begin with an example.

Suppose you were considering investment in a new solar technology that would reduce your company's expenditures on fuel in the upcoming year. The actual dollar savings would depend both on the success of the technology (how much fuel could actually be saved) and on the price of fuel during the next year. After some analysis, your staff has estimated that there are only four possible outcomes, which are detailed in Panel A of Table 5–1 on page 132, where *C* is the cash flow (cost savings).

Discrete random variable—a variable that can take on a finite number of possible values.

In the terminology of statistics, the cash flow, *C*, is a **discrete random variable**— a variable that can take on a finite number of possible values. In this case, *C* can be $1,000, $2,000, $3,000, or $4,000. Panel A of Table 5–1 is a discrete **probability distribution**—a function that assigns probabilities to possible values of a random variable. Note that in this example, *C* can take on only four values, while in other cases a random variable could take on 5, 1,000, or any number of values.

Probability distribution—a function that assigns probabilities to the possible values of a random variable.

Table 5–1

Possible Cost Savings of Solar Technology

Panel A

Possible Outcome	Value of Cost Savings (C) (dollars)	Probability of Outcome (proportion of total)
1	1,000	1/10 = 0.1
2	2,000	2/10 = 0.2
3	3,000	4/10 = 0.4
4	4,000	3/10 = 0.3

Panel B

Possible Outcome, j	Value of C (dollars), C_j	Probability (proportion of total), p_j
1	$C_1 = 1,000$	$p_1 = 0.1$
2	$C_2 = 2,000$	$p_2 = 0.2$
3	$C_3 = 3,000$	$p_3 = 0.4$
4	$C_4 = 4,000$	$p_4 = 0.3$
		$\sum_{j=1}^{M} p_j = 1.0$

Panel B of Table 5–1 develops a bit of general notation to describe what a probability distribution looks like. Specifically, j is the number assigned to each outcome ($j = 1, 2, 3, 4$); M is the number of possible outcomes ($M = 4$); C_j is the amount of the cash flow in outcome j; p_j is the probability of outcome j.

The probability distribution is nothing more than a way to characterize the uncertainty associated with this cash flow. There is only a 30 percent chance of a cost savings of $4,000, but there is also a 10 percent chance that only $1,000 may be saved. Figure 5–2 is a line chart that gives a graphical display of the same probability distribution.

The probabilities for the four possible outcomes must add up to one; that is,

$$0.1 + 0.2 + 0.4 + 0.3 = 1.0.$$

In general, the sum of the probabilities of all possible outcomes must equal one:

$$\sum_{j=1}^{M} p_j = 1$$

where j = the number of the outcome, M = the number of possible outcomes, and p_j = the probability of outcome j.

In other words, it is certain that one of the outcomes will occur. Note that if there were no uncertainty, there would be only one possible outcome, and it would have a probability of 1.0.

Developing a probability distribution is sometimes easy. For example, given a fair coin, on any given flip there is a 50 percent chance of heads and a 50 percent

Figure 5–2
Possible Cost Savings of Solar Technology

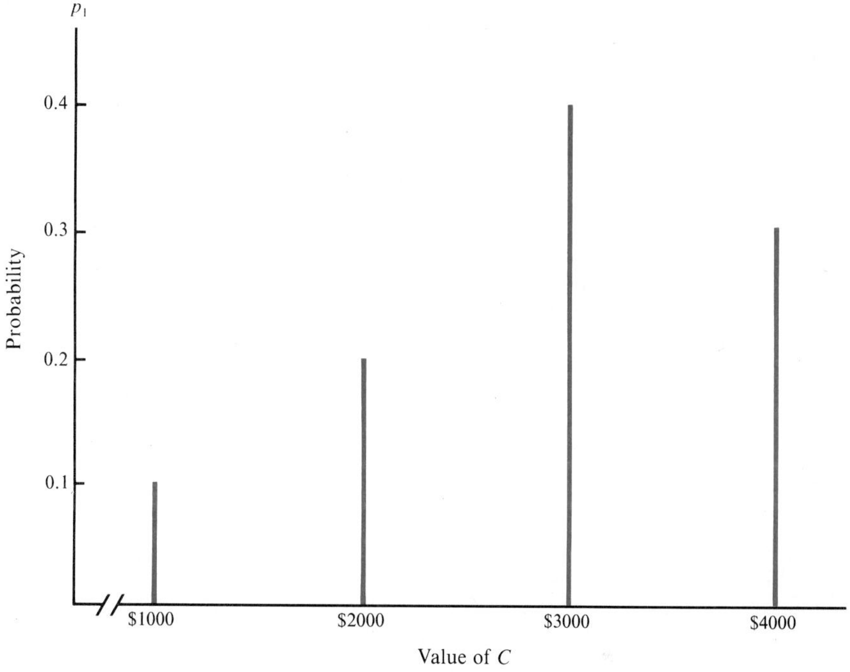

chance of tails. In most financial problems, however, our estimates are necessarily subjective and involve predictions about a whole array of future events. While the difficulty of making these estimates should not be underestimated, a probability distribution nevertheless gives us a useful way to organize our thoughts about uncertain events.

Looking at Table 5–1 and Figure 5–2, we get some rough idea of the range of likely cost savings and the uncertainty in those flows. One of the primary benefits of statistics is that it allows us to develop measures that summarize the information contained in a probability distribution. We can obtain summary measures of the cash flows we expect and of the uncertainty associated with those flows.

A probability distribution is a useful way to organize estimates about uncertain events.

Measuring Probable Outcomes: Expected Values

Expected value, or mean— the weighted average of the possible outcomes, where the weights are the probabilities of the outcomes; provides a measure of the expected outcome of a random variable.

The **expected value,** or **mean**, of a random variable is a measure of an expected cash flow. As Equation (1) indicates, the expected value is nothing more than a weighted average of the possible outcomes where the weights are the probabilities of the outcome.

The expected value, $E(C)$, of a cash flow, can be expressed as

$$E(C) = \sum_{j=1}^{M} p_j C_j \qquad (1)$$

where j = the outcome number, p_j = the probability of outcome j, C_j = the cash flow that results from outcome j, M = the number of possible outcomes, and $E(C)$ = the expected value of the random variable, C.

From the data in Table 5–1, we can calculate the expected value of the cost savings, using Equation (1), as

$$E(C) = 0.1(\$1,000) + 0.2(\$2,000) + 0.4(\$3,000) + 0.3(\$4,000)$$

$$= \$2,900 .$$

Expected-value operator (the letter E in the expected-value equation)—a signal to take the probability-weighted average of the outcomes.

As used above, the capital letter E is frequently called an **expected-value operator** and simply says to take the probability-weighted average. Note that the expected value allows different outcomes to have different probabilities—the p_j terms need not all be equal. If each of M possible outcomes was equally probable, each probability would be $1/M$. The expected value of a cash flow, when each of the possible outcomes is equally probable, can be expressed as

$$E(C) = \sum_{j=1}^{M} \frac{1}{M} C_j = \frac{1}{M} \sum_{j=1}^{M} C_j$$

Arithmetic average—a summary measure obtained by adding the values observed and dividing their sum by the number of values.

where $1/M$ = the probability of each equally probable outcome. An examination of this equation shows that this calculation produces the normal **arithmetic average.**

The expected value, or mean, is a measure of the expected outcome of a random variable. In our specific case of cost savings, the mean of $2,900 weighs all the possible outcomes given their probabilities and can be used as the single number that characterizes the likely outcome. This $2,900 figure is precisely the type of number we should use as a cash flow in DCF applications.

The expected value summarizes one bit of information about a distribution—the *average* outcome. As a summary measure, the mean does not give us any indication of how dispersed the outcomes are likely to be. For example, suppose someone offers you the following bet. A fair coin will be flipped. If it comes up heads (a 50 percent chance), you win $1.00. If it comes up tails (a 50 percent chance), you lose $1.00. The expected value of the bet is $0. Now suppose the bet is changed, and you either win $1,000.00 or lose $1,000.00. The expected value of the bet is still $0, but you probably would have different attitudes about the two bets because the outcomes of the second gamble are much more dispersed. Without some measure of this dispersion, we have no idea of how confident we can be that the cash flow that actually occurs will be close to the expected value. We need some measure of the variability of possible outcomes.

One shortcoming of the expected value as a summary measure is that it gives no indication of the dispersion of outcomes.

Measuring Variability of Outcomes

Suppose that in addition to the estimates in Table 5–1, your staff has provided cost-savings estimates for another technology (hydroelectric), as shown in Table 5–2. Table 5–2 indicates that the mean cost savings, $E(C)$, is equal to $2,900—the same expected value as that for solar technology in Table 5–1. It is obvious, however, that there is much less chance of being very far from our expected value with the hydroelectric technology (data in Table 5–2) than there is with the solar technology (data in Table 5–1). In Table 5–2, we can at worst be

Table 5–2

Possible Cost Savings of Hydroelectric Technology

Possible Outcome, j	Value of C (dollars), C_j	Probability (proportion of total), p_j
1	2700	0.25
2	2900	0.5
3	3100	0.25

$$E(C) = \sum_{j=1}^{3} p_j C_j$$
$$= 0.25(\$2700) + 0.5(\$2900) + 0.25(\$3100)$$
$$E(C) = \$2900$$

above or below our mean by $200. In Table 5–1, we have a 1 in 10 chance of being below the mean by a full $1,900, because $2,900 − $1,000 = $1,900. In a real sense, there is more variability for one of the probability distributions even if the two distributions have the same expected value—$2,900.

One statistical measure of variability is the **standard deviation.** The standard deviation, σ, is simply a probability-weighted measure of the dispersion of possible outcomes around the expected value and can be expressed as shown in Equation (2).

Standard deviation—the probability-weighted measure of the dispersion of possible outcomes around an expected value; a statistical measure of variability, or risk.

$$\sigma = \sqrt{\sum_{j=1}^{M} p_j [C_j - E(C)]^2} \tag{2}$$

where M = the number of possible outcomes, j = the outcome number, p_j = the probability of outcome j, C_j = the cash flow that results from outcome j, and $E(C)$ = the expected value of the random variable, C.

In words, the standard deviation says subtract the expected value of C from the value that C takes on with outcome j; square this difference; add up these squared terms, weighting by the probability of the outcome; finally, take the square root of the sum you have just created. Taking the square root is useful because it gives the standard deviation the same units of measurement as the random variable. In our example, the squared difference between C_j and $E(C)$ would be expressed in terms of dollars squared, whereas taking the square root of the entire sum converts units back to dollars.

We can use Equation (2) to calculate the standard deviations for the data in Tables 5–1 and 5–2. The standard deviation of possible outcomes around the expected value in the case of hydroelectric power (Table 5–2) can be calculated as

$$\sigma =$$
$$\sqrt{0.25(\$2,700 - \$2,900)^2 + 0.50(\$2,900 - \$2,900)^2 + 0.25(\$3,100 - \$2,900)^2}$$
$$= \sqrt{0.25(-\$200)^2 + 0.50(\$0)^2 + 0.25(\$200)^2}$$
$$= \sqrt{\$20,000}$$
$$= \$141.42$$

Figure 5–3
Possible Cost Savings

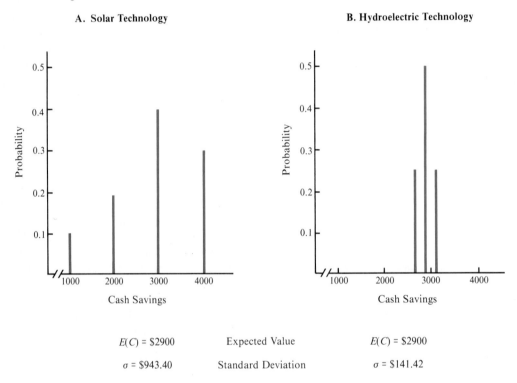

A. Solar Technology   B. Hydroelectric Technology

$E(C) = \$2900$	Expected Value	$E(C) = \$2900$
$\sigma = \$943.40$	Standard Deviation	$\sigma = \$141.42$

Following a similar procedure, we can calculate the standard deviation for the solar technology from the data in Table 5–1 to be $\sigma = \$943.40$.

As the line charts in Figure 5–3 show, the hydroelectric technology has much less variability than does the solar technology. The outcomes for hydroelectric technology are clustered between $2,700 and $3,100, while the cost savings for solar technology may be as low as $1,000 or as high as $4,000. Clearly, the outcome for solar technology is subject to much more variation. And as the calculations show, the standard deviation is much higher for the solar technology than for its hydroelectric counterpart. The larger standard deviation of $943.40 for solar technology (versus a standard deviation of $141.42 for hydroelectric) is simply a numerical measure of the dispersion that Figure 5–3 displays graphically. The higher the standard deviation, the more dispersed the possible outcomes and, as a result, the larger the chance that the actual outcome will be substantially different from the expected value. In this sense, standard deviation can serve as a measure of the risks, or uncertainty, associated with an outcome. Standard deviation is simply a summary measure of variability.

The mean and standard deviation are two extremely useful bits of summary information about a probability distribution. In our example, the mean, or

The mean indicates the likely *magnitude* of an expected outcome; the standard deviation indicates the potential *variability,* or risk, associated with an outcome.

expected value, tells us the likely *magnitude* of the dollar flows, while the standard deviation reflects the potential *variability* associated with those flows. Of course these two measures don't always tell us everything we would like to know, and other statistical measures can be developed. For many purposes in finance, however, these two measures can be useful.

For example, the expected cash flow to put in a DCF calculation can be measured by the expected value of the probability distribution of that cash flow. As we calculated earlier, the possible cost savings of solar technology displayed in Table 5–1 can be summarized as an expected cost savings of $2,900.

In our example of solar and hydroelectric technologies in Figure 5–3, the standard deviation of the cost savings for the hydroelectric technology is less than the standard deviation for the solar technology. We can, thus, speak of the solar technology as being the riskier of the two choices. The higher the standard deviation, the more dispersed the possible outcomes and, as a result, the greater the chance that the actual outcome will be substantially different from the expected value.

Coefficient of variation— the standard deviation divided by the expected value; a measure of risk relative to return.

When it is necessary to compare situations with very different levels of expected outcome, it is sometimes useful to look at the **coefficient of variation,** which is the standard deviation divided by the expected value. For example, the solar technology has a coefficient of variation equal to $943.40/$2,900 = 0.3253. The higher the coefficient of variation, the higher the risk relative to the expected outcome.

To this point, we have used the expected value and standard deviation to measure attributes of projected cash flows. These statistical measures can be applied to all kinds of random variables, including past events which we already observed.

Suppose we thought annual returns on IBM stock would be the same in the future as they have been in the past. If so, we might assume that the past distribution of returns on IBM's stock is a good guess about what the future probability distribution for that stock looks like. Table 5–3 shows IBM's record for the 10-year period from 1977 to 1986. Annual returns have ranged from −20 percent in 1986 to a whopping 75 percent in 1982. If we assume that each year's return is equally likely (that is, the probability of each year is the same) we can compute the expected return and standard deviation as illustrated in the caption to Table 5–3. Thus, we find an expected return of 10.82 percent with a standard deviation of 27.59 percent.

Past data may help with projections for the future, but the future may be different from the past.

An important cautionary word is in order. Note that we computed this expected return and standard deviation from past data. As a result, they are useful predictions about future return and risk *only* if we think the future will be like the past. In many cases, past data may help with future projections, but always remember that there is no rule that says history must repeat itself. For purposes of making most financial decisions, we must think in terms of the future course of events.

Portfolios and Risk

The basic insight that assets can be combined into portfolios has long been recognized in finance. Beginning in the 1950s, significant contributions were made in finance

Table 5–3
Annual Rate of Return from Owning Stock in IBM, 1977–1986

Year, j	Rate of Return (percent), R_j	Year, j	Rate of Return (percent), R_j
1977	1.0	1982	75.3
1978	10.1	1983	30.1
1979	−23.1	1984	4.3
1980	11.7	1985	29.9
1981	−11.1	1986	−20.0

$$E(R) = \sum_{j=1}^{M} p_j R_j$$

$$= \frac{1}{M} \sum_{j=1}^{M} R_j = 10.82\% \text{ assuming each year's return is equally likely } (M = 10)$$

$$\sigma = \sqrt{\sum_{j=1}^{M} p_j (R_j - E(R))^2} = 27.59\%$$

by applying statistical and quantitative techniques to formalize what happens in such portfolio combinations. Perhaps the most influential contribution was made by Harry Markowitz, one of the founders of modern portfolio theory.[1] While Markowitz's work and that which has followed it has been developed through rather complicated mathematics, the basic concepts are straightforward.

Diversification

Diversification—investing in more than one type of asset in order to reduce risk. When risky assets are combined in a portfolio, risk reduction is achieved through diversification.

There is an old piece of advice that says, "Don't put all your eggs in one basket." That advice is especially applicable to financial management because it tells us that risk can be reduced by **diversification**, or investing in more than one type of asset. A simple sort of diversification would be to put half your money in one stock — say, Sunglasses, Inc. — and half in another — say, Umbrellas, Inc. If the weather were especially rainy during a particular year, the earnings of Sunglasses, Inc., would decline. With a decline in earnings, the stock price and return to stockholders would decline. On the other hand, in a rainy year, the return to stockholders of Umbrellas, Inc., would be up. In a sunny year, the situation would be reversed.

[1]Markowitz's work appeared in a famous 1952 article, H. M. Markowitz, "Portfolio Selection," *Journal of Finance* (March 1952): 77–91. Many of his early contributions are in his book, *Portfolio Selection: Efficient Diversification of Investments* (New York: John Wiley & Sons, 1959). Many financial texts, such as *Investment: Concepts, Analysis, and Strategy* by Robert Radcliffe (Glenview, Ill.: Scott, Foresman and Company, 1986), provide extensive treatment of portfolio theory. See also J. Pringle and R. Harris, *Essentials of Managerial Finance* (2nd ed.), Scott, Foresman, 1987, for a more detailed discussion.

Portfolio—the combination of securities held by any one investor.

With diversification, risky assets can be put together and made into a portfolio that has less risk than the individual assets.

While the return on each individual stock might vary quite a bit, depending on the weather, the return on your **portfolio** of the two stocks could be quite stable. Bad returns on one stock are offset by good returns on the other.

In fact, at least in theory, the offsetting process could eliminate risk entirely. Consider, for example, the situation depicted in Table 5–4. With half your money in each stock, 50 percent of your money would earn R_s (the return on Sunglasses, Inc.) and 50 percent of your money would earn R_u (the return on Umbrellas, Inc.). Your portfolio rate of return (R_p) could, thus, be calculated for each possible outcome (sunny weather, normal weather, or rainy weather). The portfolio rate of return for sunny weather would be

$$R_p = 0.5R_s + 0.5R_u = 0.5(0.2) + 0.5(0) = 10 \text{ percent;}$$

the portfolio rate of return for normal weather would be

$$R_p = 0.5R_s + 0.5R_u = 0.5(0.1) + 0.5(0.1) = 10 \text{ percent;}$$

the portfolio return for rainy weather would be

$$R_p = 0.5R_s + 0.5R_u = 0.5(0) + 0.5(0.2) = 10 \text{ percent.}$$

Note that the portfolio earns 10 percent no matter what the weather is. Through diversification, two risky stocks (note R_s and R_u both depend on the weather) can be combined to make a riskless portfolio.

This effect of diversification alerts us to an important fact. Even if variability, as measured by standard deviation, is a good measure of risk, it can be quite misleading to look at the standard deviation of returns on any single asset as a measure of the asset's risk *if* that asset can be placed in a portfolio. Let us return to our example in Table 5–4. Assuming rainy, normal, and sunny weather are equally likely events (that each will happen one third of the time), we can calculate the expected return and standard deviation of returns on (1) the return, R_s, on Sunglasses, Inc., (2) the return, R_u, on Umbrellas, Inc., and (3) the return, R_p, on the portfolio of the two stocks. Table 5–5 uses Equations (1) and (2) to make these calculations. Because the portfolio is risk-free, its standard deviation—our measure of risk—is equal to zero, even though each stock in the portfolio has a stan-

It can be quite misleading to look at the standard deviation of returns on any single asset as a measure of that asset's risk if the asset can be placed in a portfolio.

Table 5–4

Effects of Diversification on Rates of Return

Weather Conditions	Return on Sunglasses, Inc. (percent), R_s	Return on Umbrellas, Inc. (percent), R_u	Return on Portfolio (percent) $R_p = 0.5R_s + 0.5R_u$
Rainy Weather	0	20	10
Normal Weather	10	10	10
Sunny Weather	20	0	10

Table 5–5
Expected Returns and Standard Deviations

Sunglasses, Inc. (R_s)

$$E(R_s) = \tfrac{1}{3}(0\%) + \tfrac{1}{3}(10\%) + \tfrac{1}{3}(20\%) = 10\%$$

$$\sigma_s = \sqrt{66.67} = 8.16\%$$

Umbrellas, Inc. (R_u)

$$E(R_u) = \tfrac{1}{3}(20\%) + \tfrac{1}{3}(10\%) + \tfrac{1}{3}(0\%) = 10\%$$

$$\sigma_u = \sqrt{66.67} = 8.16\%$$

Portfolio (R_p)

$$R_p = \tfrac{1}{3}(10\%) + \tfrac{1}{3}(10\%) + \tfrac{1}{3}(10\%) = 10\%$$

$$\sigma_p = \sqrt{0} = 0\%$$

---

dard deviation of 8.16 percent. As the calculations in Table 5–5 show, by combining two stocks in a portfolio we can reduce risk, as measured by standard deviation.

In practice, one can seldom find assets like our hypothetical Umbrellas and Sunglasses that perfectly offset one another. The returns on these two companies are said to be perfectly negatively correlated since they always move in opposite directions. For example, if two companies operated in the same industry, they both would benefit from a drop in input prices or protection from foreign competition, and we would expect their stock returns to move up and down in the same direction, at least most of the time; this is called positive correlation. And, it is even theoretically possible that two stocks would always go up together and down together. This would be perfect positive correlation, but it is not likely to be found in practice because each company is somewhat different. All stocks, practically speaking, have some degree of positive **correlation** and tend to, on average, rise and fall together because all are influenced to some extent by general economic conditions. Fluctuations in economic activity tend to affect nearly everyone.

But the good news is that we do not have to have perfect negative correlation in order to reduce risk through diversification. All we need is for stocks not to move up and down *exactly* together — in other words, all we need is the absence of perfect positive correlation.

As long as the returns of different stocks do not move in perfect lockstep, we can combine those stocks into a portfolio and achieve some risk reduction. We find in practice that returns on different stocks normally do show some association (because of the influence of the business cycle), but because it is not perfect correlation, we can achieve significant risk reduction by diversifying.

The risk-reduction effects of diversification are important both for financial managers and for investors in stocks or bonds. After all, the market value of a firm to shareholders is determined by investors buying and selling a company's stock. It is this market value that financial managers are attempting to maximize.

All stocks tend to have some degree of positive correlation (they rise and fall together) because all are influenced to some extent by general economic conditions.

Correlation — the relationship between variables indicating how they move relative to each other.

In practice, returns on different stocks show some association but it is not perfect, meaning that significant risk reduction can be obtained by diversification.

International Focus

Portfolio Diversification — Buying International Stocks

Can portfolio diversification actually reduce risk? Practitioners certainly believe so and many point to opportunities to diversify portfolios by buying stocks in other countries such as Japan, England, and West Germany. As an example, let us look at some forecasts made by First Chicago Investment Advisors. In late 1985 they forecast the following expected returns and standard deviations for investments in U.S. stocks (larger firms) and stocks abroad (returns converted to $ figures).

	Expected Return	*Standard Deviation*
U.S. Stocks	13.3%	16.5%
International Stocks	13.9%	20.5%

As might be expected, the higher expected returns on foreign stocks are accompanied by higher risk, as reflected in the 20.5% standard deviation.

But what about a portfolio formed by buying both U.S. and international stocks? First Chicago Investment Advisors projected that the correlation between returns on U.S. and international stocks would be positive but less than perfect. (Technically they projected a correlation coefficient of 0.55, whereas perfect positive correlation would be 1.0.) Using the statistics of portfolio theory, we can calculate the expected return and standard deviation for a portfolio — say 30% of our money in international stocks and 70% in U.S. stocks. The resulting portfolio has an expected return of 13.48% and a standard deviation of 15.79%. Note that this standard deviation is less than either of the standard deviations shown earlier (16.5% and 20.5%). So the portfolio actually has lower risk than either U.S. or international stocks! This clearly demonstrates the benefits of diversification when returns are not perfectly correlated. We have diversified risk away by putting some of our money in foreign stocks.

One note of caution: Before rushing out to invest in international stocks, remember that all the above calculations are based on estimates. As is usually the case in a risky world, there may be unpleasant surprises.

Source: R. Carr, "The Rationale for Investing in International Bonds and Currencies — Historical Returns, Risk, and Diversification," in R. McEnally (ed.), *International Bonds and Currencies*, Dow Jones-Irwin, Homewood, Ill., 1986, for the Institute of Chartered Financial Analysts.

Diversifiable and Nondiversifiable Risk

The fact that returns on stocks do not move in lockstep means that risk can be reduced by diversification. But the fact that there is *some* association among the returns means that risk cannot be reduced to zero. Even a very well-diversified portfolio will show some variability of return as economic conditions change and as stock prices in general fluctuate. For example, stock prices declined by 12 percent from December 1983 through June 1984 and then rose by 19 percent over the next 15 months.[2] Few portfolios, no matter how well diversified, escaped the decline in early 1984, and most benefited from the subsequent rise.

So there is a limit to the amount by which risk can be reduced by diversifying, and that limit depends on how closely the returns on the stocks are associated with one another. In technical terms, the amount of risk reduction depends on the degree of positive correlation between stocks. The lower the degree of correlation, the greater the amount of risk reduction that is possible.

The common element linking returns on stocks is their degree of association with general economic activity and the stock market overall. The extent to which a stock or a group of stocks moves with the market in general sets the lower limit on the amount of risk reduction possible through diversification. Risk that is unique to an individual firm or industry can be eliminated by diversifying, while risk arising from the link to the general market cannot. This notion of a common link suggests that the risk of any individual stock can be separated into two components: **nondiversifiable risk** and **diversifiable risk.**

Nondiversifiable risk is that part of the total risk that is related to the general economy or the stock market as a whole and, hence, *cannot* be eliminated by diversification. Nondiversifiable risk is also known as *market risk,* or *systematic risk.*

Diversifiable risk is that part of total risk that is unique to the company or industry and that, therefore, *can* be eliminated by diversification. Diversifiable risk is sometimes also referred to as *unsystematic risk,* or *specific risk.*

Table 5–6 gives some examples of factors that give rise to diversifiable and nondiversifiable risk.

The Number of Stocks in the Portfolio

The amount of risk reduction achieved by diversification depends not only on the degree of correlation with the general market, but also on the number of stocks in the portfolio. As the number of stocks increases, the diversifying effect of each additional stock diminishes, as shown in Figure 5–4.

As Figure 5–4 indicates, the major benefits of diversification are obtained with the first couple of dozen stocks, provided they are drawn from industries that are not closely related. Increases beyond this point continue to reduce risk, but the benefits are diminishing. Since the remaining risk is nearly all market-related, diversified portfolios tend to move together and in step with the stock market as a whole. The widely followed stock-market averages, such as the Dow Jones Industrial Average and the Standard & Poor's 500 stock index, are themselves diversified portfolios and tend to move together. These indices often are used as surrogates for the market as a whole. Thus, any reasonably well diversified portfolio tends to move with market indices.

Risk of Stocks in a Portfolio

Discussion of portfolio combinations, thus, provides us with a further insight into measurement of risk. We can think of a portfolio's standard deviation (a measure

The lower the degree of positive correlation between stocks in a portfolio, the greater the amount of risk reduction possible.

In a diversified portfolio, the investor must bear the nondiversifiable risk.

Nondiversifiable risk, or *market risk* — the part of total risk that is related to the general economy or to the stock market as a whole; the risk that *cannot* be eliminated by diversification.

Diversifiable risk, or *specific risk* — the part of total risk that is unique to the company or asset; the risk that *can* be eliminated by diversification.

As the number of stocks increases, the diversifying effect of each additional stock diminishes.

---

[2]These percentage changes were measured by the Dow Jones Industrial Average.

Table 5—6
Examples of Risk Factors

Nondiversifiable (Market) Risk Factors

A major change in tax rates
A war
An increase or decrease in inflation rates
An increase in international oil prices
A significant change in monetary policy by the Federal Reserve

Diversifiable (Specific) Risk Factors

A labor contract that grants above-average wage increases
A strike
Bankruptcy of a major supplier
Death of a key company officer
Unexpected entry of a new competitor into the market

Source: Based on D. W. Mullins, Jr., "Does the Capital Asset Pricing Model Work?" *Harvard Business Review* 60 (Jan./Feb. 1982): 105–114.

Figure 5—4
Risk Reduction through Diversification

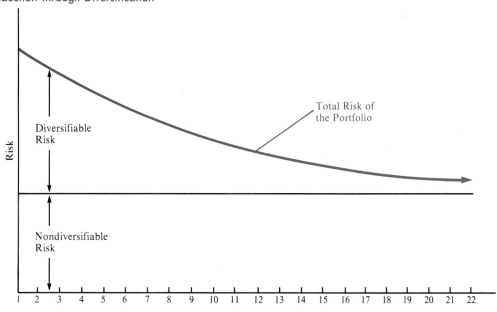

Sources: Based on D. W. Mullins, Jr., "Does the Capital Asset Pricing Model Work?" *Harvard Business Review* 60 (Jan./Feb. 1982): 105–14; J. L. Evans and S. H. Archer, "Diversification of the Reduction of Dispersion," *Journal of Finance* 23 (December 1968): 29–40.

A measure of a stock's risk is the risk it adds to a portfolio.

of variability) as a good indicator of the risk of a portfolio; to the extent that adding a stock to that portfolio increases the portfolio's standard deviation, the stock adds risk. Such addition of risk must be considered in analyzing the value of the stock to the purchaser.

If an investor were to hold only one stock, his or her risk would be the standard deviation of that stock. An important insight of portfolio theory is that if an investor holds a number of stocks, not all of an individual stock's standard deviation will ultimately be added to portfolio risk — some of it will be diversified away. In practice, holding a number of stocks is made quite easy because investors can buy shares of mutual funds, which are themselves portfolios containing many stocks.

The risk a stock adds to a portfolio will depend not only on the stock's *total risk* — its standard deviation — but also on how that risk breaks down into diversifiable risk and nondiversifiable risk. Ultimately, it is the nondiversifiable risk that an investor must bear.

As a result, when we speak of a risk/return trade-off, such as the one displayed in Figure 5–1, risk (as measured along the horizontal axis) is appropriately defined as the risk actually borne by the investor. If an investor owns only one stock, he or she has no diversification, and risk is, therefore, the standard deviation of the stock. For a diversified investor, the risk of a stock is only that portion of the stock's standard deviation that cannot be diversified away.

These comments about stocks also apply to corporate projections about future cash flows, such as the ones we used in the discounted-cash-flow model. Only when the risk associated with corporate cash flows is evaluated on the basis of how much risk the cash flows add to the holdings of the corporation's owners will managers have an appropriate measure of risk.

In evaluating a prospective investment project, financial managers should not be satisfied with looking only at the variability of the project's cash flow as a measure of risk. It is also important to determine how the project affects the risks facing the corporation's owners. The answer to this question depends not only on the variability of the project's cash flows but also on how these cash flows are correlated with returns to other assets of the corporation's owners. These assets may include existing projects in the corporation as well as stocks and bonds in other corporations, because many shareholders hold a wide variety of assets in their personal investment portfolio.

The Capital-Asset-Pricing Model

Our earlier discussion of portfolios shows that risk can be measured by the standard deviation of portfolio returns and that the relevant risk for each individual asset (whether a stock or an investment project) is the amount of risk it contributes to an investor's portfolio. These points add to our conceptual understanding of the risk/return trade-off.

Capital-asset-pricing model (CAPM) — provides useful insights about how market values and discount rates are determined in financial markets, describes the valuation process in a portfolio context, and analyzes how risk/return trade-offs work in financial markets.

The CAPM describes the valuation process in a portfolio context.

Further headway can be made by looking at the implications of the **capital-asset-pricing model (CAPM).**[3] The CAPM is one of the major developments in financial theory, and despite its shortcomings provides extremely useful insights into how market values and discount rates are determined in financial markets. Rather than viewing the return and value of each security in isolation, the capital-asset-pricing model sets the valuation process in a *portfolio* context on the assumption that an investor usually holds securities in a portfolio.

Assumptions

As are most theories, the CAPM is based on a list of critical assumptions, including those that follow.

1. Investors are risk-averse and use the expected value of return and standard deviation of return as the appropriate measures of return and risk for their portfolio. In other words, the greater the perceived risk of a portfolio, the higher the expected return on the portfolio for a risk-averse individual.
2. Investors make their investment decisions based on a single-period horizon. The risk and return they foresee for the next time period facing them drives their decisions.
3. Financial markets are essentially *frictionless;* that is, transactions costs (for example, commissions on stock sales and purchases) are low enough to ignore, and assets can be bought and sold in any unit desired. Any investor has the ability to buy any asset at the going market price and is limited only by his or her wealth and the price of the asset.
4. All returns are taxed in exactly the same fashion in a way such that taxes do not affect the choice of buying one asset versus another.
5. All individuals can borrow and lend unlimited amounts of money at a single-period riskless rate of interest.
6. All individuals assume that they can buy assets at the going market price, and they all agree on the nature of the return and risk associated with each investment.

Some of these assumptions don't fit reality and require a bit of discussion. Looking at the first three assumptions, we can agree that most people *are* risk-averse and that well-developed financial markets don't involve large transactions costs. In addition, looking only one period into the future may not be too bad an approximation as long as we remember that the return we expect for the next period (say, the next year) depends on the price we expect one period (year) from

---

[3]The capital-asset-pricing model was developed by three principal researchers: William F. Sharpe, "Capital Asset Prices: A Theory of Market Equilibrium Under Conditions of Risk," *Journal of Finance* 19 (1964): 425–42; John Lintner, "The Evaluation of Risky Assets and the Selection of Risky Investments in Stock Portfolios and Capital Budgets," *Review of Economics Statistics* 47 (February 1965): 13–77; and Jan Mossin, "Equilibrium in a Capital Asset Market," *Econometrics* 34 (October 1966): 768–75. For an excellent discussion of the model and its practical applications, see D. W. Mullins, Jr., "Does the Capital Asset Pricing Model Work?" *Harvard Business Review* 60 (Jan./Feb. 1982): 105–14.

today, which should reflect our opinion about events in the more distant future (two, three, and more periods hence).

The last three major assumptions are, admittedly, harder to square with the real world. Assumption 4 downplays the role of what is a rather complicated tax system, as we discussed in Chapter 2. Assumption 5 says there is some **riskless rate of interest** at which persons can borrow and lend money. As a first approximation, lending money to the U.S. government (say, by buying a U.S. Treasury obligation) may be close to risk-free. But if we don't know what future prices will be we can't be sure even on Treasury bills what *real return* (adjusted for inflation) we'll get because of purchasing-power risk. Borrowing money at a riskless rate is impossible; at best, individuals and corporations pay interest at a rate commensurate with the perceived risk of the loan. Finally, assumption 6 says that everyone agrees — a result that is almost never an accurate description of what a group of people manage to do. For example, assumption 6 means that if the president of IBM (an investor himself) thinks that IBM stock will have an 18 percent return in the next year with a standard deviation of 25 percent, all other investors agree with him. While no one is certain of what the return will be (the standard deviation is not zero), assumption 6 implies that everyone would at least agree on the nature of the uncertainty.

Goals

The assumptions listed above are limiting, but they do allow us to develop a very useful set of results. Namely, the CAPM lets us be much more precise about how risk/return trade-offs are determined in financial markets.[4]

The general idea of the CAPM is that in **frictionless markets,** people will buy and sell securities until an equilibrium is reached where current market prices of assets reflect people's assessments about the cash flow they might receive from owning those assets. In theory, this equilibrium requires that trade-offs be established between *all* possible assets — stocks, bonds, real estate, gold, etc. In such an equilibrium, we would expect risk-averse investors to require higher expected returns to compensate them for owning assets that are riskier. A 20 percent return on a very risky asset might be just as good to an investor as a 10 percent return on a fairly safe asset. The strength of the CAPM is that it specifies how this risk/expected-return trade-off will work. Here we concentrate on the main results of the theory.

The Market Risk Premium

In the CAPM, an expected return can also be thought of as a *required return,* the minimum acceptable return defined in Chapter 4, because of the nature of market equilibrium. The CAPM assumes that investors buy and sell securities and that

---

Riskless rate of return — the rate of return that would be received on a riskless asset; it is estimated using a current interest rate on a U.S. Treasury bond or note — the closest available approximation of a riskless asset.

Frictionless market — a market in which there are no costs, such as commissions or information costs, involved in financial transactions.

---

[4]A number of scholars have relaxed some of the assumptions of the CAPM, producing different variations of asset-pricing models. The CAPM is by far the most widely used of these models. For a discussion of some of the variants of the CAPM, see T. Copeland and F. Weston, *Financial Theory and Corporate Policy,* 3rd edition (Reading, Mass.: Addison-Wesley, 1988).

In equilibrium, demand and supply pressures will assure us that expected returns will be the same as required returns.

Market portfolio — the portfolio that includes all risky assets.

Risk premium — the difference between the required rate of return on a particular risky asset and the rate of return on a riskless asset with the same expected life; or the additional return that compensates an investor for bearing additional risk.

market prices adjust until they are in equilibrium. In equilibrium, demand and supply pressures will ensure that expected returns and required returns will be one and the same. If the expected return on an asset exceeded the required return, there would be extra demand to buy the asset. As the price was driven up, the expected return would fall. Given the same future cash flows from owning an asset, one's expected rate of return is lower the higher the price one has to pay for that asset. If expected returns were lower than required returns, prices would fall and expected rates of return would rise. Thus, in equilibrium, the expected return is equal to the required return.

A key reference point for the CAPM is the **market portfolio** of all risky assets. This portfolio represents the most diversified portfolio of risky assets an investor could buy since it includes *all* risky assets. Because investors are risk-averse, they will require a **risk premium** to invest in the market portfolio rather than in a riskless asset. We can express this risk premium expected to be earned on the market portfolio as

$$\text{Market risk premium} = K_m - R_f$$

where R_f = the risk-free rate of return and K_m = the required rate of return on the market portfolio. Remember, in market equilibrium the required return will equal the expected return.

Required Returns for Individual Assets

Now let's look at the implications of the CAPM for the individual assets (e.g., stocks) that are traded in the market. If a stock were as risky as the market portfolio, we would expect investors to require the same risk premium on that stock as they do on the market portfolio. By the same line of thought, if a stock were more risky than the market portfolio, risk-averse investors would require a higher risk premium on the stock than they do on the market portfolio. The CAPM develops these ideas by defining the risk of a stock as the risk of the stock relative to the risk of the market portfolio. This relative-risk measure has come to be known as the asset's β (beta coefficient) as defined in Equation (3).

The relative risk associated with any individual asset (or portfolio) j, as measured in relation to the risk of the market portfolio, can be expressed as

$$\beta_j = \frac{\text{nondiversifiable risk of asset } j}{\text{risk of market portfolio}} \tag{3}$$

The beta coefficient is a measure of the nondiversifiable risk of an asset relative to that of the market portfolio. A beta of 1.0 indicates an asset of average risk. A beta coefficient greater than 1.0 indicates above-average risk — stocks whose returns tend to be more risky than the market. Stocks with beta coefficients less than 1.0 are of below-average risk.

An important feature of Equation (3) is that β depends only upon the asset's nondiversifiable risk, that risk which can't be diversified away. In the case of the market portfolio, we have done all the diversification possible (since the market portfolio includes all risky assets); thus, the risk of the market portfolio is all nondiversifiable — risk that an investor can't avoid. We know, however, that some of the variability of returns on individual assets can be diversified away so that the standard deviation of an asset is *not* an appropriate measure of the risk it adds to a portfolio. As long as the asset's returns are not perfectly positively correlated with other assets, there will be some way to diversify away some of the individual asset's risk. As a result, β depends only on nondiversifiable risks.

Now we can understand the basic result of the CAPM as the market reaches equilibrium. Investors will buy and sell individual securities based on the risks of each security. Once equilibrium is reached, the only way an investor will be satisfied to hold a high-risk stock (beta greater than one) is for that stock to provide a higher rate of return than the market. This result is expressed as Equation (4). According to the capital-asset-pricing model, the expected rate of return, K_j, on asset j in market equilibrium can be expressed as

$$K_j = R_f + [(K_m - R_f)(\beta_j)]. \tag{4}$$

In Equation (4), K_j is the required rate of return on asset j in equilibrium. It is made up of two components: the risk-free rate of return, R_f, plus a risk premium. The risk premium is the product of the risk premium required on the market portfolio ($K_m - R_f$) and the relative risk, or beta coefficient, of asset j (β_j).

This beta coefficient, which we expressed earlier in Equation (3), is the nondiversifiable risk of the asset relative to the risk of the market. If the asset is greater in risk than the market, the beta coefficient exceeds 1.0, and Equation (4) tells us to assign a higher risk premium to asset j than to the market. For example, suppose that a chemical company had a beta coefficient of 1.20, that the required rate of return on the market (K_m) was 15 percent per year, and that the risk-free interest rate (R_f) was 6 percent per year. We can use Equation (4) to estimate the required return on the stock as

$$K_j = 0.06 + [(0.15 - 0.06)(1.20)]$$

$$= 0.06 + 0.108$$

$$= 0.168$$

$$= 16.8 \text{ percent}.$$

The preceding calculations show that the required return on this stock would be 16.8 percent — the sum of the 6 percent risk-free rate and a 10.8 percent risk premium. This 16.8 percent is larger than the 15 percent required return on the market because the chemical stock is riskier than the market. As a result, investors require a larger risk premium on the stock than on the market in general. The capital-asset-pricing model provides a specific estimate of how much larger this risk premium is.

The Market Line

Market line — shows the relationship between required return and risk.

We can plot the relationship between required return and nondiversifiable risk, as expressed in Equation (4), to produce a graph of the **market line,** as shown in Figure 5–5.

Figure 5–5
The Market Line

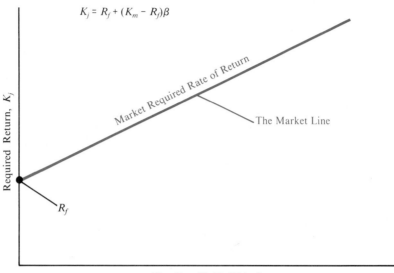

$$K_j = R_f + (K_m - R_f)\beta$$

Required Return, K_j

Market Required Rate of Return

The Market Line

R_f

Nondiversifiable Risk, β

In equilibrium, the required return of any security (K_j) depends on its nondiversifiable risk.

In equilibrium, all securities would plot on the market line.

According to the capital-asset-pricing model, in equilibrium, the required return of any security depends on its nondiversifiable risk.

The vertical axis of the figure measures required return, and the horizontal axis measures nondiversifiable risk. Figure 5–5 tells us in graphic form the same thing that Equation (4) tells us — namely, that in equilibrium the required return on any security, K_j, depends on its nondiversifiable risk. The market line in Figure 5–5 is simply the risk/return trade-off implied by the capital-asset-pricing model. It measures risk and return more precisely than does the general model of the risk/return trade-off depicted in Chapter 4 and earlier in this chapter. In equilibrium, all securities would lie along the upward-sloping line. High-risk securities would lie on the upper part of the line, and low-risk securities would lie along the lower part.[5] Figure 5–5 shows that only nondiversifiable risk is important in determining required return. Because the capital-asset-pricing model assumes that all diversifiable risk can be diversified away by holding portfolios and need not be borne by investors, there is no need for the market to "pay" for bearing diversifiable risk by granting a higher expected return. Only nondiversifiable risk is important.

Risk and Beta Coefficients

In Equation (4), the beta coefficient, β_j, is a measure of an asset's nondiversifiable risk relative to the market. If an asset has a beta coefficient of 2.0, it is twice as risky as the market, and according to Equation (4), investors will require twice as large a risk premium on this asset as on the market. It is important to remember

---

[5]Technically, the line in Figure 5–5 is called the *security market line*. For a discussion, see W. F. Sharpe, *Portfolio Theory and Capital Markets* (New York: McGraw-Hill, 1970).

that the beta coefficient reflects nondiversifiable risk—that part of total risk that cannot be eliminated by diversification. Because beta coefficients already reflect the benefits of diversification, the beta coefficient of any portfolio can be calculated as the average of the beta coefficients of the individual assets in that portfolio. As an example, if you invested 30 percent of your money in Risky Business Inc. (with a beta coefficient of 2.0) and the remaining 70 percent in No Frills Limited (with a beta coefficient of 0.5), the beta coefficient of your portfolio would be calculated as

$$\beta_p = 0.30(2.0) + 0.70(0.5) = 0.60 + 0.35 = 0.95 \, .$$

By combining a risky and a safe asset, you have created a portfolio with nondiversifiable risk only slightly lower than the market's beta coefficient of 1.0.

Beta coefficients can be estimated using the statistical technique of *regression analysis*. Returns for a particular stock would be obtained for specific time periods—normally months or weeks—and related using regression analysis to returns for identical periods on a widely diversified portfolio, such as the Standard & Poor's 500 stock index, which is a proxy for the market portfolio.[6] Beta coefficients also are available from many investment-brokerage firms and advisory services, such as the Value Line Investment Survey. Often it is safe to assume that a beta coefficient estimated using a company's past stock returns is a good indicator of future risks. If, however, a major change in the operation or risks of a company takes place, there would be a need for further care in estimating beta. For example, if an oil company purchases an electronics firm, the postmerger firm will be likely to have a level of beta risk that reflects an average of risks in both the oil and electronics industries. The risk relevant to investors is *future risk*.

Table 5–7 gives examples of beta coefficients for selected industries. Airlines head the list of high-risk stocks, with an average beta coefficient for the industry of 1.80. Airlines have revenues that fluctuate considerably with economic activity. This basic variability is amplified by high fixed costs, including interest payments, that result from corporate borrowing. At the other end of the spectrum are telephone and electric utilities. Electric utilities are regulated, and the demand for electricity tends to grow in a steady manner. Because the revenues and earnings of electric-utility companies are very stable, they have low beta coefficients. Gold-mining stocks have the lowest beta coefficients of all at 0.35. The nonferrous metals, agriculture, and food industries fall in the middle of the risk spectrum, with beta coefficients of 1.00.

Sample Problem 5–1
Calculating the Required Return on WPNA Stock

Word Processors of North America (WPNA) has a beta coefficient (relative-risk ratio) of 1.2. If the required return on the market (K_m) is 0.17 and the risk-free in-

---

[6]We noted earlier that the market portfolio theoretically consists of *all* risky assets, but because of the difficulty of obtaining data, a proxy for the market portfolio must be used in practice. All-equity portfolios, such as the Standard & Poor's 500 stock index, or the New York Stock Exchange Index, are widely used as surrogates in practice.

Table 5–7
Examples of Beta Coefficients

	Industry	Beta Coefficient
High Risk	Airlines	1.80
	Electronics	1.60
	Consumer durables	1.45
	Producer goods	1.30
	Chemicals	1.25
	Shipping	1.20
Medium Risk	Steel	1.05
	Containers	1.05
	Nonferrous metals	1.00
	Agriculture	1.00
	Food	1.00
	Liquor	0.90
Low Risk	Banks	0.85
	International oil	0.85
	Tobacco	0.80
	Telephone utilities	0.75
	Energy utilities	0.60
	Gold	0.35

Source: D. W. Mullins, Jr., "Does the Capital Asset Pricing Model Work?" *Harvard Business Review* 60 (Jan./Feb. 1982): 105–114.

terest rate (R_f) is 0.09, apply Equation (4) to calculate the market's required rate of return on WPNA stock.

Solution

According to Equation (4), the required return on a capital asset equals the risk-free rate plus a risk premium:

$$K_j = 0.09 + (0.17 - 0.09)(1.2)$$

$$= 0.09 + 0.096$$

$$= 0.186 = 18.6 \text{ percent}.$$

The market requires a 0.096 risk premium on WPNA stock. When this risk premium is added to the risk-free rate of return, the result is a required rate of return on WPNA stock of 18.6 percent.

Implementing the Capital-Asset-Pricing Model

In Sample Problem 5–1, we made a number of important assumptions to implement Equation (4). *First,* we assumed a value for the beta coefficient. In practice, this value is often estimated using past data on returns to a particular stock relative to returns on some market index. Estimated betas were given in Table 5–7. There

Finance in Practice 5—1

Where Do Betas Come From?

Beta coefficients have come into use in a number of applications where future returns on financial assets must be estimated. Analysts and executives are using beta coefficients:

- as an input to the CAPM to estimate expected returns on stocks.
- in public-utility rate cases as a basis for setting the rates that electric, telephone, and other utilities can charge the public.
- to aid in setting return targets—that is, minimum acceptable returns—for capital-investment projects.
- to identify overvalued and undervalued stocks.
- in portfolio management (by institutions such as insurance companies, pension funds, and mutual funds) to construct portfolios with particular risk characteristics.

The standard way to estimate a beta coefficient on a particular stock is to use historical data on the stock and some index of general market performance. Commonly used indexes are the Standard & Poor's 500 stock index and the New York Stock Exchange Composite index. The S&P 500 measures the total return—dividends plus capital gains (or losses!)—on a portfolio of 500 common stocks broadly diversified across many industries. The NYSE Composite index measures returns on all stocks listed on the NYSE, approximately 1,600 companies.

Whichever index is chosen plays the role of the "market portfolio" in the capital-asset-pricing model. To estimate a company's beta coefficient, actual returns are gathered for a large historical period—most commonly, by monthly intervals.

Data are also gathered on returns on the index. For each month, the analyst has a pair of returns: a return for the stock in question and a return for the index.

The next step is to use statistical *regression analysis* to determine the relationship between the returns on the stock and the returns on the index. The slope coefficient out of that regression is an estimate of the stock's beta coefficient. (See Appendix 5A at the end of this chapter.) As noted earlier, a beta coefficient is a measure of the volatility of a particular stock *relative to* the market. Some analysts go further to adjust the regression results to get an "improved" value for beta.

Every time a security analyst or a portfolio manager needs a beta coefficient, does he or she go off and do some regression analysis? The answer is no. A number of firms provide beta coefficients commercially as a service. As of this writing, beta coefficients are available on a large number of stocks from The Value Line Investment Survey, Merrill Lynch, Drexel Burnham Lambert, and Barr Rosenberg Associates.

The good news is that there are a number of sources for beta coefficients. The bad news is that the beta coefficients for a given company often vary, depending on which source one picks. In calculating the beta coefficient, a number of options exist with respect to the statistical technique used, the time period covered by the analysis, the interval chosen (such as monthly or quarterly), and the index used as a market proxy. Different choices for these parameters can give rise to different results. The different firms offering beta coefficients don't all do things the same way, so beta coefficients from different sources often vary. In using commercially available beta coefficients, a financial manager must pay attention to the details and be sure that the particular beta chosen fits the job at hand.

Source: Adapted from D. R. Harrington, "Whose Beta Is Best?" *Financial Analysts Journal,* July–August 1983, pp. 67–73.

One problem with using beta coefficients is that betas are often estimated using past data, but there is no assurance that past data will be good indicators of future risks.

In practice, probably the best guidance for choosing the risk-free rate is to use a time period that approximates the time period of the investment you are considering.

is no assurance, however, that past relationships are good indicators of future risks. Frequently, the basic nature of a company does not change, so measurement of past risk in such cases is a good indication of future risk. On the other hand, we have to be especially careful to see if there is any reason to believe that the future pattern of risk will differ from the past since only future risk is important to investors.

Second, to calculate required returns using the capital-asset-pricing model's Equation (4), we need estimates of both a risk-free rate of return, R_f, and a market risk premium, $K_m - R_f$. Typically, the risk-free rate of return is estimated using a current interest rate on U.S. government Treasury obligations because these are probably the closest things to riskless assets that one can find. Even then, however, the choice of the appropriate interest rate is not an easy one. For example, what happens if short-term U.S. government notes yield 11 percent interest but long-term U.S. government bonds yield 14 percent interest? Which is the best estimate of the risk-free rate — 11 percent or 14 percent? The capital-asset-pricing model doesn't help us out here because it considers only one time horizon, while the 11 percent and 14 percent rates are for two very different periods of time. In practice, probably the best advice is to use a time period for choosing the risk-free rate of return that approximates the time period for which you are considering investment in an asset. Thus, if you as an investor are considering a stock as a long-term investment, you might use a long-term government-bond rate as your risk-free interest rate.

The estimate of the market risk premium is also difficult. One starting point is to look at past market risk premiums, such as those that are displayed in Table 5–8. Panel A shows average returns for a long period of time, while

Table 5–8
Past Returns in U.S. Financial Markets

Panel A: Annual Rates of Return, 1926–1986

Series	Arithmetic Mean (percent)	Standard Deviation (percent)
Common stocks	12.1	21.2
Long-term corporate bonds	5.3	8.5
Long-term government bonds	4.7	8.6
U.S. Treasury bills	3.5	3.4
Inflation	3.1	4.9

Panel B: Annual Market Risk Premium (for Common Stocks)

	Arithmetic Mean (percent)
Common stocks minus long-term U.S. government bonds	7.4
Common stocks minus U.S. Treasury bills	8.6

Source: Data in Panel A from Ibbotson Associates, Chicago.

Finance in Practice 5–2

Stock Markets and Interest Rates

An investor always has the ability to invest money in either stocks or bonds. Since the two types of securities are substitutes we would expect changes in the stock market not to go unnoticed in the bond market. Do markets actually reflect these considerations? You bet!

Consider the stock-market crash of 1987. On Monday, October 19, the Dow Jones Average tumbled by over 20 percent on a single day. The table below shows selected interest rates (yields) on U.S. government debt obligations.

All the interest rates dropped dramatically after the 19th. For example, yields on 1-year maturity obligations dropped from 8.42 percent on October 15 to only 7.03 percent on October 21.

What caused the drop? The answer is that as the stock market fell, investors were selling their stocks and many of them bought bonds, pushing up bond prices. At the higher prices the bonds provide a lower yield to an investor.

Of course, one doesn't hope for more stock-market drops like those in October 1987, but these changes do provide a powerful illustration of the relationship between bond and equity markets.

Maturity	Oct. 15	Oct. 16	Oct. 19	Oct. 20	Oct. 21
3 month	7.07	6.93	6.39	5.86	5.60
1 year	8.42	8.38	7.98	7.15	7.03
5 year	9.82	9.84	9.70	8.93	8.80
30 year	10.24	10.24	10.25	9.49	9.44

Panel B converts these returns into risk-premium form by subtracting an estimate of the risk-free rate of return from each type of market return. Note that the market risk premium on common stocks has stayed between 7 percent and 9 percent as measured by the arithmetic average of annual returns. If the future is like the past, shareholders might require similar risk premiums, but there is no assurance. We will return to problems of estimating required returns in Chapters 12 and 13.

Validity of the Capital-Asset-Pricing Model

Obviously, there are many difficulties in attempting to use the capital-asset-pricing model. In addition, the model has been extensively tested with mixed results.

Some researchers have found evidence that returns do seem to be related to non-diversifiable risks, as the theory suggests. Others studying the problem have cast doubts on the model's validity.[7] Whether the model perfectly explains relationships between return and risk (which it does not), however, is not a fair test of the theory's usefulness. The capital-asset-pricing model is important for the number of qualitative insights it brings to light:

1. The values (prices) placed on financial assets are determined in the financial market by the actions of investors, lenders, and borrowers competing against one another.
2. Expected returns and perceived risk are related. The market is dominated by risk-averse investors who demand higher expected returns on riskier investments.
3. The market as a whole functions so that all financial assets are, roughly speaking, "equally good buys"; that is, prices are set so the reward/risk ratio is the same for all financial assets.
4. The market standard developed in the model is useful for evaluating investments in physical assets just as it is for evaluating financial assets. Investors require extra return for bearing nondiversifiable risk.

The capital-asset-pricing model is a theory about the way risk and required return should be related. Given its assumptions, the CAPM leads to a very useful risk/return equation—Equation (4)—that allows one to estimate required rates of return.

In practice we'll find that the CAPM is only one way to "skin the cat" in dealing with risk. In Appendix 5B we will discuss another theory of how risk affects required return, called Arbitrage Pricing Theory. Practitioners also deal with risk in other ways, as Chapter 13 will discuss.

The capital-asset-pricing model provides many useful insights for the financial manager attempting to maximize the value of the firm. The model shows the type of risk (nondiversifiable) for which shareholders require compensation in the form of a higher risk premium and, hence, a higher required return. Because financial managers are investing funds on behalf of shareholders (for example, by building a new plant), managers must keep sight of the returns shareholders will require as a result of the project's risks.

---

[7]For a review of much of the testing of the CAPM, see T. Copeland and F. Weston, *Financial Theory and Corporate Policy,* 3rd edition (Reading, Mass.: Addison-Wesley, 1988). For a critique of empirical tests of the CAPM, see R. Roll, "A Critique of the Capital Asset Pricing Theory's Tests," *Journal of Financial Economics* 4 (March 1977): 129–76. For a pragmatic discussion of the shortcomings of the CAPM, see Mullins, "Does the CAPM Work?" As an outgrowth of criticism of the CAPM, a new theory of asset pricing, called the *arbitrage-pricing theory (APT),* has been developed. Like the CAPM, the APT relies on competition among investors to produce a market equilibrium. Its appeal lies in the fact that its assumptions are less restrictive than those of the CAPM, and it allows for more than one source of risk. Unfortunately, APT offers no economic insight into what the sources of risk ought to be. Research is under way to put APT to the test, and it is too early to tell what its ultimate impact will be. The seminal work on APT was done by S. A. Ross in "The Arbitrage Theory of Capital Asset Pricing," *Journal of Economic Theory* 13 (December 1976): 341–60. Copeland and Weston review some of the work on APT, but much of it is still coming to press in academic circles. See Appendix 5B.

KEY CONCEPTS

1. Financial management provides tools for dealing with two difficult problems involved in most management decisions: time and risk.

2. In placing a value on an asset, the basic discounted-cash-flow model must reflect the fact that the value of a future cash-flow stream depends on its size, its timing, and its risk. The greater the risk, the higher the discount rate used to calculate its present value.

3. Statistical techniques allow us to provide summary measures of return and risk. *Expected value* can be used as a measure of the size of a cash flow or return. The *standard deviation,* the statistical measure of variability, can be used as a measure of the amount of risk associated with an outcome.

4. When risky assets are combined in a portfolio, some risk can be diversified away. An appropriate measure of an individual asset's risk is the risk it adds to a portfolio.

5. The total risk of any asset can be thought of as the sum of diversifiable risk and nondiversifiable risk.

6. The capital-asset-pricing model (CAPM) is a theory about how risky assets are valued in financial markets. It shows us the specific relationship between required return and risk that can exist in financial markets. Thus, it provides insight about the risk/return trade-off.

SUMMARY

A major problem in finance is dealing with risk. The standard deviation is a statistical tool that can be used to measure variability, or the amount of risk associated with an outcome.

When we extend our analysis of risk to portfolios of assets, we find that some risk can be diversified away if investors hold a number of assets in a portfolio. As a result, it is important to focus on that nondiversifiable component of risk that an investor must ultimately bear.

The capital-asset-pricing model (CAPM) provides a specific way to relate risk to required return. It shows that required returns should depend only on nondiversifiable risk. There are, however, many questions about the validity of the CAPM. We should, thus, view its insights with a grain of salt as we attempt to apply them to real-world problems. The model does, however, provide useful insights for financial managers about risk/return trade-offs.

QUESTIONS

1. What are some shortcomings of expected value and the standard deviation as a measure of risk?

2. How does the correlation between two stocks affect the risk of a portfolio formed by investing money in the two stocks? Discuss the implications of a perfect negative correlation and perfect positive correlation.

3. What is the capital-asset-pricing model (CAPM)? Why is it important to financial management?

4. Explain the difference between diversifiable and nondiversifiable risk.

5. The capital-asset-pricing model implies that investors are compensated by means of a risk premium only for bearing nondiversifiable risk and that diversifiable risk is not reflected in market required rates of return. Why should this be so?

6. Give some examples of factors that could increase (or decrease) diversifiable risk for a firm. Do the same for nondiversifiable risk.

7. What is a *beta coefficient?* How can beta coefficients be used by an investor?

Problems

1. You own rights to a lottery with the probabilities and payoffs shown in Table A. Someone has offered to buy your rights to the lottery for cash. What is the minimum amount you would accept? (Note: your answer depends upon your individual attitude about risk.)

2. Repeat Problem (1) for each of the lotteries given in Table B. Based on your results, what can you say about your own attitude toward risk?

3. Suppose that 5 individuals are offered a lottery ticket that pays either $0 or $1,000 and that each of these outcomes is equally likely. The 5 individuals are willing to pay the amounts for this lottery ticket that are indicated in Table C. What may we conclude about the attitude toward risk held by each of these individuals?

4. Consider the investment opportunities in Table D, each of which requires the same outlay.

   a. Rank the four investments in order of riskiness.
   b. Rank the four investments in descending order of value, assuming that a risk-averse investor is valuing them.
   c. Repeat part (b) assuming that a risk-neutral investor is valuing the investments.

Table C

Individual	Amount Individual Is Willing to Pay for Lottery Ticket (dollars)
1	376
2	515
3	500
4	478
5	189

Table D

Opportunity	Anticipated Cash Inflow (dollars)	Probability (percent)
A	0	0.333
	500	0.333
	1000	0.333
B	0	0.05
	500	0.90
	1000	0.05
C	0	0.15
	500	0.70
	1000	0.15
D	0	0.0
	500	1.0
	1000	0.0

5. Two investments, A and B, have the probability distributions of returns given in Table E. Calculate the expected return and standard deviation for each investment. Which is the riskier investment? What can you say about the expected return relative to the riskiness of each investment?

Table A

Lottery 1 Payoff (dollars)	Profitability (percent)	Weighted Outcome (dollars)
400	0.5	200
600	0.5	300
	Expected value	500

Table B

Lottery	Payoff (dollars)	Probabilities (percent)	Expected Value (dollars)	Sale Price (dollars)
2	0 or 1000	0.5/0.5		
3	−1000 or 2000	0.5/0.5		
4	−25000 or 26000	0.5/0.5		

Table E

A		B	
Probability	Return	Probability	Return
0.10	0.10	0.15	0.08
0.20	0.12	0.15	0.10
0.30	0.15	0.15	0.18
0.40	0.20	0.55	0.24

6. An analyst calculates the beta coefficient for XYZ Corporation to be 1.3. Suppose $K_m = 0.17$ and $R_f = 0.09$. Suppose further that the analyst calculates the expected return on XYZ's shares to be 22 percent. Is XYZ a good buy?

7. Suppose that a shareholder had just paid $50 per share for XYZ company stock. The stock will pay a $2.00 per share dividend in the upcoming year, and this dividend is expected to grow at an annual rate of 10 percent for the indefinite future. The shareholder felt that the price paid was an appropriate price given an assessment of XYZ's risks.

a. What is the annual required rate of return of this shareholder?

b. Assume that the capital-asset-pricing model holds and that the expected return on the market portfolio was 12 percent and the risk-free rate was 8 percent. What is the beta coefficient of XYZ's stock?

8. Calculate the expected rate of return (K_j) for the companies listed in Table F. Assume the government-bond rate (R_f) is 11 percent and the expected return on the market portfolio (K_m) is 19 percent.

Table F

Industry	Beta Coefficient
Airline	1.75
Electronics manufacturer	1.62
Shipping company	1.18
Packaged-food producer	1.00
Liquor distiller	0.93
Tobacco company	0.82
Telephone utility	0.77
Electric utility	0.64

REFERENCES

Copeland, T., and F. Weston. *Financial Theory and Corporate Policy*. 3rd ed. Reading, Mass.: Addison-Wesley, 1988.

Evans, J. L., and S. H. Archer, "Diversification and the Reduction of Dispersion." *Journal of Finance* 23 (Dec. 1968): 29–40.

Fama, E. F., "Efficient Capital Markets — A Review of Theory and Empirical Work." *Journal of Finance* 25 (May 1970): 383–417.

Fama, E. F., and J. D. Macbeth, "Risk, Return and Equilibrium: Empirical Tests." *Journal of Political Economy* 81 (May 1973): 607–631.

Lintner, J., "The Evaluation of Risk Assets and the Selection of Risky Investments in Stock Portfolios and Capital Budgets." *Review of Economics and Statistics 47* (Feb. 1965): 13–77.

Markowitz, H. M., "Portfolio Selection." *Journal of Finance* (Mar. 1952): 77–91.

Markowitz, H. M. *Portfolio Selection: Efficient Diversification of Investments*. New York: John Wiley & Sons, Inc., 1959.

Mossin, J., "Equilibrium in a Capital Asset Market." *Econometrics* 34, 4 (Oct. 1966): 768–775.

Mullins, D. W., Jr., "Does the Capital Asset Pricing Model Work?" *Harvard Business Review* (Jan./Feb. 1982): 105–114.

Radcliffe, R. *Investment*. 2nd ed. Glenview, Illinois: Scott, Foresman and Company, 1987.

Roll, R. W., and S. A. Ross, "The Arbitrage Pricing Theory Approach to Strategic Portfolio Planning." *Financial Analysts Journal* (May–June 1984): 14–26.

Roll, R. W., "A Critique of the Capital Asset Pricing Theory's Tests." *Journal of Financial Economics* (March 1977): 129–176.

Roll, R. W., and S. A. Ross, "An Empirical Investigation of Arbitrage Pricing Theory." *Journal of Finance* 35 (December 1980): 1073–1104.

Ross, S. A., "The Arbitrage Theory of Capital Asset Pricing." *Journal of Economic Theory* 13 (Dec. 1976): 341–360.

Shanken, J., "The Arbitrage Pricing Theory: Is It Testable?" *Journal of Finance* 37 (December 1982): 1129–1140.

Sharpe, W. F., "Capital Asset Prices: A Theory of Market Equilibrium Under Conditions of Risk." *Journal of Finance,* 19, 3 (1964): 425–442.

Sharpe, W. F. *Investments.* 3rd ed. Englewood Cliffs, New Jersey: Prentice-Hall, Inc., 1985.

Sharpe, W. F. *Portfolio Theory and Capital Markets.* New York: McGraw-Hill, 1970.

Appendix 5A

Estimating Betas

Finance in Practice 5–1 discusses the estimation of betas. This Appendix discusses the basic idea behind the standard procedures for estimating beta.

It is useful to think of beta as measuring a stock's sensitivity to changes in the market. For example, if a stock has a beta of 2, the return on the stock will tend to move twice as much as the return on the market portfolio. So on a given day for a stock with a beta of 2.0, a 10 percent change in the market portfolio's return would be translated into a 20 percent change in the return on the stock. Similarly, if a stock had a beta of 0.50, a 10 percent change in the market portfolio's return would translate into only a 5 percent change in the stock's return.

As these two examples show, the higher beta is, the more risk there is associated with a stock. Furthermore, the relationship is not perfect. Beta only gives the average relationship between a stock and the market. For instance, even if a stock has a beta of 2.0, it may decline on a day when the market goes up if some bad news is released about the firm. This bad news would be diversifiable risk that would be offset, on average, by good news on some other stock if the portfolio is well diversified. But suppose we don't know a stock's beta. We can estimate it by looking at the past patterns of changes in returns for the stock graphed against changes in returns for the market. Remember that beta should tell us the ratio of these changes.

To illustrate, suppose we gathered the data (hypothetical) in Table 5A–1 for XYZ stock and the market index. The data are plotted in Figure 5A–1. Point (1) in Figure 5A–1 corresponds to the first month in Table 5A–1, in which the market return was 8% and the return on XYZ stock was 14%. Using Figure 5A–1, we could sketch in a straight line that best fits the six points, as shown in Figure 5A–2. The slope of the line turns out to be 1.50 and tells us that for every one percent change

Table 5A–1
Hypothetical Data for Estimating Beta of XYZ Stock

Month	Return on XYZ (percent)	Return on Market (percent)
1	14	8
2	2	2
3	−7.5	−5
4	2	0
5	13	10
6	10	4

Figure 5A–1
Plot of Returns on XYZ Stock and Market

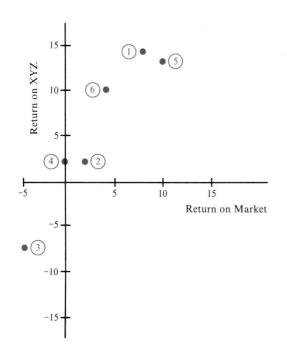

Figure 5A–2
Estimate of Beta

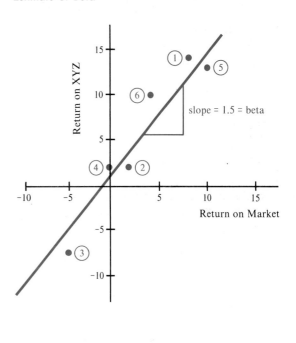

in the market return, on average, we experience a 1.5 percent change in XYZ's return. That is, on average, every time the market return changed 10 percent the return on XYZ changed ($1.5 \times 10 =$) 15 percent. Thus the slope of the line is precisely the stock's beta! The beta for XYZ is therefore 1.5.

Looking at Figure 5A–2 we see also that all the points don't lie on the line; the line only gives the average relationship. The fact that points fall off the line shows that stocks also have some diversifiable risk. This risk is not related to the market and in theory can be diversified away in a large portfolio. Beta measures the risk that can't be eliminated by diversification.

In practice we would need to use much more than six observations of data in our example (either more months or use of weekly or daily returns), and fitting a line is not always easy. Regression analysis is simply a statistical technique to fit the best straight line to a set of points. The slope from that line is an estimate of a stock's beta. Finance in Practice 5–1 discusses beta estimates in more detail.

Appendix 5B

Arbitrage Pricing Theory

Given the unrealistic assumptions of the CAPM, it will come as no surprise that many finance scholars have worked to develop other theories relating risk and required return. The most popular alternative to the CAPM is called *arbitrage pricing theory (APT)*.[1] Unlike the CAPM, in which only risk relative to the market portfolio is of concern, APT claims that a number of distinct and separate risk premiums emerge in the market. Thus, APT says that the expected rate of return on a security will be the risk-free rate *plus* a number of separate risk premiums.

To understand APT let's recall Equation (4) from Chapter 5, which stated the CAPM:

$$K_j = R_f + (K_m - R_f)\beta_j \tag{4}$$

In Equation (4) there is only one source of risk, the market portfolio, that is priced in the market and hence affects a security's risk premium. The market portfolio has a risk premium $(K_m - R_f)$, and a security's risk premium is just the market risk premium times the security's β, which shows the security's risk in relation to the market. Effectively, the CAPM says that the market portfolio captures *all* relevant sources of risk including things such as political factors, inflation, and economic fluctuations.

Now suppose that, in contrast to the CAPM, there were two sources of risk priced separately in the market. For instance, let us assume the two risk factors were unexpected inflation and unexpected changes in unemployment. If this were the case, expected returns would depend on both risk factors and could be written as Equation (5):

$$K_j = R_f + (K_1 - R_f)B_1 + (K_2 - R_f)B_2 \tag{5}$$

where K_1 stands for required return associated with unexpected inflation, K_2 stands for required return associated with unexpected unemployment, B_1 stands for a security's risk related to unexpected inflation, and B_2 stands for a security's risk related to unexpected unemployment. In Equation (5) there would be two risk factors for a stock, and a stock's final required return would depend on the *sum* of the stock's risk premiums on each of the two factors. For example, some stocks might have high sensitivity to unexpected inflation (a high B_1) and others a high sensitivity to unemployment (a high B_2). The important difference between Equations (4) and (5) is that in Equation (5) we need to know two risk measures for each stock, B_1 and B_2, not a single beta measure (β) as in the CAPM.

---

[1] See Stephen Ross, "The Arbitrage Theory of Capital Asset Pricing," *Journal of Economic Theory,* December 1976.

APT is a generalization of Equation (5) that allows for any number of risk factors, not just one or two. APT can be written as Equation (6):

$$K_j = R_f + F_1 B_1 + F_2 B_2 + \cdots + F_N B_N \tag{6}$$

where F stands for one of N possible types of risk and B stands for a security's risk relative to a risk factor.

Equation (6) says that in equilibrium the required return on a security will be the risk-free rate *plus* a number of separate risk premiums. In equilibrium, this required return will be equal to investors' expected return since prices will have adjusted. Comparing Equations (4) and (6), one can view the CAPM as a special case of APT in which there is only one relevant risk factor, the market portfolio.

While APT is intuitively appealing, its use has been limited because the theory itself, unlike the CAPM, offers no guidance on exactly what the relevant risk factors should be. As a result, there is extensive research to identify relevant factors. Early work suggests that perhaps as few as three to five factors are separately priced in the market and that, not surprisingly, these factors are related to economic variables such as inflation, interest rates, and gross national product. Unfortunately, however, widespread use of APT cannot proceed until (and unless) research is able to provide better insights into the important risk factors. For the present, we will continue to focus on the CAPM as a means of relating risk to required return.

Part 3 / Financial Analysis and Planning

Part One examined the role of financial management and the environment in which firms operate. Part Two explored time and risk and their relation to value in financial markets. The basic discounted-cash-flow model provides a way to measure the value of an asset (such as a bond) in a way that takes both time and risk into account. To use such a model, however, we need information. In the case of a U.S. government bond, we may only need to read the *Wall Street Journal* to get the relevant

information about the cash flows we should expect if we buy the bond and hold it to maturity.

For corporate financial managers, however, the problems of obtaining usable information are much more difficult. What will be the effects of an investment in a new computer? For that matter, how efficient are the company's current methods of operation? We need to be able to predict the future effects of possible courses of action among which we must choose in order to make good decisions.

In practice, we often build our predictions about future events on what we know about the present and the past. The chapters in Part Three examine some of the basic ways in which corporate managers measure and evaluate the past, present, and future results of a corporation's activity. Such techniques are also widely used by people outside the corporation, such as bank loan officers and investors, who may be trying to evaluate a company.

We begin our analysis in Chapter 6 by discussing the basic financial statements of a corporation — balance sheets, income statements, and source-and-use-of-funds statements. These provide the basic framework for measuring the profit or cash flow of a corporation.

Chapter 7 outlines the basic techniques of *financial analysis* for evaluating the health of a firm or other organization. Is the firm profitable? What have been the trends in profitability? How does profitability compare with that of the industry or other similar companies? Chapter 8 then discusses fixed and variable costs and relationships between costs, sales volume, and profits.

Chapter 9 turns to the future and a discussion of *financial planning*. The primary focus in Chapter 9 is on near-term financial planning (a time horizon of one to two years), but it also examines long-run financial planning. Financial planning is important for all firms and especially critical for small firms with small amounts of cash and with heavy borrowing. In Chapter 9, we will learn how to estimate financial requirements and to prepare a comprehensive financial plan, including pro-forma income statements, balance sheets, and cash budgets. These plans provide the type of information we need to begin analyzing corporate decisions in more detail.

6

Measuring Profit and Cash Flow

This chapter describes the basic financial statements of a corporation—balance sheets, income statements, and source-and-use-of-funds statements. These statements provide a basic framework for developing information about a company, including data on profit and cash flow.

The income to an economic unit, an individual, or a firm during any period of time is the change in that unit's wealth during the period.

Under accrual accounting, income is considered earned in the time period during which goods are shipped. Under cash accounting, income is earned only when the customer's payment is received.

Economic income — the change in the net worth of an economic unit during a period of time.

Accounting income — the income figure that results from the application of generally accepted accounting principles to the problem of allocating receipts and expenditures to particular time periods.

Economic income and accounting income converge over long time periods. Over short time periods, the difference between the two can be substantial.

Part Two focused on how financial markets place *values* on assets, such as a firm's common stock. We saw that investors in these markets valued assets based on the future cash flows that those assets might provide. To make projections about the future, however, we need to develop and interpret information. What is the future financial performance of a company likely to be? We can start answering this question only if we can evaluate what the company has done in the past and is doing currently. From this base, we are in a much better position to make projections about the future.

One of the main sources of information on business entities is accounting data. A basic concern of accounting is measurement. For example, one of the most difficult problems facing the accountant is measurement of income. In economic terms, **economic income** equals the change in wealth. The income to an economic unit, an individual, or a firm during any period of time is the change in that unit's wealth during the period. For example, suppose you bought a share of stock for $100 at the end of 1988. Suppose also that during 1989 the stock paid you a dividend of $5 and that its price increased to $120 by year-end 1989. As a result of owning that stock, your wealth went up from $100 to $125 ($120 stock price plus $5 dividend). This increase of $25 is the *economic income* earned from owning the stock in 1989.

In the case of the stock price, the economic income is fairly easy to calculate. When we turn to the actual operations of the firm, however, the problem becomes more complicated. We can think of income as the difference between revenues and expenses during a time period, but making specific judgments can be difficult. As a result we must draw a distinction between *accounting income* and economic income.[1] **Accounting income** refers to the income figure resulting from the application of generally accepted accounting principles. This figure, however, is the product of a number of essentially arbitrary judgments. The amount of an economic unit's accounting income depends on how receipts and expenditures are allocated to particular time periods as revenue or expense. As goods are sold, when is the revenue earned? Is it earned when the order is placed by the customer, when the goods are shipped, when the invoice is mailed, or when the customer's check is received? Most firms keep their books using an **accrual accounting system;** that is, they recognize the sale as a transaction and record the revenue as earned in the accounting period during which the goods are shipped. Some smaller firms keep books using a **cash accounting system;** that is, they recognize the sale only when the customer's payment is received.

Over long time periods, economic income and accounting income converge, because problems of allocation to particular time periods disappear. Over short time periods, the differences between the two can be substantial. An objective of accounting should be to measure the true economic income of the firm; however, the state of the art is not adequate to deal with all the problems involved. Later in this chapter we will discuss some of the problems of measurement with which accountants must deal in practice. For now, let us realize that the accounting records

[1]For further discussion of this distinction, see R. K. Jaedicke and R. T. Sprouse, *Accounting Flows: Income, Funds, Cash* (Englewood Cliffs, N.J.: Prentice-Hall, 1965).

kept by a firm provide important information about the firm's past and current operations. As such, these records (reported in financial statements) provide useful information for developing assumptions about what might happen in the future.

Financial Statements

Large firms typically have quite thorough accounting systems that provide a wide array of information to corporate managers. With the increasing sophistication of computers, such accounting services are also becoming available to smaller firms. This chapter will focus on the three basic financial statements used by a firm: the income statement, the balance sheet, and the source-and-use-of-funds statement. These statements provide a type of financial model for the firm that provides the starting point for both the analysis of the past and the prediction of the future.

Consider the income statement in Table 6–1 and balance sheet in Table 6–2 for Sparta Manufacturing Company, a manufacturer of paints and varnishes. We will work here with these two statements and turn to the source-and-use-of-funds statement later in this chapter.

The **income statement** (which is also known as a *profit-and-loss statement*) represents a record of events between two points in time, in this case December 31, 1987, and December 31, 1988. The **balance sheet** represents a "snapshot" of the firm's position at a single point in time: December 31, 1988. The income statement measures *flows* of dollars per unit of time, because income is a **flow variable.** In contrast, the items in the balance sheet are **stock variables;** that is, they represent dollar values at a given point in time.

Accounting ground rules govern the construction of financial statements. One way to think of the distinction between the income statement and the balance sheet is to focus on the effect of a particular transaction on the firm's owners, the shareholders. In accounting, a measure of a firm's worth to shareholders is represented

The income statement records events during a *period* of time. The balance sheet represents a "snapshot" at a *point* in time.

Income statement, or *profit-and-loss statement* — a record of financial events between two points in time. The income statement is an attempt to measure the change in net worth over time.

Balance sheet — a "snapshot" summary of the firm's financial position at a single point in time.

Flow variable — a variable whose value is measured during a period of time.

Stock variable — a variable whose value is measured at a given moment in time.

Table 6–1

Sparta Manufacturing Company Income Statement, Calendar Year 1988

Sales	$1,140,000
Cost of goods sold	(730,000)
Gross profit	$ 410,000
Depreciation	(15,000)
Selling, general, and administrative expense	(340,100)
Operating profit	$ 54,900
Interest	(12,900)
Profit before taxes	42,000
Income taxes	(8,400)
Profit after taxes	$ 33,600

Note: Figures in parentheses represent expenses which are to be subtracted.

Table 6–2

Sparta Manufacturing Company Balance Sheet, December 31, 1988

Cash	$ 2,500
Accounts receivable	152,500
Inventory	420,000
Total current assets	$575,000
Fixed assets, net of depreciation	112,500
Other assets	35,000
Total assets	**$722,500**
Note payable (bank)	$144,100
Accounts payable	122,500
Taxes payable	7,500
Miscellaneous accruals	50,000
Total current liabilities	$324,100
Mortgage payable	26,000
Total liabilities	$350,100
Common stock	155,000
Retained earnings	217,400
Total liabilities and net worth	**$722,500**

Net worth—the value of total assets minus total liabilities, or the value of the owners' claim on assets.

by the **net worth** of the corporation. The net worth is simply the total assets of the company minus the total liabilities of the company—that is, net worth is the shareholders' claim on the company after all other claims have been settled. Transactions that would increase or decrease net worth appear in the income statement. The income statement is, thus, an attempt to measure the change in the wealth of owners over a period of time—that is, it measures income.

For example, looking at Table 6–1 we see that in 1988 Sparta Manufacturing sold goods in exchange for $1,140,000, but those goods cost Sparta $730,000. The sales revenue increased net worth while the cost of the goods sold decreased net worth. The transaction of the sales increased net worth on balance by $410,000—the difference between the revenue ($1,140,000) and the cost ($730,000). Both types of transactions are recorded in the income statement. If the firm is doing well, the increases in net worth (for example, sales revenues) exceed the decreases in net worth (for example, salaries paid), so the shareholders experience an increase in wealth, at least as measured by accounting standards. This increase in wealth represents an accounting profit earned on income. In 1988, Sparta had a profit after taxes—that is, an increase in net worth—of $33,600, as shown in Table 6–1.

The balance sheet catalogs all the assets and liabilities of the company at a single point in time. At year-end 1988, Table 6–2 shows that Sparta had $722,500 worth of assets and $350,100 worth of total liabilities. The difference between the two figures of $372,400 is the claim of shareholders, which is precisely the net

The balance sheet shows the net worth (total assets minus total liabilities) of shareholders at a point in time, while the income statement measures *changes* in net worth.

The retained-earnings account in the balance sheet plays the critical role of linking the balance sheet with the income statement.

Expenditures — all cash outflows.

Expenses — only those expenditures that affect net worth and thus appear in the income statement.

Receipts — all cash inflows.

Revenues — only those receipts that affect net worth and thus appear in the income statement.

worth of Sparta. Thus, the balance sheet shows the net worth of shareholders at a point in time, while the income statement measures *changes* in net worth.

Note that in Table 6–2 this net worth is broken into two categories — common stock and retained earnings. These two accounts add up to net worth for Sparta ($155,000 + $217,400 = $372,400). The *common-stock account* represents amounts of money received from shareholders who have put money directly into the business by buying shares of the firm's stock; the *retained-earnings account* represents profits that have been earned in the past and retained in the business rather than being paid out to owners. For example, to raise money, Sparta may have originally sold 10,000 shares of stock for $15.50 a share to generate a common-stock figure of $10,000 × $15.50 = $155,000, as reported in Table 6–2.

The retained-earnings account in the balance sheet plays a critical role in linking the balance sheet and the income statement. If Sparta kept all of its profits in the business and paid out no dividends, balance-sheet retained earnings as of year-end 1988 would be retained earnings as of year-end 1987 plus profits after taxes earned during 1988. Assuming no dividends, in this case, we can infer that Sparta's 1987 balance-sheet retained earnings were $183,800 because Sparta's profits in 1988 were $33,600 (from the Table 6–1 income statement), Sparta's 1988 retained earnings were $217,400 (from the Table 6–2 balance sheet), and $217,400 − $33,600 = $183,800. Assuming the shareholders make no further actual contributions to Sparta in 1988 (assuming, in other words, that the common-stock account would be unchanged), Sparta's net worth on the balance sheet would thus increase by $33,600 in 1988 — precisely the figure of profits after taxes found in the income statement.

If dividends are paid, retained earnings would increase in a year by only the amount of profits actually retained — that is, by profit after taxes minus dividends. Thus, the net worth on the balance sheet would go up by less than profit after taxes from the income statement. The shareholders would, however, have received the dividend payment so their wealth (at least as measured by accounting data) would be increased by the full amount of profits after taxes. For example, if profits after taxes were $100,000 and dividends were $40,000, shareholders would see balance-sheet net worth increase by $60,000 (which is $100,000 − $40,000), but they would also get dividends of $40,000 for a total dollar figure of $100,000. As a result, the $100,000 profit-after-tax figure is still a measure of the effect of the year's operation on shareholder wealth. The important point for our purposes is that the income statement feeds into the balance sheet.

To understand the distinction between income-statement and balance-sheet transactions, it is important to understand the accounting meaning of the names of various categories in the statements.

All cash outflows are **expenditures**, but only those expenditures that affect net worth and, therefore, appear in the income statement are **expenses**. All cash inflows are **receipts**, but only those receipts that appear in the income statement are **revenues**.

For example, suppose a company borrows $1 million from a bank, receiving a check for the full amount. While the $1 million is certainly a *receipt* of cash, it is not *revenue*. The cash receipt is offset by the firm's owing the bank $1 million. Shareholder net worth is not changed.

Working Capital

Working capital — composed of the firm's current assets, normally with maturities of less than one year.

Within the balance-sheet total it is useful to distinguish between **current**, or circulating, **assets** and **fixed assets.** Current assets include the firm's holdings of cash, accounts receivable, and the inventory of raw materials, goods in process, and finished goods. The term **working capital** often is used to refer to the firm's current assets, and the term **net working capital** is used to refer to current assets less current liabilities. Short-term assets, such as accounts receivable and inventories, are considered working capital because they are part of the basic workings of the company's day-to-day business. Using these definitions, we can see from Table 6–2 that Sparta Manufacturing Company had $575,000 worth of working capital as of December 31, 1988. Table 6–2 also tells us that the company's **current liabilities** on that date amounted to $324,100. Subtracting this figure from total current assets of $575,000 gives us net working capital of $250,900. By "netting out" current liabilities against current assets, we can restate Sparta's balance sheet as shown in Table 6–3.

Net working capital — the firm's current assets minus its current liabilities.

Net working capital — that portion of current assets not financed by current liabilities — must of necessity be financed by long-term funds, such as common stock or long-term borrowing. If the firm is a growing one, both the net working capital and its attendant financing requirement also increase.

Current liabilities — the short-term debt obligations of a firm, with maturities of less than one year.

Income Measurement

A basic concern of accounting is measurement.

As we discussed at the beginning of this chapter, a basic concern of accounting is measurement. Measuring income is extremely difficult. Already we have distinguished between economic and accounting income. The figures in Table 6–1 show us that Sparta Manufacturing earned profits of $33,600 after taxes in 1988.

As do practically all firms, Sparta uses an accrual accounting system, rather than a cash accounting system, so it recognizes sales as transactions and records the revenue as earned in the accounting period during which the goods are shipped.

Table 6–3
Sparta Manufacturing Company Balance Sheet, December 31, 1988

Assets		Liabilities and Net Worth	
Net working capital	$250,900	Mortgage payable	$ 26,000
Net fixed assets	112,500	Common stock	155,000
Other assets	35,000	Retained earnings	217,400
Total assets	$398,400	**Total liabilities and net worth**	$398,400

Determining the Appropriate Accounting Period

There are a number of difficult problems in calculating a measured income, as Table 6–1 does for Sparta. When a firm purchases materials, it must determine in which particular time period the expenditure should be recorded as an expense. Is the expense incurred when the materials are ordered, received, consumed, or paid for? Again, the answer depends on whether the firm is using a cash or an accrual system of accounting. The firm also needs to determine whether the outlay is to be treated as a *product cost* and recognized when the product is sold or as a *period cost* that is assigned to a time period.

One of the major problems in recording accounting information is deciding how the costs of long-lived assets, such as equipment, are to be treated. Suppose a company purchased a machine for $100,000 that was expected to last five years and then be worthless. While there is a cash expenditure of $100,000 now, the company also has an asset worth $100,000 so it has not incurred a cost. It simply traded one asset (cash) for another (the machine). As the machine wears out (or becomes technologically obsolete) in the next five years, however, the company does incur a depreciation cost—the erosion of the value of a valuable asset. But at what rate does this value decrease? Is it spread evenly over five years? Does it occur mostly in the first few years? Accountants deal with this problem by calculating **depreciation** allowances that allocate the cost of the asset to different time periods. While, ideally, accountants would use economic depreciation (the reduction in the machine's value), practical difficulties in applying the concept of economic depreciation have led to the adoption of mechanical calculations of depreciation. For example, the *straight-line* method of depreciation allocates the historical cost of a machine evenly over its useful life. In the example above, the annual depreciation allowance by the straight-line method would be ($100,000 − $0)/5 = $20,000. This $20,000 figure implicitly assumes that the machine loses $20,000 of its value each year until it has zero value in five years.

To produce financial statements, many other judgments are required that affect the allocation of revenue and expense to particular time periods. A number of options usually are open with respect to the treatment of depreciation. For example, straight-line depreciation spreads the original cost of an asset evenly over a number of years, while accelerated methods of depreciation allocate a larger percentage of the asset's cost to early time periods. Research-and-development (R&D) expenditures generally are expensed as they occur, but in some cases they are treated as an asset and *amortized* (depreciated) over several accounting periods. For example, suppose a company had made total cash outlays of $200,000 on research and development to produce new products. Since the benefits of these outlays will be spread out over future time periods, the company may treat the outlays as creating an asset (that is, they may *capitalize* the outlay as an asset) and subsequently spread the $200,000 out as costs over a number of time periods in the same way depreciation allowances spread the cost of a machine over its useful life. Likewise, the acquisition of patents and goodwill (value that cannot be attributed to any specific tangible asset or assets) may be capitalized and subsequently amortized over several accounting periods. Taxes may be treated one way

Depreciation—the allocation of the cost of an asset to different time periods.

In producing financial statements, numerous judgments are made that affect the allocation of revenue and expense to particular time periods.

for reporting to the Internal Revenue Service (IRS) and another for financial reporting to investors. In all these cases, the question is not the total amount involved over the life of a transaction, but the time period to which the receipt or expenditure is to be allocated as revenue or expense.

Reflecting Changes in Market Value and Inflation

Other difficulties in measurement arise from changes in market value. If the securities owned by a firm rise in value during a particular period, should the increase be treated as income? In an economic sense, assuming no inflation, the increase does constitute income, and a decline in value would constitute a real economic loss. For accounting purposes, however, such gains and losses usually are not recognized until the securities are sold.

The treatment of inflation is a major problem in financial accounting.

A problem of major proportion in income measurement is the treatment of inflation. Inflation affects the market value of all the firm's assets. During inflationary periods, "profits" are earned on inventories while held by the firm. Fixed assets rise in value. Replacement costs of new fixed assets to maintain the firm's earning power can exceed depreciation allowances, because the depreciation allowances are based on historical cost. When price levels are rising, the use of historical-cost depreciation and the emergence of inventory profits (the gain due to inflation on inventories while held by the firm) can overstate earnings. On the other hand, if a firm had debt outstanding, the real value of this debt declines during inflationary periods because the firm will eventually repay the debt in cheaper dollars. Because historical-cost accounting conventions do not recognize this debt effect, the firm's reported earnings will tend to understate its economic income when price levels rise. The net effect of these several forces of overstatement and understatement will depend, of course, on the particular mix of assets and liabilities in the individual balance sheet under consideration. To determine the true change in the firm's net worth during any period under such circumstances is a difficult problem indeed.

In numerous cases, the question is to what time period revenue or expenses should be allocated, not the total amount involved over the life of a transaction.

While on the subject of income, let us note that income to a corporate firm is not the same as income to the firm's shareholders. Income to shareholders consists of dividends paid on the shares plus capital gains (or losses) that result from changes in the market value of the shares. In theory, in the case of a firm with shares that are publicly traded, the market value of the firm's shares should reflect all elements of value—those not measured directly by traditional financial statements as well as those that are. *Market value of a firm* often deviates substantially from the figure for *book net worth of a firm* (assets minus liabilities) given in a financial statement.

Income to a corporate firm is not the same as income to the firm's shareholders.

To compute market value, all the firm's outstanding shares are valued at the market quotation of the shares on the stock exchange where they are traded. If market value at any point in time is a good estimate of the firm's true value (in other words, if the market value of the stock is an *unbiased estimate*), then the change in market value between two points in time along with changes in dividends paid should represent a good, or unbiased, estimate of the firm's economic income for the period.

Operating Cash Flow

It is important to distinguish between profit as reported and cash flow.

Profit — the excess of revenues over expenses during a given time period.

Cash flow — the total change in the firm's cash account, the actual cash flowing into and out of a firm over a particular time period, measured as operating cash flow plus all balance-sheet changes.

Operating cash flows — the flows of cash arising from the operation of the firm, normally defined as profit after taxes plus noncash charges such as depreciation.

A firm must also distinguish between **profit** as reported and **cash flow** in recording information about the firm. Let us first consider **operating cash flow** — cash flow generated by the firm's operations. In most cases, cash flow from operations during any period will exceed profit after tax by the amount of noncash expenses charged during the period — mainly depreciation — but part of the difference between profit and cash flow may also include the amortization of goodwill, patents, or research-and-development expenditures previously capitalized. In the case of Sparta Manufacturing Company, we have only depreciation to consider. As noted above, depreciation is the process of allocating the cost of a long-lived asset to the time periods during which it is used up. Cash changes hands at the time the machine is purchased, but subsequent depreciation charges represent *noncash* expenses. To determine the cash flow generated by a firm's operations during any period, we must adjust the profit figure by *adding back* depreciation. Consider Sparta Manufacturing's profit-and-loss statement for 1986, given in Table 6–4.

Column (1) in Table 6–4 shows the results of profit-and-loss calculations using accrual accounting. Profit after taxes for Sparta is $33,600. Column (2) enters only cash items. Note that because depreciation is a noncash expense, no depreciation figure is entered in column (2). Doing the arithmetic in column (2), we see that cash flow from operations is $48,600. This cash-flow figure is precisely the amount of the depreciation expense plus the profit after taxes ($15,000 + $33,000 = $48,600) because depreciation is a noncash item and, hence, is not subtracted in column (2). The last entries in column (1) show that we can also get this cash-flow number ($48,600) by adding the depreciation expense back to profits after taxes.

Table 6–4

Profit-and-Loss Statement for Sparta Manufacturing Company, 1988

	Profit and Loss (Accrual) (1)	Cash Flow (Cash Only) (2)
Sales	$1,140,000	$1,140,000
minus Cost of goods sold	− 730,000	− 730,000
minus Depreciation	− 15,000	—
minus Selling, general, and administrative expense	− 340,100	− 340,100
minus Interest	− 12,900	− 12,900
minus Taxes	− 8,400	− 8,400
equals Profit after taxes	$ 33,600	
plus Depreciation	+ 15,000	
equals After-tax cash flow from operations	$ 48,600	$ 48,600

Adding back depreciation to profit after tax, as is done in column (1), is a handy way to arrive at an approximate measure of cash flow from operations. In some cases — for example, when a capital asset is sold — correctly identifying all the noncash charges can be confusing. We can always arrive at the right answer simply by starting with cash revenues and subtracting all cash expenses (including taxes) required to generate those revenues, as is done in column (2). Because taxes are figured as a percentage of profits, however, the accrual-accounting figures in column (1) are needed to know what taxes will be entered in column (2).

Profit Versus Cash Flow

Let us examine more closely the distinction between operating cash flow and profit. In principle, the profit figure is intended to measure change in value, albeit imperfectly. The operating-cash-flow figure measures funds generated by the firm's operations and available for expenditure. The funds might be used to expand the investment in fixed assets, to pay dividends, to expand working capital, to retire debt, or for a variety of other purposes.

Taking a long view, however, there are claims against operating cash flow that must be met. To sustain its earning power, the firm must reinvest to replace assets that wear out. Let us suppose that a particular firm reinvests exactly enough to sustain its real earning power — that is, its earning power adjusted for inflation. If we subtract the reinvestment requirement from operating cash flow, the remainder over the long run should approximately equal the firm's earnings. To generate a growing earnings stream (again, in real terms, adjusted for inflation), the firm must reinvest an amount over and above replacement requirements.

Our interpretation of operating cash flow and its uses thus depends on our time frame, whether we take a short or long view. In the short run, operating cash flow can be used for any purpose. In the long run, a large part must be earmarked for reinvestment if the cash flow itself is to be sustained.

Sample Problem 6–1
Operating Cash Flow and Profit for Montana Lumber

Montana Lumber Company raises timber and manufactures lumber products and furniture components. Projected 1989 sales are $530 million, with cost of goods sold amounting to 76 percent of sales. Selling, administrative, and research expenses should reach $50 million. Montana Lumber pays 8.5 percent interest on $5 million worth of long-term debt. Annual depreciation on fixed assets is $8 million. The 1988 balance sheet reflected a $530 million balance in the lumber and timber account. It is expected that 4 percent of this balance will be depleted in 1989. The company pays 46 percent corporate income taxes. What amount of funds generated by Montana Lumber's operations should management consider to be available for expenditure? (*Note: Depletion* of timber is a noncash charge analogous to depreciation of machinery or other fixed assets.)

Solution

This problem illustrates the difference between operating cash flow and account-ing profit. After arranging the given revenue and expense information into profit-and-loss-statement format, those figures that represent cash items are combined to find the operating cash flow. Depreciation and depletion are noncash expenses. We can arrive at the cash-flow figure in two ways: by adding noncash expenses to the profit-after-tax figure, as in column (1) of Table 6–5, or by starting with cash revenues and subtracting all cash expenses required to generate those revenues, as in column (2). As Table 6–5 shows, the cash flow from operations is $54,890, as calculated in either column (1) or column (2). ▪

Total Cash Flow Versus Operating Cash Flow

The firm's total cash flow (the total change in the firm's cash account) during a time period, as distinct from operating cash flow, is affected by balance-sheet changes.

The firm's total cash flow — the total change in the firm's cash account — during a period, as distinct from operating cash flow, is affected by balance-sheet changes. Let us examine the balance-sheet data for Sparta Manufacturing Company for two successive years, as given in Table 6–6. In Table 6–4, we calculated Sparta's cash flow from *operations* during 1988 as $48,600. Yet Table 6–6 shows that the cash balance *declined* by $7,500, from $10,000 in 1987 to $2,500 in 1988. The differ-ence arises from the fact that cash flow from operations is only part of the picture. The firm's cash balance is affected by other changes taking place in the balance sheet. To see all of these changes we need to examine the **source-and-use-of-funds statement,** the third major type of financial statement.

Source-and-use-of-funds statement — a summary of the flow of the financial activity of the firm, as recorded in the income statement and the balance sheet, that shows where a firm obtains cash and how it uses it.

Table 6–5
Profit-and-Loss Statement for Montana Lumber Company

	Profit and Loss (thousands of dollars) (1)	Cash Flow (thousands of dollars) (2)
Sales	530,000	530,000
minus Cost of goods sold	−402,800	−402,800
equals Gross profit	127,200	127,200
minus Expenses		
Selling, administrative, research	− 50,000	− 50,000
Interest	− 425	− 425
Depreciation	− 8,000	——
Depletion	− 21,200	——
equals Pretax profit	47,575	
minus Taxes (46 percent)	− 21,885	− 21,885
equals Profit after tax	25,690	
plus Noncash expense	+ 29,200	
equals After-tax cash flow from operations	54,890	54,890

Table 6–6

Sparta Manufacturing Company Year-End Balance Sheets, 1987 and 1988

	December 31, 1987	December 31, 1988
Cash	$ 10,000	$ 2,500
Accounts receivable	147,500	152,500
Inventories	410,000	420,000
Total current assets	$567,500	$575,000
Fixed assets, net of depreciation	55,000	112,500
Other assets	15,000	35,000
Total assets	$637,500	$722,500
Notes payable (bank)	$ 88,100	$144,100
Accounts payable	117,500	122,500
Taxes payable	7,600	7,500
Miscellaneous accruals	57,500	50,000
Total current liabilities	$270,700	$324,100
Mortgage payable	28,000	26,000
Total liabilities	$298,700	$350,100
Common stock	155,000	155,000
Retained earnings	183,800	217,400
Total liabilities and net worth	$637,500	$722,500

Sources and Uses of Funds

To produce goods and services, firms acquire assets and put these assets to work productively. Assets are paid for initially by using capital funds provided by owners or by issuing liabilities (such as bonds) in exchange for cash and then using the cash to acquire assets. As the goods and services produced by the firm are sold, more assets are acquired, and a cycle is established. We can view the cyclical flow of cash in the simplified terms illustrated in Figure 6–1. A useful first step in analyzing a firm's performance often is to use the income statement and balance sheet to prepare a source-and-use-of-funds statement. Here, we are defining *funds* to mean cash, although the term is not always so defined.[2] Through **source-and-use-of-funds analysis,** we can determine over any period of time where a firm obtained its funds and what it did with them — in other words, what has been going on financially in a firm.

Source-and-use-of-funds analysis — analysis of the flow of cash through the income statement and balance sheet, in order to determine where a firm obtained its cash and what it did with it.

Balance-Sheet Changes

Source-and-use analysis begins with an analysis of balance-sheet changes over the period of time in which we are interested. Tables 6–7 and 6–8 (pp. 178–179)

[2]An alternative is to define *funds* as working capital. Our purposes here are better served by defining funds as cash.

Figure 6–1
The Flow of Cash from a Firm

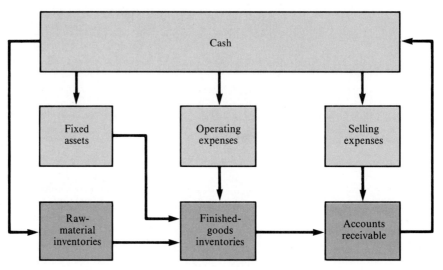

Table 6–7
Sparta Manufacturing Company Income Statements, 1983–1988

	1983	1984	1985	1986	1987	1988
Sales	$515,000	$557,500	$647,500	$930,000	$990,000	$1,140,000
Cost of goods sold	335,000	355,000	387,500	592,500	622,500	730,000
Material	167,500	177,500	192,500	300,000	317,500	375,000
Labor	77,500	80,000	90,000	147,500	157,500	205,000
Overhead	90,000	97,500	105,000	145,000	147,500	150,000
Gross profit	$180,000	$202,500	$260,000	$337,500	$367,500	$ 410,000
Depreciation	7,500	5,000	5,000	5,000	10,000	15,000
Selling, general, and administrative expense	149,400	181,100	190,600	282,400	307,900	340,100
Operating profit before taxes	$ 23,100	$ 16,400	$ 64,400	$ 50,100	$ 49,600	$ 54,900
Interest	8,100	3,900	4,400	5,100	9,600	12,900
Net profit before taxes	$ 15,000	$ 12,500	$ 60,000	$ 45,000	$ 40,000	$ 42,000
Taxes	3,000	2,500	12,000	9,000	8,000	8,400
Profit after taxes	$ 12,000	$ 10,000	$ 48,000	$ 36,000	$ 32,000	$ 33,600

Note: Taxes are computed at a tax rate of 20 percent.

Table 6–8
Sparta Manufacturing Company Year-End Balance Sheets, 1983–1988

	1983	1984	1985	1986	1987	1988
Assets						
Cash	$ 1,000	$ 1,000	$ 2,500	$ 12,500	$ 10,000	$ 2,500
Accounts receivable	125,000	90,000	95,000	107,500	147,500	152,500
Inventory	187,500	180,000	250,000	325,000	410,000	420,000
Total current assets	$313,500	$271,000	$347,500	$445,000	$567,500	$575,000
Fixed assets, net of depreciation	55,000	50,000	45,000	52,500	55,000	112,500
Other assets	17,500	15,000	15,000	17,500	15,000	35,000
Total assets	$386,000	$336,000	$407,500	$515,000	$637,500	$722,500
Liabilities and net worth						
Notes payable (bank)	$ 66,200	$ 16,400	$ 28,200	$ 34,700	$ 88,100	$144,100
Accounts payable (trade)	52,500	42,500	42,500	110,000	117,500	122,500
Taxes payable	3,500	2,800	14,000	8,500	7,600	7,500
Miscellaneous accruals	15,000	17,500	20,000	25,000	57,500	50,000
Total current liabilities	$137,200	$ 79,200	$104,700	$178,200	$270,700	$324,100
Mortgage payable	36,000	34,000	32,000	30,000	28,000	26,000
Total liabilities	$173,200	$113,200	$136,700	$208,200	$298,700	$350,100
Common stock	155,000	155,000	155,000	155,000	155,000	155,000
Retained earnings	57,800	67,800	115,800	151,800	183,800	217,400
Total liabilities and net worth	$386,000	$336,000	$407,500	$515,000	$637,500	$722,500

Source-and-use analysis begins with analysis of balance-sheet changes.

present six years of Sparta's financial history as captured by its income statements and balance sheets. Using balance-sheet data from Table 6–8, we can prepare a statement of balance-sheet changes for the Sparta Manufacturing Company over the period of December 31, 1983, to December 31, 1988, as in Table 6–9.

The Source-and-Use-of-Funds Statement

Table 6–9 (p. 180) can be reorganized into a statement of the sources and uses of Sparta's funds. In addition to acquisition of assets, funds may be used to reduce liabilities. Sources of funds include reductions in assets as well as increases in liabilities. **Sources of funds** can be defined as

Sources of funds—
(1) increases in liabilities,
(2) increases in net worth through retained earnings or additional capital contributions by owners, and
(3) reductions in assets.

1. increases in liabilities (for example, through additional bank borrowing or an increase in accounts payable);
2. increases in net worth achieved through retained earnings or additional capital contributions by owners;
3. reductions in assets (for example, through the liquidation of inventory or the sale of plant).

Table 6–9

Sparta Manufacturing Company Balance-Sheet Changes, December 31, 1983–December 31, 1988

	1983	1988	Change
Assets			
Cash	$ 1,000	$ 2,500	+$ 1,500
Accounts receivable	125,000	152,500	+ 27,500
Inventory	187,500	420,000	+ 232,500
Total current assets	$313,500	$575,000	+$261,500
Fixed assets, net of depreciation	55,000	112,500	+ 57,500
Other assets	17,500	35,000	+ 17,500
Total assets	$386,000	$722,500	+$336,500
Liabilities and net worth			
Notes payable (bank)	$ 66,200	$144,100	+$ 77,900
Accounts payable (trade)	52,500	122,500	+ 70,000
Tax payable	3,500	7,500	+ 4,000
Miscellaneous accruals	15,000	50,000	+ 35,000
Total current liabilities	$137,200	$324,100	+$186,900
Mortgage payable	36,000	26,000	− 10,000
Total liabilities	$173,200	$350,100	+$176,900
Common stock	155,000	155,000	——
Retained earnings	57,800	217,400	+ 159,600
Total liabilities and net worth	$386,000	$722,500	+$336,500

Uses of funds — (1) reductions in liabilities, (2) reductions in net worth through the payment of dividends, retirement of stock, or operating losses, and (3) increases in assets.

Uses of funds can be defined as

1. reductions in liabilities (for example, the payment of debt);
2. reductions in net worth resulting from the payment of dividends, the retirement of stock, or operating losses (the latter can also be viewed as a negative source);
3. increases in assets (for example, the purchase of fixed assets, the extension of more credit to customers, or expansion of inventories).

Reorganizing the changes in the balance sheet into this format gives us the source-and-use-of-funds statement of Table 6–10. In Table 6–10, cash is treated as the residual item. Since Sparta's sources exceed its uses, the statement shows an increase in cash. As an alternative to this format, we could interpret the change in cash as a use or a source, depending on whether it increases or decreases — in which case total uses would equal total sources. In Sparta's case, the increase in cash would then be classified as a $1,500 use (increase in assets) of funds.

In Table 6–10, all of Sparta's asset accounts increased over the period 1983–1988, so all of these changes represented *uses* of funds. This was not the case for the year 1984, viewed individually, as we can see by constructing a source-and-use statement for the period December 31, 1983, to December 31, 1984.

Table 6–10

Sparta Manufacturing Company Source-and-Use-of-Funds Statement, December 31, 1983–December 31, 1988

Sources	
Bank borrowing	$ 77,900
Increase in accounts payable	70,000
Increase in taxes payable	4,000
Increase in miscellaneous accruals	35,000
Retained earnings	159,600
Total sources	$346,500
Uses	
Increase in accounts receivable	$ 27,500
Increase in inventories	232,500
Net increase in fixed assets	57,500
Increase in other assets	17,500
Reduction in mortgage	10,000
Total uses	$345,000
Increase in cash	$ 1,500

Table 6–11 (p. 182) shows that changes in accounts receivable, inventories, and fixed assets during 1984 represented *sources* of funds rather than uses as in Table 6–10. When an asset account increases, it uses funds; when it decreases, it releases, or *provides,* funds and hence becomes a source.

Similarly, when a liability account increases, it provides funds (acts as a source), as does the accounts-payable category in Table 6–10. But in Table 6–11, accounts payable is a *use* of funds because $10,000 in funds had to be used to reduce the amount owed to trade creditors. Likewise, bank debt was reduced by $49,800 (a use), and the mortgage was reduced by $2,000 (another use). When a liability account increases, it provides funds (it is a source); when it decreases, funds are required to make the reduction (the account is a use).

Sample Problem 6–2

Alamance Corporation's Sources and Uses of Funds

Alamance Corporation's balance sheet for the period from December 31, 1987, to December 31, 1988, is given in Table 6–12 (p. 182).

A. Compute the balance-sheet changes for Alamance Corporation from year-end 1987 to year-end 1988.

B. List the various sources and uses of funds for 1988.

C. Construct a source-and-use-of-funds statement similar to the one in Table 6–10.

Table 6–11

Sparta Manufacturing Company Source-and-Use-of-Funds Statement, December 31, 1983–December 31, 1984

Sources	
Reduction in accounts receivable	$35,000
Reduction in inventory	7,500
Reduction in fixed assets	5,000
Reduction in other assets	2,500
Increase in miscellaneous accruals	2,500
Retained earnings	10,000
Total sources	**$62,500**
Uses	
Reduction in bank borrowing	$49,800
Reduction in accounts payable	10,000
Reduction in mortgage	2,000
Reduction in taxes payable	700
Total uses	**$62,500**
Change in cash balance	$ 0

Table 6–12

Alamance Corporation's Balance Sheet, Year-End 1987 and Year-End 1988 (thousands of dollars)

	December 31, 1987	December 31, 1988
Assets		
Cash	435	239
Marketable securities	648	378
Accounts receivable	1,079	1,459
Inventory	3,593	4,253
Other current assets	435	525
Total current assets	6,190	6,854
Net fixed assets	6,765	7,336
Total assets	**12,955**	**14,190**
Liabilities		
Accounts payable (trade)	3,537	3,932
Taxes payable	340	189
Other current liabilities	1,200	1,220
Total current liabilities	5,077	5,341
Long-term debt	3,012	3,000
Preferred stock	900	800
Common stock	1,500	1,700
Retained earnings	2,466	3,349
Total liabilities and owners' equity	**12,955**	**14,190**

Solution

A. The balance-sheet changes are given in Table 6–13.

B. The various sources and uses of funds are listed in Table 6–14.

C. The source-and-use-of-funds statement is given as Table 6–15 (p. 184).

As Tables 6–13 to 6–15 show, in 1988 Alamance Corporation had total sources of funds of $1,768,000 and total uses of funds of $1,964,000. Because uses exceeded sources, Alamance experienced a decrease in cash of $196,000.

Interpreting the Source-and-Use-of-Funds Statement

What do we learn from the source-and-use analysis? Let us again examine the data in Table 6–10 for Sparta Manufacturing for the entire period 1983–1988. First, we see that the largest use of funds by far was to expand inventories. Was the increase due to growth of the firm, or are inventories being managed ineffectively? We

Table 6–13

Balance-Sheet Changes for Alamance Corporation (thousands of dollars)

Assets	*Change*	*Liabilities*	*Change*
Cash	− 196	Accounts payable	+ 395
Marketable securities	− 270	Taxes payable	− 151
Accounts receivable	+ 380	Other current liabilities	+ 20
Inventory	+ 660	Long-term debt	− 12
Other current assets	+ 90	Preferred stock	− 100
Fixed assets	+ 571	Common stock	+ 200
		Retained earnings	+ 883
Total assets	+1,235	**Total liabilities and net worth**	+1,235

Table 6–14

Alamance Corporation's Sources and Uses of Funds

Sources	*Uses*
Changes in liabilities	Changes in liabilities
Increase in accounts payable	Decrease in taxes payable
Increase in other current liabilities	Decrease in long-term debt
Changes in assets	Changes in assets
Decrease in cash	Increase in accounts receivable
Decrease in marketable securities	Increase in inventory
	Increase in other current assets
	Increase in fixed assets
Changes in net worth	Changes in net worth
Increase in common stock	Decrease in preferred stock
Increase in retained earnings	

Table 6—15

Source-and-Use-of-Funds Statement for Alamance Corporation (thousands of dollars)

Sources	
Increase in accounts payable	395
Increase in other current liabilities	20
Decrease in marketable securities	270
Increase in common stock	200
Increase in retained earnings	883
Total sources	1,768
Uses	
Decrease in taxes payable	151
Decrease in long-term debt	12
Increase in accounts receivable	380
Increase in inventory	660
Increase in other current assets	90
Increase in fixed assets	571
Decrease in preferred stock	100
Total uses	1,964
Decrease in cash	196

cannot tell from the data in Table 6–10, but we can put inventory management on our list for further investigation. We see also that that increase in cash was quite small relative to other asset categories. Has the firm's ability to come up with cash (liquidity) declined? If so, that decline could be dangerous if the firm faces unexpected costs — another question for our list. With respect to sources, we see retained earnings providing the largest single source, with bank borrowing and accounts payable also providing large amounts. Has Sparta Manufacturing Company borrowed too heavily? Is trade credit being used to the point that relations with suppliers might be damaged? More questions for our list. Techniques for answering some of these questions will be developed in the next chapter.

The source-and-use statement provides valuable insights into a firm's operations.

We can see that the source-and-use statement provides valuable insights into the firm's operations. In addition to the questions raised above, we can examine the expansion of accounts receivable and fixed assets, the mix of internal versus external financing, and the mix of short-term versus long-term financing relative to the kinds of assets being financed. If, for example, we were to find a large expansion in fixed assets financed primarily by short-term sources of funds, we would want to investigate further. Perhaps the company will have trouble paying off short-term debt before the expansion becomes profitable. The source-and-use statement thus provides valuable information. Information about how a company has raised and used its funds in the past is extremely useful in trying to make "good" decisions in the present. Should a bank loan officer lend money to a company? Should a company be interested in buying another company in a merger? The source-and-use statement presents information in concise, accessible form that can be useful in answering such questions.

Source-and-use analysis can be done over any time frame.

The source-and-use analysis should be performed over that particular time period in which we are interested. It may be any length, from a month or even a shorter period up to several years. The relevant period may be defined by events in the life of the firm, such as a period of growth or a period of decline. Sometimes it is useful to break the time period into two or more smaller periods to determine whether there were significant differences in fund flows. In addition to being useful for analyzing historical performance, source-and-use analysis may be useful in connection with planning for the future. (Chapter 9 will discuss financial planning.)

Some Refinements

Some refinements of the source-and-use statement are often desirable under certain conditions. The payment of dividends, for example, is sometimes an important use of funds that we would not detect by examining only the changes in the retained-earnings account on the balance sheet. If we cannot obtain data on dividend payments directly, we may be able to draw some inferences from the income-statement and balance-sheet data we have available. We know that the transfer to retained earnings each year, in the absence of other complicating transactions, will equal profit after taxes for the year minus dividends paid. If we examine the change in the retained-earnings account for Sparta Manufacturing Company from December 31, 1983, to December 31, 1984, we find it to be $10,000 — exactly the amount of profit after taxes in 1984. Thus, we infer that Sparta paid no dividends in 1984. Repeating this analysis over the remaining years indicates that no dividends were paid over the period 1983–1988.

We also may wish to look further into the fixed-asset account. In our balance sheet for Sparta, fixed assets are measured after depreciation. Our source-and-use statement, therefore, gives the expenditures on fixed assets, *net* of depreciation over the period. We know from the income statements in Table 6–7 that depreciation charges during 1984–1988 totaled $40,000. Thus, we can infer that Sparta's total expenditures for fixed assets from December 31, 1983, to December 31, 1988, were $97,500, rather than $57,500, as indicated by the net figure in Table 6–10.

Let us now revise our source-and-use statement to take into account the refinement just discussed. Under the heading of *Sources,* we will list *Funds from operations* rather than *Increase in retained earnings.* Funds from operations is equal to profit after taxes plus depreciation for the period. Under *Uses,* we will list *Gross* (rather than *Net*) *increase in fixed assets,* expenditures and dividends (even though Sparta paid no dividends). The result is shown in Table 6–16 (p. 186).

In addition to taking into account dividends and expenditures for fixed assets, other refinements sometimes may be appropriate, such as the sale of stock, sales of fixed assets, and payment of stock dividends.[3]

---

[3]For a discussion of these and other refinements of the source-and-use statement, see Erich A. Helfert, *Techniques of Financial Analysis,* 6th ed. (Homewood, Ill.: Richard D. Irwin, 1987). Dividends are typically cash payments to shareholders. Stock dividends, in contrast, are distributions of additional shares of stock (not cash) to the existing shareholders. Cash and stock dividends are discussed in Chapter 15.

Table 6—16

Sparta Manufacturing Company Revised Source-and-Use Statement, December 31, 1983–December 31, 1988

Sources		
Bank borrowing		$ 77,900
Increase accounts payable		70,000
Increase taxes payable		4,000
Increase miscellaneous accruals		35,000
Funds from operations		
Profit after taxes	$159,600	
Depreciation	40,000	199,600
Total sources		$386,500
Uses		
Increase in accounts receivable		$ 27,500
Increase in inventories		232,500
Gross increase in fixed assets		97,500
Increase in other assets		17,500
Reduction in mortgage		10,000
Dividends		0
Total uses		$385,000
Increase in cash		$ 1,500

Where longer-term changes in the balance-sheet account, rather than changes in current assets and liabilities, are of primary importance, we can prepare a statement of sources and uses of *working capital*. Net working capital is equal to current assets *less* current liabilities. By the same token, *changes* in net working capital (or sources and uses of net working capital) are obtained by adding

Table 6—17

Sparta Manufacturing Company's Sources and Uses of Working Capital, December 31, 1983–December 31, 1988

Sources of working capital	
Funds from operations	$199,600
Uses of working capital	
Gross increase in fixed assets	97,500
Increase in other assets	17,500
Reduction in mortgage	10,000
Dividends	0
Total uses	$125,000
Increase in net working capital	$ 74,600

changes in the current-asset accounts and subtracting *changes* in the current-liability accounts. In Table 6–16, we can see that current assets increased by $261,500, which is the sum of the $1,500 cash increase, the $27,500 change in accounts receivable, and the $232,500 change in inventories. Over the same period, current liabilities increased by $184,480, which is the sum of the $77,900 change in bank borrowing, the $70,000 change in accounts payable, the $4,000 change in taxes payable, and the $35,000 change in miscellaneous accruals. Thus, net working capital increased by $261,500 *less* $186,900, or by $74,600.

We can, therefore, recast the data in Table 6–16 according to the format shown in Table 6–17. Table 6–17 simply records in net form the working-capital elements shown in detail in Table 6–16. All current-asset and current-liability items are combined into the single net figure of $74,600 shown at the bottom of Table 6–17.

In addition to giving a financial picture of a firm's activities, source-and-use analysis identifies potential trouble spots that may need further investigation. Source-and-use analysis is thus an important tool in developing information to be used in financial decisions. The next chapter now turns to an exploration of techniques for analyzing financial performance.

Finance in Practice 6–1

Credit Ratings

A number of organizations rate the credit-worthiness of firms or governments that want to borrow money. For example, Standard & Poor's Corporation rates corporate and municipal bonds in various categories ranging from *AAA* (the rating given bond-issuing organizations whose capacity to pay interest and repay principal is extremely strong) to *D* (the rating given to bond-issuing organizations whose debt is in default and whose payment of interest and/or repayment of principal is in arrears). Such ratings, according to Standard & Poor's, "help investors by providing an easily recognizable, simple tool that couples a possibly unknown issuer with an informative and meaningful symbol of credit quality." These ratings are of particular importance to financial managers because the better the ratings (*AAA* being the best), the lower the interest rate charged on borrowing.

How do credit rating agencies determine their ratings? According to Standard & Poor's, "a funds statement provides information which is of central importance in credit analysis . . . examination of sources and uses of cash is basic to an evaluation. Such examination aids in identifying the financial nature of an enterprise (fixed versus working capital intensive), in evaluating historical financial performance, and in projecting future financial direction."

While Standard & Poor's uses many other ways to develop information, a source-and-use-of-funds statement is clearly one important tool. Chapter 10 will mention credit ratings again in discussing characteristics of debt used by corporations.

Source: Standard & Poor's Corporation, *Credit Overview: Corporate and International Ratings.*

KEY CONCEPTS

1. Financial statements are the basic raw material of financial analysis.

2. *Net working capital* is the difference between current assets and current liabilities.

3. Operating cash flow is the total cash generated by the firm's operations, or the sum of profit after tax and depreciation.

4. The total cash flow of a firm during any period can be determined as operating cash flow plus the effects of balance-sheet changes.

5. A source-and-use-of-funds statement shows where a firm's money came from and where it went. It provides a useful framework for learning about a company's activity and is a good beginning point for financial analysis.

SUMMARY

The firm's financial statements provide a starting point for developing information about a company. The income statement presents a record of events between two points in time, while the balance sheet presents a "snapshot" of the firm's position at a particular point in time. The source-and-use-of-funds statement shows where the firm obtained and used its money.

A basic concern of accounting is measurement. Measurement of income requires allocation of receipts and expenditures to particular time periods. Recognition of income and expense often involves arbitrary judgments. Inflation greatly complicates the measurement problem. For these and other reasons, accounting income often is an imperfect measure of economic income.

An important distinction in financial analysis is that between profit and cash flow. Operating cash flow is cash revenues less cash expenses. A shorthand way of calculating operating cash flow is by adding depreciation back to after-tax profits. Total cash flow during any period includes balance-sheet changes in addition to operating cash flow.

The source-and-use statement shows patterns in total cash flow and gives a good picture of what has been going on financially in a firm. It is therefore a good beginning point for financial analysis.

QUESTIONS

1. What is the general rule for determining whether an accounting transaction appears in the income statement as opposed to the balance sheet?

2. What is the difference between an *expenditure* and an *expense?* What is the difference between a *receipt* and *revenue?*

3. Define *working capital* and *operating cash flow*.

4. Contrast *accounting profit* and *operating cash flow*.

5. In terms of balance-sheet changes, what are the principal sources of funds for a firm? What are the principal uses of funds?

6. What balance-sheet ledger accounts make up the common shareholders equity? Why might the *market* value of the common shareholders equity be different from the *accounting* or *book* value?

7. Why is depreciation added to PAT to compute cash flow from operations?

FINANCIAL TOOL KIT ASSIGNMENT

A. Review the balance sheets listed under the Chapter 6 menu followed by the net working-capital model. If increased inventories are financed by retained earnings, what happens to the level of NWC? Why?

B. Review the balance sheets and income statements in the model, followed by the calculation of the source-and-use-of-funds statement. What are the primary sources and uses for the sample firm? Increase fixed assets by $30,000 per year and lower the PAT level each year by $1,000 (by increasing expenses). If profits (retained-earnings growth) are reduced, what must finance the rapid growth in fixed assets? Would you use short- or long-term sources of funds to finance fixed-asset growth?

Problems

1. Calculate the amount of working capital and the amount of net working capital for the Wentz Manufacturing Corporation for each of the four years given the data in the income statement and balance sheet shown in Table A below and Table B (p. 190).

2. Wentz Manufacturing's sales are expected to increase by 15 percent in year 5 over year 4. Assuming that the relationship between net working capital and sales remains the same in year 5 as in year 4, how much additional net working capital will Wentz Manufacturing require in year 5?

3. Calculate the after-tax cash flow from operations for Wentz Manufacturing for each of the four years. Use both the long method of subtracting all cash expenses from revenues and the shortcut method of adding back noncash expenses to profit after tax.

4. Consider the balance-sheet data for the Greynolds Company for the last two years in Table C.

   a. Compute working capital and net working capital for each year.

   b. Suppose you are told that profit after taxes for the Greynolds Company was $38,000 in

Table A

	Year 1 (thousands of dollars)	Year 2 (thousands of dollars)	Year 3 (thousands of dollars)	Year 4 (thousands of dollars)
Sales	48,200	60,600	72,500	81,400
Cost of goods sold	35,600	46,000	56,200	63,100
Gross profit	12,600	14,600	16,300	18,300
Depreciation	2,200	2,400	2,400	2,900
Amortization of goodwill*	200	200	200	200
Selling, general, and administrative expense	4,100	5,500	7,100	7,700
Income from operations	6,100	6,500	6,600	7,500
Interest	1,525	1,650	1,530	1,686
Profit before taxes	4,575	4,850	5,070	5,814
Taxes	2,100	2,200	2,400	2,700
Profit after taxes	2,475	2,650	2,670	3,114

*Amortization of goodwill is not deducted in computing taxes.

Table B

	Year End as of December 31 (thousands of dollars)			
	1	*2*	*3*	*4*
Cash	1,900	2,800	4,600	2,700
Accounts receivable	7,900	9,600	11,400	13,600
Inventory	5,000	6,600	7,200	8,900
Other	1,000	1,100	1,100	1,200
Current assets	15,800	20,100	24,300	26,400
Plant and equipment	42,000	45,500	45,500	54,500
Less: Accumulated depreciation	12,900	15,300	17,700	20,000
Net fixed assets	29,100	30,200	27,800	34,500
Goodwill	6,600	6,400	6,200	6,000
Total assets	51,500	56,700	58,300	66,900
Notes payable	5,550	5,700	4,500	5,600
Accounts payable	6,500	6,300	7,400	8,900
Accruals	2,600	2,900	3,000	3,200
Tax payable	900	1,200	1,000	1,800
Current liabilities	15,550	16,100	15,900	19,500
Debentures	7,000	9,000	9,000	9,000
Subordinated debentures	7,000	7,000	7,000	8,000
Common stock ($5 par)	7,000	7,000	7,000	8,000
Capital surplus	3,500	3,500	3,500	4,500
Retained earnings	11,450	14,100	15,900	17,900
Total liabilities and net worth	51,500	56,700	58,300	66,900

year 2. How much was paid out as dividends in that year?

c. Suppose you are told that profit after taxes in year 1 was $27,000 and that $8,000 in dividends were paid in that year. What were the company's retained earnings one year earlier at the end of year 0?

d. Prepare a source-and-use-of-funds statement for the Greynolds Company for year 2.

e. Summarize in a few sentences what you have learned about Greynolds operations.

5. In Table D are year-end balance-sheet data for Irvin Motors, Inc. Arrange the data in a source-and-use format like that used in Table 6–10.

6. A balance sheet for the Williams Hardware Company is given in Table E.

a. Prepare a statement of balance-sheet changes.

b. Organize the results of Part (a) into a source-and-use format like that used in Table 6–10.

c. What further action does the source-and-use statement suggest?

Table C

	Year 1	Year 2
Cash	$ 15,000	$ 7,000
Marketable securities	11,000	0
Accounts receivable	22,000	30,000
Inventories	53,000	75,000
Total current assets	$101,000	$112,000
Gross fixed assets	$ 75,000	$150,000
Less depreciation	26,000	41,000
Net fixed assets	$ 49,000	$109,000
Total assets	$150,000	$221,000
Accounts payable	$ 15,000	$ 18,000
Notes payable	15,000	3,000
Taxes payable	7,000	15,000
Total current liabilities	$ 37,000	$ 36,000
Long-term debt	8,000	26,000
Common stock	38,000	64,000
Retained earnings	67,000	95,000
Total liabilities and net worth	$150,000	$221,000

Table D

	Year 1	Year 2	Change
Assets			
Cash	$ 434,400	$ 234,200	−$ 200,200
Marketable securities	647,800	371,700	− 276,100
Accounts receivable	1,078,800	1,457,100	+ 378,300
Inventory	3,592,700	4,253,000	+ 660,300
Other current assets	435,800	525,200	+ 89,400
Total current assets	$ 6,189,500	$ 6,841,200	+$ 651,700
Net buildings and equipment	5,192,700	5,684,000	+ 491,300
Other assets	1,571,800	1,648,400	+ 76,600
Total assets	$12,954,000	$14,173,600	+$1,219,600
Liabilities			
Accounts payable	$ 3,537,100	$ 3,932,300	+$ 395,200
Taxes payable	340,100	189,300	− 150,800
Other current liabilities	651,800	1,219,300	+ 567,500
Total current liabilities	$ 4,529,000	$ 5,340,900	+$ 811,900
Accrued liabilities	921,300	1,087,500	+ 166,200
Deferred income tax	121,600	27,200	− 94,400
Long-term debt	977,000	1,476,700	+ 499,700
Total liabilities	$ 6,548,900	$ 7,932,300	+$1,383,400
Owners' equity			
Common stock	$ 628,500	$ 595,900	−$ 32,600
Retained earnings	5,776,600	5,645,400	− 131,200
Liabilities and owners' equity	$12,954,000	$14,173,600	+$1,219,600

Table E

	December 31, Year 1	December 31, Year 2
Cash	$ 60	$ 1,420
Accounts receivable	60,290	118,826
Inventory	92,305	233,568
Total current assets	$152,655	$353,814
Net fixed assets	6,500	10,560
Total assets	$159,155	$364,374
Notes payable	$ 30,000	$ 51,000
Accounts payable	52,640	215,685
Accrued expense	1,500	2,110
Total current liabilities	$ 84,140	$268,795
Net worth	75,015	95,579
Total liabilities and net worth	$159,155	$364,374

7. A balance sheet for the Madison Company is shown in Table F (p. 192). Prepare a source-and-use statement for the Madison Company for the end of year 2. Interpret the results.

Table F

	December 31, Year 1		December 31, Year 2	
Cash		$ 10,850		$ 431
Accounts receivable		41,614		68,313
Inventory		82,892		80,710
Miscellaneous current assets		7,681		6,413
Total current assets		$143,037		$155,867
Land		42,000		42,000
Plant and equipment	$217,575		$231,820	
Less depreciation	−36,816	180,759	−42,015	189,805
Total assets		$365,796		$387,672
Accounts payable		$ 52,218		$ 50,946
Taxes payable		18,416		22,840
Accrued expenses		15,823		13,908
Total current liabilities		$ 86,457		$ 87,694
Mortgage payable		110,000		103,500
Paid-in capital		95,000		105,000
Retained earnings		74,339		91,478
Total liabilities and net worth		$365,796		$387,672

REFERENCES

For a more comprehensive treatment of financial analysis of financial statements see

  Helfert, E. A. *Techniques of Financial Analysis*. 6th ed. Homewood, Ill.: Richard D. Irwin, 1987.

Harrington, Diana R., and Brent D. Wilson. *Corporate Financial Analysis*. 2nd ed. Plano, Texas: Business Publications, Inc., 1986.

7

Analyzing Financial Performance

This chapter develops the basic tools for evaluating the financial condition of a company and for measuring its performance, past and future. The chapter explains how to measure profitability, return on investment, activity rates and turnover, liquidity, and indebtedness. We will look at some of the key measures used by investors in the stock market.

Financial analysis is never a simple task. In order to understand a company, either from the outside or the inside, it is necessary to go through the investigations of a financial detective. The clues include various financial ratios for a company — at least 20 of them and in some cases more. The ratios are compared with the company's own past and also against those of other companies in the same or similar industries.

The Requirements of Financial Analysis

As with any dissection of data, the purpose of financial analysis is to develop an underlying understanding of what is going on. Students frequently wonder if this effort is really necessary. Later, when they serve as security analysts, commercial-bank loan officers, hospital administrators, investment-banking executives, or assistants to corporate management, they invariably find that the effort is not only worthwhile but also essential.

Although the analysis of past events cannot, in itself, provide an accurate forecast of the future, it can provide a warning about difficulties that might lie ahead. The bankruptcy of the Penn Central Railroad and of W. T. Grant and Company, as well as Chrysler Corporation's financial problems, were all foreshadowed by trends in their balance sheets and income statements.

For decision makers, the future is usually of more interest than the past. But analysis of the future often begins with analyzing trends of the past.

For decision makers — whether managers, investors, or creditors — the future usually is of more interest than the past. However, analysis of the future often begins with analysis of the past to uncover trends. The question then becomes: Will the trends continue? This chapter focuses on history. Chapter 9 will look ahead and develop a financial plan. The performance-measurement techniques developed here can be applied to a forward-looking financial plan as well as to historical data.

Financial Statements and Ratio Analysis

The starting points for analyzing financial performance are the basic financial statements of the firm: income statement, balance sheet, and source-and-use-of-funds statement.

The starting points for analyzing financial performance are the basic financial statements of the firm: the income statement, the balance sheet, and the source-and-use-of-funds statement.

Chapter 6 showed how the source-and-use-of-funds statement revealed important information about Sparta Manufacturing's activities in past years. This statement is one of the tools needed by a financial manager.

Ratio analysis — the analysis of financial performance based on the comparison of one financial variable to another.

We need not stop with the basic forms of the financial statements because we can often repackage the information to reveal new and important features about a company's past — features that may improve our ability to evaluate its future. One of the primary ways of repacking the information is to use **ratio analysis.** *Ratios* simply measure one variable in relation to another. For example, to know whether a company is highly profitable, a financial manager needs to look not just at the dollar amount of its profits but at its dollar profits relative to the assets used in the business. This ratio (profits divided by assets) shows how profitable the company is per dollar of assets invested in the business. As we'll see in this chapter, many such ratios can aid in doing the detective work required in financial analysis.

Table 7–1

Sparta Manufacturing Company Income Statements, 1983–1988

	1983	1984	1985	1986	1987	1988
Sales	$515,000	$557,500	$647,500	$930,000	$990,000	$1,140,000
Cost of goods sold	$335,000	$355,000	$387,500	$592,500	$622,500	$ 730,000
Gross profit	$180,000	$202,500	$260,000	$337,500	$367,500	$ 410,000
Depreciation	7,500	5,000	5,000	5,000	10,000	15,000
Selling, general, and administrative expense	149,400	181,100	190,600	282,400	307,900	340,100
Operating profit before taxes	$ 23,100	$ 16,400	$ 64,400	$ 50,100	$ 49,600	$ 54,900
Interest	8,100	3,900	4,400	5,100	9,600	12,900
Net profit before taxes	$ 15,000	$ 12,500	$ 60,000	$ 45,000	$ 40,000	$ 42,000
Taxes	3,000	2,500	12,000	9,000	8,000	8,400
Profit after taxes	$ 12,000	$ 10,000	$ 48,000	$ 36,000	$ 32,000	$ 33,600

Note: Taxes are computed at a tax rate of 20 percent.

Tables 7–1 and 7–2 (on p. 196) duplicate the income statements and balance sheets for Sparta Manufacturing that we used in the last chapter. The information contained in these statements can be manipulated to reveal different dimensions of corporate activity, such as profitability to shareholders, return on investment, liquidity, and indebtedness.

While all of these dimensions are related and important, different financial investigators may focus on different characteristics. For example, a prospective shareholder might focus primarily on whether the company will be *profitable* and, hence, able to benefit shareholders. In analyzing whether to make a short-term loan, a bank loan officer might focus on the company's *liquidity* because liquid assets might be turned into cash to repay loans. The loan officer would also look at existing borrowing, or indebtedness, to see whether the company has to repay other existing loans before the bank could get its money back. An analyst evaluating another company as a potential merger candidate might place equal emphasis on all dimensions.

As we will see, there are a number of ways to measure each facet of a corporation. While we will restrict our focus here to private-sector firms, the same techniques can be used for other types of organizations as well, including not-for-profit organizations.

Measuring Profits and Profitability

Chapter 6 noted the importance of profits as a measure of performance and described some of the difficulties of measuring profits and the possible divergence between true economic profit and measured accounting profit. Here we will be using the terms *profit, income,* and *earnings* as synonyms.

Table 7–2

Sparta Manufacturing Company Year-End Balance Sheets, 1983–1988

	1983	1984	1985	1986	1987	1988
Assets						
Cash	$ 1,000	$ 1,000	$ 2,500	$ 12,500	$ 10,000	$ 2,500
Accounts receivable	125,000	90,000	95,000	107,500	147,500	152,500
Inventory	187,500	180,000	250,000	325,000	410,000	420,000
Total current assets	$313,500	$271,000	$347,500	$445,000	$567,500	$575,000
Fixed assets, net of depreciation	55,000	50,000	45,000	52,500	55,000	112,500
Other assets	17,500	15,000	15,000	17,500	15,000	35,000
Total assets	$386,000	$336,000	$407,500	$515,000	$637,500	$722,500
Liabilities and net worth						
Notes payable (bank)	$ 66,200	$ 16,400	$ 28,200	$ 34,700	$ 88,100	$144,100
Accounts payable (trade)	52,500	42,500	42,500	110,000	117,500	122,500
Miscellaneous accruals	18,500	20,300	34,000	33,500	65,100	57,500
Total current liabilities	$137,200	$ 79,200	$104,700	$178,200	$270,700	$324,100
Mortgage payable	36,000	34,000	32,000	30,000	28,000	26,000
Total liabilities	$173,200	$113,200	$136,700	$208,200	$298,700	$350,100
Net worth	212,800	222,800	270,800	306,800	338,800	372,400
Total liabilities and net worth	$386,000	$336,000	$407,500	$515,000	$637,500	$722,500

Dollar Profits

Let us return now to the Sparta Manufacturing Company, analyzed in Chapter 6. From Table 7–1, we see that Sparta earned $33,600 after taxes in 1988. From this figure alone, we can draw few conclusions about whether Sparta's performance was good or bad. Dollar profit figures for another similar company or for the relevant industry grouping would be of little additional help. One way of evaluating the flow of profits is to compare the 1988 profit to corresponding figures from prior years. From such comparisons we can determine *trends*.

Several different measures of profit are available in Table 7–1. On the bottom line, we have *profit after taxes (PAT)*, which takes into account all factors influencing earnings. We see that Sparta's profit after taxes increased rapidly from 1983 to 1985, then declined somewhat and remained essentially flat from 1986 to 1988. In the next section, when we measure *profitability* — profits in relation to sales — we will see a different picture.

Operating profit, or **earnings before interest and taxes (EBIT)** — measures the firm's performance before the effects of financing or taxes.

Tax rates are beyond the control of management. To factor out the effects of taxes, we can look at *profit before taxes (PBT)*. **Operating profit** measures the performance of the firm's commercial activities without regard to financing. Operating profit gives us an indication of the success of the basic operations of the company before we analyze how the company chose to finance these operations.

(We'll examine the financing issues later in this chapter.) In 1984, operating profit declined by 29 percent relative to 1983, while profit after taxes declined by only about 17 percent. In 1988, operating profit rose, while profit after taxes remained essentially flat. Operating profit often is referred to as **earnings before interest and taxes (EBIT).**

Another widely used earnings measure is **earnings per share (EPS),** which is profit after taxes divided by the number of shares of stock outstanding. EPS figures allow a shareholder to keep track of his or her claim on the company's total earnings. When the number of shares remains constant, earnings per share and profit after taxes tell the same story.

The Normalized Income Statement

We can learn still more about a firm's performance by measuring profits in relation to the sales necessary to generate those profits. **Profits per dollar of sales** is a measure of *profitability*. A convenient way to analyze profitability is to prepare a **normalized income statement** in which all items are expressed as percentages of sales. We then can examine the behavior of various elements of cost as well as the behavior of profits. Table 7–3 shows normalized income statements for Sparta Manufacturing Company, prepared from the data in Table 7–1. What conclusions can we draw from the data in Table 7–3? As before, single figures mean little; we need a standard of comparison.

We can look at the figures over time to identify trends. Sparta's profit after tax per dollar of sales declined from 3.2 percent in 1987 to 2.9 percent in 1988; dollar profits rose in absolute terms. Gross profit and operating profit both rose during

Earnings per share (EPS) — profit after taxes (PAT) divided by the number of shares of stock outstanding; a widely used performance measure.

Profits per dollar of sales — a useful measure of a firm's performance that measures profits in relation to the sales necessary to generate those profits.

Normalized income statement — income statement in which all items are expressed as percentages of sales.

Table 7–3

Sparta Manufacturing Company Normalized Income Statement, 1983–1988

	1983 *(percent)*	1984 *(percent)*	1985 *(percent)*	1986 *(percent)*	1987 *(percent)*	1988 *(percent)*
Sales	100.0	100.0	100.0	100.0	100.0	100.0
Cost of goods sold	65.0	63.7	59.8	63.7	62.9	64.0
Gross profit	35.0	36.3	40.2	36.3	37.1	36.0
Depreciation	1.5	0.9	0.8	0.5	1.0	1.3
Selling, general, and administrative expense	29.0	32.5	29.4	30.4	31.1	29.8
Operating profit	4.5	2.9	9.9	5.4	5.0	4.8
Interest	1.6	0.7	0.7	0.5	1.0	1.1
Profit before taxes	2.9	2.2	9.3	4.8	4.0	3.7
Taxes	0.6	0.4	1.9	1.0	0.8	0.7
Profit after taxes	2.3	1.8	7.4	3.9	3.2	2.9

Note: Details may not add to totals because of rounding.

1983–1985, then fell during 1985–1988. By looking at trends, we cannot tell whether a particular element is too high or too low, but we can tell whether it is getting better or worse. Trouble spots can be identified, and management can determine causes. Normalized income statements can be prepared in any format and at any level of detail for which data are available.

To make a judgment as to whether an element of cost or profit in a given year is too high or too low, we can compare Sparta to another firm with similar characteristics or to an industry average. Sparta manufactures a wide variety of paints and varnishes, some of which are produced to specifications set forth by customers. We may have some difficulty finding comparable firms or groupings of firms. In the case of a department store or a lumber wholesaler or an electric utility, interfirm comparisons may be more meaningful.

Industry averages are available from at least two sources: Dun & Bradstreet and Robert Morris Associates (RMA), a national association of bank lending and credit officers. The RMA industry grouping that best fits Sparta is the paint, varnish, and lacquer industry. RMA data for this industry indicate a profit-before-taxes-per-dollar-of-sales figure of 2.9 percent, somewhat lower than Sparta's recent experience.[1] We must make such comparisons cautiously, however, because the firms in the RMA sample may not be exactly comparable to Sparta.

> To judge whether an element of cost or profit is too high or low, we can compare the firm with a similar firm or with an industry average.

Measuring Return on Investment

It is also useful to relate profits and sales to the investment required to generate these flows. Capital is one of society's scarce resources. A measure of the efficiency with which these resources are being utilized is return per dollar of investment, known as **return on investment (ROI).** Return on investment is widely used as a measure of financial performance.

> **Return on investment (ROI)** — the return per dollar of investment per unit of time; a measure of the efficiency with which the firm utilizes capital.

Return on Investment (ROI)

Return on investment can be calculated in many ways. Some are based on standard accounting data and others on discounted-cash-flow techniques, which we discussed in Chapters 3 and 4. Accounting-based measures of ROI involve some measure of profit or return divided by some measure of outlay or investment. The resulting ratio is usually expressed in percentage terms. The general expression for calculating return on investment using accounting data is given in Equation (1).

$$\text{ROI} = \frac{\text{Return}}{\text{Investment}}. \tag{1}$$

For example, suppose a bank advertises savings accounts that pay interest of 6 percent per year. A deposit, or investment, of $100 today would yield $106 in 1 year, of which $6 is interest and $100 is the original principal. In this case, ROI would be calculated, using Equation (1), as

$$\text{ROI} = \$6/\$100 = 0.06 = 6 \text{ percent per year}.$$

[1]For an example of Robert Morris Associates data, see Finance in Practice 7–4 in this chapter.

In Equation (1), the numerator, *Return,* has a time dimension—dollars per unit of time—in this case, dollars per year. The denominator is in dollars. The quotient, ROI, is therefore a rate or percentage per unit of time—in this case, percent per year.

Return on investment based on accounting data sometimes is referred to as the *accounting rate of return.* Both the numerator and the denominator can be calculated in a number of ways. These alternatives provide flexibility but can result in ambiguity. Let us consider another example. Suppose an investment of $1,000 made at time 0 generates the earnings listed in Table 7–4 over its 4-year life.

To calculate accounting ROI, we first must determine the return. We can choose profits either before tax or after tax. We also see that profit is different each year. Which profit figure do we pick? We can calculate an average over the 4 years, or we can calculate ROI for each year if we wish.

Now for the investment. Should we define it as the initial outlay of $1,000? Alternatively, we might argue that the funds actually devoted to the project decline over time as the outlay is recovered through depreciation. In each year, we subtract depreciation allowances in calculating profit after tax and also reduce the **book value** (as opposed to the **market value**) of the asset on the balance sheet by the amount of the annual depreciation charge. The book value of the investment is $1,000 just after the investment is made, but falls to $750 at the end of year 1, and $500, $250, and $0 at the ends of years 2, 3, and 4, respectively. We might define the investment as the average of these book values over the life of the investment for an *average* investment of $500.

Thus, we see that there are many ways to calculate accounting ROI. We can calculate it before or after tax. We can calculate ROI for each year or an average over the 4 years. If we calculate an average, we still have alternative ways to define the investment. Which method of calculating ROI is correct? All are correct—that is, each answers a different question. There is no standard, generally agreed-upon calculation. Therefore, when we use accounting ROI, in order to avoid confusion, we must specify exactly how it is calculated.

Book value—a measure of asset value, at historical cost, net of depreciation.

There are many ways to calculate accounting ROI.

Table 7–4
Return on an Investment Project over Its 4-Year Life

	Return			
	Year 1	*Year 2*	*Year 3*	*Year 4*
Revenue	$670	$700	$730	$750
Cash expenses	200	200	200	200
Depreciation	250	250	250	250
Profit before taxes	$220	$250	$280	$300
Taxes at 46 percent	101	115	129	138
Profit after taxes	$119	$135	$151	$162
Investment (book value)	$750	$500	$250	$ 0

International Focus

Doing Business with the Soviets

Mikhail Gorbachev is the most dynamic leader in the Soviet Union in a very long time. He has captured the attention of the world press with his policy of *glasnost,* or "openness," and has embarked on a major program of restructuring to modernize the Soviet economy. Farsighted Westerners wish him well, for they know that a Soviet Union that feels good about itself will make a better neighbor.

As part of his program, Gorbachev pushed through a new Soviet law permitting joint ventures with Western firms. The new law is aimed at introducing Western technology, capital, and management know-how into the struggling Soviet economy.

Westerners saw great opportunity in the huge Soviet market and were enthusiastic about the new law at first, until they read the fine print. The law mandates that the Soviets have no less than 51 percent ownership in each venture, a Soviet majority on the board of directors, a Soviet chairman, and a Soviet director general in charge of operations. All documents had to be translated into Russian and there were restrictions on repatriation of profits. Western business people began to see examples of bureaucratic delays and intransigence by "turf-conscious" Soviet agencies. Because of these and other impediments, early hopes were not fulfilled.

Now both sides have lowered their expectations and progress is being made. Ways are being found around the more onerous rules and restrictions. In October 1987 the joint venture law was modified by the Soviets to make it more flexible. Soviet negotiators are becoming easier to deal with. Dedicated communists managing the joint ventures are getting used to the idea of referring their production and marketing plans, not to a state central planning board, but to a Western capitalist who is a co-owner of the enterprise.

The Soviets seem determined to do more business with the West, an objective that seems certain to benefit East-West relations.

Source: Adapted from Theodore Sorensen, "The West Can Do Business With the Soviets," *The Wall Street Journal,* December 28, 1987.

Return on assets (ROA)—one measure of return on investment in which investment is defined as the total assets of the firm. ROA is calculated as profit after taxes divided by total assets.

Return on equity (ROE)—a measure of return on investment in which investment is defined as the net worth of the firm. ROE is calculated as profit after taxes divided by net worth.

Calculating Return on Investment for a Firm

How do we measure a firm's overall return on investment? One alternative is to define investment as the total assets of the firm and then calculate the firm's **return on assets (ROA),** as shown in Equation (2):

$$ROA = \frac{\text{Profit after taxes}}{\text{Total assets}}. \tag{2}$$

Another alternative for calculating a firm's overall return on investment is to calculate **return on equity (ROE),** as shown in Equation (3):

$$ROE = \frac{\text{Profit after taxes}}{\text{Net worth}} \tag{3}$$

where net worth is the book value of the shareholder's equity claim on the balance sheet.

Return on equity explicitly takes into account the effects of the firm's use of debt, or financial leverage, while the various return-on-assets measures described above do so only indirectly (when profit is measured after interest). By incurring debt, a firm can affect its return on equity.

For example, suppose a company earned operating profit before taxes and interest of $12 on assets of $100, which were financed by borrowing $60 at 6 percent and by $40 of equity (net worth). By subtracting interest charges of 0.06($60) = $3.60, we could calculate profits before taxes to be $12 − $3.60 = $8.40. Assuming no taxes for simplicity, profit after taxes would also be $8.40. Now we can see the effects of using debt. While operating return on assets would be $12/$100 = 12 percent, return on equity would be $8.40/$40 = 21 percent. Clearly, the use of debt makes a difference.

We will discuss in depth the effects of using debt (financial leverage) in Part Five, where we will find that, although an increase in financial leverage (use of more debt) typically increases return on equity, it also increases *risk*. For now, let us note that the return-on-equity measure must be used with great caution as a performance measure. Return on equity gives us a measure of return but ignores the riskiness, or variability, of that return.

The various measures of return on investment are calculated for the Sparta Manufacturing Company in Table 7–5, using data from Tables 7–1 and 7–2.

Each of the four return-on-investment measures answers a different question, but all tell much the same story. Sparta's return on investment rose from 1983 to 1985 and then declined from 1985 to 1988. This downward trend after 1986 suggests that the company may be having difficulties. In practice, financial analysts would look further to see why profitability has declined. Has the company lost control of its costs? Are Sparta's markets becoming more competitive, putting

An increase in financial leverage (use of debt) typically increases return on equity (ROE), but it also increases risk.

Table 7–5
Sparta Manufacturing Company Return on Investment, 1983–1988

	1983	1984	1985	1986	1987	1988
Profit after taxes	$ 12,000	$ 10,000	$ 48,000	$ 36,000	$ 32,000	$ 33,600
Net worth	$212,800	$222,800	$270,800	$306,800	$338,800	$372,400
Total assets	$386,000	$336,000	$407,500	$515,000	$637,500	$722,500
Return on Assets (ROA)						
$ROA = \dfrac{\text{Profit after taxes}}{\text{Total assets}}$	3.1%	3.0%	11.8%	7.0%	5.0%	4.7%
Return on Equity (ROE)						
$ROE = \dfrac{\text{Profit after taxes}}{\text{Net worth}}$	5.6%	4.5%	17.7%	11.7%	9.4%	9.0%

downward pressure on prices and profits? Have other firms in the industry experienced the same decrease in profits? Answers to these and other questions are necessary before financial managers can make forecasts about how Sparta is likely to do in the future.

Finance in Practice 7–1

The Return on Equity of the *Fortune 500*

During the five-year period from 1976 to 1980, the return on equity (ROE) for the 500 largest industrial companies in the United States averaged 14.3 percent per year. For the first time since the average was first calculated in 1958, ROE exceeded 12 percent over a five-year period. The 14.3 percent figure compared to 9.7 percent on *A*-rated industrial bonds. (*AAA* is the top bond rating using the Standard & Poor's rating scale. An *A* rating would be more typical for the majority of companies in the *Fortune 500* list.)

During the early 1960s, return on equity had substantially exceeded the return on bonds. As inflation increased during the late 1960s and early 1970s, corporate ROE did not rise commensurately. Rather, ROE seemed to get stuck at about 12 percent, while bond yields rose to that level and above. In the 1976–1980 period, the companies in the *Fortune 500* list collectively improved their returns and sustained that improvement over a five-year period. Returns then declined somewhat in 1982 and 1983 but were up to 13.6 percent in 1984.

Data for return on equity (in percent) for selected industries are given in the accompanying table. As indicated, the 1987 return varied from a low of 7.0 percent for mining and crude oil production to 22.7 percent for the pharmaceuticals industry.

Source: Data for table adapted from C. J. Loomis, "Profitability Goes Through a Ceiling," *Fortune*, May 4, 1981. Copyright © 1981 by *Fortune* Magazine. Data subsequent to 1981 updated by the authors from annual articles on "The *Fortune* 500," *Fortune* Magazine. Reprinted by permission.

	Return on Stockholders' Equity (percent)								
	1971–75	*1976–80*	*1981*	*1982*	*1983*	*1984*	*1985*	*1986*	*1987*
Aerospace	10.4	16.0	15.0	11.7	13.4	13.9	13.1	12.4	11.3
Apparel	8.3	13.1	16.2	12.3	13.0	13.9	12.0	12.2	14.1
Computers (including office equip.)	9.5	14.2	13.3	12.1	11.1	12.6	11.0	10.8	14.6
Textiles	6.4	10.1	7.8	6.3	8.7	8.2	5.6	8.1	12.8
Petroleum refining	12.1	15.6	16.4	12.5	9.5	9.5	9.9	5.8	10.2
Chemicals	11.3	13.9	13.5	8.9	9.8	12.2	8.3	11.8	14.2
Food	12.0	13.7	14.4	15.3	14.5	16.2	15.0	15.8	16.1
Pharmaceuticals	16.4	17.2	18.0	16.9	17.5	18.1	15.6	23.6	22.7
Beverages	14.1	13.9	19.2	16.7	16.9	15.7	17.5	18.8	14.0
Mining & crude-oil production	15.6	15.3	17.6	9.0	9.8	13.8	11.0	7.7	7.0
Rubber products	10.0	8.5	10.4	1.9	10.0	12.1	9.3	10.8	13.1
Average, all industries	**11.4**	**14.3**	**13.8**	**10.9**	**10.7**	**13.6**	**11.6**	**11.6**	**13.2**

Margin Versus Turnover

Profit margin — the
difference between revenues
and total expenses (including
taxes) divided by sales.

The return generated by a firm's assets represents the difference between revenues and total expenses, including taxes. This difference, when divided by the firm's level of sales, often is referred to as the firm's **profit margin.** Over a period of time — say, a year — the total return depends not only on the profit margin per dollar of sales but also on the rate at which sales are generated. The rate of sales in relation to assets often is called the **sales turnover** rate. Thus, Equation (4) can represent return on assets (ROA) as the product of two components, margin and turnover.

$$\text{ROA} = \text{profit margin} \times \text{sales turnover}.$$

Sales turnover — the rate of
sales in relation to assets.

In other words,

$$\frac{\text{Profit}}{\text{Assets}} = \frac{\text{Profit}}{\text{Sales}} \times \frac{\text{Sales}}{\text{Assets}}. \tag{4}$$

For example, we can apply Equation (4) to Sparta Manufacturing's 1988 data found in Sparta's income statement and balance sheet (Tables 7–1 and 7–2) to determine Sparta's return on assets:

$$\text{ROA} = \frac{\$33,600}{\$1,140,000} \times \frac{\$1,140,000}{\$722,500}$$

$$= 0.0295 \times 1.58 = 0.0466 = 4.66 \text{ percent}.$$

As the calculations show, Sparta had a profit margin of 2.95 percent. Since it had $1.58 worth of sales for each dollar of assets (a turnover rate of 1.58), this profit margin translated into a 4.66 percent return on assets.

By decomposing ROA into
margin and turnover
components, it is easier to
analyze changes in a
company's performance over
time.

By decomposing ROA into margin and turnover components, we can better analyze changes over time. If ROA is decreasing, for example, we can determine whether the decrease is a result of a declining profit margin or a declining turnover rate. Such information is useful for planning corrective action. We also can compare data on margin and turnover with industry averages. Table 7–6 (p. 204) breaks down ROA into profit margin and sales turnover for each year from 1983 to 1988 for Sparta Manufacturing Company. Note that column (3) is the product of columns (1) and (2), with differences due to rounding. Now some new conclusions emerge. The big increase in ROA in 1985 resulted primarily from improved profit margins. The big drop in ROA in 1986 resulted from a sharp decline in margins, offset somewhat by an increase in sales turnover. With the exception of 1986, sales turnover remained more or less constant from 1982 to 1986. Differences in ROA were thus attributable to variations in margin. Of particular significance is the conclusion that the deterioration of ROA from 1984 to 1988 is a result of a decline in profit margin, not sales turnover. Knowing this, Sparta's management can focus its efforts to improve ROA.

The principal factors that determine the profit margin and the sales turnover rate can themselves be traced to more detailed changes in subfactors. A system of financial analysis and control designed to pinpoint the salient elements underlying the ROA achieved during any given period was developed by the DuPont Com-

Table 7–6

Sparta Manufacturing Company Profit Margin and Sales Turnover, 1983–1988

Year	Profit Margin $\left(\dfrac{\text{Profit after Taxes}}{\text{Sales}}\right)$ (percent) (1)	Sales Turnover $\left(\dfrac{\text{Sales}}{\text{Assets}}\right)$ (2)	Return on Assets (percent) (3) = (1) × (2)
1983	2.33	1.33	3.11
1984	1.79	1.66	2.98
1985	7.41	1.59	11.78
1986	3.87	1.81	7.00
1987	3.23	1.55	5.01
1988	2.95	1.58	4.66

pany many decades ago. It is a summary presentation that captures in one page (or one photographic slide) a concise picture of how and why ROA changes from one period to another. This system, adapted to suit the particular needs of individual companies, is widely used today to present results, both by major divisions and for the company as a whole, at periodic board meetings.

Figure 7–1 presents one adaptation of the DuPont system to report the results for Sparta Manufacturing for 1988. Each figure used in calculating ROA is broken down in detail. Compared with a similar presentation for the preceding year or several preceding years, it helps us determine why ROA for Sparta fell between 1985 and 1988.

In Figure 7–1, we can trace through the determinants of ROA. For example, by looking at the right portion of Figure 7–1, we see that Sparta's 1988 cost of goods sold was $730,000, or about $730,000/$1,140,000 = 64 percent of sales. To determine if this percentage is high in relation to sales, financial managers could look at data from past years to see if the decline in ROA was the result of a higher cost of goods sold. By looking at other figures compared to past years, we could continue our detective work in analyzing what has been going on at Sparta and what is likely to happen in the future.

Measuring Activity and Turnover

Turnover ratios give some indication of how efficiently managers use assets.

This section explores some measures of turnover other than the sales turnover rate discussed above. Such turnover ratios give some indication of how efficiently managers use assets. The measures discussed below pertain to three specific areas of managerial performance: accounts receivable, inventory, and accounts payable.

Accounts-Receivable Turnover

The majority of firms sell on credit. Credit terms often are viewed as a marketing tool to be used to increase the firm's profits. Sales transacted but not collected

Figure 7–1
DuPont System of Financial Control Applied to Sparta Manufacturing Company, 1988

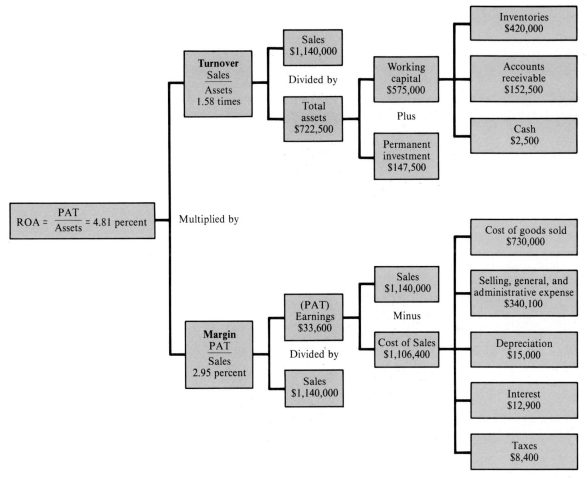

Note: Permanent assets are here considered fixed assets plus other assets.

appear on the balance sheet as accounts receivable. Accounts receivable must be financed. A loose credit policy may increase sales and operating profits, but it also increases accounts receivable and, therefore, the firm's financing costs. For example, if a company has to borrow money from a bank to finance its accounts receivable, there will be interest costs on this borrowing. The objective of credit policy should be to trade off costs and benefits and, thus, to maximize the value of the firm.

The discussion in this section will be limited to techniques for measuring the effectiveness with which receivables are being collected. We will measure collection experience against credit terms, but we will not discuss how credit terms should be set; credit policy will be discussed in Part Six.

Days sales outstanding (DSO) — the ratio of accounts receivable to credit sales per day; also called the *average collection period*.

One useful measure of collection experience is the number of **days sales outstanding (DSO)** at any point in time, which is determined as shown in Equation (5).

The average number of days it takes to receive payment from sales made on credit, or days sales outstanding (DSO), is calculated as

$$DSO = \frac{\text{Accounts receivable}}{\text{Credit sales per day}}. \tag{5}$$

The DSO figure is also referred to as the *average collection period*. To calculate DSO, we consider only sales made on credit, excluding sales for cash. Sometimes accounts receivable will be reported on a net basis, after subtracting a reserve for bad debts; other times both the gross receivables outstanding and the reserve will be given. When available, the gross receivables figure should be used to calculate DSO.

Selecting the period over which to calculate sales per day also is important. Usually it is best to use the shortest and most recent period for which data are available — say, a quarter or even a month. Managers must be especially careful in selecting the averaging period when sales are seasonal or growing rapidly. Where a seasonal sales pattern exists, variations in the sales rate over the year will cause the DSO figure to vary even when there is no change in the underlying collection rate; the DSO figures computed at different points during the year, therefore, must be interpreted with caution. Where the firm is growing rapidly, managers should select a short averaging period to reflect the most recent sales rate. Part Six will present more refined techniques for monitoring accounts receivable.

With seasonal sales patterns, variations in the sales rate over the year will cause the DSO figure to vary; DSO figures computed at different points during the year must be interpreted with caution.

For Sparta Manufacturing Company, we have only annual sales data, so we must use a year as our averaging period. Using Equation (5), we can calculate DSO figures for Sparta Manufacturing Company for December 31, 1988, as

$$DSO = \frac{\$152,500}{\$1,140,000/365 \text{ days}} = \frac{\$152,500}{\$3,123/\text{day}} = 49 \text{ days}.$$

Assuming all sales were on credit, Sparta's average daily sales rate during 1988 was \$3,123 per day. Thus, the receivables balance of \$152,500 on December 31, 1988, represented about 49 days of sales.

As financial analysts, our principal objective in calculating DSO is to determine whether Sparta is managing its receivables effectively. To answer this question, we must compare Sparta's DSO with its terms of sale. Sparta sells on two different terms, depending on competition and the bargaining power of customers. Some sales are on a *net 30* basis; that is, payment is due within 30 days. Other sales are on a *net 60* basis.[2] If all sales were net 30, a DSO figure of 49 would indicate laxity in Sparta's collection procedures. In this case, Sparta's sales are approximately half net 30 and half net 60. We would, therefore, expect a DSO figure of about 45 if all customers were paying exactly on time. If data are available, we might compare Sparta's DSO figure against an industry average.

It is useful also to examine the DSO data over time, as given in Table 7–7, to identify any trends in collection experience. We find some variability but, excluding 1983, no clear trend. The variability might result either from variations in the

[2]Chapter 20 provides a more detailed discussion of credit terms.

Table 7–7

Sparta Manufacturing Company Year-End Days Sales Outstanding, 1983–1988

Year	Days Sales Outstanding (DSO)
1983	89
1984	59
1985	54
1986	42
1987	54
1988	49

sales mix, from changes in economic conditions, or from some inconsistency on Sparta's part in managing its receivables.

The DSO figure is useful in part because it can be compared to credit terms. We converted sales to a daily basis in calculating DSO. If we had not converted sales to a daily basis, we would obtain an alternative measure relevant for analyzing the firm. This measure, the **receivables/sales ratio,** can be calculated and expressed as a percentage. While this ratio bears no intuitive relationship to credit terms, for analyzing trends it serves about as well as DSO. The reciprocal figure — the ratio of sales to receivables — is referred to as the **receivables turnover rate.** Note that the average collection period divided into 365 also gives us the turnover rate in annual terms. All of these calculations convey basically the same information. Since the DSO figure can be compared to credit terms, it is the most useful figure.

Another technique for analyzing accounts receivable is to prepare an **aging schedule.** To do this, the financial manager must categorize the receivables outstanding at any point in time according to the length of time outstanding. Table 7–8 breaks down Sparta's receivables on December 31, 1988. The aging schedule,

Comparing days sales outstanding (DSO) to credit terms indicates whether or not a firm is effectively managing its accounts receivable.

Receivables/sales ratio — a tool for analyzing collection trends; calculated as accounts receivable divided by sales.

Receivables turnover rate — sales divided by accounts receivable.

Aging schedule — a technique for analyzing accounts receivable by categorizing receivables outstanding by the length of time outstanding.

Table 7–8

Sparta Manufacturing Company Accounts-Receivable Aging Schedule, December 31, 1988

Month of Sale	Age of Account (days)	Proportion of Total Receivables (percent)
December	0–30	40
November	31–60	30
October	61–90	17
September	91–120	10
Before September	Over 120	3
		100

therefore, gives us considerably more information than the DSO figure. The DSO figure of 49 days masks the fact that 30 percent of Sparta's receivables on December 31, 1988, were more than 60 days old. The aging schedule tells Sparta's management to look further at collection procedures.

Inventory Turnover

An important aspect of managerial performance is the efficiency with which inventories are utilized. The basic function of inventories is to decouple the production process from purchases on the one hand and from sales on the other. To reduce purchasing costs, firms buy raw materials in quantity and hold them until needed. Since sales and production seldom are exactly synchronized on a daily basis, inventories of finished goods are held to avoid lost sales due to lack of stocks. Inventory policy requires a trade-off between the costs of purchasing and the cost of lost sales on the one hand and inventory-carrying costs (primarily storage and financing) on the other. Chapter 23 will address the issue of how much to invest in inventory. Here, we are concerned only with measuring inventory utilization.

Inventory management must be judged relative to some overall measure of firm output. A widely used measure is the **inventory-turnover ratio,** defined in Equation (6).

The efficiency of inventory utilization, as measured by the inventory-turnover ratio is

$$\text{Inventory turnover} = \frac{\text{Cost of goods sold}}{\text{Average inventory}}. \tag{6}$$

Cost of goods sold, rather than sales, is the appropriate activity measure because it contains elements of cost comparable to those included in the inventory figure. We can pick any period over which to measure turnover—a month, a quarter, or a year. Here again, we must be careful to take into account seasonal patterns. The average-inventory figure often must be calculated as simply the average of beginning and ending figures for the period in question. Sometimes it is necessary to settle for only a beginning or an ending inventory figure.

We can compare turnover to industry averages or examine it over time. The inventory-turnover figure for Sparta Manufacturing for December 31, 1988, would be calculated, using Equation (6), as

$$\text{Inventory turnover} = \frac{\$730,000}{(\$410,000 + \$420,000)/2}$$

$$= \frac{\$730,000}{\$415,000}$$

$$= 1.76 \text{ times}.$$

Sparta's inventory-turnover figures for the period 1984–1988 are given in Table 7–9. In our discussion of source-and-use analysis in the previous chapter, we found inventories to be the largest single user of funds. Now we can see why.

Inventory policy trades off the costs of purchasing and lost sales versus the costs of carrying inventory (primarily storage and financing).

Inventory-turnover ratio— a measure of the efficiency with which inventories are utilized; calculated as the cost of goods sold divided by average inventory.

Table 7—9
Sparta Manufacturing Company Inventory Turnover, 1984–1988

Year	Inventory Turnover
1984	1.93
1985	1.80
1986	2.06
1987	1.69
1988	1.76

Sparta is turning over its inventory less than twice a year, far below the industry average, which we find from Robert Morris Associates data to be 5.4 times per year in 1987 and much more than 5 times per year during previous years. Another interpretation is that on average, materials are remaining in inventory for more than 6 months. In addition, the data in Table 7–9 indicate a worsening trend. Inventory management seems to be a major problem area for Sparta.

Finance in Practice 7—2

Inventories and Sales

What happens to inventories during recessions? Does inventory turnover increase or decrease? What about during economic booms?

The chart on p. 210 provides some answers. As shown, during the 1974 recession, inventories rose from about 1.42 times monthly sales to about 1.64 times. These figures are totals for all firms engaged in manufacturing and trade (i.e., wholesaling and retailing) in the United States. After the recession ended, inventories gradually declined to 1.44 times monthly sales by 1980, then jumped up again during the 1980 recession, declined again, then jumped way up to 1.68 times sales in the

1981–82 recession. Then they declined again as the economy improved during 1983–86, and by the end of 1987 stood at about 1.5 times sales.

Why do inventories rise during recessions? One would think that firms would want to cut back during a recession. The answer is that one way firms and others determine that the economy is slowing is by a rise in inventories. Sales slow during the early stages of a recession, but no one can tell exactly what is happening. Firms continue to produce, so inventories rise. By the time it's clear that a recession is under way, inventories have risen significantly. Firms then try to cut back, but often sales slow down more rapidly than firms can cut production, so inventories continue to rise. After the recession ends, firms tend to keep a tight rein on production, so as sales recover, inventories fall.

Historically, inventories throughout the economy have been a good indicator of economic activity. When we see aggregate inventories rising for the whole economy, we ought to become suspicious that economic activity is slowing down, and a recession may be on the way.

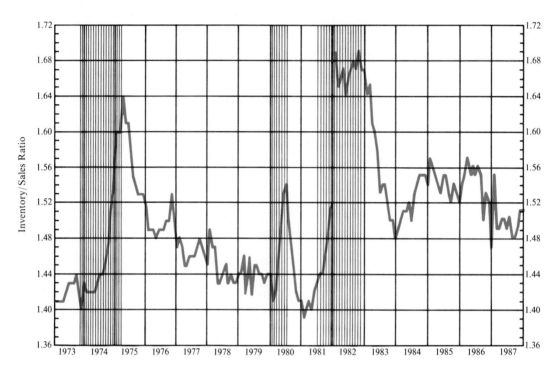

Inventories Compared with Monthly Sales, Manufacturing and Trade (seasonally adjusted)

*Beginning in 1982, inventory data reflect changes in estimation procedures. Shaded areas represent periods of business recessions. Latest data plotted: November preliminary.

Source: U.S. Department of Commerce. Prepared by the Federal Reserve Bank of St. Louis.

Payment Period

Days purchases outstanding (DPO) — a measure of how promptly a firm pays its bills. DPO is calculated as accounts payable divided by purchases per day (also known as the *average payment period*).

Creditors, especially trade creditors, are interested in how promptly a firm pays its bills. If a firm is known for paying its bills promptly, it is more likely to obtain credit and to obtain it on more favorable terms. We can calculate the number of **days purchases outstanding (DPO),** also known as the *payment period,* as shown in Equation (7).

The average number of days it takes for a firm to make payments for purchases it makes on credit, or days purchases outstanding (DPO), is calculated as

$$\text{DPO} = \frac{\text{Accounts payable}}{\text{Purchases per day}}.$$ (7)

If we do not have data on purchases, we may have to improvise. In the case of Sparta Manufacturing Company, we have (in Table 7–1) data on the materials component of cost of goods sold. If usage and purchasing rates were about the same, and if selling, general, and administrative expense does not include significant purchases (for office supplies, etc.), we can then use the cost of material as a proxy for purchases. The payment period for Sparta for December 31, 1988, can then be calculated, using Equation (7), as

$$DPO = \frac{\$122,500}{\$375,000/365 \text{ days}}$$

$$= \frac{\$122,500}{\$1,027/\text{day}}$$

$$= 119 \text{ days}.$$

Table 7–10 gives the results of calculating the payment period for each of the other years.

Days purchases outstanding can also be interpreted as the average payment period. Since Sparta's terms of purchase are net 30 in most cases, we find Sparta far overdue on its trade credit. Our earlier source-and-use analysis raised the question of whether Sparta was relying too heavily on trade credit to finance its operations. Analysis of Sparta's payment period confirms that this indeed is the case.

Sparta's management should immediately look further into the accounts-payable situation to determine the reason for the slow payment and to plan corrective action. A potential lender or supplier should look much more deeply into Sparta's treatment of its trade creditors before advancing credit. One technique for looking further is the aging schedule, constructed in the same manner as that for accounts receivable in Table 7–8. As before, seasonal patterns and growth can seriously distort the calculation of the payment period. To avoid such distortion, it is best to use purchase data for the shortest and most recent period available.

Days purchases outstanding can also be interpreted as the average payment period.

Table 7–10

Sparta Manufacturing Company Year-End Days Purchases Outstanding, 1983–1988

Year	Days Purchases Outstanding (DPO)
1983	114
1984	87
1985	81
1986	134
1987	135
1988	119

Measuring Liquidity

Liquidity — a firm's ability to come up with cash quickly to meet expected and unexpected cash requirements.

The **liquidity** of a firm measures its ability to meet expected and unexpected cash requirements, expand its assets, reduce its liabilities, or cover any operating losses. Liquidity measures the company's ability to come up with cash quickly. The most obvious way to achieve liquidity is to have cash on hand, but liquidity is also increased by holding assets that can be easily turned into cash.

Ratio Measures of Liquidity

Current ratio — liquidity measure calculated as current assets divided by current liabilities.

One of the most widely used liquidity measures is the **current ratio,** defined in Equation (8):

$$\text{Current ratio} = \frac{\text{Current assets}}{\text{Current liabilities}}. \tag{8}$$

Current assets and current liabilities, according to standard accounting convention, have maturities shorter than one year. The ratio of the one to the other, thus, gives a measure of the firm's ability to make ends meet in the short run. The current ratio for Sparta for December 31, 1988, can be calculated, using Equation (8), as

$$\text{Current ratio} = \frac{\$575,000}{\$324,100} = 1.77.$$

The current ratio is a crude measure of liquidity, however, because it does not take into account differences among categories of assets. Inventories, for example, may not be as quickly and readily turned into cash as accounts receivable. The **acid-test ratio,** or *quick ratio* — defined in Equation (9) — is a more stringent measure because it includes only the most liquid of current assets:

Acid-test ratio, or *quick ratio* — a more stringent measure of liquidity than the current ratio because it includes only the most liquid of current assets; calculated as cash plus marketable securities plus receivables, divided by current liabilities.

$$\text{Acid-test ratio} = \frac{\text{Cash} + \text{Marketable securities} + \text{Receivables}}{\text{Current liabilities}}. \tag{9}$$

For Sparta, which has no marketable securities, the acid-test ratio for December 31, 1988, can be calculated from Equation (9) as

$$\text{Acid-test ratio} = \frac{\$155,000}{\$324,100} = 0.48.$$

The same calculation for the year 1987 shows that in that year Sparta's acid-test ratio was 0.58.

The industry's average value for the acid-test ratio has been 1.0 or 1.1 for each year from 1983 to 1987. The fact that Sparta's acid-test ratio is substantially less than average may indicate that Sparta is not as liquid as other firms and would have difficulty coming up with cash in an emergency. Before we could know whether Sparta does have a liquidity problem, more detective work would be needed.

Dollar Measures of Liquidity

Net working capital (NWC) — a dollar measure of liquidity; calculated as current assets minus current liabilities.

In some cases, it is useful to measure liquidity in dollar terms. One widely used dollar measure is simply **net working capital (NWC),** defined as current assets minus current liabilities. Dividing by sales yields *net working capital per dollar of sales*.

The principal liquidity measures for the Sparta Manufacturing Company have been calculated and listed in Table 7–11. The net-liquid-assets measure has been omitted because Sparta holds no marketable securities. According to our ratio measures, Sparta's liquidity has declined steadily since 1984. Net working capital increased moderately in dollar terms through 1987 but has declined steadily in relation to sales except in 1985. Overall, we see a picture of declining liquidity. Our analysis of liquidity, therefore, confirms the suspicion raised earlier in our source-and-use analysis.

Liquidity may be declining, but is it too low? Perhaps Sparta had excess liquidity during the mid-1980s. Small growing firms have excess liquidity so infrequently that we can dismiss this as a possibility. We may be able to get a better feel for Sparta's liquidity by comparing its current and acid-test ratios with industry standards, but we must take care that the industry data are from similar firms.

In measuring liquidity as well as other aspects of financial performance, it is important to avoid being too mechanical. Financial managers should be less concerned with standard labels and methods of calculation and more concerned with what they are trying to measure. Sometimes financial managers may find that they can devise their own tailor-made measures in situations that standard measures do not fit.

Measuring Indebtedness

Indebtedness, or **financial leverage** — the mix of debt and equity used to finance a firm's activities.

It is often of interest to creditors, investors, or management to measure a firm's indebtedness. **Indebtedness,** sometimes called **financial leverage,** represents the amount of money a corporation owes to various parties and can be measured in

Table 7–11
Sparta Manufacturing Company Liquidity Measures, 1983–1988

Year	Current Ratio	Acid-Test Ratio	Net Working Capital (thousands of dollars)	Net Working Capital / Sales
1983	2.28	0.92	176	0.34
1984	3.42	1.15	192	0.34
1985	3.32	0.93	243	0.38
1986	2.50	0.67	267	0.29
1987	2.10	0.58	297	0.30
1988	1.77	0.48	251	0.22

Debt ratios—indebtedness calculated using balance-sheet data; reflect the degree to which creditors are protected in the event of the liquidation of the firm.

Coverage ratios— indebtedness calculated using income-statement data; reflect a firm's ability to meet periodic payments due on its debt obligations.

Ratio of debt to total assets—the percentage of total assets financed by creditors; calculated as total liabilities (current liabilities plus long-term debt) divided by total assets.

Debt/net worth ratio, or *debt/equity ratio*—a variation of the ratio of debt to total assets; calculated as total liabilities divided by net worth.

two ways. **Debt ratios** are based on the balance-sheet relationships between debt and asset value and are of particular concern in the event of liquidation. The higher the level of debt relative to the liquidating or sale value of assets, the less likely it is that all creditors will receive all payments due them in the event of liquidation. **Coverage ratios** are based on income-statement relationships between debt and income. They measure the ability of a firm to meet periodic payments due on its debt obligations. The larger the annual debt burden (the sum of interest and partial return of capital due each year) relative to the size and stability of the annual income flow, the higher the probability that a fall in income might push the firm into default.

Debt Ratios

The **ratio of debt to total assets** measures the percentage of total assets financed by creditors. Debt includes all current liabilities plus long-term debt. A variation on the debt/assets ratio is the **debt/net worth ratio,** also known as the *debt/equity ratio*. The debt/assets ratio is defined in Equation (10), and the debt/net worth ratio is defined in Equation (11):

$$\frac{\text{Debt}}{\text{Net worth}} = \frac{\text{Total liabilities}}{\text{Total assets}} \tag{10}$$

$$\frac{\text{Debt}}{\text{Net worth}} = \frac{\text{Total liabilities}}{\text{Common stock} + \text{Retained earnings}}. \tag{11}$$

For Sparta, these two debt ratios for December 31, 1988, can be calculated using the balance-sheet data in Table 7–2 as

$$\frac{\text{Debt}}{\text{Total assets}} = \frac{\$350,100}{\$722,500} = 0.48$$

$$\frac{\text{Debt}}{\text{Net worth}} = \frac{\$350,100}{(\$155,000 + \$217,400)}$$

$$= \frac{\$350,100}{\$372,400} = 0.94.$$

The debt/assets and debt/net worth ratios tell essentially the same story, because net worth is total assets less debt. Both ratios measure the protection afforded to creditors in the event of liquidation. A debt/assets ratio of 0.50 (debt/net worth of 1.0) indicates that assets need bring only $0.50 on the dollar in liquidation to fully protect creditors. The market value of assets in liquidation, however, may be substantially less than book value. When using debt ratios to measure protection in liquidation, it is usually wise to eliminate from the balance sheet any intangible assets, such as goodwill.

Table 7–12 lists the calculated values of the two debt ratios just discussed for each of the six years from 1983–1988 for Sparta Manufacturing Company. Beginning in 1985, Sparta's total debt has been increasing relative to assets and net

Table 7–12

Sparta Manufacturing Company Year-End Debt Ratios, 1983–1988

Year	$\dfrac{Debt}{Total\ Assets}$	$\dfrac{Debt}{Net\ Worth}$	$\dfrac{Long\text{-}Term\text{-}Debt}{Capital}$
1983	0.45	0.81	0.14
1984	0.34	0.51	0.13
1985	0.34	0.50	0.11
1986	0.40	0.68	0.09
1987	0.47	0.88	0.08
1988	0.48	0.94	0.07

worth. The increase has been in short-term debt, with the long-term debt ratio declining as the mortgage was paid down. From the standpoint of creditors, the trends are in the wrong direction, since the firm is becoming more leveraged and therefore more risky. Some additional conclusions might be drawn from a comparison of Sparta's debt ratios against industry standards.

Coverage Ratios

Coverage ratios examine indebtedness in terms of *flows* — that is, using income-statement relationships. In contrast to balance-sheet debt ratios, which measure protection of creditors in the event of liquidation, coverage ratios examine the ability of the firm to meet its debt obligations as a going concern.

Times-interest-earned ratio — the margin by which current earnings cover interest charges on debt; calculated as current earnings divided by interest charges.

The **times-interest-earned ratio** measures the margin by which current earnings cover interest charges and the extent to which operating earnings can decline before interest is threatened. The higher the ratio, the greater the margin of safety for creditors. One version of this ratio, shown as Equation (12), is calculated by dividing earnings before interest and taxes (EBIT) by interest charges on all debt, both short-term and long-term.

Interest coverage can be determined by calculating the times-interest-earned ratio, which measures the margin by which earnings cover interest charges, as

$$\text{Times interest earned} = \text{EBIT}/\text{Interest} \qquad (12)$$

where EBIT is earnings before interest and taxes.

For Sparta in 1988, we find that the times-interest-earned ratio can be calculated from income-statement data as

$$\text{Times interest earned} = \frac{\$54,900}{\$12,900} = 4.3 \text{ times}.$$

When a firm has several debt issues outstanding and some are senior to others, we may wish to calculate coverage of each issue separately because senior debt must be paid before junior debt can receive its interest payments. Here we must proceed with care. Suppose a firm has outstanding two bond issues, A and B; A is senior to B, meaning that A's interest is paid in full before any of B's. We calculate the interest coverage for issue A using Equation (12) with only the interest on A in the denominator. To determine coverage on B, we include total interest (on both A and B) in the denominator because senior debt must be paid before junior. If we (mistakenly) calculated the coverage of B as earnings available after payment of interest on A, divided by interest on B, B would appear to have a higher coverage than A. The correct calculation gives B's coverage as the same as overall coverage of both issues.

To illustrate, assume (hypothetically) that Sparta's total interest payments of $12,900 in 1988 consist of a *senior* obligation of $8,000 that must be satisfied in full before any other interest payments may be made and a *junior* obligation of $4,900. The times-interest-earned ratio for the first obligation would be $54,900/$8,000, or 6.9 times. For the junior obligation it is *not* ($54,900 − $8,000)/$4,900, which would give 9.6 times and would wrongly suggest that the junior obligation is safer than the senior; rather, the times-interest-earned ratio for the junior obligation is $54,900/$12,900, or 4.3 times—exactly the same as the overall coverage of both issues together.

A more comprehensive coverage measure is **fixed-charge coverage (FCC),** which includes all contractual obligations rather than interest alone. Other contractual obligations include rent, lease payments, and principal repayments on long-term debt. The latter often are referred to as *sinking-fund payments,* about which we will have more to say in Part Five. There are two complications involved in calculating fixed-charge coverage, which is given in Equation (13). Because lease payments and rent are *subtracted* before we arrive at EBIT, we have to add them back both to the numerator and to the denominator of the ratio. Also, because principal repayments on fixed debt are not deductible for tax purposes, we have to convert this number to a before-tax basis when we include it in the calculation by dividing by the factor $(1 − T)$, where T is the marginal income tax rate (which is 20 percent for Sparta).

Coverage of debt and other contractual obligations can be measured by the fixed-charge-coverage (FCC) ratio, which is calculated as

$$\text{FCC} = \frac{\text{EBIT} + \text{Lease} + \text{Rent}}{\text{Lease} + \text{Rent} + \text{Interest} + [\text{Principal}/(1 − T)]} \tag{13}$$

where T = the firm's marginal tax rate.

With these two factors included, the fixed-charge coverage for Sparta for 1988 can be calculated as

$$\text{FCC} = \frac{\$54,900 + \$0 + \$0}{\$0 + \$0 + \$12,900 + (\$2,000/0.80)}$$

$$= \frac{\$54,900}{\$15,400}$$

$$= 3.6 \text{ times}.$$

Fixed-charge-coverage (FCC) ratio—a more comprehensive coverage measure than the times-interest-earned ratio because it measures the margin by which a firm's current earnings can cover debt and all other contractual obligations, including lease payments.

Note that Sparta has neither lease payments nor rental payments.

A variation on Equation (13) is to add depreciation and other noncash charges to the numerator, thus providing a coverage measure in terms of operating cash flow rather than earnings. Over the long run, however, fixed charges must be covered by earnings.

The concept of coverage can be extended to dividends on preferred and common stock. Although dividends are not contractual, unlike interest and principal payments, dividends are an important obligation that should be covered except in times of serious financial difficulty. Coverage of dividends by earnings gives a measure of the likelihood of their being discontinued or reduced during hard times. The usual procedure in calculating dividend coverage is to add the before-tax equivalent of the dividend—dividend divided by $(1 - T)$—to the denominator of Equation (13).

Table 7–13 lists the coverage ratios for each year from 1983 to 1988 for Sparta Manufacturing Company.[3] Sparta's principal payments on the outstanding mortgage amounted to $2,000 per year. We see from Table 7–13 that Sparta still is covering interest and fixed charges with some margin to spare, but a bad earnings year could put fixed charges in jeopardy. Also, the trend since 1985 is worrisome. Industry comparisons again might be helpful.

Sparta Manufacturing Company is a privately owned company, which means that its stock does not trade in public stock markets. Many companies are publicly owned, and for these companies there are some additional performance measures that are of interest. Some of these measures use a company's stock price as well as its financial-statement data to provide further insights. Finance in Practice 7–3 shows how indicators such as the **price/earnings (P/E) ratio** or the **market/book ratio** can provide valuable information about the performance of a company. Table 7–14 on pp. 218–219 summarizes many of the key performance measures used to analyze a company.

A limitation of coverage ratios is that they consider only operating earnings and cash flows. Other sources of cash can be tapped in a financial emergency to cover fixed charges. Another limitation of coverage ratios is that they say nothing about the likelihood of a drop in earnings sufficient to leave fixed charges uncovered.

Price/earnings (P/E) ratio—the ratio of current market price per share to the most recently reported annual earnings per share; gives an indication of the market's assessment of a company's growth prospects and riskiness.

Market/book ratio—the ratio of share price to book value per share; relates the value to shareholders of the firm's future cash flows (market value) to the historical costs to shareholders of acquiring the firm's assets.

Table 7–13

Sparta Manufacturing Company Coverage Ratios, 1983–1988

Year	Times-Interest-Earned Ratio	Fixed-Charge-Coverage Ratio
1983	2.9	2.2
1984	4.2	2.6
1985	14.6	9.3
1986	9.8	6.6
1987	5.2	4.1
1988	4.3	3.6

[3]For a critique of alternative coverage ratios, see M. C. Findlay III and E. E. Williams, "Toward More Adequate Debt Service Coverage Ratios," *Financial Analysts Journal* 31 (Nov./Dec. 1975): 58–61.

Table 7–14

Summary of Performance Measures

Measure	Calculation
Profits	
1. Dollar profits	Profit after taxes (PAT); profit before taxes (PBT); operating profit
2. Earnings per share	$\dfrac{\text{PAT} - \text{Preferred dividends}}{\text{Average common shares outstanding}}$
Profitability	
3. Gross margin	$\dfrac{\text{Sales} - \text{Cost of goods sold}}{\text{Sales}}$
4. Operating expenses	$\dfrac{\text{Operating expenses}}{\text{Sales}}$
5. Net margin	$\dfrac{\text{PAT}}{\text{Sales}}$
6. Normalized income statement	$100 \times \dfrac{\text{Each item in income statement}}{\text{Sales}}$
Return on Investment (ROI)	
7. Accounting rate of return	$\dfrac{\text{PAT}}{\text{Average investment}}$ (typically)
8. Return on assets (ROA)	$\dfrac{\text{PAT}}{\text{Total assets}} = \dfrac{\text{PAT}}{\text{Sales}} \times \dfrac{\text{Sales}}{\text{Total assets}}$
9. Return on equity (ROE)	$\dfrac{\text{PAT}}{\text{Net worth}} = \dfrac{\text{PAT}}{\text{Sales}} \times \dfrac{\text{Sales}}{\text{Net worth}}$
Activity and Turnover	
10. Days sales outstanding (DSO) (also *average collection period*)	$\dfrac{\text{Accounts receivable}}{\text{Average credit sales per day}}$

Finance in Practice 7–3

Performance Measures for IBM Corporation

The exhibit on p. 220 is reproduced from the *Value Line Investment Survey.* Value Line, Inc., publishes on a regular basis similar data on about 1,700 companies and is used by many investors, professional and amateur alike.

The first six rows under the diagram on the sample page give annual data for key indicators on a per-share basis: revenues per share, earnings per share, book value per share, and so on. The figures are computed by taking the total figure for, say, earnings and dividing it by the number of shares of common stock outstanding. Most shareholders in IBM, with the exception of a few large institutional investors, such as pension funds, own only a small percentage of

Measure	Calculation
11. Inventory turnover rate	$\dfrac{\text{Cost of goods sold}}{\text{Average inventory}}$
12. Days purchases outstanding (also *average payment period*)	$\dfrac{\text{Accounts payable}}{\text{Average purchases per day}}$

Liquidity

13. Current ratio	$\dfrac{\text{Current assets}}{\text{Current liabilities}}$
14. Acid-test ratio	$\dfrac{\text{Cash} + \text{Marketable securities} + \text{Receivables}}{\text{Current liabilities}}$
15. Net working capital to sales	$\dfrac{\text{Current assets} - \text{Current liabilities}}{\text{Sales}}$

Indebtedness

16. Debt to total assets	$\dfrac{\text{Total liabilities}}{\text{Total assets}}$
17. Debt to net worth	$\dfrac{\text{Total liabilities}}{\text{Net worth}}$
18. Times interest earned	$\dfrac{\text{Earnings before interest and taxes (EBIT)}}{\text{Interest}}$
19. Fixed-charge coverage	$\dfrac{\text{EBIT} + \text{Lease} + \text{Rent}}{\text{Lease} + \text{Rent} + \text{Interest} + \text{Principal}/(1 - T)}$

the company. Thus, each shareholder has an interest in knowing his or her share of the total earnings. The *earnings per share (EPS)* number, multiplied by the number of shares owned, gives the shareholder's share of earnings. In 1987, IBM had 597.33 million shares of stock outstanding and earnings per share of $8.72.

A firm's EPS is widely watched as a performance measure. Also widely watched is the stock price, which is quoted on a per-share basis. After all, the value of the holding of stock is really what matters to most investors. As we found in our discussions of valuation in

Chapters 4 and 5, the market value of a stock is the present value of all the cash flow that investors expect to receive on the stock in the future. The trend in EPS is one important factor investors take into account in forecasting future cash flows. Note that Value Line forecasts cash flow along with sales revenue, earnings, dividends, and book value.

Value Line also forecasts future stock price. Later in the book we will talk about just how difficult it is to forecast stock prices. In the aggregate, all investors can receive returns equal to only what firms actually earn. Although some

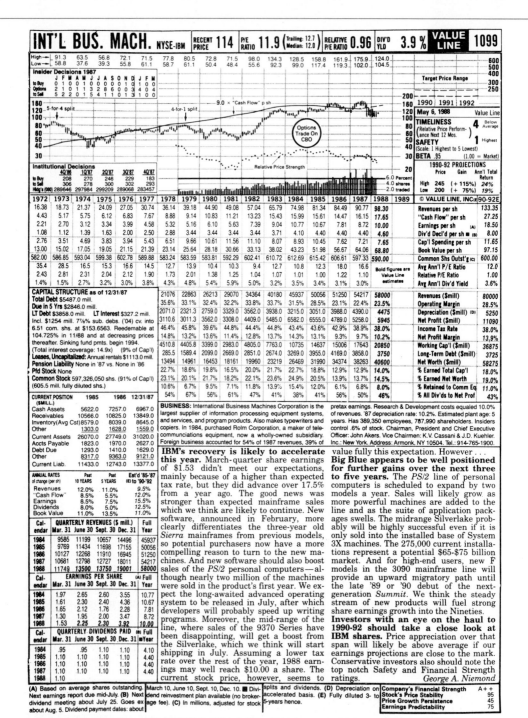

Value Line report for International Business Machines (INT'L BUS. MACH., NYSE-IBM), RECENT PRICE 114, P/E RATIO 11.9 (Trailing: 12.7, Median: 12.0), RELATIVE P/E RATIO 0.96, DIV'D YLD 3.9%, VALUE LINE 1099, May 6, 1988.

BUSINESS: International Business Machines Corporation is the largest supplier of information processing equipment systems, and services, and program products. Also makes typewriters and copiers. In 1984, purchased Rolm Corporation, a maker of telecommunications equipment, now a wholly-owned subsidiary. Foreign business accounted for 54% of 1987 revenues, 39% of pretax earnings. Research & Development costs equaled 10.0% of revenues. '87 depreciation rate: 10.2%. Estimated plant age: 5 years. Has 389,350 employees, 787,990 shareholders. Insiders control .6% of stock. Chairman, President and Chief Executive Officer: John Akers. Vice Chairman: K.V. Cassani & J.D. Kuehler. Inc.: New York. Address: Armonk, NY 10504. Tel.: 914-765-1900.

IBM's recovery is likely to accelerate this year. March-quarter share earnings of $1.53 didn't meet our expectations, mainly because of a higher than expected tax rate, but they did advance over 17.5% from a year ago. The good news was stronger than expected mainframe sales which we think are likely to continue. New software, announced in February, more clearly differentiates the three-year old *Sierra* mainframes from previous models, so potential purchasers now have a more compelling reason to turn to the new machines. And new software should also boost sales of the *PS/2* personal computers—although nearly two million of the machines were sold in the product's first year. We expect the long-awaited advanced operating system to be released in July, after which developers will probably speed up writing programs. Moreover, the mid-range of the line, where sales of the 9370 Series have been disappointing, will get a boost from the Silverlake, which we think will start shipping in July. Assuming a lower tax rate over the rest of the year, 1988 earnings may well reach $10.00 a share. The current stock price, however, seems to value fully this expectation. However . . .

Big Blue appears to be well positioned for further gains over the next three to five years. The *PS/2* line of personal computers is scheduled to expand by two models a year. Sales will likely grow as more powerful machines are added to the line and as the suite of application packages swells. The midrange Silverlake probably will be highly successful even if it is only sold into the installed base of System 3X machines. The 275,000 current installations represent a potential $65-$75 billion market. And for high-end users, new F models in the 3090 mainframe line will provide an upward migratory path until the late '89 or '90 debut of the next-generation *Summit*. We think the steady stream of new products will fuel strong share earnings growth into the Nineties. **Investors with an eye on the haul to 1990-92 should take a close look at IBM shares.** Price appreciation over that span will likely be above average if our earnings projections are close to the mark. Conservative investors also should note the top notch Safety and Financial Strength ratings.

George A. Niemond

Factual material is obtained from sources believed to be reliable, but the publisher is not responsible for any errors or omissions contained herein.

investors may forecast better than others, the number of investors who can "outforecast" all others consistently over extended periods is very small.

Another widely used indicator is the *price/earnings (P/E) ratio,* the ratio of current market price per share to the most recently reported annual earnings per share. If a company is growing rapidly in sales and, more important, in earnings, it is likely to have a higher stock price (present value of future cash flows to shareholders) than a similar company growing less rapidly. Thus, other factors equal, higher growth normally results in a higher P/E ratio. So, a high P/E may indicate that the market expects the company to grow rapidly.

A second important factor in interpreting P/E ratios is *risk*. Other factors equal, lower risk will result in a lower market required rate of return, or discount rate (the denominator in our valuation models in Chapters 4 and 5), and hence in a higher stock price. So a high P/E ratio could indicate an assessment of relatively low risk or high expected growth or both.

Book value per share and the *market/book ratio*—the ratio of share price to book value per share—also are useful indicators. Market value, in principle, is the present value of the future cash flows the company is expected to generate for shareholders. Book value, on the other hand, represents the cost of the assets financed by shareholders to produce those cash flows. Book value has many shortcomings as a measure of cost, especially in an inflationary world, but in a rough sense, book value represents the cost of inputs used by the firm, and market price represents the value of the outputs it produces. Using the market/book ratio as a guide, the market seems to be telling IBM that they have done a good job. In May 1988, the time of the Value Line data in the accompanying entry, IBM's stock price was $114 and its 1987 book value $64.06, a market/book ratio of 1.78. It would be nice for investors if all firms did so well.

Source: Value Line Investment Survey, Value Line, Inc., New York, May 1988.

Finance in Practice 7–4

Sources of Data on Firms and Industries

This chapter has emphasized the necessity for benchmarks, or standards of comparison, in analyzing performance. A single figure for a single period or point in time is of little use unless it can be compared either to data for the same firm over time or to data for other similar firms.

Firm Data. Publicly owned firms are required by the Securities and Exchange Commission (SEC) to report financial data to investors on a regular basis. A firm's annual report to stockholders is the primary reporting vehicle and is often supplemented by quarterly reports. Even more detail is provided in the annual 10-K and quarterly 10-Q reports that must be filed with the SEC. Such reports contain the basic financial information that is the starting point for financial analysis. Annual reports are sometimes collected by libraries and can usually be obtained directly from the firm.

Publications issued by Moody's Investors Service and Standard & Poor's Corp. can also be found in many libraries. Moody's Investors Service publishes financial data on thousands of publicly owned firms organized by type of business. Moody's data go back many years and provide a valuable historical source. Standard & Poor's also publishes data on individual firms. In addition, the Standard & Poor's Compustat Tapes provide a machine-readable source of standard financial data on a large number of public companies.

Another widely used source is the *Value Line Investment Survey*. Recall the data for IBM presented earlier in Finance in Practice 7–3, which shows a page from a recent edition of the *Survey*. Note that the extensive tabular data is accompanied by additional comments. The *Value Line Investment Survey* is aimed primarily at investors, and one can see this orientation both in the choice of data presented and in the nature of the comments, which present Value Line's opinion regarding the likely future returns from investing in IBM stock. Value Line provides data on approximately 1,700 companies along with summary data on a number of major industries. The *Survey* represents a compact and useful source for certain data. Like the publications of Moody's Investors Service and Standard & Poor's, the *Value Line Investment Survey* is relatively expensive but normally can be found in libraries with a good business section.

Industry Data. As noted earlier, Robert Morris Associates (RMA) compiles data for a large number of different industries. Included in RMA data are basic balance-sheet and income-statement information and standard ratios of the type discussed in this chapter, broken down by size of firm. A sample of data available from RMA covering the paints, varnish, and lacquer segment of industry (in which Sparta Manufacturing would belong) is reproduced in the sample entry on p. 223. In the entry, the firms are broken into size categories based on dollar value of assets for purposes of reporting current data. Sparta would fall in the smallest category since its assets are less than $1 million. (*MM* in the table denotes millions of dollars.)

The entry reports normalized income statements and balance sheets for the firms in the industry. In addition, Robert Morris Associates provides a number of calculated ratios. Three values are given for each ratio. For example, the current ratio in Sparta's size class ($0 to $1 million in assets) is given as 2.9, 1.8, and 1.3. The middle number, 1.8, represents the *median* current ratio of the reporting firms; that is, there are as many firms with current ratios above 1.8 as there are firms with current ratios below 1.8. Looking back at Table 7–11 in the chapter, we see that Sparta's current ratio for 1986 is 2.50. This puts Sparta above the industry median figure for the current ratio. The other two numbers give further information on how different current ratios are among firms. For example, 25 percent have current ratios below 1.3.

Dun & Bradstreet compiles data on both individual firms and industries. They compile and publish 14 key financial ratios on 125 different lines of business, including manufacturing, wholesaling, and retailing.

The Federal Trade Commission (FTC) and the SEC jointly publish the *Quarterly Financial Report for Manufacturing Corporations*. The report contains balance-sheet and income-statement data broken down by industry group and by asset size.

Trade associations represent another source of industry data. Many industries maintain trade associations with a staff that collects data and makes the data available on request.

Fortune magazine, *Forbes* magazine, and *Business Week* also provide summary data on the largest corporations.

A word of warning is in order regarding the use of industry data. Industry averages and data on other individual companies reflect what other

MANUFACTURERS - PAINT, VARNISH & LACQUER   SIC# 2851

	Current Data						Comparative Historical Data				
	37(6/30-9/30/83)			93(10/1/83-3/31/84)			6/30/79 3/31/80	6/30/80 3/31/81	6/30/81 3/31/82	6/30/82 3/31/83	6/30/83 3/31/84
	0-1MM 31	1-10MM 73	10-50MM 19	50-100MM 7	ALL 130	ASSET SIZE NUMBER OF STATEMENTS	ALL 148	ALL 155	ALL 142	ALL 136	ALL 130
	%	%	%	%	%	ASSETS	%	%	%	%	%
	6.4	8.8	8.2		8.6	Cash & Equivalents	6.5	7.6	6.7	8.3	8.6
	29.5	30.4	30.4		29.8	Accts & Notes Rec - Trade(net)	29.4	29.6	28.6	29.1	29.8
	29.9	29.8	28.9		29.2	Inventory	33.1	31.4	30.9	29.3	29.2
	3.7	.9	1.2		1.6	All Other Current	1.2	1.4	2.1	1.9	1.6
	69.6	69.9	68.7		69.2	Total Current	70.2	70.0	68.3	68.5	69.2
	22.9	22.9	23.8		23.6	Fixed Assets (net)	21.9	22.1	23.3	22.0	23.6
	.5	.2	.7		.4	Intangibles (net)	.9	.6	.6	.8	.4
	7.0	7.0	6.8		6.9	All Other Non-Current	7.1	7.2	7.8	8.7	6.9
	100.0	100.0	100.0		100.0	Total	100.0	100.0	100.0	100.0	100.0
						LIABILITIES					
	8.2	8.2	3.7		7.1	Notes Payable-Short Term	6.6	6.3	6.7	6.8	7.1
	4.6	2.7	2.1		3.0	Cur. Mat-L/T/D	2.2	2.0	2.6	2.5	3.0
	18.4	17.5	17.5		17.4	Accts & Notes Payable - Trade	19.3	17.3	17.3	16.9	17.4
	4.0	6.4	8.3		6.3	Accrued Expenses	6.5	7.2	6.4	5.6	6.3
	3.5	2.1	2.9		2.5	All Other Current	3.6	2.7	3.2	2.9	2.5
	38.8	36.9	34.4		36.3	Total Current	38.3	35.5	36.2	34.7	36.3
	13.9	14.2	9.9		13.1	Long Term Debt	12.8	12.5	15.0	12.7	13.1
	2.9	1.9	2.7		2.4	All Other Non-Current	2.3	2.5	1.7	1.8	2.4
	44.5	47.0	53.0		48.2	Net Worth	46.6	49.5	47.1	50.8	48.2
	100.0	100.0	100.0		100.0	Total Liabilities & Net Worth	100.0	100.0	100.0	100.0	100.0
						INCOME DATA					
	100.0	100.0	100.0		100.0	Net Sales	100.0	100.0	100.0	100.0	100.0
	69.2	69.9	66.9		68.7	Cost Of Sales	71.1	70.4	70.1	69.3	68.7
	30.8	30.1	33.1		31.3	Gross Profit	28.9	29.6	29.9	30.7	31.3
	27.9	26.6	28.2		27.5	Operating Expenses	24.3	25.0	25.3	27.2	27.5
	2.9	3.5	4.9		3.8	Operating Profit	4.6	4.6	4.6	3.4	3.8
	1.6	.8	.4		.9	All Other Expenses (net)	.8	.7	1.3	1.0	.9
	1.2	2.7	4.5		2.9	Profit Before Taxes	3.8	4.0	3.3	2.5	2.9
						RATIOS					
	2.9	2.9	2.5		2.8		2.5	2.7	2.9	3.1	2.8
	1.8	2.0	2.2		2.1	Current	2.0	2.1	2.2	2.2	2.1
	1.3	1.4	2.0		1.5		1.4	1.6	1.5	1.6	1.5
	1.5	1.8	1.4		1.7		1.3	1.6	1.5	1.7	1.7
(30)	1.0	1.1	1.3	(129)	1.1	Quick	1.0	1.1	1.0	1.1 (129)	1.1
	.7	.7	1.0		.7		.7	.8	.7	.8	.8
35	10.5	38 9.7	44 8.3	39 9.4		Sales/Receivables	35 10.5	35 10.3	32 11.5	34 10.7	39 9.4
49	7.4	49 7.5	51 7.2	49 7.4			42 8.6	43 8.4	41 8.8	45 8.1	49 7.4
58	6.3	59 6.2	58 6.3	59 6.2			55 6.6	54 6.7	54 6.7	54 6.8	59 6.2
36	10.2	45 8.1	48 7.6	45 8.2		Cost of Sales/Inventory	51 7.2	48 7.6	50 7.3	49 7.5	45 8.2
60	6.1	69 5.3	83 4.4	68 5.4			69 5.3	66 5.5	66 5.5	66 5.5	68 5.4
91	4.0	101 3.6	91 4.0	94 3.9			96 3.8	96 3.8	89 4.1	91 4.0	94 3.9
20	18.4	25 14.6	31 11.8	26 14.3		Cost of Sales/Payables	26 14.3	21 17.2	19 18.9	22 16.7	26 14.3
46	8.0	37 9.9	41 8.8	40 9.1			36 10.2	32 11.3	30 12.0	33 11.1	40 9.1
63	5.8	51 7.2	54 6.8	54 6.8			51 7.1	49 7.5	48 7.6	49 7.4	54 6.8
	4.8	4.6	4.7		4.8	Sales/Working Capital	4.7	4.8	5.2	4.8	4.8
	6.4	7.2	5.5		6.4		7.6	7.0	7.4	6.9	6.4
	16.0	11.8	7.3		10.6		12.1	10.6	11.6	9.2	10.6
	6.8	8.7	9.9		8.7	EBIT/Interest	8.6	8.4	7.8	6.3	8.7
(23)	2.2	(58) 3.0	(14) 7.2	(99) 3.2			(112) 4.5	(131) 4.1	(113) 3.4	(110) 2.6	(99) 3.2
	-1.0	2.0	2.6		1.9		1.5	1.8	1.3	.8	1.9
	9.5	8.4	16.4		10.3	Cash Flow/Cur. Mat. L/T/D	9.1	9.8	10.8	9.3	10.3
(25)	2.2	(47) 3.6	(17) 7.5	(96) 5.0			(90) 3.7	(100) 3.1	(96) 4.3	(91) 3.3	(96) 5.0
	-.3	2.2	2.9		2.0		1.7	1.9	1.6	1.2	2.0
	.3	.3	.4		.3	Fixed/Worth	.3	.3	.3	.3	.3
	.4	.5	.4		.5		.5	.4	.5	.4	.5
	.8	.7	.6		.7		.7	.7	.8	.7	.7
	.6	.5	.6		.5	Debt/Worth	.6	.6	.6	.5	.5
	1.2	1.1	.8		1.0		1.1	1.0	1.2	.9	1.0
	3.0	1.9	1.0		1.8		2.0	1.9	1.9	2.1	1.8
	21.5	27.9	30.8		28.4	% Profit Before Taxes/Tangible Net Worth	31.3	30.2	31.8	23.6	28.4
(29)	11.3	(72) 14.8	18.4	(127) 14.7			(145) 19.2	(154) 16.2	(140) 19.9	(133) 11.0	(127) 14.7
	-4.9	7.9	10.4		7.1		5.8	6.8	5.8	3.2	7.1
	11.4	10.6	16.6		13.0	% Profit Before Taxes/Total Assets	15.4	15.8	15.1	11.0	13.0
	3.8	6.7	9.6		6.8		8.7	8.6	7.9	5.6	6.8
	-2.1	3.2	3.8		2.8		2.7	2.5	2.0	.7	2.8
	23.2	19.6	11.1		19.4	Sales/Net Fixed Assets	19.6	20.3	17.3	17.3	19.4
	14.6	11.9	8.6		11.3		11.2	10.3	11.1	11.8	11.3
	7.5	6.5	6.5		6.4		7.8	7.1	7.4	7.4	6.4
	2.8	2.7	2.5		2.7	Sales/Total Assets	2.8	2.7	3.0	2.7	2.7
	2.5	2.2	2.2		2.3		2.3	2.3	2.4	2.3	2.3
	2.0	1.8	1.7		1.9		1.9	1.8	1.8	1.8	1.9
	1.1	1.1	1.1		1.2	% Depr., Dep., Amort./Sales	.9	.8	.8	1.1	1.2
(28)	1.5	(65) 1.7	(18) 1.7	(118) 1.6			(131) 1.3	(141) 1.3	(130) 1.4	(126) 1.5 (118)	1.6
	2.1	2.3	2.4		2.3		1.6	1.8	1.9	2.0	2.3
	.8	.5			.7	% Lease & Rental Exp/Sales	.6	.6	.7		.7
(12)	1.8	(24) 1.0		(47) 1.4			(55) 1.1	(70) 1.2	(69) 1.1	(63) 1.5	(47) 1.4
	2.1	2.0			2.0		1.9	2.4	1.9	2.4	2.0
	2.8	1.5			2.0	% Officers' Comp/Sales	1.5	1.2	1.3	2.3	2.0
(13)	4.2	(18) 3.3		(31) 3.4			(44) 3.2	(43) 2.7	(47) 3.1	(38) 3.6	(31) 3.4
	10.2	4.7			5.5		4.9	4.5	4.7	4.6	5.5
	40010M	576520M	695043M	811625M	2123198M	Net Sales (#)	1793129M	3189046M	2836601M	2275690M	2123198M
	16883M	271627M	339272M	446682M	1074444M	Total Assets (#)	807121M	1411596M	1314517M	1064171M	1074444M

M = #thousand   MM = $million.

companies *have done* and *are doing*, but not necessarily what they *should be doing*. In no sense should industry averages be viewed as targets toward which a company should aspire.

Source: Excerpted page Copyright © 1984 by Robert Morris Associates. Reprinted by permission. *Disclaimer*

Statement: RMA cautions that the studies be regarded only as a general guideline and not as an absolute industry norm. This is due to limited samples within categories, the categorization of companies by their primary Standard Industrial Classification (SIC) number only, and different methods of operations by companies within the same industry. For these reasons, RMA recommends that the figures be used only as general guidelines in addition to other methods of financial analysis.

KEY CONCEPTS

1. Profitability can be analyzed effectively using the normalized income statement, which measures elements relative to sales.

2. Return on investment, or profit per dollar of capital invested, is an efficiency measure.

3. The turnover rates for inventory, accounts receivable, and accounts payable are measures of activity and efficiency.

4. Liquidity measures are useful in assessing a firm's ability to meet its cash obligations in the short run.

5. Measures of indebtedness give an indication of a firm's ability to meet obligations over the longer term.

SUMMARY

Financial analysis begins with the examination of information to determine past trends. Fundamentally, financial analysis seeks to use the knowledge of the past to improve decisions for the future. The income statement, balance sheet, and source-and-use statement provide basic data for analyzing financial performance.

Profits are measured in dollar terms by the income statement. Profitability (profit per dollar of sales) is measured by the normalized income statement. Such a statement also is useful for examining the behavior of costs over time in relation to sales. Return on investment (ROI) measures profit per dollar of investment. There are many different ways to calculate ROI, so care must be taken to avoid ambiguity. Often it is useful to decompose ROI into two components, profit margin and sales turnover. Margin and turnover themselves can be decomposed using the DuPont system of financial control. The effectiveness of accounts-receivable management

can be measured by calculating *days sales outstanding,* also knows as the *average collection period,* or by constructing an accounts-receivable aging schedule. Inventory management can be analyzed by calculating an inventory turnover ratio. Accounts payable can be analyzed by calculating *days purchases outstanding.* Activity and turnover measures must be interpreted very carefully where seasonal patterns and growth trends are present.

The ability of a firm to meet its obligations as they come due can be judged through the use of liquidity ratios. The *current ratio* (current assets divided by current liabilities) and the *acid-test ratio* are the most widely used liquidity ratios. Dollar measures of liquidity are net working capital per dollar of sales and net liquid assets. Indebtedness can be measured both in stock terms, using various ratios of debt to other balance-sheet data, and in flow terms, using coverage ratios calculated from income-statement data. Two widely used coverage ratios are *times interest earned* and *fixed-charge coverage*. For publicly owned companies, market performance measures are also useful tools in financial analysis.

Benchmarks, or standards of comparison, are necessary for analyzing financial performance. Single figures for a single point in time are of little use by themselves and must be compared either to data for the same firm over time (to identify trends) or to data for other similar firms (to make industry comparisons).

QUESTIONS

1. The areas of financial analysis in this chapter included profitability, activity, liquidity, and indebtedness. A financial analysis assumes a specific interest and perspective of the analyst. Which of the areas of financial analysis above and two specific ratios for the area, plotted over time, might the following calculate from a firm's financial statements?

   A. A supplier of inventory on open account.
   B. A bank lending officer with a short-term loan request to finance working capital.
   C. A bank lending officer with an eight-year loan request to finance plant modernization.
   D. A prospective shareholder of the firm.
   E. A prospective employee of the firm.

2. Compare and contrast profits versus profitability.

3. How does the normalized income statement provide a detailed analysis of a company's net profit margin?

4. Activity ratios utilize one or two common values from the income statement and relate these values to balance-sheet ledger items. Name these income-statement values often used in activity ratios. List three activity ratios and the components of each.

5. What management policies and decisions might cause the net margin to increase, and at the same time, cause the asset turnover to decrease? Give an example.

6. How have McDonald's and Wendy's been able to increase their total asset turnover throughout the years? What suggestions do you have for them to continue the improvement in this ratio?

7. The manager of Dango Retail Boots has taken specific actions which have increased the average inventory and accounts receivable in the store, and the ROA as well. What policy changes and decisions has he apparently made?

8. What might happen to the indebtedness ratios if the following takes place over time in a firm?

   > Sales growth per year is 15%
   > Earnings growth per year is 6%
   > Asset growth per year is 12%
   > Dividend growth per year is 4%

   Explain your answer.

9. Why is return on investment (ROI) sometimes ambiguous as a measure of performance?

10. Return on assets can be viewed as a product of which two components?

11. What are the problems of measuring the performance of accounts receivable and inventory management in a firm with a seasonal sales pattern?

12. What sources of information are available that provide data on firms? On industries?

13. Is it possible for a firm to earn a profit consistently and yet always be short of cash?

14. Can you imagine a firm having difficulty paying its bills when its current ratio is between 2.0 and 3.0? Can you think of a firm that could operate successfully with an acid-test ratio considerably lower than 1.0?

15. What might explain the following in a firm: reasonable sales growth rate, high total-asset and earnings-per-share growth rate, higher than average ROA, exceptionally high ROE, *but* a falling stock price?

FINANCIAL TOOL KIT APPLICATIONS

From the program menu, select Chapter Seven—Analyzing Financial Statements.

A. Review the first program entitled Income Statements, Balance Sheets, Normalized Income Statements, and Selected Ratios. Review these statements for the five years, especially the normalized statements and selected ratios. Make up, name, and describe a specific, fictitious firm, the type of business, its decisions, and the economic events that might produce the results found in these financial statements. Write up your case description and analyses. Support your description and explanation.

B. How well do you recognize and know the ratios discussed in the chapter? To review your learning to this point, and to enhance your understanding, take the Ratio Quiz and Ratio Interpretation review. Select a specific year to analyze, enter the appropriate values, and check your learning to this point. While selecting the appropriate numbers for each ratio, define and describe the situation where the financial analyst would want to calculate the ratio. What does the ratio indicate about the financial condition and/or performance of a firm? The description and use of the ratio will appear on the screen as well as a plot of the ratio for the five-year period. What might have caused the trend of each ratio? If more practice is needed, select another year's financial statements and begin your review.

Problems

1. The Winick Company has been suffering a severe decline in return on assets over the last 5 years and management has asked you to recommend corrective action. Based on the preliminary information in Table A, where would you begin your initial investigative efforts?

Table A

	Return on Assets (percent)	Sales (thousands of dollars)	Profit After Taxes (thousands of dollars)
Year 1	8.4	3,500	175
Year 2	8.0	4,600	225
Year 3	7.2	6,000	280
Year 4	4.8	9,200	415
Year 5	3.1	11,000	465

2. The year-end balance sheet and income statement for Harrington Incorporated for this year along

Table B

Year-End Balance Sheet (thousands of dollars)

Cash	230	Notes payable	1,015
Accounts receivable	9,380	Accounts payable	3,545
Inventories	7,515	Accrued taxes	225
Current assets	17,125	Current liabilities	4,784
Net fixed assets	34,125	Long-term debt	18,036
Total assets	51,250	Deferred income taxes	2,840
		Total liabilities	20,876
		Common stock (par)	575
		Capital in excess of par	7,945
		Retained earnings	17,070
		Common equity	25,590
		Total liabilities and net worth	51,250

with various financial ratios for the industry in which Harrington operates are given in Tables B, C and D.

a. Compute the Table D ratios for the Harrington Company. The inventories were $6,800,000 and the receivables were $8,400,000 for Harrington at year end.

Table C

Income Statement (thousands of dollars), Year-End	
Net sales (credit)	46,235
Cost of goods sold	33,167
Gross profit	13,068
General and administrative expense	9,590
Operating income	3,478
Interest expense	1,120
Net income before taxes	2,358
Income taxes	1,130
Net income	1,228

Table D

Current ratio	4.02
Acid-test ratio	3.00
Inventory turnover	7.50 times
Average collection period	63.10 days
Profit margin (pretax)	5.0%
Return on assets (ROA)	2.5%
Debt-to-total-assets ratio	30.0%
Times-interest-earned ratio	3.90

b. Discuss briefly the liquidity and indebtedness position of Harrington in relation to the industry norms. Compare its profitability to that of the industry.

3. The ABC Company has enjoyed rapid growth in assets over the last 5 years although profits have been declining since year 1. Eight key ratios are shown in Table E for the years 1, 2, and 3. The median ratios for the industry are shown in a separate column.

a. Evaluate the company's situation and list the major problem areas.

b. What problems do you see in relying on a strict comparison with median ratios for the industry? What may cause the difference?

4. Selected information from the Cool Breeze Fan Company's financial records for the last three years is summarized in Table F (p. 228). Using ratios discussed in this chapter, analyze the company's financial condition and performance. Does the analysis reveal any problems?

5. The balance sheet and income statement for the Clone Computer Co. (CCC) and its industry average for the latest year are given in Tables G, H, and I (pp. 228–229).

a. Calculate the ratios for which CCC's industry averages are given in Table I (p. 229).

b. Outline CCC's strengths and weaknesses as revealed by your analysis.

Table E

	Ratios			Industry
	Year 1	Year 2	Year 3	Norm
Days sales outstanding (DSO)	31	34	32	33
Inventory-turnover ratio	4.1 times	3.6 times	3.2 times	4.0 times
Days purchases outstanding (DPO)	25	32	41	26
Current ratio	2.04	1.88	1.64	2.11
Acid-test ratio	1.18	1.14	1.06	1.24
Debt/total assets ratio	0.46	0.49	0.54	0.44
Debt/net worth ratio	1.15	1.17	1.18	1.13
Times-interest-earned ratio	11 times	9 times	7 times	9 times

Table F

	Year 1	Year 2	Year 3
Sales	$10,385,000	$10,750,000	$9,495,000
Cost of goods sold	$ 8,100,000	$ 9,000,000	$8,450,000
Net profit	$ 750,000	$ 500,000	$ 250,000
Cash	$ 83,000	$ 50,000	$ 35,500
Accounts receivable	500,000	650,000	725,000
Inventory	1,000,000	1,200,000	1,500,000
Net fixed assets	2,000,000	2,000,000	2,000,000
Total assets	$ 3,583,000	$ 3,900,000	$4,260,500
Accounts payable	$ 583,000	$ 750,000	$ 973,000
Miscellaneous accruals	500,000	525,000	562,500
Short-term bank loan	250,000	250,000	350,000
Long-term debt	750,000	750,000	750,000
Common stock	250,000	250,000	250,000
Retained earnings	1,250,000	$ 1,375,000	$1,375,000
Total liabilities and owners' equity	$ 3,583,000	$ 3,900,000	$4,260,500

Table G

Balance Sheet (thousands of dollars), Year End	
Cash	220
Accounts receivable	275
Inventory	825
Total current assets	1,320
Net fixed assets	605
Total assets	1,925
Accounts payable	165
Notes payable	220
Other current liabilities	110
Total current liabilities	495
Long-term debt	220
Common equity	1,210
Total claims on assets	1,925

c. Suppose CCC had doubled its sales and also its inventories, accounts receivable, and common equity during this last year. How would that information affect the validity of your ratio analysis?

6. Note the impact (+ increase or − decrease, or no change) of the following on the current ratio, net working capital, and profits. Assume the starting current ratio is greater than one.

Table H

Income Statement, Year End		
Sales		$2,750,000
Cost of goods sold		
Materials	$1,045,000	
Labor	660,000	
Heat, light, and power	99,000	
Indirect labor	165,000	
Depreciation	60,500	2,029,500
Gross profit		$ 720,000
Selling expenses		275,000
General and administrative expenses		316,800
Earnings before interest and taxes		$ 128,700
Less interest expense		−13,200
Net profit before taxes		$ 115,500
Less federal income taxes (at 50 percent)		57,570
Profit after taxes		$ 57,750

(1) The purchase of inventory from a supplier on credit.

(2) The sale of inventory on account (credit).

(3) The payment of a cash dividend.

(4) The payment of accounts payable.

(5) Financing inventory with a short-term vs. a long-term bank loan.

(6) Financing fixed assets with a short-term loan.

(7) Sale of common stock.

(8) Purchase of fixed assets for cash.

Table I

Performance Measure	Industry Average
Current ratio	2.4
Average collection period	43 days
Sales/inventories	9.8
Sales/total assets	2
Profit margin	3.3%
Return on assets	6.6%
Return on equity	18.1%
Debt to total assets	63.5%

Worksheet — Note + or − or No Change (NC)

	Current Ratio	Net Working Capital	Profits
1.			
2.			
3.			
4.			
5.			
6.			
7.			
8.			

REFERENCES

Findlay, M. C., and E. E. Williams, "Toward More Adequate Debt Service Coverage Ratios." *Financial Analysts Journal* (Nov./Dec. 1975): 58–61.

Harrington, Diana R., and Brent D. Wilson. *Corporate Financial Analysis*. 2nd ed. Plano, Texas: Business Publications, Inc., 1986.

Helfert, E. A. *Techniques of Financial Analysis*. 6th ed. Homewood, Ill.: Richard D. Irwin, 1987.

Lev, B. *Financial Statement Analysis: A New Approach*. Englewood Cliffs, N.J.: Prentice-Hall, 1974.

Chapter 8

Cost/Volume/Profit Relationships

This chapter explores the nature of fixed costs and relationships between costs, volume, and profits. We will learn how to do break-even analysis and discuss the concept of operating leverage.

Chapter 7 examined various techniques for measuring financial performance. We looked at measures of income, return on investment, activity, liquidity, and indebtedness. In this chapter we take the analysis a step further and explore relationships between level of output (sales volume), costs, and profits.

To understand the effects of various actions on profit, one must use techniques for analyzing the reponse of revenues, costs, and profits to changes in sales volume.

For planning and decision making, a further understanding of the effects of various actions on profits is clearly important. Such an understanding requires techniques for analyzing the response of revenues, costs, and profits to changes in sales volume. We will begin with costs.

Fixed Versus Variable Costs

Variable costs—costs that vary directly with changes in production volume.

Fixed costs—costs that remain the same over a given range of production.

How do costs respond to changes in sales volume? Some costs, known as **variable costs,** vary directly with production volume, and their variations are roughly proportionate to changes in production volume. For example, every passenger car that General Motors builds needs five tires; thus, the *cost* of this component of the final product rises either in proportion or almost in proportion to the total number of cars built in a period. In contrast, the total cost of tools and dies used for stamping the body parts for a new model would be a **fixed cost** because it does *not* change with the volume of bodies produced but remains *fixed* over a very wide range of production levels. In a wholesale or retail business, variable costs would include the cost of goods purchased for resale and commissions paid to salespersons. In a manufacturing firm, variable costs include materials used in the manufacturing process, direct labor, supplies, energy costs, packaging, freight, and sales commissions.

What costs are fixed with respect to sales volume? Here we must be cautious. We might begin by identifying such costs as executive salaries, depreciation, rent, property taxes, insurance, and interest. The next section will have more to say about how fixed a fixed cost really is.

Accepting for the moment that some costs vary with sales volume and that some do not, we can define the concept of *contribution*. Suppose a manufacturing firm makes a product that is priced at $10 per unit. If variable cost per unit is $6, then each unit sold contributes $4 toward payment of fixed costs. If enough units are sold, total fixed costs will be covered. Sales above that **break-even point** contribute to profits.

Break-even point—the quantity of firm output at which sales revenues just cover total fixed costs, or the quantity of output at which revenue equals operating costs and operating profit is zero.

How Fixed Are Fixed Costs?

Returning to our discussion of fixed costs, suppose a pencil-manufacturing firm operates a plant that has the capacity to produce 50,000 pencils per year. Suppose further that adequate managerial and supervisory personnel are available to produce at full plant capacity and that the accounting department, sales department, and company cafeteria are also staffed to support that level of operation. At any production level below 50,000 pencils per year, all these support or overhead costs remain fixed in total dollars per unit of time.

Suppose production is to be expanded above 50,000 units. New plant capacity is required, and another supervisor may be needed to oversee additional production personnel. Additional personnel may also be needed in the accounting department, and the cafeteria may have to be expanded.

Finance in Practice 8–1

Costs and Revenues at IBM

*F*ortune magazine recently called Thomas J. Watson, Jr., the "most successful capitalist in history," and told the story of how Watson made IBM a "money machine" for shareholders. Many would agree with *Fortune* that IBM indeed is one of the most successful business enterprises in history.

But even mighty IBM has its problems. The current chairman and chief executive, John Akers, is engaged in a massive effort to restructure the computer giant to make it more profitable. In the third quarter of 1986, IBM announced a 27 percent drop in profits compared to a year earlier. The company still expected to make a profit of $5.4 billion for the year—not bad by most standards, but nevertheless a decline from earlier years. And IBM was not used to declines in earnings.

Akers announced plans for major moves in cost cutting, new products, more streamlined management, better marketing, and a revised long-term strategy. Many of the short-term moves were aimed squarely at the topic of this chapter—costs, volume and profit. IBM had suffered a major decline in profit margins during 1985 and 1986, and to correct the problem, planned to cut $2.25 billion from 1987 expenses. The cuts would come via reductions in capital expenditures, early retirement, attrition as employees retired (IBM has a policy prohibiting layoffs), and reductions in travel and consultants.

A big part of the expense reduction was expected to come through streamlined management. The company was studying ways to cut layers of management and to reduce some of its 40,000 managers worldwide. By eliminating bureaucracy and redeploying people, IBM hoped to inject new life into its management process.

IBM also planned to attack the revenue side with a flood of new products scheduled for 1987 and 1988 in all of its product lines, from mainframes to minicomputers to PCs. By 1988, IBM hoped the new products would permit it to improve margins the old-fashioned way: by charging higher prices. Historically, IBM has done this by keeping up a steady stream of new products popular with users, who were willing to pay premium prices for the "Big Blue" label. IBM had been a very well-managed company for a long time, and many observers were betting that the record would continue.

Sources: "The Greatest Capitalist in History," *Fortune*, August 31, 1987; "How IBM Is Fighting Back," *Business Week*, November 17, 1986.

When we say that a particular element of cost is fixed, we mean that it is fixed over some *range* of sales volume. In the long run, all costs are variable. In the long run, the firm can go out of business and eventually eliminate all costs. It is necessary, therefore, when speaking of fixed costs to specify the relevant range of output. When output goes beyond the relevant range, types of costs that previously did not change with output increase, often as a step function, as shown in Figure 8–1 (p. 234). The costs depicted in Figure 8–1 are *fixed* (constant) for volumes less than Q_1, but they increase when output exceeds Q_1 and increase again when output exceeds Q_2.

Figure 8–1
Behavior of Costs

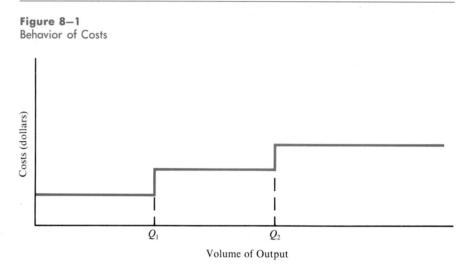

Even over the relevant range of output, any classification of costs as either fixed or variable often is an oversimplification of reality. Some costs contain both fixed and variable components. Part of the electric-power bill, for example, may be fixed, but part may vary with the level of output.

Break-Even Analysis

Break-even analysis—a technique for analyzing the relationship between revenue and profit that examines the proportion of fixed costs to total costs.

The ratio of fixed costs to total costs is an important factor in the relationship between revenue and profit. **Break-even analysis** is a technique for analyzing this relationship by examining the ratio of fixed costs to total costs. At this point, we will restrict our attention to the relationship between revenue and *operating profit*, often referred to as earnings before interest and taxes, or EBIT. In this way, we can separate the effects of operating and financial leverage, both of which we will discuss shortly.

Figure 8–2 shows a break-even diagram constructed for a product with a selling price of $3.00 and variable costs of $1.20 per unit. Fixed operating costs are $180,000 per year and plot as a horizontal line that intersects the vertical axis at $180,000. Because the selling price for the product in question is $3.00 per unit, the total revenue produced at each level of output, Q, can be calculated as $3Q$. The total-revenue line is constructed by plotting each output level against each total-revenue amount ($3Q$) associated with that output level. Because variable cost is $1.20 per unit, total variable cost is calculated as $1.2Q$ for each level of output, Q. Total cost for each level of output is calculated by adding the variable cost, $1.20Q$, for each level of output to the fixed cost of $180,000, and then plotting the result to get the total-cost line in the diagram. In cases where it would be

Figure 8–2
A Typical Break-Even Chart

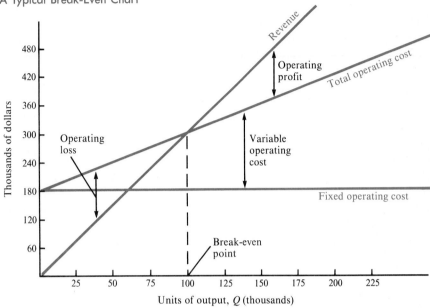

useful, we can construct a break-even chart with sales dollars or percent of production capacity, rather than units of output, on the horizontal axis.

The *break-even point* is the level of production at which sales just cover fixed costs. The break-even point in this case is 100,000 units of production. At that output level, sales revenue is $300,000, variable costs are $120,000, fixed costs are $180,000, and operating profit is zero.

We can also calculate the break-even point algebraically. At the break-even point, we know that total fixed costs are covered. Each unit sold can contribute to covering these costs to the extent that the unit sells for a price (P) more than its unit variable cost (VC). In this example, the contribution of each unit sold is $P - VC = \$3.00 - \$1.20 = \$1.80$. If Q_b is break-even volume, $\$1.80\,(Q_b)$ must equal fixed costs (FC) of $180,000. Algebraically, break-even volume of output can be calculated as shown in Equation (1):

$$(P - VC)Q_b = FC$$

$$Q_b = FC/(P - VC) \qquad (1)$$

where P = price per unit sold, VC = variable cost per unit, and FC = fixed cost.

In our example, the break-even volume of output (Q_b) would be

$$Q_b = \frac{\$180,000}{(\$3.00 - \$1.20)} = \frac{\$180,000}{\$1.80} = 100,000 \text{ units per year}.$$

At the break-even point,
total fixed costs are covered.

Break-Even Analysis on a Cash Basis

It is often useful to know a product's break-even point on a cash basis because companies are concerned with cash flow.

Since companies are concerned with cash flow, it is often useful to know the point at which a product will break even on a cash basis. To perform the analysis on a cash basis, we subtract all noncash expenses — in most cases, only depreciation — from operating costs. In the case of the product analyzed in Figure 8–2, let us assume that the fixed-cost figure of $180,000 included $60,000 in depreciation. Figure 8–3 shows the new fixed-*cash*-cost line at $120,000 and the new break-even diagram that results.

Break-even volume on a cash basis (Q_c) is calculated algebraically as shown in Equation (2):

$$Q_c = FC_c/(P - VC) \qquad (2)$$

where FC_c = fixed cash operating cost, P = price per unit, and VC = variable cost per unit.

In our example, break-even volume, determined on a cash basis, would be

$$Q_c = \frac{\$120{,}000}{(\$3.00 - \$1.20)} = \frac{\$120{,}000}{\$1.80} = 66.67 \text{ units per year}.$$

To cover total cash expenses, the firm must sell only 66,667 units versus 100,000 to cover all costs.

Figure 8–3
Break-Even Analysis on a Cash Basis

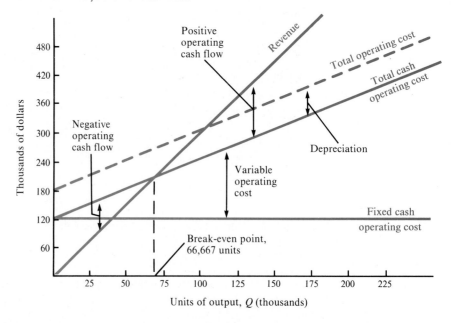

Sample Problem 8–1
Break-Even Analysis for Benchmark Corporation

Benchmark Corporation sells a single product for $30.00 with variable costs per unit of $18.00. If fixed costs are $3 million, calculate the break-even point in units. If fixed costs include $900,000 of noncash expenses (depreciation and amortization), what is the break-even point on a cash basis?

Solution

Using Equation (1), the break-even volume of output would be

$$Q_b = \frac{\$3,000,000}{(\$30 - \$18)} = 250,000 \text{ units}.$$

On a cash basis, the break-even volume of output would be determined, using Equation (2), as

$$Q_c = \frac{\$2,100,000}{(\$30 - \$18)} = \$175,000 \text{ units}. \quad \blacksquare$$

Some Limitations of Break-Even Analysis

Break-even analysis is a very useful tool, but it is important to keep its limitations firmly in mind. First, let us recall our earlier conclusion that fixed costs usually are fixed only over some relevant range of output. Our analysis, therefore, is valid only over that range. Second, we assumed in the earlier discussion that selling price is constant over the range of output analyzed. In practice, output and price are often related.

Third, simple break-even analysis ignores the time value of money. It treats costs and revenues as if they all occur at the same time. For analysis of relatively short time periods, ignoring the time value of money may not cause large problems. For long-range analysis, however, the time value of money can be an important factor.

Fourth, problems may be encountered in obtaining the data necessary for a break-even analysis. Some elements of cost may be uncertain. Cost relationships may change over time, and historical data may not always provide good estimates of future costs. Problems in using historical data are especially troublesome when rates of inflation are high.

Operating Leverage and Financial Leverage

In Figure 8–2, we can see that above the break-even point, operating profits rise rapidly. At output levels above the break-even point, a given change in volume of output produces a larger percentage change in operating profit. For example, a 10 percent change in volume, from 125,000 units to 137,500 units, produces a

Finance in Practice 8–2

Making Profits at Chrysler

In 1980, the Chrysler Corporation was in deep trouble. Losses over the preceding three years totaled $3 billion, and Chrysler symbolized all the ills of the U.S. automobile industry. Bureaucracy and inefficiency were widespread, costs were out of control, and customers were not buying its products. Lee Iacocca, just recently fired by Henry Ford, was hired by Chrysler's board to turn the company around.

Chrysler's comeback is legendary. From 1980 to 1986 the company made $5.6 million in profits, repaid $1.2 billion in government-backed loans and reclaimed some of its lost market share.

One of the first things Iacocca did was to lower Chrysler's break-even point. Prior to 1980, Chrysler's break-even volume was about 2.3 million vehicles per year. Iacocca's new

management team cut it to 1.1 million. It since has creeped back to 1.25 million units, but the company says it has no intention of permitting any further increase.

One way Chrysler keeps the break-even low is by not building new plants. One approach has been to rent plants from competitors. In 1986, Chrysler hired American Motors to build some of its cars in AMC's Kenosha, Wisconsin, plant, one of the nation's oldest automobile factories. Iacocca figured that increasing foreign competition, including capacity built by Japanese companies in the United States, would leave the country with substantial excess capacity. To avoid trouble, Iacocca planned to rent rather than buy.

Looking ahead, Chrysler in 1986 embarked on a new "Liberty Project," aimed at cutting manufacturing costs by 30 percent, or about $2,500 per car, by 1995. Only part of the savings are expected to come from lower fixed costs. The majority will come from lower labor content, better assembly methods, and greater use of components pre-assembled by outside suppliers. Chrysler also achieves savings by purchasing a higher proportion of components from outside than do GM and Ford, rather than making them in-house.

Source: "The Next Act at Chrysler," *Business Week,* November 3, 1986.

---

10 percent change in sales revenue. Operating profit, however, increases by 50 percent, from $45,000 at 125,000 units to $67,500 at 137,500 units. Below break-even volume, we have the same relationship, but in the opposite direction.

Operating leverage— measures the sensitivity of operating profit to changes in sales; can be calculated as the percentage change in operating profits divided by the percentage change in sales.

Operating Leverage

Operating leverage is the sensitivity of operating profit to changes in sales. Earlier in the book, Chapter 4 discussed a firm's operating risk as the risk to shareholders that results from the nature of a firm's product markets and production facilities. Shortly, we will define operating risk more carefully and show how overall operating risk depends in part on operating leverage. The framework of break-even analysis provides a useful way to see the relationship. The degree of operating leverage (DOL) at any level of output is given in Equation (3):

$$DOL = \frac{\text{Percentage change in operating profits}}{\text{Percentage change in sales}}. \tag{3}$$

Operating leverage is a function of the firm's cost structure, specifically the ratio of fixed operating costs to total operating costs. If a firm had no fixed costs, it would have operating leverage equal to 1.0, and a given change in sales would produce the same percentage change in operating profit. Where fixed costs do exist, the firm has operating leverage greater than 1.0, and a given change in sales produces a larger percentage change in operating profit. The higher the ratio of fixed to total operating costs, the greater the degree of operating leverage.

For example, as we stated earlier, Figure 8–2 depicts a 10 percent change in sales (from 125,000 to 137,500 units), which produced a 50 percent change in operating profit (from $45,000 to $67,500). Using Equation (3), we calculate the degree of operating leverage in this case as

$$DOL = \frac{50 \text{ percent}}{10 \text{ percent}} = 5.0.$$

This degree of operating leverage exceeds 1.0 because the firm has fixed costs.

The concept of operating leverage is illustrated in Figure 8–4, which plots the data from Table 8–1 (p. 240). Panel B of the figure repeats the break-even dia-

> Operating leverage is a function of the firm's cost structure (the ratio of fixed operating costs to total operating costs).

Figure 8–4
Operating Leverage

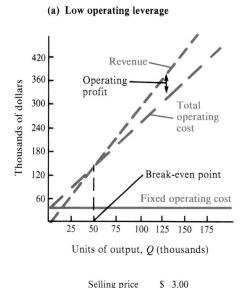

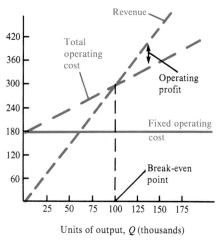

(a) Low operating leverage

(b) High operating leverage

	Selling price	$ 3.00
	Variable cost	2.20
	Fixed cost	$40,000

	Selling price	$ 3.00
	Variable cost	1.20
	Fixed cost	$180,000

Note: This figure plots the data from Table 8–1, p. 240.

Table 8–1

Comparison of Low Operating Leverage with High Operating Leverage

Panel A: Low Operating Leverage

Units *(thousands)*	Sales *(thousands of dollars)*	Variable Cost *(thousands of dollars)*	Total Cost *(thousands of dollars)*	Operating Profit *(thousands of dollars)*
25	75	55	95	−20
50	150	110	150	0
75	225	165	205	20
100	300	220	260	40
125	375	275	315	60
150	450	330	370	80
175	525	385	425	100

Panel B: High Operating Leverage

Units *(thousands)*	Sales *(thousands of dollars)*	Variable Cost *(thousands of dollars)*	Total Cost *(thousands of dollars)*	Operating Profit *(thousands of dollars)*
25	75	30	210	−135
50	150	60	240	−90
75	225	90	270	−45
100	300	120	300	0
125	375	150	330	45
150	450	180	360	90
175	525	210	390	135

Note: Panel A assumptions include a selling price of $3.00, a variable cost of $2.20, and a fixed cost of $40,000. Panel B assumptions include a selling price of $3.00, a variable cost of $1.20, and a fixed cost of $180,000.

gram presented earlier in Figure 8–2. The diagram in Panel B was constructed for a product with a selling price of $3.00, variable costs of $1.20 per unit, and fixed operating costs of $180,000 per year. Panel A of Figure 8–4 is constructed for a product with a selling price of $3.00, variable costs of $2.20 per unit, and fixed operating costs of $40,000 per year. Panel A illustrates low operating leverage; Panel B illustrates high operating leverage. Any given change in sales produces a much larger percentage change in B's operating profit than in A's. When sales are rising, high operating leverage is desirable; when sales are falling, high operating leverage is not desirable. The sword has two edges.

The degree of operating leverage (DOL) at any level of sales can be expressed directly in terms of the cost structure as shown in Equation (4):

$$\text{DOL} = \frac{(S - VC)}{(S - VC - FC)} \qquad (4)$$

where S = sales in dollars, VC = total variable cost in dollars, and FC = total fixed cost in dollars.

Using data from Figure 8–4 as an example, at a sales level of \$450,000, the DOL for the firms in Panel A and B would be calculated as

$$DOL_A = \frac{\$450,000 - \$330,000}{\$450,000 - \$330,000 - \$40,000} = 1.5$$

$$DOL_B = \frac{\$450,000 - \$180,000}{\$450,000 - \$180,000 - \$180,000} = 3.0.$$

The degree of operating leverage is different at different levels of operations.

Equation (4) makes it clear that the DOL for a given firm is different at different levels of operations.

A good example of a firm with high operating leverage is an airline. Fixed operating costs are very high and primarily include salaries, fuel, maintenance, and depreciation. All these costs are incurred no matter how many passengers are carried. Variable costs are minimal, perhaps involving not much more than the cost of in-flight meals and ticket blanks. Once above the break-even passenger load, each additional dollar of revenue is practically all operating profit. Operating profit is very sensitive to the number of passengers carried.

A typical retail business, on the other hand, has much lower operating leverage. Variable costs are high and are, primarily, the cost of goods purchased for resale. A wholesaler might have even lower operating leverage, with fixed salaries a smaller proportion of total costs.

Operating risk (or *business risk*)— the risk inherent in the firm's commercial activities. Operating risk affects the variability of operating profits over time.

In an uncertain world, sales revenue is likely to vary over time and will be uncertain for any period in the future. Variable sales result in variable operating profits. Variability of operating profits over time, and uncertainty as to what future operating profits will be, is referred to as **operating risk,** or *business risk.* Chapter 4 discussed operating risk and its relation to financial risk. We can see from Figure 8–4 that operating leverage is an important determinant of operating risk. For any given level of variability of sales, the higher the operating leverage, the more variable is operating profit and, thus, the higher is the operating risk. We will find in later chapters that the degree of operating risk is an important consideration in formulating many financial policies.

Financial Leverage

Thus far, this chapter has focused on operating costs and operating profits, with interest excluded from consideration, in order to draw a distinction between *operating leverage* and *financial leverage*.

Operating leverage is determined by the firm's cost structure and, therefore, by the nature of the business. The firm's commercial strategy dictates the markets in which it operates and, therefore, the technology of its production and marketing operations and their resulting cost structures.

Financial leverage, on the other hand, is determined by the mix of debt and equity funds used to finance the firm's assets. We discussed financial leverage briefly in Chapter 4 and will return to this important concept later in this book.

Operating leverage is determined by the firm's cost structure and, therefore, by the nature of the firm's business. Financial leverage is determined by the mix of debt and equity funds used to finance the firm's assets.

Here we make only a few brief observations. If a company uses debt, interest is subtracted from operating profit to obtain net profit before taxes. The more debt a firm employs, the more interest it pays. Interest cost is fixed with respect to output and, therefore, is directly analogous to fixed operating costs. In the presence of financial leverage, a given change in operating profit produces a larger percentage change in net profit before taxes. The analogy with operating leverage is direct. The sensitivity of net profits before (and after) taxes to changes in sales, thus, depends on the combined effects of both operating and financial leverage. Operating leverage affects the sensitivity of operating profit to changes in sales. In turn, financial leverage affects the sensitivity of net profit before (and after) taxes to changes in operating profit.

Applications of Cost/Volume/Profit Analysis

Cost/volume/profit analysis has many applications. It is useful in making projections of cash flow and profits for the period ahead. It is also helpful in analyzing decisions regarding new products or decisions to expand or contract or drop existing products. Another application is in make-or-buy decisions. Break-even analysis also may be useful in decisions involving equipment selection and replacement, especially where fixed costs are being substituted for variable costs through automation. It may find use also in marketing decisions involving pricing, promotion and advertising, and distribution channels.

KEY CONCEPTS

1. Separating costs into fixed and variable components is necessary in order to calculate break-even volumes.

2. Operating leverage depends on the relationship between a firm's fixed and variable costs.

3. Financial leverage depends on the mix of debt and equity funds used to finance the firm's as-

sets. The greater the use of debt, the higher the financial leverage.

4. The sensitivity of profits after taxes to changes in sales depends on the combined effects of both operating leverage and financial leverage.

SUMMARY

Break-even analysis is a technique for examining the relationship between operating profit and sales volume. Its usefulness, however, is sometimes limited where costs cannot be separated into fixed and variable components or where joint costs are attributable to more than one product.

Operating leverage is the sensitivity of a firm's operating profit to changes in sales. The degree of

operating leverage of a firm is a function of its cost structure (the ratio of fixed to total operating costs) and, hence, is determined by the nature of its business. *Financial leverage*, the subject of Part Five of this book, depends on the mix of debt and equity used to finance the firm's assets.

QUESTIONS

1. Define the terms *fixed costs* and *variable costs*. Is a fixed cost constant over all ranges of output?
2. What are some of the limitations of break-even analysis?
3. Why would a firm's break-even point (BEP) for operating profit differ from its break-even point on a cash basis?
4. What is *operating leverage?* What causes operating leverage to be present in the firm? Give examples of types of businesses with relatively high or low operating leverage. Is the extent of operating leverage a management decision?
5. How does financial leverage differ from operating leverage? How is it similar?
6. What happens to the DOL as production and sales increase from the BEP? Decrease toward the BEP? Relate these changing DOLs to changes in the operating risk of the firm.

Problems

1. Able Corporation sells a single product for $30.00 with variable costs per unit of $18.00. If fixed costs are $3,000,000, calculate the break-even point in units. If fixed costs include $900,000 of noncash expenses (depreciation and amortization), what is the break-even point on a cash basis?
2. Using the data in problem 1 and graph paper, prepare a break-even chart following the format of Figure 8–3 in the text.
3. If we assume that the information given in problem 1 remains valid over all levels of output, would you expect the degree of operating leverage to remain constant over all levels of output? Calculate the degree of operating leverage at sales levels of 300,000 units and 400,000 units in order to answer the question. What does the DOL measure?
4. Assume the Able Corporation, referred to in problem 1, decides to automate its production process by replacing some of the manual production tasks with a robot. If fixed costs increase to $3,300,000 because of the added depreciation while variable costs decrease to $17 per unit because of the lower labor expense, what is the effect on the break-even point? What would be the effect on operating profit at an output of 400,000 units?

5. The Erie Manufacturing Company is determining its budget for 1989. There is some concern about expected profits. Three alternatives that may improve profits are being considered. The proposed budget, in thousands of dollars, is given in Table A on p. 244.

   a. Compute the break-even point using graph paper. Make a break-even chart. Check your answer arithmetically.
   b. Alternative 1 for improving profits requires a 5 percent increase in sales prices. Evaluate the impact on EBIT and the break-even point assuming the number of units sold is unchanged. Note the percentage change in EBIT.
   c. Alternative 2 would reduce fixed costs by 5 percent. Evaluate the effect on EBIT and the break-even point, assuming alternative 1 is not put into effect.
   d. Alternative 3 would reduce variable costs by 5 percent. Evaluate the effect on EBIT and the break-even point when neither alternative 1 nor alternative 2 is put into effect.

   Evaluate the effect on EBIT and the break-even point when all three alternatives are implemented simultaneously.

Table A

Sales (14,000,000 units at $1)		$14,000
Cost of goods sold		
Fixed	$5,325	
Variable	3,150	8,475
Gross margin		$ 5,525
Selling and general expenses		
Fixed	$2,800	
Variable	2,500	5,300
EBIT		$ 225

Table B

	Estimated Costs (dollars)		
	Current	Plan 1	Plan 2
Raw materials	440,000	390,000	265,000
Factory labor	615,000	500,000	215,000
Depreciation on fixed assets	800,000	980,000	1,257,500
Salary expense	640,000	700,000	775,000
Variable selling expense	70,600	72,012	70,600
Property taxes	36,000	45,000	63,000
Other fixed expenses	52,000	75,000	103,000

6. Competition in the small-kitchen-appliance industry has forced MorPower Appliance Company to consider two different product-line strategies. Plan 1 involves the elimination of two of the four existing food-processor models. This would result in decreased start-up and packaging costs. Plan 2 would retain all four models but would replace the current hand assembly of the three-piece body with a one-piece, injection-molded body. A large initial investment for the molds would pay off in the form of lower labor and material costs. The costs for the current sales volume and the projected costs of each plan are given in Table B.

The current annual sales level is about 60,000 units. Half of these are sold at $40 each and half at $60 each. Plan 1 would eliminate one $40 and one $60 model. It is expected that unit sales would remain at 60,000, with sales of the $40 model comprising 45 percent of unit sales. Management is primarily concerned with the relative riskiness of profits under each plan.

a. Compute the degree of operating leverage at current volume (60,000 units) for each of the three possibilities.
b. What is the effect on profit of a 5 percent decrease in dollar sales?

Rank the possibilities according to their degree of riskiness, as measured by operating leverage.

7. The income statement of Leigh Corporation for 1988 is given in Table C. Leigh plans an expansion of its production facilities to allow for projected sales of $20,000,000 (at $1 per unit) for

Table C

Sales (12,200,000 units at $1)	$12,200,000
Cost of sales	
Fixed	$ 3,910,000
Variable	4,240,000
Gross margin	4,050,000
Selling and general expenses	
Fixed	1,500,000
Variable	1,950,000
Income	$ 600,000

Table D

	(Thousands of dollars)
Advertising expense	275
Depreciation and insurance on plant	450
Interest expense	120
Fixed factory overhead	150
Salaries expense	500

1989. The expansion is expected to increase expenses by the amounts shown in Table D.

a. Prepare a projected income statement for the expected (1989) sales and expenses.

b. Compare break-even points at present (1988) and projected (1989) operating levels.

c. Compare profits before and after expansion if sales remain at the 1988 level.

REFERENCES

Levin, R. I., and C. A. Kirkpatrick. *Quantitative Approaches to Management*. 3rd ed. New York: McGraw-Hill, 1975, Chapter 2.

Chapter 9

Financial Planning

This chapter discusses techniques for developing and using financial plans and explains how to estimate requirements for funds using pro-forma analysis. The chapter examines different financing patterns, including seasonal and long-term growth patterns, and shows how to develop a cash budget. As we will see, financial plans can be used for communications and control in addition to decision making.

Chapters 6 and 7 were concerned primarily with analyzing past and current performance. The tools developed there, such as source-and-use analysis and ratio analysis, were diagnostic in purpose, and the orientation was mainly historical, although we noted that the same analytical tools could be applied to plans for the future as well.

Financial plan — describes in dollar terms the activities that the firm intends to engage in over some future period. An income statement and a balance sheet are key components of the financial plan.

Another task of financial management is to look ahead — *to plan*. In simplest terms, a **financial plan** is a statement of what is to be done in some future period and of effective ways of doing it. Why should a firm plan? Planning requires effort and, therefore, is not without cost. In an uncertain world, events are likely to deviate from even the most carefully formulated plan. Are the benefits of planning worth the cost? For most firms, planning of the type discussed in this chapter very definitely is worth the cost. A planning system improves coordination in an organization and encourages the kind of thinking that identifies difficulties before they occur. Many potential problems can be avoided and significant operating and financing economies achieved. A rather modest planning system usually will pay for itself many times over in terms of efficiency and lower costs.

Commercial strategy — the firm's definition of the products and services it will produce and the markets it will serve.

A complete planning system begins with a statement of the firm's basic goal or purpose. From this statement of purpose is derived the firm's **commercial strategy,** defining the products or services it will produce and the markets it will serve. Supporting policies then are developed in production, marketing, research and development, accounting, finance, and personnel. The extent to which the system is formalized with detailed planning and budgeting systems in each area depends in part on the firm's size and on the complexity of its operations. A planning system might be represented schematically as in Figure 9–1 on p. 248.

Financial planning — part of a larger planning process within an organization; the complete planning system begins at the highest policy level with the statement of the firm's key goal or purpose.

Financial planning can be viewed as the representation of an overall plan for the firm in financial terms. The basic elements of the financial plan are the *projected income statement* and the *projected balance sheet*. Supporting elements may include a cash budget, personnel budget, production budget, purchasing budget, income and expense budget, and so on. These may be prepared by various organizational units within the firm and may be stated in terms of dollars, physical units, or people. These detailed budgets represent time-phased schedules of the expenditures, people, materials, and activities required to accomplish the objectives set forth in the overall financial plan.

Operating plan — describes in detail the activities in which the firm plans to engage and consists of the sales, production, marketing, research-and-development, and personnel plans required to carry out the firm's commercial strategy.

The starting point for the financial-planning process is the firm's commercial strategy and the associated production, marketing, and research-and-development plans. We will refer to these plans collectively as the firm's **operating plan** because they describe the activities in which the firm plans to engage. Initially, we will take the operating plan as given, although later we will see that operating plans sometimes must be modified in light of financing implications. In addition to the operating plan, we will also take as given the firm's capital expenditure plan and its long-term liabilities. Decisions with respect to these areas are taken up later in this book.

Given the firm's plan for fixed assets, its long-term liabilities (such as mortgage loans), and its operating plan, our objective is to represent its plans in financial terms and at the same time to determine financing requirements. As our vehicle for discussion and illustration, we will leave our old friend, Sparta Manufacturing

Figure 9–1

An Example of a Firm's Financial Planning System

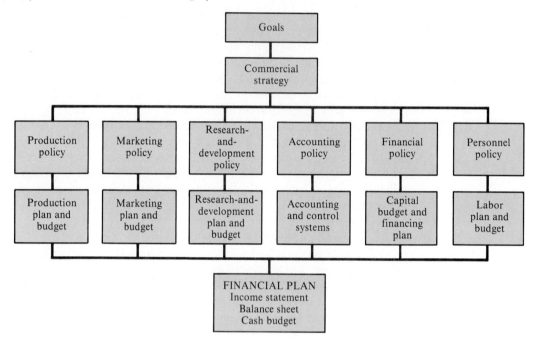

Table 9–1

Mercury Tool Company Income Statement, 1988

	Actual 1988 (thousands of dollars)
Sales	5,000
Cost of goods sold	3,350
Gross profit	1,650
Depreciation	260
Selling and administrative expense	600
Profit before taxes	790
Taxes @ 0.25	198
Profit after taxes	593
Dividends	240
Transfer to retained earnings	353

Table 9–2

Mercury Tool Company Balance Sheet, 1988

	Actual 1988 (thousands of dollars)
Cash	50
Accounts receivable	500
Inventory	1,100
Total current assets	1,650
Gross plant and equipment	4,960
less Accumulated depreciation	1,850
Net plant and equipment	3,110
Total assets	4,760
Notes payable — Bank	61
Other current liabilities	250
Mortgage loan	960
Net worth	3,489
Total liabilities and net worth	4,760

Company, and use a new firm, the Mercury Tool Company, Inc., a manufacturer of hand tools such as hammers, pliers, wrenches, and small manual drills. Financial statements for the year ending December 31, 1988, are given in Tables 9–1 and 9–2.

Seasonality — the annually recurring pattern of changes within a year.

Mercury's sales pattern was one of slow but steady growth, with little **seasonality.** More than 90 percent of sales were in standard products, and Mercury followed a policy of level production throughout the year. Financial statements for 1988 are given in Tables 9–1 and 9–2. As shown, the company has a mortgage on existing property of $960,000 and an outstanding bank loan of $61,000. Principal payments on the mortgage are $100,000 per year paid semiannually. The company has undertaken an expansion program that will require $500,000 in capital expenditures in 1989 and another $600,000 in 1990. In 1988 the company paid $240,000 in dividends and plans to continue the dividend payout at that level in 1989 and 1990.

Estimating Requirements for Funds

Mercury normally begins its annual planning cycle each October and develops a financial plan for the upcoming two years. For purposes of illustration, we will assume that the time is now early January 1989. Given Mercury's capital expenditure plan and its current mortgage loan of $960,000, what are the requirements for financing its operating plan over the next two years? Will additional outside financing, from the bank or elsewhere, be required? If so, how much, and when? When will it be repaid? The best way to answer such questions is to project the balance sheet to each date in question. The loan required to make the balance sheet balance is the answer to our question. The process requires painstaking work, but it is essential to good financial management.

The technique we will use often is referred to as **pro-forma analysis.** As used in finance, the term *pro forma* can be translated to mean "as if." Pro-forma analysis is projecting an income statement or balance sheet or cash budget into the future to depict the firm's financial condition *as if* certain prospective events—namely, a given sales and production plan—had taken place. The term *pro forma* usually pertains to projections, but the concept is equally applicable to current or prior periods. A pro-forma balance sheet could be constructed for some prior date depicting the state of affairs as if a prospective merger had taken place, or as if a particular division or subsidiary had been sold. Pro-forma analysis is a very useful concept, with applications beyond those discussed in this chapter.

Pro-forma analysis—the projection into the future or past of a firm's financial statements to depict a firm's financial condition *as if* certain prospective events (such as a given sales and production plan) had taken place.

Pro-Forma Statements: The Percentage-of-Sales Method

We have actual data for Mercury for 1988. The company anticipates that sales will grow by 8 percent over the next two years. This would produce sales of $5.4 million in 1989 and a little over $5.8 million in 1990. How do we go about estimating the income statement and balance sheet for 1989 and 1990? One widely used method is the **percentage-of-sales** method. In this approach the **sales plan** is the starting point and other key items are estimated as a percentage of the sales figure in each year. In many companies, the sales plan plays the critical role of providing the basis for the production levels, marketing programs, and a variety of activities within the firm. In a firm with good management controls, particularly on expenses, most of the uncertainty about future profits results from uncertainty about future sales. If actual sales deviate significantly from planned levels, the effects on the firm's financial condition are likely to be substantial.

Sales plan—the projection of sales into the future for a specified period; forms the basis for planning production levels, marketing programs, and other firm activities.

The sales plan plays a critical role in financial planning in many firms, forming the basis for other supporting plans.

Table 9–3 shows historical percentages of sales for key items in the income statement and balance sheet. As indicated, cost of goods sold (COGS) was 67 percent of sales in 1988. We can use this same percentage to estimate COGS in 1989 and 1990. It would be better to have several years of history and perhaps to take an *average* of the percentage in prior years. To keep things simple, we will use only the one year of history, 1988.

Table 9–3 shows that, in 1988, selling and administrative expense amounted to 12 percent of sales. Suppose sales are estimated to be $5.4 million in 1989. Let's use the 1988 data we have on COGS and S&A to estimate these figures for 1989:

		(Thousands of dollars)
Projected sales for 1989		5,400
Projected COGS	0.67 × sales	3,618
Projected S&A	0.12 × sales	1,648

Table 9–3

Mercury Tool Company Percentage of Sales for Key Items, 1988

	Actual 1988 (thousands of dollars)	*Percentage of Sales*
Sales	5,000	100
Cost of goods sold	3,350	67
Selling and administrative expense	600	12
Accounts receivable	500	10
Inventory	1,100	22
Other current liabilities	250	5

We will use the figures in Table 9–3 in projecting the pro-forma income statements and balance sheet using the percentage-of-sales method.

The percentage-of-sales method is useful in many situations, but not in all. If relationships are expected to change in the future, the method might be applicable, but the historical percentages might have to be modified. In other situations, a completely different method might be necessary. For example, in a company with a highly seasonal sales pattern with a lot of month-to-month variation, sometimes it is useful to project monthly income statements and balance sheets in order to estimate monthly financing requirements. In such a situation the percentage-of-sales method cannot be used to estimate accounts receivable and inventories. Receivables must be estimated by looking at anticipated sales and collections in each month, and the relationship to sales will vary over the year. Similarly, inventory must be estimated by looking at anticipated production rates and cost of goods sold.

Pro-Forma Income Statement

To construct pro-forma financial statements, one starts with the income statement: to do the balance sheet we need the transfer to retained earnings, and to get this we must use the profit-after-tax figure in the income statement.

Pro-forma income statement — an income statement constructed by projecting as if a certain sales and production plan had taken place.

We now have the information necessary to construct pro-forma financial statements for Mercury Tool Company for 1989 and 1990. It is necessary to begin with the **pro-forma income statement,** because in order to do the balance sheet we need the transfer to retained earnings, and to get this figure we must know the profit after tax (PAT). We will use the same format as in Table 9–1.

We begin with sales. The company estimates that sales will grow by 8 percent in each of the next two years, producing sales of $5,400,000 in 1989 and $5,832,000 in 1990. We then estimate COGS and selling and administrative expenses using the percentage-of-sales method, as described above. The two remaining items to be estimated in the income statement are depreciation and taxes. Depreciation we must estimate based on past history plus knowledge of the company's plans for capital expenditures in the future. From Table 9–1, we see that depreciation was $260,000 in 1988. Based on the planned new capital expenditures for 1989 and 1990 ($500,000 and $600,000, respectively), depreciation is estimated to be $300,000 in 1989 and $360,000 in 1990. Taxes are estimated at 25 percent of pretax profit (not exactly the actual rate applicable to a company of this size, but close enough for purposes of illustration). The complete pro-forma income statements are given in Table 9–4.

To get the transfer to retained earnings each month, we subtract dividends from PAT. Dividends normally are not included in the pro-forma income statement because they are not expenses, but we have shown them in Table 9–4 for convenience. This transfer to retained earnings will become an input to our pro-forma balance sheet.

Sample Problem 9–1

Developing a Pro-Forma Income Statement for Madison International

Prepare a pro-forma income statement for 1989 for Madison International assuming that (1) projected sales are $19.5 million, (2) the cost of goods sold is 58 percent of sales, (3) selling and administrative expenses are $2.5 million a year, (4) depreciation is $80,000 a month, (5) interest expense is $200,000 a year, and (6) the tax rate is 30 percent.

Solution

Madison International's completed pro-forma income statement for 1989 is given in Table 9–5.

Pro-Forma Balance Sheet

Our objective is to determine the amount of financing required to carry out the operating plan over the next two years. Our procedure will be to project all items in

Table 9–4

Mercury Tool Company Pro-Forma Income Statements, 1989–1990

	Actual	*Pro-Forma*	
	1988	*1989*	*1990*
		(thousands of dollars)	
Sales	5,000	5,400	5,832
Cost of goods sold	3,350	3,618	3,907
Gross profit	1,650	1,782	1,925
Depreciation	260	300	360
Selling and administrative expense	600	648	700
Profit before taxes	790	834	865
Taxes @ 0.25	198	209	216
Profit after taxes	593	625	649
Dividends	240	240	240
Transfer to retained earnings	353	385	409

Table 9–5

Madison International Pro-Forma Income Statement, 1989

Sales		$19,500,000
Cost of goods sold		11,310,000
Gross margin		$ 8,190,000
Selling and administrative expense	$2,500,000	
Depreciation ($80,000 × 12)	960,000	3,460,000
Earnings before interest and taxes (EBIT)		$ 4,730,000
Interest		200,000
Profit before taxes (PBT)		$ 4,530,000
Taxes		1,359,000
Net profit		3,171,000

the balance sheet other than the bank loan, leaving the loan as our balancing or "plug" figure. If the plug turns out to be positive, this will tell us how much additional financing is required. If it turns out to be negative, we will know that Mercury will have excess cash and will not have to borrow.

The items to be projected are determined either directly or indirectly by the operating plan or by external commitment (taxes and mortgage payments). We will proceed item by item to create a **pro-forma balance sheet,** using the format in Table 9–2.

We begin with cash. Mercury's treasurer believes that the $50,000 cash balance on hand on December 31, 1988, is the minimum balance needed for the company's operating needs. As our initial estimate for cash, we will use $50,000. The company believes that accounts receivable and inventories will maintain about the same relationship to sales in the future as in the past, so we can estimate these items using the percentage-of-sales method:

Pro-forma balance sheet — a balance sheet constructed by projecting the firm's financial condition as if a certain sales and production plan had taken place.

		(Thousands of dollars)	
		1989	1990
Projected sales		5,400	5,832
Projected AR	0.10 × sales	1,540	4,583
Projected INV	0.22 × sales	1,188	1,283

Plant and equipment should be estimated in a different way. Plant and equipment expenditures come in large "blocks," and we need to take account of the planned expenditures in each year. In 1989, the company plans capital expenditures of $500,000, and $600,000 in 1990. To project plant and equipment expenditures, we add the planned outlays in 1989 to gross plant and equipment at the end of 1988 to get gross plant and equipment at the end of 1989. Then we add planned depreciation for 1989 to accumulated depreciation at the end of 1988 to get accumulated depreciation at the end of 1989. Subtracting accumulated depreciation from gross plant and equipment gives net plant and equipment. The calculations are summarized below for 1989:

| | *(Thousands of dollars)* | | |
	Year-end 1988	Planned 1989	Year-end 1989
Gross plant and equipment	4,960	500	5,460
Accumulated depreciation	1,850	300	2,150
Net plant and equipment	3,110		3,310

Now we have estimated all major asset categories. Where will funds come from to finance these assets? As noted earlier, our procedure is to estimate everything except the bank loan, and to let the loan be the balancing or plug figure. Other liabilities we can estimate at 5 percent of 1989 sales, or $0.05 \times \$5,400,000 = \$270,000$. We know that the company pays $100,000 per year on its mortgage, so we can estimate the outstanding mortage loan balance as $960,000 − $100,000 = $860,000 at the end of 1989. Net worth we estimate as beginning net worth, plus profits, minus planned dividends, equals ending net worth, as follows:

	(Thousands of dollars)
Beginning net worth, 1989	3,489
plus estimated profits, 1989	1,625
minus planned dividends, 1989	1,240
Ending net worth, 1989	3,874

Now we are ready to calculate the plug figure. Assets and liabilities estimated thus far for 1989 are summarized below:

	(Thousands of dollars) 1989
Assets required	
Cash	50
Accounts receivable	540
Inventory	1,188
Net plant and equipment	3,310
Total assets	5,088
Financing provided	
Other current liabilities	270
Mortgage loan	860
Net worth	3,874
Total	5,004
BALANCING (PLUG) FIGURE	84

This tells us that we need $5,088,000 in operating assets by the end of 1989, but will have financing for only $5,004,000. The shortfall is $84,000, which Mercury plans to borrow from the bank. The complete balance sheets for 1989 and 1990 are given in Table 9–6. The balancing figure in 1990 is shown to be $131,000. Thus, in order to finance its operating plan, Mercury must increase its bank borrowing from $61,000 at the end of 1988, to $84,000 at the end of 1989, and further, to $131,000 at the end of 1990. If the balancing figures had been negative, it would have meant that Mercury would not need to borrow, but instead would have excess cash above the $50,000 minimum working-cash balance.

Sample Problem 9–2
Developing a Pro-Forma Balance Sheet for Madison International

Madison International's balance sheet for December 31, 1988, is shown in Table 9–7 on p. 256. Use the information from Sample Problem 9–1 plus the data in Table 9–7 to construct a December 31, 1989, pro-forma balance sheet (round off all numbers to the nearest thousand). Assume that:

1. The collection period for accounts receivable is 61 days, and all sales are on credit.
2. Inventory turnover is projected to be 6.5 times.
3. Dividends of $1.5 million will be paid on December 31, 1989.
4. Accrued labor expense is expected to be $950,000, and taxes payable will be $800,000.

Table 9–6
Mercury Tool Company Pro-Forma Balance Sheets, 1989–1990

	Actual 1988	Pro-Forma 1989	Pro-Forma 1990
		(thousands of dollars)	
Cash	50	50	50
Accounts receivable	500	540	583
Inventory	1,100	1,188	1,283
Total current assets	1,650	1,778	1,916
Gross plant and equipment	4,960	5,460	6,060
less Accumulated depreciation	1,850	2,150	2,510
Net plant and equipment	3,110	3,310	3,550
Total assets	4,760	5,088	5,466
Notes payable — Bank (Plug)	61	84	131
Other current liabilities	250	270	292
Mortgage loan	960	860	760
Net worth	3,489	3,874	4,283
Total liabilities and net worth	4,760	5,088	5,466

Table 9–7
Madison International Balance Sheet, December 31, 1988

Assets		
Cash		$2,290,000
Accounts receivable		2,850,000
Inventory		1,900,000
Total current assets		$7,040,000
Gross plant and equipment	$6,400,000	
Less accumulated depreciation	−3,860,000	
Net plant and equipment		2,540,000
Total assets		**$9,580,000**
Liabilities and net worth		
Accounts payable	$1,100,000	
Accrued labor	870,000	
Taxes payable	760,000	
Total current liabilities		$2,730,000
Bonds at 10 percent		2,000,000
Common stock		1,500,000
Retained earnings		3,350,000
Total liabilities and net worth		**$9,580,000**

5. Purchases equal 75 percent of the cost of goods sold, and the company's payment period is expected to be 36.5 days.
6. No changes are expected in the common-stock account, in the plant-and-equipment account, or in bonds.

Solution
The accounts on the balance sheet can be calculated one item at a time.

1. The collection period for accounts receivable is 61 days, which is ⅙ of a year, and sales are $19.5 million. Therefore, the ending balance for accounts receivable is $19.5 million/6 = $3.25 million.
2. With turnover of 6.5 times, and cost of goods sold equaling $11,310,000, the average inventory during 1989 will be $11,310,000/6.5 = $1,740,000. With beginning inventory equal to $1,900,000, ending inventory will be ($1,740,000 × 2) − $1,900,000 = $1,580,000.
3. The gross amount for plant and equipment will not change, but the net amount will be $960,000 less than in 1988 due to 1988 depreciation; that is, $2,540,000 − $960,000 = $1,580,000.
4. Because purchases equal 75 percent of the cost of goods sold, or $8,482,500, ending accounts payable equals purchases per day times 36.5 days purchases outstanding, or ($8,482,500/365) × 36.5 = $848,000 (rounded).
5. Accrued labor and taxes payable are given as $950,000 and $800,000.

Table 9–8

Madison International Pro-Forma Balance Sheet, December 31, 1989

Assets		
Cash	$4,709,000	
Accounts receivable	3,250,000	
Inventory	1,580,000	
Total current assets		$ 9,539,000
Gross plant and equipment	6,400,000	
Less accumulated depreciation	−4,820,000	
Net plant and equipment		1,580,000
Total assets		$11,119,000
Liabilities and net worth		
Accounts payable	$1,848,000	
Accrued labor	950,000	
Taxes payable	800,000	
Total current liabilities		$ 2,598,000
Bonds at 10 percent		2,000,000
Common stock		1,500,000
Retained earnings		5,021,000
Total liabilities and net worth		$11,119,000

6. Bonds will remain at $2 million.
7. Common stock will remain at $1.5 million.
8. Retained earnings will be $3,350,000 (beginning balance) + $3,171,000 (earnings) − $1,500,000 (dividends) = $5,021,000.
9. Cash can be calculated by finding the value that will balance the balance sheet. The completed pro-forma balance sheet is given in Table 9–8.

Pro-Forma Source-and-Use-of-Funds Statement

A source-and-use statement quickly reveals any changes in balance-sheet relationships resulting from the financial plan.

Following procedures discussed in Chapter 6, we can construct a source-and-use statement for the years 1989–1990, as shown in Table 9–9 on p. 258.

A source-and-use statement quickly reveals any changes in balance-sheet relationships resulting from the financial plan. Although it is not always necessary in connection with a financial plan, a source-and-use analysis sometimes reveals aspects of the plan that are not otherwise apparent.

The Cash Budget of Receipts and Disbursements

As noted above, the pro-forma balance sheet for 1989 shows that bank borrowing must rise from $61,000 at year-end 1988 to $84,000 by year-end 1989. What goes on *during* 1989? The annual pro-formas shed no light on this question. We could

Table 9—9

Mercury Tool Company Sources and Uses of Funds, Pro-Forma, 1989–1990 (thousands of dollars)

	1989	1990
Sources		
Increase in bank loan	23	47
Increase in other current liabilities	20	22
Profits	625	649
Depreciation	300	360
Total sources	968	1,078
Uses		
Increase accounts receivable	40	43
Increase inventory	88	95
Capital expenditures	500	600
Mortgage loan payment	100	100
Dividends	240	240
Total uses	968	1,078
Increase in cash balance	0	0

Budget—a time-phased schedule of activities, events, or transactions, usually in dollar terms.

Cash budget—a time-phased schedule of cash receipts and disbursements.

do monthly pro-forma statements to see what happens, but another helpful technique we could use is called the *cash budget*.

The cash budget is one of several specialized supporting components of the overall financial plan. Others include the advertising budget, the materials budget, the capital-expenditures budget, the income-and-expense budget by organizational unit, and so on. A **budget** is simply a time-phased schedule of activities or events or transactions, usually in dollar terms. A budget can be prepared for any activity of the firm to describe exactly what is to be done and when.

The **cash budget** is a time-phased schedule of cash receipts and disbursements. Its primary purpose is to provide control of cash at a level of detail not possible with the balance sheet alone. With a complete schedule of all planned receipts and disbursements, deviations from the plan can be detected promptly and the reasons for the deviations can be ascertained. The balance sheet will tell us when cash levels are higher or lower than planned; the cash budget will pinpoint the reason for the variance.

The cash budget is similar to the income statement in that it is constructed in flow terms and describes activities that are to take place during some specified period of time. It differs from the income statement in that it includes *cash items only* and is prepared on a cash basis, whereas the income statement is prepared on an accrual basis. The criterion for deciding whether a particular item belongs in the cash budget is whether it affects the cash balance. If it goes into the cash drawer or is deposited to the checking account, or if a check is written for it, then it goes in the cash budget. Depreciation has no place in a cash budget, nor do other noncash charges or accruals of any sort, revenue or expense. Only *cash received* or *cash disbursed* is taken into account.

Preparing the Cash Budget

We will now prepare a cash budget for Mercury Tool Company, Inc. Whereas we did the income statement and balance sheet for annual periods, we will do the cash budget for *each month* of 1989. Looking first at cash *receipts,* we see that the only receipts in this case will come from collection of accounts receivable and increases in the bank loan. We will handle the bank loan as a balancing figure to maintain the cash balance at the appropriate figure.

In the balance sheet, we were concerned with estimating accounts receivable. In the cash budget, we are concerned with *collection* of those receivables. We saw earlier that Mercury's accounts receivable average 10 percent of sales. Days sales outstanding for 1989 then equals

$$\text{DSO} = \frac{\text{Accounts receivable}}{\text{Sales per day}}$$

$$= \frac{\$540,000}{\$5,400,000/365}$$

$$= 36.5 \text{ days}.$$

This means that, on average, Mercury's customers take 36.5 days to pay. We can look at the problem as if, each day, Mercury collects sales made 36.5 days earlier. Daily sales = $5,400,000/365 = $14,794.52. Collecting that much each day means that, in a month (which averages 30.42 days), the company collects $450,000. So, assuming that sales don't vary month to month (a simplifying assumption that will not hold in many cases in practice, but is acceptable here for purposes of illustration), Mercury's collections will run $450,000 per month for March through December of 1989.

For January and February, collections will be lower because sales were lower in 1988, and collections lag sales by over one month. It takes a little arithmetic to figure it out, but collections in January will run $417,000, and in February $443,000. These are the figures that appear for collections in the cash budget, Table 9–10.

There is an important relationship between collections, sales, and receivables. If you know any two, you can calculate the third. They are related as follows:

	(Thousands of dollars)
Receivables 12/31/88	500
plus January sales	450
minus January collections	417
equals Receivables 1/31/89	533

Similarly, February month-end receivables will be $533 + 450 − 443 = $540. Thus, as sales increase in 1989, receivables also increase from $500,000 at the end of 1988 to $540,000 by the end of February. Since we are assuming that sales are steady at $450,000 per month for the balance of 1989, receivables will remain at that level through December.

Disbursements

Now let us focus on *cash disbursements*. Payments must be made each month for a large number of items, including raw materials, labor, selling and administrative (S&A) expense, and so on. Most firms use **accrual** accounting, and payments for supplies or labor often take place after the expense is actually incurred. For example, a firm may order raw materials in January, use them in February, and pay for them in March. Under accrual accounting, the expense shows up in the income statement when the materials are used. The cash budget, however, shows the *payment* for the materials. In general, payments in the cash budget lag behind expenses in the income statement for firms using accrual accounting (for firms on "cash basis" accounting, expenses and payments are one and the same).

Dealing with all these time lags gets a bit complicated, so here we will make some simplifying assumptions. We will assume that Mercury pays for materials and labor in the month they are used. For materials and labor that make up cost of goods sold, we can calculate the monthly payment by looking at cost of goods sold for the year. However, we must adjust for the fact that inventories are going to increase during 1989 from $1,100,000 to $1,188,000, an increase of $88,000. So production for the year must equal COGS, $3,618,000 (see Table 9–4), *plus* $88,000, or a total of $3,706,000. Dividing this by 12 gives $3,706,000/12 = $308,833 per month in materials and labor. We will round this off to $309,000, and this is our monthly payment for manufacturing materials and labor in the cash budget (in Table 9–10, we use $309,000 for ten months and $308,000 for the final two months to give the correct total, $3,706,000, for the year).

Selling and administrative expense is projected at $648,000 for 1989 (Table 9–4), or $54,000 per month. Again, we will simplify things by assuming that payments are made in the same month as the expense is incurred. So we have $54,000 per month for S&A in the cash budget.

Plant and equipment expenditures, tax payments, mortgage payments, and dividend payments are not made each month, but only in particular months. Plant and equipment expenditures are scheduled for $250,000 in January and again in February. Mortgage payments are scheduled to be made in June and December, $50,000 each. Dividend payments are made quarterly in March, June, September, and December, $60,000 each.

Tax payments are a bit more complicated. The tax liability for the year is $209,000, and the Internal Revenue Service requires that payments of estimated taxes be made in advance. But not all of the $209,000 needs to be paid in 1989. Note that "other current liabilities" on the pro-forma balance sheet (Table 9–6) is projected to increase by $20,000 during 1989. To simplify matters, let's assume that all of this $20,000 increase is in taxes payable — in other words, that taxes payable increase by $20,000 during the year. This would mean that only $189,000 in tax payments would be made during the year, and the remaining $20,000 of the $209,000 would be added to taxes payable and paid sometime in 1990. Dividing

Table 9–10

Mercury Tool Company Cash Budget by Month, 1989 (thousands of dollars)

	JAN	FEB	MAR	APR	MAY	JUN	JUL	AUG	SEP	OCT	NOV	DEC
Ending accounts receivable	533	540	540	540	540	540	540	540	540	540	540	540
Receipts												
Collection of accounts receivable	417	443	450	450	450	450	450	450	450	450	450	450
Disbursements												
Manufacturing materials and labor	309	309	309	309	309	309	309	309	309	309	308	308
Selling and administrative expense	54	54	54	54	54	54	54	54	54	54	54	54
Plant and equipment	250	250										
Tax payments				47		47			47			48
Mortgage principal						50						50
Dividends	—	—	60	—	—	60	—	—	60	—	—	60
Total disbursements	613	613	423	410	363	520	363	363	470	363	362	520
Receipts *minus* Disbursements	(196)	(170)	27	40	87	(70)	87	87	(20)	87	88	(70)
Beginning cash	50	50	50	50	50	50	50	50	50	50	50	50
plus Loan increase	196	170	(27)	(40)	(87)	70	(87)	(87)	20	(87)	(88)	70
Ending cash	50	50	50	50	50	50	50	50	50	50	50	50
Ending loan	257	427	400	360	273	343	256	169	189	102	14	84

the $189,000 by 4 gives $47,250 to be made in four payments in April, June, September, and December. We will use $47,000 for the first three payments and $48,000 for the final payment to give the correct total, $189,000, for the year.

The complete cash budget is shown in Table 9–10. As shown, disbursements total $613,000 in January and February, dropping to $423,000 in March, and so on. The "Receipts — Disbursements" line shows the cash surplus or (deficit) each month. As shown, large deficits are run in January and February, followed by surpluses in March, April, and May, another deficit in June, and so on.

Since the working-cash balance must be maintained at $50,000, there is no excess cash to draw down. This means that any deficit each month must be financed by increasing the bank loan. The bank loan increase therefore equals "receipts minus disbursements." Thus the bank loan starts out the year at $61,000 (the 12/31/88 figure in Table 9–2) and increases by $196,000 in January to $257,000 by the end of that month, and then by another $170,000 in February to $427,000. The loan then declines over the next three months to $273,000 by the end of May, back up some in June, down again in July, and so on. By the end of December, the loan has been paid down to $84,000, which matches (as it must) the figure in the pro-forma balance sheet for year-end 1988 (Table 9–6).

The cash budget gives us some very valuable information. Looking only at the pro-forma annual balance sheets in Table 9–6, one might conclude that the bank loan need only increase gradually from $61,000 at year-end 1988 to $84,000 by year-end 1989. Not so. The cash budget shows that the loan must increase dramatically in January and February and that *total borrowing of $427,000* will be needed. This is absolutely critical information for negotiating the loan with the bank. The bank needs to know how much is required and when. The cash budget provides the answer.

The same answer also could be provided by monthly pro-forma balance sheets. Leaving the bank loan as the "plug" figure, the balance sheet would show exactly the same loan total required at the end of each month as shown in the cash budget. Sometimes a pro-forma balance sheet actually may be easier to construct in a firm that uses accrual accounting. The cash budget, however, provides additional useful details about the timing of cash payments.

In this case, the only receipts were collections of accounts receivable and borrowings from the bank; the latter appear toward the end of Table 9–10 rather than under "Receipts." In other situations, other types of receipts may be encountered. Some part of a firm's sales may be for cash, although sales by Mercury Tool Company were all for credit. Fixed assets sometimes are sold, in which case the proceeds are treated as a receipt and any change in tax payments is treated as an increase or decrease in disbursements for taxes. Cash discounts received on purchases are sometimes treated as a receipt. Finally, proceeds of any issues of long-term securities by the firm—stock or long-term debt—should be included as receipts.

Relationships of Cash Budget to Other Pro-Forma Statements

It is important to base all projected financial statements on a single *consistent* set of assumptions.

The cash budget, the pro-forma income statement, and the pro-forma balance sheet are all interdependent.

We noted above that if a pro-forma balance sheet is done by month, the ending cash and loan figures in the cash budget should match those in the balance sheet and that the collections figure must be consistent with the sales and receivables figures. It is apparent that the cash budget, the pro-forma income statement, and the pro-forma balance sheet are all interdependent. With consistent assumptions and accurate preparation, all the figures will mesh. If they do not, an error exists somewhere. Errors often become apparent when the ending cash and loan figures are calculated in the cash budget and the figures do not match those in the balance sheet. The cash and loan figures constitute our controls in preparing the statements.

A cash budget can be prepared to cover any time period. In the case of Mercury Tool Company, we prepared a monthly cash budget covering the entire year. In practice, Mercury might prepare a cash budget for only those months in which the loan is high and control of cash is most critical. At other times during the year, the pro-forma balance sheet, coupled with an income-and-expense budget, might provide adequate control. Firms with especially acute cash shortages may find it useful to prepare a cash budget by week or even by day. Firms that employ detailed income-and-expense budgets by organizational units may find a cash budget unnecessary.

Using the Financial Plan

The pro-forma income statement, the pro-forma balance sheet, and the cash budget constitute the basic elements of the firm's financial plan. Some of the uses of the financial plan are apparent from the discussion thus far. Here we will elaborate a bit.

Planning

Planning, essentially, is making decisions in advance about what is to be done in the future. As a plan is developed, decisions are made. Hence, the very process of developing the plan yields a major part of the overall benefits, regardless of what is done with the final product.

Development of a financial plan requires good coordination and communication throughout the firm. To support the sales plan, programs and budgets are developed in production, marketing, personnel, and finance. During the process, the feasibility of alternative operating plans can be examined. Performance measures, such as those discussed in Chapter 7, can be applied, and judgments can be made as to the plan's acceptability with respect to **profitability**, return on investment, inventory and receivables management, liquidity, and debt coverage. The feasibility of obtaining financing can be ascertained. Where necessary, the operating plan can be modified, and performance and feasibility tests can be applied again. Sometimes a firm may find it desirable to develop one or more alternative plans to allow for certain outcomes. To deal with uncertainty, a firm might develop one set of plans representing the most favorable set of circumstances and another representing the least favorable.

The amounts, timing, and nature of the financing requirement can be determined from the financial plan. Appropriate sources of funds can be selected, and borrowing and repayment schedules can be prepared. Chapter 21 will discuss sources of short-term and intermediate financing in more detail.

Besides providing a record of decisions made, the financial plan has other important uses.

Communications

One such use is in communications with outside parties, including investors and other suppliers of funds. After the management of Mercury Tool Company completes the financial plan, we can imagine the financial vice-president going to the bank to negotiate the loan arrangement for 1989. The plan contained in Tables 9–4, 9–6, and 9–10 would be discussed in detail with the loan officer. The vice-president would be able to tell the loan officer exactly how much money Mercury needs, when it is needed, how it will be used, and when and how the bank will be repaid.

Contrast the above bargaining session with one in which a potential borrower approaches a bank for a loan without a detailed financial plan. The borrower is unable to be specific with respect to how much, when it is needed, how it will be used, and when and how it will be repaid.

By coming to the bargaining table equipped with a comprehensive financial plan, a firm's management sends an important message to the supplier of funds: "This management is in control of its business and knows what it is doing." Lenders and investors like to do business with such firms. The specific numbers

---

Because developing a plan necessitates the making of decisions, the very process of developing a plan yields a major part in the overall benefits of financial planning.

Profitability — profits per dollar of sales.

Sometimes financing requirements may become a constraint on the operating plan or may necessitate modification of the plan.

The final product of the financial-planning process is a description in financial terms of what the firm intends to accomplish over the period of time in question.

In practice, it is often necessary to formulate an operating plan, then calculate its financing requirement, and then determine whether the financing is feasible.

The financial plan is used to communicate with outside parties, including investors and other suppliers of funds such as banks.

can be less important to the supplier of funds than the fact that a comprehensive plan has been developed.

By coming in with a plan, a firm's management is likely to gain a psychological advantage in the bargaining process. A feeling of confidence in the firm may lead the lender to assign a lower risk and, therefore, a lower interest rate to the loan. Thus, an important use of the financial plan is as a communications device.

Control

Control — making the plan come true.

The financial plan also is useful for purposes of **control** — that is, for seeing that the plans in fact are carried out. We should not allow the precise appearance of the numbers in Tables 9–4, 9–6, and 9–10 to lead us to forget about uncertainty. The elements of the plan that depend directly or indirectly on revenue and expense estimates are subject to uncertainty. Usually, the plan represents our best guess as to the most likely set of outcomes, or the outcomes that management hopes to achieve. Deviations above or below the plan are bound to occur and should be expected. When they do occur, we want to find out immediately and determine the reasons.

Most management-control systems are based on comparisons of actual data versus plans. Such comparisons can be made at any level of detail and with any frequency. Expense-control systems often compare actual versus plan data on a monthly basis. In decentralized firms, reporting systems using computers often are designed to provide information by organizational unit in a timely manner. Subordinate managers are able to identify problems quickly in their own areas of responsibility.

For the firm as a whole, progress against the operating plan can be monitored using the consolidated pro-forma income statement and pro-forma balance sheet. Each month, or each quarter, actual income statements and balance sheets are compared to the plan, item by item, and deviations are calculated. The effects of a deviation from the sales plan will be seen in accounts receivable, inventories, cash, the bank loan (if any), profits, tax accruals, and perhaps other areas. Sometimes it is useful to examine deviations in a source-and-use format, categorizing balance-sheet changes as providing or using more or less funds than planned.

By comparing actual versus plan data at frequent intervals, deviations can be detected and corrective action taken.

By comparing actual versus plan data at frequent intervals, deviations can be detected as events unfold, and corrective action can be taken in a timely manner. The control system tells management that things are off track and identifies the problem areas. Production schedules can be modified, advertising budgets increased or decreased, collection efforts intensified, or expenses cut. As a control device, pro-forma financial statements are very useful. Indeed, there is no way of achieving good control without them.

Applicability of Financial-Planning Techniques

The financial-planning techniques discussed in this chapter are applicable to any type of business firm, regardless of its line of business. Pro-forma financial statements are always useful and usually necessary to the successful operation of any

International Focus

Exporting Hondas to Japan

On March 7, 1988, the Honda Motor Company did something interesting: it shipped a load of Honda Accord automobiles to Japan. What made it interesting was the fact that the cars were manufactured in Marysville, Ohio. Honda has a plant in Marysville, and this shipment marked the first time a Japanese firm had ever manufactured a car in the United States and shipped it to Japan for sale. A Chrysler executive quipped that the Japanese would be obliged to pitch American quality in selling the cars.

U.S. automobile manufacturers have tried for years to sell cars in Japan, with little success. The "big three" U.S. manufacturers taken together have sold only a few thousand cars annually in Japan, partly because they have no dealer networks there and partly because their products have not been competitive. Other foreign manufacturers also have had little success. In 1987, only 2.7 percent of the 3.3 million automobiles sold in Japan were imported, versus almost one-third imports in the United States.

The Honda shipment is part of a new Japanese program to encourage sale of American goods in Japan. Honda staged the event for maximum public relations impact, holding flashy ceremonies and press conferences on the ship's departure and on its arrival in Japan. The United States agrees with the objective of increasing exports to Japan. In 1987, the United States ran a trade deficit of $60 billion with Japan (i.e., Japan sold $60 billion more in goods and services here than U.S. companies sold in Japan), $22 billion of which was in automobiles. Toyota alone sold $11.5 *billion* worth of automobiles and trucks in the United States in that year.

Cars are not the only thing the big Japanese automobile manufacturers are exporting from the United States back to Japan. After delivering a load of automobiles to the United States, Honda for some time has been filling its ships for the return voyage with a variety of American products, including aluminum scrap, soybeans, hay, small aircraft, and cattle. The Honda Motor Company, in fact, was the largest U.S. exporter of live cattle to Japan in 1987. Along with Honda, Toyota and Mazda also are exporting U.S. goods back to Japan. The value of these export goods currently runs to $100–200 million or so for each company, small in relation to the total U.S. trade deficit with Japan of $60 billion, but a step in the right direction.

Source: John Bussey, "Japanese Auto Makers Are Buying American," *The Wall Street Journal*, March 7, 1988.

business, whether it is a manufacturer, a retailer, a wholesaler, a service establishment, or a financial institution. Any firm is likely to benefit from the process of developing a plan — from the improvement in internal communications, the requirement to think ahead and anticipate problems, the discipline of having to be specific, and the commitment to carry out the plan once it has been formulated. The appropriate level of detail and sophistication will vary widely from one situation to another, as will procedures and the format for organizing and presenting information. The planning system appropriate for an appliance retailer will differ markedly from that appropriate for a manufacturer or a commercial bank. All, however, are likely to benefit from a financial-planning system of some sort.

Is the usefulness of financial planning confined to profit-making enterprises? Nonprofit organizations also must plan and make decisions. Such organizations sometimes have no revenues, but nearly always have expenses and expenditures. A pro-forma income statement may not be applicable, but a pro-forma balance sheet and expense budget usually are. A cash budget often is very useful. Hospitals, schools, churches, and charitable organizations do not earn profits, but they do expend resources, handle large amounts of money, and invariably require financing. Although the procedures and details may differ, the basic techniques of financial planning and controls are just as applicable to such organizations as they are to business firms.

> Nonprofit organizations must plan and make decisions because they, like profit-making enterprises, typically have both expenditures and receipts.

Long-Range Financial Planning

Thus far we have discussed financial planning over the relatively near term, only as far as two years into the future. We took the commercial strategy and long-term asset/liability structure of Mercury Tool Company as given. Our emphasis was on the operating and financing necessary to support the longer-term strategy.

Commercial Strategy

Over the long run, the firm's *commercial strategy* is not fixed. A major purpose of long-range planning is to examine alternative commercial strategies and to select the one most appropriate to the firm's overall goals. Should Mercury Tool Company begin manufacturing a line of electric power tools such as drills and saws? Such products are related to the hand tools now being manufactured, but different manufacturing and marketing skills are required. What about diversifying into much larger machine tools such as lathes and drill presses? Such questions have long-range strategic implications, and the answers determine the nature of the business. The firm's prosperity and survival depend on wise choices by management in these areas, and mistakes can be very costly.

The purposes of long-range planning, thus, differ from those of short-range planning. More emphasis is placed on analysis of alternatives and decision making and less on communications and control. To draw an analogy, the focus is on deciding the ship's course rather than on tuning the engine for optimal fuel economy.

> Long-range planning differs from short-range planning in that more emphasis is placed on analysis of alternatives and on decision making, and less on communications and control.

Long-range financial planning plays the same role in formulating commercial strategy that short-range financial planning does in formulating the operating plan. The financing requirements of alternative commercial strategies are examined, performance measures are applied, financing feasibility is examined, sources of financing are investigated, and the strategy is modified if necessary. The final product, as before, is a description in financial terms of what the firm intends to accomplish over the period in question.

Over the long run, the firm's long-term asset/liability structure is not given. An important part of the long-range planning process is to develop the long-term **investment plan** necessary to execute the firm's commercial strategy. What products is the firm to offer? What kind of manufacturing process is to be used? What facilities are needed? What equipment is appropriate? Decisions of this sort involve acquisition of assets with long lives. Alternatives often involve complex patterns of cash flows spread over many time periods. Techniques for analyzing such investment decisions will be our principal concern in Part Four.

Investment plan—the set of decisions a firm makes about what products to produce, what manufacturing process to use, and what plant and equipment will be required as these questions relate to the acquisition of assets.

Preparing the Long-Range Financial Plan

Given a commercial strategy and its associated long-term investment plan, the approach to financial planning is essentially the same as that used for Mercury Tool Company in the short run. The basic technique is pro-forma analysis, with the income statement and balance sheet again used as the basic planning vehicles. As before, the sales plan is the critical element, and financing requirements are determined by the commercial strategy and operating plan.

Uncertainty is usually greater over long time periods than over short periods. Some random elements may average out, but new elements of uncertainty enter. Consumer preferences change, new technologies develop, costs change, competition emerges, and entire industries rise and fall.

Given these greater uncertainties, different techniques are necessary for projecting sales and other uncertain elements of a long-range plan. Long-term trends and historical relationships between firm variables and general economic variables become more important. An economist may be better equipped to forecast sales over long periods than a sales manager. Sales of color television sets, for example, are likely to depend more on population and per-capita income in the long run than on advertising and sales effort. Statistical techniques, such as correlation and regression analysis, may be useful in developing sales-forecasting models. The economic technique of *input/output analysis* may be useful. Techniques of demand analysis, marketing research, and in-depth studies of markets may be appropriate in evaluating new products. Finally, computer-assisted planning models can be very useful in applying all of the approaches.

Once the long-range sales and production plans and other elements of the operating plan are determined, financing requirements can be evaluated. Over the long run, financing choices are much wider than before, and the decisions are more difficult. The appropriate mix of debt and equity must be determined, depending on the nature of the firm's business. The firm must choose between internal and external sources and, thereby, set its dividend policy. Once the appropriate debt policy is determined, a choice must be made with respect to maturity or the appropriate mix of short-term versus long-term debt. Where outside financing is necessary, a plan must be developed that indicates the types and amounts of securities to be sold and the timing of the issues. These difficult questions of long-term financing policy will occupy us in later chapters.

Over the long run, financing choices are much wider than in the short run, and decisions are more difficult.

KEY CONCEPTS

1. Financial planning is part of a larger planning process that begins with corporate strategy and includes planning all phases of the business.
2. Pro-forma analysis is a useful technique for evaluating the effects of actions before the actions are taken.
3. The operating plan is a description of what the company intends to do, with emphasis on sales and production.

4. Pro-forma financial statements (income statement, balance sheet, and cash budget) are determined essentia   by the operating plan. The financial statemeนts are a financial representation of the activities the firm intends to carry out.
5. The financial plan is very useful as a communications device both inside and outside the company and as a control device against which actual performance can be measured.

SUMMARY

Planning is a major function of management. Financial planning is a part of the larger planning process within an organization. The basic elements of the financial plan are the income statement and the balance sheet. The starting point is the operating plan, which describes the activities in which the firm intends to engage. In developing short-term financial plans that cover a 12- to 24-month horizon, the operating plan and the long-term asset/liability structure are taken as given. The objective of the planning process is to represent the operating plan in financial terms and to determine short-term financing requirements.

The pro-forma (projected) balance sheet is the basic tool for estimating funds requirements. A standard approach is to project all items of the balance sheet except cash and the bank loan, which are left as balancing figures. The figure that brings the balance sheet into balance is the required loan or, alternatively, the excess cash balance. To project the balance sheet, the income statement must be projected first in order to provide the transfer to retained earnings. The operating plan (sales plan, production plan, and expenditures for plant, equipment, materials, labor, overhead, marketing, research and development, and administration) provides the basis for the income projection. The operating plan also determines the levels of current

operating assets and liabilities (working-cash balance, accounts receivable, inventories, accounts payable, and various accrual accounts). Projection of these items along with the addition to retained earnings and long-term assets and liabilities (taken as given) completes the balance sheet. Once the balance sheet has been projected, a pro-forma source-and-use statement can be prepared if necessary. In general, the sales plan is of central importance in financial planning because of the effect of sales on many income-statement and balance-sheet items.

The cash budget is one of several specialized supporting components of the financial plan and consists of a time-phased schedule of cash receipts and expenditures. Its purpose is to control cash at a level of detail not possible with the pro-forma balance sheet alone. With consistent assumptions, all figures in the cash budget, in the pro-forma income statement, and in the pro-forma balance sheet will mesh.

A major benefit of financial planning is the process of preparing the plan itself because, once prepared, the plan is very useful for communicating with outside parties, especially suppliers of funds. It is also useful as a control device for monitoring the firm's progress in executing the plan. Financial planning is essential not only for business firms but also for nonprofit organizations.

QUESTIONS

1. How does financial planning fit into a larger planning process within a firm?
2. Why are the sales and production plans so important to financial planning?
3. What are the basic assumptions employed when using the percentage-of-sales method for financial planning?
4. In a rapidly growing firm, sales and assets often grow faster than net worth. What is the likely result if this situation continues?

5. What is the relationship between operating plans and financing requirements?
6. What is a cash budget? What is the criterion for determining what goes into a cash budget?
7. What is the relationship of the cash budget to the pro-forma income statement and to the pro-forma balance sheet?
8. What are the major uses of the financial plan?

Problems

(* Denotes more challenging problems.)

1. The 1988 average balance sheet of Hawk Corp. is listed below.

Hawk Corp. Average Monthly Balance Sheet, 1988

Current Assets	$100,000	Current Liabilities (accruals and payables)	$ 75,000
Net Fixed Assets	300,000	Stockholders' Equity	325,000
Total Assets	$400,000	Total Liabilities and Equity	

a. Sales were $800,000 in 1988. Using the balance-sheet figures above, calculate the percent of sales of current assets, fixed assets, total assets, and current liabilities. Mark to the right of each ledger item in the balance sheet. For example, $400/$800 = 50% total asset to sales relationship.

b. Assuming a constant-percentage relationship between sales and the balance-sheet items above, except stockholders' equity, calculate the average added external funds needed for 1989 if sales increase by 10 percent. Assume the net margin (net income/sales) is 6 percent and 50 percent of net earnings are paid out in cash dividends.

Hawk Pro-Forma Average Balance Sheet, 1989
(10% Sales Growth, 6% Net Margin)

Current Assets	$	Current Liabilities	$
Fixed Assets	$	Funds Needed	$
Total Assets	$	Stockholders' Equity	$
		Total Liab. & Equity	$

2. a. With reference to Problem 1 above, but assuming a 20 percent sales increase, what amount of added funds are needed in 1989?

b. What happens to the amount of external funds needed (increase or decrease) for each of the situations below?

1) Increased rate of sales growth.
2) Increased technology requiring more fixed assets relative to sales.
3) A change in working capital policy giving longer credit terms.
4) A decrease in the number of each inventory item carried along with fewer lines of inventory carried.
5) A reduction in the net terms granted by suppliers (payables).
6) A reduction in the net margin.
7) An increase in the proportion of net income paid out in dividends.

3. The Whidden Corp. would like you to assist them in their financial planning, using the percentage-of-sales method to determine a rough estimate of funds needed. The recent balance sheet and income statement of Whidden Corp. is listed below. Whidden Corp. plans to increase net sales to $60,000,000 in 1989. Further, assume that Whidden's management assumes that all its asset, current liability, and deferred income-tax accounts will have the same relationship to sales as they had in 1988. Further assume that none of the long-term debt is due in 1989.

a. Assuming that Whidden has the same net profit margin as it had in 1988, what amount of new external financing will Whidden Corp. need in 1989? Construct a pro-forma balance sheet as part of your answer, using funds needed (or excess) to balance the right-hand side of the pro-forma balance sheet.

Whidden Corp.
Income Statement (thousands of dollars), Year-End 1988

Net sales (credit)	46,235
Cost of goods sold	33,167
Gross profit	13,068
General and administrative expense	9,590
Operating income	3,478
Interest expense	1,120
Net income before taxes	2,358
Income taxes	1,130
Net income	1,228

4. a. What after-tax profit margin would Whidden Corp. (Problem 3) need in 1989 to support the $60,000,000 sales figure without new external financing?
   b. If Whidden paid dividends, how would this affect your answers above?
   c. What dangers do you see in using a year-end pro-forma balance sheet to project financing needs?

5. Prepare a pro-forma income statement for 1989 for Hi-Tech Manufacturing Company using the following information:

Whidden Corp.
Balance Sheet (thousands of dollars), 12/31/88

Cash	230	Notes payable		1,015
Accounts receivable	9,380	Accounts payable		3,545
Inventories	7,515	Accrued taxes		225
Current assets	17,125	Current liab.		4,784
Net fixed assets	34,125	Long-term debt		18,036
Total assets	51,250	Deferred income taxes		2,840
		Total liab.		20,876
		Common stock (par)		575
		Capital in excess of par		7,945
		Retained earnings		17,070
		Common equity		25,590
		Total liab. & net worth		51,250

a. Projected sales: $2,025,000
b. Cost of goods sold: 65.92 percent of sales
c. Selling and administrative expense: $20,000 per month
d. Depreciation: $10,000 per month January–April; $12,000 per month May–December
e. Interest expense: $40,000
f. Tax rate: 46 percent

Recent balance-sheet data for Hi-Tech are shown in the following table:

Hi-Tech Mnfr. Co., 12/31/88

Assets	
Cash	$ 20,000
Accounts receivable	292,500
Inventory	118,000
Total current assets	$ 430,500
Gross plant and equipment	$1,800,000
Less accumulated depreciation	−963,000
Net plant and equipment	837,000
Total assets	$1,267,500
Liabilities and net worth	
Bank loan	$ 50,000
Accounts payable	54,000
Accrued labor	54,000
Taxes payable	5,000
Accrued overhead	10,000
Total current liabilities	$ 173,000
Debentures	500,000
Common stock	300,000
Retained earnings	294,500
Total liabilities and net worth	$1,267,500

6. Whittenberg Medical Company has recently merged with Bailey and Lowe, Incorporated, producer of a specialized line of sports equipment, to form a new industrial concern — Wolf Group Enterprises (WG). Under president Jim Valvoline's guidance, WG has recently introduced its products into the western portions of the United States under a new name — "Destiny Products." Satisfied with this new marketing concept, Valvoline plans an additional marketing push into the Southwest. WG is attempting to project funding needs for this new expansion. Income and balance sheets for last year,

1988, are reproduced below. WG feels that asset and current liability accounts, as well as costs, will remain constant percentages of sales as they have in the past. The company also plans to maintain its policy of paying out 70 percent of its earnings in the form of dividends. Valvoline projects 1989 sales of $150. Prepare an analysis of WG's needs for external financing in 1989.

Wolf Group Enterprises, 12/31/88

Assets	
Current assets	$20
Net fixed assets	30
Total assets	$50
Liabilities and owners' equity	
Accounts payable	$10
Long-term debt	20
Common stock	5
Retained earnings	15
Total liabilities and owners' equity	$50

Wolf Group Enterprises
Income Statement, Year-End 1988

Sales	$100
Cost of goods sold	80
Profit before taxes	$ 20
Taxes at 40 percent	8
Profit after tax	$ 12

7. Utilize all the information from problem (5) including the balance sheet for December 31, 1988, and the following information to construct a pro-forma balance sheet for Hi-Tech Manufacturing Company for December 31, 1989.

a. An addition to plant and equipment of $175,000 is due on April 15. The depreciation figure in problem (1) above already includes the depreciation charges for this addition.
b. The company maintains an open line of credit with a local bank and was carrying an outstanding loan balance of $50,000 on December 31, 1988.

c. The minimum cash balance desired by the company is $20,000.

d. The accounts-receivable collection period (days sales outstanding) is projected to be 55 days, the year having 365 days.

e. Inventory turnover is projected to be 10.75 times.

f. Purchases amount to 45.5 percent of cost of goods sold, and the company's payment period (days purchases outstanding) at year end is expected to be 36 days.

g. At December 31, 1989, accrued labor expense is expected to be $60,000, taxes payable zero, and accrued overhead expense $10,000.

h. No change is expected in debentures or common stock.

8. Prepare a quarterly cash budget for the Chapel-on-the-Hill Church utilizing the following information and including any required borrowing. All annual receipts and disbursements are received or made in equal quarterly amounts unless otherwise noted.

a. Annual expenditures are projected as follows:

Salary, allowances, and expenses (Rector)	$24,480
Salary, allowances, and expenses (Asst. Rector)	$16,500
Clerical and janitorial expense	$32,160
Building maintenance and taxes	$12,800
Supplies and programs	$11,600
Work outside the parish	$25,000

b. In addition to the above expenditures, the church must make principal payments on the church mortgage of $2,000 in the second and fourth quarters, and interest payments of $700 per quarter.

c. Receipts are projected as $7,800 for plate collections and $121,000 for pledge payments, with plate collections evenly distributed throughout the year, and 40 percent of pledge payments to be received in the fourth quarter and 20 percent in each of the other three quarters.

d. The cash balance at the beginning of the year is $4,200.

*9. Compute the projected accounts-receivable balance on December 31, 1989, for Transylvania Corporation from the following information (round to the nearest $10):

a. The December 31, 1988, accounts-receivable balance is $83,210.

b. All sales are on credit, and are projected for 1989 below.

c. Accounts receivable are collected as follows: 35 percent in the month following the sale; 50 percent in the second month after the sale; and 15 percent in the third month after the sale.

Transylvania Corp.
Projected Sales, 1989

January	$36,300
February	$39,850
March	$45,700
April	$51,540
May	$48,390
June	$54,400
July	$52,230
August	$57,230
September	$53,710
October	$47,930
November	$44,260
December	$41,000

10. Playtime Toy Company has projected sales as shown in the following table. The company's gross-profit percentage is 40 percent. Seventy-five percent of costs of goods sold are materials that are purchased, and 25 percent are labor. Parts must be ordered two months before they are assembled and sold. They are received one month after being ordered. Playtime pays all of its bills 30 days after they are received, and bills arrive when the parts are delivered.

a. Compute the accounts-payable balance for each month in 1989.

b. Compute the parts inventory for each month in 1989. The inventory balance on December 31, 1988, was $6,200.

Playtime Toy Company
Projected Sales

January 1989	$5,400
February	$4,800
March	$4,100
April	$4,300
May	$3,600
June	$3,700
July	$2,200
August	$2,300
September	$3,900
October	$4,500
November	$6,600
December	$8,200
January 1990	$6,000

11. Prepare monthly pro-forma income statements and a cash budget for Hi-Tech Manufacturing Company for 1989, and a monthly cash budget using the information given in problems (5) and (7) plus the following information:

a. The monthly sales forecast for 1989 is shown in the following table.

b. A total of 90 percent of sales are on credit terms of net 45 and the remaining 10 percent are for cash. Credit sales have historically been collected on the basis of 50 percent in the month following sale and the remaining 50 percent in the second month after sale. Bad-debt losses are negligible.

c. Monthly production is scheduled at the level of forecasted sales for the following month. Materials expense and labor expense each average 30 percent of sales. Both ex-penses are payable in the month following production.

d. Overhead expense of $10,000 per month is paid in the following month.

e. Interest on bonds of $20,000 is due on June 5 and December 5.

f. Selling and administrative expenses average $20,000 per month and are paid in the month incurred.

g. Tax payments are due on April 15, June 15, September 15, and December 15, and are equal to the tax liability through the month of payment.

h. No dividends will be paid.

Hi-Tech Mnfr. Co.
Sales Forecast, 1988–89 (thousands of dollars)

1988	actual	
	November	$190
	December	$230
1989	forecasted	
	January	$180
	February	$150
	March	$130
	April	$120
	May	$130
	June	$160
	July	$175
	August	$200
	September	$180
	October	$160
	November	$200
	December	$240
1990	forecasted	
	January	$200

Each year business firms commit huge sums of money for capital expenditures. In 1986, aggregate expenditures by U.S. firms for plant and equipment totaled about $379 billion. General Motors alone invested almost $8 billion. While GM's total was the largest for any single firm, many other individual firms also invested large sums. Table IV–1 gives estimates of capital expenditures for 1988 from the *Value Line Investment Survey*.

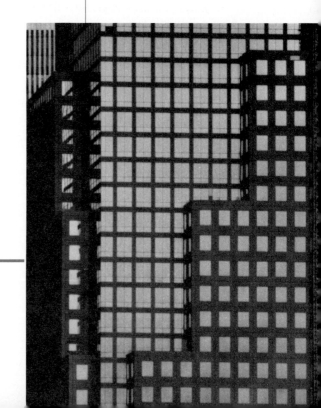

Table IV–1

Capital Investment by U.S. Firms
(millions of dollars)

Firm	1988 (estimated)
Exxon	6,008
GM	6,000
IBM	5,490
ATT	3,981
Ford	2,993
Mobil	2,410
GE	1,834
Texaco	1,798

Source: Value Line Investment Survey

Business firms compete among themselves for the funds necessary to finance their investments. The business sector also competes for funds against other sectors: individuals who wish to build houses and buy automobiles and refrigerators; governments that wish to build schools, roads, and military aircraft; nonprofit organizations that wish to build universities or hospitals; foreigners who wish to invest in the United States.

Just as firms must compete among themselves and against other sectors of the economy for capital funds, so too must individual projects or proposals compete for funds within a single firm. The decision to select one investment over another is an important one — not just for the firm making the decision, but for society as a whole. Because investment decisions consume scarce capital, a steadily increasing standard of living depends very much on wise investment decisions by firms, governments, and other organizations.

As we will see, a key characteristic of capital-investment projects typically is that they have an impact over long periods of time — years or even decades. How should long-term investment opportunities be analyzed? Which opportunities represent wise and efficient uses of capital funds and which do not? As we develop our approach, the factors that we considered earlier in Parts Two and Three — time, risk, and information — will occupy center stage. We will devote four chapters in Part Four to the question of analyzing investment opportunities. Chapter 10 develops our basic approach. Chapter 11 concentrates on estimating cash flows. Chapters 12 and 13 then deal with the problem of setting performance standards — that is, minimum acceptable rates of return.

10

Fundamentals of Capital Budgeting

In this chapter, we will learn to analyze long-term investment opportunities using the basic techniques of capital budgeting. First we will discuss alternative decision criteria and their strengths and weaknesses. Then we will develop in detail the discounted-cash-flow approach. Finally, we will discuss some practical problems in applying capital-budgeting techniques.

What Is Capital Budgeting?

Suppose a company has three investment opportunities under consideration: (1) building a new plant in Europe, (2) replacing its computer with a new generation of more advanced equipment, or (3) buying out one of its suppliers to ensure a source of raw materials.

Should the company undertake any of the three projects? All of them? Some subset of them? The firm must *budget* its funds (capital) among them. The term **capital budgeting** describes this process of *analyzing* capital-investment opportunities and *deciding* which (if any) to undertake.

We will assume that, in making such capital-budgeting decisions, managers attempt to maximize the value of the firm to existing shareholders. With such an objective, managers need some way to estimate the value a project might provide. If a project creates value, it will further the manager's pursuit of shareholder-wealth maximization and should be undertaken.

In this chapter, we focus on capital budgeting at the project level and show how to evaluate specific investment opportunities. Through this process, we can relate decisions directly to the value they may create for shareholders. The cumulative effect of undertaking specific projects ultimately defines a firm's assets and capabilities. This "bottom-up" project appraisal should be complemented with the type of financial planning discussed in the previous chapters, which analyzes the firm as a whole, typically through the use of pro-forma financial statements. By viewing the firm in its entirety, managers can make sure that the collection of projects undertaken fits into a unified whole. Before we begin analysis of capital budgeting in detail, however, it is best to take one step back and look at the capital-budgeting *process* as it faces a firm. Table 10–1 outlines the three basic steps in the process.

Capital budgeting—the process of analyzing capital investment opportunities and deciding which (if any) to undertake; it includes the creative search for investment opportunities, the gathering of data and making of forecasts, the economic analysis, the decision, and the implementation.

Determination of Alternatives and Strategic Analysis

First, investment alternatives don't arrive in neat bundles for managers to evaluate—the alternatives must be defined. The founders of Apple Computer had the insight to see that the opportunity to produce home computers was worth their consideration. In fact, many fortunes are made (or lost) at the initial stages of realizing what alternatives are even worth considering. In practice, a lot of the determination of alternatives takes place in the context of **strategic analysis** where a firm makes fundamental choices about its commercial strategy. Such strategic analysis may not consider the detailed attributes of each alternative.

Strategic analysis—the process of making fundamental decisions about a firm's basic goal or purpose and about the products or services it will produce and the markets it will serve.

Table 10–1

Steps in the Capital-Budgeting Process

A. Determination of alternatives and strategic analysis
B. Economic analysis of remaining alternatives
C. Implementation of chosen alternatives (including performance assessment)

Well-managed companies often impose a strategic test before they ever get to the economic analysis. A firm that builds aircraft is unlikely to be interested in opening a string of ice-cream parlors, no matter what the numbers look like. "We build airplanes," the chief executive would say, and a proposal to build ice-cream parlors would never make it to the economic-analysis stage.

In a world in which all information and analysis were costless, managers could quantitatively analyze every conceivable alternative. Given the costs in both dollars and time of gathering and analyzing information, managers are forced to eliminate many alternatives based on strategic grounds without a full economic evaluation of the investment.

Economic Analysis of Remaining Alternatives

After alternatives are determined and some are eliminated on strategic grounds, the remaining investments should be subjected to a detailed scrutiny, or **economic analysis,** which is the step of the capital-budgeting process on which we will focus in detail.

Since managers are attempting to maximize the value of the firm to shareholders, they need some guidance as to what value a potential investment might have. The economic analysis is a gathering of specific quantitative information about a project. Suppose a textile firm is considering the purchase of a new loom versus the repair of an old one: should the new loom be purchased?

Answering this question involves measuring and weighing costs and benefits of each alternative to determine which (if either) alternative will best serve the shareholders of the company. We'll have much more to say about the steps in the economic analysis of projects later in the chapter.

Implementation of Chosen Alternatives

Once an investment decision is made, it still must be implemented. The investment decision to build a new plant is only the beginning. Next the plant must be built and efficiently operated. Implementation involves communicating what is to be done in often complex organizations and being sure that the best efforts are made to carry out plans. Unexpected events occur, and original plans may have to be modified. Obviously, implementation is no trivial matter and absorbs the time and talents of corporate employees ranging from the executive level to manual labor.

In addition, it is important to evaluate the project after it is adopted. Did the project live up to expectations? If not, why? Answers to such questions provide critical information the firm needs to evaluate its existing employees and gain knowledge useful for future decisions. Information about why one project failed may spark an idea for a new alternative, and the whole capital-budgeting process then begins again. The three phases of capital budgeting depicted in Table 10–1 are interdependent.

Though we will focus here on economic analysis, it is important to remember that economic analysis is only part of the process. No amount of economic analy-

Finance in Practice 10–1

Innovation in the Mail Business

Need a package delivered halfway across the United States overnight? If you call Federal Express, the Memphis-based air courier, they will pick it up, take it to a company-owned plane, and deliver it to the destination the next morning. If for some reason it doesn't get there the next day, you get a reduced rate, but that doesn't happen often. Federal Express claims that more than 99 percent of its shipments arrive overnight.

This type of service is the result of a major innovation in the mail business. Until the last few years, alternatives for mailing packages were limited to the U.S. Postal Service and a few other private package carriers. All of these private carriers picked up your package and promised delivery, but they used only scheduled airplane service. This method of operation kept capital requirements down — no hangars or airplanes had to be purchased.

Enter Federal Express, founded by chairman Fred Smith. Smith decided to concentrate on delivery of small packages, but instead of relying on scheduled airline service, he decided to invest in company-owned planes to ensure control over shipments and thus to improve the speed and reliability of service. Packages are flown to a central location in Memphis, sorted during the night, and shipped to their destinations aboard company planes.

The capital outlay for the planes and other facilities was large, but it has paid off. For example, earnings grew at an almost incredible 76 percent annual rate for the five-year period beginning in 1976, the company's stock price went from $6 to $65 a share (between 1978 and 1981), and Fred Smith's holdings of that stock grew in value to about $150 million by mid-1981 — not a bad investment for Mr. Smith.

The key to this success was finding a new potentially profitable investment, analyzing its potential, and then carrying the project through — all basic steps in the capital-budgeting process. Clearly, a key was Smith's innovative idea of how to change the mail business by making a capital investment in planes and creating a dependable overnight service.

Source: Adapted from G. Colvin, "Federal Express Dives into Air Mail," *Fortune,* June 15, 1981, pp. 106–108.

sis can salvage a company that never comes up with decent alternatives to analyze. And poor implementation can foil the best-laid plans. On the other hand, economic analysis can improve decisions for all companies.

Economic Analysis of Investment Proposals

We need a method to determine if a project adds value to a firm.

Given the framework depicted in Table 10–1, let's focus on economic analysis of specific proposals. If a manager's objective is to maximize the value of the firm to existing shareholders, we need a way to determine whether or not a project adds value to the firm. In short, we need a method to determine whether a project is or is not a good investment proposal. A number of methods are often used by firms, including the payback period, accounting return on investment, net present value, internal rate of return, and profitability index. Let us examine each of these five methods.

Payback Period

■■■

Payback approach — a method of analyzing investment opportunities that determines how long it will take the cash inflows expected from an investment to repay (pay back) the initial outlay.

One simple and widely used method of analyzing investment opportunities is known as the **payback approach.** This approach addresses the question of how long a time it will take the cash inflows expected from an investment to repay the initial outlay. Suppose an investment of $1,000 is expected to generate after-tax cash inflows of $500, $400, and $300 over a three-year period. As we can see in Table 10–2, the investment would be recovered partway through the third year.

As Table 10–2 shows, the investment has "paid back" all but $100 by the end of year 2. Since year 3 produces a cash inflow of $300, the final $100 will be paid back about one third of the way through year 3. So the payback period for this hypothetical investment is 2.33 years.

A company might use the payback period in investment analysis by establishing the criterion for investments of accepting projects that had payback periods of less than some critical value. For example, if a company's maximum acceptable payback period were 3 years, the project in Table 10–2 with a payback period of 2.33 years would be acceptable, whereas another project with a payback of 4 years would be rejected.

In making investments, it is often useful to know just how long it is going to take to recover the outlay. In general, the shorter the better. However, as a criterion for judging the economic worth of an investment, or its worth relative to other investments, the payback approach has some serious shortcomings.

First, the payback approach does not take into account differences in the *time pattern* of cash flows. Consider the two hypothetical investments in Table 10–3. Both investments have the same payback period — namely, 2 years. But most people would prefer investment A for two reasons. First, while the total flows in the first two years are equal, A has a larger flow in year 1. Anyone for whom money has time value (and that includes almost everyone) would prefer a pattern of $600 sooner and $400 later to a pattern of $400 sooner and $600 later. Second, although both investments have the same total payback for the first two years, A promises $800 in year 3 and B promises only $100 in year 3. Thus, as a criterion

■■■

Payback has two serious shortcomings as a criterion for judging economic worth: it ignores the time value of money, and it ignores the cash flows that occur after the end of the payback period.

■■■

Table 10–2

Payback Period for a Hypothetical Investment

	Year 0	Year 1	Year 2	Year 3
Cash out	1000	0	0	0
Cash in	0	500	400	300
Net cash to date	(1000)	(500)	(100)	200

Table 10–3

Time Pattern of Cash Flows for Two Investment Alternatives

		Cash In		
Investment	Cash Out	Year 1	Year 2	Year 3
A	1000	600	400	800
B	1000	400	600	100

for judging economic worth, the payback approach has two serious shortcomings: it ignores the time value of money, and it ignores cash flows occurring beyond the end of the payback period.

In addition, setting a maximum acceptable payback period is essentially an arbitrary decision: there is no easy way to relate payback period to more general criteria, such as profit maximization or value maximization.

In spite of its shortcomings, the payback approach is still widely used because it answers an important question: how long is it expected to take to get the investment back? While the approach is useful for these purposes, most firms find it necessary to go beyond the simple payback measure before arriving at final decisions on important investments.[1] Thus, the payback approach is generally used in conjunction with other methods of analyzing projects.

Accounting Return on Investment (AROI)

AROI approach — a method of analyzing capital investments that relies on an accounting-based measure of return on investment, calculated as some measure of accounting profit divided by some measure of accounting investment.

The **AROI approach** to economic analysis of cash flows uses accounting-based return-on-investment calculations. Measures of *accounting-based return on investment (AROI),* as we discovered in Chapter 7, are calculated as some measure of accounting profit divided by some measure of accounting investment. Herein lies one of the problems with accounting-based ROI measures: ambiguity. There are many ways return can be measured — accounting profit, cash flow, before tax, after tax, and perhaps others we could devise. Likewise, investment can be measured in many ways — initial outlay, book value, average book value, and so on. ROI calculated with each of these different quantities would yield a different result. Even if we settled on particular choices for return and investment, these quantities themselves would be affected by accounting conventions, such as choice of depreciation method. So, there are many ways to calculate accounting ROI, none of which is any more or less "correct" than the others.

Putting aside these ambiguities for a moment, let us calculate AROI for the proposed project detailed in Table 10–4 on p. 282. The project requires investment in early 1989 and is expected to last through year-end 1991. (The assumed tax rate is 40 percent.)

[1]For an analysis of the payback criterion and some arguments in favor of its use, see J. M. Blatt, "Investment Evaluation Under Uncertainty," *Financial Management* 8 (Summer 1979): 66–81.

Table 10–4

Accounting Return on Investment (AROI) for a Proposed Project, 1989–1991

	Return (thousands of dollars)		Investment (thousands of dollars)				Return on Investment (percent)	
Year (1)	Net Profit Before Tax (2)	Net Profit After Tax (3)	Beginning Book Value (4)	Gross Investment (5)	Depreciation (6)	Ending Book Value (7) = (4) + (5) − (6)	AROI Before Tax (8) = (2) ÷ (7)	AROI After Tax (9) = (3) ÷ (7)
1989	−50	−30	0	320	100	220	−23	−14
1990	100	60	220	0	100	120	83	50
1991	100	60	120	0	100	20	500	300

Note the differences in the before-tax and after-tax calculations. Note also that the calculations were performed using *ending book value* in each year. They just as easily could have been performed using *beginning book value* or *average book value* in each year. And, of course, each of these methods would yield a different answer.

Another interesting observation can be made about the AROI numbers in Table 10–4: they are different in each year. After-tax AROI starts out at −14 percent in 1989, rises first to 50 percent the following year and then to 300 percent in 1991. Is the project a good investment? It is difficult to tell by looking only at the AROI numbers. Suppose our required return for the project—that is, the minimum return we would accept—was 15 percent after taxes. The return in Table 10–4 falls short of the target in 1989 but exceeds it in 1990 and 1991 by substantial margins. Should we undertake an investment whose projected return is inadequate in some years and very attractive in others? The answer is that we need a better measure.

One possibility is to compute the *average* AROI over the three-year period. One method of averaging is to divide average profit for the period by average investment. Averaging the figures in column (3) of Table 10–4, we see that average profit after tax (PAT) is $30,000, and using ending book values in column (7), average investment is $120,000. Average AROI would then be $30,000/$120,000 = 25 percent.

By *averaging* AROI over the three years, we have solved part of the ambiguity problem, but alas we have created another problem—we are not taking into account the time value of money. As Table 10–4 shows, the large cash outflow takes place in the early years, as reflected in column (5) of Table 10–4, whereas the cash inflows (the rewards) do not become large until the later years. Averaging the AROI figures over the three years does not take into account this timing difference, which can be very important, as it is in this case.

Thus, it turns out that the AROI method forces us to choose between the problem of ambiguity (if we calculate AROI in each year) and the problem of not considering the time value of money (if we average it). In view of these shortcomings, why use the AROI method? What questions does it answer? The AROI method gives a measure of accounting profit per dollar of investment, often a useful piece of information in measuring performance, especially over a relatively short time pe-

Annual AROI numbers can differ for each year of a project's life.

Averaging AROI over the time span resolves some ambiguity but still does not take account of the time value of money.

AROI is especially useful in measuring performance, but with investment possibilities the need is to make a decision, not to measure performance.

riod (say, a year). The AROI method is especially useful in measuring the performance of firms and industries. But our goal in the case of this project is to *make a decision,* not to measure performance.

Discounted Cash Flow and Investment Decisions

As we've seen, the payback method and the AROI method have shortcomings as means for deciding on investment projects. While useful in some respects, neither measure directly addresses the issue of what value a project adds to the firm. If managers are to maximize the value of the firm, they need such value estimates to make good decisions about investment projects.

Fortunately, some of the tools we developed earlier will help in providing such estimates of value. Our basic discounted-cash-flow (DCF) model from Part Two showed how we might value a set of cash flows. The value is determined as the present value of future cash flows—discounted back to the present. We can thus think of investment projects as packages of cash flows and use DCF techniques to determine their value.

> If we think of investment projects as bundles of cash flows, we can use discounted-cash-flow techniques to determine their value.

In actually implementing the DCF valuation concepts, firms typically use one or both of two techniques: the net-present-value (*NPV*) technique and the internal-rate-of-return (*IRR*) technique.

Net Present Value (*NPV*)

> To implement DCF valuation concepts for investment decisions, firms typically use net-present-value (*NPV*) techniques or internal-rate-of-return (*IRR*) techniques, or both.

The net-present-value (*NPV*) technique is a direct application of DCF techniques and states that the value a project adds to the firm is simply the present value of the future cash benefits of the project minus the present value of any cash costs. In other words,

$$NPV = PV \text{ cash benefits } - PV \text{ cash costs}.$$

We can write this relationship out in terms of the discounted-cash-flow techniques developed earlier, as is shown in Equation (1):

$$NPV = C_0 + \frac{C_1}{(1 + K)} + \frac{C_2}{(1 + K)^2} + \ldots + \frac{C_n}{(1 + K)^n} \tag{1}$$

$$NPV = C_0 + \sum_{t=1}^{n} \frac{C_t}{(1 + K)^t}$$

where C_t = expected cash flow the project contributes in time t, K = the required rate of return on the cash flow, and n = life of the project.

Cash inflows in Equation (1) will be positive values of C_t and cash outflows will be negative values. Thus C_0 will generally be a negative value showing that initial investment in the project requires the firm to spend money, such as on plant or equipment. The Σ (sigma) notation is a shorthand way of saying to add the present value of all cash flows from time 1 through time n, where n would be the date of the last expected cash flow associated with the project. This sum is the present

Net present value (NPV)— the present value of the cash inflows of an investment less (net of) the required outlay.

The *NPV* investment rule is: in general, accept any investment that has a positive net present value when evaluated at the appropriate required rate of return.

value of the project's cash benefits before subtracting out the initial outlay. In finding these present values, we should use a required return K that will penalize cash flows for both time delay and greater risk. Remember that we have to wait to receive some of the cash flows and that the cash flows might not materialize at all if our projections about the future are wrong.

The **net present value (NPV)** of an investment is simply the present value of the inflows less (net of) the required outlay. If *NPV* is positive, the project has a positive value (the benefits outweigh the costs) and should be accepted. Such a positive value will increase the value of the firm to shareholders and, thus, further the objective of maximizing shareholder wealth.

Sample Problem 10–1
Calculation of Net Present Value for a Hypothetical Investment

Consider a hypothetical investment of $100 that is expected to yield cash inflows of $30, $50, and $40 over the next three years. Suppose the required rate of return (K) is 15 percent. Should the firm undertake the project?

Solution
Table 10–5 lays out the calculation of net present value. Note that the initial cash flow, C_0, is a negative number showing cash outlay. Because *NPV* is negative, the project should not be accepted.

The calculations in Table 10–5 are simply the application of DCF analysis in the context of an investment proposal. It is useful here to think for a moment of the project as a financial asset. It offers cash flows of $30, $50, and $40 in each of the next three years, respectively. At a required rate of return of 15 percent per year, these flows have a present value of $90.22, which can be calculated as

$$PV = \$30/(1 + 0.15)^1 + \$50/(1 + 0.15)^2 + \$40/(1 + 0.15)^3$$
$$= \$30(0.870) + \$50(0.756) + \$40(0.658)$$
$$= \$90.22$$

Table 10–5
Calculating Net Present Value (NPV)—General Form

Period, t	Cash Flow, C_t (dollars)	Present-Value Factor at 15 Percent, $\left[\dfrac{1}{(1+K)^t}\right]$	Present Value, $\left[\dfrac{C_t}{(1+K)^t}\right]$ (dollars)
0	−100	1.000	−100.00
1	30	0.870	26.10
2	50	0.756	37.80
3	40	0.658	26.32
			$NPV = -\;9.78$

In other words, it would take $90.22 today in a bank account earning interest at 15 percent per year to enable us to make bank-account withdrawals of $30, $50, and $40 in each of the next three years. The catch is that the project requires an outlay of $100 to get the cash flows. Why pay $100 for the project if $90.22 invested at 15 percent (your required return) will get you the same future cash flows? The answer is that you should *not* invest in the project; it has a negative value. Specifically, it has a net present value of $90.22 − $100 = −$9.78, as calculated in Table 10–5.

Internal Rate of Return (*IRR*)

Net present value is a dollar measure of the net value of any project and is thus a direct application of DCF techniques developed earlier. For some purposes, however, rather than a dollar value, managers would prefer to estimate the *percentage* rate of return they expect to earn on an investment. For example, Chapter 4 showed how to calculate the yield to maturity on a bond. That yield was simply the DCF measure of the percentage rate of return you would earn on the bond if you purchased it and held it to maturity (assuming, of course, that the issuer of the bond did not default). This yield could be compared to your required rate of return to see if the bond was a desirable purchase.

Internal rate of return (*IRR*)—the rate that discounts all of the cash flows of an investment, including all outlays, to exactly zero; it is the discount rate that makes the net present value of the project equal to zero; it is the discounted-cash-flow measure of the expected rate of return to be earned on an investment.

In the analysis of investment projects within the firm, the rate of return analogous to a bond's yield to maturity is called an **internal rate of return (*IRR*)** and is simply the DCF measure of the rate of return expected to be earned on the investment in the project if the estimated cash flows actually materialize. In simplest terms, the *IRR* is the interest rate that discounts the future expected cash inflows to be exactly equal to the cash outlay. That is, an *IRR* is that discount rate which would make the net present value of the project equal to zero, as shown in Equation (2):

$$0 = C_0 + \frac{C_1}{(1 + R)} + \frac{C_2}{(1 + R)^2} + \ldots + \frac{C_n}{(1 + R)^n}$$

$$0 = C_0 + \sum_{t=1}^{n} \frac{C_t}{(1 + R)^n} \tag{2}$$

where $R = IRR$ and where C_0 will generally be a negative number showing the outlay in time period 0.

The great virtue of the *IRR* is that it is a time-adjusted rate of return, and therefore takes account of the time value of money.

The *IRR* is a *time-adjusted* rate of return. Its great virtue is that it takes into account the time value of money. In addition, its definition is standard, with no ambiguity as to the method of calculation as was true of the AROI method.

How do we use the internal rate of return to evaluate investment opportunities? We simply compare the *IRR* to the required rate of return. The *IRR* investment rule is: in general, undertake any project that has an internal rate of return greater than the required rate of return.

The *IRR* investment rule is: in general, undertake any project that has an internal rate of return greater than the required rate of return.

Like the *NPV* investment rule, the *IRR* investment rule is a general guide that should not be followed blindly. Some investments with an internal rate of return greater than the target rate may be unwise for other reasons, and some with an *IRR* below target may be necessary or desirable. For example, an investment in pollution-control equipment may have a low indicated *IRR* but may be essential to comply with the law or simply with good citizenship.

Sample Problem 10–2
Calculating the Internal Rate of Return for an Investment Proposal

Let us consider an investment proposal that is expected to yield cash inflows of $40, $50, and $30 in the next three years, respectively. The project requires an investment today of $100. Should the project be undertaken if the required rate of return is 15 percent?

Solution

Using the definition of *IRR* in Equation (2), we can set up the problem as follows:

$$\$100 = -\$100 + \frac{\$40}{(1+R)} + \frac{\$50}{(1+R)^2} + \frac{\$30}{(1+R)^3}$$

$$\$100 = \frac{\$40}{(1+R)} + \frac{\$50}{(1+R)^2} + \frac{\$30}{(1+R)^3}$$

The rate, *R*, that solves this equation—the rate that discounts the cash inflows to exactly equal the outlay of $100—is the internal rate of return of the investment.

When we calculated net present value, we started with a given discount rate and solved for the present value of the flows. To calculate the internal rate of return, we do the opposite—we start with the present value of the flows (the outlay) and solve for the discount rate. But how do we actually find *R*? The answer is by trial and error, unless we have a calculator with a solution method for *IRR* programmed into it.

Let us illustrate the method using the problem above. First we simply guess at the correct rate. Let us try 12 percent, a bit below our required return of 15 percent. Using the present-value tables, Appendix Table I at the back of the book, we get the result in the *First Try* columns of Table 10–6.

On our first try, at 12 percent, we get a present value of $96.93. At 12 percent, we have penalized the future cash flows too much because $96.93 is less than the

Table 10–6
Finding the Internal Rate of Return (*IRR*) of a Hypothetical Investment Proposal

Year	Cash Flow (dollars)	First Try Present-Value Factor at 12 Percent	First Try Present Value (dollars)	Second Try Present-Value Factor at 8 Percent	Second Try Present Value (dollars)
1	40	0.893	35.72	0.926	37.04
2	50	0.797	39.85	0.857	42.85
3	30	0.712	21.26	0.794	23.82
			96.93		103.71

outlay of $100. So we know we set the discount rate too high and need to use a figure less than 12 percent. For our second try, let us use 8 percent. Now we get $103.71, so we know 8 percent is too low. If we try 10 percent, we get $100.19; if we try 11 percent, we get $98.57. Hence, the internal rate of return lies between 10 percent and 11 percent. In many cases, it is sufficient to state that the internal rate of return is "about 10 percent," or "between 10 percent and 11 percent." Clearly, the internal rate of return is less than the required rate of return of 15 percent, so the project should be rejected.

If we need greater accuracy, we can use a computer or calculator with DCF capability. As it turns out, the *IRR* for this project is 10.12 percent. ▪

Sample Problem 10–3
Calculating the Internal Rate of Return with Equal Cash Inflows

If the cash inflows are equal and the outlay occurs only in the initial year, there is a shortcut in calculating *IRR* that uses annuity tables.

An investment of $1,000 yields $176.99 for 10 years. What is its internal rate of return?

Solution

Using Equation (2) and utilizing annuity factors for present values, we have

$$0 = -\$1,000 + \$176.99 \, PVAF(R, 10)$$

$$\frac{\$1,000}{\$176.99} = PVAF(R, 10)$$

$$5.65 = PVAF(R, 10).$$

Looking in Appendix Table II at the back of the book, we search in the row for year 10 until we find 5.650 in the column for 12 percent, which tells us that the investment has an *IRR* of 12 percent. ▪

Profitability Index

Profitability index (PI) — a ratio measure of an investment's benefits in relation to its costs that is calculated using discounted-cash-flow techniques.

In addition to net present value and internal rate of return, the **profitability index** is a third discounted-cash-flow technique used to evaluate investment projects. The profitability index is actually only a rearrangement of our net-present-value equation to put things in ratio form, as shown in Equation (3):

$$PI = \frac{PV \text{ of future cash benefits}}{\text{Dollar investment}}$$

$$PI = \frac{\sum_{t=1}^{n} C_t/(1 + K)^t}{-C_0}. \tag{3}$$

As Equation (3) shows, the profitability index is a look at the present value of future cash flows from $t = 1$ onward relative to the cash costs of undertaking the project. Just as in the *NPV* calculation, K is the required return on the project. The minus sign before C_0 in the denominator converts a cash outflow to a positive dollar cost (a minus in front of a negative number makes it a positive number). For example, for the project in Table 10–5, the profitability index (at $K = 15$ percent) can be calculated as

$$PI = \frac{\$30/(1.15) + \$50/(1.15)^2 + \$40/(1.15)^3}{-(-\$100)}$$

$$= \frac{\$30(0.870) + \$50(0.756) + \$40(0.658)}{\$100}$$

$$= \frac{\$90.22}{\$100} = 0.9022 .$$

The profitability index gives a ratio of benefits to costs.

This profitability index gives us the ratio of benefits to costs. If $PI < 1$, the benefits (in present-value terms) are less than the costs, and the project should be rejected. If $PI > 1$, the project's benefits exceed its costs, and the project should be accepted.

The *PI* investment rule is: in general, undertake those investment projects with a profitability index greater than 1.

Note that whenever $NPV > 0$, the profitability index exceeds 1 and whenever $NPV < 0$, the profitability index is less than 1. As a result, the NPV and PI investment rules always give us the same accept/reject decision on projects. The only difference is that the profitability index gives the benefits per dollar of costs, while net present value gives the dollar value of benefits minus costs. As our earlier calculations show, the project in Table 10–5 has a net present value of $-\$9.78$ and a profitability index of 0.9022. Both calculations tell us to reject the project. The profitability index tells us that we get only about 90 cents of benefits per dollar invested, which makes the decision a bad one. Because of the similarities between net present value and the profitability index, we will not carry PI through further discussions in this chapter. In addition, the PI rule is not used in practice nearly as much as is the NPV rule or the IRR rule. We will use the internal rate of return and net present value as our basic discounted-cash-flow techniques for analyzing projects.

Sample Problem 10–4
Decision Criteria for an Investment in Project Q

An investment in project Q requires an initial $15,000 cash outlay and will return $8,000 in year 1, $7,000 in year 2, and $5,000 in year 3. Calculate

A. the internal rate of return (*IRR*),
B. the payback period,
C. the net present value (*NPV*), using a 10 percent discount rate, and
D. the profitability index (*PI*), using a 10 percent discount rate.

Solution
A. Solving for the *IRR* involves a trial-and-error process. We want to find the rate, R, that will solve the equation

$$0 = -\$15,000 + \frac{\$8,000}{(1 + R)} + \frac{\$7,000}{(1 + R)^2} + \frac{\$5,000}{(1 + R)^3} .$$

In words, we want the total present value of the 3 cash flows that come after year 0 to be equal to $15,000.

Using the present-value factors from Appendix Table I at the back of the book, we can try a rate of 15 percent. Using 15 percent for R results in a present value of $15,542:

$$\$8,000\,(0.870) + \$7,000\,(0.756) + \$5,000\,(0.658) = \$15,542\,.$$

With a 15 percent rate, the present value of the future cash streams exceeds the initial outlay of $15,000 by the net present value of $542 (the *IRR* is the rate that equates present value and the amount of the investment outlay), so we know that the 15 percent rate is too low. When we try higher discount rates, we find that the net present value is $77 at a discount rate of 17 percent but is $-\$153$ at a discount rate of 18 percent. Thus, we know that the *IRR* is between 17 and 18 percent.

B. The payback period can be found by constructing Table 10–7. The payback period is 2 years. At that point, total payments received equal the outlay.

C. The net present value, using a 10 percent discount rate, can be found by using the present-value factors given in Appendix Table I at the back of this book as

$$NPV = -\$15,000 + \$8,000\,(0.909) + \$7,000\,(0.826) + \$5,000\,(0.751)$$

$$= -\$15,000 + \$16,809$$

$$= \$1,809\,.$$

D. The profitability index is calculated as follows:

$$PI = PV \text{ inflows/Dollar investment}$$

$$PI = \frac{\$8000\,(0.909) + \$7000\,(0.826) + \$5000\,(0.751)}{\$15,000}$$

$$= \frac{\$16,809}{\$15,000}$$

$$= 1.12\,.$$

Comparing Net Present Value and Internal Rate of Return

We now have two widely used measures of investment worth based on discounted cash flow. Net present value is a dollar measure; internal rate of return is a

Table 10–7
Payback Period for an Investment

| | Payback (dollars) | | | |
	Year 0	Year 1	Year 2	Year 3
Cash flow	(15,000)	8,000	7,000	5,000
Cumulative cash flow	(15,000)	(7,000)	0	5,000

percentage-return measure. Which is better? Both have their uses, and in many cases either will serve to measure investment worth. *IRR* is easy to interpret even by those unfamiliar with discounted cash flow, whereas *NPV* is reliable in some situations that *IRR* is not. Let us examine the two measures a bit more closely.

Investment decisions can be classified into two general categories:

1. *accept/reject decisions,* where the issue is whether to undertake a given investment opportunity, and
2. *ranking decisions,* where two or more investment opportunities exist but not all can be undertaken.

Accept/Reject Decisions

For accept/reject investment decisions, both *NPV* and *IRR* provide the same signal.

For normal cash-flow patterns having a single internal rate of return, the *NPV* and *IRR* investment rules give identical signals in the case of accept/reject decisions.
If *IRR* = *K*, then *NPV* = 0.
If *IRR* > *K*, then *NPV* > 0.
If *IRR* < *K*, then *NPV* < 0.

For accept/reject decisions, we can use either the *NPV* rule or the *IRR* rule and get the same signal. The result is the same because if the internal rate of return exceeds the required rate of return (*K*), net present value will be greater than zero, so both rules signal a decision to accept the investment. If the internal rate of return is less than the required rate of return, then net present value is less than zero, so both rules call for a decision to reject the investment.

To see the equivalence of these two rules, let us consider an investment of $100 that yields inflows of $50, $60, and $40 over a three-year period, with net present value plotted against the required rate of return (*K*), as shown in Figure 10–1. For example, at a required return of 10 percent, we can calculate the net present value as

$$NPV = -\$100 + \frac{\$50}{(1 + 0.10)} + \frac{\$60}{(1 + 0.10)^2} + \frac{\$40}{(1 + 0.10)^3}$$

$$= -\$100 + \$50\,(0.909) + \$60\,(0.826) + \$40\,(0.751)$$

$$= \$25.05 .$$

Figure 10–1
NPV at Different Discount Rates

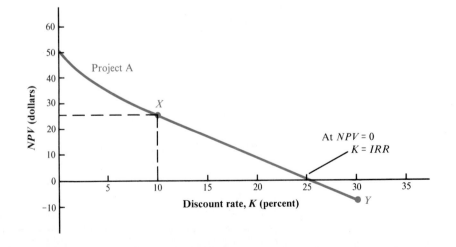

In Figure 10–1, point X represents a net present value of $25.05 at a required return of 10 percent. The other points on the line represent the *NPV* of project A calculated at other discount rates. Point Y shows a net present value of −$8 at a required return of 30 percent. By looking at the figure, we can see that *NPV* is greater than 0 for any discount rate less than 25 percent, which is project A's internal rate of return (the point in Figure 10–1 where the graph crosses the horizontal axis making *NPV* equal to 0 at 25 percent). For example, at point X, the discount rate is 10 percent, which is less than the *IRR* of 25 percent. As a result, the *NPV* at point X is greater than zero. At point Y, however, the discount rate is 30 percent, which is above the *IRR* of 25 percent, and the *NPV* at Y is less than zero.

There is a technical difficulty with the *IRR* investment rule that deserves brief mention. Certain types of cash-flow patterns may have more than one positive discount rate that produces a zero *NPV*; that is, certain cash-flow patterns have more than one *IRR*. It turns out that the number of solutions may be as great as the number of sign reversals in the cash-flow stream. A stream with a pattern of −, +, +, +, + has only one sign reversal and, therefore, no more than one positive *IRR*. A pattern of −, +, −, +, +, + may have as many as three positive solutions.

Where multiple solutions occur, which solution is correct? The answer is that none is correct. Each solution discounts the cash flows to zero, but none is a meaningful measure of project return. In practice, cash-flow patterns that yield multiple *IRR* s are rare. Even patterns with more than one sign reversal usually have only one *IRR*, because it takes extreme cases to produce multiple solutions. Thus, usually the possibility of multiple solutions can be ignored, except for one important group of investments known as *acceleration projects*.

An example of an acceleration project is one in which a petroleum or mining company invests funds in order to accelerate the recovery of a body of oil or minerals. In these situations, the typical cash flow associated with the investment always involves a major reversal of cash flows with the pattern −, +, −; that is, outlays now produce incremental positive flows in the near future (as recovery is accelerated relative to the status quo) followed by negative incremental flows (as the reserves are exhausted earlier than they would have been if the acceleration investment had not been made). The attempt to measure the *IRR* for such projects frequently yields multiple, and hence meaningless, solutions. In such cases, use of the *NPV* investment rule is recommended.

> Though it is possible that cash-flow patterns will yield multiple *IRR*s because of sign reversals in cash-flow streams, in practice this is rare.

Ranking Decisions

> Ranking decisions are necessary where capital is rationed (where capital funds are limited and there are more good investment opportunities than funds) and where two or more opportunities are mutually exclusive.

In practice, investment opportunities often unfold over time in a way that presents each one as a decision to accept or not. Ranking becomes necessary in two situations: (1) where capital is *rationed*—that is, where capital funds are limited in amount and there are more investment opportunities than funds; and (2) where two or more opportunities are *mutually exclusive*. Examples of mutually exclusive investments would be two machines to do the same job, two alternative plants to produce the same product, or two or more alternatives to accomplish any given objective.

Mutually Exclusive Projects. If forced to rank mutually exclusive projects, should we take the project with the higher net present value (as long as its *NPV* is greater than 0), or should we take the project with the higher internal rate of return? Fortunately, in most cases the project with the higher *NPV* also has the higher *IRR*, so there is no great difficulty involved in the decision. However, when projects differ greatly in their scale or useful life, the decision may become complicated.

Let us look at an example where mutually exclusive projects differ in scale. To simplify matters, we look at two projects that each last only one time period. Project X requires an initial cash outlay of $100 and promises an expected cash flow of $120 in one year. Project Y requires a larger initial outlay of $200 but has an expected cash flow of $236 in one year. The company feels the projects are equally risky and requires a return of 10 percent on both projects. Using Equations (1) and (2), we can calculate the net present value (at $K = 10$ percent) and internal rate of return for each project, as summarized in Table 10–8.

As Table 10–8 reveals, project Y has the higher net present value, but project X has the higher internal rate of return. Which project should we choose? The answer is project Y. Because project Y has the higher net present value, it should contribute more to the value of the company and be the better choice in furthering the objective of value maximization. The *NPV* investment rule provides the right signal to select Y.

But how can project Y be better than X if Y has a lower internal rate of return (18 percent versus 20 percent)? The reason project Y is a better choice can be seen if we remember that the company feels that 10 percent is the appropriate discount rate. We must earn at least 10 percent to justify the investment. Now let us compare the results of selecting X or Y. If we adopt project X, we invest $100 today. Just to break even (earn only 10 percent), we will need to have a cash flow of $100(1 + 0.10) = $110 in one year. Fortunately, we expect to get $120 from project X so we expect to come out $10 ahead ($120 − $110 = $10) in year 1 with project X. Project Y, on the other hand, is of larger scale and allows us to invest $200. To earn 10 percent we will need a cash flow of $200(1 + 0.10) = $220 in one year. Since we expect $236, we come out $16 ahead ($236 − $220 = $16) in year 1 with project Y. As the calculations show, project Y is expected to give us more money beyond our 10 percent requirement than project X. That is, $16 is larger than $10. As a result, project Y is the better choice. Project Y allowed us to earn an internal rate of return of 18 percent on a *larger* investment than the invest-

Table 10–8

Comparison of Two Investment Projects Based on Net Present Value and Internal Rate of Return

Project	Net Present Value at 10 Percent (dollars)	Internal Rate of Return (percent)
X	9.09	20
Y	14.55	18

ment on which we could earn the 20 percent *IRR* in project X. As a result, project Y gave us more extra value. The *NPV* calculations we did earlier already took this process into account. Note that the *NPV*s of projects X and Y are simply the present values (at 10 percent) of the $10 and $16 figures we calculated earlier.

Even if two projects are similar in scale, however, the *NPV* and *IRR* investment rules may rank them differently because of differences in the timing of the cash flows associated with the projects. To see this difference, let us compare two projects, one of which lasts longer than the other.

Earlier (in Figure 10–1) we considered an investment project A involving an outlay of $100 followed by inflows of $50, $60, and $40 over a three-year period. Let us now consider an alternative, project B, involving an outlay of $100 that generates inflows of $20, $30, $45, and $70 over a four-year period. Let us calculate the net present value of project B at different discount rates and plot its profile in Figure 10–2 as we did with project A in Figure 10–1. Now, the *IRR* rule tells us that project A is superior to project B because A's internal rate of return is 25 percent and B's *IRR* is about 19 percent. At a required return of, say, 15 percent, the *NPV* rule tells us the same thing: A is superior because A's *NPV* at 15 percent is greater than B's at 15 percent.

Suppose, however, that the required rate is not 15 percent but 8 percent. The *IRR* rule still tells us that A is superior, but now the *NPV* rule tells us that B is superior because it has a net present value of $31.41 at 8 percent versus A's *NPV* of $29.49 at 8 percent. At any required rate of return less than approximately 10 percent — the point at which the net present value of A and B are approximately equal — the *IRR* and *NPV* rules give conflicting signals.

Why is this so? Because the time patterns of the cash-flow streams are different. Project B's cash inflows are greater in total than project A's, but they occur later in time. At low discount rates, the greater total outweighs later receipts, and project B is the more desirable project. If, on the other hand, the investor has opportu-

Figure 10–2
Ranking Projects Using DCF Techniques

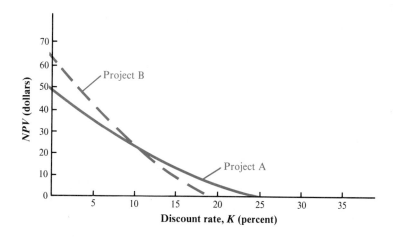

nities to reinvest cash flows at high rates and, hence, has a higher required rate of return, project A is better because it delivers the cash flows sooner. So, the relative desirability of project A versus project B depends in part on the rate at which cash inflows can be reinvested. In Figure 10–2, we see that project B is better at low discount rates, while project A is better at high rates.

Mutually exclusive projects may be ranked differently by *NPV* and *IRR* when the scales of the projects differ or when time patterns of the cash-flow streams differ.

The *NPV* rule and the *IRR* rule may give different signals for mutually exclusive projects when the scales of the projects are different or when time patterns of the cash-flow streams are different. In ranking mutually exclusive projects, if the signals given by the *NPV* and *IRR* rules conflict, the project chosen should be the one with the highest net present value.

If *NPV* and *IRR* give different signals for mutually exclusive projects, the choice should be the project with the highest *NPV*.

The problem of conflicting signals is related to the *reinvestment of intermediate cash flows*. By definition, the required rate of return is the rate at which we assume we have opportunities to reinvest. We use this rate as the discount rate in applying the *NPV* rule, as Equation (1) shows. So when we rank projects using the *NPV* rule, we automatically take the reinvestment rate into account (provided we use the reinvestment rate as the discount rate, as we should). If we rank using the *IRR* rule, on the other hand, we do not even need to know the reinvestment rate; we simply compare internal rates of return as calculated by Equation (2). Since it does not consider opportunities to reinvest, the *IRR* rule can (sometimes) give misleading signals in ranking projects with different time patterns of flows. We must simply remember that, when there is a conflict, the *NPV* rule gives the correct ranking.

Unequal Lives. How do we rank two or more mutually exclusive investments that have unequal lives? Project A described earlier had a life of 3 years, while B had a life of 4 years. Can the projects be directly compared? It depends.

If the useful life of the projects equals the time horizon over which they are being evaluated, we can compare them directly using the *NPV* rule. We evaluate both projects over a 4-year horizon and simply assume that project A generates an inflow of $0 in the fourth year.

In analyzing mutually exclusive projects with unequal lives, difficulties arise when one is faced with analyzing activities that are expected to continue beyond the time horizon of the analysis.

Problems with unequal lives arise when we analyze activities that are expected to continue beyond the time horizon of the analysis. Cash flows may be expected to continue indefinitely, but for reasons of practicality we have to cut off our analysis at some point. If we are comparing two machines to do the same job and the machines have unequal useful lives, then one of the alternatives will require an additional outflow for replacement before the other.

One way to handle such problems is to analyze both alternatives over a period equal to the shorter of the useful lives. The longer-lived project will still have some value remaining at that point. That remaining value should be estimated and treated as a cash inflow in the final period of the analysis.

Sample Problem 10–5
Ranking Mutually Exclusive Projects

Sam Legree is considering two uses for his land holdings for the next five years. The first is to continue leasing the land to a local merchant for $10,000 a year. The second is to convert the land to a parking lot. This will require a current outlay of

Finance in Practice 10–2

Replacement Decisions

▌n the 1980s, many businesses were on the brink of what has been called the next industrial revolution—the use of new computer-age production techniques to replace older manufacturing processes. These new systems of production are called *flexible manufacturing systems (FMS)* because of the flexibility companies have in changing the amount and nature of the output produced at a given location.

These new systems consist of robots, remotely guided carts, and computer-controlled machines, all linked and controlled by computer systems that dictate what will happen at each stage of the manufacturing process. For example, General Electric decided to transform a locomotive-frame factory into a modern automated manufacturing plant. With the old

techniques, building a batch of locomotive frames took 16 days and 70 skilled machine operators. The new facility is designed to produce these frames in one day, untouched by human hands. The catch is that GE planned to invest $300 million to convert to the new technology.

Was GE's decision a good one? Clearly, the decision involves trading off large current expenditures for benefits in the future. This trade-off can be analyzed using the techniques we have discussed in this chapter. More important, the decision also involves tough, sometimes nonquantifiable issues. For example, what about the 70 displaced machinists in the GE plant? In GE's case, these workers were retrained for other jobs. Sometimes, however, a company may be unable to provide employment for all displaced workers. U.S. machine-tool companies face tough competition from Japanese firms that have adopted automated systems and, as a result, have lower costs. In the next few years these companies will find it essential to analyze these investments in new production techniques.

Source: Adapted from G. Bylinsky, "The Race to the Automatic Factory," *Fortune*, February 21, 1983, pp. 52–64.

$100,000 but will generate net cash flows of $30,000 a year for the next five years. Sam isn't concerned about the land's value after the five-year period since he has already committed to sell at a fixed price to a land developer at that time. Which alternative should Sam pick if his required return is 15 percent per year?

Solution
Sam should pick the alternative with the higher present value as calculated below.

Leasing

$$NPV = \$10,000 \; PVAF(0.15, 5)$$

$$= \$10,000 \, (3.352)$$

$$= \$33,520$$

Parking Lot

$$NPV = -\$100{,}000 + \$30{,}000 \; PVAF(0.15, 5)$$
$$= -\$100{,}000 + \$30{,}000 \,(3.352)$$
$$= -\$100{,}000 + \$100{,}560$$
$$= \$560\,.$$

Therefore, Sam should continue to lease the land to the merchant. ▨

Capital Rationing

In principle, the *NPV* rule tells us that a firm should undertake all investments that are attractive — that is, all investments that meet the test of increasing the firm's net present value. In practice, top management, for other policy reasons, might want to restrain the growth (or decline) of the firm's assets to a different rate from the rate that would occur if the *NPV* rule is followed. One device that is frequently used to achieve growth (or orderly withdrawal from uneconomic activities) is to ration capital. Under a capital-rationing system, the top management of the firm decides on the size of the annual capital-expenditure budget. This size projection might be based on the volume of funds available to it for investment (without recourse to further long-term stock issues or borrowing), or it might be based on other considerations. In either case, the approach deviates from that suggested by the *NPV* rule — namely, that we should begin with the opportunities available, add up the total-funds requirements of all those that will increase the firm's net present value, and arrange for all these requirements to be financed in whatever way seems best.

Table 10–9 illustrates a capital-rationing situation when the company has decided to spend only $250,000 on projects in the current year. A quick look at Table 10–9 shows that all four projects have a positive net present value; the problem is that adopting all four projects would cost $500,000 and only $250,000 is available.

▨

Table 10–9
Investment Projects Under Consideration by a Firm with a Capital Rationing System (thousands of dollars)

Project	Required Investment in Current Year	Net Present Value
A	200	60
B	125	35
C	125	35
D	50	5

Note: Capital spending is rationed to $250,000 in the current year.

When capital is rationed, pick the set of projects that in combination have the highest total *NPV*.

Under a capital-rationing system, it is no longer feasible to make simple accept/reject decisions for each project individually. The firm must rank the available projects and select the most attractive set of projects that can be financed within the predetermined budget. To do this, it should still use a variant of the broader *NPV* rule; in other words, it should select that subset of projects that contribute the highest combined net present value to the firm.

In Table 10–9, we see that application of this rule would result in selecting projects B and C. In combination, they provide a net present value of $70,000, which is the highest possible *NPV* given the available budget and projects. Note that project A will not be chosen, even though it has the highest net present value ($60,000) of any individual project, because A would cost $200,000 of the $250,000 available. With the remaining $50,000, project D could be financed but the combined *NPV* of projects A and D would be only $65,000 — which is $5,000 lower than the combined *NPV* of projects B and C.

Table 10–9 has provided a very simple illustration. Capital-rationing problems can become much more complicated. *The basic rule, however, remains the same: select the set of projects that in combination add the most to the value of the firm.* We might pause for a moment to ask why capital rationing is used in the first place. Why does management put a limit on capital spending even if discounted-cash-flow analysis indicates that such spending will increase value? In a world of perfect information, we should not reject a project with a positive net present value as long as it is not mutually exclusive to a project with an even higher net present value. We should raise the funds necessary for the investment. A problem is that in practice we may not know what other projects will be available to the firm in the upcoming years. In practice, investment opportunities often unfold more or less continuously through time. If a particular project is undertaken when it arises, it may preclude an even better project next quarter or next year. There is no good solution to this problem. Sometimes it may be feasible to postpone decisions and save up a list of projects for consideration all at once. This approach is often used, but it can delay projects where time might be an important factor for competitive or other reasons. In such a case, managers may preserve flexibility by limiting capital spending in the current period (rationing capital) as a way to increase their ability to take advantage of projects that they hope will appear in future periods but about which they do not currently have detailed information for formal evaluation.

In many small firms and especially young firms, the need to ration capital arises sometimes not from overriding policy considerations, but simply from the nonavailability of funds. In a world of imperfect information, a firm may not be able to get funds for projects it thinks are good ones. A small, young firm with good investment opportunities may have low current cash inflows, may have no access to the regular capital markets, and, at the same time, may be reluctant to bring in outsiders as equity partners. In such cases, there may be only limited sources of outside funds and the sources offer debt funds only. With no access to outside equity funds, such a firm would have a definite limit on total external financing.

In addition, the complex organizational structures in a firm may lead to forms of capital rationing. For example, a division may be limited to a certain annual allotment of capital funds by top management at the corporate level. Given the complexities and costs of information, the top levels of management can never analyze each and every investment proposal in a large firm. Decision-making authorities are delegated. Top management may exercise some control over the general direction in which investments will go by allocating certain dollar amounts to different segments of the business. For a division manager facing such a limit, the challenge is to be effective in making decisions where capital is rationed.

Where the firm has more investment opportunities than it can accommodate within the financing limit, it must ration capital and rank its projects. The costs of doing so are the opportunities forgone.

Capital Budgeting in Practice

So far the basic message of finance is clear: managers should pick projects according to the net present value rule. This *NPV* rule is consistent with the general criterion of value maximization. In the long run, value created by means of wise investment decisions at some point will be reflected in the value of a firm's shares.

Take the case of Apple Computer, Inc., a manufacturer of microcomputers for personal and professional use. The company did not exist prior to 1975. Two young men, Steven Jobs, then age 20, and Stephen Wozniak, 24, began to build small computers. Over the next five years, the decisions they made and the activities they initiated gave birth to an enterprise worth hundreds of millions of dollars. In fact, when stock was first sold to the public in December 1980, the market placed an aggregate value on the company of $1.2 billion! The value that Jobs, Wozniak, and others working with them created through their decisions and efforts ultimately was reflected in market value—a nice example for all budding entrepreneurs.

While many investments do work out, everything is not as simple as the *NPV* rule might suggest. In an uncertain world, estimating cash flows expected in the future often is an exceedingly difficult task—as we'll discuss in Chapter 11. Additionally, finding an appropriate required return is itself a complicated job that we tackle in Chapter 12.

In addition, we've focused on the *economic analysis* of investment opportunities, but as we discussed at the outset of this chapter, there is more to capital budgeting than economic analysis.

The capital-budgeting process involves several major activities, including the creative search for investment opportunities, the gathering of data and the making of forecasts, economic analysis, decision making, and implementation.

▆ The capital-budgeting process includes the creative search for investment opportunities, the gathering of data and forecasts, economic analysis, the decision, and implementation.

As noted earlier, the kind of economic analysis described in this chapter should take place only *after* a prospective investment has been judged consistent with the firm's commercial strategy. If, for example, a firm is in business to manufacture and market industrial chemicals, it is not likely to spend much time analyzing proposals to go into the restaurant business. After all, if a firm has no competitive advantage in an area, it is unlikely to be able to generate positive net present values on investments in that area.

▆ Strategic considerations enter into the process of investment analysis and selection.

Following up on a decision is also important in capital budgeting. At some future date—say, two to three years after implementation—the performance of a project

It is important to follow up after a decision is made.

should be reviewed in order to compare actual results with initial projections. Such *post audits* are a vital part of the capital-budgeting process.

Although we have assumed that managers act to maximize the value of the firm to shareholders, it is important to remember that managers often face conflicting forces. Suppose for a moment that a division manager's compensation is based (at least in part) on some short-term accounting figure, like AROI. Indeed such accounting schemes are quite common. The question then is whether an individual manager who may have only a few more years on the job will also look past the next few years. It is a challenge to the corporation to make sure that managers are motivated to channel their actions toward shareholder wealth maximization.

One must remember that managers often face conflicting forces, and may not always act to maximize the value of the firm to shareholders.

In addition to factors relating directly to the interests of the firm and its owners, modern managers must consider other constituencies as well, including employees, customers, suppliers, creditors, the government, and the public at large. At the same time, qualitative considerations of ethics, social responsibility, relationships with local communities, and many other factors enter into investment decisions; and these factors often cannot be quantified in the economic analysis.

As well as the interests of the firm and its owners, managers must also consider the interests of employees, customers, suppliers, creditors, the government, and the public at large.

Finally, decision making usually involves many different people. In a small firm, all of these activities may be carried out by one or a few individuals. In large firms, however, many individuals and organizational units are likely to be involved. Furthermore, the review process in large organizations is likely to be complex. A proposal may be reviewed by executives in marketing, production, engineering, personnel, and legal departments as well as by staff officers in control and finance departments. The responsibility for the final decision may lie with a division executive, with the president or chairman of the board, or with the board of directors itself.

Finance in Practice 10–3

The Capital-Budgeting Techniques of 200 Firms

What capital-budgeting techniques do companies actually use in practice? The table on page 300 shows the responses of about 200 large U.S. firms to a survey that asked that question.

Most firms use a number of techniques at the same time, so the table doesn't give the full story. For example, more than 86 percent of the respondents used either the *NPV* rule or the *IRR* rule or both. However, only 16 percent of the firms use the *IRR* or *NPV* rule without also using the payback or accounting-rate-of-return methods. More than 40 percent of the firms use capital-budgeting techniques for all investment decisions, while almost 60 percent use them for only certain types of investment decisions. Based on dollar value, however, most of the dollars invested by the firms are analyzed using capital-budgeting techniques. The average firm responding to the survey uses capital-budgeting techniques for 82 percent of its investment decisions (based on dollar value).

Techniques	Percentage of Firms
NPV rule	56
IRR rule	65
Payback approach	74
AROI approach	58

Why don't all firms use the *NPV* or *IRR* rule? Why don't the firms that adopt the *NPV* or *IRR* rule use them on all decisions? There are many possible answers, but a couple of key factors stand out. First, for small, routine investment projects, it doesn't always pay to go through detailed DCF analysis. For example, if a piece of machinery critical to a production process wears out, it is replaced. The managers don't go through a formal DCF analysis because they know without doing any analysis that they will get a large positive net present value if the alternative is to shut down operations. In the long run, however, assessment of such replacement investment is necessary. Other investments may be mandated by law (for example, environmental quality control) and are required for the firm to remain in operation. Another important factor to consider is the difficulty of applying the *NPV* and *IRR* rules, especially when very uncertain cash flows need to be projected. Some firms that are reluctant to project cash flows beyond a few years in the future use the payback method of evaluation.

What is clear is that the *NPV* and *IRR* rules are becoming more widely used. A similar survey in an earlier period (1970) found that only 57 percent of firms used the *NPV* or *IRR* rule—considerably less than the 86 percent observed in the more recent survey. In addition, it appears that larger companies tend to use DCF techniques more frequently than their smaller counterparts. With the increased level of management education and ease of using computers, DCF techniques, like the *NPV* rule or the *IRR* rule, have become a standard tool of financial management.

Source: Adapted from L. D. Schall, G. L. Sundem, and W. R. Geijsbeck, Jr., "Survey and Analysis of Capital-Budgeting Methods," *Journal of Finance,* March 1978, pp. 281–87.

 International Focus

Bits and Bytes in the Soviet Union

Personal computers have become commonplace in the United States and in many other parts of the world, but they are still relatively rare in the Soviet Union. One recent estimate put the Soviet total at fewer than 100,000 units, a fraction of the U.S. total. Demand for PCs in the Soviet Union is now becoming stronger, largely from Soviet industry, but to some extent from consumers as well. The A. A. Zhdanov Vladimir Tractor Works outside Moscow recently bought a number of IBM PS/2 microcomputers for use in inventory control and other applications.

The problem for the Soviets is that they have no personal computer industry and must build it from scratch. They have designed their own IBM PC-compatible machines, but have had difficulty producing the machines in quantity because of quality-control problems.

To deal with the bottleneck, the Soviets are turning to joint ventures with Western companies. The first of these, called Dialogue, joins the Soviets with a group in Chicago, Management Partnerships International. Dialogue plans to manufacture Soviet-designed IBM PC/XT "clones" (machines that are compatible with and mimic the standard IBM PC design) for sale in the Soviet Union. Dialogue hopes to produce 5,000 computers in 1989.

A second joint venture links the Soviet trade agency for computers with three U.S. partners.

This group plans to ship easily assembled IBM PC-compatible kits to the Soviet Union. The Soviets then will assemble the kits at a plant in Moscow. The plan called for 3,000 computers in 1988 and 18,000 in 1989.

The Soviets need personal computers, and U.S. firms are beginning to give them some help in manufacturing them.

Source: "The Soviets Start Learning Their Bits and Bytes," *Business Week,* February 29, 1988.

KEY CONCEPTS

1. Capital budgeting is a process for analyzing investment opportunities.
2. Determining the payback period and determining accounting return on investment (AROI) are two methods often used in capital budgeting, but each method has some important shortcomings.
3. Using discounted-cash-flow techniques, complex cash-flow patterns can be reduced to single dollar (*NPV*), ratio (*PI*), or percentage (*IRR*) figures that can be more easily evaluated than the payback period or AROI.
4. The *NPV* rule is the general criterion that is consistent with the objective of value maximization.
5. Projects with positive net present values pass the economic test of acceptance as sound investment proposals that will add to the value of the firm. Equivalently, projects with internal rates of return exceeding the required rate of return pass this test.
6. The *NPV* rule should be used to rank mutually exclusive projects, with the acceptable project being the one with the highest net present value.
7. If capital rationing is used, the firm should select the set of feasible projects with the highest combined net present value.
8. Capital budgeting is part of a larger system of planning that includes strategic as well as economic analysis.

SUMMARY

This chapter examined *capital budgeting,* or the process of making investment decisions in firms and other organizations, including nonprofit organizations. The process of investing is very important, because when firms and other organizations invest wisely, new value is created, meaning that the outputs of the investment are worth more than the cost of the inputs.

Capital budgeting is part of a larger planning process that includes strategic and other qualitative considerations as well as economic analysis. Economic analysis of investment opportunities, the major focus of this chapter, requires that we select a method of evaluating projects.

Criteria for investment decisions can be separated into two broad classes: those that are based on discounted-cash-flow (DCF) methods and those that are not. The two most widely used DCF criteria are the *NPV* rule and the *IRR* rule, both of which take into account the time value of money. The *NPV* rule has the additional advantage of always being consistent with the general objective of maximizing the value of the firm. Applied to investments, the *NPV* and *IRR* rules constitute economic tests of investment worth. Both require that a required return — a minimum acceptable return on the investment — be established (a topic taken up in a future chapter). Investments pass the economic test if net present value is positive or, equivalently, if the internal rate of return exceeds the required return. Both rules give the same signals in accept/reject decisions but can sometimes give conflicting signals in ranking decisions. Where they do conflict, the *NPV* rule gives the correct ranking.

DCF criteria encourage managers to take a long view and to make decisions that are best over the long run. A potential for conflict exists when DCF criteria, such as the *NPV* rule or the *IRR* rule, are used for decisions while performance is measured using accounting measures, such as current profits or accounting return on investment.

Capital budgeting is part of a larger planning system. The *NPV* and *IRR* rules are decision criteria to be applied after a prospective investment has been judged consistent with the firm's commercial strategy. The firm's commercial strategy tells it where to look for attractive investment opportunities, and the *NPV* and *IRR* rules tell the firm which of those opportunities to select.

QUESTIONS

1. Define capital budgeting. Why are capital-budgeting decisions important for shareholders?

2. How does each of the following affect (increase or decrease) the *NPV* of an investment project?
   a. Increase the amount of cash inflows per period.
   b. Increase the amount of the net outlay.
   c. Decrease the salvage value of the new investment in its final year.
   d. Lengthen the delay before positive net cash inflows occur.
   e. Decrease the required rate of return.

3. In *NPV* analysis, if the *PV* calculated is the maximum one would pay for the project and the outlay is what one must pay, what is the meaning of the *NPV* amount?

4. Define the internal rate of return of an investment opportunity.

5. Why is it sometimes necessary to rank investment opportunities?

6. Why are projects with negative *NPV*'s rejected?

7. What are the shortcomings of the payback period as an investment criterion?

8. Why do the *NPV* and *IRR* rules sometimes give conflicting ranking signals?

Problems

1. Calculate the *NPV*, profitability index, and payback period of the following project. State the decision rules. The minimum rate of return or discount rate is 12 percent.

	Cash Flows				
Net Outlay	1	2	3	4	5
$10,000	$3,000	$3,000	$3,000	$3,000	$3,000

2. Calculate the *IRR* for the project in problem (1). Should the project be accepted? State the *IRR* decision rule.

3. A firm is considering two competing proposals for the purchase of new equipment described in Table A.
   a. Calculate the net present value of each alternative at a discount rate of 10 percent.

Table A

Proposal	Net Cash Outlay at Year 0 (dollars)	Salvage Value (dollars)	Estimated Life (years)	Net Cash Savings *(cash flow)* (dollars) Years 1–3	Years 4–5
A	10,000	0	5	3,000	2,500
B	7,500	1,000	5	2,000	2,000

b. If 10 percent is the required rate of return, which alternative should be selected? Why? State the decision rule.

4. Suppose that machine B in problem (3) is expected to have a salvage value of $1,000 at the end of year 5.

a. Determine the effect of the salvage value on the net present value (NPV) at 10 percent.

b. Does this change the decision reached in problem (3), part (b)? Why or why not?

5. Calculate the *NPV* for each of the following three investments if the required rate of return is 12 percent. Which of the three investments would you accept?

a. An investment of $27,000 promising a return of $4,000 per year for 13 years.

b. An investment of $27,000 promising a return of $3,000 per year for 16 years.

c. An investment of $7,070 promising a return of $1,400 per year for 16 years.

6. Calculate the *NPV* for investment projects X and Y based on the cash flows shown in Table B. Project X requires an initial outlay of $12,000, and project Y requires an outlay of $16,500. Assume a required rate of return of 10 percent. Which of the two would you accept?

7. Calculate the internal rate of return (*IRR*) for the three projects in problem (5). State the *IRR* rule. Are your results consistent with the *NPV* decisions in problem (5)?

8. Calculate the *IRR* for each of the two investments in problem (6). Are your results consistent with the *NPV* analysis in problem (6)?

9. An investment requires an initial outlay of $1,000 and an additional outlay of $500 at the

Table B

	Cash Flows (dollars)	
Year	Project X	Project Y
1	1,000	4,000
2	1,500	6,000
3	4,000	6,000
4	4,000	5,000
5	6,000	5,000

end of year 1. The investment generates cash inflows of $600, $800, and $800 at the ends of years 2, 3, and 4, respectively.

a. Calculate the *NPV* of the investment at a discount rate of 10 percent.

b. Calculate the *IRR* of the investment.

c. Should the project be accepted? State the decision rule.

10. A bank lends $10,000 to a company to purchase a piece of equipment and requires the borrower to repay $2,637.97 per year (at year end) for 5 years.

a. Viewing the transaction as an investment decision from the standpoint of the bank, what is the internal rate of return to the bank?

b. Viewing the transaction from the standpoint of the borrower, calculate the effective interest cost of the loan.

11. You have arranged to borrow $1,000 from a bank. The bank offers two repayment plans: $402.09 per year for 3 years (payable at year end) or a single lump-sum repayment of $1,259.45 at the end of the third year.

a. Calculate the effective interest cost (the rate that discounts cash flows to zero) of each alternative.

b. Which alternative would you prefer? Why?

12. You have an opportunity to purchase a bond for $912 which promises to pay $40 semiannually for 6 years and $1,000 at maturity. What is the bond's yield to maturity?

13. A building contractor has estimated that using a higher grade of insulating material in your new home could save you $650 a year in heating costs over the next 10 years. If your required rate of return on such investments is 15 percent, what is the maximum amount you would be willing to pay for the higher-grade material? (Ignore any possible tax credits, assume that after 10 years the savings differential between grades disappears, and assume that the contractor's estimates are accurate.)

14. A company is trying to decide which of two machines to purchase for a new plant. Each machine requires an investment of $15,000. The after-tax cash flows and the net income figures are listed in Table C.

a. Calculate the payback period for each investment.

b. Calculate the AROI for each investment.

c. If machine B also had an after-tax cash flow of $5,000 at the end of years 4, 5, and 6, would the payback period change? Why?

Table C

| | Machine A | | Machine B | |
| | Cash Flow | Net Income | Cash Flow | Net Income |
Year	(dollars)	(dollars)	(dollars)	(dollars)
1	3,000	1,000	6,000	2,000
2	4,000	2,000	7,000	3,000
3	5,000	3,000	8,000	4,000
4	6,000	4,000		
5	7,000	5,000		
6	8,000	6,000		

15. An investment of $1,000 generates cash inflows of $301.93 per year for 4 years.

a. Calculate the payback period of the investment.

b. Calculate the net present value of the investment at a discount rate of 8 percent.

c. Note that the payback period and the present value of annuity interest factors used in part (b) are equal. Suggest a way to interpret the present value of annuity interest factors as payback periods.

16. An equipment manufacturer has marketed a new machine that promises to provide your company cash savings of $2,000 after taxes for each year the machine is operated. The useful life of this machine is not known with certainty. The machine will cost your firm $15,000.

a. If your firm's required rate of return on such investments is 14 percent, what is the minimum number of full years of life the machine must operate to make this investment acceptable? Ignore any tax effects that may result from the purchase or sale.

b. What would be the payback period for the machine?

c. Suppose your firm requires a payback period of 10 years for new equipment, and your production manager estimates this machine's useful life to be 12 years. Would you recommend purchasing the machine?

17. The Walters Company is considering the three mutually exclusive investments referred to in Table D.

a. Calculate the payback period and *IRR* for each investment.

b. If the firm's required rate of return is 15 percent, which investment would you recommend, using *NPV* analysis? If the firm selected the investment with the highest *IRR*, would it choose the investment you recommended using *NPV* as your decision criterion?

18. The Downtown Development Corporation plans to sell a vacant lot and receives two offers: the first, an offer of $800,000 cash; the second, an offer of $900,000 with $225,000 to be paid immediately and the balance in equal installments over 5 years (at year end). Which offer should

Table D

| | Cash Flow (dollars) | | | |
Investment	Period 0	Period 1	Period 2	Period 3
A	(10,000)	6,000	4,000	3,000
B	(5,000)	(2,000)	5,000	6,000
C	(15,000)	7,120	7,120	7,120

be accepted? Assume that opportunities exist to invest in riskless U.S. government bonds returning 12 percent.

19. Suppose you are asked to rank a number of investment alternatives for which you have calculated the data shown in Table E. Each project is of approximately the same risk, and thus you think 10 percent is an appropriate required rate of return for each project.

a. Suppose that only one of the four projects (W, X, Y, Z) could be undertaken because all involve the use of the same land. Which of the projects would you choose?
b. Suppose that you could spend no more than $300 on the projects but that this was the only constraint (that is, the projects are not mutually exclusive for physical reasons). What would be your decision?

Table E

Project	Net Present Value (dollars)	Internal Rate of Return (percent)	Initial Outlay (dollars)
W	15	11	150
X	70	30	200
Y	40	33	150
Z	−10	8	100

REFERENCES

Blatt, J. M., "Investment Evaluation Under Uncertainty." *Financial Management* 8 (Summer 1979): 66–81.

Hertz, D. B., "Investment Policies That Pay Off." *Harvard Business Review* 46 (Jan/Feb 1968): 96–108.

McInness, M., and W. T. Carleton, "Theory, Models, and Implementation in Financial Management." *Management Science* (Sept 1982): 957–78.

For extensive treatments of capital budgeting see:

Berman, H., and S. Smidt. *The Capital Budgeting Decision.* 6th ed. New York: Macmillan Publishing Co., Inc., 1984.

Clark, J., T. Hindelang, and R. Pritchard. *Capital Budgeting.* 2nd ed. Englewood Cliffs, N.J.: Prentice-Hall, Inc., 1984.

Helfert, E. A. *Techniques of Financial Analysis.* 6th ed. Homewood, Ill.: Irwin, 1987.

For more advanced issues see:

Brealey, R., and S. Myers. *Principles of Corporate Finance.* 2nd ed. New York: McGraw-Hill Book Co., 1984.

Chapter 11

Estimating Cash Flows

In the last chapter, we discussed the steps in the capital-budgeting process and developed the net present value rule as a way to evaluate investment proposals. If a project has a positive net present value (*NPV*), it should be undertaken. A positive *NPV* is a direct estimate of value creation for shareholders and is thus an operational way of carrying through on the strategy of trying to maximize shareholder wealth.

To calculate *NPV*, however, we need to estimate the cash costs and benefits of any decision. These cash flows can then be discounted at a required return appropriate for the riskiness of the particular decision at hand. In this chapter we discuss the estimation of cash flows for evaluating investment proposals.

Unfortunately, such cash flows do not come in neatly labeled packages. For example, what are the costs and benefits of building a tunnel under the English Channel to connect Britain and France? This is not just a hypothetical question, since such a venture is under way as discussed in Finance in Practice 11–1.

Finance in Practice 11–1

The Channel Tunnel

Care to sink money in a hole in the ground? That is precisely the choice being made in building the Channel Tunnel — a tunnel under the English Channel to connect Britain and France. For over a century, plans to build such a tunnel have ended in failure, but now the parliaments of both nations have licensed their private sectors to dig. In return, the diggers will have sole title to a fixed link under the channel until the year 2020, a potentially profitable monopoly.

The project itself calls for a multipurpose rail tunnel. Half of the capacity will go to national railways — freight and passenger trains. The other half will be taken by the private-sector diggers, who plan to operate special shuttle-trains carrying trucks and cars between new terminals in France and Britain.

The tunnel will be 50 kilometers long, 38 kilometers of which will be undersea, making it the longest underwater tunnel stretch in the world. Fortunately, the tunnel can take advantage of friendly tunneling conditions — a section of softish, watertight "chalk marl" that runs under the channel. It is estimated that over 7 million cubic meters of chalk will come out of the tunnel — enough to cover London's Hyde Park 15 feet deep.

Eurotunnel, an Anglo-French company, will finance and manage the tunnel. Planned spending on the project, including terminals and the shuttle system, is 4.9 billion pounds — around $8 billion, based on exchange rates in late 1987. With a planned opening date of 1993, the tunnel is trying to profit from grabbing a large share of cross-channel traffic. But what will the traffic be? And how will it translate into cash for Eurotunnel? Answers to these questions are major unknowns to Eurotunnel investors. As of late 1987, basic forecasts are that the tunnel will take 46% of passenger travel across the channel and 17% of freight. This translates into 29.7 million passengers in 1993 and 39.5 million in 2003 and over 21 million tons of freight by 2003. But these forecasts are only informed guesses about the future. You can't test market a tunnel the same way you could soft-batch cookies.

Will the tunnel be completed? Will it be profitable for investors if it is? Only time will tell. To make any reasonable decisions about pursuing the project requires estimation of future cash flows.

Source: Adapted from "The Channel Tunnel," *The Economist,* October 10, 1987, pp. 21–24.

While most projects don't have the scope of drilling under the English Channel, any project requires making projections about the future. And these projections may draw on expertise throughout a company. The marketing staff may project sales revenues based on the market for a product and prospective competition from other firms, both domestic and foreign. Production and engineering specialists will need to come up with data on material and labor requirements of production as well as costs of proposed construction. And these projections may cover five, ten, or more years into the future. The contribution of financial analysis of a project is to draw all these projections together into a unified framework in order to assess the merits of the proposal.

Cash Flows: Basic Concepts

As we've discussed above, the method we will apply to the economic analysis of projects is discounted cash flow. By calculating a project's net present value, we will be able to estimate whether the project will add to the value of the firm — that is, have a positive net present value. The cash flows that we will use in our DCF analysis are **incremental after-tax cash flows.** The *incremental-cash-flow rule* is that the cash flows relevant in analyzing an investment opportunity are those after-tax cash flows and only those after-tax cash flows *directly attributable to the investment*.

The words *incremental, after-tax,* and *cash* are critical. The term *cash* calls attention to the fact that we are interested in *cash flow* and not accounting profits. This important distinction was discussed in some detail back in Part Three. Ultimately, financial transactions must be carried out with cash, not profits, so we look to cash as the source of value.

The term *after-tax* emphasizes that we get to keep the cash only after payment of taxes. As we will see, we are interested in *all* cash flows affected by a decision under evaluation, no matter how those cash flows are classified for accounting purposes. If it is a cash item and it is affected by the decision we are analyzing, we are interested in it. Noncash items, such as depreciation, are important only if they affect cash flow — for example, by means of tax payments.

The word *incremental* is important because in deciding whether or not to do something, or whether to pick alternative A or alternative B, *differences* in outcomes are of interest. What changes as a result of the decision? If a firm replaces a piece of machinery, will the firm's insurance costs change? If not, we can ignore the insurance premiums in our schedule of cash flows to analyze the decision about replacing the machinery.

The concept of **incremental analysis** has wide applicability in decision making. Incremental analysis applies not just to investment decisions or to financial-management decisions, but to all decisions faced by individuals and firms. Only differences *resulting from the decision* need to be considered. Other factors may be important, but not to the decision at hand.

> The *incremental-cash-flow rule* is that the cash flows relevant in analyzing an investment opportunity are *only* those after-tax cash flows *directly attributable to the investment*.

> Discounted-cash-flow analysis is an investment decision rule that must be applied to cash flows, not profits.

> **Incremental analysis** — the evaluation of an investment decision that focuses only on differences in after-tax cash flows that result from the decision in question.

Sample Problem 11–1
Incremental Cash Cost of Going to Summer School

Suppose you were living near a college campus and were considering the choice between going to a summer school session for a month or continuing in your current summer job at a local bank. The bank pays you a salary of $1,000 a month. Rent for your apartment is $300 per month and you budget $400 for food and other miscellaneous expenses. You calculate that tuition, fees, and books for the summer session will be $500, and you contemplate no other changes in your living expenses as a result of going to school. Finally, assume you will not earn enough during the year to owe any income taxes. What is the incremental cash cost of going to summer school?

Solution

The relevant cost is $1,500. You lose $1,000 because you will not be working at the bank and, in addition, you must pay $500 in school fees. Your rent and other expenses will not change whether you go to the summer session or not and are therefore not incremental cash costs. Your decision to go to school must be based on weighing the $1,500 cash costs against your perceived net benefits of going to school. ▆▆

Incremental Cash Flows

While the incremental after-tax cash flow rule is quite straightforward conceptually, a number of details require careful attention. To provide an illustration of cash flows, let us develop an extended example: a proposal to build a new facility. Zippo Corporation, a manufacturer of specialized computer parts, is thinking about building a facility to manufacture components for a new generation of personal computers. The company is already producing the components at its main location but has run short of capacity. Zippo's marketing staff believes that Zippo could increase sales by $1.0 million a year if they build the new plant.

However, the plant capacity will probably only be needed for five years since the market for the components will likely disappear after that period as new technologies are introduced. After a few months' study and an expenditure of $20,000, Zippo has found a suitable location and received bids on construction and equipment. These are summarized in Table 11–1. Zippo would build the plant in 1989, with the plant being fully operational in 1990.

Zippo's experience with this type of product suggests that cost of goods sold would be about 60 percent of sales and that there would be an additional $50,000 a year in operating expenses. Zippo plans to depreciate (straight-line) the building and equipment to a book value of zero by the end of 5 years. The company feels, however, that land values in this area will appreciate and that in 5 years it could sell the plant (including the land and equipment) for $500,000. Table 11–2 (p. 310) summarizes Zippo's projected annual operating flows for the new facility based on a 40 percent tax rate. Note that Table 11–2 is just a pro-forma income statement that incorporates only the operating flows resulting from the proposed facility.

▆▆

Table 11–1

Cash Outlays for New Plant (thousands of dollars)

	1989
Land	50
Building	300
Equipment	500
Site Study	20 (study already completed)

Table 11–2

Estimated Annual Operating Flows (thousands of dollars)

	1990	1991	1992	1993	1994
Sales	1,000	1,000	1,000	1,000	1,000
minus Cost of Goods Sold (60%)	−600	−600	−600	−600	−600
minus Operating Expenses	−50	−50	−50	−50	−50
Gross Profit	350	350	350	350	350
minus Depreciation*	−160	−160	−160	−160	−160
Profit Before Tax	190	190	190	190	190
minus Taxes (40%)	−76	−76	−76	−76	−76
Profit After Tax	114	114	114	114	114

*To simplify, depreciation is calculated by the straight-line method over 5 years, resulting in annual depreciation expense of $800 ÷ 5 = $160. The actual rules covering depreciation are complex and provide for different depreciation lines for buildings and equipment. Note that land is not depreciated.

Should Zippo build the facility? Are the expected benefits in the 1990s large enough to justify expenditures in 1989? This is exactly the kind of question capital-budgeting techniques are designed to answer. Our task is to relate these details to incremental after-tax cash flows. Then we can use the net present value rule to see what Zippo's decision should be.

To estimate incremental cash flows for a project, it is often useful to break the flows into three stages: initial investment, operating flows, and terminal values.

In evaluating incremental after-tax cash flows, it is often useful to break the project into three stages as shown in Figure 11–1: initial cash flows, operating cash flows, and terminal cash flows. Initial cash flows reflect start-up costs associated with the project, operating cash flows result from the ongoing operations of the project, and terminal cash flows pick up any special benefits or costs at the end of the planning horizon. Let us consider each of these categories for Zippo.

Figure 11–1

Time Profile of Incremental Cash Flows

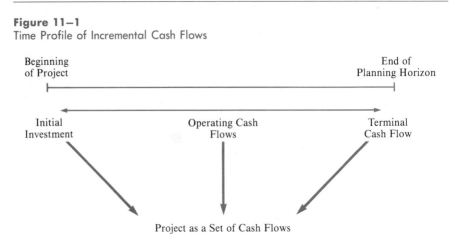

Initial-Investment Cash Flows

Initial-investment cash flows — one-time outlays necessary to acquire the land, buildings, and equipment necessary to implement an investment project.

Initial-investment cash flows are the one-time outlays necessary to undertake a project. As Table 11–1 shows, Zippo will spend money on land, building, and equipment in 1989 in starting the new facility. These expenditures total $850,000.

The site study during early 1989 cost a total of $20,000. Should this expenditure be included in our analysis? The answer is no — the money for the study has already been spent. This expenditure is a **sunk cost.** Because the site-study outlay has already been made, it cannot be affected by our decision now, so the incremental-cash-flow rule tells us that it is not relevant to the analysis of the decision at hand.

Sunk cost — an expenditure that was made before a decision has been made and that is unaffected by the decision under evaluation; it is not part of an investment's capital outlay and, in general, should be ignored in analyzing the investment.

Thus, the initial cash outlay for the new facility is $850,000, all to be spent in 1989. In other situations, projects may require cash outlays for a couple of years and may involve expenditures on a wide array of items.

Operating Cash Flows

Operating cash flows — the cash flows, such as sales, cost of goods sold, advertising, and taxes, generated by the operations associated with an investment project.

Operating cash flows — the cash flows generated by the operations associated with the project — are the next category of cash flows to consider. Table 11–2 lists the operating flows. Note carefully the word *estimated* in the table title. The items in the table represent management's best estimate of the flows that will be generated *if* the facility is built. If the facility is not built, none of the flows in Table 11–2 will take place. These flows are directly attributable to the project, so they are relevant to the decision.

Note that Table 11–2 reports the estimated operating results using accrual-accounting methods, not cash-accounting methods. Companies often base their analysis of cash flows on projections of accrual-accounting figures, such as those found in the pro-forma income statements that appear in Table 11–2. We must be careful to remember, however, that for purposes of our present evaluation, we are interested in estimating cash flows, not profits — and many of the revenues and expenses recognized in accrual accounting do not present cash going in or out of the company. Cash flows, not profits, are required to apply discounted-cash-flow analysis to an investment decision such as Zippo's proposed expansion.

Because depreciation is the major noncash item for most companies, let us assume for the moment that all the items in Table 11–2 are cash expenses and cash revenues except for the noncash expense of depreciation. Table 11–3 (p. 312) shows the calculation of both profit after taxes (PAT) using accrual-accounting methods and operating cash flow for 1990. The cash flow is calculated in the last column considering only cash items. Cash expenses (cost of goods sold plus operating expense) total $650,000 ($600 + $50 = $650). Note in Table 11–3 that the operating cash-flow total in 1990 is $274,000, whereas the total profit after tax is only $114,000. This difference results from the subtraction of the depreciation figure of $160,000 in calculating 1990 PAT (using accrual accounting) even though depreciation is not a cash item. The cash flow associated with depreciation occurred when the assets were purchased, not each year when the depreciation expense is subtracted in calculating profits.

Table 11–3

Comparison of Accrual-Accounting Figures and Cash-Flow Estimates for 1990 (thousands of dollars)

	Calculation of Profit After Taxes by Accrual-Accounting Method	Calculation of Operating Cash Flows by Cash-Accounting Method
Cash revenues	1,000	1,000
Cash expenses	−650	−650
Depreciation (Noncash)	−160	NA
Profit before taxes	190	NA
Taxes (at 40 percent)	−76	−76
	Profit after taxes = 114	Cash flow = 274

Note: This example assumes all accounting revenues and expenses except depreciation are cash items. NA means this item is not applicable since it is not cash.

When depreciation is the only noncash charge, operating cash flow can be estimated as the sum of profit after taxes and depreciation.

As Table 11–3 shows, the operating cash flow in 1990 of $274,000 is exactly $160,000 (the amount of depreciation subtracted) higher than profit after tax. In fact, when depreciation is the only noncash item, we can estimate cash flow by simply adding depreciation back to PAT—that is, we add back the noncash item that was subtracted in calculating PAT:

$$\text{Cash flow} = \text{Profit after taxes} + \text{Depreciation}$$

$$\text{Cash flow} = \$114,000 + \$160,000 = \$274,000.$$

Even though depreciation is a noncash charge, it does affect cash flow through its effect on taxes. Taxes are a cash flow, and taxes are calculated based on a profit figure—after the subtraction of depreciation. Also, there may be other noncash items besides depreciation relevant for a project's cash flows. We'll discuss these topics in more detail later in this chapter. For Zippo, however, the key result is that after-tax operating cash flow is $274,000 per year and can be estimated as the sum of PAT and depreciation.

In Zippo's case the operating cash flow is the same each year, but in many instances we would need to calculate a new cash flow each year as sales and expense levels changed. We would, however, use the same approach as applied to Zippo.

Terminal Values

In connection with many capital-budgeting projects, special steps must be taken to analyze cash flows in the final year. We noted earlier that Zippo's management expected the market for this computer component to last only five years. In many situations sales and profits begin to decline as a product enters the later stages of its life cycle. And, even if a product is expected to continue indefinitely, it still is necessary to pick a finite period over which to analyze it. The appropriate period depends on the nature of the decision, its size and complexity, and the amount of time management wishes to devote to its analysis. If a project is expected to continue to generate cash flows beyond the terminal point of the analysis, some estimate of the value of those subsequent cash flows should be made. This **terminal value** should be treated as a cash inflow in the final year of the product.

Terminal value — an estimate of the value of the cash flows of an investment project generated beyond the terminal point of the analysis and treated as a cash inflow in the final year of the analysis.

In Zippo's case, management projected that the facility (land, building, and equipment) could be sold for $500,000 at the end of 1994, the fifth and final year of the planning horizon. Zippo would not, however, get to keep the full $500,000 because the U.S. government would, as usual, ask for its share. In general, when an asset is sold, the Internal Revenue Service requires Zippo to recognize a taxable gain based on the difference between the selling price and the book value of the asset. In 1994, when the assets are sold, the book value will be the original purchase price less five years of depreciation. As shown in Table 11–4, Zippo will get to keep $320,000, or $500,000 minus $180,000 paid in taxes. This $180,000 is the tax rate (40%) times the gain of $450,000 realized by Zippo.

As a general rule, the terminal cash flow is the proceeds of the sale minus any tax obligation. In some cases, if the asset is sold at a loss, the sale may actually result in tax savings, as shown in Sample Problem 11–2 on p. 314.

Table 11–4
Terminal Cash Flows, 1994 (thousands of dollars)

After-Tax Cash Flow = Pretax Cash Flow − Taxes Paid

A. Book Value of Assets

	(1) Original (1988)	(2) Depreciation (1989–1994)	(3) = (1) − (2) Book Value (1994)
Land	50	0	50
Building	500	500	0
Equipment	300	300	0
Total	$850	$800	$50

B. Gain on Sale of Assets

Selling Price − Book Value = Taxable Gain

$500 − $50 = $450

C. Taxes on Gain

(Tax Rate) (Taxable Gain) = Taxes Paid

(0.40) ($450) = $180

D. After-Tax Cash Flow in 1994

Selling Price − Taxes Paid = After-Tax Cash Flow

$500 − $180 = $320

Sample Problem 11–2
Calculating Terminal Cash Flows

Suppose a company purchased an asset in 1990 for $300 and depreciated it over ten years using the straight-line method, towards a zero book value. The first year of depreciation is 1991. The company is subject to a 30% tax rate.

A. What would be the terminal cash flow if the asset could be sold for $290 at year-end 1993?

B. What would be the terminal cash flow if the asset could be sold for $290 at year-end 1996?

C. What would be the terminal cash flow if the asset could be sold for $10 at year-end 1996?

Solution

A. Depreciation will be $30 per year ($300 ÷ 10), and thus we can calculate the book value in 1993 based on 3 years' depreciation.

$$Original\ Book\ Value - Accumulated\ Depreciation = Book\ Value$$
$$\$300 \quad\quad - \quad\quad 3(\$30) \quad\quad = \quad\quad \$210$$

The gain on the sale will be $290 − $210 = $80. This gain means a tax bill for the company of $24 = 0.30 ($80). Thus our terminal value is the sale price of $290 minus the tax obligation of $24:

$$Terminal\ value = \$290 - \$24$$
$$= \$266.$$

B. The 1996 book value would reflect six years of depreciation and can be calculated to be $120 = $300 − 6 ($30). The gain on the sale will be $170 = $290 − $120. This results in taxes of 0.30 ($170) = $51. Finally we can calculate the terminal value:

$$Terminal\ value = \$290 - \$51$$
$$= \$239.$$

Note that the answer in part B is lower than that in part A because the company realized a larger gain and had to pay more taxes.

C. From part B the book value in 1996 is $120. The sale thus results in a gain of $10 − $120 = −$110. A negative gain is a loss. This loss will allow the company to save taxes by offsetting other tax obligations (assuming that the company is in a taxpaying position). The savings will be (0.30) ($110) = $33. Thus the terminal value will be the $10 sale price *plus* a tax savings of $33.

$$Terminal\ value = \$10 + \$33 = \$43.$$

Summary of Incremental Cash Flows

Table 11–5 summarizes our results of estimating cash flows for Zippo's proposed facility. It brings together the initial investment (determined in Table 11–1), the operating cash flows (Table 11–3), and the terminal value (Table 11–4).

The last column of Table 11–5 is a representation of the project as a package of incremental after-tax cash flows. These cash flows are precisely the type of information necessary to use our DCF methods of evaluating the merits of the proposed investment.

Applying Discounted Cash Flow

Now that we have the incremental after-tax cash flows, we can apply the concepts discussed in the last chapter. Is the new facility a desirable investment if Zippo has a required rate of return of 15 percent for this investment?

To answer this question we must recall the basic definition of net present value. Table 11–5 provides the estimated cash flows $[C(t)]$ and the required return, K, is 15 percent. Table 11–6 (p. 316) shows the results of using DCF techniques to calculate the net present value.

The *NPV* analysis tells us that the cash flows associated with the new facility, net of the required outlays, are worth $227,000 today. The *NPV* rule tells us to accept any investment project with a positive net present value. Using *NPV* analysis, we have reduced a very complex pattern of cash flows to a single time-adjusted figure that tells us whether the proposed passes the economic test and, therefore, represents a wise use of funds.

The information in Table 11–5 also allows us to calculate the profitability index (*PI*) and internal rate of return (*IRR*). From our earlier discussion we know that if the net present value at a 15 percent required rate of return is positive, we will find that the *IRR* exceeds 15 percent. We will also find that the *PI* at 15 percent is greater than one.

We can use *NPV* to reduce a complex pattern of cash flows to a single time-adjusted figure.

Table 11–5

Cash Flows for New Facility (thousands of dollars)

Year	(1) Initial Investment (Table 11–1)	(2) Operating Cash Flow (Table 11–3)	(3) Terminal Value (Table 11–4)	(4) = (1) + (2) + (3) Net Cash Flow
1989	−850	0	0	−850
1990		274	0	274
1991		274	0	274
1992		274	0	274
1993		274	0	274
1994		274	320	594

Table 11–6

Net Present Value (NPV) of Facility

Period, t	Year End	Cash Flow (C_t) (thousands of dollars) (1)	Present-Value Factor at 15 Percent (2)	Present Value (thousands of dollars) (3) = (1) × (2)
0	1989	−850		−850
1	1990	274	0.870	238
2	1991	274	0.756	207
3	1992	274	0.658	180
4	1993	274	0.572	157
5	1994	594	0.497	295
			NPV =	227
			NPV > 0, accept	

Table 11–7 recaps the results of all three DCF calculations. To calculate the profitability index, we use the information in Table 11–6. The present value of cash costs is $850,000, shown at time 0, whereas the present value of cash benefits is the sum of present values for years 1990 through 1994. The profitability index, then, is just the ratio of cash benefits to costs where all figures are in present-value terms:

$$PI = \frac{PV \text{ cash benefits}}{PV \text{ cash costs}}$$

$$PI = \frac{\$1,077}{\$850} = 1.27 .$$

The internal rate of return requires trial-and-error solution until the NPV at that rate equals zero. We know that 15 percent is too low because we obtained a positive NPV at 15 percent. Using the cash flows in Table 11–6 and a required return of 30 percent, we get a NPV of −$96,000, less than zero, so we know the internal rate of return lies between 15 percent and 30 percent. With repeated trials we can close in on the answer, which we find to be approximately 24.6 percent. Doing

Table 11–7

Discounted-Cash-Flow Evaluation of New Facility (at 15% Required Return)

Criteria	Value	Decision
Net Present Value (K = 15%)	$227	NPV > 0, accept
Profitability Index (K = 15%)	1.27	PI > 1.0, accept
Internal Rate of Return	24.6%	IRR > K, accept

K = Required return.

this by hand is a lot of work, so a calculator (or computer) with DCF capability can come in handy!

Table 11–7 gives the important bottom line calculations on Zippo's proposal. Should Zippo build the new facility? The answer is a resounding yes! Zippo stands to earn well in excess of its 15 percent required return, which leads to a positive *NPV*. This positive *NPV* is a direct measure of value creation to Zippo's shareholders. Our DCF calculations have quantified the value of Zippo's opportunity to exploit further its position in the computer business. Evidently, Zippo's expertise has given it a competitive advantage in the market, an advantage that translates into value creation for shareholders.

Positive-NPV projects create value for shareholders.

Before we leave the Zippo example, a few words of caution are appropriate. Remember that the estimated cash flows are Zippo's best estimates. There is no guarantee that the *IRR* of 24.6 percent will actually materialize. What the calculations show is that the investment is well worth the risk involved, but the project may actually turn out better or worse than forecast. Second, Zippo still has to build the facility and get the product to market. The DCF analysis is the beginning of more hard work on this investment opportunity.

Separating Operating Flows and Financing Flows

Based on our calculations of net present value and internal rate of return, Zippo's new facility looks like a good investment. Before we end our discussion, however, we must underscore an important principle we adopted in calculating cash flows for the proposal: *operating flows and financing flows should be separated*. Recall that in our calculations we did not subtract any interest payments on debt or repayments on loans.

Financing cash flows — the cash flows, such as interest, principal payments, and dividends to stockholders, arising from the financing arrangements associated with an investment project.

Suppose the facility is to be financed in part by a bank loan. Should the interest and principal payments on the loan be included among the cash flows to be analyzed? The answer is no. In most cases, the best approach is to analyze the *operating* cash flows of the project and to exclude **financing cash flows,** such as interest, principal payments, and dividends, from that analysis. Operating flows are those arising from the project itself, without regard to the way the project is financed. By separating operating and financing flows, we can view all the firm's sources of funds together. Then we can charge projects with an average of the various interest and dividend costs. Thus financing costs are brought into our analysis by means of the required rate of return (K), sometimes called the **target return,** that we set for the project, as outlined below.

In most cases, operating cash flows should be considered in the analysis of an investment project, and the financing flows should be excluded from consideration. These financing flows will be reflected in the required rate of return.

Suppose we have an investment opportunity, such as Zippo's facility, and we need money to finance the construction and equipment. The money will come from some combination of lenders and stockholders, all of whom expect a return on their investment. Will the project return enough to satisfy those providing the funds? To find out, we compare the *project return* — the *IRR* — to the *target* return demanded by the suppliers of funds. We calculate the project return looking only at the operating flows generated by the project itself and compare this return

Target return — the rate of return required by the suppliers of funds to the investment project.

To determine whether a project will return enough to satisfy those providing the funds, compare the project's return to the target return demanded by the suppliers of funds.

to the target rate of return. All the financing flows enter through the vehicle of the target return, K.

For example, in the case of Zippo's proposal, we calculated the *IRR*, which is the project return, to be 24.6 percent using operating flows. We compared this 24.6 percent to a required *target* return of 15 percent, which reflected the required returns of the suppliers of funds. Because the project return exceeded the target return, we concluded that the facility was a good investment.

Mixing operating and financing flows complicates the analysis. For one thing, most firms obtain their funds from many sources, and it is often hard to tell exactly from where the dollars for a particular outlay — say, equipment — came: whether from a bank loan negotiated last month, from profits earned this month, or from a mortgage arranged six months ago. In the case of Zippo, we would not know whether to charge interest at the rate on the bank loan or on the mortgage or what the appropriate mix of interest and dividends should be.

Our approach of separating financing and operating flows is especially useful in a corporation when money for an investment comes from a pool of corporate funds. Sometimes, however, projects arise in which financing arrangements are an integral part of the investment opportunity itself. A good example is a real-estate project, such as a shopping-center development, where a specially tailored mortgage loan will provide a major part of the financing. In such special cases, it sometimes proves necessary to analyze operating and financing flows together.[1] For our purposes here, however, the general rule is to analyze the project's operating flows distinct from its financing flows and to bring in financing considerations by means of the required rate of return.

Sample Problem 11–3
Preparing an Economic Analysis for an Investment in a New Machine

Your firm is considering replacing an existing machine with a newer piece of equipment. The existing machine has a book value of $4,000, annual depreciation charges of $800, and a remaining useful life of 5 years with an expected $0 salvage value. The machine could be sold today for $1,000. The new machine would cost $8,000, and it has an expected life of 5 years with a $0 salvage value. This new machine is expected to save $1,500 annually in operating expenses. The machine will be depreciated on a straight-line basis. That is, the annual depreciation on the new machine will be ($8,000 − 0)/5 = $1,600.

A. Assuming a tax rate of 30 percent, construct a table of the relevant incremental cash flows for the replacement decision.

B. If the firm's required rate of return on such investments is 10 percent, would you recommend replacement of the existing machine by the newer one?

---

[1] For an analysis of alternative methods of dealing with financing mix in investment analysis, see D. R. Chambers, R. S. Harris, and J. J. Pringle, "Treatment of Financing Mix in Analyzing Investment Opportunities," *Financial Management,* Summer 1982, pp. 24–41.

Solution

A. Let us calculate initial, operating, and terminal cash flows.

1. The initial cash flow is $-\$6,100$ and involves an expenditure of $8,000 for the new machine, adjusted for proceeds of selling the old machine (adjusted for taxes).

Proceeds from Sale of Old Machine	$1,000
Tax Savings from Sale of Old Machine (see below)	+ 900
	$1,900
Purchase of New Machine	− 8,000
Net Initial Cash Flow	−$6,100

The tax savings is calculated as follows:

Book Value of Old Machine	$4,000
Sale of Old Machine	$1,000
Loss on Sale	$4,000 − $1,000 = $3,000
Tax Savings on Loss	0.30 ($3,000) = $900

2. The annual operating cash flows depend on three key figures: (1) the $1,500 annual savings in operating expense, (2) the new depreciation charges due to the new machine, and (3) the elimination of depreciation charges on the old machine (they are eliminated when the company has a gain or loss on disposal of the equipment).

The net (incremental) change in depreciation is annual depreciation on the new machine minus depreciation on the old machine as calculated below:

$$\text{Incremental depreciation} = \$1,600 - \$800 = \$800.$$

Thus the effect on pretax profits of the replacement will be to increase pretax profits by $1,500 − $800 = $700. That is, operating expenses will decrease by $1,500 but depreciation will increase by $800 for a net savings of $700. Now we can estimate operating cash flow:

$$CF = PAT + DEP$$
$$= PBT(1 - \text{tax rate}) + DEP$$
$$= \$700(1 - 0.30) + \$800$$
$$= \$490 + \$800 = \$1,290.$$

3. The terminal value is $0 since there is no salvage value in 5 years on either the new or old machine.

Table 11–8 summarizes the after-tax cash flows generated by the decision to purchase new equipment.

B. Using the *NPV* rule as our decision criterion, we would purchase the new machine if the net present value of the investment is greater than zero. Table 11–8 (p. 320) provides the relevant cash flows. Because the cash flows in years 1–5 are

Table 11–8

After-Tax Cash Flows Generated by Decision to Purchase New Equipment

			Year		
0	1	2	3	4	5
−$6,100	$1,290	$1,290	$1,290	$1,290	$1,290

equal, we can use the annuity present-value factors (for 5 years and 10 percent) given in Appendix Table II to discount the cash flows:

$$NPV = -\$6,100 + \$1,290(3.791)$$

$$= -\$6,100 + \$4,890.39$$

$$= -\$1,209.61 .$$

Because the net present value is less than zero, we would not recommend purchase of the new machine.

Allocated Overhead and Use of Existing Facilities

The incremental-cash-flow rule says we should measure only those cash flows directly attributable to an investment proposal. There are two areas in which we must be especially careful when applying this rule — the treatment of allocated overhead and the use of existing facilities.

In many situations, accountants may allocate part of general corporate costs, overhead, to a project. These overhead costs may include salaries for top management, headquarters expenses, and so forth. Is allocated overhead an incremental cash flow attributable to a project? Typically, the answer is no. If the project itself causes no increase in the company's overall overhead expenditures, the company has no *incremental* cash flow due to overhead costs. The allocation is simply spreading these fixed costs out over the company's activities. Only if the project itself were to increase the company's overhead would allocated overhead be relevant for the cash-flow analysis of the project.

Allocated overhead does not represent an incremental cash cost unless the project actually causes the company's total overhead costs to change.

A second area where care must be taken is one in which a project will use existing facilities (or other existing assets) of the firm. Suppose a company currently has excess warehouse space which could be used for a new project. Should the use of existing warehouse space create a cash cost attributable to the project? To answer this question, we need to ask another question. What are the alternative uses of the excess warehouse space? If there are none and the space would otherwise lie vacant, there is no incremental cost of using the space for the new project. In this case use of an existing facility would not create an incremental cash outflow. On the other hand, suppose the excess warehouse space could be sold to net $50,000 after taxes if it is not used for the project. Then going ahead with the pro-

If existing facilities are used in a project, the incremental cash cost depends on alternative uses of the facility. If the facility has no alternative use, there is no incremental cash cost attributable to the project.

ject causes the firm to forgo $50,000. This is an incremental cash cost of $50,000 for doing the project, which should be incorporated in the incremental cash flows. In general, use of existing facilities creates cash costs only if the facility has some alternative use.

Sample Problem 11–4
Incremental Cash Costs

Franklin Corporation is currently analyzing expansion of its manufacturing operation. Franklin has a vacant building that it could sell for its book value of $30,000. Alternatively, the building could be used to house the expanded manufacturing operation. If Franklin undertakes the new manufacturing, the project will be charged with allocated overhead of $10,000 a year (pretax). This represents an allocation of corporate costs that are not expected to change as a result of undertaking the project. Franklin pays taxes at a 40 percent rate.

A. What is the *incremental* after-tax cash flow associated with the building that should be included in the evaluation of the expansion of manufacturing?

B. What is the incremental after-tax cash flow associated with allocated overhead?

Solution

A. In this case the building has an alternative use (sale), so the initial cash investment in the project should include a cash outflow of $30,000 to represent the cash forgone by not selling the facility. This is an incremental cost. Since the building is sold at book value, there is no gain or loss for tax purposes.

B. The $10,000 is not an incremental cash cost. Franklin, as a company, would have these costs whether it undertakes the project or not. As a result, the incremental cash cost is $0.

Tax Laws

In our examples we have used simplified assumptions about taxes. In principle the message is simple: in determining incremental after-tax cash flows, we need to subtract the taxes paid. These taxes are calculated based on existing laws. In practice, however, the calculation of taxes can become quite complicated and may change over time as the tax code is altered. Here we mention a few key features about taxes.

First, many companies are subject to both state and federal taxes. Both should be subtracted in determining after-tax cash flows. There also may be property taxes and other sorts of taxes levied by municipal governments. In practice, all these tax payments must be subtracted in calculating after-tax cash flows.

Second, in our examples we assume a company is in a taxpaying position. As a result, a project increases the company's tax bill if the project generates profits or creates a tax savings if it generates losses. If a company is not paying taxes and has substantial losses for tax purposes, profits from a new project may not push the company into a taxpaying position. If this is the case, no taxes are attributable to the project and none need to be subtracted in calculating cash flows in that time period.[2] In such a situation, since no taxes are paid, there is no incremental cash outflow due to taxes.

Third, companies actually pay taxes throughout the year, usually on a quarterly basis. It is usually convenient to assume they are all paid at the end of the year, as we have done in our examples.

Fourth, the tax code can be quite complicated and includes many specialized provisions. For example, during a large part of U.S. history Congress has provided a special incentive for investment known as an *investment tax credit*. An investment tax credit allows a company to reduce (take a credit against) its taxes by a specified percentage of the amount of money spent on new equipment. For example, if Zippo's 1989 expenditure of $300,000 on equipment had a 10 percent investment tax credit, this would allow Zippo to reduce its 1989 taxes by $30,000 [0.10($300) = $30]. This $30,000 is cash Zippo will not have to pay the government. As a result, the equipment would only cost Zippo $300,000 − $30,000 = $270,000 on an after-tax basis. Unfortunately for Zippo, these investment tax credits were completely eliminated by Congress in 1986. However, the laws on investment tax credits (both as to the allowable percentage of credit and the investments to which credits apply) may change. In practice, one has to check the current tax code to see if investment tax credits or other special tax breaks are available. A major tax feature important for capital budgeting is the tax treatment of depreciation. This topic is sufficiently important that we will discuss it in more detail in the next section.

Fifth, in estimating future cash flows, a company must project the tax rate that will be applicable in the future. Usually, the best guess is to assume the current rates will remain in effect, but tax laws do change. For example, prior to passage of the 1986 Tax Reform Act, the marginal tax rate for most large taxpaying corporations was 46 percent. The 1986 Act lowered this rate dramatically so that all income over $335,000 is taxed at a 34 percent rate. Given the large federal deficits of the 1980s, there will certainly be pressure for increases in taxes. Financial managers must continually stay abreast of new developments.

Depreciation

Even though depreciation is a noncash charge, it does affect cash flow through its effect on taxes. Taxes are a cash flow, and taxes are calculated based on a profit figure—after the subtraction of depreciation. If 40 percent is the marginal tax rate, every dollar of depreciation reduces taxes by $0.40. When companies that pay taxes include depreciation in their income calculation, they reduce their tax bills. For example, in our analysis of Zippo Corporation's proposal to build a new

[2]The presence of carryback and carryforward provisions may, however, mean that the project's profits today have implications for taxes in future periods.

facility, we saw (Table 11–3) that Zippo expects to pay taxes of $76,000 a year — which is equal to its tax rate of 40 percent times profit before taxes (PBT) of $190,000. If depreciation of $160,000 had not been tax-deductible, Zippo would have had PBT of $350,000 and, as a result, owed taxes of $350,000(0.40) = $140,000. The depreciation charge thus saved Zippo $64,000 in taxes ($140,000 − $76,000 = $64,000). This tax savings is often referred to as the **depreciation tax shield** and is equal to the tax rate times the amount of the depreciation charge. In this case, the depreciation tax shield is equal to (0.40)($160,000) = $64,000.

Depreciation tax shield — the tax savings resulting from the subtraction of depreciation in calculating taxable income; can be calculated as the tax rate multiplied by the amount of the depreciation charge.

In our Zippo example, we used straight-line depreciation, which gives the same depreciation charge per year. In practice, the appropriate depreciation figure is that which is actually reported to the Internal Revenue Service (IRS). Currently, the IRS allows a form of accelerated depreciation that allocates relatively more of an asset's cost to the early years and less to later years. While this doesn't affect the logic of our treatment of depreciation, it does make the calculations more tedious. It is worth the extra effort, however, to do the additional calculations, since because of the time value of money, corporations find it advantageous to use accelerated methods of depreciation and take their depreciation tax savings earlier rather than later. Appendix 11A provides a detailed discussion of the tax treatment of depreciation as outlined in the Tax Reform Act of 1986.

Finance in Practice 11–2

Tax Benefits of Accelerated Depreciation

Whenever there is talk in Congress of tax reform, businesses pay very close attention to proposals about depreciation of assets. Lobbyists emphasize the importance of short depreciation lives and accelerated depreciation rates for spurring business investment. Spokespersons on the other side talk about the tax burden on consumers if corporations are given the depreciation schedules they desire. Heated debate was evident throughout the consideration of the last major tax reform, which culminated in the Tax Reform Act of 1986.

To see why businesses are concerned, let us examine the tax effects of depreciation and the time value of money as they apply to two proposals. Proposal A calls for depreciating computers on a straight-line basis over 10 years. Proposal B provides for a 5-year useful life for computers and an accelerated rate of depreciation allowing for 35 percent in year 1, 25 percent in year 2, 20 percent in year 3, 15 percent in year 4, and the remaining 5 percent in year 5. Note that the difference in the "tax" useful life between the two proposals has nothing to do with any difference in the technological durability of the computers; it is simply a tax rule.

Consider a company in a 34 percent tax bracket that is considering the purchase of a $100,000 computer and has a 15 percent required return. Let's analyze the difference in tax benefits of the two proposals. Proposal A calls for $10,000 of depreciation each year ($100,000 ÷ 10 = $10,000). At a tax rate of 34 percent, this results in a depreciation tax shield

	(1)	(2)	(3) = (1) × (2)	(4) = (0.34) × (3)	(5)	
	Depre-	Depre-	Depre-		Present-Value	
	ciation	ciation	ciation	Tax Shield on	Factor	(6) = (4) × (5)
Year	Base	Rate	Charge	Depreciation Charge	at 15%	PV
1	$100	0.35	$35	$11.9	0.870	$10.35
2	100	0.25	25	8.5	0.756	6.43
3	100	0.20	20	6.8	0.658	4.47
4	100	0.15	15	5.1	0.572	2.92
5	100	0.05	5	1.7	0.497	0.85
		1.0	100			PV = $25.02

Note: Dollar figures are in thousands.

of 0.34($10,000) = $3,400 each year for the next 10 years. At a 15 percent required return, we can calculate the present value of this annuity of tax savings to be just over $17,000 as shown in the following equations:

$$PV = \$3,400 \; PVAF \, (0.15, 10)$$

$$PV = \$3,400 \times (5.019) = \$17,060 \,.$$

Proposal A thus has a depreciation-tax-shield benefit worth about $17,000 to a corporation.

The calculations for Proposal B follow the same pattern: we calculate the depreciation tax shield per year and then find its present value.

As these calculations show, Proposal B provides a series of tax shields worth over $25,000. This is almost half again as valuable as the $17,000 value of Proposal A. Note that this $8,000 benefit ($25,000 − $17,000 = $8,000) occurs even though both proposals have total depreciation charges of $100,000. The difference is that Proposal B gets the depreciation charges and the resultant tax benefits earlier and hence allows the company to benefit from the time value of money.

This tax benefit of shorter useful lives and accelerated depreciation is real. In some cases it may make the difference in whether the business should make the investment or not. This will show up in net-present-value analyses and can have real effects on investment. In any case, it is clear why business lobbies desire faster forms of depreciation. These accelerated methods allow them to take advantage of the time value of money. In terms of tax benefits, the faster an asset can be depreciated, the better!

Working Capital

In analyzing Zippo's investment in a new facility, we discussed the estimation of initial, operating, and terminal cash flows. To simplify matters we dealt with a situation in which Zippo's investment would not involve any increases in its net working capital. However, in many cases, if an investment is expected to increase sales, it is likely that an increase will be required in current assets such as accounts receivable, inventory, and perhaps cash. Part of this increase may be offset by increases in current liabilities such as accounts payable and miscellaneous accruals.

The part that is not offset, the *increase* in net working capital, should be treated as an incremental cash *outflow* attributable to the project. Increases in net working capital often represent a significant portion of total investment in a project. If a project has a definite life span and is terminated at some point, net working capital *recaptured* in the final period should be treated as a cash inflow.

To illustrate the treatment of working capital, consider a project that, exclusive of working-capital requirements, has the incremental flows shown in Table 11–9. At a 15 percent required return, the project has a net present value of $29 and is a good investment.

Now let us consider the effects of working capital. Suppose that some sales are on credit, and thus there will be accounts-receivable requirements equal to 20 percent of sales. Assume inventory requirements will be 10 percent of sales. On the current-liability side, assume accounts payable will be 5 percent of sales. For every $100 increase in sales, accounts receivable will increase by $20 ($20 = 0.20 × $100) and inventories by $10 ($10 = 0.10 × $100). The company must provide $30 to finance these increases in current assets. Fortunately, accounts payable will increase by $5 ($5 = 0.05 × $100). This represents a source (increase in liability) of $5 financing, so the net financing the company needs is $25 = $30 − $5. This $25 is an incremental cash *outflow* the company has as a result of its net-working-capital requirements. Note that the $25 can be thought of as a net-working-capital requirement of 25 percent on a sales increase of $100. The 25 percent requirement is the difference between the current-asset requirements of 30 percent (20 percent accounts receivable plus 10 percent inventory) minus the current-liability sources of 5 percent (5 percent accounts payable).

Table 11–10 (on p. 326) traces through the implications of these working-capital requirements for the project in Table 11–9. Net working capital goes to $25 in the

Table 11–9
Projected Flows of Project (thousands of dollars)

		Year		
A. Flows	*0*	*1*	*2*	*3*
Sales		100	160	160
Cash Flows				
Initial Investment	−60			
PAT + DEP		30	35	35
Terminal Cash Flow				20
Cash Flows	−60	30	35	55

B. Net Present Value at 15%

$$NPV = -\$60 + \$30\ PVF(0.15, 1) + \$35\ PVF(0.15, 2) + \$55\ PVF(0.15, 3)$$
$$= -\$60 + \$30(0.870) + \$35(0.756) + \$55(0.658)$$
$$= -\$60 + \$89$$
$$= \$29$$

Table 11–10

Net-Working-Capital Requirements (thousands of dollars)

	Year			
	0	*1*	*2*	*3*
(1) Sales	0	100	160	160
(2) Accounts Receivable (20% Sales)	0	20	32	32
(3) Inventory (10% Sales)	0	10	16	16
(4) Accounts Payable (5% Sales)	0	5	8	8
(5) Net Working Capital (2) + (3) − (4)	0	25	40	40
(6) Increase in Net Working Capital (relative to prior year)	0	25	15	0

first year and reaches $40 by year 2. This represents a cash outflow of $25 in year 1 and $15 in year 2 ($15 = $40 − $25). Note it is only the *increase* in net working capital that requires financing. In our example we have calculated that the first need for working capital is a $25 outflow in year 1. In reality, working capital will probably be needed throughout the first year, and some projects may require working capital (such as inventories) at the initial investment stage (time 0).

Can we stop here? No, two further steps are necessary. First, we need to discuss working-capital recapture. In year 3 we show $40 of net working capital on the books. This will have some value when we end the project, since we can collect receivables and use or sell inventory. Assuming that the project ends in year 3 (and there will be no sales in year 4), and assuming that we can recognize the full book value of $40, then we will *recapture* $40, which should be added to our terminal cash flows. This recapture is just a decrease in net working capital, which represents a cash inflow — the other side of the coin from cash outflows associated with increases in net working capital.

Second, we need to trace through the full implications of working-capital requirements for our example. Table 11–11 shows the results assuming a required return of 15 percent. Table 11–11 shows a positive net present value of $22, so the project is acceptable. However, comparing the results to those in Table 11–9, which ignored working capital, we see that the net present value has dropped from $29 (Table 11–9) to $22 (Table 11–11). In effect, working-capital requirements demand more cash outflows during the early years of a project and reduce its value.

The general rule for handling net working capital is that increases in net working capital must be subtracted in calculating incremental cash flows; decreases in net working capital (such as recapture) must be added in calculating incremental cash flows:

Increases in net working capital (NWC) should be subtracted in calculating operating cash flows. Decreases in NWC, such as recapture of NWC, must be added to cash flow.

$$\text{Cash Flow} = \text{Profit After Taxes} + \text{Depreciation}$$
$$- \text{Increase in Net Working Capital}$$

Sample Problem 11–5
Calculating Working-Capital Requirements

Return to Zippo's decision about building a new manufacturing facility (see Tables 11–1 through 11–6). Now suppose that Zippo felt that net working capital must be kept at 20 percent of sales.

A. Show the effects on incremental after-tax cash flows for the proposal.

B. Show the effect on net present value.

Solution

From Table 11–2, sales are projected to be $1,000 a year for the five years 1990–1994. At a 20 percent net-working-capital requirement, this implies the following figures for increases in net working capital:

	1989	1990	1991	1992	1993	1994
			Year (thousands of dollars)			
Sales	0	1,000	1,000	1,000	1,000	1,000
NWC (20% Sales)	0	200	200	200	200	200
Increase in NWC (outflow)	0	−200	0	0	0	0
Recapture of NWC (inflow)	0	0	0	0	0	+200
Effect on Cash Flow	0	−200	0	0	0	+200

Table 11–11
Cash Flows Adjusted for Net Working Capital (thousands of dollars)

	0	1	2	3
			Year	
A. Cash Flows				
(1) Initial Investment	−60			
(2) PAT + DEP		30	35	35
(3) Increase in NWC (increase = outflow)	0	25	15	0
(4) Recapture of NWC				40
(5) Terminal Cash Flow				20
(6) Incremental Cash Flow	−60	5	20	95
(6) = (1) + (2) − (3) + (4) + (5)				

B. Net Present Value

$$NPV = -\$60 + \$5\ PVF\,(0.15, 1) + \$20\ PVF\,(0.15, 2) + \$95\ PVF\,(0.15, 3)$$
$$= -\$60 + \$5(0.870) + \$20(0.756) + \$95(0.658)$$
$$= -\$60 + \$82 = \$22$$

These calculations show that cash flow will be reduced by $200,000 in 1990 and increased by $200,000 in 1994 (due to recapture).

B. We can now restate the cash flows for the proposal:

	Year (thousands of dollars)					
	1989	1990	1991	1992	1993	1994
Cash Flow (no NWC require-ment) (Table 11–5)	−850	274	274	274	274	594
Adjustments (from previous table) due to NWC	0	−200	0	0	0	+200
Net Cash Flow	−850	74	274	274	274	794

Using a required return of 15 percent on these cash flows we calculate the *NPV* to be equal to $152,000. This is less than the previously calculated *NPV* of $227,000 (Table 11–6) when no working-capital requirements were assumed. ▬▬

Changes in Prices

When estimating cash flows, it is important to project the future flows, taking into account any anticipated changes in prices. For example, suppose you think a machine can produce 1,000 units of output a year, output which is currently priced at $500 a unit. This means that anticipated dollar sales revenues are $500 × (1,000) = $500,000 at current prices. But as is often the case, suppose you expect the price to go up at a rate of, say, 10 percent a year. One year later the price will go to $550 = $500(1 + 0.10), and the same machine producing the same physical output (1,000 units) will now generate sales revenues of $550,000. It is this $550,000 sales figure that should enter the cash-flow estimation in the future year.

Normally, prices are subject to general economic and competitive pressures. Overall inflation may cause many prices to rise but intense competition (often from foreign suppliers) may force prices of other goods down. Other revenues or costs (such as depreciation) may not change at all. The rule of thumb is that any fore-casted changes in prices of outputs (leading to cash inflows) or inputs (leading to cash outflows) should be built into cash-flow estimates.

▬▬
Forecasted changes in prices should be built into incremental-cash-flow estimates.

Sample Problem 11–6
Cash Flows and Inflation

Return to Zippo's new facility (Tables 11–1 through 11–6). Suppose Zippo's pro-jected sales of $1 million a year were based on no changes in product prices. As-sume that Zippo now believes general inflation will allow it to raise its prices by 3 percent a year after the first year of operation. Cost of goods sold is still an-ticipated to remain at 60 percent of dollar sales, and operating expenses are ex-pected to remain at $50,000 a year.

A. What is the effect of 3 percent inflation on Zippo's projected sales and operating cash flows?

B. What is the effect of 3 percent inflation on the net present value of the proposal, assuming no change in the required return of 15 percent?

Solution

A. Sales in 1991 will be $1,000(1 + 0.03) = $1,030,000, reflecting one year of inflation. Sales in 1992 will be $1,000(1 + 0.03)^2 = $1,061,000. Table 11–12 reports the operating cash flows for the facility based on the new sales forecast.

B. The net present value is $270,000, as is shown in Table 11–12. This is an increase in *NPV* (from $227,000 to $270,000) due to increased revenues as the output price goes up. It is important to remember that expectation of general inflation is also likely to *increase* required rates of return because investors will need to be compensated for the reduced purchasing power of a dollar. Such an increase in required return will have the effect of reducing a project's *NPV*. In practice, then, whether expected inflation increases or decreases a project's *NPV* depends on the effects on both cash flows and required returns. In the next chapter, we'll discuss possible effects of inflation on required returns.

Table 11–12

Operating Cash Flows Given 3 Percent Inflation (thousands of dollars)

	1990	1991	1992	1993	1994
Sales	$1,000	$1,030	$1,061	$1,093	$1,126
minus Cost of goods sold (60%)	−600	−618	−637	−656	−676
minus Operating Expenses	−50	−50	−50	−50	−50
minus Depreciation	−160	−160	−160	−160	−160
Profit Before Tax	190	202	214	227	240
minus Taxes (40%)	−76	−81	−86	−91	−96
Profit After Taxes	114	121	128	136	144
Operating Cash Flow (PAT + DEP)	274	281	288	296	304

Zippo's cash flows are higher than those in Table 11–6 because of the increased sales revenue.

B. The net present value is calculated using the initial outlay of $850,000 (Table 11–6), the terminal cash flow of $320,000 (Table 11–5), and the operating cash flows given above.

$$NPV = -\$850 + \$274\, PVF(0.15, 1) + \$281\, PVF(0.15, 2) + \$288\, PVF(0.15, 3)$$
$$+ \$296\, PVF(0.15, 4) + (\$304 + \$320)PVF(0.15, 5)$$
$$= \$270$$

International Focus

Kuwait's Overseas Holdings

We have focused on cash-flow estimates denominated in dollars. In a global economy, however, many investments cross national boundaries and involve many different currencies. Consider the case of Kuwait.

The stock-market crash of October 1987 was bad news for many investors. For some, however, it created opportunities. One investor that took advantage of the fall in prices was the Kingdom of Kuwait, an "oil sheikdom" on the Persian Gulf. Investment by Kuwait was nothing new — the tiny country had been quietly investing its oil surpluses in Western industry for many years. By 1987, its foreign assets were estimated at $90 billion, perhaps considerably higher.

After the October crash, Kuwait went after a new target: British Petroleum PLC, the third largest oil company in the world. In November of 1987, the Kuwaitis purchased 10 percent of BP, and by the following February had increased their holdings to 20 percent, making Kuwait far and away BP's largest shareholder. According to Kuwait's managing director of investments, lower stock prices following the crash "offered BP to us on a silver platter."

Kuwait had been buying shares of companies all over the world for many years, reportedly including DuPont, IBM, Ford, West Germany's Deutsche Bank, automaker Daimler-Benz (maker of the automobile that many aspire to own, the Mercedes-Benz), the giant chemical company Hoechst, and the mining company Metallgesellschaft. Kuwait has also acquired shares in several British banks and insurance companies and recently acquired Santa Fe International Corporation, a California oil-exploration company. Kuwait also owns a large portfolio of real-estate investments in the United States and Europe, including London Bridge City, a complex of restaurants and shops along the Thames River. The Kuwaitis are reported to have taken positions in the top 70 industrial companies on the New York Stock Exchange and to be considering investments in Singapore, Malaysia, Hong Kong, and Australia.

The facts of Kuwait's investment activities are not well known because the country itself has released little information about its activities. Some estimates place the value of its worldwide holdings as high as $200 billion. One thing is certain: tiny Kuwait is a major player on the international investment scene.

Source: "Kuwait's Money Machine Comes Out Buying," *Business Week,* March 7, 1988.

Cash-Flow Estimation in Practice

In this chapter we have discussed important features of estimating future cash flows. The objective is to get the best estimates of after-tax cash flows that are attributable to any investment proposal. In practice, such estimation is an exceedingly difficult job and by its very nature often involves consulting one's own crystal ball. While there are objective sources of information available, including engineering studies, test-marketing results, and macroeconomic forecasts on general price levels, one is often forced to make difficult choices. What will be consumers' attitudes about purchasing goods? How long will IBM be able to keep competitors from developing an effective duplicate (clone) of a computer product and becoming intense competitors? There are no easy answers to questions such as these; best guesses must be made.

Will you be right in making cash-flow forecasts? Making best guesses means you'll almost always be wrong. After the fact, sales revenues will ultimately be higher or lower than projected. That is the nature of decision making in a risky environment. Success just means making the right decision more often than not.

There is, however, one source of cash-flow misestimation that requires further comment—human nature. Recall that the components of cash-flow estimates ultimately come from people who supply their estimates of the future. In any situation where people are competing for resources (such as in capital budgeting), some people may consciously overstate cash inflows or understate costs. For example, a division manager may have a strong incentive to put the best light on a pet project so that the "numbers" justify the division's getting money for the proposed investment. If such conscious overoptimism (or conscious pessimism, for that matter) creeps into a company's cash-flow estimation, there is real potential to distort investment decisions.

What can be done? In practice, a good procedure is to follow up on accepted projects. If a division's projects consistently underperform the cash-flow estimates made at the project-evaluation stage, financial managers need to investigate. If it turns out that conscious exaggeration was at work, steps need to be taken. A crude procedure would be to reduce the division manager's estimates by some fraction when evaluating his or her requests. The best solution would be to get all decision makers to supply their best estimates, rather than misuse the capital-budgeting process. Such a solution can be difficult, however, in a world of ambitious individuals—just one of the problems that makes financial management a challenging career.

All sales and expense figures for the future are estimates, and therefore are subject to uncertainty. All are likely to turn out different from the projections.

KEY CONCEPTS

1. The incremental-cash-flow rule is a general guide for estimating cash flows. The cash flows relevant in analyzing an investment opportunity are those after-tax cash flows and only those after-tax cash flows directly attributable to the investment.

2. Depreciation is a noncash charge relevant to the calculation of cash flows to the extent that it must be added back to accrual-accounting figures.

3. Operating flows and financing flows should be kept separate in the analysis of an investment project.

4. Tax laws are subject to change, and financial managers must apply the current tax code in calculating cash flows.

5. Depreciation provides a tax shield in the form of reduced taxes. This is true because subtraction of depreciation reduces taxable income and hence reduces taxes.

6. Increases in net working capital should be subtracted in calculating incremental after-tax operating cash flows.

7. Forecasted changes in prices should be built into incremental-cash-flow estimates.

8. In most situations, estimating cash flows for investment decisions is a very difficult job. The payoff is improved decision making.

SUMMARY

Discounted-cash-flow (DCF) criteria, such as net present value, are very useful in evaluating investment decisions. If the net present value is positive, the investment decision is a good one that should contribute to shareholder wealth. To implement such DCF methods, it is necessary to project cash flows that will result from an investment decision.

In using DCF decision criteria, it is cash flow that matters, rather than accounting profits. Careful cash-flow estimates are essential for good decisions. The incremental-cash-flow rule states that the cash flows that should be considered in analyzing an investment are those flows directly attributable to the investment. Cash flows that must be considered typi-

cally include the initial outlay, revenues and cash expenses, and taxes. The effect of depreciation on taxes must also be considered.

Sunk costs — that is, costs already incurred and unaffected by the decision under evaluation — are irrelevant in the economic analysis of an investment decision. The end objective of the cash-flow estimating process is the determination of *operating cash flows after taxes*. Financial flows (interest, principal, and dividends) in most cases should be kept out of the cash-flow analysis and taken into account in the required return (to be discussed in the next chapter).

QUESTIONS

1. Define and discuss the important elements of the incremental-cash-flow rule.

2. Why are cash-flow estimates rather than accounting-income estimates preferred in capital-budgeting analysis?

3. Five thousand dollars was paid to a consultant to study the lighting adequacy in a plant. Later, it was decided to purchase new lights. Should the consultant's fee be included in the capital-budgeting evaluation of the various new lighting proposals? Why?

4. Differentiate initial investment cash flows from operating cash flows.

5. What are the factors to be considered when calculating an estimated terminal value associated with a project?

6. Why does the profitability-index-decision rule give the same accept or reject decision as the *NPV* rule?

7. Why is it best to separate financing flows from an evaluation of the after-tax operating cash flows of an investment?

8. In a replacement decision, what data related to the replaced, old equipment does the analyst need when studying the feasibility of the replacement?

9. How should allocated expenses, such as managers' salaries, be treated when analyzing investment opportunities?

10. In capital-budgeting cash-flow analysis, when does the marginal tax rate of the firm enter the analysis?

11. Why are net-working-capital changes considered in capital budgeting? Give an example. What about at the end of the project life?

12. How do analysts incorporate expected inflation into a capital-budgeting analysis? Give an example.

13. In some cases, investment opportunities involve outlays over several time periods. In such cases, what procedures should be followed to identify the "initial investment"?

14. A nonprofit organization not subject to income tax is considering an investment opportunity involving a labor-saving machine. How should depreciation be treated in the analysis?

15. How should sunk costs be treated in analyzing investment opportunities?

16. When an investment opportunity makes use of existing facilities, how should costs associated with those existing facilities be treated in the analysis?

Problems

1. The marginal tax rate of Lennert Corp. is 34 percent. Calculate the after-tax cash flows of the following capital-budgeting cash-flow examples. Consider each separately.

   a. Added EBIT per year of $20,000.
   b. Cash labor savings of $30,000 per year.
   c. Initial cost of $50,000 for the computer.
   d. Estimated terminal value of $10,000, $2,000 below estimated accounting book value.
   e. Added depreciation of $15,000 per period.
   f. Added net working capital of $25,000.

2. Deemer Corp., a highly profitable enterprise, is looking at two mutually exclusive investment projects — project A and project B. Each of the projects has an expected useful life of 3 years after which there will be zero salvage value. Information has been estimated for these projects and appears in Table A. Assume that Deemer faces a cost of capital of 10 percent based on its operations in the food industry, and that projects A and B are in the food industry. Which (if either) would you recommend for acceptance by Deemer?

3. V. B. Smith Inc. is considering the purchase of a dump truck for $70,000. Analysts for the Smith project combined labor savings and added taxable revenue of $18,000 per year for five years. Assuming straight-line depreciation, no terminal value, and a 34 percent marginal tax rate,

   a. Calculate the estimated after-tax annual cash flows.

   b. Calculate the NPV assuming a 15 percent minimum required rate of return.
   c. What is the maximum that V. B. Smith should pay for the truck?

4. International Company is considering replacing an old stamping machine with a newer and more efficient model. The old machine had an accounting book value of $12,000 and a projected life of 20 years when it was purchased 10 years ago. The projected salvage value was $2,000 at the time of purchase. The machine has recently begun causing problems with breakdowns and is costing the company $1,000 per year in maintenance expenses. The company has been offered $5,000 for the old machine as a trade-in on a newer model which has a delivered price (before allowance for trade-in) of $11,000. It has a projected life of 10 years and a projected salvage value of $1,000. The new machine will require installation modifications of $2,000 to existing facilities, but it is projected to have a cost savings in production materials of $4,000 per year. Maintenance costs are included in the purchase contract and are borne by the machine manufacturer. Assuming a marginal tax rate of 40 percent and all depreciation via the straight-line method, construct a summary table of relevant cash flows. For simplicity, assume that installation costs will be depreciated over the life of the asset.

Table A

Project	Initial Cash Outlay (dollars)	Annual Cash Revenues Before Taxes (dollars)	Annual Expenses* (dollars)	Tax Rate (percent)
A	1,500	2,000	1,500	40
B	2,100	2,300	1,600	40

*These expenses include both cash expenses and depreciation charges. Deemer depreciates on a straight-line basis. All of the initial cash outlays are to purchase items that will be depreciated.

5. Chatham Manufacturing Corporation purchased an old building in Washington, D.C., 12 days ago and immediately contracted for $50,000 in exterior renovation. The building has a projected life of 30 years with zero salvage value. Chatham paid $3,610,000 for it. Annual upkeep on the building is estimated at $25,000 and annual property taxes are $50,000. Chatham is now considering using the building as a warehousing outlet to reduce current annual storage expenses by $400,000 per year. Alternatively, another firm has offered to lease the building for 30 years at $300,000 per year and assume all required maintenance expense. Assuming a marginal tax rate of 40 percent and all depreciation via the straight-line method, construct a summary table of relevant cash flows. Do you have enough information to be able to recommend what Chatham should do? If not, what additional information do you need?

6. The Cleveland Company is using an automated bench lathe that cost $120,000 five years ago. Its current market (salvage) value is only $10,000 due to the present marketing of a computerized bench lathe that is more economical and efficient. The old lathe had been depreciated on a straight-line basis over a ten-year life toward a zero salvage value. Management can purchase the new machine at a cost of $100,000. This new machine would be depreciated over a five-year life to a zero salvage value. Expected cash savings from the new machine are $7,000 a year (before tax) and the company's required rate of return is 10 percent per year (for projects of this risk). Assume a 40 percent tax rate and an estimated income of over $62,000 in either case.

   a. What will be the net cash outflow if the old lathe is sold and the new one is purchased?
   b. What is the present value of the net cash inflows?
   c. What do you think management should do?

7. Orange Manufacturing Company has an opportunity to replace an existing piece of equipment with a new machine that performs a particular manufacturing operation more efficiently. The purchase price of the new machine is $16,500. Shipping charges will be $900 and installation $600. Because of a high rate of technological obsolescence, the machine is expected to have a life of only three years and to have no salvage value. Direct savings from use of the new machine are expected to be $9,600 in the first year and $8,400 in each of the next two years. The old machine has a remaining book value of $2,100 and is being depreciated at a rate of $700 per year. Its remaining useful life is three years, at the end of which time it will have no salvage value. If sold now, it will bring $3,000. The applicable tax rate is 40 percent on both income and on gains on sales of equipment. The company uses straight-line depreciation and depreciates shipping and installation costs over the life of an asset.

   a. Calculate the net present value of the investment opportunity at a discount rate of 10 percent. Calculate the internal rate of return. If 10 percent is the minimum acceptable rate of return on the investment opportunity, should the old machine be replaced?
   b. Suppose that the new machine has an estimated salvage value of $3,000 at the end of the third year, and that straight-line depreciation is calculated on this assumption. If all other assumptions are as in part (a), what are the NPV at 10 percent and the internal rate of return?
   c. Suppose that use of the new machine required an immediate investment in additional inventory of $2,500, and that this extra inventory can be liquidated at the end of year 3. If all other assumptions are those of part (a), what is the internal rate of return?

8. Brown Bag Brewery is contemplating replacing one of its bottling machines with a newer and more efficient machine. The old machine has a book value of $500,000 and a remaining useful life of five years. The firm does not expect to realize any return from scrapping the old machine in five years, but if it is sold now to another firm in the industry, Brown Bag would receive $300,000 for it. The new machine has a

purchase price of $1.1 million, an estimated useful life of five years, and an estimated salvage value of $100,000. The new machine is expected to economize on electric-power usage, labor, and repair costs, and also to reduce defective bottles; in total, an annual pretax cash savings of $200,000 will be realized if the new machine is installed. (Note: To calculate depreciation, assume that the salvage value is deducted from cost to get the depreciable cost.) The company is in the 40 percent tax bracket and uses straight-line depreciation. Brown Bag considers this a fairly safe project and feels it should earn at least 10 percent to justify its investment.

a. What is the incremental cash outlay (at time 0) necessary for the replacement?

b. What is the incremental annual cash flow (year 2) as a result of the replacement? (Hint: Consider only changes in depreciation per year.)

c. Should Brown Bag purchase the new machine?

d. How would your analysis be affected if the expected life of the existing machine was shorter than the expected life of the new machine?

9. Your firm is considering an expansion project that will increase annual sales by $1 million. Aside from the usual project cash flows, you also recognize that working capital will have to be increased in order to support the new sales volume. Given the balance-sheet breakdown shown in Table B, expressed as a percentage of sales, and assuming that these percentages are expected to remain constant at the new sales level, what cash flow would you budget for the net increase in working capital? In what period would this outflow occur?

10. The Cartwright Company is considering replacing one of its existing machines with a new, more automated, more efficient machine. The existing machine was purchased for $93,800 (installed) four years ago and is being depreciated on a straight-line basis over a 14-year life to a zero salvage value. The machine could be sold

Table B

Assets	(percent of sales)	Liabilities	(percent of sales)
Cash	3	Accounts payable	12
Receivables	15	Accrued taxes	2
Inventories	22	Bonds	21
Net fixed assets	45	Common stock	20
		Retained earnings	20

today for $20,000. The new machine could be purchased for $95,000. Installation costs would be an additional $3,000. It is estimated that the new machine could increase output by 10 percent, increasing operating revenue by $15,000 per year. In addition, the machine is expected to reduce operating costs by $18,000 annually. The machine has an expected ten-year life with a $13,000 salvage value and will be depreciated on a straight-line basis. Cartwright's required rate of return on such investments is 14 percent, and the firm's tax rate is 50 percent.

a. Should Cartwright purchase the new machine?

b. If the new machine did not reduce any costs but only increased output, what would be your recommendation?

c. If you do not advocate purchasing the new machine, what would the purchase price have to be to change your recommendation?

11. The Allen Company, a manufacturer of inexpensive perfumes and toiletries, is considering an investment in a new perfume, Jasper. The company has spent $75,000 in developing and testing the new fragrance, and the final chemical formula and marketing plans have been decided upon. If Jasper is introduced, it will replace the Rosalyn product line, which has experienced declining sales over the past few years. Jasper can be manufactured and bottled using the same equipment and labor force currently used for Rosalyn without any adjustments or modifications. The equipment being used has a remaining book value of $160,000 and is being depreciated at a rate of $20,000 per year. An additional packaging machine will be required for the Jasper line to accommodate the product's more

sophisticated package design. The machine required will cost $50,000 (delivered and installed) and has a projected life of five years with no salvage value. The machine is fully automated and will not require any additional personnel for operation. It is expected that this machine will increase overhead maintenance and power expenses by $1,000 per year. The raw material costs of Jasper are expected to be 15 cents per bottle compared to Rosalyn's cost of 10 cents per bottle. Labeling and packaging costs for Jasper are expected to be 20 cents per bottle compared to Rosalyn's 10 cents per bottle. The marketing department has provided projected sales levels and marketing expenses for the Jasper and Rosalyn lines for the next five years, which are shown in Table C. These forecasts assume that if Jasper is not introduced, Rosalyn will stay on the market, and if Jasper is introduced, Rosalyn will be taken off the market. At the end of five years, it is expected that either product will have exhausted its sales potential and will be taken off the market. No increases in working capital are expected to be needed to support the Jasper line.

a. Assuming a 50 percent tax rate and straight-line depreciation, construct a summary table of relevant cash flows for making the decision of introducing Jasper or keeping Rosalyn.

b. If Allen's required rate of return is 20 percent, what is the incremental NPV of introducing Jasper? (For simplicity, assume all cash flows occur at the end of the year.)

12. Your firm is considering the purchase of a tractor. It has been established that this tractor will cost $32,000, will produce annual cash revenues in the neighborhood of $10,000 (before tax), and will be depreciated using the straight-line approach to zero in eight years. The board of directors, however, is having a heated debate as to whether the tractor can be expected to last eight years. Specifically, Wayne Seus insists he knows of some that have lasted only five years. Tom Smith agrees with Wayne but argues that it is more likely that the tractor will give eight

Table C

Year	Sales (number of bottles)	Price per Bottle (dollars)	Marketing Expenses (dollars)
	Jasper Market Forecasts		
1	100,000	5.00	200,000
2	100,000	5.00	200,000
3	75,000	5.00	120,000
4	60,000	4.00	50,000
5	30,000	4.00	20,000
	Rosalyn Market Forecasts		
1	75,000	4.00	50,000
2	75,000	4.00	40,000
3	50,000	3.50	40,000
4	30,000	3.50	0
5	20,000	3.00	0

years of service. Wayne agrees. Finally, Ralph Evans says he has seen some last as long as ten years. Given the discussion, the board asks you to prepare a sensitivity analysis to ascertain how important the uncertainty about the life of the tractor is. Assume a 40 percent tax rate on both income and capital gains, zero salvage value, and a required rate of return of 10 percent.

a. Calculate the NPV if the tractor lasts 8 years.

b. Calculate the NPV if the tractor lasts only 5 years and then must be scrapped for zero salvage value.

Table D

Project	Net Present Value (NPV) (thousands of dollars)	Internal Rate of Return (IRR) (percent)	Required Initial Outlay (thousands of dollars)
A	30	28	100
B	10	20	75
C	8	14	75
D	40	15	300
E	8	13	100
F	5	17	50

c. Calculate the *NPV* if the tractor lasts 10 years and then is scrapped for zero salvage value.

d. Comment on the sensitivity of the purchase proposal to the life of the tractor.

13. After careful analysis, you have calculated *NPV* and *IRR* figures on a number of investment projects as shown in Table D. As division manager, you have authority to choose any of the projects you desire. But there is a catch. While the projects are not mutually exclusive, the chief financial officer of the company has decided that your division can spend no more than $350,000 on capital projects during the coming year. What set of projects would you choose? Why?

REFERENCES

Blatt, J. M., "Investment Evaluation Under Uncertainty." *Financial Management* 8 (Summer 1979): 66–81.

Chambers, D., R. Harris, and J. Pringle, "Treatment of Financing Mix in Analyzing Investment Opportunities." *Financial Management* (Summer 1982): 24–41.

Hertz, D. B., "Investment Policies That Pay Off." *Harvard Business Review* 46 (Jan/Feb 1968): 96–108.

Johnson, R. *Issues and Readings in Managerial Finance.* 3rd ed. New York: Dryden Press, 1987.

McInness, M., and W. T. Carleton, "Theory, Models, and Implementation in Financial Management." *Management Science* (Sept 1982): 957–78.

For extensive treatments of capital budgeting see:

Berman, H., and S. Smidt. *The Capital Budgeting Decision.* 6th ed. New York: Macmillan Publishing Co., Inc., 1984.

Clark, J., T. Hindelang, and R. Pritchard. *Capital Budgeting.* 2nd ed. Englewood Cliffs, N.J.: Prentice-Hall, Inc., 1984.

Helfert, E. A. *Techniques of Financial Analysis.* 6th ed. Homewood, Ill.: Irwin, 1987.

For more advanced issues see:

Brealey, R., and S. Myers. *Principles of Corporate Finance.* 2nd ed. New York: McGraw-Hill Book Co., 1984.

Appendix 11A

Accelerated Depreciation Under the Tax Reform Act of 1986

The Tax Reform Act of 1986 changed many features of the tax laws for both individuals and corporations. In this Appendix we focus on the Act's treatment of depreciation due to the importance of depreciation charges in estimating operating cash flows.

The Act changed depreciation in three fundamental ways. The first major change was the reclassification of asset lives. In general, asset lives were lengthened for depreciation purposes. This is generally costly to businesses because it postpones the tax savings due to the depreciation tax shield. The second major change in depreciation was allowing a faster percentage depreciation rate. The third major change was the adoption of an assumption about when assets are placed in service. The 1986 Act assumes they are placed in service at mid-year, so it only allows a portion of the initial year's depreciation expense to be taken in the initial year. Table 11A–1 summarizes the Act's rules for determining the depreciable lives of major asset categories.

To compute the depreciation expenses for an asset requires knowledge of the depreciable life of the asset, the depreciable value of the asset, and the proportion of the value that can be depreciated during each year of the asset's life. The new depreciation rules assume that an asset is placed in service at mid-year, so the initial year's depreciation is only half the normal amount. To reflect this convention, in this Appendix we assume that the first depreciation expense is at period 0. This reflects the 1986 Act's approach to determining the depreciation expenses. Note that this allows depreciation to be taken during year 0. In the text our examples have assumed one must wait a full year to get depreciation benefits. This reflects one of the complexities of working with an often complicated tax code, but it does not change the basic logic of figuring out cash flows.

The Act allows for a switching to straight-line depreciation at any time. Table 11A–2 gives the depreciation percentages for different classes of property and reflects a switching to straight-line at the time that makes the depreciation as fast as possible. Under the rules in Table 11A–2, the full price of an asset is depreciated with no allowance for salvage value.

Table 11A–1
Asset Lives for Depreciation Tax Reform Act of 1986

3-Year Property

Special handling devices for the manufacture of food and beverages, tools for the manufacture of rubber and finished plastic products, fabricated metal products or motor vehicles, breeding hogs, and racehorses more than 2 years old when placed in service.

5-Year Property

Computers, typewriters, copiers, duplicating equipment, heavy trucks, trailers, cargo containers, cars, light trucks, computer-based telephone switching equipment, semiconductor-manufacturing equipment, research-and-experimentation equipment.

7-Year Property

Office furniture, fixtures and equipment, railroad track, agricultural and horticultural structures.

10-Year Property

Assets used in petroleum refining and the manufacture of tobacco products.

Other Categories

There are also 15-year and 20-year categories for such items as municipal sewage-treatment plants. In addition, certain kinds of real estate must be depreciated for 27.5 or 31.5 years.

warehouse   apartments

Table 11A–2
Depreciation Rates: Tax Reform Act of 1986

Recovery Year	Type of Asset (percent)			
	3-Year	*5-Year*	*7-Year*	*10-Year*
0	33.00	20.00	14.28	10.00
1	45.00	32.00	24.49	18.00
2	15.00	19.20	17.49	14.40
3	7.00	11.52	12.49	11.52
4		11.52	8.93	9.22
5		5.76	8.93	7.37
6			8.93	6.55
7			4.46	6.55
8				6.55
9				6.55
10				3.29

Sample Problem 11A–1
Calculating Depreciation Under the 1986 Tax Act

A contractor buys a truck for $20,000 in 1988. What are the depreciation expenses generated by the truck for each year?

Solution

A truck would be classified as 5-year property as shown in Table 11A–1. The depreciation would be calculated as shown in the following table:

Recovery Year	Calendar Year	Depreciation Percentage (Table 11A–2)	Depreciation* Expense
0	1988	20.00	$4,000.00
1	1989	32.00	6,400.00
2	1990	19.20	3,840.00
3	1991	11.52	2,304.00
4	1992	11.52	2,304.00
5	1993	5.76	1,152.00
		100.00	$20,000.00

*$20,000 times depreciation percentage

There are other special complications about depreciation. For example, the law allows the expensing of costs up to $10,000 per year and has special penalties attached to it if too high a percentage of an asset category is placed in service at year end.

The practical advice for financial managers is that they must be sure to check the tax code carefully or to consult a tax specialist. This is especially true since tax laws will undoubtedly change over time.

Appendix 11B

Tax Effects

Nonprofit organizations excluded, taxes are relevant to almost every financial decision that a firm or individual makes.

Taxes are relevant to almost every financial decision a firm or individual makes, unless the firm or individual is not subject to taxation. The incremental-cash-flow rule tells us that, if the decision at hand affects tax payments, those tax effects should be considered. In the final analysis, we are interested in the *net cash flow after taxes*.

While the details of tax laws change over time, tax effects remain very important in business decisions. For example, if the marginal tax rate is 40 percent, a dollar's worth of revenue becomes $0.60 after taxes, and a dollar's worth of depreciation saves $0.40 in taxes. Tax effects are also important to individuals because they often face high tax rates.

There are two general approaches to dealing with tax effects in calculating cash flows. One way is to use an income-statement format and determine taxes on net profit.

There are two general approaches to dealing with tax effects in investment decisions. One is to put financial information in income-statement format and determine taxes on net profit. This method was used earlier in this chapter. In a simple case, where depreciation is the only noncash item, we can represent this method symbolically, as shown in Equation (B–1). Net operating cash flow (C) after taxes can be calculated from income-statement data as

$$C = PAT + DEP \qquad\qquad (B\text{–}1)$$
$$= (CR - CE - DEP)(1 - T) + DEP$$

where CR = cash revenues, CE = cash expenses, PAT = profit after taxes, DEP = depreciation, and T = the corporate tax rate.

In Equation (B–1), we have simply stated that profit after taxes can be written as $(CR - CE - DEP)(1 - T)$ and that cash flow is profit after taxes plus depreciation. For example, using the 1990 date for Zippo (from Table 11–2), we see that CR = $1,000,000, CE = $600,000 + $50,000 = $650,000, and DEP = $160,000. Using Equation (B–1), we can calculate operating cash flow after taxes as

$$C = (\$1,000,000 - \$650,000 - \$160,000)(1 - 0.40) + \$160,000$$
$$= \$274,000.$$

The second way is to convert each cash flow to its after-tax equivalent flow.

This same result was given in the second column of Table 11–5 in the body of Chapter 11.

A second method for calculating operating cash flow after taxes that many find useful can be expressed by rearranging Equation (B–1) as shown in Equation (B–2). Net operating cash flow after taxes (C) can also be calculated, by converting each component cash flow to its after-tax equivalent flow, as

$$C = CR(1 - T) - CE(1 - T) - DEP(1 - T) + DEP \qquad (B-2)$$

$$= CR(1 - T) - CE(1 - T) + DEP(T)$$

where variables are defined as in Equation (B–1). Note that Equation (B–2) is mathematically equivalent to Equation (B–1) — our first method of calculating after-tax operating cash flows — so we'll always get the same answer whether we use Equation (B–1) or Equation (B–2). The approach suggested in Equation (B–2) is to convert each cash flow to its after-tax equivalent flow. A cash revenue (for example, a sales figure) of $1,000 becomes $600, for that is the amount left over after the tax collector leaves. At a tax rate of 40 percent, $600 is the *after-tax equivalent* of the $1,000 revenue figure. In Equation (B–2), the after-tax equivalent of cash revenues is expressed as $CR(1 - T)$. Similarly, the after-tax equivalent of $600 in expenses is $CE(1 - T) = \$600(1 - 0.40) = \$360$.

As noted earlier, each dollar of depreciation saves taxes. This tax saving is called the *depreciation tax shield* and is the last term in Equation (B–2). To illustrate, $400 in depreciation generates a depreciation tax shield, or tax savings, of $(DEP \times T) = \$400 \times 0.40 = \$160$. Let us illustrate this method by applying it to Zippo's proposed facility. We will use 1990 data from Table 11–2 as reproduced in the first column of Table 11B–1. Using Equation (B–2), net operating cash flow can be calculated as

$$C = \$1,000,000(1 - 0.40) - \$650,000(1 - 0.40) + \$160,000(0.40)$$

$$= \$274,000 .$$

Table 11B–1 demonstrates this result in more detail. Note that the result using the second method is the same as the one we obtained using the first method, $274,000. Note also that Table 11B–1 deals only with the pretax cash-flow items, plus depreciation. Note also that while depreciation is an expense, the depreciation tax shield is a cash inflow because it reduces taxes. Table 11B–2 outlines the general rules we followed in constructing Table 11B–1.

It is important to keep in mind that tax effects could be quite different if the firm were losing money at the time and, therefore, were paying no taxes. Negative taxes are not paid to the firm by the government! Tax losses may be carried forward and applied against future income or may be carried back against prior years. Thus, even when a firm is losing money, tax effects can still be important, but the actual cash flows resulting from tax effects might take place in years other than the current one.

In addition, for a nonprofit organization such as a university or a church that pays no taxes, the tax rate, T, is 0 percent. Thus, while we could still use either approach — Equation (B–1) or Equation (B–2) — for calculating the nonprofit organization's operating cash flows, we would have to set T equal to zero.

One final note on depreciation: depreciation can be calculated on a straight-line basis, or using one of several accelerated methods, such as the declining-balance method or the sum-of-the-year's-digits method. (See Appendix 11A for further

Tax effects may be quite different if the firm is losing money and therefore paying no taxes.

For nonprofit organizations, the effective tax rate is zero.

Table 11B–1

Calculating After-Tax Equivalent Cash Flows

	1990 Pretax Cash Flow Item (thousands of dollars) (1)	Tax Effect (2)	After-Tax Equivalent (thousands of dollars) (3) = (1) × (2)
Sales (CR)	1,000	(1 − 0.40)	+600
Cost of goods sold (CE)	−600	(1 − 0.40)	−360
Operating expense (CE)	−50	(1 − 0.40)	−30
Depreciation tax shield, (DEP) × T	160	0.40)	+64
Cash flow from operations after taxes			274

Table 11B–2

Rules to Apply in Calculating After-Tax Equivalent Cash Flows

Type of Item	Calculation Rule
For cash items (sales, cash expenses, etc.)	Pretax amount × (1 − T) = After-tax equivalent
For noncash items (depreciation, etc.)	Pretax amount × T = Tax shield

Deferring taxes by means of accelerated depreciation is advantageous because of the time value of money.

discussion of depreciation expenses.) The more rapid the depreciation, the lower the taxes in early years and the higher the taxes in later years. Deferring taxes by means of accelerated depreciation is advantageous because of the time value of money.

Sample Problem 11B–1

Determining the Net Operating Cash Flow and the Net Present Value of an Investment in a New Machine

Camino Industries is considering replacing an old machine with a newer model having lower maintenance expense. The old machine has a current book value of $2,000, depreciation charges of $500 per year, and a remaining life of 4 years, at which time it will have no salvage value. If the machine were sold today, proceeds would be $1,500. Annual maintenance is $1,500.

The new machine has a purchase price of $6,000, a life of 4 years, a salvage value at the end of 4 years of $2,000, and annual maintenance expense of $200. Assuming a tax rate of 46 percent, straight-line depreciation, and no investment tax credit, prepare a table of the relevant after-tax cash flows associated with the replacement. Calculate the net present value of the replacement assuming a required return of 10 percent.

Table 11B–3

Comparison of Incremental Cash Flows for New and Old Machines, Camino Industries

Rule (from Table 11B–2)	*Existing* *(1)*	*Replacement* *(2)*	*Incremental* *(3) = (2) − (1)*
Maintenance			
Cash item:	−$1,500(1 − 0.46) = −$810	−$200(1 − 0.46) = −$108	$702
Pretax amount × (1 − T)			
Depreciation			
Noncash item:	$500(0.46) = $230	$1,000(0.46) = $460	$230
Pretax amount × T		*Total*	$932

Solution

As the first step, let us calculate the depreciation charge on the new machine. Assuming straight-line depreciation, we can calculate the annual depreciation expense as

$$\text{Depreciation} = \frac{\text{Amount to be depreciated}}{\text{Useful life}}$$

$$= \frac{\$6{,}000 - \$2{,}000}{4} = \$1{,}000 \text{ per year}.$$

Table 11B–3 shows the results of calculating the annual change in operating cash flow using the rules in Table 11B–2. Note that Table 11B–3 gives the *incremental* maintenance and depreciation flows determined by comparing the new machine with the old. As Table 11B–3 shows, there will be an annual after-tax cash savings of $932. Table 11B–4 shows the results of adding to the new operating cash flows the initial and terminal cash flows associated with the replacement.

Table 11B–4

Total Cash Flows Generated by a New Machine Purchase

	Cash Flows				
	Year 0	*Year 1*	*Year 2*	*Year 3*	*Year 4*
Purchase of new machine	$(6,000)				
Salvage value of old machine	$ 1,500				$2,000
Salvage tax shield*	230				
Annual new cash flow	0	$932	$932	$932	932
Total	**$(4,270)**	**$932**	**$932**	**$932**	**$2,932**

*Current book value of old machine is $2,000. Selling it today for $1,500 yields a book loss of $500 and thus a tax shield of $500 × 0.46 = $230. Salvage value of new machine equals book value at the end of year 4 ($2,000), so no tax shield is generated in year 4.

The net present value at 10 percent can be calculated using the figures in Table 11B–4:

$$NPV = -\$4{,}270 + \frac{\$932}{(1.1)} + \frac{\$932}{(1.1)^2} + \frac{\$932}{(1.1)^3} + \frac{\$2{,}932}{(1.1)^4}$$

$$= -\$4{,}270 + \$932(0.909) + \$932(0.826) + \$932(0.751)$$

$$+ \$2{,}932(0.683)$$

$$= \$49.51\,.$$

Because net present value is greater than 0, the replacement is a good decision, although it does not give an extremely large *NPV*.

Chapter 12

Required Rates of Return and the Cost of Capital

In this chapter we will discuss how companies and other organizations establish required returns for capital-investment projects. We will explore the relationship between required returns inside the firm and returns earned by investors in financial markets outside the firm. After learning how to calculate required returns, we will then discuss how these returns are actually used in evaluating projects.

In Chapters 10 and 11, we discussed two important steps in analyzing investment opportunities: (1) choosing a decision criterion and (2) estimating cash flows. We settled on the discounted-cash-flow calculations of net present value (*NPV*) and internal rate of return (*IRR*) as the most useful criteria because they take into account the time value of money. We also discussed the calculation of incremental after-tax cash flows. Now we come to step (3): choosing an appropriate required rate of return.

Required rate of return — the minimum acceptable return on any investment; the rate forgone on the next best alternative investment opportunity of comparable risk; it is an *opportunity rate*.

In using the *NPV* rule, what do we use for a required rate of return? If the expected internal rate of return is, say, 12 percent, is the investment acceptable? To answer this question, we must establish a **required rate of return,** which is the minimum acceptable expected return on the investment.

In this chapter, we will discuss the concept of required returns for projects and develop our basic approach to determining appropriate required returns. Refinements to the basic approach will be saved for the next chapter.

How Required Returns Are Determined in Financial Markets ✳

At the outset let us establish a basic framework for approaching the problem of required returns for capital investments. The required return for any project depends on the opportunities to invest elsewhere in financial markets.

Required Returns and Investors' Opportunities

Because the funds used by a firm to make investments are supplied by others, the investments must earn a return sufficient to compensate these suppliers of capital.

Where does a firm get the funds to invest? When a firm invests, it uses capital funds supplied by others — namely, lenders and investors. Therefore, investments undertaken by a firm must earn a return sufficient to compensate suppliers of capital.

What return do investors expect on their additional investment? To be satisfied, they must expect a return at least equal to what they could earn on alternative investments of comparable risk. When an investment decision is to be made, the investor — whether an individual or a manager acting on behalf of shareholders — always has alternative opportunities in which to invest the funds. If not, there is no decision to be made.

Consider the problem of an investor analyzing a new investment opportunity, called Project X. Project X requires an outlay of $10,000 now and promises cash inflows in the future. If the investor undertakes Project X, he or she must forgo the opportunity to do something else with the money. Hence, by undertaking Project X, the investor incurs an **opportunity cost** — namely, whatever rate of return could have been earned on an alternative investment.

Opportunity cost — the return an investor could have earned on the next best alternative investment forgone.

The concept of opportunity cost is a general and very useful one. The true economic cost of any action includes all that one must give up in order to undertake the action. The $5 spent on a movie means $5 less available for something else. The money provided to a corporation is unavailable for other investments that might have returned more.

Finance in Practice 12–1

Who Should Pay for Power-Plant Duds?

An article in the *Wall Street Journal* raised the question of who should pay for power-plant duds in connection with electric-utility plants. The article was written by Alfred Kahn, a Cornell economist, former chairman of the Civil Aeronautics Board, champion of airline deregulation during the Carter Administration, and noted authority on regulated industries. The article began, "The New York Public Service Commission decided in June to disallow, on grounds of imprudence, the passing on to consumers of $1.35 billion of Long Island Lighting Company's $4.2 billion-plus investment in its Shoreham nuclear plant. This is only the latest and most dramatic of a series of similar decisions confronting utility commissions all over the country—what to do with the billions of dollars sunk in nuclear generating plants that have either been abandoned or threaten, upon coming into service, to require rate increases in the 20–60 percent range."

The struggle over who should pay for nuclear power plants that cost more than originally envisioned or that were never completed is peculiar to the electric-utility industry. But the dilemma illustrates one of the basic concepts of finance—namely, that capital investments must earn a return sufficient to compensate those who put up the funds to finance them.

Electric utilities are regulated, and electricity rates supposedly are set so that utility investors earn a fair rate of return on their investment—a fair rate being defined as a return roughly equal to that of other investments of comparable risk. This chapter will define this rate as the "market required rate of return." During the 1950s and

For an individual, it is clear that the required return on a prospective investment should be set in relation to other opportunities available. What about the case of a professionally managed firm? Whose required rate of return is appropriate? Management's? The shareholders'?

Value maximization for shareholders is our decision criterion, and value ultimately is determined in the financial marketplace by investors. Thus, in evaluating investment opportunities, management acts as the **agent** of shareholders. In setting return targets, management should base decisions on *shareholders'* required returns—*that is, on the rates the shareholders would use if they were performing the evaluation themselves*.

This proposition is basic to the operation of a market economy, but it is not always applied in practice. Firms sometimes find themselves pressed to put too much emphasis on profits and earnings per share in the short run, to the neglect of long-run return on investment. Such preoccupation with near-term profits can lead to a failure to earn an adequate return on invested capital.

Systematic failure to earn the market required rate of return over an extended period can lead only to serious financial difficulty. Managers sometimes lay the blame on the capital markets for their inability to raise capital at reasonable rates when, in fact, the markets are performing exactly as they should be in disciplining firms that fail to earn the market rate of return.

Agent (in economic terms)—an individual or organization that acts in behalf of and to promote the interests of another party, usually referred to as the *principal*.

Systematic failure to earn the market required rate of return can only lead to serious financial difficulty.

1960s, utilities consistently earned more than the market required rate of return. At the same time, because of falling costs, customer prices for electricity dropped by 12 percent from 1950 to 1970. Allowing for inflation, the drop in real terms was much greater. Through the rate-setting process, utility commissions saw to it that many cost reductions were passed along to customers. But in the 1970s the situation reversed, and utilities on average earned much less than the market required rate of return on nuclear plants opened during that period, partly because of cost overruns, delays in construction, and other factors related to public controversy over nuclear power.

With respect to these nuclear plants that have not paid their way, the question is, who foots the bill? Some utility commissions, such as New York's in the Kahn article, are saying that it must be the investors. But in taking this position, the regulators are trying to have it both ways — setting rates so that utility investors earn no more than the market required rate of return

on successful projects but earn less than the required rate of return on failures. Consumers get the benefits of good investments, and investors foot the bill for bad ones. Such an arrangement will hardly be acceptable to those asked to supply the funds.

No one knows in advance which investments will turn out to be successful and which will not. One way to proceed would be to allow utilities to earn the market required rate of return on all investments, successes and failures alike. An alternative would be to allow more on successes, by allowing utilities to keep returns above the market rate, and less on failures, by forcing utilities to pay for them. This latter arrangement is essentially the situation in unregulated firms.

No matter how the problem of nuclear plants finally is resolved, the lesson pertinent to this chapter is clear: investments that fail to earn the market required rate of return are going to mean trouble for someone.

Source: Alfred E. Kahn, "Who Should Pay for Power Plant Duds?" *Wall Street Journal,* August 15, 1985.

The Role of Markets

The expected return required by investors and lenders can be inferred from market data on stocks and bonds.

Market opportunities available to investors outside the firm set the minimum standard for investment by management inside the firm.

Suppose there are thousands of shareholders. Must management ask each for his or her required rate of return? Fortunately, the answer is no. *Financial markets* provide a solution to this problem. In financial markets, investors express their preferences by their own actions.

Returns in organized public financial markets, such as the markets described in Chapter 2, are available at low transaction costs and relatively little effort (almost anyone can call a stockbroker or buy a mutual fund). Market returns, then, represent the minimum that an investor should accept on any investment opportunity. Organized markets, therefore, establish the required rate of return for managers to use in evaluating investment opportunities. Since everyone faces essentially the same set of investment opportunities in markets, we need not worry about a different rate for each shareholder; opportunity rates are the same for everyone.

Setting required returns need not involve complex mathematics. The proper approach stems directly from the fundamental premise that management's job is to act as agent of shareholders in investing shareholder funds. In effect, suppliers of funds say to the management of any firm: "These are the rates we can expect to earn outside the firm in other investments. If you cannot equal or exceed these rates, pay the funds out to us and we will do the investing ourselves somewhere else."

Required rates of return are not set by management, nor are they set by negotiation between management and suppliers of funds. Rather, they are set impersonally in the financial markets by the actions of investors and lenders competing against one another. Managers must examine market data to determine what those required rates are and then use the rates in evaluating capital investments.

Return and Risk

Risk-averse investors expect a risk premium on risky investments.

Required returns should include a risk premium; the greater the risk, the higher the required return.

Risk premium — the difference between the required rate of return on a particular risky asset and the rate of return on a riskless asset with the same expected life.

In evaluating projects, managers are acting as agents of shareholders who are risk-averse. Those shareholders expect management to take risk into account and to set required returns that vary with risk. In Chapters 4 and 5, we discussed the relationship between risk and risk aversion and concluded that risk-averse investors will expect a **risk premium** on risky investments. The greater the risk, the higher the required rate of return. Figure 12–1 diagrams a market risk/return schedule.

At the low end of the risk spectrum are savings accounts and, for those with sufficient funds, U.S. government securities. Money-market mutual funds offer low-cost investment in a diversified portfolio of very low-risk assets. Next in risk come corporate bonds, followed by common stocks, which vary widely in risk from stable and well-established firms, such as telephone and electric companies, to new or high-technology firms, such as Apple Computer. Markets for all of these assets are public and highly organized; information is readily available to participants, and the cost of transacting is low. Other markets for investment assets, such

Figure 12–1
The Market Risk/Return Schedule

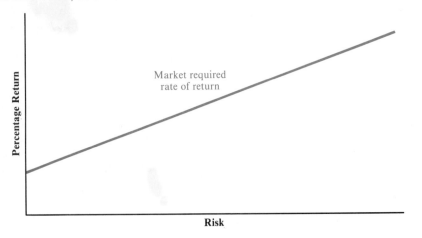

as real estate, present additional opportunities on the risk/return spectrum but are less highly organized.

Let us summarize our discussion to this point:

1. Management acts as the agent of shareholders in analyzing investment opportunities and making investment decisions.
2. A firm's investments must be expected to earn a return adequate to compensate suppliers of funds.
3. Management must set required returns that ensure this result.
4. Required returns are opportunity rates derived from data on market opportunities available to investors in financial markets.
5. Required returns should include a premium for risk.

Required Returns, Return Targets, and the Cost of Capital

Before we go further, we need to say a few words about terminology. So far, we have used the term **required return** to describe the minimum expected rate of return we will accept on a project. In finance circles, this concept goes by many names, including marginal cost of capital, hurdle rate, return target, and target return. You may wonder why there are so many names for the same thing. Is it just a conspiracy against students? Not really. Each term is intended to emphasize a different aspect of the concept.

The phrase **return target** (or **target return**) emphasizes that a required return is the return targeted as a minimum for a new investment. Similarly, **hurdle rate** implies that a project's internal rate of return must exceed the required return hurdle before it is a desirable investment.

A widely used term is the **marginal cost of capital.** The discussion so far has emphasized that a required rate of return for a project reflects opportunity costs of investors as the firm uses additional capital for investment. The flipside of this discussion is the interpretation of the required return as the cost of using capital. Hence required return is often referred to as the marginal cost of capital. The term *marginal* reflects the fact that the required return should be determined on *incremental* investment leading to incremental cash flows. Such incremental investment occurs *now* — not in the past — and has its own risk characteristics. The term *cost* reflects the fact that capital is not free.

The cost of capital is the rate of return required by those who supply the capital. It is defined in the same way as the cost of anything else. If $0.50 is the price of a cup of coffee, then $0.50 is the amount required by the restaurant in exchange for the coffee. Similarly, if 15 percent per year is the cost of capital to a firm, those supplying the capital are saying they require a return of 15 percent per year for the use of the capital. They set this requirement because, presumably, 15 percent is the rate they can earn elsewhere on other investments of comparable risk.

Return target or **target return**—the minimum acceptable expected return on an investment.

Hurdle rate—the return target to which an investment project's internal rate of return is compared in determining whether or not the investment project is acceptable to the firm.

Marginal cost of capital—another name for the *return target* for an investment project.

The terms *required rate of return* and *cost of capital* can be used interchangeably, provided one is aware of the latter term's implications. One difficulty with the term *cost of capital* is that it may imply to the unwary that there is some cost (rate) at which capital can be raised, and that this rate is independent of the way the capital is to be used. Such a view is incorrect. The capital being employed is provided by lenders and investors who expect management, acting as agent on their behalf, to take into account their opportunities to invest the capital elsewhere. Because suppliers of capital are risk-averse, the cost of capital depends on the way it is to be used—that is, on the riskiness of the investments it is to finance. It is important to remember that the *cost of capital,* when applied to investment decisions, is a marginal cost. It must reflect the costs of funds for the new investment proposal under consideration. The riskier the investment, the higher the cost of capital.

While the term *cost of capital* is useful and widely used, it carries with it the potential for confusion. To avoid this confusion and to emphasize the link between the required rate of return and investment risk, we will continue to use the terms *required rate of return* and *return targets* throughout this book.

Required Returns on a Firm's Securities

To apply our basic approach to establishing required returns for investments by a firm, we need to have some idea of how investors perceive the risk of the firm. We can get this information by looking at the stocks and bonds that firms issue to finance their assets.

Required Returns on Equity and Debt

Consider a firm that has financed its assets by issuing common stock and debt. Given the firm's history and financial policies, the investments it has made in the past, and the nature of its business, the market will have a set of expectations regarding the magnitude and riskiness of the firm's future earnings. The market will require a return on the firm's stock commensurate with the perceived risk. We can represent the **required return on equity** as K_e. K_e varies with risk; the greater the risk, the higher K_e is.

Required return on equity—equates the price of a stock to the present value of the expected future cash benefits of owning the stock; also known as the *cost of equity capital*.

Recall from Chapter 4 that K_e sometimes is called the **capitalization rate** (yet another term for required return!) of the firm's equity because K_e is the discount rate at which the market *capitalizes* the expected future cash flows to equity holders in order to determine the present value of its stock.

Capitalization rate—another name for the *discount rate*.

Now consider the firm's debt financing. Suppose it issues some bonds with a 20-year maturity and an interest rate of 12 percent. Each $1,000 bond pays its holder $120 per year in interest. At the time of issue, 12 percent is the market required rate of return on the bonds because this rate is required in order to induce bondholders to buy. In terms of the bond market, 12 percent is the yield to maturity on the bond. Bonds are only one type of debt. The firm also might borrow from a bank or an insurance company. If a bank charges the firm 15 percent interest, we can say that the bank's required return is 15 percent. We can represent the **required return on debt** as K_d.

Required return on debt—the internal rate of return that equates the price of a bond (or debt instrument) to the present value of the expected future cash benefits of owning the bond (or debt instrument).

As we discussed in Chapter 4 and will discuss again in Part Five, we expect the required return on debt to be lower than the shareholders' required return for any firm because the debt owners bear less risk. In the event of financial difficulty, the debt owners have first claim. Shareholders, on the other hand, bear the residual risk. That is, shareholders bear financial risk introduced by the use of debt in addition to the firm's underlying operating risk.

Variations Among Firms

Because equity is more risky than debt, for a given firm the required return on equity is greater than the required return on debt; that is, $K_e > K_d$.

What about variations in K_e from one firm to another? Apple Computer Inc., a company we mentioned earlier, is a manufacturer of microcomputers for personal and professional use. Apple is likely to be perceived by the market as relatively risky. The company was born in 1975 and is still young as companies go. It is part of a high-technology industry subject to rapid technical advances, rapid obsolescence, and fierce competition. It is true that the microcomputer industry is growing rapidly, but in a firm of Apple's size one big mistake can mean trouble, especially when it is competing against IBM. Thus, while investors hope their rate of return on Apple stock will be high because of the prospect of rapid growth, the *required return* is also high because of the high risk. Other high-risk companies include airlines and electronics firms.

Contrast Apple Computer with General Mills, the packaged-foods company with multibillion-dollar-per-year revenues. Although the growth of General Mills is slower than that of Apple Computer, General Mills is able to count on cash flows generated by products such as Gold Medal flour (marketed for more than 100 years) and Wheaties, the "breakfast of champions," and thus its revenues are subject to far less uncertainty than Apple's. Because the risk is lower, we would expect the General Mills K_e to be less than the Apple Computer K_e. Because investors are risk-averse, K_e is a function of risk and varies from one firm to another.

Since risk varies from firm to firm, the required return on equity varies from firm to firm.

The required return on debt varies from firm to firm.

How about required returns on debt? Required return on debt, K_d, also varies from one firm to another for exactly the same reasons. U.S. government bonds are generally considered to be the least risky debt of all. Corporate bonds are somewhat riskier. Although low in risk, the bonds of large corporations are by no means riskless. One need only point to the bankruptcy of the Penn Central railroad in 1970, the troubles of Chrysler in 1980, and the bankruptcy filing of New Hampshire Public Service in 1988 in order to prove the point. While Chrysler never formally declared bankruptcy, it was unable to meet its contractual financial obligations at one time or another, and required federal-government guarantees of its debt in order to induce banks and others to lend. In the absence of the guarantees, Chrysler would have been likely to go bankrupt.

Bonds of many large corporations are rated according to their degree of default risk by rating services, such as Moody's Investors Service and Standard & Poor's. Moody's rates the very safest bonds as *Aaa,* the next safest as *Aa,* the next as *A,* and the relatively risky bonds as *Baa.* Standard & Poor's uses the ratings *AAA,*

Table 12–1

Interest Rates by Category of Long-Term Bonds

	Yield to Maturity as of December 25, 1987 (percent)
U.S. government bonds	8.95
Corporate bonds:	
Aaa	10.08
Aa	10.31
A	10.59
Baa	11.28

Source: Federal Reserve Bulletin.

AA, A, and *BBB.* Both services have yet other ratings for even more risky debt. Table 12–1 gives the yields for some rating categories. The bonds in Table 12–1 are all of roughly the same maturity. The differences in yields result primarily from differences in perceived risk.

Inflation

Nominal rate of return — the contract or observed rate of return.

Real rate of return — the difference between the nominal rate and the inflation rate.

Inflation premium — an addition to the real rate of return required by investors to compensate them for the change in the value of the investment that results from anticipated inflation.

All market required rates of return include an inflation premium approximately equal to the rate of inflation expected in the future.

Table 12–1 shows a yield of 8.95 percent on U.S. government bonds. This rate may seem a bit high for a *default-free* investment, but the reason the rate is not lower has to do with market expectations of inflation.

Lenders who expect inflation in the coming year of, say, 6 percent are going to seek a return on a loan of more than 6 percent in order to protect themselves against inflation. If inflation is 6 percent, lenders will be repaid in dollars that will buy 6 percent less. Thus, if the **nominal rate of return** on the loan were set at 6 percent, the lender's **real rate of return,** net of inflation, would be zero. At a nominal return of 9 percent, the real return would be 9 percent − 6 percent, or 3 percent. In general, the real return is the difference between the nominal return and the inflation rate.

In the absence of inflation, the yield on U.S. government bonds would be much lower than those presented in Table 12–1, as would yields on corporate *Aaa* bonds. So the yields in Table 12–1 all contain an **inflation premium.**

Required rates of return on equities likewise contain an inflation premium. Suppose the market required return (K_e) on the stock of General Mills Inc. were, say, 8 percent in the absence of inflation. Then with an expected inflation rate of 6 percent, the K_e for General Mills would be about 14 percent (8 + 6 = 14). Although this figure may sound high, a large part of the return is due to an inflation premium.

Return targets set by management, therefore, must include an inflation premium. We will shortly explore ways to include this inflation premium in return targets. *Future expectations of inflation,* not past inflation, are the determining factor in establishing an inflation premium. Of course, past inflation provides a basis for future estimates.

The Weighted-Average Required Return (*WARR*)

Weighted-average required return (*WARR*)—the required return for an average-risk investment project based on an average of equity and debt returns, where the weights are the respective proportions of equity and of debt used by the firm.

The preceding section discussed the market required return on equity and debt. Most firms finance their assets with some combination of equity and debt. Figure 12–2 illustrates the situation. For purposes of analyzing investment opportunities, it is often easier to use an *average* of the equity and debt returns rather than to apply the equity and debt required returns separately. In effect, we lump all suppliers of funds together and calculate a **weighted-average required return (*WARR*)**. The same concept is often referred to as the *weighted-average cost of capital* since investors' required returns are the cost to the firm of raising capital.

Table 12–2 (p. 356) outlines our calculations of the *WARR*. The *WARR* is simply the weighted average of the required returns on equity (K_e) and debt (K_d), where the weights are the proportion of financing done by equity (W_e) and debt (W_d). These weights add up to 1.0 since we must finance the entire project from either debt or equity sources. Importantly, the required return on debt is adjusted to its after-tax equivalent to reflect the tax deductibility of interest payments. We will discuss this tax adjustment shortly.

To illustrate the calculation of *WARR* and its use, let us consider the hypothetical case of Mattari, Inc., a manufacturer of electronic games. The market

Figure 12–2
Suppliers of Capital and Corporate Investment

A. Projects Are Funded by Suppliers of Capital

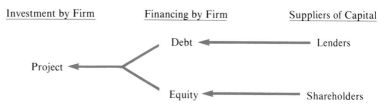

B. Required Returns Are Determined by Demands of Suppliers of Capital

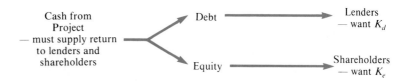

Table 12-2

Summary of Symbols Used in Calculating the Weighted-Average Required Return (WARR)

Symbol	Meaning
K_e	The rate of return required by equity holders
K_d	The rate of return required by debt holders
$K_d(1-T)$	The after-tax equivalent of the debt required return
T	The corporate marginal tax rate
K_w	The WARR on equity and debt
W_e	Target equity proportion, $E/(E+D)$
W_d	Target debt proportion, $D/(E+D)$

$$WARR = K_w = W_e K_e + W_d K_d(1-T)$$

might require a return of, say, 17 percent on Mattari's equity and 11 percent on Mattari's debt. For the moment, we will just make up these required returns. Later on we will examine how to estimate values of K_e and K_d.

The Mix of Equity and Debt

In addition to values of K_e and K_d, we also need the weights for financing with equity (W_e) and debt (W_d). Summary data from Mattari's balance sheet of December 31, 1988, are given in Table 12–3. The Mattari balance sheet is highly simplified to permit us to concentrate first on the basics. We will return later in this chapter to the question of how to deal with details such as accounts payable, accruals, capital stock, and retained earnings.

As a first step in calculating the weighted-average required return, we must calculate the proportion of total financing provided by each source. Table 12–4 shows the proportion of total financing provided by each source as the amount of financing done by each source divided by the total amount of financing. For example, the debt weight is calculated as $W_d = 1,500/5,000 = 0.30$.

Tax-Deductibility of Interest

If we know that 70 percent of Mattari's capital is supplied by equity investors requiring a 17 percent return and that the remaining 30 percent is supplied by

Table 12-3

Summary Balance Sheet for Mattari, Inc. (thousands of dollars)

Current assets	2,000	Long-term debt	1,500
Fixed assets	3,000	Equity	3,500
Total assets	5,000	**Total capital**	5,000

Table 12–4
Relative Weight of Capital Items in Mattari's Balance Sheet

Capital Item	Amount (thousands of dollars)	Weight (proportion)
Long-term debt	1,500	$0.30 = W_d$
Equity	3,500	$0.70 = W_e$
Total	5,000	1.00

debt holders requiring an 11 percent return, we should be able to calculate our weighted-average required return. Before making this calculation, however, we must first recognize a critical factor: taxes. Interest on debt is tax-deductible. If the corporate marginal tax rate is, say, 40 percent, then each dollar of interest generates a tax saving, or **interest tax shield**, of $0.40. Mattari pays interest of 11 percent annually on $1.5 million in long-term debt for a total of $165,000 in interest. Deducting this $165,000 from taxable income saves $165,000 × 0.40 = $66,000 in taxes. The net interest cost to Mattari, after taxes, is $99,000, or $165,000 minus tax savings of $66,000. In percentage terms, Mattari's after-tax interest cost is $99,000/$1,500,000, or 6.60 percent. We can calculate the after-tax cost of debt more simply by multiplying K_d times $(1 - T)$, where T is the tax rate. In the case of Mattari, this after-tax cost of debt would be $0.11 \times (1 - 0.40) = 0.066$, or 6.60 percent. The figure of 6.60 percent represents the *after-tax equivalent* of the required return on debt, which is the cost of debt to the firm.

Interest tax shield — the tax saving a firm generates by using debt because interest on debt is tax-deductible.

Sample Problem 12–1
Calculating the Weighted-Average Required Return for Mattari, Inc.

Calculate the weighted-average required return for Mattari, Inc., from the data in Tables 12–3 and 12–4.

Solution

Equity holders supply 70 percent of Mattari's capital and require a return of 17 percent; debt holders supply 30 percent of the capital and require a return of 11 percent, which comes to 6.60 percent after taxes. We can calculate the weighted average as shown in Table 12–5 (p. 358). As the calculations show, Mattari's weighted-average required return is found by first multiplying the required returns on debt and equity by their respective weights in the firm's financing plan. The results are then added together to get Mattari's *WARR* of 0.0198 + 0.1190 = 0.1388, or 13.88 percent.

Summary of *WARR* Calculations

Table 12–2 outlined our procedure for calculating the *WARR*. In calculating the weighted-average required return, it is important to keep in mind the following points:

Table 12–5

Calculating the Weighted-Average Required Return (WARR) for Mattari, Inc.

	Required Return (1)	Weight (2)	Weighted Required Return (3) = (1) × (2)
Debt, $K_d(1 - T)$	$0.11(1 - 0.4) = 0.066$	0.30	0.0198
Equity, K_e	0.170	0.70	0.1190
Weighted average			0.1388

$$\text{Mattari's } WARR = W_e K_e + W_d K_d(1 - T)$$
$$= 0.70(0.17) + 0.30(0.11)(1 - 0.4)$$
$$= 0.0198 + 0.1190$$
$$= 0.1388 = 13.88 \text{ percent}$$

1. We ignore accounts payable, accruals, and other short-term liabilities arising in the course of doing business because normally no interest is paid on these liabilities.

2. We include all sources of funds that require an explicit return. If the firm uses bank debt as a permanent part of its financing, it would be included and treated the same way as long-term debt. Likewise, preferred stock would be included as an additional source with its own required return.

3. The required returns on sources of financing (K_d and K_e) are based on current financial-market conditions. For example, K_d is the interest rate on *new* borrowing, not the coupon rate on a company's existing debt that was issued in the past.

4. The weights in the *WARR* calculation are *targets* — that is, the planned proportions of debt and equity in the future.

5. In considering equity, we do not distinguish between new stock issues and retained earnings. Strictly speaking, equity obtained through stock issues is slightly more costly than retained earnings because of flotation (issue) costs, but this difference can be ignored in nearly all cases in practice.[1]

6. In theory, the weights (W_e and W_d) used to calculate the *WARR* should be based on market values of debt and equity rather than book values. In practice, however, book values are frequently used, mainly because market values can vary considerably from period to period.

The Weighted-Average Required Return as a Return Target

How can we use the *WARR* in evaluating investment opportunities? We can use it as the return target for evaluating average-risk investments.

The *WARR* is used as the return target for evaluating investments of average risk for the firm.

[1]One exception is rate setting in utility companies. Utility regulatory commissions typically do consider flotation costs in connection with equity obtained through stock issues. Flotation costs are the cash costs associated with issuance of a company's new stock or long-term debt.

Suppose Mattari is evaluating a prospective investment that has an expected *operating return* — the internal rate of return calculated considering only after-tax operating cash flows — of exactly 13.88 percent after taxes. Financing flows (interest, principal, and dividends) are excluded from the project flows and instead enter the analysis through the weighted-average required return.

Suppose the investment requires an outlay of $100,000. To keep our example simple, suppose the investment generates a *perpetuity* — that is, level cash flows indefinitely into the future. (Some projects in practice approximate this pattern as depreciation flows are reinvested.) With an operating return of 13.88 percent, the project will generate a cash-flow stream of $13,880 annually.

Table 12–6 shows how this stream is divided up. Debt holders provide $30,000 at a rate of 11 percent, so they collect $3,300. Deducting the interest saves $1,320 in taxes (0.40 × $3,300), so there is left for equity holders $13,880 − $3,300 + $1,320 = $11,900. On the equity holders' investment of $70,000, a return of $11,900 represents 17 percent, exactly their required rate.

We find that if the investment has a return exactly equal to the *WARR* (13.88 percent in this case), it will exactly compensate all the suppliers of capital at their respective required rates. Therefore, we can use the weighted-average required return as a target, either as the discount rate in calculating net present value or as the rate to beat in calculating internal rate of return. If the expected *IRR* exceeds the *WARR*, we would anticipate — if things work out as planned — that all suppliers of capital can be repaid at their required returns, with some left over. This excess normally accrues to the benefit of the equity holders. If the expected *IRR* falls short of the *WARR*, the project return is inadequate and someone — most likely the equity holders — will come up short because the project will have failed the economic test.

Now we can see more clearly why in Chapter 11 we included only operating flows in the project's cash-flow schedule: we incorporate financing requirements in the return target and evaluate the project to see whether it returns enough to compensate suppliers of funds. The appropriate return target for evaluating projects of average risk is the weighted-average required return (*WARR*) on the firm's securities.

If an investment produces a return exactly equal to the *WARR*, it will exactly compensate all of the suppliers of capital at their respective required rates.

The appropriate return target for evaluating projects of average risk is the weighted-average required return (*WARR*) on the firm's securities.

Table 12–6
Compensation of Capital Suppliers for a Hypothetical Investment

Operating cash flow	$13,880
minus	
Interest to debt holders	−3,300
plus	
Interest tax shield	+1,320
equals	
Return available for equity holders	$11,900
Return to debt holders	$3,300/$30,000 = 11 percent
Return to equity holders	$11,900/$70,000 = 17 percent

What do we mean by *average-risk* projects? We mean projects whose risk is approximately equal to the overall risk of the firm—that is, projects at about the middle of the risk spectrum, considering all of the firm's investments. Because the *WARR* represents the market required return on the firm as it now exists, it is appropriate for the current overall risk of the firm and is thus appropriate only for projects that have this same level of risk. Projects that are more risky than average should have a higher required return, and less risky projects should have a lower required return. Measuring risk and dealing with risk differences are difficult problems that we will defer to the next chapter. In this chapter, we will consider only projects of average risk. For average-risk projects, the *WARR* is the appropriate target.

Financing Mix and the Weights Used in Calculating the *WARR*

As stated earlier, theory suggests the use of market-value weights in calculating W_d and W_e to reflect the fact that it is the market value of the firm that managers are attempting to maximize. In addition, the required returns of shareholders and bondholders are based on the market values of their claims on the company. Because market values of stock and debt can vary widely, however, managers in practice often set target ratios for financing that they monitor by using book values. For example, management may plan that one third of funds would be raised by equity and two thirds by debt—that is, $W_e = \frac{1}{3}$ and $W_d = \frac{2}{3}$. When new funds are raised, the market values of debt and equity funds obtained are often approximately equal to book values, so at least at the margin, for additional funding, book-value weights may represent how funds are being raised to finance projects. We must recognize that the use of book-value weights is only a pragmatic way to apply concepts based on market values and is one of the problems of attempting to apply theory in an imperfect world.

Note that the weights to be used in calculating *WARR* are long-run weights to reflect the mix of financing over a number of years. At any one time, the company may have just raised money by borrowing—it is understood that at some time additional equity financing will be used to keep the long-run mix of debt and equity in line with the weights W_e and W_d. (Choosing the appropriate mix of financing is a topic we will discuss in Part Five.)

> Because market values of stock and debt can vary widely, managers often set target ratios for financing which they monitor using book values.

Sample Problem 12–2
Calculating Market-Value Weights

Suppose Mattari, Inc., has 1,000,000 shares of stock outstanding selling at a price of $5 a share. Also assume the current market interest rates are equal to the coupon rates on Mattari's existing debt so that its debt would sell in the market at a price equal to its book value. Using this information, calculate the market value weights of Mattari's debt and equity financing. Data from Table 12–3 will be needed.

Solution

First, we calculate the market value of Mattari's equity to be $5 \times 1,000,000 =$ $5,000,000. From Table 12–3, Mattari's debt has a book value of $1,500,000, so the debt's market value is also $1,500,000. Total capital at market value is thus $5,000,000 + $1,500,000 = $6,500,000.

We can now calculate the market-value weights as

$$(\text{equity}) \ W_e = \frac{\$5,000,000}{\$6,500,000} = 0.77$$

$$(\text{debt}) \ W_d = \frac{\$1,500,000}{\$6,500,000} = 0.23 \ .$$

Comparing these results to the book-value weights in Table 12–4, we see that the market-value weight of equity is higher than the book-value weight of 0.70. This is the case because Mattari's stock is selling at a market value which exceeds its book value.

Estimating Required Returns: Using Market Data

For debt, the required return is the market rate of interest on new debt.

How do we determine the return expected by the market on a firm's equity and debt? For debt, the required return is the market rate of interest on new debt. For example, in the case of bonds, K_d is the *yield to maturity* the company would have to pay if it issued new debt selling it at face value. As a first approximation, this yield would be equal to the yield to maturity on existing debt.

Unfortunately, we cannot directly observe a comparable figure for equity for two reasons: first, equity is not a contractual claim as debt is; second, equity has no maturity. Knowing the maturity of a bond, we can compute its yield to maturity, defined as the internal rate of return of an investment in the bond. To make a comparable computation for equity requires that we make some assumptions.

If the market price of a company's stock is set in competitive financial markets, the expected return on the stock should be equal to the required return of shareholders.

In principle, what we desire is the required return of equity owners in the firm. Unfortunately, it is not feasible to ask the shareholders directly, so we must infer such a required return. One method of doing so is to try to find what return shareholders seem to expect given the current market price of the company's stock. If the market price is set in competitive financial markets, this expected return should be equal to the required return of shareholders. For example, if expected return exceeded required return, there would be increased demand for the stock, driving its price up and its expected return down. The process would continue until expected return and required return were equal. Fortunately, the materials we covered in Chapters 3, 4, and 5 provide exactly the tools to calculate such a required return, K_e.

The Dividend-Growth Model

The dividend-valuation model can be used to measure K_e, the required return on equity.

One approach to measuring K_e is the dividend-valuation model explained in Chapter 4. This model says that at time 0 the current share price (P_0) is the present value of expected future dividends (D_t).

Sometimes it is reasonable to predict that dividends will grow at a constant rate, g, indefinitely. As we saw in Chapter 4, in this constant-growth case, we can write out a specific expression for shareholder required return, K_e.

The required return that equates the present value of a share of stock, P_0, and the streams of all future benefits expected, assuming that the dividend will grow at a constant rate, can be calculated as:

$$K_e = D_1/(P_0) + g \tag{1}$$

where

Capital gain—a gain that results from the increase in the value of an asset, or the difference between the purchase price and the sale price.

D_1 = dividend expected in the next period,
P_0 = current price per share,
g = expected growth rate in dividends,
K_e = the shareholder required return on the firm's stock.

That is, the required return of equity holders can be thought of as a given dividend rate, D_1/P_0, plus a growth rate, g. This shows that a shareholder expects some current income in the form of dividends plus a capital gain as the stock price rises due to dividend growth.

In practice, it is quite difficult to obtain estimates of dividend-growth rates or future share prices.

As we'll discuss later, obtaining estimates of dividend-growth rates is quite difficult. We should remember that estimates of K_e are only that—estimates. The result of using any model must be checked to see if it is at all reasonable. One way to check the reasonableness of estimated equity required returns is to compare them to similar estimates for stocks believed to be of similar risk. In efficient financial markets, investments of comparable risk will have similar required rates of return.

Sample Problem 12–3
Calculating Shareholder Required Return for Jefferson Company

Jefferson Company just paid its dividend of $1.00 per common share, each share of which sells for $10.00. Jefferson dividends per share are expected to grow at 12 percent per year indefinitely. What is the required rate of return on Jefferson stock?

Solution
Before solving this problem, we must note that applying Equation (1) requires an estimate of D_1—the dividend expected to be paid one year hence. In this example, dividends are expected to grow at 12 percent annually, so $D_1 = \$1.00(1 + 0.12) = \$1.12$. Now using Equation (1), we can solve for K_e as $\$1.12/\$10.00 + 0.12 = 0.232$. Jefferson stockholders appear to have a required return of more than 23 percent. ■

Risk-Premium Approach

The **risk-premium approach** bases estimates of required returns on risk-premium data.

Another approach to estimating shareholder return requirements is to look at the risk premiums that equities provide over and above returns on debt.

To illustrate how we might use this **risk-premium approach** in estimating required returns, let us focus on calculating the required return on a common stock. We can make our estimate of the market required return on common stock as shown in Equation (2):

$$K_e = i + \text{risk premium} \tag{2}$$

where i = the current market required return on long-term government bonds.

We use the long-term U.S. government rate in Equation (2) because government bonds are one of the safest investments one can make over a relatively long time period.

The size of the risk premium will depend on the risk of the stock and reflects the risk-return trade-off we have discussed before. Risk-averse investors require a risk premium on risky investments.

The practical difficulty in applying Equation (2) is finding an estimate of a risk premium, as we'll discuss later. But for now let's illustrate the approach. Suppose government bonds were currently yielding 10 percent and investors required a risk premium of 8 percent on IBM stock. Using Equation (2), the market-required return on IBM stock would be calculated as

$$K_e = 0.10 + 0.08$$

$$= 0.18 = 18 \text{ percent}.$$

This 18 percent figure would reflect the risks that investors see from investing in IBM stock.

We mentioned earlier that return targets must include an inflation premium. By using the government-bond rate, i, as the base for calculating K_e, we *automatically* include the market inflation premium because i includes the market's consensus judgment regarding the appropriate inflation premium. A government-bond rate of, say, 10 percent already includes an inflation premium. So when we add the risk premium to i to get K_e, an inflation premium has been built into K_e.

Appendix 12A shows how we might further refine our estimates of risk premiums.

Sources of Estimates

Now we have introduced two approaches to estimating shareholder required returns: the dividend-growth model and risk-premium approach. In practice, a primary difficulty is obtaining estimates of growth (g) for use in the dividend-growth model, Equation (1), or estimates of risk premiums for use in Equation (2). Let's discuss some of the sources for such estimates.

The estimate of g for use in the dividend-growth model should reflect market expectations of future performance. One source of such expectations is financial

One source of
dividend-growth estimates is
financial analysts' forecasts.

analysts' forecasts of corporate earnings and dividend performance. Financial analysts working for investment advisory services, such as Value Line, Merrill Lynch, and Goldman, regularly publish their own estimates of future corporate performance. In recent years, investor interest in such forecasts has led to services that collect and publish such forecasts from hundreds of analysts on thousands of stocks. For example, IBES (Institutional Brokers' Estimate System) provides clients with earnings-per-share estimates made by about 2,000 individual analysts from 100 brokerage firms on more than 3,000 corporations. Zacks provides a similar service. This sort of data enables one to estimate for a particular stock the type of growth figure that Equation (1) calls for. These data reflect the expectations of market participants about the future.[2]

Using the forecasts of financial analysts goes a long way in reducing the problems of applying the dividend-valuation model. Such forecasts are not, however, foolproof. In practice, growth estimates are typically available for horizons of about five years. People just don't often look into their crystal balls for longer periods. In addition, at least currently, the organized collections of analyst data cover earnings rather than dividend-growth forecasts. While these features do not exactly fit the requirements of the dividend-valuation model, for large groups of stocks they may not cause too many difficulties. In the long run, dividend growth is dependent on earnings growth. Furthermore, without compelling evidence to the contrary, there is no reason to believe that investors somehow feel that growth will dramatically change after five years. The virtue of analyst forecasts is that they are direct measures of the type of expectations that determine value in markets.

Table 12–7 shows the results of using an average of analysts' forecasts to estimate shareholder required returns and risk premiums for stocks in general as proxied by the Standard & Poor's 500 stock index, a widely followed index of stock performance in the United States. As the estimates show, shareholders do require a risk premium over returns on safer government bonds. For the 1982–87 period, the estimated risk premium has averaged slightly more than 6 percent. This risk premium also appears to change over time with changing conditions in financial markets.

The dividend-growth model
can be used to estimate risk
premiums.

The figures in Table 12–7 are averages for the stock market. As such, they are an average of data for hundreds of stocks combining both low- and high-growth securities. At the same time, the data reflect the average risk of equity investments. For an individual stock, risks may well differ from average and as a result shareholder required returns will differ from average. In such a case, the dividend-valuation model could be applied to the individual stock or to a select group of stocks deemed to be of comparable risk. The difficulty in working with smaller groups of stocks is that the constant-growth version of the dividend-valuation model given in Equation (1) may not fit the pattern of expected growth.

---

[2]IBES is a product of Lynch, Jones and Ryan, a major brokerage firm. In recent years, a growing body of research has shown that market prices are related to analyst forecasts, thus strengthening the case for their use. For a discussion of the use of analysts' forecasts in estimating required returns, see R. Harris, "Using Analysts' Growth Forecasts to Estimate Shareholder Required Returns," *Financial Management*, Spring 1986.

Table 12–7

Required Returns and Risk Premiums for Standard and Poor's (S&P) 500 Stocks, 1982–1987

Year	Government Bond Yield (percent) (1)	S&P 500 Required Return (percent) (2)	S&P 500 Risk Premium (percent) (3) = (2) − (1)
1982	12.92	20.08	7.16
1983	11.34	17.89	6.55
1984	12.48	17.26	4.78
1985	10.97	16.33	5.35
1986	7.85	15.09	7.24
1987	8.58	14.71	6.13
Average 1982–1987	**10.69**	**16.89**	**6.20**

Note: Government bond yield is the yield to maturity on long-term U.S. Treasury obligations. Required return is estimated as the sum of dividend yield plus expected growth where expected growth is average of analysts' growth forecast (5-year earnings per share) from Institutional Brokers' Estimate System. Standard & Poor's figures are market-value weighted averages of required returns for all dividend-paying stocks in the S&P 500. Annual values are averages of monthly figures.

Source: R. Harris, "Using Analysts' Growth Forecasts to Estimate Shareholder Required Returns," *Financial Management,* Spring 1986. Updated by author.

As Table 12–7 illustrates, one can get an estimate of a risk premium by using the dividend-growth model and analysts' forecasts.

Another source of data for risk premiums is the past history of returns on financial securities. Table 12–8 (p. 366) presents the results of one study covering more than 60 years of U.S. financial history. Panel A shows the arithmetic mean (the average) of the annual returns over the 1926–1986 period. The returns on common stocks include both dividends and capital gains—that is, increases or decreases in the price of stocks.

Another source of risk-premium estimates is the past history of returns on financial assets.

Panel B shows the historical-average market risk premium on corporate equities—that is, the premium return to equities over and above rates of return on various forms of debt. From row (6), we see that stocks have on average returned about 6.8 percent more than bonds of the same firms. In row (7), we see that stocks have returned 7.4 percent more than long-term U.S. government bonds. Finally, in row (8) we see the risk premium on stocks relative to short-term Treasury bills has been around 8.6 percent.

Historically, stocks have returned, on average, more per year than have long-term U.S. government bonds.

What do these data on historical returns tell us? They tell us that, on average, the market requires a higher return on equity than it does on bonds. They also tell us how large that premium has been for one long period in U.S. financial history.

Do these results necessarily mean that these risk premiums will be demanded in the future? Unfortunately, the answer to that question involves predictions about which we can at best speculate; only time will tell. We can, however, use these past data as another way to estimate a required return on equity and to compare it to results we might obtain using, for example, a dividend-growth model.

Table 12–8
Past Returns in U.S. Financial Markets

Panel A: Basic Series, Investment Total Annual Returns, 1926–1986

Series	Arithmetic Mean (percent)
1. Common stocks	12.1
2. Long-term corporate bonds	5.3
3. Long-term government bonds	4.7
4. U.S. treasury bills	3.5
5. Inflation	3.1

Panel B: Annual Risk Premiums for Common Stocks

Series	Arithmetic Mean (percent)
6. Common stocks compared to long-term corporate bonds	6.8
7. Common stocks compared to long-term U.S. government bonds	7.4
8. Common stocks compared to U.S. Treasury bills	8.6

Source: R. Ibbotson and R. A. Sinquefield, *Stocks, Bonds, Bills and Inflation: The Past and the Future*. The Financial Analysis Research Foundation.

To use these results for estimating required returns, we must assume that the average risk premiums actually earned over very long periods in the past represent a good measure of the normal risk premiums expected by investors. This assumption represents a leap of faith, but making estimates of future dividends and growth rates in using a dividend-growth model is also such a leap. To obtain information for use in making decisions, we must often pay the price of adopting rather strong assumptions.

As our discussion indicates, getting estimates for determination of required returns is not an easy task. The financial manager must use judgment in the process and, in practice, it is prudent to try a number of different approaches.

Estimating required returns is not an easy task: it involves judgment and it is often helpful to try a number of approaches.

Sample Problem 12–4
Calculating a Required Return and Weighted-Average Required Return for Largo Enterprises

Largo Enterprises, at year-end 1988, is currently reevaluating its return target for analyzing investment proposals. Largo has already decided that it will finance its investments 25 percent by debt and 75 percent by equity. In recent conversations with an investment banker, Largo has determined it can issue new bonds with a yield to maturity of 10 percent, which is 1 percent above the present long-term government-bond rate of 9 percent. Largo management feels comfortable that its current dividend (expected to be $2 per share in 1989) can grow at 6 percent per year in the foreseeable future. Largo's stock price currently (year-end 1988) is $20 per share. In addition, Largo has received a recent report showing that stocks have averaged returns of 7.4 percent per year over and above interest rates on long-term government debt. Largo management feels that all of these assumptions are consistent with shareholders' expectations and are in keeping with Largo's reputation as an aggressive but sound company. Largo is quite proud that, despite its success, its stock is viewed as no more risky than average by the financial community. Largo pays taxes at a rate of 40 percent. What is an appropriate figure to use for the required return, K_e, of Largo's shareholders? What is Largo's weighted-average required return?

Solution

To estimate K_e, we can apply two methods. We can (A) use the dividend-valuation model assuming constant growth of dividends and (B) use the historical risk premium on stocks.

A. Applying the dividend-growth model, we can use Equation (1) to calculate K_e as

$$K_e = \frac{2.00}{(20.00)} + 0.06$$

$$= 0.10 + 0.06 = 0.16.$$

B. Using the historical risk premium, we can calculate K_e as

$$K_e = i + 0.074$$

$$= 0.09 + 0.074 = 0.164.$$

The two calculations of K_e provide answers that are quite close. In practice we will not always be so lucky given the type of estimates and assumptions we have to make to use these models. Given the data in the problem, a required return in the 16–17 percent range appears appropriate. This figure is consistent with dividend-growth expectations and fits fairly well with the historical risk premium for average-risk common stocks.

If we adopt $K_e = 16$ percent as a working assumption, we can now calculate the weighted-average required return as

$$WARR = 0.75K_e + 0.25K_d(1 - 0.40)$$

$$= 0.75(0.16) + 0.25(0.10)(1 - 0.40)$$

$$= 0.135 = 13.5 \text{ percent}.$$

These figures, therefore, suggest that Largo should use a return target of 13.5 percent on its average-risk investments. Note, however, the sorts of judgments we must make in coming up with such a figure. ▪

Using Return Targets

Let us now tie our discussion back to that of Chapter 10 by asking ourselves what to do with the answer—the return target for an investment opportunity—once we

Finance in Practice 12–2

How the Market Required Return Changes Over Time

This chapter has looked at financial-market data. We used these data as the basis for deriving required rates of return on a firm's securities and also on capital-investment projects.

What we found is that all market required rates of return are scaled upward from the U.S.-government-bond rate as a base. The rates on government bonds are the base rate because they are almost default-free and, hence, represent the least-risk investment for any given maturity.

Suppose the government-bond rate changes over time. Do market required rates change also? The government-bond rate *does* change over time, as do other market rates, including required rates on firms' stocks and bonds as well as return targets for capital-investment projects, as the data in the accompanying table show.

	Interest Rate on Long-Term U.S. Government Bonds (percent)	Interest Rate on Corporate AAA Bonds (percent)
1962	4.0	4.3
1972	6.0	7.2
1975	8.0	8.7
Feb. 1980	12.2	13.0
Aug. 1981	14.0	15.0
1985	10.8	11.4
1986	8.1	9.0
1987	8.6	9.4

Earlier in the chapter, we calculated the weighted-average required return for Largo Enterprises as 13.5 percent. That calculation was based on required returns when the government-bond rate was 9 percent. Suppose the government rate was 15 percent instead, a figure it approached in early 1982. Had we calculated Largo's *WARR* at that time, following the procedure we used before, we would have obtained a very different answer. For example, if Largo could borrow at 1 percent above the government rate of 15 percent, its required return on debt (K_d) would be 16 percent. Requirements of equity holders would also be different. Using the historical-risk-premium approach, we would obtain a required return on equity (K_e) of 15 percent + 7.4 percent = 22.4 percent. In an environment of 15 percent government-bond rates, we would have expected stock prices and expected-dividend-growth rates to have adjusted, so that the use of dividend-growth models would produce a similar estimate (22 to 23 percent) of K_e. We would have calculated *WARR* to be 18.7 percent rather than 13.5 percent. (For simplicity, assume no changes in Largo's capital structure or tax rates.) The 6-percentage-point increase in the government-bond rate (from 9 percent to 15 percent) increased the *WARR* by less than 6 percent. In general, the change in *WARR* is going to be less than the change in government rates because of the tax-deductibility of interest. If Largo's *WARR* had been figured in 1962 when the government-bond rate was 4 percent, the result would have been a *WARR* of around 9 percent.

So we see that market required rates of return rise and fall over time as conditions in the financial markets change — which is as it should be. Financial-market rates reflect investors' expectations about future inflation, risk, and other market conditions. When investors expect high inflation, they demand a high inflation premium to compensate for the loss of purchasing power in future returns. Managers, in setting return targets for use in evaluating capital-investment projects, must take those expectations into account.

Source: Table data from Federal Reserve Bank of St. Louis and Federal Reserve Bulletin.

The return target can be used as the discount rate in a net-present-value (*NPV*) calculation or as the hurdle rate to compare with the project's internal rate of return (*IRR*).

have it. We can use it one of two basic ways: as the discount rate in a net present value (*NPV*) calculation or as the hurdle rate to which the project's internal rate of return (*IRR*) is compared. Sample Problem 12–5 illustrates the use of return targets with an example.

Sample Problem 12–5
Evaluating an Average-Risk Investment for Integrated Systems, Inc.

Integrated Systems, Inc. (ISI) is considering the possibility of expanding its production facilities for integrated-circuit boards, which are components used in the manufacturing of electronic equipment. The project involves expansion of an existing product, and management judges it to be of average risk compared to ISI's other projects. ISI follows a policy of financing with 35 percent long-term debt and 65 percent equity. The government-bond rate currently is 10 percent, and the yield to maturity of ISI's bonds currently outstanding is 11 percent. ISI estimates its cost of equity to be 18 percent, and the tax rate is 40 percent. Should the investment be undertaken?

Solution
Table 12–9 outlines the process for calculating the weighted-average required return for ISI. Rounding off the result in Table 12–9, we will take 14 percent as ISI's *WARR*. The project requires an immediate outlay of $350,000 and produces the cash flows shown in Table 12–10 (p. 370). Sales and profits from the product build in the early years, peak, and then begin to decline, reflecting the likelihood that new and better products will come along to replace this one. The cash inflow of $105,000 in year 10 reflects management's estimate of the salvage value of the plant and equipment in that year. The *NPV* calculation shown in Table 12–10 was calculated using ISI's *WARR* of 14 percent as the return target for discounting the cash flows.

We see the project has a negative *NPV* when evaluated at the company's *WARR* of 14 percent. Because *NPV* is negative at 14 percent, we know that the project's internal rate of return must lie below 14 percent, and in fact it turns out to be about 11.6 percent—well below the target. Thus, the project does not pass the economic test and cannot be said to constitute a wise use of capital funds. Unless

Table 12–9
Calculating Integrated Systems' Weighted-Average Required Return (WARR)

	Required Return (percent) (1)	Weight (2)	Weighted Return (percent) (3) = (1) × (2)
Long-term debt, after taxes	6.60	0.35	2.31
Equity	18.0	0.65	11.70
			WARR = 14.01

Note: $K_e = 18$ percent; $K_d = 11$ percent; after-tax $K_d = 11.0(1 - 0.40) = 6.6$ percent.

Table 12–10

Net Present Value of Expansion Project at Integrated Systems, Inc.

Year	After-Tax Cash Flow (1)	Present-Value Factor at 14 Percent (2)	Present Value (3) = (1) × (2)
0	−$350,000	1.000	−$350,000
1	− 15,000	0.877	− 13,155
2	40,000	0.769	30,760
3	60,000	0.675	40,500
4	85,000	0.592	50,320
5	95,000	0.519	49,305
6	95,000	0.456	43,320
7	80,000	0.400	32,000
8	75,000	0.351	26,325
9	70,000	0.308	21,560
10	105,000	0.270	28,350

Net present value at 14 percent = −$ 40,715

there are compelling reasons for the project that are not reflected in the economic analysis, the project should be rejected.

Using the *WARR* as a Target

In this chapter, we have developed an approach to calculating the weighted-average required return, and we have discussed its use in evaluating investment opportunities. We noted at several points that the *WARR* is the correct target for evaluating investment opportunities of average risk.[3]

Some firms use the *WARR* for evaluating all capital-investment projects. Such an approach is correct in principle only if all the firm's projects are equally risky — seldom the case in practice. For example, cost-reduction projects usually are subject to much less uncertainty than are new products and, hence, are much less risky.

Most firms face investment opportunities that vary across the risk spectrum, and in such cases, the use of the *WARR* as a target for all projects is not correct theoretically. One might defend the use of the *WARR* as a single target for all projects on grounds that all projects should return at least the firm average. This argument may sound plausible, but it is not correct because suppliers of capital are risk-averse and demand higher rates of return for greater risk. Investors might require a weighted-average return of, say, 15 percent on the securities of a given

Since most firms face investment opportunities that vary across the risk spectrum, the use of the *WARR* as a target for all projects is not correct theoretically.

[3]Approaches other than the weighted-average required return will be discussed in Chapter 13. For evaluating average-risk projects, the *WARR* has both theoretical and practical advantages over alternative methods and is the simplest to use. See D. R. Chambers, R. S. Harris, and J. J. Pringle, "Treatment of Financing Mix in Analyzing Investment Opportunities," *Financial Management*, Summer 1982, pp. 24–41.

firm. But on funds for a particular project that has a risk greater than the firm's average risk, they would require a higher return.

Setting different targets for individual projects depending on their risk, however, brings us face to face with a problem of great difficulty: measuring risk *quantitatively* is not just being able to say that Project A is more risky than Project B, but *how much* more risky. As we will see in Chapter 13, measuring risk quantitatively is extremely difficult, and even when carefully done, the results may not always be credible to managers and investors.

Given the difficulty of measuring risk quantitatively, some firms adopt the approach of using the same target for all projects, and in effect treat all projects as equally risky. The single target most often used is the target appropriate for an average-risk project, the *WARR*. While some firms use the *WARR* as a general-purpose target, others go on to refine this basic approach by setting targets for individual projects or categories of projects to take account of differences in risk. We will discuss these refinements in the next chapter.

Setting different targets for different projects depending on their risk requires some way of measuring risk.

Because of the difficulty in measuring risk quantitatively, some firms use the same target for all projects, treating all projects as equally risky. The single target most often used is the *WARR*.

Finance in Practice 12–3

Required Returns, Capital Spending, and the Economy

In the early spring of 1982, many firms were cutting back on their capital-spending plans, much to the disappointment of the government and of others concerned about the economy. A survey of capital-spending plans of major business firms conducted by McGraw-Hill Inc. in November 1981 showed firms planning to increase their 1982 capital outlays by 9.6 percent over 1981. In March 1982, a second survey found that plans had been cut back and now called for only a 6.9 percent increase over 1981. Once inflation was taken into account, the 6.9 percent increase projected for 1982 became hardly any increase at all. Table A on p. 372 gives data for selected industry groups.

The Economic Recovery Act of 1981 had put in place substantial tax reductions for business on the premise that tax reductions would stimulate capital spending, yet just the opposite was taking place. Why? The answer is that business executives were expecting a weak economy in 1982. As one executive stated, "It made sense to batten down the hatches and hold on to our cash." Said another: "Interest rates, excess capacity, and poor profits have more than offset the incentive provided by the tax bill."

Firms responded to the expectation of weak economic activity by cutting back capital expenditures along with operating expenses. Halliburton Company, a Dallas-based supplier of oil-field equipment, planned to keep 1982 spending constant at the 1981 figure. Armco Steel Company delayed indefinitely plans to construct a new mill for $671 million. Champion International Corporation cut 1982 capital spending to $250 million from $600 million in 1981. Aggregate plant-and-equipment spending for the whole economy in the early 1980s is given in Table B on p. 372.

Table A

| | 1982 Capital Spending Plans as a Percentage Change from 1981 | |
	November 1981	March 1982
All business	**9.6**	**6.9**
Mining	24.8	−3.1
Railroads	23.4	3.1
Rubber	21.2	11.5
Food and beverages	20.6	2.7
Nonferrous metals	18.2	−4.6
Petroleum	16.8	8.2
Communications and other	12.2	7.8
Electrical machinery	10.4	6.2
Autos, trucks, and parts	10.2	2.6
Gas utilities	8.7	−3.5
Textiles	2.5	−0.9

Table B

Year	Expenditure for Nonresidential Plant and Equipment (billions of dollars)
1980	308.8
1981	352.2
1982	348.3
1983	352.9

Rather than increasing in response to the 1981 tax cuts, capital spending actually declined in 1982. As a percentage of gross national product, it declined in 1982 and again in 1983.

How can we interpret these reactions in light of financial theory? Our capital-budgeting model discussed in this and earlier chapters tells us to evaluate investment opportunities by discounting expected future cash flows to their present value using a market required return. What happens when the economy weakens or a recession begins? The answer is that estimates of future cash flows become lower. If a project that looked attractive in the fall of 1981 is reevaluated in the spring of 1982, and lower cash-flow estimates are the result, the project may no longer look attractive.

In 1981 and 1982, firms were also faced with extremely high interest rates. For example, in August 1981 the interest rate on corporate *AAA* bonds was 15 percent. As we have seen from our earlier calculations, such high interest rates increase required returns on projects, not only because of the higher interest costs themselves but also because higher interest rates mean higher required returns on equity as well.

As a result, in 1982 many U.S. firms faced a double whammy: lower estimated cash flows resulting from economic recession and higher required returns resulting from capital-market conditions. Both of these effects reduced net present values on projects and made investments look less attractive. While the 1982 cutbacks in capital spending may have surprised tax planners at the time, the cutbacks can readily be interpreted in light of financial theory.

Source: "Capital Spending Takes a Dive," *Business Week,* March 22, 1982, p. 24, updated with subsequent data from the Federal Reserve Bulletin.

KEY CONCEPTS

1. Setting return targets is an important step in evaluating investment opportunities. Return targets should be set by management based on market required rates of return. These required rates of return can then be used in discounted-cash-flow analysis of the desirability of individual investment projects.

2. Required rates of return are opportunity rates that are determined in the financial markets by the competitive interactions of suppliers of funds. In effect, the required return of investors is the marginal cost of capital to the firm.

3. Management acts as the agent of shareholders in setting return targets.

4. Return targets must include both a risk premium and an inflation premium. The risk premium should depend on the risk of the incremental investment being made.

5. The weighted-average required return ($WARR$), also called the *weighted-average cost of capital,*

is a weighted average of the return required by the market on debt (K_d) and on equity (K_e), with K_d adjusted for the tax-deductibility of interest. For a given firm, K_e is greater than K_d.

6. The weighted-average required return is the appropriate return target for evaluating projects of average risk.

7. Market data are useful in estimating values for K_e and K_d. Estimates of K_e, however, are necessarily somewhat imprecise.

8. A weighted-average required return for individual firms can be calculated using market required returns on each future source of funds (K_e, K_d, plus returns on bank debt and preferred stock if used) along with data on future financing proportions (W_e, W_d).

9. Using the weighted-average required return as a return target for all projects is not correct theoretically because projects differ in risk.

SUMMARY

The third step in evaluating investment opportunities, after estimating cash flows and choosing an investment criterion, such as the *NPV* rule or the *IRR* rule (Chapter 10), is to set a return target. The return target is the minimum acceptable return on the investment. It is an *opportunity rate* — the rate forgone on the next best alternative investment opportunity of comparable risk. In evaluating investments, management acts as the agent of shareholders, setting return targets based on the shareholders' required return.

The purpose of return targets is to impose an economic test to ensure that prospective investment opportunities constitute wise and efficient uses of shareholder capital funds. The economic analysis of a project is a second step in the overall planning process of the firm, the first step being a strategic test to make certain that a prospective investment is consistent with the firm's commercial strategy. Its

commercial strategy tells the firm where to look for profitable investment opportunities; return targets tell which of those opportunities to select. In addition to these strategic and economic tests, the evaluation process must take into account the risk preferences of shareholders and managers, interactions among various parts of the firm, constraints on managerial and technical personnel, impact on local communities, environmental factors, and other qualitative considerations.

Although not sufficient by itself, an economic test is wise in nearly all cases because if a prospective investment is not likely to earn the market return, suppliers of capital will not wish it to be undertaken. Going ahead with a project that has little chance of earning a satisfactory return is likely to lead to shareholder unhappiness.

Required rates of return are *market-determined* by the actions of suppliers of capital competing against one another. These market rates represent opportunities available to investors outside the firm and, hence, the minimum return acceptable on investments inside the firm.

The simplest and most basic approach to setting return targets is to calculate a weighted-average required return for the firm individually. Such a *WARR* is a weighted average of the market required returns of all the suppliers of capital. The weights reflect the proportion of total financing coming from each source. In calculating the *WARR,* we must take care to use the after-tax cost of debt to take into account the tax-deductibility of interest. Calculating required returns on equity can be a difficult task. A number of different methods can be used (for exam-

ple, dividend-growth models or historical risk premiums), but the process of estimating the required return on equity involves a number of educated guesses. Once estimated, the *WARR* is appropriate for evaluating projects whose risk is approximately equal to the overall risk of the firm.

The most refined approach is to set targets individually for projects or for categories of projects. This kind of specific target setting requires quantitative measures of project risk, a difficult thing to measure. Many firms stop short of attempting to measure project risk explicitly and instead use the *WARR* as a target for all projects. The next chapter will discuss refinements in target setting to measure project risk and set project targets.

QUESTIONS

1. Why can the required rate of return be viewed as an opportunity rate?
2. Does management determine or interpret the required rates of return of the financial markets?
3. "The required rate of return of any investment opportunity is the rate that could be earned on the next best investment opportunity that must be forgone by the firm." Is this statement true or false? Explain.
4. Why does the required return of an investment opportunity depend on its riskiness?
5. What role is played by the financial markets in establishing required rates of return?
6. "The required rate of return on a firm's stock is always greater than the return on its bonds or other debt." Is this statement true or false? Explain.
7. What is the effect of inflation on rates of return in the financial markets?
8. Why must inflation be taken into account in evaluating investment opportunities in a firm?

9. Under what circumstances would the required return on a new investment opportunity equal the weighted-average return required by the market on the firm's outstanding securities (stocks and bonds)?
10. Define the term *cost of capital* and explain its relationship to the market required rate of return.
11. What is the best source of information regarding current returns required by investors?
12. Are historical market rates of return relevant when determining the current required rate of return? Discuss.
13. Explain the steps in calculating a firm's weighted-average required return.
14. What problems do you see in a firm using the WARR on its securities as the return target for evaluating all of its capital-investment projects?
15. What are some of the problems in calculating the required return on equity?

Problems

Note: Problems preceded by an asterisk (*) are more challenging.

1. Assume that a firm can borrow from its bank at 14 percent annual interest, and it can issue long-

term debt at an interest rate of 12.5 percent and preferred stock at 13.5 percent. Calculate the after-tax equivalent required return on each of these sources of funds, assuming a tax rate of 46 percent.

2. The recent balance sheet of Alamo Corporation is shown in Table A. The company can borrow new long-term funds at 12 percent. Preferred stockholders require a 13.5 percent return. The company's stock is presently selling for $10 a share based on next year's expected annual dividend of $1 per share and growth in dividends of 9 percent a year after that. Assuming a corporate tax rate of 46 percent, calculate Alamo's weighted-average required return (*WARR*). Assume book-value weights are approximately equal to market-value weights.

3. During the past five years, the dividends of Ditka Inc. have grown at an annual rate of 5 percent, leading to a current dividend per share of $.60. Ditka's stock is presently selling for $10 a share.

   a. Suppose you assumed that past dividend growth was expected to continue indefinitely into the future. What would be your estimate of the required return of Ditka stock (K_e)?

   b. If the government long-term bond rates were 12 percent, how would you feel about the validity of your answers as calculated in part (a)?

4. Consider the data on Durham Industries (DI) in Table B, showing company dividends for the years 1981 through 1988. At the year-end 1980, DI stock was quoted at $25.00, and at year-end 1988, $35.00.

   a. Calculate the return realized by investors over the period 1981–1988 assuming the stock was purchased at the end of 1980 and sold at the end of 1988 (the solution requires trial and error or an *IRR* calculator).

   b. Discuss the use of these data as a basis for estimating K_e, the required return on DI's stock as of early 1987. Suppose the U.S.-government-bond rate was 11 percent.

Table B

Year	Dividend
1981	$1.25
1982	$1.25
1983	$1.35
1984	$1.35
1985	$1.35
1986	$1.35
1987	$1.50
1988	$1.50

5. Skeleton Enterprises has the balance-sheet items listed in Table C (p. 376). The company is paying 12 percent on borrowing from the bank (and expects that rate to continue). Skeleton can issue new long-term debt at 10.7 percent. Preferred stock, being more risky, has a higher required return. In Skeleton's case it is 11.5 percent. Skeleton plans to maintain its current capital structure (book and market values are approximately equal). Management is proud of the fact that Skeleton stock is currently selling for $20 per share based on an expected annual dividend growth rate of 6.4 percent, leading to a dividend for next year of $2 per share. Assuming a 46 percent tax rate, calculate Skeleton's *WARR*.

Table A

Assets		Liabilities	
Current assets	$6,854,000	Current liabilities	$5,341,000
Fixed assets	7,336,000	Long-term debt	3,000,000
Total	$14,190,000	Preferred stock	800,000
		Common stock	1,700,000
		Retained earnings	3,349,000
		Total	$14,190,000

Table C

Category	Amount
Accounts payable	$ 6,000
Accruals	4,000
Notes payable (bank)	8,000
Long-term debt	7,000
Preferred stock	4,000
Common stock	8,000
Retained earnings	25,000
Total liabilities and net worth	$62,000

6. In problem (5), if Skeleton Enterprises earns an internal rate of return equal to the *WARR*, what is the return to common-equity funds contributed to the project? (Hint: Determine the after-tax return on a $100,000 investment, then deduct the tax-adjusted interest and preferred dividends, leaving an amount available for common equity.)

7. If the *IRR* for the Skeleton Enterprise project in problem (5) is 20 percent, what is the return to the preferred stock and common-equity funds? If the *IRR* were 7 percent, what is the return to debt, preferred, and common-equity funds?

*8. Jane Dixie of Shallow Vineyards, Inc., has taken a close look at her firm's required rate of return. It seems as if some aspiring finance student has convinced her that the financial complexity of her holdings make the calculation of her "cost of capital" an intriguing project. Consequently, the recent balance sheet shown in Table D (with figures in millions of dollars) is being closely scrutinized. In addition to the balance sheet, you have learned that new long-term debt can be sold at face value ($1,000) if the coupon rate is 8 percent. This explains why the existing bonds (3 percent coupon) have a market value of only $16,014,000 compared to their book value of $20 million. New preferred stock can be sold at par (100) if a 9 percent dividend payment is stipulated. Shallow Vineyards presently has one million shares of common stock outstanding. The market price of this stock has been roughly constant at $72 per share. Dixie feels that this is a fair price. The firm is expected to pay a dividend of $8 per share in the next year, and dividends (per share) and earnings (per share) of Shallow Vineyards are expected to grow at 4 percent per year for the foreseeable future. Assume that the corporate tax rate is 40 percent. Dixie views her capital structure as the best financial mix for Shallow Vineyards. She bases this upon market-value calculations. Now that the hard work has been done—gathering the data and making estimates—Dixie requires a discount rate to use in evaluation of some small investment proposals. What rate would you suggest? Under what conditions might the rate that you calculate be an improper discount rate to use in net-present-value calculations?

Table D

Assets		Liabilities and Owner's Equity	
Cash	10	Accounts payable	20
Accounts receivable	10	Long-term debt	
Plant and equipment	60	(3% coupon)	20
Other assets	20	Preferred stock (9%)	10
		Common stock	20
Total assets	100	Retained earnings	30
		Total liabilities and owner's equity	100

REFERENCES

Chambers, D. R., R. S. Harris, and J. J. Pringle, "Treatment of Financing Mix in Analyzing Investment Opportunities." *Financial Management* (Summer 1982): 24–41.

Harris, R., "Using Analysts' Growth Forecasts to Estimate Shareholder Required Returns." *Financial Management* (Spring 1986).

Harris, R. S., and J. J. Pringle, "A Note on the Implications of Miller's Argument for Capital Budgeting." *Journal of Financial Research*. (Spring 1983): 13–23.

Hastie, K. L., "One Businessman's View of Capital Budgeting." *Financial Management* 4 (Winter 1974): 36–44.

Johnson, R. *Issues and Readings in Managerial Finance*. 3rd ed. New York: Dryden Press, 1987.

Miles, J. A., and J. R. Ezzell, "The Weighted Average Cost of Capital, Perfect Capital Markets and Project Life: A Clarification." *Journal of Financial and Quantitative Analysis* (September 1980).

Appendix 12A

Using the Capital-Asset-Pricing Model to Calculate Required Returns on Equity

In Chapter 12, we focused on the risk-premium approach and dividend-growth models to calculate the required return on equity, K_e. Another method sometimes used to estimate K_e is the capital-asset-pricing model (CAPM), discussed in Chapter 5. There we saw that, according to the CAPM, the required return on any asset (for example, a share of stock) could be calculated as shown in Equation (A–1):

$$K_j = R_f + \beta_j(K_m - R_f) \qquad \text{(A–1)}$$

where K_j = the required rate of return on asset j, R_f = the risk-free rate of return, K_m = the required rate of return on the market portfolio, and β_j = the beta coefficient of asset j (a measure of nondiversifiable risk).

If we think of the stock of a company as just another asset, we can use Equation (A–1) to estimate K_e. In Equation (A–1), K_j can stand for K_e.

The CAPM risk/return relationship states that the required return, K_j, on any asset, j, is equal to a least-risk rate, R_f, plus a risk premium. In theory, R_f is a risk-free rate of interest. In practice, the interest rate (yield to maturity) on long-term U.S. government bonds is often used as a value for R_f when looking at long-term rates of return. While U.S. government bonds are not risk-free, they are perhaps the least risky of long-term investments.

The risk premium of any asset is the result of taking the market risk premium $(K_m - R_f)$ and multiplying it by a measure of the nondiversifiable risk of the asset relative to the risk of the market (β_j). The "market" is, in theory, the portfolio of all risky assets in the economy. In practice, a widely diversified portfolio, such as the Standard & Poor's 500 stock index, is often used as a proxy for the market portfolio.

The most frequently used measure of nondiversifiable risk is the beta coefficient, β_j, shown in Equation (A–1). As we saw in Chapter 5, the beta coefficient is a measure of how returns on an asset move *relative* to returns on the market portfolio. A beta of 1.0 indicates an asset of average risk. A beta greater than 1.0 indicates an asset of above-average risk, whose returns tend to be more risky than the market. For example, the stocks of high-risk firms, such as airlines, typically have estimated beta coefficients well above 1.0.

The higher the beta, the higher the nondiversifiable risk of the firm and, as a result, the higher the risk premium.

Sample Problem 12A–1
Estimating the Required Return on Equity for Malta Mining Company

Suppose that stock in Malta Mining Company has an estimated beta coefficient of 1.1 and that Malta Mining management thinks that the market risk premium $(K_m - R_f)$, given current financial-market conditions, is 7.5 percent. Assume that the long-term government-bond rate is 10 percent. Estimate the required return on equity, K_e, for Malta Mining using the capital-asset-pricing model.

Solution

Using Equation (A–1), we can calculate Malta Mining's required return on debt as

$$K_e = 0.10 + (1.1)(0.075)$$

$$= 0.10 + 0.0825 = 0.1825 = 18.25 \text{ percent}.$$

Note that the capital-asset-pricing model adds a risk premium of 8.25 percent to calculate Malta Mining's K_e. This risk premium is larger than the market risk premium of 7.5 percent because Malta Mining is riskier than average (the beta coefficient of Malta Mining is greater than 1.0). This estimate of the required return on equity can now be used to calculate the weighted-average required return for Malta Mining.

Sample Problem 12A–2
Estimating the Weighted-Average Required Return for Rendleman Enterprises

Rendleman Enterprises uses a large amount of debt financing. Sixty percent of its financing is done with debt, compared to the industry average of 25 percent. As a result of the extra financial risk, Rendleman's stock has a beta of 1.50, well above the industry average. Rendleman faces a 40 percent tax rate and can issue new debt at a yield to maturity of 9 percent, which is above the yield on U.S. government bonds of 7.5 percent. Rendleman management feels that investors require a 6 percent risk premium to invest in stocks (a broad market portfolio) rather than government bonds. What is the required return of shareholders in Rendleman? What is the weighted-average required return for Rendleman?

Solution

To calculate shareholder's required return, we can use the CAPM. In this $R_f = 0.075$, $(K_m - R_f) = 0.06$ and $\beta = 1.5$:

$$K_e = R_f + \beta(K_m - R_f)$$

$$= 0.075 + 1.5(0.06) = 0.075 + 0.09$$

$$= 0.165 = 16.5 \text{ percent}.$$

Note that Rendleman's stock has a risk premium of 9 percent due to its beta of 1.5, whereas the market risk premium ($\beta = 1$) is only 6 percent.

Using our results for K_e, we can now calculate Rendleman's *WARR:*

$$WARR = W_e K_e + W_d K_d (1 - T)$$
$$= 0.4(0.165) + 0.6(0.09)(1 - 0.4)$$
$$= 0.0984 = 9.84 \text{ percent}.$$

Rendleman's *WARR* is 9.84 percent or approximately 10 percent. This would be an appropriate required return to use in evaluating projects of average risk for Rendleman. ▮

Chapter 13

Dealing with Risk in Capital Budgeting

In this chapter, we will learn how to deal with risk in capital budgeting. We will use sensitivity analysis to determine the impact of different cash-flow assumptions. Then we will discuss risk-adjusted discount rates and learn how to set the return target for a project on the basis of its risk. Finally, we will summarize the approach developed in Part Four of the book to analyzing capital-investment opportunities.

Risk—the degree of uncertainty about future events or outcomes; very difficult to measure accurately or quantitatively.

If we use the weighted-average required return, *WARR*, to evaluate all investment projects, we are treating all projects as if they are equally risky.

In this chapter, we address the thorny problem of how to deal with **risk**—uncertainty about future events or outcomes. In Chapter 12, we discussed the calculation of a weighted-average required return (*WARR*), which is appropriate for evaluating projects of average risk for a firm. If we use the *WARR* for evaluating all projects, we are in effect treating all projects as if they are equally risky. For most firms, however, all projects are not equally risky. Some prospective investments may involve new products and untried technologies. In these cases, risks are likely to be high. On the other hand, when an existing machine wears out and is replaced by essentially the same type of equipment, risks are likely to be relatively small.

From our earlier discussion, we know that there is a trade-off between risk and investors' required rate of return. This trade-off is just as applicable to investment projects considered by a firm as it is to individual investors' decisions about investments (stocks and bonds) in financial markets. The higher the risk, the higher the required rate of return should be. Remember that the firm is ultimately interested in creating value for shareholders. Consequently, managers must take into account investors' dislike of risk. The problem is finding practical ways to implement such risk adjustments.

Measuring risk accurately in a manner that has credibility with executives is so difficult, in fact, that some firms do not attempt it and simply use the weighted-average required return as the return target for all projects. Others adjust the *WARR* "up a bit" for high-risk projects and "down a bit" for low-risk projects. In many situations, it is desirable to deal more rigorously with risk. Ways of doing so are the topic of this chapter. Before grappling with techniques for dealing with

Finance in Practice 13–1

The Alaska Gas Pipeline

In the summer of 1981, John McMillian, chairman of the Northwest Energy Company, a natural-gas-transmission company, faced a problem: how to raise $22 billion. Companies do not often set out to raise this kind of money, but McMillian's company needed it for an unusual purpose: to finance a pipeline across Alaska and

Canada to carry natural gas from the Prudhoe Bay oil fields on Alaska's north slope to users in the United States. The idea for the gas pipeline grew out of the success of a similar pipeline built during the 1970s to carry oil from Prudhoe Bay south across the state to Valdez, Alaska, where it was loaded onto tankers for shipment to other parts of the United States.

The gas-pipeline project was mind-boggling in its scope and complexity. When completed, the line was to carry 2.5 billion cubic feet of gas daily, about 5 percent of current U.S. consumption, south through part of Alaska and across western Canada to a point in southern Alberta. There the line was to split, with one leg running to Chicago and the other to San Francisco. The finished line was to involve a total of 4,800 miles of pipe and was expected, ultimately, to cost between $35 and $50 billion.

risk, let us consider the problem of risk in connection with a large and interesting project—the Alaska gas pipeline.

Techniques for Dealing with Risk

For the Alaska gas pipeline to be privately financed, prospective investors and lenders had to analyze it as an investment opportunity. This analysis required estimating future cash flows and dealing with uncertainties. The gas pipeline is by no means a typical project, but the same techniques used in analyzing it would be applicable to the more usual investments undertaken by firms.

What are those techniques? The two techniques for dealing with risk that find the widest use are **sensitivity analysis** and the **risk-adjusted discount rate.** Equation (1) restates the basic formula for calculating net present value that we have used in analyzing investment opportunities, originally presented in Chapter 10:

Sensitivity analysis—a technique for examining the impact on return and net present value of variations in underlying factors; can show the consequences of different possible outcomes.

Risk-adjusted discount rate—a return target that reflects the risk of the investment being analyzed.

$$NPV = C_0 + \frac{C_1}{1 + K} + \frac{C_2}{(1 + K)^2} + \ldots + \frac{C_n}{(1 + K)^n}$$

$$= C_0 + \sum_{t=1}^{n} \frac{C_t}{(1 + K)^t} \tag{1}$$

where C_t = the expected cash flow in period t and K = the required rate of return. Cash outlays mean negative values for cash flows.

Some who studied the project concluded that it was so large and faced so many unknowns that private companies would not risk putting up the money and that only the federal government would be able to take the risk. Others, including McMillian, believed that private capital could do the job. McMillian's plan was to put together a consortium of 100 banks—50 domestic and 50 foreign—to put up about $9.5 billion in the form of loans. Insurance companies would be asked to lend $2.25 billion, and equipment and material suppliers would be asked for about $4.5 billion. The remainder of the initial $22 billion, which would finance the 745-mile segment across Alaska, would come from the sale of bonds. Later, after the Alaska segment was completed, financing would be arranged for the segments across Canada and the United States.

Consider the risks in the project, both from the standpoint of the 11 sponsoring firms putting up the equity capital (about 30 percent of the total) and from the standpoint of the lenders putting up the balance. No one knew for certain how much the pipeline ultimately would cost or exactly how long it would take to build. Unforeseen problems might be encountered. Costs might run higher than anticipated because of technical problems, weather, or inflation. Before the pipeline could be completed, alternative sources of energy, such as coal, solar, or nuclear power, might drive down the price of natural gas to the point where the pipeline was a losing proposition. To McMillian and others contemplating the Alaska gas pipeline in the summer of 1981, the word *risk* had real significance.

Source: Adapted from the *Wall Street Journal,* July 2, 1981.

Sensitivity analysis focuses on cash flows—the numerator in the net-present-value calculation. The *risk-adjusted discount rate* focuses on the required return—the denominator in the *NPV* calculation.

In sensitivity analysis, we focus on the cash flow, C_t—the *numerator* of the *NPV* calculation. We can ask ourselves *what if* cash flows turn out to be different from those anticipated—that is, what if cash flows do not turn out to be the most likely flows. In using risk-adjusted discount rates, we focus on the required return, K—the *denominator* of the *NPV* calculation. We incorporate the uncertainty surrounding the cash flows into the discount rate used to calculate present value. We will explore these two techniques in more depth.

Sensitivity Analysis

To illustrate the use of sensitivity analysis, let us return to Zippo Corporation's proposal to build a new facility to manufacture computer components, which we examined in Chapter 11. Data for the project are repeated in Table 13–1.

The figures in Table 13–1 are all expected cash flows, but in most cases there is no assurance that these cash flows will actually materialize. No one knows for sure that sales of computer components will turn out to be $1 million in 1990. Sales in any year will depend on many factors, including technological changes in computers, the state of the economy, advertising effectiveness, and competition from other suppliers. Actual sales in 1990 may turn out to be lower or higher than $1 million. So the sales figure for the Zippo proposal should be thought of as a *range* of possible outcomes. The single best guess for sales, according to Zippo's

Table 13–1
Incremental Cash Flows for Zippo Proposal (thousands of dollars)

A. Operating Cash Flows

	1990	1991	1992	1993	1994
Sales	1,000	1,000	1,000	1,000	1,000
minus Cost of Goods Sold	−600	−600	−600	−600	−600
minus Operating Expense	− 50	− 50	− 50	− 50	− 50
minus Depreciation	−160	−160	−160	−160	−160
Profit Before Tax	190	190	190	190	190
minus Taxes (40%)	− 76	− 76	− 76	− 76	− 76
Profit After Tax	114	114	114	114	114
Operating Cash Flow (PAT + DEP)	**274**	**274**	**274**	**274**	**274**

B. Total Cash Flows

	1989	1990	1991	1992	1993	1994
Initial Cash Flow	−850	0	0	0	0	0
Operating Cash Flow	0	274	274	274	274	274
Terminal Cash Flow	0	0	0	0	0	320
Total Cash Flow	**−850**	**274**	**274**	**274**	**274**	**594**

management, is $1 million, so that figure appears in Table 13–1 and is used in our calculation of the internal rate of return on the project.

As we proceed further out into the future, the uncertainties surrounding the sales estimates increase. The estimate of $1 million for 1994 is very speculative; indeed, it is management's best guess as to the most likely outcome in that year, with a wide range of possibilities above and below.

The sales estimate is not the only component of cash flow subject to uncertainty. Raw-material costs, manufacturing costs, and energy costs are all subject to uncertainty. As with sales, the figures for cost of goods sold and operating expenses in Table 13–1 are management's estimates of *most likely* figures.[1]

Thus, the final set of cash flows from which the project's internal rate of return is calculated, labeled "Total Cash Flow" in Table 13–1, is composed of the *most likely* figures from a range of possible outcomes. In a world characterized by unpredictability, no amount of analysis can eliminate entirely the uncertainty surrounding estimates of future cash flows.

What can management do to deal with such uncertainties? It can do little to control outside events, but it can prepare itself by anticipating outcomes other than the single most likely one. By using the technique of sensitivity analysis, management can examine the impact on return and net present value of variations in the underlying factors.

In a world of uncertainty, no amount of analysis can eliminate the uncertainty surrounding cash-flow estimates in the future. Analysis can, however, help one to be prepared.

What If?

Sensitivity analysis is a "What if?" technique. What if the sales of Zippo's computer component turn out lower than expected? This could happen if there is more competition in the market than Zippo projects. What if costs of goods sold are higher? On a more positive note, Zippo may get lucky and sales may be higher than expected, or costs lower. Sensitivity analysis simply traces through the effects of different scenarios on an investment proposal.

We can apply sensitivity analysis to Zippo's decision by examining the effects of different assumptions on the project's internal rate of return. Let us examine the impact of a shortfall in sales — say, 10 percent below the most likely figures in Table 13–1. To do so, we multiply all the sales figures in Table 13–1 by 0.90, yielding annual sales of $900,000. We then recalculate profits, cash flows, and internal rate of return. We find that the internal rate of return falls to 21.2 percent from 24.6. If sales are 20 percent below the most likely level in each year, return drops to 17.8 percent. If, on the other hand, sales run 10 percent above the most likely level, return will be 27.9 percent. The results of these various assumptions about sales are displayed in Table 13–2 on p. 386.

We can also perform sensitivity analysis on cost of goods sold. What if costs of production run 10 percent above the most likely level even though sales are $1 million as expected? Return drops from 24.6 to 19.5 percent. Results of sensitivity analysis on cost of goods sold are displayed in Table 13–3 on p. 386.

[1]As we stated in Chapter 5, technically speaking there can be a difference between the *expected value* of an outcome and the *most likely outcome*. We will not make that distinction here. In doing *NPV* and *IRR* analysis without sensitivity analysis, it would be appropriate to use expected cash flows.

Table 13–2

Sensitivity Analysis on Sales — Zippo Proposal

Sales as Percent of Most Likely *Value*	Internal Rate of Return *(percent)*
120	31.1
110	27.9
100	24.6 ←— Most likely
90	21.2
80	17.8

Table 13–3

Sensitivity Analysis on Cost of Goods Sold — Zippo Proposal

Cost of Goods Sold as Percent *of* Most Likely *Value*	Internal Rate of Return *(percent)*
120	14.4
110	19.5
100	24.6 ←— Most likely
90	29.5
80	34.4

Often it is useful to graph the results of sensitivity analysis, as shown in Figure 13–1.

In addition to looking at changes in sales and cost of goods sold separately, we may want to vary both at the same time. After all, increased sales volume may allow the company to reduce costs of goods sold as a percentage of sales. And, on the downside, if sales are disappointing, costs may run high. Table 13–4 shows the results when both sales and costs are allowed to change. The internal rate of return of 24.6 percent in the middle of Table 13–4 is the result when both costs and sales are as expected. But, as the table shows, if costs are 20 percent higher [that is, cost of goods sold is 72 percent of sales rather than the expected value of 60 percent: 72 = 60(1.20)] and sales only 80 percent of expected, the return drops to 9.5 percent — well below Zippo's hopes for the project. If things go well, the return may be as high as 42.6 percent, shown in the bottom right of the table. Figures such as those in Table 13–4 can be a tremendous aid to a manager in seeing exactly how sensitive a decision is to changes in assumptions.

Worst-Case Analysis

Worst-case analysis — tells management how low a return could fall under adverse circumstances; the return target for evaluating the worst case should not include a risk premium for bearing risk.

Figures such as those in Table 13–4 are extremely valuable for **worst-case analysis.** In a worst-case analysis, we are dealing with uncertainty by looking at cash

Figure 13–1
Sensitivity Analysis for Zippo Proposal

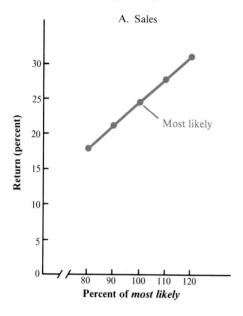

A. Sales

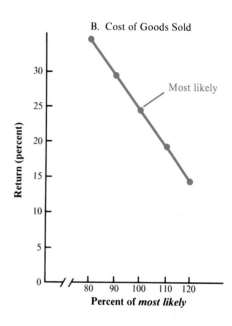

B. Cost of Goods Sold

Table 13–4
Sensitivity Analysis of Internal Rate of Return to Changes in Sales and Cost of Goods Sold*

		Sales (% of most likely)				
		80	90	100	110	120
Cost of	120	9.5	12.0	14.4	16.8	19.2
Goods Sold	110	13.7	16.6	19.5	22.4	25.2
(% of most likely)	100	17.8	21.2	24.6	27.9	31.1	← Expected
	90	21.9	25.7	29.5	33.2	36.9
	80	25.9	30.2	34.4	38.5	42.6

↑
Expected

*Entries in table are internal rate of return.

flows under adverse conditions. In Zippo's case this might correspond to sales shortfalls of 20 percent and cost of goods sold being 20 percent higher than expected. As shown in Table 13–4, this produces a return of only 9.5 percent. How do we evaluate whether the 9.5 percent is high enough to justify investing in the project? If we compare 9.5 percent to a return target that includes a risk premium, we would "double count" with respect to risk. As a result, the return target for

The return target for evaluating the "worst case" should not include a risk premium for bearing risk.

evaluating the worst case should not include a risk premium to compensate equity owners for bearing risk. If we have truly identified the worst case, we need not add a risk premium to the required return. Risk has already been taken into account by the fact that the cash flows we are analyzing (in the worst case) are typically much lower than the cash flows we expect.

To illustrate, let us assume that at the time Zippo management is analyzing the new facility, the long-term government-bond rate is 8 percent. For our purposes, this 8 percent figure can be taken as shareholders' required return without any added risk premium. As noted above, a shortfall in sales to 80 percent of the most likely level, coupled with costs of 120 percent of the most likely level, would produce a return of 9.5 percent. In this situation, the project would return more than enough to satisfy a return target of 8 percent.[2] If this were the worst possible outcome, the facility would be an excellent investment. If, as seems more likely, management concluded that sales could fall below 80 percent and that, simultaneously, costs could go above 120 percent, the case would be less clear. In any event, the technique of worst-case analysis tells management just how low the return could fall under adverse circumstances.

Computer-Assisted Financial Modeling

Sensitivity analysis requires a great deal of calculation, a requirement that can inhibit the use of the technique. To examine the impact of a shortfall in sales to 90 percent of the most likely level, we must recalculate the entire income statement for each year, refigure cash flow, and recalculate the internal rate of return. These calculations can be done by hand using present-value tables, but someone forced to do it this way will not perform many sensitivity analyses. An easier way is to use an electronic calculator equipped to do discounted cash flow.

Financial-modeling programs — computer programs specially designed to do *what if* analysis by calculating the consequences of changing assumptions.

Still a better way is to use a computer program specially designed to do *what if* analysis. Programs of this type generally are referred to as **financial-modeling programs.** Rapid technological advances in computers during the 1980s made quite powerful financial-modeling programs, the most popular of which were labeled *spreadsheet programs,* available on desktop microcomputers sometimes costing less than $1,000. This development has made financial-modeling technology available to the smallest firms and to private individuals. All the data in Tables 13–1 through 13–4 (and in fact many of the tables in this book) were developed using a spreadsheet program on a small desktop computer.

Once the model of a project's cash flows is developed, it is a simple matter to ask the computer *what if* sales are only 90 percent of the most likely level. The computer then recalculates all the figures in the tables, including the internal rate of return, in a few seconds. Such computer models also make it easy to do sensi-

---

[2]In the general case where the company has a policy to finance W_d percentage of investment with debt and W_e percentage with equity, we would calculate a weighted-average required return as we did in Chapter 12 using the government-bond rate as our estimate of K_e (without a risk premium). This calculation would assure that we recognize the after-tax cost of debt, $K_d(1 - T)$, with shareholders evaluating their residual claim at a risk-free required rate of K_e = the government-bond rate. Note that we should not add a risk premium to K_e because risk has already been taken into account in the cash flows when we do worst-case analysis.

tivity analysis using changes in many variables (such as sales, operating costs, or tax laws).

Using Sensitivity Analysis

Sensitivity analysis is a powerful planning technique useful in virtually any situation involving uncertain future events. Computer-based modeling programs take the drudgery out of the calculations, so that sensitivity analysis now can be done quickly and inexpensively.

Consider the uncertainties involved in planning the Alaska gas-pipeline venture. Given the long planning and construction period, inflation can have a major impact on costs and financing requirements. What if the inflation rate runs 1 or 2 percentage points higher than anticipated? Is the viability of the project threatened? Using sensitivity analysis, planners and executives can ascertain the financial impact of a wide range of inflation rates. Similarly, they can examine the impact of ranges of construction costs, prices for natural gas and competing fuels, or any other variable about which there is uncertainty.

It is a safe bet that, during the planning period of the gas-pipeline project, questions such as these were being examined carefully. Sensitivity analysis could not tell those responsible what would happen in the future, and it certainly could not make the decision for them, but it could show them the consequences of many possible outcomes and help them prepare by reducing surprises. Sensitivity analysis can show what key variables dramatically affect the success of the project and give managers guidance as to where they might best spend time in further analysis or planning.

Sample Problem 13–1
Sensitivity Analysis of Zippo Proposal

Zippo's management is concerned about possible sales shortfalls and cost overruns associated with its proposed facility. In particular, management feels that in a worst case sales might drop to $700,000 a year, cost of goods sold may rise to 75 percent of sales (compared to the most likely value of 60 percent), and annual operating expenses may run $100,000. Note that this worst case is different from any of the entries in Table 13–4 and reflects new information.

Solution

Using the same format as Table 13–1, we can recalculate the cash flows for the worst-case scenario as shown in Table 13–5 on p. 390. Note that sales are $700,000, cost of goods sold is 75 percent, and operating expenses are $100,000. Since Zippo has a loss on the facility, there is actually a tax savings of $34,000 a year, reflecting taxes that Zippo will no longer have to pay on profits from its other operations.

Now we can find the IRR based on the last line of cash flows in Table 13–5:

$$-\$850 + \$109 \, PVAF(IRR, 4) + \$429 \, PVF(IRR, 5) = 0.$$

By trial and error, $IRR = 0.005 = 0.5$ percent.

Table 13–5
Worst-Case Analysis of Proposed Facility (thousands of dollars)

A. Operating Cash Flows		1990	1991	1992	1993	1994
Sales		700	700	700	700	700
minus Cost of Goods Sold (0.75)		−525	−525	−525	−525	−525
minus Operating Expenses		−100	−100	−100	−100	−100
minus Depreciation		−160	−160	−160	−160	−160
Profit Before Tax		− 85	− 85	− 85	− 85	− 85
minus Taxes (40%)		(34)	(34)	(34)	(34)	(34)
Profit After Tax		− 51	− 51	− 51	− 51	− 51
Operating Cash Flow (PAT + DEP)		**109**	**109**	**109**	**109**	**109**

B. Total Cash Flows	1989	1990	1991	1992	1993	1994
Initial Cash Flows	−850	0	0	0	0	0
Operating Cash Flow	0	109	109	109	109	109
Terminal Cash Flow	0	0	0	0	0	320
Total Cash Flow	−850	109	109	109	109	429

Since the *IRR* is less than one percent, it is clear that the facility will not be desirable if the worst case occurs because one percent is less than even a risk-free required rate of return. The worst case represents a clear risk and must be weighed against the better outcomes. Of key importance will be the likelihood that the worst case could actually occur.

Using Risk-Adjusted Discount Rates

The more uncertain (risky) the cash flows, the higher the required rate of return, *K*, that we use as the discount rate to calculate net present value or as the target against which to compare the internal rate of return. The lower the risk, the lower the required rate of return used in the *NPV* or *IRR* analysis.

We noted earlier that sensitivity analysis is one of two main techniques for dealing with risk in capital-investment analysis. Sensitivity analysis focuses on the impact of changes in cash flows — the *numerator* in the *NPV* and *IRR* calculation. The second approach is to formulate risk-adjusted discount rates. In formulating risk-adjusted discount rates, we use only the expected cash flows in the numerator of the *NPV* or *IRR* calculation and focus instead on the discount rate in the *denominator*. We can attempt to take into account the uncertainty surrounding the cash flows by adjusting the discount rate to reflect the degree of risk. The more uncertain (risky) the cash flows, the higher the required rate of return, *K*, that we use as the discount rate to calculate net present value or as the target against which to compare the internal rate of return. The lower the risk, the lower the required rate of return used in the *NPV* or *IRR* calculation.

For example, in Chapter 12 we calculated the weighted-average required return for Mattari to be 13.88 percent (see Table 12–5). This 13.88 percent required return would be appropriate as a discount rate to evaluate projects of average risk for Mattari. For projects of higher-than-average risk, Mattari should use a higher discount rate — say, 16 percent. One of our goals in this chapter is to see how we would go about determining such a 16 percent figure.

This risk-adjusted-discount-rate technique simply applies the risk/return trade-off concept to the analysis of investment proposals. An example can highlight the difference between the two techniques of *sensitivity analysis* and *risk-adjusted discount rates*.

Look carefully at the flows in Table 13–6. In Period 1, Project A's flows will fall somewhere between $140 and $260, with a most likely value of $200. For Project B, the range of possible outcomes is much wider, from −$250 to $550, but the most likely figure is the same, $200. Similarly, in each period the *range* of possible outcomes is much wider for Project B than for Project A.

In Table 13–7, the data for Projects A and B are displayed the same way as in earlier chapters — that is, showing only the most likely cash flow in each year.

Table 13–6

Uncertainty of Cash Flows Expected for Two Hypothetical Projects

			Cash Flows		
	Period 0	*Period 1*	*Period 2*	*Period 3*	*Period 4*
Project A					
Outlay	−$1,000				
Possible inflows					
Maximum value		$260	$500	$ 800	$ 800
Most likely value		$200	$400	$ 600	$ 600
Minimum value		$140	$300	$ 450	$ 450
Project B					
Outlay	−$1,000				
Possible inflows					
Maximum value		$550	$750	$1,050	$1,050
Most likely value		$200	$400	$ 600	$ 600
Minimum value		−$250	$ 50	$ 200	$ 200

Table 13–7

Most Likely Cash Flows for Two Hypothetical Projects

			Cash Flows		
	Period 0	*Period 1*	*Period 2*	*Period 3*	*Period 4*
Project A	−$1,000	$200	$400	$600	$600
Project B	−$1,000	$200	$400	$600	$600

As Table 13–6 makes clear, Project B's flows are far more uncertain (risky) than are Project A's. Yet the presentation in Table 13–7, looking only at most likely values, obscures the differences in uncertainty between the two projects. Sensitivity analysis, along lines outlined earlier in this chapter, would make clear the difference in uncertainty and permit us to deal with it.

The second approach, using risk-adjusted discount rates, deals only with the most likely cash flows (those listed in Table 13–7), but *discounts them at different rates.* The flows for Project B, being more risky, would be discounted at a higher rate. Low-risk and high-risk projects will have different discount rates — the rates adjusted for the risk of the project. Table 13–8 gives illustrative calculations using risk-adjusted discount rates for Projects A and B. Here, Project B is evaluated using a higher required return (assumed 18 percent), reflecting that it is more risky than Project A, which has an assumed required return of 10 percent. As the calculations show, Project B has a lower net present value ($131) than Project A ($373), even though the two projects have the same expected cash flows. The lower net present value for Project B reflects the higher penalty for risk imposed on that project through a higher required return.

> Though the risk-adjusted discount rate technique deals only with the most likely cash flows, it discounts them at different rates depending on the risk of the cash flows.

Grouping Investments by Risk Category

In principle, investment opportunities of a given firm will vary in risk over a wide range. In theory, this variation would require determining a separate required rate of return for each investment proposal. Such an attempt would, however, ignore the costs and difficulties in estimating required returns. One practical solution to this problem is to group investment opportunities into **risk categories.** For example, a company might divide projects into three possible risk categories: cost-reduction projects, expansion projects, and new products.

> **Risk categories** — groups of investment projects of similar risk.

Cost-reduction projects might include a variety of investment opportunities, such as the substitution of equipment for labor, the substitution of a new machine for an older, less efficient one, or the substitution of a completely new manufacturing facility for an old, outmoded one. Cash flows attributable to such projects often, though not always, can be estimated with reasonable accuracy, at least during the first several years.

A second project category might include projects that would expand existing product lines. Such projects might include expansion of existing facilities or addi-

Table 13–8

Application of Risk-Adjusted Discount Rates

Projected A: Low Risk Required Return, $K = 0.10$	Project B: High Risk Required Return, $K = 0.18$
$NPV = -\$1,000 + \dfrac{\$200}{(1.10)} + \dfrac{\$400}{(1.10)^2} + \dfrac{\$600}{(1.10)^3} + \dfrac{\$600}{(1.10)^4}$	$NPV = -\$1,000 + \dfrac{\$200}{(1.18)} + \dfrac{\$400}{(1.18)^2} + \dfrac{\$600}{(1.18)^3} + \dfrac{\$600}{(1.18)^4}$
$= -\$1,000 + \$1,373 = \$373$	$= -\$1,000 + \$1,131 = \$131$

tion of new facilities to manufacture existing products. Because expansion projects generate additional sales revenue, cash flows attributable to such projects usually are more uncertain and, hence, more risky than those of cost-reduction projects.

A third and still more risky project category includes the introduction of new products. Such projects may involve new technology for manufacturing, packaging, or marketing. Judgments may be required as to the likelihood that the firm will be able to solve complex engineering and manufacturing problems. The effects of inflation may be very uncertain. The possibility of shifts in consumer preferences, countermoves by competitors, and technological obsolescence must be taken into account. Because of these and other considerations, both the sales revenue and cost estimates associated with new products usually are subject to considerably greater uncertainty than those associated with the expansion of existing products. Within the new-products category itself, there may be considerable variation in uncertainty.

As a practical approach to capital budgeting, a firm might establish investment categories along the lines just described. Required rates of return then could be set by category rather than for each new project individually. Any number of risk categories might be established. For each category, a measure of risk would have to be estimated.

If expansion projects, for example, were considered to be of average risk for the firm as a whole, then the required return of expansion projects, K_{exp} would be the firm's weighted-average required return that we calculated in the last chapter; that is, $K_{exp} = WARR$. Cost-reduction projects would probably be less risky, and projects involving new products would be more risky. The relationships might be represented as in Figure 13–2, where K symbolizes the required rate of return.

Because we are grouping projects into risk categories, Figure 13–2 shows only a crude risk adjustment. All cost-reduction projects would be treated as equally

> Grouping investment projects by risk categories is a practical response to the difficult problem of measuring risk.

Figure 13–2
Required Return by Risk Category

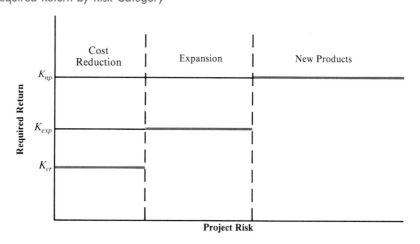

risky, and all would be evaluated using a required return of K_{cr}. All new products would be evaluated using a required return of K_{np}. In practice, we know that some new products may be more risky than others, but the risk adjustment shown in Figure 13–2 would not make this distinction. Figure 13–2 represents an improvement over using a single discount rate for all projects, but it is still a crude form of risk adjustment.

In practice, risk adjustments may use the *WARR* as a baseline for return targets, as demonstrated in Sample Problem 13–2.

Sample Problem 13–2
Setting Return Targets by Project Category for Menlo Corporation

Kim Park, the financial vice-president of Menlo Corporation, has decided to establish a system for setting return targets for capital-investment projects. The company regularly undertakes projects that involve installation of labor-saving machinery. The company operates 12 manufacturing plants located in the United States and frequently receives recommendations from division executives that manufacturing facilities be expanded. Over the past five years, the company has built three new plants and marketed a total of eight entirely new products. By gathering data on past investment projects, Park has determined that most cost-reduction projects are about half as risky as expansion projects. New products, on the other hand, are two to three times as risky.

Set up a system of return targets for Menlo Corporation, assuming that the U.S.-government-bond rate is 8 percent and that Menlo's weighted-average required return is 13 percent.

Solution
The simplest system for a firm such as Menlo is to establish several risk categories for capital-investment projects. In this case, three categories — cost reduction, expansion, and new products — seem to fit the situation. Taking expansion projects to be approximately average in risk, Park has decided to establish a target return of 13 percent for those projects — a target return that is equal to the company's *WARR*. The risk premium for this category would then be 5 percent — which is the weighted-average required return minus the U.S.-government-bond rate. Cost-reduction projects would be assigned a premium of $0.5 \times 5 = 2.5$ percent over the bond rate. Although new products vary somewhat in risk (two to three times as risky as expansion), it would be acceptable as a first approximation to establish a single category for new products with a risk premium of $2.5 \times 5 = 12.5$ percent. The complete system is shown in Table 13–9, where the risk premium is added to the 8 percent government-bond rate to get the required return. ▬

Multidivision Firms and Risk Adjustments

One particularly important application of risk-adjusted required rates of return occurs in multidivision firms. Consider R. J. Reynolds, the consumer-products giant with almost $20 billion worth of sales after its 1985 acquisition of Nabisco. In ad-

Table 13–9

Three Risk Categories Established for Menlo Corporation

Category	Risk Premium (percent)	Required Return (percent)
Cost reduction	2.5	10.5
Expansion	5.0	13.0
New products	12.5	20.5

dition to its tobacco operations, R. J. Reynolds markets Kentucky Fried Chicken, Del Monte food products, and Nabisco brands, such as Oreo cookies. How should R. J. Reynolds allocate capital among its different divisions that produce quite different sorts of products? One mechanism is to use divisional required rates of return that reflect the differing risks of the various lines of business. The risks of investment in cigarette production are quite different from those in the fast-food business, for example. Required rates of return should reflect these differences in risk. It would not be appropriate to apply one single rate (the company's *WARR*) to all lines of business.

Risk-Adjusted Discount Rates and Future Risks

In our calculation of a weighted-average required return and in formulating risk-adjusted discount rates, we have used a single rate that will then be applied to all future periods. We used exactly the same procedure in our discussion of the time value of money. In using this method, we need to be aware of the implicit assumption it makes about the riskiness of future cash flows. Specifically, this method imposes a greater penalty for risk on cash flows the further into the future these cash flows occur.

An example will illustrate. Suppose a project was expected to have a cash flow of $1,000 in each of the next three years. Assume further that, given the risk of the project, we have decided to use a required rate of return of 14 percent when U.S. government bonds are yielding only 10 percent. In other words, the risk premium on the project is 4 percent, using the government-bond yield as a proxy for a risk-free rate. Table 13–10 on p. 396 shows the present values of these future cash flows both at 10 percent and at 14 percent. We can interpret the present values at 10 percent as adjusting only for the time value of money (including a premium for expected inflation). The present values at 14 percent are lower, reflecting an extra penalty for the risk of the project.

The last column of Table 13–10 reports the differences between the present-value figures. These differences are the penalty for risk in dollar terms. For example, for the cash flow expected in year 1, the 4 percent risk premium in the discount rate translates into a $32 reduction in present value. As the figures in the last column show, the dollar penalty for risk gets larger the further the cash flow is in the future. The lesson from this example is that using the same discount

Table 13–10

Risk-Adjusted Discount Rates and Penalties for Risk

Year	Expected Cash Flow	Present Value at 10 Percent (1)	Present Value at 14 Percent (2)	Penalty for Risk (3) = (1) − (2)
1	$1,000	$909	$877	$32
2	$1,000	$826	$769	$57
3	$1,000	$751	$675	$76

Using the same discount rate for all future periods provides a larger and larger dollar penalty for risk the further in the future the projected cash flow occurs—typically a reasonable assumption since uncertainty tends to increase the further into the future we have to forecast.

rate for all future periods provides a larger and larger dollar penalty for risk the further in the future the projected cash flow occurs.

Is this a reasonable result? In many cases the answer is yes. The further in the future we have to project cash flows, the more likely we are to encounter uncertainties in making those estimates. It is typically easier to predict sales for the next year than for five years from now. In these cases, applying the same discount rate to all time periods is exactly what is needed. But we may sometimes encounter investments that don't fit this scenario. Perhaps the speed with which a new product can penetrate a market is highly uncertain, but the company is relatively confident that the product will ultimately be successful; the chief uncertainty is how long it will take. In this case, cash flows in the first few years might be more uncertain than those in later years. How do we handle such a situation? One way would be to establish different required rates of return for different phases of the project. During the early high-risk phase, we might require 15 percent; for cash flows after that phase, we might apply only 13 percent. The difficulty here, as with risk-adjusted discount rates in general, is coming up with specific ways to develop such rates. As a practical matter, it is usually appropriate to obtain a single required return for a project and then apply it to all future cash flows. We should, however, be aware of the implicit assumption this procedure makes about risk in case we find specific situations that do not fit this assumption.

Developing Specific Risk-Adjusted Discount Rates

How can we develop risk-adjusted required returns? The place to start is to recall our calculation of the weighted-average required return. As stated in Chapter 12, the *WARR* is a rate that reflects the average-risk investment for a firm. Firms with different risks will have different *WARR*s. For example, Apple Computer, a firm in the highly volatile personal-computer industry, is more risky than Duke Power Company, a largely regulated provider of electricity in the southeastern United States. As a result, if we calculated *WARR*s for the two firms, we would expect a higher figure for Apple Computer. This higher figure for Apple Computer would reflect the market's distaste for risk. In other words, the market requires higher returns the higher the risk.

The difficulty is that we often need required returns for projects or divisions of companies that will not be traded separately in financial markets. Take the case of

R. J. Reynolds: its debt and stock reflect the risk characteristics of its entire port-folio of activities. Thus, its traded securities do not have the same risk as one of its divisions. In fact, there is no separate set of securities that show ownership in just one of the R. J. Reynolds divisions. If there were, and we needed a required rate of return for one division, we could just treat these securities as a separate company and use the techniques discussed in Chapter 12 to calculate the weighted-average required return based on those securities. The division *WARR* would be the appropriate required return for that division.

If different divisions had different risks, we would get different required returns for each division. The market would do our risk adjusting for us. Unfortunately, life is not so easy. Divisions or projects are not traded as separate companies in financial markets. While this makes our job of risk adjustment more difficult, we still can use market information to help. The principle we will use is: *invest-ments of equal risk should have the same required return*. One way to use this basic principle and take advantage of financial-market information is the **pure-play technique.**

The Pure-Play Technique

The pure-play technique calls for matching a particular investment proposal under consideration to some traded company (or group of companies) based on risk. The idea is to find two situations in which the risks are equal and calculate the required return (*WARR*) for the case where market data are available — that is, for the com-pany whose stock is publicly traded. This rate will also be appropriate for the in-vestment proposal, provided it has approximately the same risk.

To illustrate, consider the American Telephone & Telegraph (AT&T) divesti-ture in 1984, in which the parent company (AT&T) and its operating subsidiaries (the local telephone companies) were split into separate corporations. After the divestiture, the new AT&T provided long-distance phone service, produced telecommunications equipment, and was entering new information-processing markets. This last entry involved introducing its own line of computers in direct competition with IBM. How might AT&T decide on an appropriate required re-turn for investments in the computer business? The pure-play technique might be applied by finding a set of companies whose predominant activities were in the computer field.

A practical way of selecting such companies is to use the system of **standard industrial codes (SICs)** developed to classify companies by their primary line of business. According to these codes, the computer group would include IBM, Bur-roughs Corporation, Control Data Corporation, Hewlett-Packard, Apple Com-puter, Honeywell, NCR Corporation, and Sperry Corporation, plus others. A weighted-average required return could be calculated for each of these companies and the resultant figures averaged to produce an *industry required return*. This in-dustry figure would then serve as an estimate of the required return appropriate for investment in the computer business. AT&T would now have a risk-adjusted re-quired return for its computer operations. This rate would be based on the risks of that business, as reflected in market required rates of return on companies in that business.

Investments of equal risk should have the same required return.

Pure-play technique — calculates the risk-adjusted discount rates by matching a particular investment to one or more publicly traded companies that have risks comparable to those of the investment.

Standard industrial codes (SICs) — a system for classifying companies by their primary line of business.

Using Entry into the Computer Industry as an Example. To see how this risk-adjusted required return could be formulated, we can attempt to find a required rate of return for AT&T's investments in the computer industry. The first step is to gather some data from financial markets. Table 13–11 shows data collected in November 1985. At that time, yields on long-term government bonds were slightly above 10 percent; we will round to 10 percent for this illustration. In addition, suppose that the market risk premium on stocks in general was 7 percent. This figure is based on our discussion of risk premiums on equity in Chapter 12. Finally, assume for simplicity that all of the firms could issue new long-term debt at a yield to maturity of 11 percent. With extra effort, we could get borrowing costs for each of the individual companies based on the market's assessment of the risk of each company's debt. Assume a 50 percent tax rate for this example.

Company Data. For this illustration, we have limited ourselves to data on four companies, though in practice one might choose more. In addition to AT&T, we have selected three firms who are classified by Value Line as being in the computer business. The beta coefficient and proportions of equity financing and debt financing as of late 1985 are given in Table 13–12 (see Chapter 5 for a discussion of beta coefficients and the capital-asset-pricing model).

Calculating the Weighted-Average Required Return. First, let us calculate the *WARR* for AT&T. Using the capital-asset-pricing model and rounding to the nearest percent, we can calculate AT&T's required return on equity as

Table 13–11
Selected Financial Data

Category	Rate (percent)
Long-term interest rate for government bonds	10.0
Market risk premium on stocks	7.0
Firms' interest rate on new debt	11.0
Tax rate	50.0

Table 13–12
Beta Coefficients and Financing Mix for Selected Firms

Firm	Beta Coefficient	Proportion of Financing Done with Equity, W_e	Proportion of Financing Done with Debt, W_d
AT&T	0.80	0.63	0.37
Apple	1.70	1.00	0.00
Amdahl	1.55	0.81	0.19
IBM	1.05	0.89	0.11

Source: Value Line Investment Survey.

$$K_e = R_f + (K_m - R_f)(\beta)$$

$AT\&T$

$$= 0.10 + (0.07)(0.80) = 0.10 + 0.06 = 0.16.$$

Note that according to Value Line's estimate of the beta coefficient, stock in AT&T is less risky than the average stock. Therefore it receives a risk premium of 6 percent, which is below the assumed market risk premium of 7 percent.

We can now calculate AT&T's weighted-average required return, using our earlier assumptions and the data from Table 13–12, as

$$WARR = W_e K_e + W_d K_d(1 - T)$$

$AT\&T$

$$= (0.63)(0.16) + 0.37(0.11)(1 - 0.5) = 0.1212.$$

Based on this *WARR*, AT&T's average-risk project should have a required rate of return of approximately 12 percent. Is this rate appropriate for its computer investments? No. A look at the data for the three computer firms tells us that the computer business is riskier. Each of the computer stocks has a beta coefficient greater than 1.0, indicating that these stocks are riskier than AT&T's stock. The computer business is riskier, even though the computer firms use very little debt financing compared to AT&T. Remember that the use of debt exposes shareholders to extra risks over and above the operating risks of the company. So if the operating risk of AT&T and the computer firms were the same, we would expect the computer stocks to be less risky than AT&T stock because AT&T uses more debt. The data show this is not the case: despite their lower use of debt, the computer stocks are riskier. Therefore, the operating risks associated with the computer business are greater compared to AT&T's average risk.

To estimate the required return associated with the computer business, we can calculate the weighted-average required return for each of the three computer firms. First, we use the capital-asset-pricing model to estimate the shareholders' required return. From these calculated required returns on equity, we can then calculate the weighted-average required return, as shown in Table 13–13.

Interpreting the Results. In each case, the required return is substantially above AT&T's *WARR* of 12 percent. There are, however, variations even within the computer industry. For example, the relatively new entrant, Apple Computer, appears to have a higher *WARR* than the computer giant, IBM. This higher *WARR*

Table 13–13

Calculating Required Return on Equity and Weighted-Average Required Returns for Three Firms in the Computer Industry

	$R_f + (K_m - R_f)\beta = K_e$	$W_e K_e + W_d K_d(1 - T) = WARR$
Apple Computer	$0.10 + (0.07)(1.7) = 0.2119$	$1.0(0.2119) + 0(0.11)(1 - 0.5) = 0.2119$
Amdahl Corp.	$0.10 + (0.07)(1.55) = 0.2085$	$0.81(0.2085) + 0.19(0.11)(1 - 0.5) = 0.1793$
IBM Corp.	$0.10 + (0.07)(1.05) = 0.1735$	$0.89(0.1735) + 0.11(0.11)(1 - 0.5) = 0.1605$
		Average $= 0.1839$

undoubtedly reflects the higher risks to Apple Computer as it tries to establish its long-term presence in the market.

What rate should AT&T use? One approach is to take an average for the three computer companies. As shown in Table 13–13, averaging the three *WARR* figures calculated above gives us an industry average of 0.1839, or approximately 18 percent. If AT&T felt it had risks comparable to this average for the industry, it could use an 18 percent required return for its computer investments. The 18 percent figure is higher than AT&T's *WARR* of 12 percent to reflect the extra risks of the computer business. We have adjusted for risk by using a higher required rate of return.

Before leaving this example, remember that we have made some very specific assumptions in deriving the figure of 18 percent. To test the reasonableness of our results, we might do alternative calculations of K_e using the dividend-growth model. In addition, the 18 percent is a simple average of three *WARR*s. If we thought AT&T was more like IBM in terms of its risk in the computer business, we would give more weight to IBM's *WARR* in determining the average. One way to calculate such a weighted average would be to weight the *WARR*s by the market values of the companies, because IBM is much larger than either Apple or Amdahl. On the other hand, AT&T is a new entrant into the computer business, which might make it riskier than IBM and more like Apple. As we can see, the process of risk adjustment is not easy. Often there are no simple answers, and a good deal of judgment is required.

The illustration above shows one way to apply the pure-play technique. Such an application would provide important insights into the relative risks of the computer business as compared to AT&T's overall risks. At least in the environment of the mid-1980s, the computer business is probably riskier than AT&T's long-distance phone operations. The above application of the pure-play technique would give an idea of how required rates of return should be adjusted to reflect such differences in risk.

Problems in Obtaining Data. The pure-play technique does not solve all our problems, however. First, we have the difficulty of defining comparable risks. The industry classifications may be a useful start, but they may not capture all dimensions of risk. As an example, what, if any, additional risk would AT&T bear as a new entrant into the computer field? It is possible to use other criteria for picking comparable-risk companies, such as financial ratios, past variability of returns, or measures of nondiversifiable risk (such as beta coefficients). It may be difficult or impractical, however, to develop such measures for the investment proposal under consideration. Second, the pure-play approach relies on finding traded companies that have risks directly comparable to the investment in question. Sometimes such companies do not exist, possibly because all the firms producing a product are themselves significantly involved in other product lines. In other cases, the proposed investment may represent a completely new product or technology. As is usually the case, the manager's job is not an easy one. In practice, many difficult judgments must be made. The key is to make the best use of the information that is available.

The process of risk adjustment is not easy; a good deal of judgment is often required.

Finance in Practice 13–2

Methods of Dealing with Risk

As we have discussed, there are different ways to deal with risk in capital budgeting, such as sensitivity analysis and using risk-adjusted discount rates. What methods do firms actually use in practice?

By looking at the results of a survey of 189 large U.S. firms conducted in the 1970s, we can get some idea of what many firms do. Of the 143 firms responding to questions about how they deal with risk, 90 percent of the firms assign a higher required rate of return on the project for higher risk. That is, they use risk-adjusted discount rates. About 10 percent of the firms used a shortened payback period as their only means of risk adjustment. About 31 percent of the firms combine a shortening of the payback period with a raising of the required return.

While the firms often raise required returns, many of them do so based only on a subjective evaluation of risk. In the sample, more than 57 percent of the firms responded that they either assess project riskiness based only on a subjective evaluation or ignore risk differences altogether. Another 23 percent of the firms assigned projects to risk categories. About 35 percent of the firms used sensitivity analysis or some other method incorporating a probability distribution of cash flows rather than a single best guess at a projected cash flow.

Why aren't more firms making sophisticated risk adjustments? Don't managers know about the methods? Are the methods wrong? The answers lie in the standard logic of a cost/benefit trade-off. It's not that the techniques for risk adjustment are wrong, nor is it true that the techniques are not widely known. The fact is that dealing with risk is extremely difficult. The information required to use many formal risk-adjustment techniques is sometimes very costly, if not impossible, to come by. Facing such a situation, managers often must deal with risk subjectively.

The fact that there are problems of applying the techniques does not mean that studying risk-adjustment techniques is a fruitless exercise. In some cases, the techniques can be applied. In many more instances, the basic insights attained from studying risk-adjustment methods are extremely useful in improving a person's ability to deal subjectively with risk.

Source: Adapted from L. D. Schall, G. L. Sundem, and W. R. Geijsbeck, Jr., "Survey and Analysis of Capital Budgeting Methods," *Journal of Finance,* March 1978, pp. 281–87.

Using Theoretical Models of the Risk/Return Trade-Off

A basic principle in determining risk-adjusted discount rates is that investments of the same risk should have the same required rate of return.

The pure-play technique makes use of the basic principle that investments of equal risk should have the same required rate of return. It implements this principle by identifying traded companies with risks comparable to those of the investment in question. In the example above, we made direct use of theoretical models to carry out our risk adjustments. In particular, we used the capital-asset-pricing model

(CAPM) in estimating the required return on the stocks of AT&T and the three computer companies. The CAPM provided one way to quantify the risks of stock ownership in the individual companies.

Suppose, however, that we could not find traded companies comparable in risk to the investment under consideration. Can we apply the capital-asset-pricing model or other models directly to the project? In theory, the answer is yes. We can view the project as another asset. Given the risks of that asset, investors will have a particular required rate of return. The difficulty is that we typically have no independent financial market data on the project. We don't have a "project" share price or dividend, so we can't calculate a dividend yield to use a dividend-growth model tailored to the project. There is no such thing as stock in the project, so we can't use standard techniques to estimate a project beta coefficient. As a result, we must typically make subjective risk estimates.

The important message is that, despite its difficulties, risk adjustment is critical to making sound investment decisions. Even when theory does not give explicit guidance on how to quantify risks, the insights about the risk/return trade-off can offer substantial benefits in adjusting for risk.

Unresolved Issues

In this chapter, we have focused on ways to deal with risk. The two techniques we have discussed are sensitivity analysis and the formulation of risk-adjusted discount rates. Before closing our discussion, we want to point out two key difficulties in doing risk adjustments.

The first difficulty is conceptual in nature and goes back to the basic problem of measuring risk. For example, the capital-asset-pricing model (CAPM) says that the only type of risk that matters to investors is **nondiversifiable risk**—risk relative to the market. The rationale for looking only at nondiversifiable risk is that, in the CAPM, investors are well diversified, holding many stocks and bonds. The only risk such investors care about is the risk a project will add to their total portfolio. Such nondiversifiable risk depends on how the cash flows on the project are related to changes in general market conditions, such as interest rates, GNP growth, and inflation. Nondiversifiable risk does not depend on project-specific risk, such as whether there is a chance for the unexpected entry of a new competitor, a strike, or a sudden technological development that affects a key product. These types of uncertainty would be examples of **diversifiable risk.** We discussed diversifiable and nondiversifiable risk in Chapter 5.

Nondiversifiable risk—market-related risk, the risk that cannot be eliminated by diversification. It depends on how a project's cash flows are related to changes in general economic and market conditions, such as interest rates, GNP growth, or inflation.

Diversifiable risk—project-specific risk, such as that deriving from uncertainty over entry of competitors, strikes, or technological advances.

Now we can see a potential problem. Can we distinguish between types of risk—nondiversifiable and diversifiable—associated with a project and the types of risks they pose to investors? Unfortunately, there is no easy answer. It is probably the case that nondiversifiable risk should be given more weight in determining a risk premium than diversifiable risk, but as yet we have no well-developed theory that allows us to know what weights we should give to the two types of risk. It is probably safe to say that diversifiable risk would be much less important

International Focus

International Investment and Risks in Capital Budgeting

Suppose you work for an American company that is planning to build a plant in Germany to produce goods for sale in Europe. As we have emphasized, an important part of the analysis will be projection and evaluation of cash flows. And those cash flows will be subject to numerous risks, including labor costs, sales volumes, competition from other suppliers, and so forth. The evaluation will be complicated by the actions of foreign governments in terms of tax and export policy. A major item for analysis will be the European Economic Community's plan to turn its 12 member countries (including Germany) into one barrier-free market by the end of 1992. Will project "1992" actually be completed on schedule, and what effects will it have on doing business in Europe? In addition, unlike a capital-budgeting project in the United States, the European project has yet another uncertainty — exchange rates.

From the perspective of an American company you are very interested in projecting *dollar* cash flows, not just cash flows in German marks (D-marks). And to further complicate the evaluation, exchange rates between the D-mark and the dollar move up and down with market forces (we will discuss this in Chapter 24).

The problem is that if you are projecting dollar cash flows five years hence, you need to project not only cash flows in D-marks but the exchange rate at which those D-marks can be converted to dollars. In late summer 1988, the D-mark stood at around 1.90 per dollar — that is, for every dollar you could buy 1.90 D-marks. But will that rate change? According to one school of thought at the time, the dollar should get stronger, moving toward 2.20 D-marks per dollar. This prediction of a strengthening of the dollar was based on the presumption that the dollar was undervalued in relation to the D-mark. The undervaluation argument was a result of the notion that eventually goods and services should cost the same in all countries and that in late summer 1988 (at prevailing exchange rates), goods purchased in Germany were more expensive than similar goods purchased in the United States.

At the same time, however, other economists looking at trade deficits calculated that the dollar was overvalued and should move toward a range of 1.66–1.84 D-marks per dollar.

Which forecast is correct? Only time will tell. Clearly, the uncertainty about exchange rates introduces yet another risk to be considered in evaluating the investment proposal. In Chapter 24, we will discuss further some of the risks of doing business internationally. The message for now is that investment across national boundaries presents additional risks that must be handled in evaluating a project.

Source: Material on exchange rates adapted from *The Economist*, August 27, 1988, p. 59.

for large companies whose stock is held by well-diversified investors than it is for small firms owned by a few individuals.

A second major difficulty that we found in dealing with risk is coming up with the numbers to use to quantify risk adjustments. The costs and difficulties of developing information are not small ones, and these costs will affect the types of risk adjustments that firms decide to apply in practice. As is true in making any financial decision, firms must evaluate whether or not the benefits of adopting a particular form of risk adjustment outweigh the costs. As a result, it may be prudent for a firm to apply detailed risk adjustments to large projects while placing many smaller projects in one of a number of risk categories with no further analysis of the project's risk.

Do these problems mean that we should not consider risk adjustments in making investment decisions? The answer is no. Investors in financial markets require extra returns for bearing risk and incorporate these requirements in determining the value of shares of stock in a company. If managers pursue the objective of value maximization, they must grapple with the problems of adjusting for risk, even though it is an extremely difficult task. The techniques we have discussed in this chapter provide some guidance in this difficult job.

> The CAPM gives no weight to diversifiable risk in determining risk adjustments, but diversifiable risk may be important to investors who are not well diversified.

> Attempts to quantify risk adjustments come up against the difficulty of obtaining realistic numbers.

Summary of Part Four

We have reached a point where we can summarize the basic approach to analyzing investment opportunities that has been developed. As we discussed in Chapter 10, we use discounted-cash-flow techniques to calculate the net present value and the internal rate of return for an investment project.

A positive net present value signals that an investment opportunity passes the economic test. In the case of a positive *NPV*, the present value of the cash benefits of the project exceeds the present value of the cash costs. In other words, the outputs are worth more than the inputs. As a result, projects with a positive net present value create value for the firm. By accepting such projects, managers further the objective of value maximization. If forced to rank mutually exclusive projects, managers should pick the project with the highest net present value — that is, the project that adds the most value.

To use *NPV* analysis, we need to calculate expected cash flows, C_t, and an appropriate required rate of return, K, at which to discount these cash flows. We have taken the approach of looking at operating cash flows and letting the discount rate reflect the financing mix of the corporation. In Chapter 11, we saw that the cash flows appropriate to use in calculating net present value are the firm's *incremental after-tax operating cash flows* that result from adopting the project.

The required return, K, is based on the required returns of the suppliers of capital to the firm. As a result, we look to financial markets to determine required returns. In Chapter 12, we saw that, for a firm's average-risk project, the weighted-average required return could be used as a discount rate. The *WARR* is a

> A positive *NPV* signals that an investment opportunity passes the economic test.

> Our approach has been to look at operating cash flows and to let the discount rate reflect financing mix.

weighted average of the required returns of the suppliers of capital to the firm. In the simple case where a firm uses only debt and common stock, we can calculate *WARR* as

$$WARR = K_w = W_d\,K_d(1 - T) + W_e\,K_e\,.$$

Note that because of the tax-deductibility of interest, we use the *after-tax* cost of debt, $K_d(1 - T)$, in calculating *WARR*.

In Chapter 13 we addressed the problems of adjusting our analysis for differences in project risk. Remember that the *WARR* is an appropriate discount rate only if the project is of average risk for the firm.

Because investors in financial markets require higher returns for bearing higher risk, it is important to adjust for risk. The two most widely used techniques for dealing with risk are (1) sensitivity analysis and (2) risk-adjusted discount rates. Sensitivity analysis focuses on the numerator of our *NPV* calculation and allows managers to ask: what if cash flows differ from what is expected? Techniques for adjusting discount rates to take risk into account focus on the denominator of the *NPV* calculation. Required returns are changed as risk changes. The higher the risk of a project, the higher the required return used as a discount rate.

The four chapters of Part Four have developed the tools necessary to analyze investment projects. It is important to remember, however, that being successful at capital budgeting requires much more than applying the tools of finance. Someone has to come up with ideas for new investments. As we mentioned earlier, investment alternatives don't arrive in neat bundles for managers to evaluate — the alternatives must be thought up and defined. In addition, once an investment decision is made, it still must be implemented. That implementation involves the time and talents of many managers in addition to other corporate employees.

Chapters 10 through 13 have focused on the basic economic analysis of investment decisions — the tools of finance. It is important to remember that these tools are only part of the process of making investment decisions. No amount of sophistication with discounted-cash-flow techniques can salvage a company that never comes up with good investment alternatives to analyze. On the other hand, the tools we have developed can help improve decisions for all companies.

For a firm's average-risk project, the weighted-average required return (WARR) could be used as a discount rate.

The two main techniques for dealing with risk are (1) sensitivity analysis and (2) risk-adjusted discount rate.

To be successful at capital budgeting, there is more to be done than applying the tools of finance: someone must produce ideas for new investments.

Once an investment decision is made, it still must be implemented.

KEY CONCEPTS

1. The two main practical techniques for dealing with risk in capital-investment analysis are sensitivity analysis and risk-adjusted discount rates.
2. Sensitivity analysis is a *what if* technique useful for examining the impact of variations in underlying factors (such as sales and costs) on a project's internal rate of return.

3. Risk-adjusted discount rates (required rates of return) can be used as return targets for projects that are not of average risk. The higher the risk, the higher the required rate of return.
4. Classifying projects by risk category is a useful way of simplifying the capital-budgeting process.

5. A basic principle in setting risk-adjusted discount rates is that investments of equal risk should have the same required return.

6. One way to estimate risk-adjusted discount rates is to use *WARR*s for companies that are similar in risk to the investment proposal under consideration.

SUMMARY

Dealing with risk is one of the most difficult problems a manager faces. Two techniques for dealing with risk in capital-investment analysis are sensitivity analysis and use of risk-adjusted discount rates. Using sensitivity analysis, the manager can ask *what if* important factors turn out different from what is expected. Using risk-adjusted discount rates, the manager can incorporate risk into the return target rather than in the cash-flow estimates.

Projects can be classified into risk categories—such as cost-reduction projects, expansion projects, and new products—as a way of simplifying the capital-budgeting process. Return targets can then be set by category rather than for each project individually. Return targets may also be determined at the division level to provide for effective allocation

of capital in multidivision firms. A basic principle in estimating risk-adjusted discount rates is that investments of the same risk should have the same required rate of return.

Adjusting for risk is not an easy task. Each specific tool we have suggested for risk adjustment has its strengths and weaknesses. It is important to remember, however, that investors in financial markets require extra returns for bearing risk. The higher required returns affect the value of the stocks and bonds that are traded in financial markets.

To pursue the objective of maximizing the value of the firm, financial managers must deal with the problem of adjusting the risk in analyzing investment opportunities.

QUESTIONS

1. Explain the two general approaches to dealing with risk in capital budgeting.

2. How can sensitivity analysis be used in capital budgeting?

3. Discuss the considerations in setting the return target for a worst-case analysis.

4. Explain the basic differences between risk-adjusted discount rates and sensitivity analysis as techniques for dealing with risk.

5. Explain how the notion of risk categories can be used to simplify capital budgeting in a firm.

6. Describe the pure-play technique. How can it be used to determine risk-adjusted discount rates?

7. If a firm uses a single return target to evaluate projects of widely varying risk characteristics, what is the likely outcome over an extended period of time?

8. How can a firm undertake a high-risk investment opportunity without increasing overall risk to its shareholders?

Problems

1. The community hospital is planning to expand its facilities. Capacity for 50 new beds is needed immediately and for another 50 in 5 years. A contractor submits a bid to build the entire 100-bed facility for $500,000. Maintenance and utilities on the 100-bed facility will run $10,000 per year. As an alternative, the contractor is willing to build a 50-bed facility now for $300,000 and to agree to build the remaining 50-bed facility in 5 years for an additional $350,000 under a fixed-price contract. Maintenance and utilities on the 50-bed facility will run $5,000 per year. Assume that the yield to maturity on long-term U.S. government bonds is 10 percent and that the hospital is not subject to taxation. Which alternative should the hospital elect?

2. The Downtown Municipal Hospital is considering installing an automatic dishwashing facility as a labor-saving measure. The hospital is municipally owned and not subject to taxation. The dishwasher, conveyor system, and other ancillary equipment require an outlay of $45,000 and have an expected life of 8 years, at the end of which time they are expected to have zero salvage value. Electrical power, supplies, and maintenance are expected to cost $1,300 per year. Direct labor savings are expected to be $11,500 annually (one full-time employee). At the time the project is being considered, the yield to maturity on long-term U.S. government bonds is 11 percent. The rate on an issue of bonds sold recently by the city was 9 percent.

   a. Can discounted-cash-flow techniques be used to analyze the decision? If so, what discount rate should be used?

   b. What decision should the hospital make?

3. The Orion Company has decided to categorize its investment opportunities by degree of risk and to set return targets by risk category. Orion's management has conducted a study of past investment projects to measure their relative risk. A large amount of data has been gathered to permit calculation of relative risk ratios. Results of the study are given in Table A. Develop a system of return targets for Orion. Use a government-bond rate of 10 percent. Assume Orion is an all-equity firm and the market risk premium is 7.2 percent.

Table A

Category	Relative Risk Ratio
Cost reduction	0.40
Expansion — existing product lines	1.00
New products — existing industries	1.75
New products — new industries	3.00

4. The Saki Camera Company, manufacturer of high-quality cameras and photographic equipment, feels that the time is right to enter the photocopier business. After three years of research and development, company engineers have designed a copy machine that they feel will be able to compete effectively with three established manufacturers, for whom selected financial data appear in Table B on p. 408.

   a. Using the dividend-valuation model of Chapter 4, calculate the shareholders' required rate of return, K_e, for each of the photocopy companies listed in Table B.

   b. Calculate the weighted-average required return ($WARR$) for each of these potential competitors, and suggest a $WARR$ suitable for Saki to evaluate the manufacturing and marketing of photocopy machines. Assume that all of these firms are subject to a marginal tax rate of 40 percent.

5. McIntyre Industries is considering a plan to establish return targets for investment decisions in its various divisions. A study of past data indicates that projects in different categories are not uniformly risky from one division to another. For

Table B

	Dividend-Growth Rate (percent)	Current Dividend (dollars)	Current Share Price (dollars)	Proportion of Financing Done by Debt, W_d (percent)	Required Return on Debt, K_d (percent)
Imitations, Inc.	5	4.40	54.00 $+ 5\%$	40	11
Images Corp.	8	3.25	42.00	55	14
Copy-Rite Co.	3	6.30	86.00	30	8

example, cost-reduction projects in the Electric Motors Division were found to be generally less risky than cost-reduction projects in the Microelectronics Division. These risk differences were due primarily to differences in technology among divisions. Data gathered on relative risk were as shown in Table C. Assume McIntyre is an all-equity firm and the market risk premium is 7.2 percent. Develop a system of return targets for each division, assuming a government-bond rate of 11 percent.

6. Estimate the required rate of return on equity (K_e) for the stocks listed in Table D, assuming a government-bond rate of 11 percent and a market risk premium of 7.2 percent. Are the rates appropriate as required rates of return to be used on the "typical project" in each firm? Explain.

7. Atlantic Leasing Company is considering an investment opportunity involving the construction of a plant and the subsequent rental of the facility to a user, the Ajax Manufacturing Corporation. The total outlay for construction would be $1 million. The plant would be leased to Ajax for a period of 10 years. Atlantic would take the depreciation and pay for property taxes and insurance. The net after-tax operating cash inflow to Atlan-

Table D

Stock	Beta Coefficient
A	0.80
B	0.95
C	1.25
D	1.45

tic during years 1 through 10, including the lease payment, insurance, and all taxes, would be $115,000 per year. At the end of the 10 years, Atlantic would own the plant. Its market value at that time, net of all taxes, is estimated to be $1 million. Calculate the net present value (NPV) of the operating cash flows and the terminal value. Assume that, even though the lease payment from Ajax is contractual, it is not riskless because of the possibility, though small, that Ajax might default. Given this risk, Atlantic has determined the required rate of return for the operating cash flows ($115,000 per year) to be 13 percent. The terminal value is subject to greater uncertainty and is to be evaluated using an 18 percent required rate of return. What decision should Atlantic make?

Table C

Division	Relative Risk in Various Project Categories		
	Cost Reduction	Expansion	New Products
Electric Motors	0.5	1.0	2.0
Electrical Components	0.3	1.0	1.5
Microelectronics	0.8	1.5	3.5

REFERENCES

Bower, R. S., and J. M. Jenks, "Divisional Screening Rates." *Financial Management* 4 (Autumn 1975): 42–49.

Bower, R. S., and D. R. Lessard, "An Operational Approach to Risk Screening." *Journal of Finance* 28 (May 1973): 321–328.

Chambers, D. R., R. S. Harris, and J. J. Pringle, "Treatment of Financing Mix in Analyzing Investment Opportunities." *Financial Management* (Summer 1982): 24–41.

Haley, C. W., and L. D. Schall, "Problems with the Concept of the Cost of Capital." *Journal of Financial and Quantitative Analysis* 13 (Dec. 1978): 847–871.

Hastie, K. L., "One Businessman's View of Capital Budgeting." *Financial Management* 4 (Winter 1974): 36–44.

Hertz, D. B., "Risk Analysis in Capital Investment." *Harvard Business Review* 42 (Jan.–Feb. 1964): 95–106.

Myers, S. C., "Interaction of Corporate Financing and Investment Decisions — Implications for Capital Budgeting." *Journal of Finance* 29 (Mar. 1974): 1–25.

Myers, S. C., and S. M. Turnbull, "Capital Budgeting and the Capital Asset Pricing Model — Good News and Bad News." *Journal of Finance* 32 (May 1977): 321–333.

Part 5 / Financing the Firm's Assets

In the last few chapters, we have discussed ways of analyzing investment decisions—perhaps the most critical set of decisions a financial manager has to make. We must realize, however, that all the money a firm spends has to come from somewhere. In other words, investment has to be financed. In this portion of the book, we analyze the sources of long-term financing available to corporations.

It is useful at this stage to look back at Figure 1–1 in Chapter 1, which gave an

overview of the role of financial management. In each part of the book we have analyzed key topics necessary for fulfilling that role. In Part One, we provided background on the objectives of financial management and the nature of the financial environment. Basic tools of dealing with time and risk were developed in Part Two, while in Part Three we focused on developing information and used some principles of accounting. In Part Four, we applied these tools to the firm's investment decision—a *use* of corporate funds. We now focus on decisions about *sources* of funds. How can money be raised in financial markets? What are the best forms in which to raise money?

In addressing these questions, we will discuss many of the numerous methods that corporations can use to obtain funds. In addition, we will discuss ways to analyze whether one means of financing is better than another and whether there is some best financing policy for the firm. Not surprisingly, we will find that we must give careful attention to the matter of risk. In an uncertain world, adverse things can happen and probably will. In almost every business decision, there is the opportunity to increase the potential return at the price of uncertainty, and financing decisions are no exception.

We will find many of the tools developed in Parts Two, Three, and Four useful. In Chapter 14, we will consider the main sources of long-term funds available to firms: debt, preferred stock, common stock, and specialized sources. We will also discuss the efficiency of the financial markets in which these funds are raised. In Chapter 15, we will begin a discussion of one of the major decisions facing financial managers—whether to borrow money (use debt) or to raise funds from shareholders (use equity). As we will see in Chapter 15, the use of debt (financial leverage) can affect the expected returns and risk to shareholders and ultimately the value of the firm. In Chapter 16 we will develop specific analytical tools for determining the appropriate level of debt for a firm, and in Chapter 17 we will examine dividend policy. The payment of dividends ultimately is a financing decision because funds used to pay dividends are unavailable for other uses in the firm. Chapter 18 discusses options and financial futures, and Chapter 19 discusses leasing. Chapter 20 focuses on the management of outstanding stock and bond issues.

In Part Six, we will give more attention to short-term financing. Our focus in Part Five will be on raising long-term funds. What are the best sources for the funds a corporation needs for investment? The following chapters will provide some answers to that question.

Chapter 14

Sources of Long-Term Financing

In this chapter, we will learn about the basic methods of raising long-term outside funds to finance investments. We will discuss the characteristics of the financing instruments that firms use to raise money, including basic instruments such as debt, preferred stock, and common stock, as well as more specialized types. We also will discuss the efficiency of the financial markets in which these financing instruments are traded.

A glance at the balance sheet of most major corporations will show that corporations typically get money in a wide variety of ways. But no matter what the specific form of financing, the money is ultimately supplied by investors. In return for their money, these suppliers of funds (investors) expect future benefits of ownership. For example, shareholders expect dividends or increases in share price. We saw earlier how these shareholder expectations can be translated into a required rate of return using the dividend-growth model. This general feature is true for all forms of financing. Suppliers of capital require a return on their investment. These required returns ultimately affect the way a financial manager makes decisions. If the firm's investments can't earn returns high enough to meet the required returns of investors, the firm's market value will drop, and shareholder interests will not be served. This is why we used investor required rates of return in determining discount rates to evaluate capital-budgeting projects.

But why do companies use so many forms of financing? What are the relative advantages of each? To make some headway in answering these questions, a working knowledge of the forms of financing available is needed. In fact, understanding all the financial channels available for obtaining funds is a never-ending challenge for a financial manager because new financing methods appear as financial markets change.

Corporate Financing Overview

Table 14–1 on p. 414 is a starting point for getting some idea of the major sorts of funding used by corporations. Table 14–1 gives a breakdown of the liabilities of nonfinancial corporations in the United States as of December 31, 1986. From these figures we can get a picture of the sources of financing — other than equity — used by the major producers of goods and services in our economy.

Of the total of $2,427.5 billion worth of financing broken down in Table 14–1, about 21 percent was derived from sources that arise spontaneously out of normal business operations — primarily trade credit and wage and tax accruals. The remaining 79 percent, about $1,920.1 billion, was derived from credit markets ($1,710.8 billion) and foreign sources ($209.3 billion).

Bonds — long-term debt claims entitling the holder to periodic interest and principal.

Bonds accounted for about 46 percent of the funds raised through the credit markets and constituted the single largest source of debt funds for nonfinancial firms. The bond total includes funds raised through public issues and private placements. It also includes $119.1 billion worth of tax-exempt bonds. For particular socially desirable purposes, such as environmental-pollution control, the U.S. tax laws allow state and local governments to pass on their tax-exempt status to industrial bonds issued by profit-seeking enterprises.

Mortgage — a bond that has particular assets — usually buildings or equipment — pledged as security against default on interest or principal payments.

Mortgages, another major form of long-term borrowing, provided $83.8 billion worth of the total in Table 14–1. In recent years, a growing part of corporate mortgage financing has been devoted to the construction and financing of homes, apartments, and residential developments. However, the bulk of mortgage borrowing by nonfinancial companies still finances industrial and commercial properties.

Table 14–1

Financial Liabilities of All Nonfinancial Corporations, December 31, 1986 (billions of dollars)

Credit market instruments		
Corporate bonds	664.6	
Tax-exempt bonds	119.1	
Mortgages		
Residential	53.3	
Commercial	30.5	
Bank loans (other than mortgages)	582.2	
Commercial paper	62.9	
Bankers' acceptances	14.1	
Finance company loans	169.3	
United States government loans	14.8	
Total credit market		1,710.8
Other sources		
Spontaneous sources		
Trade credit	497.2	
Taxes payable	10.2	
Foreign direct investments in U.S. corporations	209.3	
Total other sources		716.7
Total financial liabilities		2,427.5

Source: Board of Governors, Federal Reserve System, Flow of Funds Accounts (Sept. 1987).

Commercial loan — money borrowed by a business from a bank or lending institution in exchange for a promise to repay at a specified schedule and rate of interest.

Equity — ownership in a firm — specifically, the claims of preferred and common stockholders.

Debt — the contractual liability of a firm to lenders; consists of a promise to make periodic interest payments and to repay the principal according to an agreed-upon schedule.

Commercial loans provided the third major source of funds for nonfinancial corporations. According to Table 14–1, bank loans financed about 34 percent of the total funds raised in the credit markets.

Equity Versus Debt

Table 14–1 includes only sources of **debt** funds and excludes **equity**. Reliable figures on the value of equity are more difficult to obtain. The data on equity values in Table 14–2 are for all corporations, rather than only nonfinancial firms, and are not directly comparable to the debt figures in Table 14–1. They do, however, communicate a sense of the relative importance of debt and equity sources.

Sources of Long-Term Funds

Table 14–3 shows the sources of long-term funds to nonfinancial firms. The figures shown are amounts raised during 1984 and estimated figures for 1987. The figures show that pension funds have become important sources of long-term funds and that individuals were net sellers of equities rather than buyers. Over the past two decades, there has been an increasing trend toward institutional owner-

Table 14–2

Corporate Debt Versus Corporate Equity, 1950–1986

Year (as of December 31)	Total Liabilities of Nonfinancial Corporations (billions of dollars)	Total Market Value of Equities of All Corporations (billions of dollars)
1950	124	146
1955	174	317
1960	239	451
1965	351	749
1970	542	906
1975	767	893
1980	1377	1634
1981	1532	1565
1982	1609	1798
1983	1731	2134
1984	1990	2158
1985	2213	2825
1986	2427	3362

Source: Board of Governors, Federal Reserve System, Flow of Funds Accounts (Sept. 1987).

Table 14–3

Sources of Long-Term Funds, 1984 and 1987

	Net Purchases (billions of dollars)					
	Bonds		Equities		Mortgages	
	1984	1987	1984	1987	1984	1987
Thrifts	(1.5)	(3.1)	(0.2)	(0.5)	86.6	21.5
Insurance and Pensions	49.6	73.0	11.3	11.2	6.7	15.4
Investment Companies	3.6	8.5	5.9	4.6	0.8	1.0
Other Nonbank Finance	2.8	0.8	2.8	(3.0)	5.4	3.1
Total Nonbank Finance	54.5	79.2	19.8	12.3	99.5	41.0
Commercial Banks	4.2	29.4	(0.1)	0.0	44.2	69.1
Foreign Investors	0.2	7.0	(3.0)	30.0	—	—
Households Direct	36.9	(5.3)	(98.4)	(94.3)	(4.3)	20.7
Total	95.8	110.3	(81.7)	(52.0)	139.4	130.8

Note: Figures for 1987 are estimations.

Source: Prospects for Financial Markets in 1988, Salomon Brothers Inc.

ship of equities (insurance companies, pension funds, and the like), while individuals have reduced their holdings.

Characteristics of Financing Instruments

Having described recent trends in long-term financing in the aggregate, we turn now to a more detailed discussion of the principal types of claims issued by firms in order to acquire funds.

Preferred stock — long-term equity that pays a fixed dividend. Preferred stock is senior to common stock with respect to both income (preferred dividends come ahead of common) and assets.

Financing instruments issued by a firm represent claims against the firm's income and assets. Suppliers of capital exchange their funds for these claims against the firm. The principal types of long-term claims issued by firms are debt, **preferred stock,** and **common stock.** In addition, firms may lease assets or issue convertible securities. We will describe each of these forms of financing.

It is useful to outline the different characteristics of financing instruments before describing how the major types of financing instruments differ with respect to these characteristics.

Common stock — a perpetual ownership claim that has no maturity.

Maturity. First, financing instruments may differ with respect to **maturity**. Maturity refers to the time at which the principal amount of the claim is to be paid. If a loan requires payments of interest at the end of each year for three years and the principal amount repaid at the end of the third year, such a loan is said to have a three-year maturity. In the case of a mortgage loan, where equal payments are made over the life of the loan, each payment includes some interest and some principal. Here the term *maturity* is somewhat ambiguous; it might refer to the entire time span over which payments are made or to the average maturity of the payments. As we will see later, some claims — notably common stock and most preferred stock — have no maturity date; they are *perpetual claims*.

Maturity — the time at which the principal amount of the claim is to be paid.

Priority, or **seniority** — the order in which types of financial claims are satisfied.

Seniority. In an uncertain world, there is always a chance that the income or assets of the firm will be inadequate to satisfy all claimants. Hence, there must be agreement in advance as to whose claim comes first. In short, the **priority**, or **seniority**, of the claims must be established.

To understand this priority characteristic of a financial instrument, one must understand the distinction between **contractual claims** and **residual claims.** Contractual claims are *debt* and involve an agreement by the obligor, firm or individual, to make certain payments of interest and principal at certain times. The agreement is an enforceable contract; if the obligor fails to make the specified payments, the claim holder can take legal action to enforce the claim. Such legal action includes forcing a company into bankruptcy. Residual claims, such as common stock, on the other hand, involve no enforceable agreement; rather, they entitle the claimant to what is left after higher-priority contractual claims are paid. Contractual claims are usually fixed in amount, and residual claims by their nature are variable. Hence, in any given firm, payments to residual claimants are inherently more uncertain than payments to contractual claimants.

Contractual claim — a claim that is an enforceable contract, such as debt.

Residual claim — a claim, such as common stock, to what is left after contractual claims are settled.

Priorities also may be established within major categories. Some contractual claims may be junior to others; such claims are often referred to as *subordinated claims.* Some residual claims may be senior to others; preferred stock is senior to common stock.

As we have noted, financial claims against firms represent claims against both income and assets. In many cases, the claim is against all income and all assets, subject to the priorities established. In some cases, however, specific assets are pledged as *collateral* to secure specific claims. We will discuss secured and unsecured debt in more detail shortly.

Tax Treatment. Another important difference in claims of different types is tax treatment. Under present law, interest paid on contractual claims is deductible for income-tax purposes to the firm or individual paying it. Payments made on residual claims, normally called *dividends* rather than interest, are not deductible under present law.

Risk. Different claims also vary with respect to the return required by the claimants. These differences result primarily from variances in risk, or the uncertainty about whether the agreed-upon payments will be made. Risk-averse investors require a higher return in exchange for a higher degree of risk. Hence, the more subordinated the claim on the firm, the higher the required return on that claim.

Voice in management — the extent to which various financial-claim holders can influence the policies of a firm.

Voice in Management. A final important distinction among claims of different types concerns the extent to which claim holders can influence the policies of the firm. We will refer to this influence as the **voice in management.** This right may include the right to choose the firm's board of directors and the right to vote on other matters of importance.

Debt

Short-term debt — debt with a maturity of less than one year.

Intermediate-term debt — debt with a maturity of between one year and five to seven years.

Long-term debt — debt with a maturity of eight to ten years or longer.

Short-term debt usually refers to debt with a maturity shorter than 1 year. **Intermediate-term debt** has no generally agreed-upon definition but ordinarily refers to maturities between 1 and 5–7 years. **Long-term debt,** usually given the label *bonds,* refers to debt with maturities of 8–10 years or longer. Sources of short-term debt funds will be discussed in Chapter 21. In this chapter, we will consider primarily long-term debt and provide a brief look at intermediate-term debt.

A long-term debt contract is a loan of a specified principal amount made in exchange for a promise to make periodic interest payments and to repay the principal according to an agreed-upon schedule. Repayment schedules are negotiable and may call for the principal to be repaid in one lump sum, in equal installments, or in amounts such that the sum of the interest and principal payment each period is constant. The latter type of schedule is typical of mortgage loans.

The agreement between lenders and borrowers, called the *indenture,* usually includes a number of provisions in addition to the interest rate and repayment schedule. The provisions typically encountered require the borrower to maintain certain financial standards with respect to liquidity and working capital. Restrictions may be placed on payment of dividends, capital expenditures, or repurchase of common or preferred stock. Such **protective covenants** are designed to protect the position of lenders by giving them certain rights (discussed later) in the event the covenants are violated. In a way, the covenants act as an early warning system to signal trouble. Some covenants are relatively short and simple; others run into hundreds of pages.

Bondholders are represented by a *trustee* whose function is to administer the agreement and to see that the borrower lives up to its provisions. In the event of *default* on any provision, the trustee generally is required to report the violation to bondholders. The trustee usually is empowered to take legal action to force compliance. Where the firm is unable to comply, the trustee can force bankruptcy proceedings.

Bondholders normally do not have a direct voice in the affairs of the firm or in the voting for directors. They may influence policies indirectly through the protective covenants in the indenture. In the event of default, bondholders come to have a much larger voice through the trustee. In the event of a bankruptcy proceeding, bondholders and other contractual claim holders are in virtually complete control, with common stockholders having little say in the settlement.

Claim on Income and Assets

The rate of interest on a bond is fixed by contract and often is referred to as the **coupon rate.** Interest on most bonds is paid semiannually, although different schedules are sometimes encountered. In terms of seniority, bondholders have first claim on the firm's income. Interest always is paid on debt before dividends can be paid on preferred and common stock. Even where income is not sufficient to cover interest, firms go to great lengths to avoid defaulting on an interest payment.

As in the case of the claim on income, the claim of bondholders against assets is senior to that of preferred and common shareholders. With respect to other contractual-claim holders, the seniority of a particular claim depends on the terms of the agreement. Where several debt issues are outstanding, there usually is a clearly specified priority.

Seniority also depends on whether the bonds are secured by particular assets. Mortgage bonds have specific assets, usually buildings or equipment, pledged as security against default on interest or principal payments. In the event of default, mortgage holders are entitled to liquidate the asset(s) to settle their claim, with any excess returned to settle claims of unsecured creditors. Unsecured bonds, having no particular assets pledged as security, are called **debentures**. In the event of trouble, debenture holders stand in line with other unsecured creditors, such as trade creditors and banks, behind secured creditors but ahead of shareholders. When the claims against a firm include both secured and unsecured creditors (and in the latter category, there may be both senior and subordinated creditors), the determination of how to divide funds received from liquidation of assets becomes a very complex matter.

Par value of a bond — the value that is equal to the principal amount.

As we can see, the type of bonds — debenture, mortgage bond, subordinated bond — is often defined in terms of the nature of the claim against assets. Many specialized types of bonds exist that are not discussed in detail here. There are, for example, *collateral-trust bonds* secured by the stocks and bonds of other firms, and *equipment-trust certificates* used to finance certain types of equipment. Discussions of these more specialized financing vehicles may be found in the references at the end of this chapter.

Risk Associated with Bonds

Default Risk. Because debt is a contractual claim, debt obligations of a given firm are less risky than the preferred or common stock of the same firm. In an uncertain world, however, default can and does occur. From the standpoint of lenders, debt obligations of firms are not riskless. From the firm's standpoint, on the other hand, interest and principal payments of debt can be viewed as certain if the firm is to remain in business.

Default risk — the risk that the firm will not make specified contractual payments at the specified times.

Default risk is the risk that the firm will not make its specified contractual payments at the specified times. Bonds of many large corporations are rated according to default risk by rating services.

The two major bond-rating agencies are Moody's Investors Service and Standard & Poor's Corporation (S&P). The former uses the rating of *Aaa* for the very best bonds, *Aa* for the next category, *A* for the next, and *Baa* for relatively risky bonds. Bonds rated below *Baa* are those with severe exposure to possible default. Standard & Poor's uses *AAA, AA, A,* and *BBB* for its classifications. The two agencies do not always agree with each other, so dozens of bond issues are *split-rated* — that is, rated differently by the two.

Prior to the onset of high inflation in the 1970s, bond rating was mainly an objective skill. It rested heavily on capital-structure analysis, the adequacy of operating income relative to fixed charges (known as the *fixed-charge-coverage ratio*), and the general trends and fluctuations in the company's earnings. This analysis employs many of the techniques we discussed in Part Three, such as ratio analysis and source-and-use-of-funds analysis. Over the past years of severe inflation (and the steep rise in the cost of energy), bond-rating agencies have had to move to broader measures and more subjective judgment. As a result, the number of split ratings has increased dramatically.

For the most part, bond yields are inversely related to their ratings.

By and large, the yield on bonds is inversely related to their ratings. How much difference does a rating make as far as yield is concerned? The data in Table 14–4 (p. 420) reveal three important facts:

1. Long-term bond yields have risen sharply since inflation began in 1965. New highs were reached in the early 1980s with rates well into double digits.
2. There is clearly a spread between upper and lower ranges of bond yields, which reflects quality differentials. Safer bonds (*Aaa*) are less risky; thus investors have a lower rate of return on them than on higher-risk bonds.

Table 14—4

Interest Rates on Long-Term Utility Bonds, 1965–September 1987

Year	Bond Rating Interest Rate (percent)			
	Aaa	Aa	A	Baa
1965	4.50	4.52	4.58	4.78
1966	5.19	5.25	5.39	5.60
1967	5.58	5.66	5.87	6.15
1968	6.22	6.35	6.51	6.87
1969	7.12	7.34	7.54	7.93
1970	8.31	8.52	8.69	9.18
1971	7.72	8.00	8.16	8.63
1972	7.46	7.60	7.72	8.17
1973	7.60	7.72	7.84	8.17
1974	8.71	9.04	9.50	9.84
1975	9.03	9.44	10.09	10.96
1976	8.63	8.92	9.29	9.82
1977	8.19	8.43	8.61	9.06
1978	8.87	9.10	9.29	9.62
1979	9.86	10.22	10.49	10.96
1980	12.30	13.00	13.34	13.95
1981	14.64	15.30	15.95	16.60
1982	14.22	14.79	15.86	16.46
1983	12.52	12.83	13.66	14.20
1984	12.72	13.66	14.03	14.53
1985	11.68	12.06	12.47	12.96
1986	8.92	9.30	9.58	10.00
1987**	9.14	9.42	9.78	10.17

**Average from Jan. '87–Sept. '87.

Source: Moody's Public Utility Manual, Vol. 1 (1987).

3. The spread rises during periods of general financial stress. For example, the spreads rose sharply in the early 1980s when *Baa* yields were 2 percent above *Aaa* rates.

Interest-Rate Risk. Obligations of the U.S. government are considered default-free, because the payments are essentially certain to be made. However, government bonds are not totally riskless, for they are subject to a second type of risk: **interest-rate risk,** or uncertainty about future interest rates.

We showed the effects of interest-rate risk on bond prices earlier, in Chapter 4. Suppose you buy a 20-year bond and sell it one year later. Your actual return over the year will depend on the price of the bond in one year. For a government bond, if we know with certainty that we will hold the bond to maturity, there is no default risk and no interest-rate risk. If we are uncertain about the future rate of inflation, we still cannot be certain of the real rate of return on the bond.

Interest-rate risk—the risk arising because bond prices change as market interest rates change; the risk that a bond may have to be sold before maturity at a price lower than the price paid for it because of changing interest rates.

Interest Cost to the Borrower

The interest cost to the borrower is the return required by lenders. In simplest terms, it is the **interest rate.** On short-term debt, the cost of the debt is simply the rate of interest on the loan. On a long-term bond issue, if the bonds are issued at par (face value), which is typical, the cost to the firm is the **coupon** rate on the bonds. At the time of issue, the coupon rate and the **yield to maturity** are equal. If the bonds later rise or fall in price, the yield to maturity will change and will no longer equal the coupon rate. We discussed yield to maturity in Chapter 4.

The rate of return required by lenders, which we defined in earlier chapters as K_d, is the pretax cost of debt to the firm. As we noted earlier in Chapter 12, current tax laws permit firms to deduct interest expense in figuring their income taxes. The after-tax equivalent of the interest cost then is $K_d(1 - T)$. This is the figure we used in calculating a firm's weighted-average cost of capital in Chapter 12. Deductibility of interest is an important advantage of debt that we will discuss in more detail in Chapter 15.

The 1986 Tax Bill

As we have noted at many points in this book, in 1986 Congress passed a sweeping overhaul of the nation's tax code. We discussed the new law in Chapter 2. One important feature of the bill was a reduction in maximum marginal federal income-tax rates, from 46 percent to 34 percent for corporations, and from 50 percent to 28 percent for individuals.

The reduction in tax rates has important implications for financing decisions, especially choices between debt and equity. Since interest on debt is tax-deductible, lowering the tax rate makes the deduction worth less and thereby reduces the tax benefit of debt financing. Hence, under the new law, debt becomes somewhat less advantageous *relative to equity* for some firms. We will discuss the tax advantages of debt in more detail in the next chapter.

Foreign Bonds and Eurobonds

With the increasingly international nature of business and financial activity, U.S. companies have also turned outside the United States to issue bonds. In the international bond market, bonds are sold outside the country of the borrower, often in many countries. A **foreign bond** is a bond sold in a foreign country by a home-country borrower and is denominated in the currency of that foreign country. For example, a U.S. company might borrow money in West Germany and promise to pay interest and principal in the West German currency, the mark.

Some companies also issue **Eurobonds**, or bonds that are sold mainly in countries other than the country in whose currency the interest and principal payments are denominated. For example, if a U.S. company borrowed money in West Germany but promised to make payments in U.S. dollars rather than German marks, the bond issue would be a Eurobond. In Chapter 24, we will discuss some

Yield to maturity (YTM) on a bond is the internal rate of return on a bond earned by an investor if the bond is bought now and held to maturity. The YTM is the required rate of return on the bond.

The tax-deductibility of interest is an important advantage of debt.

Foreign bond—a bond sold in a foreign country by a home-country borrower, denominated in the currency of the foreign country.

Eurobonds—bonds sold mainly in countries other than the country in whose currency the interest and principal payments are to be denominated.

of the important features of the international financial markets as they affect U.S. companies.

Preferred Stock

Preferred shareholders are owners, not creditors.

The second of the three major types of claims issued by firms is preferred stock. Preferred shareholders are owners, not creditors. However, their claim differs in important respects from that of the residual claimants, the common shareholders.

Claim on Income and Assets

In terms of seniority, preferred claims stand behind all contractual claims of creditors and ahead of claims of common shareholders. Payments on preferred stock are usually called *dividends.* Such payments are fixed in amount, usually as a percentage of par value. A 12 percent preferred stock, for example, would pay a dividend of $12 per year if its par value were $100.

Dividends on preferred stock are typically fixed in amount but not contractual.

Although fixed in amount, preferred dividends are not contractual. Each time they are due to be paid, they must be declared by the board of directors. If for some reason a preferred dividend is not paid, preferred shareholders have no right to take legal action. The agreement between the firm and the preferred shareholders provides only that dividends will be paid in the agreed amounts prior to any payments to common shareholders. In a sense, preferred stock is a hybrid security. Like debt, payments are fixed in amount. Unlike debt, payments are not contractual, and failure to make a payment does not bring insolvency or bankruptcy. Because they are not contractual, preferred dividends are not deductible by the firm for income-tax purposes.

Nearly all preferred-stock issues are *cumulative,* in that dividends passed without payment accumulate and must be cleared completely before any payments can be made to common shareholders. For example, suppose you owned a share of 12 percent preferred stock ($100 par value). If last year the company did not pay you the $12 preferred dividend, it would have to pay you $24 this year before making any payments to common shareholders.

Other protective covenants similar to those found in long-term-debt and term-loan contracts also are often included. For example, common dividends might be restricted to amounts that will maintain a specified current ratio or working-capital position. By restricting common dividends, the preferred shareholders, who have claims senior to those of common stockholders, reduce their risk. The claim of preferred shareholders against the assets of the firm, like that of common shareholders, is general rather than specific, with no particular assets set aside to settle preferred claims.

Voting rights of preferred shareholders are specified in the corporate charter. Such rights normally concern payment of common dividends and issuance of other classes of securities of equal or higher seniority. In addition, preferred agreements usually provide for election of a specified number of directors by preferred shareholders in the event that the provisions of the preferred agreement are not met.

Cost of Preferred Stock to the Firm

The cost of preferred stock to the firm is the **dividend rate** on the preferred stock. The preferred dividend can be expressed either as a percentage, equivalent to an interest rate, or as a dollar amount. For example, suppose a firm could sell preferred stock with a dividend of $10 per share (to be paid indefinitely) and the preferred stock sold for $80 per share. The dividend rate then would be $10/$80 = 12.5 percent.

As is true of all financing instruments, the cost of preferred stock to the firm issuing it is the rate of return required by the market, i.e., those investors who will buy the preferred stock. The preferred-dividend rate is the market required rate of return. As always, the rate of return required by the market (preferred shareholders in this case) depends to a great extent on the degree of risk perceived by investors.

Because preferred dividends are not tax-deductible, the preferred dividend rate is both the before-tax and the after-tax cost of preferred stock to the firm. There is no tax adjustment.

Use of Preferred Stock

Preferred stock does not have debt's advantage of the tax-deductibility of interest, but preferred stock provides the corporation with more flexibility.

It was noted earlier that tax-deductibility of interest is a major attraction of long-term debt. Preferred stock does not have this advantage. Relative to debt, an advantage of preferred stock is its flexibility. If earnings fall below expectations, or if the firm encounters difficulties for other reasons, the preferred dividend can be omitted without the threat of legal action, including bankruptcy. Contractual claims do not offer such flexibility.

Though more flexible than debt, preferred stock is less flexible than common stock. Protective covenants exist on preferred stock, and omission of a preferred dividend normally is viewed by the financial markets as a more serious matter than omission of a common dividend. In addition, the payment of preferred dividends, just as in the case of dividends on common stock, does not lead to tax deductions. As a result, the use of preferred stock in addition to common stock is suitable only under special circumstances. Over the six-year period 1979–1984, new issues of preferred stock by U.S. corporations averaged only $3.9 billion a year compared to new bond issues (including private placements) of $36.0 billion a year and annual new common-stock offerings of $21.3 billion.[1]

Public utilities have been among the major issuers of preferred stock, at least partly in response to regulatory restrictions on the design of utility capital structures. Another specialized use has been in connection with mergers and acquisitions where tax considerations may make preferred stock advantageous as a vehicle for acquiring another firm. Finally, for some corporations, a combination of two circumstances may give preferred financing an edge over both bond financing and financing through a new issue of common stock. The first circumstance is a depressed market price for a firm's common stock in relation to past and future

[1]Salomon Brothers, *1985 Prospects for Financial Markets.*

expected levels, in which case a new common issue would dilute its per-share earnings — a development most managers would prefer to avoid and can avoid by issuing preferred stock. The second circumstance is the case in which a company's tax bracket is significantly below the normal percentage rate (as might be true if it has a large investment tax credit or heavy investment outlays that can be expensed for tax purposes), in which case the fact that bond interest payments are tax-deductible may be a less important factor than the greater flexibility associated with preferred-stock financing.

We can gain further insight into the use of preferred stock by looking at the *demand side* of the equation: who wants to buy preferred stock and why? As we noted in looking at the supply of this form of security, preferred stock is a hybrid that combines the fixity of return normally associated with a bond and the owner-ship normally associated with common stock. Because it is such a hybrid, there is a demand for preferred stock only under special circumstances:

Preferred stock typically offers higher current yields than common stock.

1. Some investors desire large and dependable amounts of current income, which are often not available from common stock whose returns may come largely from capital gains. Preferred stock typically offers higher *current yields* (dividends divided by price) than common stock and, hence, would be more attractive than common stock to such investors. Preferred stock may also be more attractive than bonds because some types of preferred stock, such as *convertible preferred stock,* offer the potential for capital gains, in addition to current income. Convertible preferred stock can be converted into common stock on specified terms, and its price goes up if the common-stock price rises substantially. In recent years, many preferred-stock issues have been convertible.

2. Corporations receiving preferred-stock dividends (other than dividends paid by public utilities) are allowed under current law to exempt 80 percent of such receipts in computing their taxable income. (The exemption on public-utility preferred dividends is lower.) This feature increases the after-tax yield on preferred stock relative to the yield on bonds. As a consequence, for many fire- and casualty-insurance companies, which pay normal corporate tax rates on taxable investment income, preferred stock offers a better yield than bonds.

These specialized and, hence, competing demands for preferred stocks *as investments* lead to a lowering of the gross yields that preferred-stock issuers have to pay when they raise funds through this instrument. As a result, such issuers may then find it worthwhile in some situations to use preferred-stock financing as opposed to other types of financing.

Common Stock

In any commercial enterprise, some person or some group must have final responsibility for policy and a residual claim to income and assets. In a corporation, common shareholders play this role and are entitled only to what remains after

In any commercial enterprise, someone or some group must have a residual claim to income and assets.

creditors and preferred-stock owners are compensated. In an uncertain world, the residual claim is inherently uncertain as to amount. Sometimes residual returns are greater than anticipated; sometimes they are less.

Returns to common shareholders have two components: dividends and capital gains (or losses). Capital gains arise through changes in the price of the firm's stock. As a firm reinvests and grows, its value presumably increases, and the increase is reflected in a higher stock price. Dividends are declared by action of the board of directors and are not contractual; shareholders cannot take legal action to force payment. Because they are not contractual, dividends on common stock are not deductible for income-tax purposes under current law.

In this section, we will concentrate on the characteristics of common stock and the rights of its holders. We defer to Chapter 20 a discussion of the problems of issuing common stock.

In the U.S., the liability of common shareholders is limited to the amount of their investment in the corporation.

In the United States, common stockholders have limited liability; that is, their liability is limited to the amount of their investment. If the corporation's liabilities exceed its assets, the common stockholders cannot be held liable for the difference, as can a sole proprietor or a member of a partnership.

Common stock is a perpetual claim; it has no maturity. An individual shareholder can typically liquidate an investment in the firm only by selling shares to another investor. The value of a share at any point in time is, in the final analysis, a function of the dividends that all investors expect to receive, whether in the immediate or distant future.

A corporation's charter specifies the number of shares of common stock the directors are authorized to issue. The number of authorized shares normally can be changed by a vote of the shareholders. *Issued shares* are those shares of stock that have been sold to investors. *Outstanding shares* are those shares of stock held at any point in time by the public. If a firm repurchases previously issued shares, such *treasury shares* are issued but not outstanding.

Par value of stock — the nominal or face value of the share of stock.

Stock can be issued with or without **par value;** this term has some historical, legal, and accounting significance, but little economic significance. In many states, shareholders are liable to creditors for the difference between the price at which the stock originally was issued and the par value, if the latter is greater. For that reason, par value normally is set at a figure lower than the price at which the stock is to be issued. To illustrate, consider the sale of 100,000 shares of $1-par-value stock at an issue price to the public of $10 per share. The accounting entries, ignoring issue costs, are displayed in Table 14–5.

Table 14–5

Par Value in Accounting Records

Debit		Credit	
Cash	$1,000,000	Common stock $1 par	$100,000
		Paid-in surplus	900,000

Book value of stock—the total of book value of net assets available for common shareholders after subtracting claims of creditors and preferred shareholders.

Market value of stock—the price at which stock is being traded in the marketplace.

The **book value of stock** per share at any point in time is simply net assets available for common shareholders, after subtracting claims of creditors and preferred shareholders, divided by the number of shares. As noted earlier, **market value** for publicly traded stocks is the price at which transactions are taking place. Stocks are bought and sold on the *stock exchanges* and in the *over-the-counter (OTC) market,* about which we will have more to say in Chapter 20.

Sometimes a firm will issue more than one *class* of common stock, often referred to as *Class A* and *Class B* stock. One of the classes usually has a larger voice in management and a junior claim to income. The senior class takes on some of the characteristics of preferred stock.

Roughly speaking, the term *equity* means "ownership," so it is correct to speak of *preferred equity* or *common equity*. Where a firm has no preferred stock outstanding, *equity* refers to the entire claim of the common stockholders, including retained earnings. Where preferred stock is involved, it is important to be clear as to which type of equity is meant.

Rights of Residual Owners

The rights of common shareholders are established by the laws of the state in which the corporation is chartered. Many of these rights are spelled out in the charter itself. Some rights belong to the shareholders as a group and usually are exercised by a vote. Such collective rights normally include: amending the corporation's charter (usually with the approval of designated state officials), adopting and amending bylaws, electing directors, entering into mergers with other firms, and authorizing the issuance of senior claims such as preferred stock and long-term debt. In addition, shareholders have a number of rights they may exercise as individuals, including the right to sell their shares to others and the right to inspect the records of the firm.

Shareholders normally exercise their collective rights by voting. Most corporations hold a regular annual meeting of shareholders, at which voting takes place on issues presented to the shareholders by the directors. Special meetings are sometimes held to vote on specific issues, such as approval for a merger. A shareholder unable to attend may vote by means of a *proxy* — that is, by giving written authorization to someone to represent him or her at the meeting. Election of directors is by majority vote in many states, but some states permit an alternative system called *cumulative voting,* which makes it easier for minority interests to gain representation on the board of directors. Cumulative voting permits multiple votes for a single director. For example, if you owned 100 shares of stock in a company that was electing five directors, you would get 500 votes and could cast all of them for a *single* candidate instead of spreading them out over five candidates.

The claim on the income and assets of the firm is also a right. We noted earlier that the residual owners are last in line with respect to both income and assets. Creditors and preferred shareholders must receive their interest and dividends before dividends are paid on common stock. In the event of serious difficulty leading to bankruptcy, claims of common shareholders are settled last. In the unhappy event of dissolution of a firm, common shareholders have claim to whatever assets remain after creditors and preferred shareholders are satisfied in full.

In connection with new issues of common stock, laws of many states give existing shareholders the *preemptive right* to maintain their current percentage claim on the income and assets of the firm. Under this provision, existing shareholders must be offered first refusal on any new offering of stock prior to sale to the general public. Each existing shareholder has the preemptive right to purchase new shares in the amount necessary to maintain his or her current share in the firm. For example, suppose you owned 100 shares of the 1,000 presently outstanding shares of stock in a company. You currently own $100/1,000 = 10$ percent of the firm. If the firm issues 500 new shares (for a total of 1,500 total shares after the new issue), you would have to own 150 shares of stock to maintain your 10 percent share of ownership. This would require that you purchase 50 additional shares. A preemptive right would give you the privilege to buy these 50 shares prior to the sale of stock to the general public. *Rights offerings* are discussed in more detail in Chapter 20.

In principle, common stockholders control the policies of the firm by means of their rights to establish bylaws and to elect directors to represent them. Directors then appoint the executive officers of the firm, generally referred to as *management*. Management's job, therefore, is to act as agent of the firm and to work in the best interests of shareholders. This statement is a normative one—it describes the way things *should* be and the way professional managers *should* behave. In practice, it would be naive to suppose that all managers always act only in the interests of shareholders. There are many instances in corporations where the interests of managers and shareholders may diverge. Managerial behavior under such circumstances raises important moral, ethical, and perhaps even legal questions, but full discussion of these questions is beyond the scope of this book. The primary responsibility of professional managers is clear: to manage the firm to serve the best interests of shareholders.

Cost of Common Stock to the Firm

Because common stock is a residual claim, its return is subject to greater uncertainty than the return to preferred shareholders and creditors.

Because common stock is a residual claim, its return is subject to greater uncertainty than the return to preferred shareholders and creditors. Because investors as a group are risk-averse, we would expect common shareholders to require a higher rate of return than preferred shareholders and creditors, and, indeed, common shareholders do require a higher return. In terms of a probability distribution, the return to common stock has a higher expected value, but also higher dispersion.

The cost of common stock to the firm is the return required by the investors who hold the common stock. If the market requires 15 percent on a firm's stock, then 15 percent is the cost of common equity to the firm. That is the figure we would use as one input in calculating the firm's weighted-average cost of capital. In earlier chapters we defined the cost of common equity as K_e and discussed (in Chapter 12) some approaches to estimating it.

Convertible Securities

Convertible security—a claim that begins as a debenture or as preferred stock but that can later be converted *at the holder's option* and at a specified rate into shares of the issuing company's common stock.

A **convertible security** is a claim that begins as a debenture or as preferred stock but can later be *converted* at the holder's option (and at a specified rate) into shares of the issuing company's common stock. Convertible securities represent a specialized form of financing, so we defer a discussion of them to Chapter 18.

Intermediate-Term Financing

Thus far in this chapter, we have discussed sources of long-term funds — debt usually involving maturities of eight to ten years or more and equity which never matures. In Chapter 21, we will discuss sources of short-term funds, usually involving maturities of one year or less. Let us now consider sources of financing over intermediate periods, usually defined as longer than one year but no more than five to seven years.

Intermediate-term financing normally is used to finance fixed assets or permanent additions to working capital. Repayment usually must come from profits rather than from liquidation of the assets financed, as in the case of seasonal short-term loans. For this reason, intermediate-term lenders, along with long-term lenders, are more concerned with earning power than short-term lenders.

Term Loans from Banks

Seasonal loans — funds borrowed for use during a part of a year and repaid out of seasonal inflows of funds.

Term loans — secured loans made by banks, insurance companies, or other lending institutions that must be repaid usually within three to seven years.

Collateral — property pledged by a borrower to protect the interests of the lender.

Historically, bankers have preferred short-term **seasonal loans** to **term loans.** Seasonal loans are to be used for only a few months to fund seasonal needs but generally must be paid off in full during the course of a year. Term loans, on the other hand, obligate the bank's funds for a longer period of time. In recent years, banks have expanded their term lending significantly. Maturities normally range from three to seven years, seldom going beyond ten years. Banks nearly always require security on term loans; the most commonly used **collateral** is equipment or real estate.

Since repayment is to come from operating profits, term loans nearly always are *amortized,* or repaid in installments. The amortization requirement encourages the borrower to earmark a portion of the firm's earnings for debt repayment and avoids leaving the lender dependent on the borrower's asset structure at the end of the loan's term. Home mortgages are amortized for precisely this same reason.

Interest rates on term loans usually run higher than on short-term loans of similar size and riskiness. Because of large shifts in the general level of interest rates during the last ten years, many banks have moved to a variable-rate arrangement, whereby the rate on the term loan is tied to the prime rate. Compensating-balance requirements make the effective cost of both term loans and short-term loans higher than the stated rate of interest on the loan because the borrower gets to use only a portion of the money borrowed while paying interest on the full amount.

Term loans usually include restrictive covenants similar to those used in long-term debt agreements. To ensure that the borrower maintains an adequate degree of liquidity, restrictions may be included on minimum net working capital and current ratio. Restrictions also may be placed on the payment of dividends and on the purchase and sale of fixed assets. Pledging assets to others is often prohibited by a *negative-pledge clause.* Additional borrowings senior to the term loan in question may also be prohibited. In smaller firms with less depth in management, insurance is often required on the lives of the principal officers. In all cases, periodic financial statements are required of the borrower.

Term Loans from Insurance Companies

Insurance companies also represent a source of intermediate-term financing to business. To the insurance company, the loan is simply an investment, rather than a part of a larger and continuing customer relationship, as it is to a bank. Insurance companies tend to prefer larger loans and often are unwilling to lend to smaller firms.

Because of the longer maturity of their liabilities, insurance companies prefer maturities of 10 years or longer and often are not interested in those shorter than 7 or 8 years. Prepayment penalties are more common on loans by insurance companies, though other restrictive covenants are similar to those imposed by banks.

Loans Against Equipment

Chattel mortgage — a security claim against equipment (or anything other than land or buildings) used in providing collateral for a loan.

Equipment is frequently pledged as collateral against a term loan from a bank or insurance company. The proceeds of the loan may be used to purchase the equipment itself or for other purposes. Title to the equipment rests with the borrower, whose balance sheet will show both asset and loan. A security interest in the equipment is given to the lender by means of a **chattel mortgage,** which gives the lender the right to seize and sell the equipment in the event of default on the loan by the borrower. Public notice of this right, referred to as a *lien,* is filed in the state in which the equipment is located. The word *chattel* literally means "thing" and indicates that the lien is on something other than real property, such as land or a building.

Commercial finance companies also represent an important source of equipment financing. Two methods of equipment financing normally are used: conditional sales contracts and leasing.

Conditional Sales Contracts

Conditional sales contract — an installment equipment-purchase contract under which title to the equipment remains with the lender until all payments are made.

A **conditional sales contract** is an installment purchase contract under which title to the equipment remains with the lender until all payments are made. Consummation of the contract by passage of title is conditioned on the borrower making all payments. A *down payment* is nearly always required, and the borrower signs a *promissory note* for the balance. Under present accounting guidelines, both equipment and loan appear on the borrower's balance sheet. For accounting and tax purposes, borrowers treat the equipment as if they own it, taking depreciation and deducting only the interest portion of the payment to the lender. The amount of the down payment and the maturity of the contract are set so that the unpaid balance is always below the resale value of the equipment. If the borrower defaults, the lender sells the equipment to satisfy the contract. Maturities usually range from 1 to 4 years.

Leasing

Lease—a contractual arrangement for financing equipment under which the lessee (the firm) has the right to use the equipment in return for making periodic payments to the lessor (the owner of the equipment).

A second method of financing equipment is via a **lease**. A lease is a contractual arrangement under which the *lessee* has the right to use the equipment, and in return makes periodic payments to the owner, or *lessor*. The lessor retains title to the equipment. Accounting and tax treatment of leases is very complex, and the applicable rules have undergone significant change in recent years. Normally, the lessor carries the equipment on its balance sheet as an asset and takes the depreciation on it. The lessee shows nothing on the balance sheet and deducts the full amount of the lease payment as an expense. Thus, the party providing the financing, rather than the user, is treated as the owner for accounting and tax purposes, whereas it is the other way around in the case of the conditional sales contract. To qualify for this treatment, however, certain conditions must be met, and the Internal Revenue Service goes to great lengths to distinguish leases from conditional sales contracts. In recent years the accounting profession has tightened its guidelines regarding disclosure of lease contracts in financial statements. In some cases, a lessee is required to capitalize a lease and to show both asset and lease obligation on the balance sheet. Sometimes the accounting treatment may be handled one way for financial-reporting purposes and another way for tax purposes.

Lease contracts to finance equipment usually are written for periods of one to five years. Commercial banks and finance companies most often act as lessors. On longer-lived assets, such as building and land, lease contracts are written over longer time periods, with insurance companies and pension funds more often acting as lessors. Leases on real estate typically provide that maintenance, taxes, and insurance expenses are borne by the lessee rather than the lessor. In the case of equipment leases, the lessor often bears these maintenance, tax, and insurance costs.

Leasing is a very important means of both intermediate-term and long-term financing. We will discuss leasing in more depth in Chapter 19.

Borrowing Abroad

Just as U.S. companies can issue long-term bonds in other countries, intermediate-term financing can be arranged from sources outside the United States. In Chapter 24, we'll discuss international financial markets in more detail.

Recent Financing Innovations

For most of the period since World War II, the nation's leading companies raised most of their capital by issuing straight equity and straight debt. Convertible securities, *warrants* (special contracts giving the buyer of a bond the right to buy stock), floating-rate notes, and other such features were used only in unusual circumstances. Beginning in the late 1970s, however, financing innovations arose primarily as a result of three main factors: a decade of high inflation, the greatly increased volatility of interest rates, and the deregulation of financial institutions. These changes produced a number of new and innovative financing instruments.

Response to Inflation

Not only did inflation drive rates upward, it increased the *uncertainty* about what future rates would be. High inflation and high interest rates gave rise to several innovations, including *original-issue, deep-discount bonds, zero-coupon bonds, convertibles,* and *exchangeables*.

Original-issue, deep-discount bonds (OIDs) — bonds issued at prices well below face value with very low coupon rates; they have appealed to buyers who believe interest rates will trend downward.

Original-Issue, Deep-Discount Bonds. For buyers who believed that rates would trend downward, there arose considerable interest in the **original-issue, deep-discount bond (OID).** These securities typically are issued at 40 to 55 percent of face value, with very low coupon rates of interest — say, 6 to 7 percent at a time when standard issues carried rates of 14 to 16 percent. A major feature of OIDs is that much of the return comes in the form of the final principal payment — less of the return is in the form of coupon payments. As a result, owners of OIDs need not worry as much as owners of regular bonds about reinvesting coupon payments in future periods. Of course, the way to eliminate the reinvestment problem completely is to have a bond with *no* coupon payments, and just such bonds appeared in the financial markets of the early 1980s.

Zero-coupon bond — a bond that pays no interest but is issued at a large discount and later redeemed at face value.

Zero-Coupon Bonds. Taking the OID one step further, Pepsico in 1981 placed privately a **zero-coupon bond** — that is, a bond paying no interest at all. Like a U.S. savings bond, the zero-coupon bond is bought at a discount and later redeemed at face value. J. C. Penney followed soon thereafter with a public issue of zero-coupon bonds. In Chapter 4, we discussed the General Mills zero-coupon money-multiplier notes issued in summer 1982.

OIDs and zero-coupon bonds also exploited a provision in the tax laws at that time that was favorable to the issuing firm. A revision of the tax laws in 1982 spoiled the fun, and corporate issues of OIDs and zero-coupon bonds dropped sharply. Both types still find occasional use by corporations, and there is some activity in zero-coupon Eurodollar bonds (see Chapter 24 for a discussion of Eurodollars).

There also remains considerable activity in special zero-coupon securities (with names like CATS and TIGERS) that are derived from United States government bonds. These securities are widely used in portfolios that are either tax-exempt or subject to a low tax rate. One use of these securities is in setting aside funds for college educations years in the future.

Finance in Practice 14–1

Inflation Bonds

Suppose an investor is worried about future inflation. The answer might be to invest in Real Yield Securities, or REALs. REALs are bonds with their interest payments linked to changes in consumer prices.

Consider the case of REALs issued by Franklin Savings Association in early 1988. Franklin, a thrift institution based in Kansas, sold $170 million worth of 20-year REALs and another $100 million worth of REALs with 15-year maturities.

Inflation-linked bonds such as REALs are floating-rate securities with their interest rates tied to the consumer price index (CPI). The rate on Franklin's REAL issues is reset quarterly. The 20-year issue is priced at 3 percent over increases in the CPI, the 15-year issue at 2 ½ percent over the CPI. So if the CPI goes up by 5 percent annually, Franklin pays 8 percent on its 20-year REALs and 7 ½ percent on its 15-year REALs.

By purchasing a REAL, an investor knows that interest income will always stay ahead of inflation (assuming the issuer doesn't default!). But what advantage does a REAL have for the issuer? According to industry experts, the primary value of inflation-linked securities for corporate issuers is added diversification. By using a variety of indexes for its floating-rate debt — Treasuries, the prime rate, and the CPI — a company is less likely to be hurt by a distortion in any one index that would send its interest payments skyrocketing. For example, in the early 1980s short-term interest rates, such as the prime rate, shot up much more than inflation. An additional advantage of inflation-linked bonds is that they provide a closer match to fluctuations in prices of commodities that a company uses or sells.

As of mid-1988, only a handful of issuers had used inflation-linked debt, but investment bankers like First Boston were working to increase the market. REALs represent yet another innovation in financial markets to deal with uncertain inflation.

Source: Some of this material is adapted from *Corporate Finance,* July 1988, p. 29.

Convertibles and Exchangeables. Financing by means of convertible bonds (discussed in detail in Chapter 18) increased in the mid-1980s, perhaps in part because of a perception by management in many companies that their common stock was undervalued in the stock market, making the issuance of "debt now, stock later" more attractive. At the same time there was born a new security — the **exchangeable bond** — resulting primarily from the high-interest-rate environment of the late 1970s and early 1980s. Whereas convertibility is at the option of the *holder* of the bond, exchangeability is at the option of the *issuer,* giving the issuer the right to exchange the bond for another issue of securities. Exchangeability is an attrac-

Exchangeable bond — a bond that can be exchanged for another type of security *at the option of the issuer.*

tive option to management in the event of a decline in interest rates or a change in the firm's situation.

Response to Market Volatility

The second major factor resulting in financial innovation was a significant increase in the volatility of financial markets, especially in interest rates. Take a look back at Figure 2–3 and its text description in Chapter 2. The violent gyrations in interest rates during the 1970s and 1980s were unprecedented for most participants in the markets at that time. Both issuers and buyers of securities were

---

Finance in Practice 14–2

A New Word: Securitization

The 1980s added lots of new words to the dictionary. One of these was *securitization,* a term referring to the transformation into securities of assets that began as loans or leases. The distinction is that securities are tradeable — i.e., they can be traded in financial markets — whereas loans and leases typically are not.

The technical term for the new securities is *asset-backed securities*. Mortgage loans were the first major class of loans to be securitized. This was done back in the 1970s when the Government National Mortgage Association, known affectionately as "Ginny Mae," created the first so-called pass-through certificates. Through this process a group of mortgages held by a bank or savings-and-loan association were packaged up and sold publicly. A trust was created to own the mortgages, and certificates were issued against the trust. As payments were made on the mortgages, the cash was "passed

through" the trust to the holders of the certificates. The certificates were tradeable, so they became "securities." Hence the mortgages had been "securitized" — i.e., they had been transformed into securities. Whereas the mortgages had once been loans in a bank's portfolio, now they were, in effect, securities that traded publicly.

The significance of this transformation has been to reduce total financing costs. Competitive national and international capital markets are more efficient than banks for providing large amounts of capital. By packaging mortgages from different parts of the country, the trust can gain greater diversification than banks typically have in their mortgage portfolios. Also, the trust is not subject to the capital and reserve requirements of a bank. These factors combine to permit a lower financing cost through securitization than is possible through financial institutions.

Securitized mortgages, known as *mortgage-backed securities,* or MBS, grew rapidly during the early 1980s and reached a total of over $600 billion by year-end 1987. The idea caught on, and other types of financial assets began to be securitized. After mortgages, next came leases, first done in 1985. Automobile loans also were first securitized in 1985, and by December 1987 over $17 billion of "automobile paper" had been securitized and financed in

Asset-Backed Securities Cumulative Issuance, January 1985 through December 1987

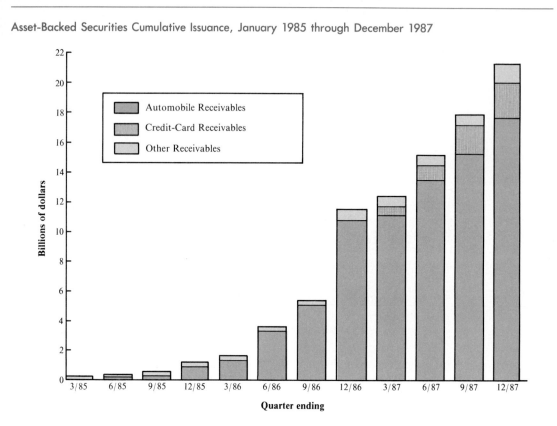

Source: Goldman-Sachs, Inc.

public capital markets (see chart). Credit-card receivables followed in 1987 and by year end about $2.4 billion had been securitized.

By year-end 1987, asset-backed securities excluding mortgages totaled $21 billion. Essentially all of this growth took place over a two-year period. If these trends continue, we can expect to see financial institutions such as banks and savings-and-loan associations continue to originate the loans, that is, do the credit analysis and paperwork and make the loan to the borrower. Once the loan is made, it is packaged up along with others of like kind, sold to a trust, and thereby "securitized" and financed in national capital markets. The bank or savings and loan receives the cash in payment for the loans and goes out to repeat the process.

What this process suggests is that banks and other financial institutions are very good at originating loans and leases, but that permanent financing may be cheaper via national and international capital markets. It certainly appears that the new asset-backed securities will become a very important financing tool.

Source: Asset-Backed Securities Quarterly, Goldman-Sachs, Inc., January 1988.

scarred by that experience and sought protection from the ravages of interest-rate risk. The markets, true to form, brought forth new products to fill the need, including floating-rate notes, financial futures contracts, and interest-rate swaps.

Floating-Rate Notes. The interest rates of **floating-rate notes (FRNs)** are adjusted periodically with the rise and fall of rates generally. Typically, FRNs have their rates tied to a widely representative market rate, such as the Treasury-bill rate. FRNs appeal to investors who believe that rates will fluctuate and who do not wish to be exposed to changes in market value. Because the interest rate on the FRN is altered with market rates, its value does not rise and fall with changes in rates as does that of a fixed-rate instrument.

Citicorp pioneered the floating-rate note in 1974, and FRNs became increasingly popular as rates became more volatile later in the decade. Many of these issues had rates adjusted every six months and in some cases even less frequently. Such infrequent adjustment became inadequate in the super-volatile early 1980s as rates moved quickly through wide ranges. (During one 12-month period in 1981, the Treasury-bill rate went from 16 percent to 7 percent and back to 16 percent!)

To deal with such changes, more frequent adjustment of rates was needed, and in 1984 American Express responded with a new security called a *money-market preferred stock,* a $150 million preferred-stock issue with a dividend rate that was reset every seven weeks. U.S. Steel issued $62.5 million worth of money-market preferred stock with a seven-week adjustment period in 1985, and American Express issued $100 million worth of money-market notes with a five-week reset also in 1985. Adjustable-rate mortgages have become very important also, accounting for 55–65 percent of new mortgages during 1984 and 1985. In 1983, Chemical Bank in New York introduced floating-rate automobile loans. Floating-rate notes have maintained their popularity in recent years.

Financial Futures. The **financial futures contract** represents another major innovation, resulting directly from the high volatility of the late 1970s and early 1980s. A **futures contract** is an agreement between a buyer and a seller to buy or sell something at some future date, with the price set at the present — that is, at the time of the contract. Futures contracts have been widely used in commodities markets, such as wheat, corn, or cocoa, for a long time, allowing a farmer, for example, to sell wheat in December for delivery in March at a price fixed in December. The farmer then worried about growing the wheat and let someone else worry about the risk of price changes. Producers (such as farmers) and consumers (such as flour or chocolate manufacturers) have used futures contracts for many years to hedge their risk.

Futures contracts came to the financial world in 1976 with the advent of Treasury-bill futures. Consider a company in December anticipating completion of a major contract the following March. Using T-bill futures, the company can invest in December the funds to be received in March *at a rate agreed upon in December.* By appropriately buying or selling bill futures, both holders and issuers of financial obligations can hedge away the risk of fluctuations in interest rates.

Since 1976, futures contracts have been introduced on Treasury bonds, bank certificates of deposit, Eurodollars, several major international currencies, and even on the Standard & Poor's 500 stock index and the New York Stock Exchange index. Some suspect that stock-index futures are being used more for speculating than for hedging risk, but that is another story. In 1985, a futures contract on the U.S. dollar was introduced, and for those worried about uncertain inflation rates, a contract on the consumer price index was introduced!

We will discuss financial futures in more detail in Chapter 18.

Interest-rate swap—an agreement between two companies in which each takes on the obligation of paying interest on the debt of the other company.

Interest-Rate Swaps. Another important innovation of the early 1980s growing out of interest-rate volatility is the **interest-rate swap.** Basically, two companies get together and agree to swap interest payments, X paying interest on Y's debt and Y paying interest on X's debt. What is the advantage? Consider a company that issued long-term debt but, after changes in market conditions, finds that it would prefer to have short-term debt. A savings-and-loan association has long-term mortgages financed by short-term deposits but would prefer to use long-term financing. Both can benefit by making each other's interest payments. In effect, each is adjusting the maturity of its liabilities to better fit changing circumstances.

Corporate Restructuring

The combination of a decade of inflation and high financial volatility also led to widespread corporate restructuring during the early and mid-1980s. Some of this activity took the form of multibillion-dollar *leveraged buyouts,* in which venture capitalists often working with a firm's management bought out the public share-holders and took the firm private. There were many large and celebrated *takeovers* in which a firm, or in some cases an individual, would buy another company, some-times against the will of management. Chevron bought Gulf Oil for $13.2 billion. Mesa Petroleum, headed by T. Boone Pickens, a renowned corporate raider, at-tempted unsuccessfully to buy both the Gulf Oil Company and Phillips Petroleum, and succeeded in buying Cities Service. Texaco bought Getty Oil for $10.1 billion.

Junk bonds—bonds with low credit ratings and high interest rates that play a role in corporate buyouts and takeovers.

We will discuss leveraged buyouts and takeovers in more depth in Chapter 25. We mention them briefly here because many of these and other acquisitions were financed by securities that came to be known as **junk bonds,** a reference to their low credit ratings and high interest rates. The corporate restructuring of this period also involved extensive repurchase of their own shares by some companies. We will discuss stock repurchase in Chapter 20.

Market Efficiency

One consideration that managers often face is the timing of new issues. Firms natu-rally prefer to sell new securities when prices are high. The real question is whether managers, or any investors for that matter, can identify when market prices are high or low in relation to their true economic value. For investors, an attractive path to a plush retirement is to buy low and sell high. Financial managers for companies want to make sure they don't sell securities for too low a price. Doing so would deprive existing shareholders of funds that could be invested profitably.

What are the real benefits of timing? How easy is it to make money buying and selling securities? The answers depend on how good financial markets are at pricing securities. Can individuals do a better job of pinpointing an asset's true economic value than financial markets, made up of thousands of presumably well-informed individuals?

Efficient market—one in which market prices fully reflect all the information available about the assets being traded.

An **efficient market** is one in which market prices fully reflect all the information available about the assets being traded. In such a market, prices will reflect the cumulative wisdom of all market participants. Robert Higgins provides a graphic description of the forces that could lead to market efficiency:

The arrival of new information to a competitive market can be likened to the arrival of a lamb chop to a school of flesh-eating piranha, where investors are plausibly enough the piranha. The instant the lamb chop hits the water, there is turmoil as the fish devour the meat. Very soon the meat is gone, leaving only the worthless bone behind, and the water returns to normal. Similarly, when new information reaches a competitive market there is much turmoil as investors buy and sell securities in response to the news, causing prices to change. Once prices adjust, all that is left of the information is the worthless bone. No amount of gnawing on the bone will yield any more meat, and no further study of old information will yield any more valuable intelligence.[2]

In essence, a competitive financial market will incorporate information into prices very rapidly as a result of the competition among thousands of buyers and sellers. If the market is efficient, such information is fully reflected in prices, so no further study of the existing information will give us a better estimate of true economic value than the one already given by the market price.

Whether or not financial markets are efficient is one of the most controversial topics in finance, and a few preliminary comments are important before it is discussed further. First, some parts of the financial markets may be efficient while others are not. Highly organized and competitive markets for U.S. government securities may turn out to be reasonably efficient, whereas markets for the trading of stocks in new smaller companies may not. Second, efficiency is in the eye of the beholder and depends on the type of information available to a particular investor or manager. Market prices may reflect all the information known by an aspiring millionaire who doesn't yet know the difference between profits and cash flow. At the same time, the market can be inefficient to a corporate executive who happens to know about as-yet-undisclosed merger plans.

[2]R. C. Higgins, *Analysis for Financial Management* (Homewood, Ill.: R. D. Irwin, 1984), p. 133.

The Case of Sam Q. Public

To gain a better understanding of the processes that could lead to market efficiency, let's take a look at a hypothetical series of events. Rambo, Inc., recently had its stock begin to trade publicly. Based on the limited information available, Rambo's stock price was $10 per share at the beginning of trading one Monday morning. That afternoon, the U.S. government announced that it was awarding the company a highly lucrative contract. Monday afternoon the announcement was carried over the major news wires and by evening made all the network television newscasts. On Tuesday, the contract made headlines in the *Wall Street Journal*.

Sam Q. Public happened to hear about the contract as he lounged in front of the TV Monday night and went to bed with a smile on his face dreaming of a vacation in the Bahamas. Sam planned to finance the trip by buying Rambo stock first thing Tuesday morning and then cashing in later when Rambo's stock price went up. Sam called his broker Tuesday morning just as the market opened with instructions to buy 1,000 shares of Rambo, but first he asked about the price. His broker noted that Rambo was selling for only $5 a share two months ago but had gone up by $2 a share Monday to close at $12. Undaunted, Sam purchased the stock and waited for the big profit.

Weeks go by and Sam begins to frown. Rambo's price has moved up and down with general market conditions, but the big profit just hasn't materialized. Disappointed, Sam sells at $12.25 a share, and his vacation dreams fade. His profit turns out to be a meager rate of return considering the brokerage fees and the fact that he pulled the money out of an interest-bearing bank account to finance the stock purchase.

What went wrong for Sam? He was right in his conclusion that the government contract was a bonanza for Rambo, Inc. The trouble was that he was just too late to cash in. The stock price had already adjusted by the time Sam got the information because other investors got the information earlier and bid up the stock price. In Sam's case, on Tuesday morning the market was efficient in that Rambo's stock price fully reflected the information about the contract.

Now consider Sam's cousin Ernest, who happens to work for the government-contract office. Ernest knew that Rambo was going to get the contract a full two months before the announcement. At that time, the stock was still selling for only $5 a share. Ernest also knew that the contract information had not yet leaked out. Could Ernest have made money? You bet. By purchasing at $5 per share based on his inside information, he could have profited from the price run-up to $12 a share, more than doubling his money in a couple of months. Two months before the announcement the market was not efficient with respect to Ernest's information. The stock price was too low because investors had yet to find out about the contract. As it turned out, Ernest, realizing his conflict of interest as a public servant, could not take advantage of his inside information. In fact, it would have been a violation of the law for him to do so. So, like Sam, he doesn't have any big vacations planned either.

Forms of Market Efficiency

The preceding scenario illustrates an important point: efficiency depends on the nature of information available. Three forms of market efficiency can be defined, each making use of a different definition of available information.

1. A market is *weak-form efficient* if current prices fully reflect all information about past security prices and returns.
2. A market is *semistrong-form efficient* if current prices fully reflect all publicly available information.
3. A market is *strong-form efficient* if current prices fully reflect *all* information, both public and private.

Table 14–6 defines the three types of market efficiency and gives examples of each type of information. Note that a market can be weak-form efficient but not efficient in the semistrong form. If this were the case, an investor might be able to find underpriced stocks by diligent research of material in a company's financial statements and in the financial press. If the investor has in truth identified such underpriced securities, he or she should be able to make lots of money by purchasing them while they are still cheap and profiting from sales at higher prices when the market finally does adjust to the information. On the other hand, no amount of studying past prices would yield such profitable investment opportunities if the market is weak-form efficient. If a market is weak-form efficient, all the information contained in past prices will already be reflected in the asset's market price, so it is already too late to use the information to pick underpriced stocks. For example, if the information found was good news about the company's future profitability, the stock price would have already gone up before an investor had a chance to purchase it.

Table 14–6

Type of Information and Market Efficiency

Type of Information Fully Reflected in Prices	Examples of Information	Form of Market Efficiency
Past prices and returns	Price of IBM stock last year Whether IBM stock price increased last month	Weak
All publicly available information, including past prices and returns	Article in *Wall Street Journal* Financial Statements Information on the CBS Evening News	Semistrong
All information, including all public information	Unannounced plan to acquire another company Quarterly earnings figure before it is announced	Strong

Findings on Market Efficiency

Are financial markets actually efficient? An immense amount of research has been devoted to exactly this question, mostly focusing on the stock market. Most studies approach the problem by trying to see if one could make abnormally high returns (relative to returns generally available in the market) by buying and selling stocks based on a particular type of information. Similar approaches have been used to study the efficiency of markets for assets other than stocks.

For example, suppose you followed Sam's strategy and bought stocks based on the TV evening news. If, based on such information, you could make abnormally high returns, this outcome would be evidence that the stock market was not semistrong-form efficient. Television news is public information, and semistrong-form efficiency requires that such public information already be reflected in stock prices. To control for getting lucky on a single day, it would be necessary to follow the results of applying the strategy based on a number of different news telecasts. If Sam's experience is typical and no abnormal returns are earned based on the TV information, the market is truly characterized by semistrong-form efficiency.

While the evidence is not crystal clear, there are some useful lessons that emerge from the findings.[3] First, it is very difficult, if not impossible, to consistently find underpriced securities based solely on information about past prices or returns. There will always be the exception to the rule, but U.S. financial markets appear to satisfy the requirements for weak-form efficiency. If some weak-form inefficiencies can be found, they are likely to involve quite complicated patterns that have yet to be unearthed and tested rigorously.

Second, market prices adjust quite rapidly to new information that comes into the public domain. In fact, the market often anticipates many public announcements, such as a company's intention to raise its dividend or its announcement of a particularly good year in terms of earnings.

Third, the market is definitely not efficient with respect to types of inside information sometimes held by corporate managers. In our example about Rambo, Inc., the market was not efficient with respect to Ernest's inside information on the government contract. A number of studies have shown that managers acting on inside information could make substantial profits by buying and selling stock in the companies for which they work because managers sometimes have important information that has not yet been made available to the public. For example, a manager in the oil business might know that his or her company has just made a major find of new oil reserves. If the manager bought stock in the company before the news became public, he or she would stand to reap a handsome profit as the stock price increased. As noted earlier, the use of such inside information is illegal, but there is evidence that it does occur. The celebrated cases of Ivan Boesky and others involved in the insider-trading scandal of 1987–1988 are cases in point.

[3]For a useful review and interpretation of much of the research on market efficiency, see B. Boldt and H. Arbit, "Efficient Markets and the Professional Investor," *Financial Analysts Journal,* July–August 1984.

Sources of Market Inefficiencies

The preceding discussion has stressed the relative efficiency of U.S. financial markets, especially with respect to public information, an emphasis that we believe is warranted. Corporate managers are likely to serve their shareholders best in the long run by focusing on the investments and commercial strategy of the company, rather than investing large blocks of time trying to spot market inefficiencies. That conclusion does not imply, however, that financial markets are infallible. There are intriguing findings that reveal apparent inefficiencies, and more will probably be discovered in the future. One such finding concerns the reaction of a company's stock price to an announcement of higher-than-expected earnings. Stock prices go up as would be expected. The puzzling finding in terms of market efficiency is that the adjustment is relatively slow. This slow adjustment means that someone could consistently make money by buying stocks after the earnings announcement is public. Apparently, at least for a while, the market price does not fully reflect the "earnings surprise."

One difficulty with spotting a market inefficiency is that bringing it to investors' attention is likely to make it disappear. A quick way to get a stock price to stop being undervalued is for investors to believe that it really is priced too low. The buy orders will hit the market in a hurry if people think there is money to be made. The message from studies of market efficiency is that there aren't many free lunches in financial markets.

Implications for Financial Decisions

Relatively efficient markets have some important implications for both investors and managers. For investors, market efficiency means that earning above-average returns in the financial markets is not an easy business. Just looking at past price trends and reading the financial press is not likely to produce a highly profitable way to pick underpriced stocks. The key to amassing a fortune is getting information before it is already impounded in prices. This task isn't necessarily hopeless, but it is difficult—just the type of result you would expect in competitive financial markets. For the vast majority of individual investors who don't have the resources or time to uncover new information, the best prescription is probably to pick a preferred level of risk, invest in a well-diversified portfolio of assets that fit that risk profile, and be satisfied to earn the market (average) return. Instead of devoting considerable expense in trying to pick winners, most investors should diversify their portfolios and trust that market prices already reflect the information they might uncover. This approach might be less glamorous than hunting for the next IBM, but it will probably turn out to be a more sound investment strategy in the long run.

Findings on market efficiency also have important lessons for managers. One of them is not, however, to trade for personal gain based on inside information. As noted above, such insider trading is illegal and for good reasons. The managers' charge is to work in the best interests of shareholders, not to take advantage of them by using inside information. A first lesson is that financial markets will react quickly to new information. One of the jobs of corporate management is to be sure that it communicates such information to the market in a careful and responsible manner. For a company's stock price to reflect the value of the investments managers have made, the market must have relevant and reliable information. We will have more to say on communications with the market when we discuss dividend policy in Chapter 17 and managing outstanding securities in Chapter 20.

A second lesson is that market prices already reflect a great deal of information. Unless a manager has some comparative advantage in gathering and processing information about a particular asset, he or she is unlikely to identify any pricing error made in the market. As a result, speculating in marketable securities or stocks is not a prudent or productive course of action for corporate managers. After all, there are major banks, large brokerage firms, and savvy private investors already trading in those securities. For the same reasons, trying to time debt issues to outguess the market about interest-rate trends is usually unwarranted.

A third lesson is that markets are not strong-form efficient. As a result, managers may sometimes know inside information that the market does not. Usually it is best to go ahead and relay this information to the financial markets, but there are times — for example, when disclosure would give away a major competitive advantage — when relaying this information may not be possible. The last thing a company wants to do is let competitors know the details of a new technology that can't be protected by patent laws. The manager faces a dilemma in such a situation. The current stock price may not reflect the inside information, but releasing that information may destroy long-run value. If managers make decisions for the long run, ultimately that economic value will surface in the prices of the firms' securities.

In summary, a lesson of market efficiency is that managers should focus their efforts on making the company a sound, profitable enterprise. If they succeed, stock prices will go up, and shareholders will reap the economic rewards.

KEY CONCEPTS

1. Firms can choose from among a wide variety of long-term financing methods to raise money.

2. Three principal forms of financial instruments are debt, preferred stock, and common stock. These types of securities issued by firms are valued in financial markets.

3. Debt is the most senior claim on the firm and gives the owner the legal right to receive interest and principal payments.

4. Preferred stockholders, though junior to debt holders, have prior claim to common shareholders. Preferred stockholders receive preferred dividends.

5. Common stockholders are the residual owners of the corporation. They have the most risky claim on the corporation and, as a result, require a higher rate of return than owners of the company's debt and preferred stock.

6. Firms use intermediate-term financing (maturities of two to seven years) in addition to long-term (maturities of eight to ten years or longer)

and short-term (maturities of less than one year) financing.

7. In recent years, firms have come to rely more on innovative financing schemes as financial markets have changed.

8. An efficient financial market is one in which current market prices fully reflect all available information.

9. The three forms of market efficiency are weak-form, semistrong-form, and strong-form efficiency.

10. U.S. financial markets are at least reasonably efficient with respect to publicly available information.

11. The research on market efficiency shows the importance of information in determining market values.

SUMMARY

The major types of long-term financing available to firms are debt, preferred stock, common stock, leases, and convertible securities. Financing instruments differ with respect to maturity, seniority, whether they are contractual or residual, the use of collateral, tax treatment, cost, and the right to a voice in management.

Long-term debt is a contractual claim that normally has a maturity of eight to ten years or longer. Protective covenants in the debt contract are designed primarily to protect lenders. The claim of bondholders against income and assets is senior to that of preferred and common stockholders. In addition to default risk, debt holders are subject to interest-rate risk and purchasing-power risk. Deductibility of interest lowers the effective cost of debt to the borrower.

Preferred stockholders are owners, not creditors. Preferred dividends are fixed in amount but are not contractual and are not deductible by the firm for tax purposes. In seniority, preferred claims come after those of bondholders but ahead of those of common stockholders.

Common stockholders have final responsibility for policy and residual claim to income and assets. Common stockholders bear the ultimate risks of commercial enterprise, receiving more return than bondholders and preferred stockholders in good times and less in bad times. The return to common stockholders is made up of two components: dividends and capital gains. Dividends are not deductible for tax purposes under present law. The liability of common stockholders is limited to the amount of their investment.

In addition to long-term and short-term sources of financing, firms can also obtain funds from intermediate-term sources with maturities of more than one year and up to five to seven years. Term loans from banks and insurance companies, loans against equipment, conditional sales agreements, leases, and foreign loans are all sources of intermediate-term financing.

Recent innovations in long-term financing include issuance of bonds with very low coupon rates (and in some cases no coupon payments at all) as well as floating-rate and adjustable-rate notes.

An efficient financial market is one in which market prices fully reflect all available information about the assets being traded. The three forms of market efficiency relate to different definitions of information. Weak-form efficiency requires only that prices fully reflect the information contained in past prices and returns. Semistrong-form efficiency means that all public information is fully reflected in prices, while strong-form efficiency requires that all information (both public and private) be fully reflected in market prices.

Though not efficient in the strong-form sense, U.S. financial markets do seem to meet the basic requirements of weak-form efficiency. In addition, prices react quickly to the revelation of new public information. As a result, most investors and managers are not likely to be able to profit by trying to outguess the market and find mispriced assets.

QUESTIONS

1. In what important respects do the major types of financial claims issued by firms differ?

2. How do contractual differences among financial claims affect investor risk and required rates of return? Give examples.

3. In connection with debt claims, what is meant by the term *contractual?*

4. What is a residual claim?

5. What is a subordinated claim?

6. What is the purpose of protective covenants in a debt contract?

7. How does a mortgage bond differ from a debenture?

8. In general, a bondholder is exposed to three different types of risk. What are they, and how do they differ?

9. What determines the yield to maturity of a bond?

10. Contrast preferred stock with debt and common stock. What are the similarities and differences?

11. What are the key characteristics of common stock?

12. How do common stockholders receive their financial return?

13. Compare and contrast intermediate versus seasonal bank loans in terms of what is financed and the means of repayment. Why are intermediate-term loans amortized?

14. What is meant by the term *preemptive rights?*

15. Define the three forms of market efficiency.

16. Suppose that, in response to quarterly earnings reports, the price of a company's stock increases dramatically within a few hours but levels off by the end of the trading day. What type of market efficiency does this represent?

17. Does semistrong-form efficiency imply weak-form efficiency? Does it imply strong-form efficiency?

REFERENCES

Brigham, E. F., "An Analysis of Convertible Debentures: Theory and Some Empirical Evidence." *Journal of Finance* 21 (Mar. 1966): 35–54.

Buse, A., "Expectations, Prices, Coupons and Yields." *Journal of Finance* 25 (Sept. 1970): 809–818.

Business Week (March 1, 1982).

Cohan, A. B. *Yields on Corporate Debt Directly Placed.* (New York: National Bureau of Economic Research, 1967.)

Donaldson, G., "In Defense of Preferred Stock." *Harvard Business Review* 40 (July–Aug. 1962): 123–136.

Gritta, R. D., "The Impact of Lease Capitalization." *Financial Analysts Journal* 30 (Mar.–Apr. 1974): 47–52.

Hayes, S. L., III, "New Interest in Incentive Financing." *Harvard Business Review* 44 (July–Aug. 1966): 99–112.

Hayes, S. L., III, and H. B. Reiling, "Sophisticated Financing Tool: The Warrant." *Harvard Business Review* 47 (Jan.–Feb. 1969): 137–150.

Pinches, G. E., "Financing with Convertible Preferred Stock, 1960–67." *Journal of Finance* 25 (Mar. 1970): 53–64.

Pogue, T. F., and R. M. Soldofsky, "What's in a Bond Rating?" *Journal of Financial and Quantitative Analysis* 4 (July 1969): 201–228.

Werner, G. F., and J. J. Weygandt, "Convertible Debt and Earnings Per Share: Pragmatism vs. Good Theory." *Accounting Review* 40 (Apr. 1970): 280–289.

West, R. R., "An Alternative Approach to Predicting Corporate Bond Ratings." *Journal of Accounting Research* 8 (Spring 1970): 118–125.

15

The Effects of Financial Leverage

In this chapter, we will investigate the effects of using debt (financial leverage) on the returns and risks to shareholders. We show that financial managers should attempt to maximize value when using debt. This value maximization requires trading off the benefits of debt, including the tax-deductibility of interest payments made by a corporation, against its costs, including agency costs and the costs of financial distress.

In the last chapter we discussed the many types of long-term and intermediate-term financing that a corporation can use. Now we can address the questions of what *mix* of these financing sources a firm should use to obtain funds. Just as the firm tries to increase its value by making good investment decisions, can the firm increase its value by making wise financing decisions? If so, how should financial managers go about making choices about the firm's financing mix?

Financial leverage — the use of debt.

Financing mix — the proportion of debt and equity used to finance investments.

In this chapter, we focus on **financial leverage** — the use of debt. In Chapter 12, in which we calculated a weighted-average required return for use in analyzing investment projects, the weights we used assumed some financing mix for the firm — a certain percentage of debt and a certain percentage of equity. We now want to explore how this **financing mix** is determined. In this chapter, we will discuss the effects of financial leverage on the value of the firm in order to provide qualitative guidance and a way of thinking about financing decisions. In the next chapter, we will discuss practical applications of these concepts.

Leverage and Required Returns

One way to evaluate the firm's financial choice is to look for the financing mix that will lower the firm's overall required rate of return, given the risk of its investments. This required return is what suppliers of capital require on their investment for any given level of risk. The lower this rate is, the higher the *value* of the firm's future cash flows will be because the value of a given future cash flow increases as the discount rate drops.

To see the nature of the problem, let's suppose a firm currently does its financing with equal amounts of debt and equity and faces a 40 percent tax rate. Given the underlying operating risk of the company and its current total financing mix, shareholders require a 16 percent return, and the firm can borrow long-term funds at an interest rate of 10 percent. Using these data and the techniques developed in Chapter 12, we can calculate the weighted-average required return (*WARR*) of suppliers of capital as:

$$WARR = W_e K_e + W_d K_d (1 - T)$$

$$= 0.5(0.16) + 0.5(0.10)(1 - 0.4) = 0.11 .$$

This 11 percent return requirement can be used as a discount rate to analyze projects that are of average risk for the firm.

Now suppose a new analyst for the company suggests: "Why don't we just do more financing with debt? Because it has a lower required rate of return, switching more of our financing to debt will lower our *WARR*. In essence, we can lower our cost of capital."

The Problem of Risk

The goal of lowering the *WARR* is a laudable one, but there is a major problem with the analyst's recommendation. The analyst has forgotten about the effects of financial leverage on the risks to shareholders. Remember that the shareholders' return requirement of 16 percent is based on the firm's current financing mix of 50 percent debt. If the firm tries to use more debt — say, raising the debt financing to 60 percent — shareholders will face higher risks and, as a result, will increase their required return to more than 16 percent. This extra risk to shareholders arises from the fact that, with higher borrowing, the firm will have to pay more in interest and principal before shareholders receive any returns. In addition, an increase in the firm's use of debt might push borrowing costs above a 10 percent interest rate if lenders believe there are extra risks that the company might default on the promised (now higher) debt payments.

To illustrate these effects, let's use some hypothetical numbers. Suppose shareholders and lenders were told of the change in financing, and as a result increased their required returns to 18 percent and 11 percent, respectively. We can calculate the *WARR* at the proposed new financing mix of 60 percent debt and 40 percent equity as

$$WARR = 0.4(0.18) + 0.6(0.11)(1 - 0.4) = 0.1116 .$$

The new *WARR* is 11.16 percent, which is actually *higher* than the original *WARR* of 11 percent. We can see the problem with the analyst's recommendation. Even though debt has a lower required return than equity, increasing the use of debt doesn't necessarily lower the *WARR*. Although in some instances the *WARR* might drop as more debt is used (we will return to this point later), in our example the *WARR* actually went up when the firm increased its use of debt. Changing the financing mix affects the risks borne by suppliers of capital and, in particular, affects risks to shareholders. In financial markets, shareholders will demand a **risk premium** for any additional risk. In choosing any financing mix, financial managers must be aware of these effects on risk.

To examine more carefully the relationship between required return and leverage, let us define K_0 as the return shareholders would require if the firm used no debt. In such a case, the firm uses no financial leverage, and its common shares are referred to as **unlevered shares.** We will let K_e represent the return required on equity at any given level of financial leverage, or the required return on **levered shares.** Now imagine what happens when leverage is increased, with everything else held constant. Such a controlled situation would be very difficult to achieve in practice, but for purposes of understanding the relationships, we can imagine that it is achieved by issuing debt and using the proceeds to repurchase equity.

As leverage increases, risk increases, and investors demand a higher return, so K_e rises. Equation (1) expresses this relationship symbolically and is diagrammed in Figure 15–1 on p. 448.

The relationship between the required return on levered equity, K_e, and the required return on unlevered, K_0, can be expressed as

$$K_e = K_0 + \text{risk premium for financial risk} . \tag{1}$$

The increased risk to shareholders that arises from the use of debt is **financial risk.** Because of the increased risk, investors demand a higher return.

Looking at Figure 15–1, a number of questions arise. What determines the risk premium for **operating risk,** where operating risk is the business risk inherent in

Risk premium — the difference between the required rate of return on a relatively riskless asset and that on a risky asset of the same expected life.

Unlevered shares — shares of stock in a company that uses no debt.

Levered shares — shares of stock in a company that uses debt.

As financial leverage increases, risk also increases, and risk-averse investors demand a higher return as compensation for the higher level of risk. The required rate of return on the firm's shares rises with leverage, other things being equal.

Operating risk — the uncertainty about future profitability that arises from the basic nature of the business and operation of a company; the business risk inherent in the firm's operations.

Figure 15–1
Leverage and the Required Rate of Return

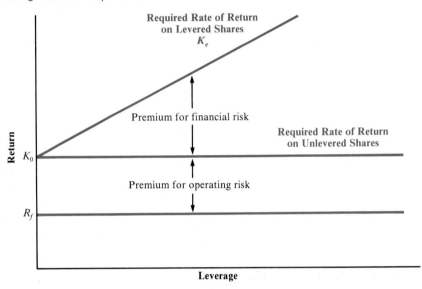

the firm's operations? In the figure, the premium for operating risk is measured as the vertical distance between the **risk-free rate of interest,** R_f, and the required return on unlevered shares, K_0. What is the nature of the extra risk premium shareholders demand as the firm increases its use of financial leverage? What criteria can financial managers use to pick the best mix of financing given that shareholders require an additional risk premium when more financial leverage is used? As will be discussed later, the appropriate criterion for choosing the firm's financial mix is to make decisions to maximize the market value of the firm. This is the same criterion we used to analyze investment decisions.

Although our focus in this chapter is on the effects of financial leverage, let us begin our analysis by recalling a second type of leverage, operating leverage.

Operating Leverage and Financial Leverage

In Chapter 8, we defined **operating leverage** in terms of the relationship between fixed and variable operating expenses. The term *operating* expenses refers to expenses related to the firm's operations, or to its commercial activities, and includes all expenses except interest and taxes.

The higher a firm's ratio of fixed to variable operating costs, the higher its operating leverage. An example of a firm with high operating leverage is an airline. In the short run, few of an airline's costs vary with the level of passenger traffic, perhaps only the cost of meals served in flight. Above its break-even passenger load factor, its operating profits rise very rapidly with increases in the number of passengers. Below the break-even point, the opposite occurs. Contrast this behav-

Risk-free rate of interest — the interest rate on a relatively riskless asset.

Operating leverage — the relationship between fixed and variable operating expenses that measures the sensitivity of operating profit to changes in sales.

ior with that of a wholesaler, the majority of whose operating leverage and operating profits are much less sensitive to changes in revenues, up or down. The degree of operating leverage of a firm thus has a pronounced effect on the sensitivity of its EBIT (earnings before interest and taxes) to changes in revenue.

As contrasted with operating leverage, *financial leverage* refers to the mix of debt and equity used to finance the firm's activities. A firm that uses a lot of debt is said to be *highly levered*.

We can see from the preceding definitions that operating leverage determines the extent to which a change in sales revenue affects EBIT. On the other hand, financial leverage does not affect EBIT since interest payments on debt come after the calculation of EBIT on the income statement. This does not mean that financial leverage has no effect. Financial leverage determines the extent to which changes in EBIT affect shareholders. From the shareholders' perspective, interest charges on debt are fixed costs. The higher the financial leverage, the more sensitive shareholder returns (for example, profits after taxes or earnings per share) will be to changes in EBIT. As a result, shareholders are affected by both operating leverage (determining the relationship between sales revenue and EBIT) and financial leverage (determining the relationship between EBIT and shareholder profits). The effects of this leverage can be dramatic.

> Financial leverage determines the extent to which changes in EBIT (earnings before interest and taxes) affect shareholders.

The Effects of Financial Leverage on Return and Risk

Let's now focus on the effects of financial leverage on return to shareholders. In analyzing financial leverage from this point on, we will take EBIT as our point of departure, though we must remember that EBIT itself will depend on sales levels and operating leverages.

Magnitude of Returns

Let us first examine the effects of different degrees of financial leverage at a given level of EBIT. Consider a firm with assets of $1,000 and imagine that this might be financed one of three ways: *A*, entirely by equity (common stock); *B*, 70 percent by equity and 30 percent by debt; and *C*, 40 percent by equity and 60 percent by debt. Assume that debt requires an interest rate of 8 percent and equity has a market price of $10 per share. Assume also that the $1,000 in assets generates EBIT of $240. We then have the figures listed in Table 15–1 (p. 450) for the three levels of leverage. A 50 percent tax rate is used for simplicity.

From Table 15–1 we see that the effect of leverage is quite significant. When financed 30 percent by debt (case *B*), the firm earns $1.54 per share, 28 percent more than the $1.20 earned with no leverage. Return on equity (ROE) is greater by the same percentage. At 60 percent debt, (case *C*), EPS and ROE are double what they are with no leverage.

Table 15–1 assumes that the firm earns 24 percent before interest and taxes on its assets ($240 on assets of $1,000). The effects of leverage depend very much on the relationship between the firm's ability to earn, or its rate of return on assets, and the interest cost of debt. In the preceding example, the firm obtains debt funds

> The effects of financial leverage depend on the relationship between the firm's ability to earn (its rate of return on assets), and the interest cost of debt. When the return on assets exceeds the interest cost of debt, leverage has a favorable impact on ROE (and EPS), and vice versa.

Table 15-1

Effect of Leverage on Earnings per Share for a "Normal" Year

	Leverage		
	A	B	C
Assets	$1,000	$1,000	$1,000
Debt	0	$ 300	$ 600
Equity	$1,000	$ 700	$ 400
Leverage ratio (percent of debt)	0	30	60
EBIT	$ 240	$ 240	$ 240
Interest @ 8 percent	0	$ 24	$ 48
Profit before taxes	$ 240	$ 216	$ 192
Tax @ 50 percent	$ 120	$ 108	$ 96
Profit after taxes	$ 120	$ 108	$ 96
Shares	100	70	40
Earnings per share (EPS)	$ 1.20	$ 1.54	$ 2.40
Return on equity (ROE, percent)	12.0	15.4	24.0

at a cost of 8 percent and puts those funds to work to earn 24 percent. The more debt it uses, the more favorable the impact. The more the return exceeds the cost of debt, the more pronounced the effects. If, on the other hand, the firm could earn only 8 percent on assets, there would be no advantage to the use of debt. In Table 15-1, if EBIT were $80 (8 percent of $1,000 assets), EPS would be $0.40 no matter how much debt was used, and ROE would be 4 percent. If the firm's return were less than the cost of debt, the effects of leverage would be unfavorable.

Do we conclude that, when the return/cost relationship is favorable, the more debt the better? The "no free lunch" rule should make us skeptical. The reason for the favorable leverage effect is that debt represents a fixed, prior claim on income. When times are good, debt is advantageous, but what happens if times are not good? Suppose the return/cost relationship suddenly turns from favorable to unfavorable, and EBIT drops? The fixed claim is a two-edged sword! Let us now see what happens when EBIT varies.

Variability of Returns

Earnings before interest and taxes in any given firm are subject to many influences, some peculiar to the firm, some common to all firms in the industry, and some related to general economic conditions that affect all firms. In an uncertain world, EBIT in any period can turn out to be higher or lower than expected. Uncertainty with respect to EBIT often is referred to as **operating risk.**

One major source of operating risk is the business cycle — that is, the possibility of a recession. Other sources may be due to the possibility of technological obso-

Because debt is a fixed, prior claim on income, financial leverage may produce a favorable effect when times are good but an unfavorable one when times are bad. The fixed claim is a double-edged sword.

Operating risk — uncertainty with regard to EBIT.

lescence, actions of competitors, shifts in consumer preferences, changes in supply prices (such as the sharp increase in oil prices during the 1970s and the subsequent sharp decline in the early 1980s), and so on. Let us simplify matters by assuming that events of this kind can produce three possible outcomes: a normal year for EBIT, a good year, or a bad year. For example, suppose EBIT will be $240 in a normal year, $60 in a bad year, and $400 in a good year. As in Table 15–1, we examine the results at each of three levels of leverage — zero, 30 percent, and 60 percent debt — in Table 15–2. In Tables 15–3 and 15–4 (p. 452) we then summarize the results in terms of impact on EPS. Finally, Figure 15–2 (p. 452) dis-

Table 15–2

Leverage Effect with Variable EBIT

	State of the World		
	Bad	Normal	Good
A, No Leverage			
EBIT	$ 60	$240	$400
Interest @ 8 percent	0	0	0
Profit before taxes	$ 60	$240	$400
Tax @ 50 percent	$ 30	$120	$200
Profit after taxes	$ 30	$120	$200
Shares	100	100	100
Earnings per share (EPS)	$ 0.30	$ 1.20	$ 2.00
Return on equity (ROE, percent)	3.0	12.0	20.0
B, 30 Percent Debt			
EBIT	$ 60	$240	$400
Interest @ 8 percent	$ 24	$ 24	$ 24
Profit before taxes	$ 36	$216	$376
Tax @ 50 percent	$ 18	$108	$188
Profit after taxes	$ 18	$108	$188
Shares	70	70	70
Earnings per share (EPS)	$ 0.26	$ 1.54	$ 2.69
Return on equity (ROE, percent)	$ 2.6	15.4	26.9
C, 60 Percent Debt			
EBIT	$ 60	$240	$400
Interest @ 8 percent	$ 48	$ 48	$ 48
Profit before taxes	$ 12	$192	$352
Tax @ 50 percent	$ 6	$ 96	$176
Profit after taxes	$ 6	$ 96	$176
Shares	40	40	40
Earnings per share (EPS)	$ 0.15	$ 2.40	$ 4.40
Return on equity (ROE, percent)	1.5	24.0	44.0

Table 15—3

Earnings per Share

	State of the World		
	Bad	*Normal*	*Good*
No leverage	$0.30	$1.20	$2.00
30 percent debt	0.26	1.54	2.69
60 percent debt	0.15	2.40	4.40

Table 15—4

Percentage Change in Earnings per Share Compared to Normal Year

	State of the World	
	Bad	*Good*
No leverage	−75	+67
30 percent debt	−83	+75
60 percent debt	−94	+83

Figure 15—2
The Effects of Changes in EBIT on Earnings per Share

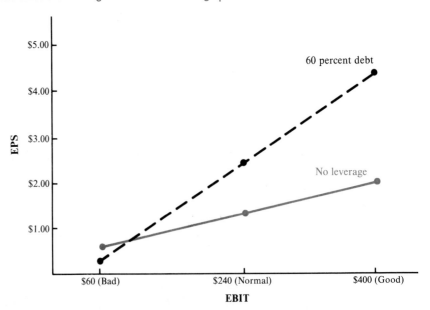

plays the results graphically by plotting EPS versus EBIT for the two extreme plans; first, no leverage, and second, 60 percent debt.

Look carefully at Table 15–2. The top panel, Panel A, shows the figures for the no-leverage case. Panel B shows the effects of 30 percent debt, and Panel C 60 percent debt. Focus on the center column, a "normal" year. With no leverage, return on equity (ROE) is 12 percent. With 30 percent debt, ROE rises to 15.4 percent, and with 60 percent debt, to 24 percent. These are the figures from Table 15–1. In a normal year, the effect of leverage is favorable. The same is true in a "good" year, where ROE is much higher if the firm levers up.

The results of Table 15–2 are summarized in Tables 15–3 and 15–4. We see that, in normal and good years, use of more leverage increases EPS. In a bad year, EPS is lower with debt, and the more we use, the worse off we are. We also see in Table 15–3 that the greater the leverage, the wider the range over which EPS varies from bad year to good. It is interesting also to look at the results in terms of percentage changes that are listed in Table 15–4.

From Table 15–4, we see that when leverage is used, EPS rises more in good years and falls more in bad years. When EBIT is rising, the more leverage we use the faster EPS rises. When EBIT is falling, greater leverage causes EPS to fall faster.

From this analysis, we arrive at the general proposition that *financial leverage increases the variability of EPS and of percentage ROE.*

The increase in risk caused by using financial leverage is often referred to as **financial risk.** Why does this increase in risk occur? It occurs because debt constitutes a fixed, prior claim against earnings. No matter what happens to EBIT, a fixed amount of interest must be paid. When EBIT falls, all the decline is deducted from the portion going to equity. As a result, the greater the use of financial leverage, the more sensitive EPS is to changes in EBIT. Figure 15–2 shows this result graphically.

Suppose EBIT declines to a level below that required to pay interest. This can happen — and does. In that case, the firm shows a loss. However, it does not necessarily go bankrupt, because it can make the interest payment by drawing down cash or other liquid assets, by borrowing, or, in extreme cases, by selling off operating assets. Where the shortfall is so great that these options are unavailable or inadequate, the firm faces possible bankruptcy if it defaults on its contract to pay interest. So we see that debt brings blessings when times are good, and dangers when times are bad.[1]

We conclude that for a given degree of variability of EBIT, the more leverage the firm uses the more variable will be its earnings, both in total and per share. It is clear that variability of earnings stems from two factors: variability of EBIT (operating risk) and the extent to which financial leverage is employed (financial risk). The degree of variability of EBIT is an important factor in deciding the extent to which leverage should be used. We will return to this conclusion later in this chapter.

The greater the financial leverage, the wider the range over which EPS (earnings per share) varies from bad year to good.

Financial risk — extra risk due to the use of financial leverage.

Variability of earnings to shareholders arises from both the variability of EBIT and the degree of financial leverage.

---

[1] A good example of the effect of financial leverage on variability of returns is provided by the airline industry. See R. D. Gritta, "The Effect of Financial Leverage on Air Carrier Earnings: A Break-Even Analysis," *Financial Management* 8 (Summer 1979), 53–60.

Sample Problem 15–1

Leverage Effects

The Osgood Company has assets of $4 million that are expected to generate $800,000 next year before interest and taxes.

A. Assume that Osgood's assets could be financed in one of three ways:

Policy	Debt (percent)	Equity (percent)
A	0	100
B	20	80
C	50	50

Assume that debt requires an interest of 10 percent and that equity has a market price of $20 per share. Also assume that the market price per share of stock is equal to the book (balance-sheet) value per share under each of the alternatives, and that the firm's tax rate is 50 percent. What will be the expected earnings per share and return on equity under each of these plans at next year's expected level of EBIT?

B. In a bad year, Osgood's EBIT may fall as low as $400,000, and in a good year, EBIT may rise to $1,000,000. Calculate the expected earnings per share and return on equity for the high and low EBIT for the financing plans discussed in Part A.

Solution

A. This problem can be approached by constructing tables similar to Tables 15–1 and 15–2.

	Policy (thousands of dollars, unless otherwise noted)		
	A	B	C
Assets	$4,000	$4,000	$4,000
Debt	0	800	2,000
Equity	4,000	3,200	2,000
Leverage ratio (percent of debt)	0	20	50
EBIT	800	800	800
Interest @ 10 percent	0	80	200
Profit before taxes	800	720	600
Taxes @ 50 percent	400	360	300
Profit after taxes	400	360	300
Shares (thousands)	200	160	100
Earnings per share (EPS, dollars)	$ 2.00	$ 2.25	$ 3.00
Return on equity (ROE, percent)	10.00	11.25	15.00

Osgood's assets and EBIT are not affected by the choice of a financing plan and will be the same under either plan. Policy A is 100 percent equity financed so debt will, of course, equal 0 and equity will equal $4 million. Since there is no debt in Policy A, there will be no interest expense associated with Policy A. The number of shares of stock outstanding for Policy A is 200,000 shares (the amount of equity, $4 million, divided by the market price per share, $20). Note that the equity figure is the stock required to finance the $4 million dollars of assets at the beginning of the year. EPS under A is $2.00 and the return on equity equals 10 percent. Policy B, 20 percent debt, has debt of $800,000 ($4 million times 20 percent) and equity of $3,200,000. Interest expense is $80,000, reducing profit before taxes to $720,000. The number of shares outstanding in this plan equals 160,000, resulting in EPS of $2.25 and ROE of 11.25 percent. For Policy C, debt and equity equal $2,000,000 each, resulting in $3.00 EPS and ROE of 15 percent.

B. The approach here is the same as in Part A, using the different EBIT levels. The table that follows shows the results.

	State of the World (thousands of dollars, unless otherwise noted)	
	Bad	Good
Policy A, 0 percent debt		
EBIT	$ 400	$1,000
Interest @ 10 percent	0	0
Profit before taxes	400	1,000
Taxes @ 50 percent	200	500
Profit after taxes	200	500
Shares (thousands)	200	200
EPS (dollars)	$1.00	$ 2.50
ROE (percent)	5	12.5
Policy B, 20 percent debt		
EBIT	400	1,000
Interest @ 10 percent	80	80
Profit before taxes	320	920
Taxes @ 50 percent	160	460
Profit after taxes	160	460
Shares (thousands)	160	160
EPS (dollars)	$1.00	$ 2.88
ROE (percent)	5	14.4
Policy C, 50 percent debt		
EBIT	400	1,000
Interest @ 10 percent	200	200
Profit before taxes	200	800
Taxes @ 50 percent	100	400
Profit after taxes	100	400
Shares (thousands)	100	100
EPS (dollars)	$1.00	$ 4.00
ROE (percent)	5	20

Note that if the state of the world is "bad," EPS and ROE are the same under all three financing alternatives. This result occurs because, in state "bad," Osgood's operating earnings are $0.10 per dollar of assets ($400,000 on $4 million assets), exactly the same as the interest rate on debt funds. Since the percentage rate of operating earnings (0.10) is exactly equal to the rate of interest, the use of leverage does not raise or lower EPS or ROE.

The Risk/Return Trade-Off

The foregoing analysis makes clear that there is a *trade-off* between return and risk. With increased leverage, the return in normal and good years is likely to be better than without debt, but the return in bad years is likely to be worse. By using debt, the firm gains an advantage in normal and good years, but it pays a price: the risk of low returns in bad years. **So the use of debt represents a gamble: more return if things turn out well, less return if things turn out badly.** If we only knew the future, the debt decision would be easy — we could determine just how much to use. But we don't know the future, and those who go too far in using debt may regret it.

> Financial leverage increases the expected return on a firm's equity at the expense of increased risk.

How then do we make the decision regarding how much debt to use? Unfortunately the final answer does not lie in Table 15–1 or 15–2 or Figure 15–2. These kinds of illustrations are very useful because they show us outcomes *if* EBIT turns out to be such and such. But we do not know what EBIT will be. We need a decision criterion to help us deal with the trade-offs.

Criteria for Financing Decisions

To make a choice between alternative financial plans in the face of a risk/return trade-off, we need a criterion for determining whether gains in expected return to shareholders by using more leverage are sufficient to justify the extra risks. Our decision criterion must therefore be able to incorporate the effects of changes in both risk and return.

> EPS has some serious shortcomings as a decision criterion to be used in answering the question: what should the firm do?

Sometimes accounting measures of shareholder interest, such as return on equity (ROE) or earnings per share (EPS), are suggested as decision criteria for financial decisions. Unfortunately, they are not adequate for the job because they measure return but not risk. Projecting what ROE or EPS might be at future EBIT levels gives us a useful display of possible outcomes, but it doesn't resolve the risk/return trade-off. To pick a financing plan with the highest ROE or EPS at expected EBIT levels is to ignore the critical factor of extra risks if EBIT drops below the expected outcome. Often a firm can continue to improve *expected* earnings per share or return on equity by increasing debt, but this decision could lead to a decline in the market price of the firm's stock as investors become concerned about greater risks — clearly an undesirable outcome.

Another suggested decision criterion is to pick the source of financing with the lowest cost, where the cost of any source of funds is the rate of return required by those who supply the funds. While such a rule may sound appealing, it ignores the changes in risk that occur when a firm changes its financial leverage.

In the case of firms to whom both equity and debt are available, debt is always the cheaper of the two. This being so, why use any equity at all? Using cost as our only criterion would always lead to a choice of debt, right up to the point of going bankrupt! Here, as before, using cost as the criterion considers only half of the issue: it ignores risk. Equity costs more — that is, has a higher required rate of return — because it does more: it bears risk. A bicycle costs less than an automobile, and both provide transportation, but to choose the bicycle because it is cheaper is to ignore some rather obvious differences between the two. Likewise, it is misleading to compare the cost of debt to the cost of equity because the use of additional debt (increasing financial leverage) without adding more equity increases risks to shareholders, and shareholders demand compensation for this additional risk.

We have looked at a number of criteria and found serious shortcomings with each. What about market value? Is our general criterion for financial-management decisions — value maximization — applicable to financing decisions as well as to investment decisions? Indeed it is.

The best criterion for choosing a financing plan is to pick the financing alternative that maximizes the value of the firm.

In principle, the use of value as our criterion solves our problems with respect to both time and risk. A value criterion can be used to compare the effects of alternative plans over many future periods rather than only near-term periods. A value criterion not only takes into account expected value, but also recognizes the risk/return trade-off. Although a value criterion accomplishes these goals in principle, application of value as a criterion is not easy. To develop valuation as a criterion for financing decisions, we need to know more about the way in which changes in leverage affect value.

Finance in Practice 15–1

Increased Use of Debt

Frequently during the 1980s, stories have appeared in the financial press about the rise in debt on corporate balance sheets in the United States. In 1960, total liabilities of the *Fortune* 500 industrial companies (the 500 largest industrial companies as identified each year by *Fortune* magazine) averaged 35 percent of assets, with the other 65 percent of assets financed by equity. By the end of 1984, liabilities of the *Fortune* 500 had risen to 55 percent of assets. Total debt of all nonfinancial firms was $1.3 trillion. Over the 1960–1984 period, interest rose from about 8 percent of total cash flow to about 20 percent. Table A on p. 458 shows the debt burden by industry for 15 industries.

Are these trends alarming? Certain factors suggest that they are less serious than they first appear. Many years of inflation have left assets, especially real property and inventories, undervalued on corporate balance sheets. Real property has increased greatly in value over the years, but in many cases the increases are not reflected on balance sheets. Under the LIFO (last in, first out) method of inventory accounting, inventories become progressively more understated over time relative to replacement value. Even measuring interest as a percentage of cash flow can be misleading because of the

Table A

Liabilities as Percentage of Assets		
	1984	*1974*
Retailing	68.8	58.6
Utilities	64.3	62.6
Transportation	64.0	63.6
Metals	61.4	48.6
Aerospace	61.1	62.0
Petroleum refining	59.5	49.9
Drugs	58.6	41.7
Motor vehicles and parts	58.6	50.4
Food	56.4	56.0
Electronics	54.0	55.5
Forest products	52.6	51.6
Chemicals	52.2	50.3
Rubber	51.8	57.0
Textiles	45.9	50.5
Computers	44.9	42.9

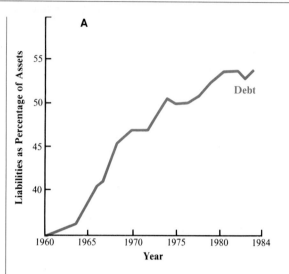

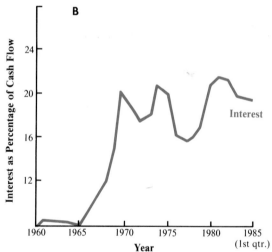

dramatic rise in interest rates during the 1970s and early 1980s, again under the influence of inflation. Much of that higher interest expense is attributable to the inflation premium, which is actually not a true expense, even though the accounting system treats it as such, but rather a payment to debt holders to maintain the purchasing power of the debt.

This is not to say that some companies didn't overdo it. Some that borrowed heavily and then went bankrupt were Baldwin-United, Charter Company, Lionel, Saxon Industries, Wickes, and Wheeling Pittsburgh Steel. Phelps Dodge, a copper producer, borrowed extensively during the 1970s and early 1980s to finance capital investment and subsequently had to sell parts of the business when it got into difficulty.

Mergers also account for an important share of the increase in debt. Chevron borrowed $12 billion to finance its acquisition of Gulf Oil. Martin Marietta borrowed heavily in a celebrated case during the early 1980s to escape a takeover attempt by Bendix Corporation. Phillips Petroleum and Unocal likewise used heavy borrowing to thwart takeover attempts by rearranging their capital structures. All in all,

mergers during the late 1970s and early 1980s did contribute significantly to total corporate use of debt financing.

While not as alarming as they first appear, the figures in the accompanying table and diagrams nevertheless are not to be taken lightly. As Figure A shows, debt levels are higher than they were two decades ago, and Figure B shows that a higher proportion of corporate cash flow must be allocated to making interest payments.

Source: Adapted from K. Labich, "Is Business Taking On Too Much Debt?" *Fortune,* July 22, 1985.

How Leverage Affects Firm Value

If we view a firm as a going concern, its value depends on future cash flows.

If we view a firm as a going concern, its value depends on the cash flows it can generate in the future. The firm's pretax operating profit, or EBIT, is divided among three principal claimants. Debt holders (D) receive their share in the form of interest, the government (G) receives its share in taxes, and equity holders (E) receive what is left. Thus, we can think of EBIT as a pie to be divided among the three claimants, as illustrated in Figure 15–3.

Investment decisions determine the size of EBIT, while financing decisions determine how EBIT is to be divided among debt holders, equity holders, and the government (taxes).

Investment decisions determine the size of the EBIT pie, while financing decisions determine how it is to be sliced. The total value of the firm is its value to owners and creditors together and is determined by the combined slice going to equity holders and debt holders together in Figure 15–3. Investment decisions increase the value of the firm by increasing the size of the pie. Financing decisions can increase firm value by reducing the share of the pie going to the government—that is, by reducing the taxes paid by the firm.

Tax Effects

Financial friction—the additional cost of financial transactions, such as commissions paid by investors to buy or sell securities, flotation costs of issuing new securities, information costs of financial decision making, and costs associated with financial distress.

Financing decisions affect the firm's tax liability because interest on debt is tax-deductible. To simplify the analysis, we will discuss tax effects as they would work in well-developed financial markets without the **financial friction** that makes it more difficult or more costly to undertake financial transactions. Financial friction includes the commissions paid by investors when they buy or sell stocks and bonds, the flotation costs of issuing new securities, and the information costs, in time and effort, required by investors to gather and analyze information

Figure 15–3
Division of Earnings Before Interest and Taxes (EBIT)

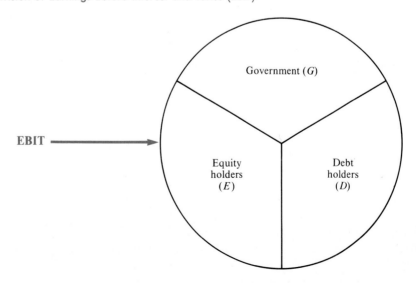

Because interest is tax-deductible, an increase in debt produces a tax shield and the government's share of EBIT is reduced.

in making financial decisions. Markets without friction would be efficient in the sense that market values would reflect all available information. By ignoring financial friction, we can focus on the tax effects of leverage without adding other complications (such as transactions or information costs). Even if some of these complications are added (as we do later), the same basic message remains: financing decisions affect the firm's tax liability because interest on debt is tax-deductible.

If interest were not deductible, a change in the firm's debt/equity mix would have no effect on taxes. Let us examine the slicing of the EBIT pie with and without deductibility of interest. In Table 15–5, the firm's EBIT each period is represented by the symbol O to emphasize that EBIT is a result of operations. Assume for simplicity that the firm pays interest at a rate, i, on total debt, D. Total interest payments each period are iD. With interest not deductible, the firm pays taxes of OT, where T is the tax rate. As leverage is increased, the share to debt holders increases, the share to equity holders decreases by a like amount, and the share to the government remains unchanged. Thus, the share to debt and equity holders together is fixed at $O(1 - T)$ and does not vary with changes in leverage.

If interest were not tax-deductible, the increase in risk due to greater leverage would offset the increase in expected return, and market valuation would not increase.

With interest tax-deductible, the government's share each period is lowered by iDT, sometimes called the **interest tax shield** on interest. The combined share to debt and equity together is higher by iDT. Table 15–6 illustrates this effect for a firm that has EBIT of $1,000, faces a 40 percent tax rate, and uses $3,000 of debt financing with an interest rate of 10 percent.

The firm's cash flows to owners increase with leverage because of the *interest tax shield* provided by the use of debt.

As a comparison of the rows in Table 15–6 shows, the use of debt increases the combined share to debt and equity together from $600 to $720. This increase of $120 is exactly the amount of the tax shield on interest: $iDT = 0.10(\$3,000)(0.4) = \$120$. As shown in the table, the $120 increase to debt and equity owners comes at the expense of the government whose tax revenues decline by $120, from $400 to $280.

Interest tax shield — the reduction in taxes that results from the tax-deductibility of interest.

From the preceding analysis, we can conclude that interest deductibility is an important benefit of debt financing. With interest not deductible, the use of debt financing in lieu of equity does not make the firm more valuable. The portion of the EBIT pie to be shared by debt and equity holders, $O(1 - T)$ in Table 15–5, is fixed in total, and leverage affects only the way the portion is sliced between debt

Table 15–5

Division of Earnings Before Interest and Taxes (EBIT) Among Claimants

		Claimant's Share When	
		Interest Is Not Deductible	Interest Is Deductible
EBIT (O) →	Debt holders	iD	iD
	Government	OT	$OT - iDT$
	Equity holders	$O - iD - OT$	$O - iD - OT + iDT$
Debt and equity together		$O(1 - T)$	$O(1 - T) + iDT$

Table 15—6
Effect of Tax-Deductibility of Interest on Cash Flows to Owners

	Earnings Before Interest and Taxes, O (1)	Interest on Debt, iD (2)	Pretax Profits (3) = (1) − (2)	Taxes, T (at 40 percent) (4)	Profits after Tax (5) = (3) − (4)	Money to Debt and Equity (6) = (2) + (5)
Company having no debt	$1,000	$ 0	$1,000	$400	$600	$600
Company with debt of $3,000 at interest of 10 percent	$1,000	$300 ↓ Debt holders	$ 700	$280 ↓ Government	$420 ↓ Equity holders	$720

and equity holders. An increase in the size of the slice to one group must come at the expense of the other. Hence, in frictionless, well-developed financial markets, with interest not deductible, leverage cannot increase the combined value of debt and equity.

To see this point more clearly, consider a firm whose debt and equity are entirely held by a single individual. With interest not deductible, for a given level of EBIT total payments to debt and equity are fixed, and changes in the split between the two cannot make the holder better or worse off. Given the existence of organized financial markets, the same conclusion holds if there are many holders of the firm's debt and equity.

Although when interest is not deductible leverage does not increase the total value of the debt and equity, it does affect characteristics of the cash-flow streams going to the two groups. An increase in leverage increases the expected rate of return to equity in percentage terms but, as we found earlier in this chapter, simultaneously increases the riskiness of that return. As risk increases, risk-averse investors demand a higher return. The increase in risk offsets the increase in expected return, and the value of a share of stock remains unchanged. In other words, while leverage increases the expected return, because of the accompanying increase in risk the market does not place a higher valuation on that return.

When interest is tax-deductible, the picture changes. An increase in leverage decreases the share of EBIT going to the government and increases the share going to debt and equity. In effect the government is providing a tax subsidy.

Value of the Tax Subsidy

What value does the market place on this tax subsidy? If the firm had no debt, it would provide to investors a cash-flow stream equal to $O(1 - T)$, from

Table 15–5, in each period. This cash-flow stream has a value that we will label V_U, where the subscript U signifies "unlevered."

With debt present, the stream shared by debt and equity holders with interest deductible is $O(1 - T) + iDT$. The value of this stream is therefore V_U plus the value of the tax shield, iDT. For simplicity, we will assume that the firm plans to borrow for the indefinite future, so that iDT is a perpetuity. We can determine the present value of this tax shield by discounting. When this problem was first worked out in the early 1960s, it was argued that the tax shield is of approximately the same degree of risk as the interest payments themselves and should be discounted at the same rate, i. Thus, the present value of the tax shield of iDT per period was then calculated as $iDT/i = DT$, and the value of the firm with interest deductible was calculated as shown in Equation (2).[2] The value, V_L, of the cash flows of the levered firm, with interest tax-deductible, can be calculated as:

$$V_L = V_U + DT \tag{2}$$

where $V_U =$ the value of the cash flows with no debt and $DT =$ the present value of the tax shield.

Graphically, we can represent the relationship in Equation (2) as shown in Figure 15–4. Equation (2) states that the value of the levered firm, V_L, is larger than

[2]Equation (2) was first worked out by Modigliani and Miller, "Corporate Income Taxes and the Cost of Capital—a Correction," *American Economic Review* 53 (June 1963): 433–43. The analysis in this article did not consider the effects of differences in personal taxes paid by stockholders and bondholders. Personal taxes are discussed in the next section of the book.

The value of a firm that is levered is larger than the value the same firm would have if it were unlevered by the present value of the interest tax shield.

Figure 15–4
Leverage and Value Considering Only Corporate Taxes

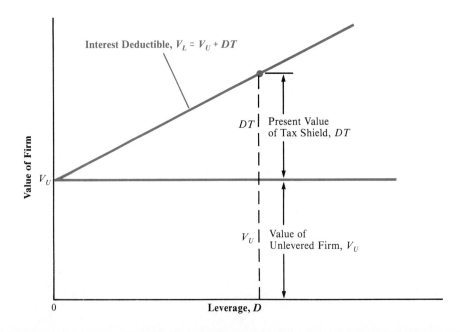

the value of the unlevered firm, V_U, by the present value of the tax shield, DT, provided by the interest payments made by the levered firm.

Sample Problem 15–2
The Effects of Corporate Taxes on Zetatronics, Inc.

Zetatronics, Inc., is financed entirely by equity that has a current market value of $16 million. The company is considering replacing some of its equity with debt by issuing bonds and using the proceeds to repurchase stock. Determine the theoretical value of the tax subsidy (considering corporate taxes only) if the amount of the swap is $4 million ($4 million in bonds replacing a like amount of stock). Assume a tax rate of 46 percent.

Solution
Assuming the change to be permanent and treating its cash flow as perpetuities, the value of the tax subsidy, from Equation (2), is

$$DT = \$4 \text{ million} \times 0.46 = \$1.84 \text{ million}.$$

So, from Equation (2), the value of the firm after the transaction theoretically would be $16 million + $1.84 million = $17.84 million.

To this point we have focused on the effects of leverage on value in light of the tax-deductibility of interest at the corporate level. We have seen that leverage can increase value because of the tax shield on interest. But, as one would suspect, there is more to the story. Let us consider some complicating factors—personal taxes and financial distress.

Personal Taxes

The tax benefits considered in Figure 15–4 and Equation (2) take into account only taxes paid by the firm. It is clear that an increase in debt reduces the firm's tax liability and thereby increases total cash flows accruing to debt and equity holders together.

But corporate taxes are not the whole story. Bondholders and stockholders themselves must pay taxes on the returns they receive from the firm. These personal taxes may act to offset part of the saving in the firm's taxes. Some economists have argued that the offset is total and that, in general, there is no tax benefit to the use of debt at all. This extreme view of no net tax benefit of debt was proposed when (prior to 1987) capital gains were taxed at a lower rate than ordinary income.

According to this view, the personal tax rate was effectively higher on returns to bondholders than on returns to shareholders because capital gains provide a large portion of a shareholder's return and were taxed at a lower rate than ordinary income, such as interest and dividends. Interest rates adjust to reflect the fact that bondholders must pay taxes on the interest they receive. The interest rate that the firm must pay on debt is therefore higher by an amount sufficient to pay the bondholders' tax compared to what it would be if no taxes existed. This extra interest paid by the firm comes out of the stockholders' pockets. The net effect, so this ar-

Corporate taxes are not the only taxes to consider in determining financing mix.

gument goes, is that the taxes saved by shareholders due to deductibility of corporate interest are offset by the taxes paid by bondholders. An increase in debt by a firm would increase its after-tax cash flows, as indicated by Table 15–5. But this increase is offset by personal taxes paid by bondholders and stockholders (which are not shown in Table 15–5). In other words, while the *firm's* cash flows are altered by leverage, the net flows to *investors* are not. In the final analysis, when all taxes at all levels are taken into account, the use of debt by a firm provides no net tax benefit to its shareholders. The value of the firm, according to this argument, would be unaffected by changes in leverage, and V_L would always equal V_U.

The elimination of the favorable treatment of capital gains by the Tax Reform Act of 1986 reduced the personal tax advantage of equity. And, even prior to that, the weight of the evidence suggested that there is, on balance, some net tax benefit to the use of debt. It seems safe to bet, however, that the net benefit is less than that suggested by the corporate tax alone. To the extent that personal taxes do offset the corporate tax saving, the upper line in Figure 15–4 would rise less steeply.

Financial Distress

Figure 15–4 implies that the value of the firm continues to rise with leverage no matter how much is used and, therefore, that the firm should use as much debt as possible. We have considered the benefits of debt, but not the costs. Since EBIT is uncertain, there is always the possibility that it may drop too low to permit the firm to meet its contractual obligations. Thus, an increase in debt increases the probability of **financial distress.**

Financial distress — occurs when a firm has difficulty meeting contractual obligations to its creditors.

Financial distress is usually a matter of degree, with a declaration of **bankruptcy** the extreme form. Milder forms of financial distress occur when a firm's cash flows fall below expectations. In such a case, liquidity falls and the firm may have difficulty in meeting contractual obligations to its creditors. The costs of such financial distress are the modifications of investment and financing strategies made necessary by the distress condition. If a firm is forced to forgo desirable investments, significant opportunity costs may be incurred. Other costs may be incurred because of the inability of the distressed firm to negotiate effectively with suppliers, to ensure prompt delivery for customers, and to guarantee future availability of parts and service. During distress, creditors may restrict the firm's operations, thereby possibly reducing profitability. Dividend payments to shareholders also may be interrupted. Other kinds of opportunity costs may be incurred simply because of the diversion of management time from operating to financial matters.

Bankruptcy — a legal procedure for reorganizing or liquidating a firm that is in financial difficulty, carried out under the supervision of the courts.

Because EBIT may drop too low to permit a firm to meet its contractual obligations, an increase in debt increases the probability of financial distress.

Firms often encounter conditions of financial distress — sometimes mild, sometimes not so mild. Bankruptcy involves legal action and occurs much less often. Bankruptcy costs include costs of accountants, lawyers, and lost time of managers overseeing the bankruptcy proceedings. Even more important may be the opportunity costs of lost output resulting from underutilization of the firm's labor, management, and physical plant during the bankruptcy proceedings. Losses may be incurred on sale of assets under distress conditions. There also may be psychological costs in the minds of investors, creditors, and managers. There has been little research on the magnitude of costs associated with bankruptcy, but it seems rea-

The costs associated with bankruptcy may be significant in relation to the value of the firm.

sonable to suppose that they may be significant in relation to the value of the firm. Certainly, the consequences of bankruptcy are significant in the minds of the firm's managers.

In addition to costs incurred under conditions of distress, the use of debt may involve other opportunity costs that are more subtle but no less important. One of the important conclusions of this analysis is that the optimal amount of debt depends on the firm's operating risk and, therefore, on the nature of its business. Any use of debt, therefore, reduces a firm's flexibility to alter its commercial strategy in the direction of higher risk. Consider, for example, a firm contemplating a new venture that promises high returns but also involves high risk. If the firm's preexisting capital structure included a level of debt that would be imprudent if the new venture were undertaken, three options would be available. The firm could:

> The optimal amount of debt depends on the firm's operating risk and, therefore, on the nature of its business.

1. alter the capital structure,
2. undertake the new venture and operate with too much debt, or
3. forgo the new venture.

Each of these options has its costs. Taking such costs into account is difficult because the need to alter the commercial strategy may not be foreseen at the time the debt policy must be set. Nevertheless, the reduction in the firm's commercial flexibility must be counted as a cost of using debt.

Leverage and Value

We can conclude that debt has both benefits and costs. The benefits arise from the deductibility of interest payments, and the costs arise from the possibility of financial distress and reduced commercial flexibility. Choosing the appropriate debt level therefore involves a trade-off.

> As leverage increases, the firm reaches a point where the expected costs of financial distress and reduced flexibility begin to outweigh the benefits of the tax subsidy. At that point, the value of the firm stops rising with leverage, and the optimal debt/equity ratio has been reached.

Pushing debt beyond the optimal point would result in a decline in value. We can represent the relationships graphically as in Figure 15–5 (p. 466), in which D^* represents the optimal debt level for the firm. This debt level would correspond to an optimal debt/equity ratio, D/E^*, for financing the firm's operations.

Another important consideration is the possible loss of tax credits in bankruptcy. If a firm goes bankrupt, tax credits arising from losses normally cannot be recovered from the government, unless the firm merges with another firm or manages to carry the tax credits forward after bankruptcy. Thus, higher debt levels reduce the firm's tax liability during periods when profits are earned, but at the same time increase the likelihood of losing tax benefits during other periods if the firm goes bankrupt. These offsetting effects reduce the value of the tax subsidy below the theoretical maximum of DT in Equation (2) and cause the value of the firm to decline at high levels of debt, as depicted in Figure 15–5.

From the preceding discussion, we can conclude that theories explaining the relationship between leverage and firm value are not yet completely developed. A number of important factors have been identified, but their relative importance is not yet perfectly understood. The exact size of the tax subsidy is open to considerable question. Nevertheless, enough is known to suggest that the relationship be-

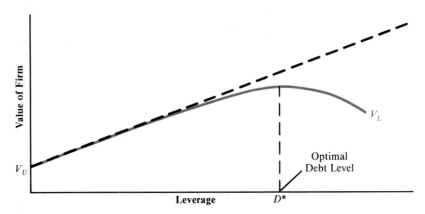

Figure 15–5
Leverage and Firm Value

The value of a firm rises with leverage up to a point and then declines.

tween leverage and value is more or less as depicted in Figure 15–5. The value of the firm rises with leverage up to a point, and then begins to decline.

Figure 15–5 suggests that managers should, in practice, be careful in choosing their financial policies concerning financial leverage. By judicious use of debt, the firm may be able to create extra value for shareholders. Thought of another way, judicious choice of financing mix can lower investors' overall weighted-average required return (*WARR*) for supplying capital to the firm. For a given set of future operating cash flows, lower return requirements translate into higher values. Before talking about the practical aspects of using the insights from Figure 15–5, we need to discuss briefly some additional factors, other than tax effects and costs of financial distress, that also play roles in understanding debt policy.

Other Considerations in Using Debt

A full understanding of debt policies requires consideration of factors that are not fully reflected in the trade-off shown in Figure 15–5. These include issuance costs (especially for smaller firms), considerations of voting control, agency relationships, and possible differences in information. These factors in a sense all represent deviations from the ideal frictionless-market assumptions that we used earlier in discussing the tax benefits of debt financing.

Issuance and Financing Costs

In our discussion so far we have assumed that the corporation has easy and low-cost access to sources of debt and equity capital. Financing sources are considered low in cost if the cost of issuing the debt or equity is relatively minor in proportion to the funds raised. This assumption is usually valid in the case of larger firms

International Focus

The Euroequity Market

Traditionally, when a company wanted to raise money by selling shares of its common stock, it did so in its home country. For example, U.S. companies sold new shares in New York and British companies sold shares in London. Now there is another alternative—the Euroequity market.

A Euroequity issue is a new share issue by a company outside its home-country exchange. While many Euroequity issues are made by U.S. companies in Europe, the name would also apply if a British firm issued shares in the United States. A Euroequity issue in New York by a British firm means that the firm is receiving new funds directly from American buyers. In 1987 alone, there were over $17 billion worth of Euroequity issues—more than three times the volume in 1984.

The growth of the Euroequity market for new issues has been made possible by the huge expansion of investor interest in owning foreign stocks. This has been further spurred by lifting of foreign-exchange controls in such countries as Japan and Britain.

The largest single trading place for international shares is London, where the estimated daily volume in trading such international shares often exceeds the trading in British shares. In the United States many foreign shares are traded in the form of American Depository Receipts (ADRs). Trading in these ADRs is estimated to run about 5 percent of total New York Stock Exchange volume. And on some days the single most actively traded issue on the American exchanges has been an ADR such as that of British companies Jaguar, Glaxo, and ICI.

The major investors in international shares are large pension funds seeking to diversify their portfolios internationally. While many funds still don't buy such foreign shares, they are likely to do so in the future. This represents another source of growth for global equity markets.

Source: Adapted from "International Shares Go Down—But Not Out," *The Economist,* December 26, 1987, pp. 75–76.

---

raising large amounts of debt or equity. Debt either may be sold directly in public financial markets (as in the case of a bond issue) or may come in the form of a loan from a financial intermediary, such as a bank. New equity funds may come from the sale of new stock or the retention of profits.

For smaller firms, however, access to public markets for debt and equity is typically quite expensive. As an alternative, they rely more heavily on financial intermediaries as sources of funding. As we discussed in Chapter 2, such intermediaries include commercial banks, insurance companies, and savings-and-loan associations.

Consider what would happen if a small or little-known firm needed to raise $1 million worth of external funds. If it tried to issue stock or bonds for this amount in public financial markets, the process would probably be very expensive because it would require a substantial amount of information processing and credit analysis by hundreds or even thousands of different individuals. On the other

Financing costs are another motive for using debt: for many firms, especially small firms, debt raised via financial intermediaries is much cheaper than debt or equity raised via public financial markets.

hand, a commercial bank could perform this credit analysis and information-processing function — a major role of a financial intermediary — on behalf of all these individuals at much lower costs. By law, however, commercial banks can provide only debt financing to firms. As a result, for smaller firms, use of debt through a commercial bank may have added advantages over equity that are not captured in Figure 15–5. Commercial banks are primary suppliers of funds to smaller firms.

Larger firms also often find that debt obtained from financial intermediaries has certain advantages. By dealing with a financial intermediary, the firm raises the required funds conveniently in a single transaction and avoids some of the legal procedures, filings, and disclosure of information that come with public sales of securities. We will have more to say on these issues in Chapter 20.

Voting Control

In large, publicly held firms, stock ownership is typically dispersed among a wide array of individuals and institutions (such as pension funds). In such cases, no unified group of shareholders has voting control (50 percent or more) of the company and hence is in a position to dictate the future membership of the corporation's board of directors and its choice of management. In such instances, sale of new shares of stock typically has no appreciable effect on the concentration of voting control.

Voting control is sometimes an important issue in financing decisions.

In some circumstances, however, issuance of new stock to raise funds may have important implications for control of the company. A prime example is the family-owned firm that is usually a relatively small enterprise, at least relative to major multibillion-dollar corporations. If such a firm were to raise large amounts of money by new equity sales, the original family owners (assuming they don't have the money to buy the newly issued stock too!) may eventually lose control of a majority of the voting shares. This dispersion of shares exposes them to the possibility that some other individual could buy up more than 50 percent of the stock and effectively take control of the company. This takeover could result in dramatic shifts in both corporate strategy and personnel. While these kinds of developments are not necessarily bad, the family owners may be reluctant to expose themselves to such prospects for change. Such a company would have a preference for issuing debt rather than equity if new funds are needed. Such debt does not give up any voting rights to its owners.

Agency Relationships

Sometimes the interests of managers and shareholders diverge.

We have noted at many points throughout this book that management's job is to act as agent of the stockholders. Unfortunately, this agency relationship is not costless, for sometimes situations arise in which the interests of managers and stockholders diverge. Conflicts can also arise between stockholders and bondholders. Sometimes these problems emerge because managers are unable to reveal full information to bondholders and stockholders regarding the firm's prospects without at the same time giving competitors an advantage. The limited liability of stockholders can motivate them to press for projects more risky than either the bondholders or the managers desire to undertake. Hired managers sometimes are known to allocate to themselves benefits in the form of salaries and *perquisites,* such as country-club memberships, travel, or company cars, over and above what they would allocate if they were the sole owners of the enterprise.

Agency costs — costs arising from the separation of ownership and management by the hiring of professional managers.

Collectively, these costs arising from the separation of ownership and management by the hiring of professional managers are known as **agency costs.** Some agency costs result from the use of debt in the capital structure, but others would exist whether debt were used or not. Because of the potential for conflict, stockholders and bondholders monitor and control the firm's activities by means of required reporting and covenants in agreements. All such arrangements involve some costs.

Competitive markets and innovative financing techniques help reduce agency costs but cannot eliminate them completely. Those agency costs that remain must be counted as another cost of doing business. Those related to the use of debt must be included along with the costs of financial distress in evaluating the wisdom of alternative debt policies.

Differences in Information

Managers who are making the financial decisions may well possess some inside knowledge about the firm's prospects — information not yet reflected in market prices. In such a case, a manager may well feel that the company's stock is not properly priced in the market. For example, if the manager knows about a new technology the company has developed, but the news has not yet become public, he or she may feel the current stock price is undervalued because the financial market has not yet placed a value on the technology. The manager may be reluctant to issue stock because it will allow new shareholders to buy into the company at a relatively low price, thus depriving existing shareholders of the full-value gains when the market finally does give value to the technology. What is a manager to do in such a situation?

Full disclosure is important in financing decisions.

Our first advice is that, whenever possible, managers should communicate information to financial-market participants so that their firm's securities will be fairly valued. In Chapter 20, we will discuss such communication policy in detail. But suppose for competitive reasons such information cannot be disclosed fully. One solution is for managers to avoid equity financing and use debt. Thus, one motive for using debt is simply to gain the advantage of financial leverage that accrues to shareholders if things turn out well. If management is convinced that operating returns on assets in the future will exceed the interest rate on debt, the use of debt makes sense. In addition, management's willingness to take on debt may actually signal to the market that the firm does have a bright future. Such a signal through use of debt may therefore increase firm value.

The wisdom of this kind of "betting on the future" must be considered carefully. Any time debt is used, there is the prospect for higher returns to shareholders if operating results are good. But if operating results are not good, shareholders will suffer. Managers who bet on the future should do so only if they have a much better idea of the odds of winning than the market does. While this knowledge of odds may come with inside information, managers must be careful not to underestimate the potential risks to shareholders. Large doses of debt can threaten the very existence of the company if economic conditions turn sour.

Practical Implications

As we have seen, there are a number of motives for borrowing by firms. One motive is to capture the tax benefits of deductibility of interest. Just how large these benefits are to shareholders after personal taxes is open to some question. Firms may also use debt when the sale of stock may dilute existing control of the firm or involve large issuance costs.

Even if there were no tax benefit at all, many firms would borrow for other reasons. Firms with access to either debt or equity through the public markets might choose to borrow in order to exploit the effects of financial leverage. Firms that cannot economically raise equity choose debt because it is the only economical source of external funds.

Much of the material in this chapter is conceptual and theoretical. What guidance can it provide to decision makers in practice? Does an understanding of the effects of leverage on returns, risk, and value tell managers whether to use debt and, if so, how much? The answer is no, for our understanding of many of the key relationships is not sufficiently developed to permit exact quantitative application. The theory does, however, provide a useful way of thinking about the relationships and yields insights and qualitative guidance that are valuable.

One motive for using debt is to gain the advantage of financial leverage if things turn out well.

One conclusion that emerges is that it is useful to consider debt in terms of its impact on firm value rather than only on earnings. By using value as the framework, we focus on what counts most to shareholders. Shareholders receive their return in the form of dividends and stock-price appreciation, not earnings per share. The valuation framework makes clear the fact that excessive use of debt can lower stock price and thereby reduce returns to shareholders, even though expected earnings per share may increase.

Should the effects of leverage on earnings be ignored? They should not, because earnings figures, such as EPS, are important and closely watched indicators of performance. Investors usually do not have access to projections of future earnings and cash flows and must rely heavily on historical data. In evaluating financing alternatives, management should analyze carefully the impact of each alternative on EPS and on *coverage* (how large the company's earnings are in relation to fixed charges, such as interest payments). Useful techniques for such analysis are the EBIT/EPS chart and coverage ratios that we will discuss in the next chapter. If the alternative to be picked has an adverse impact on near-term EPS, management should communicate carefully and completely to investors the reasons why a plan that adversely affects near-term earnings is nonetheless best in the long run.

Finance in Practice 15—2

The Billion Dollar Club

Corporate Issuer	Stock Offering (billions of dollars)	Year
AT&T	3.263	1981–83
Consolidated Rail	1.645	1987
Henley Group	1.190	1986
Coca-Cola Enterprises	1.178	1986
Occidental Petroleum	1.157	1987
Citicorp	1.000 est.	1987

Source: Fortune, September 14, 1987.

On August 19, 1987, Citicorp announced plans to make a worldwide offering of 17 million new shares of common stock in September. With that decision, Citicorp joined the "Billion Dollar Club," a select group of only five other firms that had raised a billion dollars or more of common stock in a single offering. The list is headed by AT&T, whose $3.3 billion offering in 1983 still holds the record.

The day before the August 19 announcement, Citicorp stock closed at $65 ⅝, slightly below its high for the year of $68 ¼. Along with the general market, the stock had climbed from about $50 throughout the spring to its summer peak. The new issue came out on September 21 at $58 ¼ per share. A total of 20 million shares were sold, 15 million in the United States, 1.5 million in Canada, and 3.5 million in international equity markets. Citicorp raised about $1.1 billion of new equity in the offering.

In retrospect, Citi's timing was exquisite. The market as a whole had dropped about 7 percent between the August 19 announcement and the September 21 offering date. The market continued to slide during September and October, culminating in the "Crash of '87" on October 19. After the dust had settled, Citicorp stock was trading at about $40 dollars per share. Citi had indeed done well to sell the new issue at $58 before the Crash. Four of the other six firms in the Billion Dollar Club likewise had sold stock during the great bull market of 1986–87 (see chart).

Sources: "Citicorp to Issue About $1 Billion of Common," *Wall Street Journal,* August 19, 1987; Offering Announcement, *Wall Street Journal,* September 21, 1987; "The Never-Sleeping Precedent Setter," *Fortune,* September 14, 1987.

The optimal debt/equity mix depends on the nature of the business and, therefore, on the kinds of investments that the firm makes.

The valuation analysis indicates that the optimal financing mix depends on the risk of bankruptcy and financial distress. The risk of bankruptcy and financial distress depends to an important extent on the *operating risk,* or business risk, of the firm. Thus, the optimal debt/equity mix depends on the nature of the business and, therefore, on the kinds of investments the firm makes. The more risky the firm's investments — that is, the higher its operating risk — the less debt it should use.

When the firm maintains a more or less stable commercial strategy and remains in the industry in which it historically has operated, it probably will routinely invest in projects covering a wide spectrum of risk. In such cases, high-risk and

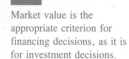
Market value is the appropriate criterion for financing decisions, as it is for investment decisions.

low-risk projects may average out over time and leave the overall operating risk of the firm and, therefore, its optimal debt/equity mix unchanged. Where a series of investments does have a cumulative effect on the firm's overall operating risk, the optimal debt/equity mix may change enough so that a revision in the actual debt/equity mix may become desirable.

Because the optimal debt/equity mix depends critically on operating risk, it is clear that the optimal mix is not static but is likely to vary, perhaps widely, over time. A debt level considered prudent one day may suddenly become too high.

Market value is the appropriate criterion for financing decisions, as it is for investment decisions. In this chapter, we have used the valuation criterion to provide qualitative guidance and a way of thinking about capital-structure decisions. We will turn to the difficult task of applying these concepts in the next chapter.

KEY CONCEPTS

1. Financial leverage increases the return to equity if return on assets exceeds the interest rate.

2. Financial leverage magnifies the variability of operating income and thereby increases the riskiness of the return to equity.

3. As financial leverage increases, risk increases, and the return required by equity holders increases.

4. Earnings per share is useful as a performance measure but not as a criterion for financing decisions because it does not take risk into account.

5. Financial leverage affects the value of the firm because the tax-deductibility of interest acts as a subsidy to the firm.

6. Offsetting the tax benefits of debt are the costs of financial distress, agency problems, and reduced flexibility. In principle, an optimal debt level exists beyond which the tax benefits of additional debt are outweighed by its costs.

SUMMARY

Financial leverage refers to the mix of debt and equity funds used to finance a firm's activities. Financial leverage affects both the magnitude and the variability of earnings per share (EPS) and return on equity (ROE). For any given level of operating return (EBIT), the effect of an increase in leverage is favorable if the percentage rate of operating return on assets is greater than the interest cost of debt and is unfavorable if the rate of operating return is less than the interest cost of debt. When EBIT varies over time, financial leverage magnifies the variation in EPS and ROE. Variability of EPS and ROE, therefore, stems from two factors: the variability of EBIT (operating risk) and the degree of financial

leverage employed (financial risk). Thus, in general, the use of financial leverage increases both the expected return to shareholders and the variability of that return and presents the financial manager with the fundamental trade-off between return and risk: more return if things go well, less return if things go poorly.

To analyze financing alternatives, a decision criterion is needed that takes into account both sides of the risk/return trade-off. Earnings per share, while very useful as a performance measure, is not satisfactory as a decision criterion because it considers only return and ignores risk. As decision criteria, ROE and cost suffer from the same shortcoming.

The criterion that does deal with the future and with both sides of the risk/return trade-off is the market-value criterion.

Financial leverage affects the value of the firm in several ways. Because interest on debt is tax-deductible, an increase in leverage reduces the firm's tax liability and thereby increases the share of EBIT going to debt and equity owners. At the same time, increased leverage reduces commercial flexibility and increases the probability of financial distress. Choosing the appropriate level of debt requires a trade-off among these opposing factors. The opti-mal debt level is that which maximizes the total value of the firm, equity and debt together. A critical determinant of the optimal debt level is the degree of operating risk inherent in the firm's commercial strategy.

The effect of personal taxes may negate some of the benefit of the tax-deductibility of interest to the firm. Motives for borrowing — other than tax bene-fits — include exploiting the favorable effect of fi-nancial leverage and reducing total financing costs by using debt supplied by financial intermediaries.

QUESTIONS

*Indicates more challenging questions.

1. Explain the distinction between financial lever-age and operating leverage.

2. How does financial leverage affect earnings after taxes, earnings per share, and percentage return on equity?

3. How does financial leverage affect the variabil-ity of dollar returns?

4. Why does the presence of financial leverage re-sult in lower earnings per share and lower re-turn on equity when EBIT falls to low levels?

5. Why is earnings per share unsuitable as a crite-rion for financing decisions?

6. Why is using financial leverage a risk/return trade-off?

* 7. Distinguish between accounting return on equity and return to shareholders. Can you think of an action that increases return on equity but simul-taneously reduces return to shareholders?

* 8. What is the cost of debt funds? What is the cost of equity funds? How are the costs of debt and equity funds related for a given firm?

* 9. Discuss the use of cost as a criterion for financ-ing decisions.

*10. In choosing between debt and equity, how should the relationship between the market value and the book value of a firm's stock be taken into account?

11. How does market value as a criterion deal with the risk/return trade-off in financing decisions?

12. How do financing decisions affect the division of EBIT going to the various claimants?

13. What effect does the tax-deductibility of interest have on the shares of EBIT going to the various claimants?

14. How can the use of debt increase the value of the firm?

15. If interest were not tax-deductible, what advan-tage would there be in using debt?

16. How is a firm's optimal debt/equity ratio related to its operating risk?

Problems

1. Mr. Bandy, President of Bandy Enterprises, re-cently attended a seminar on the benefits of fi-nancial leverage. Bandy Enterprises has assets of $2 million financed entirely with 100,000 shares

of common stock currently selling at $20 per share. Mr. Bandy is considering retiring some of the stock with borrowed funds, which he can obtain at an interest rate of 10 percent. He expects the company to earn $440,000 next year before interest and taxes. The company's tax rate is 50 percent.

a. What will be expected earnings per share (EPS) and return on equity (ROE) at next year's expected level of EBIT?

b. What would be the effect of increased leverage on expected EPS and ROE? Why?

c. Mr. Bandy is considering two alternative leverage ratios, 25 percent debt and 50 percent debt (percent debt to total assets). Calculate expected EPS and ROE for each of these debt ratios at next year's expected EBIT.

d. Mr. Bandy thought that, in a bad year, Bandy Enterprises' EBIT could fall as low as $100,000, and in a good year could rise as high as $750,000. He wondered what effect this might have at the leverage ratios he was considering. Calculate expected EPS and ROE at the low and high EBIT levels for debt ratios of 0 percent, 25 percent, and 50 percent, and compare the results with those of part (c).

e. Analyze the potential variability of EPS and ROE. Which option would you recommend to Mr. Bandy? Why?

2. Assume that a firm has a market value of $10 million if financed entirely with equity. Calculate the value of the firm if $1 million, $3 million, and $5 million in debt are used to replace equal amounts of equity. Assume a tax rate of 40 percent, and ignore the effects of personal taxes.

Would the value of the firm continue to increase as more debt is used to replace equity? Why or why not?

3. Assume a firm is considering expanding assets by $5 million and has determined that it can finance the expansion either through a bond issue carrying a 10 percent interest rate or through a new issue of common stock which can be sold to net the company $20 per share. The firm currently has 400,000 shares of stock outstanding and $6 million of bonds with an 8 percent coupon. The tax rate is 48 percent.

a. Calculate the earnings per share (EPS) for each alternative at EBIT levels of $1 million, $2 million, $3 million, and $4 million.

b. What can be said from this analysis regarding the choice between bonds and stock?

4. Suppose a firm used no debt and its value was $1,000. Now suppose the same firm issued $300 of debt with an interest rate of 10 percent. Assume this debt is perpetual, so it pays interest payments for the indefinite future. Also assume that interest is tax-deductible and the corporate tax rate is 40 percent.

a. What would be the value (debt plus equity) of the firm after the debt was issued if both personal taxes and any costs of financial distress were ignored? Explain.

b. What would be the value of the stock after the debt was issued?

c. Suppose the beta of the unlevered (no debt) firm's stock was 1.0. What would you expect to be true about the beta of the stock after the debt was issued? Give a written explanation.

REFERENCES

Asquith, P., and D. W. Mullins, Jr., "Equity Issues and Stock Price Dilution." Working paper, Harvard Business School (May 1983).

Beaver, W., and D. Morse, "What Determines Price-Earnings Ratios." *Financial Analysts Journal* (July–Aug. 1978): 65–76.

Bernea, A., R. A. Haugen, and L. W. Senbet, "Market Imperfections, Agency Problems and Capital Structure: A Review." *Financial Management* 10 (Summer 1981): 7–22.

Dearborn, D. C., and R. I. Levin, "Error Visibility as a Factor in Executive Performance." *Southern Journal of Business* 6 (Jan. 1972): 65–70.

Ezzell, J. R., and J. A. Miles, "Capital Project Analysis and the Debt Transaction Plan." *Journal of Financial Research* VI, no. 1, 25–31 (Spring 1983).

Fama, E. F., "Efficient Capital Markets: A Review of Theory and Empirical Work." *Journal of Finance* 25 (May 1970): 383–417.

Gritta, R. D., "The Effect of Financial Leverage on Air Carrier Earnings: A Break-Even Analysis." *Financial Management* 8 (Summer 1979): 53–60.

Jensen, M., and W. Meckling, "Theory of the Firm: Managerial Behavior, Agency Costs, and Ownership Structure." *Journal of Financial Economics* 2 (October 1976): 305–360.

Litzenberger, R. H., and H. B. Sosin, "A Comparison of Capital Structure Decisions of Regulated and Non-Regulated Firms." *Financial Management* 8 (Autumn 1979): 17–21.

Miller, M. H., "Debt and Taxes." *Journal of Finance* 32 (May 1977): 261–276.

Modigliani, F., and M. H. Miller, "Corporate Income Taxes and the Cost of Capital: A Correction." *American Economic Review* 53 (June 1963): 433–443.

Modigliani, F., and M. H. Miller, "The Cost of Capital, Corporation Finance, and the Theory of Investment." *American Economic Review* 48 (July 1958): 261–297.

Moyer, R. C., "Forecasting Financial Failure: A Reexamination." *Financial Management* 6 (Spring 1977): 9–17.

Pringle, J. J., "Price/Earnings Ratios, Earnings per Share, and Financial Management." *Financial Management* 2 (Spring, 1973): 34–40.

16

Choosing the Appropriate Debt Level

In this chapter, we will examine the choice of an appropriate debt level for a firm. We will first discuss key qualitative factors in setting debt policy before learning how to analyze alternative financing plans. We will explore the use of EBIT/EPS analysis, interest coverage ratios, and cash-flow analysis under recession conditions. Finally, we will tie our discussion to the firm's overall policy and commercial strategy.

In Chapter 15, we analyzed the effect of financial leverage on return and risk. We concluded that leverage has costs as well as benefits, and thus we found ourselves face to face with the basic question of the trade-off between risk and return. We turned to valuation as a criterion for resolving the trade-off question and found that it provided some useful insights and guidance. In particular, we identified certain factors as relevant to the leverage decision and eliminated some that are not. However, the guidance that we found was entirely qualitative, and we did not develop an approach to actually determining how much debt a firm should use.

Now it is time to apply the theory. Our problem is to determine the appropriate mix of debt and equity the firm should use. Let us keep in mind the motives for using debt. Some firms may find debt advantageous because of its tax benefits. Others may use debt to increase prospective returns to shareholders, recognizing that the price for the increase in prospective returns is increased risk. Still others may find debt obtained through financial intermediaries, such as banks, to be a less expensive and more convenient way to satisfy investment requirements. Some firms do not have access to equity markets, and, for them, debt is the only available source of outside capital. Whatever the motive, users of debt need a way to decide how much debt to use.

Tailoring Financing Mix to Commercial Strategy

We found in Chapter 15 that a firm's total risk, as measured by variability of earnings, depends partly on its operating risk and partly on the amount of financial leverage used. Operating risk can be measured in terms of variability of earnings before interest and taxes (EBIT). For any given operating risk, an increase in financial leverage increases the variability of net earnings. We concluded that the appropriate degree of financial leverage for a firm depends on its operating risk. The higher the operating risk, the less debt the firm should use. The same reasoning applies to individuals: the more variable or uncertain one's income is, the more risky it is to use debt.

The appropriate degree of financial leverage for a firm depends on its operating risk.

Understanding the relationship between leverage and variability still does not tell us how much leverage to use. At what point do the terms of the risk/return trade-off become unfavorable? To help resolve this question, we turned in Chapter 15 to our general criterion of value maximization. Because investors are risk-averse, value depends on both expected return and risk. Hence, in principle, we resolve the risk/return trade-off by pushing leverage to the point where the value of the firm is maximized.

The optimal debt ratio is achieved by trading off the benefits of debt against the expected costs of financial distress and reduced commercial flexibility.

We found that finding the optimal debt ratio requires trading off the benefits of debt (including tax-deductibility of interest and leverage effects) against the expected costs of financial distress, which includes a broad range of problems from relatively minor liquidity shortages all the way to the extreme case of bankruptcy. All these problems are assumed to involve some costs to the firm — the more serious the problem, the higher the cost. Such costs are borne by the shareholders up to the full amount of their investment; above that point, costs are borne by creditors. The expected cost of financial distress can be thought of as the magnitude of the cost times the likelihood (probability) of its being incurred.

Using valuation as a criterion for leverage policy clarifies the relationship between leverage and operating risk. At zero leverage, we start with some probability of encountering financial distress of one form or another. Increasing leverage increases that probability. Starting from zero leverage, the use of the first dollars of debt adds less to the expected costs of financial distress than it adds to benefits. Use of such debt provides a net benefit and increases the value of the firm. There comes a point, however, where the use of any additional debt will increase the expected costs of financial distress by *more* than it will increase the expected benefits of using this extra debt. At that point, the debt ratio is optimal. We can see that the extent to which leverage should be used depends on how high the firm's operating risk was to begin with.

> The appropriate debt ratio for a firm depends on the nature of its business. In other words, the financing mix and commercial strategy of a firm must support each other.

Theory tells us that the optimal debt ratio for a firm depends on its operating risk.

Although, in general, firms make their investment and financing plans jointly, in this chapter, for simplicity, we will take the firm's investment policy as given. The question is: given a set of investments, what is the appropriate mix of debt and equity for financing them? Financial theory gives valuable qualitative guidance but is quite difficult to apply quantitatively.

In this chapter, we will focus only on the appropriate mix of debt and equity. For now, we will draw no distinction between long-term and short-term debt; in order to determine the appropriate debt ratio, we will view all debt as the same.

Analyzing Financing Plans Using Accounting Data

Suppose a firm has decided to raise a given amount of money by issuing either common stock or bonds. How does it make the choice? We know from our earlier discussion that market value is the appropriate decision criterion, so our job is to find methods of analysis that will give some insights into effects on market value. Because investors often analyze the firm in terms of accounting data, we begin with an examination of the impact of alternative financing plans on earnings and other key indicators, such as interest coverage. Let us begin with earnings.

> With financial leverage, EPS becomes more sensitive to changes in EBIT.

EBIT/EPS Analysis

> EBIT/EPS analysis — an examination of the impact on earnings per share of a given financing alternative at different levels of earnings before interest and taxes.

Given the importance of earnings per share (EPS) as a measure of a firm's performance, analysis of the impact of financing alternatives on EPS is an important first step in analyzing financing plans. Because earnings before interest and taxes (EBIT) is uncertain, it is useful to examine the impact of financing alternatives at levels of EBIT. One technique for doing so is to perform an **EBIT/EPS analysis** and to diagram the results.

An **EBIT/EPS chart** is a graph of the relationship between operating outcomes (as measured by EBIT) and financial results to shareholders (as measured by EPS)

EBIT/EPS chart—a graph of the relationship between operating outcomes (as measured by earnings before interest and taxes) and financial results to shareholders (as measured by earnings per share) for a given financing alternative.

for a given financing plan. Such a chart provides a clear display of some of the merits of alternative financing plans.

Analyzing a Financing Alternative. Suppose a firm has decided to finance a $10 million expansion of its manufacturing facilities by issuing either common stock or bonds. Currently, the firm's stock is selling at $20 per share, and it has 2.5 million shares outstanding. Ignoring issue costs, the firm would have to issue 500,000 new shares if it were to raise the needed funds by means of a stock issue. The firm has no existing debt. Alternatively, the firm could issue 20-year bonds at 8 percent interest.

Let us assume that EBIT in the upcoming year is expected to be $6 million, including the earnings from the expanded facilities. However, EBIT in past years has been highly variable and could turn out to be considerably above or below the most likely level. Following the procedure used in the last chapter, we can calculate EPS at an EBIT of $6 million as in Table 16–1.

Our objective is to develop a chart that shows the behavior of EPS in response to variations in EBIT—that is, a chart that graphs EPS as a function of EBIT. Because EPS is PAT (profit after taxes) divided by the number of common shares, and because PAT is EBIT less interest and taxes (at a constant tax rate for practical purposes), EPS is a linear function of EBIT. There is one point on an EBIT/EPS line for each financing plan from Table 16–1. One more point on each line is all we need to draw the EBIT/EPS line. Often, it is convenient to pick as the second point the intercept of the EPS line and the EBIT axis. This point corresponds to the EBIT level required to produce EPS of zero. For the stock plan, EPS of zero requires that EBIT = 0. For the bond plan, EBIT of $800,000 is required to cover interest and, hence, produce EPS = 0. Now we have two points on each EBIT/EPS line and can plot the lines in Figure 16–1 on p. 480.

Table 16–1

Earnings Per Share (EPS) at the Expected Level of Earnings Before Interest and Taxes (EBIT) for Two Financing Alternatives

	Stock Plan	*Bond Plan*
EBIT	$6,000	$6,000
Interest	0	800
Profit before taxes	$6,000	$5,200
Tax at 50 percent	3,000	2,600
Profit after taxes	$3,000	$2,600
Shares	3,000	2,500
EPS	$ 1.00	$ 1.04

Figure 16–1
EBIT/EPS Analysis

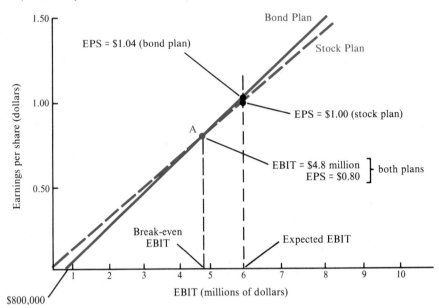

In Figure 16–1, we see that the break-even EBIT (point *A*) is just under $5 million (we will calculate it later as exactly $4.8 million). At that point, EPS is equal under the two plans. If EBIT turns out to be above $4.8 million, EPS will be higher under the bond plan. If EBIT turns out to be below $4.8 million, the stock plan produces higher EPS. The expected EBIT level of $6 million is above the break-even point.

Here we see in graphic form the effects of leverage that we found earlier. The slope of the bond line is steeper than that of the stock line, indicating that, with leverage, EPS is more sensitive to changes in EBIT. The steeper slope is advantageous if EBIT rises and disadvantageous if EBIT falls.

In our example above, we assumed for simplicity that the firm had no other debt outstanding. Often this is not the case. Where other debt is outstanding, the interest payments from that debt, if any, must be included. The old interest payments are added to the new, and the total is used to calculate the points necessary to plot the graphs. Note that old interest payments are made under both the stock financing and the bond financing alternatives when a firm already uses debt.

We also assumed that the firm had no preferred stock outstanding. The term *earnings per share* is interpreted as *earnings available to common stock* per share. If a firm did use preferred stock, in calculating EPS we would subtract any preferred-dividend requirement before dividing by the number of common shares.

EPS break-even level of EBIT—the level of earnings before interest and taxes that equates earnings per share for two financing alternatives.

Calculating Break-Even Points. Sometimes it is useful to calculate EPS break-even points algebraically. We know that EPS for the two plans are equal to each other at the break-even level of EBIT. To determine the **EPS break-even level of EBIT** under each plan, we set the EPS expressions equal to each other and solve for EBIT, as shown in Equation (1). If the firm has no existing debt prior to the financing plans being analyzed, under the stock plan interest payments will be zero.

$$EPS_{Bond\ Plan} = EPS_{Stock\ Plan}$$

$$\frac{(EBIT - I_B)\ (1 - T)}{N_B} = \frac{(EBIT - I_S)\ (1 - T)}{N_S} \tag{1}$$

where N_B = the number of shares of stock outstanding under the bond plan, N_S = the number of shares of stock outstanding under the stock plan, I_B = the firm's total interest payment under the bond plan, I_S = the interest payment under the stock plan, and T = the tax rate.

For our example, using a 50 percent tax rate, we can calculate the EPS break-even level of EBIT as:

$$\frac{(EBIT - \$800,000)\ (1 - 0.5)}{2,500,000} = \frac{(EBIT - 0)\ (1 - 0.5)}{3,000,000}$$

$$EBIT = \$4.8\ million\ .$$

Thus, at a level of EBIT of $4.8 million, EPS for the two plans are equal at $0.80 per share.

We should note again that if the firm had had other debt issues outstanding, interest and payments on those issues should be considered in calculating break-even points. In calculating the EPS break-even level of EBIT, old interest payments would be figured in on both sides of Equation (1). In addition, to simplify matters, we did not incorporate preferred stock in the equations. If preferred stock were outstanding, its dividend requirements would be subtracted before dividing by N_B and N_S.

Sample Problem 16–1
EBIT/EPS Analysis for the Franklin Corporation

The Franklin Corporation has decided to finance a $4 million expansion program by issuing either common stock or bonds. Currently, the firm has 200,000 shares outstanding and no long-term debt. Common stock can be sold to net $40 per share. The bond issue will be a 25-year issue at 12 percent interest with sinking-fund payments of $200,000 per year starting in year 5. Franklin's tax rate is 50 percent.

A. Assume that Franklin's EBIT next year is expected to be $1.5 million. Calculate the expected EPS next year for the two alternative financing plans.

B. Determine the EPS break-even EBIT level.

Solution

A. This type of problem is best attacked by constructing a table similar to Table 16–2, which shows the derivation of EPS for each alternative.

B. To determine the EPS break-even EBIT level, we can use Equation (1), after determining that $I_B = (0.12)\ (\$4,000,000) = \$480,000$, $N_B = 200,000$, $I_S = 0$, and $N_S = 200,000 + (\$4,000,000/\$40) = 200,000 + 100,000 = 300,000$ shares.

$$\frac{(\text{EBIT} - \$480,000)\ (1 - 0.5)}{200,000} = \frac{(\text{EBIT} - 0)\ (1 - 0.5)}{300,000}$$

$$\text{EBIT} = \$1,440,000.$$

Thus, the EPS break-even level of EBIT is $1,440,000. █████

Coverage Ratios

Another useful analytical technique for comparing financing alternatives is to calculate **interest coverage ratios.** The interest coverage ratio is the number of times interest payments are covered by EBIT and is calculated as shown in Equation (2):

$$\text{Interest coverage ratio} = \frac{\text{EBIT}}{I} \tag{2}$$

where I = the pretax interest payment.

For the bond alternative graphed in Figure 16–1, we can calculate coverage as:

$$\text{Interest coverage ratio} = \frac{\$6,000,000}{\$800,000} = 7.5.$$

What do coverage ratios tell us? They provide a measure of the safety of the interest payment or of whatever specific commitment is being considered. The

█████

Table 16–2

Derivation of Expected Earnings per Share (EPS) for Two Financing Alternatives Available to the Franklin Corporation

	Stock Plan	Debt Plan
Earnings before interest and taxes (EBIT)	$1,500,000	$1,500,000
Interest	—	480,000
Profit before tax	$1,500,000	$1,020,000
Tax at 50 percent	750,000	510,000
Profit after tax	$ 750,000	$ 510,000
Shares	300,000	200,000
EPS	$2.50	$2.55

greater the coverage, the more secure the payment. Thus, an interest coverage ratio of 7.5 tells us that EBIT must fall well short of its expected level of $6 million before the interest payment is in jeopardy.

Interest coverage ratios measure the size of the interest payment relative to EBIT.

The variability of EBIT points up a major shortcoming of coverage ratios in general. Which EBIT do we use to calculate coverage? In the example above, we calculated coverage at the expected (most likely) level of EBIT. To draw meaningful conclusions regarding the safety of various payments that the firm is committed to make would require some knowledge of the likelihood of a decline in EBIT to levels at which the payments are threatened. We can calculate coverage at several different levels of EBIT. If we could construct a probability distribution over all possible values of EBIT, we then would have a better sense of the adequacy of various coverage levels.

A major shortcoming of coverage ratios is that they are based on EBIT, which is variable.

Sample Problem 16–2
Coverage Ratios for the Franklin Corporation

Calculate coverage ratios for the debt financing being contemplated by Franklin Corporation in Sample Problem 16–1.

Solution

Using the data from Sample Problem 16–1 and Equation (2), we can calculate interest coverage as:

$$\text{EBIT}/I = \$1,500,000/\$480,000 = 3.125 \text{ times}.$$

Note that we have used Franklin's expected EBIT level of $1,500,000. Actual results could differ.

 International Focus

The Problem of Third-World Debt

During the 1970s and early 1980s, "third-world" countries borrowed billions of dollars from United States and other banks. "Third-world" is another name for less-developed countries, including countries in Latin America, Asia, and Africa. Some of the money was borrowed by private companies, some by

governments. By 1986, borrowers in these countries had run up big bills, as shown in the accompanying table.

Third World Debtors (billions of dollars)	
Brazil	108.0
Mexico	100.3
South Korea	51.6
Argentina	49.8
Indonesia	42.7
India	39.7
Egypt	36.8
Venezuela	35.3
Turkey	30.3

Source: Wall Street Journal, Jan. 9, 1987.

(continued)

By the early 1980s, many economists and bankers had begun to worry about the ability of the countries to repay the loans. Countries, like individuals and families, can repay external debt only by spending less than they earn, i.e., running a surplus, and using the difference to pay off the debt. The trouble was, most of these countries were running deficits. When they had difficulty meeting payments, the banks simply lent them the additional money to make the payments, a dubious practice. The loans got bigger and bigger.

In 1982, Mexico threw a big scare into the international markets by nearly defaulting on $82 billion in foreign debt. The creditors got together and "solved" the problem by "restructuring" the debt—a euphemism for extending maturities and lowering interest payments. In 1986, Mexico again got into serious difficulty, and the banks responded by lending an additional $6 billion. By that time, the U.S. government, banks around the world, and the debtor nations themselves knew they had a big problem. Brazil brought the problems to the international headlines in February 1987 by suspending interest payments on $67 billion in foreign debt. The total foreign debt of the 15 largest third-world debtors by that time added up to about $435 billion. Brazil headed the list with $78.6 billion, followed closely by Mexico with $76.3 billion. Of the $435 billion total, $86 billion was owed to banks in the United States.

Sometime in 1983 or 1984, a few banks, mostly in Europe, began to try to get some of the debt off their books by selling it. They found buyers, but at prices well below face value. The big banks, including those in the United States,

ignored these transactions and continued to carry the debt on their books at face value, but knowledgeable people knew that its true market value was far less. In October 1986, the *Wall Street Journal* carried an article in which it was estimated that the market value of the third-world loans ranged from 60 to 75 cents on the dollar for most countries, down to 24 cents per dollar for Peru's debt.

By May 1987, prices according to *Business Week* had dropped another 10 cents per dollar, to 58 cents for Mexican debt, 61 cents for Brazil, and 13 cents for Peru. Citibank, America's biggest bank, finally decided in May to recognize reality by adding $3 billion to its reserves for losses on third-world debt. It was fitting for Citibank to be the first bank to adopt a realistic stance because it had been one of the leaders in lending to third-world nations and it had the largest exposure, some $15 billion.

By November 1987, market prices had dropped to 37–41 cents per dollar for Brazil's debt, 48–52 for Mexico's, and 2–7 cents for Peru's. Just how the problems eventually would be resolved remained unclear. In late 1987, the banks and the debtor nations were working on a plan to swap some of the debt for equity. The details of this debt-for-equity swap and its full implications had not yet been fully worked out. One thing did seem clear, however: the dispassionate financial markets placed a low probability on the money ever being fully repaid.

Sources: Wall Street Journal, October 7, 1986, January 9, 1987, February 4, 1987, March 3, 1987, and November 16, 1987; "John Reed's Bold Stroke," *Fortune,* June 22, 1987; "The Citi Squeezes Its Lemons," *Business Week,* June 15, 1987.

Setting Debt Policy and Defining Debt Capacity

Now let us return to the policy question of choosing an appropriate debt policy. Our analysis of earnings and coverage outlined the nature of the risk/return trade-off facing the firm. If investors believe the firm has gone too far in its use of debt, they will judge that the prospective return was not enough to compensate for the added risk, and we would expect the market value of the firm to fall. While useful, our analysis so far still leaves unanswered questions. Even if we had a probability distribution over all possible EBIT levels, could we say how much coverage is enough? Can we examine the EBIT/EPS chart in Figure 16–1 and decide which plan is best? We cannot, because to say that one plan is best requires an unambiguous criterion on which to make the comparison. EBIT/EPS analysis and coverage ratios are very useful in making explicit the impact of leverage on EPS and on the firm's ability to meet its commitments at various levels of EBIT. However, we still face the risk/return trade-off: should we accept greater risk in order to gain a higher expected return?

One approach to the problem of setting debt policy is to rely on industry standards. ABC Corporation might calculate the equity or debt ratios for other firms in its industry and set its own ratio equal to the industry average. The logic of the use of industry standards is that debt ratios appropriate for other firms in a similar line of business should be appropriate for ABC Corporation as well. Also, this approach ensures that ABC Corporation appears to lenders and investors to be right in line with industry averages.

To illustrate, suppose ABC Corporation was an integrated oil company. ABC Corporation management might gather the data listed in Table 16–3. The difficulty with the use of industry standards in this way is that it relies on the judgment of others. Can we be sure the managements of the other firms in the industry will not err? Also, in many cases, there may be no well-defined industry — that is, no group of firms whose structure and commercial strategy are similar enough to provide a good comparison. Industry standards, when available, certainly provide a useful benchmark. If a firm is out of line, it should know the reasons why and be satisfied that they are good reasons. But a comparison with industry standards should be the final step, not the beginning point in the analysis.

Another approach to setting debt policy is to seek the opinion of lenders and investment bankers. ABC Corporation might ask the advice of investment-banking firms, who regularly participate in marketing debt issues, and of institutional

One approach to setting debt policy is to rely on industry standards.

Table 16–3
Ratio of Equity to Total Assets for Selected Oil Companies, December 31, 1985

	Total Assets (milions of dollars)	Stockholders' Equity (millions of dollars)	Equity Ratio (percent)
Exxon	69,160	36,238	52.40
Mobil Oil	41,752	14,689	33.74
Texaco	37,703	15,253	40.46
Chevron	38,899	15,554	39.99
Sunoco	12,923	6,065	46.93
		Average	**42.70**

Source: Moody's Industrial Manual, 1986.

buyers of debt issues, such as insurance companies. Commercial banks may provide useful advice. Investment rating services, such as Moody's Investors Service or Standard & Poor's Corporation, also might be helpful. A firm whose debt has already been rated by such services might be able to draw some inferences from the ratings themselves. If more recent debt issues were rated lower than older issues, indicating a rise in risk, the firm might view this trend as an indication of having pushed its debt far enough.

The opinions of prospective lenders are likely to be very useful, but if the firm relies on them too heavily, it runs the risk of answering the wrong question. The firm may learn how much the lenders would like to lend — or the maximum that the lenders would be willing to lend. But just because lenders are willing to lend does not mean the firm should take them up on it. Lenders err also — many firms have encountered serious difficulties because of using too much debt, with once-willing lenders a party to the arrangement. The responsibility for debt policy belongs to management, and the central question is how much debt should be used, not how much the lenders are willing to lend.

The notion that there is some absolute dollar ceiling on the amount lenders will lend is vague. In practice, such a ceiling may exist. In principle, the amount lenders will lend should depend on the interest rate the firm is prepared to pay. By paying a sufficiently high rate, a firm should be able to induce lenders to lend well beyond the debt ratio that is optimal for shareholders.

Debt Capacity and Cash Flows

A firm's **debt capacity,** then, should be defined as the optimal amount of debt from the standpoint of shareholders, which is the amount of debt the firm *should* use and not necessarily the maximum that lenders will lend.

Defining debt capacity as optimal debt provides a useful framework for analyzing policy options. For example, sometimes it is suggested that the use of leases to finance assets increases the firm's total debt capacity because the leases do not appear on the balance sheet. Here, debt capacity refers to the willingness of lenders to lend. Even if lenders were fooled by the leases, which is doubtful, should the firm borrow more just because the lenders are willing? In many cases, it should not. If we analyze the leasing decision in the context of the theory of optimal financial leverage, we will conclude that leases are quite similar to debt. Therefore, the use of leases does not necessarily increase the optimal debt ratio — the total that the firm should use. Hence, by viewing debt capacity and optimal debt as one and the same, we are able to analyze the leasing decision more effectively.

To determine a firm's debt capacity, then, requires a method of evaluating the effect of different debt policies on the firm's risk of financial distress. This evaluation will provide an operational way to link our debt-policy decisions to the valuation framework we outlined in the last chapter. There we saw how the benefits of debt were traded off against the costs of financial distress. We can develop such a method for looking at the risk of financial distress by looking at cash flows. As we will see later, for purposes of understanding the risks of financial distress, the use of cash-flow analysis has major advantages over analysis of accounting numbers, such as earnings or coverage ratios.

To simplify matters, let us ignore milder financial difficulties for the moment and consider only the risk of bankruptcy. The principal factor in avoiding bankruptcy is maintaining the ability to meet contractual interest and principal payments that must be made in cash. Hence, it is more useful to view debt capacity in terms of cash flows than in terms of balance-sheet ratios of debt to equity or accrual-accounting estimates of earnings per share. This point becomes all the more clear when we consider that just knowing the principal amount of debt tells us nothing about the repayment schedule and the firm's ability to meet it.

For example, suppose we see that a firm has $1 million in long-term debt outstanding and an equity base of $4 million. The debt/equity ratio is 0.25 — not an alarming figure at first glance. But the principal may be due in 2 years or in 20 years. Clearly, maturity makes a big difference to the firm's ability to meet the payments.

Suppose we find that repayment is to be made over 4 years. We now know a good deal more than before but still not everything we need to know. Consider the repayment schedules listed in Table 16–4, assuming interest at 12 percent. From this table, we see that even knowing the amount of debt and the maturity does not tell us whether the firm can meet the payments. The firm's ability to meet its payments depends on the total payments required — interest and principal — in relation to the cash flow available to meet them. In Table 16–4, we see only three of an infinite number of possible repayment schedules. It is clear that the cash flow required to service a given amount of debt can cover a wide range. Conversely, a given cash flow can service widely varying principal amounts of debt, depending on the repayment schedule.

The repayment schedule on the firm's debt is only half of the picture. We also must examine the firm's ability to meet the schedule. Normally, principal and interest payments are met out of cash flows from operations. During emergencies, however, other sources are available. Marketable securities held for liquidity purposes might be sold, or cash may be drawn down. Other current assets, such as inventories and receivables, might be reduced, and current liabilities might be increased. Certain discretionary expenditures might be reduced or postponed, such as those for capital improvements, dividends, or research and development.

To determine the impact of alternative debt policies on the risk of bankruptcy requires a careful analysis of how the firm's cash flows might be affected by adverse developments in the future.

Table 16–4

Alternative Repayment Schedules for $1 Million over 4 Years at 12 Percent (thousands of dollars)

Year	A: Principal at Maturity			B: Equal Annual Payments			C: Principal in Equal Installments		
	Interest	Principal	Total	Interest	Principal	Total	Interest	Principal	Total
1	120	—	120	120	209	329	120	250	370
2	120	—	120	95	234	329	90	250	340
3	120	—	120	67	262	329	60	250	310
4	120	1,000	1,120	35	294	329	30	250	280

Cash-flow analysis (of debt capacity)—the comparison of cash-flow patterns under adverse, or recession, conditions at various levels of leverage in order to determine the level of debt that will allow the firm to meet its contractual obligations in a recession.

The best way to explain how **cash-flow analysis** works is to examine a specific example. Because many variables are involved, cash-flow projections can be tedious, but the procedures are essential to good financial planning.

In the following section, the effects of alternative debt policies on the risk of bankruptcy are analyzed in terms of specific numbers. The risk of bankruptcy, however, is not the only consideration in setting debt policy. The optimal debt policy also provides for a reserve for contingencies and commercial flexibility. We will consider these latter factors in a separate section following the basic cash-flow analysis.

Finance in Practice 16–1

A Survey of Financing Policies

How do managers actually go about setting financial policies? How is financial leverage measured? How do managers choose the right amount of financial leverage?

In response to a survey, 212 large U.S. corporations provided some answers to these questions. To measure financial leverage, most financial managers look at balance-sheet figures (for example, debt/equity ratios) and income-statement figures (for example, times-interest-earned ratios). The accompanying Table A shows the basic types of leverage measures used by the companies responding to the survey.

Perhaps more interesting were the managers' perceptions of the benefits of using financial leverage and the factors that shape their financing policies. The vast majority of managers (well over 90 percent) thought that the value of the firm could be increased by using leverage but that, after some point, using too much leverage

Table A

Type of Measure	Companies (percent)
Balance sheet only	17
Income statement only	0
Both types of measures	80
Other	2
Total	100

would reduce the value of the firm. As a result, managers think it is important to pick an appropriate amount of debt. In selecting the amount, about 87 percent of the respondents explicitly stated that their firm used the notion of a debt capacity of the firm—a maximum amount of borrowing. The firms wanted to use financial leverage, but not too much.

The firms also revealed the types of influences that shaped their financial policies. The accompanying Table B shows the rankings given by managers of various influences on their choice of a target financial structure.

As the responses show, managers are actively engaged in choosing target financial policies and subscribe to the concept of an optimal capital structure.

Source: Adapted from D. F. Scott and D. J. Johnson, "Financing Policies and Practices in Large Corporations," *Financial Management,* Summer 1982, pp. 51–58.

Table B

Type of Influence	Ranked as Most Important Influence (percent)	Ranked as Second Most Important Influence (percent)
Internal management and staff analysts	85	7
Investment bankers	3	39
Commercial bankers	0	9
Trade creditors	1	0
Security analysts	1	4
Comparative industry ratios	3	23
Other	7	18
Total	100	100

Analyzing Cash Flows

To illustrate the approach of using cash-flow analysis to analyze debt capacity, let us consider a specific example. The time is late 1988, and Reliance Manufacturing Corporation is reviewing its financial structure. Currently, Reliance's ratio of debt to total capital (debt plus equity) is 35 percent. Management is concerned that the current debt ratio may be too high.

Management knows that, when times are good, debt is no problem. It is when business is bad that debt becomes burdensome or even dangerous. Management wants to analyze the company's cash flows under recession conditions.

Reliance manufactures a variety of industrial products. Its sales are moderately sensitive to the business cycle. During the early 1980s, Reliance had a very good year in 1981, then suffered a decline in sales in the 1982 recession, and experienced a sharp recovery in 1983. The company made a profit in each year during the recession, but experienced cash-flow problems in 1983 due to large capital outlays needed for a new manufacturing facility and working-capital requirements to support the 1983 sales recovery.

Recession Behavior

Reliance management did not consider the behavior of company sales during the 1982 recession to be typical. A study of company data revealed that, in previous recessions, sales volume usually declined for two years in a row, then recovered in the third year. Total declines ranged from 12 percent to 16 percent. For purposes of establishing debt capacity, management decided to err on the side of conservatism and to assume that the effect of a recession on sales could last a year longer, with recovery only in the fourth year, and that the total decline could reach 20 percent.

In prior recessions, prices of some of Reliance's products had fallen somewhat, but the declines had not been significant. To be conservative, however, management decided to assume that prices of products would decline by 3 percent and recover in year 4. Prices of all cost elements were assumed to remain constant.

Reliance management was now ready to prepare forecasts of the cash flows under recession conditions. It was decided to group cash flows into four categories: operating cash flows, plant-and-equipment expenditures, working capital, and financing flows.

Projections for these categories were made by management and are shown in Table 16–5. The cash flow from operations reflects the decline in sales and prices discussed earlier. Plant-and-equipment expenditures normally ran about $10 million per year. If a recession hit, management's plan was to cut P&E to $3 million per year, considered the absolute minimum required level. However, because of the long-term nature of construction and equipment contracts, there would be a time lag in implementing the cuts, and the $3 million level could be reached only by the third year of the recession. Assuming recovery from the recession in year 4, P&E would be restored to $7 million, and to the normal $10 million thereafter. P&E expenditures under these assumptions are given in Table 16–5.

The company made a detailed projection of working-capital flows under recession conditions. Marketable securities would be sold and balances drawn down to

Cash flows in debt-capacity analysis can usefully be grouped into four categories: operating cash flows, investment cash flows, working-capital flows, and financing flows.

Table 16–5

Reliance Manufacturing Corporation Cash-Flow Projections Under Recession Conditions

	Year Prior 0	(millions of dollars)			
		Recession Year ⟶			
		1	2	3	4
Sources					
Cash flow from operations	24.9	19.8	13.8	15.6	24.9
Uses					
Plant-and-equipment expenditures	−10.0	−10.0	−5.0	−3.0	−7.0
Additions to working capital	−1.5	−0.4	0.8	−1.5	−6.4
Financial flows*	−12.3	−11.5	−10.8	−11.1	−11.5
Total Uses	−23.8	−21.9	−15.0	−15.6	−24.9
Change in Cash Balance					
Year-by-year change	1.1	−2.1	−1.2	0.0	0.0
Cumulative change	1.1	−1.0	−2.2	−2.2	−2.2

*Financial flows include lease payments, interest on debt, principal on debt, dividends, and taxes.

absolute minimum levels at commercial banks. Receivables and inventories first would rise, then fall as sales declined, then rise again during recovery from the recession. Accounts payable would also vary considerably. Management made detailed projections of each of these items and combined them to get the overall projection for working capital shown in Table 16–5.

Financial flows include lease payments, interest and principal on debt, dividends on common stock, and taxes. Lease payments and debt service are contractual and must be maintained, whereas dividends are discretionary. Although discretionary, dividends were viewed by Reliance management as being very high priority. The total projection for financing flows in Table 16–5 assumes that dividends are maintained at their current level.

Although discretionary, dividends should be viewed as having high priority.

Changes in Cash Balance

The final two lines in Table 16–5 show the effect of a recession on Reliance's cash position. As shown on the line labeled "year-by-year change," the company runs a deficit of −$2.1 million in year 1 and −$1.2 million in year 2, then breaks even in years 3 and 4. On a cumulative basis, the company is $1 million in the hole at the end of year 1, and $2.2 million at the end of year 2. The cash balance is graphed in Figure 16–2.

Figure 16–2
Reliance Manufacturing Corporation Change in Cash Balance During a Recession

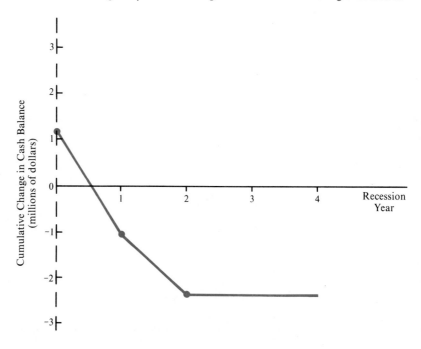

Since the projections already take into account all possible reductions in cash balances and other assets, the results in Table 16–5 mean that the company probably cannot make it through a serious recession without changing something. What should be changed? There are two obvious possibilities: dividend payout and the debt ratio. The company has been paying $3 million a year in dividends on its common stock. Table 16–5 indicates that the company probably could make it through the recession if it cut its total dividend by $1 million beginning in year 1 of the recession. If it then maintained the dividend at the reduced level, it would save a total of $4 million over the four years.

If management did not wish to be forced into a dividend cut in a recession, debt would have to be reduced. This would reduce the financial flows for interest and principal. To analyze this possibility, management repeated the cash-flow analysis with debt at 20 percent rather than the present 35 percent. The results indicated that, at a debt level of 20 percent, the company could maintain its dividend during a recession.

Conclusions of the Cash-Flow Analysis

Recessions sometimes are difficult to diagnose in their very early stages, and hard to forecast.

Recessions sometimes are difficult to diagnose in their very early stages and are even more difficult to forecast. Reliance management would probably not have sufficient evidence to implement its recession plan until well into year 1. At that point, sales would be declining and action would be taken to cut back expenses. Action also would be taken to cut back the capital-expenditure program in the manner described earlier.

Reliance management had established a dividend policy that treats dividends as a long-run residual and sets the dollar payout to be non-decreasing.[1] The dollar payout was set at a level that was thought to give a high probability of avoiding subsequent cuts, although it was recognized that circumstances could arise in which cuts clearly might become necessary. During temporary difficulties, management was willing to postpone, though not to forgo, certain types of capital-investment projects. Management had decided not to rely on temporary short-term borrowing to maintain either the capital-investment program or the dividend during adverse financial circumstances. While management had no objection to such a policy, there was always a possibility that short-term funds would not be available during a recession. Basing policy on an assumption that short-term borrowing would be possible, therefore, seemed unwise.

One should not assume that short-term borrowing will always be possible.

The alternative debt policies then were evaluated in light of these and other policies. With the current capital structure of 35 percent debt, we saw from Table 16–5 that Reliance could not survive the recession without cutting the dividend on common stock. If the dividend is to be maintained, debt must be reduced to about 20 percent.

What can we conclude from the analysis? Which policies are safe and which are not? By asking this question, we can see some of the limitations of financial theory when the practical realities of the world are considered. The current policy

---

[1]The concept of treating dividends as a long-run residual is discussed in Chapter 17.

permits Reliance to survive the recession, provided management is willing to cut the dividend during the recession. The choice is clear: the higher debt level (35 percent) provides higher returns during normal times (because of the additional leverage and tax benefits) but would force management to make a painful decision (cutting the dividend) during a recession. The lower debt level eliminates the problem of the dividend cut in a bad year, but produces lower returns in normal years. The risk/return tradeoff is ever-present.

Does the cash-flow analysis tell management which choice to make? Clearly it does not. It does tell management what will happen under each alternative. The decision must be made by management. That is what they are paid to do.

Advantages of Cash-Flow Analysis. Compared to EBIT/EPS analysis and coverage ratios, cash-flow analysis provides a number of additional insights for the critical task of setting debt policy.

First, cash-flow analysis focuses on the **solvency** of the firm during *adverse* circumstances rather than on the effects of leverage under *normal* circumstances. Cash-flow analysis also considers balance-sheet changes and other cash flows that do not appear in the income statement (such as capital expenditures), whereas EBIT/EPS and coverage analysis do not. Cash-flow analysis also gives an *inventory of financial reserves* available in the event of recession.

Cash-flow analysis identifies discretionary cash flows and develops a plan of action in advance. Nothing precludes the development of such a plan in connection with EBIT/EPS analysis, but cash-flow analysis views the problem over several years, whereas EBIT/EPS and coverage analysis normally consider only a single year.

Cash-flow analysis is consistent with financial theory. The theory of optimal financial leverage tells us that debt should be used up to the point at which its benefits are outweighed by the expected cost of financial distress and reduced commercial flexibility. Cash-flow analysis evaluates the risk of financial distress. We will consider the factors omitted by cash-flow analysis in the next section.

Cash-flow analysis also has its weaknesses. The analysis may give an illusion of precision that is not justified on the basis of the underlying information. In an uncertain world, the numbers may not capture all the relevant factors. Cash-flow analysis, as we have described it here, considers an economic recession as the main source of uncertainty. What about technological developments, or shifts in consumer preferences, or political changes? The cash-flow procedure can be adapted to include factors of this sort. The main point is that recessions are not the only source of economic unhappiness.

Allowing for Reserve Borrowing Capacity

As noted earlier, the theory developed in Chapter 15 tells us that the optimal debt level includes a reserve for contingencies and commercial flexibility. The cash-flow analysis outlined above does not include these factors, mainly because they are very difficult to quantify.

Solvency — the ability to pay all legal debts.

Compared to EBIT/EPS analysis and coverage ratios, cash-flow analysis yields additional insights to setting debt policy.

The cash-flow procedure can be adapted to include factors of uncertainty other than recessions.

The optimal debt level includes a reserve for contingencies and commercial flexibility, which should be allowed for when examining the cash-flow analysis.

Reserve for Contingencies. Cash-flow analysis tells us approximately how much debt a firm can use without running a significant risk of bankruptcy. Should we assume that the risk of bankruptcy is constant through time? We should not. We noted earlier that, in an uncertain world, there are factors in addition to investment policy that can change a firm's operating risk.

A good case can be made, therefore, for backing away from the maximum safe debt level indicated by the cash-flow analysis. By such a reduction, the firm obtains a margin to allow for error and for changes over time and a cushion to provide flexibility to deal with problems that cannot be foreseen.

Inflation provides further reason for caution. In the cash-flow analysis, cash flows are estimated in nominal terms, with the effects of inflation included. Considerable uncertainty may exist, however, about the future rate of inflation. Even though the earlier cash-flow estimate is a best guess, uncertainty regarding the rate of inflation suggests that we should back away still further from the point of maximum debt indicated by the cash-flow analysis.

Maintaining Flexibility for Commercial Strategy. Another reason for operating below the maximum safe debt level is to preserve operating flexibility. A debt policy that might force a firm subsequently to make an undesirable change in its commercial strategy or to forgo a desirable change would be costly. An aggressive debt policy might look good at one point, but later—because of changes in technology that make products obsolete or because of rapid increases in the prices of key inputs—that same policy might threaten the firm's existence. Faced with such a situation, a firm might find it necessary to forgo investments it would otherwise have made or to alter its strategy in other important ways. Similarly, a firm faced with unexpected and attractive new opportunities might wish to alter its commercial strategy to take advantage of them. If it is unable to do so because of a debt policy adopted earlier, the opportunity cost could be high.

Considerations such as these suggest a cautious approach to debt policy that leaves room for operating flexibility. In the long run, firms succeed primarily because of their commercial strategies rather than because of debt/equity or dividend policies. Management should avoid too much emphasis on the right-hand side of the balance sheet and not lose sight of the fact that successful commercial strategy comes first and that financing policies play a supporting role.

To preserve operating flexibility, the firm should operate with leverage which is below the maximum safe debt level.

In the long run, firms succeed primarily because of their commercial strategies rather than because of debt/equity or dividend policies.

Choosing the Appropriate Debt Policy

How much should a firm back away from the maximum safe debt level indicated by cash-flow analysis because of factors discussed above? We cannot be precise in answering this question, because the answer requires far more knowledge of the costs of financial distress and reduced flexibility than we have at present. Our theories provide qualitative guidance, and we can answer some questions with cash-flow analysis, but the final decision is a subjective one.

The concept of a reserve for contingencies is especially relevant to firms whose operating risk is especially high because of size or technology or length of experience. In many cases, the optimal debt ratio may well be zero.

Finance in Practice 16–2

Notable Examples of Leveraged Buyouts

During the 1980s, one of the most interesting of a number of new developments in finance was the *leveraged buyout* — a transaction in which a firm is purchased using borrowed funds, with the firm's own assets or stock pledged as collateral to secure the loan and with the firm's own cash flows used to pay it off. The buyers often are the firm's own top management, sometimes acting in concert with venture capitalists. The technique has been used to purchase privately held companies from their former owner(s) as well as to purchase publicly held companies and thereby "take them private." Using the leveraged buyout, a group of individuals can purchase a sizable company without putting up very much of their own capital, sometimes none at all. The trick is to use the firm itself to secure the debt.

For example, suppose four members of the top management of a manufacturer of desk calendars decided to purchase the company from its long-time owner. The owner decided to retire and sell the company, and rather than see it sold to outsiders, members of management decided to purchase it themselves. The owner asked $10 million, with at least $8 million in cash. The four prospective buyers, all of whom had been with the company for many years as members of management, between them raised $250,000 of their own money. Where was the remaining $9.75 million to come from?

The answer, as the term *leveraged buyout* implies, was debt. The former owner agreed to take a *seller's note* for $2 million. A large bank agreed to lend $3 million in the form of a term loan. The remainder came from a venture capitalist, who agreed to put up the $4.75 million in the form of debt, with part of it convertible into common stock.

Working out all the details of the seniority and other arrangements among the various suppliers of funds was very complicated. For purposes of our present discussion of financial leverage, the main point is that a small group of people bought a $10 million company with $250,000 in equity and $9.75 million in debt.

The company just described was privately owned. A recent example of a buyout of a public company is the buyout of the Beatrice Company, a large food and consumer-products company based in Chicago. The total purchase price was $6.2 billion, making it at the time the largest leveraged buyout ever proposed. This time the buyers were former members of Beatrice management, acting in concert with the firm of Kohlberg Kravis Roberts & Company, a New York investment partnership specializing in leveraged buyouts. Kohlberg Kravis played the role of the investment venture capitalist in this transaction. Beatrice was a public company that was taken private by means of a leveraged buyout. During 1985, there were a number of other well-known firms taken private, among them Storer Communications, Levi Strauss & Company, Northwest Industries, Uniroyal, Inc., and Scovill, Inc. A name familiar to many is that of R. H. Macy & Company, the nation's tenth largest retailer and sponsor of New York City's annual Thanksgiving Day parade. A group of Macy executives proposed in October 1985 to buy the firm in a transaction valued at $3.58 billion.

The buyouts we have just discussed involve members of management and venture capitalists as buyers. Another interesting class of leveraged buyout during the 1980s were buyouts by employees. These nearly always involved the use of Employee Stock Ownership Plans (ESOPs), under which substantial tax incentives are made available to encourage employee ownership of stock. ESOPs have been encouraged by legislation beginning in the early 1970s as a way to improve worker morale, increase productivity, and improve labor/management relations. The largest employee buyout as of 1985 was that of Blue Bell, Inc., a North Carolina textile manufacturer with sales of $1.2 billion and 25,000 employees. Other well-known companies purchased by their employees were Rath Packing in 1982 and Weirton Steel, a division of National Steel, in 1982.

Leveraged buyouts are interesting and exciting transactions, especially to the buyers. Some of the numbers are very large. Very large companies can be bought with relatively small equity bases, and therein lies the focus of our interest in this chapter that discusses how far to go with the use of financial leverage. Most leveraged buyouts appear to go *much* further than would seem prudent following the guidelines discussed in this chapter. In explanation, two points are important: first, leveraged buyouts are attempted only with companies that meet special criteria, such as low debt to begin with, very stable operating cash flows, profit margins sufficient to finance growth internally with funds left over to service the new

debt, and assets for use as collateral. It is very unlikely that anyone could get financing to do a leveraged buyout of a high-growth, high-risk company. Second, the fact is that the transactions indeed are risky and go well beyond the risk levels that would be acceptable in typical situations. The operating risk of the firms is low, but once all the new debt is put in place, the residual cash flow available for equity holders is very risky indeed. The new owners in fact are taking a big gamble.

Leveraged buyouts on the scale of those occurring during the 1980s are a new phenomenon. Have they exceeded the bounds of prudence and gone too far in the use of debt? Some would say yes, and as noted earlier, they go much further in the use of debt than conventional wisdom suggests is prudent. Time will tell, and as of the time of this writing, the test — namely, the next recession — has not yet come. One can only wish the owners and lenders good fortune and recommend hard work to keep those operating cash flows coming in.

Sources: J. K. Butters *et al.* "Harrington Corporation," *Case Problems in Finance,* 8th ed. (Homewood, Ill.: R. D. Irwin, 1981); articles on Beatrice Corporation buyout, *Wall Street Journal,* November 15, October 17, October 18, October 21, and October 22, 1985; "Firms Have Two Avenues for Going Private," *Wall Street Journal,* August 12, 1985.

Leveraged buyout— a transaction in which a firm is purchased using borrowed funds, with the firm's own assets or stock pledged as collateral to secure the loan and with the firm's own cash flows used to pay off the loan.

Finance in Practice 16–1 looks at how financial managers of 212 firms make their decisions about debt policy. Finance in Practice 16–2 examines the 1980s phenomenon of the **leveraged buyout** and its relationship to setting debt policy. When a firm uses debt, it takes more risk in hopes of earning higher future returns. Debt has advantages, but to go too far in exploiting them can be costly. The use of debt represents essentially a gamble that the benefits of debt will exceed the costs. Such bets should be placed with caution.

KEY CONCEPTS

1. Financing mix should be tailored to commercial strategy. The higher the operating risk, the less debt the firm should use.

2. EBIT/EPS analysis is very useful for analyzing the impact of alternative financing plans on earnings.

3. Coverage ratios, which measure the margin of safety by which earnings and cash flows cover debt service, are useful in measuring risk.

4. Debt capacity is best defined as the optimal level of debt for the firm from the perspective of shareholders — not as how much lenders are willing to lend.

5. A useful approach to determining the appropriate debt level in practice is to analyze the firm's cash flows under conditions of recession.

6. Good financial planning requires that some reserve borrowing capacity be maintained to allow for contingencies and to provide operating flexibility.

SUMMARY

In planning its financial structure, the first major policy decision facing the firm is that of determining the appropriate level of debt. For some firms, the decision involves a choice between long-term debt and equity. Firms without access to the public equity markets also must decide how much debt they prudently should use.

The choice of an appropriate debt policy involves a trade-off between benefits and costs of financial leverage. The optimal debt level depends to an important extent on the firm's operating risk. The greater the operating risk, the less debt the firm should use. Therefore, a firm's financing policy should be tailored to its commercial strategy.

Alternative financing plans should be analyzed along several dimensions. EBIT/EPS analysis is useful for evaluating the sensitivity of earnings per share (EPS) to changes in EBIT. EPS break-even levels of EBIT can be calculated to determine the EBIT level at which EPS for two alternative plans is equal. Coverage ratios provide a measure of the security of interest payments. None of these measures, however, tells the firm how far it should go in using

debt. The firm's debt capacity is best defined, not as the maximum amount that lenders are willing to lend, but as the amount of debt that is optimal for shareholders.

A determination of debt capacity requires an analysis of the likelihood of financial distress, which depends on the firm's ability to meet its financial obligations. Analysis of cash flows expected under adverse conditions (for example, recession or loss of market due to a change in technology) provides information about the effects of alternative financing plans on the risk of insolvency. Cash-flow analysis considers balance-sheet changes as well as operating flows, provides an inventory of financial reserves, and outlines a plan of action in the event of recession. However, cash-flow analysis does not automatically provide a reserve for contingencies and commercial flexibility. In setting debt policy, a firm should allow for these factors by backing away from the maximum safe debt level indicated by cash-flow analysis. Determining the appropriate amount of such reserve borrowing capacity is largely a matter of subjective judgment.

QUESTIONS

1. What are the principal determinants of a firm's operating risk?

2. Discuss the relationship between the optimal financial structure of a firm and its commercial strategy.

3. Should short-term debt be considered in determining the optimal level of debt?

4. How should a firm's debt capacity be defined?

5. What can be said about a firm's exposure to the risk of financial distress, knowing only the total level of debt (principal amount) in its financial structure?

6. What information is provided by a complete analysis of cash flows that normally is not provided by EBIT/EPS or coverage analysis?

7. Should a firm extend its debt level to the point indicated as safe by a cash-flow analysis?

Problems

*Indicates more challenging problems.

1. Utilize the information in problem (3) in Chapter 15 to construct an EBIT/EPS chart. Use graph paper. Which financing alternative would you recommend? Why?

2. Utilize the information given in problem (3) in Chapter 15 to calculate the EPS break-even point using Equation (1) of this chapter. (Hint: Be sure to include old interest payments.)

3. The current balance sheet for Rafferty Corporation shows $10 million of 8 percent bonds and $7.2 million of $4.00 par-value common stock. Total current sales of $45.5 million per year are to the United States Navy on a 10-year contract. The Air Force has offered a similar 10-year contract for $13.0 million per year. The company has accepted the new contract and now must raise $7.5 million from external sources in order to expand its production facilities. The financing could be accomplished through a debt issue carrying a 13 percent coupon rate or by selling shares of common stock to net the company $6.25 per share. EBIT is 3.3 percent of sales and the tax rate is 45 percent.

a. Calculate the EPS break-even level of EBIT — that is, the level of EBIT at which the EPS-figures for the two financing alternatives are equal.

b. Analyze the coverage ratios for Rafferty Corporation under each of the two financing alternatives. What conclusions can you draw?

*4. The Bengston Corporation has undertaken a five-year plant-expansion program, which will require $5 million in external capital in year 1 and $6 million in year 2. The company has several alternative financing plans available to it to meet its financing needs. Plan A is to issue $11 million in new common stock in year 1. Plan B is to issue $5 million in new common stock in year 1 and $6 million in 25-year bonds in year 2. Plan C is to issue $5 million in 20-year bonds in year 1 and $6 million in stock in year 2. Currently, the firm has 500,000 shares of stock outstanding and $3 million of 6 percent bonds. The new bond issues in year 1 or year 2 will carry 12 percent interest. Bengston's EBIT this year (year 0) was $3.5 million. Management expects EBIT to grow 10 percent annually over the next 10 years. New common stock can be issued now to net $50 per share.

Table A

Hill Brothers, Balance Sheet, December 31, 1988			
(thousands of dollars)			
Current assets	3,200	Current liabilities	2,850
Net plant & equip.	5,320	Long-term debt	2,000
Other	480	Total liabilities	4,850
		Equity	
		Common stock — 200,000	
		shares at $1 par	200
		Additional paid-in	
		capital	2,800
		Retained earnings	1,150
Total assets	9,000	Total liab. and equity	9,000

Table B

Hills Brothers, Income Statement, 1988 *(thousands of dollars)*	
Sales	2,030
Cost of goods sold	1,624
Gross margin	406
Interest*	165
Profit before tax	281
Tax at 48%	135
Profit after tax	146

*Long-term debt was $2,125,000 at the beginning of 1988. A sinking-fund payment of $125,000 was made on June 30, 1988. Interest for the year, therefore, is [($2,125,000 + 2,000,000)/2] × 0.08 = $165,000.

a. Calculate the EPS at the end of year 2 and at the end of year 6 for each of the financing alternatives. Assume that stock can be issued at the beginning of year 2 to net $50 per share. Also assume a 50 percent tax rate.

b. Calculate the EPS break-even point for plan A compared with plan B for the end of year 2.

c. Analyze the coverage ratios under each of the three plans at the end of year 2.

d. Which alternative would you recommend? What factors do you consider important in making these recommendations?

5. As a new financial analyst for Hill Brothers, Inc., you have been asked to help evaluate the alternative financing plans for the corporation's expansion program. The firm's balance sheet and income statement as of December 31, 1988 (in thousands of dollars) are summarized in Tables A and B. One alternative financing plan is a new stock issue of $4 million. Stock can be issued to net $25 per share. The other alternative is a 20-year, 9 percent, $4 million bond issue.

a. The company has maintained a 50-cent annual dividend in the past and wishes to continue this annual dividend payment regardless of the financing plan chosen. What level of EBIT would be required in the first year in order to cover interest and dividend payments? (Hint: Start with net income and work up to EBIT.)

b. Calculate EPS break-even points for the bond plan compared with the stock plan for year 1.

c. Suppose Hill Brothers expects the EBIT level in year 1 to be $1,033,000 with a two-thirds probability that it will be between $833,000 and $1,233,000. Which financing alternative would you recommend and why?

REFERENCES

Donaldson, G. *Corporate Debt Capacity*. Boston, Mass.: Division of Research, Harvard Business School, 1961.

Donaldson, G. *Strategy for Financial Mobility*. Homewood, Ill.: Richard D. Irwin, 1971.

Moyer, R. C., "Forecasting Financial Failure: A Reexamination." *Financial Management* 6 (Spring 1977): 9–17.

Pringle, J. J., "Price/Earnings Ratios, Earnings per Share, and Financial Management." *Financial Management* 2 (Spring 1973): 34–40.

17

Dividend Policy

In this chapter we address the important issue of dividend policy. We will first discuss the underlying theories and concepts of dividend policy to learn how dividends affect the value of the firm. We will explore the effects of taxes, financial friction, and information, followed by a discussion of the linkages between dividends, investment decisions, debt levels, and external financing. We will learn how to set a firm's dividend-payout ratio in practice. Finally, we will explore some of the procedural and legal questions in connection with paying dividends.

In the last two chapters, we examined financial-leverage policy—the choice of debt versus equity in financing a corporation. There we saw that, used prudently, some debt financing can increase the value of the firm and that managers should strive to pick the amount of leverage that will maximize the value of the firm. Now we focus our attention on the equity financing of a corporation from internal sources, with particular emphasis on the issue of dividend policy.

In addition to making investment decisions and planning the firm's financial structure, a firm's management has a decision to make about dividend policy—whether the earnings of the firm should be retained for reinvestment in the firm or paid out to shareholders. The earnings belong entirely to the owners, but if retained they can be invested in future projects. If paid out in dividends, the funds are unavailable for investment inside the firm. If paid out immediately, the current return or yield to investors is increased; if retained and invested profitably, future returns to stockholders are increased. The dividend decision basically is a decision between return now and larger expected returns later. In public corporations, stockholders hire managers to make this decision in their behalf. In this chapter, we will consider only dividends on common stock because preferred dividends are stipulated and fixed in amount.

The dividend decision is a choice between return now versus larger expected returns later.

Finance in Practice 17–1

How Important Are Dividends?

Financial managers attempt to maximize the value of the firm to shareholders. Such shareholder value is determined in financial markets and is based on shareholders' expectations of future dividends and of increases in share price (capital gains). Basic questions for financial managers are: How do stock prices react to dividends? If increasing current dividends will reduce the dividends per share shareholders expect to receive in the future, how should financial managers evaluate whether such an increase in dividends is good or bad?

In fact, one of the most controversial topics in finance is the issue of the effect of dividends on stock prices. Many argue that most investors prefer the security of dividends to the vague prospect of future capital gains. Many corporations seem to feel that the best way to win favor with the financial markets is to increase dividends every year.

Some companies go to great lengths to avoid skipping or even cutting a dividend. Both Ford and General Motors, for example, continued to pay dividends in 1980 despite record losses. A number of other companies on *Fortune*'s list of the 500 largest U.S. firms, including Republic Steel and Weyerhaeuser Corporation, also continued to pay dividends during 1980 while incurring losses.

Over recent years a number of studies by financial economists have raised questions about the wisdom of the apparent preoccupation with dividends on the part of corporate treasurers. As long as a firm can reinvest internally at rates of return higher than those available to investors outside in the financial markets, the firm should retain the funds and reinvest them—or so goes the argument.

Data from the 1981 *Fortune* 500 (*Fortune* magazine's list of the 500 largest firms) provide some ammunition to those who argue that some firms give too much emphasis to dividends. The accompanying Table A gives total-return figures for 12 firms from the *Fortune* list that paid no dividends during the period 1971–1980. Out of these 12 firms, 4 rank in the top 20 in terms of total return to shareholders, and 8 are above the median.

The accompanying Table B lists 19 companies from the 1981 *Fortune* 500 that had the opposite experience: they increased their dividends every year during the period 1971–1980, yet still experienced a decline in stock price over the period. To take one example, Avon Products increased its dividend at an average rate of 10 percent per year over the period, yet its stock price fell more than 60 percent. Coca-Cola's dividends grew at 11.8 percent per year, but its stock price fell 21 percent. The median return

for the group of 19 firms in Table B was 1.2 percent, versus 9.4 percent for the *Fortune* 500 as a whole. These 19 firms represent the extreme cases among the group of companies that followed a policy of steady dividend increases. Of the 500 companies on the *Fortune* list, a total of 115 raised their dividends each year during 1971–1980; the median return of this group of 115 was 10.7 percent, slightly above that of the *Fortune* 500 as a whole. As the experience over the decade of the 1970s shows, increases in dividends certainly do not guarantee good returns for shareholders.

The academic studies of the topic, along with data such as that from *Fortune,* do raise the question of whether dividends are as important a factor in stock prices as some believe. Certainly, the data in Tables A and B demonstrate that dividends are not necessary for high returns to shareholders.

Source: "Fresh Evidence That Dividends Don't Matter," *Fortune,* May 4, 1981, pp. 351–54. Copyright ©1981 by *Fortune* Magazine. Reprinted by permission.

Table A

Firms That Paid No Dividends, 1971–1980	Total Return to Investors, 1971–80	
	Annual Average, Compounded (percent)	Rank among Other Fortune 500 Firms
NVE	41.7	2
National Semiconductor*	33.3	7
Teledyne*	32.2	9
Tosco*	28.9	17
Data General*	25.3	34
Penn Central	19.9	78
Digital Equipment*	17.4	98
Lockheed	13.9	143
Median for 500	9.4	
LTV	6.9	284
Crown Cork & Seal	4.6	342
DPF*	(5.7)	451
Memorex*	(13.9)	463

*Company has never paid a cash dividend.

Table B

Firms That Increased Their Dividends, 1971–1980	Average Annual Rate of Growth in Cash Dividends Compounded, 1971–80 (percent)	Decline in Stock Price, 1970–80 (percent)	Total Return to Investors, 1970–80	
			Annual Average Compounded (percent)	Rank among Other Fortune 500 Firms
Burroughs	26.6	(1.4)	1.2	398
Brunswick	24.7	(17.3)	1.3	396
Economics Laboratory	16.7	(13.2)	0.8	404
Jim Walter	16.3	(16.4)	1.9	386
Georgia-Pacific	14.0	(4.1)	2.4	381
Nashua	13.5	(16.8)	1.5	392
Coca-Cola	11.8	(21.2)	1.0	402
Brockway Glass	10.4	(36.4)	0.7	411
Avon Products	10.0	(61.4)	(5.2)	449
Colgate-Palmolive	9.9	(8.1)	3.0	375
Quaker Oats	9.0	(6.4)	2.9	376
Warner-Lambert	8.7	(41.2)	(1.8)	432
ITT	8.5	(40.7)	0.5	413
Owens-Illinois	8.4	(10.5)	3.3	370
Champion Spark Plug	8.0	(11.5)	4.2	350
Heublein	7.7	(38.3)	(1.3)	428
National Service Industries	7.3	(9.3)	5.0	324
Sybron	6.8	(45.4)	(1.7)	431
Squibb	4.9	(17.9)	0.8	405

How Dividends Affect Firm Value

We use the value of the firm as the criterion for financial-management decisions and as the yardstick to judge those decisions.

Throughout this book our basic organizing framework has been *valuation*. We use the value of the firm as the criterion for financial-management decisions as well as the yardstick against which we judge those decisions. We found in our earlier discussions that investment decisions affect value; indeed, it is through its investment decisions that a firm creates value and thus benefits its shareholders. We found that financing (debt versus equity) decisions also affect value, primarily because of the tax-deductibility of interest payments on debt.

What about dividend decisions? Can a firm make itself more valuable by manipulating the proportion of earnings paid out? Because this question is a complex one, let us attack it by first assuming away many of the complexities in order to understand the underlying relationships. Later, we will add back the complexities.

Financial friction — the cost of financial transactions, such as commissions on trading stocks and bonds, flotation costs, and the time and effort spent to analyze information concerning investment decisions.

Assumptions That Simplify the Analysis

Taxes often complicate matters, so we will begin by assuming them away. We will assume there is no **financial friction** — costs involved in financial transactions,

Information effects — the change in stock price that results from the market's knowledge that the dividend is to change.

such as commissions on the trading of stocks and bonds by investors, flotation (issue) costs on new issues of stocks and bonds by firms, and the time and effort by investors to gather and analyze information necessary to make decisions regarding their investments. Let us also assume that dividend decisions have no **information effects** — that is, that investors draw no inferences from dividend decisions regarding the firm's earning prospects, investment opportunities, or debt/equity policy. We will come back to information effects shortly.

In our simplified world of no taxes, friction, or information effects, shareholders would be indifferent between dividends and capital gains. Shareholders would wish the firm to undertake all attractive investment opportunities — defined as projects with positive net present values. Such attractive opportunities promise returns greater than those available to investors outside the firm. Hence, the shareholder prefers to forgo a dividend now in order to receive a larger dividend in the future, larger by more than enough to compensate for time and risk.

If internal funds were insufficient to finance all attractive projects, the firm would issue new securities, incurring no issue costs in the process. In the opposite case, when internal funds were more than adequate to undertake all attractive projects, the excess would be paid out to shareholders as dividends. In this case, payout would be preferable to retention because the firm, having exhausted all attractive investment opportunities, could invest the remaining funds only at rates below what shareholders themselves could earn outside. Note that under our assumptions, no costs are incurred in paying the dividend. If the firm erred and paid out too much, it would simply issue new securities to get the funds back. It would incur no costs in this process either.

In our simple taxless and frictionless world, the firm treats dividends as a residual. Investment policy is king because the firm creates value through its investment decisions. Each year, the firm undertakes all attractive investments, issuing new securities if necessary in order to finance them. Where earnings and investment opportunities vary from year to year, as they do in practice, the firm's dividend would also be highly variable from year to year. Such variations would cause no discomfort to investors in our hypothetical world, because they could alter their investment portfolios as often as they wish at no cost to themselves in either time or money. If they were dissatisfied with a particular firm's dividend payout, they would simply sell its shares and buy those of another firm whose policy is more to their liking.

In a simplified world of no taxes, friction, or information effects, shareholders would be indifferent between dividends and capital gains, and the firm would treat dividends as a residual.

Dividend policy in a simplified world is straightforward: pay out what funds are left after making all attractive investments. In practice, taxes, friction, and information effects do exist. The purpose of trying to analyze the problem in the absence of factors known to exist is to isolate these factors as the ones that matter.

Before leaving our hypothetical world, let us point out that at the time a dividend is paid, we would expect the price of a share to fall by exactly the amount of the dividend. For example, suppose a shareholder pays $60 for a share of stock that is going to pay a $10-per-share dividend immediately. In essence, the shareholder is paying $50 for any ownership benefits the stock will produce after the $10 dividend payment, and paying $10 for the dividend. Immediately after the dividend payment, the shareholder has a stock worth only $50 — the value of the future benefits of stock ownership. The shareholder still has $60 of value ($10 in hand from the dividend and $50 worth of stock), but the stock price has dropped from $60 to $50. Hence, when we say that dividend policy does not affect firm value in our hypothetical world, strictly speaking we mean that it does not affect shareholder wealth. We will have more to say later in this chapter about the price behavior of common stock upon payment of a dividend.

Taxes

Let us now reintroduce taxes in our analysis of dividend policy. Here, we will focus on the *personal* taxes paid by investors, not on corporate taxes paid by the firm itself. Prior to 1987, capital gains were taxed to individuals at lower rates than ordinary income (wages, salary, interest, dividends, etc.). A capital gain is an increase in the value of a stock from one point in time to some future date. A decrease in value is a capital loss. This *differential* in personal tax rates induced a bias in favor of retention as opposed to payment of dividends.

The 1986 tax bill changed all this. Now capital gains and ordinary income are taxed at the same rates. In addition, all dividends received by individuals are now taxable, whereas prior to 1987 the first $100 of dividends was excluded.

These changes have gone a long way toward removing any bias in dividend policy caused by personal taxes. With both dividends and capital gains taxed at the same rate, shareholders theoretically should not care which way they receive their return, in the form of a dividend or a price appreciation (capital gain). Here we are still assuming no transaction costs on dividend payments, stock sales, etc. If management can invest the shareholders' money at higher rates of return inside the firm than the shareholders can get themselves outside the firm, shareholders should prefer retention and reinvestment. Otherwise, they should prefer payment of dividends. The important point here is that personal *taxes* do not influence the decision.

There is just one complicating factor. Even though capital gains are now taxed at the same *rate* as dividends, they are treated differently: the capital-gains tax is not paid until the stock is sold, whereas taxes on dividends must be paid in the year the dividend is received (this was true under the old law as well). In effect, payment of capital-gains taxes can be deferred by holding on to the stock. This somewhat more favorable treatment may introduce a slight bias in favor of retention by firms rather than dividend payout, but the bias probably is not significant.

One other factor is worth mentioning: not all shareholders pay taxes in the first place. Pension trusts, tax-exempt foundations, and a few individuals pay no taxes at all. Although individual shareholders outnumber institutional holders, the proportion of total market value owned by tax-exempt institutions has increased markedly in recent years. Although fewer in number, institutional holders may exert more influence on market prices because they have greater analytical resources and do more trading. Corporations, such as insurance companies, pay federal income taxes on only 20 percent of their dividend income. As in the case of individual taxes, the biases introduced by these considerations are small for most firms and can be ignored in setting dividend policy.

Differences in personal-income-tax treatment are no longer a major factor in dividend decisions in publicly held firms.

Financial Friction

Let us now reintroduce financial friction. One element of friction is commissions on purchases and sales of securities. Such commissions are paid to brokers for executing the transactions and handling related bookkeeping. In percentage terms, commissions vary inversely with the size of the transaction, from 1 percent to 1.5 percent on a transaction of several thousand dollars up to 10 percent or more on transactions of less than $100.

Such commissions tend to exert a bias in favor of payout rather than retention for some shareholders. Shareholders can no longer sell a portion of their holdings without cost when they need cash. In addition to commissions, the necessity of periodically selling small amounts of stock is inconvenient and involves time and effort. Reevaluation of holdings made necessary by periodic sales also involves effort. Taken together, commissions and these inconvenience costs may be significant on small, periodic sales. In such cases, other factors being equal, shareholders needing income would prefer the payment of at least some dividend.

These same commissions may exert a bias in favor of retention rather than payout for other shareholders who do not desire current income. For example, individuals with high salaries may be investing in stocks to accumulate wealth for future retirement because their current salaries provide more than enough money for their current needs. In such a case, individuals may prefer the company to retain funds rather than pay out dividends that individuals will then have to reinvest (with the resultant transactions costs and payment of further tax on the dividends).

Flotation costs—cash costs associated with the issuance of a company's new long-term debt or stock issue.

A second type of transaction cost is incurred in the issuance of new securities. **Flotation costs,** which are the compensation of investment bankers for assisting in issuing the securities, can be significant. Given such costs, a firm no longer can err in calculating funds available for dividends and expect to get the money back later at no cost by selling securities.

Some elements of friction exert a bias in favor of higher payout, while other frictions bias toward retention and lower payout.

Given taxes and friction, we see that a firm's dividend policy does matter and that shareholders are not likely to be indifferent toward it. The existence of transaction costs to shareholders—commissions as well as inconvenience costs—suggests the desirability of minimizing the transactions shareholders must make. The existence of flotation costs on new issues suggests the need to avoid overpaying in one year and selling securities the next. When friction costs are incurred unnecessarily, shareholder wealth is adversely affected. We will come back to these points again later.

Information Effects

Information effects play a role in dividend policy.

In practice, there is ample evidence that announcements of dividend actions by firms affect the market prices of their shares. Often, the magnitude of the effect goes beyond what can be attributed to friction costs. In the second quarter of 1974, for example, Consolidated Edison, an electric utility serving New York City, omitted its regular quarterly dividend of $0.45 per share. The price of its stock immediately dropped from $18 to about $12 and declined to $8 within two weeks. How can we explain this behavior? In terms of information effects, the dividend action sent a message to investors that motivated them to revise sharply downward their estimate of the value of Consolidated Edison common stock.

What was the nature of the message? For some time prior to its dividend cut, Consolidated Edison and other electric utilities had been encountering increasing financial difficulties because of the impact of inflation on costs, the reluctance of regulatory officials to grant rate increases, and pressures to take expensive measures to protect the environment. Share prices had been declining as the outlook for utility earnings worsened. The omission of the first-quarter (1974) dividend was taken by investors to mean that the board of directors and management expected things to get even worse. In short, investors thought those in the best position to know were saying that things did not look good. The impact on share prices was immediate and dramatic.

Something similar happened to ITT Corporation in July 1984. Late in the afternoon of July 10, ITT's chairman, Rand Araskog, stunned Wall Street by announcing a cut in the company's dividend by nearly two thirds, from $2.76 per share to $1.00 annually. The next morning, the opening of trading in ITT stock was delayed for more than an hour, and by the end of the day ITT stock had lost nearly a third of its value. As in the Consolidated Edison case, the dividend cut sent a message to the market that things did not look good, and ITT's stock reacted immediately.[1]

Contrast the preceding examples with the experience of RCA Corporation in the spring of 1982. On March 3, RCA announced a cut in its quarterly dividend from $0.50 per share to $0.225. RCA had been paying a dividend regularly since 1937, and this was the first time in the company's history that its board of directors had reduced it. Although the dividend was cut in half, RCA's stock fell only $1 per share on the announcement, from $18 to $17. Why was the reaction in RCA's stock price so much milder than in the cases of ITT and Consolidated Edison? The answer is that the RCA cut was not a surprise. Financial analysts familiar with the RCA situation had anticipated the cut, and the effects of a prospective cut had already been reflected in RCA's stock price prior to the announcement. One analyst commented that the cut was a "sound management decision."[2]

While RCA cut its dividend in half during early 1982, the Ford Motor Company omitted its first-quarter 1982 dividend entirely. In July of 1980, Ford's directors had cut the quarterly payment from $1 to $0.30, but the 1982 action constituted the first time the dividend had been omitted since Ford had become a public company in 1956. Following a temporary halt in trading, Ford's shares the day of the announcement closed down $0.50. As in the RCA case, the reaction was mild in relation to the change in the dividend, which was cut by 100 percent. The reason for the mild reaction was the same: the market had already anticipated the action. One analyst commented that the action "shows some good hard realism by Ford management."[3]

A surprise change in dividend policy tends to have a greater effect than an anticipated change.

---

[1]"The Troubles That Led To ITT's Dividend Shocker," *Business Week*, July 23, 1984.

[2]The RCA dividend cut was reported in the *Wall Street Journal* of March 4, 1982.

[3]*Wall Street Journal*, January 15, 1982.

Let us consider a different, and this time hypothetical, situation. Consider a firm, ABC Corporation, that historically has paid out a significant portion of earnings and has increased its dividend payment as earnings have grown. ABC is known to have under development a new family of products that appear quite promising but will require considerable capital investment. Suddenly ABC's directors announce that, in order to conserve cash, dividends will no longer be increased each quarter and may even be reduced. What impact might be expected on the firm's stock price? It is possible that investors would interpret the announcement as evidence that investment opportunities did indeed look very attractive. Its stock price might well rise upon the announcement that dividends no longer will be increased each quarter.

Contrast ABC's situation with that of Consolidated Edison. Both firms announced a dividend lower than that previously expected by investors. In both cases conserving cash was the immediate objective. Why did the stock prices in the two cases behave in exactly opposite ways? *Investors drew different inferences* regarding the firms' respective investment opportunities. In Consolidated Edison's case, investors believed the dividend action signaled a situation worse than previously envisioned; in ABC's case, investors felt the dividend action signaled a better situation.

Consider another hypothetical case, that of DEF Corporation. DEF has a history of above-average return on investment and above-average earnings growth, coupled with a very low dividend payout averaging about 5 percent of earnings. Suddenly DEF's board of directors announces that the payout will be increased to approximately 25 percent of earnings. How might the stock price react? It might well fall if investors inferred from the dividend action that DEF's management believed it was running out of high-return investment opportunities.

In the ABC and DEF cases, as well as in the ITT and Consolidated Edison cases, a common element is that the dividend action was unexpected; that is, the change in policy was a surprise. A change in policy that had been anticipated—as in the cases of RCA and Ford—probably would have little or no impact on price, because such impact would have already been felt. Where the action is unexpected, investors draw an inference from the dividend action about the firm's investment and earnings prospects. As a result, investors revise their estimates of the value of the firm's stock, and stock price moves quickly to a new equilibrium level. Such a role for the information effects of dividend announcements suggests that managers possess inside information which is signaled to the market by means of dividends.

What conclusions can we draw about the information effects of dividend actions? We can say that the magnitude of the information effect can be quite large; but what about the direction? Do dividend increases always lead to an increase in stock price? Not always. In one of the earlier examples, a dividend increase led to a drop in stock price, and in another case a dividend reduction led to a price increase. We can make no general statement at all regarding the direction of the information effect of a dividend decision. It depends on the inferences drawn by investors, and many different inferences are possible.

A decision to cut dividends can have various effects on share price, depending on the inference drawn by investors concerning the firm's investment opportunities.

The empirical evidence regarding the effects of dividend actions on stock price is mixed. Most recent studies find a relationship between dividends and value, but expert opinions differ as to the reasons. Some researchers have concluded that the effect is primarily tax-related — that is, resulting from the difference between ordinary income and capital-gains tax rates when such a difference existed. These studies conclude that "tax clienteles" exist — that high-payout firms tend to attract low-tax-bracket investors, and vice versa. They conclude further that payment of dividends in lieu of capital gains through retention of earnings has a negative effect on firm value in the long run.

Other researchers believe that the relationship between dividends and stock value can be explained almost entirely in terms of information effects. This argument rests on the proposition that investors can avoid taxes on dividend income by means of various tax shelters permitted under the tax code. If the effective tax rate on dividends really is low, the observed impact of dividends on stock values must operate through information effects. Announcements of unexpected dividend increases are often followed by share-price increases.

How Investment, Financing, and Dividend Decisions Are Interrelated

Dividend, investment, and financing decisions are interdependent.

It is apparent from our earlier discussion that dividend, investment, and financing decisions are interdependent. Funds paid out in dividends are unavailable for investment, unless they are replaced through external financing. Let us briefly explore these interdependencies.

Suppose a firm has attractive new investment opportunities — defined as opportunities having a positive net present value. If its earnings are sufficient, the firm can finance its capital investments entirely from retained earnings. Otherwise, it may have to borrow or sell additional stock.

If the firm finances its investments out of earnings, those earnings are not available for dividends. Each dollar invested is a dollar that cannot be paid out to shareholders, unless it is replaced by outside financing. If the firm wants to make capital investments and maintain its dividend, it may have to borrow. More borrowing would permit higher investment or higher dividends or both. So the firm has a number of alternatives:

1. Increase investment and cut dividends, holding borrowing (or sales of stock) constant.
2. Increase investment and increase borrowing, holding dividends constant.
3. Increase borrowing and increase dividends, holding investment constant.
4. The reverse, or some combination, of any of the above.

The important point is that the three major elements the firm can vary — investment, borrowing and stock sales, and dividends — are interrelated. The firm cannot change one without changing at least one of the others. In setting dividend policy, management must take account of these interrelationships.

In choosing among these various trade-offs, management should keep its attention focused on *valuation* as the guiding principal. If it forgoes attractive investments, it is probably making the firm less valuable. If it operates with too much debt, or perhaps with too little, it may also reduce the firm's value. Apart from information effects, in most cases dividends should have no effect on value, holding other factors constant. This suggests that management should set investment and debt policy to their optimal levels, and use dividends as the "slack" variable. Such a policy amounts to treating dividends as a "residual," to be paid if funds exist. We will return later in this chapter to the idea of dividends as a residual.

Finance in Practice 17–2

Interdependencies of Financing and Investment

Ford Motor Company's actions during 1980 and 1981 provide a good example of the dilemma posed by the interactions of major policy decisions. In the face of a seriously deteriorating market share, Ford planned capital outlays totaling $16 billion over the period 1981–85. Issuing common stock was not attractive to Ford's management because the company had lost more than $1 billion during the first three quarters of 1980, and taking such a record to the financial markets would not be easy. Debt also looked unpromising because Ford's bonds had been downgraded twice during 1980 by the Standard & Poor's rating service. In the face of these constraints, Ford chose to do three things: reduce its dividend, reduce its liquidity, and borrow heavily short-term. During the period September 1979 to May 1981, Ford borrowed nearly $2 billion at rates in the neighborhood of 20 percent. Thus, Ford resolved the dilemma in favor of its capital-investment program, but it did opt to maintain some dividend payout during

1981 even at the expense of higher borrowing. Ford subsequently cut out its dividend entirely in January 1982.

General Motors resolved a similar dilemma in the spring of 1981 by postponing parts of its investment plan. GM announced in May of that year that it was deferring for at least a year construction of a $500 million automobile-assembly plant in Kansas City, Missouri, and putting off for a year a decision on whether to build a plant in Flint, Michigan. The company explained that these plans were part of an overall $40 billion, five-year capital-spending program and that all of the spending eventually would take place, although portions would be delayed.

GM's decision to postpone parts of its capital program was made against a backdrop of its first full-year loss in nearly six decades, a loss of $763 million in 1980. At the same time that the postponement of spending plans was announced, in May 1981, GM's board of directors voted to pay the regular quarterly dividend of $0.60 per share. GM's board and management evidently concluded that in the face of the cash shortage caused by the 1980 loss, maintaining the regular dividend had a higher priority than keeping the capital-investment program on schedule.

Sources: J. Carson-Parker, "The Capital Cloud Over Smoke-Stack America," *Fortune,* February 23, 1981, pp. 70–80; "GM Says Cash Crunch Is Forcing Delay in Parts of $40 Billion, 5-Year Outlay Plan," *Wall Street Journal,* May 5, 1981.

Setting Dividend Policy

We have laid the groundwork for our analysis of dividend policy with our discussion of theory and interdependence. Let us now turn to specific factors a firm should consider in establishing dividend policy.[4]

Internal Investment Opportunities

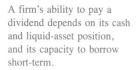

Opportunities to invest are a major consideration in setting dividend policy.

From our earlier discussions, it is apparent that opportunities to invest are a major consideration in setting dividend policy. Other considerations aside, when the firm has opportunities to earn returns greater than those available to shareholders outside the firm, retention and reinvestment are appropriate.

Earnings, Cash Flow, and Liquidity

A firm's ability to pay a dividend depends on its cash and liquid-asset position, and its capacity to borrow short-term.

The firm's ability to generate earnings and cash flow is also a factor in determining dividend policy. When other factors are equal, the more profitable the firm is, the more earnings are available for payout. Dividends are paid with cash, so at any given moment a firm's ability to pay a dividend depends on its cash and liquid-asset position and its capacity for short-term borrowing.

[4]For research concluding that the effect of dividends on value is primarily by means of taxes, see R. H. Litzenberger and K. Ramaswamy, "Dividends, Short-Selling Restrictions, Tax-Induced Investor Clienteles, and Market Equilibrium," *Journal of Finance* 35 (May 1980): 469–82. For an opposing argument—namely, that tax effects are minimal and that the dividend impact operates primarily by means of information effects—see M. Miller and M. Scholes, "Dividends and Taxes," *Journal of Financial Economics* 6 (December 1978): 333–64 and "Dividends and Taxes: Some Empirical Evidence," *Journal of Political Economy*, December 1982, pp. 1118–41.

 International Focus

Hungary's Bond-Market Horrors

We have discussed financial policy focusing on U.S. firms, but what goes on in communist countries?

Communists panic, too. Barely a month after Black Monday of October 1987 when the U.S. and other major stock markets fell dramatically,

Hungary's domestic corporate-bond market—which had cruised to a value of $500 million in only five years—collapsed. Many of the 100,000 bondholders stampeded the Budapest Bank with sell orders. The crash, and the subsequent recovery, showed the value of Hungary's budding capital market to its budget-cutting government.

The trigger was Hungary's new austerity program for 1988, announced in November 1987. The government planned to cut subsidies on consumer goods. That was expected to push the official rate of inflation up to 14 to 15 percent for 1988. Holders of the bonds—most of which carry an interest rate of only 9 to 11 percent—rushed to sell and plough the proceeds into jewelry, consumer durables, and property.

The throng of sellers pushed the banks and some companies into offering an interest bonus of 1 to 4 percent to loyal investors. This seemed to help, as did the emptiness of the shops. By mid-December the bond market had returned to normal, and the public was buying again.

The government breathed a sigh of relief, since it hoped to issue bills itself. It was keen to cut subsidies to Hungary's loss-making companies, and hoped that the bond market could provide more than its present 10 percent share of industrial investment. Shares could also help: plans were that soon employees would be able to buy shares in their companies, which would pay a dividend based on company performance. But the difficult ideological question of allowing people to buy shares in a company they did not work for was unresolved.

Source: The Economist, December 26, 1987, p. 79.

External Financing Needs

In a world with taxes, inflation effects, and transaction costs, a firm must plan its program of external financing. For any firm there exists an optimal debt/equity ratio that depends in part on the nature of its business and its operating risk. That ratio should be established as a target. When not at its target debt/equity mix, the firm should take steps to reach it. In our discussion in the preceding section, we found dividend payout to be interdependent with the debt/equity ratio and with external financing requirements. As a result, changes in dividend policy are one means of altering (or maintaining) a firm's debt/equity ratio.

Changes in dividend policy are one means of altering or maintaining a firm's debt/equity ratio.

Earnings Record and Prospects

Of major importance to dividend policy is the firm's earnings record, its prospects for future earnings, and the market's perceptions of those prospects. Both the growth trend and the stability of earnings are also important. To be credible, the dividend pattern must be consistent with the earnings pattern. Consider the data for the two firms listed in Table 17–1. Firm A's earnings have shown steady

Table 17–1
Patterns Likely to Influence the Credibility of Dividend Policies for Two Firms over a 5-Year Period

	Firm A			Firm B		
Year	Earnings per Share	Dividend	Payout Ratio	Earnings per Share	Dividend	Payout Ratio
1	$1.38	$0.72	0.52	$1.26	$0.72	0.57
2	$1.62	$0.72	0.44	$1.10	$0.72	0.65
3	$1.92	$0.96	0.50	$1.32	$0.96	0.73
4	$2.08	$0.96	0.46	$1.12	$0.96	0.86
5	$2.46	$1.20	0.49	$1.20	$1.20	1.00

growth, and its dividend policy has been in line with that growth. Investors are likely to feel confident that the historical dividend pattern will be continued—subject, of course, to the firm's ability to continue its growth in earnings. Firm B's earnings, on the other hand, have been erratic around a flat trend, while the dividend has been steadily increased. In view of the earnings record, investors are likely to doubt B's ability to continue the historical pattern of steady dividend increases. Firm B's dividend pattern does not appear to be sustainable. The actual dividend payments in the two cases are identical, but A's pattern is more credible.

The credibility of dividend policy is important: the dividend pattern must be consistent with the earnings pattern.

Clientele

There is some evidence that different dividend policies attract different types of investors, or different **investor clienteles.** This argument suggests that firms with high and stable payouts attract investors who prefer a large proportion of their total return in current income. Such investors may well depend on dividends for current consumption and, therefore, may prefer a dividend that is stable and predictable. On the other hand, low-payout growth companies might attract investors interested mainly in capital gains. In short, investors may attempt to match their own income needs with the magnitude and stability of the firm's payout.

Investor clientele—a group of investors attracted to a certain stock investment because of a particular characteristic, such as the company's dividend policy.

The clientele argument had more force prior to 1987 when capital gains were taxed at lower rates than ordinary income. The argument was plausible, and most studies found at least some evidence of a clientele effect. With the change in the tax law in 1986, the argument for clienteles is less strong, but it still remains plausible that some investors may prefer high-payout stocks and others low-payout stocks. Until the matter is studied carefully with the new tax rules in place, managements would be prudent to assume that clienteles do exist.

Some evidence suggests that different dividend policies attract different types of investors, or clienteles.

Of what significance is the clientele argument? One might argue that if the firm's clientele were used to a particular dividend policy, that policy should not be changed. Most firms for which dividend policy is important are publicly traded. If the firm wished to change its dividend policy, those shareholders not satisfied with the new policy could simply sell their shares and buy those of another firm with a policy suited to their needs. The firm would lose one clientele and attract another. However, in making portfolio shifts, shareholders incur transaction costs and also costs in time and effort to gather and analyze information and make decisions. Thus, because of friction in the markets, a change in dividend policy can impose costs on shareholders that are real and potentially significant in magnitude, especially to small shareholders. As a result, companies should consider carefully changes in dividend policy.

Investors incur costs in changing their investment portfolios because of frictions in the system.

Legal and Regulatory Restrictions

Certain institutional investors, particularly insurance companies, are subject to a variety of legal and regulatory restrictions with respect to their investment policies. In some states, laws or regulations stipulate that for a firm's stock to qualify for certain institutional portfolios, an uninterrupted dividend record is required over some minimum number of years. Some states prohibit certain institutions, such as savings banks and certain trustees, from holding the bonds of a corporation unless there exists an uninterrupted dividend record on the underlying common stock over some minimum period. Omission of a dividend by a firm thus might result in removal of its stock or bonds or both from the legal list of investments of some institutions. It is difficult to judge the true significance of such a development, but it is plausible that institutional interest in a firm's securities may give it a broader, more liquid market and facilitate new issues of securities.

Universities and other endowed educational institutions sometimes are restricted in their use of capital gains on their securities. Since such institutions are generally not taxed, they might have a preference for stocks with a high payout.

Control

In some cases, control of the firm may be a factor in setting dividend policy. Suppose an individual or group owns a significant interest in a firm, the remainder of the stock being publicly held. The higher the payout, the greater the chance that a subsequent issue of common stock might be required—perhaps because of a change in commercial strategy requiring greater investment. Those in control might prefer to minimize the likelihood of a requirement for new outside capital by opting for low payout and a high liquid-asset position.

This argument applies also to firms that, because of size or reputation or other factors, might find their access to public equity markets limited. The lower the payout, the less likely it is that outside capital will be needed.

Dividend-Policy Goals

We now have developed a basic framework of analysis and have discussed the major factors pertinent to setting dividend policy. No two firms are exactly alike, and the policy for a firm must be tailored to its own unique circumstances. Let us attempt, however, to set down some general policy goals that are applicable to most firms.

A Long-Run Residual

It is apparent that dividend policy depends on many factors that are often confusing and sometimes conflicting. In such situations, we must look to basic principles for guidance. What are those basic principles?

1. We know that valuation is the central organizing framework and that financial-management decisions should be analyzed in terms of their effect on the value of the firm rather than on earnings or other yardsticks.
2. We know it is through its investments that the firm executes its commercial strategy. Investments create value, and when a firm forgoes an attractive investment, shareholders incur an opportunity loss.
3. We know that the debt/equity mix also affects the value of the firm.

4. We know that friction exists in the system and that real costs are incurred when the firm issues securities and when shareholders make changes in their holdings.

5. We know that dividend, investment, and financing decisions are interdependent, and that trade-offs must be made.

Let us examine these trade-offs in a long-run setting. As a matter of *long-run policy,* does it make sense for the firm to plan consciously to forgo attractive investments, or to operate at a nonoptimal debt/equity ratio, or to finance dividend payments by selling stock? We conclude that none of these options is sensible as a long-run policy. The policy that avoids all of these choices is to treat dividends as a *long-run residual*.

Short-Run Constraints

In the short run, however, the firm faces a number of constraints that make a strictly residual dividend policy not feasible. Since investment requirements and earnings in most firms vary from year to year, treating dividends as a residual each year is likely to lead to a highly variable dividend that may even fall to zero in some years. From our earlier discussion, we know that a variable dividend is undesirable. Investors would have a difficult time interpreting the frequent changes in the dividend, and information effects would be likely to lead to wide fluctuations in stock price. Even if they averaged out over time, such fluctuations would benefit some shareholders at the expense of others who would be forced to sell at low points; therefore, it would be a highly unfair policy. In addition, fluctuations in price and dividends would cause shifts in the shareholder group, or clientele, that could impose significant costs on those shareholders who are induced by that policy to alter their holdings. If the residual policy dictated a dividend of zero in any year, the firm's dividend record would be broken and regulatory restrictions might force removal of the firm's securities from the approved buy lists of some institutions.

A Long-Run Residual Managed in the Short Run

Although a policy of treating dividends as a residual in the short run is unworkable, a feasible compromise is to treat dividends as a long-run residual, but to constrain it in the short run in order to avoid undesirable variations in payout. To implement such an approach requires financial planning over a fairly long time horizon — probably five years.

First, investment requirements must be estimated, with the estimate providing for all attractive opportunities that the firm expects to face. Next, funds expected to be available internally from earnings and depreciation should be estimated. A target debt/equity ratio then should be set, based on the firm's operating risk and other relevant considerations. Given investment requirements, funds from internal sources, and a target debt/equity ratio, the firm can then determine whether, over the planning horizon, residual funds will be available for payout. If so, the ratio of

---

Dividend, investment, and financing decisions are interdependent, and trade-offs must be made.

Treating dividends as a long-run residual allows the firm to avoid forgoing attractive investments or adopting unsound financing plans.

In the short run, there are a number of constraints against a strictly residual dividend policy.

To implement a policy of treating dividends as a long-run residual, a long time horizon is needed.

In planning dividends as a long-run residual, the ratio of residual funds to total earnings after taxes should become a firm's long-run target payout ratio.

Long-run target payout ratio—the ratio of residual funds to total earnings after taxes over a relatively long planning horizon.

residual funds to total earnings after taxes becomes the firm's **long-run target payout ratio.**

If no residual earnings remain after financing is provided for all attractive investment opportunities, this approach suggests a policy of no dividend at all. External equity financing would be required to make up any shortfall in internal funds. No dividends at all would be a problem for some institutions that are required to hold only dividend-paying stocks. Where institutional ownership of the firm's securities seems desirable, the firm might wish to compromise by paying a small token dividend with the intention of leaving it fixed over the planning horizon. Where the long-run analysis shows that residual funds will be available, the plan would suggest some dividends and no external equity financing.

The long planning horizon is necessary because the world is uncertain and not frictionless. Investment opportunities cannot be foreseen with complete accuracy each year, nor can earnings be accurately forecast each year. In effect, we plan the long-run dividend-payout target based on *trend* values. Needed external financing can be planned in more economical amounts to avoid high issue costs associated with small financings. Also, the long horizon allows time to anticipate changes in commercial strategy or debt/equity policy.

The long-run target is stated in *percentage* terms—that is, dividends to be paid as a percentage of earnings. But if the firm paid that same percentage of earnings as dividends each quarter, short-term variations in earnings would cause dividends to fluctuate, and that would be undesirable. So the firm should control the *dollar* dividend payout in the short term and set it to average out to the target percentage over the longer term. As earnings fluctuate from period to period, the percentage payout will fluctuate, but the dollar payout will not. In some years, the percentage payout will be below the target, and in other years this percentage will be above the target. In effect, the firm saves during fat years in order to maintain the dividend during lean years.

Let us illustrate the approach with an example. ABC Corporation is making its financial plan over a five-year horizon. The company foresees investment opportunities requiring net new investment, over and above depreciation charges, of $4 million per year, or $20 million over the five years. This investment requirement includes expenditures for plant and equipment plus additions to working capital. Aggregate earnings after taxes over the period are expected to be $25 million. The company's target debt/assets ratio is 0.25.

The company plans to invest an additional $20 million. Applying the debt/assets ratio shows that the company can finance 25 percent of this amount using debt and 75 percent using equity; that is,

$$\text{New debt} = 0.25 \times 20 = \$5 \text{ million}$$

$$\text{Equity} = 20 - 5 = \$15 \text{ million}.$$

If $5 million of the $20 million comes from debt, the remaining $15 million of equity must come from retained earnings or issuing new shares. Since the company expects to earn $25 million over the five years, retaining $15 million for investment leaves $10 million available for dividends. Hence the target average payout over the five years would be $10/$25 = 40 percent of earnings.

The company would then set 40 percent as its *average* target payout, but it would not try to pay out exactly 40 percent each year. The goal is to pay out $10 million over five years. One alternative would be to set annual payout at $2 million and hold to that dollar figure. A more conservative approach would be initially to set dollar payout below $2 million, say $1.75 million for the first two years, then $2 million in year 3, then $2.25 million in years 4 and 5.

There are many possible combinations. The objective would be to set a target percentage payout based on trend values over a long horizon, and then control dollar payout in the short run so that dividends would not fluctuate and the target could be reached.

Communicating the Policy

It is important for a firm to communicate clearly to investors the dividend policy it adopts.

Whatever specific policies the firm adopts, it is important that the policy be communicated clearly to investors. Investors should not have to guess what policy management intends to follow. Investors are then better prepared to decide whether the policy suits their own preferences and needs. Good communication also reduces the chances of misinterpretation.

Changing the Dividend Policy

Consistency in dividend policy is important, given information effects, friction, and clienteles.

Given information effects, friction, and a clientele, consistency in policy is important. Erratic changes are costly and should be avoided. Sometimes, however, a policy change will become necessary—perhaps because of a change in commercial strategy, investment opportunities, or debt/equity policy. Changes in general economic conditions might also necessitate a change in policy. Or management simply might find that it had wrongly estimated one or more of the determinants of dividend policy, which in an uncertain world can happen to even the most capable and farsighted managers.

When a policy change is indicated, management should not shrink from the task. Dividend reductions are painful, but if a reduction is in the shareholders' best interests, it should be made. In such cases, communication becomes all the more important. If the reasons are sensible, investors will understand them. A dividend cut may well lead to a fall in stock price, but careful communications will increase the likelihood that stock price will adjust to the underlying economic realities.[5]

If a lower average payout became necessary, it might be possible to move to the new target gradually. Where a firm's earnings are growing, the dollar payout could be held constant and the average payout ratio allowed to decline over time.

---

[5]For an analysis of management attitudes about changes in dividend policy, see E. F. Fama and H. Babiak, "Dividend Policy: An Empirical Analysis," *Journal of the American Statistical Association* 63 (December 1968): 1132–61. Fama and Babiak conclude that managers generally believe investors prefer a stable dividend policy. See also R. W. Kolb, "Predicting Dividend Changes," unpublished doctoral dissertation, School of Business Administration, University of North Carolina at Chapel Hill, 1978. Kolb found a marked reluctance among managers to cut dividends. When cuts finally were made, they tended to be large. Increases, on the other hand, tended to be small—the average increase being about 3 percent. This finding supports the notion that managers make dividend increases only when they are reasonably sure they can be sustained.

Finance in Practice 17–3

What Managers Consider in Setting Dividend Policy

In 1983, three business-school professors surveyed a group of firms to find out what they considered important in setting dividend policy.

They sent questionnaires to the chief financial officers of 562 firms listed on the New York Stock Exchange, asking them to rank the factors they considered most important. They divided the firms into three categories: manufacturing, wholesale/retail, and utilities. The survey yielded 318 usable responses, and the results are summarized in the accompanying table.

The results produced no surprises, but the differences in rankings are interesting. After what happened to Consolidated Edison, it is not surprising that utility executives think a lot about stock price.

Source: H. K. Baker, G. E. Farrelly, and R. B. Edelman, "A Survey of Management Views on Dividend Policy," *Financial Management,* Autumn 1985, pp. 78–84.

	Rank of Factor		
Factor	*Manufacturing*	*Wholesale/Retail*	*Utilities*
Anticipated level of future earnings	1	1	1
Pattern of past dividends	2	2	3
Availability of cash	3	4	4
Concern about maintaining or increasing stock price	4	3	2

Such an approach would avoid a reduction in dollar payout, which could be inconvenient or costly to some shareholders. The policy change and the reasons for it should also be communicated to shareholders.

Procedural and Legal Considerations in Paying Dividends

Each dividend payment must be declared by a vote of the board of directors. Suppose the directors of XYZ Corporation meet on Tuesday, January 21, and declare that the regular first-quarter dividend of $0.25 per share is to be paid on March 12 to all investors who hold the firm's stock on Wednesday, February 12. February 12 becomes the *record date,* and holders on that date become *holders of record.*

To account for the time required to record transfer of ownership, the major stock exchanges subtract four business days from the record date to establish the **ex-dividend date**—in this case, Thursday, February 6. Any investor purchasing XYZ stock on or before February 5 would become a holder of record on February 12 and would, therefore, receive the first-quarter dividend. Investors purchasing on February 6 and thereafter would not receive the dividend. On February 6,

Ex-dividend date — date on which the right to the next dividend payment stops accompanying the purchase of a share of stock. The stock price drops on the ex-dividend date.

the stock thus sells *ex-dividend*. We would expect its price to drop on that date by the amount of the dividend to show that buyers that day will not receive the dividend. Testing this proposition is difficult because of the many factors, other than dividends, affecting prices. Carefully controlled empirical studies indicate that price does adjust on the ex-dividend date, but by something less than the full amount. Prior to 1987, the difference is at least in part due to the difference in tax rates on dividends and capital gains.

Once declared by the board, dividends payable become a current liability of the firm. If XYZ had 1 million shares outstanding, the accounting entries on the day of declaration would be a $250,000 credit (increase) in current liabilities and a $250,000 debit (decrease) in retained earnings. When the checks are paid, the current liability is eliminated and cash declines by $250,000. The net effect of paying the dividend is a reduction in cash and an offsetting reduction in retained earnings.

In many cases, common-stock dividends are limited by restrictions placed in long-term-debt indentures and preferred-stock agreements.

In many cases, long-term-debt and preferred-stock agreements contain restrictions on the maximum common-stock dividend that can be paid by a firm. Such covenants are designed to protect senior claim holders from excessive withdrawals by residual owners. Though frequently encountered, restrictions usually are not troublesome during normal times because they are consistent with what good financial management would require anyway.

In addition to covenants in debt and preferred-stock agreements, many state laws place restrictions on dividend payments designed to give further protection to senior claim holders. Many states require that dividends be paid only out of retained earnings. The effect of such a restriction is to permit dividend payments only when retained earnings is a positive figure. The intent of the provision is to permit withdrawal of earnings but not withdrawal of the original capital contribution. Some states define the original capital contribution as including only the par value of the stock, while others include paid-in capital as well. A few states permit dividends if current earnings, usually over the most recent 12 months, are positive, even if total cumulative retained earnings are negative.

Dividends in Closely Held Firms

Much of our dividend discussion does not apply to firms which are not publicly held.

The discussion to this point has concentrated on the formulation of dividend policy in publicly held corporations. Much of the discussion does not apply to firms that are not publicly held. In privately held firms, there are no problems with information effects or clientele.

Taxes are of major importance in establishing policy in private companies with respect to withdrawals by owners.

Taxes, however, are a factor, and tax considerations are of major importance in establishing policy in private companies with respect to withdrawals by owners. The form of organization — whether proprietorship, partnership, or corporation — significantly affects the firm's tax status. If certain conditions are met, a corporation having a small number of shareholders may be taxed as a partnership. If the firm is taxed as a corporation, long-range planning of investment and financing needs becomes essential. If funds are paid out and later returned, taxes would have been paid unnecessarily. The long-range residual approach to planning withdrawals would be appropriate. In many cases, the appropriate policy depends heavily on the income needs and tax brackets of the principals. In some cases, a policy of total retention may be best, but Internal Revenue Service regulations prohibit excessive retention as a means of avoiding income taxes. Given the complexity of the applicable tax laws, expert accounting and legal advice is necessary in most cases.

KEY CONCEPTS

1. In the absence of information effects, financial friction, and differential tax rates, dividend policy would not affect firm value.

2. Commissions on stock trades exert a bias in favor of higher payouts on the part of some investors and a bias in favor of lower payouts on the part of other investors. Issue costs exert a bias in favor of lower payouts.

3. Information effects on the price of stock resulting from dividend actions can be quite pro-

nounced, but there is no general rule regarding the direction of the effect.

4. Investment, financing, and dividend decisions are interdependent. It is not possible to set policies in all three areas independently.

5. Dividend policy is best set as a long-run residual managed in the short run.

SUMMARY

In analyzing dividend policy from the standpoint of firm value and shareholder interests, one should focus attention on financial friction and information effects. Friction costs include commissions, issue costs, and costs of analysis by investors. Information effects occur when, on the basis of dividend decisions by the firm, investors draw inferences regarding other important events or policies, such as investment opportunities in the future, earnings prospects, or changes in financing policy. Information effects result from unexpected dividend actions and can have a significant impact on stock price in either direction. The potential for undesirable information effects points up the need for careful communication by management to the financial markets.

In setting its dividend policy, a firm must consider many factors in addition to friction costs and information effects. It must consider interdependen-

cies among investment, financing, and dividend policies; earnings prospects; liquidity requirements; the makeup of the stockholder group; and legal and regulatory restrictions.

When dividend policy is analyzed in a valuation framework, it becomes clear that, in general, dividends should be treated as a long-run residual. Although they can be treated as a residual in the long run, dividends must also be managed carefully in the short run to avoid undesirable variations in payout that impose real costs on shareholders. In setting policy, a firm must recognize the importance of consistency and careful communication.

In closely held firms, tax considerations usually are a central factor in determining a payout or withdrawal policy that best serves the interests of owners.

QUESTIONS

1. "In a world of no taxes and no financial friction, a firm cannot make itself more valuable by manipulating the dividend-payout ratio." Is this statement true or false? Explain.

2. What is the relationship between sales and asset growth, optimal debt levels and dividend-payout ratios?

3. What types of transaction costs must be considered in setting dividend policy?

4. Describe the information effects that can be induced by dividend actions.

5. Why are investment, financing, and dividend decisions interdependent?

6. What are the principal factors a firm should consider in setting its dividend policy?

7. Over the long run, which of the three major financial policy variables — investment policy, debt/equity policy, or dividend policy — should be treated as residual?

8. In practice, what constraints operate to prevent a firm from treating dividends as a residual in the short run?

9. Why must dividend policies be planned over a relatively long time horizon?

Problems

Note: To work problems preceded by an asterisk (*) requires knowledge of material in Appendix 17A.

1. Suppose that the board of directors of Orange Computer Company meets on April 16, 1988, and decides that the regular quarterly dividend of $4.00 per share will be raised to $5.00 per share beginning with the second-quarter 1988 dividend. At the same meeting, the board declares that the second-quarter dividend will be paid on Thursday, June 18, 1988, to holders of record on Monday, May 18, 1988. The results of this meeting, including the dividend-policy revision and the declaration of the second-quarter dividend, appear in an article in the *Wall Street Journal* on April 17, 1988. Orange's stock price is observed to fluctuate as shown in Table A.

   a. In the context of this dividend decision, when is the declaration date, the record date, the ex-dividend date, and the payment date?

   b. Please refer to the stock prices listed in Table A. How might you explain the increases in stock price observed on April 16 and April 17? Why did the stock price drop on

Table A

Date	Stock Price
April 10, 1988	$439.50
April 16, 1988	440.50
April 17, 1988	442.00
April 30, 1988	441.80
May 6, 1988	442.30
May 11, 1988	441.65
May 12, 1988	436.85
May 28, 1988	436.90
June 10, 1988	439.10
June 15, 1988	436.30
June 19, 1988	436.20

May 12? What can you say about the magnitude of the decline? Given the second-quarter dividend, what sort of stock-price movement would you have expected in June? Do your observations of a decline in price around the middle of June coincide with your expectations? Can this decline be explained in relation to the dividend payment?

2. Suppose that an individual stockholder of Payton Plastics, Inc., is taxed at a rate of 28 percent. The

McMahon Metals Company also holds stock in Payton; the income of McMahon is taxed at a rate of 34 percent and is taxed on only 20 percent of its dividend income.

a. Assuming that this is the only stock owned by an individual, how much would he or she have on an after-tax basis of pretax dividends from Payton totaling $1,000?

b. On an after-tax basis, how much would the same $1,000 in dividends be worth to McMahon Metals?

c. Does the individual or the corporation face a larger tax disincentive on dividend income?

3. Troxler Manufacturing Company produces components for heavy machine tools. For the past 15 years, Troxler has experienced moderate sales and earnings growth. Currently, Troxler is considering expanding its production facilities and product line to include components for sensitive testing equipment. This is a new area of component manufacturing with no dominant firm in the market. Expansion into this line has met Troxler's economic and qualitative criteria for acceptance. The expansion program will require an investment of $30 million in the next year to set up operations. Troxler has 4 million shares of common stock outstanding and has maintained a stable annual dollar dividend of $2.50 per share. Troxler's board of directors is reluctant to make any sudden changes in this dividend level. The firm has a target debt/equity ratio of 0.35. Total earnings after taxes for the past year were $25 million. Earnings are expected to remain constant over the next year. Troxler's balance sheet for the past year indicates the capital structure (in thousands of dollars) shown in Table B.

a. What is Troxler's current dividend-payout ratio?

b. If Troxler undertakes the new investment and maintains its current dividend-payout ratio, how much external financing will be required? To maintain its target debt/equity ratio, how much must be raised in new equity? If new common stock can be issued to net $40 per share, how many new shares must be issued and what will be the effect of this issue on the dollar dividend per share if the current dividend-payout ratio is maintained?

c. Suppose the directors of Troxler are unwilling to undertake a new common stock issue at this time to finance the new investment. What policies could you suggest to the directors so that the new investment could be made? Discuss the advantages and disadvantages of each of your policies.

4. You are the president of a large manufacturing corporation that views dividends as a long-run residual. Currently, the dividend-payout ratio is 35 percent. The debt/equity ratio of 40 percent is considered to be optimal. You are reviewing the five-year strategic plan in order to decide whether the current dividend-payout ratio of 35 percent should be revised. The plan anticipates investment opportunities of $5 million per year for five years, including plant and equipment plus additions to working capital. In keeping with the target debt/equity ratio, new debt will be issued in year 4. Assume that earnings over the five years are expected to vary as shown in Table C.

Table B

Debt	14,000
Equity: 4,000,000 shares of common stock at $1 par	4,000
Additional paid-in capital	6,000
Retained earnings	30,000

Table C

Year	Expected Earnings
1	$7,000,000
2	$8,000,000
3	$6,000,000
4	$5,000,000
5	$6,000,000

a. How much debt must be issued over the five years in order to maintain the target debt/equity ratio of 40 percent? (Hint: new debt = 0.4 RE.)

b. If the firm did not view dividends as a long-run residual, what would dividend payments be in each of the next five years? What are the potential problems with such a policy?

c. Given that the firm does set dividend policy as a long-run residual, what annual dividends are indicated by the five-year plan?

d. If a change in the dividend-payout ratio is indicated, what issues should be considered before such a change is enacted?

*5. The stockholders' equity account of the Stevens Manufacturing Company is given in Table D. The

Table D

Common stock (2,000,000 shares at $2 par value)	$ 4,000,000
Paid-in surplus	16,000,000
Retained earnings	28,000,000
Net worth	$48,000,000

firm's common stock has a current market price of $45 per share.

a. Show the results of a 10 percent stock dividend.

b. Show the results of a 20 percent stock dividend.

c. Show the results of a two-for-one stock split.

d. Given your answers to the preceding analyses, explain the effects of stock dividends and stock splits on net worth and shareholder value.

REFERENCES

Bhattacharya, S., "Imperfect Information, Dividend Policy, and the Bird-in-the-Hand Fallacy." *Bell Journal of Economics* 10 (Spring 1979): 259–70.

Black, F., and M. Scholes, "The Effects of Dividend Yield and Dividend Policy on Common Stock Prices and Returns." *Journal of Financial Economics* 1 (1974): 1–22.

Carson-Parker, J., "The Capital Cloud Over Smoke-Stack America." *Fortune* (Feb. 23, 1981): 70–80.

Elton, E. J., and M. J. Gruber, "Marginal Stockholder Tax Rates and the Clientele Effect." *Review of Economics and Statistics* 52 (Feb. 1970): 68–74.

Fama, E. F., and H. Babiak, "Dividend Policy: An Empirical Analysis." *Journal of the American Statistical Association* 63 (Dec. 1968): 1132–61.

Finnerty, J. E., "Corporate Stock Issue and Repurchase." *Financial Management* 4 (Oct. 1975): 62–66.

"Fresh Evidence That Dividends Don't Matter." *Fortune* (May 4, 1981): 351–54.

Friend, I., and M. Puckett, "Dividends and Stock Prices." *American Economic Review* 54 (Sept. 1964): 656–82.

"GM Says Cash Crunch Is Forcing Delay In Parts of $40 Billion, 5-Year Outlay Plan," *Wall Street Journal* (May 5, 1981).

Higgins, R. C., "The Corporate Dividend-Saving Decision." *Journal of Financial and Quantitative Analysis* 7 (Mar. 1972): 1527–1541.

John, K., and J. Williams, "Dividends, Dilution and Taxes: A Signalling Equilibrium." *Journal of Finance* (September 1985): 1053–1070.

Kolb, R. W. "Predicting Dividend Changes." Unpublished doctoral dissertation, Graduate School of Business Administration, University of North Carolina at Chapel Hill, 1978.

Lakonishok, J., and B. Lev, "Stock Splits and Stock Dividends: Why, Who, and When." *Journal of Finance* (Sept. 1987): 913–31.

Lakonishok, J., and T. Vermaelen, "Tax-Induced Trading Around Ex-Dividend Days." *Journal of Financial Economics* (July 1986): 287–319.

Lewellen, W. G., et al., "Some Direct Evidence on the Dividend Clientele Phenomenon." *Journal of Finance* 33 (Dec. 1978): 1385–1400.

Litzenberger, R. H., and K. Ramaswamy, "Dividends, Short Selling Restrictions, Tax-Induced Investor Clienteles and Market Equilibrium." *Journal of Finance* 35 (May 1980): 469–482.

Litzenberger, R. H., and K. Ramaswamy, "The Effect of Personal Taxes and Dividends on Capital Asset Prices." *Journal of Financial Economics* 7 (1979): 163–195.

Litzenberger, R. H., and J. C. Van Horne, "Elimination of the Double Taxation of Dividends and Corporate Financial Policy." *Journal of Finance* 33 (June 1978): 737–49.

Miller, M. H., and F. Modigliani, "Dividend Policy, Growth, and the Valuation of Shares." *Journal of Business* 34 (October 1961): 411–33.

Miller, M., and M. Scholes. "Dividends and Taxes," *Journal of Financial Economics* 6 (1978): 333–64.

Myers, S. C., "Interactions of Corporate Financing and Investment Decisions — Implications for Capital Budgeting." *Journal of Finance* (March 1974): 433–43.

Pettit, R. R., "Dividend Announcements, Security Performance, and Market Efficiency." *Journal of Finance* 27 (Dec. 1972): 993–1007.

Pettit, R. R., "Taxes, Transactions Costs and the Clientele Effect of Dividends." *Journal of Finance* 5 (Dec. 1977): 419–36.

Ross, S. A., "The Determination of Financial Structure: The Incentive-Signalling Approach." *Bell Journal of Economics* 8 (1977): 23–40.

Van Horne, J. C., and J. G. McDonald, "Dividend Policy and New Equity Financing." *Journal of Finance* 26 (May 1971): 507–19.

Watts, R., "The Information Content of Dividends." *Journal of Business* 46 (Apr. 1973): 191–211.

Appendix 17A

Stock Dividends and Stock Splits

This appendix discusses two topics—stock dividends and stock splits—that do not involve a distribution of earnings and, therefore, are not cash dividends. Each is more properly considered a recapitalization, or a restructuring, of capital accounts of the firm. We discuss these topics here because the motives for paying stock dividends are related to those of distributing cash dividends. We include a discussion of stock splits because they are very similar in effect to stock dividends. In Chapter 20, we will discuss yet another related topic—the repurchase of shares of stock as an alternative to paying such dividends.

Stock dividends and stock splits are essentially a recapitalization of the firm's capital accounts, not a dividend.

Stock Dividends

Some firms pay a **stock dividend** in lieu of, or in combination with, a cash dividend. Stock dividends usually take the form of shares of common stock. Consider a firm whose stock has a par value at $1, was originally sold at $10 per share, and now has a market price of $20. When a 10 percent stock dividend is paid, the balance sheet, before and after the stock dividend is paid, would appear as shown in Table 17A–1 on p. 526.

The number of shares outstanding increases by 100,000 (10 percent) to 1,100,000. However, net worth remains the same and no cash has been paid out. The issue of the additional shares has been accompanied by a restructuring—or a relabeling—of accounting entries in the net-worth section of the balance sheet. Retained earnings have been reduced by $2,000,000 (100,000 shares times the market price of $20), with $1,900,000 transferred to paid-in surplus and $100,000 transferred to common stock (based on par value).

Stock dividends are accompanied by a restructuring of accounting entries in the net-worth section of the balance sheet.

Each shareholder now has 10 percent more shares than before. Is the shareholder better off? One firm justified a stock dividend on grounds that it "should enable stockholders to benefit from the improving earnings outlook." However, total earnings are unchanged, so earnings per share decline by 10 percent, and each shareholder's proportional share in earnings is the same as before.

To illustrate, consider a shareholder who owned 100 shares before the stock dividend, and assume that total earnings after taxes were $2,000,000, or $2.00 per share before the stock dividend, as shown in Table 17A–2 (p. 526). Because the claim on earnings is unchanged, if the shareholders are better off, it must be because the firm is worth more. Such would be the case if market price per share de-

Table 17A-1

Balance Sheets, Both Before and After the Payment of Stock Dividends, for a Hypothetical Firm

	Before	
Cash $1,000,000	Common stock (1,000,000 shares at $1 par value)	$ 1,000,000
	Paid-in surplus	9,000,000
	Retained earnings	15,000,000
	Net worth	$25,000,000

	After	
Cash $1,000,000	Common stock (1,100,000 shares at $1 par value)	$ 1,100,000
	Paid-in surplus	10,900,000
	Retained earnings	13,000,000
	Net worth	$25,000,000

Table 17A-2

Changes for an Individual Shareholder after a Firm's Payment of a Stock Dividend

	Shares Owned	Earnings per Share	Total Claim on Earnings
Before	100	$2.00	$200
After	110	$1.82	$200

clined by less than 10 percent. Empirical evidence suggests, however, that prices on average do adjust by the same amount as the stock dividend. A direct analogy is that of two pies, both the same size, with one sliced ten ways and the other sliced eleven ways. It seems doubtful that the pie with eleven slices would command a higher price in the market place. Likewise, to argue that a stock dividend alone can permanently affect the value of a firm requires an assumption of irrationality on the part of investors, not a very comfortable basis for making financial policy. As a final bit of evidence on the true value of stock dividends, we might note that the Internal Revenue Service views them as nontaxable.[1]

With the economic benefits of stock dividends in doubt, what about their cost? The firm incurs costs in connection with issuing the new stock certificates. In addition, owners of small amounts of stock receive fractional shares and must either sell the fractional shares or *round up* by buying more fractional shares to obtain full shares. The cost to the firm of handling these transactions may be significant. There also are costs to shareholders in terms of inconvenience and additional recordkeeping.

When paying stock dividends, firms incur costs in issuing new stock certificates.

[1]For a discussion of stock splits and dividends see J. Lakonishok and B. Lev, "Stock Splits and Stock Dividends: Why, Who, and When," *Journal of Finance* (Sept. 1987): 913–31.

Table 17A–3

Changes Occurring When a Hypothetical Firm Recapitalizes with a Two-for-One Stock Split

	Before	
Cash $1,000,000	Common stock (1,000,000 shares at $1 par value)	$ 1,000,000
	Paid-in surplus	9,000,000
	Retained earnings	15,000,000
	Net worth	$25,000,000

	After	
Cash $1,000,000	Common stock (2,000,000 shares at $0.50 par value)	$ 1,000,000
	Paid-in surplus	9,000,000
	Retained earnings	15,000,000
	Net worth	$25,000,000

Occasionally, a firm may use a stock dividend as a mechanism for increasing cash-dividend payout. If the dollar dividend per share is held constant, a stock dividend has the effect of increasing the aggregate cash-dividend payout by the firm. Chapter 17 discussed the effects of such an increase in cash dividends.

Stock Splits

We noted above that a stock dividend is not a distribution of earnings, but a recapitalization of sorts. A closely related type of recapitalization is the **stock split.** A stock split involves different accounting entries from a stock dividend and usually can be accomplished at lower cost because fractional shares can be avoided. Consider the illustration given in Table 17A–3 of a two-for-one split, using the same firm described earlier as an example.

In this case, one million new shares are issued, and the par value is cut in half. No transfer is made from the retained-earnings account. Earnings per share are cut in half. We would expect market price also to be cut in half, if the stock split is purely a cosmetic change. There is some evidence, however, that stock splits may be interpreted as signals of good news about the company's future prospects. This is because in a two-for-one split the market share price doesn't quite get cut in half. Just as cash dividends may be a signal to shareholders, stock splits may signal some information but the signal is much weaker. After all, there is no cash payment in a stock split.

Motives for a stock split: to increase the number of shares and thereby to broaden the market for the stock, and to reduce the price to a more favorable trading range.

A frequently cited motive for a stock split is to increase the number of shares outstanding and thereby broaden the market for the stock. Another motive is to reduce the price to a more favorable trading range. Reducing the price, therefore, may increase the stock's appeal to investors with small amounts to invest. There is no evidence, however, that a broadening of the market, if it does occur, has any significant impact on the total value of the firm.

Chapter 18

Options, Futures, and Specialized Forms of Financing

In this chapter we will discuss two types of specialized financial contracts that have become increasingly important—options and futures contracts. Both types of contracts have specialized uses for both individual investors and corporate managers. In addition, we will discuss convertible bonds and warrants, which can provide a company with a useful means of financing in the right situations. Both convertibles and warrants involve types of options contracts.

Options

Basic Features

An **option** is a contract conveying the right to buy or sell designated securities or commodities at a specified price during a stipulated period of time. Such a contract is an agreement between two parties. The option buyer has the right to exercise the option but does not have an obligation to buy or sell the security. The option seller, sometimes referred to as the *writer* of the option, must stand ready to honor the buyer's choice.

In recent years, the variety of options on financial securities has increased tremendously, as have their uses. Now there are options on stocks, interest rates, stock indexes, and foreign currencies, to name a few examples. All options have the same basic elements: (1) the option buyer has a right, not an obligation; (2) the price of the underlying security is specified when the option is originally sold; (3) there is a time frame in which the option must be exercised. There are, however, many important differences among options. *European options,* for example, may be exercised only at maturity. *American options* may be exercised at any time up through the expiration date.

Options on Common Stock

There are three basic categories of options allowing investors to purchase stock: (1) warrants, (2) stock options given to employees, and (3) call and put options. *Warrants* are sold by the company to outside investors and are sold to raise money for the company. **Stock options** are similar to warrants but are granted by the company to selected managers as part of the managers' compensation to allow them to share in the company's good fortune if share prices go up. The last category, call and put options, are traded between outside investors in organized exchanges.

A **call option** gives the owner the right to buy a specified number of shares of stock for a specified price for a specified period of time. Call options differ from warrants and stock options given to managers in that the call option is sold by another investor (not the corporation), so that if the call option is exercised, its owner does not purchase new stock from the company. Rather, there would be a financial transaction between two investors with no cash flow to the company. Call options typically cover a shorter time period for exercise (up to nine months) than warrants or stock options given to managers. Call options are attractive investments to individuals who are betting on large increases in stock prices. Similarly, a **put option** gives the owner of the option the right to *sell* at a specified

price for a specified period of time. Thus, a put option might be an attractive investment for someone who thinks the stock price is likely to fall.

Call and put options have existed for decades, but large-scale trading activity began only in the 1970s. In April 1973 the Chicago Board Options Exchange (CBOE) began trading call options on stocks. With the advent of standardized contracts and published prices, the markets for options on common stock have flourished. Now calls and puts are a standard part of the investment menu in U.S. financial markets.

Options in the Financial Pages

Exercise price — the price specified in an option contract, also called the strike price.

Table 18–1 shows how American call options on IBM stock are recorded in the *Wall Street Journal*. In each call option there is an **exercise price,** also known as the *strike price,* that specifies the price at which the owner of the call can purchase the stock. Second, there is a *maturity date,* also known as the *expiration date,* which gives the last time the option can be used. Let us focus on a specific IBM call option, one with a strike price of $115 and a maturity date of January 1988. Table 18–1 shows that this call option was selling for 6¼ = $6.25 in late 1987. This option price is often called the "premium"; that is, a buyer would have to pay a "premium" of $6.25 to buy the right to purchase one share of IBM stock for $115 a share. In fact, though the financial pages quote options as if the call were for a single share of IBM stock, call options are typically for 100 shares, so buying this call would actually cost $6.25 × 100 = $625. As is done by participants in the options markets, in the remainder of our discussion we will describe the situation as if the call were for a single share. Just remember to multiply all figures by 100 if you plan to get into this market!

The other calls in Table 18–1 involve different strike prices (set in multiples of five dollars) and different maturity dates. For example, calls with a strike price of $110 maturing in April 1988 have a price of $12.50. Notice that the closing price of IBM *stock* is $118 no matter which call we look at. This is the case because all of the calls are just different options to buy the same thing — common stock in IBM.

The figures in Table 18–1 are interesting, but they pose a basic question. Why do call options have value? And why would some call options have higher prices than others?

Table 18–1
Wall Street Journal Call-Options Listing, December 23, 1987

Option & NY Close	Strike Price	Calls — Last		
		Jan	Feb	Apr
IBM				
118	100	18	s	20¼
118	105	14	s	r
118	110	10	r	12½
→ 118	115	6¼	7½	10
118	120	3½	4⅞	7⅛
118	125	1⅝	s	5¾

r = not traded.
s = no option.

Valuation of Call Options

The variables that affect option prices can be divided into two categories: (1) variables associated with the underlying asset and (2) variables contained in the option contract itself.[1]

1. *Variables associated with the underlying asset:*
   a. *Price* of the underlying asset. For a call option on IBM stock this is the price of IBM stock. All other things equal, the higher the stock price, the higher the value of a call option.
   b. *Volatility* of the underlying asset. The more volatile IBM's stock price is, the greater the chance that IBM's stock price will go up, thus making the call option more valuable.
2. *Variables in the option contract:*
   a. *Exercise price* (strike price). Since the exercise price is the price a call owner would have to pay per share of stock, the lower the exercise price, the higher the value of the call.
   b. *Maturity.* The longer the time before the option expires, the greater the chance the stock price may increase, and thus the greater the value of the call.

The main variables affecting the value of an option are the price of the underlying asset, the volatility of the underlying asset, the exercise (strike) price specified in the option, and the maturity of the option.

We can relate some of these key variables by focusing on the value of a call option just as it is about to expire. To do this, let us create a "payoff" table that shows the value of a call option with an exercise price of $3 per share of common stock.

Price of Stock at Maturity	−	Exercise Price	=	Payoff
$8	−	$3	=	$5
$4	−	$3	=	$1
$3	−	$3	=	$0
$2		don't exercise	=	$0
$1		don't exercise	=	$0

The "payoff" at maturity is simply the price of the stock (the price at which the shares could be sold) minus the exercise price (the price one must pay to get the stock) if it makes sense to exercise. If the stock price is below the exercise price of $3, however, the payoff is zero since it would be best to just let the option expire worthless. Remember, a call option is the right but not the obligation to buy stock.

These payoffs are the "maturity value" of the call option and can be formalized as shown in Equation (1):

$$V_c = N(P - E) \quad \text{if } P > E$$

$$\text{or } V_c = 0 \qquad\qquad \text{if } P \le E \tag{1}$$

[1]More technical valuation considerations show that the value of a call also depends on the interest rate in the market (due to the time value of money) and whether a company will pay dividends over the life of the option. See S. Turnbull, *Option Valuation,* for some advanced models of option valuation.

where V_c = the maturity of the call, N = the number of shares of common stock that can be purchased with one call, P = the market price of the common stock per share, and E = the exercise price of the common stock per share that has been stipulated in the call option.

Equation (1) states that if the stock is selling for more than the exercise price (if P is greater than E), the call has a value equal to the difference between the market price and exercise price of the stock times the number of shares of stock the call allows you to buy at the exercise price. For example, if P = \$5, E = \$3, and N = 1, Equation (1) indicates that the value of the call = 1(\$5 − \$3) = \$2. The call would be worth \$2 because the holder could immediately make a \$2 profit by purchasing a share of stock for \$3 a share and selling it in the market at \$5 a share. Equation (1) also indicates, however, that if the market price is less than or equal to the exercise price, the call is worthless.

Note that Equation (1) was developed assuming the call option was about to expire, so that an owner could either exercise the call by buying stock at the lower price and selling this stock at the prevailing market price or see the call expire and become worthless. In fact, as long as a call option has an extended time period left before expiration, there is some chance that the stock's market price will go higher and the call will be worth even more than indicated by Equation (1). As a result, calls normally sell for more than the "value at maturity" given in Equation (1). Figure 18–1 displays the situation graphically. The magnitude of the premium over maturity value depends primarily on the time remaining to expiration, the volatility of the common stock, and the opportunity cost of funds to investors.[2]

Let us interpret the data on IBM call options found in Table 18–1 in terms of Equation (1) and Figure 18–1. Consider the call maturing in January with an exercise (strike) price of \$115, so E = \$115. Also assume the call was for a single share, N = 1. If the option matured in December, IBM's stock price, P (its closing price on the date of the WSJ quotes), would be \$118 in Equation (1). Putting these facts together, we can calculate the value of the call if it matured immediately:

$$V_c = N(P - E) \quad \text{since } P = \$118 > E = \$115$$

$$V_c = 1(\$118 - \$115)$$

$$V_c = \$3 \,.$$

The maturity value of the call is thus \$3.00. In fact, however, the call sold for \$6.25 in December. The "excess" over maturity value in this case is \$3.25 (\$6.25 − \$3.00 = \$3.25). This \$3.25 is the extra value associated with the fact that the option matures in January — not immediately. During the life of the option, the share price of IBM may go even higher than \$118.

Two features about the prices in Table 18–1 are worth noting at this point. First, for a given maturity, the lower the exercise (strike) price, the higher the

[2] A voluminous literature exists on valuing options. The path-breaking work is the option pricing formula developed by F. Black and M. Scholes in "The Pricing of Options and Corporate Liabilities," *Journal of Political Economy*, May/June 1975. Although its detail is beyond the scope of this book, the Black-Scholes formula (and variations) for valuing options is widely used in the investment community. For a readable development of options pricing see W. Sharpe, *Investments*, 3rd edition, Englewood Cliffs, N.J.: Prentice-Hall, 1985.

Figure 18–1
Valuation of a Call Option

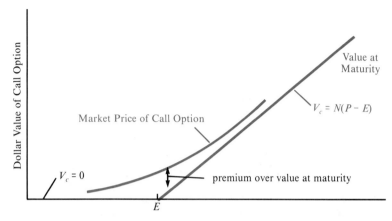

Market Price per Share of Common Stock, P

price of the call option. For example, January calls with an exercise price of $125 sell for $1⅝, whereas January calls with an exercise price of $105 sell for $14. This is the case because lower exercise prices are a benefit to the owner of a call option. Second, for a given exercise price, the longer the maturity of the option, the greater the value of the option. For example, at an exercise price of $115 January calls sell at $6¼, while April calls sell at $10. The longer maturity gives IBM stock more time to rise in price and makes the option more valuable.

Sample Problem 18–1
Value of Call Option on Franklin Stock

A call option on Franklin Mint stock has an exercise price of $100 and expires in exactly three months. Franklin stock currently sells for $103 a share. (Assume the call is for one share of stock.)

A. What would the value of the call option be if the option expired today?

B. Would you expect the current price of the call option to be worth more or less than the number calculated in part A?

C. What would the price of the call option be at the end of three months if Franklin's stock at that time was trading for $95 a share?

Solution
A. The "maturity" value of the call option can be determined from Equation (1) as follows:

$$V_c = N(P - E)$$

$$= 1(\$103 - \$100) = \$3.00.$$

B. Today, the call would sell for more than the maturity value of $3.00, because there is a chance the stock price will go even higher than $103 in the next three months.

C. In this case, the option is about to expire, so its price would be equal to its maturity value. Since the stock price is less than the exercise price, we know from Equation (1) the call option will have a zero value.   ▨

Leverage Available from Purchasing Options

The valuation concepts we have presented imply a tremendous potential profit from owning call options if the price per share of stock goes up. To understand this, suppose you thought IBM stock would go from $118 (the closing price in December 1987 in Table 18–1) to $140 by April 1988. One strategy would be to buy the stock for $118 and, if you're right, reap a $22-per-share profit for a $22/$118 = 0.186 = 18.6 percent rate of return. But suppose instead you had bought an April call with a strike price of $115. This would cost $10 in December. If you are right, and IBM stock goes to $140, the call will be worth $25 in April at maturity ($V_c = P - E = \$140 - \$115 = \$25$). Thus you'd have earned a $15 profit ($25 − $10) on an investment of only $10 — a 150 percent rate of return in a few months. Not bad!

> *Call options have tremendous profit potential if stock prices increase.*

Of course, there's no free lunch, and the upside potential of call options has its risks. Just consider what happens if IBM stock ends April at $115. If you had bought a share of stock in December at $118, you would have lost $3 on your investment — a bit less than a 3 percent loss — not fun but not a disaster. On the other hand, if you'd bought the April call with an exercise price of $115 it would be worthless in April. You would lose 100 percent of your money invested in calls! The message is clear: purchased alone, call options can have high potential

> *But, call options involve high risks.*

rewards but involve high risks.

Options and Risk of the Underlying Stock

Before leaving our discussion of call options, it is important to stress a basic point in option valuation: the more volatility there is associated with a stock, the more valuable the option is. Think about the preceding sentence, because it may at first seem to fly in the face of risk-averse behavior by investors. We have said that the riskier the underlying stock is, the more valuable a call option is. Doesn't this go against our statements that investors dislike risk? No, because of the particular way a call option works. With more volatility, there is a greater chance a stock price will go up (or down) in the future. If you own a call option, you get to benefit from the full range of price increases above the exercise price, and on the downside you can just let your option expire worthless. In short, the call option picks up the upside in stock price movements but has limited losses on the downside. As a result, call-option prices actually go up as the volatility of the underlying stock increases.

> *The value of an option increases as the volatility of the underlying asset increases.*

Put-Option Valuation

Just as call options allow you to profit from upward movements in share price, put options allow profits if share prices fall, because the put allows you to sell stock at a specified price. Consider the payoffs at maturity from owning a put option with a $3 exercise price. The payoff results because you could buy a share of stock (at the market price) and then turn around and sell it at the exercise price specified in the put.

Exercise Price	−	Stock Price	=	Payoff
$3		$8		don't exercise, $0
$3		$4		don't exercise, $0
$3	−	$3		$0
$3	−	$2		$1
$3	−	$1		$2

Figure 18–2 graphs the value (payoff) of the put, V_p, at maturity, given an exercise price, E, of $3.00. As in our example, we assume the put is for a single share $(N = 1)$.

Figure 18–2
Valuation of a Put Option

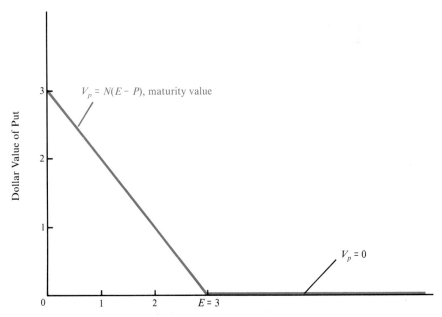

$V_p = N(E − P)$, maturity value

$V_p = 0$

Dollar Value of Put

$E = 3$

Market Price per Share of Common Stock, P

This valuation relationship is reminiscent of valuation of a call and can be expressed as Equation (2), where V_p is the value of the put at maturity:

$$V_p = N(E - P) \quad \text{if } P < E \tag{2}$$

$$V_p = 0 \quad \text{if } P \geq E$$

where N = number of shares of common stock that can be purchased with one put, P = the market price of the common stock per share, and E = the exercise price of the common stock per share that has been stipulated in the put option.

As the preceding discussion shows, a put option is useful when a share price drops in value.

Call options allow the owner to profit from price increases in the underlying asset. Put options allow the owner to profit from price decreases in the underlying asset.

Sample Problem 18–2
Valuing a Put Option on XYZ Stock

A put option on XYZ stock has an exercise price of $10 and XYZ stock is currently selling for $11 a share. The put expires in one month and is for one share of stock.

A. What would be the maturity value (in one month) of the put if XYZ's stock price remains at $11.00?

B. Would you expect the current price of the put to be higher or lower than the figure calculated in part A?

C. What would be the price of the put at the end of one month (just before expiration) if XYZ's stock price was $7 a share at that time?

Solution

A. From Equation (2) the put would have zero value since the price of the stock exceeds the exercise price. It would not make sense to exercise the put and sell the stock at $10 if the stock can be sold at $11.00 in the market.

B. The current price of the put would be higher than zero since there is some chance XYZ's stock price will fall below $10 in the next month.

C. The put should sell at its maturity value, which from Equation (2) is

$$V_p = N(E - P)$$

$$= 1(\$10 - \$7) = \$3.00.$$

Options Pricing Theory

As we have seen, an option's value depends on the price of the underlying asset, the exercise price, the volatility of the underlying asset, and the maturity of the option. These last two factors, volatility and maturity, mean that prior to maturity an option will sell for more than its maturity value. But how much more? We can always find out by looking at option prices in the financial press, but it would be helpful to have a formula to calculate what these prices should be. Developing such formulas is the challenge of **options pricing theory.** In recent years finance scholars have developed models that do quite well in explaining observed option prices. The most famous of these valuation theories is the Black-Scholes theory of option pricing. For an option about to expire, this theory gives the same answer as the maturity value given in Equation (1) for a call option. The benefit of the Black-Scholes formula is that it also calculates values for calls prior to maturity. The difficulty of the formula is that using it requires estimates of a stock's volatility. Do people actually use such a formula? You bet. There are even calculators available with a "Black-Scholes" key. While a full treatment of the theory of option pricing is beyond the scope of this text, the message is that because of the importance of options (and the profit potential!), practitioners routinely use advanced models of option pricing.

Options pricing theory— theories to explain option values before maturity; most famous is Black-Scholes formula.

Combining Positions

Owning a call or put option can be advantageous in many situations, some of which involve combining options with positions in the underlying stock. For example, suppose you already owned shares of IBM stock but wanted to protect yourself from a major loss on the investment. A made-to-order solution is to also buy a put option on IBM. To see this, let's look at the payoffs from owning one share of IBM and one put option on IBM at an exercise price of $110.

Price of IBM Stock at Maturity of Put	Value of Put with E = $110	Value of Stock Plus Put
$130	0	$130
$120	0	$120
$110	0	$110
$100	$10	$110
$ 90	$20	$110

Portfolio insurance— an investment strategy to guarantee the minimum value of a portfolio; can be accomplished by buying put options on stocks you own.

If IBM stock ends up being worth more than $110, your put expires worthless. But if IBM stock drops below $110, your put has value. In fact, for every dollar below $110 IBM stock drops, your put goes up in value by a dollar! This ensures that your portfolio (stock plus put) will be worth at least $110 no matter what happens. This basic type of strategy is sometimes known as **portfolio insurance.** The cost of the insurance is the price you pay to buy the put.

Figure 18–3
Portfolio Insurance by Owning a Put Option

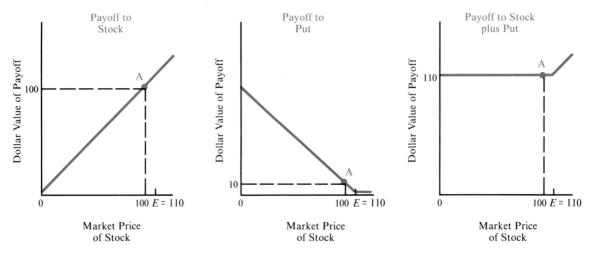

At A, price of stock is $100, stock is worth $100, put is
worth $10 ($110 − $100); so portfolio is worth $100 + $10 = $110.

We can see the effects of portfolio insurance graphically in Figure 18–3 by combining a payoff from the stock plus a payoff from the put. For example, point A in the three graphs corresponds to a price of $100 for IBM when the put expires. The stock will be worth $100, the put will be worth $10 ($110 − $100), so the portfolio of the stock plus the put will be worth $110.[3]

There are many other positions one can take in options. Instead of owning a call, you can sell a call. In options terminology this is *writing* a call. In this case your payoff is just the reverse of that of the owner of the calls. Table 18–2 (pp. 540–541) provides more detail on many of the terms associated with the options markets.

By owning portfolios of options and the underlying assets, investors can reduce risks.

Other Types of Options

Thus far we have discussed options where the underlying asset is the common stock of a particular company. For example, an investor anticipating a large rise in IBM's stock price might buy a call option on IBM stock. Not all options are based on stock of individual companies, however.

Foreign-Currency Options. Each day in the financial press (for example, the *Wall Street Journal*), you can find price quotations to buy options on various for-

[3]It is interesting to note that the payoff to the portfolio of the stock plus put looks very similar to the payoff to a call option. This technically can be formalized as an equivalence known as put-call parity but is beyond the scope of this text.

eign currencies, such as the British pound or Japanese yen. These foreign-currency options are similar to stock options but the underlying asset is a specified currency. A buyer of a foreign-currency option can "lock in" the right to buy the foreign currency for a specified price in dollars. Such options might be quite useful to a financial manager whose company is considering doing business abroad but does not know whether the business will actually materialize. (In Chapter 24, we will discuss other ways of dealing with exchange-rate fluctuations between currencies.)

Stock-Index Options. In addition to options on individual stocks, there are now index options based on the level of a particular stock-price index. Though the technical details are more complicated, index options are essentially ways to take advantage of movements in a stock index rather than movements in just a single stock.

Some index options are based on broad stock-market aggregates, while others are related to particular industries. Index options have been offered on the Standard and Poor's 500 stock index, the New York Stock Exchange Composite index (which is based on approximately 1,500 stocks), and the American Stock Exchange Major Market Value Index, to name only a few.

Interest-Rate Options. Options are available on debt securities, including bills, notes, and bonds issued by the U.S. Treasury. Because the prices of such debt securities change with changes in prevailing market interest rates, these options are referred to as interest-rate options. Such options give individuals and corporate managers ways to take advantage of swings in interest rates.

Options are available on many types of securities and have become increasingly important for financial managers.

As the preceding discussion shows, there are many types of options already traded in financial markets, and we have covered only a subset of those. In theory, one can create options on almost any underlying asset. If investors find such options attractive, innovators in financial markets will design and trade them. The options markets will become an increasingly important part of the environment facing financial managers.

Options and Financial Management

As we've already mentioned, foreign-currency options and interest-rate options offer direct advantages to a financial manager in dealings in either foreign currency or debt markets. In practice, the applicability of options to corporate financial management is quite broad. In this section we'll discuss three dimensions of applying options to corporate finance. The first is a conceptual framework of viewing the stock of the firm as a call option on the underlying assets. The second and third dimensions involve direct applications of options in specialized financing arrangements—warrants and convertible securities.

Table 18-2

A Glossary of Terms in the Options Market

The jargon of the options markets is similar to that of the other securities markets. Some terms, however, are unique to the options markets, and an options trader or investor would do well to know them.

At-the-money

A put or call is at-the-money when the underlying stock sells at the same price as the exercise price of the option.

Call

An option which gives its owner, or holder, the right to buy 100 shares (usually) of the underlying stock at a specified price within a specified time period.

Class of Options

A class of options consists of a group of puts or calls (i.e., one or the other) on the same security.

Combination

A strategy. Combinations involve buying or selling both a put and a call on the same stock.

Covered Call Writer

The writer of a call who owns the shares of stock on which he or she has written a call.

Covered Put Writer

The writer of a put who holds an identical put on the same class of stock, and one in

which the exercise, or striking price, of the put held is equal to or greater than that of the written put.

Exercise Price

Also the *Striking Price*. The price at which the holder may purchase (in the case of call options), or sell (in the case of put options), an underlying stock.

Expiration Date

The last date on which an option may be exercised at the striking or exercise price.

In-the-money

An option is in-the-money when it has intrinsic value. A call is in-the-money when the underlying stock's price is greater than the option's exercise price. A put is in-the-money when the underlying stock's price is lower than the option's exercise price.

Intrinsic Value

The value of the option if exercised immediately. This would be the maturity value if the current price of the underlying asset remains unchanged.

Option

A contract giving its holder the right to buy or sell 100 shares (generally) of a particular stock at a predetermined price and predetermined time period, i.e., expiration date.

A Firm's Equity as a Call Option on the Underlying Assets

The equity of a company can be thought of as an option on the underlying assets where the exercise price is the amount of money owed to debt holders.

Because shareholders have limited liability, it is possible to view equity as a call option on the firm's assets. To illustrate, consider a firm with only one asset, which has been financed in part by borrowings of $1,000 at 10 percent interest. To simplify matters, suppose the principal and interest on the debt (a total of $1,100) is due in one year. The firm's single asset will produce operating cash flow (prior to financial charges) only at the end of the next year, but the amount is uncertain. The following table shows payoffs to equity owners for various operating outcomes. Note that if the operating cash flow is less than $1,100, the firm will be forced into bankruptcy, and the debt owners will get the entire operating cash flow.

Options Clearing Corp.
The actual issuer of options. Moreover, in the event of an exercise, it is the corporation, as the ultimate obligor, that becomes the source of securities for buyers of calls who exercise their options; and the one to whom the put holder sells his or her shares.

Out-of-the-money
An option with no intrinsic value. A call is out-of-the-money when the exercise price is higher than the underlying stock's price. A put is out-of-the-money when the exercise price is lower than the current market value of the stock.

Premium
The price paid by a buyer to the writer of an option. It is quoted on a per-share basis.

Put
An option which gives its owner, or holder, the right to sell 100 shares (generally) at a specified price within a specified time period.

Spreads
A strategy in which an investor or speculator buys one option and sells another on the same underlying stock, but with a different expiration date and/or a different strike price.

Straddle
Another strategy. A straddle involves writing a put as well as a call on the same stock. Both options also carry the same striking price and the same expiration date.

Striking Price
The *Exercise Price,* or the price at which the holder may purchase (a call), or sell (a put) an underlying stock.

Time-Spread
The purchase and sale of options with the same exercise price on the same stock, but with different expiration dates. Also known as calendar and horizontal spreads.

Time-Value
Or *Time-Premium.* The portion of the premium that reflects the remaining life of an option. The amount over the option's intrinsic value.

Underlying Security
The security underlying an option. It would be purchased or sold were the option exercised.

Writer
A person or organization that sells an option.

Source: Adapted from *The ABC's of Option Trading,* Dow Jones & Company, 1984.

Possible Cash Flow from Operations	−	Cash Flow to Debt	=	Cash Flow to Shareholders
$2,000	−	$1,100	=	$900
$1,500	−	$1,100	=	$400
$1,100	−	$1,100	=	$ 0
$1,000	−	$1,000 (bankruptcy)	=	$ 0
$ 500	−	$ 500 (bankruptcy)	=	$ 0

Look at the payoffs to shareholders in the last column. They are exactly like the payoffs to the owner of a call option on the firm's operating assets with an exer-

Finance in Practice 18—1

Stock Options to Executives

As the stock market rose in the 1980s, many companies made more widespread use of stock options as part of executive compensation packages. In 1981 stock-option programs were worth 57 percent of a top manager's salary, but by 1986 the options were worth 140 percent of salary. According to one industry expert, the average stock-option grant to a chief executive of a *Fortune* 200 company was $1 million in 1986. Perhaps the most noteworthy case was Lee Iacocca, chairman of Chrysler Corporation. When Iacocca took over the struggling auto firm in 1980, he took a lot of stock options rather than salary. Iacocca wanted to show his confidence in Chrysler's ability to turn the corner and return to profitability. Chrysler did rise from the brink of bankruptcy, and so did its share price. In 1986 Iacocca's compensation was $20.6

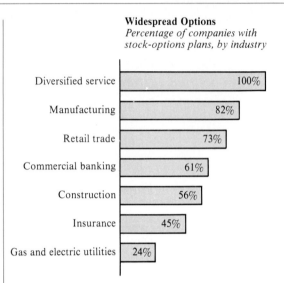

Widespread Options
Percentage of companies with stock-options plans, by industry

Source: The Conference Board.

million—largely cashing in on stock options he had received a few years earlier.

The logic of using stock options is to link management compensation to the fortunes of shareholders. If share prices rise so do managers' wealth, but if there is no share price increase the option is worthless. The accompanying table shows the widespread use of options in selected industries.

Source: Adapted from "Executives See Stock Options Drop in Value," *Wall Street Journal,* October 21, 1987.

cise price of $1,100. As long as the operating cash flow is above $1,100, the shareholders exercise the option to stay in business by paying the promised amount to debt owners. If the operating cash flow is below $1,100, however, the shareholders in this example will not exercise their option, but rather will let it expire worthless. The key is that shareholders' limited liability means they don't have to come up with their own personal funds to pay off corporate debt.

Admittedly, the preceding example is simplified. Firms have many assets with cash flows for many future periods. In addition, there are usually many forms of corporate debt of varying maturities. These complications do not, however, change the main insight of the example. The limited liability of shareholders means that the equity of a corporation can be viewed as a call option on the firm's assets. While this insight may not provide day-to-day guidance in financial management, it can provide insights into possible behavior by corporate managers. For example, our earlier discussion of options showed that increases in the volatility of the underlying asset increase the value of a call option on that asset. As a result, a manager trying to increase the value of the firm's common stock (the call option on the assets) would have some incentive to increase the riskiness of the firm's assets. This might be done by maintaining low levels of liquidity or taking on high-risk projects. It is precisely for this reason that many bonds have bond covenants restricting the actions of management.

Since common stock can be viewed as a call option on the firm's assets, there may be incentives to increase the riskiness of the firm's assets.

Warrants

One of the most straightforward uses of options concepts in financial management is the use of warrants in raising funds. A **warrant** is an option to purchase a specified number of shares of common stock at a specified price for a specified period of time. Warrants typically are issued in connection with bonds and usually are detachable, but not always. If detachable, the warrants can be detached from the bonds and sold separately. Markets exist for detachable warrants; many are listed on the American Stock Exchange, and a few are listed on the New York Stock Exchange.

Warrant — an option to purchase a number of shares of common stock at a specified price for a specified period of time, typically issued in connection with bonds, and usually detachable.

The warrant itself sets forth the terms of the option, which include the number of shares that can be purchased with each warrant, the exercise price, and the time period over which the warrant can be exercised. Most warrants can be exercised over a number of years, and most have a stated expiration date. Sometimes the terms — either the exercise price or the shares per warrant — may change over time. When the warrant is exercised, it is exchanged along with an appropriate sum of money for the specified number of shares of common stock. In essence, the warrant is a type of long-term call option, since its maturity is much longer than the maturity of a typical call option. A key feature of the warrant is that the company actually issues new shares of stock and receives money when investors exercise their warrants.

Warrants give the holder an option of an equity claim and, therefore, a chance to share in a firm's good fortunes. Warrants usually are issued in connection with debt securities and can be sold privately or publicly, but sometimes they may be issued by themselves. When issued in connection with debt securities, the motive usually is to "sweeten the deal" and thereby to make the issue easier to sell or make a lower rate of interest on the debt possible. In exchange for the option, the buyer accepts the lower rate. A firm with a marginal credit rating faced with an embarrassingly high interest rate might use warrants to lower the rate. A firm unable to sell a standard debt issue at any rate, presumably because of risk or the lack of a track record, might find that warrants would make the issue salable. Venture capitalists might find warrants an attractive alternative as a means of providing funds to a fledgling firm, with the security of a debt claim and also an option on the equity.

Convertible Securities

Convertible security — a security that can be converted at the option of the holder into a security of the same firm but of another type.

A **convertible security** is one that can be converted at the option of the holder into a security of the same firm but of another type. Both bonds and preferred stock are issued as convertible securities and in nearly all cases are convertible into shares of common stock. Once the conversion has been made, the process cannot be reversed. Holders of convertible bonds thus give up their position as creditors to become owners. Rather than paying cash as the holder of a standard call option does, the owner of a convertible gives up a financial asset (e.g., a bond) to acquire shares of stock.

As with a warrant, the option to convert a bond into common stock can be quite attractive if an investor anticipates an increase in share price. A convertible bond also has the "downside protection" of paying interest and principal even if the stock price does not go up.

The use of convertible securities has varied over time. During the period 1960–1981, about 10 percent of all new corporate-bond offerings were convertible, and more than 20 percent of preferred-stock issues were convertible. In the late 1960s, convertible securities saw their largest use when many were employed to finance corporate acquisitions. In the three-year period 1966–1968, about 25 percent of all corporate-bond issues were convertible, and the comparable figure for convertible preferred stock was almost 50 percent.[4]

A firm may issue convertible securities as a means of obtaining a lower interest rate on debt or a lower dividend on preferred stock than would be possible with a nonconvertible issue. Another motive might arise in a situation in which management felt that its prospects were not being fairly evaluated by the stock market. A convertible issue offers an opportunity to sell common stock at a premium over current market rates, assuming that conversion eventually takes place. Rapidly growing firms might find this possibility especially appealing.

Convertible securities also might be attractive in more specialized financing situations. Consider, for example, a relatively young firm with no track record that is attempting to raise outside capital. In such high-risk situations, investors might wish to participate, provided they share in the firm's good fortunes as equity investors should the outcome be favorable. A convertible bond gives them an option on an equity position but at the same time provides a senior debt claim against assets during the early, more uncertain period. Other specialized situations in which convertible securities might be attractive include mergers and acquisitions. Appendix 18A discusses the valuation of convertibles in more detail.

Though convertibles and warrants both have option features, they differ in several important respects. Even when originally issued with bonds, warrants are detachable and can thus stand separately as a long-term option to buy stock. A convertible bond, on the other hand, has the bond and option features bound together. The combination of bond and warrant is thus more flexible than a convertible bond from the standpoint of the holder. A second and major difference is that the firm receives additional funds when warrants are exercised, whereas it does not when convertibles are converted. Accounting entries in the capital section of the balance sheet differ accordingly. Third, from the firm's standpoint, warrants may

Convertibles may be attractive in specialized financing situations.

Convertibles and warrants differ in several important respects.

---

[4]Data on the use of convertible securities are from J. Hannum, *Convertible Bond Financing,* unpublished dissertation, University of North Carolina at Chapel Hill, 1983. The data describe new convertible financing as a proportion of underwritten public offerings. The numbers reported are averages of annual percentages.

provide less control than convertible securities, because the firm cannot force holders of warrants to exercise them. Most convertibles, on the other hand, have call features whereby the issuer, at its option, can call the issue for redemption. (See Appendix 18A for more detail.)

Financing in Competitive Markets

While the use of convertible bonds or warrants can lower the rate of interest to the firm, this lower interest rate comes at a cost — the cost of giving up a claim on the firm's equity.

The use of convertible securities and warrants does indeed lower the rate of interest (or preferred dividends) to the firm, but at a price. In return for the lower rate, the buyers of convertible securities or warrants obtain a claim against the firm's equity. If things turn out favorably, they will later be able to buy the firm's stock at a bargain price. In the case of firms with marginal credit ratings or unproven records, convertible securities and warrants may provide sources of financing not otherwise available. Here again, the firm pays for the accommodation with a claim on its equity.

A lower interest rate does not necessarily mean that existing shareholders will obtain a net benefit (increase in value) as the result of the firm's use of convertible securities or warrants.

If a firm issuing convertible securities or warrants fully discloses all material information, as it typically should, we would expect a competitive market to evaluate the firm's prospects in an unbiased manner. The market is likely to value the option on the common stock properly, meaning that overvaluation and undervaluation are about equally likely. In a competitive market, we would expect investors to reduce the dividend or interest rate on the securities by an amount that correctly reflects the value of the option to buy the firm's stock. Thus, the firm pays for the lower interest or dividend rate approximately what it is worth.

What then do we conclude with respect to the use of convertible securities and warrants? For reasons discussed earlier, convertible securities and warrants do not often offer advantages for which the firm does not pay full price. Both are complex securities requiring considerable expertise to market. Thus, convertible securities and warrants find their main application in quite specialized financing situations.

Futures and Forwards

Futures contract — contract to buy (or sell) an asset at a specified price at a specified time; unlike an option, the future *requires* the holder to buy (or sell) the asset.

A financial **futures contract** is a contract to buy or sell a stated financial claim (such as a U.S. Treasury bond) at a specified price at a specified time. Unlike an option, a futures contract *requires* the holder to buy or sell the asset at a specified date; the holder doesn't have an option. Just as in the case of options, it is possible to trade futures contracts on many different types of underlying assets. Financial futures are simply futures where the underlying asset is some type of financial security.

For decades, there had been futures contracts on commodities, such as wheat, corn, and cocoa, but not until the 1970s and early 1980s did financial futures become an integral part of financial markets. Trading in financial futures contracts has skyrocketed in recent years. As an example, in 1984 daily trading in U.S. Treasury-bond futures represented claims on about $15 billion in securities — more than twice the trading volume in Treasury bonds themselves. Other financial futures cover foreign currencies, Treasury bills, and stock-market indices. In 1985, a

Forward contract—
contract to buy or sell an
asset at a specified price at a
specified future date; differs
from future in that it does
not involve cash settlement
prior to the maturity date.

futures contract on the U.S. dollar was introduced, and for those worried about uncertain inflation rates, a contract on the consumer price index was introduced!

Forward contracts are quite similar to futures contracts. A **forward contract** also requires the holder to buy (or sell) an asset at specified price at a specified future date. Futures contracts are standardized and tradeable, whereas forward contracts are normally not tradeable in the secondary markets. The main difference between forward and futures contracts is that the futures contract typically involves some cash settlements prior to the future date as if the owner were to buy the asset each trading day. The forward contract involves cash settlement only on the date specified in the contract.

Payoffs to Forward Contracts and Futures Contracts

Let us begin with forward contracts since their payoffs occur on a single date—the cash settlement date. Suppose today is January 2, 1989. Consider a forward contract that involves the purchase of an asset for $100 one month hence, on February 2. Figure 18–4 shows a time line of the events if you were to buy such a contract. Note that although you agree on the price today, January 2, you don't pay until February 2, nor do you get the asset until February 2. The uncertainty involved is what the asset will actually be worth on February 2. Let us look at the payoffs to owning the forward contract, given different possible market prices the asset might have on February 2. Remember, because you own the forward contract, you buy at $100 no matter what the market price is.

Market Price of Asset (Feb. 2)	−	Your Purchase Price (Forward)		Payoff to Forward Contract
$110	−	$100	=	$ 10
$105	−	$100	=	$ 5
$100	−	$100	=	$ 0
$ 95	−	$100	=	$ −5
$ 90	−	$100	=	$−10

Futures and forward
contracts involve an
obligation (not an option) to
buy (or sell) an asset at a
fixed price.

As the payoffs show, your forward contract is valuable if the asset price increases above $100, but if its price drops below $100 you actually have a loss. While an option gives you the *right* to buy an asset, a forward contract *requires* that you buy the asset. Figure 18–4 graphs the payoffs to a forward position; note how it differs from Figure 18–1 for a call option. As Figure 18–4 shows, a forward contract can be a very risky investment if market prices of the asset drop.

The payoffs for futures contracts are determined by the same logic as that for forwards, but now there are settlements prior to the last date. For example, suppose there were a forward contract for two days with a forward price of $100. Assume also that a futures contract had the same specified price ($100) and was for two days. The following table illustrates the payoffs for a particular assumption about the price of the asset for the next two days.

Figure 18–4
Payoff at Maturity to a Forward Contract

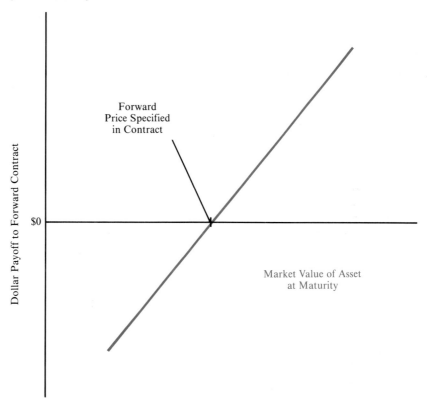

	Price of Asset	Payoff to Forward	Payoff to Future	
Day 1	$103	no payoff	$3	= (103 − 100)
Day 2	$105	$5 = (105 − 100)	$2	= (105 − 103)
Total		$5	$5	

As the table shows, the two contracts give the same total payment ($5). The difference is that the futures contract is "marked to market" each day so that the owner of the future takes part of his or her gain (or loss) each day. While this payment feature on futures can be a bit tedious, it should not hide the key forces at work. Just as in a forward contract, the owner of a futures contract will profit from increases in the price of the underlying asset and suffer losses if the underlying asset drops in price.

So far we have discussed payoffs to buyers of forward and futures contracts. If you sell such a contract, your payoffs are exactly the opposite. For example, if you've sold a futures contract with a specified price of $100 and the market price of the asset drops to $95, you'll actually make a profit of $5. Your profit comes from being able to sell at $100 something you can buy at $95 — not a bad deal if you can get it!

Sample Problem 18–3
Payoffs on Forwards and Call Options

In April you buy a forward contract to purchase British pounds in May (one month hence) and agree on a price of $1.70 per pound. For simplicity assume the contract is for one pound.

A. If the exchange rate in May is $1.80 per pound, what is your payoff on the forward contract?

B. If the exchange rate in May is $1.65 per pound, what is your payoff on the forward contract? How does this compare to the payoff on a call option to buy pounds in May that has a strike price of $1.70?

Solution

A. You buy the pound for $1.70 and can resell the pound for $1.80 in the market, so your payoff is $1.80 − $1.70 = $0.10.

B. You buy the pound for $1.70 but can resell it for only $1.65 in the market, so your payoff is $1.65 − $1.70 = −$0.05. You have a loss. If you had owned a call option, you would not have been obligated to exercise the right to buy and could have let the option expire worthless with a payoff of $0. If you had an option and wanted pounds, you would just buy the pounds in the market for $1.65 rather than exercising the call option.   ▮

Using Futures and Forward Contracts in Financial Management

Given the payoffs noted earlier, a financial manager who wanted to speculate on movements in prices could use forward or futures contracts. Some managers use contracts in this way. The more widespread and prudent use of such contracts is, however, to *reduce* risks and not to take them. This can be done by means of hedging. **Hedging** is the process of reducing risk by taking more than a single bet on an outcome. Suppose, for example, that you bet $5.00 that a particular college basketball team would win the national championship, but afterwards felt unhappy about the bet.[5] If you put down an additional $5.00 bet that the same team would

Hedging — reducing risk by taking offsetting positions.

[5]Our advice is to put your money on the UNC Tarheels.

not win the championship, you would have created a hedge. No matter what happens you'll break even — not very exciting but at least there is no risk.

By using futures it is possible to hedge risks related to interest rates, prices of commodities, or foreign currencies. For example, let's consider a situation of hedging interest rates. Suppose you are a corporate manager with a temporary surplus of funds and have used them to purchase a long-term U.S. Treasury bond. You will need to sell the bond in six months, however, to obtain cash. Your problem is that if interest rates go up, the value of the bond will drop. You are exposed to interest-rate risk, as we discussed in Chapter 4. To hedge this risk you may take a position in Treasury-bond futures and agree to sell Treasury bonds in six months at a specified price. In effect, your position in the Treasury-bond future gains money whenever interest rates go up unexpectedly. By selling the future, you have locked in a selling price now even though the market value of the Treasury bond may drop as interest rates rise. The two positions, owning a Treasury bond and effectively selling in the futures market, create a hedge. One position makes money whenever the other loses money.

In practice, the details of hedging become more complicated, but the potential benefits can be large. Hedging can be used to reduce the risks associated with borrowing costs as well as returns on investments. Hedging interest-rate risks with financial futures has become another tool for sophisticated financial management.[6]

> Futures contracts offer useful opportunities for managers to hedge risks.

[6]For an account of the growth in the use of financial futures see "Big Players in Financial Futures," *Fortune,* September 17, 1984. For a useful introduction to the topic see R. Kolb, *Understanding Futures Markets* (Glenview, Ill.: Scott, Foresman, 1985).

Finance in Practice 18–2

The Hot New World of Stock-Index Futures Trading

The age of computer investing opened a vast new territory in the early 1980s with the introduction of the stock-index future.

One of the first, and by far the most popular, is the Standard & Poor's 500 futures contract, traded on the Chicago Mercantile Exchange (the Merc). The S&P contract traded at the rate of 20.9 million contracts in 1987, compared with 8.7 million in 1983, its first full year of trading.

Each contract is worth the current level of the index times 500. For example, in mid-August 1988, the S&P index closed at 260.24 — that's $130,120 per contract. At 1988 volumes, that comes to about $5.5 billion traded per day. Total value of stocks traded on the New York Stock Exchange on a typical day during that period came to barely more, at $5.6 billion.

Of course, money managers don't actually lay out that much to buy a contract, which is part of the reason for its popularity. They like S&P futures because transaction costs are cheap and margins, or the amount paid in cash, are low, currently about $10,000 per contract.

Many money managers who handle large sums of money for pension funds and other big institutions are evaluated on how well they perform in comparison to the S&P 500 index. As a result, it is very important for them to keep track of how the index is doing and to try to match or outperform it. S&P futures make it easier for money managers to match the performance of the index. To be just like the index, they must have all their money invested in the index stocks at all times. But it's not efficient to buy little slices of the index every time cash builds up. Instead, by buying and selling index futures to hedge that cash until there's enough to invest efficiently, managers can get almost the same return without the expense of a lot of little stock transactions.

No one, not even the Merc, foresaw the popularity of the index future when the Merc introduced it in the early 1980s. "There's no question that the acceptance of stock-index futures went beyond anyone's early expectations," said William Brodsky, president of the Merc. "No one expected it to be so well accepted so quickly."

Index futures also opened the way for new computer trading strategies. Originally, program trading meant the buying or selling of a basket of stocks — usually the S&P stocks — at once, with the help of a computer. Once stock-index futures started trading, index arbitrageurs started using computers to trade on discrepancies between the price of the futures and the prices of the underlying stocks.

Source: Adapted from the *Washington Post,* August 21, 1988, page H4.

Finance in Practice 18–3

Portfolio Insurance

In the early 1980s, two finance professors and a finance practitioner started a new company, called LOR for short, reflecting the names of the three founders, Hayne Leland, John O'Brien, and Mark Rubinstein. By 1987 fund managers (e.g., pension funds) investing in stocks had upwards of $60 billion managed using LOR's methods — not a bad track record for a six-year-old company. And in 1987 the three men were featured in *Fortune* magazine among the business people of the year. What was the product that brought LOR such attention? The answer: portfolio insurance.

In concept, portfolio insurance can be thought of as combining put options with stock ownership to lock in a minimum value for the portfolio. If stock prices fall, the put option has value. In practice, however, suitable put options are not readily available for many stocks. LOR's technique was to develop portfolio insurance by selling Standard & Poor's 500 index futures — that is, agreeing to sell the stocks in the S&P 500 index at a specified price on a specified future date. Such a contract has the effect of locking in the value of the stock portfolio if stock prices fall. And due in part to the low cost and ease of dealing in index futures, portfolio insurance took off as a product.

The implementation of this investment strategy can become quite complicated, and that's what clients paid LOR to carry out. The aim was to make sure stock portfolios went down by no more than a predetermined amount over a future period—say, 5 percent over two years.

But 1987 was not all glory for LOR. The stock-market crash of October 19, when the Dow lost 508 points, caught LOR off guard. LOR actually stopped selling index futures during that day, in opposition to the dictates of their technique. One client claimed he lost more in a day than he was supposed to lose in three years. And LOR and other portfolio insurers came under heavy fire as being among those responsible for the severity of the crash. After all, LOR's methods call for *selling* stock-index futures as stock prices are going down. Such sales may put further downward pressure on prices. According to *Fortune* estimates, only about half of the $60 billion remained covered by year-end 1987.

October 19 provided a stern lesson about the types of risks possible in financial markets, but John O'Brien, LOR's chief executive officer, also saw some possible bright spots: "The events of October 19 didn't reduce people's concern with risk." And businesses such as LOR develop products in hopes of controlling risks.

Source: Adapted from Andrew Kupfer, "The Guys Who Gave Us Portfolio Insurance," *Fortune,* January 4, 1988, pp. 30–31.

KEY CONCEPTS

1. Options have become increasingly important to financial managers in recent years.

2. The main variables affecting the value of an option are the price of the underlying asset, the volatility of the underlying asset, the exercise (strike) price specified in the option, and the maturity of the option.

3. At any time prior to maturity, an option will sell for more than its maturity value since there are still opportunities for changes in the price of the underlying asset.

4. The value of an option increases as the volatility of the underlying asset increases.

5. Call options allow the owner to profit from price increases in the underlying asset. Put options allow the owner to profit from price decreases in the underlying asset.

6. By owning portfolios of options and the underlying assets, investors can reduce risks.

7. The equity of a company can be thought of as an option on the underlying assets where the exercise price is the amount of money owed to debt holders.

8. Convertible securities and warrants are specialized securities that provide varying combinations of contractual claims with options on equity.

9. Warrants can be used as an extra incentive to lenders when a company issues debt.

10. While the use of convertible bonds or warrants can lower the rate of interest to the firm, this lower interest rate comes at a cost—the cost of giving up a claim on the firm's equity. In competitive financial markets, the firm pays for the lower interest rate approximately what it is worth. As a result, the lower interest rate does not necessarily mean that existing shareholders will obtain a net benefit (increase in value) as the result of the firm's use of convertible securities or warrants.

11. Futures and forward contracts involve an obligation (not an option) to buy (or sell) an asset at a fixed price.

12. Futures contracts offer useful opportunities for managers to hedge risks.

SUMMARY

Options have become an important part of financial markets and offer an important tool to financial managers. Options give the owner the right but not the obligation to buy (or sell) an asset at a specified price for a specified period of time. As such they allow the owners to profit from future price changes in the asset. They also can be used to reduce risks.

The equity of a firm can be thought of as an option on the firm's assets where the exercise price is the amount of money owed to debt holders. At a more practical level, financial managers can use warrants and convertible securities to raise outside money. Both of these financing vehicles involve option features. Warrants are long-term call options to buy stock and are normally issued in combination with debt. Convertible securities (bonds and pre-

ferred stock) normally carry a lower interest rate or dividend rate than nonconvertible securities of the same firm, reflecting the value of the option to convert the security to common stock. Both convertible securities and warrants find their main application in specialized situations.

Financial futures have become increasingly important in recent years. Unlike options, they involve an obligation (not an option) to buy (or sell) an asset at a specified price. Futures and forward contracts are available on a wide variety of assets, including bonds, stock indexes, and foreign currencies. A primary use of futures and forward contracts is to hedge risks by combining a position in the underlying asset (e.g., a bond) with another position on the financial future on that asset.

QUESTIONS

Note: To answer questions preceded by an asterisk (*) requires knowledge of material in Appendix 18A.

1. Discuss the basic features and terminology of an option contract.

2. What is it that gives an option value?

3. If an investor thought a stock's price would decrease in the future, would the investor buy a call or put option? Explain.

4. The lower the exercise or strike price, the (less/more) valuable the option. Discuss.

5. If the market price (P) is less than the exercise price (E) for an option with a 30-day maturity, why might the option trade at a positive value?

6. What is meant by "leveraging" when investing in options?

7. "A warrant is a type of long-term call option." Explain.

8. What is a convertible security? Is it an option contract?

9. What is the function of the call feature of a convertible security?

*10. What is the conversion premium of a convertible bond or preferred stock issue?

11. Define and discuss the basic features of a futures contract.

12. Compare and contrast an option contract with a futures contract.

13. Compare and contrast a forward contract with a futures contract.

14. How can a financial manager hedge risks with futures contracts? Give a specific example.

Problems

*Problems preceded by an asterisk (*) require knowledge of material in Appendix 18A.

1. With reference to Table 18–1 in the chapter, answer the following questions.
   a. What is the price of an option maturing in January at the strike price of $120? In February? In April? Why does the value increase with time?
   b. What was the closing price of IBM?
   c. If an April option is purchased at a strike price of $110, what is the break-even stock price?
   d. When would an investor exercise the call option [part (c) above]?

2. A call option for Apex stock has an exercise price of $50 and expires in three months. The stock currently sells for $54. Assuming the call is for one share,
   a. What is the approximate value of the call option if the option expired today?
   b. Why would you expect the option to trade at a value above your answer on part (a)?
   c. What would be the price of the option at the end of three months if the stock were trading at $48?
   d. If the stock were trading at $58 at the end of three months, what would be the price of the option?

3. The 100-share call-option-payoff matrix of Zip Products is listed in Table A with several values missing. Fill in the blank values and explain their computation.

4. Construct the same payoff table for Problem (3) if the 100-share call option costs the investor $200.

5. The 100-share put-option-payoff matrix of Buchtel Services is listed in Table B with several values missing. The put option costs the investor $200 today. Fill in the blank values and explain their computation.

Table A

Price of Stock at Maturity	Exercise Price	Payoff
$20	_____	$1,100
16	_____	_____
12	_____	_____
8	_____	_____
4	_____	_____
2	_____	$0

Table B

Price of Stock at Maturity	Exercise Price	Payoff
$29	_____	_____
25	_____	_____
21	_____	$0
18	_____	_____
15	_____	_____
10	_____	_____

6. Suppose you are considering purchasing a call option on 100 shares of Robinson Industries common stock at a price of $43.50 per share. The option expires three months from today. The stock is currently selling for $36.125 per share.
   a. Does this call have any value? Why or why not?
   b. In order for this to be an attractive investment for you, how would you expect the stock price to behave in the future (rise or fall)?
   c. Suppose that you decide to purchase the contract. One month later, you need cash and would like to sell the contract to another investor. At that time, the stock price happens to be $36.125 per share. Would there be a market for the contract? If so, what would you expect the price of the contract to be relative to the price that you paid for the contract one month ago?

d. Now suppose that you still hold the call, and it is due to expire in one week. The stock price has jumped around considerably and is now $42.00. If you decide to sell the contract at this time, would anyone be willing to buy it? If so, what considerations would be important in determining a fair price for the call-option contract?

e. Suppose that on the expiration date of the call, the stock price is $45.25 per share. What is the value of the contract?

f. Now suppose that on the expiration date of the contract, the stock price is $39.75 per share. What is the value of the contract?

*7. Levy Industries has determined that holders of the company's convertible bonds would convert the issue if it were called. The company therefore has decided to force the conversion of the 10,000 out-standing bonds in order to increase its equity base in preparation for future bond issues. The $1,000 par bonds mature in 20 years and carry an 11 per-cent coupon. Each bond is convertible into 50 shares of common stock. The firm currently has 1.7 million shares of stock outstanding. The tax rate is 46 percent.

a. Assuming that the market rate of interest on nonconvertible bonds of comparable risk is 13 percent, calculate the bond value of Levy's convertible issue.

b. Levy's stock is currently selling for $22 per share. Calculate the conversion value of the convertible bonds.

c. Calculate the effect of conversion on earnings per share (EPS) at an expected earnings before interest and taxes (EBIT) of $8 million.

REFERENCES

R. Kolb. *Understanding Futures Markets*. Glenview, Ill.: Scott, Foresman, 1985.

C. W. Smithson, "A Lego Approach to Financial Engineering." *Midland Corporate Finance Journal* (Winter 1987): 16–28.

S. M. Turnbull. *Option Valuation*. Dryden Press, 1987. This book contains many computer programs for option valuation.

Appendix 18A

Valuation of Convertible Securities

In this appendix we discuss in detail the valuation of convertible securities.

Terms of Conversion

The conversion privilege can be stated in terms of either a conversion price or a conversion ratio. For example, in August 1981, MCI Telecommunications Corporation, a competitor of AT&T in offering long-distance telephone service, issued $100 million worth of 20-year convertible subordinated debentures at an interest rate of 10.25 percent. The debentures were convertible into MCI common stock at $25.65 per share (the conversion price); that is, each $1,000 bond could be exchanged, at the holder's option, into $1,000/$25.65 = 38.986 shares of common stock (the conversion ratio). At the time of the debenture issue, MCI stock was selling at $21.75 per share. Thus, the conversion price was set about 18 percent above the then market price of the common stock.

Convertible securities nearly always include a *call feature* whereby the issuer, at its option, can call the issue for redemption. However, the purpose of the call feature usually is not to force redemption but to force conversion. When the value of the common shares into which the security is convertible exceeds the call price, holders opt to convert rather than to redeem. Convertible securities usually are issued with the expectation that they will convert. The call feature provides the issuer some control over the timing of the conversion. We will return to the matter of forced conversion later.

Valuation of Convertible Securities

A convertible security derives value from two sources: its value as a bond or preferred stock and its potential value as common stock if converted. The same general valuation principles apply in the case of both convertible bonds and convertible preferred stock. In the case of a convertible bond, we can label the two components of value the *bond value* and the *conversion value*. The convertible bond can be thought of as a combination of a bond plus an option to buy the firm's common stock. If the value of the common stock rises, the value of the option and, hence, that of the convertible bond, will rise. If the value of the stock falls, the value of the convertible as a bond provides a floor below which the price of the convertible will not fall. The **bond value of a convertible bond** can be thought of as the

555

present value of future interest and principal payments and can be expressed as shown in Equation A–1:

$$V_B = \left[\sum_{t=1}^{n} \frac{I}{(1 + K_d)^t} \right] + \frac{P}{(1 + K_d)^n} \qquad (A–1)$$

where I = the annual interest payment, P = the principal amount due at maturity, n = number of years to maturity, and K_d = the yield to maturity on a nonconvertible bond of the same company or same risk class.

Equation (A–1) represents the standard valuation equation for a bond. For simplicity, the expression assumes annual interest payments rather than the semiannual payments more often encountered in practice.

Consider the MCI convertible debenture mentioned earlier. It offered a 10.25 percent interest rate, or $102.50 a year per $1,000 bond at a time when the market interest rate on a straight (nonconvertible) bond for this company, according to company officials, would have been around 18 percent.[1] Applying Equation (A–1), we find the bond value of such a convertible bond to be

$$V_B = \left[\sum_{t=1}^{20} \frac{\$102.50}{(1.18)^t} \right] + \frac{\$1,000}{(1.18)^{20}}$$

$$= \$548.66 + \$36.51$$

$$= \$585.17 .$$

Conversion value of a convertible bond — the market value of the common stock into which the bond is convertible.

The **conversion value of a convertible bond** is the market value of the common stock into which the bond is convertible. The bond described before is convertible into 38.986 shares of common stock, and the market price per share of stock was $21.75. The conversion value of each bond was, therefore, 38.986 × $21.75 = $847.95.

The value of a convertible bond depends on both its bond value and its conversion value.

Because the convertible security has value as a bond (or as preferred stock), its market price will not fall below its bond value. Because of the value of this downside protection, a convertible security nearly always sells at a premium over its exact conversion value. For example, if the MCI convertible debenture were sold for $1,000, the premium over its exact conversion value would be $1,000 − $847.95 = $152.05. The magnitude of this premium depends on the likelihood that conversion value will drop below bond value.

Conversion premium — the amount by which a convertible bond's market price exceeds the higher of its bond value or its conversion value.

The **conversion premium,** therefore, is a function of the difference between conversion value and bond value and also of the volatility of the conversion value, which depends on the volatility of the price of the underlying stock. As noted earlier, the bond value of a convertible bond provides a floor below which its price will not fall. A convertible bond usually sells at a premium over bond value because of the value of the conversion privilege. Thus, the conversion premium of

---

[1]See "Funding Fast Growth at MCI," *Business Week,* October 5, 1981. The MCI bonds were sold in August 1981, a time of unusually high interest rates in the long-term bond market. At the time, the rate on *AAA* corporate bonds was about 15.2 percent.

Figure 18A–1
Relationship of Convertible-Bond Price to Common-Stock Price

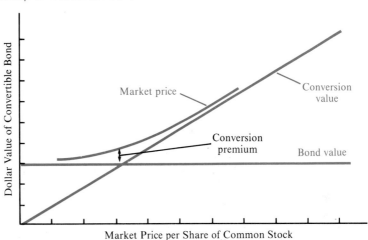

the bond is the amount by which its market price exceeds the higher of its bond value or its conversion value. Figure 18A–1 diagrams these price relationships.

When the conversion value of the bond is below bond value, the conversion premium over bond value can be ascribed to the value of the conversion privilege. When conversion value exceeds bond value, the premium over conversion value can be ascribed to the downside protection of the floor. As the stock price rises, the conversion value rises, and the value of the downside protection declines. Also, the probability of a call of the issue increases, and if called, the bond is worth only its conversion value. On the other side, the further conversion value falls below bond value, the less the conversion privilege is worth. Consequently, as indicated in Figure 18A–1, the conversion premium narrows at both ends of the spectrum of stock prices.

The diagram in Figure 18A–1 assumes that the bond value is constant. In fact, the floor provided by the bond value is not fixed, and in practice it may vary because of the same factors that affect stock price. The element K_d in Equation (A–1) represents the rate of return required by the market on a straight debt issue of the firm in question. This required rate of return may change either in response to a change in the general level of interest rates or in response to a change in the perceived riskiness of the particular firm's cash flows. For example, an increase in the required rate of return on the firm's debt from 18 to 19 percent would cause the bond value in the example cited earlier to drop from $585.17 to $553.68. Thus, a decline in the firm's prospects might give rise to a decline in the bond value of its convertible bonds just at the time when the bond value is most needed as downside protection against a stock price that is also declining for the same reason. The floor provided by the bond value is not a fixed floor, but one that can vary.

Accounting Treatment

Conversion of a convertible security into common stock affects earnings per share for two reasons: first, the requirement to pay interest (or dividends, in the case of preferred stock) is eliminated, and second, the number of common shares is increased. For example, assume a company issues $6 million of 9 percent convertible bonds and that each bond is convertible into 20 shares of stock. Assume further that expected earnings before interest and taxes (EBIT) is $5 million, that the tax rate is 50 percent, and that 500,000 shares of common stock are outstanding before conversion. Earnings per share before and after conversion are shown in Table 18A–1.

As indicated, conversion causes the firm's earnings per share to decline. Whether the stock price also will decline depends on circumstances. Conversion reduced expected earnings per share from $4.46 to $4.03 (that is, by 9.6 percent), but at the same time it also reduced the firm's debt/equity ratio, thereby reducing the riskiness of earnings per share (EPS). The reduction in risk offsets at least in part the reduction in expected EPS. Applying the theory of financial leverage developed in Chapter 15, we know that the effect on the value of the firm's shares should depend on the effect of the conversion on taxes and bankruptcy risk. If the firm were significantly below its optimal debt ratio, conversion would reduce the total value of the firm by the amount of the net tax benefits forgone, considering both corporate and personal taxes of investors (see discussion in Chapter 15). If the firm were above its optimal debt ratio, conversion theoretically should increase firm value. In the latter case, the reduction in risk would more than offset the reduction in expected EPS.

To assist investors in evaluating the impact of convertible securities, current accounting guidelines require reporting of two EPS figures: primary EPS and fully diluted EPS. The fully diluted figure shows on a pro-forma basis what EPS would be if all outstanding convertible securities were converted to common stock.

Table 18A–1

Effect of Conversion on Earnings per Share at a Hypothetical Firm
(thousands of dollars)

	Before Conversion	After Conversion
Expected earnings before interest and taxes (EBIT)	5,000	5,000
Interest on bonds at 9 percent	−540	—
Profit before taxes	4,460	5,000
Taxes at 50 percent	−2,230	−2,500
Profit after taxes	2,230	2,500
Common shares outstanding (thousands)	500	620
Expected earnings per share (dollars)	4.46	4.03

Financing with Convertible Securities

Convertible securities are usually issued at a premium over current conversion value. Consider a 9 percent convertible bond issued by ABC Corporation at $1,000 with a conversion price of $50 (conversion ratio is 20 shares of common stock per bond) and a call price of $1,090. If the market price of the common stock at the time the bonds are issued is $44 per share, the conversion value of the bonds is $20 \times \$44 = \$880$. The issue price of $1,000 thus represents a premium of 13.6 percent over the conversion value. The premium also can be calculated by comparing the conversion price, $50, to the market price at the time of issue, $44 — a premium of $(\$50 - \$44)/\$44 = 13.6$ percent.

The conversion premium set at time of issue varies from one issue to another but usually lies between 10 percent and 20 percent. The premium is set by adjusting the conversion ratio. In general, the faster the firm is growing, the higher the premium is set. Most convertible securities are issued with the expectation that they will convert in the not-too-distant future — say, a period of a few years. A convertible issue, therefore, can be viewed as a deferred common-stock issue, with the stock sold for future delivery at a price above current market price. Compared to a sale of common stock now, the firm obtains a higher price for the stock, issues fewer shares, and subjects existing shareholders to less earnings dilution. As compared to a straight-debt issue, the convertible issue can be sold at a lower interest rate — sometimes substantially lower, as in the MCI case. Similarly, convertible preferred stock can be sold at a lower dividend rate than straight preferred stock.

In order to induce complete conversion, the issue usually must be called by the issuing firm. Calling the issue would force conversion, provided the conversion value of the bonds was sufficiently above the call price. If ABC Corporation called its convertible bonds at $1,090 at a time when its stock was selling for $60, holders would be forced to choose between $1,090 in cash or stock worth $1,200. Most, undoubtedly, would convert. Because some reasonable period must be allowed for the transaction to be consummated, firms usually find it wise to wait until conversion value is 10 percent to 20 percent above the call price before calling the issue. Such a margin gives some protection against unexpected drops in the stock price during the conversion period.

On June 3, 1981, Wang Laboratories, a manufacturer of computer equipment based in Massachusetts, announced the call of its 9 percent convertible subordinated debentures due in 2005. The debentures were convertible into Wang Class B common stock at a conversion price of $32, so each $1,000 debenture could be exchanged for 31.25 shares of common stock. At the time the debentures were called, Wang Class B common stock was selling for $40.625 per share. Wang wanted the bondholders to convert, but they would not do so voluntarily even though they could exchange a bond with a face value of $1,000 for 31.25 shares of stock worth $1269.53. Why wouldn't the bondholders convert? The dividend on Wang Class B common stock was only $0.12 per share at that time. Thus, a bondholder would give up a bond paying $90 per year in interest for stock paying only $0.12 \times 31.25 = \$3.75$ — not a good bargain. So Wang had to *force* bond-

Most convertible securities are issued with the expectation that they will be converted in the not-too-distant future.

A convertible issue can be sold at a lower interest rate than a straight debt issue.

To induce complete conversion, the issue usually must be called by the issuing firm.

holders to convert. According to the original terms of issue, each bond was callable at *Wang's* option at a price of $1,090 (a premium of one year's interest) plus accrued interest to the date of the call—a total of $1,124.25 per bond. Thus, by calling the issue, the company forced holders of a bond to choose either $1,124.25 in cash or stock worth $1,269.53. One would anticipate that all would choose to convert into stock, as desired by the company.

When a firm that has issued convertible securities does not perform as well as had been expected, its stock price may not rise sufficiently to permit a forced conversion. If this situation persists, the convertible issue is said to be *hung,* or *overhanging*. The existence of a hung convertible issue in a firm's capital structure usually is taken as evidence that things have not gone as planned. Often the firm's flexibility with respect to external financing is reduced considerably, because any new issue may be difficult as long as the uncertainty over the convertible issue is unresolved. If the financing constraint motivates the firm to alter its commercial strategy—perhaps by forgoing investments that it otherwise would have made—the cost of a hung convertible issue to the shareholders may be very high. Such potential complications in the event of unfavorable developments constitute an important disadvantage of convertible securities. A firm issuing convertible securities, therefore, must be prepared to see the issue remain as debt or preferred stock for an indefinite period.

When a firm's stock price does not rise sufficiently to permit a forced conversion, the convertible issue is said to be overhanging or hung.

Chapter 19

Leasing

In this chapter we examine the use of leases to obtain the use of an asset. We explain the motivations for leases as well as how to use discounted-cash-flow analysis to evaluate whether leasing is desirable.

Leasing—a specialized means of acquiring the use of assets without owning the assets.

Lease—a contractual arrangement whereby the *lessee* has the right to use the asset in return for making periodic payments to the owner, or *lessor*.

Firms often raise funds in order to acquire income-producing assets. In the case of physical (nonfinancial) assets, firms that are in business to produce goods and services usually are more interested in *using* the asset than in *owning* it per se. A specialized means of acquiring the use of assets without ownership is **leasing**. Because it represents an alternative to ownership, leasing can be viewed as a specialized means of obtaining funds—one of a number of financing alternatives open to a firm.

A **lease** is a contractual arrangement under which the *lessee* has the right to use the equipment and, in return, makes periodic payments to the owner, or *lessor*. The lessor retains title to the equipment. Figure 19–1 diagrams the difference between leasing and ownership for Firm X. Firm X wants to use a particular asset. One alternative, displayed in Panel A, is to purchase the asset from the manufacturer and obtain the necessary funds by using debt or equity financing. For example, Firm X might borrow money from a bank.

Another alternative, shown in Panel B, is to lease the asset from a lessor who has bought the asset from the manufacturer. As a lessee, Firm X uses the asset even though the lessor owns the asset. In essence, the lessor performs the role of a financial intermediary. The lessor raises the funds for purchasing the asset and then provides the asset to the lessee in exchange for lease payments.

A specific example of the situation shown in Figure 19–1 often occurs in the airline industry. Firm X could be an airline company that flies the plane, but the lessor may be a large bank that actually owns the plane, which was manufactured by yet another company.

Figure 19–1
Leasing Versus Owning an Asset

A. Purchase and Ownership: Firm *X* owns and uses the asset.
The money for the purchase is raised by debt or equity.

B. Lease: Firm *X* (lessee) uses the asset and in return makes lease payments.
The lessor owns the asset.

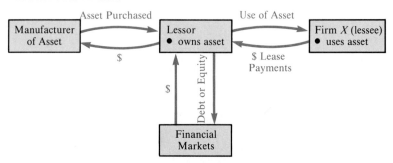

Leasing experienced a rapid rise in popularity in the 1960s and 1970s. During this period, many new firms, including a large number of commercial banks, entered the leasing field as lessors. Now leasing has become an important means of asset financing. A firm can issue a claim against its future cash flows by means of long-term debt, equity, or a lease obligation. Each of these claims would allow the firm to obtain use of an asset. Issuing debt or equity provides funds to purchase the asset. The lease provides an alternative way for the lessee to use the asset even though the lessor retains ownership.

Types of Leases

Operating lease — a contract covering intermediate to short terms whereby the lessor (owner) typically is responsible for maintenance, insurance, and property taxes; also known as a *maintenance lease* or *service lease*.

Financial lease — a noncancelable, fully amortized contract typically covering intermediate to long terms whereby the lessee (user) normally is responsible for maintenance, insurance, and taxes; also known as a *net lease*.

Figure 19–1 shows a simple type of lease arrangement. In practice, there are many types of leases, some of which become quite complicated. The two most frequently encountered types of leases are the **operating lease** and the **financial lease.** Under an operating lease, sometimes called a *maintenance lease,* or *service lease,* the lessor (owner) typically is responsible for maintenance, insurance, and property taxes. Compensation for providing these services is included in the lease payment. Assets leased under operating leases include computers, office equipment, automobiles, trucks, and a wide variety of other types of equipment. Contracts typically are intermediate- to short-term. Computers, for example, typically are leased for three to five years, and automobiles are leased for one to three years. Other types of equipment may be leased or rented on a daily or even hourly basis. Contracts covering intermediate periods usually are cancelable. Because they usually cover a period considerably shorter than the useful life of the asset, operating leases normally do not fully amortize the original cost of the asset. Rather, the lessor expects either to lease the asset again or to sell it at the expiration of the original contract. Because contracts are short- to intermediate-term and are cancelable, the lessor bears the risk of technological obsolescence of the asset.

Financial leases are noncancelable contracts typically covering intermediate to long terms. Provision often is made for renewal or purchase of the asset at expiration. The lessee (user) normally is responsible for maintenance, insurance, and taxes, and for this reason financial leases are often called *net leases*. Types of assets leased under financial leases include aircraft, rail cars, land, and buildings. Ordinarily, the payments under a financial lease fully amortize the original cost of the asset over the term of the lease, which usually approximates the useful life of the asset. Full amortization and noncancelability are the key features that distinguish financial leases from operating leases. Noncancelability implies that lessees are legally obligated to make all the lease payments regardless of whether they continue to use the asset and, thus, can cancel only by paying off the entire contract. Default by the lessee can lead to bankruptcy, just as in the case of a debt contract.

As shown in Figure 19–1, the asset may be acquired from the manufacturer by a lessor who then leases it to the user. Lessors entering into such transactions include finance companies, commercial banks, specialized leasing companies, and individuals. Individual lessors usually are high-tax-bracket investors who can re-

Finance companies, commercial banks, specialized leasing companies, and individuals have acted as lessors when an asset is acquired from the manufacturer.

Sale-and-leaseback agreement — an arrangement in which a firm or individual owning an asset sells it to another party and then leases it back.

Leveraged lease — a lease agreement in which the lessor borrows a substantial part of the purchase price of the asset to be leased.

ceive large tax benefits from being the owner of the asset for tax purposes (depreciation tax shields and sometimes investment tax credits). We will discuss these tax benefits shortly. Alternatively, the manufacturer may itself serve as the lessor, as is often done with computers and office equipment.

Yet another variation on leasing is the **sale-and-leaseback agreement.** Under a sale-and-leaseback agreement, a firm or individual owning an asset sells it to another party and then leases it back. The seller gives up title to the asset but retains its use. The selling price usually approximates the fair market value of the asset, and the lease contract is nearly always written as a financial lease. In essence, the sale-and-leaseback agreement allows a firm to obtain cash by selling an asset but to retain use of the asset by becoming a lessee.

A **leveraged lease** is a lease in which the lessor borrows a substantial part of the purchase price of the asset to be leased. The lessor has used financial leverage (debt) to obtain the asset to be leased. The lender — often an insurance company or pension fund — typically takes a mortgage on the asset for security. The lender also may require that the lessors assign their interests in the lease. Under this arrangement lease payments would go directly to the lender, who would deduct principal and interest payments due on the loan and then send the balance to the lessor. Risk to the lender, therefore, is the risk of default by the lessee, even though the loan was made to the lessor.[1]

As the preceding discussion shows, leases can take on many forms. A basic question is, what advantages do such leases have over direct ownership? Before we can address that question, however, we need to look at the accounting and tax treatment of lease arrangements. As it turns out, this treatment has direct bearing on the decision to lease an asset rather than to purchase it directly.

Tax and Accounting Treatment of Leases

As the owner, the lessor is entitled to the tax benefits of ownership, including any investment tax credit and depreciation associated with the purchase of an asset. The lessee is allowed to deduct lease payments as tax-deductible expenses.

Accounting and tax treatment of leases can become quite complex, and the applicable rules have undergone significant change in recent years. For tax purposes, the lessee is typically allowed to deduct lease payments as tax-deductible expenses. The lessor is typically designated as the owner of the asset. As the owner, the lessor is entitled to the tax benefits of ownership, including the depreciation tax shield associated with the asset. The lessor may also be entitled to an investment tax credit if such credits are allowed under the tax law in effect.

If they are in effect, investment tax credits (ITCs) can provide an important benefit because they allow the lessor (owner) to get an immediate reduction in his or her tax bill when the asset is purchased. To illustrate, suppose a 10 percent ITC were in effect and a corporation purchased an asset for $300,000. The ITC would provide a $30,000 = 0.10($300,000) direct reduction from the company's tax bill. This would reduce the effective after-tax cash cost of the asset to $270,000. As a result, ITCs can provide a considerable incentive for investment.

[1]For a discussion of leveraged leases, see P. J. Athanasopoulos and P. W. Bacon, "The Evaluation of Leveraged Leases," *Financial Management* 9 (Spring 1980): 76–80.

In 1986, through passage of the Tax Reform Act of 1986, Congress eliminated ITCs completely. As a result, as of this printing the ITC is not available and thus is not a relevant tax benefit to a lessor (owner). ITCs may, however, be reinstituted by a future session of Congress.

In determining the tax treatment of a lease, the Internal Revenue Service goes to great lengths to distinguish between a lease and a **conditional sales agreement,** which details the sale of an asset. If a transaction is declared a conditional sale by the IRS, payments for use of the assets will not be allowed as tax-deductible items but will be treated as payments toward the purchase of the asset. The details of the tax treatment of specific leases are beyond the scope of our present discussion. In practice, tax experts scrutinize leases to make sure of the treatment of the transaction by the IRS. For our present purposes, the important tax implication is that the owner-lessor for tax purposes will get the tax benefits of ownership (any investment tax credits and depreciation tax shields), whereas the lessee will be allowed to treat lease payments as tax-deductible expenses. Before analyzing any lease, financial managers should check carefully to see exactly what the tax treatment of a specific lease will be.

The accounting treatment of leases has been the subject of considerable debate. As a lessee, a firm does not own an asset. Hence, one could argue that the asset should not appear on the company's balance sheet as an asset and that lease payments, just like other costs of doing business, should be deducted as expenses on the income statement. For most operating leases, which cover a period considerably shorter than the useful life of the asset, the accounting is done in this way. Lessees show nothing on their balance sheets and deduct the full amount of the lease payment as an expense.

In the case of long-term financial leases, matters are not so clear-cut. If a lease lasts for the effective life of the asset, one could argue that the company ought to show the asset on its balance sheet and at the same time somehow recognize future lease payments as an obligation reflected in a liability on the balance sheet. The accounting profession has established rules, detailed by the Financial Accounting Standards Board in Financial Accounting Standard No. 13, whereby certain leases are classified as **capital leases.** If a lease is a capital lease, it must be capitalized by the lessee on its balance sheet as an asset and as an obligation. In essence, a lease will be classified as a capital lease if the terms of the lease last for more than 75 percent of the estimated useful life of the asset or involve any provisions that effectively transfer ownership of the asset to the lessee by the end of the lease term.[2]

Just as the tax laws affecting leases can become complicated, so can the accounting treatment. And to make matters more complex, sometimes the accounting may be handled one way for financial-reporting purposes and another way for

Conditional sales agreement — an installment contract for the purchase of equipment in which title to the equipment remains with the lender until all payments are made.

For most operating leases, which cover a period considerably shorter than the useful life of the asset, leases are not shown on the balance sheet, and the full amount of the lease payment is deducted as an expense.

Capital lease — a lease that, for accounting purposes, must be capitalized on the lessee's balance sheet as an asset and as an obligation.

---

[2]The details of FASB No. 13 classify a lease as a capital lease if the lease has any one of the following four elements: (1) the lease transfers ownership of the property to the lessee by the end of the lease term, (2) the lease contains an option to buy the property at a bargain price, (3) the lease term is equal to 75 percent or more of the estimated economic life of the property, or (4) the present value of the rentals and other minimum lease payments is equal to 90 percent or more of the fair value of the leased property less any related investment tax credit retained by the lessor.

tax purposes. The important point to note is that for short-term operating leases, the leased asset typically will not appear on the lessee's balance sheet, whereas with long-term financial leases, the lessee will show the lease on the balance sheet as both a leased asset and a lease obligation. Whether leases are on the balance sheets of lessees or not, lease payments constitute a fixed, contractual claim against a firm's cash flows and, hence, affect risk in much the same way as debt does.

Sometimes the accounting treatment of leases may be one way for financial reporting purposes and another way for tax purposes.

Motives for Leasing

Now we turn to the question of what motivates firms to lease assets rather than buy them directly. Leases have both advantages and disadvantages to both lessee and lessor.

The major motive for many leases has to do with taxes.

The major motive for many leases is tax treatment. When a company buys an asset, it can receive two major tax benefits: a depreciation tax shield and, if applicable under current law, an investment tax credit. Normally both of these tax features reduce a firm's tax bill. But if a firm has suffered losses and isn't paying taxes in the first place, investment tax credits and depreciation tax shields are of little immediate value.[3] Certainly the tax benefits of ownership would be worth more to a profitable firm that has a large taxable income or to a private individual in a high tax bracket.

The lease offers a made-to-order financial arrangement. Suppose an airline needed a new plane but currently had losses for tax purposes. The airline itself could gain little or no immediate tax benefit from any investment tax credit or depreciation on the plane. Enter a highly profitable bank, which could use those tax benefits of ownership. The bank buys the plane and acts as a lessor. The airline — the lessee — uses the plane but the bank gets the tax benefits of ownership. In the process of the lease arrangement, there has been a tax savings. Tax benefits that might have gone unused by the airline are utilized by the bank. The airline shares in the tax savings to the extent that the bank requires lower lease payments for use of the asset because of the tax benefits it reaps. In effect, the lease arrangement allows the tax savings related to owning an asset to be used by the entity that can benefit most from those savings. It thus comes as no surprise that many lessors are profitable firms or wealthy individuals in high tax brackets. Since the Tax Reform Act of 1986 eliminated one of the tax benefits of ownership (the investment tax credit), the Act reduced some of the tax benefits for lessors.

In effect, the lease arrangement allows the tax savings related to owning an asset to be used by the entity that can benefit most from those savings.

One often-cited advantage of leasing is that it may provide 100 percent financing.

One often-cited advantage of leasing is that it may provide 100 percent financing. Elimination of the requirement for a down payment may indeed be a real ad-

---

[3]Using the provisions of the tax laws, such tax benefits might be used in future periods if and when the firm had taxable income. Because of the time value of money, however, tax savings in the future are worth less than tax savings taken today.

vantage to a lessee who has no cash. However, we should not lose sight of the fact that lease payments are contractual, and the lease, therefore, provides the equivalent of debt financing. The financing is not free. Furthermore, for practically all firms, cash to purchase an asset can be obtained from financial markets — for example, by borrowing money.

Operating leases may give a firm greater flexibility than ownership by shifting the risk of obsolescence to the lessor. The same is not true of financial leases, because they are noncancelable and normally cover the useful life of the asset. Where the risk is shifted, we can expect the lessor to require compensation for bearing it, usually incorporating the compensation directly in the lease payment. Taking such risks into account is central to the leasing business, and in general lessors are likely to be more expert than lessees at judging the risks. While flexibility with respect to obsolescence is indeed an advantage of the operating lease, it is one for which the lessee pays. In effect, the lessee buys insurance against obsolescence.

> Operating leases may provide a firm greater flexibility than ownership by shifting the risk of obsolescence to the lessor. Where risk is shifted, we can expect the lessor to require compensation for bearing it.

In situations of bankruptcy or reorganization, whether a lease contract is advantageous as compared to ownership depends on circumstances. Under ownership with a mortgage, in the event of default, the mortgagee (lender) is entitled to seize the asset and sell it to satisfy the debt. Any excess accrues to the firm, and any deficiency usually becomes an unsecured general obligation of the firm. Under a lease, the owner may repossess the asset and file a claim against the lessee for lost rent, with the maximum allowable claim depending on the type of asset and the nature of the proceeding. For example, in the case of real property, a claim for lost rent in bankruptcy is limited to a maximum of one year's rent. Whether the lessee is better off leasing or owning in the event of distress thus depends on the relationship between the current market value of the asset at the time and the remaining lease or debt obligation, and also on the ability of the lessor to find a new lessee. Because these considerations regarding bankruptcy and reorganization mean nothing as long as the firm remains a going concern, they are usually of secondary importance in leasing decisions.

A major consideration in many leasing decisions concerns the *residual value* of the asset at the end of the lease period. By opting for leasing rather than owning, the lessee gives up any claim to residual value. The lessor, on the other hand, benefits from any residual value. If residual values are correctly taken into account and markets for leasing are reasonably competitive, the anticipated residual value should be reflected in lower lease payments. Where residual values are significant, as in real-estate projects, they can significantly affect the return to the lessor and the cost to the lessee. We will deal explicitly with residual values in developing an approach to lease analysis later in this chapter.

> The residual value of the asset at the end of the lease period is a major consideration in many leasing decisions.

In summary, being a lessee and leasing an asset has certain advantages (often tax-related) and disadvantages (for example, loss of residual value) relative to owning the asset directly. To make the decision whether or not to lease requires an economic evaluation of whether the advantages of leasing outweigh the disadvantages.

Finance in Practice 19–1

The Anaconda Company's Leasing Decision

In 1973, the Anaconda Company entered into an agreement to lease a new aluminum-reduction mill from a consortium of five banks and one commercial finance company. The mill cost $110.7 million. Anaconda agreed to make 40 semiannual payments over a 20-year period. The first 21 payments were to be $3.985 million each, and the last 19 payments $5.460 million each. The lessors were to have title to the mill at the end of the lease in 1993 and also would get the investment tax credit and the depreciation tax shield. Anaconda was to be responsible for all operating cash flows, including maintenance and insurance.

The Anaconda lease illustrates the central importance of taxes in lease financing. The lease turned out to be advantageous to both lessor and lessee at the same time because of taxes. Because the Chilean government had expropriated some of Anaconda's properties in Chile, Anaconda had a large tax loss to carry forward and, therefore, a very low marginal tax rate for a period several years beyond 1973. If Anaconda had purchased the aluminum-reduction mill, it could not have used the depreciation tax shield to full advantage or the investment tax credit. By means of the lease, Anaconda transferred the tax shields that it could not use to the lessors, who could use them. By properly designing the lease terms, Anaconda and the lessors reduced their combined tax liability. So, the lease left both Anaconda and the lessors better off, with the tax collector footing the bill. Although now dated, the Anaconda lease remains a classic example of a lease designed around tax factors.

Sources: P. Vanderwicken, "The Powerful Logic of the Leasing Boom," *Fortune* 88 (November 1973): 132–36; S. C. Myers, D. A. Dill, and J. A. Bautista, "Valuation of Financial Lease Contracts," *Journal of Finance* 31 (June 1976): 799–820; and J. R. Franks and S. C. Hodges, "Valuation of Financial Lease Contracts: A Note," *Journal of Finance* 33 (May 1978): 657–69.

Economic Evaluation of Leases

If the asset is to be used, the problem then becomes: lease or borrow?

In its most general form, the leasing decision can be viewed as a choice among three mutually exclusive alternatives: (1) leasing the asset, (2) purchasing the asset, or (3) not using the asset at all. If we assume that the decision has already been made to use the asset, our decision about leasing can be usefully simplified by viewing the problem as leasing versus borrowing.[4] That is, we view leasing as

[4] In practice, this is often the case. For example, if a company needs a new truck to continue its delivery operation, the question is whether to lease the truck or to purchase it. In theory, one must consider all three alternatives, including the do-not-use option. See R. Brealey and S. Myers, *Principles of Corporate Finance* (New York: McGraw-Hill, 1984) for further discussion of these issues. They also discuss the assumptions behind comparing leasing to borrowing. In our book, essentially we have assumed that leases will typically displace debt dollar for dollar and, hence, that leasing can be compared to 100 percent debt financing.

a means of financing to be compared to debt financing. The reason for comparing leasing to debt financing is that a lease is a contractual arrangement under which the owner of an asset (the lessor) permits another party (the lessee) to use the asset for a specified period of time in return for a specified payment. Lease payments are fixed and contractual, just as are payments on debt. Thus, a lease can be viewed as a specialized form of debt financing. Here we will consider only financial leases, which are noncancelable and, therefore, essentially equivalent to debt in their effect on firm risk.

Leases should be compared to debt financing because lease payments are typically fixed and contractual, just as are payments on debt.

Our general approach to lease evaluation will be the same one we have used before—discounted-cash-flow techniques. We will specify the incremental cash flows associated with (1) leasing the asset versus (2) purchasing the asset with borrowed funds. Then we will discount these cash flows at the required return appropriate for the riskiness of the decision at hand. If the present value of the benefits of leasing exceeds the present value of the costs, the firm should lease.

We can apply DCF techniques to leasing.

Incremental Cash Flows Attributable to Leasing

To apply the incremental-cash-flow rule, we need to identify all cash flows attributable to leasing—that is, those cash flows that will be different if leasing is selected rather than owning. By leasing, the firm avoids the cash outlay required to purchase the asset, incurs an obligation to make lease payments, forgoes the depreciation tax shield, and forgoes the residual (salvage) value of the asset at the expiration of the lease. Costs of operation, maintenance, insurance, property taxes, and the like are often the same under leasing, but if they were different, the difference would represent an incremental cash flow. In the case of all cash flows, associated tax effects must be taken into account.

Some of the incremental cash flows attributable to leasing are inflows (the outlay avoided), and some are outflows (any investment tax credit forgone, the lease payment, depreciation tax shield forgone, and terminal value forgone).

Generally, five categories of cash flows are involved:

1. the acquisition cost of the asset (adjusted for any investment tax credit),
2. the lease payment,
3. the depreciation tax shield,
4. the operating and maintenance costs, and
5. the residual (salvage) value.

The first item—the acquisition cost of the asset—is the outlay that will be avoided if the asset is leased rather than purchased. Because it is an outlay avoided, it is treated as a net cash inflow attributable to the lease. The timing of the inflow is the point at which the outlay would have been made. The outlay avoided is usually the purchase price of the asset reduced by any investment tax credit.

The lease payment is the cash payment that will be made to the lessor in each period over the term of the lease, net of taxes. Assuming that the lessee will make a profit in each period, its after-tax lease payment is the pretax payment times (1 − the marginal tax rate).

The depreciation tax shield is the tax saving forgone by the lessee because depreciation cannot be taken for tax purposes (but is taken by the lessor instead). The tax shield in each period is a cash outflow and is calculated as the depreciation in each period times the marginal tax rate.

In some cases, certain costs of operation, maintenance, insurance, property taxes, or similar items may be different if the asset is leased rather than owned. If these costs are greater under leasing, they should be treated as a cash outflow; if they are less, they should be treated as inflow. Tax effects should be included. If the amounts are uncertain, strictly speaking, they should be adjusted for uncertainty. We will ignore this problem in our discussion here.

When an asset is leased rather than purchased, the lessor has title to it at the expiration of the lease. Hence, as compared to owning, the lessee forgoes the benefit of whatever value the asset might have at expiration. This residual value must be treated as a cash outflow attributable to the decision to lease. In many cases, it may be small enough to ignore. In others — notably in connection with leases involving real estate — residual values may be very significant and may have a significant impact on the cost of leasing as compared to owning. The higher the residual value forgone, the higher the cost of leasing relative to owning.

Let us illustrate the calculation of incremental cash flows with an example. Suppose a firm has decided that it needs a particular machine. The machine can be purchased for $50,000 or leased from the manufacturer for $12,000 per year under a five-year noncancelable lease. Lease payments would be due at year end. The firm uses straight-line depreciation, and Internal Revenue Service regulations permit depreciation of the machine over five years. The combined federal and state tax rate is assumed to be 40 percent. The firm's interest rate on five-year debt is 10 percent, before taxes. The operating, maintenance, and insurance costs of the financial lease are the same as under ownership. Currently tax laws allow no investment tax credit.

Panel A of Table 19–1 outlines the incremental cash flows attributable to leasing. By leasing, the firm avoids an immediate outlay of $50,000. The lease thus provides an inflow of $50,000 in period 0. The annual lease payment net of taxes is $12,000(1 − 0.40) = $7,200 due at the end of each of the five years.[5] Depreciation forgone is $50,000/5 = $10,000 per year, so the tax shield forgone is $10,000(0.40) = $4,000 per year. This depreciation tax shield lost is precisely the tax savings that depreciation would have provided had the asset been purchased. We discussed such tax shields earlier in Chapter 11.

The firm feels confident that the market value of the machine at the end of year 5 will be $5,000. Because book value at the end of year 5 will be zero, if the firm owns the machine, it will have a tax liability against the market value of ($5,000 − 0)(0.40) = $2,000. The adjusted residual value at the end of year 5, net of the tax liability, is $3,000. As Table 19–1 shows, leasing leads to a cash savings of $50,000 today (a cash inflow) but results in cash outflows in years 1 through 5. Should the company lease? The answer depends on whether today's

---

[5]Leases often have payments due at the beginning of each period. Year-end flows are assumed here to simplify the analysis.

Table 19–1

Economic Evaluation of a Hypothetical Lease

A. Incremental Cash Flows Attributable to Lease (dollars)

Year	Acquisition Cost	After-Tax Lease Payments	Depreciation Tax Shield	After-Tax Residual Value	Total Cash Flow
0	50,000				50,000
1		−7,200	−4,000		−11,200
2		−7,200	−4,000		−11,200
3		−7,200	−4,000		−11,200
4		−7,200	−4,000		−11,200
5		−7,200	−4,000	−3,000	−14,200

B. Net Present Value of Leasing Versus Borrowing

Required Return $= 0.10(1 - 0.4) = 0.06$ after-tax cost of debt

$$
\begin{aligned}
NPV &= \$50,000 - \$11,200\ PVAF(0.06, 4) - \$14,200\ PVF(0.06, 5) \\
&= \$50,000 - \$11,200(3.465) - \$14,200(0.747) \\
&= \$50,000 - \$49,420 \\
&= \$580; \text{ leasing is preferred to borrowing}
\end{aligned}
$$

cash benefits are worth more than the present value of future cash costs. To complete our analysis, we need to specify a required rate of return so that we can evaluate the present value of the future cash flows associated with the lease.

Required Rate of Return for Lease Analysis

We use the after-tax cost of debt as the discount rate in lease analysis.

As we've discussed earlier, the required rate of return should depend on the riskiness of the project. For the firm's average-risk project, we saw in Chapter 12 that we should use the weighted-average required return. Is a lease an average-risk project? The answer is no! As Table 19–1 shows, the future cash flows are largely contractual lease payments and depreciation tax shields. These are much safer than projected sales and costs figures for a typical project. As a result, we need a lower required return to reflect lower risk. As a first approximation, we can view the cash outflows associated with a lease as essentially equivalent in risk to interest and principal payments on debt. This means that the required return would be the after-tax interest cost on debt. In this case, since the company can borrow at 10 percent, the after-tax cost of debt — $10(1 - 0.4) = 6$ percent — should be used to evaluate the lease. In using this rate, we are assuming that since an after-tax interest rate of 6 percent is appropriate for cash flows on debt, it is also appropriate to use on a lease with cash flows equal in risk to those on debt.

Net Present Value of Lease Versus Borrow

Using a 6 percent required return, Panel B of Table 19–1 evaluates the cash flows of leasing. There we see that the cash outflows have a present value of $49,420;

thus the lease provides a positive net present value of $580 relative to borrowing—the difference between the $50,000 savings and the $49,420. As a result, given our assumption, the company would find it advantageous to lease the asset. The lease decision has a positive *NPV* and thus creates value for shareholders.

We illustrated the evaluation of leases using a simple example. In practice, leasing decisions often involve a more complex set of cash flows, longer time periods, accelerated depreciation, purchase and renewal options at the expiration of the lease, and so on. Occasionally, situations may be encountered in which an asset can be used only if it is leased because no option to purchase exists. In such cases, the investment and financing decisions are made together.

All these complications can be handled using DCF techniques. The computations are more tedious, but the logic is the same.

Further Complications in Lease Analysis

In our application of DCF techniques to a financial lease, we argued that the after-tax cost of debt was an appropriate required return because the cash flows being discounted (e.g., lease payments and depreciation tax shields) were comparable in risk to cash flows on debt (interest and principal payments). In many situations this assumption about risk is valid. But, as is often the case, suppose that the salvage value of the asset is subject to a great deal more uncertainty than lease payments and depreciation tax shields. After all, salvage value depends on many unknown factors, whereas the other cash flows are highly predictable. How do we proceed in this case? A reasonable approach is to use a higher required return for discounting the salvage value while still using the after-tax debt cost for the more predictable flows. This procedure would penalize the salvage value due to risk and is perfectly consistent with investors' dislike of risk. In practice, choosing the appropriate discount rate for the salvage value is difficult but would be based on the general principles we discussed earlier in Chapters 12 and 13. An alternative approach to handling a highly uncertain salvage value would be to do sensitivity analysis, allowing the salvage value of the asset to vary.

Our approach to evaluating a lease requires that we quantify the benefits and costs of a lease in terms of incremental cash flows. If the net present value of the lease decision is positive, leasing looks like a desirable investment. A negative *NPV* means that borrowing money and purchasing the asset is preferable to leasing. In practice it may not be possible to quantify all costs and benefits; however, the DCF calculations are still important. Qualitative advantages of a lease may cause a firm to lease even if it calculates a negative *NPV,* but the *NPV* tells management just how large a premium it is paying to get this qualitative feature. For example, if a DCF analysis shows a *NPV* of −$500, the lease must have qualitative advantages worth more than $500 before the lease should be accepted.

Sample Problem 19–1
Evaluating the Leasing Alternative for Ozark Printing Company

The Ozark Printing Company has decided to acquire a new printing press and is trying to decide between leasing and buying the machine. The press can be purchased from the manufacturer for $100,000 (delivered). The investment tax credit

Table 19–2

Evaluation of Proposed Lease for Ozark Printing

A. Incremental Cash Flows Attributable to Lease (dollars)

Year	Acquisition Cost	After-Tax Lease Payment	Depreciation Tax Shield	After-Tax Residual Value	Total Cash Flow
0	92,000*				92,000
1		−18,000	−8,000		−26,000
2		−18,000	−8,000		−26,000
3		−18,000	−8,000		−26,000
4		−18,000	−8,000		−26,000
5		−18,000	−8,000	0	−26,000

B. Net Present Value of Leasing Versus Borrowing

Required Return = $0.10(1 - 0.4) = 0.06$ after-tax cost of debt

$$
\begin{aligned}
NPV &= \$92,000 - \$26,000 \; PVAF(0.06, 5) \\
&= \$92,000 - \$26,000(4.212) \\
&= \$92,000 - \$109,512 \\
&= -\$17,512 < 0; \text{ don't lease}
\end{aligned}
$$

*Adjusted for investment tax credit of $0.08(\$100,000) = \$8,000$.

is 8 percent. (As we've said, the Tax Reform Act of 1986 eliminated tax credits; we include an ITC here only as an illustration in case ITCs are reinstituted in the future.) The machine will be depreciated over a five-year life, using straight-line depreciation to a zero salvage value. Ozark could lease the machine from the manufacturer for $30,000 per year for five years. All operating, maintenance, and insurance costs for the new machine will be borne by Ozark. Ozark has a 40 percent tax rate and a before-tax interest rate on long-term debt of 10 percent. Which financing alternative do you recommend (assuming there is no residual value of the machine in year 5)?

Solution

This problem can be approached by examining the incremental cash flow associated with leasing rather than purchasing. Table 19–2 traces the cash-flow patterns. The investment tax credit is $0.08 \times \$100,000 = \$8,000$. Thus, on an after-tax basis it would cost $92,000 to purchase the machine ($100,000 minus the tax savings of $8,000 due to the investment tax credit). By leasing rather than purchasing, Ozark saves $92,000, an incremental cash inflow in year 0. The after-tax lease payments equal $(\$30,000)(1 - 0.40) = \$18,000$ per year, representing incremental cash outflows in years 1 through 5. The depreciation tax shield forgone by leasing equals $(\$100,000/5)(0.40) = \$8,000$ per year. We have assumed there is no residual or salvage value.

Panel B of Table 19–2 shows that the net present value of the incremental cash flows is −$17,512. This negative value means that Ozark should not lease the printing press, since it would be better to purchase the press. In Panel B a required return of 6 percent has been used since that is Ozark's after-tax cost of debt.

Finance in Practice 19—2

Leasing and the Tax Laws

A lease is often a way for a company effectively to sell tax benefits to another company. This exchange can be advantageous when the lessor can make better use of the tax benefits of ownership than can the lessee. By shifting tax benefits from the lessee to the lessor, the lease lowers the total taxes paid by the corporations to the government.

This tax effect of leasing has not gone unnoticed by Congress. In fact, in the Economic Recovery Act of 1981, Congress actually encouraged the use of leasing to save taxes as part of a series of measures (primarily shortening of periods over which capital equipment could be depreciated) to reduce corporate taxes and spur investment. Prior to the 1981 Tax Act, any lease that appeared to be designed to pass tax credits from one firm to another was resisted by the Internal Revenue Service, usually successfully. The 1981 law actually encouraged this practice, and the mechanism was simple: the lessee was a firm with low or negative profits and thus low taxes. The lessor was paying taxes. The lessor purchased the equipment needed by the lessee, took advantage of the new short depreciation

periods, and passed most of the tax savings along to the lessee in the form of lower lease payments. Competition forced this outcome, for if the lessor tried to retain too large a share of the tax savings, another lessor would offer the lessee a lower lease rate.

Firms, along with their investment bankers, lawyers, and accountants, jumped to take advantage of the new law. By means of a lease, Ford Motor Company sold the tax credits on virtually its entire 1981 domestic capital-spending program to IBM for a price reported to be between $100 million and $200 million. B. F. Goodrich sold tax credits to IBM for $60 million, and Chrysler used this strategy to raise $26 million from General Electric Credit Corporation. During the first 90 days after passage of the 1981 law, some $2 billion in tax credits, involving equipment worth $15 billion, changed hands by means of the new leasing mechanism. The 1981 Tax Act was the biggest development in leasing in some time.

In fact, the use of these leases to avoid taxes became a prime target for criticism in times of large federal deficits. In 1982, Congress passed legislation restricting the generous lease treatment in the 1981 Act. Leasing still remained a way to shift tax benefits, but it was subject to tighter regulations. What will be the tax treatment of leases in the future? Only time and the actions of tax authorities will tell. Financial managers must continually monitor the tax treatment of leases because tax benefits often play a key role. Changes in laws governing investment tax credits and depreciation schedules can dramatically affect incentives for leasing.

KEY CONCEPTS

1. By leasing, a firm can obtain use of an asset without owning the asset.

2. Leases are forms of financing that are similar to debt financing.

3. Much of the motivation for leases arises from tax considerations.

4. To analyze the desirability of leasing, one can estimate the incremental cash flows associated with a lease. If the net present value of these cash flows is positive, leasing is preferable to borrowing.

SUMMARY

Leasing has become an important means of financing in special situations. Leasing allows a lessee to use an asset even though the asset is owned by the lessor.

There are many forms of leases patterned after the needs of different lessees and lessors. Operating leases are short-to-intermediate term contracts and are usually cancelable. Such operating leases cover a period considerably shorter than the useful life of the asset. In contrast, financial leases are noncancelable contracts typically covering intermediate to long terms.

The major motive for many leases is tax treatment. The lease arrangement allows the tax savings related to owning an asset (depreciation tax shields and any investment tax credits) to be used by the entity that can benefit most from those savings. Thus a firm that isn't currently paying taxes may become a lessee, passing along the tax benefits of ownership to a tax-paying lessor. The ability to transfer these tax savings will depend on the current tax code.

Being a lessee and leasing an asset has certain advantages (often tax-related) and disadvantages (for example, loss of residual value) relative to owning the asset directly. To evaluate whether a lease is desirable, discounted-cash-flow techniques can be applied to the incremental cash flows attributable to a lease. Such cash flows normally include the avoided outlay for the asset, any lost investment tax credit, the lease payment, the depreciation tax shield, and the residual value of the asset. Given estimates of these cash flows for a financial lease, we can determine if the present value of cash savings exceeds the present value of cash costs. If a positive net present value exists, the lease is a desirable financing alternative. In evaluating a financial lease, we use a required return equal to the after-tax interest cost of debt, because the cash flows associated with a financial lease are contractual and roughly equivalent in risk to cash flows on debt. In making a final decision about whether to lease, it is important to weigh any nonquantifiable aspects of the lease that have not been incorporated in the cash-flow analysis.

QUESTIONS

1. Describe the function and role of the lessor and lessee in a lease arrangement.
2. Discuss the reasons for the significant development of leasing.
3. Compare and contrast an operating lease with a financial lease.
4. How is leasing like borrowing?
5. Why might a business sell and then lease back its plant and equipment?
6. Summarize the current approach to accounting for leases.
7. What are the significant variables used in a cash-flow analysis of a lease/borrow comparison?
8. What discount rate is used to analyze the cash flows of a lease proposal?
9. In a lease analysis, discuss the meaning of a positive versus a negative net-present-value calculation.

10. Which of the following is (A) a leasing benefit or (B) a leasing cost? Explain each.
    a. Cost of leased item
    b. Investment tax credit
    c. Depreciation and maintenance expenses
    d. Residual value

Problems

1. Determine the after-tax value of the following lease evaluation cash flows. Assume a marginal tax rate of 34 percent.
   a. $350,000 cost of equipment leased
   b. $60,000-per-year lease payment
   c. $24,000-per-year depreciation amount (no salvage value assumed)
   d. $500 maintenance cost per year paid by lessor
   e. $20,000 residual or salvage value

2. In problem (1), if the after-tax cost of debt is 6 percent and the lease is written for a 10-year term, should the firm lease or borrow? Use the *NPV* decision rule. (Hint: the maintenance cost paid by the lessor is an amount, net of taxes that the lessee does not pay because of leasing.)

3. Queens Manufacturing Company has decided to acquire a new pressing machine and is trying to decide between the leasing and buying alternatives. The machine can be purchased from the manufacturer for a delivered price of $85,000. The machine will be depreciated over a 10-year period to a zero salvage value although the firm estimates that it could be sold for a minimum of $5,000 at the end of 10 years. Alternatively, the manufacturer has offered a financial lease at $11,000 per year for the 10 years with all operating, maintenance, and insurance expense to be borne by the lessee. The firm's before-tax interest rate on long-term debt is 10 percent, all depreciation is straight-line, and the tax rate is 45 percent. Which financial alternative would you recommend?

4. The Mudville public school system plans to install a computer to cut expenses for recordkeeping, payroll, and other clerical functions. The manufacturer offers two options: purchase or a noncancelable lease. Outright purchase would require an outlay of $150,000, and maintenance and insurance would run $1,000 per month. Alternatively, Mudville could lease the computer for an initial term of 4 years at $4,000 per month, maintenance and insurance included. At the end of 4 years, Mudville would have the option of purchasing the computer for $40,000 (the estimated fair market price at that time), leasing for a second 4-year term for $2,500 per month, or terminating the arrangement. At the end of year 8, the computer is expected to have zero salvage value. Lease contracts would be noncancelable in both years 1–4 and 5–8. Operating costs other than maintenance and insurance would be the same under either purchase or lease. The interest rate on long-term U.S. government bonds is 10 percent, and Mudville's borrowing rate (on tax-free municipal bonds) is 9 percent. How should Mudville finance the computer?

5. The Schlotterbeck Manufacturing Company has decided to acquire a new automated drilling machine for its plant in Portland, Maine. The firm can purchase the machine from the manufacturer for a delivered price of $125,000. If purchased, the machine qualifies for an investment tax credit of 10 percent. The incremental servicing and maintenance costs of the new machine are estimated to be $5,000 annually. These costs would not be incurred if the machine is leased. If purchased, the machine will be depreciated over a 10-year period to a zero salvage value using the straight-line method. Even though depreciation will be based on a zero salvage value, the company anticipates being able to sell the machine for a minimum of $6,000 at the end of the 10 years. Alternatively, Schlotterbeck could lease the machine for an initial term of 5 years at $3,000 per month with the option of purchasing the machine at the end of year 5 for $50,000 (the

estimated fair market value at that time) or renew the lease for another 5-year term for $2,000 per month. At the end of year 10, all rights to the machine would revert back to the leasing company, and Schlotterbeck would not be given a purchase option. The monthly lease payments include all servicing and maintenance costs for the machine. The firm's tax rate is 46 percent, and its before-tax interest rate on long-term debt is 12 percent.

after-tax in back answers

a. Which plan would you recommend? [For simplicity, in your calculations use annual year-end lease payments of $36,000 (years 1–5) and $24,000 (years 6–10) rather than the monthly payments.]

b. Suppose this industry is subject to rapid technological changes in production methods which make existing equipment obsolete relatively quickly. Would this change your recommendation in part (a)?

REFERENCES

Athanasopoulos, P. J., and P. W. Bacon, "The Evaluation of Leveraged Leases." *Financial Management* 9 (Spring 1980): 76–80.

Bower, R. S., "Issues in Lease Financing." *Financial Management* 2 (Winter 1973): 25–34.

Franks, J. R., and S. C. Hodges, "Valuation of Financial Lease Contracts: A Note." *Journal of Finance* 33 (May 1978): 657–69.

Meyers, S. C., D. A. Dill, and J. A. Bautista, "Valuation of Financial Lease Contracts." *Journal of Finance* 31 (June 1976): 799–820.

Roenfeldt, R. L., and J. S. Osteryoung, "Analysis of Financial Leases." *Financial Management* 2 (Spring 1973): 34–40.

20

Issuing and Managing Long-Term Securities

In this chapter, we discuss two main topics: first, the policies and procedures that firms follow in actually issuing new equity and debt securities to investors; and second, the responsibilities of the firm in managing its outstanding securities after they have been issued. We will learn about public offerings versus private placements, the use of privileged subscriptions, disclosure requirements in connection with new issues, and considerations in deciding the exact timing of new issues. We will then discuss the unhappy matter of financial distress and failure, including reorganization and liquidation under the bankruptcy laws.

Financial securities— financial claims, such as bonds and stocks.

The material in this chapter is, for the most part, applicable to firms that have reached a stage in their development that permits access to the public capital markets. The financial claims we shall discuss usually are referred to as **financial securities.** Firms that are too small or too new to have their securities accepted by the capital markets usually acquire their external funds by means of *loans,* the label normally given to debt contracts negotiated with financial intermediaries, such as commercial banks, finance companies, and insurance companies.

Issuing Long-Term Securities

Firms normally use one of three methods to issue debt and equity securities to the public: public offerings through investment bankers, public offerings via privileged subscription, and private placements.

Firms normally issue debt and equity securities to the public using one of three methods: public offerings through investment bankers, public offerings through privileged subscription, and private placements. We will discuss each of these methods. We then will discuss government regulation of securities issues, especially requirements for disclosure of information. Finally, we will take up considerations such as issue costs and timing that are pertinent to all types of issues.

Methods of Issuing Securities

Firms that sell securities directly to the public tend to be large companies. For example, on June 27, 1985, Eastern Airlines sold stock worth $88 million to the public. Only a few weeks later, Beatrice Companies sold more than $400 million worth of stock. Though certainly large, these stock offerings are not close to record sizes. In the early 1980s, American Telephone and Telegraph Company (AT&T) had three separate stock issues, each of which was worth about $1 billion. These issues predated the breakup of AT&T into eight smaller companies in January 1984.

Single buyers, such as insurance companies or banks, are ordinarily unable to supply such large sums, and are unwilling to concentrate their investments to such an extent because of risk considerations. Large amounts, therefore, are usually sold to large numbers of buyers in **public offerings.** To assist firms in public sales of securities, the specialized institution of investment banking has been developed.

Public offerings— security offerings in which securities are made available to the public and are sold to large numbers of buyers.

In public offerings, investment bankers bring together the sellers of securities (firms) and the buyers (the public).

Public Offerings Through Investment Bankers. Investment bankers are essentially intermediaries who bring together the seller of securities—namely, the firm—and the buyers—namely, the public. The largest investment banking firms, such as Morgan Stanley, Salomon Brothers, and Goldman Sachs, are found in New York City, but many regional firms also exist. The specialized function performed by the investment banker is directly analogous to that of the retailer of goods. The investment banker has the expertise and specialized sales organization to do an effective marketing job. Because of this specialization, the investment banker generally can perform the distribution job at lower cost than can the firm itself, which normally would issue securities rather infrequently.

One of the most important functions of the investment banker is to *underwrite* the issue. The underwriter actually buys the securities from the selling firm and resells them to the public. Thus, a good part of the risk of issuing the securities—for example, the risk of adverse reception because of overpricing or adverse general market fluctuations during the distribution period—is borne by the underwriter. In large issues, a number of underwriters often will join together in a *syndicate* to spread the risk.

The second major function of the investment banker is that of *selling* the securities to investors. The selling and risk-bearing functions are separable, and the investment banker is compensated for both. The total compensation to the investment banker is the difference between the price paid to the issuing firm and the resale price to the public. The total spread usually is divided into an *underwriting profit*, which compensates for risk-bearing, and the *selling concession*, which compensates for the service function of selling.

Not all securities sold through investment bankers are underwritten. Sometimes an issue is sold on a *best-efforts basis*, an arrangement under which the investment banker acts as *agent* of the seller and sells as many securities as possible at an agreed-upon price. In this situation, the investment banker has no responsibility for unsold securities and thus bears no risk. Compensation to the investment banker includes only the selling concession.

Another major function of the investment banker is to advise the issuing firm with respect to *pricing* the issue. When the firm has securities of the same class already outstanding, the issue price is likely to be set slightly below the market price of the then outstanding securities. Pricing is most critical in connection with **new issues**—the initial public offering of securities of a given class. For example, when a firm issues common stock for the first time, there is no established market price to serve as a benchmark.

In pricing a new issue, it is in the interests of all parties that the securities be priced fairly—neither too high nor too low. Too high an offering price benefits existing holders at the expense of new holders, whose interests are soon to become a responsibility of the management by virtue of the transaction; too low a price hurts existing holders. Pricing a new issue is part art and part science, and the judgment of the investment banker, a feel for the market, and experience with similar firms in the past play a key role.

An offering that is underwritten may be sold either on a negotiated or a competitive-bid basis. In the former case, the seller and the underwriter mutually agree on the price to be paid for the securities by the underwriter. Under competitive bidding, the seller invites bids from several firms and awards the issue to the highest bidder. Bids are based on the anticipated resale price to the public and the desired spread.

Another important function of the investment banker is to assist the seller and its lawyers in preparing the offering circular, or **prospectus**, which provides important information about the securities to potential buyers. We will discuss the prospectus in more detail below in connection with government regulation.

Public Offerings Through Privileged Subscription.

When new common shares are sold to the general public, the proportionate ownership share of existing shareholders is reduced. For this reason, when new common stock or securities con-

---

Investment bankers often perform the important function of underwriting a securities offering—investment bankers buy all of the securities offered and then resell them, thereby relieving the firm of the risk of adverse reception or adverse price fluctuations.

Investment bankers advise the issuing firm with respect to the pricing of the issue.

New issues—the initial public offering of a security of a given class.

Investment bankers assist the firm in preparing the prospectus for the securities offered.

Prospectus—a document filed with the SEC providing a summary of the financial and commercial-strategy information contained in a registration statement and composed when securities are being issued by a firm.

Finance in Practice 20—1

Going Public

One way for entrepreneurs to cash in on their success is to sell shares to the public after their company establishes itself. In the five years ending mid-1986, more than 1,500 U.S. companies "went public" by making their first public sale of shares. In the process, quite a few fortunes took shape. Take the case of Bill Gates, a computer-software prodigy who helped found Microsoft.

Founded in 1975, Microsoft emerged as a leader in producing software for personal computers. The company's major successes included operating systems that run millions of personal computers and fast-selling applications programs that could be used on those same computers. By spring of 1986, the company's revenues were approaching $200 million a year. In addition, Microsoft's pretax profits were running as high as 34 percent of revenues. Unlike many companies, Microsoft generated sufficient cash flow to finance its growth without needing external financing.

To attract top managers and programmers, Gates had been offering them shares in Microsoft as well as stock options. These provided a powerful incentive for these employees to work in the interest of the firm. As the firm grew, the number of shareholders grew until it was expected to hit 500 by 1987. This 500 level would require Microsoft to register with the Securities and Exchange Commission. Furthermore, to give employees a chance to cash in on Microsoft's success, a public market for the stock would be desirable.

The stage was set for going public and in March 1986 Microsoft offered shares to the public at $21 per share. Shares were traded in the over-the-counter market, and the price shot to more than $30, representing a price/earnings ratio of well over 20 times. It was apparent that the market anticipated a bright future for Microsoft, and the company raised more than $60 million even though employees still retained the vast majority of shares.

How did Bill Gates make out? He got $1.6 million from the shares he sold personally, but that was only the tip of the iceberg. He retained 45 percent ownership of the company. At the going market price, this holding had a market value of $350 million, making Gates, at age 30, probably one of the 100 richest Americans. Despite his immense personal gain, Gates still had concerns that too much emphasis on the firm's share price might distract managers and programmers from doing what made Microsoft a success in the first place: excelling in the computer-software business. A few weeks after the offering, Gates noticed a chart of Microsoft's stock price on a programmer's door. Gates queried the programmer, "Is this a distraction?"

Source: Adapted from B. Uttal, "Inside the Deal That Made Bill Gates $350,000,000," *Fortune,* July 21, 1986, pp. 23–33.

Privileged subscription—
the practice of offering new securities to existing shareholders first, before any public offering is made.

vertible into common stock are to be issued, some firms follow a practice of first offering the new securities to existing shareholders on the basis of **privileged subscription.** The right of shareholders to have first chance at purchasing new shares is called a **preemptive right** and is supported by some state laws as well as by the corporate charters of some firms.

When a firm undertakes a **rights offering,** as privileged subscriptions often are called, it mails directly to shareholders one right for each share held. The terms of the offering specify the subscription price and number of rights required to purchase an additional share. For example, if a firm had 1 million shares outstanding and wished to offer 100,000 new shares, it would mail out 1 million rights and require 10 rights to purchase an additional share.

The subscription period during which the rights can be exercised generally runs 20–30 days. During that period, the rights have value because the subscription price is set below the current market price of the stock at the beginning of the subscription period. Shareholders, therefore, have several options: they can exercise their rights and purchase their prorated share of the new securities; they can sell their rights; they can buy additional rights from others not wishing to exercise them and subscribe to more than their prorated share; they can do nothing. They must, however, choose one of these alternatives prior to the end of the subscription period, because at that point the rights become valueless.

When a rights offering is announced, the firm establishes a *date of record.* Owners of the stock on that date will receive rights to subscribe to the new offering. Prior to the record date, the stock sells *rights on,* which means that a purchaser of existing shares in the market prior to the record date will receive rights to the new offering. On the record date, the price of existing shares drops and the stock sells *ex rights,* meaning that purchasers of the stock after the record date do not receive rights to subscribe to the new offering. By the end of the subscription period, the firm has collected the rights and the subscription proceeds, and any unexercised rights become worthless. Certificates for the new shares are issued at some later date. Appendix 20A discusses the valuation of rights.

To ensure a successful offering, it is important that the market price of the stock not fall below the subscription price. If market price were below subscription price, no one would buy the new shares because old shares could be bought at a lower price in the open market. Because the subscription price does not affect the net worth of existing shareholders, it can be set low in relation to current market price in order to reduce the likelihood that the rights would not be exercised. The more volatile the market price, the greater the discount. The lower the subscription price is set, however, the greater is the number of new shares that must be issued to raise a given amount of money. In deciding this question, the firm must take into account the implications for dividend policy. For example, if a firm desires to maintain a given level of dividends per share, a larger total dollar payment of dividends will be required as the firm issues more shares.

Some rights offerings are undertaken by the issuing firm without the assistance of an investment banker. The success of such offerings depends in part on factors under the control of management, such as the relationship between subscription price and market price and the size of the issue, and also on factors that management cannot control, such as general economic and market developments. To protect against unfavorable developments that might jeopardize the success of an offering, many firms find it wise to obtain a standby commitment from an investment banker, or group of investment bankers, to underwrite any unsubscribed portion of the issue. In this way, the firm ensures that it will receive the funds. For this insurance, the firm pays a fee to the investment banker.

In recent years, the use of rights offerings has fallen off markedly. Many corporations have changed their charters to eliminate the preemptive right previously given to shareholders. The firms are thus free to go directly to the market.

Private Placements. Firms often sell securities directly to one investor or to a small group of investors, rather than to the public, through **private placements.** The great majority of private placements are debt issues; common stock is placed privately rather infrequently. Buyers of private placements are nearly always financial intermediaries, such as insurance companies and pension funds.

A firm may opt for a private placement rather than a public offering for any of several reasons. Firms that have not yet reached a sufficient size or established a sufficient track record to permit a public offering may find a private placement feasible. In fact, a major function of the private-placement market is to serve as a source of long-term debt financing for smaller, less financially secure firms. In a private placement, a financial intermediary (say, an insurance company) performs the necessary tasks of information gathering and analysis at much less expense than would be the case in a public offering. Smaller amounts of funds — say, in the range of several hundred thousand to several million dollars — can be raised through private placement, whereas such amounts would usually be judged too small for a public offering. Registration by the Securities and Exchange Commission is not required, so private placements generally can be consummated more quickly than public offerings. Terms can be negotiated directly by lender and borrower without the involvement of an investment banker, although the latter often plays a role both in bringing borrower and lender together and in the negotiations. Because terms are negotiated and the time frame usually is shorter, timing problems arising from market fluctuations are less troublesome than in the case of public offerings. Another advantage of a private placement is that the borrower can obtain a forward commitment by the lender to deliver funds in the future at a known rate.

Because registration is not required and because no underwriting and selling expenses are involved, the direct expenses of private placements tend to be lower than those of public offerings, thereby reducing effective borrowing costs from as much as one percentage point for small offerings ($1 million or less) to 0.10 percentage point for large offerings. Interest costs, on the other hand, tend to be slightly higher on private placements. The rate differential depends on the financial strength of the borrower, ranging from essentially no differential for stronger firms to 0.30 percentage points for less secure firms.[1]

The major borrower categories — public utilities, finance companies, and industrial companies — have exhibited markedly different patterns of reliance on the private-placement market. Public utilities have sold their debt almost entirely in the public markets. Large finance companies have sold a majority of their debt in the public markets. Small finance companies have sold most of their debt in the private markets.

Private placements — offerings of new securities in which firms sell securities directly to one investor or to a small group of investors rather than to the public.

Since registration with the SEC is not required and no underwriting and selling expenses are involved, the direct expenses of private placements tend to be lower than those of public offerings.

---

[1]See Eli Shapiro and Charles R. Wolf, *The Role of Private Placements in Corporate Finance* (Cambridge, Mass.: Graduate School of Business Administration, Harvard University, 1972).

Other Methods of Security Issuance

Dividend-Reinvestment Plans. One method corporations have devised to ensure a steady inflow of new equity capital is to allow shareholders to apply their periodic dividend receipts automatically to the purchase of new shares. Under this procedure, dividend payments never actually go to the shareholder but rather are applied directly by the company to a purchase of new shares. One unfortunate disadvantage of such plans is that the Internal Revenue Service taxes the dividend as usual, even though the shareholder never actually receives the cash. In spite of this drawback, **dividend-reinvestment plans** have grown in popularity, especially among utility companies during periods when they face large needs for new capital.

Dividend-reinvestment plan — the policy of allowing shareholders to apply their periodic dividend receipts automatically to the purchase of new shares.

Direct Sales to the Public. Yet another innovation in financial markets is direct sale of securities to the public without the use of an investment-banker intermediary. The innovator was Exxon Corporation, which bypassed Wall Street in late 1976 by offering a $50 million issue of new debt securities to the public. In order to bring in small as well as large investors, Exxon used the so-called *Dutch auction method.* Under this system, prospective investors submitted individual bids (prices) to purchase selected amounts of the issue, but every successful bidder eventually paid the *same price* — which was the lowest price Exxon had to accept in order to sell the stated $50 million amount of the issue.

Disclosure Requirements

Both the federal and state governments regulate the sale of securities to the public. The principal objective of such regulation is to ensure that adequate information is provided to prospective buyers of the securities and to protect buyers against misinformation and fraud.

The Securities Act of 1933, passed in the aftermath of the Great Depression and in response to stock-market abuses of earlier years, sets forth federal regulatory requirements for new security issues. The Securities Exchange Act of 1934 regulates securities already outstanding. The Securities and Exchange Commission (SEC) administers both sets of requirements.

Under the provisions of the 1933 act as administered by the SEC, a firm wishing to sell securities to the public must register the issue with the SEC. Smaller issues are subject to considerably less detailed disclosure requirements. Certain specialized types of firms, such as railroads, are exempt from SEC registration requirements because they are regulated by other government agencies.

Registration statement — statement of information a company must file with the SEC when new securities are issued.

The **registration statement** filed with the SEC contains information on the firm's history, its management, financial data, a description of the securities to be offered, uses to which proceeds will be put, and legal and accounting opinions. The firm also must file a *prospectus,* a summary of the information provided in the registration statement. A copy of the first page of the prospectus for an issue of Microsoft Corporation common stock is shown in Figure 20–1. The prospectus is the primary vehicle by which information is communicated to prospective investors. The prospectus is made available to investors by the investment banker or by the issuing firm if no investment banker is involved.

Figure 20–1
An Example of a Prospectus

2,795,000 Shares

Microsoft Corporation

Common Stock

Of the 2,795,000 shares of Common Stock offered hereby, 2,000,000 shares are being sold by the Company and 795,000 shares are being sold by the Selling Stockholders. See "Principal and Selling Stockholders." The Company will not receive any of the proceeds from the sale of shares by the Selling Stockholders.

Prior to this offering, there has been no public market for the Common Stock of the Company. For the factors which were considered in determining the initial public offering price, see "Underwriting."

See "Certain Factors" for a discussion of certain factors which should be considered by prospective purchasers of the Common Stock offered hereby.

THESE SECURITIES HAVE NOT BEEN APPROVED OR DISAPPROVED BY THE SECURITIES AND EXCHANGE COMMISSION NOR HAS THE COMMISSION PASSED UPON THE ACCURACY OR ADEQUACY OF THIS PROSPECTUS. ANY REPRESENTATION TO THE CONTRARY IS A CRIMINAL OFFENSE.

	Initial Public Offering Price	Underwriting Discount(1)	Proceeds to Company(2)	Proceeds to Selling Stockholders(2)
Per Share	$21.00	$1.31	$19.69	$19.69
Total(3)	$58,695,000	$3,661,450	$39,380,000	$15,653,550

(1) The Company and the Selling Stockholders have agreed to indemnify the Underwriters against certain liabilities, including liabilities under the Securities Act of 1933.

(2) Before deducting expenses of the offering estimated at $541,000, of which $452,000 will be paid by the Company and $89,000 by the Selling Stockholders.

(3) The Company has granted to the Underwriters an option to purchase up to an additional 300,000 shares at the initial public offering price, less the underwriting discount, solely to cover over-allotments. If such option is exercised in full, the total Initial Public Offering Price, Underwriting Discount and Proceeds to Company will be $64,995,000, $4,054,450 and $45,287,000, respectively.

The shares are offered severally by the Underwriters, as specified herein, subject to receipt and acceptance by them and subject to their right to reject any order in whole or in part. It is expected that the certificates for the shares will be ready for delivery at the offices of Goldman, Sachs & Co., New York, New York on or about March 20, 1986.

Goldman, Sachs & Co.   Alex. Brown & Sons
Incorporated

The date of this Prospectus is March 13, 1986.

All parties to a securities offering have an interest in full disclosure of relevant information. The evidence indicates that the securities markets in general do an effective job of processing information and incorporating it into security prices. One of the most important objectives in a new issue is to see that it is priced so that neither new buyers nor existing holders are treated unfairly. Given the evidence regarding market efficiency, a firm's management can rely on the impersonal action of the marketplace to see that the information is evaluated in an unbiased manner. A policy of full disclosure coupled with the market's efficiency is management's best guarantee that new securities will be issued at fair prices.

Beginning in 1982, the SEC authorized a type of registration statement that allows a firm, if it desires, to prepare all the registration and legal documents for a financing and then "put it on the shelf" to await favorable market conditions. When conditions were favorable, the firm could proceed with the offering in a matter of days without having to repeat the steps in the registration process. After a successful trial period, in late 1983 **shelf registration** was permanently authorized under Rule 415 for large firms. Rule 415 allows a firm to register all securities it expects to sell over the upcoming 24 months and then sell them over that period whenever it chooses.[2]

Shelf registration — method of selling securities allowing a firm flexibility in timing the issuance.

Costs of Issuing Securities

In addition to the returns paid to the suppliers of capital, such as interest payments to bondholders, a company has flotation costs when it issues securities. Direct expenses include underwriting commissions, selling expenses, legal fees, printing expenses, and mailing expenses.

Table 20–1 shows flotation costs associated with public issues of bonds, preferred stocks, and common stocks. Two trends are evident in the table. First, the larger the size of the issue, the lower the percentage flotation costs because certain flotation costs are fixed and have to be borne no matter how small the issue. As a result, smaller firms that would have smaller issues are subject to higher flotation

Because some issue costs are fixed, raising small amounts of money is uneconomical: firms try to limit the frequency of trips to the markets and to finance in blocks.

Table 20–1

Flotation Costs of Bonds, Preferred Stock, and Common Stock

Size of Issue (millions of dollars)	Flotation Costs as a Percentage of Issue's Total Dollar Value		
	Bonds	Preferred Stock	Common Stock
Under 0.5		NA	23.7
0.5–0.9	Average 13.3	NA	20.9
1.0–1.9		11.8	16.9
2.0–4.9	6.2	NA	12.4
5.0–9.9	3.2	2.6	8.1
10.0–19.9	1.9	1.8	5.9
20.0–49.9	1.4	1.7	4.6
50.0 and over	1.1	1.6	3.5

NA: Information is not available.

Source: Securities and Exchange Commission.

[2]For studies of the effects of shelf registration, see D. Kidwell, M. Marr, and G. Thompson, "SEC Rule 415: The Ultimate Competitive Bid," *Journal of Financial and Quantitative Analysis,* June 1984, pp. 183–95; and S. Bhagat, M. Marr, and G. Thompson, "The Rule 415 Experiment: Equity Markets," *Journal of Finance,* December 1985, pp. 1385–1401.

costs. Second, percentage flotation costs are typically lower for bond issues than for preferred-stock issues. Raising new common stock has the highest percentage flotation costs. Though there are no organized data to report on flotation costs of bank loans, they are lower than the percentage costs of bond issues.

In addition to the costs shown in Table 20–1, another significant expense is the management time that must be devoted to planning and negotiating an issue. Since issue costs as a percentage of funds raised vary inversely with the size of issue, raising small amounts of money is uneconomical. As a result, firms generally attempt to limit the frequency of trips to the financial markets and to finance in blocks. This lumpiness may impose short-run constraints on a firm's investment policy.

Dealing with Variable Interest Rates

A major problem for both borrowers and lenders is high and variable interest rates. Many long-term lenders, such as insurance companies, suffered heavy losses during the late 1970s when, believing that interest rates were near their peaks, they placed long-term debt issues in their portfolios only to see rates go higher still. When rates rose, bond prices dropped; losses ran into hundreds of millions of dollars.

In the face of these losses, lenders became increasingly reluctant to purchase long-term issues. At the same time, borrowers worried about issuing long-term bonds at historically high rates when lower rates might be just ahead. To resolve these problems, some lenders and borrowers turned to issues with variable interest rates (variable-rate notes were discussed in Chapter 14). The technique gained popularity at the beginning of the 1980s. In November 1980, General Motors Acceptance Corporation sold publicly a 10-year $250 million issue with an adjustable rate tied to the rate on 10-year Treasury bonds. Chemical New York Corporation and Citicorp followed shortly thereafter with private placements totaling $150 million worth of adjustable-rate preferred stock and notes. Variable-rate financing is now one of the financing tools available for corporate managers. Another technique for dealing with unanticipated swings in interest rates is hedging with financial futures contracts, as discussed in Chapter 18.

Timing of New Issues of Securities

From the standpoint of existing shareholders, it would be desirable to issue new stock when stock prices are relatively high and to issue new bonds when long-term interest rates are relatively low. Should managers devote significant effort to an attempt to time new issues for stock-price highs and interest-rate lows? The timing issue is a controversial one.

As discussed earlier in Chapter 14, the benefits of timing depend on the efficiency of financial markets. The theory of market efficiency holds that prices and interest rates reflect all public information in an unbiased manner. In such an efficient market, current prices and rates would reflect a consensus forecast of future prices and rates by the best-informed and best-financed investors. Everyone knows that the consensus forecast could be inaccurate and that the future might well turn out to be different from the expectation. But the error is about as likely to be in one direction as in the other, and most attempts to outguess the market will have only about a 50/50 chance of success. If managers operate in efficient financial markets and face such odds, firms should not attempt to time issues, but rather should adopt a general policy of raising funds when needed.

What is the evidence? Research on the subject, mostly by academic researchers, suggests that financial markets are reasonably efficient.[3] This finding suggests that consistently superior timing is very difficult — so difficult that most firms should not waste effort trying. Frequently, conditions that appear to be depressed will turn out, in retrospect, to be not so depressed after all. Deferral of security issues is likely to mean deferral of investment decisions and interference with the firm's commercial strategy. Given the odds of success, a policy of attempting to exploit market movements is unlikely to provide gains that consistently outweigh the costs of interruptions in investment plans. The best policy, therefore, is to let the commercial strategy dictate the timing of external financings and to rely on full disclosure and market efficiency to ensure fair pricing of these financings.

Many practicing managers reject the suggestion that timing is too difficult to be worthwhile. Data on new issues of securities indicate that the volume of new stock issues increases after a significant rise in stock prices and falls after a decline.[4]

It is not hard to imagine why a manager would attempt to time new security issues. A new stock issue at a market low does not look good to the existing shareholders — that is, those who were shareholders prior to the new issue. They feel that newcomers will capture a part of an increase in value that is rightfully theirs. Much better, they would say, to wait until *after* the price rise to issue the new stock. Then fewer new shares must be issued to raise a given amount of money, and the position of the old shareholders is diluted less. The same would hold for new bond issues. A manager looks much better if he or she issues new bonds *before* a rise in interest rates rather than after.

A new stock issue after an increase in stock prices reduces the risk of appearing to misjudge the market. If prices go back down, the manager is a hero for catching the peak. Even if prices continue to rise, he or she has captured at least part of the increase for the old shareholders. If, on the other hand, a manager issues stock when the market is low in relation to the recent past or issues bonds when interest rates are high, he or she runs the risk of appearing to be imprudent.

There are also situations in which managers have important information about a company's future earnings prospects that they do not wish to make public for competitive reasons. Issuing stock before the new information is released could be disadvantageous to existing shareholders because they would not capture for them-

Because it is difficult to time the issuance of new securities consistently to capture stock-price highs or interest-rate lows, the best policy is to let the commercial strategy dictate the timing of external financings and to let market efficiency ensure fair pricing.

[3]See Chapter 14 for a discussion of evidence on market efficiency. There we also distinguish between three forms of market efficiency.

[4]See R. A. Taggart, "A Model of Corporate Financing Decisions," *Journal of Finance,* December 1977, pp. 1467–84. For further evidence that companies time security issues, see A. Jalilvand and R. Harris, "Corporate Behavior in Adjusting to Capital Structure and Dividend Targets," *Journal of Finance,* March 1984, pp. 127–45.

selves the resulting increase in the value of the firm. In this case, the firm may choose to issue debt to raise needed new funds and wait until the information can be made public at an advantageous time before issuing new stock.[5]

In sum, managers have good reason to attempt to time new issues of stocks and bonds to take advantage of market conditions. The question is not over the wisdom of doing so, but rather over the chances of success. The weight of the research evidence suggests that the odds of *consistently* timing new issues to advantage are not good, and that managers' time is better spent concentrating on other matters. Most likely, however, managers will continue to try.

Other Considerations in Issuing Securities

At this point, it is appropriate to remind ourselves of several other considerations that we have discussed at other points in this book. One such consideration is *control*. Maintenance of control usually is a major consideration in closely held firms when external financing is contemplated. In order to maintain control, a firm may impose restrictions on financing alternatives, which in turn may constrain its investment policy. Control is very important in some situations, but maintaining it is likely to entail costs in terms of reduced access to the financial markets and constraints on commercial strategy.

To maintain control, a closely held firm may restrict its financing alternatives, which may constrain its investment policy.

Another important consideration is the sequencing of issues when a series of external financings is in prospect. A major objective in planning sequential issues is to maintain flexibility with respect to alternative sources.

Some financial economists have argued that new stock and bond issues have the potential for inducing significant information effects of the sort discussed in connection with dividend policy in Chapter 17. The potential for information effects could exist when managers have inside information not yet reflected in market prices. Suppose a firm's management has significant and favorable information about its firm's future prospects that investors do not have. In order to preserve the benefits for existing shareholders, the management issues debt instead of equity, planning to issue equity later after the good news has been reflected in the stock price. If investors begin to see such actions as a typical pattern, they may interpret a decision *not to issue* stock as evidence of good news. A decision *to issue* stock might imply that there existed no future prospects sufficiently favorable to justify preserving them for existing shareholders by issuing debt. Hence, a debt issue might signal good news, and a stock issue might signal bad news, or at least news that is less good. Such reasoning might explain why stock prices often fall upon the announcement of a stock issue.[6]

Managers should be conscious of any such information effects that new security issues might have. As our discussion has indicated, the manager's job is not sim-

---

[5]In this situation the financial market is not efficient in the strong form because it does not reflect inside information (see Chapter 14 for discussion) known by the manager. In practice, markets are not strong-form efficient, so such situations may arise.

[6]For an analysis of this argument, see S. C. Myers and N. J. Majluf, "Stock Issues and Investment Policy When Firms Have Information That Investors Do Not Have," *Journal of Financial Economics* 13 (1984): 187–221.

ply to choose whether to issue one type of security or another. The actual process of issuing the securities requires management time and consideration.

Managing Securities After Issuance

Once a firm has issued securities to the public, it incurs some responsibilities for managing the securities after issuance. The discussion in this section pertains primarily to publicly traded issues, although parts of the discussion, such as that pertaining to communications, are pertinent to privately held issues as well.

Trading of Securities After Issuance

Stock exchanges — formal organizations that act as auction markets in the trading of financial securities.

If holders of the bonds or stock of a firm wish to liquidate their investment, they must sell their securities to someone else. They cannot return them to the issuing firm for redemption. In the case of closely held firms, finding an interested buyer may be difficult. In the case of more widely held firms, public markets exist in which shares can be freely bought and sold. Public markets in the United States are of two general types: the organized **stock exchanges** and the **over-the-counter (OTC) market.**

Over-the-counter (OTC) markets — markets for trading in securities not listed on organized security exchanges.

The best-known stock exchanges are the New York Stock Exchange and the American Stock Exchange, both located in New York City. There also exist a number of regional exchanges elsewhere in the United States. The exchanges are an **auction market** where buyers and sellers state their terms. Specialists act as brokers to bring buyers and sellers together, sometimes buying and selling for their own account.

Auction market — a market in which buyers and sellers state their terms publicly.

The over-the-counter market is made up of a larger number of investment firms that act as dealers. Dealers *make a market* in the shares of a particular firm by quoting *bid* and *asked* prices at which they stand ready to buy or sell. The dealer is compensated by the spread between the bid and asked prices.

Communication with the Markets

Heading the list of important responsibilities in connection with outstanding issues is *communication*. Earlier in this chapter we discussed the importance of full disclosure of all pertinent information to prospective buyers of new issues. Here we focus on communication with holders of existing issues.

Regular Financial Reporting. Because management acts as agent of the owners of the firm, keeping those owners informed clearly is an important management responsibility. In the case of publicly held firms, SEC regulations require regular reporting, at least annually, to shareholders. Larger firms also are required to report to shareholders quarterly. The New York Stock Exchange requires both annual and quarterly reports by firms whose stock is traded on the exchange.

The format and content of such published financial reports are prescribed by the SEC in cooperation with the accounting profession. Quarterly reports generally are brief and cover the most recent quarterly and year-to-date information. Annual reports usually are much more comprehensive; they often include extensive historical statistical data as well as narrative information on the firm's operations and plans. Financial statements in annual reports are audited by a certified-public-accounting firm.

Besides these published reports, firms are also required to file certain regular reports directly with the SEC. These reports include standard financial information as well as reports of special events such as changes in directors and principal officers, mergers and acquisitions, lawsuits, large losses, and the like. Information of this sort also should be reported to shareholders and the investing public, and most firms follow a policy of doing so.

Firms are further required to hold a general meeting of shareholders at least annually, at which time directors are elected and other business is conducted. In addition to regularly scheduled communications through meetings and reports, firms typically communicate a variety of routine information through press releases.

In addition to reporting historical information, firms should keep investors fully informed with respect to strategy and policy. Owners and potential investors are entitled to know what basic goals management has set, the general outline of the commercial strategy, and the major policies that will be followed. With respect to financial management specifically, investors are entitled to know management's target debt/equity ratio, what policies will be followed with respect to debt maturity, and the target dividend-payout ratio. To the extent that competitive considerations permit, future investment opportunities and plans should also be communicated. With respect to all such policies, the objective is to tell investors what is going on rather than force them to guess. Complete disclosure is good practice not only because owners are entitled to the information, but also because better disclosure promotes fairer pricing of securities. In general, comprehensive disclosure on a regular basis contributes to smaller price fluctuations and avoids surprises.

Regular reporting also lays the groundwork for future securities issues. Where a firm has publicly traded securities, their market price is a major factor in setting the price of a new issue. Hence, the price at which new securities are offered is largely determined by holders of existing securities. For this reason, comprehensive disclosure on a regular basis provides the best assurance of fair prices for new issues.

Reporting in Connection with Extraordinary Events. Even with a comprehensive program of disclosure on a regular basis, special effort is required in connection with extraordinary events such as new security offerings or major new investment plans. Security prices are determined by future-oriented factors: future cash flows and the riskiness of those cash flows. When only historical information is reported, the market is forced to draw inferences from management actions and whatever data are reported. The announcement of investment, financing, and dividend decisions can thus produce significant and possibly undesirable information effects as the market attempts to draw inferences regarding the future.

For example, announcement of a financing decision may convey information regarding investment opportunities. If the market interprets the announcement of a new financing as a signal that management sees more attractive investment opportunities ahead than had previously been anticipated, the stock price may rise. If the market sees no such attractive opportunities, the price may fall. In either case, the market is using the financing decision as the basis for drawing an inference about investment opportunities. Rather than relying on the market to draw the proper inference, it is better to communicate the facts directly.

A similar situation might arise in connection with a change in dividend policy. A cut in dividends, for example, might indicate that management sees attractive investment opportunities ahead and is conserving funds for investment. Alternatively, the market might infer that management sees bad times ahead and is conserving cash for emergency use. The first inference is likely to cause a rise in stock price; the second is likely to cause a fall in stock price. To avoid the possibility of incorrect interpretations, management should communicate the reasons for the change carefully and clearly. If the news is bad, owners and prospective investors are entitled to know it.

The preceding examples illustrate situations in which the market draws inferences from management actions. It is clear that straightforward communication is desirable so that the market bases its actions on facts rather than inferences. A related situation can occur when a firm's management is contemplating an action that is believed to be in the shareholders' interests, but that may be misinterpreted by the market. If funds are needed for investment and the firm is at or near its debt capacity, equity may be the right choice. Will the resulting dilution of earnings per share reduce stock price? Suppose equity is needed at a time when market price is below book value. Will a sale of equity at a price below book value be viewed negatively by the market? A third situation can occur in the case of an investment opportunity with a very high rate of return but low cash flows in early years and, therefore, adverse implications for near-term accounting profits. Fear of misinterpretation and an adverse reception by the market may lead a firm's management to forgo actions that in fact are in the shareholders' interests.

Problems of this sort usually can be minimized by careful communication. Investors are rational and entirely capable of understanding their own self-interests. If a particular decision is in the interests of shareholders, it is likely that they will agree. If a dividend cut really is needed, it should be made and the reasons carefully communicated. If an investment really does have attractive long-run returns, investors will be quite prepared to ignore an adverse impact on near-term profits. Forgoing such investments does shareholders no favor. If an equity issue is needed, investors can be persuaded. In fact, firms that issue debt instead of equity for fear of earnings dilution and thereby exceed their debt capacity ultimately will receive a message of disapproval from the market in the form of a low price/earnings (P/E) ratio.

Communication Policy. From the foregoing discussion of communications, what can we conclude with respect to appropriate policies? In general, firms should make financial-management decisions using value maximization as their criterion. Insofar as possible in an uncertain world, a firm's management can be confident that decisions reached in this way are in the shareholders' interests. Once the appropriate action has been chosen, the reasoning behind it should be communicated as completely as possible. Often, competitive considerations will make complete disclosure unwise. In such cases, the benefits of disclosure have to be weighed against loss of competitive advantages, with the interests of existing shareholders the guiding criterion. Difficulties with controversial decisions often center on adverse near-term impact on earnings per share. Communications should deal with this problem by explaining long-run implications. Good communication helps management take a long view, which, after all, is management's job.

Because management's role is to act as the agent of the firm's owners, managers have the responsibility of keeping owners and investors fully informed about the firm's strategy and policy. In the long run, full disclosure promotes the fair pricing of securities.

Listing of Shares

Shares that trade on an exchange, such as the New York or the American Stock Exchange, are said to be *listed* on the exchange. Exchanges have certain requirements with respect to size, years in business, number of shares outstanding, trading volume, market value, and earnings record that must be met before a firm will be accepted for listing. The reporting requirements of the exchanges over and above those already imposed by the SEC are not great in the case of nonfinancial firms, although there historically have been differences in the case of banks.

Most firms, therefore, begin their existence as public companies in the over-the-counter market and graduate to an exchange at a later stage in their development. Listed firms make up only a small percentage of the total number of business firms in the United States, but include the great majority of the larger nonfinancial firms. Banks and insurance companies historically have had their shares traded on an over-the-counter basis, but recently there has been a strong trend toward listing of bank holding company shares.

Advantages of exchange listing that typically are cited include a better market for shareholders wishing to buy and sell, better accommodation of large transactions, facilitation of future financings, and an improvement in the firm's status. While these indeed may be real advantages, studies of listing have found no evidence that exchange listing itself adds permanently to a firm's value.[7]

Retiring Outstanding Securities

Long-term debt issues of firms almost without exception have a final maturity date by which the principal must be repaid.[8] Maturities range from a few years to about 25 years. Maturities beyond 25 years are rare, because over longer periods the nature of a business and its environment can change radically; and lenders usually want an opportunity to reevaluate the risk from time to time.

Unlike debt, common stock is a perpetual claim with no provision for retirement, although retirement can be accomplished by means of repurchase. Preferred stock usually carries a provision for retirement but sometimes does not.

[7]See James C. Van Horne, "New Listings and Their Price Behavior," *Journal of Finance* 25 (September 1970): 783–94. See also Susan M. Phillips and J. Richard Zecher, "Exchange Listing and the Cost of Equity Capital," Capital Market Working Paper #8 (U.S. Securities and Exchange Commission, March 1982).

[8]An exception is the Canadian Pacific 4 percent perpetual bonds, which are consoles having no maturity.

—an
arrangement in which firms
make periodic repayments of
principal to the trustees of a
bond issue, who retire a
specified number of bonds
by open-market purchases or
by calling certain bonds at a
previously agreed-upon
price.

Serial redemption—the
retirement each year as they
mature of bonds that have
been issued with serial
maturity dates.

The most frequent motive
for calling a debt issue is to
refund it (to issue a new set
of bonds in its place).

Retirement of Long-Term Debt. Long-term debt can be retired in a number of ways. One way is simply to repay the entire principal at maturity. Most issues, however, require periodic repayment either by means of a **sinking fund** or through **serial redemption.** Some bond issues can be called at the option of the issuer. Convertible bonds are retired by conversion into common stock.

Under a sinking-fund arrangement, the terms of which are set forth in the bond indenture, the firm makes periodic payments, usually annually or semiannually, to the trustee of the bond issue. The trustee uses the funds to retire a specified number of bonds in one of two ways: by open-market purchases or by calling certain bonds at a previously agreed-upon price. The trustee will purchase in the open market as long as the market price is less than the call price. When market price is above the call price, the call provision will be exercised. Bonds to be called are usually selected on a lottery basis using their serial numbers to identify them.[9]

The proportion of the total issue to be retired at each sinking-fund payment date is set forth in the indenture. The amount of the periodic sinking-fund payment is usually fixed so that the same number of bonds is retired each time. Some issues provide for retirement of the entire issue by the final maturity date, whereas others may provide for only partial retirement with a *balloon payment* at maturity.

Sinking-fund bonds all have the same maturity date, although a portion of the bonds are retired in advance of maturity under procedures described above. *Serial bonds,* on the other hand, have sequential maturity dates. A $50 million issue, for example, may have $2.5 million in bonds maturing each year for 20 years. Over the life of the issue, bonds are redeemed each year as they mature.

Under a sinking-fund arrangement, the trustee is empowered to call a portion of the bonds each year. Most corporate-bond issues also provide for calling the entire issue at the option of the issuer. Some issues permit call at any time, although more typically the call privilege is not effective for five to ten years after issuance.

Retirement by means of a sinking fund or through serial redemption usually is a provision sought by lenders. The option to call the entire issue is a provision sought by the borrower. Call of an entire issue might be advantageous to a firm either to permit changes in capital structure or to permit refunding of the issue at a lower interest rate. The latter reason probably is more often the principal motive for the call provision from the borrowers' standpoint. In an uncertain world in which interest rates vary, having the option to retire a bond issue and reborrow at a lower rate is clearly advantageous. The advantage accrues to the shareholders, who would benefit from the reduction in interest costs. To the extent that the call privilege is advantageous to shareholders, it is usually disadvantageous to holders of the bonds, for in the event the privilege is exercised, bondholders must give up a security paying an interest rate above the prevailing market rate.[10] As one would

---

[9] For a theoretical analysis of callable bonds, see J. E. Ingersoll, "A Contingent-Claims Valuation of Convertible Securities," *Journal of Financial Economics* 2 (May 1977): 289–322.

[10] Differential tax rates between lenders and borrowers can sometimes create an economic incentive for a call feature beneficial to both borrower and lender. For an analysis of tax incentives for call features, see W. M. Boyce and A. J. Kalotay, "Tax Differentials and Callable Bonds," *Journal of Finance* 34 (September 1979): 825–38. The tax-incentive argument sheds light on why corporate bonds nearly always have a call feature and why Treasury bonds almost never have one.

expect in a competitive market, bondholders insist on being compensated for the call privilege. Other factors being equal, the interest rate on a callable issue will be higher. Also, the price at which the bonds are callable is set above par value. In short, the shareholders must pay for the flexibility afforded by the call privilege.

As noted earlier, the most frequent motive for calling an issue is to refund it — that is, to issue a new set of bonds in its place. The usual motive is to refund at a lower interest rate, although sometimes renegotiation of restrictive covenants is also a consideration. Considering only the interest-rate motive, the decision of whether to refund can be analyzed using discounted-cash-flow techniques. To identify the relevant cash flows, we apply the incremental-cash-flow rule. The firm makes an outlay — essentially, the difference between the amount required to call the old issue and the proceeds of the new issue — and receives a stream of inflows consisting mainly of the annual interest savings. Other incremental cash flows include expenses of the transaction and tax effects. Because the interest savings are known with certainty and the expenses and tax effects are subject to little uncertainty, the appropriate discount rate is the after-tax equivalent of the interest rate on the new bonds.[11]

Sample Problem 20–1
Bond Refunding for Geoffrey Enterprises

Geoffrey Enterprises is considering the refunding of an issue of 12 percent coupon, 25-year bonds issued five years ago. The bonds have a call price of $1,120 (per $1,000 of face value) and were originally sold at face value for $50 million. The initial flotation costs were $500,000. Interest rates have fallen, and Geoffrey can now issue $50 million of new 20-year bonds with a coupon rate of 10 percent and sell them at face value. There will also be a $500,000 flotation cost involved in issuing the new bonds. Geoffrey faces a 40 percent corporate tax rate. Flotation costs must be amortized over the life of the bond for tax purposes. Should the bond be refunded?

Solution
The task is to estimate the relevant cash flows and then determine if they have a positive net present value. Do interest savings outweigh the costs of the refunding operation? The cash flows associated with the refunding are shown in Table 20–2 (p. 596). The flotation costs are assumed to be amortized straight-line over the life of the bond. For example, when the old bond was issued five years ago, the flotation cost of $500,000 would have been spread over the 25-year life of the bond for an annual tax-deductible noncash expense of $500,000/25 = $20,000. After five years, only $100,000 of the expense would have been taken, so the company could deduct the remaining $400,000 for tax purposes when the bond was refunded. This deduction would produce a tax savings of 0.4($400,000) = $160,000, as shown in row (3) of Table 20–2. On the new bond, flotation costs would be

---

[11]Use of the after-tax equivalent of the interest rate on the new bond is one method of analyzing refundings. For an analysis of the assumptions of this method, see Aharon R. Offer and R. A. Taggart, "Bond Refunding: A Clarifying Analysis," *Journal of Finance,* March 1977, pp. 21–30.

Table 20–2
Cash Flows Associated with Bond Refunding at Geoffrey Enteprises

Initial outlay:
Cost of calling old bonds (50,000 bonds at $1,120 each)	$-\$56,000,000$
Receipts from new bond issue	$+ \ 50,000,000$
(1) Net outlay	$-\$ \ 6,000,000$
Expenses	
(2) Flotation cost on new bonds	$- \ \ \ \ \ 500,000$
Tax Savings*	
(3) Unamortized flotation cost on old bonds, 0.4($400,000)	$+ \ \ \ \ \ 160,000$
Net cash flow, (1) + (2) + (3)	$-\$ \ 6,340,000$

Annual cash flows (for 20 years):
(4) After-tax interest expense on new bonds (10 percent),	
0.10(1 − 0.4)($50,000,000)	$-\$ \ 3,000,000$
(5) After-tax interest savings having retired old bonds (12 percent),	
0.12(1 − 0.4)($50,000,000)	$+ \ \ \ 3,600,000$
(6) Net after-tax interest savings, (4) + (5)	$+\$ \ \ \ 600,000$
Tax effects of flotation costs*	
(7) Loss of tax shield on amortization of old bond, 0.4($20,000)	$-\$ \ \ \ \ \ \ \ 8,000$
(8) Tax shield on amortization of flotation costs on new bonds,	
0.4($25,000)	$+ \ \ \ \ \ \ 10,000$
(9) Net savings, (7) + (8)	$+\$ \ \ \ \ \ \ 2,000$
Total annual cash flow, (6) + (9)	$+\$ \ \ \ 602,000$

*See text for explanation of the treatment of flotation costs.

amortized over the 20-year life of the bond to be $500,000/20 = $25,000 per year. Note that these amortized charges are *noncash* charges, which give rise to tax shields perfectly analogous to tax shields created by depreciation charges, which were discussed in Chapter 11.

Looking at the data in Table 20–2, we see that for an initial outlay of $6,340,000, the company can obtain an annual after-tax cash flow of $602,000 for 20 years. The after-tax cost of new debt is 6 percent: $K_d(1 − T) = 0.10(1 − 0.4) = 0.06$. Using this discount rate and Appendix Table II at the end of the book, we can calculate the net present value of the refunding as

$$NPV = -\$6,340,000 + \left[\sum_{t=1}^{t=20} \frac{\$602,000}{(1 + 0.06)^t} \right]$$

$$= -\$6,340,000 + [\$602,000(11.47)]$$

$$= \$564,940.$$

The positive net present value suggests that the old bond should be refunded.

Bond-refunding problems can become much more complicated than the one worked out in Sample Problem 20–1. For simplicity, we assumed that the new bonds had maturity equal to the maturity of the old bond. In addition, we assumed away any bond discounts (selling a bond at less than face value) that add additional tax complications. Perhaps more fundamentally, we have not considered whether it is best to refund now or to wait a few more months to refund if interest rates are expected to decline further.[12] Despite all these qualifications, however, we have shown the basic nature of the refunding problem: are the costs of refunding justified by future cash savings?

Retirement of Preferred Stock. Although preferred stock has no maturity date and the preferred shareholders' investment is considered permanent, preferred issues nearly always include some provision for retirement. Some issues provide for periodic retirement by means of a sinking fund, although many do not. Where used, the procedure is essentially the same as that in the case of bond sinking funds.

Nearly all preferred issues include a call privilege. As in the case of callable debt issues, the call price is above par value. Buyers of preferred issues charge for the call privilege by demanding a higher dividend rate. The usual motives for calling a preferred issue are to refinance at a lower dividend rate, to alter the firm's capital structure, or to renegotiate restrictive covenants.

Many preferred issues are convertible into common stock and are subject to retirement in that manner.

Repurchase of Common Stock. Common stock has no maturity and never includes provisions either for periodic retirement or for call. The only means by which common stock can be retired is by repurchase of outstanding shares — either through open-market purchases or through an invitation to *tender*. In the latter case, a firm invites shareholders to offer, or tender, their shares to the firm at a specified price. Usually, the firm specifies a minimum and maximum number of shares that will be repurchased.

Common stock can be retired only by repurchase of outstanding shares, through either open-market purchases or an invitation to tender.

The incidence of repurchasing by firms of their own shares seems to ebb and flow, becoming more prevalent in some periods and then declining again in other periods. Several motives may be cited by a firm for repurchasing, one of which is as an alternative to paying dividends. If a firm wishes to distribute a given amount of cash to its shareholders, in lieu of a cash dividend it can simply repurchase an appropriate number of its own shares. Cash received by shareholders upon sale of stock normally would be taxed at capital-gain rates, whereas a dividend would have been taxed as ordinary income. Prior to the 1986 Tax Act (and perhaps again in the future if tax laws change), capital gains were taxed at lower rates than ordinary income. As a result, repurchase had the potential to transform ordinary income into a capital gain and save the shareholders some taxes. However, the Internal Revenue Service (IRS) has long since noticed the tax advantage to share-

---

[12]See E. J. Elton and M. J. Gruber, *Finance As A Dynamic Process* (Englewood Cliffs, N.J.: Prentice-Hall, 1975), Chapter 2, for a more thorough discussion of the analysis of bond refundings considering the set of possible future decisions on capital structure.

holders and has ruled against it. Any repurchase deemed to be in lieu of a dividend is likely to be treated as such by the IRS.

Repurchase, therefore, usually is justified on grounds other than as an alternative to a dividend. Sometimes repurchase is justified as an investment, or a means of improving earnings per share. However, it is improper to view repurchase as a new investment. In fact, it is nothing more or less than a stock issue in reverse. It is true that earnings per share rise, but only in proportion to the reduction in the number of shares. If the shares are repurchased at less than their true value, those shareholders who do not sell realize a gain, but it represents a transfer of wealth from selling shareholders, not new value created, and raises serious questions of ethics.

Sometimes repurchase is justified as a means of accumulating shares for use in future acquisitions or for employee stock options. Here, too, the advantage is illusory, for the purpose is served equally well by issuing new shares.

One motive for repurchase that does make economic sense is to return capital—that is, to achieve a partial liquidation of the firm. If a firm's markets have eroded and a reduction in scale is appropriate, a part of the shareholders' investment can be returned through repurchase. This reason for repurchase is not often used, however, because the managers of most firms prefer the alternative of seeking other investments to a partial liquidation. Another motive for repurchase that is defensible is to effect a change in the firm's debt/equity ratio. If a firm wishes to increase its debt ratio quickly, it can issue new debt and use the proceeds to retire common stock. Again, this motive is not often used in practice.

Because of potential ethical questions involved in a stock repurchase, management should consider carefully the benefits and costs.

Whatever the motive for repurchase, management should be especially careful to communicate fully to investors its reasons for the repurchase. Because some shareholders give up all or a part of their interest in the firm, it is especially important as a matter of fairness and ethics that all shareholders have all pertinent information on which to base their decisions, including information regarding the firm's future prospects. As a practical matter, it is essentially impossible for a management to communicate all relevant information. Therefore, being entirely fair to both selling and nonselling shareholders is difficult indeed.

Of the motives usually given for repurchase discussed above, one motive (repurchase in lieu of a dividend) is not permitted under IRS regulations. Two others (repurchase as an investment and repurchase to obtain shares for other purposes) rest on questionable economic logic. The two that do make economic sense (repurchase as partial liquidation and repurchase to increase the debt ratio) are applicable in situations that do not often occur. In view of the potential ethical questions involved in repurchase, a management contemplating repurchase should consider carefully the benefits and costs and make certain that repurchase is the best vehicle for accomplishing the objectives at hand.

Business Failure and Reorganization

Thus far we have discussed issuing and managing securities under more or less normal circumstances. Unhappily, firms are not always as successful as their owners, managers, and creditors hope. Many firms encounter difficulty of one degree

Finance in Practice 20–2

How Stock Repurchase Affects Return to Investors

During the early 1980s, companies began to be more and more interested in buying back their own shares, and repurchase activity increased significantly. According to the New York investment-banking firm Merrill Lynch, in 1984 some 600 companies announced programs to repurchase their own shares—a new record. A total of about $26 billion went into repurchases.

How does repurchase affect investors? To shed some light on this issue, *Fortune* magazine conducted a study using the 1,660 firms in the *Value Line Investment Survey. Fortune* identified those companies in the Value Line list that had engaged in significant repurchase activity during the 10-year period from 1974 through 1983. They then calculated the total annual return to shareholders (dividends plus capital gains) for companies in this group, and compared them to returns on the Standard & Poor's 500 stock index, a widely followed index of general stock-market performance. They found that return on the buy-back companies averaged 22.6 percent per year compounded over the 10 years, while the S&P 500 companies averaged only 14.1 percent—a big difference.

Critics of stock repurchase feel that repurchase programs accomplish little of value. A repurchase of stock is not an investment, but rather a stock issue in reverse. In and of itself it cannot create value. Can repurchase make a firm's shareholders better off? For some shareholders, the answer is yes. If a firm's stock is undervalued at the time of the repurchase, those who hold their shares and do not sell back to the firm definitely are made better off, because they have "bought out" other shareholders at less than true value. But those who sell are worse off than they would have been had they not sold. Hence, benefits to shareholders who don't sell come at the expense of those who do. It is a wealth transfer, not new value created. This situation presents a problem, because the action is benefiting some shareholders at the expense of others. Proponents of repurchase point out that selling shareholders do so willingly and that the choice of whether or not to sell back lies entirely with them. Nevertheless, repurchase does put management in the position potentially of favoring one group of shareholders over another.

Another problem with repurchase is that it diverts management time from activities that truly do create new value. One critic stated that it is regrettable to see managers spending so much time worrying about the stock market "instead of finding good business opportunities, competing against the Japanese, and minding the store." Some feel that the market should regard repurchase as a negative signal, indicating that the firm has run out of profitable investment opportunities. Indeed, firms sell stock when they need money, and because repurchase is a stock issue in reverse, presumably they would repurchase when they have excess cash.

In spite of questions about repurchase, it has become an important phenomenon in the 1980s, and companies continue to announce repurchase programs. Ford Motor Company, for example, completed a 10-million-share buy-back program in the fall of 1985. In November of that year, the company announced a second repurchase program even bigger than the first, involving 20 million shares and $1 billion. Repurchases under the two programs, when completed, would account for approximately 15 percent of Ford's common-stock capitalization.

(continued)

Many analysts attribute much of the buy-back activity in the early 1980s to a perception on the part of managers that their stocks were undervalued. If so, a major upward move in stock prices should reduce the repurchase activity.

Source: Adapted from C. J. Loomis, "Beating the Market by Buying Back Stock," *Fortune,* April 29, 1985; "Ford Plans $1 Billion Stock Buy-Back," *Wall Street Journal,* November 15, 1985.

---

or another during their lives, and some fail. Here we consider failure and reorganization as a special case of managing relationships with suppliers of funds.

The reasons that firms encounter distress are varied. Sometimes distress is caused by external factors, such as changes in technology or markets. In an uncertain world, even the most capably managed firm is not immune to unexpected difficulties.

A frequent reason for serious financial difficulty is poor management.

A more frequent reason for serious financial difficulty is poor management. A good example is W. T. Grant and Co., a giant retailing chain of over 1,000 stores that went into bankruptcy proceedings in 1975. As the court-appointed trustees explored the reasons for Grant's failure, the evidence clearly pointed to one over-riding cause — bad management, exemplified by totally inadequate budgetary, inventory, and credit controls.[13]

In some cases, financial difficulty may represent a signal that society wishes a reduction in resources allocated to the activity in question.

In still other cases, financial difficulty may represent a signal that society wishes a reduction in the resources allocated to the activity in question. In a market economy, profits are the ultimate measure of whether resources are being allocated appropriately and managed efficiently.

Financial difficulties vary widely in severity, from relatively minor liquidity problems to complete failure. The number of firms having difficulties severe enough to file bankruptcy petitions is relatively small. The number encountering less severe forms of financial distress is much larger. The more severe the difficulty, the more drastic the remedy required and usually the more formal the procedure for adjustment. In all cases, the rights of creditors and owners and their claims against the assets and earnings of the firm must be spelled out clearly. To begin our discussion, let us define business failure more clearly.

Business Failure

Business failure — the situation that results (1) when the firm is unable to meet its contractual financial obligations even though the value of the firm's assets exceeds its liabilities (also known as *technical insolvency*) or (2) when the firm's liabilities exceed the value of its assets as a going concern.

Under what conditions should a firm be considered to have failed? We must distinguish between two different situations of **business failure.** In the first situation, the value of the firm's assets exceeds its liabilities; that is, its net worth is greater than zero, but it is unable to meet its contractual financial obligations. These obligations might include interest or principal payments on debt, lease payments, or payments on installment sales contracts. The firm's cash flows are not sufficient to

---

[13]For a discussion of the application of standard ratio analysis to the Grant case, see "Cash Flows, Ratio Analysis, and the W. T. Grant Bankruptcy," *Financial Analysts Journal,* July/August 1980, pp. 51–54.

meet the contractual payments. Essentially, the problem is one of maturity; the firm's liabilities are maturing faster than its assets.

Such situations involving a shortage of liquidity are sometimes referred to as *technical insolvency*. Where the firm's prospects remain favorable, as implied by a positive net worth, the difficulties often can be resolved by means short of legal bankruptcy. Such adjustments are worked out voluntarily by the firm and its creditors. Where the difficulties are so resolved, the term *failure* probably overstates the case a bit, even though the situation initially involved a default on a financial obligation.

The second type of failure is one in which the firm's liabilities exceed the value of its assets as a going concern; that is, its net worth is zero. Often this type of failure is accompanied by the first type (a liquidity crisis), but the two are separable. In some cases, there may be uncertainty about the eventual value of the assets if the firm is liquidated, and the market price of the firm's stock may not fall entirely to zero. Where it is clear that liabilities exceed the firm's going-concern value, the ultimate outcome is likely to be bankruptcy, unless action can be taken to improve the firm's earnings prospects.

Voluntary Adjustments

In the first type of business failure, creditors are usually better off if they accommodate the firm's short-run difficulties and allow it to remain in operation.

In a crisis of the first type—where the difficulty is one of cash flow and liquidity—the firm's value as a going concern exceeds its liabilities. In such situations, creditors are usually better off if they accommodate the firm's short-run difficulties and allow it to remain in operation, especially if the costs associated with bankruptcy are significant. In some cases, the firm may be able to adjust its cash flows to meet its financial obligations, with no changes in the terms of the latter. Adjustments of this sort usually involve a sale of assets. For example, accounts receivable or a part of the firm's plant and equipment might be sold. Such sales of assets are likely to be painful, but perhaps less so than the available alternatives.

When cash-flow adjustments cannot be made, financial obligations might be adjusted to fit the available cash flow.

Where cash-flow adjustments are not feasible or are inadequate, a second alternative is to adjust the financial obligations to fit the available cash flow. Often such adjustments are worked out between firm and creditors without recourse to the bankruptcy statutes and without the involvement of the courts. One possible adjustment is called an *extension,* whereby the maturity of one or more obligations is extended to give the firm more time to meet it. Another is called a *composition,* under which all creditors agree to accept a partial payment. Where the basic difficulty results from a liquidity shortage, an extension is usually the appropriate remedy.

An example of the use of *voluntary adjustments* comes from the International Harvester Company. Harvester lost $393 million during fiscal 1981 (with its fiscal year ending October 31, 1981). The loss from continuing operations actually was much higher, totaling $635 million, but was offset in part by a special nonrecurring gain, mainly on the sale of its solar turbines division. Late in 1981, International Harvester concluded a $4.2 billion debt restructuring plan with its creditors requiring that net worth be maintained above $1 billion. At that point, all parties seemed to agree that voluntary adjustments were preferable to bankruptcy proceedings. By 1986 the company had sold off some of its businesses and changed its name to Navistar.

Braniff Airways provides another case in point. Braniff lost $128 million during 1980, a bad year for nearly all airline companies. By July 1981, Braniff was in such difficulty that it could not meet payments coming due on its debt, which totaled about $540 million. Braniff's lenders agreed to accept a deferral of some $45 million in interest charges and to negotiate a complete restructuring of the company's debt. Unfortunately for Braniff, even this arrangement was not enough. Within a year, Braniff was bankrupt.[14]

Bankruptcy

Bankruptcy — the failure to meet contractual obligations that results in court action to have the firm administered for the benefit of the firm's creditors.

Where the appropriate remedy cannot be agreed upon informally, relief can be sought by either the firm or its creditors in the courts in **bankruptcy** proceedings. Bankruptcies are governed by federal law. Federal bankruptcy laws were first enacted in the late nineteenth century and most recently were changed by the Bankruptcy Reform Act of 1984. Under the act, a debtor may petition the court for reorganization. Alternatively, under certain circumstances, creditors may petition to have a firm adjudged bankrupt. Under either case, a basic purpose of the Bankruptcy Reform Act is to maintain the status quo so that no one group of creditors can gain at the expense of another. Time is thus made available to study the situation and determine the appropriate remedy.

When a bankruptcy petition is filed, it usually means that the firm's liabilities exceed its value as a going concern, at least in the eyes of creditors or owners, or both. The question of whether the firm should be reorganized and allowed to continue in operation, or liquidated, still remains.

Reorganization — the restructuring of liabilities so that a firm's anticipated cash flows are sufficient to meet them.

Most **reorganizations** take place under Chapter 11 of the Bankruptcy Reform Act. The objective of the reorganization is to restructure the liabilities so that the firm's anticipated cash flows are sufficient to meet them. Reorganization may involve extension or composition of debt obligations or creation of new classes of securities. During the reorganization, the firm continues to operate, either under its old management or under a trustee appointed by the court.

Liquidation — the dissolution of a firm by selling its assets and distributing the proceeds to creditors and shareholders on the basis of seniority.

If the liquidation value of the firm is greater than its going-concern value, then **liquidation** of the firm's assets is probably the best remedy. Liquidation is conducted under procedures spelled out in Chapter 7 of the Bankruptcy Reform Act. Such liquidation may take place if no reorganization can be worked out under Chapter 11. Assets are converted to cash, and the proceeds are distributed to claim holders. Liquidation is usually lengthy and costly.

No matter what the outcome of bankruptcy, there are often large costs involved, including explicit costs, such as lawyers' fees, and indirect costs, such as forgone business opportunities.

---

[14]For International Harvester, see the *Wall Street Journal*, February 25, 1982. For Braniff, see the *Wall Street Journal*, July 2, 1981.

KEY CONCEPTS

1. Firms normally issue debt and equity securities to the public using one of three methods: public offerings through investment bankers, public offerings through privileged subscriptions, and private placements.

2. Investment bankers serve as intermediaries who bring together the seller of securities (namely, the firm) and the buyers (namely, the public).

3. Both the federal and state governments regulate the sale of securities to the public and require that the seller of the securities disclose certain types of information.

4. Firms incur flotation costs when new securities are issued.

5. While there are understandable motives for timing the issuance of securities to take advantage of capital-market conditions, the odds of *consistently* timing new issues to advantage are not good.

6. Keeping the owners of a firm's securities informed about the firm is an important responsibility of management. It is important to have a good communications policy with the owners of a firm.

7. Sometimes firms retire long-term securities before the securities actually become due, as in the case of bond refunding.

8. Stock repurchases must be analyzed carefully to make sure that the stated objectives of the repurchase actually have sound economic foundations.

9. Business failure, often induced by poor management, can lead to bankruptcy.

SUMMARY

Firms have important responsibilities to their suppliers of funds, both creditors and investors. These responsibilities begin with the issuance of new securities and continue as long as the securities remain outstanding.

Firms normally issue new debt and equity securities to the public using one of three methods: public offerings through investment bankers, public offerings by means of privileged subscription, and private placements. Investment bankers are intermediaries who perform a number of important functions in the issuance of new securities, including underwriting, pricing, and selling. Some firms follow a practice of offering new common stock to existing shareholders by means of privileged subscription before offering it to the public at large. All public offerings are subject to government regulation, especially with respect to disclosure of pertinent information.

An alternative to a public offering, normally used only for debt issues, is a private placement with one or a small group of investors — usually insurance companies or pension funds. Private placements are usually simpler and quicker than public offerings and represent an important source of long-term financing to smaller, less financially secure firms.

In developing financing plans, the timing of new issues is an important consideration, especially when a sequence of issues is in prospect. Market conditions must be taken into account even though forecasting changes in conditions is very difficult.

One of the most important of the firm's continuing responsibilities after issuance of securities is communication. Comprehensive disclosure of developments within the firm and of management policies facilitates relations with the financial markets. Especially important is careful communication in connection with extraordinary events or changes in major policies so that investors and creditors can base decisions on facts rather than on inferences.

Long-term debt issues nearly always provide for gradual retirement (repayment) prior to maturity, either through a sinking-fund arrangement or by means of serial redemption. Many bond issues also include provisions for calling the issue at the option of management. Some preferred-stock issues include a sinking-fund provision, and nearly all include a call privilege. Common stock does not include provision for periodic retirement or for call and can be retired only through repurchase by the firm. Because of the potential for conflict between different groups of shareholders, repurchase should be considered only when it can accomplish clear economic objectives equitably.

The responsibility of a firm to investors and creditors includes provisions for dealing with financial distress. Liquidation of assets is appropriate only if liquidation value exceeds the value of the firm as a going concern.

QUESTIONS

Note: To answer questions preceded by an asterisk (*) requires knowledge of material in Appendix 20A.

1. What are the three principal methods of issuing securities to the public?

2. What are the major functions of investment bankers?

*3. What is a privileged-subscription, or rights, offering?

*4. In a rights offering, how does the subscription price of the offering affect the net worth of shareholders?

5. What is the purpose of federal and state regulation of the securities markets?

6. What is a private placement of securities? What are the advantages of private placements?

7. Why do issue costs affect the size and frequency of financing?

8. What responsibilities do firms have to provide information to investors and other participants in the financial markets?

9. Why is it desirable for firms to keep investors informed regarding future plans to the greatest extent possible? How does such information affect the price of the firm's securities?

10. How are long-term debt issues retired?

11. What is a sinking fund in connection with bonds or preferred stock?

12. How do serial bonds differ from sinking-fund bonds?

13. Why do borrowers normally wish to have the option to call a bond issue before maturity?

14. How can common stock be retired?

15. What motives exist for the repurchase by a firm of its own common stock?

16. What potential ethical questions do you see in a decision to repurchase stock?

17. In what way does financial difficulty represent a judgment by society regarding a firm's performance?

18. What is technical insolvency?

19. What steps are required when a firm encounters financial difficulty?

Problems

Note: To work problems preceded by an asterisk (*) requires knowledge of material in Appendix 20A.

1. Dave D. works for A. U. Gold and is in the process of collecting data related to possibly refunding a bond issue of A. U. Gold. All of the relevant data are listed below, but Dave has not had a chance to (a) sort out the numbers as to initial outlay or periodic savings, or to (b) determine the after-tax amounts, assuming a 34 percent tax rate. Please sort out this data, compute the after-tax computations where needed, and set up the annual cash flows.

$18 million — amount of old bonds outstanding
$1000 — face value of old bonds

14 percent — coupon rate of old bonds

25 years — original term of old bonds, five years ago

$1140 — call price of old bonds

$150,000 — flotation costs of old bonds

$18 million — amount of new bonds, $1000 face value

10.5 percent — coupon rate on new bonds

$1,050 — call price of new bonds

20 years — term of new bonds

$200,000 — flotation costs of new bonds

34 percent — marginal tax rate of A. U. Gold

$28,000 — Dave's salary for next year

9 percent — estimated bond rate next year

2. Using *NPV* analysis and the data from Problem 1, what should Dave recommend to the management of A. U. Gold? Use 7 percent as an approximate after-tax rate of debt.

3. Fan Attics Corporation has an outstanding issue of 16 percent 25-year bonds which have 15 years left to maturity. They have a call price of $1,160 (per $1,000 of face value) and were sold at face value for $40 million dollars. Fan feels it could issue new bonds for $40 million at face value, with a 15-year life and a coupon of 12 percent. The flotation costs on the old issue were $500,000, which have been partially amortized on a straight-line basis. Flotation costs on the new issue would be $450,000 and would be amortized over the life of the bond. The corporate tax rate is 46 percent. Should the bond be refunded?

*4. Akron, Inc., plans to raise $10,000,000 in new equity by means of a rights offering with a sub-scription price of $80 per share. The stock currently sells for $100 per share and there are 1 million shares outstanding.

a. How many new shares will Akron issue?
b. How many rights will be required to buy one share?
c. At what price will the stock sell when it goes *ex rights* if the total value of all stock increases by the amount of the new funds?
d. What is the theoretical value of one right?

*5. Suppose you have the income information shown in Table A for the firm in Problem 4 before the rights offering. Suppose the market price does fall to the level determined in part (d) of the preceding problem when the stock goes *ex rights*.

a. If the firm's total earnings remain at $10,000,000, what will be the new earnings per share (EPS)?
b. What will happen to the P/E ratio (price per share divided by earnings per share)?
c. By how much must total earnings rise so that EPS remains the same before and after the rights offering?

Table A

Total earnings	$10,000,000
Interest on debt	2,000,000
Income before taxes	$ 8,000,000
Taxes at 46 percent	3,680,000
Earnings after taxes	$ 4,320,000
Earnings per share	$4.32

REFERENCES

Bhagat, S., M. Marr, and G. Thompson. "The Rule 415 Experiment: Equity Markets." *Journal of Finance* (December 1985): 1385–1401.

"Cash Flows, Ratio Analysis, and W. T. Grant Bankruptcy." *Financial Analysts Journal* (July–Aug. 1980): 51–54.

Elton, E. J. and M. J. Gruber. "The Effect of Share Repurchase on the Value of the Firm." *Journal of Finance* 23 (Mar. 1968): 135–150.

Ingersoll, J. E. "A Contingent Claims Valuation of Convertible Securities." *Journal of Financial Economics* 2 (May 1977): 289–322.

Jalilvand, A., and R. Harris. "Corporate Behavior in Adjusting to Capital Structure and Dividend Targets." *Journal of Finance* (March 1984): 127–145.

Johnson, K. B., T. G. Morton, and M. C. Findlay, III. "An Empirical Analysis of the Flotation Cost of Corporate Securities." *Journal of Finance* 30 (Sept. 1975): 1129–1134.

Kolb, R. *Understanding Futures Markets*. Glenview, Ill.: Scott, Foresman, 1987.

Kalotay, A. J. "Sinking Funds and the Realized Cost of Debt." *Financial Management* 11 (Spring 1982): 43–54.

Kidwell, D., M. Marr, and G. Thompson, "SEC Rule 415: The Ultimate Competitive Bid." *Journal of Financial and Quantitative Analysis*, June 1984, pp. 183–195.

Myers, S. C., and N. J. Majluf. "Stock Issues and Investment Policy When Firms Have Information That Investors Do Not Have." *Journal of Financial Economics* 13 (1984): 187–221.

Offer, A. R., and R. A. Taggart. "Bond Refunding: A Clarifying Analysis." *Journal of Finance* (March 1977): 21–30.

Phillips, S. M., and J. R. Zecher, "Exchange Listing and the Cost of Equity Capital." U.S. Securities and Exchange Commission — Capital Market Working Paper #8 (March 1982).

Securities and Exchange Commission, *Annual Reports*. Washington, D.C.: U.S. Government Printing Office.

Shapiro, E., and C. R. Wolf. *The Role of Private Placements in Corporate Finance*. Boston: Graduate School of Business Administration, Harvard University, 1972.

Taggart, R. A., "A Model of Corporate Financing Decisions." *Journal of Finance* (Dec. 1977): 1467–84.

Van Horne, James C., "New Listings and Their Price Behavior." *Journal of Finance* (Sept. 1970): 783–94.

Appendix 20A

The Valuation of Rights

In the body of the chapter we discussed the rights offering, a means of issuing new shares of stock.

Let us explore these price relationships in more detail. To simplify our discussion, we will assume that the market price would remain constant at P_0 without the rights offering, and we will ignore the time value of money for the short time period surrounding the rights offering. Suppose a firm has Y shares of stock outstanding selling at a price of P_0. A rights offering of X new shares is planned. Thus, a total of Y rights will be issued to shareholders, and the number of rights, N, required to purchase one new share is Y/X. The subscription price is set at S, so the shareholder will exchange N rights plus $\$S$ for one new share.

Let us assume that the total value of the firm is unchanged by the announcement of the offering; in other words, we will assume there are no *information effects*. When the new shares actually are issued, total value will increase by the amount of new funds obtained, SX. Total value after the offering is completed will thus be value before the offering plus SX, as indicated in Equation (A–1).

The value of the firm, V_1, after a rights offering is completed can be calculated as

$$V_1 = P_0 Y + SX \qquad (A–1)$$

where P_0 = the market price of the firm's stock before the rights offering, Y = the number of shares of stock outstanding before the rights offering, X = the number of shares being offered on a privileged-subscription basis, and S = the subscription price for shares offered on a privileged-subscription basis.

Value per share after the offering, P_1, will be the total value, V_1, divided by the total number of shares $(Y + X)$, as shown in Equation (A–2). To get the last part of Equation (A–2), we use Equation (A–1) to express V and then divide through by X. Value per share, P_1, after a rights offering can be calculated as

$$P_1 = \frac{V_1}{Y + X} = \frac{P_0 Y + SX}{Y + X} = \frac{P_0 N + S}{N + 1} \qquad (A–2)$$

where V_1 = the value of the firm after the rights offering, N = the number of rights required to purchase one new share = Y/X, and Y, S, and X are as defined in Equation (A–1).

Equation (A–2) establishes the price per share after the offering. Now let us move back in time from a point after the offering to the period before the issue date but after the record date. Because the stock sells *ex rights*, the buyer will pay only P_1 for a share of the stock. P_1 represents the value of the one share that will be owned after the offering. Thus we expect the market price of the stock to change from P_0 to P_1 when the stock goes *ex rights* (even before the offering). Thus, P_1 is the price during the *ex rights* period as well as after the offering.

Continuing back in time, the record date is the date on which the rights take on value independently of the stock. Investors know that on the issue date they will be able to purchase a share of stock for $\$S + N$ rights. During the subscription period, the value of one right, therefore, can be determined as shown in Equation (A–3).

The value of one privileged-subscription right, R, during the subscription period, can be calculated as

$$R = \frac{P_1 - S}{N} \tag{A–3}$$

where P_1 = the value per share after the rights offering, S = the subscription price for shares offered on a privileged-subscription basis, and N = the number of rights required to purchase one new share = Y/X.

While the stock is selling ex rights, the total value of the firm is the value of the stock plus the value of the rights, or $P_1 Y + RY$. Prior to the record date, total value was $P_0 Y$. Because the total value of the firm remains unchanged on the record date, we see that $P_1 Y + RY = P_0 Y$ and that the market price of the stock on the record date can be calculated as shown in Equation (A–4):

$$P_1 = P_0 - R \tag{A–4}$$

where P_0 = the market price of the firm's stock before the rights offering, and R = the value of one right during the subscription period.

The market price of the stock thus drops on the record date by the amount of the value of one right.

▆▆▆▆

In theory, the market price of a stock drops on the record date by the amount of the value of one right.

Let us illustrate these relationships with an example. ABC Corporation has 100,000 shares outstanding at $50 per share and plans a rights offering of 25,000 shares. The subscription price is set at $40, and 100,000 rights are to be issued. Purchase of one new share will thus require $40 + 4 rights. Applying Equation (A–2), we find that the value per share after the rights offering is

$$P_1 = [(50 \times 4) + 40]/(4 + 1) = \$48 \,.$$

Applying Equation (A–3), we find that the value of one right during the subscription period is

$$R = (48 - 40)/4 = \$2 \,.$$

On the record date, the price of ABC drops from $50 to $48, and the rights take on an independent value of $2. A holder of a share previously worth $50 now holds a share worth $48 and rights worth $2. On the date of issue, 25,000 new shares are issued at $40. The total value of the firm becomes ($50 × 100,000) + ($40 × 25,000), or $6 million. With 125,000 shares outstanding, the price per share is $48. These various price and value relationships are illustrated in Figure 20A–1.

Figure 20A–1
Chronology of a Rights Offering

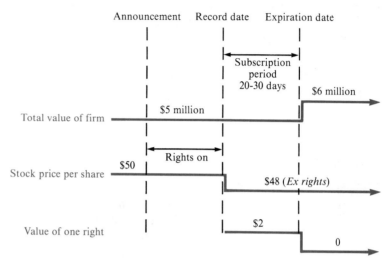

The value given by Equation (A–3) is the theoretical value of one right. In practice, the value of rights during the subscription period may deviate somewhat from the theoretical figure because of transaction costs and speculative pressures. Also, the value of both stock and rights may fluctuate because of changes in investor expectations regarding the firm or the economy.

It is important to note that, even though rights have value, the net worth of a shareholder is unchanged by a rights offering as long as the shareholder exercises or sells the rights. Consider an individual holding four shares of ABC Corporation stock (worth $200) and $40 in cash prior to the offering. If the rights are exercised, the shareholder winds up with five shares worth $48 each, a total of $240. If the four rights are sold, the shareholder winds up with four shares worth $48 each plus $48 in cash, again $240. Note also that to purchase one of the new shares, a nonshareholder must buy four rights at $2 each and put up $40 in addition for a total of $48.

Because the offering itself does not affect shareholder wealth, the subscription price can be set at any figure, provided that it is less than the current market price. The lower subscription price does not permit outsiders to buy in at a lower figure because outsiders must purchase the rights.

The value of rights during a subscription period may vary from the theoretical figure because of transaction costs and speculative pressures.

The net worth of a shareholder is unchanged by a rights offering as long as the shareholder exercises or sells the rights.

Since a rights offering does not affect shareholder wealth, the subscription price can be set at any figure less than the current market price.

Part 6 / Managing Working Capital

In Part Five, we discussed some basic long-term financing decisions facing a firm: What is the appropriate amount of debt financing? What is the best dividend policy for a firm to choose? In that discussion, we focused on long-term sources of funds.

In addition to these long-term financing decisions, corporations face many decisions involving short-term financing and short-term asset management. Short-term assets and liabilities are normally those that last less than one

year. For example, firms have many current assets (such as cash, marketable securities, and inventories) that are usually replaced within a year. Similarly, there are many current liabilities (primarily accounts payable, accruals of various types, and short-term borrowing) that represent short-term financing for the corporation.

We now turn our attention to a firm's decisions about managing its short-term assets and liabilities. Conceptually, the problems are the same as those we considered in discussing long-term investment and financing decisions. A current asset represents a type of investment and as such should provide a return to justify the investment. These assets consume cash that has been left in the business. For example, many large companies have substantial investments in inventories. In fact, any long-term project, such as the introduction of a new product, typically involves a buildup of inventory in the early phases of the project and is likely to cause a buildup of accounts receivable as sales increase.

Short-term liabilities are sources of funds, just as long-term debt and equity are. They often have explicit (or implicit) interest costs and involve risks. Financial managers must decide what mix of short-term and long-term financing should be used, and this decision requires analyzing the costs and risks of each funding source.

In Chapter 21, we will focus on short-term sources of finance and the general issues involved in choosing short-term versus long-term financing. In Chapters 22 and 23, we will turn our attention to short-term assets. In Chapter 22, we will focus on the important topic of cash management, while in Chapter 23 we will consider management of accounts receivable and inventory.

Working capital refers to the firm's current assets. *Net working capital* is current assets minus current liabilities. Current assets are called *working capital* because most of these assets vary closely with the level of the firm's operations — that is, with the level of production and sales. Most decisions with respect to working capital and its components have their impact over weeks and months rather than years. For this reason, short-term finance — managing the firm's short-term assets and liabilities — is often referred to as *working-capital management.*

The topics covered in Part Six are important to the management of any firm. Short-term finance is especially important to the small or new firm, where survival and growth are matters of continuous concern. In any growing firm, we will find that financing a growing working-capital requirement is a major problem. Short-term finance is especially important in retail and wholesale businesses and in many service businesses where the major investment is in short-term rather than long-term assets.

Chapter

21

Short-Term Financing

In this chapter, we will explore methods of providing short-term funds to the firm, including trade credit, loans from various types of financial institutions, and commercial paper issued by the borrower directly to investors.

To obtain funds, a firm issues claims against its income and assets. Liabilities are contractual claims; equities are ownership claims. Liabilities are obligations, but they also represent sources of funds. Some liabilities, such as accounts payable and accrual accounts of various kinds, arise naturally out of the firm's operations because of the lag between the time the liability is incurred and the time it is discharged or paid. Other liabilities, such as loans, are incurred at management's discretion.

Short-term funds—funds borrowed for less than one year.

Earlier, in Part Five, we discussed the major sources of long-term funds. Here we turn to **short-term funds** and **intermediate-term funds**. The words *short-term* and *intermediate-term* refer to the maturity of the claim against the firm—that is, the time horizon over which the principal amount remains outstanding. The short term is usually a period of less than a year; the intermediate term is usually a period between one and perhaps five to seven years. These definitions are more or less arbitrary, and there often is no clear distinction between a short-term and an intermediate-term loan. A loan that begins as short-term may become intermediate-term if the borrower is unable to repay on schedule or renews it for other reasons.

Intermediate-term funds—funds borrowed for periods between 1 and perhaps 5 to 7 years.

Short-term loans are often made to finance seasonal working-capital requirements, while intermediate-term loans are usually made to finance permanent additions to working capital or to fixed assets.

Perhaps more useful distinctions can be drawn with respect to the purpose of the loan and the means of repaying it. Short-term loans often are made to finance seasonal working-capital requirements, such as the buildup of inventories that might occur for a company that stockpiled goods for sale at Christmas. Such seasonal loans might be repaid with the cash generated from sale of the goods and the resultant reduction of inventory. Intermediate-term loans, on the other hand, usually are made to finance permanent additions to working capital or fixed assets. Funds to repay such loans usually come from profits or cash flows generated from operations over a period of several years and not from liquidation of the assets being financed, as in the case of a seasonal working-capital loan. Short-term lenders are thus concerned mainly with the strength of the firm's balance sheet, the quality of assets, and other claims against the assets. Intermediate-term and long-term lenders are concerned more with the income statement, looking for their security to the firm's earning power over sustained periods of time.

We discussed the financial environment in Chapter 2. Finance in Practice 21–1 describes in more detail some recent developments in the interest-rate environment in which managers must operate.

Suppliers of Short-Term and Intermediate-Term Funds

Trade credit—short-term credit extended by a supplier in connection with goods purchased for ultimate resale; used by nearly all firms to some extent as a source of short-term funds.

Business firms obtain funds from a variety of sources—from other business firms, from banks, and from the money market. Nearly all firms rely to some extent on **trade credit** as a source of short-term funds. Trade credit is short-term credit extended by a supplier in connection with goods purchased for ultimate resale. The credit appears on the supplier's balance sheet as an account receivable. Thus, although the trade creditor is the direct supplier of funds, ultimately the funds come from those who finance the trade creditor.

Wage and tax accruals provide another source of short-term financing, although one over which management has little control. Such accruals represent expenses

Finance in Practice 21–1

Roller-Coaster Interest Rates

In April 1980, the prime rate — the benchmark rate used in banking as the rate for the most creditworthy customers — reached 20 percent, the highest rate in more than 60 years. It had risen irregularly over the preceding eight months from 11.5 percent in July 1979 to the April high. After peaking at 20 percent, the prime rate then fell nine percentage points over the next four months to 11 percent in August. Most observers of the economy thought that the economy was slowing down and that interest rates would follow the classic pattern of climbing irregularly from the August low back to high levels over a period roughly corresponding to a typical business cycle — that is, two to four years. That was the pattern interest-rate cycles historically had followed.

It was not to be. After bottoming out in August, rates began climbing again, but very rapidly, not slowly. By late December, only *four months* after the August low, rates had surpassed even the peak of the previous April. After topping out at 21.5 percent in early January of 1981, the prime bank rate again fell rapidly and by April was back down to 17 percent.

In a space of less than a year, short-term rates had risen rapidly to a peak and then declined not once but twice. In April 1981, most observers expected the decline to continue, but instead more gyrations were to come. Rates climbed very rapidly again in May, and by the end of that month the prime rate was back at 20

percent! It stayed at the 20 percent level until September and then declined rapidly to 15.75 percent by December.

Long-term bond rates, while not nearly so volatile as short-term rates, nevertheless had gyrated over the preceding 18 months to an extent unknown in recent memory. Over a period of 20 months, the *AAA* corporate bond rate went from 9.5 percent up to 13 percent, back down to 10.5 percent, and up again to 15.5 percent. Movements of this magnitude produced very large changes in the price of long-term bonds. The initial move from 9.5 percent to 13 percent, for example, produced a drop of as much as 25 percent in the prices of 20-year bonds over a six-month period. Between June 1979 and the peak in October 1981, long-term bonds lost more than a third of their market value.

The financial markets were in a state of shock. Corporate treasurers responsible for raising funds threw up their hands at the thought of trying to forecast interest rates. Insurance companies and banks owning hundreds of millions of dollars worth of long-term bonds saw the market value of their holdings fluctuate by tens of millions of dollars over periods of several weeks. The bond markets in 1981–82 were dominated by a pervasive sense of gloom.

After declining throughout 1982, rates bottomed out in the spring of 1983 and then climbed slowly but steadily to mid-1984. They then began gradually dropping again in July 1984, and by mid-1985 the *AAA* corporate rate was about 11 percent and the prime bank rate was about 9.5 percent. The rate declines continued throughout 1986 and into early 1987, and by March 1987, the *AAA* corporate rate stood at 8.4 percent, compared to 15.5 percent in September 1981.

In April 1987, interest rates began to rise again. They rose rapidly during the spring and summer of 1987, with the *AAA* rate going from 8.4 percent in March to 10.5 percent by October.

Normally, rising interest rates are bad for the stock market, but this time the market seemed oblivious. It rocketed up from January through August, setting the stage for the now famous "Crash of '87" (see Finance in Practice 4–2).

After the "Crash" of October 1987, interest rates declined again, with the *AAA* corporate rate going from 10.5 percent in October to about 8.4 percent in February 1988, a decline of two percentage points in just four months. They began another rise in March, and in May 1988 stood at just over 9 percent.

The ups and downs of 1986–88, while significant, nevertheless are still mild compared to those of the 1979–82 period, a period of volatility unprecedented for most participants in the financial markets. Figure 2–4 in Chapter 2 showed the pattern of rates over this period. Some economists attribute much of the greater volatility during the earlier period to a change in the operating procedure of the Federal Reserve late in 1979 that placed greater emphasis on growth rates of the money supply and less emphasis on interest rates themselves. The "Fed" abandoned this policy in 1982. The particularly sharp drop in short-term rates from April to August of 1980 is attributed by some to the imposition of credit controls on commercial-bank lending by the Federal Reserve from March to July of that year (cynics don't miss the opportunity to note that 1980 was a presidential election year).

Although the interest-rate swings of recent years appear less violent than those of 1979–82, there has nevertheless been plenty of excitement in the financial markets.

Sources: Wall Street Journal, various issues; Federal Reserve Bank of St. Louis, various publications.

incurred but not yet paid. For example, if a company pays its workers every two weeks, a balance sheet prepared the day before payday would show accrued wages owed to workers. Since any liability is a source of funds, workers are providing part of the firm's financing by agreeing to be paid every two weeks rather than every day. Likewise, accrued taxes constitute a source of financing. While accruals must be taken into account in financial planning, they are not usually the subject of decision making because their amounts are determined by the timing of wage and tax payments and, hence, are not subject to management control.

Bank loans are a major source of short-term and intermediate-term financing.

Bank loans provide a major source of short-term and intermediate-term financing. Although commercial banks are the most important of the intermediaries that finance business firms, other financial institutions also supply short-term and intermediate-term funds. Finance companies make specialized loans to finance working capital and equipment, and insurance companies make intermediate-term and long-term loans to business firms.

Commercial paper — unsecured short-term promissory notes issued by firms with the highest credit ratings.

Firms, especially the larger, more creditworthy corporations, also obtain short-term funds by issuing interest-bearing unsecured promissory notes — known as **commercial paper** — in the open money market. Thus, the immediate suppliers of short-term and intermediate-term funds to business firms are other business firms, commercial banks, finance companies, insurance companies, and pension funds. It is important to note, however, that all these suppliers of funds are themselves only intermediaries in the chain of finance, because they require financing also.

A portion of total investment capital is provided by individuals who have excess funds to save and invest. Firms themselves also provide investment funds via their

The immediate suppliers of short-term and intermediate-term funds to business firms include other business firms, commercial banks, finance companies, insurance companies, and pension funds. In the final analysis, the ultimate suppliers of all business funds are individuals who save.

own earnings retention and depreciation charges, but ultimately firms are owned by individuals, or by financial intermediaries (e.g., pension funds) that are owned by individuals. Thus, in the final analysis, the suppliers of all business funds are individuals, who, by consuming less than they earn, provide the savings necessary to finance investment. These funds are channeled from savers to firms and other investors through the specialized financial markets and financial intermediaries in our system. Figure 21–1 illustrates the chain of finance.

Some of the direct suppliers of funds make more than one type of loan. Business firms supply trade credit and are major purchasers of commercial paper. Commercial banks make both unsecured and secured short-term loans as well as *term loans* with maturities of up to seven to ten years. Finance companies make short-term working-capital loans and intermediate-term loans to finance equipment. The financing instruments discussed below are organized according to the type of maturity and collateral, rather than by source.

Figure 21–1
The Chain of Finance

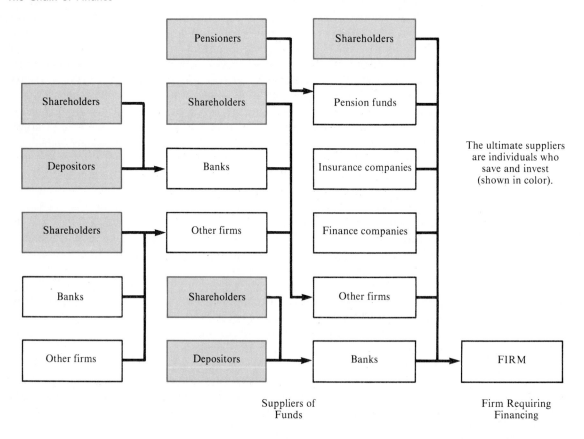

The ultimate suppliers
are individuals who
save and invest
(shown in color).

Suppliers of
Funds

Firm Requiring
Financing

Trade Credit

Earlier, we defined trade credit extended in connection with goods purchased for resale. This qualification—that goods be purchased for resale—distinguishes trade credit from other related forms. Machinery and equipment, for example, may be purchased on credit by means of an installment-purchase contract of some sort. But if the equipment is used by the firm in its production process rather than resold to others, the financing usually is not called trade credit. Trade credit is credit extended in connection with goods purchased for resale by a retailer or wholesaler or with raw materials purchased by a manufacturer for producing its products. Thus, we also exclude *consumer credit,* which is credit extended to individuals for purchase of goods for ultimate use rather than for resale.

Trade credit arises from the firm's normal operations, specifically from the time lag between receipt of goods and payment for them. The sum total of a firm's obligations to its trade creditors at any point in time is normally listed as *accounts payable* on the balance sheet. As we found in Chapter 6, an increase in accounts payable represents a source of funds to the firm; a decrease in accounts payable is a use of funds.

The extent to which trade credit is used as a source of funds varies widely among firms. In general, manufacturers, retailers, and wholesalers make extensive use of trade credit. Service firms purchase less and, therefore, rely less on trade credit. There is also considerable variation with respect to firm size; small firms generally use trade credit more extensively than large firms. When monetary policy is tight and credit is difficult to obtain, small firms tend to increase their reliance on trade credit. Large firms often have better access to financial markets and more bargaining power relative to commercial banks and other intermediaries than small firms do. During periods of tight money, small firms unable to obtain sufficient funds through normal channels may obtain financing indirectly from large suppliers by stretching their payment periods and expanding accounts payable. Large firms are often willing to finance their smaller customers in this manner in order to preserve their markets.

Within certain limits, a firm has discretion with respect to the extent to which it uses trade credit as a source of funds. By altering its payment period, a firm can expand or contract its accounts payable. In theory, a firm could reduce accounts payable to zero and not use trade credit simply by paying each invoice on the day received. However, because trade credit is not interest-bearing, it represents a desirable source of financing; if used beyond certain limits, though, it can entail significant costs. Our concern here is with the use of trade credit extended by suppliers. In Chapter 23, we will discuss the other side of the coin—that is, the granting of trade credit to customers.

Because trade credit is not interest-bearing, it represents a desirable source of financing.

Forms of Trade Credit

Most trade is extended by means of an **open account.** Under this arrangement, goods are shipped and an invoice is sent to the purchaser, but the purchaser nor-

Open account—a credit arrangement under which no promissory note is normally given and the purchaser agrees to make payment at a later date under terms specified in the agreement.

Promissory note — a document specifying the conditions of a loan, including amount, interest rate, and repayment schedule; a legally enforceable "promise to pay."

mally does not acknowledge the debt in writing. Payment is made later according to the terms of the agreement (discussed later). The major advantage of the open account is its simplicity and low administrative cost. Before granting credit through an open account, most suppliers perform a credit check.

A less common form of trade credit is the **promissory note,** usually listed as *note(s) payable, trade* on the balance sheet. The note is a written promise to pay that must be signed by the purchaser. Such notes usually bear interest and have specific maturity dates. They are used most often in situations in which the purchaser has failed to meet the terms of an open credit agreement, and the supplier wishes a formal acknowledgment of the debt and a specific agreement regarding payment date.

Terms of Payment

Net period — the period within which an invoice is to be paid.

Because the open account is by far the most common, we will restrict our discussion of payment terms to this form. A common arrangement is to specify a **net period** within which the invoice is to be paid. Terms of *net 30* indicate that the payment is due within 30 days of the date of the invoice.

Prompt-payment discounts — discounts given for prompt payment of an invoice, within a specified time period.

Suppliers often give cash discounts for payment within a specified period. Terms of *2/10, net 30* indicate that a discount of 2 percent may be taken if the invoice is paid within 10 days of the invoice date; otherwise, the net (full) amount is due within 30 days. Such **prompt-payment discounts** are to be distinguished from *quantity discounts* given for purchase in large quantities and also from *trade discounts* given at different points in the distribution chain (such as wholesale versus retail). Prompt-payment discounts are very common.

Cost of Trade Credit as a Source of Funds

Trade credit on open accounts normally bears no interest, but its use involves costs.

Effective interest rate — the rate compounded once per interest period (usually per year) that provides the same dollar payoff as the stated rate.

In the final analysis, the principal consideration in the use of trade credit is cost. Trade credit on an open account normally bears no interest, but its use does involve costs. If prompt-payment discounts are allowed by the supplier, a cost is incurred if the discount is not taken. For example, suppose a firm purchases goods on terms of 2/10, net 30. If the invoice is for $1,000, the firm can take a discount of $20 and pay only $980 if payment is made within 10 days. If the firm forgoes the discount, it pays $1,000 by day 30, assuming it maintains its accounts on a current basis, as it should. By forgoing the discount, the firm has the use of $980 for 20 days, for which it pays interest of $20. This interest rate is $20/$980 = 2.05 percent for a 20-day period. Annualized, the **effective interest rate** is

$$\frac{\$20}{\$980} \times \frac{365 \text{ days}}{20 \text{ days}} = 0.372 = 37.2 \,.$$

We find that in this case, not taking the discount is equivalent to borrowing at 37.2 percent per year, a rather expensive financing arrangement.[1] Equation (1) shows how to calculate the approximate cost of forgoing cash discounts.

$$\text{Cost} = \frac{\text{Percentage discount}}{(100 \text{ percent} - \text{Percentage discount})} \times \frac{365 \text{ days}}{(\text{Net period} - \text{Discount period})}.$$

(1)

Applying Equation (1) to our example, we can calculate the cost to be:

$$\text{Cost} = \frac{2 \text{ percent}}{100 \text{ percent} - 2 \text{ percent}} \times \frac{365 \text{ days}}{30 \text{ days} - 10 \text{ days}}$$

$$= 0.372 = 37.2 \text{ percent}.$$

Sample Problem 21–1
Calculating the Cost of Trade Credit

Calculate the cost of trade credit for the following discount periods:

A. 1/10, net 30;   B. 2/10, net 20;   C. 2/20, net 45.

Solution
A. Applying Equation (1) to the terms 1/10, net 30, we find that

$$\text{Cost} = \frac{1 \text{ percent}}{100 \text{ percent} - 1 \text{ percent}} \times \frac{365 \text{ days}}{30 \text{ days} - 10 \text{ days}}$$

$$= 0.184 = 18.4 \text{ percent}.$$

B. Using this procedure for terms of 2/10, net 20, we find that cost equals 74.5 percent.

C. Similarly, applying Equation (1) to terms of 2/20, net 45, we see that cost equals 29.8 percent.

The costs indicated represent the equivalent financing cost of forgoing cash discounts and then paying the full amount on the due date. In the case of 1/10, net 30, the preceding calculation assumes that the full amount of the invoice is paid on day 30.   ▮

---

[1]Note that the calculation in the text assumes only annual compounding. In fact, allowing for compounding every 20 days, the effective annualized interest cost, r_a, would be calculated as

$$1 + r_a = (1 + \$20/\$980)^{365/20}$$

$$r_a = (1 + 0.0205)^{18.25} - 1 = 44.82 \text{ percent}.$$

In Chapter 3, we cover the effects of compounding many times during the year. The 44.82 percent figure is in fact the true effective annual cost of the trade credit.

Other Considerations in Using Trade Credit

If there is no discount offered and if the firm pays during the net period, trade credit still is not free. The supplier must operate a credit department to conduct credit analysis, maintain records, and proceed against overdue accounts. The accounts receivable on the supplier's books must be financed. These administrative and financing costs, like all costs of doing business, in the long run are borne by the buyers of the supplier's output. We should note, however, that the purchaser is bearing these costs whether credit granted by the supplier is used or not.

Another element of cost is incurred if the firm delays payment beyond the net period. When a firm becomes overdue in its payments, its relationships with suppliers are bound to suffer. Some suppliers can be stretched more than others, and a given supplier may be more tolerant of late payment at some times than at others. Just how far a firm can push its suppliers depends on circumstances. A policy of late payment, however, is bad business practice, and in the long run is likely to be costly. At the least, late payment damages a firm's credit reputation, which is a valuable asset and, once lost, is difficult to regain. At worst, late payment can cost a firm its sources of supply. During times of severe financial difficulty, a firm may be unable to avoid late payment. As a matter of long-run policy, however, obligations to suppliers should be discharged on schedule.

While late payment is dangerous and costly in the long run, early payment is uneconomical. Where prompt-payment discounts are offered, they should be taken if attractive, as they nearly always are. Otherwise, payment should be made within the net period. In either case, the full extent of the credit period should be utilized.

Sample Problem 21–2
Effect of Trade Credit on Financial Statements for the Perry Company

Table 21–1 shows the balance sheet of the Perry Company. Perry currently purchases a total of $120,000 per month on terms of 2/10, net 30, and is forgoing all cash discounts and paying invoices at face amount on day 30. Calculate the effect on Perry's financial statements of a change in policy to begin taking cash discounts.

Solution
Perry is purchasing $120,000 of materials per month, or $4,000 per day. Because the company is taking the full 30 days to pay each invoice, it has at any point in time 30 *days purchases outstanding* (DPO) in the form of accounts payable — a total of 30 × $4,000 = $120,000. To take cash discounts, Perry must pay within 10 days. Under this policy, accounts payable would amount to 10 days purchases outstanding, or 10 × $4,000 = $40,000.

If accounts payable were reduced from $120,000 to $40,000, what would make up the difference? Balance sheets, after all, must balance. One answer is bank credit. Something must replace the $80,000 in accounts payable, and if a bank loan were used, the balance sheet would show accounts payable of $40,000 and bank loans of $80,000.

Table 21–1

Year-End Balance Sheet for the Perry Company (thousands of dollars)

Cash	$ 40	Accounts payable	$ 120
Receivables	300	Bank loan	0
Inventory	450	Accruals	50
Fixed assets	400	Mortgage loan	300
Other assets	50	Common stock	770
Total assets	**$1,240**	**Total liabilities and net worth**	**$1,240**

What about the effect on the income statement? Perry now takes a total of $28,800 in cash discounts: $120,000/month × 12 months × 2 percent = $28,800. Offsetting this amount is interest on the bank loan, let's say at 12 percent: $80,000 × 12 percent = $9,600.

So Perry takes in an additional $28,800 per year in cash discounts and pays out an additional $9,600 to the bank, a gain in pretax profit of $19,200 per year. The gain arises from the fact that the cost of the bank loan is only 12 percent, while the cost of forgoing the cash discount is 37.2 percent on an annual basis. Given this effect on profits, firms should think carefully about a policy of forgoing cash discounts.

Forgoing cash discounts is an expensive form of financing.

Unsecured Short-Term Loans

Unsecured loan — a loan against which no specific assets are pledged as collateral.

An **unsecured loan** is one against which no specific assets are pledged as collateral. Secured loans will be discussed in a later section. Commercial banks are by far the largest suppliers of unsecured loans to business firms, so in this section we will restrict our discussion to bank loans.

Whereas nearly all firms use trade credit to some extent as a source of funds, not all firms use bank credit. Bank credit is, however, a very important source of credit for many businesses. At the end of 1986, aggregate trade credit outstanding was $520 billion for nonfinancial firms; commercial and industrial loans by banks totaled $544 billion.[2]

Arranging Bank Financing

A comprehensive financial plan, including a pro-forma income statement and balance sheet and perhaps a cash budget, will prove very valuable to management when negotiating a bank loan.

Most commercial banks view a relationship with a customer as involving more than just a loan. A loan is only one of a number of services a bank will normally attempt to sell a business customer. Others are a checking account, time certificates of deposit, payroll and other accounting services, cash-flow analysis, lock-box services (discussed in Chapter 22) for speeding collections, investment services, pension and profit-sharing services, and corporate trust services pertain-

[2]Board of Governors, Federal Reserve System.

ing to shareholder records and payment of dividends. The bank, in short, thinks in terms of a total customer relationship, not just a loan.

Before approving a loan, the bank will want detailed information regarding the nature of the financing requirement, the amounts and timing of the need, the uses to which the funds will be put, and when and how the bank will be repaid. Here is where the financial plan, developed along lines that we discussed in Chapter 9, comes in. A comprehensive plan, including a pro-forma income statement and balance sheet and perhaps a cash budget, will prove very valuable to any firm's management when it is negotiating a bank loan. The financial plan not only communicates the information sought by the bank regarding the financing requirement; it also tells the bank that the firm's management is competent and knows its business.

Good communications are also important after the loan is made. Few financial plans are executed exactly as planned. In an uncertain world, we would be surprised if deviations did not occur. When deviations do occur that affect the financing requirement or the firm's overall financial condition, the bank should be informed. By this approach, the firm shares the problems with the bank and gives the bank an opportunity to respond. Banks expect their customers to have problems (banks have problems, too) and usually are pleased to learn that the problems have been recognized and are being acted upon even if the banks prefer (as does the firm) that the problems never arise.

Types of Bank Loans

Line of credit—a noncontractual loan agreement between a bank or other lender and a firm in which the firm can borrow up to an agreed-upon maximum at any time during a specified period.

Short-term unsecured bank loans usually take one of three forms: a line of credit, a revolving-credit agreement, or a simple single-transaction loan. A **line of credit** is an agreement under which a firm can borrow up to an agreed-upon maximum amount at any time during an agreed-upon period—often one year. Lines of credit are not contractual and are not legally binding upon the bank, but they are nearly always honored. A major advantage of the line of credit is its convenience and administrative simplicity.

A line of credit is often used to finance seasonal working-capital requirements or other temporary needs. Banks typically require an annual paying up of the loan—a period of usually one or two months during which the loan is completely paid off, or "off the books." If a firm is unable to pay up, the bank will be alerted that the financing requirement may not be entirely seasonal. Lines of credit are renegotiated periodically, often annually, at which time the bank conducts a full review of the customer relationship, the financing requirement, and the firm's plans for the coming year.

Revolving-credit agreement—a contractual agreement by the bank to provide funds.

A **revolving-credit agreement**, unlike the line of credit, involves a contractual and binding commitment by the bank to provide funds. In return for this commitment, the borrower usually pays a fee of 0.25 to 0.5 percent per year on the average unused portion of the commitment. The size of the fee depends on credit conditions at the time—that is, the availability of funds in the banking system—and on the relative bargaining power of the bank and the borrower. Like the line of credit, the revolving-credit agreement permits the borrower to borrow any

The line of credit and revolving-credit agreement are well suited to firms that need financing frequently and in varying amounts.

amount up to some maximum at any time. Revolving credit often is negotiated for periods longer than a year, and during the period of the contract is not subject to pay-up provisions or to renegotiation or cancelation by the bank because of tight credit conditions.

The line of credit and revolving-credit agreement are well suited to firms that need financing frequently and in varying amounts. Where a firm needs financing only occasionally for specific purposes, banks typically treat each request individually.

Interest Rates on Bank Loans

Prime rate—the benchmark rate set by the banking industry as the rate for the class of borrowers deemed most creditworthy.

Interest rates on bank loans to firms are typically scaled upward from the **prime rate,** the benchmark rate set by the banking industry for borrowers with the highest credit rating. Rates for other than prime borrowers may exceed the prime rate by several percentage points. On the other hand, some borrowers may be able to obtain bank loans at below the prevailing prime rate. Although banks continue to refer to the prime rate as the best short-term rate, it became increasingly evident during the early 1980s that some bank customers were able to negotiate loan rates below prime.

Interest rates vary from loan to loan and from borrower to borrower for a number of reasons. Slight variations occur from region to region and from state to state, the latter depending to some extent on statutory rate ceilings. Rates vary with the riskiness of the loan, the size of the loan, and often the size of the borrower. The size of the borrower is often related to risk, and the size of the loan is a factor in the bank's administrative costs. For example, it does not take 100 times as much work to negotiate and administer a $1,000,000 loan as it does a $10,000 loan; in fact, the large loan may even take less work if the borrower is well known and an established customer.

There are several methods for computing the interest charge on bank loans.

When a lender quotes the nominal or stated interest rate on a loan, the borrower still cannot be sure how much interest he or she will pay. There are several methods of computing the interest charge, and each gives a different *effective interest rate*. Suppose we want to borrow $1,000 for one year. The lender quotes a rate of 8 percent. If we pay *interest in arrears on the unpaid balance,* we pay the lender $1,080 in one year—$1,000 principal and $80 interest.[3] The effective interest rate is $80/$1,000, or 8 percent.

Interest in arrears

Amount borrowed	$1,000
Interest due in 1 year @ 8%	80
Total due in 1 year	1,080

Effective interest rate = $80/1,000 = 0.08 = 8.00%

---

[3]The term *in arrears* in this context does not imply that the borrower is delinquent, but only that interest is paid at the end of the period on the balance outstanding during the period.

Discount method

Amount borrowed	$1,000
Discount, 8%	80
Net proceeds to borrower	920
Interest due in 1 year	80
Principal due in 1 year	920
Total due in 1 year	1,000

Effective interest rate = $80/920 = 0.0870 = 8.70\%$

If interest is computed using the *discount method,* the lender advances us $1,000 − $80 = $920, and we repay $1,000 in one year. We pay interest of $80 for the use of $920 for one year. The effective rate is $80/$920, or 8.70 percent.

Suppose now that the loan must be repaid in *monthly installments.* Interest on consumer installment loans often is computed using the *add-on method.* Using this method, one year's interest of $80 is added on to the principal, and the result— $1,080—is divided by 12 to get the monthly payment of $90.00. Here, the effective rate is considerably higher than 8 percent because we are paying off the loan over the year. In effect, over the year we have the use on average of only about half the principal, for which we pay interest of $80. Thus, the effective rate is almost double the stated rate. To compute the effective rate exactly (which in this case is 14.44 percent) requires the use of discounted-cash-flow techniques, which were discussed in Chapter 3.

Compensating Balances

In addition to the interest rate, banks often impose other conditions for obtaining a loan. A condition nearly always encountered is that the firm maintain a *compensating balance,* which is the agreed-upon minimum balance to be maintained in the checking account. The minimum balance compensates the bank for clearing checks and other services and for any standby commitment to lend under a line of credit. The amount of the compensating balance is usually determined as a percentage, normally between 10 and 20 percent, of either the amount of the bank's commitment or of the loan outstanding. Under a $1 million line of credit, for example, a firm might be required to maintain a minimum deposit balance of $150,000 (15 percent of the line) at all times. An additional requirement might be imposed to compensate for other services.

By adjusting the compensating-balance requirement, banks can vary the price of credit without changing nominal interest rates.

From the bank's standpoint, the compensating balance, if in addition to balances otherwise maintained, has the effect of increasing the rate of return on the price of credit without changing nominal interest rates. This effect is sometimes an important consideration in the face of interest-rate ceilings or political pressures for lower rates. From the firm's standpoint, the compensating balance increases the effective interest rate.

Sample Problem 21–3

Effective Interest Cost for the Boyd Machinery Company

A. The Boyd Machinery Company needs $100,000 and plans to borrow the funds from a bank. The bank requires a compensating balance of 15 percent. How much will Boyd have to borrow? If the stated interest rate is 12 percent, what will be the effective rate?

B. Rework the problem described in part (A) assuming that the bank pays 10 percent annual interest on the compensating balance.

Solution

A. The amount to be borrowed, X, must be such that X minus the 15 percent compensating balance equals $100,000. Algebraically, we can write this relationship as

$$X - 0.15X = \$100,000$$

$$X(1 - 0.15) = \$100,000$$

$$X = \frac{\$100,000}{1 - 0.15} = \frac{\$100,000}{0.85}$$

$$= \$117,647 \,.$$

The net funds available are $117,647 − 0.15($117,647) = $100,000. On this loan of $117,647, interest will be calculated as $0.12 \times \$117,647 = \$14,118$.

Because the company has only $100,000 available for use (the loan minus the compensating balance), the $14,118 of interest represents an effective interest rate of $14,118/$100,000 = 14.1 percent. Thus, the compensating-balance requirement requires that Boyd borrow $17,647 more than actually needed and increases the effective interest rate on the loan to 14.1 percent versus the stated rate of 12 percent.

B. Here we need to calculate the *net* interest charge the bank makes. As we calculated in part (A), there is an interest charge of $14,118 on the loan. On the other hand, the bank will pay interest of 0.10($17,647) = $1764.70 on the compensating balance. The *net* interest charge would be $14,118 − $1764.70 = $12,353.30. That is, the firm would owe the bank $12,353.30 over and above the interest the bank paid the firm on the compensating balance. The firm thus pays net interest of $12,353.30 to use $100,000 for a year. The effective interest rate is calculated as $12,353.30/$100,000 = 0.124 = 12.4 percent.

Although the 12.4 percent is still higher than the stated 12 percent on the loan, it is substantially lower than the 14.1 percent effective interest rate we calculated when the bank paid no interest on the compensating balance.

When the bank does pay such interest, the effective interest cost of the loan is reduced. Because the interest paid by the bank on the compensating balance will typically be less than the interest charged on the loan, however, the effective interest rate on the loan is still higher than the stated interest rate.   ▬

Secured Short-Term Loans

Unsecured loans provide maximum flexibility for the borrower and are less expensive to administer than a secured loan.

Secured loan — a loan against which specific assets are pledged as collateral by the borrower.

Borrowers and lenders alike would prefer to do business on an unsecured basis. An unsecured loan provides maximum flexibility for the borrower and is less expensive to administer than a secured loan. However, in many situations the risk of default is sufficiently high that lenders are unwilling to lend on an unsecured basis.

A **secured loan** is one against which specific assets are pledged as **collateral** by the borrower. In the case of short-term loans, lenders usually insist on collateral that is reasonably liquid — that is, assets that can be sold and, thereby, converted to cash without great difficulty. Inventory and accounts receivable are most often used. Marketable securities would serve nicely as collateral but seldom are available to firms needing secured loans. Fixed assets, such as equipment and buildings, are sometimes pledged against short-term loans but are more often pledged to obtain long-term funds. Since accounts receivable and inventory are the most common collateral for short-term loans, we will discuss these in more detail.

Commercial banks often require collateral under any of the lending arrangements discussed above. In addition to banks, commercial finance companies also make secured loans to business firms, with accounts receivable and inventories usually providing the collateral. The procedure for securing a loan is covered by the Uniform Commercial Code, adopted by all states during the 1960s. An agreement between lender and borrower identifying the collateral is filed in the public records. If the borrower defaults on the terms of the agreement, the lender may seize the collateral and sell it to satisfy the claim. Any excess proceeds are returned to the borrowing firm. If the proceeds are insufficient to satisfy the claim, the lender must share the remaining assets of the firm with unsecured creditors.

It is important to understand the function of collateral from the lender's standpoint. Collateral protects the lender in the event of default, but it does not lead to indifference to the prospect of default. There comes a point on the risk spectrum where lenders refuse the loan even with collateral. Lenders are in business to provide funds, not to liquidate inventories of electronic parts or garments or to collect accounts receivable. The real function of collateral is to induce the lender to make a loan that, if unsecured, is too risky in relation to the rate that can be charged and yet still has reasonable prospects of being repaid.

In considering secured financing, we should not lose sight of the effect of pledging a firm's assets on its other creditors. Trade creditors and other general creditors look to the firm's assets for protection in the event of financial difficulty. If particular assets are suddenly pledged, the position of these unsecured creditors is weakened. Such changes are not likely to go unnoticed and may be taken into account by the affected parties in future transactions.

We will consider security arrangements in more detail in Appendix 21A, which follows this chapter. Finance in Practice 21–2 relates an example of the hazards to which a lender can be exposed, even when security is provided for a loan.

Finance in Practice 21–2

The Great Salad-Oil Swindle

Requiring collateral by no means provides complete security to lenders. The Great Salad-Oil Swindle of the early 1960s provides a classic, if extreme, case of what can go wrong if the borrower is determined, ingenious, and dishonest.

In the late 1950s, a man named Anthony De Angelis established the Allied Crude Oil Vegetable Refining Corporation. Allied was in the business of processing crude vegetable oil, mainly soybean and cottonseed oils, into salad oil.

The oil was stored in large tanks at Bayonne, New Jersey. A number of well-known banks, exporters, and Wall Street investment-banking firms lent money to Allied against the oil as collateral. The oil was controlled under a field warehousing arrangement supervised by the American Express Field Warehousing Corporation, a subsidiary of the American Express Company.

The job of the Field Warehousing Company was to supervise the storage of oil and certify that it was indeed on hand in the amounts specified (see Appendix 21A for a discussion of field warehousing). American Express issued field-warehouse receipts, which Allied then used as collateral for loans.

Over the period of 1957–1963, Allied managed to steal hundreds of millions of dollars worth of oil without the Field Warehousing Company's knowledge. The tanks were connected by a complex system of pipes and valves. Allied personnel would pump out the oil in a tank and pump in seawater, leaving a foot or two of oil floating on top of perhaps 40 feet of seawater. Inspectors of the Field Warehousing Company would look into the tank and see only oil. Special devices lowered through ports in the tops of the tanks verified that oil extended to the bottom. Indeed, the oil did extend to the bottom, but only inside special narrow cylindrical chambers installed directly under the ports by Allied personnel. The seawater remained undetected.

When the swindle was finally uncovered, warehouse receipts were outstanding for 1.988 billion pounds of oil. Only 134 million pounds were actually on hand in the Bayonne tanks. The rest had either disappeared over the period 1957–1963 or had never existed in the first place. The amount of soybean oil certified to be in the Bayonne tanks by the warehouse receipts actually exceeded the total soybean-oil stocks in the entire United States in 1963 as reported by the U.S. government! The total shortage was 1.854 billion pounds, valued at about $175 million.

A total of 51 companies and banks that had loaned money to Allied using warehouse receipts as collateral suffered losses totaling $175 million. Two Wall Street investment-banking firms went bankrupt, as did the American Express Field Warehousing subsidiary. The list of banks that lost money included nearly every major bank in New York City, as well as major banks in Chicago, on the West Coast, and abroad. The parent American Express Company incurred large losses in making good a portion of the claims.

De Angelis eventually went to prison for masterminding the swindle. Little of the $175 million was ever recovered, and just where it all went remains a mystery to this day. The salad-oil case remains the classic object lesson in making loans against inventory.

Source: N. C. Miller, *The Great Salad Oil Swindle* (Baltimore: Penguin Books, 1965).

Commercial Paper

Commercial paper is unsecured short-term promissory notes issued by borrowers to investors. Commercial paper distributed through organized financial markets is known as a *money-market instrument* (along with other short-term highly liquid securities, such as U.S. Treasury bills and bank certificates of deposit).

Because commercial paper is unsecured, it can be issued only by firms with the highest credit ratings, which usually means only relatively large firms. Although a wide variety of firms use the commercial-paper market as a source of funds, the big borrowers are finance companies, financing subsidiaries of large manufacturers such as General Motors Acceptance Corporation and Chrysler Financial Corporation, and commercial banks and bank-holding companies that jointly account for 75 percent of the funds borrowed in this form. Major buyers of commercial paper include nonbank financial institutions, such as insurance companies, pension funds, and mutual funds, and business firms with temporary excess cash.

> Commercial paper is unsecured and, therefore, can be issued only by firms with the highest credit ratings.

Commercial-Paper Market

The commercial-paper market has grown rapidly since the 1960s, and as of October 31, 1987, some $360 billion worth was outstanding.[4] The minimum denomination is $25,000, although denominations of $100,000 up to several million dollars are much more common. Maturities usually range from 30 to 180 days but may go up to 270 days. Under current regulations, an issue of maturity longer than 270 days would have to be registered with the Securities and Exchange Commission.

The commercial-paper market is highly organized, with paper sold both directly and through dealers. Dealers typically charge a commission of 0.12 to 0.25 percent. The interest rate on commercial paper usually runs about 1 percent less than the prime lending rate at commercial banks, although in recent years this spread has sometimes widened to around 1.5 percent.

Commercial Paper as a Source of Funds

We noted earlier that ordinarily only large firms with the highest credit ratings have access to the commercial-paper market. For such firms, the principal advantage of commercial paper is its lower cost compared to the cost of alternative sources, such as bank loans. Offsetting this cost advantage somewhat is the fact that borrowers in the commercial-paper market have to maintain backup lines of credit or revolving-credit agreements at commercial banks.

> The principal advantage of commercial paper is its lower cost compared to the cost of alternative sources such as bank loans.

For lending agreements to backstop commercial paper, banks typically charge a commitment fee of between 0.25 and 0.5 percent. Even with this cost included, commercial paper is usually less expensive than bank loans because the commercial-paper market is generally more price-competitive than bank-loan markets. The more competitive the market, the lower the price to the buyer — in this case the buyer of funds.

[4]Federal Reserve *Bulletin,* February 1988. For a good discussion of the commercial-paper market, see E. M. Hurley, "The Commercial Paper Market," Federal Reserve *Bulletin,* June 1977.

KEY CONCEPTS

1. The immediate suppliers of short-term and intermediate-term funds to business firms include other business firms, commercial banks, finance companies, insurance companies, and pension funds. In the final analysis, the ultimate suppliers of all business funds are individuals who save.

2. The principal factor determining the appropriate use of trade credit is cost.

3. The true interest cost of a bank loan depends on the timing and pattern of interest payments.

4. Compensating balances have the effect of increasing the effective interest rate on bank loans.

SUMMARY

The direct suppliers of short-term and intermediate-term funds to business firms are other business firms, commercial banks, finance companies, insurance companies, and pension funds. These suppliers are themselves only intermediaries in the chain of finance. Ultimately, the suppliers of all business funds are individuals with funds to save and invest.

Trade credit is credit extended in connection with goods purchased for resale. Nearly all firms rely on trade credit to provide some financing, though the extent of its use varies widely among industries. Although trade credit is interest-free, its use does involve costs. In general, firms should take prompt-payment discounts when offered and otherwise pay within the specified credit period.

Commercial banks are the largest suppliers of unsecured short-term loans to business firms. A comprehensive financial plan is very useful during the process of negotiating the bank financing. In addition to the contracted interest rate, the effective cost of bank credit includes the cost of compensating-balance requirements and any fees that are charged.

A secured loan is one against which specific assets are pledged as collateral by the borrower. Commercial banks and commercial-finance companies make the majority of secured loans to business firms. Accounts receivable and inventory are the most commonly used collateral.

Commercial paper is unsecured short-term promissory notes issued by a borrowing firm directly to a lender. Because it is unsecured and marketable, commercial paper normally can be issued by only the largest and most creditworthy firms.

QUESTIONS

1. Who are the major suppliers of short-term and intermediate-term funds to business firms? Who are the ultimate suppliers of funds? (See Figure 21–1.)

2. What are the costs of using trade credit as a source of funds?

3. How is the financial plan used in arranging bank financing?

4. Describe the major types of short-term unsecured bank loans.

5. What is the purpose of collateral, from the lender's standpoint?

6. How might the standards of creditworthiness applied by a bank differ from those applied by a trade creditor?

7. Why might short-term lenders be less concerned with earning power than intermediate-term lenders?

8. Why do secured loans often carry higher rates of interest than unsecured loans?

Problems

1. Calculate for the following credit situations the effective annual interest rate that would be lost if a firm paid on the final net due date rather than taking the cash discount. Assume a 365-day year and compounding once per year.
   a. 2/15, net 45.
   b. 3/10, net 30.
   c. 1/15, net 40.
   d. 2/10, net 40.

2. Repeat problem (1) allowing for multiple compoundings per year. See footnote 1 in the chapter to calculate the effective annual cost. (Hint: Work problem with your present-value calculator using PV, FV, and $n/365$.)

3. Suppose a firm faced credit terms of 2/15, net 45. Since it was running short of cash, the firm passed up the trade discount. In fact, it stretched its credit and paid the bill ten days late (on day 55 rather than day 45). Fortunately, the creditor was lenient and imposed no penalties for the late payment.
   a. What was the effective annual interest rate on the credit, given that the firm paid late? (Assume a 365-day year and compounding once per year.)
   b. How does the rate in part (a) compare to the effective annual interest cost if the bill were paid on time?

4. Calculate the effective annual interest rate on the following discounted loans: (Hint: Calculate the interest using the discount method.)
   a. $100,000 loan at 14 percent.
   b. $50,000 loan at 14 ½ percent.
   c. $25,000 loan at 15 percent.

5. Calculate the effective annual interest rate for the following loans:
   a. The firm needs $10,000, and the lending bank charges 15 percent and requires a 10 percent compensating balance.
   b. The firm needs $250,000, and the lending bank charges 16 percent and requires a 15 percent compensating balance.

6. Repeat problem (5) assuming that the bank pays 8 percent interest on money left in the bank as a compensating balance.

7. MSM, Incorporated, has been paying its major supplier approximately 20 days after the materials are received. The supplier offers terms of 1/10, net 45, on all open accounts. (For simplicity, assume compounding once per year.)
   a. What is the annual rate that MSM is giving up by not paying by the tenth day?
   b. Assuming that a local bank has offered to lend MSM the funds needed to purchase these materials at an effective annual rate of 16 percent, what strategy do you see as optimal for MSM?

8. Bland Corporation needs an immediate increase in short-term funds and has determined that four sources are available for the required $1,500,000:
   a. a 14 percent discount loan from the bank with a required compensating balance of 10 percent;
   b. commercial paper at 15 percent with a placement fee of $20,000 per year payable at the start of the year;
   c. foregoing discounts from suppliers at terms of 1/15, net 35;
   d. a bank loan quoted at an effective annual rate of 15 percent but requiring the pledging of accounts receivable.

   Calculate the effective annual interest cost of each alternative. Which alternative should Bland choose? (Assume a 365-day year and, for simplicity, compounding once per year.)

9. DLM Enterprises needs to increase its short-term funds by $2,000,000 and has found two possible loan arrangements. Loan A is a 16 percent discount loan with no compensating balance. Loan B is a 16 percent nondiscount loan with a 10 percent compensating balance. Which loan should DLM choose?

10. Refer to problem (9) to calculate:

    a. the nominal interest rate (discount basis) on loan A that would make its effective interest rate equal to loan B's effective interest rate; and

    b. the nominal interest rate on loan B that would make its effective interest rate equal 16 percent.

REFERENCES

Board of Governors, Federal Reserve System. *Flow of Funds Accounts*. Washington, D.C.: various dates.

Brealey, R., and S. Myers. *Principles of Corporate Finance*. 2nd ed. New York: McGraw-Hill, 1984.

Lazere, M. R., ed. *Commercial Financing*. New York: Ronald Press, 1968.

Sinkey, J. F., Jr. *Commercial Bank Financial Management*. New York: Macmillan, 1983.

Vander Weide, J., and S. F. Maier. *Managing Corporate Liquidity*. New York: John Wiley & Sons, 1985.

Appendix 21A

Secured Loans

Loans Against Accounts Receivable

Both banks and commercial-finance companies regularly make loans against accounts receivable as collateral. All or part of a firm's receivables may be pledged. Those pledged constitute a *pool* of collateral, with new receivables continuously feeding into the pool and payments made by customers reducing it.

Typically, the borrower retains responsibility for credit analysis of its customers and certifies to the lender that customers whose accounts are pledged are solvent. The lender judges the quality of the receivables and often has the option of rejecting any individual accounts. Because the borrower retains title to the receivables, defaults are the borrower's responsibility.

The lender and borrower agree upon a fixed percentage that will be advanced against the receivables. The percentage may vary from 60 to 90 percent, depending on the lender, an evaluation of the riskiness of the receivables, and the administrative costs of the arrangement. Commercial-finance companies are usually willing to advance somewhat more than banks.

As the borrowing firm makes sales, the new receivables are assigned to the lender, who advances the agreed-upon percentage of the face amount to the borrower. The customers usually are not notified that the account has been assigned and make their payments to the borrowing firm. Many agreements specify that the full amount of payments be sent immediately to the lender to be applied against the loan balance. If the assigned receivables and the loan are in the agreed-upon-percentage relationship, the lender usually deducts the loan percentage and returns the balance to the borrower.

Loans secured by receivables usually involve high administrative costs to the lender. Charges are sometimes separated into two components, a service charge and an interest rate. The total of these charges varies from a minimum of 2 to 3 percent above the prime rate to figures considerably higher for small or marginal customers, depending on risk and administrative costs.

A major advantage of receivables financing to the borrowing firm is the link between the loan and the assets to be financed. If sales and receivables are seasonal, the loan varies automatically. Besides the relatively high cost, a disadvantage of receivables financing is its administrative complexity.

Factoring

When a firm *factors* its accounts receivable, it sells them to another party — a factor — for cash. Title to the receivables passes to the factor, and the receivables are replaced by cash on the firm's balance sheet. In contrast, when a firm borrows against its receivables as collateral, it retains title, and both receivables and the loan appear on the balance sheet. Many commercial-finance companies, along with some commercial banks, engage in factoring, although banks usually conduct their factoring operations as separate subsidiaries of the bank or of a parent holding company.

Sale of the receivables to the factor normally is *without recourse* — meaning that the factor absorbs bad-debt losses and cannot look to the seller in the event of default. Occasionally, receivables are sold *with recourse,* in which case uncollectable receivables are returned to the seller, who absorbs the bad-debt expense.

The factor normally approves each order and reserves the right to reject individual accounts or orders. Once the order is approved by the factor, the goods are shipped, and the firm's customer is notified to remit directly to the factor. Because the customer is notified that the account has been sold to a factor, some firms may be inhibited from using factoring. In industries in which factoring is widely used — notably textiles, shoes, and furniture — there is no stigma attached.

Services performed by the factor include credit analysis, collection, and absorption of bad debts. The fee charged varies with the specific services and ranges between 1 and 3 percent of the face amount of the receivables purchased. If funds are advanced to the seller before the receivables are collected by the factor, an additional interest charge is levied that is normally tied to, and is above, the prime bank rate.

In some situations, factoring offers significant advantages. With a factoring arrangement, a firm avoids the expense of bad debts and also may avoid the necessity of operating a credit department for analysis and collection. Firms that are small or have seasonal sales patterns may realize substantial savings. Costs avoided by the firm are borne by the factor, but because the factor serves many customers, the aggregate cost may be lower. By serving firms with different seasonal patterns, the credit analysis and collection workload may be spread more evenly over the year. By serving a large number of accounts, the factor can realize economies of scale and can also achieve better diversification with respect to default risk. For these reasons, in some industries, a factor can perform the services in question more economically than firms can individually.

To evaluate factoring as a financing arrangement requires a careful analysis of activities and costs and a comparison of the resulting savings with the fee charged by the factor.

Loans Against Inventory

Inventory is also often used as collateral for loans by both banks and commercial-finance companies. The nature of the inventory is an important factor in determining the attractiveness of the loan to a lender and the percentage to be advanced. The more readily salable the inventory, the higher the loan percentage. A lumber wholesaler's inventory, for example, readily salable as is, would probably justify a higher loan percentage than an inventory of specialized electronic parts or half-completed electronic instruments. Loan percentages against inventory typically vary from 50 to 90 percent.

The security arrangement is a critical factor in inventory loans and greatly affects the administrative costs. A number of methods are in common use; some leave the inventory in the possession of the borrower, and some place it under the control of a third party.

The simplest arrangement by which a borrower can retain control of the inventory is a *blanket,* or *floating, lien.* The Uniform Commercial Code includes a provision whereby a borrower may pledge inventory "in general," without specifying the exact items involved. The floating lien is inexpensive to administer but difficult to police.

Considerably more security is afforded the lender under a *trust-receipt loan.* This arrangement is often used to finance automobiles, consumer durable goods, and certain types of equipment. In these applications, the arrangement is referred to as *floor planning.* Under such an arrangement, the lender advances the funds to purchase the inventory. The borrower signs a trust receipt, and each item is identified individually by serial number. Usually, title to the goods rests with the lender until sold. After sale, the proceeds belong to the lender and are forwarded immediately by the borrower. As inventory is sold, new inventory is entered into the arrangement and is controlled individually by serial numbers. Lenders usually audit the inventory periodically to ensure that items supposed to be in the inventory, identified by serial number, are in fact there.

With goods in the hands of the borrower, the lender is not protected against fraud or misapplication. To gain complete protection, the goods may be placed under the control of a third party, or *warehouser.* The *warehouser* is given physical control of the inventory and issues a warehouse receipt assigning the security interest to the lender. The warehouser releases the inventory to the borrowing firm upon authorization of the lender, which usually requires that some portion of the loan be repaid.

There are two principal types of warehouse arrangements. A *terminal warehouse* is a public warehouse facility to and from which the inventory must be physically transported. Often a more convenient arrangement is the *field warehouse,* operated by the warehouse company on the premises of the borrower. Under this arrangement, a suitable facility is established providing storage under lock and key with direct control by the warehouser. The arrangement between Allied Crude Oil Company and American Express described in Finance in Practice

21–2 is a good example of a field-warehousing arrangement—albeit one that ultimately did not perform its function.

Because inventory must be controlled item by item, administrative costs are high under a warehouse arrangement. Floor-planning arrangements are normally somewhat less costly but provide less security and are not suitable for all types of goods. On warehouse loans, interest and service charges are usually listed separately. Interest charges are imposed by the lender and depend on the creditworthiness of the borrower, the nature of the inventory, the loan percentage, and the amount of the loan. Service charges are levied by the warehouse company and depend on the nature of the inventory, the handling required, and the rate of turnover of the goods under control. Warehouse-receipt loans are an expensive method of financing, but in some cases involving firms in financial difficulty, with no established credit record, or in risky lines of business, they may be the only source available.

22

Managing Cash

In this chapter, we will focus on how firms can keep their investment in cash to a minimum while still operating the firm effectively. The overall problem of cash management can be divided into three steps: (1) collecting and disbursing funds efficiently, (2) determining the appropriate working-cash balance, and (3) investing the remaining excess cash. As we will see, subject to the constraint of honoring its commitments to customers and suppliers, a firm should make it a policy to collect early and pay late because money has a time value. Because of the high costs of financing and the attractive interest rates on investments in marketable securities, many firms are actively engaged in sophisticated cash management to reduce their investment in working-cash balances.

In the last chapter, we focused on sources of short-term and intermediate-term financing. Obtaining such financing is costly to the firm because the suppliers of funds must be compensated. For example, a bank requires the firm to pay interest on the amount it borrows. One way to reduce these costs is to keep the amount of financing needed as low as possible while still operating the firm effectively. Managers can reduce financing needs by reducing the assets that the firm uses.

Current assets — assets with a maturity of less than one year, normally cash, accounts receivable, and inventories.

In this chapter and the next, we will focus on the **current assets** of the firm — mainly cash, inventories, and accounts receivable. For many firms, current assets represent a large portion of total investment, and, like long-term assets, current assets must be financed. As an example, in 1986 Xerox Corporation had over $4 billion in current assets out of total assets of $10.6 billion. That $4 billion investment in current assets had to be financed by Xerox. In this chapter, we will focus on one major current asset — cash — then move on to accounts receivable and inventories in the next chapter.

Many firms actively try to keep cash to a minimum. It is not that firms do not want cash flow. In fact, getting large positive cash flows is what undertaking good investment opportunities is all about. But once cash comes in, there is good reason not to leave it idle in a cash account. Interest in cash management has risen to the extent that there now exists a national organization called the National Corporate Cash Managers' Association, which sponsors a journal and holds annual meetings devoted to topics in working-capital management.

Cash for purposes of cash management is total liquid assets: cash plus near-cash.

Liquid assets — assets that can easily be converted to cash on short notice.

Working-cash balance — currency plus checking-account balances.

The term **cash** sometimes refers to currency plus checking-account balances held at commercial banks and sometimes also includes *near-cash assets,* such as marketable securities or bank time deposits. Earlier, we used the term **liquid assets** to refer to the total of cash plus near-cash. In this chapter, however, we will use the term *cash* in its broader sense — that is, as total liquid assets. We will use the term **working-cash balances** to refer to the subset of liquid assets that includes only currency plus checking-account balances. We will not distinguish between currency and checking-account balances because for most firms the checking account is far more important than currency as a working balance.

Motives for Holding Cash

The **transactions motive** for holding cash concerns the use of cash to pay bills.

The **precautionary motive** for holding cash concerns the use of liquid assets as a reserve for contingencies in an uncertain world.

Firms have two main motives for holding cash, or liquid assets: a **transactions motive,** and a **precautionary motive.** The transactions motive refers to cash balances required in the ordinary course of business — a pool from which the firm makes payments to suppliers, employees, and creditors and into which it places payments received from customers. These receipts and disbursements constitute a continuous flow through the firm's working-cash balance. The precautionary motive refers to cash held for unexpected problems or opportunities requiring funds on short notice. Precautionary cash balances are usually held in liquid assets that earn interest. In seasonal firms, a part of the transaction balance also may be stored temporarily in near-cash form — such as in marketable securities — during parts of the year. In addition to the transactions and precautionary motives, firms may sometimes build up liquid assets because of a *speculative motive* while they are waiting to decide on the long-term use of funds. For example, a buildup of liquid assets might provide some of the resources necessary to acquire another firm in the future. We will not discuss the speculative motive further in this chapter. In Chapter 25, we discuss mergers in detail.

Cash-management policy—the set of decisions related to (1) managing collections and disbursements of cash, (2) determining the appropriate working-cash balance, and (3) investing idle cash.

In order to concentrate on cash management, we will take as given all aspects of the firm's operating plan except those that directly affect its cash position. Inventory levels, for example, will be assumed to be already determined, as will trade credit policy and the level of accounts receivable.

Cash-management policy addresses three basic questions:

1. How should working-cash balances be stored, collected, and disbursed?
2. Given a total pool of cash, how should the appropriate working balance be determined?
3. How should any temporarily idle funds be invested in interest-bearing assets?

Managing Collections and Disbursements

Cash cycle—the process whereby cash is used to purchase materials from which are produced goods that are then sold to customers, who later pay their bills.

To size up our problem of cash management, let us examine the flow of cash through a firm's accounts. It is useful to think of the process as a **cash cycle** whereby cash is used to purchase materials from which are produced goods, which are then sold to customers, who later pay their bills. The firm receives cash from its customers, and the cycle repeats. We can represent the cash cycle as shown in Figure 22–1.

Figure 22–1
Overview of the Cash Cycle

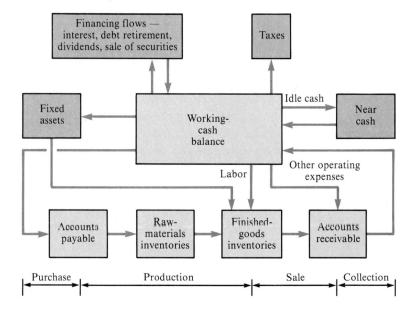

Figure 22–2
Details of the Cash Cycle

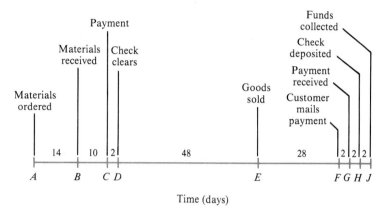

Time (days)

Opportunities to improve efficiency in collecting and disbursing funds center on flows through the current section of the balance sheet, depicted in the bottom part of Figure 22–1. We diagram these flows in more detail in Figure 22–2, which shows the steps along the way as funds flow through the firm's accounts. Let us assume that XYZ Corporation orders raw materials at point A in Figure 22–2 and receives them 14 days later at point B. Terms of 2/10, net 30 are offered, so the firm pays the invoice in time for the check to get to the supplier 10 days later at point C. However, it takes 2 days for the check to clear, and XYZ's bank account is not charged until point D. XYZ turns over its inventory six times per year, so 60 days after the materials are received, the product is sold and the customer is billed. The collection period is 30 days — 28 days for the customer to pay and 2 days for the check to arrive by mail, bringing us to point G. XYZ processes the payment and deposits it 2 days later at point H. Another 2 days elapse while XYZ's bank collects the funds from the customer's bank, bringing us to point J.

In viewing Figure 22–2, the manager sees cash effectively leaving the firm's bank account at D and entering the account at J. Because money has a time value, it would benefit the firm to speed up the collection of funds (move J to the left in the figure) and slow down the disbursement of funds (move D to the right). Such steps would reduce the firm's costs — either the direct interest cost of having to borrow funds to bridge the gap between D and J or the opportunity costs of not being able to earn interest by investing surplus cash. Again, subject to the constraint of honoring its commitments to customers and suppliers, the company should make it a policy to collect early and pay late.

Another way to view this process is to note that the firm's total financing requirement is affected by the total time lag from point B to point J. The firm itself can control some factors that determine the various lags, but some factors it cannot control. Some of the lags affect the cash balance, while others affect other components of working capital, such as accounts receivable and inventory. In addressing ourselves to cash management, we are concerned with time periods

By speeding collections and controlling disbursements, firms can reduce their requirements for working-cash balances.

Subject to the constraint of honoring its commitments to customers and suppliers, a firm's policy should be to collect early and to pay late.

BCD and *FGHJ*. Time period *AB* is beyond the firm's control and does not directly affect its financial statements, although it may affect production schedules. Time period *DE* is determined by the firm's production process and inventory policy and affects the total investment in inventory. Time period *EF* is determined by the firm's credit terms and the payment policies of its customers and affects the total investment in accounts receivable. We will examine the management of inventory and accounts receivable in the next chapter. Our present task is to examine what can be done to improve the efficiency of a firm's cash management. We will focus on three areas: concentrating working balances, speeding collections, and controlling disbursements. In each case, we will examine policies that reduce the amount of cash that a firm has to maintain.

One bank described the objectives of cash management in these terms: "Companies use cash-management services basically for two reasons—to maximize earnings from the investment of idle cash and to reduce the need for borrowing to finance daily operations. In addition, our cash-management services provide companies greater control through improved information, while helping to feed internal accounting and information systems."[1]

Speeding Collections

One important way firms conserve cash is by reducing the lag between the time the customer mails the check and the time the funds are collected—that is, from point *F* to point *J* in Figure 22–2. Of the six-day lag in Figure 22–2, two days are mail time, two days are processing time within XYZ Corporation, and two days are collection time within the banking system.

Float—the product of the time delay in collecting funds and the dollars collected.

These delays in collection create **float**, which is the product of the time delay and the dollars collected. For example, a firm that collects $1.5 million per day and experiences a six-day lag in collecting the funds would have total float of $1.5 million per day × 6 days = $9 million. Reducing collection time by two days would reduce float by $3 million, and each dollar so released would be available for investment. If the firm could earn, say, 10 percent on such an investment, it would have $300,000 per year in additional earnings. It's easy to see why firms work hard to reduce collection float.

The firm can control some factors that determine various lags in the cash cycle, but some it cannot. Some lags affect the cash balance, others affect other components of working capital.

Total float can be broken down into mail float, processing float, and availability float. Availability float refers to collection time in the banking system, to which we will return later. For now, let's focus on mail and processing float caused by the four-day lag from point *F* to point *H* in Figure 22–2.

Internal processing of collections should be speeded up to the point at which the costs of further improvement exceed any additional savings.

Small firms that operate in limited geographical areas can do little to reduce mail time. However, improvements often can be made in processing time within the firm. Suppose XYZ Corporation has credit sales of $5 million per year. With approximately 250 working days per year, XYZ's collections average $20,000 per working day. If XYZ could reduce its processing time from two days to one day and thereby get the checks to the bank one day sooner, its accounts receivable balance would be reduced by $20,000. XYZ's financing requirements would,

[1]NCNB Corporation, *First Quarter Report to Shareholders*, 1985.

therefore, be reduced by $20,000. If XYZ's borrowing costs were 9 percent, it would realize savings of about $1,800 per year. These potential savings could be compared to the cost of faster processing to determine whether the change in processing should be made. We can conclude that internal processing should be speeded up to the point at which the costs of further improvement exceed the additional savings.

Now let us consider a larger firm that receives remittances from customers over a wide geographical area. Opportunities may exist to reduce both mail time and processing time. One way to reduce mail time is by operating a number of strategically located collection centers to which customer payments are mailed.

Lockbox system—a collection system in which payments are mailed to a post office box, which is emptied several times a day by a bank, which then deposits the payments and updates accounting records.

A major advantage of speeding collections is to free cash and thereby reduce the firm's total financing requirement.

Lockbox Systems. Many firms find it advantageous to engage the services of commercial banks to operate collection centers for them as part of a **lockbox system.** The firm first establishes a number of collection points, taking into account customer locations and mail schedules. Often the bank provides technical assistance in selecting the most advantageous locations for collection centers.[2] At each location, the firm rents a post office box and instructs its customers to remit to the box. The firm's local bank is authorized to pick up mail directly from the box. The bank does so, perhaps several times a day, and deposits the checks in the firm's account. The bank records names and amounts and other data needed by the firm for internal accounting purposes and immediately enters the checks for collection.

The lockbox system results in two benefits to the firm. First, the bank performs the clerical tasks of handling the remittances prior to deposit, services that the bank may be able to perform at lower cost. Second, and often more important, the process of collection through the banking system begins immediately upon receipt of the remittance and does not have to wait until the firm completes its processing for internal accounting purposes. In terms of the activities in Figure 22–2, the activity represented by *HJ* now takes place simultaneously with *GH*. The firm processes remittances for internal accounting purposes, using data supplied by the bank, and can schedule this processing at any time without delaying collection. Using a lockbox system saves as much as four days in mailing and processing time. The cost saving to the firm from such a system can be significant.

For example, assume Ajax Manufacturing Company handles collections of $10 million a year and has an opportunity to use a bank lockbox system that offers to save two days of processing time on each check received. If the company's cost of short-term funds is 10 percent per annum, its *gross* saving would be the product of annual remittances times number of days saved times cost of funds times 1/365, or

$10 million × 2 days × 10 percent per year × 1/365 = $5,479 per year.

The first lockbox system was set up in 1947 by RCA with the help of the First National Bank of Chicago and Bankers Trust Company. Since that time the use of

---

[2]Determining optimal locations for collection points in a large lockbox system is highly technical and can be formulated and solved as a linear-programming problem. See J. Vander Weide and S. F. Maier, *Managing Corporate Liquidity* (New York: John Wiley & Sons, 1985), Chapter 3.

lockbox systems has become commonplace. However, the use of a lockbox system is not without cost. The bank will either charge a flat amount for its services or ask that the firm maintain a compensating balance at the bank in exchange for the service. In the case of Ajax Company, as long as these costs are less than $5,479 a year, the system produces a net gain to the company. Whether the savings will outweigh the costs for a particular company depends mainly on the geographical dispersion of customers, the dollar amount of the average remittance, and the firm's cost of financing.

We see that a major advantage of speeding collections is to free cash and thereby reduce the firm's total financing requirement. There are other advantages as well. By transferring clerical functions to the bank, the firm may reduce its costs, improve internal control, and reduce the possibility of fraud. By getting checks sooner to the banks on which they are written, the incidence of checks dishonored for insufficient funds may be reduced.

Collection Time in the Banking System. The time required to collect a check through the banking system is represented by *HJ* in Figure 22–2. Suppose a customer in Chapel Hill, North Carolina, purchases electronics equipment from a firm in Palo Alto, California, and remits with a check drawn on a Chapel Hill bank. The seller deposits the check in a bank in Palo Alto, but the funds are not available for use until the check has been presented physically to the Chapel Hill bank, a process that depends on mail service between the two cities and may take several days. A very extensive clearing network has been established in the United States that involves the commercial banks and the Federal Reserve System. In the majority of cases, clearing times have been reduced to two days or less using the facilities of the Fed or direct interbank clearings. The availability of funds to depositors was further improved by the Expedited Funds Availability Act, which became effective September 1, 1988. In the matter of check clearing, the banks are the experts, and firms usually can rely on their banks to minimize the time requirements.

Controlling Disbursements

Just as speeding collections turns accounts receivable into cash and thereby reduces the firm's financing requirements, slowing disbursements does the same. In Chapter 21, we discussed trade credit as a source of funds. There we concluded that the proper policy was to pay within the terms agreed upon, taking cash discounts when the terms offered were favorable. We concluded also that there is no point in paying sooner than agreed. By waiting as long as possible, the firm maximizes the extent to which accounts payable are used as a source of funds, a source which requires no interest payment.

Consider the effect of a one-day change in payment period. Engineered Systems, Inc., planned to purchase about $1.5 million worth of raw materials in 1989, which comes to about $4,100 per day. The company followed a policy of paying within credit terms offered by suppliers. Suppose ESI paid one day earlier than necessary. Accounts payable would decline by one day's purchases, or by about $4,100. These funds would have to be replaced by bank debt, and at an interest rate of 9 percent, ESI's interest costs would rise by $370 per year.

By waiting as long as possible to pay its bills (as determined by the terms of payment already agreed upon), the firm maximizes the extent to which accounts payable are used as a source of funds, a source which requires no interest payment.

Firms with expense-generating activities that cover a wide area often find it advantageous to make disbursements from a single central account. In that way, schedules can be tightly controlled and disbursements can be made on exactly the right day. An alternative arrangement is to disburse from decentralized locations, but to wire transfer the exact amount needed in each local account for all disbursements scheduled that day.

Some firms find it advantageous to exploit the *checkbook float,* or *disbursement float,* which is the time between the writing of a check and its presentation for collection, represented by segment *CD* in Figure 22–2. If this lag can be exploited, it offsets at least partially the lag in the other direction in collecting checks from customers (*HJ*). Because of lag *CD,* a firm's balance on the bank's books is higher than that in its own checkbook. Knowing this, a firm may be able to reduce its working-cash requirements. Banks also understand checkbook float and can be expected to set compensating balances and fees based on balances on their (the banks') books. If a firm exploits checkbook float too far, it increases the likelihood of checks being dishonored for insufficient funds and the accompanying displeasure of both bank and payee.

Going beyond merely taking into account disbursement float, it has become common practice in recent years for aggressively managed firms to actually increase disbursement float by extending the lag from *C* to *D* in Figure 22–2. Mail time can be increased by mailing the check from a distant office; presentation time can be extended by drawing the check on a distant bank. In recent years, the matter of selecting disbursement centers to accomplish these aims has received as much attention as selection of the collection centers discussed earlier.[3] The Federal Reserve, however, discourages such practices because it sees its own mission as that of reducing, not increasing, collection time. Vendors likewise disapprove of aggressive disbursement practices because the payer's disbursement float is the payee's collection float. Firms that go too far in extending disbursement float are simply taking advantage of their suppliers, and such practices are not conducive to good business relationships.

Concentration Banking

Many firms need only a single checking account. Larger firms that operate over wide geographical areas usually need more than one, sometimes dozens. Where many accounts are needed, **concentration accounts** can be used to minimize the total requirement for working balances.

Suppose a company has a number of branch offices, each with a local bank account. Branches collect accounts receivable and make deposits in their local accounts. Each day, funds above a certain predetermined minimum are transferred to a central concentration account, usually at the firm's headquarters. For example, a fast-food chain with 200 locations might make deposits of $2,000 per day on average per store and might have collected balances of $5,000 in each store's local bank account. Such a small amount could not be invested advantageously, especially on an overnight basis. On the other hand, if the franchise concentrates its

Sidenote 1: Firms with expense-generating activities over a wide geographic area often find it advantageous to make disbursements from a single central account.

Sidenote 2: **Concentration account** — a centralized bank account in which disbursement funds from different branches, divisions, or franchises of a company can be pooled so that the firm's aggregate working-balance requirement is lower than if balances were maintained at each branch.

[3]See Vander Weide and Maier, *Managing Corporate Liquidity,* Chapter 4.

funds at the close of business each day by transferring collected balances from all 200 local accounts to a single central account, it will have a pool of $1 million available for investing. Thus, the motivation for concentration banking is to maximize the amount of investable funds.

Methods of Funds Transfer. The daily transfer of funds can be made using one of three methods: by *depository transfer check (DTC),* by *wire transfer,* or by an *automated clearinghouse (ACH).* The DTC is the most widely used and least expensive but usually the slowest because it is performed with a piece of paper. Wire transfer is virtually instantaneous but is expensive.

The automated clearinghouse has grown over recent years out of the universal desire of banks and their customers to reduce the avalanche of paper required to execute payment transactions in the United States. The ACH system today, with the exception of that in New York City, is run by the Federal Reserve. Its basis is computer-to-computer transmission of payment instructions without paper ever being created. ACH, unlike wire transfer, is not intended for immediate transfer of funds, but normally involves a one-day delay.[4]

Regardless of the transfer method used, the funds transferred to the concentration account are available for disbursement for other purposes. As we will see later, the more variable a firm's cash flows, the higher the requirement for working-cash balances. If funds are pooled for disbursement in a single account, the aggregate requirement for working balances is lower than it would be if balances were maintained at each branch office. Concentration, in short, permits the firm to store its cash more efficiently. Concentration banking has become widely used by firms with many retail outlets, such as fast-food franchises or department stores.

Electronic Banking. The automated clearinghouse is a form of electronic banking because payments are transferred electronically, with no paper involved. Banks also are experimenting with other forms of electronic funds transfer, among them:

1. *point-of-sale terminals* located on a merchant's premises that permit direct transfer of funds from a customer's account to that of the merchant;
2. *automatic teller machines (ATMs)* that permit bank customers to execute a number of typical banking transactions at convenient locations 24 hours a day;
3. *telephone-instructed transactions* performed with a personal computer or terminal from the home or office of a customer to the bank.[5]

Although the venerable check remains the preferred means of payment for the majority of transactions, we can expect electronic banking to grow rapidly in coming years as technology advances. The impetus toward electronic banking is being stimulated also by the drive of the Federal Reserve to reduce float, specifically the availability float resulting from collection time within the banking system. In 1980

---

[4]For a discussion of the automated clearinghouse and of concentration banking in general, see Vander Weide and Maier, *Managing Corporate Liquidity,* Chapter 5.

[5]See Vander Weide and Maier, *Managing Corporate Liquidity,* Chapter 2.

Finance in Practice 22–1

Integrated Cash-Management Systems

Many banks offer integrated cash-management systems designed especially for large firms with extensive collection and disbursement activities. Such systems rely heavily on the technology of computers and high-speed data transmission. A system offered by many banks features lockboxes and remote *zero-balance accounts* linked by wire to a centralized master-control account where working balances are pooled. The zero-balance accounts are used for decentralized collection and disbursement, with funds transferred in and out each day to achieve a zero balance at the day's end. Extensive reports are generated to provide data to the firm for control purposes. Such systems are costly but provide substantial benefits for firms that can utilize them. One major regional bank includes the following services in its cash-management program:

1. cash-management consulting that uses computer models to help identify ways in which companies can increase income from investments and reduce borrowing;
2. a lockbox to speed the collection of payments by having a company's receipts mailed directly to the bank;
3. a controlled-disbursing service that allows firms to identify daily cash requirements precisely, enabling them to make timely, accurate investment and borrowing decisions;
4. account-reconciliation services, ranging from a paid-item listing to full reconciliation reports;
5. automated-clearinghouse capabilities, including electronic transfer of funds, direct debit and credit, corporate trade payments (the electronic payment of suppliers), and direct deposit of payroll;
6. concentration of receipts from regional locations in a single bank account for greater investment potential and better cash control;
7. a treasury-management system that enables corporate treasurers to use personal computers to receive and process information for improved management of cash flow, debts, and investments;
8. a freight-payment plan that handles the administrative details of paying bills for freight shipments through preauthorized withdrawals from a company's account; and
9. information services, including the sending and receiving of balance and related financial information worldwide through electronic networks.

Source: NCNB Corporation, *Report to Shareholders,* 1985.

---

the Fed began charging banks for excess float, and in response to this change and to improved operating procedures, total availability float in the banking system declined from a daily average of $6.3 billion in 1979 to $1.8 billion in early 1983.[6] The increased pressure by the Fed to reduce float is making electronic funds transfer relatively more attractive.

[6]"Companies Learn to Live Without the Float," *Business Week,* September 26, 1983, p. 134.

Sample Problem 22–1
Collecting Cash Quickly in the Omark Corporation

The Omark Corporation has a centralized billing system at its headquarters in Chicago to handle average daily collections of $200,000. The collection float for Omark averages six days.

A. How much money does Omark have tied up in collection float?

B. If Omark's opportunity cost on short-term funds is 6 percent, how much does this float cost the company?

C. Omark's treasurer is considering a concentration-banking system, which, she estimates, will reduce float by two days. What is the largest total amount of required compensating balances Omark should be willing to accept with the concentration system? (Assume there are no cost savings from the system other than the reduced collection float.)

Solution
A. The total amount of funds tied up in collection float is equal to the firm's average daily collections times the number of days required for collection. For Omark, average daily collections are $200,000, and float is 6 days, so the total amount of funds tied up is:

$$\$200{,}000 \text{ per day} \times 6 \text{ days} = \$1{,}200{,}000 \,.$$

B. The cost of float to the firm equals the amount of funds tied up in float times the opportunity rate at which these funds could be invested. Because Omark can invest the short-term funds to yield 6 percent, the opportunity cost of having $1,200,000 tied up in float is:

$$\$1{,}200{,}000 \times 6 \text{ percent} = \$72{,}000 \text{ per year} \,.$$

C. The concentration-banking system would reduce Omark's cost by reducing the opportunity cost of float. The system will reduce Omark's float by $200,000/day × 2 days = $400,000, reducing Omark's float costs by

$$\$400{,}000 \times 6 \text{ percent} = \$24{,}000 \text{ per year} \,.$$

The opportunity cost to Omark of compensating balances equals the required compensating balance times the opportunity cost of short-term funds. The maximum acceptable required compensating balance for Omark is found by equating the opportunity cost of the compensating balance to the savings from the concentration banking system, which we found to be $24,000.

$$\text{Compensating balance} \times 6 \text{ percent} = \$24{,}000 \,.$$

Therefore,

$$\text{Compensating balance} = \$24{,}000/0.06 = \$400{,}000 \,.$$

Note that if Omark maintained a $400,000 compensating balance, this would exactly offset the $400,000 of reduced float provided by the concentration-banking system. ▇▇▇

Determining the Appropriate Working-Cash Balance

Let us assume the firm is now collecting, storing, and disbursing its cash as efficiently as possible. Given its long-term financial structure — fixed assets, long-term liabilities, and equity — its total cash position at any time is determined by its operating plan. Suppose total cash is more than the firm needs for operating purposes, if disbursements are made according to plan. Should all these funds be kept in the firm's checking account? No. Because checking accounts earn interest at lower rates than various interest-bearing liquid assets, such as marketable securities, it is to the firm's advantage to leave in the checking account only the amount necessary to operate and invest the remainder elsewhere until needed.

It is to the firm's advantage to leave in the checking account only the amount necessary to operate.

The second major step in managing cash is to determine how much cash a firm should maintain in its checking account as a working balance. We will address this question here, and in the next section we will discuss the investment of amounts above the working balance.

The working balance is maintained for *transactions purposes* — for paying bills and collecting payments on accounts receivable. If the firm maintains too small a working balance, it runs out of cash. It then must liquidate marketable securities, if available, or borrow. Liquidating marketable securities and borrowing both involve transaction costs. If, on the other hand, the firm maintains too high a working balance, it forgoes the opportunity to earn higher interest rates on marketable securities — that is, it incurs an opportunity cost. Thus, we are seeking the *optimal* working balance, rather than the minimum working balance.

The working balance is maintained for transactions purposes (paying bills and collecting payments on accounts receivable).

Compensating-Balance Requirements

If a firm uses bank credit as a source of financing, the question of the optimal checking-account balance may have a very simple answer: it may be dictated by compensating-balance requirements imposed by the bank. As we found in Chapter 21, banks typically impose minimum-balance requirements to compensate for various services, such as processing checks and standby commitments to lend. The amount of the compensating balance may be determined as a percentage of the loan outstanding or of the line of credit. Alternatively, if there is no loan involved and the balance requirement is strictly to compensate the bank for services rendered, such as clearing of checks, the amount may simply be some minimum dollar balance. The bank might require, for example, that the firm's balance not fall below $100,000, and in return, the bank would agree to process a certain number of transactions each month without charge. The bank, of course, is compensated in the form of what it can earn by lending or investing the minimum balance.

If a firm uses bank credit as a source of financing, the optimal checking-account balance may be dictated by compensating-balance requirements imposed by the bank.

In some cases, a firm may determine with little analysis that its optimal working balance is below the bank's compensating-balance requirement. In such cases, the latter figure becomes the firm's minimum checking-account balance. In other cases, where the answer is not so clear or where compensating balances are not required, we must put pencil to paper to determine the appropriate working balance.

Finding the Optimal Working Balance

Having done all we can to improve our collection and disbursement procedures, let us now take the pattern of receipts and disbursements as given. How much cash should the firm maintain as a working balance? As noted earlier, if the bank requires a compensating balance, the issue is settled: the compensating balance becomes the minimum balance.

In other cases, where there is no compensating balance or the working balance is higher, the problem requires some study. Many attempts have been made to apply sophisticated mathematical models to the problem of cash management, with mixed results.[7] For the majority of firms, sophisticated models are too complex and the benefits unclear. The decision regarding the working-cash balance usually boils down to a judgment call. If the firm keeps too little, it might find itself buying and selling marketable securities too often and thereby incurring excessive transaction costs. Worse, it might spend each day worrying about whether checks written the day before will bounce. If the working balance is set too high, the firm loses earnings that could be made by investing the excess funds. The firm should set the working balance at the minimum that will permit it to operate effectively.

> Because receipts and disbursements are variable and uncertain, financial managers face a challenging task in finding an optimal working-cash balance.

The checking-account balance the firm should maintain is the compensating-balance requirement or the optimal working balance, whichever is greater. Some firms, especially those with seasonal sales patterns, may find that the appropriate working balance varies somewhat over the year. As a firm grows, the appropriate working-cash balance will also grow, although probably not proportionally.

Once we have settled on the appropriate balance to be maintained in the checking account, we can integrate cash management into the financial-planning process. The projected checking-account balance goes into the pro-forma balance sheet. Any excess cash over that figure may then be invested in interest-bearing assets.

Investing Idle Cash

> Excess cash normally is invested in interest-bearing assets readily convertible to cash.

Cash in excess of requirements for working balances normally is invested in interest-bearing assets that can be converted readily to cash. A firm might hold excess cash for two principal reasons. First, the firm's working-capital requirements may vary over the year, perhaps in a fairly predictable manner if the variation is the result of recurring seasonal factors. For example, a toy manufacturer would probably have inventory and accounts receivable requirements that would vary in a seasonal pattern. Excess cash would build up during seasonal lows in accounts

[7]See Vander Weide and Maier.

receivable and inventory and would be needed later to finance a reexpansion of receivables and inventory during the next seasonal high. We can view the excess cash as a part of the firm's *transaction balances*. Even though the cash is temporarily idle, there is a predictable requirement for it later.

Second, excess cash may be held to cover unpredictable financing requirements. In a world of uncertainty, cash flows can never be predicted with complete accuracy. Competitors act, technology changes, products fail, strikes occur, and economic conditions vary. On the positive side, attractive investment opportunities may suddenly appear. A firm may choose to hold excess cash to finance such needs if and when they occur. We noted earlier that cash held for such purposes is referred to as a *precautionary balance* and is usually invested in interest-bearing assets until needed.

An alternative exists to the holding of excess cash for either of the two purposes described above. The firm can simply borrow short-term funds to finance variable requirements as they arise. Under such a policy, the firm would never hold excess cash. A firm's choice between short-term borrowing versus liquid assets as a means of financing variable requirements will depend on policy decisions with respect to the firm's long-term financial structure, particularly the mix of short-term and long-term funds. Here, we take as given the long-term structure and the amount available for investment in interest-bearing assets.

For many companies, especially larger ones, investing idle cash is a very important matter indeed. Table 22–1 shows the holdings of cash and marketable se-

Excess cash may be held to cover unpredictable financing requirements.

Table 22–1

Cash Positions of Selected Companies, Year-End 1986

Company	Cash and Short-Term Securities, Year-End 1986 (millions of dollars)
Ford	8,553
American Express	7,369
IBM	7,257
Boeing	4,172
GM	4,019
USX	3,915
Exxon	3,816
Texaco	3,000
GE	1,919
Phillips Petroleum	1,141
RJR Nabisco	863
Eastman Kodak	613
Westinghouse	598
Du Pont	584
Standard Oil, Ohio	413
Xerox	402
GTE	226

Source: Moody's Manuals and Annual Reports for 1986.

International Focus

The Four Tigers

The "global economy" has been much in the news in the 1980s. International trade was once the province of larger companies. Now all firms must think in global terms and consider foreign countries as a part of their natural market.

Japan has done a superb job in this. The feats of the Japanese automobile and electronics industries are legendary, and it is the rare American who has not used a Japanese product. Japan has succeeded in taking away from U.S. manufacturers most of the consumer electronics market and large shares of personal computing, construction equipment, automobiles, and other industries. In recent years Japan has exported to the United States far more than it has imported, and the U.S. trade deficit with Japan has received much attention. The Japanese have done it with hard work, good product design, favorable government export policies, a high savings rate, and heavy investment.

Now, in the late '80s, other countries are about to do the same thing to Japan. Japanese export growth is slowing down because the exchange rate of yen for dollars changed substantially in favor of the United States during 1985–87 (see Finance in Practice 24–1, "The Value of the Dollar"). South Korea, Singapore, Hong Kong, and Taiwan—known to some as the "four tigers"—have become the world's fastest-growing exporters and now are breathing down the necks of the Japanese. Since 1973, the tigers have averaged 6 percent annual growth in per-capita income, compared to 3 percent in Japan and under 2 percent in the United States and Western Europe.

Government policies differ in the four countries, but they have key characteristics in common. Poor in natural resources and dependent on others for technology and energy, the tigers have succeeded through thrift, a high savings rate, a high rate of investment, and determination to become and remain competitive. Taiwan, a small island nation near mainland China, currently is investing nearly 20 percent of its national income outside its own country, and has amassed $60 billion in foreign assets. A measure of the success of the four is that they are now beginning to worry about trade retaliation by other countries.

The four tigers have set a good example for us all. They, like Japan before them, have shown that with hard work and determination, small companies in small countries can compete in a global marketplace.

Source: Adapted from Peter Passell, "Made in Singapore," *New York Times,* October 2, 1987.

curities of some major companies as of December 31, 1986. These numbers are very big. Ford alone held more than $8.5 billion, an impressive sum for a single company. On a portfolio of this size, an increase of half a percentage point in yield could add more than $42.5 million to the firm's pretax profits! Companies with much more modest holdings of cash and marketable securities find that the potential from careful management can be extremely attractive.

Investment Criteria

A firm might invest excess cash in many types of interest-bearing assets. To choose among the alternatives, we must establish criteria based on our reasons for investing excess cash in the first place. We are investing either temporary transaction balances or precautionary balances or both. When we need the cash, we want to be able to obtain it — all of it — quickly. Given these objectives, we can rule out common stocks and other investments with returns that are not contractual and with prices that often vary widely. Debt securities, with a contractual obligation to pay, are our best candidates. In selecting among debt securities, there are three principal characteristics we should examine: default risk, maturity, and marketability.

Default risk refers to the possibility that interest or principal might not be paid on time and in the amount promised. If the financial markets suddenly perceive a significant risk of default on a particular security, the price of the security is likely to fall substantially, even though default may not actually have occurred. Because investors in general are averse to risk, even the possibility of default is sufficient to depress the price. Given our purposes in investing excess cash, we want to steer clear of securities that stand any significant chance of defaulting. In an uncertain world, there is no guarantee that is absolutely certain — except perhaps that of the U.S. government, with its capacity to create money. However, the default risk on some securities is sufficiently low to be almost negligible. In selecting securities, we must keep in mind that risk and return are related and that low-risk securities provide the lowest returns. We must give up some return in order to purchase safety.

Maturity refers to the time period over which interest and principal payments are to be made. A 20-year bond might promise interest semiannually and principal at the end of the twentieth year. A six-month bank **certificate of deposit** would promise interest and principal at the end of the sixth month.

When interest rates vary, the prices of fixed-income securities vary. A rise in market rates produces a fall in price, and vice versa. Because of this relationship, debt securities are subject to a second type of risk — **interest-rate risk** — in addition to default risk. A U.S. government bond, though free of default risk, is not immune to interest-rate risk. The longer the maturity of a security, the more sensitive its price will be to interest-rate changes and the greater its exposure will be to interest-rate risk. For this reason, short maturities are generally best for investing excess cash.

Marketability refers to the ease with which an asset can be converted to cash. With reference to financial assets, the terms *marketability* and *liquidity* are often used synonymously. Marketability has two principal, and interrelated, dimensions: price and time. If an asset can be sold quickly in large amounts at a price that can be determined in advance within narrow limits, the asset is said to be highly marketable or highly liquid. Perhaps the most liquid of all financial assets are U.S. Treasury bills (discussed later). On the other hand, if the price that can be realized depends significantly on the time available to sell the asset, the asset is said to be

Criteria for selecting the best vehicle for investing idle cash include the amount of money available and the default risk, maturity, and marketability of the investment.

Default risk — the possibility that interest or principal might not be paid on time and in the amount promised.

Because risk and return are related, we must give up some return in order to gain safety.

Maturity — the time period over which interest and principal payments are to be made.

Certificates of deposit (CD) — a fixed-maturity time deposit.

Interest-rate risk — the risk that the price of a security may fall due to a rise in the level of interest rates.

Marketability — the ease with which an asset can be converted to cash on short notice (also known as *liquidity*).

An asset that can be sold quickly in large amounts at a price that can be determined in advance within narrow limits is said to be highly marketable or highly liquid.

Money-market securities — interest-bearing assets with low default risk, short maturity, and ready marketability.

U.S. Treasury bills and notes — short-term obligations of the U.S. government.

Federal-agency issues — short-term obligations of agencies of the federal government.

Commercial paper — short-term unsecured promissory notes of large corporations.

illiquid. The more independent of time the price is, the more liquid the asset. A Van Gogh painting appraised at $100,000 would be likely to fetch far less if the owner were forced to sell it quickly on short notice. Besides price and time, a third attribute of marketability is low transaction costs.

Investment Alternatives

Here we discuss briefly the principal types of interest-bearing assets that meet the criteria of low-default risk, short maturity, and ready marketability. Such securities are often referred to as **money-market securities.**

U.S. Treasury bills and notes are obligations of the U.S. government. Treasury bills are one of the most widely used mediums for the temporary investment of excess cash. Bills are issued weekly by the government, are readily marketable, and have maturities at issue ranging from 91 to 360 days. Treasury notes have initial maturities of one to five years. Because Treasury securities are default-free, they have somewhat lower yields than other marketable securities.

Federal-agency issues are obligations of agencies of the federal government rather than the U.S. Treasury. Such agencies include the Federal Home Loan Bank, the Federal Land Bank, the Federal National Mortgage Association, and several others. These agencies are closely associated in the minds of investors with the federal government — although their obligations, strictly speaking, are not guaranteed by the government. Normally, yields on federal-agency issues are slightly higher than those on Treasury securities, and maturities range from one month to more than ten years.

Bank **certificates of deposit (CDs)** are fixed-maturity time deposits placed with leading commercial banks. CDs in denominations over $100,000 usually are negotiable, meaning they can be sold in a secondary market prior to maturity. Maturities generally range from 90 to 360 days. CDs of the largest banks are generally considered to be money-market instruments and are marketable. Many banks issue CDs in denominations less than $100,000, although such certificates are usually not negotiable, and penalties are imposed if they are not held to maturity. Default risk is quite low, but not entirely absent, as evidenced by the failures of some large banks in recent years. Yields on CDs are higher than those on Treasury securities and usually about equal to those on commercial paper (discussed below). Certificates of deposit have become the most widely used vehicle for temporarily storing idle cash funds.

Commercial paper is short-term unsecured promissory notes of large corporations. We discussed commercial paper as a source of funds in Chapter 21. As an investment medium, we are interested in the commercial paper of other firms. Commercial paper is regularly issued by major finance companies, banks and bank-holding companies, and some nonfinancial firms. Denominations are usually larger than $100,000, and maturities range up to 270 days. Commercial paper is usually held to maturity because the secondary market is not well developed.

Besides the principal alternatives just discussed, there are several others that meet our criteria but are less widely used. *Banker's acceptances* are drafts drawn against deposits in commercial banks. They are used as financing instruments in certain specialized lines of domestic and foreign trade. The draft has a specific payment date and, once accepted by the bank, becomes an obligation of the bank rather than of the initiating firm. By accepting the draft, the bank has guaranteed its payment at maturity. Yields are comparable to those on bank CDs, and maturities are usually less than 180 days.

Repurchase agreements are contracts whereby a firm lends by purchasing marketable securities (usually Treasury bills) from a borrower (often a bond dealer), with the agreement that the borrower will repurchase the securities at a specified price and time. The price difference represents interest earned by the lender. The arrangement provides great flexibility with respect to maturity, which usually is for periods of a few days to a week. Yields are comparable to those on Treasury bills.

State and local governments also issue debt securities that often meet our requirements. Income from such securities under present law is not taxable by the federal government. Yields are lower to reflect the tax advantage but often are higher on an after-tax basis than those on taxable securities. For example, suppose a firm was paying taxes at a 34 percent tax rate. If the firm bought a security paying 10 percent interest that was taxed, the firm would receive only $0.10(1 - 0.34) = 0.066$, or 6.6 percent, on an after-tax basis. A local-government debt security that was tax-exempt would have to pay only 6 percent to provide this same after-tax yield to the firm.

Eurodollars—deposits denominated in U.S. dollars but held in banks outside the United States.

Eurodollar deposits are deposits (CDs of various maturities) denominated in U.S. dollars but held at branches of U.S. banks or other banks located *outside* the United States, principally in London but also in other European financial centers, the Caribbean, and Singapore. These deposits yield rates slightly above domestic U.S. CD rates; thus, this market is widely used by multinational corporations as a medium for placing temporarily idle funds. The principal reason for the higher rate on Eurodollar deposits is that the depository banks face fewer regulations and restrictions on these deposits than on deposits in the United States. In short, their costs are lower, which allows them to offer depositors somewhat higher rates than domestic U.S. banks can offer. On the other hand, depositors require a slightly higher rate because the potential risks are also slightly higher. Among these risks are: (1) there is no federal insurance on funds deposited outside the United States; (2) there is no *legal* requirement for a U.S. parent bank to come to the aid of an overseas branch that may get into trouble; (3) no central bank is obligated to function as a lender of last resort should many Eurobanks get into trouble during periods of credit stringency or panic.

Money-market mutual funds—funds set up to allow small investors to pool their funds to invest in money-market instruments in the required large denominations.

The **money-market mutual fund** is an important development in recent years. Money placed in such funds by shareholders is invested in money-market instruments of just the sort we are discussing here—U.S. Treasury bills, bank certificates of deposit, and commercial paper. Before the availability of the money-market funds, investments in high-yield money-market instruments were not available to small investors. The minimum denomination available in Treasury bills is $10,000 and in commercial paper is $100,000. Bank CDs are available in smaller denominations, but to get a true money-market yield requires a minimum purchase of $100,000 — well beyond the means of most private individuals and small firms.

By means of the money-market fund, however, small investors can pool their funds and buy in the required large denominations. The funds also give the investor good diversification by holding a large number of different instruments.

The success of the money-market funds is evident from their dramatic growth. Starting at essentially zero in early 1978, the money-market funds grew to about $10 billion in assets by the end of that year, to $47 billion by the end of 1979, and to more than $230 billion by December 1982. At that time federally insured banks and thrift institutions first began to pay interest on demand deposits, and many experts predicted that money-market funds would no longer serve a purpose and would vanish. They did decline by 20 percent in 1983 but staged a comeback in 1984. In March 1988, money-market-fund assets stood at $280 billion.[8]

Yields

Default risk, maturity, and marketability affect yield. In general, the lower the default risk and the better the marketability, the lower the yield.

All the characteristics we have discussed — default risk, maturity, and marketability — affect yields. In general, the lower the default risk and the better the marketability, the lower the yield. Securities with these desirable characteristics have higher prices and (because price and yield are inversely related) lower yields.

The relationship between maturity and yield is more complex and changes over time. On average, short maturities yield less, other factors being equal, because they are subject to less interest-rate risk. Rates on short maturities, however, are more volatile than those on longer maturities and at times exceed the latter.

At any point in time, rates on the major types of money-market securities we have discussed are fairly close to one another. For equal maturities, the differentials are usually small and are due to small differences in default risk and marketability.

Over time, the entire structure of short-term rates varies significantly.

Over time, the entire structure of short-term rates varies significantly. Such variations are related to the business and monetary cycles, the demand for funds by individuals and firms, and the credit policies of the Federal Reserve, but the single most important factor is the rate of inflation. At the peak of the interest-rate cycle reached in 1974, money-market rates for business borrowers were close to 12 percent. Thereafter, rates fell rapidly to just under 5 percent at the end of 1976. After that, rates again rose, and during 1980 and 1981 the federal-funds rate was well into double digits. Since that time, rates have declined substantially, and by early 1988, money-market rates were down in the 6 to 7 percent range. It is clear that rising inflation rates played a key role in the rise of interest rates generally throughout the 1960s and 1970s, as indicated by Figure 22–3. Similarly, the relatively low level of inflation observed in recent years has been accompanied by declining interest rates.

The single most important factor affecting the variation in interest rates is the rate of inflation.

Yields on money-market instruments tend to move together with a high degree of correlation for like maturities. Table 22–2 presents yield data as of one particu-

[8]*Wall Street Journal,* March 13, 1981, April 22, 1983, and July 26, 1985; *Business Week,* July 29, 1985.

Figure 22–3
Inflation and Nominal Interest Rates

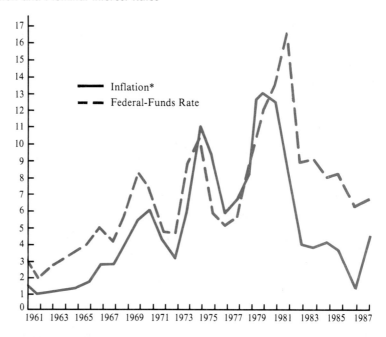

*Annual rate of change of the consumer price index.

Source: Salomon Brothers, *Comments on Credit,* August 17, 1979; and Federal Reserve Bank of St. Louis.

Table 22–2
Yields on Selected Money-Market Instruments, February 12, 1988

Money-Market Instruments	Yield on February 12, 1988 (percent)
90-day CDs	6.54
Prime commercial paper	6.47
Banker acceptances	6.43
Federal funds	6.38
3-month Treasury bills	5.65
6-month Treasury bonds	5.85
1-year Treasury bills	6.16

Source: Federal Reserve Bank of St. Louis, U.S. Financial Data, February 18, 1988.

lar date—February 12, 1988. On other dates, the general level of rates would differ, but yields on these money-market securities would be quite close together.

As we have seen, the late 1970s and early 1980s brought significantly greater volatility to financial markets. Interest rates rose and fell with a frequency and magnitude not seen in recent history. Many managers of short-term funds began to see a need to protect themselves against changes in interest rates. A new tool appeared to serve this need: the **interest-rate futures contract.** Basically, the interest-rate futures contract gives a manager a way to contract to buy or sell debt instruments in the present at agreed-upon interest rates for future settlement. By using interest-rate futures, managers can hedge against the uncertainty of future changes in rates. We discussed financial futures in detail in Chapter 18.

Interest-rate futures contract—an agreement to buy or sell a financial security in the future at an agreed-upon price; allows a manager to hedge against the risk of future rises or falls in interest rates by locking in today the price that must be paid in the future.

Finance in Practice 22–2

E. F. Hutton: Taking Cash Management Too Far

In May of 1985, E. F. Hutton, known to many as the stock brokerage firm to which "people listen," pleaded guilty to 2,000 counts of mail and wire fraud involving overdrafts at as many as 400 banks where the firm had accounts between July 1980 and February 1982. Hutton's customers, employees, and many members of the investment community and the public at large were shocked. Fraud? E. F. Hutton?

The story made big news in both the general and financial press over the next several months. At first it appeared that the practices, while widespread at many Hutton branch offices, were carried out by overzealous local branch controllers without the sanction of top management. As the facts continued to unfold, however, allegations began to surface in the press that members of Hutton's top management had indeed known of the practices.

Many firms use zero-balance accounts, which are checking accounts at branch locations that are drawn to zero at the close of business each day. Hutton, according to press reports, was going much further and systematically *overdrawing* its bank accounts as part of its everyday operating procedure. The drawdown formula was intended to increase daily withdrawals in order to compensate Hutton for weekends and other times when it didn't have access to certain deposits. Such a practice might not be illegal, but Hutton apparently went even further by withdrawing from local accounts funds it *expected* local customers to deposit during the next few days. Further, according to Hutton's plea filed with the Justice Department, company officials illegally transferred funds between branch offices by using some 50 elaborate chains around the country with the aim of delaying check clearing and increasing float. The objective of both the drawdown formula and the chaining, according to prosecutors, was to obtain interest-free loans amounting to hundreds of millions of dollars.

In May 1985, the Justice Department fined E. F. Hutton $2 million, as the company pleaded guilty to 2,000 counts of defrauding banks through checking-account overdrafts. Two senior executives resigned, another retired, and eleven mid-level managers were disciplined.

In all, E. F. Hutton had to pay fines and legal fees amounting to $2.75 million. Hutton had

taken cash management too far and paid a heavy price for its transgression.

Sources: The Wall Street Journal, July 5, 1985, p. 3, and July 25, 1985, p. 6; *Time,* September 16, 1985; *Business Week,* September 23, 1985; *Fortune,* September 30, 1985; D. S. Kidwell and R. L. Peterson, *Financial Institutions, Markets and Money,* p. 142.

KEY CONCEPTS

1. Firms have two primary motives for holding cash and liquid assets: a transactions motive and a precautionary motive.
2. By speeding collections and controlling disbursements, firms can reduce their investment in working-cash balances. Such a reduction allows the firm either to invest in interest-bearing marketable securities or to reduce its total financing needs and, hence, to save on financing costs.
3. The optimal working-cash balance is the mini-

mum that will permit the firm to operate effectively.
4. Criteria for selecting the best vehicle for investing idle cash include the amount of money available and the default risk, maturity, and marketability of the investment.
5. Yields on most short-term money-market instruments move together. The most important factor affecting the level of yields generally is inflation.

SUMMARY

The term *cash* in this chapter refers to total liquid assets, made up of working-cash balances plus interest-bearing marketable securities and deposits. Firms hold cash (liquid assets) for two primary reasons: to execute financial transactions and for precautionary purposes. The overall task of cash management comprises three steps: (1) collecting and disbursing funds efficiently, (2) determining the appropriate working-cash balance, and (3) investing the remaining excess cash.

Steps to improve the efficiency of collection and disbursement must focus on the cash cycle of the firm. Concentration accounts can be used to reduce the requirement for working balances. Collection time can be reduced by the use of a lockbox system. Disbursements should be made within credit terms but no sooner than required.

A working-cash balance is required for transaction purposes. In some cases, bank compensating-balance requirements may determine the minimum working balance. Where this is not the case, the optimal working-cash balance is the minimum that will permit the firm to operate effectively.

Firms hold liquid assets over and above working-balance requirements for two main reasons: as temporarily idle transaction balances and as precautionary balances. Vehicles for investing such cash reserves should be evaluated on the basis of default risk, maturity, and marketability. Many alternatives exist, including U.S. Treasury bills, federal-agency issues, bank certificates of deposit, and commercial paper. Yields on such short-term money-market instruments vary over the business cycle and tend to average slightly less than those of longer-maturity issues.

QUESTIONS

1. What are the principal motives for holding cash and liquid assets?

2. From the standpoint of cash management, on what parts of the cash cycle (diagrammed in Figures 22–1 and 22–2) should attention focus?

3. What are the advantages of concentration banking?

4. How can a firm speed the collection of cash?

5. As a firm's cash cycle increases, does the amount of working capital increase or decrease? Explain.

6. Note the impact (increase or decrease) of the following actions on the length of the cash cycle and on specific current-asset balances.
   a. Changing credit terms from 2/10, n/30 to n/30.
   b. Adding a new line of expensive specialty clothing in a clothing store.
   c. Adopting a lockbox cash-collection system.
   d. Developing a concentration-banking system.
   e. Adding products with longer production times.

7. Why might a firm have idle cash?

8. Discuss the criteria a firm should use in choosing assets in which to invest idle cash.

Problems

1. The Uptown Supply Company has credit sales of $2 million per year. Collections average $8,000 per day with 250 working days assumed per year. Suppose Uptown could reduce its internal processing time by one day. What would be its annual savings, assuming a cost of funds of 12 percent?

2. The Monogram Company is a national retailing concern that sells primarily on a credit basis. Collections from the southern region average $100,000 a day, and the total *float* (amount of time it takes from payment mailing to the time Monogram obtains the use of the funds) is averaging 5 days for customers in this area. The opportunity cost on short-term funds is considered to be 10 percent.
   a. An Atlanta bank has offered to set up a lockbox system which will reduce float by 3 days but requires a compensating balance of $200,000. Would you recommend that Monogram accept the offer?
   b. The bank also proposes an alternative to the compensating-balance requirement of a flat annual fee of $10,000. Which option should Monogram prefer?

3. The Celec Company purchases $3 million of raw materials each year on terms of net 30. The purchasing agent is currently paying each invoice 20 working days after its date to make sure that payment is received by suppliers in 30 days. A study shows that payment could be delayed until the 25th working day and still leave enough time for receipt by the 30th day. How much would the company save annually by making this change, assuming an 11 percent cost of funds?

4. The MHF Company currently maintains an account with a Washington, D.C., bank for collections in the southeastern marketing area. The bank handles collections of $500,000 per day in return for a compensating balance of $300,000. The company is considering an alternative of opening two separate accounts in the southeastern area. It has been projected that total processing time could be reduced by 1 ½ days if accounts are maintained in a Richmond bank and an Atlanta bank, each requiring a $300,000 compensating balance. Would you recommend the two-bank system to the MHF Company?

5. The Rice Company currently maintains a centralized billing system at its home office to handle

average daily collections of $300,000. The total time for mailing, processing, and clearing has been estimated at 5 days.

a. If the firm's opportunity cost on short-term funds is 12 percent, how much is this time lag of 5 days costing the company?

b. If management has designed a system of lockboxes with regional banks that would reduce float by 2 ½ days and home-office credit-department expenses by $30,000 annually, what is the largest amount of required compensating balances that the firm should be willing to accept with the lockbox arrangement?

6. Creative Papers Inc., a nationwide wholesaler of paper supplies, currently has a centralized billing system costing $70,000 annually in recordkeeping expenses with a collection float of 7 days. As the new treasurer of Creative Papers, you have been asked to evaluate two proposed cash-management systems. The concentration-banking system would establish five regional banks to handle Creative's accounts and would require a minimum total compensating balance of $2 million. Collection float for this system is estimated to be 5 days. The lockbox system would establish 10 lockboxes throughout the country with collection float of 3 days. This system would require $3.5 million in compensating balances plus a $0.02 charge per check processed. Your assistant reports that the average check from your customers is for $500, and the firm's opportunity costs on short-term funds is 8 percent. All sales are on credit. Assume 250 working days per year.

a. If average daily collections are $200,000, what is the annual cost of Creative's current system?

b. What must Creative's average daily collections be for the concentration system to be preferred to the current system? For the lockbox system to be preferred to the current system?

7. The Flyer Manufacturing Company has an account with a Philadelphia bank for collections in Flyer's northeast sales region. The bank charges the firm a flat annual fee of $20,000 plus a charge of $0.05 per check processed. Presently, annual credit sales are $50 million, and the typical check from customers is for $1,000. Flyer's opportunity cost on short-term funds is 11 percent. The Philadelphia bank has offered to set up a system of four lockboxes in return for $300,000 in compensating balances plus a charge of $0.03 per check processed. The boxes would be emptied three times daily and would reduce collection float by two days:

a. Would you recommend that Flyer accept the bank's offer? (Assume 250 working days per year.)

b. What is the largest total amount of required compensating balances that Flyer should be willing to accept for this new arrangement?

REFERENCES

"Companies Learn to Live Without the Float." *Business Week* (September 26, 1983): 134.

Donaldson, G. *Strategy for Financial Mobility,* Homewood, Ill.: Richard D. Irwin, 1969.

Donoghue, W. E. *The Cash Management Manual.* Holliston, Mass.: Cash Management Institute, 1978.

Dufey, G., and I. H. Giddy. *The International Money Market.* Englewood Cliffs, N.J.: Prentice-Hall, 1978.

Kolb, R. W. *Understanding Futures Markets.* Chapter 5. Glenview, Illinois: Scott, Foresman and Company, 1985.

Stigum, M. *The Money Market,* 2nd ed. Homewood, Ill.: R. D. Irwin, Inc., 1983.

Vander Weide, J., and S. F. Maier. *Managing Corporate Liquidity.* New York: John Wiley and Sons, 1985.

23

Managing Inventory and Accounts Receivable

In this chapter we apply the perspective of the financial manager to the task of managing two categories of assets that are vital to many firms: inventories and accounts receivable. First we discuss the functions of inventory. We then calculate expected return on the investment in inventory and see how return varies with changes in the inventory level. Then, after discussing the relationship between expected return and required return for inventory investment, we turn to receivables. Here we calculate the expected return on the firm's investment in receivables and see how changes in credit policy affect that return. Finally, we apply this same technique to an individual account.

Inventories and accounts receivable are investments because both represent a commitment of funds the firm can expect to liquidate only at some later periods in time.

In the last chapter we discussed a firm's cash-management policy. Two other important current assets for many firms are inventories and accounts receivable. The stock of inventories held by a firm and the amount of trade credit extended by a firm are *investments* in the sense that each represents a commitment of corporate funds (either of the firm's own capital or of borrowed funds) that the firm can expect to liquidate only at some later point or points in time. These working-capital investments differ from a firm's investment in fixed assets, such as plant and equipment, in only one respect: the average time lag between investment in working capital and its later recoupment is fairly short—a year or less—whereas the corresponding time lag for investment in fixed assets is considerably longer. In spite of this difference, funds committed to working-capital assets are investments; financial management, therefore, has a responsibility to analyze these investments as carefully as it analyzes longer-term commitments to fixed assets. The benefits expected from any proposed increase in working-capital assets must be weighed against the cost to the firm of holding extra assets, including an allowance for the cost of any additional capital required. As a result, we can apply the principles developed in Part Four for analyzing these investments in working capital.

In many situations working-capital decisions are a source of potential conflict between financial managers and operating managers who are in charge of a firm's purchasing, production, and marketing departments. Consider a situation in which the marketing manager believes the level of sales can be increased if the firm's credit policy is loosened—that is, if the firm extends credit to a wider range of customers or if it permits an easier collection policy for whatever credit it does extend. Even if the assumption is correct that such a change in credit policy will lead to an increase in sales volume, it does not necessarily follow that the firm should do what the marketing manager proposes. For a marketing department, the maximization of sales volume is a natural and legitimate objective; for the firm, sales maximization is only a means to an end, and that end, as we saw in Chapter 1, is value maximization.

The loosening of credit terms may increase sales and thus provide gross benefits to the firm, but this loosening of credit is not without cost. A likely consequence of the suggested change in credit policy is that accounts receivable will rise, and this rise imposes several kinds of cost:

1. As the firm's credit is extended to a wider group of buyers, the cost of credit analysis will rise, as will the cost of collecting; it is most likely that the cost of bad debts (credit that cannot be collected) will also rise.

2. The increase in accounts receivable has to be financed somehow. If the firm borrows the funds required, there is the out-of-pocket cost of the extra interest payments incurred.

3. If the firm finances the increase in accounts receivable out of its own funds, there is the opportunity cost that arises because funds used for this purpose cannot also be used in some other possibly lucrative way. Thus, the opportunity cost of using one extra dollar to fund an increase in accounts receivable would be the rate of return the firm has to forgo on the best alternative use available for this dollar.

The financial manager's function is to ensure that the firm's investment in accounts receivable and inventory is at its optimum level — the level that maximizes the value of the firm.

If it is estimated that these costs together will exceed the benefits to be derived from increased sales, the suggested change in credit policy would not be a wise move. On the other hand, if benefits promise to exceed costs, the change would increase the firm's value and should be pursued. The important point is that someone within the firm should be there to press the case for the firm's overall objective as opposed to subordinate objectives, such as sales maximization. Usually this function belongs to the financial manager. In this particular situation, it is his or her duty to see that credit policy and, hence, the level of trade credit extended (or the level of accounts receivable) is expanded as long as such an expansion contributes *net benefits* to the firm. It is also his or her duty to see that credit expansion does not proceed beyond this point.

Changes in the level of accounts receivable and inventory are investment decisions that affect the overall value of the firm.

Taking the viewpoint of the financial manager, we will analyze changes in the level of inventory and accounts receivable as *investment decisions* using wealth maximization for the firm as a whole as our decision criterion. Increases in inventory or accounts receivable are investments that should be undertaken only if the expected rate of return on such new investment exceeds the required rate of return.

Let us take the case of inventory first.

Investing in Inventory

A decision to expand inventories is an *investment decision*.

Inventories represent an important use of a firm's funds and are therefore an important concern of the financial manager. At any point in time, a firm has a given investment in inventory. For example, if a merchandising firm purchases $1 million worth of goods for later resale at a profit, that holding of goods should be viewed as an investment — that is, a commitment of funds now in the expectation of profits later. A decision to expand inventories is an *investment decision*. As we did with long-term assets, we will use **valuation** as our basic conceptual framework and will define the financial manager's responsibility as making sure inventories are set at the level that maximizes the value of the firm. Our analysis will show that the marginal expected return on investment in inventory declines as inventory is increased and that the optimum inventory level lies at the point at which marginal expected return equals the rate required by suppliers of funds.

Raw materials — materials, parts, and subassemblies that are purchased from others and that become part of the final product a firm sells.

Functions of Inventory

Inventories of manufacturing firms can usefully be classified in three categories: raw materials, work in process, and finished goods. **Raw materials** are materials, parts, and subassemblies that are purchased from others and that become a part of the final product. Usually excluded from raw materials are supplies, such as pencils and paper clips, that are consumed but not in the manufacturing process. **Work in process** is goods in various stages of production. **Finished goods** are completed products awaiting sale.

Work in process — goods in various stages of production.

The inventory of a wholesaler or retailer, as opposed to a manufacturer, normally would consist of only a single category — goods purchased from others for resale. Among manufacturers, the mix of the three types of inventory varies with the na-

Finished goods — completed products awaiting sale.

ture of the business. Proximity of raw-material supplies, length of the manufacturing process, and durability or perishability of the final product are all determinants. Manufacturers of machine tools or aircraft produced to customer order have large work-in-process inventories and relatively small finished-goods inventories. Manufacturers of off-the-shelf hardware items, such as hammers and screwdrivers, with short production times and low perishability and obsolescence, are likely to maintain larger finished-goods inventories.

Each of the three types of inventory performs a different though related function. Work-in-process (WIP) inventory is necessary because production is not instantaneous. It takes time to build things, and while goods are being built, but before they are completed, the partially finished product becomes WIP inventory.

Raw-material and finished-goods inventories act as *buffers* between the various activities of the firm so that all activities do not have to proceed at the same rate. Raw-material inventories act as a buffer between purchasing and production. If no raw-material inventories were maintained, materials would have to be purchased continuously at exactly the rate of usage in production. Coordinating purchasing and production in this way would be inconvenient or perhaps even impossible in some cases. Likewise, finished-goods inventories serve as a buffer between production and sales. If the most efficient production rate is faster than the rate of sales, if may be best to produce for a while, let finished-goods inventories build, and then shut down production for a while. Finished-goods inventories also absorb unexpected changes in either the production or the sales rate resulting from production delays, strikes, unanticipated demand, or other causes.

> Each of the three types of inventory performs a different function.

> The basic function of inventory is to decouple the major activities of the firm — purchasing, production, and sales — so that all do not have to proceed at the same rate.

Finance in Practice 23–1

Asset Management and Inventories

Mindful of the high cost of borrowing and the long lead time before technological investments yield payback, management has placed increased emphasis on the effective employment of assets. Internal measurements of managerial performance emphasize return on invested capital, inventory turn-over, cash flow, payback and other indices of asset management.

This quotation from IBM's 1981 annual report reflects a theme heard in many U.S. corporations in the 1980s — the importance of asset management. *Asset management* is the attempt to keep assets, such as inventories, needed for operation at an optimal level. This emphasis has been in place for all sorts of firms — publishers, retailers, manufacturers — not just high-technology firms such as IBM. Why has there been an increase in the emphasis on asset management?

Part of the answer is right out of basic finance. As market interest rates and the costs of obtaining funds go up, as they did in the United States during the 1960s and 1970s, firms must impose higher required rates of return on their investments in all sorts of assets. For many firms, inventories represent large dollar investments. For example, IBM reported 1981 inventories in excess of $2.8 billion. Cutting inventory by even a few percentage points can save large dollar amounts. Suppose a firm could reduce inventories by $200 million. At an annual 10 percent interest rate, the financing-cost savings would be $20 million a year — a tidy sum.

Figure 23–2 (p. 670) displays the finance of the situation. As market required rates of return increase, the required rate of return line in Figure 23–2 shifts upward, implying a higher required rate of return at each level of investment. The new required-return line will intersect the marginal-expected-return line at a point to the left of I^*, implying a new but lower optimal level of investment. Asset management is the process of getting to that optimal level of investment.

Costs of Holding Inventories

In discussing the functions of inventories, we have identified the major benefits of holding them. What about costs? As we saw before in discussing accounts receivable, looking only at operating costs associated with inventories will not be sufficient because having inventories also means that these inventories must be financed; this financing has costs in addition to operating costs — namely, the required returns of the suppliers of capital. As a result, we will look at the total costs of inventory, both operating and financing. Inventory costs can be grouped into two categories: those that rise as inventory increases and those that fall as inventory increases.

Carrying costs rise as inventories increase and include the costs of financing, storage, servicing, and the risk of loss in value.

Those costs that rise with increases in inventory often are referred to as **carrying costs,** which include costs of financing, storage, servicing, and risk of loss in value. Financing costs include the interest on borrowing necessary to finance the inventory as well as the required returns of any other capital supplied to finance inventories. Later, we will comment further on financing costs. Storage costs include rent on facilities and equipment (or the firm's cost of having its own facilities and equipment), property taxes, insurance, and utilities. Servicing costs include labor for handling the inventory, clerical and accounting costs for recordkeeping, and taxes on the inventory itself. Decline in value may take place because of pilferage, fire, deterioration, technological obsolescence, style obsolescence, or price decline. Some of these risks can be insured, in which case the cost of insurance becomes a component of carrying cost. Not all these costs will be incurred by every firm in every situation, and the total cost of carrying inventory varies widely from one situation to another.

Ordering costs decline as inventories increase and include the costs of placing orders and unit purchase costs.

Costs that decline as inventory increases are **ordering costs** (including unit purchase costs), production costs, and opportunity costs of lost sales. Ordering costs are often a fixed amount per order placed, regardless of the amount ordered. By ordering less frequently in larger quantities, total ordering costs are reduced, but

Some costs (carrying costs) rise as inventories are increased, while others (ordering costs, production costs, and opportunity costs of lost sales) fall as inventories are increased.

The optimal inventory level is determined by trading off carrying costs against ordering and stockout costs.

Stockout occurs when there is insufficient inventory to fill orders.

average inventories are larger. Unit costs of materials purchased may be reduced if quantity discounts can be obtained by purchasing in larger quantities. With larger stocks of raw materials and work in process, longer production runs can be made with less frequent setup, lower total setup costs, and fewer delays. Finally, larger finished-goods inventories will reduce **stockouts** (running out of inventory) and lost contribution resulting from sales forgone. This latter cost is an opportunity cost, but an important element in determining the optimal inventory level.

Figure 23–1 shows inventory costs in graphical form. As the inventory level increases, carrying costs increase. At the same time, costs of lost contribution from stockouts go down. Total inventory cost is the sum of the two, plotted as the top line in Figure 23–1. The best or "optimal" inventory level, I^*, is the level at which total inventory costs are at a minimum.

Figure 23–1 helps us understand the problem of inventories, but just drawing graphs isn't actually going to show us how to make inventory decisions in practice. To locate I^*, the optimal inventory level, we need to do some additional analysis: we calculate *return on investment* in inventory.

Calculating Expected Return

Let us illustrate the calculation of expected return on inventory investment with an example. Southeastern Motors, Inc., is a manufacturer of fractional-horsepower electric motors used in hand tools, electric fans, appliances, and other similar applications. The product line includes about 60 different models. All models are produced for stock according to a schedule jointly planned by the sales and production departments.

Southeastern Motors's sales totaled $7.8 million in 1988. In the past, inventories had been tightly controlled and were dictated to a considerable extent by pro-

Figure 23–1
Minimizing Inventory Costs

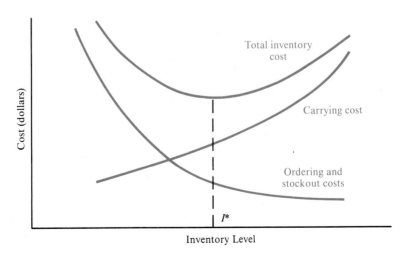

duction considerations. Inventory turnover in 1988 was 6.3 times, a figure considered quite good by industry standards. However, Southeastern management had become increasingly concerned over lost sales due to stockouts of finished-goods inventories. At year-end 1988, total inventories were $800,000, of which $200,000 was in finished goods.

Motivated by the problem of stockouts, management initiated a study to determine whether finished-goods inventories should be increased. From historical records of orders received and filled, management estimated that, at the present inventory level, lost sales due to stockouts were running at an annual rate of $625,000. What really matters is not sales but *profits,* which is equal to sales *less* variable costs. In this case, because variable costs totaled about 60 percent of sales, or $375,000, lost contribution amounted to $625,000 *less* $375,000, or about $250,000. Restating these calculations:

$$\text{Stockouts result in lost sales}$$

$$\text{Lost contribution} = \text{lost sales} - \text{variable cost}$$

$$= \$625,000 - 375,000$$

$$= \$250,000$$

The large size of the lost-contribution figure ($250,000) convinced management that further study was necessary. Lost sales were estimated at four alternative levels of finished-goods inventories associated with inventory policies A, B, C, and D, each of which represented an incremental increase over current levels. The results are listed in Table 23–1. The analysis shows that if finished-goods inventories were increased from the current level of $200,000 to $278,000, lost sales would decline from $625,000 to $475,000, and an additional contribution of $60,000 (from the last column in Table 23–1) would be realized, calculated as shown above. The additional contributions at inventory levels B, C, and D were determined in the same way.

Table 23–1

Lost Sales Estimated at Four Alternative Finished-Goods Inventory Levels at Southeastern Motors, Inc. (thousands of dollars)

Policy	Inventory Level[a]	Lost Sales	Lost Contribution[b]	Incremental Contribution
Current	200	625	250	—
A	278	475	190	60
B	414	303	121	69
C	620	153	61	60
D	868	63	25	36

[a]Finished-goods inventory only.

[b]Variable costs equal 60 percent of sales. Thus, contribution is 40 percent of sales.

The next step in the analysis of operating profit was to determine carrying costs (exclusive of financing costs) at each inventory level. These costs included warehousing, servicing, taxes, insurance, and recordkeeping, and amounted to about 5 percent of the value of the inventory. Incremental operating profit then was estimated as shown in Table 23–2. Calculations are as follows:

Carrying cost $= 0.05 \times$ inventory level

Incremental carrying cost
    for Level A $=$ Level A cost $-$ current cost

Incremental operating profit $=$ Incremental contribution (from Table 23–1)
    $-$ incremental cost

The results are shown in Table 23–2. By moving to the inventory level associated with policy A, carrying costs (excluding financing costs) would increase by $4,000. Subtracting this figure from an incremental contribution of $60,000 gives a pretax increase in operating profit of $56,000, or $28,000 after taxes (assuming a 50 percent tax rate for simplicity).

From the data in Tables 23–1 and 23–2, expected return on investment, $E(R)$, was calculated as shown in Table 23–3 (p. 668). The incremental investment at each inventory level is *additional* inventory required at that level over and above inventory at the previous level. For example, policy A requires inventory of $278,000, $78,000 more than the current policy. So $78,000 is the *incremental investment* for policy A. Calculations are as follows:

Incremental investment $=$ Additional inventory

Incremental return on investment $= \dfrac{\text{Incremental profit (from Table 23–2)}}{\text{Incremental investment}}$

Table 23–2
Estimated Incremental Operating Profit at Four Alternative Inventory Levels at Southeastern Motors, Inc. (thousands of dollars)

Policy	Inventory Level	Carrying Cost[a]	Incremental Carrying Cost	Incremental Contribution[b]	Incremental Operating Profit Before Tax	After Tax[c]
Current	200	10	—	—	—	—
A	278	14	4	60	56	28
B	414	21	7	69	62	31
C	620	31	10	60	50	25
D	868	43	12	36	24	12

[a] 5 percent of inventory level, exclusive of financing costs.
[b] From Table 23–1.
[c] Taxes at 50 percent.

Table 23–3

Expected Rate of Return, E(R), on Investment in Additional Inventory for Southeastern Motors, Inc.

Policy	Inventory Level (thousands of dollars)	Incremental Investment[a] (thousands of dollars)	Incremental After-Tax Operating Profit[b] (thousands of dollars)	Incremental After-Tax E(R) on Investment (percent)
Current	200			
A	278	78	28	35.9
B	414	136	31	22.8
C	620	206	25	12.1
D	868	248	12	4.8

[a]Out-of-pocket outlay.
[b]From Table 23–2.

To move from the current policy to policy A, Southeastern must invest an additional $78,000 in finished-goods inventory. This additional investment is expected to generate additional operating profit of $28,000 per year after taxes, yielding an expected return on the additional investment of 35.9 percent after taxes.

An important feature of the analysis above is that it examines the *incremental* return on successive *increments* of inventory. We see in Table 23–3 that, for each successive increment of inventory, the incremental, or marginal, expected return declines. As finished-goods inventories are increased, each successive increment recaptures less lost sales and, therefore, less lost contribution, as shown in the last column of Table 23–3.

This analysis examines the incremental return on successive increments of inventory.

Making the Decision

Which policy should Southeastern Motors adopt? The answer depends on the required rate of return on investment in inventories that reflects financing costs and risks. Although we will explore the required return in more detail in the next section, let us assume for the moment that Southeastern's required return is 10 percent. Looking at Table 23–3, we see that Southeastern should choose policy C and increase its inventory level to $620,000. The *expected* return of 12.1 percent in going from policy B to policy C is greater than the *required* return of 10 percent, so the move benefits the firm. On the other hand, going on to policy D is not in the firm's best interests since the expected return of 4.8 percent falls short of required return. The general rule is to keep increasing inventory investment as long as expected return exceeds required return.

There is an advantage to looking at inventory policy in terms of increments. Southeastern could have examined a single option — a major expansion of inventory from the current policy all the way to policy D. From Table 23–3, we can see that this change would require a total investment of $868,000 − $200,000 = $668,000 and would generate additional operating profit of $96,000 (found by summing the incremental operating profits in Table 23–3). The expected return of this policy change from the current policy to policy D would be $96,000/$668,000 = 14.4 percent — not bad. The expected return on the last increment from policy C to policy D, however, is only 4.8 percent.

Thus, by looking at several increments, we can better determine the point at which marginal expected return falls below the required rate. At inventory levels associated with policies A and B, expected return appears to be quite attractive. Policy D, returning only 4.8 percent after taxes compared to policy C, does not seem attractive. If management looked only at the *overall* return of 14.4 percent (previous paragraph), it might decide to go from the current policy all the way to policy D. In fact, if required return is 10 percent, it would be better to go only to policy C and not to D, because the *incremental* return from D is only 4.8 percent. By looking at increments, management can make a better-informed decision.

Even within increments, the figures in Table 23–3 represent averages. The marginal expected return on the last dollar of investment in increment B is quite a bit lower than the average expected return, 22.8 percent, on increment B as a whole.

Before discussing required return, let us note one important point. In the preceding analysis of Southeastern's inventories, we made a critical assumption about the behavior of costs. We identified the costs that vary and those that remain fixed as sales expand as a result of the recovery of lost sales. The validity of the analysis depends on our ability to correctly identify fixed and variable costs in the range of sales with which we are concerned.

> The financial manager must continually evaluate the firm's aggregate investment in inventory to ensure that, at the margin, expected return on investment in inventory is acceptable.

Required Return Versus Expected Return on Investment in Inventory

Our approach focuses on calculating expected return on the investment in inventories. This is then compared to required return. In our example for Southeastern, we made a simplifying assumption that the required return was 10 percent. Let us examine the required return in more detail.

For several different inventory levels, we determined incremental investment and operating earnings, and calculated the marginal expected rate of return. As Table 23–3 shows, expected return on investment in inventories declines as the inventory level increases. This happens because carrying costs go up, and savings from lost contribution go down. This decline in the expected return on investment is shown in Figure 23–2 on p. 670.

Also as shown in Figure 23–2, rather than remaining constant the *required* return on inventories goes up as the level of inventories increases. This happens because of risk. Investing in inventory is not riskless mainly because the recapture of lost sales is not guaranteed. As the level of inventory increases, two things happen. First, marginal expected return falls. Second, risk increases, so the required rate of return increases. Lenders and investors are risk-averse and require compensation for both time and risk. So, as risk increases, the required rate of return increases.

> As risk increases, the required rate of return increases.

Figure 23–2
Optimal Investment in Inventory

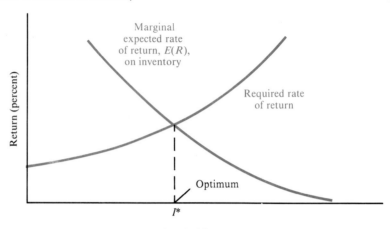

Putting expected return and required return together, Figure 23–2 shows that the optimum investment in inventory is at I^*, where the marginal expected return on investment in inventory just equals the required return. Investment at I^* is optimal because we should accept all investments when the expected return exceeds the required but not accept additional investments when expected return falls short of required return. Figure 23–2 thus provides an operational approach to finding I^*, the same I^* we saw earlier in Figure 23–1.

Inventory policy is optimal when the marginal expected return on additional investment in inventory just equals the required rate.

In practice, determining the required rate of return is not easy. We know it slopes upward from the rate on riskless investment, usually taken to be the rate on U.S. Treasury obligations. One workable approach to determining the required rate is to categorize investments into risk classes. The risk of the investment in inventory could be broken down by inventory category — raw materials, work in process, and finished goods. We discussed the required rate of return earlier in Chapter 12.

Sample Problem 23–1
Investment in Inventory for Adrianne, Inc.

Adrianne Incorporated currently has average inventory of $100,000, but management feels it has lost some sales because of occasional inventory shortages. Given the company's pretax contribution margin of 30 percent on sales (that is, variable costs are 70 percent of sales), management is concerned about lost profits. Adrianne projects that by increasing inventory to $150,000 (Policy I) it can increase sales by $30,000 a year. If inventory is increased to $200,000 (Policy II), sales would be $45,000 a year higher than they are currently. Carrying costs (exclusive of financing) will run 5 percent of inventory. Adrianne faces a 40 percent tax rate and, because of a recent drop in market rates of interest, feels that a 6 percent required rate of return is appropriate over the range of inventories being considered. What should Adrianne do in terms of inventory investment?

Solution

First we calculate the incremental investment in inventory.

	Incremental Investment
Policy I versus Current $150,000 − $100,000	$50,000
Policy II versus Policy I $200,000 − $150,000	$50,000

Note that we compare Policy II to Policy I to determine the *incremental* change.

We now need to calculate incremental profits. Our initial step is to calculate incremental contribution by multiplying additional sales by the contribution margin of 30 percent. Note that in going from Policy I to Policy II additional sales are $15,000 = $45,000 − $30,000.

	Additional Sales	Pretax Contribution Margin	Incremental Contribution
Policy I vs. Current	$30,000	0.30	$9,000
Policy II vs. Policy I	$15,000	0.30	$4,500

We now can adopt the format of Table 23–2 to calculate the incremental operating profit.

Policy	Inventory Level (dollars)	Carrying Cost[a] (dollars)	Incremental Carrying Cost (dollars)	Incremental Contribution[b] (dollars)	Incremental Operating Profit Before Tax	Incremental Operating Profit After Tax[c]
					(dollars)	(dollars)
Current	100,000	5,000	—	—		
Policy I	150,000	7,500	2,500	9,000	6,500	3,900
Policy II	200,000	10,000	2,500	4,500	2,000	1,200

7.8%
2.4%

[a]5 percent of inventory.

[b]From earlier calculations.

[c]Multiply by (1 − 0.40) where 0.40 is tax rate.

Now we can calculate marginal expected return as the ratio of incremental after-tax profit to incremental investment.

	(1) *Incremental* *After-Tax Profit* *(dollars)*	(2) *Incremental* *Investment* *(dollars)*	*(1) ÷ (2)* *Expected* *Return (percent)*
Policy I vs. Current	3,900	50,000	7.8
Policy II vs. Policy I	1,200	50,000	2.4

Given Adrianne's required rate of return of 6 percent, the company should se-lect Policy I and expand inventory to $150,000. The expected return of 7.8 percent exceeds the required return. Adrianne should not adopt Policy II since further in-creases in inventory (from $150,000 to $200,000) only provide a return of 2.4 percent, well below the required return. ▬

Managing Inventory

The financial manager usually has the primary responsibility for establishing the appropriate overall level of inventory investment.

Establishing the appropriate overall level of inventory investment usually is the primary responsibility of the financial manager. The responsibility of day-to-day management of inventory, often called *inventory control,* generally falls to the production manager in large manufacturing firms, or to someone with operating responsibilities in smaller firms or nonmanufacturing firms. Included in the pro-duction manager's responsibility is the determination of order quantities, safety stocks, and reorder points for every individual item stocked. In the case of fin-ished goods, the sales department is likely to take a strong interest in levels of safety stocks. The production manager also is responsible for ordering, receiving, handling, storing, protecting, and issuing inventory. In most firms, inventory management comprises an important set of responsibilities indeed and is a topic on which volumes have been written.[1]

The application of computers has brought major advances to inventory manage-ment. Sophisticated automated inventory-control systems are now available that integrate many necessary functions including determination of order quantities and reorder points, automatic preparation of orders, generation of accounting entries, and compilation of management information.

In most firms, policy formulation and inventory management involve an iterative process that goes on in a more or less continuous manner. Close cooperation is nec-essary between the financial manager and operating (sales and/or production) man-agers. The financial manager has the continuing responsibility of evaluating and reevaluating the firm's aggregate investment in inventory to ensure that, at the margin, expected return on investment in inventory is acceptable.

Inventory Policy in Seasonal Firms

Inventory policy in a firm with a pronounced seasonal sales pattern usually involves some additional complicating factors. A major policy question in manu-

[1]See Richard I. Levin and Charles A. Kirkpatrick, *Quantitative Approaches to Management,* 3rd ed. (New York: McGraw-Hill, 1975), Chapters 7 and 8.

facturing firms with seasonal sales is whether to produce at the same rate through the year (level production) or to gear production to seasonal sales needs. Where level production is adopted, as in the case of Mercury Tool Company from Chapter 9, inventory levels vary over the year, as inventories are built up during low sales months and are drawn down in the peak sales season.

In such situations, production and inventory policy must be considered jointly. Level production results in savings in costs of setup, hiring, training, morale, productivity, and related factors. Savings in these areas must be traded off against higher carrying costs resulting from the higher average inventory level under level production. In some situations, risk of obsolescence or deterioration may represent an important component of total carrying costs.

The return-on-investment approach is applicable to inventory decisions in seasonal firms, but the analysis is more complex. The general approach is to analyze production and inventory costs under each policy alternative. Annual expected return then can be computed using the average investment in inventory over the year.

Finance in Practice 23–2

Inventories in the Automobile Business

In 1981, General Motors executives measured their worldwide inventory and found it to be worth a whopping $9.7 billion. Facing large cash needs because of sagging profitability and needed capital expenditures, GM executives decided to cut down on inventory. As GM president F. James McDonald stated, "The incentive came from a dire need to accumulate capital without borrowing to keep our forward product schedules going." In other words, GM decided it had too much invested in inventory and decided to cut back on inventory to free funds for other investment purposes.

How could GM cut back on inventory without reducing the efficiency of the automobile production process? Part of the answer, so GM thought, was to adopt a different concept of supplier/producer relationships — the *kanban* concept proved effective by Japanese manufacturers. *Kanban,* or "just-in-time," inventory control brings parts and components to the assembly plant hours or even minutes before cars are built instead of weeks or months earlier to be stockpiled as inventory. With *kanban* inventory control, GM could have a constant stream of materials delivered with a drastic reduction in the inventory GM actually keeps on hand. One GM program manager at GM's Buick division estimated that *kanban* inventory control could reduce inventory costs by 50 percent. With multibillion-dollar inventory levels, such a reduction would represent huge dollar savings.

Moving to *kanban* inventory control could have major effects on the way GM does business. As an example, officials from GM's Buick division said that a new facility based on the *kanban* approach would need only about half the space previously required to produce a given number of cars, because less space would be required for parts storage. In addition, the *kanban* approach put a new premium on higher quality in parts. Without a stockpile of hundreds of parts to draw upon, the arrival of a supply truck full of defective parts could bring the whole automobile production facility to a standstill. The *kanban* approach also means that suppliers needed to locate closer to automobile production facilities to reduce the transportation costs of the many deliveries. According to Herb Stone, a program manager for GM, "We're working to get suppliers to build closer for three to four times daily delivery versus once a week as before." As a reflection of this need for closer location, in planning a Buick plant in Flint, Michigan, to replace outdated facilities, GM drew up its blueprints to allow for an industrial park across from the plant's loading bays where suppliers could locate.

To induce suppliers to produce higher-quality parts and locate close to automobile-production facilities, GM was prepared to give suppliers long-term contracts and to consider rewarding quality suppliers by naming them as the single source of a particular component.

In short, the *kanban* approach could change the nature of relationships with suppliers to make suppliers an integral part of the process.

The *kanban* approach to inventory control is only part of the overhaul taking place in U.S. automobile manufacture (along with the use of robots in production and the redesign of cars for fuel efficiency), but it is an important part. The decision to adopt the *kanban* approach not only reduced GM's investment in inventories, but it also required that GM change its basic business relationships with its suppliers.

Source: Adapted from J. Mateja, "'Buick City' Aims at Japanese-Style Cost-Cutting" and "GM Chief: The Dollar Made Us Do It," *Chicago Tribune,* June 26, 1983.

Investing in Accounts Receivable

We now turn our attention to accounts receivable. First we need to define some terms.

Credit Policy

Credit policy—the set of decisions made about credit standards, credit terms, and collection policy.

A firm's **credit policy** consists of the set of decisions it makes about credit standards, credit terms, and collection policy. **Credit standards** are the criteria and guidelines used by a firm to decide to which accounts it will or will not extend credit. When the standards are applied to a credit applicant, a yes or no decision can be made.

Credit terms include both the length of the credit period and the discount offered. The *credit period* is the period over which credit is granted, usually measured in days from the date of the invoice. Terms of *net 30,* for example, mean that payment is due 30 days from the date of the invoice. If a *prompt-payment discount* is offered, both the amount and the discount period must be specified. Terms of *2/10, net 30* indicate that a 2 percent cash discount may be taken if payment is made within 10 days of the invoice date; otherwise the net (full) amount is due in 30 days.

Credit terms include the length of the credit period and the discount offered.

Collection policy—the set of procedures undertaken to collect accounts that have not been paid within the specified period.

Collection policy refers to procedures undertaken to collect accounts that have not been paid within the specified period. Included might be letters, telephone calls, personal visits, and legal action. These procedures are normally the province of the credit manager and concern the financial manager only to the extent that they affect the volume of accounts receivable.

We will refer to credit standards, credit terms, and collection policy collectively as the *credit policy* of the firm. A *loosening* of credit policy is a change toward less rigorous standards in granting credit, more liberal credit terms, or less vigorous collection policies. A *tightening* of credit policy is a change in the opposite direction.

When a firm loosens its credit policy, it grants credit to additional customers who earlier would have been refused credit. As sales expand, so do accounts receivable. As receivables expand, certain costs increase, including costs of analysis and administration in the firm's credit department, costs of trying to collect doubtful accounts, and costs of accounts actually charged off as uncollectible. At the same time, as credit policy is loosened, the firm obtains new customers. Some turn out to be mistakes, as just noted; but others turn out to be good accounts and contribute to profits. So we have a trade-off: Will the profits from the new accounts that turn out to be good outweigh the losses from the new accounts that turn out bad? To answer this question, we can adopt the same approach we did to inventories. We calculate the expected return on investment in accounts receivable and then compare it to the required rate of return. First, let's look at expected return on investment in accounts receivable.

> Credit policy determines the magnitude of the firm's investment in accounts receivable and the return on that investment.

> As credit policy becomes looser, accounts receivable expand.

Calculating Expected Return on Investment in Receivables

We will illustrate the calculation of expected return on investment in accounts receivable with an example. The Delta Electric Company is a large distributor of electrical parts and equipment with facilities in 14 states. In 1988, Delta Electric's sales totaled $46 million, and after-tax profits totaled slightly more than $1 million. Delta Electric's profit margins had declined during 1987 and 1988, and the credit manager believed one reason for this was that credit policy was too loose.

To explore the credit policy question, the manager identified a group of accounts that might have been considered marginal prospects and recommended that policy be tightened to eliminate them. Sales to this group of marginal accounts amounted to about 10 percent of Delta Electric's total sales, or about $4,600,000. Sales to the remaining good accounts made up the remainder, $41,400,000.

The financial manager decided to calculate the return on investment in these accounts. The first step was to examine the behavior of Delta Electric's costs if the accounts were to be eliminated entirely, in order to get a clear comparison between a tighter credit policy and existing policies. Using historical data on costs and past knowledge of the business, the financial manager developed the data in Table 23–4. Table 23–4 (p. 676) shows the breakdown of Delta's costs into fixed and variable components.

The financial manager believed that if some of the marginal accounts were eliminated, fixed costs would remain unchanged and, hence, that only the costs identifiable as variable would decline. This manager also believed that bad debt and collection expense were almost entirely attributable to the marginal accounts. Using this information, the manager allocated Delta's income and expense between marginal accounts and good accounts as shown in Table 23–5 (p. 676).

As shown in Table 23–4, cost of goods sold is entirely variable. Hence, in Table 23–5 both good and marginal accounts have cost of goods sold of 0.87

Table 23–4

Fixed and Variable Costs for Delta Electric Company (percent of sales)

	Total Costs	Fixed Costs	Variable Costs
Cost of goods sold	87.0	—	87.0
Warehousing	5.1	2.9	2.2
Selling	4.4	0.3	4.1
Administration	1.1	1.0	0.1
Bad debts	0.13	—	0.13
Collection	0.04	—	0.04
Total costs	97.77	4.2	93.57
Operating profit	2.23		

If some marginal accounts are eliminated, fixed costs remain unchanged; only variable costs decline.

times sales. Warehousing, on the other hand, is part fixed and part variable. The fixed portion amounts to 2.9 percent of sales (from Table 23–4), or 0.029 × $46,000,000 = $1,334,000. This fixed cost presumably would not disappear if the marginal accounts were dropped, so the $1,334,000 is allocated in Table 23–5 entirely to good accounts. Variable warehousing costs of 2.2 percent are allocated

Table 23–5

Comparison of Good and Marginal Accounts at Delta Electric Company, 1988

	Fraction of Sales	All Accounts (thousands of dollars)	Good Accounts (thousands of dollars)	Marginal Accounts (thousands of dollars)
Sales		46,000	41,400	4,600
Cost of goods sold	0.87	40,020	36,018	4,002
Gross profit		5,980	5,382	598
Warehousing expense				
Fixed	0.029	1,334	1,334	—
Variable	0.022	1,012	911	101
Selling expense				
Fixed	0.003	138	138	—
Variable	0.041	1,886	1,697	189
Administration expense				
Fixed	0.001	460	460	—
Variable	0.001	46	41	5
Bad debts	0.0013	60	—	60
Collection	0.0004	20	—	20
Total operating expense		4,956	4,581	375
Operating profit		1,024	801	223

to both categories. This variable cost, then, is 0.022 × $41,400,000 = $910,800 in the case of good accounts and 0.022 × $4,600,000 = $101,200 in the case of marginal accounts. This allocation assumes that, if the marginal accounts were dropped, costs would decline by $101,200, but $910,800 of the variable costs would continue. In Table 23–5, these figures are rounded to the nearest thousand.

Selling and administrative expenses are allocated in a similar manner, with the entire fixed portion allocated to good accounts, and the variable portion allocated to both categories. Bad-debt and collection expenses are assumed to be entirely attributable to marginal accounts. Adding up the figures shows that, of the total operating expense of $4,956,000, $4,581,000 is identified with the good accounts, and $375,000 is associated with the marginal accounts.

Assuming the allocations shown in Table 23–5 are approximately correct, what conclusions should the financial manager draw from these figures? The profit margin from the two sets of accounts can be calculated as follows:

$$\text{Profit margin} = \frac{\text{Operating profit}}{\text{Sales}}.$$

These calculations are made in Table 23–6.

In other words, the marginal clients accounted for only 10 percent of sales, but they provided about 22 percent of total operating profit (from Table 23–5, $223,000/ $1,024,000 = 0.218). Because most of Delta Electric's credit-management costs are incurred anyway in order to service the good accounts, the *incremental* profits contributed by the marginal accounts provided a significant addition to the company's total operating profits.

Calculating the Investment in Receivables

In order to complete the preliminary analysis, it is necessary to estimate the level of additional *investment* the firm had to make to sell and service the so-called marginal accounts. Delta Electric's credit files indicated that the receivables balance on marginal accounts averaged $567,000 during 1988. However, this figure overstates the amount the firm had to invest in accounts receivable in order to achieve its sales to the marginal accounts, because this $567,000 figure includes a profit margin on sales, which does not constitute funds actually invested by Delta

Table 23–6

The Profit Margin on Delta Electric Company's Good Accounts and Marginal Accounts

Accounts	Sales Volume (thousands of dollars)	Operating Profit (thousands of dollars)	Profit Margin (percent)
Good	41,400	801	1.94
Marginal	4,600	223	4.85

Electric. Only the *variable-cost* component of accounts receivable on the marginal accounts represents funds actually invested, or put at risk, by Delta Electric in order to sell to the marginal accounts.

From our discussion earlier, we see that marginal accounts generated pretax profits of $223,000 on sales of $4,600,000 — a profit margin of 4.85 percent. Thus, 4.85 percent of the earnings on marginal accounts is profit, and the remaining 95.2 percent is variable cost. Hence, about 95.2 percent of $567,000 (about $540,000) represents the average amount the firm had to risk in order to sell to its marginal accounts, or the amount Delta Electric had *invested* in the marginal accounts. The calculations are as follows:

$$\text{Accounts receivable (marginal accounts)} = \$567,000.$$

The variable-cost component on marginal accounts receivable represents the firm's investment in those accounts.

Calculate investment in receivables *at cost:*

$$\text{Cost} = \text{total receivables less profit}$$

$$= 0.952 \times \$567,000$$

$$= \$540,000 = \text{investment in receivables at cost}.$$

Now let us calculate the return on the investment in receivables. The pretax return per dollar of investment is annual pretax operating profit divided by total investment, or

Incremental profit on marginal
accounts (Table 23–6)   = $223,000

Investment in marginal accounts = $540,000

Return on investment   = Profit/investment

                               = $223,000/$540,000

                               = 41.3 percent pretax.

To determine the after-tax return on investment, we can multiply this 41.3 percent times $(1 - T)$, where T is the tax rate. We assume a 40 percent tax rate for Delta Electric.

$$\text{After-tax return} = \text{pretax return} \times (1 - T)$$

$$= 0.413 \times (1 - 0.40)$$

$$= 0.248 = 24.8 \text{ percent after tax}.$$

Our calculations show that the after-tax return on the marginal accounts was 24.8 percent per year. If Delta Electric made future sales to these marginal accounts and had no reason to expect changes from past experience, the expected rate of return, $E(R)$, on such new sales would also be 24.8 percent. If Delta Electric's management views a 24.8 percent return as attractive, the preliminary analysis above indicates that the financial manager might consider a move to *loosen* credit policy still further rather than a move toward a tighter policy.

Refining the Analysis

Before a decision about Delta Electric's credit policy is made, additional refinements of the analysis are possible; indeed, in many situations such refinements are necessary.

First, our calculation of the required investment included only accounts receivable. In practice, expanding the level of sales to include the marginal accounts would probably require some increase in the level of inventories held as well as some increase in operating cash balances, and these increases are also relevant elements in estimating the total investment required. Of course, any increase in accounts payable or other accruals would provide an offset.

Second, we have also assumed that the fixed costs shown in Table 23–4 would, in fact, remain fixed even if sales to marginal accounts are expanded. (Recall that the manager had determined that they were fixed with respect to a decline in sales, but had not explicitly considered an increase in sales.)

Refining our estimates to include these two considerations would probably give us a figure somewhat below 24.8 percent per annum for the expected after-tax operating rate of return from our incremental sales to more marginal accounts.

Expected Returns Versus Required Return on Investment in Accounts Receivable

Our final step in evaluating investments in accounts receivable is to ask this critical question: Given the riskiness of the marginal accounts, is the expected after-tax rate of return adequate to justify the investment? To answer this question, we must compare expected return to required return. If the expected return exceeds the required return, the investment is a good one. In terms of Delta Electric's decision, if the required return is less than the expected return of 24.8 percent (or whatever the expected rate might be after further refinements), the company should definitely continue granting credit to the marginal accounts. Let's look at the comparison of expected and required return in general terms.

> The credit decision requires the financial manager to compare the expected return to the required return.

We noted earlier that expenses of analysis, collection, and bad debts rise at an increasing rate as credit policy is loosened. If Delta Electric were to loosen its policy, these expenses would rise in relation to the new sales generated, and the expected rate of return, $E(R)$, on the newly made investment in accounts receivable accompanying the new sales would be lower than the expected return on previous investments in accounts receivable. The expected return on the *new,* or incremental, investment is the **marginal expected return.** In general, we would expect the marginal expected return to become lower and lower as the firm loosened its credit policy. Figure 23–3 on p. 680 illustrates this fall in marginal expected return.

> **Marginal expected return** — the expected rate of return on incremental investment.

As receivables expand, accounts obtained by loosening credit policy become progressively more risky. Starting with a very tight policy, the cash flows associated with the first group of new accounts may be subject to little uncertainty, because only the very best customers are granted credit. As policy becomes progressively looser, accounts become subject to an increasing probability of de-

Figure 23–3
Optimal Investment in Receivables and Inventory

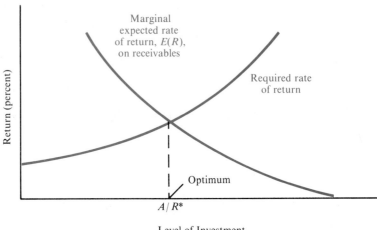

fault. So, as receivables increase, risk goes up, and as risk goes up, the required rate of return goes up, as shown in Figure 23–3.

How far should credit policy be pushed? The optimal level of investment in receivables is shown as $A/R*$ in Figure 23–3. Credit policy should be set at the point where the marginal expected return on additional investment in receivables just equals the return required by those who supply the firm's funds — the lenders and investors. At that point, the value of the firm is maximized.

Credit policy often is viewed as a marketing tool with the purpose of expanding sales. The *real* objective of credit policy is to maximize the value of the firm. Clearly, the goal is not to maximize sales, just as it is clearly not to minimize bad-debt expense. To maximize sales, the firm would sell to anyone on credit; to minimize bad-debt expense, it would sell to no one. The value-maximization policy lies somewhere in between, and analyzing return on investment gives us a method of finding it.

> The goal of credit policy is to maximize the value of the firm. The optimal policy is the one at which the marginal expected return on incremental investment in receivables equals the required rate.

Implementing Credit Policy

Once credit policy has been formulated, it must be translated into operational guidelines for use by the sales and credit departments. Of particular importance are credit standards for selecting individual accounts, because it is through individual decisions, account by account, that policy is implemented.

Selecting Individual Accounts

In principle, the correct approach to selecting accounts is to calculate expected return on each and make a judgment as to whether this expected return is above

Policy is implemented
through individual decisions,
account by account.

the required rate. Calculated expected return on an individual account follows the
same general procedure as that discussed earlier for groups of accounts. Expected
earnings are estimated over some convenient period, usually a year, and the investment necessary to generate those earnings is determined. Here again, the relevant investment amount is the out-of-pocket cash investment that the firm actually
will have at risk at any point in time.

Sample Problem 23–2

Analyzing the Tarheel Industries Account for Chatham Supply Company

Suppose Tarheel Industries requests open-account credit of $2,500 from Chatham
Supply Company for purchase of parts. Chatham estimates that the account will
turn over four times per year; that is, it will generate $10,000 per year in sales
volume. Chatham's gross margin on the parts to be sold is 20 percent, and commissions to sales representatives are 2 percent. There are no other variable
costs associated with taking on the account. What would be the pretax rate of return on the account? What would be the after-tax rate of return on the account?

Solution

We begin by estimating the profit Chatham would earn over a year's time. Gross
profit is 20 percent of sales, or $2,000; subtracting the 2 percent sales commis-
sions leaves a profit before tax of $2,000 − $200 = $1,800. To simplify things,
assume that Tarheel Industries orders $2,500 worth of parts, pays for them 45
days later, and then in another 45 days places another order, repeating this process
four times per year. While credit is outstanding, Chatham's investment would be
determined by subtracting profit of 20 percent (0.2 × $2,500 = $500) from the
$2,500 order and adding sales commissions of 2 percent (0.02 × $2,500 = $50).
Thus, $2,500 − $500 + $50 = $2,050.

During the periods when Tarheel Industries has purchased goods but has not
yet paid for them, Chatham has out-of-pocket investment at risk of $2,050. But
during 45 days of each 90-day period, Tarheel Industries owes nothing. So the
average investment over the year is only $2,050/2 = $1,025. The expected rate
of return on investment, then, is $1,800/$1,025 = 175 percent before taxes. Not
bad, and probably good enough to induce Chatham to do business with Tarheel. If
taxes are 40 percent, this return is 175(1 − 0.40) = 105 percent after taxes.

The figure of 175 percent, of course, assumes that Tarheel stays in business for
a year and pays its bills. Thus, 175 percent, or 105 percent after taxes, is the *prospective* return if everything works out as planned. If all of Chatham's accounts
actually returned this much, Chatham's owners would get very rich. The problem,
of course, is that some accounts will not pay on time or perhaps at all.

Although credit policy is
implemented by making
decisions on individual
accounts, sometimes it is
advisable to set standards
and targets for categories
of accounts.

Calculating expected return on individual accounts is expensive and often cannot
be justified on every account. If groups of accounts with similar characteristics
can be identified in terms of the product mix sold to the accounts and the rate of
sales, shortcuts may be possible. For example, it may be found that in a particular
group of accounts, the only major difference among accounts is in probability of

default. It might be possible to calculate a target default probability at which point the expected return falls below the required rate. Accounts then would be analyzed only to estimate default probability, with those above the target rejected and those below accepted.

Other more sophisticated techniques of grouping accounts are available. **Discriminant analysis** is a technique for discriminating between good and bad accounts based on certain readily available financial data such as firm size, acid-test ratio, or accounts-payable payment period. The development of a model based on discriminant analysis involves complex statistical techniques but may be worthwhile for large firms that can justify the development expense.

A similar technique, known as **credit scoring,** has been employed with some success in consumer credit. In this approach, selection criteria are developed by relating past default experience to certain characteristics of the applicant, such as age, marital status, income, net worth, house ownership, and so on. New applicants are then scored, and a decision is made based on a predetermined cutoff point. As with discriminant analysis, the objective of credit scoring is to reduce the expense of selecting accounts that have a high likelihood of meeting the return criterion.

Monitoring Payment Patterns

Payment patterns by customers affect both the investment in accounts receivable and the return on that investment. It is, therefore, necessary to monitor payment patterns closely to detect any changes that might be occurring as a result of a recession, because of a change in the application of credit policy, or for other reasons.

In Chapter 7, we discussed two measures for use in evaluating a firm's collection of receivables: **days sales outstanding (DSO)** and the accounts-receivable **aging schedule.** These two measures are widely used and are perfectly adequate in many situations, but in some they are not.

Days sales outstanding is calculated by dividing the accounts-receivable balance at any point in time by credit sales per day. The DSO figure thus depends on three main factors: sales rate, averaging period (whether the most recent month, quarter, or year), and underlying pattern of payment by customers. This third factor is the one we wish to monitor, but changes in the sales rate or averaging period can produce widely varying DSO figures even when the underlying payment pattern remains stable.[2] In a firm with a seasonal sales pattern, for example, DSO figures will vary over the year even when the payment pattern remains unchanged.

The aging schedule suffers from the same difficulty. For example, the percentage of accounts less than, say, 30 days old will increase during periods when the sales rate rises and decrease when the sales rate declines. An aging schedule in a seasonal firm will thus be different at different times during the year, even when payment patterns are stable.

In many applications, DSO and the aging schedule are adequate measures of payment patterns. Where a more refined technique is needed, a useful approach is

Discriminant analysis—a technique for discriminating between good and bad accounts based on certain readily available financial data, such as firm size, acid-test ratio, or accounts-payable payment period.

Credit scoring—a technique for discriminating between good and bad accounts in which selection criteria are developed by relating past default experience to certain characteristics of the applicant.

Days sales outstanding (DSO)—the ratio of accounts receivable to credit sales per day.

Aging schedule—a technique for analyzing accounts receivable by cataloging receivables outstanding according to due dates.

---

[2]For a good discussion of this problem, see Wilber G. Lewellen and Robert W. Johnson, "Better Way to Monitor Accounts Receivable," *Harvard Business Review* 50, 3 (May/June 1972): 101–109.

to identify receivables as to the month of origination—that is, the month in which the sale was made. In this way, the proportion of receivables arising from each prior month can be monitored. One way to organize the data is shown in Table 23–7.[3] The left-hand column of the table lists the month in which the original sales were made, and the column heads to the right indicate the calendar month in which the receivables remain outstanding. Thus, for example, the figure of 19 percent in the bottom of the January column tells us that 19 percent of the sales made in November (two months before January) were still outstanding and uncollected at the end of January. An increase in the fraction of receivables outstanding implies a corresponding *decrease* in payments received. These data indicate that Delta Electric's customers slowed their payments somewhat in February and March and then accelerated again in April. By identifying receivables balances by month of origination, changes in payment pattern can be detected.

Credit-Department Procedures

Credit-department procedures are the province of the credit manager, but because the credit function is often under the overall supervision of the financial manager, we will touch briefly on these procedures.

Activities of the credit department fall into two main categories: credit analysis and collection. Credit analysis determines the selection of account—that is, the decision of whether or not to grant credit. In establishing procedures, a benefit/cost point of view must be maintained. Analysis is expensive, and care must be taken to see that the costs of the analysis and selection procedure do not exceed the potential earnings. The extent of the effort devoted to individual accounts must be related to the size of the account or the order and to its riskiness—although the latter cannot be determined until some analysis is performed. Ideally, we would like to devote little effort to accounts of very low and very high risk and concen-

Table 23–7

Receivables as a Percent of Original Sales for Delta Electric Company

Period Used as Sales Base	Receivables Outstanding as of Month End (percent of sales base)				
	January	*February*	*March*	*April* · · ·	*December*
Same month	89	91	93	90	90
One month before	62	65	67	61	63
Two months before	19	23	27	22	21

[3]The approach discussed here is that recommended by Lewellen and Johnson, "Better Way to Monitor Accounts Receivable" (see footnote 2). See also B. K. Stone, "The Payments Approach to the Forecasting and Control of Accounts Receivable," *Financial Management* 5 (Autumn 1976): 65–82. Stone provides a good discussion of the relationship between the receivables-balance fraction outstanding (as in Table 23–7) and the payment proportion—the fraction of an account paid in each month following a sale.

trate on those in the middle. The performance measures discussed in Part Three are often useful for making preliminary judgments as to whether further analysis is justified. Where detailed analysis is appropriate, the approaches discussed earlier in this chapter are applicable.

Analysis must begin with information, and the starting point usually is the applicant's own financial statements. Also useful are specialized sources, such as Dun & Bradstreet, which provides a *credit-reference book* containing basic data on line of business, net worth, and credit rating for a large number of firms. Dun & Bradstreet *credit reports* then provide much more detailed data on individual firms. Other sources of credit information include local credit bureaus, banks, and other firms.

Collection procedures are also an important area of concern to the credit manager. Collection normally becomes an issue only after an account is past due. A basic question, therefore, is how long an account should be allowed to go past due before collection procedures are initiated. Many techniques then can be applied, including letters, telephone calls, personal visits, and finally a collection agency or legal action. The guiding principle in deciding how far to go to collect an account is benefits versus costs. Collection is expensive, and we do not want to spend $200 to collect a $100 account.

> Credit-department activities fall into two main categories: credit analysis and collection.

> Collection is expensive: to justify the expense, benefits must exceed costs.

Evaluating the Credit Function

Evaluating the credit function in a firm is an important responsibility of the financial manager. The responsibility includes both the evaluation of credit policy and the performance of the credit department itself in executing the policy.

From our earlier discussion, it is apparent that neither sales nor bad-debt expense can be used as a guide in evaluating credit policy. The proper criterion is expected return on investment, and the firm's investment in receivables must be analyzed periodically to ensure that expected-return guidelines are being met. In evaluating rate of return, the costs of the credit department itself must be taken into account.

KEY CONCEPTS

1. From the perspective of financial management, the proper level of inventory and accounts receivable should be viewed as an investment decision.

2. The basic function of inventories is to decouple the major activities of the firm — purchasing, production, and sales — so that all do not have to proceed at the same rate.

3. The optimal inventory level is determined by balancing carrying costs against ordering and stockout costs.

4. Inventory policy can be set by calculating the rate of return on the incremental investment in inventories and comparing this to the required rate of return.

5. The appropriate credit policy is determined by trading off costs of analysis, collection, and bad debts against opportunity costs of lost sales.

6. Accounts-receivable policy can be set by calculating the rate of return on the incremental investment in receivables.

7. The goal of inventory policy and credit policy is to maximize the value of the firm. This is done by expanding inventory and receivables to the point where expected return equals required return.

SUMMARY

The financial manager should view the expansion of inventories and accounts receivable as *investment decisions,* using value maximization as the decision criterion. Inventories and receivables should be expanded to the point where the marginal expected return on additional investment equals the return required by suppliers of funds.

The financial manager should be concerned with the return on investment in inventories. Inventories serve as buffers to decouple the purchasing, production, and sales activities of the firm so that all do not have to proceed at the same rate and so that unexpected events are not disruptive. Such buffers are necessary because of transaction costs (friction losses) and uncertainty. As inventories are expanded, some costs rise and others decline. Costs that rise with increases in inventory (or carrying costs) include financing costs, storage costs, servicing costs, and risk of loss in value. Costs that decline with increases in inventory include costs of ordering, production, and lost sales.

The optimal inventory policy must consider not only profit but also return on investment. The expected return on incremental investment in inventory can be calculated by identifying the various elements of operating cost associated with different inventory levels, calculating incremental operating profit, and dividing by the required incremental investment.

A firm's credit policy includes credit standards, credit terms, and collection procedures. Taken together, the three elements of credit policy determine the size of the firm's investment in accounts receivable and the return on that investment. As credit policy is loosened, accounts receivable expand. Costs of analysis, collection, and bad debts rise, while opportunity costs of lost sales decline. The expected return on incremental investment in accounts receivable can be calculated using data on costs of servicing different categories of accounts.

Once overall credit policy has been formulated using a return-on-investment approach, the policy must be implemented by means of decisions on individual accounts. A return-on-investment approach can be utilized but is often too expensive for individual accounts. Analytical techniques such as discriminant analysis and credit scoring may be useful. Payment patterns must be monitored to detect changes requiring management attention.

The objective of both credit policy and inventory policy is to maximize the value of the firm. In both cases, the policy that accomplishes this objective lies at the point where marginal expected operating return just equals the return necessary to compensate suppliers of funds.

QUESTIONS

Note: Questions preceded by an asterisk (*) require knowledge of the material in Appendix 23A.

1. Describe the three major types of inventory.

2. What are the principal costs of holding inventories?

3. With respect to inventory, how might the perspectives of the financial manager and the production manager differ?

4. What is the objective of credit policy?

5. Why is the expected return on an investment in accounts receivable subject to uncertainty? Why is the expected return on an investment in inventory subject to uncertainty?

6. Discuss the problem of monitoring payment patterns in seasonal firms.

7. Suppose that the Delta Electric Company described in this chapter and a local bank are both considering extending credit to the same customer. Why might Delta and the bank arrive at different decisions?

8. With respect to accounts receivable, how might the perspective of the financial manager differ from that of the credit manager?

*9. On what does the optimal size of the safety stock depend?

*10. "The function of the safety stock is to prevent stockouts." Is this statement true or false? Explain.

Problems

Note: Problems preceded by an asterisk (*) require knowledge of the material in Appendix 23A.

1. Jackson Manufacturing Company uses inventory turnover as one performance measure by which to evaluate its production manager. Currently, Jackson's inventory turnover (CGS/inventory) is ten times per year compared with an industry average of four times. Average sales are $450,000 per year. Variable costs have consistently remained at 70 percent of sales with fixed costs of $10,000. Carrying costs of inventory (excluding financing costs) are 5 percent annually. Jackson's sales force has complained that low inventory levels are resulting in lost sales due to stockouts. The sales manager has made the estimates based on stockout reports which appear in Table A. On the basis of these estimates, assuming a 46 percent tax rate and an after-tax required rate of return of 15 percent on investment in inventory, what inventory policy would you recommend? (Hint: Use Table A as a worksheet.)

2. The management of Bland Company is concerned about the seemingly large losses it has been experiencing in lost sales due to frequent stockouts. The company has been carrying a finished-goods inventory of $150,000 and has estimated lost sales at $525,000 per year. Variable costs have consistently remained at 75 percent of sales, and carrying costs of inventory (excluding financing costs) are 4 percent annually. Assuming a tax rate of 46 percent, an after-tax required rate of return of 15 percent on investment in inventory, and the projected figures shown in Table B (in thousands of dollars), determine the optimal level of inventory for the company.

3. Lenk, Inc., a manufacturer of office equipment, expects to have sales of $20 million under current operating policies. Variable costs comprise 80 percent of sales, and the company's cost of capital is 16 percent. Currently, Lenk's credit policy is net 25, but its average collection period is 30 days. This concerns the financial manager, who would like the company to consider tightening the credit policy in an effort to crack down on delinquent accounts. The sales manager, on the other hand, has suggested loosening the credit policy in order to increase sales volume.

Table A

									Incremental Operating Profit			E(R) of Incremental
Policy	*Turnover (times)*	*Inventory Level*	*Lost Sales*	*Cost of Goods Sold*	*Contribution*	*Incremental Contribution*	*Carrying Cost*	*Incremental Carrying Cost*	*Before Tax*	*After Tax*	*Incremental Investment*	*Investment (percent)*
Current	10	___	450	___	___	___						
A	8	___	500	___	___	___	___	___	___	___	___	___
B	6	___	540	___	___	___	___	___	___	___	___	___
C	4	___	565	___	___	___	___	___	___	___	___	___

Thousands of Dollars

Table B

							Change in Operating Profit			Incremental E(R) on Investment(%
Policy	Inventory Level	Lost Sales	Lost Contribution	Change in Contribution	Carrying Cost	Change in Carrying Cost	Before Tax	After Tax	Incremental Investment	After Tax)
Current	150	525	——		——					
A	200	375	——	——	——	——	——	——	——	——
B	250	250	——	——	——	——	——	——	——	——
C	300	150	——	——	——	——	——	——	——	——
D	350	75	——	——	——	——	——	——	——	——
E	400	25	——	——	——	——	——	——	——	——
F	450	0	——	——	——	——	——	——	——	——

In response to these arguments, the credit manager is considering two alternative proposals for changing Lenk's credit policy. Proposal A would lengthen the credit period to net 40, and is expected to increase sales by $4,350,000 and to increase days sales outstanding (DSO) on all sales to 45 days. Proposal B would shorten the credit period to net 20, and is expected to decrease sales volume by $2,750,000 and to decrease DSO to 22 days on all sales. All other costs are identical under the current and proposed policies. Which proposal should be adopted?

4. The Candee Corporation is considering liberalizing its credit policies to allow higher-risk customers to buy on credit terms of net 30. The credit department has been informed that variable costs will remain at 80 percent of sales over the new potential sales levels. All new sales will be on credit, and the projected information for each risk class is as shown in Table C. The scale of required returns reflects the increased risk perceived for each risk class of customers. Which, if any, of the risk classes should Candee allow to buy on credit? Assume a 365-day year and a 50 percent tax rate.

5. Assume the credit department for Candee Corporation realized it had failed to include all the

Table C

Risk Class	Required Return (percent)	Average Collection Period (days)	New Sales (thousands of dollars)
3	0.12	38	500
4	0.15	45	400
5	0.19	58	300
6	0.25	70	200

Table D

Risk Class	Default Rate (percent)	Increased Credit Department Expense
3	4	$5,000
4	7	$5,000
5	12	$5,000
6	20	$5,000

relevant costs in problem (4), and the additional information in Table D is submitted. Which risk classes should Candee allow to buy on credit?

6. The CBM Company currently offers credit terms of 1/10, net 30, on annual credit sales of $3,000,000. An average of 50 percent of the current customers take the discount, and the

average collection period has consistently remained at 35 days. The percentage default rate has been 1 percent. The company is considering two alternative changes in credit terms as outlined in Table E. If sales are projected to remain stable under either alternative and the required rate of return on investment in accounts receivable is 20 percent, what strategy would you recommend for CBM? (Assume a 50 percent tax rate.)

Table E

Credit Terms	Customers Taking Discount (percent)	Average Collection Period (days)	Default Rate (percent)
2/10, net 30	75	18	0.005
3/10, net 20	98	12	0.001

7. Delta Electric Company is considering a request from Bill's Electronics for open-account credit in the amount of $1,000 (figured at Delta's selling price). Delta's gross margin on the particular merchandise to be purchased by Bill's is 17 percent. Delta's salesperson expects Bill's to purchase $5,000 of merchandise annually. On all sales, Delta will incur variable expenses of 2 percent for the salesperson's commissions and 1.5 percent for warehousing.

   a. Calculate the annual expected return on the prospective account with Bill's.

   b. Suppose Delta establishes 30 percent as the required rate of return on accounts in the risk class in which Bill's falls. Is Bill's account acceptable?

8. The financial officers of MVB, Inc., are concerned that their current credit policy of 75-day terms may be too loose when compared with their competitors' 30-day credit terms. MVB's annual average sales are $1.2 million. Variable costs are 75 percent of sales with fixed costs of $100,000. MVB is considering several alternative credit policies as shown in worksheet Table F. Assuming a required rate of return on investment in accounts receivable of 20 percent, which policy would you recommend? (Assume a 360-day year and that all sales are on credit with the average collection period equal to the terms given. For simplicity, assume there are no taxes.)

*9. A firm has a $50-per-year carrying cost (including costs of financing) on each unit of inventory, an annual usage rate of 10,000 units, and an ordering cost of $100 per order. Ignore any potential stockout costs.

   a. Calculate the economic order quantity for the firm.

   b. What would be the total annual inventory costs of the firm if it orders in this quantity?

*10. Assume that the supplier for the firm in problem (7) offers a quantity discount of $0.30 per unit if the firm orders in lots of 400 units. Should the firm accept the quantity discount?

Table F

				Thousands of Dollars					
Policy	Terms	Sales	Cost of Goods Sold	Total Contribution	Change in Contribution	Average A/R	Change in A/R	Incremental Return Forgone (percent)
Current	75 days	1,200	_____	_____		_____		
A	60 days	1,130	_____	_____	_____	_____	_____	_____
B	45 days	1,050	_____	_____	_____	_____	_____	_____
C	30 days	950	_____	_____	_____	_____	_____	_____

*11. Marston Industries is reviewing its inventory policy regarding one of its essential raw materials. The production manager has compiled the following information: orders must be placed in multiples of 100 units; usage for the year is 280,000 units; the purchase price per unit is $7.50; carrying costs (including financing costs) are 30 percent of the purchasing price of the goods; order costs per order are $150,000; desired safety stock is 35,000 units, which is the amount currently in inventory; 10 days are required for delivery. The credit manager has asked you to provide the following information:

a. What is the economic order quantity?

b. How many orders should Marston place per year?

c. At what level of inventory would these orders be placed?

12. The Broyhill Finishing Company uses 1,000 gallons of dye #704 per day. The dye can be purchased in 100-gallon drums for $50 per drum or in 1,000-gallon drums for $450 per drum. Ordering costs are $10 per order. The company's accountant has estimated the following costs associated with carrying inventory: The required rate of return for funds invested in inventory is 15 percent; depreciation and property tax on warehouse space occupied are $100 per month (there is no alternative use for this warehouse space at the present time); and insurance on inventory is 5 percent of cost per year.

a. What is the economic order quantity assuming that only 100-gallon drums can be ordered? Assume 250 working days per year.

b. What is the economic order quantity assuming that only 1,000-gallon drums can be ordered?

c. Assuming that the firm must order one size or the other and not mix them, which drum size and ordering policy would you recommend?

REFERENCES

Carpenter, M. D., and J. E. Miller, "A Reliable Framework for Monitoring Accounts Receivable." *Financial Management* 8 (Winter 1979): 37–41.

Levin, R. I., and C. A. Kirkpatrick. *Quantitative Approaches to Management.* 3d ed. New York: McGraw-Hill, 1975.

Lewellen, W. G., and R. W. Johnson, "Better Way to Monitor Accounts Receivable." *Harvard Business Review* 50 (May–June 1972): 21–32.

Mehta, D. R. *Working Capital Management.* Englewood Cliffs, N.J.: Prentice-Hall, 1974.

Stone, B. K., "The Payments-Pattern Approach to the Forecasting and Control of Accounts Receivable." *Financial Management* 5 (Autumn 1976): 65–82.

Vander Weide, J., and S. F. Maier, *Managing Corporate Liquidity.* New York: John Wiley & Sons, 1985.

Appendix 23A

Inventory-Decision Models

The use of inventories as buffer stocks has been studied extensively, and a large body of inventory theory has been developed. Inventory theory has been found useful for studying a broad class of problems in addition to the problems of stocking raw materials and finished goods in a firm. Cash and liquidity, for example, can be viewed as inventories and analyzed using inventory theory.[4]

Inventory theory — the theory of how much should be ordered and when it should be ordered.

Inventory theory addresses two basic questions: (1) *How much* should be ordered? (2) *When* should it be ordered?

The first question — how much to order — arises because of "friction" in the form of ordering costs, setup costs, and the like. The second question — when to order — arises because the world is uncertain.

The Economic Order Quantity

Economic order quantity (EOQ) — the optimal quantity of goods to be ordered, determined by trading off ordering costs (or setup costs) against carrying costs.

Taking these two questions one at a time, we will deal with friction first and assume for the moment that no uncertainty exists with respect to the future. Inventory models deal with the question of how much to order by defining an **economic order quantity (EOQ)**. The EOQ is determined by trading off ordering costs (or setup costs) against carrying costs. A larger order quantity reduces the frequency of ordering and thus reduces total ordering costs but increases the average inventory level and therefore increases carrying costs. The optimal order quantity can be defined as shown in Equation (A–1):[5]

$$EOQ = \sqrt{\frac{2RO}{C}} \qquad (A-1)$$

where R = the usage per period in units, O = the ordering cost per order, and C = the carrying cost per unit per period.

[4] See William J. Baumol, "The Transactions Demand for Cash — An Inventory-Theoretic Approach," *Quarterly Journal of Economics* 65 (November 1952): 545–56; Merton H. Miller and Daniel Orr, "A Model of the Demand for Money by Firms," *Quarterly Journal of Economics* 80 (August 1966): 413–35; and Yair E. Orgler, *Cash Management* (Belmont, Cal.: Wadsworth, 1970).

[5] For a detailed development and discussion of the EOQ model, see Richard I. Levin and Charles A. Kirkpatrick, *Quantitative Approaches to Management,* 3rd ed. (New York: McGraw-Hill, 1975).

To illustrate the use of the EOQ formula, consider an item that is used at the rate of 100 units per year. Ordering costs are $25 per order, and carrying costs are $20 per unit per year. The EOQ can then be calculated as

$$\text{EOQ} = \sqrt{\frac{2(1,000)\,(25)}{20}} = 50 \text{ units} .$$

Assuming that the usage rate is uniform, we can illustrate the ordering and usage process as shown in Figure 23A–1. At time t_0, 50 units are received and consumed over the period t_0 to t_1. At t_1, another 50 units are ordered. We can see that the average inventory level is 25 units, so that total carrying costs for the year are 25 units $\times$ $20 per unit = $500. We must place a total of 1,000/50 = 20 orders per year, so total ordering costs also are $500 per year. The sum of ordering and carrying costs is $1,000 per year. With a little arithmetic, we can verify that total costs are higher at any order quantity other than 50 units.

The EOQ formula is widely used in inventory control to determine optimal order quantities. To use the EOQ formula in quantitative applications, the cost of financing must be included as a component of carrying cost. Often, this cost is approximated using the interest cost of debt. Investment in inventory is not riskless, however, so the interest rate may understate the real cost of financing, which is the return required by lenders and investors. The use of the interest rate may be

Figure 23A–1
The Economic-Order-Quantity Model

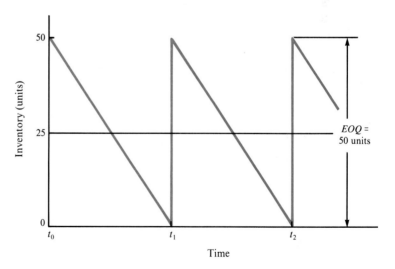

a satisfactory approximation for the production manager to use in calculating order quantities for individual items. When financial managers view inventory as an investment decision, they must take risk into account and require a return higher than the interest rate on debt.

In addition to its usefulness in quantitative applications, the EOQ model yields several useful qualitative insights. We see the importance of friction costs; if ordering costs were zero, the EOQ would be zero. The firm would order continuously at the usage rate, holding no inventory at all. We see also that the EOQ and, therefore, the average inventory level vary with the square root of usage. Thus, a doubling of usage does not double the optimal inventory level, but rather increases it by the square root of 2, or by about 1.4 times.

The basic EOQ model discussed above assumes that delivery is instantaneous when an order is placed. If delivery lead time is known with certainty, the EOQ is unchanged. The order is simply placed earlier by the number of days required for delivery. We will discuss the effects of uncertain delivery times in the next section. The availability of quantity discounts does alter the EOQ and can be handled by modifying the analysis. However, because quantity discounts are of secondary importance to our discussion here, we will not deal with them.[6]

> The economic order quantity takes into account usage rate, ordering costs, and carrying costs.

Sample Problem 23A–1
Determining the Economic Order Quantity for Tampa Building Company

Tampa Building Company sells 5,000 three-speed drills a year. The cost of holding inventory is $20 per drill per year, and ordering costs are $80 per order.

A. Determine Tampa's economic order quantity for three-speed drills, ignoring any potential stockout costs.

B. Determine the total annual inventory costs associated with this economic order quantity.

Solution

A. The economic order quantity (EOQ) can be found by applying Equation (A–1) as

$$EOQ = \sqrt{\frac{2\,(5{,}000)\,(80)}{20}} = 200 \text{ drills}.$$

[6]For a treatment of the quantity discount in EOQ models, see Levin and Kirkpatrick, *Quantitative Approaches to Management*, Chapter 7.

B. The total inventory costs are composed of ordering and carrying costs. The total ordering cost is equal to the number of orders placed times the cost per order. The total carrying cost is equal to the average number of units in inventory times the carrying cost per unit. For Tampa, the number of orders placed equals 5,000 drills/200 drills per order, or 25 orders. Total ordering costs, then, are 25 orders × $80 per order = $2,000. The average inventory is 200 drills per order/2 = 100 drills. The total carrying costs are 100 drills × $20 per drill = $2,000, and the total annual inventory costs are $2,000 total ordering costs plus $2,000 total carrying costs, or $4,000. ■■■■

Safety Stocks

In practice, uncertainty is likely to exist with respect to delivery times, production rates, and sales rates.

Safety stock — additional inventory over and above that prescribed by the EOQ formula.

The optimal size of safety stock depends on stockout costs, carrying costs, and the probability that stockouts will occur.

Now let us reintroduce uncertainty. In practice, uncertainty is likely to exist with respect to delivery times, production rates, and sales rates. Strikes occur, suppliers fail to deliver, and unexpected surges in demand appear. When delivery is delayed or usage unexpectedly increases, a *stockout* is likely to occur. To reduce the likelihood of stockouts, firms hold **safety stocks,** additional inventory over and above that prescribed by the EOQ formula.

Finding the optimal level of safety stock involves a trade-off between stockout costs and carrying costs. When a stockout occurs, several kinds of costs may be incurred, some that are out-of-pocket costs and some that are opportunity costs. A stockout in raw materials may cause production delays or stoppages and higher costs of scheduling and setup. In continuous-process industries, such as those involving paper or synthetic-fiber production, a stoppage would be very costly indeed. A stockout in finished goods probably means that sales were lost or, at a minimum, customers were inconvenienced. The relationship between on-time delivery and inventory level is not linear, and in most cases resembles the graph in Figure 23A–2 (p. 694). The lower the level of inventories held, the larger the volume of delayed deliveries on orders received.

The cost of stockouts includes lost contribution as well as damage to the firm's reputation. Calculating stockout costs is a difficult problem and one about which not much can be said of a general nature. In each situation, it is necessary to identify out-of-pocket and opportunity costs incurred because of the stockout.

The optimal size of the safety stock depends on stockout costs, carrying costs, and the probability that stockouts will occur. The optimal level of safety stock, thus, varies *directly* with:

1. stockout costs, either in lost contribution or production inefficiency,
2. uncertainty of usage or sales rates, and
3. uncertainty of delivery times.

Figure 23A–2
Inventories and On-Time Deliveries

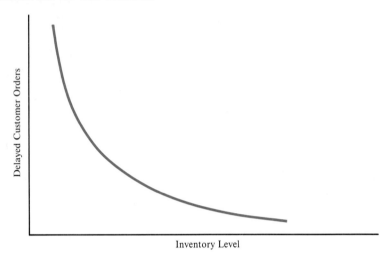

The optimal safety stock varies *inversely* with

4. inventory carrying costs.

Models incorporating safety stocks can also address the question of the appropriate *reorder point,* which is the level of inventory at which the firm should reorder new units for inventory. Such a reorder point can incorporate many factors, including the delivery time to receive the new inventory units after they have been ordered.[7]

Quantitative models for calculating reorder points and safety stocks are widely used in inventory-control systems. Having a safety stock, however, still does not eliminate the possibility of a stockout. The safety stock is intended to give a *known probability* of a stockout such that the expected cost of a stockout (cost times probability) is balanced against the inventory carrying cost. The quantitative models show us the important effect of uncertainty — the greater the uncertainty, the higher the optimal level of inventory.

Safety stocks are held to protect against uncertainty in usage rates and delivery times.

[7]For an excellent discussion of inventory models under conditions of uncertainty, see Levin and Kirkpatrick, *Quantitative Approaches to Management,* Chapter 8.

Total Inventory Costs

If we apply inventory theory as described earlier, we will be led to minimize the total costs of inventory, including opportunity costs of stockouts. Diagrammatically, we can view the relationships as shown earlier in Figure 23–1. At inventory level I^*, the total out-of-pocket and opportunity costs of inventory are minimized. If another increment of inventory is added, carrying costs exceed the ordering and stockout costs that are saved. Thus, at point I^*, the firm has chosen its optimal level of inventory.

Part 7 / Special Topics in Financial Management

We have now discussed the basics of financial management. We addressed the fundamentals of time and risk in Part Two, financial analysis and planning in Part Three, investment decisions in Part Four, financing decisions in Part Five, and working-capital management in Part Six. Thus, in these six prior parts of the book, we have covered the concepts, tools, and techniques of financial management.

In Part Seven, we take up two special topics: international

finance in Chapter 24 and mergers and acquisitions in Chapter 25. These chapters represent applications to two specialized areas of the fundamental concepts of financial management presented in Parts One through Six. With the increasing internationalization of business, international decisions are becoming important for more and more financial managers. International investment decisions are analyzed with the same tools used to analyze purely domestic investment decisions. An acquisition opportunity, also known as a merger, is analyzed using the same techniques of discounted cash flow that we use for any investment opportunity. In both of these chapters, it is the institutional and descriptive material that is specialized, not the concepts.

Chapter 24

International Financial Management

The world is becoming a much more international place. Business firms now operate "globally"; that is, they consider the entire world as their territory. Such multinational operations can take many forms, including the sale of products in foreign markets that were manufactured domestically, the manufacture of products in foreign countries and then sale in foreign or domestic markets, and the raising of funds in foreign capital markets.

Business education is becoming more international also, and in this chapter we will discuss some of the basic issues of doing business in a foreign country. We will learn about foreign-exchange markets, foreign-exchange rates, and how managers can hedge against the risk of unexpected changes in exchange rates. We will also learn how managers view investment decisions in foreign countries and how funds are raised in international capital markets.

The basic concepts and techniques of financial management are just as applicable to firms operating in foreign markets as they are to purely domestic firms.

Foreign-exchange rate — the price of one currency expressed in terms of another.

Multinational firms deal with many financial issues. Two of the most important are currency exchange rates and interest rates.

The basic concepts and techniques of financial management are just as applicable to firms operating in foreign markets as they are to purely domestic firms, but there are two important differences for the multinational firm. First, when a firm does business in a foreign country, it must operate within the laws, customs, and political institutions of that country. It must deal with local financial institutions, buy from local suppliers, hire local workers and managers, and sell to local customers. To succeed, the firm must be as well schooled in these matters as its local competitors. But these are not issues addressed by the theory and practices of financial management, so we will not discuss them in any depth in this chapter.

The multinational firms must deal with a second set of issues that are financial in character and, therefore, are addressed in this chapter. Two factors are most important: currency exchange rates and interest rates. **Foreign-exchange rates** are the conversion ratio between, say, U.S. dollars and Mexican pesos or British pounds. A firm doing business in Mexico or the United Kingdom ultimately wants to convert the proceeds of transactions into its native currency. The currency exchange rate is an important factor in determining how much ultimately will be received.

Another important financial factor is the relationship between domestic interest rates and those in the foreign country. In December 1987, interest rates on short-term certificates of deposit were around 7 percent in the United States and 4 percent in West Germany. Why do such differences exist, and what are the implications of the difference in interest rates for firms doing international business?

We will address a number of issues related to currency exchange rates and interest rates in this chapter. What causes exchange rates to behave as they do? How are exchange rates and interest rates related? How can a firm protect itself against fluctuations in exchange rates? When should firms raise needed funds in foreign capital markets rather than at home in domestic markets? What additional factors must a firm consider when it is contemplating an investment, such as building a new plant, in a foreign country? Before turning to these questions, we will briefly review the scope of international activities of U.S. firms and the history of the present international financial system.

Scope of Multinational Operations

Over the past three decades, world trade and investment have grown dramatically. In 1965, total world exports and imports amounted to about $350 billion. By the mid-1980s the total had increased more than tenfold. In the mid-1960s, the *Eurocurrency market,* which we will discuss in more depth later, totaled about $11 billion in gross liabilities.[1] By the end of 1986, it had grown to almost $3,579 billion.

International trade has become more important to the U.S. economy also. In 1965, the sum of exports and imports in the United States represented just over

[1]See R. M. Kubarych, *Foreign Exchange Markets in the United States,* Federal Reserve Bank of New York, 1978. Kubarych provides an excellent discussion of foreign-exchange markets and other aspects of international finance.

7 percent of that year's gross national product. By the end of 1986, exports and imports had grown to a point where their sum totaled 17 percent of the gross national product. The past three decades have also brought rapid growth in foreign investments by U.S. firms and in profits earned by foreign subsidiaries of U.S. companies. Table 24–1 shows the importance of foreign sales for the most active U.S. participants in foreign trade.

The Bretton Woods System

In 1949, the major trading nations of the world got together and established a system of managing exchange rates among their currencies known as the Bretton Woods system. Under this system, each nation subscribing to the agreement was required to fix the rate of exchange of its own currency against the U.S. dollar and to maintain that rate within a narrow band above and below. The dollar thus served as the linchpin of the system, and its value was tied directly to the price of gold. Gold was regarded as the ultimate store of value and was widely accepted as the proper foundation of the entire system. Thus, all currency values were tied, directly or indirectly, to the price of gold.

From time to time during this period of **fixed exchange rates,** certain member nations found they were unable to maintain the value of their currencies and were

Exchange rates ultimately must reflect the reality of the relative values of goods and services in one country versus another.

Fixed exchange rates— foreign-exchange rates set administratively by governments and changed according to agreed-upon rules.

Table 24–1
Export Sales for the Top 20 U.S. Exporting Firms, 1988

Firm	Export Sales (millions of dollars)	Percent of Total Sales
General Motors	8,731	8.6
Ford Motor	7,614	10.6
Boeing	6,286	40.9
General Electric	4,825	12.3
International Business Machines	3,994	7.4
DuPont	3,526	11.6
McDonnell Douglas	3,243	24.7
Chrysler	3,052	11.6
Eastman Kodak	2,255	17.0
Caterpillar	2,190	26.8
United Technologies	2,071	12.1
Digital Equipment	1,921	20.5
Philip Morris	1,700	7.6
Hewlett-Packard	1,596	19.7
Allied-Signal	1,416	12.2
Occidental Petroleum	1,316	7.7
Motorola	1,303	19.4
Unisys	1,198	12.3
Weyerhaeuser	1,159	16.6
General Dynamics	1,157	12.4

Source: Fortune, July 18, 1988.

Currency devaluation — a reduction in the value of a country's currency stated in terms of other currencies.

Currency revaluation — an increase in the value of a country's currency stated in terms of other currencies.

forced to *devalue* relative to the dollar. This **currency devaluation** usually happened after a sustained period of inflation at rates above those of other nations. Exchange rates ultimately must reflect the reality of the relative values of goods and services in one country versus another. So when inflation in one country ran ahead of that in other countries for an extended period, exchange rates would get out of line with prices of goods and services, and devaluation would become necessary. Devaluations took the form of changes in the official exchange rate. Only once did a **currency revaluation** — that is, a raising of the currency's value against the dollar — take place, and that revaluation occurred in the case of the West German deutsche mark.

Even with these occasional changes, most exchange rates were remarkably stable from 1949, when Bretton Woods took effect, until 1971. The exchange rate between the dollar and the Japanese yen, for example, remained unchanged for the entire 22-year period. France, West Germany, and the United Kingdom together changed their exchange rates against the dollar only a total of four times. This kind of stability was true of most other countries in Europe.

Floating Rates

Floating exchange rates — foreign-exchange rates set by free-market forces.

A big change came in 1971. In that year, the Nixon administration decided that, because of persistent inflation (at rates of 4 to 6 percent, considered intolerable at that time) and other domestic economic problems, the dollar had to be devalued against gold. After two years of futile attempts to set and maintain a new set of fixed exchange rates, the world moved in 1973 to a totally different system of **floating exchange rates.** Under this system, which has remained in effect to the present time, exchange rates were allowed to move against one another in response to market forces. The result has been continuous and sizable shifts, as illustrated in Figure 24–1 (p. 702), which shows changes in the exchange rate of the U.S. dollar against a weighted average of ten foreign currencies.

Thus, we see that, under a system of fixed exchange rates, rates are set administratively by governments and changed only infrequently according to agreed-upon rules. Under a floating system, rates are set by free-market forces. The issue of fixed versus floating rates is a very important one for managers of companies that do business internationally. Under fixed rates, during normal times a manager can negotiate a transaction with someone in another country with some assurance regarding the amount ultimately to be paid or received in units of domestic currency. Of course, this assurance would evaporate if the exchange rate were changed by one of the governments after the contract had been negotiated but before payment. But rate changes under the Bretton Woods system were relatively infrequent.

Under a floating-exchange rate system, managers face an element of uncertainty concerning future exchange rates.

Under a floating system, a manager faces an element of uncertainty in addition to the normal risks of doing business: if payment is to be made at some future date in a foreign currency, there is no assurance as to what the exchange rate will be on that date. So there is uncertainty about the amount that will ultimately be received in units of domestic currency. Later in this chapter, we will explore some of the ways managers deal with this **exchange-rate risk.**

Exchange-rate risk — risk of loss in value due to changes in foreign-exchange rates.

Figure 24—1
The Ups and Downs of the Floating Dollar

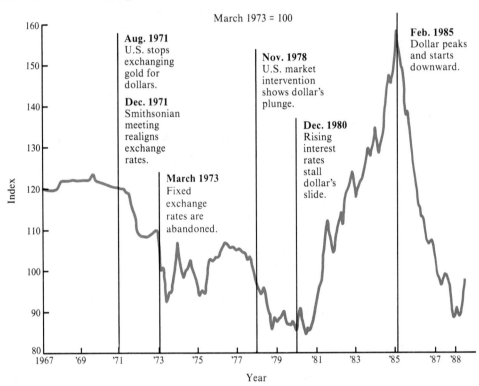

Source: The Federal Reserve System.

Finance in Practice 24—1

The Value of the Dollar

The dollar was front-page news during much of the early to mid-1980s. Measured against an average of ten other currencies, the dollar climbed steadily from a low of 88 in 1979 to a peak of 165 on February 25, 1985. Here we are measuring the dollar's value as an index with 1973 the base year; that is, its 1973 value equals 100. The rise of nearly 90 percent during 1979–85 was not only large enough to make the newspapers, it had very important effects on many Americans. Exports became more difficult as U.S. products became more expensive in foreign markets. Some U.S. firms moved production facilities overseas to take advantage of the dollar's greater purchasing power (a given number of dollars would purchase more foreign labor). Many experts argued that these two developments cost American workers thousands of jobs.

At the same time, the strong dollar made imports cheaper, and foreign products flooded into the United States. Cheaper imports had several effects — some good, some bad. On the plus side, intense foreign competition held prices down in the United States, and many experts feel that the strong dollar contributed to the favorable inflation picture in this country during the early 1980s. On the other side, the U.S. merchandise trade deficit — the excess of our imports over our exports — increased from about $25 billion in the late 1970s to more than $190 billion by 1986. The trade deficit had to be financed in part by borrowing dollars abroad, which many feel contributed to high real interest rates (adjusted for inflation) during the early 1980s. During 1984 and early 1985, rather than pointing to the strong dollar with pride as politicians sometimes do, most politicians were complaining that the dollar had gone too far, and many economists agreed.

However, looking at the period since 1980 tells only part of the story, for history did not begin in 1980. After a period of stability during the 1960s, resulting largely from the system of fixed exchange rates, the dollar went through a long period of decline from 1970 to 1980 after the world moved to a system of floating rates, falling 28 percent from 122 to 88 (see Figure 24–1) as the United States lost its leadership position in the world economy. So the rebound since 1980 started from the dollar's lowest point since World War II.

Economists point to several factors to explain the dollar's strong performance in the early 1980s. First, monetary policy was relatively tight during much of the period, as the Federal Reserve battled inflation. The resulting high interest rates made dollar investments more attractive than investments in other currencies. Second, the 1981 tax cuts initiated by the Reagan administration made business investment more profitable, raising rates of return generally. Finally, the large deficits in the federal budget during the early 1980s, projected to continue

throughout the decade, contributed to high real rates of interest, again making the dollar attractive.

After peaking in February of 1985, the dollar began to fall against other currencies. Many experts welcomed the decline, feeling that the dollar had been overvalued for some time, at least in part because of high real interest rates in the United States. At its position in the mid-1980s, the dollar stood well above its 1980 low, but some of its strong performance during the early 1980s appears to have been a correction of an earlier period of weakness during the 1970s.

The fall in the dollar continued unabated throughout 1985, 1986, and 1987. By December 1987, it had fallen 40 percent from its peak in early 1985. Against the Japanese yen, the value of the dollar fell by half, from 260 yen/dollar to 130 by December 1987. Against the West German mark it likewise fell from 3.30 DM/dollar to 1.65. The decline of the dollar against these two key currencies is shown in the accompanying chart.

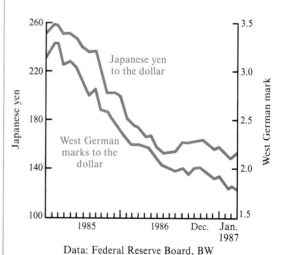

Data: Federal Reserve Board, BW

Source: Reprinted from February 12, 1987 issue of *Business Week* by special permission, copyright © 1987 by McGraw-Hill, Inc.

(*continued*)

During 1986 and 1987, there was almost universal agreement that the dollar needed to fall in order for the U.S. to correct its very serious foreign trade deficit (see Finance in Practice 24–2). As the dollar fell, imports would get more expensive and exports cheaper, thus helping to bring exports and imports into balance. But all through 1987, the trade deficit remained stubbornly high and was a source of serious concern to the government. Many economists said that the dollar needed to fall still further to correct the deficit.

A few disagreed, however, pointing out that on a *purchasing-power* basis, the dollar had fallen far enough, perhaps too far. The *Wall Street Journal* ran an article in April 1987 documenting the fact that everyday items, such as eggs, toothpaste, meat, clothes, and haircuts, by then had become considerably less expensive in the United States than in many foreign countries. Against some currencies, the dollar appeared to be 15 to 20 percent *under*valued in purchasing-power terms.

The dollar remained stable in relation to other currencies during the first half of 1988. Just where it will go in the future remains to be seen. As long as the U.S. budget and trade deficits continue at high levels, the dollar will remain a major focus of attention.

Sources: John Rutledge, "The Dollar Will Keep on Flying," *Fortune,* April 16, 1984, pp. 155–58; "Why the World Loves the Dollar," *Fortune,* February 18, 1985; the *Wall Street Journal,* September 23, 1985, February 20, 1986, April 15, 1987, and November 5, 1987; and *Business Week,* "The Risks of a Free-Fall," February 2, 1987.

Some economists and business managers believe that a fixed-rate system is preferable to a floating-rate system, although there is great disagreement on this point, even among experts. But it is certainly possible that the major trading nations of the world could return to a fixed system. We may see a good deal of discussion of the merits of returning to fixed rates in the financial press in the late 1980s. In fact, some nations have gone back a step toward a fixed system by periodically intervening in foreign-exchange markets to try to influence exchange rates. Such intervention in a system that is supposed to be floating sometimes is called a "dirty float." We will return later to the matter of central-bank intervention and its effects on foreign-exchange markets.

Because the world for the most part now operates under a system of floating rates, we will now explore in more detail just how such a system works.

The Foreign-Exchange Market

Most individuals become involved with foreign exchange in only one way: as tourists. An American tourist traveling in the United Kingdom buys British pounds with dollars, using either currency or, more likely, traveler's checks.

These pounds are usually bought at a local bank, hotel, or perhaps a store and are then used to make purchases in local markets. A tourist also might use an internationally recognized credit card to make payments abroad. The credit-card company then makes payment to the seller in the local currency and converts the amount into dollars on the cardholder's monthly statement. Individuals also purchase goods directly from abroad and pay for them using drafts (similar to checks) that are purchased from a domestic commercial bank and denominated in the ap-

In contrast to individual tourist foreign-exchange transactions, international trade and investment transactions frequently are large and recurrent.

propriate foreign currency. In all these transactions, the credit-card company, bank, or other organization that actually makes the currency conversion does so at an exchange rate that, under the system of floating rates in effect since 1973, fluctuates in response to market forces.

Foreign-exchange transactions arising out of the activities of individual tourists involve relatively small amounts and, for most individuals, occur infrequently but in the aggregate add up to substantial amounts. In contrast, transactions arising out of international trade and investment are frequently large and recurrent. A large exporter, for example, would be likely to generate a large number of transactions, some for substantial amounts, in the course of a single business day. Corporations with international operations, financial institutions, central banks, and various kinds of international organizations all generate large volumes of foreign-exchange transactions in the course of their activities.

Foreign-exchange market — a loosely connected group of major banks and foreign-exchange brokers who communicate by telephone and mail over great distances to buy and sell different currencies.

The **foreign-exchange market** is a loosely connected group of banks and foreign-exchange brokers who communicate by telephone and mail over great distances to buy and sell different currencies. Market participants are located in the major worldwide financial centers: New York, London, Zurich, Paris, Frankfurt, Tokyo, Toronto, and others.

The supply and demand for foreign currencies originates with commercial transactions between corporations, investors, importers, exporters, and tourists doing business throughout the United States and other countries. Large commercial banks in the major financial centers maintain inventories of foreign currencies and serve as wholesalers for the firms and individuals engaging in the underlying commercial transactions. These banks make the market by buying and selling currencies for their own account — that is, from their own inventories of foreign currencies. In New York, a dozen or so commercial banks trade currencies, normally going through foreign-currency brokers in order to preserve the anonymity of the transacting parties. Central banks, such as the U.S. Federal Reserve, are also active transactors in foreign currencies, as we will discuss later.

The Nature of Foreign-Exchange Transactions

Foreign exchange consists of money denominated in different currencies.

For corporations, financial institutions, and governmental units, foreign exchange consists of bank deposits denominated in different currencies.

For an individual, a foreign-exchange transaction typically involves swapping traveler's checks for local currency. For corporations, financial institutions, and governmental units, **foreign exchange** is bank deposits denominated in different currencies, and foreign-exchange transactions are executed by exchanging one bank deposit for another. All of these transactions, however, are alike in that each is simply an exchange of one country's money for that of another.

Most foreign-exchange transactions involving individuals and firms have another common feature: they are usually motivated not by a desire to trade the currencies for their own sake, but by a desire to buy or sell goods, services, or financial assets. Foreign-exchange transactions are thus a basic part of the international payments mechanism, just as transactions involving checking accounts are a part of the domestic payments mechanism. Unlike individuals and firms, as we noted earlier, central banks often do trade currencies for their own sake when they intervene to prevent exchange rates from fluctuating too much over short periods.

Most foreign-exchange transactions for both individuals and firms are undertaken in the process of buying and selling goods, services, or financial assets.

Because foreign-exchange transactions are part of the payments mechanism, individuals and firms traditionally have called on commercial banks to execute transactions for them and to make the necessary currency conversions. An importer who needs Japanese yen to pay for a shipment could try to find an exporter with just the right amount of yen for sale, but that would be inconvenient and costly. It is far more convenient and efficient for a bank to act as intermediary, just as banks do in facilitating the flow of funds between lenders and borrowers in domestic transactions. Let us now examine foreign-exchange rates in more detail.

The Spot Market

Spot rate—the price of one currency in terms of another when purchased for immediate delivery.

Table 24–2 (pp. 708–709) shows foreign-exchange rates on a particular day, December 4, 1987. The rate shown in the first column for the British pound, 1.7955, means that one pound can be purchased for $1.7955. This **spot rate** is the rate applicable for purchasing pounds for *immediate delivery*. In the spot market, "immediate delivery" normally means delivery within two business days to allow time for the necessary accounting and paperwork, although sometimes under special circumstances spot transactions are executed in one day. Just as the pound was quoted spot at $1.7955 on December 4, 1987, the Japanese yen was $0.007561, the Mexican peso was $0.0004444, the Italian lira was $0.0008143, and so on.

Table 24–2 shows four spot quotations for each currency. The first two columns give the rate in dollars. The British pound, for example, was quoted at $1.7955 per pound on Friday, December 4, 1987, and at $1.8040 per pound the day before. The two additional columns on the right state the exchange the other way, in pounds per dollar for each of the two dates—0.5569 pounds on December 4 and 0.5543 pounds the day before. The dollar/pound rate is simply the reciprocal of the pound/dollar rate.

The Forward Market

Forward rate—the price of one currency in terms of another when purchased for future delivery.

Besides the entries for spot rates in Table 24–2, there are three additional sets of **forward rates** for the British pound. Similarly, for other principal currencies, including the Canadian dollar, French franc, Japanese yen, Swiss franc, and West German mark, listings of forward rates appear. Whereas spot transactions are for immediate delivery (allowing two days for paperwork), forward transactions are made on one date for execution at some future date—normally either 30, 90, or 180 days in the future. For currencies without forward-market quotations in Table 24–2, forward-market transactions still take place, but the market is not as well developed.

Thus, on December 4, 1987, an importer might arrange to purchase British pounds 90 days hence, on March 4, 1988. According to Table 24–2, the rate would be $1.7922. In entering into the transaction, the importer has agreed on December 4, 1987, to purchase pounds on March 4, 1988. The critical point is that the exchange rate is agreed upon on the date of the transaction (December 4), rather than waiting until March 4 to execute the transaction at the spot rate on that date.

What function does the forward market serve? Suppose that on December 4, 1987, a U.S. company orders a piece of machinery from a Japanese supplier that will not be delivered until March 4. No one knows what the spot exchange rate will be on March 4. If between December 4 and March 4 the dollar declines in value against the yen, on March 4 it will take more dollars than originally anticipated to pay for the shipment. If the buying company does not want to risk having to pay more, it can fix the exchange rate at the time the order is placed by purchasing yen in the forward market for delivery on March 4. Then the buyer knows exactly what he or she will have to pay. We will talk more about such hedging transactions later in this chapter.

How Foreign-Exchange Rates Are Determined

What determines that exactly $0.6004 should be required to purchase one West German DM (deutsche mark) on December 4, 1987? One day earlier, the rate was slightly different at $0.6017. Two and a half years earlier, in July 1985, the dollar was much stronger, and the rate was about $0.3400. Then it took only about 34 cents to buy one German DM, whereas in December 1987 it took 60 cents. What factors determine spot exchange rates, and why do spot rates change over time? It is clear from Table 24–2 that forward and spot rates on a given date are different. Why should this be so, and what factors determine the *forward/spot differential?* As one might guess, the relationship between forward and spot rates is important, and understanding the various factors at work provides insights into how foreign-exchange markets work.

What factors influence the thousands of individual decisions to buy or sell a currency? Before proceeding, let us note that there are hundreds of different exchange rates. There is the dollar/DM rate, the yen/peso rate, the Swiss franc/Saudi riyal rate, and so on — an exchange rate for each pair of the currencies listed in Table 24–2, and then some. The dollar market for each currency is normally the most active, and most trading activity finds the U.S. dollar on one side of the trade. So we will confine our attention to relationships between the dollar and other currencies.

Exchange rates are determined by the same forces that determine prices in all competitive markets: the actions of market participants competing against one another — that is, by the forces of supply and demand.

The Forward/Spot Differential

Note from Table 24–2 that German marks for future delivery cost more on December 4, 1987, than marks in the spot market. On that date, the forward DM sold at a *premium* relative to the spot DM, and the longer the contract, the higher the premium. In contrast, the forward British pound sold at a *discount* in relation to the spot pound.

Why should the forward mark sell at a premium on December 4, 1987, and the forward pound at a discount? In order to explore this question, Equation (1) shows how to express the spot/forward relationship in quantitative terms.

If the forward rate exceeds the spot rate, the forward currency is said to be at a premium relative to the spot currency. If the spot rate is larger than the forward rate, the forward currency is selling at a discount relative to the spot.

$$P = \frac{F - S}{S} \times \frac{12}{n} \times 100, \tag{1}$$

1 Canadian $
= .7625 Am $

1 Am $ = 1.3114
Canadian $

Table 24—2

Foreign-Exchange Rates for Friday, December 4, 1987

reciprocals

Country	U.S. Dollar Equivalent		Currency per U.S. Dollar	
	Friday	Thursday	Friday	Thursday
Argentina (Austral)	0.2857	0.2857	3.50	3.50
Australia (Dollar)	0.6975	0.7018	1.4337	1.4249
Austria (Schilling)	0.08525	0.08569	11.73	11.67
Belgium (Franc)				
Commercial rate	0.02874	0.02874	34.80	34.80
Financial rate	0.02861	0.02871	34.95	34.83
Brazil (Cruzeiro)	0.01545	0.01570	64.73	63.69
Britain (Pound)	1.7955	1.8040	0.5569	0.5543
30-Day Forward	1.7947	1.8030	0.5572	0.5546
90-Day Forward	1.7922	1.8004	0.5580	0.5554
180-Day Forward	1.7888	1.7970	0.5590	0.5565
Canada (Dollar)	0.7625	0.7630	1.3114	1.3106
30-Day Forward	0.7630	0.7625	1.3107	1.3114
90-Day Forward	0.7647	0.7607	1.3077	1.3146
180-Day Forward	0.7670	0.7582	1.3037	1.3189
Chile (Official rate)	0.004336	0.004336	230.61	230.61
China (Yuan)	0.2693	0.2693	3.7127	3.7127
Colombia (Peso)	0.003852	0.003852	259.58	259.58
Denmark (Krone)	0.1555	0.1557	6.4300	6.4225
Ecuador (Sucre)				
Official rate	0.004000	0.004000	250.00	250.00
Floating rate	0.004728	0.004728	211.50	211.50
Finland (Mark)	0.2439	0.2446	4.1000	4.0880
France (Franc)	0.1768	0.1770	5.6550	5.6495
30-Day Forward	0.1769	0.1769	5.6520	5.6520
90-Day Forward	0.1772	0.1766	5.6430	5.6620
180-Day Forward	0.1777	0.1762	5.6275	5.6760
Greece (Drachma)	0.007613	0.007631	131.35	131.04
Hong Kong (Dollar)	0.1287	0.1287	7.7670	7.7680
India (Rupee)	0.07710	0.07716	12.97	12.96
Indonesia (Rupiah)	0.0006061	0.0006061	1650.00	1650.00
Ireland (Punt)	1.5950	1.6024	0.6270	0.6241
Israel (Shekel)	0.6357	0.6357	1.573	1.573
Italy (Lira)	0.0008143	0.0008157	1228.00	1226.00
Japan (Yen)	0.007561	0.007543	132.25	132.58
30-Day Forward	0.007585	0.007567	131.84	132.15
90-Day Forward	0.007627	0.007610	131.11	131.41
180-Day Forward	0.007692	0.007676	130.00	130.28
Jordan (Dinar)	2.8902	2.8902	0.346	0.346
Kuwait (Dinar)	3.6010	3.6010	0.2777	0.2777
Lebanon (Pound)	0.002083	0.002083	480.00	480.00

where F = the forward rate, S = the spot rate, and n = the number of months forward. As in the case of interest rates, foreign-exchange premiums and discounts are normally expressed in terms of percent per year.

Country	U.S. Dollar Equivalent		Currency per U.S. Dollar	
	Friday	Thursday	Friday	Thursday
Malaysia (Ringgit)	0.4003	0.4000	2.4980	2.5000
Malta (Lira)	3.1008	3.1008	0.3225	0.3225
Mexico (Peso)				
Floating rate	0.0004444	0.0004444	2250.00	2250.00
Netherlands (Guilder)	0.5325	0.5348	1.8780	1.8700
New Zealand (Dollar)	0.6395	0.6465	1.5637	1.5468
Norway (Krone)	0.1550	0.1554	6.4500	6.4350
Pakistan (Rupee)	0.05714	0.05714	17.50	17.50
Peru (Sol)	0.05	0.05	20.00	20.00
Philippines (Peso)	0.04739	0.04739	21.10	21.10
Portugal (Escudo)	0.007372	0.007386	135.65	135.40
Saudi Arabia (Riyal)	0.2666	0.2666	3.751	3.751
Singapore (Dollar)	0.4921	0.4929	2.0320	2.0290
South Africa (Rand)				
Commercial rate	0.5070	0.5085	1.9724	1.9666
Financial rate	0.3300	0.3300	3.0303	3.0303
South Korea (Won)	0.001254	0.001254	797.30	797.30
Spain (Peseta)	0.008857	0.008929	112.90	112.00
Sweden (Krona)	0.1658	0.1659	6.0320	6.0280
Switzerland (Franc)	0.7358	0.7361	1.3590	1.3585
30-Day Forward	0.7386	0.7388	1.3540	1.3536
90-Day Forward	0.7432	0.7435	1.3455	1.3450
180-Day Forward	0.7508	0.7513	1.3320	1.3310
Taiwan (Dollar)	0.03413	0.03409	29.30	29.33
Thailand (Baht)	0.03926	0.03926	25.47	25.47
Turkey (Lira)	0.001032	0.001032	969.065	969.065
United Arab (Dirham)	0.2723	0.2723	3.673	3.673
Uruguay (New Peso)				
Financial	0.003742	0.003742	267.25	267.25
Venezuela (Bolivar)				
Official rate	0.1333	0.1333	7.50	7.50
Floating rate	0.03578	0.03578	27.95	27.95
West Germany (Mark)	0.6004	0.6017	1.6655	1.6620
30-Day Forward	0.6031	0.6040	1.6582	1.6556
90-Day Forward	0.6068	0.6081	1.6481	1.6445
180-Day Forward	0.6127	0.6142	1.6322	1.6282

Note: The New York foreign-exchange selling rates above apply to trading among banks in amounts of $1 million and more, as quoted at 3 P.M. Eastern time by Bankers Trust Co. Retail transactions provide fewer units of foreign currency per dollar.

Source: Wall Street Journal, December 4, 1987.

In words, the percentage premium is the difference between the forward and spot rates, divided by the spot rate, then multiplied by $12/n$ to annualize it, and multiplied by 100 to put it in percentage terms.

We can now calculate the premium for the 180-day forward mark on December 4, 1987, as

$$P = \frac{0.6127 - 0.6004}{0.6004} \times \frac{12}{6} \times 100$$

$$= 4.10 \text{ percent per year}.$$

A similar calculation for the British pound would give

$$P = \frac{1.7888 - 1.7955}{1.7955} \times \frac{12}{6} \times 100$$

$$= -0.75 \text{ percent per year}.$$

Thus, the 180-day forward DM is selling at a *premium* of 4.10 percent, and the 180-day forward pound is selling at a *discount* of 0.75 percent. (A discount is a negative premium.)

Why does one currency sell at a forward premium while another simultaneously sells at a forward discount? Is it because the market expected the mark to rise against the dollar over the next six months and the pound to fall? It is possible to view the forward exchange rate in a currency as a forecast of future spot exchange rates. Also very important is the outlook for inflation in the countries involved in the rate relationship. Most important is the *difference* in inflation rates between the countries — the United States and West Germany in the case of dollar/DM exchange rates, and the United States and Great Britain in the case of the dollar/pound exchange rates.

Dealing with anticipated inflation directly is difficult because of the problem of getting reliable forecasts of future inflation rates, but we can take inflation and its relationship to forward exchange rates into account indirectly by looking at interest rates. As we know from earlier chapters, interest rates contain an inflation premium, which represents the market's consensus forecast of future inflation rates. It is therefore possible to explain a great deal about forward exchange rates by examining their relationship to interest rates. This important relationship is described by the **interest-rate-parity theorem.**

The Interest-Rate-Parity Theorem

Because the world's major financial centers are linked by telephone, the foreign-exchange market functions essentially as a single market. Therefore, an investor in New York should receive the same interest return on a six-month deposit regardless of whether the funds are invested in dollars or deutsche marks — that is the message of the interest-rate-parity theorem.

Suppose someone has money to invest in New York — say, an amount of A dollars — and is considering two options: investing in dollars or in deutsche marks. If this New York investor invests in dollars for a period of n months at an annual interest rate of $i(\$)$, the return would be calculated as

$$\text{Return} = \$A[1 + i(\$) \, n/12],$$

where $(n/12)$ represents the fraction of the year the money is invested.

Alternatively, the New York investor could invest his or her money in D-marks, as follows: (1) convert dollars to D-marks at the spot rate for DM and receive $ A/S D-marks; (2) then invest the D-marks for n months at the German annual interest rate of i(DM); and (3) then convert back to dollars at the forward rate, F. The return in this case would be calculated as

$$\text{Return} = \$A/S[1 + i(\text{DM})\, n/12]F .$$

If international currency markets work well, competition would ensure that we get the same return no matter which of these options we pick. If we equate the preceding two expressions for return and simplify, we get an expression for the interest-rate-parity theorem, as shown in Equations (2) and (3):

$$\frac{F}{S} = \frac{1 + i(\$)\,(n/12)}{1 + i(\text{DM})\,(n/12)} \qquad (2)$$

where F = the forward rate in \$/DM, S is the spot rate in \$/DM, $i(\$)$ = the annual interest rate (decimal form) on dollar-denominated deposits, $i(\text{DM})$ = the annual interest rate (decimal form) on DM-denominated deposits, and n = the number of months forward. Equation (2) can be rearranged as:

$$\frac{F - S}{S} \times \frac{12}{n} = \frac{i(\$) - i(\text{DM})}{1 + i(\text{DM})\,(n/12)} . \qquad (3)$$

When we compare Equation (3) to Equation (1), we see that the interest-rate-parity theorem tells us that the premium on the forward DM for any period of time (say, 90 days) equals the difference between the interest rates in the United States and West Germany for the same period of time divided by one plus the West German interest rate. The premium — on the left side of Equation (3) — is annualized, as are the interest rates, and the denominator of the right side is also adjusted for the time period.

Let us check the accuracy of the theorem. On December 4, 1987, we check an international newspaper such as the *Financial Times* of London and find that the rate of interest on large six-month **Eurocurrency** deposits denominated in dollars is 7.813 percent per year. (Eurocurrencies are a form of international money to which we will return later in this chapter.) The corresponding rate on deposits denominated in D-marks on December 4, 1987, is 3.688 percent per year. We calculated the left side of Equation (2) earlier (the six-month forward premium on the mark) and got 4.10 percent, or 0.0410. Calculating the right side, we get 4.05 percent, or 0.0405. Thus we see that interest-rate parity holds very closely. The difference between the 4.10 and 4.05 percent figures results partly from the fact that in our calculations we are ignoring commissions charged by foreign-exchange traders and other transaction costs.

Thus, the interest-rate-parity theorem helps us understand how interest rates and exchange rates are related. The fact that we earn a lower interest rate in DM than in dollars (3.688 percent versus 7.813 percent) is offset by the fact that there is a forward premium on the mark. As shown in Table 24–2, the mark is worth more in terms of dollars on the 180-day forward market (\$0.6127 per mark) than it is on the spot market (\$0.6004).

Eurocurrency — deposit denominated in a given country's currency and held in a bank outside that country.

Covered-interest arbitrage — the market process through which the relationships in the interest-rate-parity theorem are enforced.

The market process through which the relationships in the interest-rate-parity theorem come into being is known as **covered-interest arbitrage.** Suppose a U.S. corporation had $100,000 of excess cash on December 4, 1987, and knew that it would not need to use the funds for 180 days. It could invest the funds in a Euro-currency certificate of deposit (CD) denominated in dollars and receive interest over the 180-day period at the then-current rate of 7.813 percent, for a return of $7.813/2 = 3.907$ percent during the six-month period.[2] Alternatively, the firm's treasurer could buy DM spot and invest the proceeds in a CD denominated in DM at an interest rate of 3.688 percent, or 1.844 percent for six months. These two alternatives are outlined in Table 24–3.

At first glance the choice looks pretty clear-cut. The treasurer can earn 7.813 percent in the dollar-denominated CD and only 3.688 percent in the DM-denominated CD. The U.S. CD initially looks better as an investment, but before the treasurer can reach a final conclusion, he or she has to remember that the 3.688 percent is a return in DM. To be directly comparable to the 7.813 percent on the dollar-denominated CD, the marks must be converted to dollars.

[2]To simplify matters, we round interest rates to the nearest thousandth of a percent and assume compounding once per year.

Table 24–3
Covered-Interest Arbitrage

Panel A: Alternative A
1. Invest $100,000 in dollar-denominated certificate of deposit (CD) for 180 days at 7.813 percent per year (= 3.907 = 7.813 ÷ 2 for six months).

December 1987
1. Buy $100,000 CD.

June 1988
1. Receive $100,000(1 + 0.03907) = $103,907.

Panel B: Alternative B
1. In spot market, buy deutsche marks (DM) worth $100,000.
2. Buy CD denominated in marks, at 1.844* percent for six months.
3. In forward market, sell DM for dollars.

December 1987
1. In spot market: $100,000 × 1.6655 = 166,550 DM (exchange rate from Table 24–2).
2. Buy CD for 166,550 DM, which in 6 months will return (166,550 DM) × (1.01844) = 169,621 DM.
3. In forward market: Buy dollars for delivery in June (169,621 DM) × (0.6127) = $103,927.

June 1988
1. Collect 169,621 DM from the investment in the CD.
2. Deliver the 169,621 DM to honor the contract in the forward market, receiving (169,621 DM) × (0.6127) = $103,927 as planned.

---

*To simplify matters, the percent rate of return has been rounded. All exchange rates are for Friday, December 4, 1987, and come from Table 24–2.

The treasurer knows that the marks have to be converted back to dollars the following June when the foreign CD matures and the dollars are needed for other purposes. Suppose the exchange rate between the two currencies changed between December and June. A change in one direction would make the firm worse off, and a change in the other direction would make the firm better off. The treasurer could remove this uncertainty from the transaction by selling marks in December for delivery in June in the forward market because he or she knows in December just how much he or she will have in marks in June — that sum being the original amount plus the interest earned on the marks between December and June. Such a transaction in the forward market is known as *covering*.

Table 24–3 summarizes the results of the entire series of transactions. Panel A shows the direct investment in a dollar-denominated CD. Panel B shows the steps necessary to perform covered-interest arbitrage. Note that in Panel B, three transactions must be made in December 1987: buying marks in the spot market, buying the DM-denominated CD, and buying dollars in the forward market. In June 1988, Panel A shows a dollar return of $103,907. Panel B shows a dollar return of $103,927 in June. Note that the figures are very close, just as the interest-rate-parity theorem in Equation (2) suggests. The lower interest rate in Germany was effectively converted to a higher interest rate (in dollar terms) because the forward mark was at a premium. In other words, the interest rates shown in Panels A and B of Table 24–3 are effectively almost the same once the foreign-exchange market is considered — the interest rates are *in parity*.

What should the treasurer do? According to the calculations in Table 24–3, slightly more money can be earned by the strategy in Panel B, but this result ignores transactions costs. It is highly likely that the extra $20 earned by going from A to B would not be enough to offset the extra transactions costs, in which case the treasurer should invest the money in a dollar-denominated CD.

If the dollar/deutsche mark exchange rate and interest rates in the two countries were *not* related as in Equation (2), investors could earn a profit by entering into covered transactions similar to the one described earlier. Because all exchange rates were set at the time of the transaction, there would be no risk (ignoring the slight risk of a default or bankruptcy by one of the banks involved). But opportunities for riskless profits do not go unnoticed for long, so we can expect the relationships embodied in the interest-rate-parity theorem in Equation (2) to hold very closely.

We noted earlier that relationships between exchange rates depend on a number of factors. One of the most important factors affecting both exchange rates and interest rates is the inflation rate expected in the future. Differences between inflation rates in two countries — say, the United States and West Germany — have a great deal to do with the way exchange rates between currencies of the two countries behave over time. If the inflation rate were higher in the United States than in West Germany over an extended period, the dollar would decline relative to the mark: the spot exchange rate between the two currencies would change. Suppose the investors and companies engaged in trade between the United States and West Germany expected inflation rates in the two countries to differ in the future. Dollar/DM exchange rates would be affected, but the effects would be felt primarily in forward rates rather than in spot rates. But, as noted earlier, these expectations of future inflation are captured in interest rates, so we take anticipated inflation into account implicitly when we use the interest-rate-parity theorem.[3]

Central-Bank Intervention

Central banks, for practical purposes arms of governments, have an important influence on exchange rates.

In practice, exchange rates are not determined solely by the actions of individuals and firms. Central banks — which are, for practical purposes, arms of governments — also have an important influence. In the United States, the Federal Reserve plays the role of central bank.

Because major currencies began floating against one another in 1973, central banks of different countries have intervened in foreign-exchange markets in varying degrees and for varying reasons. Such intervention takes the form of buying and selling one currency against another. In the case of the United States, intervention by the Federal Reserve typically has been aimed at smoothing out fluctuations in exchange rates rather than trying to maintain a particular exchange rate or to push rates to a new level. This motive might be described as countering disorderly market conditions in order to stabilize the market.

Central-bank intervention takes the form of buying and selling one currency against another.

Some governments from time to time may intervene in order to resist an appreciation of their currency that could erode the position of their exports in world markets. Or a government might intervene in the other direction to resist depreciation of its currency that would cause prices of imports to rise and thereby increase domestic inflation. In the resulting "dirty float," rates are technically floating, but not freely. The extent to which governments have succeeded in resisting changes in exchange rates to new levels is open to question, although there is no doubt that trading by a central bank can dampen short-term fluctuations.

Dealing with Foreign-Exchange Exposure

Exchange-rate risk is the consequence of trading in a world where foreign-currency values fluctuate because of supply and demand forces.

Exchange-rate risk is the inevitable consequence of trading in a world in which foreign-currency values fluctuate in response to forces of supply and demand. Suppose a U.S. electronics manufacturer buys solid-state memory chips from a Japanese supplier. The sales contract could be expressed either in U.S. dollars or in Japanese yen — a matter subject to negotiation by the two parties. In a world of

[3]There is an important relationship, known as the *purchasing-power-parity theorem,* or less formally as the *law of one price,* which states that a single good must sell at the same price everywhere, adjusting for transportation costs. The theorem also implies that prices of a given good in the future should be the same everywhere. When applied to foreign-exchange markets, the purchasing-power-parity theorem implies that expected differences in inflation rates between two countries should be related in a precise way to expected changes in spot exchange rates. The expectations theory of forward rates in turn calls for a precise relationship between forward rates and expected changes in spot rates. At the same time, expected inflation rates are related to interest rates. Thus, spot exchange rates, forward rates, inflation rates, interest rates, and expectations regarding future values of these variables all are closely related. All of these various relationships can be examined independently, but for our purposes here, much of what is important in foreign-exchange markets can be discussed by focusing on just two factors — exchange rates and interest rates — by means of the interest-rate-parity theorem.

For a party bearing exchange-rate risk, it is exactly as if the final price is left uncertain.

floating rates, one of the two parties will wind up bearing the exchange-rate risk. If the contract is in dollars, the Japanese firm bears the risk; if the contract is in yen, the American firm bears the risk. For the party bearing the risk, it is exactly as if the final price to be paid is left uncertain. Let us now consider how firms and other organizations can deal with the foreign-exchange risk to which they are exposed by virtue of owning assets or liabilities denominated in another currency.[4]

Hedging

Hedging — an attempt to reduce the risk associated with future price fluctuations.

Through hedging, the risk of changes in foreign-exchange rates can be eliminated in many international transactions.

A widely used method of reducing foreign-exchange risk is **hedging** through the use of forward contracts. A hedge is an arrangement designed to reduce the risk from future price fluctuations. Hedging is widely used in connection with commodities as a way for producers and consumers to "lay off" the risk of price fluctuations. Producers of commodities, such as farmers in the case of agricultural commodities or mining companies in the case of metals, regularly hedge against future price fluctuations by selling their production for future delivery. A wheat farmer, for example, might sell wheat in January for delivery in May at a price specified in January. The farmer would then be obligated to deliver a specified amount of wheat and, hence, would be subject to business risk but has laid off the risk of price fluctuations.

Consumers of commodities also hedge by buying in the futures market. A manufacturer of chocolate candy might buy cocoa beans in the futures market in order to be assured of a supply at a known price.

In such cases the producers and consumers of the commodities are hedging: they concentrate on what they are best at — growing wheat or making candy — and let others bear the risk of price fluctuations. The risk bearers are known as **speculators** because they willingly seek to bear the risk, with the prospect of large gains if things turn out favorably for them. Speculators in commodities and foreign exchange perform a socially necessary and desirable function. Through speculation, those willing and able to bear risk do so and those who wish to avoid it have a means of meeting their objectives as well.

Speculators — people who willingly bear risk, with the prospect of large gains if things turn out favorably for them.

In foreign exchange, the uncertain future price is the exchange rate between two currencies at some future date. Consider an American automobile manufacturer that decided to sell a small foreign subsidiary located in Great Britain in order to raise needed cash for domestic use. The subsidiary was sold to a British buyer for 4.5 million British pounds. The contract was signed on December 4, 1987, with payment to be made in pounds on the closing date six months hence, on June 4, 1988.

The spot exchange rate on December 4, 1987, was $1.7955 (Table 24–2), so if payment could have been received on that date, it would have yielded $1.7955 × 4,500,000 = $8,079,750. But the funds were not available on December 4 and would not be available for six months. If, between December and June, the pound declines in relation to the dollar, the U.S. company will get less than $8,079,750;

---

[4]For a discussion of ways companies deal with foreign-exchange risk, see R. M. Rodriguez, "Corporate Exchange Risk Management," *Journal of Finance* 36 (May 1981): 427–38.

if it rises, the company will get more. The automobile company needs the money and does not wish to run the risk of an adverse movement in exchange rates. What should the management do?

The American company can lay off the uncertainty by selling 4.5 million pounds forward for delivery in six months on June 4, 1988. Such a transaction is called a *forward hedge* because it is being accomplished through the forward currency market. On December 4, the 180-day forward rate was $1.7888, so by hedging the company could be assured of receiving $1.7888 × 4,500,000 = $8,049,600 in June. The company will get less by hedging, but this difference simply reflects the fact that, in December 1987, interest rates were higher in Great Britain than in the United States. The pound was selling at a forward discount, which implies an expectation that the spot rate relative to the dollar would decline over the coming months.

The American firm has two choices. It can do nothing and simply wait until June, receive the 4.5 million British pounds, and convert to dollars at the spot rate on that date—recognizing that the most likely outlook (implied by the current forward discount in the pound) is a declining spot rate. Or the company can sell the pounds now and eliminate the uncertainty. So the choice is between a likely decline of uncertain magnitude and a certain discount now.

The automobile manufacturer was considering hedging against a decline in the price of an asset denominated in a foreign currency. Consider now the opposite case, in which an obligation exists to make a payment in a foreign currency at some future date. The Chapel of the Cross, an Episcopal church in Chapel Hill, North Carolina, was given a substantial sum with the stipulation by the donor that it be used to purchase a new organ of first quality. After a lengthy search, a contract was negotiated with a West German company to build and install the organ. Payment was to be made in deutsche marks in installments over a two-year period.

At the spot exchange rate at the time the contract was negotiated, the church had enough dollars to purchase the marks necessary to settle the contract. But what if the dollar declined relative to the mark while the organ was being constructed, a period of more than a year? At the time, the dollar looked weak, and a decline could leave the church with insufficient funds to pay the organ builder. So the church vestry decided to buy marks forward and eliminate the uncertainty. Churches are not regular participants in the foreign-exchange market, but in this case, *not* to have hedged would have been, in effect, to speculate.

In some cases, not to hedge is, in effect, to speculate.

Other Techniques for Reducing Risk

A forward hedge such as that described in the preceding section will not work in cases where there is no functioning forward market. Forward markets are well developed in only a few of the world's major currencies: the U.S. dollar, the British pound, the Canadian dollar, the French franc, the Japanese yen, the Swiss franc, and the West German deutsche mark. Table 24–2 showed forward quotes for only these currencies.

In currencies with no forward market, it is sometimes possible to arrange a special forward contract with a large financial intermediary. One cannot count on this, however, and in such cases one often must look to other methods. What other

Where well-developed forward markets do not exist, companies can reduce risk by engaging in "leading and lagging"—hastening or slowing down payments and prospective receipts depending on the likely direction of changes in exchange rates.

methods can a company use to reduce foreign-exchange risk in transactions involving currencies with no forward market?

One method, called *leading and lagging,* is simply to try to hasten or slow down payments and prospective receipts depending on the likely direction of changes in exchange rates. If an American company owed 100,000 Indian rupees (a currency for which no forward-market quotes appear in Table 24–2) in 90 days, and expected the rupee to rise relative to the dollar, the company might find it advantageous to go ahead and settle the bill sooner. If the rupee did rise, in 90 days it would take more dollars to settle the bill, so paying it sooner would be better.

Another device is to borrow or lend in the local currency. Suppose the automobile manufacturer described earlier with the subsidiary in Great Britain were instead selling a subsidiary located in Mexico. The company could not hedge the transaction by selling pesos forward. Instead it could employ a *spot hedge* involving a loan in Mexican pesos. The company would first determine how many pesos it will receive on the closing date, June 4, 1988. It could then borrow that amount from a bank in Mexico, convert the pesos it borrows to dollars in the spot market, and invest the dollars in U.S. Treasury bills or some other dollar-denominated deposit with a maturity of June 4, 1988. On the closing date, June 4, 1988, the company receives payment in pesos for its subsidiary and uses the proceeds to pay off its loan to the Mexican bank. Earlier, by investing in the dollar-denominated deposit, the company locked in the dollar amount of the transaction and so was not exposed to exchange-rate risk during the six-month period.

A third method of reducing exchange-rate risk is by means of a *parallel loan.* Suppose one company expects a payment in 60 days from a subsidiary located in a country for whose currency no forward market exists. At the same time, another company plans to begin building a new plant in that country on about the same date and must make an outlay to start construction. One company wants to sell the foreign currency in 60 days, and the other wants to buy it. The two firms could work out an arrangement that would protect them both from changes in the spot exchange rate. In effect, the two companies create their own foreign-exchange market. Such transactions require that amounts and timing match up and so are relatively rare, but the parallel-loan device can be beneficial in some cases.

Currency Options

In some situations, hedging is not possible using the spot or forward markets. There are also cases in which individuals or firms want to hedge against the risk of a move in one direction without giving up potential profits if the move is the other way.

A new device, called a **currency option,** has come into being recently to fill these needs. Under a forward contract, the buyer or seller is obligated to complete the transaction. With an option, the option buyer has the *right* but not the obligation to buy or sell the currency. We discussed options on securities in Chapter 18. Here we will focus specifically on currency options.

Consider the following case in which an option might be used. An American firm bids on a contract in the United Kingdom on August 1, 1989. The contract requires that the firm install a security system in a British factory. Most of the

---

Firms can also reduce risk by borrowing or lending in a local currency.

Currency option—a financial claim giving one the right but not the obligation to buy or sell a foreign currency.

Currency options sometimes can be used to reduce risk in cases in which hedging in the forward currency markets does not work.

materials and labor will be purchased in the United States, but payment by the British firm upon completion of the contract will be made in British pounds. Bids must be submitted by August 1, 1989; the contract will be awarded on October 1, 1989. The work must be completed by April 1, 1990; payment will be made on April 1, 1990.

If the firm wins the contract on October 1, at that point it can hedge against changes in the dollar/pound exchange rate by selling pounds forward for delivery on April 1, 1990. When the firm gets paid on April 1, it uses the pounds received from its British customer to settle the forward currency contract.

The forward contract will work fine on October 1 once the firm *knows for sure* that it has the contract. But what can it do on August 1, when winning the contract is not assured? If it sells pounds then and subsequently does not get the contract, it is at risk. If it does not sell pounds and then does get the contract, it is again at risk. There is no way using the forward currency market to hedge against risk during the period from August 1 to October 1 when there is uncertainty about the contract.

Enter the currency option. On August 1, when it submits the bid, the firm buys a put option on the pound giving it the right, *but not the obligation,* to sell pounds on or before April 1, 1990, at an agreed-upon price. If it wins the bid, it is assured of the exchange rate at the completion of the contract. If it loses the bid, it simply does not exercise the option. If it wins the bid and the pound moves to the firm's advantage, it can forgo the option and simply sell pounds in the spot market on April 1, 1990.

The option is ideal for situations in which the need for foreign currency is not certain. The buyer of the option pays a price — an option fee that normally ranges from 1.5 to 1.75 percent of the amount of the option. A company using options in its commercial operations obviously would have to build the cost of options into its bids.

Currency options are a recent innovation and only became a significant factor in commercial transactions in 1984. That year the value of contracts outstanding grew rapidly to an estimated $5 billion. Options are now available in the United States in five major foreign currencies: the pound, the deutsche mark, the yen, the Canadian dollar, and the Swiss franc. The typical option has a face amount of $5 to $10 million for three to six months. Banks reportedly have been asked to quote on options for as much as $650 million and for periods as long as two and a half years, although such transactions are unusual.[5]

Options are traded on several exchanges, including the Philadelphia Stock Exchange and the Chicago Mercantile Exchange. Commercial banks in major money centers and some major investment-banking firms are also active participants.

Other Risks

Foreign-exchange risk is not the only risk to which multinational firms are exposed. If a transaction with a foreign firm involves a loan, there is the standard **credit risk** that the borrower may default. Even if the borrower is a foreign gov-

Credit risk — the risk that a borrower will default on a loan.

[5]*Wall Street Journal,* April 20, 1984, p. 25.

ernment, credit risk may still be a factor. In 1982, the Polish government was unable to meet maturing loan obligations to Western banks. Although the loans were never declared by the banks to be in default, the fact remains that payments were not made according to schedule and loans had to be "restructured" with new maturities and interest rates. Throughout the middle 1980s, loans to Latin American countries were a major problem for U.S. banks. Although the word "default" was avoided, the terms of the loans were continually renegotiated, and most of these loans were valued at far below face value (see the International Focus in Chapter 16, "The Problem of Third-World Debt").

Country risk — the risk that a foreign government or foreign politics will interfere with international transactions. At the extreme, country risk includes the possibility that a foreign government may expropriate the firm's property or that a war may ensue.

A second important factor is **country risk.** At one time or another in its history, virtually every government has interfered with international transactions. Such interference has taken the form of regulation of the local foreign-exchange market, restrictions on amounts of currency that can be converted, restrictions on foreign investment by residents, and restrictions on *repatriation* of funds by local subsidiaries of foreign companies (restricting the payment of dividends to the parent company by the subsidiary). Such restrictions may be designed to improve control over the domestic banking system, to conserve foreign exchange, to smooth out fluctuations in the exchange rate, or even to try to influence its level. At any rate, restrictions such as these are sometimes a fact of life, and participants in international transactions must take them into account. Actions by foreign governments also affect the basic business risk of operating internationally. At the extreme, the likelihood of war or of expropriation of property affects basic business decisions made across international boundaries.

Multinational Investment and Financing Decisions

Multinational firm — a firm that operates or invests in two or more countries.

Thus far we have discussed primarily transactions between two parties — for example, one company buying something from another. Complex problems also arise in the case of a single company that operates in two or more countries, the so-called **multinational firm.** The multinational firm must make long-term investments and pay for them in local currencies. It must invest for short periods its idle cash balances held in local currencies. It may find it advantageous to raise funds in local or international capital markets (see International Focus, "The Euroequity Market"). And it must have a way of repatriating the earnings of foreign subsidiaries, back to its native country. All such transactions potentially involve foreign-exchange risk.

Long-Term Investment Decisions

Analyzing investment decisions becomes more complicated where decisions involve capital flows across international boundaries.

Multinational companies invest funds in long-term assets in many countries around the world. They build plants to produce products, replace equipment as it wears out, install new equipment to reduce costs, and invest in transportation and distribution networks. These decisions have the same basic economic characteristics that domestic investment decisions do; namely, they involve making an outlay in the present with the prospect of generating future cash flows.

International Focus

The Euroequity Market

The Eurocurrency market has been around for a good while, beginning with trading in dollars in the 1950s. Eurobonds came later, providing firms the opportunity to sell bonds denominated in dollars or other currencies in foreign capital markets.

In the mid-1980s, a new "Euro" market, called by some the "Euroequity" market, came into being. Prior to 1980, few companies issued stock outside their own domestic capital markets, in spite of the fact that Eurocurrencies and Eurobonds were used routinely. Since 1980, nearly 60 companies have issued stock simultaneously in two or more countries, and the pace is accelerating: 23 of these issues — more than a third of the total — were issued during the first five months of 1986. The accompanying table shows the development of the Euroequity market since 1983.

U.S. companies accounted for 11 of the 23 issues in 1986, compared to three issues in 1985 and one in 1984. The 11 U.S. issues raised a total of $605 million in the European capital markets. Some investment bankers are already predicting that, before too long, a part of almost every U.S. equity issue will be sold in Europe. One of the U.S. offerings in 1986 was issued by Chrysler Corporation, which sold its holdings in the French automobile manufacturer Peugeot through stock offerings in six national markets. Black and Decker recently sold 8.5 million new shares, with 2.0 million of the total going into the European market. In an earlier offering in 1983, Black and Decker had not even considered Europe, but in this latest offering, the company instructed its investment bankers "to get as much of the stock as possible into Europe."

Investment bankers state that the advantage of selling stock in multiple markets is wider distribution, increased demand, and possibly a better price for the issuing company. A company that recently issued 31 percent of its total offering in Europe stated that "the price would have been lower if we had done the deal just in the U.S." One investment banker, whose firm has tripled the size of its staff in London in the past two years, optimistically predicts that "within five years, everybody who issues equity is going to look to the European market."

Source: Adapted from "U.S. Firms Offering Stock Look Overseas," *Wall Street Journal,* June 16, 1986, p. 17.

Year	Number of Issues of Stock in the Euroequity Market	Amount of Stock Issued in the Euroequity Market (millions of dollars)
1983	4	116.6
1984	5	305.8
1985	26	3,185.6
1986 (Jan. thru May)	23	1,733.6

The analytical techniques that we discussed in Part Four apply to international investment decisions as well as to domestic ones. Discounted-cash-flow techniques can be applied, using valuation as the basic decision framework. This process involves the same steps: estimating cash flows, choosing a decision criterion, and setting a return target. However, the evaluation process is more complicated when capital flows across international boundaries.

Besides additional complexity in setting return targets for foreign investments, estimating cash flows also becomes more complex.

Short-Term Investments

Subsidiaries of international firms have temporarily idle cash balances, just as most firms do. Suppose a U.S. firm has a subsidiary in West Germany that has 1 million deutsche marks in a German bank that will not be needed for six months. The funds could be invested in a DM-denominated certificate of deposit with a six-month maturity. Alternatively, the treasurer could buy U.S. dollars on the spot market, invest in a six-month CD denominated in dollars, and sell the dollars (including the prospective interest) six months forward to hedge the transaction and eliminate exchange-rate risk. In fact, the treasurer could do the same thing with any of the major currencies for which an active forward market exists: the British pound, the Canadian dollar, the French franc, the Japanese yen, or the Swiss franc.

Financing Foreign Operations

Firms doing business in foreign countries face many alternatives for financing those activities. A U.S. firm with a subsidiary in France, for example, could raise funds in U.S. capital markets and transfer them to the subsidiary, where the funds would be converted to francs and used for local purposes. The original financing instrument would be denominated in dollars. Alternatively, the firm or its subsidiary could raise funds locally in France, with the obligation denominated in francs.

The Eurocurrency market has become very important in international trade and finance and has become an important source of financing for many multinational firms.

Still a third alternative would be to finance in the Eurocurrency market. Eurocurrencies began with Eurodollars back in the 1950s. A *Eurodollar* is simply a dollar-denominated deposit in a bank outside the United States. Such deposits began in banks in Europe — hence the name. After the Eurodollar was invented, other Eurocurrencies came into being. A Euromark, for example, is simply a deposit denominated in marks in a bank outside West Germany.

The interesting thing about Eurocurrencies is that they are not regulated by any government. In the United States, the Federal Reserve regulates the money supply and controls its size by means of reserve requirements imposed on deposits in commercial banks and by other techniques. Central banks in other countries likewise control the size of their domestic money supplies, but nobody controls Eurocurrencies. If the British government attempted to control Eurodollar deposits in British banks, the deposits would simply move to another country. To gain control of Eurocurrencies would require the collaboration of practically every government in the world — not likely any time soon.

Eurocurrencies remain an unregulated and truly international currency. No one has exact figures on just how large the Eurocurrency market is, but the total at year-end 1987 was believed to have been roughly $3,500 billion, with Eurodollars making up roughly 80 percent of the market. The Eurocurrency market has become very important in international trade and finance and an important source of financing for many multinational firms. Firms can borrow Eurodollars or other Eurocurrencies in the short term or raise long-term funds in the Eurobond market. Rates of interest parallel those in corresponding domestic markets, but deviations do occur and offer opportunities for cheaper financing to sharp-penciled treasurers.

Finance in Practice 24–2

The Foreign Trade Deficit

Like the dollar, the foreign trade deficit was front-page news during the 1980s, and indeed, the two issues are closely connected. What is the "trade deficit"? In simplest terms, it is the difference between what we sell abroad (exports) and what foreigners sell to us (imports). So the trade deficit equals exports minus imports.

There are actually several different ways to measure the deficit—the *merchandise* balance includes goods only; the *current account* balance is a broader measure that also includes services and income flows such as interest and dividends; and the *balance of payments* is broader still to include capital flows and other items. Each of these measures answers a different though related question. The first chart shows the current account balance.

The basic cause of the trade deficit was that we Americans bought more from foreigners than we sold to them. A trade deficit isn't necessarily a big problem as long as it isn't too large and we

have a way to finance it, such as with dividends and interest received on foreign investments. The deficit wasn't a problem in the early 1980s, but it began to grow larger in 1983, just after the massive tax cuts of 1981. Some economists and politicians predicted that Americans would save the extra cash they received from the 1981 tax cuts, but they didn't—they spent it. The overall savings rate of Americans dropped from an average of 6 to 7 percent of disposable income to 2 to 3 percent by the mid-1980s. Some of those same economists also predicted that the

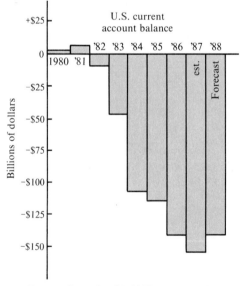

Source: Fortune, December 21, 1987.

1981 tax cuts would stimulate economic activity to such an extent that tax receipts of the U.S. Treasury would actually *rise,* but that didn't happen either. At the same time, the Reagan administration did not succeed in its goal of reducing overall federal spending, although there were shifts among categories such as defense and domestic spending. The failure to achieve spending cuts coupled with the drop in tax receipts threw the federal budget massively into deficit.

The trade deficit and the budget deficit are related. The budget deficit drove up real (inflation-adjusted) interest rates. That made investments denominated in dollars attractive, so the dollar rose in value (see Finance in Practice 24–1). The strong dollar caused foreign goods to fall in price, making them more attractive as far as Americans were concerned. With more money to spend after the 1981 tax cut, Americans went on a buying binge — Hondas, BMWs, Toyotas, VCRs, CD players, cameras, Walkmen — things that make life fun. We financed the budget deficit by borrowing the money from foreigners, and they got the money to lend us by selling us cars and VCRs. We spent, and foreigners took our IOU.

Viewed from another angle, the total claims on the U.S. economy — for consumption, investment by business, and government — were greater than the economy could produce. Total demand exceeded capacity. When that happens, only two outcomes are possible: either prices rise to reduce demand, or part of the demand is satisfied from abroad. The latter occurred.

Measured in dollars, the trade deficit remained in bad shape throughout 1987. Measured in physical units, however, the merchandise deficit actually peaked in 1986 (see the second chart). Exports began to improve, and the physical quantity of imports leveled off. But the value of the dollar had begun to decline in early 1985 (see Finance in Practice 24–1), making imports more expensive. So, even

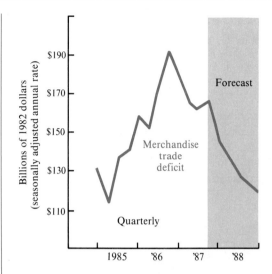

Source: *Fortune,* December 21, 1987.

though the volume of imports stopped rising in 1986, the dollar value of those imports stayed high throughout 1987.

When the United States runs a trade deficit, foreigners accumulate dollar holdings. What are those foreigners doing with all those dollars? The answer is that they are investing large amounts back into the United States. They are buying stocks, bonds, and real estate. The Japanese alone invested $4.1 billion in U.S. real estate in 1986, and another $2.2 billion during the first half of 1987. Exxon Corporation is among a number of U.S. companies that now pay rent to a foreign landlord. At the end of 1985, foreigners owned about $1 trillion of U.S. assets, 20 percent by foreign governments and 80 percent by foreign individuals, corporations and institutions. The latter breaks down as follows: $80 billion of Treasury securities, $200 billion of corporate stocks and bonds, $180 billion of direct investment in U.S. companies, and $400 billion in bank deposits.

Of course, Americans themselves own extensive foreign assets. Until the mid-1980s, Americans owned more abroad than foreigners owned in the United States, but in the mid-1980s that position was reversed. Why? Because of the trade deficit. Because of our consumption and government spending binges, we Americans had to look to foreigners to provide part of our needs. We bought foreign goods, and the foreigners used a good part of the money we paid them to buy long-term assets in the United States. We traded our shopping centers and office buildings and companies for cars and CD players. The long-term implications of continuing such a swap are worrisome indeed. As 1987 drew to a close, there were some hopeful signs that the trade deficit was slowly improving, but we still had a long way to go.

Sources: "The Selling of America," *Fortune,* December 22, 1986; "Surprising Majority Agree on the Need for Weaker Dollar," *Wall Street Journal,* November 7, 1987; "Crawling Out of the Trade Tunnel," *Fortune,* December 21, 1987.

Accounting and Reporting Requirements

As one might imagine, measuring the performance and financial position of a firm engaged in international operations gets very complicated. Added to the problem of accounting for domestic operations are all the complexities of foreign exchange and dealing with foreign-exchange gains and losses.

Translation — the conversion of accounting information denominated in one currency into accounting information denominated in another currency.

There is the problem of foreign-currency **translation**. Suppose a multinational firm has subsidiaries in several countries. To keep things simple, assume for the moment that during a particular accounting period there were no capital flows between parent and subsidiaries and no foreign-exchange transactions of any kind. The firm still must deal with foreign exchange if it wants to produce a consolidated accounting statement combining the operations of the entire multinational enterprise. The financial statements of a French subsidiary are denominated in francs; the statements of a Japanese subsidiary are denominated in yen. To produce consolidated statements, all of these figures must be converted into dollars. Translation is a very complicated and important matter, but it affects only one part of the overall problem of managing foreign operations — the preparation of consolidated financial statements by multinational firms.

KEY CONCEPTS

1. International operations have become steadily more important in the U.S. economy during the past two decades.

2. The major trading nations of the world operated under a system of fixed exchange rates, called the Bretton Woods system, from 1949 to 1971. In 1973, a system of floating rates was adopted.

3. Under a fixed-rate system, foreign-exchange rates are set administratively by governments. Under a floating-rate system, rates are set by market forces.

4. A foreign-exchange rate is the price of one currency in terms of another.

5. The *spot* foreign-exchange market is the market for immediate delivery of one currency in exchange for another. The *forward* market is the market for delivery at some future date.

6. The difference between the spot and forward rates, the *forward premium* or *forward discount,* depends on the expectations of investors regarding future changes in exchange rates and depends indirectly on relative interest rates and

inflation rates in the two countries. The relationship between spot and forward rates is formally described by the interest-rate-parity theorem.

7. Covered-interest arbitrage is the market process that results in the rate relationships described by the interest-rate-parity theorem.

8. Managers can insure against the risk of changes in exchange rates by hedging—that is, by buying or selling currencies in forward markets.

9. International investment and financing decisions involve credit risk, country risk, and foreign-exchange risk.

10. International money and capital markets offer managers additional flexibility, but at the cost of additional complexity.

SUMMARY

Firms that do business in more than one country must make transactions in currencies other than their own. Managers of such firms, therefore, must deal with the complexities of foreign-exchange rates and foreign-exchange risk.

Spot foreign-exchange rates are the prices of one currency in terms of another for immediate delivery. Forward rates are present prices for transactions at future dates—that is, funds for future delivery. One currency may sell at a forward premium or discount relative to another, depending on expectations regarding future changes in the spot rate and also on relative rates of interest in the two countries.

The interest-rate-parity theorem describes a relationship of fundamental importance in understanding foreign-exchange markets. The theorem relates the forward/spot differential for two currencies to relative rates of interest in the two countries.

Most companies doing business internationally try to insure against losses resulting from movements in exchange rates. The most common technique is to hedge using the forward markets. Both asset and liability positions can be hedged with the appropriate sales or purchases in the forward market.

International investment decisions ought to be analyzed using the same basic framework applicable to domestic decisions. When the standard procedures are applied, however, they become more complex because of the extra complication of foreign exchange.

QUESTIONS

1. How does the financial manager's task change when the company engages in foreign operations?

2. Describe the difference between a fixed-exchange-rate system and a floating-exchange-rate system.

3. Which of the two systems in question (2) is a business manager likely to prefer and why?

4. Distinguish between the spot and forward foreign-exchange markets.

5. What factors account for the forward/spot differential?

6. Describe how a corporate treasurer can hedge against the chance of an exchange-rate loss on an asset held in French francs.

7. Describe how a corporate treasurer can hedge against the chance of an exchange-rate loss on a long-term liability denominated in Swiss francs.

8. What is the interest-rate-parity theorem?

9. What is covered-interest arbitrage?

Problems

1. Refer to the exchange rates in Table 24–2 to answer the following:

a. Is the French franc at a premium or discount in relation to the U.S. dollar?

b. What is the premium/discount on an annual basis for the 180-day forward franc?

c. What does this information tell you about relative interest rates and inflation rates in France and the United States?

2. Referring again to Table 24–2, if the U.S. dollar cost of a Japanese yen were $0.004155 in July 1985, has the U.S. dollar appreciated or depreciated against the yen since mid-1985? What are the probable reasons for this change? Assuming everything the same, what would a Japanese automobile selling for $10,000 in mid-1985 cost in December 1987?

3. A U.S. firm in early December 1987 must pay a Canadian supplier $100,000 Canadian in ninety days. Which party bears the foreign-exchange risk? Which options are open to the U.S. firm? What was the market's forecast of future (90 day) U.S.-Canadian spot rates as of December 4, 1987? See Table 24–2.

4. It is December 4, 1987. Using the exchange rates quoted in Table 24–2, how would you, the firm's international-currency expert, respond to the following inquiry from your boss, the firm's treasurer: "We have agreed to advance our West German subsidiary 1,000,000 deutsche marks (DM) on March 4, 1988. My neighbor, an economist, predicts that the spot rate, for dollars per deutsche mark, will be $0.6050 at that time. That means we will need $605,000 to purchase the necessary foreign currency. What do you think?"

5. On December 4, 1987, a Canadian affiliate had to pay its Dutch (Netherlands) supplier 150,000 guilders. How many Canadian dollars were required to make the payment? See Table 24–2.

6. On January 3, 1986, the three-month Eurodollar interest rate was 7.94 percent. The spot and forward rates for West German deutsche marks (DM) per U.S. dollar are given in Table A. What rate would you expect to receive on a three-month Euro-deutsche-mark deposit? What would you do if Euro-deutsche-mark deposits were offered at 6 percent?

Table A

Foreign-Exchange Market	West German Deutsche Marks (DM) per U.S. dollar
Spot	2.4580
30-day forward	2.4504
90-day forward	2.4377
180-day forward	2.4182

7. ABC Corp. is evaluating a cost-reduction proposal by its Japanese affiliate. The project would increase the amount of funds which could be paid to ABC Corp. by the affiliate in the form of dividends. The project costs 2,383,500 yen. The increased after-tax cash flow available for dividend payments to ABC Corp. would be 476,700,000 yen per year for 10 years. ABC Corp.'s required rate of return on cost-reduction proposals is 15 percent. If the dollar/yen spot rate was currently $0.004195, would the project be acceptable? Would the project be worthwhile on December 4, 1987? See Table 24–2.

8. If the British pound/U.S. dollar spot rate were currently £0.67 (0.67 pounds per dollar) in New York, and a London currency dealer offered you pounds for $1.47, what action would you take? If other traders followed your example, what would happen to pound/dollar rates in New York and London?

9. It is December 4, 1987, and you have just come into a large inheritance. You want to invest the money at the highest-possible rate for six months while you and your financial advisers develop a long-term investment strategy. Six-month U.S.-dollar deposits in London offer an annual rate of approximately 7.6 percent. Your bank tells you that six-month Swiss-franc deposits in London offer annual rates of approximately 3.5 percent, and six-month deposits of West German marks in London offer annual rates of approximately 3.8 percent. Would you make your deposit in U.S. dollars, Swiss francs, or West German marks? The exchange rates needed to answer this question can be found in Table 24–2.

REFERENCES

Dufey, G., and I. H. Giddy. *The International Money Market*. Prentice-Hall Foundations of Finance Series. Englewood Cliffs, N.J.: Prentice-Hall, 1978.

Eiteman, D. K., and A. I. Stonehill. *Multinational Business Finance*. Reading, Mass.: Addison-Wesley, 1982.

Lessard, D. R. *International Financial Management: Theory and Application,* 2nd ed. New York: John Wiley & Sons, 1985.

Oblak, D. J., and R. J. Helm Jr. "Survey and Analysis of Capital Budgeting Methods Used by Multinationals." *Financial Management* 9 (Winter 1980): 37–41.

Rodriguez, R. M., and E. E. Carter. *International Financial Management,* 2nd ed. Englewood Cliffs, N.J.: Prentice-Hall, 1979.

Shapiro, A. *Multinational Financial Management*. Boston: Allyn & Bacon, 1986.

25

Mergers and Acquisitions

In this chapter, we will discuss corporate mergers and acquisitions. These corporate combinations have reshaped the organization of many companies both in the United State and abroad and have in recent years been the focus of considerable attention by both financial managers and government officials. We will begin with some history. Next we will discuss how and why mergers may create value for shareholders and explore various motives for merging, including creation of value. Then we will examine some evidence regarding effects of mergers on returns to shareholders of both acquiring and acquired firms. Finally, we will examine the merger phenomenon from a public-policy perspective.

Statutory merger—a combination of two or more firms in which one company survives under its own name while any others cease to exist as legal entities.

Corporate mergers have played a prominent role in shaping the structure of U.S. corporations. For example, in 1984 Chevron purchased Gulf Oil and paid more than $13 billion in cash for the privilege. In addition, Chevron and Gulf Oil paid financial advisers in excess of $60 million for advice about the merger. This large merger is one of many. In 1987 alone, over 3,700 separate acquisitions occurred in the United States,[1] involving about $170 billion in market value. In fact, mergers became such publicized events that even cartoon strips carried some of the news.

Technically speaking, there are a number of different ways two (or more) firms can combine. For example, in a **statutory merger,** when two or more firms combine, one company survives under its own name and the others cease to exist as legal entities. In a **statutory consolidation,** on the other hand, all the combining companies cease to exist as legal entities, and an entirely new, consolidated corporation is created. In addition, corporate combinations differ in their tax treatment and accounting treatment, depending upon rules laid down by the Internal Revenue Service and the accounting profession.

Hostile takeover—occurs when the acquired firm's management resists the acquisition, and the acquiring firm goes over their heads by buying stock directly from shareholders.

Tender offer—an acquiring firm's offer to pay existing shareholders some specified amount of cash or securities if these shareholders will sell (tender) their shares of stock to the acquiring firm.

Some mergers are consummated after amicable negotiation between managers of acquiring and acquired firms. Other business combinations occur despite bitter disagreement between two sets of managers. In such **hostile takeovers,** the acquiring firm often goes over the heads of the acquired firm's management to the shareholders by means of a **tender offer.** A tender offer is an offer to pay existing shareholders some specified amount of cash or securities if these shareholders will sell (tender) their shares of stock to the acquiring firm. For present purposes, we will use the broader term *merger* to refer to combinations of firms without making these detailed distinctions.

[1]The source for the number of mergers is *Mergers and Acquisitions.*

Finance in Practice 25–1

The Language of the Merger Market

No reader of the financial press in the 1980s could fail to notice the frequent accounts of one large company buying another. Corporate America had entered a merger boom sometimes likened to a feeding frenzy of sharks. The question in managers' minds was whether their company was the next deal in the merger market.

Suppose you encountered a newspaper headline reading: "Poison Pill Not Effective; White Knight to the Rescue." Although you might expect an account of a fairy tale to follow, the story would probably be about an attempted takeover being resisted by the management of the target company. Here are a few definitions to help the confused reader decipher the meaning of some of the language used to describe the merger market.

Crown jewel—the most valued asset held by an acquisition target; divestiture of this asset is frequently a sufficient defense to discourage takeover.

Greenmail — the premium paid by a targeted company to a raider in exchange for the raider's shares of the targeted company.

Maiden — the target company toward which a takeover attempt is directed.

Poison pill — a provision giving stockholders other than those involved in a hostile takeover the right to purchase securities at a very favorable price in the event of a takeover.

Raider — the person or company attempting the takeover of another company.

Shark repellants — antitakeover corporate-charter amendments.

Stripper — a successful raider who sells off some of the assets of the target company once the target is acquired.

White knight — a merger partner (solicited by management of a target) who offers an alternative merger plan to that offered by the raider and who protects the target company from attempted takeover by the raider.

Source: Mack Ott and G. J. Santoni, "Mergers and Takeovers — The Value of Predators' Information," The Federal Reserve Bank of St. Louis, December 1985.

Golden parachute — a provision in the employment contract of top-level management that provides for severance pay or other compensation should the manager lose his or her job as the result of a takeover.

Leveraged buyout (LBO) — an acquisition financed largely with new debt, typically borrowed against the assets of the acquired firm.

Mergers have provoked considerable public concern.

One of the most notorious deals of the 1980s was a four-cornered fight among Bendix, Martin Marietta, Allied, and United Technologies. Ultimately, in 1982 Allied acquired Bendix for $1.8 billion, but before the takeover could be completed, tender offers by Bendix and Martin Marietta for each other had to be unraveled. In the heat of the Bendix/Martin Marietta takeover battle, the board of Bendix voted its chairman Bill Agee a **golden parachute.** The contract guaranteed him an annual salary of $825,000 for five years if Bendix were acquired. The public fighting of such major U.S. corporations was a catalyst for many critics of hostile takeover activity, spurring an outcry for new and stronger federal legislation to control mergers. Yet the merger activity continued. Table 25–1 shows the largest deals of 1987. For example, Burlington Industries was acquired by Burlington Holdings, a newly formed company. The acquisition followed an unsuccessful attempt by a Canadian firm to buy Burlington in a hostile takeover. The Burlington takeover is an example of a **leveraged buyout (LBO),** in which the purchase is financed with large amounts of new debt. LBOs have become a mainstay of the 1980s acquisitions market in the United States.

The desirability of mergers remains a key topic of public debate. In addition, corporate managers are investing time and resources in buying firms or in fighting off unwanted suitors.

All of this activity raises basic financial questions. Do mergers create value to the owners of merging firms? As we have discussed throughout the book, financial managers should strive to make decisions that increase the value of the firm to existing shareholders. Do mergers further this objective of value maximization? Mergers also raise other questions for public-policy makers. Do mergers increase or decrease competition in U.S. markets? Do mergers allow firms to take advantage of certain cost-saving techniques? Are mergers in the best interests of society? Before we address some of these questions, let us take a look at the history of mergers.

Table 25—1

Biggest Deals of 1987

Rank	Companies/Transaction	Industry	Price Paid for Acquired Company (thousands of dollars)	Percentage of Book Value of Acquired Company
1	British Petroleum acquires Standard Oil	Oil and gas Oil and gas	7,995,213	253
2	Borg-Warner Holdings acquires Borg-Warner	Automotive parts, chemicals	4,174,579	262
3	Owens-Illinois Holdings acquires Owens-Illinois	Glass containers, plastics	3,728,748	222
4	J. T. Acquisition acquires Southland	Convenience stores, dairy products	3,712,105	215
5	Unilever acquires Chesebrough-Ponds	Food, soap Toiletries	3,096,092	294
6	National Amusements acquires Viacom International	Movie theaters Television entertainment	2,937,841	731
7	Hoechst acquires Celanese	Chemicals Chemicals	2,885,706	302
8	Burlington Holdings acquires Burlington Industries	Textiles	2,497,667	218
9	Hillsborough Holdings acquires Jim Walter Corporation	Housing	2,312,355	200
10	JMB Institutional Realty acquires Cadillac Fairview	Real estate Real estate	1,990,116	NA

NA: not available

Source: "Deals of the Year," *Fortune,* February 1, 1988.

History of Mergers in the United States

Recent merger activity is the fourth major wave of mergers in U.S. financial history.

While the current wave of mergers is certainly an important event, it is not unprecedented. In fact, today's activity is the fourth major wave of mergers in U.S. financial history. Mergers tend to occur in large waves, with lulls without significant merger activity coming between the waves. The first large mergers in U.S. history began in the late 1800s. During that period, U.S. Steel became the first billion-dollar corporation in U.S. history as the result of many smaller steel firms combining into one corporate giant. Most of the mergers during this period combined companies in the same industry, leading to one dominant firm in that particular industry.

This first merger wave ended around 1903 as the U.S. economy took a downturn. A result of that merger activity, however, was a public outcry against the formation of these large firms, sometimes called *trusts*. This factor contributed to the passage of additional antitrust laws in the first part of the twentieth century. Such laws were directed at a corporation's attempts to monopolize industries or fix prices.

The second wave of merger activity occurred after World War I, through the 1920s. Unlike those that occurred in the first wave, however, these mergers did not lead to the emergence of one dominant firm in an industry. George Stigler, Nobel Prize winner in economics, considers this second wave to have been "mergers for oligopoly." An **oligopoly** is an industry that has a few large firms rather than a single dominant firm. In the merger wave after the First World War, there were typically a number of large firms left in an industry after the mergers.

The third merger wave began after World War II and ran through the late 1960s. Looking at Figure 25–1, we can see some measures of the annual merger activity during this period. Although the data in Figure 25–1 are only for stocks traded on the American and New York Stock Exchanges, the figure still portrays the trends in overall merger activity in the United States. One major difference between mergers after World War II and earlier mergers is that mergers after World War II were largely **conglomerate mergers,** or mergers between firms in different industries. In contrast, **horizontal mergers** combine firms operating in the same business line, and **vertical mergers** combine firms that have some customer/supplier relationship. For example, a chemical company buying a sports-equipment manufacturer would be a conglomerate merger. A clothing manufacturer buying a firm that makes fabrics would be a vertical merger. This third merger wave peaked in the late 1960s, as Figure 25–1 shows.

Oligopoly — an industry that has a few large firms rather than a single large firm or numerous smaller firms and that possesses some competitive characteristics and some monopolistic ones.

Conglomerate merger — a merger that combines firms that operate in different industries.

Horizontal merger — a merger that combines firms operating in the same business line.

Vertical merger — a merger that combines firms that have some customer/supplier relationship.

Figure 25–1
Mergers of Exchange-Listed Companies, 1955–1984

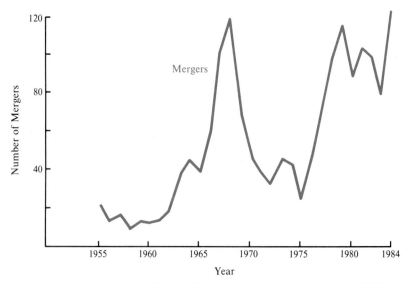

Source: J. R. Franks and R. S. Harris, "Merger Waves: Theory and Evidence," (Chapel Hill, University of North Carolina, Working Paper, 1986).

During the 1960s, merger activity was extremely hectic. In a one-month period, one firm, Automatic Sprinkler, acquired four other firms. The mergers also involved a number of innovative financing schemes. In addition, there was public outcry against the mergers. In the late 1960s, the Justice Department issued major guidelines in an attempt to designate when mergers would be in violation of antitrust laws and, thus, subject to legal action by the U.S. government. The decline in mergers, leading into the early 1970s, was a result of a combination of factors including the economic downturn in the economy and the fact that some of the mergers pursued in the 1960s appeared to have less than favorable outcomes.

As Figure 25–1 shows, mergers again started to increase in the 1970s and crescendoed into the 1980s. In 1985 alone there were over 3,000 corporate acquisitions and in 1986 the number exceeded 4,000. The most recent wave of mergers has some different characteristics from the earlier mergers.

The fourth merger wave (mid-1970s through 1980s) has had characteristics different from those of earlier merger waves.

As Table 25–2 displays, in many of the recent mergers the acquiring firm focused on the particular assets being purchased (for example, British Petroleum's purchase of the oil and gas business of Standard Oil) without an exclusive focus on earnings per share. As we will show later in the chapter, many earlier mergers appear to have been motivated by desires to manipulate earnings-per-share figures. The means of payment in recent mergers have also differed. In the 1960s, most mergers were accomplished through the payment of the acquiring firm's stock or convertible securities (for example, convertible bonds) to the acquired firm's shareholders in exchange for their stock in the acquired firm. More recently, many more mergers were accomplished with payment in cash, often raised by large new debt issues. Later in this chapter we will discuss the differences associated with means of payment. Table 25–2 also indicates that many recent mergers were unfriendly, which means that the acquired firm's management resisted the takeover, and the acquiring firm went over their heads by buying stock directly from shareholders. Such a hostile takeover differs from friendly mergers, in which managers of both firms come to terms on the details of the merger. Finally, in recent years there have been many mergers between firms in the same industry. These horizontal mergers have substantially reshaped many U.S. industries. For example, in 1984 the three largest mergers of U.S. companies all involved horizontal mergers in the oil business: Chevron acquiring Gulf, Texaco buying Getty Oil, and Mobil acquiring Superior Oil.

Table 25–2
Comparison of Merger Characteristics: The 1980s Versus the 1960s

Mergers in the 1960s	*Mergers in the 1980s*
1. Focus on earnings per share	1. Focus on underlying assets
2. Payment with stock and convertible securities	2. Payment with cash, often debt financed
3. Few hostile takeovers	3. Frequent unfriendly raids
4. Mostly conglomerate mergers	4. Many horizontal mergers

Merger Motives

A basic question to be answered is: What motivates mergers? One possible motive is that mergers create value for the owners of the acquiring and acquired firms. If such value is created, we may view mergers as being in the best interest of shareholders and consistent with good capital-budgeting decisions made by firms. On the other hand, some authorities have argued that mergers are simply ways for managers of corporations to further their own interest even at the expense of shareholders. For example, if a manager's compensation and psychic rewards are based on the size of the company, he or she would have an interest in acquiring another firm and thereby increasing the size of the corporation. If successful in carrying out these desires, he or she might acquire another company even if that acquisition cost more than the benefits it could give to shareholders. Thus, a first question is whether mergers create value or whether they are motivated by the personal interests of managers. Do merger projects have a positive net present value (*NPV*) for shareholders in the participating firms?

Even if value is created in mergers, however, we must look a bit further. We have to see if there is extra value in a merger for shareholders of both acquiring and acquired firms. That is, do mergers have a positive net present value for *both* sets of owners? It is possible that acquired-firm shareholders would receive a price in the merger that was sufficiently high to make them better off, while acquiring-firm shareholders would have paid too high a price. In this case, the merger would have a positive net present value for acquired-firm shareholders but a negative *NPV* for acquiring-firm shareholders.

An important question in evaluating mergers: Do *both* the owners of the acquiring firm *and* the owners of the acquired firm view the merger as providing a positive net present value?

How can mergers increase value? Table 25–3 lists some of the more frequently cited merger motives. One motive is that mergers sometimes enable companies to take advantage of certain cost-saving techniques that may be available only when two firms combine. For example, the merging firms may be able to consolidate some administrative functions (such as accounting staffs) and save money. A merger may also allow certain scale economies in production if prior to the merger

Mergers sometimes allow companies to take advantage of certain cost-saving techniques.

Table 25–3
Merger Motives

Cost savings
Monopoly power
Avoiding bankruptcy
Tax considerations
Retirement planning
Diversification
Increased debt capacity
Undervalued assets
Manipulating earnings per share
Management desires
Replacing inefficient management

the firms were too small to be efficient. Cost savings may also occur if firms with different strengths combine through a merger. An example might be a small firm with the latest technology that merges with a larger company that knows how to mass produce the product and market it nationwide. Alternatively, both combining companies could be small but one might have the technical know-how while the other has the sales expertise. For example, in 1982 SmithKline Corporation, a major company in the health-care industry, acquired Beckman Instruments, a firm that designed, manufactured, and marketed laboratory instruments, related chemical supplies, and industrial components. Among other things, the combination eliminated duplicate fundamental research and, through SmithKline's marketing expertise and access to the health-care distribution system, provided an improved commercial outlet for Beckman's products. Management of the two firms had hopes that the merger would create **synergy** — the result of a combination in which the combined firm is worth more than the sum of the values of the separate firms.

Synergy — the effect achieved when the whole is greater than the sum of its parts.

Value may also be increased when a combination of two firms allows them to exercise more monopoly power and keep their prices well in excess of costs. Such higher prices that increase profits and cash flow to the firm could also lead to increases in value. This benefit might be achieved when two firms in the same industry combine, reducing the number of effective competitors by one. Of course, the ability to keep higher prices in the long run depends on how easily other firms can enter the market. Unless there are barriers to entry, excess profits are not likely to persist over time. New firms will enter the market, and prices and profits will be forced down. In recent years, the potential entrants to markets have increasingly come from abroad as the world economy has become more integrated — as demonstrated by the developments in the automobile, textile, and steel industries.

In some cases, a combination of two firms allows them to exercise more monopoly power and keep their prices well in excess of costs.

There are many other reasons why individual mergers can lead to increases in value. Some mergers are the best way for one company to avoid some of the high cost associated with the failure of one firm. For example, in early 1983 United American Bank of Knoxville failed — resulting in the fourth largest bank failure in U.S. history. Instead of long and costly delays, United American was taken over by another bank, First Tennessee National Corporation, almost immediately.

Some mergers arise because they are the best way for one company to avoid bankruptcy.

Tax laws also provide merger motives in some instances. If one company has tax losses it cannot presently use (for example, it does not have income against which it can deduct taxable expenses), it may have a motive for a merger. After the merger, those tax losses can lead to tax savings when applied to the income of some other company, and these tax savings can increase value. Thus mergers, like leases discussed in Chapter 19, can provide a mechanism whereby corporations take best advantage of tax laws. As an example, Bangor Punta had substantial tax losses after the expropriation of its sugar plantations in Cuba. Because it could not use these losses, it combined with other firms that did have taxable income.[2]

Tax laws also provide a motive for mergers in some instances.

Another consideration leading to the acquisition of many smaller firms is planning for retirement by acquired-company owners or managers. An acquisition may be a

Some mergers arise because the owners or managers of smaller firms plan for retirement.

[2]The Internal Revenue Service does have rules against pursuing mergers solely to use tax losses. In practice, however, these rules allow for some tax benefits to be realized by virtue of two firms combining to take advantage of what would otherwise be unused tax losses.

perfect way for the founder of a company to cash in his or her investment. When all of an individual's wealth is tied up in one company, the person is not well diversified and does not, therefore, gain the risk-reducing benefits of portfolio diversification. When that person is vitally involved in the management of the business, he or she may be prepared to accept such a lack of diversification. In planning for retirement, however, the individual may desire to diversify. One way to achieve that diversification is to sell the company in a merger. The seller may obtain cash that could be invested elsewhere. Alternatively, he or she could receive readily marketable stock in a larger, more diversified acquiring firm.[3]

A reason often given for mergers is the benefit of diversification, but we must be careful here because the word *diversification* is sometimes used to mean two quite different things. First, managers sometimes use the term *diversification* to refer to a firm's branching out of its existing lines of business because they no longer offer new investment opportunities for expansion. As an example, a cash-rich company, but one with no new internally profitable investments, may view acquisitions of other lines of business as alternatives to paying increased dividends or repurchasing shares of its own stock. Because dividend payments may impose extra personal-income taxes on shareholders, as we discussed in Chapter 17, the acquisition route may be attractive — as long as the merger premium paid is not too high. Acquisitions may be preferable to share repurchase because the Internal Revenue Service may classify large systematic repurchases as taxable if the motive is purely to avoid the paying of personal taxes on dividend income. This type of diversification is based on basic changes in the actual cash flows involved (perhaps motivated by taxes) and may create value. This usage is not the traditional financial definition of diversification, which depends on risk.

The benefit of diversification is often cited as a motive for mergers.

The second meaning of *diversification* refers to risk. Do mergers diversify risks? In our earlier discussion of risk, we noted that as long as returns to two businesses are not perfectly correlated, the combination of the two by merger can produce a firm with lower variability of returns, as when we combined two or more stocks in a portfolio. Mergers can thus reduce the variability of a firm's returns.

Is this diversification valuable? The answer depends on how well the firm's shareholders are diversified in the first place. Suppose a shareholder already owned shares in both firms; the firm's diversification might do nothing more than the shareholder has already done. If such were the case, the diversification accomplished through a merger would provide no new diversification benefits. In general, if shareholders are already well diversified, the diversification in the merger will provide no new substantial diversification benefits. For a person who owns stock in only one company, however, the diversification in the merger might be of benefit.

In general, if shareholders are well diversified, the diversification in a merger will provide no additional diversification benefits.

In addition, an indirect benefit of diversification can result if it increases the company's ability to borrow money, allowing it to benefit further from the use of financial leverage. As we saw in Chapters 15 and 16, the use of financial leverage

---

[3]In fact, tax laws often provide an incentive for owner/managers who are selling their companies to prefer being paid in common stock rather than in cash. Under certain conditions, the capital gain on the stock received in the merger is not taxed until the stock is actually sold, whereas capital-gains taxes would be levied immediately if cash were received.

can increase the value of a firm, although firms must trade off the benefits of leverage (for example, the tax-deductibility of interest) against the risks introduced by leverage. Thus, prudence dictates using leverage only up to a point because of leverage-induced risks. Diversification by means of a merger may make the combined entity subject to less variability in operating flows than existed in either of the premerger firms. As a result, the post-merger firm may find that its best capital structure involves using more debt than the combined debt of the two pre-merger firms. The increased use of debt may increase value.[4] Certainly many leveraged buyouts are motivated by the desire to reap value by using more debt. Many of these LBOs, however, involve no real combination of firms but rather focus on the refinancing of an existing set of assets, sometimes including the sale of some assets to pay off debt.

One frequently stated reason for merger is that the earning power and assets of the acquired company are undervalued by the stock market. If so, the assets of the acquired firm can be bought at a bargain price in a merger. The question then arises: Can managers of an acquiring firm have a better idea of the value of a company than other investors who buy and sell stocks? If acquiring-firm managers have some inside information, unknown to the general public, they may in fact know when a company is undervalued. For example, if company A knows that company B is on the verge of discovering a cure for the common cold, but the general investing public does not have this information, company A may know that company B is currently undervalued in the market. There is no doubt that the stock market undervalues some companies and overvalues others relative to the cash flows the companies will eventually produce. The challenge for a potential acquiring firm is to find some way of knowing how to separate one group of firms from the other. After all, the market value represents the consensus value of thousands of well-informed investors about the current value of *expected* future outcomes.

Three last motives for merger deserve mention. First, as we will analyze later in this chapter, acquisitions may provide a means to increase earnings per share (at least in the short run). Second, acquisitions may not be motivated by shareholder interests at all but rather may be a result of managers' desire to manage larger and growing firms even if such size and growth come at the expense of shareholder value. Third, some argue that acquisitions are one way inefficient managers may be replaced. It may be very difficult, and in fact often is difficult, to replace the entire upper level of management. If managers of a company are not doing a good job, someone can buy the company and substitute better management and, in this way, increase value.

While Table 25–3 contains the major merger motives, one could find others that fit certain business combinations.[5] What is important from a financial man-

One motive for takeover is to replace inefficient managers.

The financial manager is interested in estimating whether a merger can increase value, regardless of the source of that value.

[4]This increase in debt capacity was suggested by W. G. Lewellen, "A Pure Financial Rationale for the Conglomerate Merger," *Journal of Finance,* May 1971, pp. 521–45. For a more thorough analysis of the issues, see R. C. Higgins and L. D. Schall, "Corporate Bankruptcy and Conglomerate Merger," *Journal of Finance,* March 1975, pp. 93–113.

[5]See F. M. Scherer, *Industrial Market Structure and Economic Performance,* 2nd ed. (Chicago: Rand McNally, 1982); T. E. Copeland and J. F. Weston, *Financial Theory and Corporate Policy,* 3rd ed. (Reading, Mass.: Addison-Wesley, 1988).

ager's point of view is to make an estimate of whether the merger can lead to increased value, regardless of the source of that value.

Financial Evaluation of Mergers

Viewed from the perspective of the acquiring firm, buying another firm is like investing in a new project.

From the perspective of an acquiring firm, a merger can be viewed as an investment decision for which standard discounted-cash-flow techniques can be used.

Merger premium—the difference between the value of the money or securities offered by an acquiring firm and the present value of the stock owned by the shareholders of the firm to be acquired.

Like other financial-management decisions, acquisitions are not made simply by plugging numbers into equations.

One useful way to view a merger is from the perspective of the acquiring firm. From this perspective, buying another firm is like investing in a new project. There is a certain outlay associated with the merger. This outlay will be the amount paid to the acquired firm's shareholders, or the value of the securities traded to those shareholders in exchange for obtaining the company. In exchange for this outlay, the acquiring firm will expect to receive certain cash-flow benefits from the acquired firm. These cash flows will occur in future periods as the assets and labor force of the firm that has been purchased generate cash flows from operations.

Alternatively, these cash flows could come from cost savings to the acquiring firm as a result of buying a new entity. Or these cash flows could come from selling off some of the assets of the corporation that has been bought. In any case, we can view the merger as an investment proposal. There is an initial outlay to obtain another company. There are some cash benefits, mostly in the future, of undertaking the merger. Thus, from the perspective of an acquiring firm, a merger can be viewed as an *investment decision,* and we can use the standard discounted-cash-flow techniques developed in earlier chapters to analyze such an acquisition. The questions for the acquiring managers are: Does the merger investment have a positive net present value (*NPV*)? Is the *NPV* of the merger larger than the *NPV* of other mutually exclusive investment alternatives?

Similarly, the net present value of the merger can also be analyzed from the perspective of the acquired firm. From the acquired firm's perspective, the benefits of selling out the firm are primarily in the present, whereas the costs of the merger are the forgone cash flows that might have been received in future periods. In many cases, this analysis can be simplified because the future cash flows that were expected to be received by acquired-firm shareholders have already been given a value in the market represented by the current market value of the stock of the acquired firm. In such a case, the acquired firm's shareholders must compare the value of money or securities promised by the acquiring firm to the present market value of the stock owned. The difference, the **merger premium,** is a stockholder's incentive to sell out the company. This merger premium must be weighed against whatever other factors the acquired firm's shareholders believe are involved in selling the company.

Mergers and Discounted Cash Flow

Like other financial-management decisions, acquisitions are not made simply by plugging numbers into equations. Decisions to merge involve complicated judgments about growth and profit potential of specific product markets, the quality of a company's management, and the compatibility of the two organizations planning to merge. For these reasons, many of the difficult decisions about mergers involve nonfinancial and nonquantifiable factors. Many firms first approach the subject of making acquisitions by seeing how an acquisition fits a broad corporate strategy. For example, one firm may see itself as specializing in high-technology areas and, as a result, will consider acquisitions only of other high-technology firms. Another firm may be seeking to diversify out of its existing lines of business and will, therefore, look only at certain types of corporations as potential acquisitions.

Realizing this, finance still plays a critical role in acquisitions. To decide whether buying another company makes sense, managers ultimately have to be able to set a value on a company they might buy. If the company can be purchased for less than this value, the acquisition has a positive net present value to the acquiring firm. The challenge is establishing such a value. Fortunately, the discounted-cash-flow techniques we developed in earlier chapters are useful here. An acquisition can be viewed as an investment proposal with cash traded today in hopes of receiving cash in future periods. Equation (1) restates our basic calculation of net present value developed in Chapter 10. The original outlay, C_0, is separated and is shown as a negative number to emphasize that it is money going out at time zero.

$$NPV = -C_0 + \sum_{t=1}^{N} \frac{C_t}{(1 + K)^t},$$ (1)

where C_0 = the market value of all the securities and cash paid in the acquisition plus the market value of all debt liabilities assumed as a result of the acquisition, C_t = the incremental after-tax operating cash flows ultimately available to the acquiring company as a result of buying the acquired company, and K = the required return.

In the net-present-value equation for mergers, the purchase price is the market value of all the securities and cash paid in the acquisition plus the market value of all debt liabilities assumed as a result of the acquisition.

In the context of an acquisition, each of the terms in Equation (1) must be interpreted with care.[6] First, C_0 is the dollar value to be paid to the acquired company. If the acquiring company pays in cash and assumes no liabilities as a result of the acquisition, C_0 is the amount of cash paid — but things are not always so clear-cut. For example, in 1984 General Motors (GM) acquired Electronic Data Systems (EDS) by giving cash, common stock, and notes to EDS. The total value of the securities plus cash was $2.555 billion. How would we treat this amount in Equation (1)? One useful way is to set C_0 equal to the full $2.555 billion as if it were a cash outlay, even though we know part of the payment was in common stock and notes. The rationale for this approach is that the cash equivalent of GM's offer was $2.555 billion. By using notes and common stock in this acquisition, GM gave up the opportunity to raise cash by selling those securities. Adding their value into C_0 reflects this forgone opportunity.

There may be yet another complication. Suppose GM also assumed some of EDS's debts as a result of the acquisition — a common practice when the acquiring company does not want to retire the acquired company's debt immediately but prefers to pay it off by honoring the interest and principal payments. If the acquir-

---

[6] We separate financing and investment in using Equation (1), in keeping with our development of net present value in Chapter 10. Other ways to use Equation (1) are discussed in D. Chambers, R. Harris, and J. Pringle, "Treatment of Financing Mix in Analyzing Investment Opportunities," *Financial Management*, Summer 1982, pp. 24–41.

ing company assumes these debt obligations, it receives cash flows from the acquisition only after honoring these obligations. We can incorporate this debt in Equation (1) if we define C_0 as including not only the value of the payments (cash plus securities) made by the acquiring firm but also the value of the liabilities (debt) assumed by the acquiring firm. Because the market value of debt appropriately captures this value, C_0 also includes the market value of the acquired-company debt assumed by the acquiring company as a result of the acquisition. In Equation (1), then, C_0 represents the market value of all the securities and cash paid in the acquisition plus the market value of all debt liabilities assumed as a result of the acquisition.

The cash flows in the *NPV* merger equation are incremental after-tax operating cash flows.

The cash flows, C_t, in Equation (1) also deserve attention. Just as in our capital-budgeting analysis in Chapter 11, these flows are incremental after-tax operating cash flows. In other words, they are the cash flows ultimately available to one company as a result of buying another company. These cash flows would include the cash flows from the acquired company's operations plus any special cash flows that can be realized only as a result of the acquisition. Even though the cash flows would conceivably extend indefinitely into the future if the firm is a going concern, it is often useful to project cash flows for only a number of years and then assign a lump-sum terminal value to the acquired company. (See Sample Problem 25–1.) Also, it is important to remember that these flows are operating cash flows prior to interest charges, just as we calculated in Chapter 11.

Finally, the required return, K, in Equation (1) must reflect the riskiness of the cash flows being analyzed. If these cash flows are of the same risk as the *acquiring* company's existing operations and if the acquiring company plans no change in its financing mix relative to the premerger mix, we could use the acquiring company's after-tax weighted-average required return (as calculated in Chapter 12) as the appropriate required return in Equation (1). Sometimes, this may be a reasonable assumption. For example, in a horizontal merger the business risk of the acquired firm may be essentially the same as the risk of the acquiring firm.

In most mergers, the cash flows are of risks related to the business of the acquired company, not the acquiring company.

In most cases, however, the cash flows in Equation (1) are associated with risks related to the business of the acquired company, not the acquiring company. As a result, we would expect financial markets to require a different rate of return on these than on the acquiring company. For example, when Aetna Life and Casualty, a firm primarily involved in insurance and other financial services, acquired Geosource, a company in the oil-exploration-equipment business, it would have been inappropriate to use a required return based on Aetna's existing operations to value cash flows coming from Geosource. In some cases, we could argue that the cash flows in Equation (1) are of essentially the same risk as the acquired firm and, hence, might base K on the required returns the market appears to have placed on the acquired firm's business.

In practice, a financial manager needs to pay special attention to risks associated with the cash flows that are being acquired. As discussed in Chapter 13, some of the tools for dealing with risk (for example, sensitivity analysis) need to be used in merger valuations.

Sample Problem 25–1

Calculating the Net Present Value of Union Amalgamated's Purchase of
Pearsall Manufacturing

In December 1988, Union Amalgamated was considering the purchase of Pearsall Manufacturing, Inc. Union's investment banker has advised Union's chief financial officer that Pearsall's common stock can be bought for $50 million cash plus 1 million shares of Union's stock, which is presently selling for $30 a share. In addition, Union will assume Pearsall's debt, which has a book value of $10 million and a coupon rate of 7 percent. Presently the debt has a market value of $8 million because market interest rates are above 7 percent. Union has made the projections shown in Table 25–4.

Union has also estimated that capital expenditures necessary to maintain this level of operation for Pearsall will be $8 million per year for the next three years. Finally, Union analysts project that Pearsall's assets can be sold at year-end 1991 to net the company $60 million after paying tax obligations. (In this projection we have not dealt with working capital, which is typically relevant in such a decision. We are assuming it away here to keep things simple.) Union management has traditionally used a weighted-average required return of 12 percent, but feels that because the Pearsall acquisition is somewhat riskier than current operations a 15 percent required return is appropriate. Calculate the net present value of the acquisition. Is the acquisition of Pearsall a sound investment?

Table 25–4

Pro-Forma Results for Pearsall Manufacturing, Inc., 1989–91 (millions of dollars)

	1989	1990	1991
Sales	100	130	170
minus			
Cash expenses	− 58	− 80	− 110
minus			
Depreciation	− 10	− 13	− 17
equals			
Earnings before interest and taxes (EBIT)	32	37	43
minus			
Interest	−7	−7	−7
equals			
Profit before taxes (PBT)	25	30	36
minus			
Taxes at 40 percent	−10	−12	−14.4
equals			
Profit after taxes (PAT)	15	18	21.6

Solution

We can use Equation (1) to calculate the net present value of the acquisition. First, we need to calculate the cash flows associated with the purchase of Pearsall. These cash flows are after-tax operating (pre-interest) cash flows and can be calculated as

$$C = \text{EBIT}(1 - T) + \text{Depreciation} - \text{Capital expenditures}.$$

For example in 1989 (in millions of dollars), we can use data from Table 25–4 to calculate

$$C = 32(1 - 0.4) + 10 - 8 = 21.2.$$

Note that we must subtract capital expenditures because these are dollars that must be reinvested in Pearsall to produce the cash flows in future periods and justify the estimated $60 million selling price in 1991. Using the data from the problem, we can determine that cash flow from operations will be $21.2 million in 1989, $27.2 million in 1990, and $34.8 million in 1991, and that the cash flow from sales in 1991 will be $60 million.

Note that this $60 million in 1989 would be prior to paying off Pearsall's debt. Because Pearsall's debt is going to be included in C_0 (as a liability assumed), the cash flows should include dollars available to pay off this debt as well as to yield cash to Union.

Second, we must calculate the cash-equivalent outlay for Pearsall, which is composed of three parts: the cash outlay of $50 million; the market value of the stock given to Pearsall's present stockholders, which is 10 million shares × $30 per share = $30 million; and the market value of Pearsall's debt that is assumed, which is $8 million. Thus, C_0 = $50 million + $30 million + $8 million = $88 million.

This $88 million is the amount effectively paid for the operating cash flows of Pearsall — $80 million for Pearsall's common stock plus the assumption of $8 million of debt. In essence, Union would have to pay $88 million to buy all of Pearsall's cash flows with $8 million of the total to pay off debt. Using $K = 15$ percent, we can now use Equation (1) to calculate the net present value (in millions of dollars) as:

$$NPV = -\$88 + \frac{\$21.2}{(1 + 0.15)} + \frac{\$27.2}{(1 + 0.15)^2} + \frac{\$34.8}{(1 + 0.15)^3} + \frac{\$60}{(1 + 0.15)^3}$$

$$= -\$88 + \$21.2(0.870) + \$27.2(0.756) + \$34.8(0.658) + \$60(0.658)$$

$$= -\$88 + \$101.39$$

$$= \$13.39$$

As the calculations show, the acquisition yields a positive net present value of $13.39 million and appears to be a good investment. Union is paying $88 million for cash flows worth $101.39 million. Stated another way, given current assumptions, Union could afford to pay up to $101.39 million to buy Pearsall and still have the acquisition make financial sense. This price would be $101.39 million —

$8 million = $93.39 million in excess of the $8 million debt assumed. Before making a final decision on the acquisition, Union must also make sure that no other mutually exclusive investment alternatives (for example, internal expansion to provide the same benefits as those available from acquiring Pearsall) offer a net present value greater than $13.39 million. ▨

Sample Problem 25–2
Sensitivity Analysis of Union Amalgamated's Acquisition of Pearsall Manufacturing

A. Suppose you thought Union's staff had overestimated all the cash flows from Pearsall by 20 percent. Would the acquisition still look good to you?

B. Suppose Union thought that acquisition of Pearsall, in addition to the cash flows already calculated and the adjustment in part (A), would allow Union to cut its own advertising expenditures by $500,000 a year for the next three years because of Pearsall's excellent reputation, which is expected to spill over and help Union's sales. How would this assumption affect your analysis of acquiring Pearsall?

Solution
A. We need to do a sensitivity analysis by cutting the cash flows figured in Sample Problem 25–1 by 20 percent. As a result, we get the cash flows listed in Table 25–5. Using the right-hand column of numbers we can recalculate net present value from Equation (1), in millions of dollars, as:

$$NPV = -\$88 + \frac{\$16.96}{(1 + 0.15)} + \frac{\$21.76}{(1 + 0.15)^2} + \frac{\$75.84}{(1 + 0.15)^3}$$

$$= -\$88 + \$16.96\,(0.870) + \$21.76\,(0.756) + \$75.84\,(0.658)$$

$$= -\$88 + \$81.1$$

$$= -\$6.9.$$

With these lower expected cash flows, the net present value of acquiring Pearsall is negative (−$6.9 million), so Pearsall should not be acquired. The maxi-

▨

Table 25–5
Sensitivity Analysis of Pearson Manufacturing's Estimated 1989–91 Cash Flows (millions of dollars)

Year	Original Cash Flow	Original Cash Flow Minus 20 Percent
1989	21.2	16.96
1990	27.2	21.76
1991	34.8 + 60	75.84

mum that could be paid for Pearsall, given the current assumptions, is $81.1 million, which is $73.1 million in excess of the $8 million debt assumed.

B. The $500,000 advertising savings would save Union $500,000 (1 − 0.4) = $300,000 a year on an after-tax basis for each of the next three years and would increase the calculated net present value of the acquisition by a dollar value of

$$\frac{\$300,000}{(1 + 0.15)} + \frac{\$300,000}{(1 + 0.15)^2} + \frac{\$300,000}{(1 + 0.15)^3} = \$685,200 \,.$$

Compared to the net present value of −$6.9 million found in part (A), the new net present value would be −$6,900,000 + $685,200 = −$6,214,800. Because this *NPV* is still negative, the acquisition does not look good. Note that one might argue for using a discount rate lower than 15 percent for the advertising cost savings if they are fairly safe. Even with a lower discount rate, however, these savings would not overcome the −$6.9 million net present value calculated in part (A). ▪

While discounted-cash-flow analysis provides an extremely useful tool in assessing the value of a company, it is not the only important means of assessing the financial effects of mergers. Mergers also have effects on the basic accounting information that companies present to the financial community because an acquiring company must restate its income statement and balance sheet to reflect the operations, assets, and liabilities of the company being acquired.

Mergers and Earnings per Share

One important effect of an acquisition is on the reported earnings per share (EPS) of the acquiring company. Because analysts in the financial community follow EPS, a thorough analysis of a merger should include a calculation of the impact of the acquisition on EPS.

To calculate the effects on EPS, recall that EPS is calculated as profits after taxes (PAT) divided by the number of shares of common stock. To calculate projected EPS, then, we need to project PAT and the number of shares of stock after the acquisition.

Sample Problem 25–3
EPS Effects of Franklin's Acquisition of Stove Enterprises

In December 1988, Franklin Inc. was planning an acquisition of Stove Enterprises. Franklin's financial staff had prepared the PAT projections that the two companies would have without the acquisition, as shown in Table 25–6. As a preliminary stage of analysis, Franklin is assuming that if the acquisition goes through, the post-merger profits will simply be the sum of the profits of the two companies if they had not merged. Presently, Franklin has 10 million shares of stock selling at $30 per share. Stove has 4 million shares of stock selling at $20 per share. The previous year (1987), Franklin's earnings per share were $1.54.

Sidebar notes (left margin):

Though discounted-cash-flow analysis provides an extremely useful tool in assessing the value of a company, it is not the only important means of gauging the financial effects of mergers.

One effect of an acquisition is on the reported earnings per share of the acquiring company.

Table 25—6

Projected Profit after Taxes (PAT) for Franklin Inc. and Stove Enterprises Without a Merger, 1988–91 (millions of dollars)

Year	Franklin PAT	Stove PAT
1988	20	10
1989	26	12
1990	33.8	14.4
1991	43.9	17.28

After negotiations, Franklin has offered to give one share of its stock for each share of Stove Stock. Assuming Franklin's stock price doesn't drop as a result of the offer, Franklin is offering $30 worth of stock in exchange for $20 worth of stock. This offer represents a 50 percent increase for Stove shareholders, and they are quite delighted with the prospect. Paying a 50 percent premium is not uncommon in acquisitions. Such a premium may be necessary to induce Stove shareholders to agree to the merger, especially if other firms are waiting in the wings to make a bid for Stove. What are the effects of the acquisition on Franklin's EPS?

A. Calculate Franklin's EPS without the merger.

B. Calculate Franklin's EPS with the merger.

Solution

To calculate EPS, we need to divide PAT by the number of shares of stock, N.

A. Without the merger we get the results shown in Table 25–7.

B. With the merger, the number of shares of stock (N) = Franklin's old shares + new shares issued in acquisition = 10 million + 4 million = 14 mil-

Table 25—7

Calculation of Estimated Earnings per Share (EPS) for Franklin Inc. Without a Merger, 1988–1991

Year	PAT (millions of dollars) (1)	Number of Shares of Stock, N (millions) (2)	EPS (3) = (1) ÷ (2)
1988	20	10	$2.00
1989	26	10	$2.60
1990	33.8	10	$3.38
1991	43.9	10	$4.39

lion. Note that one new share is issued for each old share of Stove. We can find Franklin's PAT (with the merger) by adding the projected PAT figures for Franklin and Stove. For example, in 1988 PAT will be $20 million + $10 million = $30 million. Summarizing, Franklin's earnings per share are projected as shown in Table 25–8 and Table 25–9.

Note that Franklin's earnings per share initially increase as a result of the acquisition (from $2.00 to $2.14 in 1988), but by 1991 Franklin finds its expected earnings per share are actually lower as a result of the acquisition ($4.37 versus $4.39). Franklin thus faces a trade-off. The acquisition initially increases EPS but lowers EPS in the more distant future.

Before leaving this example, let us ask an important question. Would Franklin's stock price be expected to drop below $30 per share once it announced its offer? The answer depends on investors' valuation of the investment Franklin is making by buying Stove Enterprises. If investors think no value is created in the takeover, they would certainly think Franklin is making a mistake offering any premium, so Franklin's stock price would drop. This drop of stock price would make the offer less attractive to Stove stockholders who have been promised a share of Franklin stock for each share of Stove they presently own.

As Sample Problem 25–3 shows, EPS can be changed as a result of an acquisition. The key to understanding the nature of the change is to look at these impor-

Table 25–8

Calculation of Estimated Earnings per Share (EPS) for Franklin Inc. With a Merger, 1988–91

Year	PAT (millions of dollars)	Number of Shares of Stock, N (millions)	EPS
1988	30	14	$2.14
1989	38	14	$2.71
1990	48.2	14	$3.44
1991	61.18	14	$4.37

Table 25–9

Comparison of Estimated Earnings per Share (EPS) for Franklin Inc. With and Without a Merger, 1988–91

Year	EPS Without Merger	EPS With Merger
1988	$2.00	$2.14
1989	$2.60	$2.71
1990	$3.38	$3.44
1991	$4.39	$4.37

tant factors: the way the acquisition is financed, the price/earnings (P/E) ratios of the acquiring and acquired firms, and the expected growth in earnings for the acquired and acquiring firms.

The financing of the acquisition has an important effect on EPS if the financing causes a shift in the mix of debt and equity financing used by the merging firms, because of the effects of financial leverage that we studied in detail in Chapters 15 and 16. For example, suppose an acquiring firm borrows cash to buy the stock of another firm and simultaneously assumes the debt of that firm. These actions would substantially increase the financial leverage of the acquiring firm. The likely effect would be to increase not only the expected EPS but also the risk of those earnings. In some cases, mergers involve large shifts in financing mix, which may have dramatic effects on reported earnings. Even without changes in financial leverage, however, acquisitions can affect EPS, as we will see later.

A second important factor is the relationship of the price/earnings (P/E) ratio of the acquiring firm to that of the acquired firm. If a company with a high P/E ratio exchanges its stock for stock of a company with a low P/E ratio, short-run EPS typically will increase. To illustrate, let's return to the data for Franklin and Stove in Sample Problem 25–3. Franklin's stock price of $30 per share based on a $2.00 EPS reflects a P/E ratio of $30/$2.00 = 15. Stove's (preacquisition) EPS is $10 million/4 million = $2.50 and, with a stock price of $20, this produces a P/E ratio of $20/$2.50 = 8. Why the difference between the P/E ratios? The likely explanation is that Franklin is expected to grow faster than Stove or is less risky than Stove. One other P/E ratio is important to examine—namely, the P/E ratio Franklin "paid" for Stove. Franklin offered one share of its stock ($30 value) for each share of Stove stock ($2.50 of earnings). As a result, the P/E ratio paid was $30/$2.50 = 12.

Now we can see the importance of the P/E ratios when a merger is consummated by an exchange of stock. Because Stove was trading at a P/E ratio of 8, or $8 of share price per $1 of earnings, Franklin would have to pay in excess of $8 to Stove's owners per dollar of earnings to make the offer attractive to Stove's shareholders. In other words, Franklin has to pay a merger premium. On the other hand, as long as Franklin pays a P/E ratio less than 15 (its current P/E), it can buy earnings relatively cheaply and see its EPS rise in the short run. By relatively cheaply, we mean that Franklin will get more earnings per $15 paid in the merger than the earnings its current shareholders get per $15 of their share price. In the actual transaction, Franklin paid a P/E ratio of 12, which gave Stove shareholders a merger premium of 50 percent but also increased Franklin's EPS.

Does this analysis mean that mergers necessarily create benefits to both acquiring and acquired firms? The answer is no. It is not EPS that is ultimately important to shareholders but the price per share of the stock they own. An increase in current EPS does not necessarily lead to an increase in share price.

To get some insight into the problem, we can graph the EPS calculations we made in Sample Problem 25–3, as shown in Figure 25–2 on p. 748.

As Figure 25–2 shows, earnings per share with the merger (colored line) are initially higher than EPS without the merger (black line), but the growth rates in EPS are lower with the merger. Looking back at the figures for Franklin and

If a company with a high P/E ratio exchanges its stock for stock of a low P/E company, short-run EPS typically will increase.

It is not EPS that is ultimately important to shareholders but the price per share of stock they own. Increases in EPS do not necessarily correspond to increases in share price.

Figure 25–2
Earnings per Share and Mergers

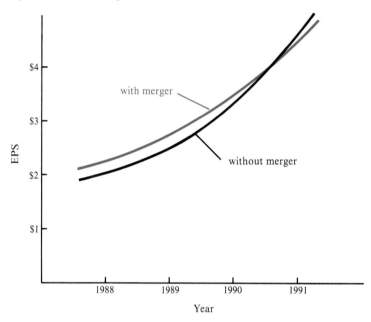

If a low-P/E company is acquired, the acquiring firm's EPS are often initially higher than EPS without the merger, but the growth rate in EPS is lower with the merger.

Stove, this result is no surprise. Franklin was expecting 30 percent annual growth in earnings, whereas Stove was expecting only 20 percent. The merged firms should reasonably expect growth somewhere between 20 percent and 30 percent. In fact, the post-merger growth turns out to be at a 27 percent annual rate.

As we know from our discussion of stock valuation, stock prices depend not only on the initial level of earnings and dividends but also on their expected growth and the risk associated with these flows.

Because Franklin shareholders expected growth in EPS to drop as a result of this merger, we would expect the P/E ratio of Franklin stock to drop. The question is: How far will the P/E ratio drop? Looking at the data, we see that 1988 EPS will go from $2 to $2.14 as a result of the merger. The P/E ratio necessary to keep Franklin's stock at its current $30 price, when multiplied by Franklin's EPS of $2.14, must equal $30.00. That is, 2.14(P/E) = $30.00. Therefore, P/E = $30.00/$2.14 = 14.02.

If Franklin's P/E ratio right after the merger (that is, the P/E of the new combined firm) remains above 14.02, Franklin's share price will go up from its current level of $30. If the share price increases, the merger has served the financial manager's objective—increasing the value of the firm to its owners.

One can pause to ask whether Franklin's current P/E is likely to stay above 14.02 and, as a result, whether the merger will increase value to Franklin's shareholders. If the merger itself creates no value, Franklin's P/E should drop below 14.02 because Franklin paid a 50 percent premium for Stove's stock. A direct way to estimate whether value will be created from Franklin is to use DCF techniques to analyze the net present value of the acquisition, just as we did earlier in this chapter. If the *NPV* is positive, the merger should benefit the acquiring firm.

Looking back at the effects of mergers on EPS, we see that one has to be very careful in analyzing EPS data for merging firms. If we had expected Franklin's EPS without the acquisition to be $2.00 in 1988 and now saw reported 1988 EPS of $2.14 after the merger, we might be tempted to conclude that Franklin had increased its growth rate in EPS from 30 percent (from 1.54 to 2.00) without the merger to 39 percent (from 1.54 to 2.14) with the merger.

In reality, Franklin did increase its *short-run* growth rate in EPS from 30 percent to 39 percent because it bought a company with a lower P/E ratio. The danger lies in extrapolating this growth rate into the future. We know from Figure 25–2 and earlier calculations that Franklin's *long-term* growth rate in EPS is actually lowered by this acquisition from 30 percent to 27 percent because Stove, as its lower P/E suggests, is not expected to grow as fast as Franklin's existing operations. In making judgments about the merger, it is critical to look beyond the short-run effect on EPS and take into account the long-run effects.

In fact, investors have not always been so careful in looking at EPS figures. In the 1960s a number of acquiring firms with high P/E ratios were able to increase short-run growth in EPS by making acquisitions of low-P/E companies. The acquiring companies made a series of acquisitions and over the course of a few years were able to produce earnings per share that were growing at outstanding rates. The acquisitions were much like a chain letter. What happened?

For a while, investors in the stock market appeared to extrapolate these short-term growth rates into the distant future. As a result, the acquiring firms maintained their high P/E ratios. The problem is that the chain letters could not go on forever and eventually earnings growth began to fall off, just as Figure 25–2 suggests will happen if Franklin acquires Stove.

Investors are not fooled forever, and in the late 1960s they caught on to the chain-letter game of short-run increases in EPS. Acquiring-company P/E ratios and stock prices plummeted, and acquisition activity came to a grinding halt. Given this earlier experience and investors' awareness of it, the chain-letter game is not played much these days. Companies and investors appear to focus on both the short-run and long-run effects of acquisitions.

Mergers and Balance Sheets

The balance sheet of the merging corporations can also be affected by mergers. The nature of these effects depends upon the treatment of complex accounting issues. The accounting profession has defined two primary ways to account for acquisitions. In a **pooling of interests,** the balance sheets of the two combining companies are simply added together to produce the balance sheet of the surviving company. In a **purchase of assets,** the assets of the acquired company are revalued to reflect the amount of money actually paid for the acquired entity, which involves taking into account differences between the current book value of assets and the amount paid for the company.

In making judgments about a merger, it is crucial to look beyond short-run effects on EPS and take account of long-run effects.

Pooling of interests — an accounting method for reporting a merger in which the balance sheets of the two combining companies are added together to produce the balance sheet of the surviving company.

Purchase of assets — an accounting method for reporting a merger in which the assets of the acquired company are revalued to reflect the amount of money actually paid for the acquired entity.

For example, consider the balance sheets for Franklin and Stove shown in Table 25–10. If the merger is treated as a pooling of interests, the premerger balance sheets are simply added together. Though the details of the requirements for pooling are lengthy, in essence, poolings occur when one company exchanges its stock for the stock of another company. The shareholders of the acquired firm now have a shareholder interest in the new firm.

In a purchase of assets, the balance sheet in Table 25–10 is adjusted for the fact that Franklin paid $120 million, which is $20 million in excess of the book value of Stove's assets. The difference of $20 million could reflect the fact that Stove's tangible assets are actually worth more than their book value — for example, as a result of increased prices of equipment carried on Stove's books at historical costs. In such a case we would have to revalue these tangible assets in producing the post-merger balance sheet.

In the example in Table 25–10, we have assumed that the entire $20 million is paid for intangible assets of Stove that are not listed on the balance sheet. These assets might include Stove's management expertise or its reputation as a producer of quality products. The $20 million is entered as a new asset account called **goodwill**.

Goodwill — the excess of the price paid for a going concern over the book value of its tangible assets; an intangible asset of the firm.

Table 25–10

Comparison of Two Major Methods of Accounting for Mergers (millions of dollars)

Panel A: Premerger Balance Sheets

Franklin Inc.

Current assets	80	Debt	10
Fixed assets	120	Equity	190
Total assets	**200**	**Total debt and equity**	**200**

Stove Enterprises

Current assets	40	Debt	0
Fixed assets	60	Equity	100
Total assets	**100**	**Total debt and equity**	**100**

Panel B: Post-Merger Balance Sheet

Pooling of Interests Method

Current assets	120	Debt	10
Fixed assets	180	Equity	290
Total assets	**300**	**Total debt and equity**	**300**

Assumes Franklin pays 4,000,000 shares at $30 share, or $120 million, and acquisition is pooling of interests.

Purchase Method

Current assets	120	Debt	10
Fixed assets	180	Equity	310
Goodwill	20		
Total assets	**320**	**Total debt and equity**	**320**

Assumes Franklin pays $120 million and acquisition is treated as a purchase of assets.

Just as other long-term assets are depreciated, this goodwill account must be amortized. This amortization must be done over a period not exceeding 40 years and reduces reported income. For example, the figures in Table 25–10 would lead to an annual amortization charge of $20,000,000/40 = $500,000, which would reduce Franklin's reported income by $500,000 for each of the next 40 years, as compared to pooling-of-interests accounting, which creates no goodwill account. As a result, many managers prefer pooling-of-interest accounting when they pay in excess of the book value of the assets.[7]

On the other hand, goodwill-amortization charges are not cash flows, nor are they tax-deductible. As a result, while affecting reported income, goodwill-amortization charges have no effect on the underlying cash flow. If they do not affect this cash flow, our DCF valuation techniques suggest that they should not affect value. Thus, the choice of pooling versus purchase accounting should not affect the value of the acquisition if it has no effect on cash flows.[8]

Effects of Mergers

Owners' Perspective

If both sets of shareholders expect a positive net present value, the merger is expected to create some value, perhaps through cost savings. We can examine past mergers to see if there is any evidence that such value has been created.

There have been a number of studies that have analyzed the effects of mergers on the shareholders of the participating firms.[9] Have shareholders in acquiring firms benefited? Have acquired-firm shareholders benefited? On balance, has there been net increase in value as a result of mergers?

There are a number of difficult issues in trying to answer such questions. For example, if we want to decide whether an acquired shareholder benefits, we need to figure out what sort of value and return such a shareholder would have had in the absence of a merger and compare those to the returns they actually did receive as a result of the merger.[10]

[7]H. Hong, G. Mandelker, and R. S. Kaplan, "Pooling vs. Purchase: The Effects of Accounting for Mergers on Stock Prices," *Accounting Review,* January 1978, pp. 31–47.

[8]Hong, Mandelker, and Kaplan, "Pooling vs. Purchase." Note that if part of the excess of purchase price over book value is allocated to tangible assets (unlike our example in Table 25–10), tax-deductible depreciation charges will be affected. The ultimate effect of this approach on value depends not only on tax deductions to the acquiring firm but also on the tax status of the selling firm and involves tax issues beyond the scope of our discussion. See B. I. Bittker and J. Eustice, *Fundamentals of Federal Income Taxation of Corporations and Shareholders* (New York: Warren, Gorham and Lamont, 1980).

[9]Two useful review articles are Paul Halpern, "Corporate Acquisitions: A Theory of Special Cases? A Review of Event Studies Applied to Acquisitions," *Journal of Finance,* May 1983, pp. 297–318; and M. Jensen and R. Ruback, "The Market for Corporate Control: The Scientific Evidence," *Journal of Financial Economics,* April 1983. For an update see G. Jarrell, J. Brickley, and J. Netter, *Journal of Economic Perspectives,* Winter 1988.

[10]Halpern, "Corporate Acquisitions"; Jensen and Ruback, "The Market for Corporate Control." Both sources discuss in detail many of the difficulties of structuring a test to see whether mergers benefit shareholders and survey past studies and the results of those studies.

■
The historical evidence suggests that shareholders of acquired firms seem to have benefited from mergers.

■
Shareholders of acquiring firms do not seem to have been harmed by mergers, but the evidence is not so clear that they have been helped.

■
In a highly competitive market, we would expect the price paid to the acquired firm's shareholders to go just high enough so that most of the benefits of the merger to the acquiring firm are eliminated.

■
The data summarized above are averages over large samples of mergers. Some mergers have not increased value for shareholders; others have.

■
Observing an increase in value is not sufficient to judge whether a merger is in the best interest of society at large.

Without going into the details of the techniques used in studies of mergers, we can briefly summarize the results. First, shareholders of acquired firms do seem to have benefited. This result is not extremely surprising because acquired-firm shareholders are typically paid a price in excess of the market price of their stock. In the last few years it has not been unusual for shareholders to be paid 50 percent in excess of the market value of their stock in a merger.

Second, shareholders of acquiring firms do not seem to have been harmed by mergers, but the evidence is not so clear that they have been helped. A final judgment involves some interpretation, and analysts differ in their conclusions. A reading of the evidence, however, suggests that acquiring firms, on average, have not received large value increases (positive *NPV*s) in mergers. One possible explanation of this result is that the market in which acquiring firms acquire other firms is quite competitive. Acquiring firms will have to pay a price to buy another firm. This price will have to be high enough to outbid other potential acquiring firms. As the price they pay goes up, the net present value to the acquiring firm goes down. In fact, in a highly competitive market, we would expect the price paid to go just high enough that most of the benefits of the merger to the acquiring firm are eliminated. This expectation seems to be consistent with the evidence. The evidence also suggests that acquiring firms should look for acquisitions in which they will have some advantage over other potential acquiring firms.

Thus, mergers seem to have created value for acquired-firm shareholders and at least have not harmed acquiring-firm shareholders. As a result, it appears that mergers in the last few decades have increased value to the shareholders of participating firms. Unfortunately, we cannot be sure that mergers in the future will also be value-increasing. In addition, the results stated earlier were averages over large samples of mergers. Clearly, some mergers have not increased value for shareholders while others have.

Public-Policy Perspective

One of the remaining issues is whether or not the increases in value that appear to have resulted from mergers are in the best interests of the economy. If the increase in value is from realization of cost savings and efficient production techniques, the merger would not only benefit the owners of the merging firms but could also potentially provide lower prices to consumers and release resources for uses elsewhere in the economy. If, on the other hand, the increase in value is the result of increased monopoly power as the merged firms charge higher prices for the goods and services they sell, the merger value would come at the expense of those consumers buying the goods and services of the firm. In short, observing an increase in value is not sufficient to judge whether the merger is in the best interest of society at large. This judgment also depends upon the motives for merger and the effects of mergers on others in the economy.

Who Gets Acquired. One possible way of getting some insight into the motives for mergers is to look at the types of firms that are acquired. From the numerous studies of the characteristics of firms that are bought, some general features have

Mergers in the United Kingdom

In the 1980s major U.S. investment-banking firms were beefing up their London operations. Why? One reason was that merger activity in the United Kingdom offered a real growth market for their mergers-and-acquisitions (M&A) groups. The prospects of attractive fees for merger advice and assistance was a powerful incentive for U.S. investment bankers. At the same time, London *merchant bankers* (the British term for investment bankers) were increasing their M&A operations. The accompanying table chronicles acquisition activity in the United Kingdom in terms of both numbers and value for the period 1963 to 1985. As the table shows, in terms of the value (in pounds) of acquisitions, merger activity increased sharply in 1984 and 1985. Adjusted for inflation, however, United Kingdom merger activity was still below its 1968 peak — as indicated in the column where all values are in terms of 1985 prices.

As the table shows, mergers have not been restricted to U.S. borders. In fact, during 1985 there were 709 acquisitions in Germany, 712 in Canada, and 318 in the Netherlands. The merger boom is an international business.

Year	Number of Firms Acquired	Value in Historic Prices (millions of pounds)	Value in 1985 Prices (millions of pounds)
1963	888	352	2,429
1964	940	505	3,371
1965	1,000	517	3,295
1966	807	500	3,077
1967	763	822	4,928
1968	946	1,946	11,145
1969	846	1,069	5,794
1970	793	1,122	5,730
1971	884	911	4,255
1972	1,210	2,532	11,023
1973	1,205	1,304	5,197
1974	504	508	1,749
1975	315	291	806
1976	353	448	1,064
1977	481	824	1,690
1978	567	1,140	2,159
1979	534	1,656	2,763
1980	469	1,475	2,087
1981	452	1,144	1,447
1982	463	2,206	2,569
1983	447	2,343	2,608
1984	568	5,474	5,806
1985	474	7,090	7,090

(continued)

Many of the concerns about mergers felt in the United States are also shared by the United Kingdom. Do mergers serve shareholders' interest? Do they reduce competition? The analysis of these and other questions is complex. One comprehensive study of benefits of British mergers to shareholders found results quite similar to those found in U.S. studies. Acquiree shareholders experienced value gains of 20 to 30 percent around the merger date and acquiror shareholders either had zero or small gains. Thus, on average, British mergers appear to

benefit shareholders at least around the merger date. Whether or not a particular acquisition is good and whether or not anticipated merger benefits will actually materialize are questions that require close study. What is clear is that financial managers around the globe are operating in a busy merger market.

Source: Data on United Kingdom mergers over time are from the British Department of Trade and Industry. Estimates of effects of mergers on shareholders are from J. Franks and R. Harris, "The Wealth Effects of Corporate Takeovers: the U.K. Experience 1955–1985" (Working paper, University of North Carolina at Chapel Hill, 1988).

emerged. Small firms are acquired more often than large firms. In addition, the lower the price/earnings ratio of a firm, the greater the probability that the firm will be acquired.[11] Unfortunately, however, further generalizations are difficult. Not all mergers are alike. There are enough differences in mergers that it is hard to characterize what sorts of firms are acquired or are not acquired. It does not appear that particularly profitable or unprofitable firms are typically bought or that firms with a lot of debt or a very small amount of debt are typically bought. Many recent mergers have been concentrated in certain industries—oil, gas, transportation, and finance. However, mergers have included everything from the 1984 acquisition of Gulf for which Chevron paid in excess of $13 billion to acquisitions of dime stores for considerably smaller dollar amounts.

Concentration ratio—the percentage of sales, production volume, or any other variable to be measured accounted for by the *x* largest firms in an industry.

Concentration in Particular Markets. Another factor to examine in assessing the motives for and effects of mergers is the concentration of producers in particular product markets. One measure of industry concentration is the **concentration ratio.** For example, a 4-firm concentration ratio would be the percentage of total sales controlled by the top four firms in an industry. If there were only four firms in the industry, of course, the 4-firm concentration ratio would be 100 percent. The higher the concentration ratio, the less likely it is that there will be competitive behavior in this particular market and the more likely it is that there would be some monopoly power and, as a result, abnormally high profits earned by firms in that industry. One criticism of certain mergers is that they increase concentration in a particular product market. The most obvious example of this is a horizontal merger of two firms in the same industry. The ability of firms to earn abnormally high profits for any prolonged period of time is, however, affected by likely entrants into a market as well as the concentration of existing producers. As long as there are no barriers to entry into the market by other firms, the exercise of monopoly power is likely to be rather short-lived.

[11]See R. Harris, J. Stewart, D. Guilkey, and W. Carleton, "Characteristics of Acquired Firms: Fixed and Random Coefficient Profit Analysis," *Southern Economic Journal,* July 1982, pp. 164–84.

International Focus

Takeovers the Japanese Way

1987 was a watershed year for Japanese takeovers: It marked the first time that Japanese firms acquired more firms outside Japan (228 takeovers) than inside Japan (219 takeovers). Some of the deals were large: Nippon Mining's $1.1 billion purchase of Gould, an American computer manufacturer; the $2.6 billion acquisition of Firestone Tire and Rubber by Tokyo-based Bridgestone Corporation; and Sony's $2 billion purchase of CBS records.

While Japanese takeovers represented only a fraction (less than 5 percent) of the value of all U.S. deals in 1987, the future is likely to see more Japanese takeovers of U.S. and other non-Japanese firms. And even if Japanese

companies do not step up their takeovers as much as expected, Japanese banks and securities houses apparently see opportunities for entry into a growing business by acting as advisers. In 1988 Nomura Securities spent $100 million for a 20 percent stake in a new mergers-and-acquisition firm set up by two leading American specialists who left First Boston, a major U.S. investment banking firm. Japanese banks are also beginning to charge fees to their Japanese clients for advice on takeovers, whereas they had previously provided free advice as part of a banking relationship.

It does not appear as likely, however, that many foreign firms will be buying Japanese companies. Any foreign buyer has to fight through cultural barriers. In addition, most big Japanese firms are controlled by big bank-centered industrial groupings with elaborate patterns of cross-shareholding, making purchase of shares more difficult. Finally, unless there is a major shift in the equity markets, Japanese companies just seem quite expensive. For example, price/earnings ratios of 50 are common in Japan but rare in other major markets such as London or New York.

Source: Adapted from *The Economist,* September 17, 1988, pp. 84–85.

Since World War II and prior to the 1980s, most of the mergers in the United States took place between firms in different industries. These conglomerate mergers do not themselves increase concentration in a particular industry. Furthermore, a number of experts have noted that concentration in particular product markets, at least as measured by average 4-firm concentration ratios, has been remarkably stable over the past few decades (through the 1970s) of U.S. economic history.[12] The recent set of mergers of firms in the same industry has renewed concern in some camps about the desirability of mergers. Some experts believe that mergers of firms in the same industry often provide cost savings and that the vigor of competition (especially given substantial competition from foreign firms in many industries) has not been diminished. These opinions appear to have won in shaping

[12]See Scherer, *Industrial Market Structure*. In addition to the 4-firm concentration ratio, investigators use other measures of industry concentration, such as the Herfindahl index.

U.S. governmental policy toward mergers, which has become more lenient in the last decade. Many horizontal mergers of the 1980s would not have gone unchallenged by antitrust authorities in the 1960s and early 1970s. On the other hand, critics of merger activity are concerned about the possible exercise of monopoly power if industries have fewer firms. Though the public debate goes on, the full evidence on who is correct is not yet in.

Aggregate Concentration. Another factor to consider in mergers is the sheer size of firms. Is being big bad? Some argue that mergers leading to large firms are not in the best interest of the economy because they tend to concentrate economic and political power. This argument against being big does not depend solely on a firm's having power in a particular product market. Some argue that very large firms are more likely to wield political power and, hence, will have an undue influence on both economic and political outcomes in the economy. Paraphrasing critics of mergers on these grounds, "Big is bad."

It is extremely difficult to measure aggregate concentration — the amount of economic activity in the hands of a few individuals or firms in the United States. One way to gauge aggregate concentration is to look at the total percentage of certain economic aggregates controlled by particular groups of firms. In a study of such aggregate concentration in the entire private sector, L. J. White showed that aggregate concentration (measured by either employment or corporate profits) was not increasing throughout the 1970s despite the large number of mergers in the last part of that decade.[13] For example, White found that in 1980 the 100 largest U.S. companies controlled 16.6 percent of private-sector employment, down from 18.2 percent in 1972.

While aggregate concentration ratios would have fallen without mergers, it appears that basing the case against mergers by arguing that they have increased aggregate concentration is not consistent with the historical evidence, at least for the 1970s. In fact, policymakers in Washington seem to have concluded that mergers are not likely to have damaging effects simply because larger firms are created. Most of the merger legislation in the 1980s assumed that big is not necessarily bad.

Mergers and Policies. A large number of government regulations apply to mergers and acquisitions. These include regulations enforced by the Securities and Exchange Commission (SEC), provisions of the Sherman and Clayton Antitrust laws in the United States, and numerous laws issued by states. The antitrust laws, in effect, state that mergers will not be allowed if their effect is to substantially lessen competition in the provision and sale of goods and services in the U.S. economy. They do not emphasize the pure size of the corporation but rather its size relative to each market.

A large number of government regulations apply to mergers and acquisitions.

[13]These data are drawn from the work of Lawrence J. White. See, for example, L. J. White, "Mergers and Aggregate Concentration," in M. Keenan and L. White, eds., *Mergers and Acquisitions* (Lexington, Mass.: Lexington Books, 1982).

In the 1980s, the Justice Department became more lenient in its policies about stopping mergers for antitrust reasons. This shift allowed both vertical and horizontal mergers to take place that would have been challenged in earlier years. As of this writing, Congress is reviewing proposals to revise some of the antitrust laws about mergers. Any fundamental changes could affect the future course of merger activity in the United States.

The SEC has important responsibilities for governing corporate conduct as it affects the well-being of shareholders. In the merger area, these responsibilities include setting standards for the nature and timing of takeover offers that one firm can make to acquire another. These standards are especially important in hostile takeovers when a potential acquiror, despite resistance from the target company's management, makes a tender offer.

Merger activity in recent years has also been affected by governmental policies to deregulate certain industries. For example, acquisitions in both the banking sector and the airline industry have been spurred by fundamental changes in those industries that have accompanied deregulation.

In addition, tax laws affect mergers in numerous ways. An acquisition is classified as either taxable or tax-free. In tax-free mergers, shareholders of the acquired firm receive shares in the post-merger firm and do not have to pay any capital-gains taxes until they choose to sell the new shares (which suggests that such mergers might better be described as "tax-deferred").

In a taxable merger, the sellers of the acquired firm must recognize any gains or losses immediately and be subject to the applicable taxes. Taxable mergers generally occur whenever shareholders in the acquired firm receive something other than shares of stock (for example, cash or bonds) in exchange for their shares of stock. The taxable versus tax-free status can also affect corporate taxes levied on the post-merger firms. The details of the tax laws are actually quite complicated on this point and are beyond the scope of this text.[14]

[14]See Bittker and Eustice, *Fundamentals of Federal Income Taxation of Corporations and Shareholders.*

KEY CONCEPTS

1. The latest wave of mergers is the fourth in U.S. history.

2. To be good investments, mergers must create value for shareholders. The basic question is whether acquisitions have positive net present values to shareholders.

3. There are many possible motives for mergers, each of which may explain at least some mergers.

4. Mergers can be viewed as investment proposals and analyzed with discounted-cash-flow techniques.

5. Companies with high P/E ratios may increase short-term earnings per share by acquiring companies with low P/E ratios. Such short-term increases in EPS may not raise share price, however, because they typically come with a reduction in the expected long-term growth of EPS.

6. Mergers have become a public-policy concern in the U.S. economy.

SUMMARY

Mergers have had a long history in U.S. business. From a financial manager's perspective, mergers can be viewed as investment proposals. The fundamental question is whether mergers can create value. While numerous motives for mergers have been suggested, most of them can be thought of as factors that could increase the value of the firm to shareholders.

From the acquiring company's perspective, discounted-cash-flow analysis is a useful way to analyze mergers because it allows the acquiring firm to see if a proposed merger is a good investment. In addition, the analysis provides useful information on the maximum price that can be paid for another company that would still make the acquisition a good investment for the acquiring company.

In addition to DCF analysis, it is also useful to calculate the effects of mergers on the firm's balance sheet and on its earnings per share. In many cases firms with high P/E ratios may be able to increase earnings per share in the short run by acquiring firms with low P/E ratios. This short-run increase usually comes at the cost of EPS growth in the future.

In addition to being of tremendous concern in the business community, mergers and acquisitions have been a focus of much public-policy debate. This debate extends to the effects of mergers on monopoly power in product markets and on aggregate concentration, in addition to the effects of mergers on shareholders of participating firms.

While each merger is different, past evidence suggests that, on average, acquired-firm shareholders have benefited from mergers because of the large premiums paid. Acquiring-firm shareholders, on the other hand, often appear to have paid a sufficiently high price such that most, if not all, of any value created in a merger goes to the acquired firm.

QUESTIONS

1. What are the differences between horizontal, vertical, and conglomerate mergers?

2. If the value of the post-merger company is larger than the combined values of the two premerger companies, does the merger have a positive net present value as an investment for the acquiring firm?

3. Is the diversification through merger likely to lead to increases in value?

4. How can companies with high P/E ratios increase earnings per share when they buy companies with low P/E ratios?

5. Do merger-induced increases in earnings per share always benefit the shareholders?

6. What is the difference between pooling of interests and purchase of assets as accounting methods for reporting on mergers?

7. In the past, have mergers benefited shareholders of acquired firms? Have mergers benefited shareholders of acquiring firms?

8. Compare mergers in the 1960s to mergers today.

9. How are acquisitions similar to other investment proposals analyzed by firms? How are they different?

Problems

1. Suppose XYZ corporation's stock is trading for $50 a share while ABC stock goes for $25 a share. XYZ has earnings per share (EPS) of $1 while ABC has EPS of $2.50. Currently neither company has debt, and each has 1,000,000 shares of stock outstanding.

   a. If the merger takes place based on an exchange of stock, which company should be the acquiring firm in order to see an increase in EPS? Explain.

b. If XYZ buys ABC and pays a premium of 20 percent (20 percent in excess of ABC's current market value), how many shares of XYZ must be given to ABC shareholders for each of their shares? (Use current market prices in your calculations.)

c. Based on your calculations in parts (a) and (b), what will be XYZ's EPS after it acquires ABC?

d. Would you expect XYZ's price/earnings ratio to remain at its current level of $50 divided by $1 = 50 if the merger goes through? Why?

e. If ABC were to acquire XYZ and offer a 20 percent premium, how many shares of stock would ABC have to offer? What would be the effect on ABC's EPS?

f. What do the preceding calculations indicate about which company should acquire the other? (Assume there is to be an acquisition.)

2. Sample Problems 25–1 and 25–2 analyze Union's acquisition of Pearsall. Answer the following questions using the data provided in those problems. (Do each part separately.)

a. Should Union buy Pearsall if it has to pay $120 million (cash plus stock) for Pearsall's common stock? Calculate net present value (NPV).

b. If Pearsall's debt had a market value of $6 million, what would be the maximum amount of money Union could pay for Pearsall?

c. How much could Union pay for Pearsall's common stock assuming that cash flows were expected to be 25 percent higher than originally projected?

d. How much could Union pay for Pearsall's common stock assuming that cash flows were expected to be 25 percent higher but the required rate of return was 18 percent rather than 15 percent?

e. Suppose that instead of assuming a sale price of $60 million in 1991, you thought Pearsall's operating cash flows in that year could be maintained indefinitely. Assuming a required rate of return of 15 percent, what would Pearsall be worth in 1988? (Hint: use a perpetuity.) Given this calculation, how would this affect the NPV of buying Pearsall?

3. You are given the premerger (1988) balance sheets for Statistical Labs Amalgamated and Dunkirk Enterprises, as shown in Table A. Statistical Labs is planning to acquire Dunkirk, paying $160 million to Dunkirk shareholders and assuming the current liabilities of $20 million for a total "cash equivalent" price of $180 million.

Table A

Dunkirk Enterprises, 1988 (millions of dollars)			
Current assets	70	Current liabilities	20
Fixed assets	80	Long-term debt	0
Total assets	150	Equity	130
		Total liabilities and debt	150

Statistical Labs, 1988 (millions of dollars)			
Current assets	200	Current liabilities	200
Fixed assets	400	Long-term debt	100
Total assets	600	Equity	300
		Total liabilities and debt	600

a. Prepare the balance sheet of a new post-merger company (called SLAM-DUNK) if the transaction is a pooling of interests.

b. Prepare a balance sheet for SLAM-DUNK if the acquisition is a purchase of assets. Assume that Dunkirk's tangible assets are not revalued as the result of acquisition.

c. Suppose SLAM-DUNK's 1989 profits after taxes were anticipated to be $5 million if pooling-of-interests accounting is used. What would the reported profits be if the acquisition is a purchase of assets? How would this affect cash flow?

4. Schubert Shoe is considering the acquisition of Lipstein Leather for $6.5 million. Schubert would also assume Lipstein's liabilities of $3.2 million. Half of the merger premium is due to the fact that Lipstein's assets are carried on the books at $6.2 million, which is below their fair market value. The remainder of the premium reflects the unusually strong reputation of Lipstein as a fine-leather manufacturer. Pro-forma analysis predicts pretax cash flows from Lipstein of $2.9 million per year for 35 years. Lipstein's assets are to be depreciated on a straight-line basis over 35 years, with zero salvage value anticipated. The goodwill arising from the merger will be amortized over a 35-year period. Schubert is taxed at a rate of 50 percent, and requires a 16 percent return on investments of a risk similar to that of the Lipstein investment.

a. If the merger must be treated as a purchase for accounting purposes, should Lipstein be acquired?

b. If the merger must be treated as a pooling of interests for accounting purposes, should Lipstein be acquired?

5. Rework Franklin's acquisition of Stove (see Sample Problem 25–3), assuming that Franklin's original share price was $20 per share [a price/earnings ratio (P/E) of 10] rather than $30 per share. Assume that Franklin still planned to pay a 50 percent premium and hence was going to offer $30 of its stock for each share of Stove's stock.

a. How many shares of Franklin stock must be offered for each share of Stove stock?

b. What will the EPS be after the merger?

c. Explain why your results are different from those in the sample problem. (Hint: focus on the relevance of Franklin's P/E ratio, the P/E ratio "paid" for Stove, and Stove's P/E ratio.)

6. Let's return to Union Amalgamated's proposed acquisition of Pearsall in Sample Problems 25–1 and 25–2. There we had projected that Pearsall, if acquired, would have profits after taxes (PAT) as shown in Table B. In addition, to buy Pearsall's common stock, Union was planning to pay $50,000,000 cash plus 1,000,000 shares of Union common stock. Now we need to supply information on Union's existing financial situation. Suppose Union had 20,000,000 shares of stock outstanding. Also suppose that Union would raise the $50,000,000 cash by issuing long-term bonds that had an interest rate of 10 percent. Also suppose that Union's PAT without the merger (and also without the borrowing) was projected to be as shown in Table C.

a. Calculate Union's PAT in each of the next three years if it acquires Pearsall.

Table B

Year	Profit after Taxes (PAT) (millions of dollars)
1989	15.0
1990	18.0
1991	21.6

Table C

Year	Profit after Taxes (PAT) (millions of dollars)
1989	40
1990	50
1991	60

b. Calculate Union's EPS in each of the next three years if Union buys Pearsall.

c. What happens to Union's EPS as a result of buying Pearsall?

REFERENCES

Bittker, B. I., and J. S. Eustice. *Fundamentals of Federal Income Taxation of Corporations and Shareholders*. New York: Warren, Gorham and Lamont, 1980.

Copeland, T. E., and J. F. Weston. *Financial Theory and Corporate Policy*. 3rd ed. Reading, Mass.: Addison-Wesley Publishing Company, 1988.

Jarrell, G. A., J. Brickley, and J. Netter, "The Market for Corporate Control: The Empirical Evidence Since 1980." *Journal of Economic Perspectives* (Winter 1988): 49–68.

Jensen, M., and R. Ruback, "The Market for Corporate Control: The Scientific Evidence." *Journal of Financial Economics* (April 1983).

Keenan, M., and L. White. ed. *Mergers and Acquisitions*. Lexington, Mass.: Lexington Books, 1982.

Scherer, F. M. *Industrial Market Structure and Economic Performance*. 2nd ed. Chicago: Rand McNally and Company, 1980.

Scherer, F. M., "Corporate Takeovers: The Efficiency Arguments." *Journal of Economic Perspectives* (Winter 1988): 69–82.

Acknowledgments

Figure 1–2 on page 11: "Certificate of Deposit" by Bank of Virginia. Courtesy of Signet (formerly Bank of Virginia). Reprinted by permission.

Table 2–1 on page 28 from *1987 Prospects for Financial Markets*. Copyright © 1987 by Salomon Brothers, Inc. Reprinted by permission.

Quoted paragraphs on pages 36–37 from "The Euromarket's Flexible Friend," *The Economist*, 8/13/88. Copyright © 1988 The Economist Newspaper Ltd. Reprinted by permission.

Figure 4–2 on page 100: "General Mills, Inc., Money Multiplier Notes." *Money Multiplier Notes* is a trademark of Salomon Brothers, Inc. Copyright © 1982 by General Mills. Reprinted by permission.

Figure 4–3 on page 101 from "Treasury Bonds, Notes & Bills," *The Wall Street Journal*, 1/18/88. Reprinted by permission of *The Wall Street Journal*. © Dow Jones & Company, Inc. 1988. All Rights Reserved.

Figure on page 117 from "Are Stocks Too High?" by John J. Curran, *Fortune*, 9/28/87. Copyright © 1987 by *Fortune* Magazine. Reprinted by permission from *Fortune* Magazine.

Figure in left-hand column on page 118 from "Are Stocks Too High?" by John J. Curran, *Fortune*, 9/28/87. Copyright © 1987 by *Fortune* Magazine. Reprinted by permission from *Fortune* Magazine.

Figure in right-hand column on page 118 and figures on page 119 from "Charting an Avalanche" by Wilton Woods, *Fortune*, 11/23/87. Copyright © 1987 by *Fortune* Magazine. Reprinted by permission from *Fortune* Magazine.

Table 4–4 on page 121 and Figure 4–7 on page 122 from Ibbotson Associates, Inc., Chicago. Reprinted by permission.

Table 5–6 and Figure 5–4 on page 143 and Table 5–7 on page 151 reprinted by permission of the *Harvard Business Review*. Exhibits from "Does the Capital Asset Pricing Model Work?" by D. W. Mullins, Jr. (Jan/Feb 1982). Copyright © 1982 by the President and Fellows of Harvard College; all rights reserved.

Table 5–8 on page 153 (data in Panel A only) from Ibbotson Associates, Inc., Chicago, 1982. Reprinted by permission.

Table on page 202 from "Profitability Goes Through a Ceiling" by C. J. Loomis, *Fortune*, 5/4/81; data updated by the authors. Copyright © 1981 by *Fortune* Magazine. Reprinted by permission from *Fortune* Magazine.

Exhibit on page 220 from *Value Line Investment Survey*, February 1988. Copyright © 1988 by Value Line, Inc.; used by permission of Value Line, Inc.

Example on page 223 from *Annual Statement Studies*, Robert Morris Associates. Copyright © 1984 by Robert Morris Associates. Reprinted by permission.

Quoted paragraph in Finance in Practice 12–1 on page 348 from "Who Should Pay for Power-Plant Duds?" by Alfred E. Kahn, *Wall Street Journal*, 8/15/85. Reprinted by permission of *The Wall Street Journal*, © Dow Jones & Company, Inc. 1985. All Rights Reserved.

Table 12–8 on page 366 from Ibbotson, Roger G., and Rex A. Sinquefield, *Stocks, Bonds, Bills and Inflation* (SBBI), updated in *SBBI 1988 Yearbook*, Ibbotson Associates, Chicago. Reprinted by permission.

Table 13–12 on page 398 from *Value Line Investment Survey*, © 1988 by Value Line, Inc.; used by permission of Value Line, Inc.

Table 14–3 on page 415 from *Prospects for Financial Markets in 1988*, Salomon Brothers, Inc. Copyright © 1988 by Salomon Brothers, Inc. Reprinted by permission.

Table 14–4 on page 420 from *Moody's Public Utility Manual*, Vol. 1, 1987. Copyright © 1987 by Moody's Investors Service, Inc. Reprinted by permission.

Figure on page 434 from *Asset-Backed Securities Quarterly*, 1/88. Copyright © 1988 by Goldman-Sachs, Inc. Reprinted by permission.

Table on page 471 from *Fortune*, 9/14/87. Copyright © 1987 *Fortune* Magazine. Reprinted by permission from *Fortune* Magazine.

Table on page 483 from *The Wall Street Journal*, 1/9/87. Reprinted by permission of *The Wall Street Journal*, © Dow Jones & Company, 1987. All Rights Reserved.

Table 16–3 on page 485 from *Moody's Industrial Manual, 1986*. Copyright © 1986 by Moody's Investors Service, Inc. Reprinted by permission.

Finance in Practice 16–1 on pages 488–489 adapted from "Financing Policies and Practices in Large Corporations" by D. F. Scott and D. J. Johnson, *Financial Management*, Summer 1982. Copyright © 1982 by Financial Management Association. Reprinted by permission.

International Focus on pages 511–512 from *The Economist*, 12/26/87. Copyright © 1987 by The Economist Newspaper Ltd.

Table 18–2 on pages 540–541 adapted from *The ABC's of Option Trading: How to Use Barron's Complete Coverage of Puts and Calls*, Dow Jones & Company, 1984. Copyright © 1984 by Dow Jones & Company. Reprinted by permission.

Table 18–1 on page 530 from *The Wall Street Journal*, 12/23/87. Reprinted by permission of *The Wall Street Journal*, © Dow Jones & Company, Inc. 1987. All Rights Reserved.

Table on page 542 from *The Wall Street Journal*, 10/21/87. Reprinted by permission of *The Wall Street Journal*, © Dow Jones & Company, Inc. 1987. All Rights Reserved.

Figure 20–1 on page 585 from Goldman-Sachs, Inc. Copyright © 1986 by Goldman-Sachs, Inc. Reprinted by permission.

Information in Finance in Practice 22–1 on page 645 from *1985 Report to Shareholders*, NCNB Corporation. Copyright © 1985 by NCNB Corporation, Charlotte, NC. Reprinted by permission.

Table 22–1 on page 649 from Moody's Manuals and Annual Reports for 1986. Copyright © 1986 by Moody's Investors Service, Inc. Reprinted by permission.

Figure 22–3 on page 655 from *Comments on Credit*, 8/17/79; updated with data from Federal Reserve Bank of St. Louis for 1979–1987. Copyright © 1979 by Salomon Brothers, Inc. Reprinted by permission.

Table 24–1 on page 700 from *Fortune*, 7/20/87. Copyright © 1987 by *Fortune* Magazine. Reprinted by permission from *Fortune* Magazine.

Table 24–2 on pages 708–709 from *The Wall Street Journal*, 12/4/87. Reprinted by permission of *The Wall Street Journal*, © Dow Jones & Company, Inc. 1987. All Rights Reserved.

Figures on pages 722–723 from "Crawling Out of the Trade Tunnel," *Fortune*, 12/21/87. Copyright © 1987 by *Fortune* Magazine. Reprinted by permission from *Fortune* Magazine.

Appendix Table I
Present Value* (at *i* per period) of $1 Received at the End of *n* Periods

0% for any n = 1 (handwritten)

n	i = 1%	2%	3%	4%	5%	6%	7%	8%	9%	10%
1	0.990	0.980	0.970	0.962	0.952	0.943	0.935	0.926	0.917	0.909
2	0.980	0.961	0.943	0.925	0.907	0.890	0.873	0.857	0.842	0.826
3	0.971	0.942	0.915	0.889	0.864	0.840	0.816	0.794	0.772	0.751
4	0.961	0.924	0.888	0.855	0.823	0.792	0.763	0.735	0.708	0.683
5	0.951	0.906	0.863	0.822	0.784	0.747	0.713	0.681	0.650	0.621
6	0.942	0.888	0.837	0.790	0.746	0.705	0.666	0.630	0.596	0.564
7	0.933	0.871	0.813	0.760	0.711	0.665	0.623	0.583	0.547	0.513
8	0.923	0.853	0.789	0.731	0.677	0.627	0.582	0.540	0.502	0.467
9	0.914	0.837	0.766	0.703	0.645	0.592	0.544	0.500	0.460	0.424
10	0.905	0.820	0.744	0.676	0.614	0.558	0.508	0.463	0.422	0.386
11	0.896	0.804	0.722	0.650	0.585	0.527	0.475	0.429	0.388	0.350
12	0.887	0.788	0.701	0.625	0.557	0.497	0.444	0.397	0.356	0.319
13	0.879	0.773	0.681	0.601	0.530	0.469	0.415	0.368	0.326	0.290
14	0.870	0.758	0.661	0.577	0.505	0.442	0.388	0.340	0.299	0.263
15	0.861	0.743	0.642	0.555	0.481	0.417	0.362	0.315	0.275	0.239
16	0.853	0.728	0.623	0.534	0.458	0.394	0.339	0.299	0.252	0.218
17	0.844	0.714	0.605	0.513	0.436	0.371	0.317	0.270	0.231	0.198
18	0.836	0.700	0.587	0.494	0.416	0.350	0.296	0.250	0.212	0.180
19	0.828	0.686	0.570	0.475	0.396	0.331	0.277	0.232	0.194	0.164
20	0.820	0.673	0.554	0.456	0.377	0.312	0.258	0.215	0.178	0.149
21	0.811	0.660	0.538	0.439	0.359	0.294	0.242	0.199	0.164	0.135
22	0.803	0.647	0.522	0.422	0.342	0.278	0.226	0.184	0.150	0.123
23	0.795	0.634	0.507	0.406	0.326	0.262	0.211	0.170	0.138	0.112
24	0.788	0.622	0.492	0.390	0.310	0.247	0.197	0.158	0.126	0.102
25	0.780	0.610	0.478	0.375	0.295	0.233	0.184	0.146	0.116	0.092
30	0.742	0.552	0.412	0.308	0.231	0.174	0.131	0.099	0.075	0.057
35	0.706	0.500	0.355	0.253	0.181	0.130	0.094	0.068	0.049	0.036
40	0.672	0.453	0.307	0.208	0.142	0.097	0.067	0.046	0.032	0.022
45	0.639	0.410	0.264	0.171	0.111	0.073	0.048	0.031	0.021	0.014
50	0.608	0.372	0.228	0.141	0.087	0.054	0.034	0.021	0.013	0.009

*Value is calculated as $\dfrac{1}{(1 + i)^n}$.

(handwritten) 1000 × .386

Appendix Table I
(continued)

n	i = 11%	12%	13%	14%	15%	16%	17%	18%	19%	20%
1	0.901	0.893	0.885	0.877	0.870	0.862	0.855	0.847	0.840	0.833
2	0.812	0.797	0.783	0.769	0.756	0.743	0.731	0.718	0.706	0.694
3	0.731	0.712	0.693	0.675	0.658	0.641	0.624	0.609	0.593	0.579
4	0.659	0.636	0.613	0.592	0.572	0.552	0.534	0.516	0.499	0.482
5	0.593	0.567	0.543	0.519	0.497	0.476	0.456	0.437	0.419	0.402
6	0.535	0.507	0.480	0.456	0.432	0.410	0.390	0.370	0.352	0.333
7	0.482	0.452	0.425	0.400	0.376	0.354	0.333	0.314	0.296	0.279
8	0.434	0.404	0.376	0.351	0.327	0.305	0.285	0.266	0.249	0.233
9	0.391	0.361	0.333	0.308	0.284	0.263	0.243	0.225	0.209	0.194
10	0.352	0.322	0.295	0.270	0.247	0.227	0.208	0.191	0.176	0.162
11	0.317	0.287	0.261	0.237	0.215	0.195	0.178	0.162	0.148	0.135
12	0.286	0.257	0.231	0.208	0.187	0.168	0.152	0.137	0.124	0.112
13	0.258	0.229	0.204	0.182	0.163	0.145	0.130	0.116	0.104	0.093
14	0.232	0.205	0.181	0.160	0.141	0.125	0.111	0.099	0.088	0.078
15	0.209	0.183	0.160	0.140	0.123	0.108	0.095	0.084	0.074	0.065
16	0.188	0.163	0.142	0.123	0.107	0.093	0.081	0.071	0.062	0.054
17	0.170	0.146	0.125	0.108	0.093	0.080	0.069	0.060	0.052	0.045
18	0.153	0.130	0.111	0.095	0.081	0.069	0.059	0.051	0.044	0.038
19	0.138	0.116	0.098	0.083	0.070	0.060	0.051	0.043	0.037	0.031
20	0.124	0.104	0.087	0.073	0.061	0.051	0.043	0.037	0.031	0.026
21	0.112	0.093	0.077	0.064	0.053	0.044	0.037	0.031	0.026	0.022
22	0.101	0.083	0.068	0.056	0.046	0.038	0.032	0.026	0.022	0.018
23	0.091	0.074	0.060	0.049	0.040	0.033	0.027	0.022	0.018	0.015
24	0.082	0.066	0.053	0.043	0.035	0.028	0.023	0.019	0.015	0.013
25	0.074	0.059	0.047	0.038	0.030	0.024	0.020	0.016	0.013	0.010
30	0.044	0.033	0.026	0.020	0.015	0.012	0.009	0.007	0.005	0.004
35	0.026	0.019	0.014	0.010	0.008	0.006	0.004	0.003	0.002	0.002
40	0.015	0.011	0.008	0.005	0.004	0.003	0.002	0.001	0.001	0.001
45	0.009	0.006	0.004	0.003	0.002	0.001	0.001	0.001	*	*
50	0.005	0.003	0.002	0.001	0.001	0.001	*	*	*	*

*Value less than 0.001.

Appendix Table I
(continued)

n	i = 21%	22%	23%	24%	25%	26%	27%	28%	29%	30%
1	0.826	0.820	0.813	0.806	0.800	0.794	0.787	0.781	0.775	0.769
2	0.683	0.672	0.661	0.650	0.640	0.630	0.620	0.610	0.601	0.592
3	0.564	0.551	0.537	0.524	0.512	0.500	0.488	0.477	0.466	0.455
4	0.467	0.451	0.437	0.423	0.410	0.397	0.384	0.373	0.361	0.350
5	0.386	0.370	0.355	0.341	0.328	0.315	0.303	0.291	0.280	0.269
6	0.319	0.303	0.289	0.275	0.262	0.250	0.238	0.227	0.217	0.207
7	0.263	0.249	0.235	0.222	0.210	0.198	0.188	0.178	0.168	0.159
8	0.218	0.204	0.191	0.179	0.168	0.157	0.148	0.139	0.130	0.123
9	0.180	0.167	0.155	0.144	0.134	0.125	0.116	0.108	0.101	0.094
10	0.149	0.137	0.126	0.116	0.107	0.099	0.092	0.085	0.078	0.073
11	0.123	0.112	0.103	0.094	0.086	0.079	0.072	0.066	0.061	0.056
12	0.102	0.092	0.083	0.076	0.069	0.062	0.057	0.052	0.047	0.043
13	0.084	0.075	0.068	0.061	0.055	0.050	0.045	0.040	0.037	0.033
14	0.069	0.062	0.055	0.049	0.044	0.039	0.035	0.032	0.028	0.025
15	0.057	0.051	0.045	0.040	0.035	0.031	0.028	0.025	0.022	0.020
16	0.047	0.042	0.036	0.032	0.028	0.025	0.022	0.019	0.017	0.015
17	0.039	0.034	0.030	0.026	0.023	0.020	0.017	0.015	0.013	0.012
18	0.032	0.028	0.024	0.021	0.018	0.016	0.014	0.012	0.010	0.009
19	0.027	0.023	0.020	0.017	0.014	0.012	0.011	0.009	0.008	0.007
20	0.022	0.019	0.016	0.014	0.012	0.010	0.008	0.007	0.006	0.005
21	0.018	0.015	0.013	0.011	0.009	0.008	0.007	0.006	0.005	0.004
22	0.015	0.013	0.011	0.009	0.007	0.006	0.005	0.004	0.004	0.003
23	0.012	0.010	0.009	0.007	0.006	0.005	0.004	0.003	0.003	0.002
24	0.010	0.008	0.007	0.006	0.005	0.004	0.003	0.003	0.002	0.002
25	0.009	0.007	0.006	0.005	0.004	0.003	0.003	0.002	0.002	0.001
30	0.003	0.003	0.002	0.002	0.001	0.001	0.001	0.001	*	*
35	0.001	0.001	0.001	0.001	*	*	*	*	*	*
40	*	*	*	*	*	*	*	*	*	*

Appendix Table I
(continued)

n	i = 31%	32%	33%	34%	35%	36%	37%	38%	39%	40%	50%
1	0.763	0.758	0.752	0.746	0.741	0.735	0.730	0.725	0.719	0.714	0.667
2	0.583	0.574	0.565	0.557	0.549	0.541	0.533	0.525	0.518	0.510	0.444
3	0.445	0.435	0.425	0.416	0.406	0.398	0.389	0.381	0.372	0.364	0.296
4	0.340	0.329	0.320	0.310	0.301	0.292	0.284	0.276	0.268	0.260	0.198
5	0.259	0.250	0.240	0.231	0.223	0.215	0.207	0.200	0.193	0.186	0.132
6	0.198	0.189	0.181	0.173	0.165	0.158	0.151	0.145	0.139	0.133	0.088
7	0.151	0.143	0.136	0.129	0.122	0.116	0.110	0.105	0.100	0.095	0.059
8	0.115	0.108	0.102	0.096	0.091	0.085	0.081	0.076	0.072	0.068	0.039
9	0.088	0.082	0.077	0.072	0.067	0.063	0.059	0.055	0.052	0.048	0.026
10	0.067	0.062	0.058	0.054	0.050	0.046	0.043	0.040	0.037	0.035	0.017
11	0.051	0.047	0.043	0.040	0.037	0.034	0.031	0.029	0.027	0.025	0.012
12	0.039	0.036	0.033	0.030	0.027	0.025	0.023	0.021	0.019	0.018	0.008
13	0.030	0.027	0.025	0.022	0.020	0.018	0.017	0.015	0.014	0.013	0.005
14	0.023	0.021	0.018	0.017	0.015	0.014	0.012	0.011	0.010	0.009	0.003
15	0.017	0.016	0.014	0.012	0.011	0.010	0.009	0.008	0.007	0.006	0.002
16	0.013	0.012	0.010	0.009	0.008	0.007	0.006	0.006	0.005	0.005	0.002
17	0.010	0.009	0.008	0.007	0.006	0.005	0.005	0.004	0.004	0.003	0.001
18	0.008	0.007	0.006	0.005	0.005	0.004	0.003	0.003	0.003	0.002	0.001
19	0.006	0.005	0.004	0.004	0.003	0.003	0.003	0.002	0.002	0.002	*
20	0.005	0.004	0.003	0.003	0.002	0.002	0.002	0.002	0.001	0.001	*
21	0.003	0.003	0.003	0.002	0.002	0.002	0.001	0.001	0.001	0.001	*
22	0.003	0.002	0.002	0.002	0.001	0.001	0.001	0.001	0.001	0.001	*
23	0.002	0.002	0.001	0.001	0.001	0.001	0.001	0.001	0.001	*	*
24	0.002	0.001	0.001	0.001	0.001	0.001	0.001	*	*	*	*
25	0.001	0.001	0.001	0.001	0.001	*	*	*	*	*	*
30	*	*	*	*	*	*	*	*	*	*	*

Appendix Table II Annuity

Present Value* (at i per period) of $1 Received per Period for Each of n Periods

n	$i = 1\%$	2%	3%	4%	5%	6%	7%			
1	0.990	0.980	0.971	0.962	0.952	0.943	0.935			
2	1.970	1.942	1.914	1.886	1.859	1.833	1.808	1.783	1.759	1.736
3	2.941	2.884	2.829	2.775	2.723	2.673	2.624	2.577	2.531	2.487
4	3.902	3.808	3.717	3.630	3.546	3.465	3.387	3.312	3.240	3.170
5	4.854	4.713	4.580	4.452	4.330	4.212	4.100	3.993	3.890	3.791
6	5.796	5.601	5.417	5.242	5.076	4.917	4.767	4.623	4.486	4.355
7	6.728	6.472	6.230	6.002	5.786	5.582	5.389	5.206	5.033	4.868
8	7.652	7.325	7.020	6.733	6.463	6.210	5.971	5.747	5.535	5.335
9	8.566	8.162	7.786	7.435	7.108	6.802	6.515	6.247	5.985	5.759
10	9.471	8.983	8.530	8.111	7.722	7.360	7.024	6.710	6.418	6.145
11	10.368	9.787	9.253	8.760	8.036	7.887	7.499	7.139	6.805	6.495
12	11.255	10.575	9.954	9.385	8.863	8.384	7.943	7.536	7.161	6.814
13	12.134	11.348	10.635	9.986	9.394	8.853	8.358	7.904	7.487	7.103
14	13.004	12.106	11.296	10.563	9.899	9.295	8.745	8.244	7.786	7.367
15	13.865	12.849	11.938	11.118	10.380	9.712	9.108	8.560	8.061	7.606
16	14.718	13.578	12.561	11.652	10.838	10.106	9.447	8.851	8.313	7.824
17	15.562	14.292	13.166	12.166	11.274	10.477	9.763	9.122	8.544	8.022
18	16.398	14.992	13.753	12.659	11.690	10.828	10.059	9.372	8.756	8.201
19	17.226	15.678	14.324	13.134	12.085	11.158	10.336	9.604	8.950	8.365
20	18.046	16.351	14.877	13.590	12.462	11.470	10.594	9.818	9.129	8.514
21	18.857	17.011	15.415	14.029	12.821	11.764	10.836	10.017	9.292	8.649
22	19.661	17.658	15.937	14.451	13.163	12.042	11.061	10.201	9.442	8.772
23	20.456	18.292	16.444	14.857	13.489	12.303	11.272	10.371	9.580	8.883
24	21.244	18.914	16.936	15.247	13.799	12.550	11.469	10.529	9.707	8.985
25	22.023	19.523	17.413	15.622	14.094	12.783	11.654	10.675	9.823	9.077
30	25.808	22.396	19.600	17.292	15.372	13.765	12.409	11.258	10.274	9.427
35	29.409	24.999	21.487	18.665	16.374	14.498	12.948	11.655	10.567	9.644
40	32.835	27.355	23.115	19.793	17.159	15.046	13.332	11.925	10.757	9.779
45	36.095	29.490	24.519	20.720	17.774	15.456	13.606	12.108	10.881	9.863
50	39.196	31.424	25.730	21.482	18.256	15.762	13.801	12.233	10.962	9.915

*Value is calculated as $\left(\dfrac{1}{(1 + i)} + \dfrac{1}{(1 + i)^2} + \cdots + \dfrac{1}{(1 + i)^n} \right)$.

Appendix Table II

(continued)

n	i = 11%	12%	13%	14%	15%	16%	17%	18%	19%	20%
1	0.901	0.893	0.885	0.377	0.870	0.862	0.855	0.848	0.840	0.833
2	1.713	1.690	1.668	1.647	1.626	1.605	1.585	1.566	1.547	1.528
3	2.444	2.402	2.361	2.322	2.283	2.246	2.210	2.174	2.140	2.107
4	3.102	3.037	2.975	2.914	2.855	2.798	2.743	2.690	2.639	2.589
5	3.696	3.605	3.517	3.433	3.352	3.274	3.199	3.127	3.058	2.991
6	4.231	4.111	3.998	3.889	3.785	3.685	3.589	3.498	3.410	3.326
7	4.712	4.564	4.423	4.288	4.160	4.029	3.922	3.812	3.706	3.605
9	5.537	5.328	5.132	4.946	4.772	4.607	4.451	4.303	4.163	4.031
10	5.889	5.650	5.426	5.216	5.019	4.833	4.659	4.404	4.339	4.193
11	6.207	5.938	5.687	5.453	5.234	5.029	4.836	4.656	4.487	4.327
12	6.492	6.194	5.918	5.660	5.421	5.197	4.988	4.793	4.611	4.439
13	6.750	6.424	6.122	5.842	5.583	5.342	5.118	4.910	4.715	4.533
14	6.982	6.628	6.303	6.002	5.725	5.468	5.229	5.008	4.802	4.611
15	7.191	6.811	6.462	6.142	5.847	5.576	5.324	5.092	4.876	4.676
16	7.379	6.974	6.604	6.265	5.954	5.669	5.405	5.162	4.938	4.730
17	7.549	7.120	6.729	6.373	6.047	5.749	5.475	5.222	4.990	4.775
18	7.702	7.250	6.840	6.467	6.128	5.818	5.534	5.273	5.033	4.812
19	7.839	7.366	6.938	6.550	6.198	5.878	5.585	5.316	5.070	4.844
20	7.963	7.469	7.025	6.623	6.259	5.929	5.628	5.353	5.101	4.870
21	8.075	7.562	7.102	6.687	6.313	5.973	5.665	5.384	5.127	4.891
22	8.176	7.534	7.170	6.743	6.359	6.011	5.696	5.410	5.149	4.909
23	8.266	7.718	7.230	6.792	6.399	6.044	5.723	5.432	5.167	4.925
24	8.348	7.784	7.283	6.835	6.434	6.073	5.747	5.451	5.182	4.937
25	8.422	7.843	7.330	6.873	6.464	6.097	5.766	5.467	5.195	4.948
30	8.694	8.055	7.496	7.003	6.566	6.177	5.829	5.517	5.235	4.979
35	8.855	8.176	7.586	7.070	6.617	6.215	5.858	5.539	5.251	4.992
40	8.951	8.244	7.634	7.105	6.642	6.233	5.871	5.548	5.258	4.997
45	9.008	8.283	7.661	7.123	6.654	6.242	5.877	5.552	5.261	4.999
50	9.042	8.304	7.675	7.133	6.661	6.246	5.880	5.554	5.262	4.999

Appendix Table II
(continued)

n	i = 21%	22%	23%	24%	25%	26%	27%	28%	29%	30%
1	0.826	0.820	0.813	0.807	0.800	0.794	0.787	0.781	0.775	0.769
2	1.510	1.492	1.474	1.457	1.440	1.424	1.407	1.392	1.376	1.361
3	2.074	2.042	2.011	1.981	1.952	1.923	1.896	1.868	1.842	1.816
4	2.540	2.494	2.448	2.404	2.362	2.320	2.280	2.241	2.203	2.166
5	2.926	2.864	2.804	2.745	2.689	2.635	2.583	2.532	2.483	2.436
6	3.245	3.167	3.092	3.021	2.951	2.885	2.821	2.759	2.700	2.643
7	3.508	3.416	3.327	3.242	3.161	3.083	3.009	2.937	2.868	2.802
8	3.726	3.619	3.518	3.421	3.329	3.241	3.156	3.076	2.999	2.925
9	3.905	3.786	3.673	3.566	3.463	3.366	3.273	3.184	3.010	3.019
10	4.054	3.923	3.799	3.682	3.571	3.465	3.364	3.269	3.178	3.092
11	4.177	4.035	3.902	3.776	3.656	3.544	3.437	3.335	3.239	3.147
12	4.279	4.127	3.985	3.851	3.725	3.606	3.493	3.387	3.286	3.190
13	4.362	4.203	4.053	3.912	3.780	3.656	3.638	3.427	3.322	3.223
14	4.432	4.265	4.108	3.962	3.824	3.695	3.573	3.459	3.351	3.249
15	4.489	4.315	4.153	4.001	3.859	3.726	3.601	3.483	3.373	3.268
16	4.536	4.357	4.189	4.033	3.887	3.751	3.623	3.503	3.390	3.283
17	4.576	4.391	4.219	4.059	3.910	3.771	3.640	3.518	3.403	3.295
18	4.608	4.419	4.243	4.080	3.928	3.786	3.654	3.529	3.413	3.304
19	4.635	4.442	4.263	4.097	3.942	3.799	3.664	3.539	3.421	3.311
20	4.657	4.460	4.279	4.110	3.954	3.808	3.673	3.546	3.427	3.316
21	4.675	4.476	4.292	4.121	3.963	3.816	3.679	3.551	3.432	3.320
22	4.690	4.488	4.302	4.130	3.971	3.822	3.684	3.556	3.436	3.323
23	4.703	4.499	4.311	4.137	3.976	3.827	3.689	3.559	3.438	3.325
24	4.713	4.507	4.318	4.143	3.981	3.831	3.692	3.562	3.441	3.327
25	4.721	4.514	4.323	4.147	3.985	3.834	3.694	3.564	3.442	3.329
30	4.746	4.534	4.339	4.160	3.995	3.842	3.701	3.569	3.447	3.332
35	4.756	4.541	4.345	4.164	3.998	3.845	3.703	3.571	3.448	3.333
40	4.760	4.544	4.347	4.166	3.999	3.846	3.703	3.571	3.448	3.333
45	4.761	4.545	4.347	4.166	4.000	3.846	3.704	3.571	3.448	3.333
50	4.762	4.545	4.348	4.167	4.000	3.846	3.704	3.571	3.448	3.333

Appendix Table II

(continued)

n	i = 31%	32%	33%	34%	35%	36%	37%	38%	39%	40%	50%
1	0.763	0.758	0.752	0.746	0.741	0.735	0.730	0.725	0.719	0.714	0.667
2	1.346	1.332	1.317	1.303	1.289	1.276	1.263	1.250	1.237	1.225	1.111
3	1.791	1.766	1.742	1.719	1.696	1.674	1.652	1.630	1.609	1.589	1.407
4	2.131	2.096	2.062	2.029	1.997	1.966	1.936	1.906	1.877	1.849	1.605
5	2.390	2.345	2.302	2.260	2.220	2.181	2.143	2.106	2.070	2.935	1.737
6	2.588	2.534	2.483	2.433	2.386	2.339	2.294	2.251	2.209	2.168	1.824
7	2.739	2.678	2.619	2.562	2.508	2.455	2.404	2.356	2.308	2.263	1.883
8	2.854	2.786	2.721	2.658	2.598	2.540	2.485	2.432	2.380	2.331	1.922
9	2.942	2.868	2.798	2.730	2.665	2.603	2.544	2.487	2.432	2.379	1.948
10	3.009	2.930	2.855	2.784	2.715	2.650	2.587	2.527	2.469	2.414	1.965
11	3.060	2.978	2.899	2.924	2.752	2.683	2.618	2.556	2.496	2.438	1.977
12	3.100	3.012	2.931	2.853	2.779	2.708	2.641	2.576	2.515	2.456	1.985
13	3.129	3.040	2.956	2.876	2.799	2.727	2.658	2.592	2.469	1.990	
14	3.152	3.061	2.974	2.892	2.814	2.740	2.670	2.603	2.539	2.478	1.993
15	3.170	3.076	2.988	2.905	2.826	2.750	2.679	2.611	2.546	2.484	1.995
16	3.183	3.088	2.999	2.914	2.834	2.758	2.685	2.616	2.551	2.489	1.997
17	3.193	3.097	3.007	2.921	2.840	2.763	2.690	2.621	2.555	2.492	1.998
18	3.201	3.104	3.012	2.926	2.844	2.767	2.693	2.624	2.557	2.494	1.999
19	3.207	3.109	3.017	2.930	2.848	2.770	2.696	2.626	2.559	2.496	1.999
20	3.211	3.113	3.020	2.933	2.850	2.772	2.698	2.627	2.561	2.497	1.999
21	3.215	3.116	3.023	2.935	2.852	2.773	2.699	2.629	2.562	2.498	2.000
22	3.217	3.118	3.025	2.937	2.853	2.775	2.700	2.629	2.562	2.499	2.000
23	3.219	3.120	3.026	2.938	2.854	2.775	2.701	2.630	2.563	2.499	2.000
24	3.221	3.121	3.027	2.939	2.855	2.776	2.701	2.630	2.563	2.499	2.000
25	3.222	3.122	3.028	2.939	2.856	2.777	2.702	2.631	2.563	2.499	2.000
30	3.225	3.124	3.030	2.941	2.857	2.778	2.702	2.631	2.564	2.500	2.000
35	3.226	3.125	3.030	2.941	2.857	2.778	2.702	2.632	2.564	2.500	2.000
40	3.226	3.125	3.030	2.941	2.857	2.778	2.702	2.632	2.564	2.500	2.000
45	3.226	3.125	3.030	2.941	2.857	2.778	2.702	2.632	2.564	2.500	2.000
50	3.226	3.125	3.030	2.941	2.857	2.778	2.702	2.632	2.564	2.500	2.000

Appendix Table III
Future Value* (at *i* per period) at the End of *n* Periods of $1 Invested Today

n	i = 1%	2%	3%	4%	5%	6%	7%	8%	9%	10%
1	1.010	1.020	1.030	1.040	1.050	1.060	1.070	1.080	1.090	1.100
2	1.020	1.040	1.061	1.082	1.103	1.124	1.145	1.166	1.188	1.210
3	1.030	1.061	1.093	1.125	1.158	1.191	1.225	1.260	1.295	1.331
4	1.041	1.082	1.126	1.170	1.216	1.263	1.311	1.361	1.417	1.464
5	1.051	1.104	1.159	1.217	1.276	1.338	1.403	1.469	1.539	1.611
6	1.062	1.126	1.194	1.265	1.340	1.519	1.501	1.587	1.677	1.772
7	1.072	1.149	1.230	1.316	1.407	1.504	1.606	1.714	1.828	1.949
8	1.083	1.172	1.267	1.369	1.478	1.594	1.718	1.851	1.993	2.144
9	1.094	1.195	1.305	1.423	1.551	1.690	1.839	1.999	2.172	2.358
10	1.105	1.219	1.344	1.480	1.629	1.791	1.967	2.159	2.367	2.594
11	1.116	1.243	1.384	1.540	1.710	1.898	2.105	2.332	2.580	2.853
12	1.127	1.268	1.426	1.602	1.796	2.012	2.252	2.518	2.813	3.138
13	1.138	1.294	1.469	1.665	1.886	2.133	2.410	2.720	3.066	3.452
14	1.150	1.320	1.513	1.732	1.980	2.261	2.579	2.927	3.342	3.798
15	1.161	1.346	1.558	1.801	2.079	2.397	2.759	3.172	3.643	4.177
16	1.173	1.373	1.605	1.873	2.183	2.540	2.952	3.426	3.970	4.595
17	1.184	1.400	1.653	1.948	2.292	2.693	3.159	3.700	4.328	5.054
18	1.196	1.428	1.702	2.026	2.407	2.854	3.380	3.996	4.717	5.560
19	1.208	1.457	1.754	2.107	2.527	3.026	3.617	4.316	5.142	6.116
20	1.220	1.486	1.806	2.191	2.653	3.207	3.870	4.661	5.604	6.728
21	1.232	1.516	1.860	2.279	2.786	3.400	4.141	5.034	6.109	7.400
22	1.245	1.546	1.916	2.370	2.925	3.604	4.430	5.437	6.659	8.140
23	1.257	1.577	1.974	2.465	3.072	3.820	4.741	5.871	7.258	8.954
24	1.270	1.608	2.033	2.563	3.225	4.049	5.072	6.341	7.911	9.850
25	1.282	1.641	2.094	2.666	3.386	4.292	5.427	6.849	8.623	10.835
30	1.348	1.811	2.427	3.243	4.322	5.743	7.612	10.063	13.268	17.449
35	1.417	2.000	2.813	3.946	5.516	7.686	10.677	14.785	20.414	28.102
40	1.489	2.208	3.262	4.801	7.040	10.286	14.974	21.725	31.409	45.259
45	1.565	2.438	3.782	5.841	8.985	13.765	21.002	31.920	48.327	72.890
50	1.645	2.692	4.384	7.107	11.467	18.420	29.457	46.902	74.357	117.391

*Value is calculated as $(1 + i)^n$.

[handwritten annotation: "$ has doubled" pointing near row 7, 10%; "tripled" pointing near row 11, 10%]

Appendix Table III

(continued)

n	i = 11%	12%	13%	14%	15%	16%	17%	18%	19%	20%
1	1.110	1.120	1.130	1.140	1.150	1.160	1.170	1.180	1.190	1.200
2	1.232	1.254	1.277	1.300	1.323	1.346	1.369	1.392	1.416	1.440
3	1.368	1.405	1.443	1.482	1.521	1.561	1.602	1.643	1.685	1.728
4	1.518	1.574	1.631	1.689	1.749	1.811	1.874	1.939	2.005	2.074
5	1.685	1.762	1.842	1.925	2.011	2.100	2.193	2.288	2.386	2.488
6	1.870	1.974	2.082	2.195	2.313	2.436	2.565	2.700	2.840	2.986
7	2.076	2.211	2.353	2.502	2.660	2.826	3.001	3.186	3.379	3.583
8	2.305	2.476	2.658	2.853	3.059	3.278	3.512	3.759	4.021	4.300
9	2.558	2.773	3.004	3.252	3.518	3.803	4.108	4.436	4.786	5.160
10	2.839	3.106	3.395	3.707	4.046	4.411	4.807	5.234	5.695	6.192
11	3.152	3.479	3.836	4.226	4.652	5.117	5.624	6.176	6.777	7.430
12	3.499	3.896	4.335	4.818	5.350	5.936	6.580	7.288	8.064	8.916
13	3.883	4.364	4.898	5.492	6.153	6.886	7.699	8.599	9.597	10.699
14	4.310	4.887	5.535	6.262	7.076	7.988	9.008	10.147	11.420	12.839
15	4.785	5.474	6.254	7.138	8.137	9.266	10.539	11.974	13.590	15.407
16	5.311	6.130	7.067	8.137	9.358	10.748	12.330	14.129	16.172	18.488
17	5.895	6.866	7.986	9.277	10.761	12.468	14.427	16.672	19.244	22.186
18	6.544	7.690	9.024	10.575	12.376	14.463	16.879	19.673	22.901	26.623
19	7.263	8.613	10.107	12.056	14.232	16.777	19.748	23.214	27.252	31.948
20	8.062	9.646	11.523	13.744	16.367	19.461	23.106	27.393	32.429	38.338
21	8.949	10.804	13.021	15.668	18.822	22.575	27.034	32.324	38.591	46.005
22	9.934	12.100	14.714	17.861	21.645	26.186	31.629	38.142	45.923	55.206
23	11.026	13.552	16.627	20.362	24.892	30.376	37.006	45.008	54.649	66.247
24	12.239	15.179	18.788	23.212	28.625	35.236	43.297	53.109	65.032	79.497
25	13.586	17.000	21.232	26.462	32.919	40.874	50.658	62.669	77.388	95.396
30	22.892	29.960	39.116	50.590	66.212	85.850	111.065	143.371	184.675	237.376
35	38.575	52.780	72.069	98.100	133.176	180.314	243.503	327.997	440.701	590.688
40	65.001	93.051	132.781	188.884	267.864	378.721	533.869	750.378	1051.668	1469.772
45	109.530	163.988	244.641	363.679	538.769	795.444	1170.479	1716.684	2509.651	3657.262
50	184.565	289.002	450.736	700.233	1083.657	1670.704	2566.215	3927.357	5988.914	9100.438

Appendix Table IV   Annuity

Future Value* (at i per period) of $1 Invested per Period for Each of n Periods FV_A

n	i = 1%	2%	3%	4%	5%	6%	7%	8%	9%	10%
1	1.000	1.000	1.000	1.000	1.000	1.000	1.000	1.000	1.000	1.000
2	2.010	2.020	2.030	2.040	2.050	2.060	2.070	2.080	2.090	2.100
3	3.030	3.060	3.091	3.122	3.153	3.183	3.214	3.246	3.278	3.310
4	4.060	4.122	4.184	4.246	4.310	4.375	4.440	4.506	4.573	4.641
5	5.101	5.204	5.309	5.416	5.526	5.637	5.718	5.866	5.984	6.105
6	6.152	6.308	6.468	6.633	6.802	6.975	7.153	7.336	7.523	7.716
7	7.214	7.434	7.663	7.898	8.142	8.393	8.654	8.923	9.200	9.487
8	8.286	8.583	8.892	9.214	9.549	9.898	10.260	10.637	11.028	11.436
9	9.369	9.755	10.159	10.583	11.027	11.491	11.978	12.488	13.021	13.579
10	10.462	10.950	11.464	12.006	12.578	13.181	13.816	14.487	15.193	15.937
11	11.567	12.169	12.808	13.486	14.207	14.972	15.784	16.645	17.560	18.531
12	12.683	13.412	14.192	15.026	15.917	16.870	17.888	18.977	20.141	21.384
13	13.809	14.680	15.618	16.627	17.713	18.882	20.141	21.495	22.953	24.523
14	14.947	15.974	17.086	18.292	19.599	21.051	22.550	24.215	26.019	27.975
15	16.097	17.293	18.599	20.024	21.579	23.276	25.129	27.152	29.361	31.772
16	17.258	18.639	20.157	21.825	23.657	25.673	27.888	30.324	33.003	35.950
17	18.430	20.012	21.762	23.698	25.840	28.213	30.840	33.750	36.973	40.545
18	19.615	21.412	23.414	25.645	28.132	30.906	33.999	37.450	41.301	45.599
19	20.811	22.841	25.117	27.671	30.539	33.760	37.379	41.446	46.019	51.159
20	22.019	24.297	26.870	29.778	33.066	36.766	40.995	45.762	51.160	57.275
21	23.239	25.783	28.676	31.969	35.719	39.993	44.865	50.423	56.764	64.002
22	24.472	27.299	30.537	34.248	38.505	42.392	49.006	55.457	62.873	71.403
23	25.716	28.845	32.453	36.618	41.430	46.996	53.436	60.893	69.532	79.543
24	26.973	30.422	34.426	39.083	44.502	50.816	58.177	66.765	76.790	88.497
25	28.243	32.030	36.459	41.646	47.727	54.865	63.249	73.106	84.701	98.347
30	34.785	40.568	45.575	56.085	66.439	79.058	94.461	113.283	136.308	164.494
35	41.660	49.995	60.462	73.652	90.320	111.435	138.237	172.317	215.711	271.024
40	48.886	60.402	75.401	95.026	120.800	154.762	199.635	259.057	337.882	442.593
45	56.481	71.893	92.720	121.030	159.700	212.744	285.749	386.506	525.859	718.905
50	64.463	84.579	112.797	152.667	209.348	290.336	406.529	573.770	815.084	1163.909

*Value is calculated as $[(1 + i)^{n-1} + (1 + i)^{n-2} + \ldots + (1 + i)^{n-n}]$.

Appendix Table IV

(continued)

n	i = 11%	12%	13%	14%	15%	16%	17%	18%	19%	20%
1	1.000	1.000	1.000	1.000	1.000	1.000	1.000	1.000	1.000	1.000
2	2.110	2.120	2.130	2.140	2.150	2.160	2.170	2.180	2.190	2.200
3	3.342	3.374	3.401	3.439	3.472	3.501	3.539	3.572	3.606	3.640
4	4.710	4.779	4.850	4.921	4.993	5.067	5.141	5.216	5.290	5.368
5	6.229	6.353	6.480	6.610	6l742	6.877	7.015	7.154	7.297	7.442
6	7.913	8.115	8.323	8.536	8.754	8.978	9.207	9.442	9.683	9.930
7	9.784	10.089	10.405	10.730	11.067	11.414	11.772	12.142	12.523	12.916
8	11.859	12.300	12.757	13.233	13.723	14.240	14.774	15.327	15.902	16.499
9	14.164	15.415	16.085	16.786	17.518	18.285	19.086	19.924	20.799	
10	16.722	17.549	18.420	19.337	20.304	21.321	22.393	23.521	24.709	25.959
11	19.562	20.655	21.815	23.044	24.349	25.733	27.200	28.755	30.404	32.150
12	22.714	24.133	25.650	27.271	29.002	30.850	32.824	34.931	37.180	39.580
13	26.212	28.029	29.985	32.089	34.352	36.786	39.404	42.219	45.245	48.497
14	30.095	32.393	34.883	37.581	40.505	43.672	47.103	50.818	54.842	59.196
15	34.405	37.280	40.418	43.842	47.581	51.659	56.112	60.965	66.263	72.035
16	39.190	42.753	46.672	50.981	55.717	60.925	66.647	72.939	79.853	87.440
17	44.501	48.883	53.739	59.118	65.073	71.675	78.984	87.067	96.021	105.931
18	50.696	55.750	61.725	68.393	75.840	84.144	93.406	103.740	115.266	128.117
19	56.939	63.440	70.054	78.971	88.213	98.606	110.285	123.414	138.166	154.740
20	64.203	72.053	80.946	91.029	102.444	115.380	130.033	146.628	165.418	186.688
21	72.265	81.709	92.469	104.768	118.810	134.841	153.139	174.021	197.847	225.026
22	81.214	92.500	105.491	120.436	137.632	157.415	180.172	206.345	236.438	271.031
23	91.145	104.603	120.205	138.297	159.276	183.601	211.801	244.487	282.362	326.237
24	102.174	118.155	136.831	158.659	184.168	213.978	248.808	289.494	337.010	392.484
25	114.413	133.334	155.620	181.871	212.793	249.214	292.105	342.603	402.042	471.981
30	199.021	241.333	293.199	356.787	434.745	530.312	647.439	790.948	966.712	1181.882
35	341.590	431.664	546.681	693.573	881.170	1120.713	1426.491	1816.652	2314.214	2948.341
40	581.826	767.091	1013.704	1342.025	1779.090	2360.757	3134.522	4163.213	5529.829	7343.858
45	986.639	1358.230	1874.165	2590.565	3585.129	4965.274	6879.291	9531.577	13,203.424	18,281.310
50	1668.771	2400.018	3459.507	4994.521	7217.716	10,435.649	15,089.502	21,813.093	31,515.336	45,497.191

Glossary

Accelerated method of depreciation depreciation method that allocates the cost of an asset over a period of years according to a schedule that allows a greater fraction of the historical cost to be allocated to earlier years and a smaller fraction of the historical cost to be allocated to later years. **(10)**

Accounting income the income figure that results from the application of generally accepted accounting principles to the problem of allocating receipts and expenditures to particular time periods. **(6)**

Accounts receivable amounts of money owed to a firm by its customers and shown as current assets on the balance sheet. **(6)**

Accrual accounting system a system of accounting that assigns revenues and expenses to particular time periods according to a predetermined set of rules. **(6)**

Acid-test ratio, or *quick ratio* a more stringent measure of liquidity than the current ratio because it includes only the most liquid of current assets; calculated as cash plus marketable securities plus receivables, divided by current liabilities. **(7)**

Agency costs costs arising from the separation of ownership and management by the hiring of professional managers. **(15)**

Agent (in economic terms) an individual or organization that acts in behalf of and to promote the interests of another party, usually referred to as the *principal*. **(12)**

Aging schedule a technique for analyzing accounts receivable by categorizing receivables outstanding by length of time outstanding. **(7, 23)**

Annuity a stream of equal payments at regular time intervals. **(3)**

Note: Chapter numbers appear in parentheses.

Arithmetic average a summary measure obtained by adding the values observed and dividing their sum by the number of values. **(5)**

AROI approach a method of analyzing capital investments that relies on an accounting-based measure of return on investment, calculated as some measure of accounting profit divided by some measure of accounting investment. **(10)**

Auction market a market in which buyers and sellers state their terms publicly. **(20)**

Average collection period *See* **Days sales outstanding (DSO)**

Average payment period *See* **Days purchases outstanding (DPO)**

Average tax rate a taxpayer's tax payment divided by taxable income. **(2)**

Bad-debt expense the cost associated with customers who default on their payments. **(23)**

Balance sheet a "snapshot" summary of a firm's financial position at a single point in time. **(6)**

Bankruptcy the failure to meet contractual obligations that results in court action to reorganize or liquidate a firm for the benefit of the firm's creditors. **(15, 20)**

Bills and notes *See* **U.S. Treasury bills and notes**

Bonds long-term debt claims entitling the holder to periodic interest and principal. **(14)** *See also* **Corporate bond; Eurobonds; Exchangeable bond; Foreign bond; Junk bonds; Original-issue, deep-discount bonds (OIDs); Par value of a bond; Zero-coupon bonds**

Bond value of a convertible bond the present value of future interest and principal payments. **(18)**

Book value a measure of asset value, at historical cost, net of depreciation. **(7)**

Book value of stock   the total of book value of net assets available for common shareholders after subtracting claims of creditors and preferred shareholders. **(14)**

Break-even analysis   a technique for analyzing the relationship between revenue and profit that examines the proportion of fixed costs to total costs. **(8)**

Break-even point   the quantity of firm output at which sales revenues just cover total fixed costs, or the quantity of output at which revenue equals operating costs and operating profit is zero. **(8)**

Budget   a time-phased schedule of activities, events, or transactions, usually in dollar terms. **(9)**

Budgeting   *See* **Capital budgeting**

Business failure   the situation that results (1) when a firm is unable to meet its contractual financial obligations even though the value of the firm's assets exceeds its liabilities (also known as *technical insolvency*) or (2) when a firm's liabilities exceed the value of its assets as a going concern. **(20)**

Business risk   *See* **Operating risk**

Buyout   *See* **Leveraged buyout**

Call option   a contract giving the owner the right (but not the obligation) to buy a specified number of shares of stock at a specified price for a specified period of time. **(17)**

Capital-asset-pricing model (CAPM)   a financial model that provides useful insights about how market values and discount rates are determined in financial markets, describes the valuation process in a portfolio context, and analyzes how risk/return trade-offs work in financial markets. **(5)**

Capital budgeting   the process of analyzing capital investment opportunities and deciding which (if any) to undertake; it includes the creative search for investment opportunities, the gathering of data and making of forecasts, the economic analysis, the decision, and the implementation. **(10)**

Capital formation   investment in real assets, such as new buildings, machinery, or technology; it is facilitated by financial markets. **(2)**

Capital gain   a gain that results from the increase in the value of an asset, or the difference between the purchase price and the sale price. **(12)**

Capital-gains tax   the tax applied to the gain on a sale of assets not used or bought and sold in the ordinary course of a firm's business. **(2)**

Capitalization rate, or *discount rate*   the rate of exchange between various time periods. **(4, 12)**

Capital lease   a lease that, for accounting purposes, must be capitalized on a lessee's balance sheet as an asset and as an obligation. **(19)**

Capital market   the market for transactions in longer-term debt issues and stock. **(2)**

Capital value   the present value of a stream of expected cash flows. **(4)**

CAPM   *See* **Capital-asset-pricing model (CAPM)**

Carrying costs   costs of financing, storage, servicing, and the risk of loss in value; carrying costs rise as inventories increase. **(23)**

Cash   for purposes of cash management, total liquid assets: cash plus near-cash. **(22)**

Cash accounting system   a system of accounting that assigns revenues and expenses to particular time periods according to the timing of receipts and expenditures. **(6)**

Cash budget   a time-phased schedule of cash receipts and disbursements. **(9)**

Cash cycle   the process whereby cash is used to purchase materials from which are produced goods that are then sold to customers, who later pay their bills. **(22)**

Cash flow   the total change in a firm's cash account, the actual cash flowing into and out of a firm over a particular time period, measured as operating cash flow plus all balance-sheet changes. **(6)** *See also* **Financing cash flows; Incremental after-tax cash flows; Initial investment cash flows; Operating cash flows**

Cash-flow analysis (of debt capacity)   the comparison of cash-flow patterns under adverse, or recession, conditions at various levels of leverage in order to determine the level of debt that will allow a firm to meet its contractual obligations in a recession (or other set of adverse circumstances). **(16)**

Cash-management policy the set of decisions related to (1) managing collections and disbursements of cash, (2) determining the appropriate working-cash balance, and (3) investing idle cash. **(22)**

CD *See* **Certificate of deposit (CD)**

Certificate of deposit (CD) a bank's promise to make certain future cash payments to the person who buys the CD for a stated price **(1)**; a fixed-maturity time deposit. **(22)**

Chattel mortgage a security claim against equipment (or anything other than land or buildings) used in providing collateral for a loan. **(14)**

Coefficient of variation the standard deviation divided by the expected value; a measure of risk relative to return. **(5)**

Collateral any asset pledged as security for a loan **(21)**; also, property pledged by a borrower to protect the interests of the lender. **(14)**

Collection policy the set of procedures undertaken to collect accounts that have not been paid within the specified period. **(23)**

Commercial bank a depository financial institution that offers checking-account services, accepts savings and other types of deposits, and makes loans. **(2)**

Commercial loan the transfer of funds from a bank to a business firm in exchange for the firm's promise to repay the funds with interest according to a specified schedule. **(2, 14)**

Commercial paper short-term borrowing, typically notes of less than six months' maturity **(2)**; unsecured short-term promissory notes issued by firms with the highest credit ratings. **(21, 22)**

Commercial strategy a firm's definition of the products and services it will produce and the markets it will serve. **(9)**

Common stock a perpetual ownership claim that has no maturity. **(14)**

Compounding the evaluation of how a certain interest rate will cause a certain present dollar amount to grow in the future. **(3)**

Compounding period the calendar period over which compounding occurs. **(3)**

Compound interest interest figured on both the initial principal and the interest earned in prior periods. Interest on interest is the key feature of compound interest. **(3)**

Concentration account a centralized bank account in which disbursement funds from different branches, divisions, or franchises of a company can be pooled so that the firm's aggregate working-balance requirement is lower than if balances were maintained at each branch. **(22)**

Concentration ratio the percentage of sales, production volume, or any other variable to be measured accounted for by the x largest firms in an industry. **(25)**

Conditional sales contract an installment contract for the purchase of equipment in which title to the equipment remains with the lender until all payments are made. **(14, 19)**

Conglomerate merger a merger that combines firms that operate in different industries. **(25)**

Constant-growth dividend-valuation model a method for valuing stock that assumes the dividend will grow at a constant rate. **(4)**

Contract *See* **Conditional sales contract; Futures contract; Interest-rate futures contract**

Contractual claim a claim that is an enforceable contract, such as debt. **(14)**

Conversion premium the amount by which a convertible bond's market price exceeds the higher of its bond value or its conversion value. **(18)**

Conversion value of a convertible bond the market value of the common stock into which a bond is convertible. **(18)**

Convertible security a claim that begins as a debenture or as preferred stock but that can later be converted *at the holder's option* and at a specified rate into shares of the issuing company's common stock. **(14, 17)**

Corporate bond a long-term debt claim representing a corporation's promise to repay with interest money borrowed from a bondholder. **(2)**

Corporation an entity created by law that owns assets, incurs liabilities, enters into contracts, and engages in ongoing activities. **(2)**

Correlation the relationship between variables indicating how they move relative to each other. **(5)**

Cost *See* **Agency costs; Carrying costs; Fixed costs; Flotation costs; Opportunity cost; Ordering costs; Sunk cost; Variable costs**

Cost minimization the goal of making a firm's costs as low as possible; it can be used as a criterion for making financial-management decisions. **(1)**

Cost of capital another name for the *required rate of return*. **(12)** *See also* **Marginal cost of capital**

Cost of equity capital *See* **Required return on equity**

Country risk the risk that a foreign government or foreign politics will interfere with international transactions. At the extreme, country risk includes the possibility that a foreign government may expropriate a firm's property or that a war may ensue. **(24)**

Coupon bond *See* **Zero-coupon bond**

Coupon rate the stated percentage of the face value of a bond or note paid in interest each period. **(4, 14)**

Coverage ratios indebtedness calculated using income-statement data; coverage ratios reflect a firm's ability to meet periodic payments due on its debt obligations. **(7)** *See also* **Interest coverage ratio; Fixed-charge-coverage (FCC) ratio**

Covered-interest arbitrage the market process through which the relationships in the interest-rate-parity theorem are enforced. **(24)**

Credit *See* **Investment tax credit (ITC); Line of credit; Trade credit**

Credit agreement *See* **Revolving-credit agreement**

Credit policy the set of decisions made about credit standards, credit terms, and collection policy. **(23)**

Credit risk the risk that a borrower will default on a loan. **(24)**

Credit scoring a technique for discriminating between good and bad accounts in which selection criteria are developed by relating past default experience to certain characteristics of the applicant. **(23)**

Credit standards criteria and guidelines used by a firm to decide to which accounts it will extend credit. **(23)**

Credit terms include the length of the credit period and the discount offered. **(23)**

Currency devaluation a reduction in the value of a country's currency stated in terms of other currencies. **(24)**

Currency option a financial claim giving one the right but not the obligation to buy or sell a foreign currency. **(24)**

Currency revaluation an increase in the value of a country's currency stated in terms of other currencies. **(24)**

Current assets assets with a maturity of less than one year, such as cash holdings, inventories of raw materials, accounts receivable, goods in process, and finished goods. **(6, 22)**

Current liabilities the short-term debt obligations of a firm, with maturities of less than one year. **(6)**

Current ratio a measure of liquidity calculated as current assets divided by current liabilities. **(7)**

Current saving any income not spent on consumption in the current period. **(2)**

Days purchases outstanding (DPO) a measure of how promptly a firm pays its bills. DPO is calculated as accounts payable divided by purchases per day (also known as the *average payment period*). **(7)**

Days sales outstanding (DSO) the ratio of accounts receivable to credit sales per day; also called the *average collection period*. **(7, 23)**

DCF *See* **Discounted cash flow (DCF)**

Debentures unsecured bonds with no particular assets pledged as security. **(14)**

Debt the contractual liability of a firm to lenders; consists of a promise to make periodic interest payments and to repay the principal according to an agreed-upon schedule. **(14)** *See also* **Intermediate-term debt; Long-term debt (LTD); Ratio of debt to total assets; Ratio of long-term debt to total capital; Required return on debt; Secured debt; Short-term debt; Unsecured debt**

Debt capacity the amount of debt that is optimal for shareholders. **(16)**

Debt/equity ratio *See* **Debt/net worth ratio**

Debt/net worth ratio, or *debt/equity ratio*   a variation of the ratio of debt to total assets; calculated as total liabilities divided by net worth. **(7)**

Debt ratios   indebtedness calculated using balance-sheet data; reflect the degree to which creditors are protected in the event of the liquidation of a firm. **(7)**

Deductible expenses   *See* **Tax-deductible expenses**

Default risk   the possibility that interest or principal might not be paid on time and in the amount promised. **(4, 14, 22)**

Deficit spending units   individuals, companies, or government bodies that need funds. **(2)**

Demand curve   a graph that shows the amounts of a good or service buyers are prepared to purchase at different prices during a specified time period. **(4)**

Deposit account   *See* **Money-market deposit account (MMDA)**

Depreciation   the allocation of the cost of a long-lived asset to different time periods over the life of the asset. **(2, 6)** *See also* **Accelerated method of depreciation; Straight-line method of depreciation**

Depreciation tax shield   the tax savings resulting from the subtraction of depreciation in calculating taxable income; can be calculated as the tax rate multiplied by the amount of the depreciation charge. **(11)**

Devaluation   *See* **Currency devaluation**

Direct finance   the direct transfer of funds from savers to investors without going through a financial intermediary. **(2)**

Discount bonds   *See* **Original-issue, deep-discount bonds**

Discounted cash flow (DCF)   a method of estimating the value of an asset by taking the cash flows associated with the asset and discounting them for time and risk. **(3)**

Discounting   the evaluation of how a certain discount rate will decrease the value of a certain future dollar amount to convert it to its present value. **(3)**

Discount rate   the rate of exchange between the future and the present time period, or the interest rate used in the discounting process. **(3)** *See also* **Capitalization rate; Risk-adjusted discount rate**

Discrete random variable   a variable that can take on a finite number of possible values. **(5)**

Discriminant analysis   a technique for discriminating between good and bad accounts based on certain readily available financial data, such as firm size, acid-test ratio, or accounts-payable payment period. **(23)**

Distress   *See* **Financial distress**

Diversifiable risk, or *specific risk*   the part of total risk that is unique to a company or asset; the risk that *can* be eliminated by diversification **(5)**; project-specific risk, such as that deriving from uncertainty over entry of competitors, strikes, or technological advances. **(13)**

Diversification   investing in more than one type of asset in order to reduce risk. When risky assets are combined in a portfolio, risk reduction is achieved through diversification. **(5)**

Dividend-reinvestment plan   the policy of allowing shareholders to apply their periodic dividend receipts automatically to the purchase of new shares. **(20)**

Dividend-valuation model   the discounted-cash-flow model applied to the valuation of stock, or equity. **(4)** *See also* **Constant-growth valuation model; Variable-growth valuation model**

DPO   *See* **Days purchases outstanding (DPO)**

DSO   *See* **Days sales outstanding (DSO)**

E   *See* **Expected-value operator**

Earnings before interest and taxes (EBIT)   a measure of operating earnings. **(15)** *See also* **Operating profit**

Earnings per share (EPS)   profit after taxes (PAT) divided by the number of shares of stock outstanding; a widely used performance measure. **(7)**

EBIT   *See* **Earnings before taxes and interest (EBIT)**

EBIT/EPS analysis   an examination of the impact on earnings per share of a given financing alternative at different levels of earnings before interest and taxes. **(16)**

EBIT/EPS chart   a graph of the relationship between operating outcomes (as measured by earnings before interest and taxes) and financial results to shareholders (as measured by earnings per share) for a given financing alternative. **(16)**

Economic analysis   the process of gathering and evaluating quantitative information about the costs and benefits of an investment project. **(10)**

Economic income   the change in the net worth of an economic unit during a period of time. **(6)**

Economic order quantity (EOQ)   the optimal quantity of goods to be ordered, determined by trading off ordering costs (or setup costs) against carrying costs. **(23)**

Effective interest rate   the rate compounded once per interest period (usually per year) that provides the same dollar payoff as the stated rate or a financial contract. **(3, 21)**

Effects   *See* **Information effects**

Efficient market   a market in which current market prices impound all available information and are a fair reflection of the true value of a financial asset. **(4, 14)**

EOQ   *See* **Economic order quantity (EOQ)**

EPS   *See* **Earning per share (EPS)**

EPS analysis   *See* **EBIT/EPS analysis**

EPS break-even level of EBIT   the level of earnings before interest and taxes that equates earnings per share for two financing alternatives. **(16)**

Equilibrium price, or *market-clearing price*   the price at which the quantity demanded of a good or service equals the quantity supplied. **(1, 4)**

Equity   ownership in a firm — specifically, the claims of preferred and common stockholders. **(14)** *See also* **Required return on equity; Return on equity (ROE)**

Eurocurrency   deposit denominated in a given country's currency and held in a bank outside that country. **(24)**

Eurobonds   bonds sold mainly in countries other than the country in whose currency the interest and principal payments are to be denominated. **(14)**

Eurodollars   deposits denominated in U.S. dollars but held in banks outside the United States. **(22)**

Exchange   *See* **Foreign exchange**

Exchangeable bond   a bond that can be exchanged for another type of security *at the option of the issuer.* **(14)**

Exchange rate   *See* **Foreign-exchange rate**

Exchange-rate risk   risk of loss in value due to changes in foreign-exchange rates. **(24)**

Exchange rates   *See* **Fixed exchange rates; Floating exchange rates**

Exchanges   actual organizations with physical locations where financial claims are bought and sold. **(2)**

Exercise price   the price specified in an option contract; also called the *strike price.* **(17)**

Expected rate of return   the rate of return an investor expects to earn from an investment. **(23)**

Expected value, or *mean*   the weighted average of possible outcomes, where the weights are the probabilities of the outcomes; provides a measure of the expected outcome of a random variable. **(4, 5)**

Expected-value operator (the letter E in the expected-value equation)   a signal to take the probability-weighted average of the outcomes. **(5)**

Expenditures   all cash outflows. **(6)**

Expenses   only those expenditures that affect net worth and therefore appear in the income statement. **(6)** *See also* **Tax-deductible expenses**

Federal-agency issues   short-term obligations of agencies of the federal government. **(22)**

Federal-funds market   the market in which excess bank reserves are borrowed and lent by federal banks. **(2)**

Financial claims   promises to pay money in the future, exchanged in financial markets for money. Examples are stocks, bonds, and loans. **(2)**

Financial distress   occurs when a firm has difficulty meeting contractual obligations to its creditors. **(15)**

Financial friction   the additional cost of financial transactions, such as commissions paid by investors to buy or sell securities, flotation costs of issuing new securities, information costs of financial decision making, and costs associated with financial distress. **(2, 15, 17)**

Financial futures contract   an agreement between a buyer and seller to buy or sell a financial security at some future date but with the price set at the time of the contract. **(14)**

Financial institution   an institution, such as an insurance company, a leasing company, a mutual fund, a savings-and-loan association, or a commercial bank, that channels funds from savers to borrowers. **(2)**

Financial intermediary   a financial go-between, such as a bank, that makes possible the easy transfer of funds from savers to spenders. Financial intermediaries gather funds, analyze credit possibilities, evaluate risk, and handle administrative and legal details for borrowers and lenders. **(2)**

Financial lease   a noncancelable, fully amortized contract typically covering intermediate to long terms whereby the lessee (user) normally is responsible for maintenance, insurance, and taxes; also known as a *net lease*. **(19)**

Financial leverage   the use of debt, or borrowing, to finance investment. **(4, 15)** *See also* **Indebtedness**

Financial market   a market where firms can raise funds and where firms may be valued; it is a vast network linking institution, instruments, and submarkets; it brings together millions of buyers and sellers of financial instruments. **(1, 2)**

Financial-modeling programs   computer programs specifically designed to do *what if* analysis by calculating the consequences of changing assumptions. **(13)**

Financial plan   a description in dollar terms of the activities a firm intends to engage in over some future period. An income statement and a balance sheet are key components of the financial plan. **(9)**

Financial planning   part of a larger planning process within an organization; a complete planning system begins at the highest policy level with the statement of a firm's key goal or purpose. **(9)**

Financial risk   the additional risk to shareholders, over and above operating risk, that results from the use of debt (or debt-like) financing. **(4, 15)**

Financial securities   financial claims, such as bonds and stocks. **(20)**

Financing cash flows   the cash flows, such as interest, principal payments, and dividends to stockholders, arising from the financing arrangements associated with an investment project. **(11)**

Financing instruments   claims against a firm's income and assets. **(14)**

Financing mix   the proportion of debt and equity used to finance investments. **(15)**

Finished goods   completed products awaiting sale. **(23)**

Firm   *See* **Multinational firm**

Fixed assets   normally defined as assets with a maturity of more than one year. **(6)**

Fixed-charge-coverage (FCC) ratio   a more comprehensive coverage measure than the times-interest-earned ratio, the FCC ratio measures the margin by which a firm's current earnings can cover debt and all other contractual obligations, including lease payments. **(7)**

Fixed costs   costs that remain the same over a given wide range of production. **(8)**

Fixed exchange rates   foreign-exchange rates set administratively by governments and changed according to agreed-upon rules. **(24)**

Float   the product of the time delay in collecting funds and the dollars collected. **(22)**

Floating exchange rates   foreign-exchange rates set by free-market forces. **(24)**

Floating-rate notes (FRNs)   debt instruments for which the interest rate is adjusted periodically with the rise and fall of interest rates generally. **(14)**

Flotation costs   cash costs associated with the issuance of a company's new long-term debt or stock issue. **(17)**

Flow variable   a variable whose value is measured during a period of time. **(6)**

Foreign bond   a bond sold in a foreign country by a home-country borrower, denominated in the currency of the foreign country. **(14)**

Foreign exchange   money denominated in different currencies. **(24)**

Foreign-exchange market   a loosely connected group of major banks and foreign-exchange brokers who communicate by telephone and mail over great distances to buy and sell different currencies. **(24)**

Foreign-exchange rate the price of one currency expressed in terms of another. **(24)**

Formation *See* **Capital formation**

Forward contract a contract to buy or sell an asset at a specified price at a specified future date; differs from future in that it does not involve cash settlement prior to the maturity date. **(17)**

Forward rate the price of one currency in terms of another when purchased for future delivery. **(24)**

Friction *See* **Financial friction**

Frictionless market a market in which there are no costs, such as commissions or information costs, involved in financial transactions. **(5)**

FRNs *See* **Floating-rate notes (FRNs)**

Funds *See* **Money-market mutual funds; Short-term funds; Sources of funds; Uses of funds**

Funds market *See* **Federal-funds market**

Future value *(FV)* the value of a certain current dollar amount compounded forward through time at an appropriate interest rate. It is the amount to which a payment or series of payments will grow by a given future date. **(3)**

Future-value factor for a single cash flow, the number by which a given present value is multiplied to determine the amount into which that present value will grow in the future (future value). A future-value factor $FVF(i, n)$ is calculated as $(1 + i)^n$. **(3)**

Futures contract an agreement between a buyer and seller to buy or sell something, such as a commodity, at some future date but with the price set at the time of the contract. Unlike an option, the future *requires* the holder to buy (or sell) the asset. **(14, 17)** *See also* **Financial futures contract; Interest-rate futures contract**

FV *See* **Future value** *(FV)*

Gain *See* **Capital gain**

General partnership a partnership in which all partners have unlimited liability for the debts and actions of a firm. **(2)**

Golden parachute a provision in the employment contract of top-level management that provides for severance pay or other compensation should the manager lose his or her job as the result of a takeover. **(25)**

Goods *See* **Finished goods**

Goodwill the excess of the price paid for a going concern over the book value of its tangible assets; an intangible asset of a firm. **(25)**

Government-bond dealers financial intermediaries that buy and sell government bonds. **(2)**

Hedging an attempt to reduce the risk associated with future price fluctuations by taking offsetting positions. **(17, 24)**

Horizontal merger a merger that combines firms operating in the same line of business. **(25)**

Hostile takeover occurs when an acquired firm's management resists the acquisition, and the acquiring firm goes over the heads of management by buying stock directly from shareholders. **(25)**

Hurdle rate the return target to which an investment project's internal rate of return is compared in determining whether or not the investment project is acceptable to a firm. **(12)**

Income *See* **Economic income; Net income**

Income statement, or *profit-and-loss statement* a record of financial events between two points in time. The income statement is an attempt to measure the change in net worth over time. **(6)** *See also* **Normalized income statement; Pro-forma income statement**

Incremental after-tax cash flows after-tax cash flows of an investment directly attributable to the investment; necessary information for performing a discounted-cash-flow analysis of an investment decision. **(11)**

Incremental analysis the evaluation of an investment decision that focuses only on differences in after-tax cash flows that result from the decision in question. **(11)**

Indebtedness, or *financial leverage* the mix of debt and equity used to finance a firm's activities. **(7)** *See also* **Financial leverage**

Industrial codes *See* **Standard industrial codes (SICs)**

Inflation   the general rate of increase in the level of prices of goods and services in the economy. (**2**)

Inflation premium   an addition to the real rate of return required by investors to compensate them for the change in the value of the investment that results from anticipated inflation. (**2, 12**)

Information effects   the change in stock price that results from the market's knowledge that the dividend is to change. (**17**)

Initial-investment cash flows   one-time outlays necessary to acquire the land, buildings, and equipment necessary to implement an investment project. (**11**)

Installment equipment-purchase contract   *See* **Conditional sales contract**

Interest arbitrage   *See* **Covered-interest arbitrage**

Interest coverage ratio   the number of times interest payments are covered by EBIT, calculated as EBIT divided by pretax interest. (**16**)

Interest period   the calendar period over which an interest rate is named. (**3**)

Interest rate   the rate at which individuals or firms will be compensated for exchanging money now for money to be received later (**3**); the price of borrowing funds over time, usually a percentage of the amount borrowed. (**2**) *See also* **Effective interest rate; Nominal interest rate; Real interest rate**

Interest-rate futures contract   an agreement to buy or sell a financial security in the future at an agreed-upon price; allows a manager to hedge against the risk of future rises or falls in interest rates by locking in today the price that must be paid in the future. (**22**)

Interest-rate-parity theorem   a theorem that shows the relationship between spot and forward exchange rates and interest rates in two currencies. (**24**)

Interest-rate risk   the risk arising because prices of securities change as market interest rates change; the risk that a security may have to be sold before maturity at a price lower than the price paid for it because of fluctuating interest rates. (**4, 14, 22**)

Interest-rate swap   an agreement between two companies in which each takes on the obligation of paying interest on the debt of the other company. (**14**)

Interest tax shield   the tax saving a firm generates by using debt because interest on debt is tax-deductible. (**12, 15**)

Intermediary   *See* **Financial intermediary**

Intermediate-term debt   debt with a maturity of between one year and five to seven years. Intermediate-term financing is usually used to finance part of a firm's fixed assets or permanent additions to working capital. (**14, 21**)

Intermediate-term funds   *See* **Intermediate-term debt**

Internal rate of return (*IRR*)   the rate that discounts all of the cash flows of an investment, including all outlays, to exactly zero; it is the discount rate that makes the net present value of the project equal to zero; it is the discounted-cash-flow measure of the expected rate of return to be earned on an investment. (**10**)

Inventory control   the determination of order quantities, safety stocks, and reorder points for every individual item stocked, along with ordering, receiving, handling, storing, protecting, and issuing inventory. (**23**)

Inventory theory   the theory of how much should be ordered and when it should be ordered. (**23**)

Inventory-turnover ratio   a measure of the efficiency with which inventories are utilized; calculated as the cost of goods sold divided by average inventory. (**7**)

Investment banker   a financial intermediary that underwrites and distributes new securities offerings and helps a business obtain financing. (**2**)

Investment cash flows   *See* **Initial-investment cash flows**

Investment plan   the set of decisions a firm makes about what products to produce, what manufacturing process to use, and what plant and equipment will be required as these questions relate to the acquisition of assets. (**9**)

Investment tax credit (ITC)   a specified percentage of capital expenditures a firm is permitted to subtract from its tax liability; eliminated by the 1986 Tax Act. (**2, 11**)

Investor clientele   a group of investors attracted to a certain stock investment because of a particular characteristic, such as the company's dividend policy. **(17)**

IRR *See* **Internal rate of return (*IRR*)**

Issues *See* **Federal-agency issues; New issues**

Issues market *See* **New-issues market**

ITC *See* **Investment tax credit (ITC)**

Junk bonds bonds with low credit ratings and high interest rates that play a role in corporate buyouts and takeovers. **(14)**

LBO *See* **Leveraged buyout (LBO)**

Lease a contractual arrangement for financing equipment under which the lessee (the firm) has the right to use the equipment in return for making periodic payments to the lessor (the owner of the equipment). **(14, 19)** *See also* **Capital lease; Financial lease; Leveraged lease; Operating lease**

Leaseback agreement *See* **Sale-and-leaseback agreement**

Leasing a specialized means of acquiring the use of assets without owning the assets. **(19)**

Level of EBIT *See* **EPS break-even level of EBIT**

Leverage *See* **Financial leverage; Operating leverage**

Leveraged buyout (LBO) a transaction in which a firm is purchased using borrowed funds, with the firm's own assets or stock pledged as collateral to secure the loan and with the firm's own cash flows used to pay off the loan. **(16, 25)**

Leveraged lease a lease agreement in which the lessor borrows a substantial part of the purchase price of the asset to be leased. **(19)**

Levered shares the shares of stock in a company that uses debt. **(15)**

Liability *See* **Tax liability**

Limited partnership a partnership in which there is at least one general partner and one or more limited partners. Limited partners contribute capital, share in the profits, have limited liability for debts, and have no voice in directing the firm. **(2)**

Line of credit a noncontractual loan agreement between a bank or other lender and a firm in which the firm can borrow up to an agreed-upon maximum at any time during a specified period. **(21)**

Liquid assets assets that can easily be converted to cash on short notice. **(22)**

Liquidation the dissolution of a firm by selling its assets and distributing the proceeds to creditors and shareholders on the basis of seniority. **(20)**

Liquidity a firm's ability to come up with cash quickly to meet expected and unexpected cash requirements. **(7)** *See also* **Marketability**

Loans *See* **Commercial loan; Seasonal loans; Secured loan; Term loans; Unsecured loan**

Lockbox system a collection system in which payments are mailed to a post office box, which is emptied several times a day by a bank, which then deposits the payments and updates accounting records. **(22)**

Long-run target payout ratio the ratio of residual funds to total earnings after taxes over a relatively long planning horizon. **(17)**

Long-term debt (LTD) secured and unsecured debt maturing beyond one year, normally with a maturity of eight to ten years or longer. **(7, 14)**

LTD *See* **Long-term debt (LTD)**

Maintenance lease *See* **Operating lease**

Marginal cost of capital another name for the *return target* for an investment project. **(12)**

Marginal expected return the expected rate of return on incremental investment. **(23)**

Marginal tax rate the tax rate on the last dollar of income, or the change in a taxpayer's tax payment divided by the change in taxable income. **(2)**

Market *See* **Auction market; Capital market; Efficient market; Federal-funds market; Financial market; Foreign-exchange market; Frictionless market; Money market; New-issues market; Over-the-counter (OTC) market; Secondary market**

Marketability the ease with which an asset can be converted to cash on short notice (also known as *liquidity*). **(22)**

Market/book ratio the ratio of share price to book value per share; relates the value to shareholders of a firm's future cash flows (market value) to the historical costs to shareholders of acquiring the firm's assets. **(7)**

Market clearing price   *See* **Equilibrium price**

Market economy   an economic system in which resources are allocated and prices are determined through the interaction of buyers and sellers in markets. **(1)**

Market line   shows the relationship between required return and risk. **(5)**

Market portfolio   the portfolio that includes all risky assets. **(5)**

Market risk   *See* **Nondiversifiable risk**

Market risk/return schedule   a schedule that shows the return required by investors at different levels of risk. **(4)**

Market value of stock   the price at which stock is being traded in the marketplace. **(14)**

Materials   *See* **Raw materials**

Maturity   the time at which, or the time period over which, interest and principal payments are to be made on a loan or bond. **(2, 14, 22)** *See also* **Yield to maturity (YTM)**

Mean   *See* **Expected value**

Merger premium   the difference between the value of the money or securities offered by an acquiring firm and the present value of the stock owned by the shareholders of the firm to be acquired. **(25)**

MMDA   *See* **Money-market deposit account (MMDA)**

Modeling programs   *See* **Financial-modeling programs**

Money market   the market for transactions in short-term loans. **(2)**

Money-market deposit account (MMDA)   a deposit account offered by a bank or depository institution that offers money-market interest rates but restricts check writing. **(2)**

Money-market mutual funds   funds set up to allow small investors to pool their funds to invest in money-market instruments in the required large denominations. **(22)**

Money-market securities   interest-bearing assets with low default risk, short maturity, and ready marketability. **(22)**

Mortgage   a loan in which designated property is pledged as security **(2)**; a bond that has particular assets — usually buildings or equipment — pledged as security against default on interest or principal payments. **(14)** *See also* **Chattel mortgage**

Mortgage banker   a financial intermediary who transfers funds from institutions that want to invest in mortgages to institutions or individuals who wish to borrow mortgage funds. **(2)**

Motive   *See* **Precautionary motive; Transactions motive**

Multinational firm   a firm that operates or invests in two or more countries. **(24)**

Mutual funds   *See* **Money-market mutual funds**

Negotiable-order-of-withdrawal (NOW) account   a type of checking account at a depository institution that pays interest. **(2)**

Net income   a firm's revenues minus its expenses. **(2)**

Net lease   *See* **Financial lease**

Net period   the period within which an invoice is to be paid. **(21)**

New issues   the initial public offering of a security of a given class. **(20)**

New-issues market, or *primary market*   the market in which issues of new securities are offered for sale by companies to investors. **(2)**

Net present value (*NPV*)   the present value of the cash inflows of an investment less (net of) the required outlay. **(10)** *See also* **Present value (*PV*)**

Net working capital (NWC)   a dollar measure of liquidity; calculated as current assets minus current liabilities. **(6, 7, 11)** *See also* **Working capital**

Net worth   the value of total assets minus total liabilities, or the value of the owners' claim on assets. **(6)**

Nominal interest rate   the interest rate observed in financial markets. **(2)**

Nominal rate of return   the contract or observed rate of return. **(12)**

Nondiversifiable risk, or *market risk*   the part of total risk that is related to the general economy or to the stock market as a whole; the risk that *cannot* be eliminated by diversification. **(5, 13)**

Normalized income statement   an income statement in which all items are expressed as percentages of sales. **(7)**

Note(s)   *See* **Floating-rate notes (FRNs); Promissory note; U.S. Treasury bills and notes**

NOW account   *See* **Negotiable-order-of-withdrawal (NOW) account**

NPV   *See* **Net present value** (*NPV*)

NWC   *See* **Net working capital (NWC)**

OIDs   *See* **Original-issue, deep-discount bonds (OIDs)**

Oligopoly   an industry that has a few large firms rather than a single large firm or numerous smaller firms and that possesses some competitive characteristics and some monopolistic ones. **(25)**

Order quantity   *See* **Economic order quantity (EOQ)**

Open account   a credit arrangement under which no promissory note is normally given and the purchaser agrees to make payment at a later date under terms specified in the agreement. **(21)**

Operating cash flows   the cash flows, such as sales, cost of goods sold, advertising, and taxes, arising from the operation of the firm, normally defined as profit after taxes plus noncash charges such as depreciation. **(6, 11)**

Operating lease   a contract covering intermediate to short terms whereby the lessor (owner) typically is responsible for maintenance, insurance, and property taxes; also known as a *maintenance lease* or *service lease*. **(19)**

Operating leverage   the relationship between fixed and variable operating expenses that measures the sensitivity of operating profit to changes in sales; can be calculated as the percentage change in operating profits divided by the percentage change in sales. **(8, 15)**

Operating plan   describes in detail the activities in which a firm plans to engage and consists of the sales, production, marketing, research-and-development, and personnel plans required to carry out the firm's commercial strategy. **(9)**

Operating profit, or *earnings before interest and taxes (EBIT)*   measures a firm's performance before the effects of financing or taxes. **(7)**

Operating return   the internal rate of return for an investment project calculated considering only operating cash flows; the ratio of operating profit to investment. **(12, 23)**

Operating risk or *business risk*   the uncertainty about future profitability that arises from the basic nature of the business and operation of a company; the business risk inherent in a firm's operations. Operating risk affects the variability of operating profits over time. **(4, 8, 15)**

Opportunity cost   the return on the best alternative investment forgone by making a chosen investment. **(3, 12)**

Opportunity rate   *See* **Required rate of return**

Option   a contract conveying the right to buy or sell designated securities or commodities at a specified price during a stipulated period of time. **(17)** *See also* **Currency option**

Ordering costs   costs of placing orders and unit purchase costs; ordering costs decline as inventories increase. **(23)**

Original-issue, deep-discount bonds (OIDs)   bonds issued at prices well below face value with very low coupon rates; they have appealed to buyers who believe interest rates will trend downward. **(14)**

OTC market   *See* **Over-the-counter (OTC) market**

Over-the-counter (OTC) market   the network of buyers, sellers, and brokers who interact by means of telecommunication and deal in securities not listed on an organized exchange. **(2, 20)**

Parachute   *See* **Golden parachute**

Parity theorem   *See* **Interest-rate-parity theorem**

Partnership   an unincorporated business owned by two or more persons. **(2)** *See also* **General partnership; Limited partnership**

Par value of a bond   the value that is equal to the principal amount. **(14)**

Par value of stock   the nominal or face value of a share of stock. **(14)**

PAT   *See* **Profit after taxes (PAT)**

Payback approach   a method of analyzing investment opportunities that determines how long it will take the cash inflows expected from an investment to repay (pay back) the initial outlay. **(10)**

P/E ratio   *See* **Price/earnings (P/E) ratio**

Perpetuity   an annuity that continues forever. **(3)**

PI   *See* **Profitability index (PI)**

Pooling of interests   an accounting method for reporting a merger in which the balance sheets of the two combining companies are added together to produce the balance sheet of the surviving company. **(25)**

Portfolio   the combination of securities held by any one investor. **(17)**

Portfolio insurance   an investment strategy to guarantee the minimum value of a portfolio; can be accomplished by buying put options on stocks in one's portfolio. **(17)**

Precautionary motive (for holding cash concerns)   the use of liquid assets as a reserve for contingencies in an uncertain world. **(22)**

Preemptive right   a provision in some corporate bylaws and charters giving existing common stockholders the right to purchase new issues of common or convertible securities on a prorated basis. **(20)**

Preferred stock   long-term equity that pays a fixed dividend. Preferred stock is senior to common stock with respect to both income (preferred dividends come ahead of common) and assets. **(14)**

Premium   the price of buying an option. **(17)** *See also* **Conversion premium; Inflation premium; Merger premium; Risk premium** (*rp*)

Present value (*PV*)   the value today of a future payment or stream of payments, discounted at the appropriate discount rate. **(1, 3)** *See also* **Net present value** (*NPV*)

Present-value factor   the number by which a given future value is multiplied to determine that future value's present value; calculated as $1/(1 + i)^n$. **(3)**

Price/earnings (P/E) ratio   the ratio of current market price per share to the most recently reported annual earnings per share; gives an indication of the market's assessments of a company's growth prospects and riskiness. **(7)**

Price system   the coordination of economic activity through free trading of goods and services at prices set in markets by producers and consumers. **(1)**

Primary market   *See* **New-issues market**

Prime rate   the benchmark rate set by the banking industry as the rate for the class of borrowers deemed most creditworthy. **(21)**

Principal   a dollar amount borrowed, loaned, or deposited upon which interest is owed or earned **(1, 3)**; a party in whose behalf an agent acts and whose interests the agent promotes. **(12)** *See also* **Agent**

Priority, or *seniority*   the order in which types of financial claims are satisfied. **(14)**

Private placements   offerings of new securities in which firms sell securities directly to one investor or to a small group of investors rather than to the public. **(20)**

Privileged subscription   the practice of offering new securities to existing shareholders first, before any public offering is made. **(20)**

Probability distribution   a function that assigns probabilities to the possible values of a random variable. **(5)**

Profit   the excess of revenues over costs for a given project or time period. **(1, 6)** *See also* **Operating profit**

Profitability   profits per dollar of sales. **(9)**

Profitability index (PI)   a ratio measure of an investment's benefits in relation to its costs that is calculated using discounted-cash-flow techniques. **(10)**

Profit after taxes (PAT)   a dollar measure of firm profit. **(15)**

Profit-and-loss statement   *See* **Income statement**

Profit margin   the difference between revenues and total expenses (including taxes) divided by sales. **(7)**

Profit maximization   the goal of making a firm's profits as large as possible. **(1)**

Profits per dollar of sales   a useful measure of a firm's performance that measures profits in relation to the sales necessary to generate those profits. **(7)**

Pro-forma analysis   the projection into the future or past of a firm's financial statements to depict a firm's financial condition *as if* certain prospective events (such as a given sales and production plan) had taken place. **(9)**

Pro-forma balance sheet   a balance sheet constructed by projecting a firm's financial condition as if a certain sales and production plan had taken place. (**9**)

Pro-forma income statement   an income statement constructed by projecting as if a certain sales and production plan had taken place. (**9**)

Progressive tax rates   tax rates in which the higher the amount of taxable income, the higher the percentage payable as taxes. (**2**)

Project-specific risk   *See* **Diversifiable risk**

Promissory note   a document specifying the conditions of a loan, including amount, interest rate, and repayment schedule; a legally enforceable "promise to pay." (**21**)

Prompt-payment discounts   discounts given for prompt payment of an invoice, within a specified time period. (**21**)

Proprietorship   *See* **Sole proprietorship**

Prospectus   a document filed with the SEC providing a summary of the financial and commercial-strategy information contained in a registration statement and composed when securities are being issued by a firm. (**20**)

Protective covenants   restrictions, made as part of a loan agreement, that are placed on dividend payments, capital expenditures, or other firm actions, designed to protect the position of lenders. (**14**)

Public offerings   security offerings in which securities are made available to the public and are sold to large numbers of buyers. (**20**)

Purchase of assets   an accounting method for reporting a merger in which the assets of the acquired company are revalued to reflect the amount of money actually paid for the acquired entity. (**25**)

Purchasing-power risk   the risk that money received in the future will not purchase the same goods and services it can today, or the risk that inflation will decrease the value of future cash flows (**4**); the risk that a bond may not bring the expected *real* rate of return because unexpected inflation will have diminished the purchasing power of dollars received. (**14**)

Pure-play technique   calculates the risk-adjusted discount rates by matching a particular investment to one or more publicly traded companies that have risks comparable to those of the investment. (**13**)

Put option   a contract giving the owner the right to sell a specified number of shares of stock at a specified price for a specified period of time. (**17**)

PV   *See* **Present value (PV)**

Quantity   *See* **Economic order quantity (EOQ)**

Quick ratio   *See* **Acid-test ratio**

Random variable   *See* **Discrete random variable**

Rate of interest   *See* **Risk-free rate of interest**

Rate of return   the percentage benefit earned per dollar invested. (**3**) *See also* **Expected rate of return; Internal rate of return; Nominal rate of return; Real rate of return; Required rate of return; Risk-free rate of return**

Ratio analysis   the analysis of financial performance based on the comparison of one financial variable to another. (**7**)

Ratio of debt to total assets   the percentage of total assets financed by creditors; calculated as total liabilities (current liabilities plus long-term debt) divided by total assets. (**7**)

Ratio of long-term debt to total capital   the proportion of total long-term funds supplied by creditors as opposed to owners; calculated as long-term debt divided by the sum of long-term debt and net worth. (**7**)

Ratios   *See* **Coverage ratios; Debt ratios**

Raw materials   materials, parts, and subassemblies that are purchased from others and that become part of the final product a firm sells. (**23**)

Real interest rate   the rate of increase in the ability to purchase goods and services, or the nominal interest rate minus the expected rate of inflation. (**2**)

Real rate of return   the difference between the nominal rate and the inflation rate. (**12**)

Receipts   all cash inflows. (**6**)

Receivables/sales ratio   a tool for analyzing collection trends; calculated as accounts receivable divided by sales. (**7**)

Receivables turnover rate   sales divided by accounts receivable. (**7**)

Reinvestment *See* **Dividend-reinvestment plan**

Reorganization the restructuring of liabilities so that a firm's anticipated cash flows are sufficient to meet them. **(20)**

Required rate of return the minimum acceptable return on any investment; the rate forgone on the next best alternative investment opportunity of comparable risk; it is an *opportunity rate*. **(4, 12, 23)** *See also* **Cost of capital**

Required return on debt the internal rate of return that equates the price of a bond (or debt instrument) to the present value of the expected future cash benefits of owning the bond (or debt instrument). **(12)** *See also* **Yield to maturity (YTM)**

Required return on equity equates the price of a stock to the present value of the expected future cash benefits of owning the stock; also known as the *cost of equity capital*. **(12)**

Residual claim a claim, such as common stock, to what is left after contractual claims are settled. **(14)**

Return on assets (ROA) one measure of return on investment in which investment is defined as the total assets of a firm. ROA is calculated as profit after taxes divided by total assets. **(7)**

Return on debt *See* **Required return on debt**

Return on equity (ROE) a measure of return on investment in which investment is defined as the net worth of a firm. ROE is calculated as profit after taxes divided by net worth. **(7)** *See also* **Required return on equity**

Return on investment (ROI) the return per dollar of investment per unit of time; a measure of the efficiency with which the firm utilizes capital. **(7)**

Return schedule *See* **Market risk/return schedule**

Return target or target return the minimum acceptable expected return on an investment. **(12)** *See also* **Marginal cost of capital; Target return**

Revaluation *See* **Currency revaluation**

Revenues only those receipts that affect net worth and therefore appear in the income statement. **(6)**

Revolving-credit agreement a contractual agreement by a bank to provide funds. **(21)**

Right *See* **Preemptive right**

Rights offering the offering of new securities on the basis of privileged subscription. **(20)**

Risk the degree of uncertainty about future events or outcomes, very difficult to measure accurately or quantitatively. **(4, 13)** *See also* **Country risk; Credit risk; Default risk; Exchange-rate risk; Financial risk; Interest-rate risk; Nondiversifiable risk; Operating risk; Purchasing-power risk**

Risk-adjusted discount rate a return target that reflects the risk of an investment being analyzed. **(13)**

Risk categories groups of investment projects of similar risk. **(13)**

Risk/expected-return trade-off the greater the risk of an investment opportunity, the greater the return required by an investor. **(4)**

Risk-free rate of interest the interest rate on a relatively riskless asset. **(15)**

Riskless rate of return the rate of return that would be received on a riskless asset; it is estimated using a current interest rate on a U.S. Treasury bond or note—the closest available approximation of a riskless asset. **(5)**

Risk premium (rp) the difference between the required rate of return on a particular risky asset and the rate of return on a riskless asset with the same expected life; or the additional return that compensates an investor for bearing additional risk. **(4, 5, 12)**

Risk-premium approach an approach that bases estimates of required returns on risk-premium data. **(12)**

Risk/return schedule *See* **Market risk/return schedule**

ROA *See* **Return on assets (ROA)**

ROE *See* **Return on equity (ROE)**

ROI *See* **Return on investment (ROI)**

rp *See* **Risk premium (rp)**

Safety stock additional inventory over and above that prescribed by the EOQ formula. **(23)**

Sale-and-leaseback agreement an arrangement in which a firm or individual owning an asset sells it to another party and then leases it back. **(19)**

Sales contract *See* **Conditional sales contract**

Sales plan the projection of sales into the future for a specified period; forms the basis for planning production levels, marketing programs, and other firm activities. **(9)**

Scoring *See* **Credit scoring**

Seasonality the annually recurring pattern of changes within a year. **(9)**

Seasonal loans funds borrowed for use during a part of a year and repaid out of seasonal inflows of funds. **(14)**

SEC *See* **Securities and Exchange Commission (SEC)**

Secondary market the market where existing financial claims (such as stocks or bonds), as compared to new claims, can be bought and sold. **(2)**

Secured debt debt against which certain property is pledged to satisfy the debt in the event of borrower default. **(7)**

Secured loan a loan against which specific assets are pledged as collateral by the borrower. **(21)**

Securities claims to ownership, such as stocks and bonds. **(1)**

Securities brokers and dealers financial intermediaries that buy and sell stocks, bonds, and other financial claims in return for a commission fee. **(2)**

Securities and Exchange Commission (SEC) a government agency that regulates (1) the markets where stocks and bonds are traded, (2) the issuance of new securities, and (3) the merger of firms. **(2)**

Seniority *See* **Priority**

Sensitivity analysis a technique for examining the impact on return and net present value of variations in underlying factors; can show the consequences of different possible outcomes. **(13)**

Serial redemption the retirement each year as they mature of bonds that have been issued with serial maturity dates. **(20)**

Service lease *See* **Operating lease**

Short-term debt debt with a maturity of less than one year. **(14)**

Short-term funds funds borrowed for less than one year. **(21)**

SICs *See* **Standard industrial codes (SICs)**

Sinking fund an arrangement in which firms make periodic repayments of principal to the trustees of a bond issue, who retire a specified number of bonds by open-market purchases or by calling certain bonds at a previously agreed-upon price. **(20)**

Sole proprietorship a business owned and operated by a single individual that is not incorporated. **(2)**

Solvency the ability to pay all legal debts. **(16)**

Source-and-use-of-funds statement a summary of the flow of the financial activity of a firm, as recorded in the income statement and the balance sheet, that shows where the firm obtains cash and how it uses it. **(6)**

Sources of funds (1) increases in liabilities, (2) increases in net worth through retained earnings or additional capital contributions by owners, and (3) reductions in assets. **(6)**

Specific risk *See* **Diversifiable risk**

Speculators investors who willingly bear risk, with the prospect of large gains if things turn out favorably for them. **(24)**

Spot rate the price of one currency in terms of another when purchased for immediate delivery. **(24)**

Standard deviation the probability-weighted measure of the dispersion of possible outcomes around an expected value; a statistical measure of variability, or risk. **(5)**

Standard industrial codes (SICs) a system for classifying companies by their primary line of business. **(13)**

Statutory consolidation a merger in which all the combining companies cease to exist as legal entities and in which a new corporation is created. **(25)**

Statutory merger a combination of two or more firms in which one company survives under its own name while any others cease to exist as legal entities. **(25)**

Stock the legal claim to ownership of a business corporation, divided into shares and represented by certificates that can be transferred from one owner to another. **(1, 2)**

Stock exchanges formal organizations that act as auction markets in the trading of financial securities. **(20)**

Stock option an option to buy a company's stock, often granted to management. **(17)**

Stockout occurs when there is insufficient inventory to fill orders. **(23)**

Stock variable a variable whose value is measured at a given moment in time. **(6)**

Straight-line method of depreciation depreciation method that allocates the cost of an asset equally over a period of years by dividing the historical cost of the asset by the number of years and allocating that equal fraction of the cost to each year in the recovery period. **(10)**

Strategic analysis the process of making fundamental decisions about a firm's basic goal or purpose and about the products or services it will produce and the markets it will serve. **(10)**

Stream of payments a series of cash payments at specified (although not necessarily regular) intervals of specified (although not always necessarily the same) amounts. **(3)**

Strike price *See* **Exercise price**

Subchapter S corporation a small corporation that may legally be treated as if it were a partnership for income-tax purposes. **(2)**

Subscription *See* **Privileged subscription**

Sunk cost an expenditure that was made before a decision has been made and that is unaffected by the decision under evaluation; it is not part of an investment's capital outlay and, in general, should be ignored in analyzing the investment. **(11)**

Supply curve a graph that shows the amounts of a good or service suppliers are willing to offer for sale at different prices during a specified time period. **(4)**

Surplus spending units individuals, companies, or government bodies that have excess funds. **(2)**

Swap *See* **Interest-rate swap**

Synergy the effect achieved when the whole is greater than the sum of its parts. **(25)**

Takeover *See* **Hostile takeover**

Target payout ratio *See* **Long-run target payout ratio**

Target return the rate of return required by suppliers of funds to an investment project; the rate with which an investment project's internal rate of return is compared to determine whether the project will return enough to satisfy those providing the funds. **(11)** *See also* **Return target; Marginal cost of capital**

Tax *See* **Capital-gains tax; Investment tax credit; Profit after taxes (PAT)**

Tax-deductible expenses expenses that can legally be subtracted from total income to determine taxable income. **(2)**

Tax liability the amount of tax a taxpayer must pay in a given period. **(2)**

Tax rate *See* **Average tax rate; Marginal tax rate; Progressive tax rates**

Technical insolvency *See* **Business failure**

Tender offer an acquiring firm's offer to pay existing shareholders some specified amount of cash or securities if these shareholders will sell (tender) their shares of stock to the acquiring firm. **(25)**

Terminal value an estimate of the cash flows of an investment project generated beyond the terminal point of the analysis and treated as a cash inflow in the final year of the analysis. **(11)**

Term loans secured loans made by banks, insurance companies, or other lending institutions that must be repaid usually within three to seven years. **(14)**

Thrift institution a financial intermediary that accepts savings deposits and makes certain types of loans. **(2)**

Times-interest-earned ratio the margin by which current earnings cover interest charges on debt; calculated as current earnings divided by interest charges. **(7)**

Time value of money the opportunity to earn interest on money one receives now rather than later. Because of the time value of money, a dollar today is worth more than a dollar in the future. **(3)**

Trade credit short-term credit extended by a supplier in connection with goods purchased for ultimate resale; used by nearly all firms to some extent as a source of short-term funds. **(21)**

Transactions motive (for holding cash) concerns the use of cash to pay bills. **(22)**

Translation the conversion of accounting information denominated in one currency into accounting information denominated in another currency. **(24)**

Treasury bills and notes *See* **U.S. Treasury bills and notes**

Unlevered shares shares of stock in a company that uses no debt. **(15)**

Unsecured debt debt that is not backed with a pledge of property. **(7)**

Unsecured loan a loan against which no specific assets are pledged as collateral. **(21)**

Uses of funds (1) reductions in liabilities; (2) reductions in net worth through the payment of dividends, retirement of stock, or operating losses; and (3) increases in assets. **(6)**

U.S. Treasury bills and notes short-term obligations of the U.S. government. **(22)**

Valuation model *See* **Constant-growth dividend-valuation model; Variable-growth dividend-valuation model**

Value the dollar amount one would have to receive today to be just as well off as one would be owning the asset. **(1)**

Value maximization the goal of making a firm's value as large as possible; it can be used as a criterion for making financial-management decisions. **(1)**

Value of stock *See* **Book value of stock; Market value of stock**

Variable costs costs that vary directly with changes in production volume. **(8)**

Variable-growth dividend-valuation model a method for valuing stock that assumes that a rapid growth in the dividend can continue for only a short period and will then decline to a more normal growth level. **(4)**

Variation *See* **Coefficient of variation**

Vertical merger a merger that combines firms that have some customer/supplier relationship. **(25)**

Voice in management the extent to which various financial-claim holders can influence the policies of a firm. **(14)**

WACC See **Weighted-average cost of capital (*WACC*)**

WARR See **Weighted-average required return (*WARR*)**

Warrant an option to purchase a number of shares of common stock at a specified price for a specified period of time, typically issued in connection with bonds, and usually detachable. **(17)**

Weighted-average cost of capital (*WACC*) another name for the *weighted-average required return (WARR)*. **(12)**

Weighted-average required return (*WARR*) the required return for an average-risk investment project based on an average of equity and debt returns, where the weights are the respective proportions of equity and of debt used by a firm. **(12)**

Working capital composed of a firm's current assets, normally with maturities of less than one year. **(6)** *See also* **Net working capital**

Working-cash balance currency plus checking-account balances. **(22)**

Work in process goods in various stages of production. **(23)**

Worst-case analysis a financial analysis that tells management how low a return could fall under adverse circumstances; the return target for evaluating the worst case should not include a risk premium for bearing risk. **(13)**

Worth *See* **Net worth**

Yield to maturity (YTM) the rate that could be earned on a bond or note if an investor bought it at the current price, held it to maturity, and received all the cash flows promised **(4)**; the internal rate of return that equates the price of a bond (or debt instrument) to the present value of the expected future cash benefits of owning the bond (or debt instrument); also known as the *required return on debt* **(12)**; the internal rate of return on a bond earned by an investor if the bond is bought now and held to maturity. The YTM is the required rate of return on the bond. **(14)**

YTM *See* **Yield to maturity (YTM)**

Zero-coupon bond a bond that pays no interest but is issued at a large discount and later redeemed at face value. **(14)**

Answers to Odd-Numbered Questions

Chapter 1

1. The role of business firms in a market economy is to produce the goods and services desired by society as efficiently as possible. Profit maximization as a practical criterion suffers from three principal shortcomings: (1) it does not take account of uncertainty, (2) it does not take account of the time value of money, and (3) it is ambiguous. Value maximization is the extension of profit maximization to a world that is uncertain and multiperiodic in nature. When the time period is short and the degree of uncertainty is not great, value maximization and profit maximization amount to essentially the same thing.

3. Because we assume that most individuals are risk-averse, a promise of return that involves greater uncertainty as to the actual amount of return will have a lower value than a comparable promise of return that is less uncertain.

5. Corporate goals and objectives identify the mission and purpose of the firm. Corporate strategy defines the markets, products, technology, etc., to advance the firm toward its goals. A decision criterion, such as profit maximization and value maximization, is the basis for making specific decisions consistent with corporate goals and strategy.

Chapter 2

1. The three basic forms of business organization are the sole proprietorship, the partnership, and the corporation. Proprietorships and partnerships represent an extension of the activities of individuals into the sphere of commerce. Except in the case of limited partnerships, proprietors and partners have unlimited liability for the acts and debts of their firms. A corporation, on the other hand, is an entity created by law that is empowered to own assets, incur liabilities, and engage in certain specified activities. The liability of owners for acts and debts of the firm is limited to their investments. The corporate form also permits easier transfer of ownership and better access to capital markets. Finally, there are important differences in the way these organizational forms are taxed.

3. Corporate income is subject to taxation, with the taxes paid by the corporation. If dividends are paid, the dividends are then subject to taxation as income received by individuals. The taxes on dividends are paid by the individuals. Triple taxation may exist when a subsidiary investment in a corporation pays taxes, pays dividends to the corporation which pays taxes on the dividends and income, and finally, pays taxable dividends to the shareholders.

5. Taxation of income affects incentives. The lower the marginal tax rate, the more of each incremental dollar of revenue an individual is able to keep, and (presumably) the harder he or she will work to earn an additional dollar. Conversely, when expenses are deductible, the net cost of each expense is only a part of the gross outlay. The lower the marginal tax rate, the greater the portion of the net expense borne by the individual and the more careful he or she will be about expenses. For example, a lower marginal tax rate might reduce the total amount spent by businesses for entertainment.

7. The next dollar more or less of taxable income will be taxed at the marginal tax rate. Total taxes divided by total taxable income is the average tax rate. Most financial decisions entail an analysis of added or less taxable income; thus the marginal, current tax bracket, is the preferred decision variable.

9. In the aggregate, the net providers of funds in the U.S. economy are households. Business firms, in the aggregate, are net users of funds. When it incurs a deficit, government (federal as well as state and local) is also a net user of funds.

11. Government regulation is designed to encourage a high degree of competition with reasonable risk assumption. Disclosure, protection for the small participant, lines-of-business exclusions, and minimum net worth ratios *may* provide a balance between safety and performance. Government regulation compliance costs money and may reallocate resources in ways different from a nonregulated market. (This is a good question to pull out varied philosophies of political economy in the class.)

13. Commercial banks, mutual-savings banks, savings-and-loan associations, and credit unions are the major types of depository financial intermediaries. Insurance companies and pension and retirement funds are the major contractual types. Also included are mutual funds, finance companies, and real-estate investment trusts.

15. If lenders anticipate a certain level of inflation, they will add an inflation premium to the interest rate they charge borrow-

ers in order to obtain their required real return. Likewise, borrowers will be willing to pay an inflation premium because they anticipate an inflated return on the money borrowed. Thus, anticipated inflation is incorporated into market interest rates.

Chapter 3

1. Money has time value because a dollar today is worth more to the holder than a dollar received at some time in the future. A dollar now can be invested over the time period to earn a profit.
3. The effective rate increases with frequency of compounding.
5. When interest is compounded daily, there will be more opportunity to earn interest on interest; therefore, the account paying 5 percent compounded daily will provide a higher effective rate of interest and should be selected.
7. The $1,000 and $1,500 are not comparable unless adjusted for time and the opportunity rate of return. One may find the value of $1,000 after five years at 8 percent and compare to $1,500, or discount the $1,500 to "present" and compare to $1,000; $1,000 $(1.08)^5$ = $1,469.33 — take the $1,500; $1,500 $(1/1.08^5)$ = $1,020.87 — again, take the $1,500. We are assuming that the $1,500 is a certainty.

Chapter 4

1. The value of a business asset is determined by the size, timing, and degree of uncertainty attached to the stream of future payments the owner expects to receive.
3. Risk aversion is the dislike for risk, whereas risk preference is the desire to take on risk. Risk neutrality is indifference to the element of risk. A risk-averse investor requires compensation for bearing risk, whereas a risk-neutral investor does not.
5. The dividend-valuation model is a discounted-cash-flow model applied to the valuation of a firm, taking into consideration the cash flows expected to be received by the owners.
7. A market is efficient when market prices reflect all available information. While financial markets may not be perfectly efficient at all times, the competition of thousands of well-informed investors ensures that market prices quickly adjust to reflect new information.
9. Not necessarily. Many risky investments are available, but the prudent investor must not assume that returns follow automatically from risk-taking. Reasonable, expected returns must be sufficient to coax the prudent investor down the risk-taking path.
11. General levels of interest rates in the economy vary directly with strength of the economy (GNP) and expected inflation, and inversely with changes in the money supply by the Federal Reserve system.

Chapter 5

1. Expected value is a probability-weighted average, mean value, or average expected outcome. It does not give any indication of the expected dispersion of outcomes. The standard deviation of returns is a measure of the variability of past returns. We cannot always assume that future variability will be the same. In addition, the standard deviation of returns on an asset does not take into account the relationships among returns on various assets. If returns on assets are not perfectly positively correlated, investors can achieve risk reduction by investing in a portfolio of assets. Therefore, a better measure of risk for a single asset may be the variability that the asset contributes to the variability of the portfolio.
3. The CAPM is a model that relates return on assets in financial markets to nondiversifiable risk. It assumes that investors are risk-averse and that market prices will reflect the relative riskiness of assets. The CAPM may be useful for evaluating investment in both physical and financial assets.
5. Because investors can purchase any assets available in the market in any unit desired and because these assets are considered risk-averse, under the assumptions of the CAPM investors can be expected to hold diversified portfolios and, therefore, to eliminate diversifiable risk. Nondiversifiable risk then becomes the only possible risk, and, in market equilibrium, securities will be priced to compensate investors for nondiversifiable risk only.
7. The beta coefficient is a measure of the volatility of the firm's return relative to that of the market portfolio. A beta greater than one indicates a firm with greater-than-average volatility in returns relative to the market. A beta of less than one indicates a firm with less volatile returns, and a beta of one indicates a firm with average volatility of returns. Under the assumptions of the CAPM, beta can be used to calculate the required rate of return on a stock as $K_j = R_f + (K_m - R_f)\beta_j$, where R_f is the risk-free rate and K_m is the required return on the market.

Chapter 6

1. Except for dividends, any transaction that changes net worth appears in the income statement.
3. *Working capital* refers to the firm's current assets outstanding; net working capital refers to current assets less current liabilities at a point in time. *Operating cash flows,* or cash flows from operations, represent the net amount of funds generated (cash flows from revenues less cash expenses) in a period of time. Net or working capital is a point-in-time balance, while operating cash flow is a cumulative total for a period of time. A positive cash flow from operations for a period increases the amount of net working capital, measured at the end of a period.

5. Principal sources of funds include increases in liabilities, increases in net worth, and reductions in assets. Principal uses of funds include reductions in liabilities, reductions in net worth, and increases in assets.

7. Depreciation expense, other noncash expenses, and noncash revenues cause net profits to vary from operating cash flows. Noncash expense deductions from revenues results in a net profit figure that understates cash flow. This is why depreciation is added to net profit to determine operating cash flow.

Chapter 7

1. A. A supplier is interested in the ability of the firm to pay its bills and turn its current assets. Liquidity (current ratio and acid test) and activity (inventory turnover and A/R turnover) ratios are likely to be calculated and studied.

   B. A short-term lender is interested in the ability to turn (activity) current assets into cash and the ability to pay. See part (A) for selected ratios.

   C. A long-term lender is interested in the cash-flow-generating ability of management (profitability—ROA, ROE) and the extent to which other creditors have claims on the firm (indebtedness—times interest earned and debt ratio), as well as the liquidity and activity level of the firm.

   D. Shareholders are concerned with the cash-flow-generating ability of management (profitability—ROA, ROE, EPS) and their risks assumed to generate the profitability (debt ratio, variability of earnings, quality of earnings). All ratio areas are of concern to the shareholder.

   E. An employee, like a shareholder, is concerned with the long-term competitiveness of the firm and should review all ratio areas.

3. A normalized income statement presents all accounts as a proportion of total or net revenue. Since the total sum of the proportions of sales equals 100 percent, the possible reasons for a change in the net income/sales (net margin) ratio may be reviewed by observing the proportional changes in the specific expense areas.

5. For an inventory business, selling more high-quality products may improve the net margin, but since few items may be sold, the sales/asset ratio may decline.

7. The purpose of this question is to associate policies and decisions with intended changes in ratio relationships. Dango might have attempted to provide more inventory per square foot of retail space—higher-quality, higher-margined inventory for a special market segment. With easy credit terms along with more inventory, the sales/asset ratio (turnover) probably fell, but if it were more than offset by increased margins per dollar of sales, the ROA would increase. There are many ways to generate an acceptable level of ROA, but taking more risk may not be in the shareholder's best interest.

9. Return on investment is sometimes an ambiguous measure of performance because it can be calculated in many ways. Return can be calculated either before or after tax, or as an average over several years. Investment can be defined either as the initial outlay or as the average book investment over the period in question.

11. In a seasonal firm, variation in the sales rate over the year will cause the days-of-sales-outstanding (DSO) figure to vary even when there is no change in the underlying collection rate. In such a firm, the averaging period of sales must be selected carefully and the results interpreted with caution. Similarly, seasonality in sales and purchasing may cause the inventory turnover rate to vary over the year.

13. Yes. If a firm is growing rapidly, all of its profits may be absorbed by necessary increases in current assets, leaving the firm always short of cash.

15. Above-average risk-taking may enhance earnings and profitability, but may turn off investors.

Chapter 8

1. *Fixed costs* refer to costs that are constant in total over some specified range of output, usually in terms of sales volume. *Variable costs* are costs that vary in total as output varies. Costs that are labeled "fixed" over some range of output usually become variable outside that range.

3. Where depreciation is included as an expense, the break-even point on a cash basis will always be lower than the break-even point on a profit basis. Less revenue is required to cover cash operating expenses than is required to cover full operating expenses, which include depreciation.

5. Operating leverage is determined by the firm's cost structure (the ratio of fixed operating costs to total operating costs) and, therefore, by the nature of the business. Financial leverage is determined by the mix of debt and equity used to finance the firm's assets. In flow terms, financial leverage depends on the portion of EBIT that is paid in interest.

Chapter 9

1. The planning process begins with the firm's basic goal or purpose. From this is derived the commercial strategy, which defines products, markets, and production technology. Supporting policies are then developed in production, marketing, research and development, accounting, finance, and personnel.

3. The percent of sales method of financial planning assumes a long-run, consistent relationship between the rate of business activity (sales) and investment in specific assets. Assets in turn must be "financed." Analysis of the sales/assets/financing relationship is an important part of financial planning. The rough, long-range planning technique may not be the most effective in short-run seasonal forecasting, but in all financial planning, activity (sales) "drives" asset needs which "drive" financing needed.

5. In principle, commercial strategy comes first, and financing is tailored to fit. Often an operating plan must be modified to

take account of availability of funds. In theory, operating plans and financing requirements should be determined jointly. In practice, however, an iterative process often is appropriate whereby an operating plan is formulated, financing feasibility determined, and the process repeated if necessary.

7. All three financial statements are interdependent. With consistent assumptions and accurate presentation, all of the figures will mesh. For example, collections must be consistent with sales and accounts receivable; accounts payable, purchases, inventory, and cost of goods sold must be consistent with each other; tax payments must be consistent with tax expense on the income statement and with taxes payable on the balance sheet.

Chapter 10

1. Capital budgeting is the process of planning and evaluating long-term investments. In some firms large amounts of funds must be committed for long periods of time with payoffs many years down the road. Because shareholders are most affected by the residual impact of these decisions, they are very concerned with this decision-making process in the firm.

3. In *NPV* analysis, the sum of the discounted cash flows, discounted at the *minimum* required rate of return, generates a present value which is the maximum one is willing to pay for the project. The *NPV* is the difference between what one must pay (outlay) and the maximum one will pay (sum of present values). A positive amount of *NPV* is the added estimated value contributed to the firm when the firm makes the investment at today's required rates of return. If the expected *NPV* is negative, the investment is expected to reduce the value of the firm.

5. Ranking is necessary when two or more investment opportunities are mutually exclusive and also when capital is rationed.

7. Payback ignores the time value of money and the cash flows beyond the end of the payback period. Establishing the required payback period is essentially an arbitrary judgment, because payback cannot be related to a more general criterion such as profit maximization or value maximization.

Chapter 11

1. Cash flows relevant to the analysis of an investment opportunity are those directly attributable to the investment. Only the incremental cash flows or the cash flow changes that will differ depending on the decision made should be considered. Thus, previous investments are sunk costs and can be ignored. Also, cash flows that will be identical under alternative decisions can be ignored.

3. No, the decision to analyze the lighting condition was made prior to and was a sunk cost prior to the light-improvement analysis.

5. Terminal or concluding net after-tax cash flows resulting from the sale, demolition, or completion at the end of a project are relevant to the analysis. One may wish to estimate the present value of remaining cash flows from a project as a terminal value. One may assign a minimal attainable value as a conservative estimate.

7. The standard procedure proposed throughout this book is to evaluate the after-tax operating cash flows of an investment, using a required rate of return that takes account of compensation required by those who supply the funds. When operating and financing flows are mixed, determining the required rate of return becomes difficult.

9. Only expenses that actually will change because of the decision being evaluated should be included. If overhead, for example, will increase or decrease because of the decision at hand, the change in overhead expense should be included in the cash-flow analysis.

11. Added current assets such as cash, accounts receivable, and inventory, net of spontaneously added payables and accruals, that is required for a project, must be included as part of the outlay (or whenever added or retracted). At the end of a project, NWC may be "returned" and included in the net terminal value.

13. Usually it is not necessary to identify a single figure as the initial investment. Net present value and internal rate of return can be calculated without such identification. Later cash outlays are represented by negative cash flows in the years in which they occur.

15. Sunk costs are costs that have already been incurred at the time the decision is to be made and, therefore, cannot be affected by the decision. In general, sunk costs are irrelevant to the analysis of investment opportunities.

Chapter 12

1. In undertaking any investment opportunity, the investor forgoes the return that could be earned on alternative investments. Rates available on alternative opportunities thus establish the minimum acceptable rate of return on any given investment.

3. False. The required rate is that on the next best opportunity forgone by the *shareholders,* rather than by the firm itself. Thus, the required return is established by the alternative opportunities of shareholders.

5. Required rates of return are established in the financial markets by the actions of investors competing among themselves. Because all investors have access to the financial markets, a standard set of opportunity rates is established that is the same for all investors. Given risk aversion, those opportunity rates increase with risk.

7. Suppliers and users of capital react to inflation in a way that incorporates anticipated inflation into all market-determined required rates of return. Required rates thus reflect the rate of inflation expected in the future.

9. The required rate of return on the firm's outstanding securities represents the required return given the overall combined risk of all investments undertaken in the past and expected by the market in the future. The required return on a single prospective investment opportunity would be the same as the required return on the firm's outstanding securities only if the riskiness of the prospective investment opportunity equaled the average risk of the firm as a whole.

11. The best source is market data on risk and return on financial assets.

13. First, determine the target financing mix — that is, the proportions of common equity, preferred stock, and various forms of debt that will provide capital to the firm in the future. Second, determine the required rate of return on each component, making certain to adjust for the tax-deductibility of interest. Third, multiply the tax-adjusted required rates of return by their proportions, and add them to obtain the *WARR*.

15. In calculating K_e, we have to make an estimate of the required return of stockholders in a company. This boils down to making some very difficult assumptions. A number of models can be used to calculate K_e, including historical risk premiums and the dividend-growth model (both finite and infinite growth). In using dividend-growth models, we have to estimate what shareholders expect to happen in the future. That is, we have to estimate future dividends. In using the historical-risk-premium approach, we have to assume that the long-run risk premiums earned in the past are expected to be earned in the future. In addition, we have to adjust the risk premium for the length of the time period because arithmetic and geometric averages differ. In short, estimating K_e is a difficult business, and, in practice, it is usually prudent to try a number of different models to calculate K_e.

Chapter 13

1. Two approaches to dealing with risk in capital budgeting are sensitivity analysis on project cash flows and risk-adjusted discount rates. Sensitivity analysis requires recalculating the internal rate of return (or net present value) for a range of possible sales levels and costs, in addition to calculating for the most likely case. This approach allows the manager to focus on how variability in certain factors may affect the success of the project. The alternative approach requires that cash flows be discounted at required rates of return that reflect their relative riskiness. Thus, higher discount rates are used for more uncertain cash flows. This approach is the risk-adjusted discount-rate method.

3. In a worst-case analysis, the riskiness of cash flows has been accounted for. Because the cash flows are likely to be higher than the worst-case projections, there is no risk that must be compensated for by requiring a higher return. Therefore, these cash flows are discounted at a required rate of return that does not include a risk premium.

5. By assigning investment projects to different categories that depend on the riskiness of the cash flows, the firm could use a modified form of the CAPM to derive an estimate of the required rate of return on an unlevered firm. Betas of 0.5, 1, and 1.5, for example, could be assigned to projects of low, average, and high risk. To adjust the required returns for debt financing, the firm could also weight the firm's debt ratio in relation to the riskiness of the project, with the riskiest project having a weight of 0 placed on the firm's debt ratio and average projects having a weight of 1 placed on the firm's debt ratio.

7. In theory, the use of a single discount rate to evaluate projects of varying risk will lead to acceptance of some high-risk projects that should be rejected and rejection of some low-risk projects that should be accepted. Over time, the firm's average risk level may be increased as a result of this bias. Also, acceptance of high-risk projects that do not provide sufficient return will, in the long run, reduce the firm's profitability and its market value.

Chapter 14

1. Financial claims issued by firms differ with respect to maturity, seniority (priority), whether they are contractual or residual, whether collateral is involved, and tax treatment. Because of differences in risks, the financial markets require different rates of return on different types of securities.

3. The agreement between a debt holder and a firm (or other borrower) represents an enforceable contract. If the obligor fails to meet the terms of the agreement with respect to repayment or other matters, the claim holder can take legal action to enforce the claim.

5. Within major categories, some contractual claims may be junior to others. In such cases, the junior claims are often referred to as subordinated.

7. A mortgage bond is normally secured by a specific asset or assets, usually buildings or equipment, that are pledged as security against default on interest or principal payments. Debentures, on the other hand, are not secured by specific assets, but rather by all the assets of the firm collectively.

9. The yield to maturity (YTM) is the rate that discounts all interest and principal payments on a bond to an amount exactly equal to the price of the bond. In the case of publicly traded bonds, price — and, therefore, yield to maturity — is determined in the financial markets.

11. Common stockholders have final responsibility for policy and a residual claim to income and assets, behind preferred shareholders and debt holders. Common stock is a perpetual claim, having no maturity. Common stockholders have limited liability. Under the laws of most states, common stockholders have the right to amend the corporate charter, adopt and amend bylaws, elect the directors, enter into mergers with other firms, change the number of authorized shares outstand-

ing, and authorize the issuance of senior claims such as preferred stock and long-term debt.

13.

	Seasonal Loan	Term Loan
Use of Funds	Temporary, seasonal asset needs	Permanent long-term need
Source of Repayment	Reduction in assets to cash	Cash flows generated from assets financed

Term loans are amortized to match the loan payments with the cash flows generated by the assets financed. The term or maturity varies to match the financing with the cash flows or assets financed.

15. Weak-form efficiency results when market prices reflect all information contained in historic prices. Semistrong-form efficiency results when market prices reflect all publicly available information. Strong-form efficiency results when market prices reflect all information — both public and private.

17. Semistrong-form efficiency does imply weak-form efficiency because past information on security prices is part of public information. Semistrong-form efficiency does not, however, imply strong-form efficiency because public information would not include inside information.

Chapter 15

1. Operating leverage is determined by the relationship between fixed and variable operating expenses, which include expenses related to the firm's operations and exclude interest and taxes. The higher the ratio of fixed operating cost to total operating cost, the higher the operating leverage. Financial leverage refers to the mix of debt and equity used to finance the firm's activities. The higher the proportion of debt funds to total funds, the higher the financial leverage. Thus, operating leverage is determined by the nature of the business and its cost structure, whereas financial leverage is determined by the financing mix.

3. Financial leverage has no effect on the variability of dollar operating returns (no effect on range or standard deviation). Financial leverage does affect the variability of earnings per share and percentage return on equity.

5. When earnings-per-share (EPS) data are used as criteria for financing decisions, the analysis is nearly always carried out in terms of expected values. Earnings per share as a criterion thus ignores risk and results in a bias toward the use of debt in lieu of equity. If applied strictly, the EPS criterion nearly always leads to the choice of debt rather than equity and can lead to excessive use of debt.

7. Accounting return on equity is defined as accounting profit (pretax or after tax) divided by book net worth. Return to shareholders is composed of dividends plus capital gains or losses. Excessive use of debt financing will simultaneously increase accounting return on equity and reduce return to shareholders by lowering stock price.

9. Since, for any given firm, debt is always cheaper than equity, strict application of the cost criterion would always lead to a choice of debt over equity. Debt and equity perform different functions, so a strict comparison of cost is insufficient for choosing between the two.

11. In theory, market value is a function of both expected return and risk. The higher the expected return, the greater the value, whereas the higher the risk, the lower the value. Since an increase in financial leverage increases both expected return and risk, market value theoretically deals with the trade-offs between the two.

13. Tax-deductibility of interest reduces the share of EBIT going to the government and increases by a like amount the share going to equity holders. The share going to debt holders is unchanged.

15. Even if interest were not tax-deductible, some firms might use debt in order to exploit potentially favorable effects of financial leverage. Firms having no access to the equity market would find debt their only source of funds and would use debt regardless of whether interest were deductible. Short-term debt would find use by firms for financing short-term requirements. Debt might also be preferred to equity to avoid dilution of ownership and control.

Chapter 16

1. A firm's operating risk manifests itself in variability of earnings before interest and taxes (EBIT). Variability of EBIT is determined by variability of sales revenue, variability of operating expenses, degree of operating leverage, and composition of the firm's assets. All these factors in turn derive from the characteristics of the industry and company and the technology of the business in which the company is engaged.

3. Yes, short-term debt should be considered. Debt increases risk regardless of whether it is short-term or long-term debt. In fact, an argument can be made that short-term debt is riskier than long-term debt. In Chapter 16, the distinction between short-term and long-term debt is ignored, and all debt is treated the same for determining the optimal level of debt. The question of maturity structure is treated in Chapter 18.

5. Very little can be said about a firm's exposure to risk of financial distress without knowing the maturity of the debt and the schedule for repayment of principal. A complete analysis also requires information on the firm's cash flows, both those from operations and those generated by changes in invest-

ment policy, asset structure, and discretionary financial payments (dividends).

7. In general, a firm should not extend the debt level indicated as safe by a cash-flow analysis. A firm should maintain a substantial reserve borrowing capacity to provide flexibility for changes in its commercial strategy and also a reserve for contingencies. Uncertainty about future rates of inflation provides a further reason for maintaining reserve borrowing power.

Chapter 17

1. True. Dividends are treated as a residual. Fluctuating dividends cause no problems for investors in a frictionless world. If the firm errs and pays out too much in dividends, it simply issues new securities to replace the funds, incurring no costs in the process.

3. Shareholders are subject to transaction costs resulting from commissions on purchases and sales of securities and from the time, effort, and inconvenience of altering their personal portfolios. The combined effect of all such costs is significant and may constitute quite a large percentage of small transactions. A second general category includes transaction costs incurred in issuing new securities by firms.

5. Investment, debt/equity, and dividend decisions cannot all be treated as active policy variables unless the firm is prepared to place no constraints on external financing. A constraint on external financing means that one of the three major policy variables must be treated as a residual.

7. Dividend policy should be treated as residual. Any other choice requires that the firm either consciously plan to forgo attractive investments, operate at a nonoptimal debt/equity ratio, or finance dividend payments by selling stock.

9. Dividend policies must be planned over a relatively long time horizon because investment opportunities cannot be foreseen with complete accuracy each year, nor can earnings be forecast accurately each year. In a world of uncertainty and considerable financial friction, dividend policy must be based on trend values over relatively long time periods.

Chapter 18

1. An option is a contract agreement between two parties conveying the right to buy or sell specific assets at a specified price during a stipulated period of time. An option buyer has the right, but not the obligation, to exercise the option. The option seller (writer) must be ready to honor the buyer's option.

3. A call option is an option to buy at a specified price; a put option is an option to sell at a specified price. If one suspects the stock price might fall, the purchase of the put will provide a gain if the stock drops below the strike price.

5. If the option is a call (option to buy), the buyer may pay an expected value price for the option, given the probability of the asset value changing in the next 30 days. If it is a put, the value is related to the opportunity to sell at the exercise price which is currently below the current market price.

7. A warrant (option) is initially attached to a bond or other contract, but subsequently trades alone. A warrant is an option (call) to buy (usually stock) at a given exercise price up to a maturity date.

9. The call option provides the ability to force conversion of the convertible security if the total market value of the "conversion" is greater than the call price.

11. A financial futures contract is a contract to buy or sell a specified financial asset at a *specified* price at a *specified* time. The contract is between the buyer/seller and an exchange where similar contracts are traded. Daily settlements of gains/losses are required to prevent default.

13. Both forward contracts and futures contracts are used by the financial manager as a means of hedging. A forward contract is a unique, negotiated contract between two parties to deliver at a specified price on a specified date, whereas a futures contract is a generic contract between one party (buyer or seller) and an exchange where the contract is traded. Delivery is usually made with the forward contract; not so with the futures contract. Daily cash settlements of gains and losses are required on futures contracts.

Chapter 19

1. In a lease agreement the owner of the asset (lessor) conveys use of the asset to the lessee in return for future lease payments. The lessor retains title to the asset and contributes or borrows funds to finance the asset.

3. Under a shorter-term operating (or *service*) lease, the owner/lessor is usually responsible for the maintenance, insurance, and taxes (operating expenses) associated with the asset. A longer-term financial (or *capital*) lease usually is a net lease, with the lessee responsible for the asset-oriented operating expenses. A financial lease may be capitalized and appear on the balance sheet.

5. A business in need of liquidity and/or earnings might sell appreciated real estate and buildings, etc., receive cash, an accounting gain, and agree to lease the assets, thus retaining "use" but giving up "ownership."

7. To the lessee evaluating a lease proposal with a benefit/cost analysis such as net present value, the relevant incremental estimated cash flows over time associated with leasing versus borrowing must set forth with cash flows as either "benefits" or "costs." *NPV* is a time-weighted analysis of the B/C's using the firm's opportunity cost of funds, or if borrowing is the likely alternative, the after-tax rate of borrowing is used as the discount rate. The following cash-flow benefits and costs may be associated with leasing:

Item	Leasing Benefit/Cost
Cost of item leased	Benefit—Do not have to pay
Investment tax credit	Cost—Benefit of owner/lessor given up by leasing
Lease payments	Cost of leasing
Maintenance, insurance, taxes on asset	Benefit or Cost—Depends on who pays
Depreciation tax shield	Cost of leasing—Retained by owner/lessor
Terminal value	Cost—Owner retains

9. In a *NPV* lease analysis one discounts the net cost cash flows at the after-tax cost of debt and subtracts the PV sum from the benefits of leasing (acquisition cost). If the benefits exceed the PV costs of leasing, the *NPV* is greater than zero and the asset should be leased. A negative *NPV* implies that leasing will reduce the value of the firm.

Chapter 20

1. The three principal methods of issuing securities to the public are public offerings through investment bankers, public offerings by a privileged subscription, and private placements.

*3. A privileged subscription is a new offering of securities in which existing security holders (usually shareholders) are given the right to purchase their prorata shares of securities before the securities are offered to the general public. The right of shareholders to have first refusal is called a *preemptive right*.

5. The primary purpose of federal and state regulation of securities markets is to protect investors against misinformation and fraud.

7. Some issue costs vary with the size of the issue and some costs are fixed. To the extent that some costs are fixed, issue costs as a percentage of funds raised will vary with the size of the issue. Raising small amounts of money, therefore, is uneconomical; firms tend to raise money in larger blocks.

9. Keeping investors and other participants in the financial markets informed about major policies, investments, and financing decisions is of great importance in the pricing of a firm's securities. The factors that determine security prices are future-oriented. The better informed the market is kept about the policies and future plans, the more the market relies on facts and substantive information and the less it is forced to draw inferences from other actions. For example, based on an announcement of a major financing decision or a change in dividend policy, the market might draw inferences about the firm's investment opportunities. Depending on the nature of the inferences, stock price may be affected in one direction or the other. Where possible, management should communicate its policies and plans to the market so that prices are based on facts and information rather than inferences.

11. The term *sinking fund* refers to an arrangement whereby a firm makes periodic payments, usually annually or semiannually, to the trustee of a bond or preferred-stock issue. The trustee then uses the funds to retire a specified number of bonds periodically either by open-market purchase or by calling certain bonds at previously agreed-upon prices.

13. The option to call an entire issue prior to maturity can be advantageous to a firm to permit changes in capital structure or to permit refunding of the issue at a lower inerest rate. Whatever advantage accrues from the call privilege accrues to shareholders and represents a corresponding disadvantage to bondholders. Bondholders normally insist on being compensated by a higher interest rate for the call privilege.

15. Four motives exist for a firm to repurchase stock. First, a firm might elect to repurchase its stock in lieu of paying a dividend. However, internal revenue regulations require that such a repurchase be taxed as a dividend. Second, repurchase is sometimes justified as a means of accumulating shares of stock for use in future acquisition or for employee stock options, but any advantage of repurchase for this purpose is illusory. A third motive is to effect a partial return of capital to the shareholders or a partial liquidation of the firm. A final motive for repurchase is to bring about a change in the firm's debt/equity ratio.

17. Financial difficulty may result from a number of causes including failures of management, changes in technology or markets, or overallocation of resources to a particular economic activity. In all three cases, profits are a yardstick for judging performance, and society is sending a message that changes are necessary. If technology or markets change, management must make the necessary adjustments. If errors were made by management in the past, they should be corrected; if excessive resources are allocated to the particular activity, resources must be withdrawn and reallocated to other uses.

19. The appropriate remedy when a firm encounters financial difficulty depends on the nature of the difficulty. In cases of technical insolvency, creditors are usually better off to accommodate the firm's short-run liquidity difficulty and to allow it to remain in operation. Such problems usually are worked out either by an extension of maturities or by a composition, under which all creditors agree to accept a partial payment. Where the appropriate remedy cannot be agreed upon informally, relief can be sought by either the firm or its creditors in the courts. Such relief usually takes the form of a reorganization under the provisions of the Bankruptcy Act. In situations in which the value of a firm as a going concern is less than its liquidation value, liquidation of assets is usually the appropriate remedy.

Chapter 21

1. The short-term and immediate-term suppliers of funds are other business firms, commercial banks, finance companies, insurance companies, pension funds, and others to whom firms may become obligated for one reason or another. All of these suppliers are themselves only intermediaries in the chain of finance, because they require financing also. Ultimately, the suppliers of all business funds are individuals who, by consuming less than they earn, have excess funds to save and invest.

3. Through the financial plan, the borrower communicates to the bank information about the nature of the financing requirement, the amount and timing of the need, the uses to which the funds will be put, and the timing and means of repayment. The fact that a financial plan has been prepared is important in that it communicates to the bank that the firm's management is competent.

5. Collateral permits a lender to make a loan that, when unsecured, is too risky in relation to the rate that can be charged, and yet still has reasonable prospects of being repaid.

7. Short-term lenders are less concerned with earning power than intermediate-term lenders because repayment of a term loan must come from profits over a period of several years rather than from liquidations of the assets financed by the loan.

Chapter 22

1. Principal motives for holding cash and liquid assets include the transactions motive, for making payments, and a precautionary motive, for responding to unexpected problems or opportunities requiring funds on short notice.

3. Concentration banking permits a firm to pool its requirements for working balances in a single account and thereby reduce the aggregate requirements.

5. As the length (number of days) of the cash cycle increases, the amount of funds tied up in working capital (inventory, accounts receivables, and cash) increases. Current assets, though we measure them at points in time (balance sheet), really flow from cash to inventory to A/R and back to cash. As with the volume of water in a pipe, the longer the pipe (cash cycle) and the greater the diameter of the pipe (sales), the greater the volume of water (working capital) in the pipe.

7. A firm might have idle cash as a matter of policy for either of two reasons: First, a seasonal firm might have temporary idle balances during parts of the year; second, a firm might hold precautionary balances to finance unpredictable requirements. In both cases, the firm would probably find it advantageous to invest the idle balances temporarily in liquid assets.

Chapter 23

1. *Raw-material inventories* serve as a buffer to decouple the purchasing and production functions. *Work-in-process (WIP) in-*
ventories are necessary because production processes are not instantaneous. WIP inventories also serve to decouple the various stages of the production process so that all stages do not have to proceed at the same rate. *Finished-goods inventories* act as buffers to decouple the production and sales functions.

3. The production manager may be concerned with the availability of inventory to keep production running at the optimum level, while the financial manager is concerned about the return from added investments in inventory. Production may want more, while finance may want less.

5. At the margin, investment in accounts receivable is risky because of the possibility of customer default. Similarly, incremental investment in inventory is risky because of uncertainty surrounding the extent to which lost sales will be recaptured by holding additional inventory.

7. The expected return to Delta Electric on an investment in trade credit would be likely to far exceed the expected return to a bank on a loan to the same customer. Thus, the expected return to Delta might well be sufficient to compensate for the risk involved, whereas the expected return to the bank might be too low given the risk. For this reason, suppliers often are willing to extend trade credit to customers considered too risky to qualify for bank credit.

*9. The optimal size of safety stock varies directly with stockout costs, uncertainty of usage or sales rates, and uncertainty of delivery times. The optimum varies inversely with inventory-carrying costs.

Chapter 24

1. The basic concepts of finance do not change. They are just as applicable for firms doing business in foreign markets. However, the financial officer will now have additional elements to consider in financial decisions — specifically, currency-exchange rates, both current and future, and interest rates applicable to those currencies.

3. The floating system creates more uncertainty (risk) for the business managers doing business in foreign countries. Even though some business managers might benefit occasionally from changes under a floating system, a fixed system is preferable — all other things being equal — because people are risk-averse. There are ways this risk can be reduced, but these methods create transactions costs in both time and money. In practice, all other things are not equal. In the long run, a floating-rate system may be more responsive to underlying economic changes around the world. In short, there is no easy answer for which system is better. It is clear, however, that a floating-rate system introduces new risks to business.

5. The most important factor that accounts for forward/spot differentials is the difference between the inflation rates of the countries involved. Differences in interest rates paid for the country's currency, to the extent those rates reflect anticipated inflation, also affect the differential. Central banks can also have an impact.

7. The treasurer would purchase forward the amount of Swiss francs needed in order to guarantee the availability at the required time. This purchase could result in the treasurer's actually paying more or less, depending on relative inflation rates, but would protect against further fluctuations.

9. Covered-interest arbitrage is the market process through which the relationships in the interest-rate-parity theorem came into being. This process is used to cover one's position by buying or selling forward the currencies involved.

Chapter 25

1. Horizontal mergers combine firms operating in the same business line. Vertical mergers combine firms that have some customer/supplier relationship. Conglomerate mergers combine firms in different industries.

3. Diversification through merger may lead to increases in value, depending on the circumstances of the merger. If the stockholders of the acquiring firm have diversified portfolios, it is not likely that the merger will create value for them. But there are circumstances, such as mergers, that actually change cash flows, increase borrowing power, or take advantage of an undervalued situation, in which value can be created.

5. Merger-induced increases in earnings per share (EPS) do not always benefit shareholders. It is not EPS that is ultimately important to shareholders but the price per share of the stock they own. The EPS increase may or may not translate into an increased share price, depending on how the market views the value of the merged firm.

7. Studies indicate that shareholders of acquired firms have benefited. The picture is not so clear for shareholders of the acquiring firm. Evidence suggests that they have not been harmed by mergers.

9. An acquisition is similar to other investment proposals, since a stream of cash flows is being purchased for some outlay. It is different from other investments only in that it may be much more complicated from a financial, tax, or business perspective. There may be more intangibles involved, and a firm may be going outside its area of expertise where there is more uncertainty.

Solutions to Odd-Numbered Problems

Chapter 2

1. For $100,000 in taxable income:

Taxable Income	Tax Rate	Tax Amount
$0–$50,000	15%	$ 7,500
$50,001–$75,000	25%	$ 6,250
$75,001–$100,000	34%	$ 8,500
Total Taxes		$22,250

For $1 million in taxable income:

Taxable Income	Tax Rate	Tax Amount
$0–$50,000	15%	$ 7,500
$50,001–$75,000	25%	$ 6,250
$75,001–$100,000	34%	$ 8,500
$100,001–$335,000	39%	$ 91,650
$335,001–$1,000,000	34%	$226,100
Total Taxes		$340,000

3. Using the marginal tax rate of 34 percent, the added $44,000 of taxable income incurs an added tax liability of $44,000 × 0.34 = $14,960, and added after-tax income of $44,000(1 − 0.34) = $29,040.
5. Calculate the pretax nominal rate.

$$4\% \quad \text{real after-tax rate}$$
$$\underline{+\ 4\%} \quad \text{expected inflation}$$
$$8\% \quad \text{after-tax rate}$$

$$\frac{8\%}{1 - 0.28} = 11.11\% \text{ pretax nominal rate}$$

Chapter 3

Problems preceded by an asterisk (*) assume knowledge of Appendixes 3A and 3B.

1. The application of Equation (1) from the text (these problems could be solved using the reciprocal from Appendix Table I at the end of the text or figures from Appendix Table III when available) provides the following results:
   a. $100(1 + 0.10)^3 = \$133.10$.
   b. $100(1 + 0.30)^3 = \$219.70$.
   c. $100(1 + 0)^3 = \$100.00$.
3. The application of the annuity present-value table (Appendix Table II at the end of the text) provides the following results:
   a. $500(2.775) = \$1,387.50$.
   b. $500(1.952) = \$976.00$.
5. The application of present-value table (Appendix Table I at the end of the text) provides the following results:
   a. $100(0.943) + \$400(0.890) + \$800(0.840) = \$1,122.30$.
   b. $100(0.833) + \$400(0.694) + \$800(0.579) = \$824.10$.
7. The solutions require the use of the compounding portion of Equation (1) to find the effective rate.

   a. $\left(1 + \dfrac{0.08}{2}\right)^2 = 1.0816$; effective rate = 8.16 percent.

   b. $\left(1 + \dfrac{0.08}{4}\right)^4 = 1.0824$; effective rate = 8.24 percent.

   c. $\left(1 + \dfrac{0.08}{12}\right)^{12} = 1.0830$; effective rate = 8.30 percent.

9. The application of Equation (2) provides the following results:

   a. $\dfrac{\$1,000}{(1 + 0.06)^2} = \dfrac{\$1,000}{1.12360} = \$890.00$.

   b. $\dfrac{\$4,000}{[1 + (0.04/4)]^4} = \dfrac{\$4,000}{1.0406} = \$3,843.94$.

   c. $\dfrac{\$1,000}{[1 + (0.12/12)]^6} = \dfrac{\$1,000}{1.0615} = \$942.06$.

   d. $\dfrac{\$3,000}{[1 + (0.08/2)]^4} = \dfrac{\$3,000}{1.1699} = \$2,564.32$.

11. Applying Equation (3) and the present-value tables at the back of the book provides the results shown in Table S–1.
13. The problem could be solved by looking up the individual present-value factors for each of the 16 periods. However, problems of this type can usually be shortened considerably

Table S–1

Period	Cash Flow (dollars)	Present-Value Factor at 4 Percent	Present Value at 4 Percent (dollars)	Present-Value Factor at 8 Percent	Present Value at 8 Percent (dollars)	Present-Value Factor at 12 Percent	Present Value at 12 Percent (dollars)
1	300	0.962	288.60	0.926	277.80	0.893	267.90
2	400	0.925	370.00	0.857	342.80	0.797	318.80
3	600	0.889	533.40	0.794	476.40	0.712	427.20
4	100	0.855	85.50	0.735	73.50	0.636	63.60
			1,277.50		1,170.50		1,077.50

by breaking them down into an annuity plus several individual inflows. One such division is given in Table S–2.

Table S–2

Year	Cash Flow (dollars)	Factor at 8 Percent	Present Value (dollars)
1–16	100 (annuity)	8.851	885.10
5	100	0.681	68.10
6	200	0.630	126.00
16	300	0.292	87.60
			1,166.80

15. This problem is intended to demonstrate the usefulness of discounted cash flow in moving cash flows around through time while maintaining value equivalence. The solutions are as follows:
 a. $100(0.090) + $300(0.826) + $200(0.751) = $488.90.
 b. $100 + $300(0.909) + $200(0.826) = $537.90.
 c. $100(1 + 0.10) + $300 + $200(0.909) = $591.80.
 d. $100(1 + 0.10)^2 + $300(1 + 0.10) + $200 = $651.00.
 Note: Solutions (b), (c), and (d) can also be found by compounding $488.90 forward for one, two, and three years, respectively, at 10 percent.

17. Instead of an ordinary annuity (end of year payments), this is an annuity due, with $600 plus the PV of a three year $600 annuity. Add one to the interest factor; subtract one year.

$$PV = [1 + (\text{annuity factor}, n = 3, i = 10 \text{ percent})]\,(\$600)$$

$$= [1 + (2.487)]\,(\$600)$$

$$= \$2092.20.$$

19. The solution requires the use of the compounding portion of Equation (1) to find the effective rate:

$$\left(1 + \frac{0.06}{4}\right)^4 = 1.0614; \quad \text{effective rate} = 6.14 \text{ percent}.$$

21. The future value of $2,000 in two years at 10 percent can be determined as follows: $2,000 (future-value factor) = $2,000(1.21) = $2,420. Your savings, thus invested, would fall short of the $2,500 required.

23. This problem requires solving for the amount of an annuity, given the present value, discount rate, and time horizon. The determination of the maximum amount requires equating the lump-sum amount to the present value of an annuity, solving for the payment:

$$(\text{Payment}) \times (\text{Annuity factor}, n = 4, r = 7 \text{ percent})$$

$$= \$8,000.00.$$

$$\text{Payment} = \$8,000.00/3.387$$

$$= \$2,361.97.$$

25. This is a fairly straightforward problem, requiring the calculation of the effective interest rate (r) on a loan as follows:

$$(\text{Annuity factor}, n = 5) \times (\$4,161) = \$15,000.$$

$$\text{Annuity factor} = \$15,000/\$4,161 = 3.605.$$

Referring to Appendix Table II at the end of the book, we see that $r = 12$ percent.

27. Assuming semiannual compounding, the market rate of interest is 4.5 percent per half year. The value of the bond, therefore, is the present value of an infinite stream of $20 per half year capitalized at 4.5 percent, or 20/0.045 = $444.44.

29. Figure S–1 graphically depicts the dividend income from this investment. It is first necessary to find a rate of return (r)

Figure S–1

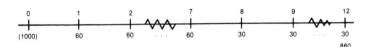

such that the present value of the dividends plus the present value of the final selling price is equal to the purchase price. The formula, using present-value (PV) factors, is as follows:

$1,000 = $60 (PV annuity factor for 7 years at r percent)

   + $30 (PV annuity factor for 5 years at r percent)

   × (PV factor for 7 years at r percent)

   + $860 (PV factor for 12 years at r percent) .

The next step is to solve by trial and error. Eventually, the use of 4 percent will yield these results: $60(6.002) + $30(4.452) (0.760) + $860(0.625) = 999.1256. The conclusion is that $r \sim 4$ percent. Notice that the five-year $30 annuity is collapsed into a single value that represents its present value at the end of the seventh year. Then this sum is discounted back to time zero by applying the seven-year present-value factor.

31. The following is an analysis of your two alternatives: Alternative 1—Keep the certificate. A deposit of $500 in a certificate earns 5 percent interest semiannually, $500(1.05)^2 = $551.25, while an average balance of $450 in a checking account earns no interest. The total funds available at year's end = $551.25 + $450.00 = $1,001.25. Alternative 2—Switch to a NOW account. A deposit of $500 in savings earns 0.055/365 in interest daily, or

$$\$500\left(1 + \frac{0.055}{365}\right)^{365} = \$500(1.05653) = \$528.27 .$$

An average balance of $450 in checking also receives 0.055/365 in interest daily, or

$$\$450\left(1 + \frac{0.055}{365}\right)^{365} = \$459(1.05653) = \$465.44 .$$

The total funds available at year's end = $528.27 + $475.44 = $1,003.71.

33. The cash flows are given in Figure S–2, a time line along which $t = 0$ corresponds to your 35th birthday, $t = 25$ corresponds to your 60th birthday, and $t = 45$ corresponds to your 80th birthday. As can be seen from the time line, there are two annuities—one with payments of $1,000 and one with withdrawals of $X. It is convenient to focus on $t = 25$ (your 60th birthday and anticipated date of retirement). We can calculate the future value of the first annuity ($1,000 payments for 25 years) and the present value (at $t = 25$) of the second annuity ($X withdrawals for 20 years). These two amounts must be equal. Note that $t = 25$ is the terminal date for the first annuity and the beginning date for the second

annuity. The calculations to determine the value of X are as follows:

$1000(future-value annuity factor for 25 years at 5 percent)

   = $X(present-value annuity factor for 20 years at 5 percent)

$$\frac{\$1000(\text{future-value annuity factor for 25 years at 5 percent})}{\text{present-value annuity factor for 20 years at 5 percent}} = X$$

$$\frac{\$1,000(47.727)}{(12.462)} = X$$

$$\$3,829.80 = X .$$

35. The problem requires calculation of the amount of an annuity necessary to produce a specified future value and consideration of the effects of inflation upon purchasing power.
   a. The calculations to determine the annuity required to produce $6,000 in year 5 are as follows:

(Amount of annuity) ×

(FV annuity factor, $n = 1, n = 6$ percent) = $6,000.00 .

Amount of annuity = $6,000.00/5.637

= $1,064.40 .

   b. The calculations to determine the annuity required to produce $6,000 in year 5, with the last payment in year 4, are as follows:

(Amount of annuity) ×

(FV annuity factor, $n = 4, r = 6$ percent) ×

(FV factor, $n = 1, r = 6$ percent) = $6,000.00 .

Amount of annuity = $6,000.00/(4.375 × 1.06)

= $6,000.00/4.6375

= $1,293.80 .

37. The calculations are as follows:

(Annuity factor for $i = 6$ percent) × $7,000 = $80,500 .

$$\text{Annuity factor} = \frac{\$80,500}{\$7,000} = 11.5 .$$

The application of the PV Annuity Table at the end of the book determines that $n =$ approximately 20 years. Consequently, Grow will be about $60 + 20 = 80$ years old when his money runs out.

Figure S–2

*39. The cash flows are given in Figure S–3. To find the effective interest rate, set the present value of the loan equal to $2,000 and solve for the monthly interest rate:

$$P_0 = \$2,000$$

$$= \$189.17 \text{ (PV annuity factor for 12 months at } r^*).$$

$$\frac{\$2,000}{\$189.17} = \text{(present-value annuity factor)} = 10.57.$$

[Note: Both the 12 and the r^* must refer to the same time period. As shown in the appendix tables at the end of the book, a factor of 10.57 corresponds to an interest rate of 2 percent monthly. On an annual basis, r_A^* is such that $(1 + 0.02)^{12} = 1 + r_A^*$ with $r_A^* = (1 + 0.02)^{12} - 1 = 26.8$ percent annually.]

___

Figure S–3

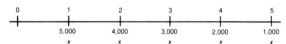

Chapter 4

1. Price = $1,000 (PV factor, $N = 5 \times 2 = 10$,

$$r = 10/2 = 5\%)$$

$$= \$1,000 \ (0.614)$$

$$= \$614.00.$$

3. Discounting the future cash flows of the bonds at 8 percent semiannually, the results are as follows:

$$\text{Price} = \left[\sum_{t=1}^{30} \frac{\$53.75}{(1 + 0.04)^t} \right] + \frac{\$1,000}{(1 + 0.04)^{30}}$$

$$= \underset{35.00}{\cancel{\$53.75}} \text{ (PV annuity factor, } n = 30, r = 4 \text{ percent)}$$
$$+ \$1,000 \text{ (PV factor, } n = 30, r = 4 \text{ percent)}$$

$$= \$53.75(17.292) + \$1,000(0.308)$$

$$= \$929.45 + \$308.00 = \$1,237.45$$

5. By discounting the expected cash flows at the minimum rate of return of 18 percent, we can calculate the maximum that Sarah is willing to pay for the stock, as follows:

$$\text{Price} = \sum_{t=1}^{4} \frac{\$4.00}{(1 + 0.18)^t} + \frac{\$60.00}{(1 + 0.18)^4}$$

$$= \$4.00(\text{PV annuity factor, } n = 4, r = 18\%)$$

$$+ \$60.00(\text{PV factor, } n = 4, r = 18\%)$$

$$= \$4.00(2.690) + \$60.00(0.516)$$

$$= \$10.76 + 30.96 = \$41.72$$

Sarah is willing to pay up to $41.72 for the stock. It is available in the market for $36.00. Her expected return at $36.00 exceeds her minimum rate of return of 18 percent.

7. $$\frac{P_0}{D_1} = \frac{P_0}{E_1} \times \frac{E_1}{D_1} = 10 \times \frac{1}{0.75} = \frac{10}{0.75}(13.33)$$

$$K = \frac{D_1}{P_0} + g = \frac{1}{13.33} + 0.04 = 0.075 + 0.04 = 0.115$$

$$= 11.5 \text{ percent}.$$

9. If the ACC bond were equal in risk to government bonds, we would expect the price to be equal to the present value of the $120 coupons and the face value of $1,000 discounted at the risk-free 9 percent rate of return for 10 years.

$$P_b = \$120(\text{PV annuity factor}) + \$1,000(\text{PV factor})$$

$$= \$120(6.418) + \$1,000(0.422)$$

$$= \$1,192.16.$$

That is, the bond sells for $192.16 less because it is more risky.

11. A review of Table 4–2 provides information for the following responses.

a. Expected return of Plan A = 0.5(0.20) + 0.5(0.5)

$$= 0.10 + 0.025$$

$$= 0.125 = 12.5 \text{ percent}.$$

b. Expected return of Plan B = 0.5(1.10) + 0.5(−0.40)

$$= 0.55 - 0.20$$

$$= 0.35.$$

c. The "better" strategy depends on each firm's risk/return trade-off. Plan B has the highest expected value, but it is also a riskier strategy because of the higher variability of possible returns.

Chapter 5

1. The purpose of problems (1) and (2) is to clarify the concepts of risk and risk aversion. The expected value of each of the four lotteries is $500. The problems put the student in the position of already owning the lottery tickets, rather than having to buy them, so as to avoid having students refuse to answer because of lack of funds. Where the gamble is very small in relation to the decision maker's wealth, the selling price if rights are already owned approximately equals the purchase price if the rights are not owned. Where the gamble is large in relation to wealth, in general the selling price would be greater than the purchase price. The manner in which the lottery tickets were obtained is, of course, unimportant; any costs are sunk. The sale price for rights to a given lottery represents the seller's certainty equivalent for the uncertain prospect. Risk-averse individuals will assign a value to the lotteries less than the expected value and risk preferent individuals a value greater. Risk-averse individuals assign progressively lower values as the lotteries become more risky. In solving this problem, the following two questions have been found useful:

a. Why would a given individual assign different values (different certainty equivalents) to different lotteries? This action would be taken because the lotteries vary in riskiness.

b. Why would different individuals assign different values to the same lottery? These actions would be taken because of differences in attitude toward risk.

By posing the questions in this way, the student can see a clear distinction between risk — a function of the investment opportunity (probabilities and payoffs) having nothing to do with the investor — and attitude toward risk — a function of the preferences of the investor. Use of expected value for decision making is inadequate, because it ignores investors' attitudes toward risk. The student can make the connection between risk, risk aversion, and the required rate of return by noting the following:

$$1 + \text{Expected return (percent)} = \frac{\text{Expected value (dollars)}}{SP}$$

where SP is the selling price set by the individual. The individual is willing to forgo an amount just under SP in order to retain rights to the lottery. By retaining the lottery, the individual establishes his or her expected return. Presumably, the SP will be set so that the expected return equals the individual's required return. Rearranging the elements of the equation yields this result:

$$SP = \text{Value} = \frac{E(V)}{1 + K}$$

where E/V is the expected value in dollars and where K is the required rate of return.

3. The expected value of this gamble is $0.5(0) + 0.5(\$1,000) = \$500$. Individual 2 is risk-preferent because he or she is willing to pay more than the expected value of the gamble. Individuals 1, 4, and 5 are risk-averse because they are willing to pay less than the expected value of the gamble. Individual 3 is risk-neutral because he or she is willing to pay exactly the expected value of the gamble.

5. The expected return and standard deviation in each case can be calculated as follows:

$$E(R_A) = 0.10(0.10) + 0.20(0.12) + 0.30(0.15) + 0.40(0.20) = 0.159$$

$$\sigma_A = \sqrt{(0.10 - 0.159)^2 0.10 + (0.12 - 0.159)^2 0.20 + (0.15 - 0.159)^2 0.30 + (0.20 - 0.159)^2 0.40} = 0.0367$$

$$E(R_B) = 0.15(0.08) + 0.15(0.10) + 0.15(0.18) + 0.55(0.24) = 0.186$$

$$\sigma_B = \sqrt{(0.08 - 0.186)^2 0.15 + (0.10 - 0.186)^2 0.15 + (0.18 - 0.186)^2 0.15 + (0.24 - 0.186)^2 0.55} = 0.0664$$

Investment B has the larger standard deviation of returns, so it appears to be riskier. The ratio of risk to return (referred to as the coefficient of variation) is also higher for B.

$$CV_A = \frac{\sigma_A}{E(R_A)} = \frac{0.0367}{0.159} = 0.23$$

$$CV_B = \frac{\sigma_B}{E(R_B)} = \frac{0.0664}{0.186} = 0.36$$

7. a. Using the constant-growth model for valuing stock from Chapter 4, we can develop the formula:

$$\text{Price} = \frac{\text{Dividend}}{K_e - g}$$

Since we know the price, dividend, and growth rate (g), we can now solve for the required rate of return (K_e).

$$K_e = \frac{\text{Dividend}}{\text{Price}} + g$$

$$= \frac{2}{50} + 0.10$$

$$= 0.14 .$$

b. The following formula is useful in determining the beta coefficient for a stock when the CAPM holds:

$$K_e = R_r + (K_m - R_r)\beta_j$$

$$14 = 8 + (12 - 8)\beta_j$$

$$14 = 8 + 4\beta_j$$

$$4\beta_j = 6$$

$$\beta_j = 1.5$$

Chapter 6

1. Knowledge of the following relationships is essential in solving this problem:

Working capital = current assets

Net working capital = current assets − current liabilities

Net operating capital = current assets − (current liabilities − notes payable)

See Table S–3 for the amounts (in thousands of dollars) attributed to capital for years 1 through 4.

Table S–3

	Year 1	Year 2	Year 3	Year 4
Working capital	15,800	20,100	24,300	26,400
Net working capital	250	4,000	8,400	6,900
Net operating capital	5,800	9,700	12,900	12,500

3. Table S–4 shows the long method, Table S–5 the short-cut method.

Table S—4

	Year 1	Year 2	Year 3	Year 4
Sales	48,200	60,600	72,500	81,400
Cost of goods sold	(35,600)	(46,000)	(56,200)	(63,100)
Selling, general, and administrative expense	(4,100)	(5,500)	(7,100)	(7,700)
Interest	(1,525)	(1,650)	(1,530)	(1,686)
Taxes	(2,100)	(2,200)	(2,400)	(2,700)
After-tax cash flow	4,875	5,250	5,270	6,214

Table S—5

	Year 1	Year 2	Year 3	Year 4
Profit after tax	2,475	2,650	2,670	3,114
Depreciation	2,200	2,400	2,400	2,900
Amortization of goodwill	200	200	200	200
After-tax cash flow	4,875	5,250	5,270	6,214

5. Table S–6 presents a source-and-use-of-funds statement for Irvin Motors Inc. for year 2.

Table S—6

Sources	
Increase in accounts payable	$ 395,200
Increase in other current liabilities	567,500
Increase in accrued liabilities	166,200
Increase in long-term debt	499,700
Decrease in marketable securities	276,100
Total sources	**$1,904,700**
Uses	
Increase in accounts receivable	$ 378,300
Increase in inventory	660,300
Increase in other current assets	89,400
Increase in net fixed assets	491,300
Increase in other assets	76,600
Decrease in taxes payable	150,800
Decrease in deferred income tax	94,400
Decrease in common stock	32,600
Decrease in retained earnings	131,200
Total uses	**$2,104,900**
Decrease in cash	**$ 200,200**

7. An analysis of balance-sheet changes over the period is the first step in determining the sources and uses of funds, as shown in Table S–7. Using the balance-sheet analysis, a source-and-use statement for year 2 can be prepared, modeled after Table 6–10, as shown in Table S–8.

Table S—7

	Year 1	Year 2	Change
Assets			
Cash	$ 10,850	$ 431	−$10,419
Accounts receivable	41,614	68,313	+ 26,699
Inventory	82,892	80,710	− 2,182
Miscellaneous current assets	7,681	6,413	− 1,268
Total current assets	$143,037	$155,867	+$12,830
Land	$ 42,000	$ 42,000	$ 0
Plant and equipment, net	180,759	189,805	+ 9,046
Total Assets	**$365,796**	**$387,672**	**+$21,876**
Liabilities and net worth			
Accounts payable	$ 52,218	$ 50,946	−$ 1,272
Taxes payable	18,416	22,840	+ 4,424
Accrued expenses	15,823	13,908	− 1,915
Total current liabilities	$ 86,457	$ 87,694	+$ 1,237
Mortgage payable	$110,000	$103,500	−$ 6,500
Paid-in capital	95,000	105,000	+ 10,000
Retained earnings	74,339	91,478	+ 17,139
Total liabilities and net worth	**$365,796**	**$387,672**	**+$21,876**

Table S–8

Sources	
Increase in taxes payable	$ 4,424
Increase in paid-in capital	10,000
Decrease in inventory	2,182
Decrease in miscellaneous current assets	1,268
Retained earnings	17,139
Total sources	**$35,013**

Uses	
Increase in accounts receivable	$26,699
Increase in net plant and equipment	9,046
Decrease in accounts payable	1,272
Decrease in accrued expenses	1,915
Decrease in mortgage payable	6,500
Total uses	**$45,432**

Decrease in cash	**$10,419**

Chapter 7

1. See Table S–9. The normalized income statement (in thousands of dollars) shows that cost of goods sold and selling, general, and administrative expenses increased in years 2 and 3. Management should investigate the reasons. The decline in interest expense may indicate less reliance on debt financing.

Table S–9

	Year 1	Year 2	Year 3	Year 4
Sales (percent)	100.0	100.0	100.0	100.0
Cost of goods sold	73.9	75.9	77.5	77.5
Gross profit	26.1	24.1	22.5	22.5
Depreciation	4.6	4.0	3.3	3.6
Amortization of goodwill	0.4	0.3	0.3	0.2
Selling, general, administrative	8.5	9.1	9.8	9.5
Income from operations	12.6	10.7	9.1	9.2
Interest	3.2	2.7	2.1	2.1
Taxable income	9.4	8.0	7.0	7.1
Taxes	4.3	3.6	3.3	3.3
New income	5.1	4.4	3.7	3.8

3. a. The troublesome ratios, in terms of both trend and comparison to the industry norms, appear to be inventory turnover (ITO), days purchases outstanding (DPO), current ratio (CR), acid-test ratio (ATR), debt to total assets (DTA), and times interest earned (TIE). The low and declining ITO indicates that the company does have an inventory problem. If we assume that sales are growing, we can conclude that inventories are too high. The truth of this conclusion is partially confirmed by the rapid decline in the CR coupled with a somewhat less severe decline in the ATR. That the ATR is also declining does hint at the possibility that some other current account is also involved, and the high and increasing DPO indicates that the accounts payable may be too high. Finally, the high and increasing DTA ratio coupled with a steady debt/net worth ratio implies that debt is expanding faster than assets. The declining TIE could be attributed to lower profits and higher debt and thus does not supply much new information. In short, the company appears to be expanding inventory too rapidly and relying too heavily on trade credit. The analysis should probably begin with these two accounts.

b. First, every company is unique, and it is difficult to set up a specific classification. Second, companies differ in a number of accounting practices such as depreciation, inventory evaluation, and recognition of income. Finally, median ratios are not necessarily optimal.

5. a. See Table S–10.

b. CCC inventories are far higher than the industry average for its sales level. These high inventory levels contribute to low asset turnover. As a result of the costs of carrying inventory and the low turnover ratio, CCC's profit margin is low, causing ROA and ROE to be well below industry averages. CCC also uses relatively little debt. As a strength, CCC's average collection period is shorter than the industry average.

c. If this growth is much higher than the industry average (which it probably is), it would make any ratio which uses both balance-sheet and income-statement figures somewhat misleading. For example, if CCC inventories doubled and ended at $825,000 (balance sheet), they must have been $412,500 at the prior year end. This result would represent an average inventory of [(825 + 412.5)/2] = $618,750 (assuming inventories grew smoothly through the year). Recalculating sales/inventory with this average figure, we would get $2,750,000/$618,750 = 4.44. While higher than our previous calculation, this is still well below the industry average. Other such ratios could also be recalculated.

Table S–10

Ratio	Industry Average	CCC
Current ratio	2.4	2.67
Average collection period (days)	43.0	36.5
Sales/inventories	9.8	3.33
Sales/total assets	2.0	1.43
Profit margin (percent)	3.3	2.1
Return on assets (percent)	6.6	3.0
Return on equity (percent)	18.1	4.8
Debt to total assets (percent)	63.5	37.14

Chapter 8

1. The break-even point in units can be calculated from Equation (1):

$$Q_b = \frac{FC}{P - VC} = \frac{\$3,000,000}{\$30 - \$18} = 250,000 \text{ units}.$$

The break-even point on a cash basis can be calculated from Equation (1):

$$Q_b = \frac{FC_c}{P - VC}$$

$$= \frac{\$3,000,000 - \$900,000}{\$30 - \$18} = 175,000 \text{ units}.$$

3. The following formula is used to solve this problem:

$$DOL = \frac{S - VC}{S - VC - FC}.$$

The calculations proceed as follows:

Sales at 300,000 units = 300,000 × $30 = $9,000,000.

Sales at 400,000 units = 400,000 × $30 = $12,000,000.

VC at 300,000 units = 300,000 × $18 = $5,400,000.

VC at 400,000 units = 400,000 × $18 = $7,200,000.

DOL at 300,000 units

$$= \frac{\$9,000,000 - \$5,400,000}{\$9,000,000 - \$5,400,000 - \$3,000,000} = 6.$$

DOL at 400,000 units

$$= \frac{\$12,000,000 - \$7,200,000}{\$12,000,000 - \$7,200,000 - \$3,000,000} = 2.67.$$

The DOL measures the volatility of earnings given the change in sales.

5. a. The break-even chart in Figure S–4 indicates a break-even volume of approximately 13,500,000 units. Using the formula provided, break-even volume is calculated as follows:

Contribution to profit = $1.00 − $0.4036

$$= \$0.5964/\text{unit}.$$

$$Q_b = \frac{FC}{P - VC} = \frac{\$8,125,000}{\$0.5964} = 13,623,407 \text{ units}.$$

b. An increase in sales price decreases break-even volume and increases the contribution to profit.

Contribution to profit = $1.05 − $0.4036

$$= \$0.6464/\text{unit}.$$

$$\text{Break-even volume} = \frac{\$8,125,000}{\$0.6464} = 12,569,616 \text{ units}.$$

Profit increases by 14 million × $0.05 = $700,000. The break-even point declines by 1,053,791 units.

Figure S–4

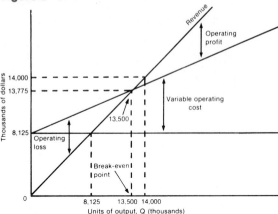

c. A decrease in fixed costs increases profits by the amount of the decrease ($406,250) and decreases break-even volume.

$$\text{Break-even volume} = \frac{\$8,125,000 - 0.05(\$8,125,000)}{\$0.5964}$$

$$= 12,942,237 \text{ units}.$$

d. A decrease in variable costs decreases break-even volume and increases the contribution to profit.

Contribution to profit

$$= \$1.00 - [\$0.4036 - 0.05(\$0.4036)]$$

$$= \$0.6166/\text{unit}.$$

$$\text{Break-even volume} = \frac{\$8,125,000}{\$0.6166} = 13,177,000 \text{ units}.$$

Profit increases by 0.05($0.4036) × (14,000,000)

$$= \$282,520.$$

All three methods, implemented simultaneously, would have the effect of decreasing break-even volume, increasing per-unit contribution to profit, and increasing profit directly.

Contribution to profit

$$= \$1.05 - [\$0.4036 - 0.05(\$0.4036)]$$

$$= \$0.6666/\text{unit}.$$

Total increase in contribution at 14,000,000 units

$$= (\$0.6666 - \$0.594) \times 14,000,000 = \$982,800.$$

$$\text{Break-even volume} = \frac{\$8,125,000 - 0.05(\$8,125,000)}{\$0.6666}$$

$$= 11,579,283 \text{ units}.$$

Direct increase in profits $= (0.05)(\$8,125,000)$

$$= \$406,250.$$

Total increase in profit $= \$406,250 + \$982,800$

$$= \$1,389,050.$$

7. a. See Table S–11 for a projected income statement for 1989. It is necessary to classify the expenses listed as either fixed or variable expenses.
   b. The break-even point at present (1988) operating levels is calculated as follows:

   $$P = \$1.00/\text{unit}.$$

   $$VC = \$0.35 + 0.16 = \$0.51/\text{unit}.$$

   $$FC = \$3,910,000 + \$1,500,000 = \$5,410,000.$$

   $$\text{Break-even volume} = \frac{FC}{P - VC} = \frac{\$5,410,000}{\$1.00 - \$0.51}$$

   $$= 11,040.816 \text{ units}.$$

   The break-even point at projected (1989) operating levels is calculated as follows:

   $$FC = \$4,060,000 + \$2,845,000 = \$6,905,000.$$

   $$\text{Break-even volume} = \frac{\$6,905,000}{\$0.49} = 14,091,837 \text{ units}.$$

   c. After expansion, the fixed costs will reduce the profit level by $1,495,000. If sales volume were to remain at the current level of 12,200,000 units, there would be a net loss of $895,000.

Chapter 9

1. a. See table *below*.
   b. If the historical relationship of average balance-sheet values relative to sales, calculated in the 1988 Hawk table, hold into the future (1989), and if sales growth is 10 percent $[800(1.10) = 880]$, the percent-of-sales estimate of Hawk Corp.'s average balance sheet is listed below. The funds-needed line is the squeeze variable representing financing needed. Stockholder's equity is increased by the amount of the six percent net margin less one-half paid to dividends, or equity increases 3 cents for every dollar of sales. The increase in sales will *increase* asset needs by 40, 7.5 $(82.5 - 75)$ of which will be financed sponta-

Table S–11

Sales		$20,000,000
Cost of sales		
Fixed	$4,060,000	
Variable[a]	7,000,000	11,060,000
Gross margin		$ 8,940,000
Selling and general expenses	$2,845,000	
Fixed		
Variable[b]	3,200,000	6,045,000
Net income		$ 2,895,000

[a]Variable cost of sales per unit $= \dfrac{\$4,240,000}{12,200,000} = \$0.35/\text{unit}.$

[b]Variable selling and general expenses $= \dfrac{\$1,950,000}{12,200,000}$

$$= \$0.16/\text{unit}.$$

neously by payables and accruals. Earnings retained (net income minus dividends) will provide $26.4, leaving $6.1 to be financed by the financial manager.

Hawk Pro-Forma Average Balance Sheet, 1989
(thousands of dollars)

Current Assets	110[a]	Current Liabilities	82.5[d]
Net Fixed Assets	330[b]	Funds Needed	6.1[f]
Total Assets	440[c]	Stockholder's Equity	351.4[e]
		Total Liab. and Equity	440

[a]12.5% × 880 = 110   [d]9.4% × 880 = 82.5
[b]37.5% × 880 = 330   [e]325 + (0.06 × 880)(0.5) = 351.4
[c]50% × 880 = 440   [f]440 − 82.5 − 351.4 = 6.1

3. The pro-forma balance sheet for December 31, 1989, is given in Table S–12. Major items were calculated as follows:

   $$\text{Assets} = [\$51,250/\$46,235] \times \$60,000 = \$66,508.$$

   $$\text{Current Liabilities} = [\$4,784/\$46,235] \times \$60,000$$

   $$= \$6,208.$$

Hawk Corp. Average Monthly Balance Sheet, 1988
(thousands of dollars)

	% Sales			% Sales	
Current Assets	100	100/800 = 12.5%	Current Liabilities	75	75/800 = 9.4%
Net Fixed Assets	300	300/800 = 37.5%	Stockholder's Equity	325	
T. Assets	400	400/800 = 50%	T. Liabilities and Equity	400	

Table S–12

Assets	Liabilities and Deferred Taxes	
	Current liabilities	$ 6,208.00
	Deferred taxes	3,685.50
	Long-term debt	18,036.00
Total assets:	Common stock par	575.00
$66,508.00	Capital (excess of par)	7,945.00
	Retained earnings	18,664.00
	Total (preliminary)	$55,113.50
	Funds needed	11,394.50
	Total liab. and deferred taxes	$66,508.00

Deferred Taxes = [$2,840/$46,235] × $60,000

$$= \$3,685.50.$$

Retained Earnings = 1986 RE + Profit after taxes (PAT)

$$= \$17,070 + \$1,594$$

$$= \$18,664$$

where PAT = [$1,228/$46,235] × $60,000 = $1,594.

5. See Table S–13 for a pro-forma income statement of Hi-Tech Manufacturing for 1989.

Table S–13

Sales	$2,025,000
Cost of goods sold	1,335,000
Gross profit	$ 690,000
Depreciation	136,000
Selling and administrative	240,000
Interest	40,000
Profit before taxes	$ 274,000
Tax at 46 percent	126,040
Net income	$ 147,960

7. See Table S–14 for a pro-forma balance sheet for Hi-Tech Manufacturing for 1989.
*9. On December 31, 1989, there will be an accounts receivable balance of $76,959 composed of:

15 percent of October sales	$ 7,190
65 percent of November sales	28,769
100 percent of December sales	41,000
Balance	$76,959

11. See Tables S–15 and S–16 for the pro-forma monthly income statements and monthly cash budget, respectively, for Hi-Tech Manufacturing Co.

Table S–14

Assets		
Cash		$ 67,042
Accounts receivable		305,137
Inventory		124,186
Total current assets		$ 496,365
Gross plant and equipment		1,975,000
Less depreciation		1,099,000
Net plant and equipment		$ 876,000
Total assets		**$1,372,365**
Liabilities and Net Worth		
Bank loan		$ 0
Accounts payable		59,905
Accrued labor		60,000
Taxes payable		0
Accrued overhead		10,000
Total current liabilities		$ 129,905
Debentures		500,000
Common stock		300,000
Retained earnings		442,460
Total liabilities and net worth		$1,372,365

Chapter 10

1.

Period	Cash Flow		PV factor (12%)		PV Sum
0	($10,000)	×	1.000	=	($8,930)
1	3,000	×	0.893	=	2,679
2	3,000	×	0.797	=	2,391
3	3,000	×	0.712	=	2,136
4	3,000	×	0.636	=	1,908
5	3,000	×	0.567	=	1,701
			NPV	=	$ 815

Present value = $10,815

Alternatively, using the PV annuity factor for five years, 12 percent:

$$NPV = (\$10,000)(1.00) + \$3,000(3.605)$$

$$= (\$10,000) + 10,815$$

$$= \$815.$$

Decision rule: NPV > 0, accept.

The profitability index is the ratio of the sum of PV of cash flows divided by the outlay, or:

$$PI = \frac{PV \text{ Sum of Cash Flows}}{Outlay}$$

$$= \frac{\$10,845}{10,000}$$

$$= 1.08.$$

Decision rule: If PI > 1, accept.

Table S–15

	January	February	March	April	May	June	July	August	September	October	November	December	1987
Sales	$ 180	$ 150	$ 130	$ 120	$130	$ 160	$ 175	$ 200	$ 180	$ 160	$ 200	$ 240	$ 2,025
Cost of goods sold													
Material expense	54	45	39	36	39	48	52.5	60	54	48	60	72	607.5
Labor expense	54	45	39	36	39	48	52.5	60	54	48	60	72	607.5
Overhead	10	10	10	10	10	10	10	10	10	10	10	10	120
Total cost goods sold	$ 118	$ 100	$ 88	$ 82	$ 88	$ 106	$ 115	$ 130	$ 118	$ 106	$ 130	$ 154	$ 1,335
Gross profit	$ 62	$ 50	$ 42	$ 38	$ 42	$ 54	$ 60	$ 70	$ 62	$ 54	$ 70	$ 86	$ 690
Depreciation	10	10	10	10	12	12	12	12	12	12	12	12	136
Selling and administrative	20	20	20	20	20	20	20	20	20	20	20	20	240
Interest	0	0	0	0	0	20	20	20	0	0	0	20	40
Profit before taxes	$ 32	$ 20	$ 12	$ 8	$ 10	$ 2	$ 28	$ 38	$ 30	$ 22	$ 38	$ 34	$ 274
Tax (at 46 percent)	14.72	9.2	5.52	3.68	4.6	0.92	12.88	17.48	13.8	10.12	17.48	15.64	126.04
Net income	$17.28	$10.8	$6.48	$4.32	$5.4	$1.08	$15.12	$20.52	$16.2	$11.88	$20.52	$18.36	$147.96

Table S–16

	January	February	March	April	May	June	July	August	September	October	November	December
Receipts												
Cash sales	$ 18	$ 15	$ 13	$ 12	$ 13	$ 16	$ 17.5	$ 20	$ 18	$ 16	$ 20	$ 24
Accounts receivable (1 month)	103.5	81	67.5	58.5	54	58.5	72	78.75	90	81	72	90
Accounts receivable (2 months)	85.5	103.5	81	67.5	58.5	54	58.5	72	78.75	90	81	72
Total receipts	$207.0	$199.5	$161.5	$138.0	$125.5	$128.5	$148.0	$170.75	$186.75	$187.0	$173.0	$186.0
Disbursements												
Payment of accounts payable	54	45	39	36	39	48	52.5	60	54	48	60	72
Payment of labor	54	45	39	36	39	48	52.5	60	54	48	60	72
Overhead	10	10	10	10	10	10	10	10	10	10	10	10
Bond interest						20						20
Capital expense				175								
Selling and administrative	20	20	20	20	20	20	20	20	20	20	20	20
Tax payments				33.12		5.52			44.16			43.24
Total disbursements	$138.0	$120.0	$108.0	$310.12	$108.0	$151.52	$135.0	$150.0	$182.16	$126.0	$150.0	$237.34
Receipts less disbursements	$ 69.0	$ 79.5	$ 53.5	($172.12)	$ 17.5	($ 23.02)	$ 13.0	$ 20.75	$ 4.59	$ 61.0	$ 23.0	($ 51.24)
Add beginning cash balance	20.0	39.0	118.5	172.0	20.0	20.0	20.0	20.0	28.11	32.76	93.76	116.70
	$ 89.0	$118.5	$172.0	($ 0.12)	$ 37.5	($ 3.02)	$ 33.0	$ 40.75	$ 32.70	$ 93.76	$116.70	$ 65.46
Loan increase (decrease)	($ 50.0)			$ 20.12	($ 17.5)	$ 23.02	($ 13.0)	($ 12.64)				
Ending cash balance	$ 39.0	$118.5	$172.0	$ 20.12	$ 20.0	$ 20.0	$ 20.0	$ 28.11	$ 32.70	$ 93.76	$116.70	$ 65.46
Ending loan	$ 0	$ 0	$ 0	$ 20.12	$ 2.62	$ 25.64	$ 12.64	$ 0	$ 0	$ 0	$ 0	$ 0

The payback period is the length of time it takes to recover the original outlay of an investment. At the rate of $3,000 per year (assuming a constant flow per year), the $10,000 outlay is recovered in $10,000/$3,000, or 3.33, years.

Decision rule: If the expected payback period is less than the minimum required, accept . . . or calculate the *NPV*!

3. a. Calculate the *NPV* for machines A and B. See Tables S–17 and S–18.
   b. Select project A, which has the higher net present value.

Table S–17

Year	Cash Flows	Present-Value Factor at 10 percent	Present Value
0	($10,000)	1.000	($10,000)
1	$ 3,000	0.909	$ 2,727
2	$ 3,000	0.826	2,478
3	$ 3,000	0.751	2,253
4	$ 2,500	0.683	1,708
5	$ 2,500	0.621	1,552
		Net present value at 10 percent =	$ 718

Table S–18

Year	Outlay	Cash Flows	Present-Value Factor (10 percent)	Present Value
0	($7,500)	($7,500)	1.000	($7,500)
1		$2,000	0.909	$1,818
2		$2,000	0.826	$1,652
3		$2,000	0.751	$1,502
4		$2,000	0.683	$1,366
5		$3,000	0.621	$1,863
			Net present value at 10 percent =	$ 701

5. The net present value (*NPV*) for the investments described is calculated as follows:

   a. *NPV* = $4,000(PV factor for 13 years at 12%)
      − $27,000

      = $4,000(6.24) − $27,000

      = $25,696 − $27,000

      = −$1,304

   b. *NPV* = $3,000(PV factor for 16 years at 12%)
      − $27,000

      = $3,000(6.974) − $27,000

      = −$6078

c. *NPV* = $1,400(PV factor for 16 years at 12%) − $7,070

   = $1,400(6.974) − $7,070

   = $2,693.60

Based on these results, the investment described in part (c) is the one that should accepted.

7. a. 0 = $27,000 + $4,000 (PV annuity factor for 13 years)

   $27,000 = $4,000 (present-value annuity factor)

   $$\frac{\$27,000}{\$4,000} = \text{present-value annuity factor}$$

   6.75 = present-value annuity factor.

   Reading across the annuity factor for 13 years in the PV annuity table enables the student to see that the annuity factor = 6.75 at 11 percent.

   Decision rule: *IRR* of 11% < *RRR* of 12%; reject

   b. $27,000 = $3,000(present-value annuity factor for 16 years)

   $$\frac{\$27,000}{\$3,000} = \text{present-value annuity factor}$$

   9 = present-value annuity factor.

   For 16 years the annuity factor is 9.447 at 7 percent and 8.851 at 8 percent. Interpolating provides the following result:

   $$\left(\frac{9.447 - 9.000}{9.447 - 8.851}\right) = \frac{0.447}{0.596} = 0.75$$

   Thus the internal rate of return = 7.75 percent.

   Decision rule: *IRR* of 7.75% < *RRR* of 12%; reject

   c. $7,070 = $1,400 (PV annuity factor for 16 years)

   $$\frac{\$7,070}{\$1,400} = \text{present-value annuity factor}$$

   5.05 = present-value annuity factor.

   For 16 years the annuity factor is 5.162 at 18 percent and 4.938 at 19 percent. Interpolating provides the following result:

   $$\left(\frac{5.162 - 5.05}{5.162 - 4.938}\right) = \frac{0.112}{0.224} = 0.5$$

   Thus the internal rate of return = 18.5%.

   Decision rule: *IRR* of 18.5% > *RRR* of 12%; accept. This is consistent with the *NPV*s above.

9. a. See Table S–19.
   b. Using part (a) as the first trial, select a higher rate because the net present value (*NPV*) > 0 at 10 percent. The use of 15 percent as the discount rate generates the results shown in Table S–20, indicating that the internal rate of return (*IRR*) is slightly over 15 percent. Interpolating

Table S–19

Year	Cash Flow	Present-Value Factor (percent)	Present Value
0	($1,000)	1.000	($1,000.00)
1	($500)	0.909	($454.50)
2	$600	0.826	$495.60
3	$800	0.751	$600.80
4	$800	0.683	$546.50
		Net present value =	$188.30

Table S–20

Present-Value Factor at 15%	Present Value
1.000	($1,000.00)
1.000	($435.00)
0.756	$453.60
0.658	$526.40
0.572	$457.60
Net present value =	$2.60

yields the following as the change in *NPV* for a 1 percent change in the discount rate:

$$\frac{\$188.30 - \$2.60}{10 - 15} = \$37.14.$$

Then solve for the *IRR* as follows:

$$IRR = 15 + \frac{\$2.60}{\$37.14} = 15.07 \text{ percent}.$$

c. The project should be accepted. The internal rate of return (15.07) exceeds the target rate of 10 percent.

11. a. This problem demonstrates the usefulness of DCF in evaluating financing decisions. The effective interest cost for the single-payment alternative is calculated as follows:

$$\$1,000 = \text{Present-value factor } (\$1,259.45)$$

Present-value factor = 0.794

See the PV table in the three-year row to learn that the effective interest cost is 8 percent.

The three-year payment loan is calculated by studying the PV annuity table in the year row three to learn that the effective interest cost is 10 percent. The effective interest cost for the annual payment alternatives is calculated as follows:

$$\$1,000 = \text{PV annuity factor } (\$402.09).$$

PV annuity factor = 2.487.

b. The single-payment alternative is preferred because it has a lower effective interest cost.

13. The maximum one should pay for the higher grade of insulation material is the present value. Use the PV annuity table to determine the present value as follows:

Present value = $650 (PV annuity factor for 10 years at 15 percent)

$$= \$650(5.019)$$

$$= \$3,262.35.$$

15. a. Figure the payback period as follows:

$$\frac{\$1,000}{\$301.93} = 3.312 \text{ years}.$$

b. The net present value is calculated as follows:

$$\$301.93(3.312) - \$1,000 = 0$$

c. The present-value factor for *R* percent and *N* years represents the maximum payback period that an *N*-year investment can have and provide an internal rate of return of *R* percent. This interpretation is possible only for investments generating level cash inflows.

17. This problem requires the student to calculate the internal rate of return (*IRR*), the net present value (*NPV*), and the payback period for three mutually exclusive investments. In this problem, *NPV* and *IRR* do not give the same ranking among investments because of differences in initial outlays and patterns of subsequent cash flows.

a. Table S–21 gives the payback period for each investment. See Tables S–22 and S–23 for the net present values at various discount rates of investment A and B. *IRR*$_A$ is between 16 and 17 percent. Interpolating yields the following result:

$$\frac{74}{141} \times 1.0 \text{ percent} = 0.52 \text{ percent}$$

$$IRR_A = 17 \text{ percent} - 0.52 \text{ percent} = 16.48 \text{ percent}.$$

IRR$_B$ is between 22 and 23 percent. Interpolating yields the following result:

$$\frac{99}{125} \times 1.0 \text{ percent} = 0.79 \text{ percent}$$

$$IRR_B = 23 \text{ percent} - 0.79 \text{ percent} = 22.21 \text{ percent}.$$

Similarly, the internal rate of return for investment C can be generated as follows:

$$\$15,000 = \$7,120 \text{ (annuity factor, } r \text{ percent, } n = 3)$$

$$\frac{\$15,000}{\$7,120} = 2.107$$

$$IRR_C = 20 \text{ percent}.$$

b. See Table S–24 for the net present value (*NPV*) for each investment at 15 percent. Investment C should be chosen, using the *NPV* criterion, since it provides the greatest

Table S-21

Investment	Payback Period (years)
A	2
B	2.33
C	2.11

Table S-22
Net Present Values at Various Discount Rates for Investment A

Discount Rate (percent)	NPV
14	$363
15	$218
16	$67
17	-$74

Table S-23
Net Present Values at Various Discount Rates for Investment B

Discount Rate (percent)	NPV
15	$988
20	$278
22	$26
23	-$99

Table S-24

Investment	Net Present Value
A	$ 218
B	$ 988
C	$1,255

NPV at the firm's required rate of return. However, if the internal-rate-of-return (IRR) criterion were used, investment B would be selected because it has the greatest IRR.

19. a. Project X should be chosen because it generates the highest net present value (NPV).

b. Project X again should be chosen. The combination of projects W and Y exhausts the $300 budget but provides a total NPV of $55, lower than the $70 provided by project X. Note that the choice of project X leaves $100 in the budget, but this $100 cannot be spent profitably. Using it to invest in project Z would decrease the value of the firm by $10. Therefore, the $100 should be invested for use in the next period or paid out to investors as a dividend.

Chapter 11

1. a. $20,000(1 - 0.34) = $13,200 after tax per year.
   b. $30,000(1 - 0.34) = $19,800 after tax. Expense reduction increases taxable income.
   c. No tax adjustment (recognition) unless there are tax credits involved.
   d. $ 12,000 book value
      $\underline{-10,000}$ cash flow sale
      $ 2,000 Accounting loss (0.34) = $680 savings in taxes in terminal year. The total terminal value is expected to be $10,680.
   e. $15,000 added noncash expense (revenue reduction)
      $\underline{\times\ 0.34}$ taxes saved per each added expense dollar
      $ 5,100 tax cash flow saved per period
   f. No tax adjustment or recognition is realized from added NWC.

3. a. Calculate after-tax annual cash flows.

$$\frac{\$70,000 \text{ cost}}{5 \text{ years}} = \$14,000 \text{ annual added depreciation expense}$$

Incremental Income Analysis

	Book	Cash Flows
$18,000	added EBIT	$18,000
$\underline{-\ 14,000}$	added Depreciation	
4,000	added Taxable income	
$\underline{-\ 1,360}$	Tax @ 34%	$-1,360$
2,640	added After-tax income	
$\underline{+\ 14,000}$	added Noncash depreciation	$\underline{\qquad}$
16,640	Net after-tax cash flows	$16,640$

Net After-Tax Analysis

	Before Tax	After Tax
$18,000 (1 - 0.34)	Added taxable income	$11,880
$14,000 (0.34)	Tax shield	$\underline{4,760}$
	Net after tax cash flow	$16,640

b.
$$(PVAN, N = 5, L = 15)$$
$$NPV = (\$70,000)(1.00) - \$16,640(3.352)$$
$$= (70,000) - \$55,777$$
$$= -\$14,223$$

c. Discounting the annual after-tax cash flows at the minimum rate of return of 15 percent ($16,640 × 3.352) indicates that V. B. Smith is willing to pay only $55,777 for the truck. If he pays more, his *IRR* will be less than 15 percent.

5. The key to this problem is to recognize that the cost of the building and the renovation expense are sunk costs, while depreciation and property taxes have no incremental influence. Thus, all these items can be ignored in the analysis. Relevant items, when one takes the warehousing alternative as the base, are generated as follows: (1) accepting the lease decreases upkeep expense by $25,000, for a cash flow of $25,000(1 − 0.40) = $15,000; (2) accepting the lease increases revenue by $300,000, for a cash flow of $300,000 × (1 − 0.40) = $180,000; and (3) accepting the lease increases costs by $400,000, for a cash flow of ($400,000)(1 − 0.40) = ($240,000), a result based on the assumption that Chatham would revert to its existing storage arrangements. In summary, the cash-flow table would show a net outflow of $15,000 + $180,000 − $240,000 = ($45,000) per year for each of the 30 years. Thus, the lease alternative would result in a net disadvantage and should be rejected.

7. a. See Table S–25 for a comparison of the cash flows and depreciation of the new and old machines. Table S–26 shows the savings attributable to the new machine, and Table S–27 provides a calculation of the net present value (*NPV*) of the investment opportunity at a discount rate of 10 percent. The internal rate of return (*IRR*) is calculated as follows:

$$NPV \text{ at } 22 \text{ percent} = 141.72$$

$$NPV \text{ at } 20 \text{ percent} = 318.72.$$

Interpolating provides the following results:

$$\frac{318.72 - 0}{318.72 - (-141.72)} \times 2 \text{ percent} = 1.38 \text{ percent}$$

$$IRR = 20 \text{ percent} + 1.38 \text{ percent} = 21.38 \text{ percent}.$$

So, if 10 percent is the minimal acceptable rate of return, the machine should be replaced.

Table S–25

Sale of old machine		
Proceeds from sale		$ 3,000
Book value		2,100
Taxable gain		$ 900
Tax at 40 percent		360
Cash flow: proceeds		3,000
		−360
Net cash flow after tax		$ 2,640
Outlay for new machine		
Purchase price		$16,500
Freight		900
Installation		600
Total outlay		$18,000
Depreciation		
Old machine, $2,100/3 years		$ 700/year
New machine, $18,000/3 years		6,000/year
Difference		$ 5,300

Table S–26

Savings Attributable to New Machine	Year 1	Years 2–3
Direct cash savings	$ 9,600	$ 8,400
Increase in depreciation	5,300	5,300
Taxable savings	$ 4,300	$ 3,100
Tax at 40 percent	$ 1,720	$ 1,240
Cash flow: Direct savings	$ 9,600	$ 8,400
Less tax	−1,720	−1,240
Net cash flow after tax	$ 7,880	$ 7,160

Table S–27

Year	Cash from Sale of Old Machine	Cash Outlay for Purchase of New Machine	Savings	Total Cash Flow	Present-Value Factor at 10 Percent (percent)	Present Value
0	$2,640	($18,000)		($15,360)	1.000	($15,360)
1			$7,880	$ 7,880	0.909	$ 7,169.92
2			$7,160	$ 7,160	0.826	$ 5,914.16
3			$7,160	$ 7,160	0.751	$ 5,377.15
					Net present value at 10 percent =	$ 3,101.24

b. See Table S–28 for a revised depreciation schedule. The savings attributable to the new machine are shown in Table S–29, and the calculation of net present value is presented in Table S–30. The *IRR* is calculated as follows:

$$NPV \text{ at 25 percent} = (\$52.48)$$

$$NPV \text{ at 24 percent} = \$177.12.$$

Interpolating provides the following results:

$$\frac{\$177.12 - 0}{\$177.12 - (-\$52.48)} \times 1\% = 0.77 \text{ percent}.$$

$$IRR \doteq 24 \text{ percent} + 0.77 \text{ percent} = 24.77 \text{ percent}.$$

Table S–28

Revised depreciation schedule	
Outlay for new machine	$18,000
Estimated salvage	3,000
Depreciation amount	$15,000
Depreciation per year ($\div 3$)	5,000
Depreciation of old machine	700
Increase in depreciation	$ 4,300

Table S–29

	Year 1	Years 2–3
Direct cash savings	$ 9,600	$ 8,400
Increase in depreciation	4,300	4,300
Taxable savings	$ 5,300	$ 4,100
Tax at 40 percent	2,120	1,640
Cash flow: Direct savings	9,600	8,400
Less tax	−2,120	−1,640
Net cash flow after tax	$ 7,480	$ 6,760

c. The cash outflow at time 0 now is $15,360 + $2,500 = $17,860. Year 3 cash flows are $7,160 + $2,500 = $9,660. Cash outflows in years 1 and 2 remain $7,880 and $7,160, respectively.

$$NPV \text{ at 18 percent} = (\$161.82)$$

$$NPV \text{ at 16 percent} = \$444.52.$$

Interpolating provides the following results:

$$\frac{\$444.52 - 0}{\$444.52 - (-161.82)} \times 2\% = 1.466 \text{ percent}$$

$$IRR = 16 \text{ percent} + 1.466 \text{ percent} = 17.466 \text{ percent}.$$

9. The purpose of this problem is to stress that the new projects frequently involve some investment for increasing working capital and that a part of the required increase in current assets often is financed by increases in current liabilities. Here, $0.40(\$1,000,000) = \$400,000$ represents the increased investment in current assets because current assets (cash plus receivables plus inventory) are 40 percent of sales. However, increases in current liabilities are estimated at $0.14(\$1,000,000) = \$140,000$. Thus, $400,000 − $140,000 = \$260,000$ is the amount of the required investment in net working capital. When this $260,000 outflow will occur depends on when the new sales are expected. This is normally budgeted in period 0, but may well be appropriately divided between period 0 and period 1.

11. This problem requires the evaluation of the information and the determination of the relevant cash flows. The $75,000 development and testing expenditures are sunk costs and, therefore, are not relevant. The $20,000 depreciation on existing equipment will be the same under either decision and, therefore, need not be included in the analysis.

   a. See Table S–31 for relevant cash flows associated with the Jasper fragrance-line introduction.

   b. Incremental net present value (*NPV*) is calculated in Table S–32.

13. Because all projects have positive net present values, you would want to select the combination of projects that has the highest combined net present value and yet still meets the $350,000 constraint. The combination of projects A, B, C, and E has a net present value of $56,000, which is the highest attainable. Assuming there are no other factors that affect the decision, this is the combination that should be accepted.

Table S–30

Year	Cash from Sale of Old Machine	Cash Outlay for Purchase of New Machine	Salvage Value	Savings	Total Cash Flow	Present-Value Factor at 10 Percent (percent)	Present Value
0	$2,640	($18,000)		—	($15,360)	1.000	($15,360)
1				$7,480	$ 7,480	0.909	$ 6,799.32
2				$6,760	$ 6,760	0.825	$ 5,583.76
3			$3,000	$6,760	$ 9,760	0.751	$ 7,329.75
						Net present value at 10 percent =	$ 4,352.84

Table S–31

	Year 0	Year 1	Year 2	Year 3	Year 4	Year 5
			Relevant Cash Flows			
Initial outlay	($50,000)	—	—	—	—	—
Change in sales	—	$200,000	$200,000	$200,000	$135,000	$60,000
Change in maintenance expenses	—	(1,000)	(1,000)	(1,000)	(1,000)	(1,000)
Change in materials and packaging expenses	—	(20,000)	(20,000)	(16,250)	(15,000)	(6,500)
Change in marketing expenses	—	(150,000)	(160,000)	(80,000)	(50,000)	(20,000)
Change in depreciation	—	(10,000)	(10,000)	(10,000)	(10,000)	(10,000)
Change in profit before taxes	—	$ 19,000	$ 9,000	$ 92,750	$ 59,000	$22,500
Taxes on incremental profit	—	$ 9,500	$ 4,500	$ 46,375	$ 29,500	$11,250
Net cash flow	($50,000)	$ 19,500	$ 14,500	$ 56,375	$ 39,500	$21,250

Table S–32

Year	Cash Flow	Present-Value Factor at 20 Percent	Present Value
0	($50,000)	1.000	($50,000)
1	$19,500	0.833	$16,244
2	$14,500	0.694	$10,063
3	$56,375	0.579	$32,641
4	$39,500	0.482	$19,039
5	$21,250	0.402	$ 8,543
		Net present value =	$36,530

Chapter 12

1. The after-tax equivalent required return (K) on each of these sources of funds is as follows:

$$K(\text{Bank debt}) = 0.14(1 - 0.46) = 0.0756$$

$$= 7.56 \text{ percent.}$$

$$K(\text{Long-term debt}) = 0.125(1 - 0.46) = 0.0675$$

$$= 6.75 \text{ percent.}$$

$$K(\text{Preferred stock}) = 0.135(1) = 0.135 = 13.5 \text{ percent.}$$

3. a. We can calculate K_e using the dividend-growth model as follows:

$$K_e = \frac{D_1}{P_0} + g.$$

In this case, the figures would be:

$$D_1 = \$0.60(1 + 0.05) = \$0.63.$$

$$P_0 = \$10.$$

$$g = 0.05.$$

$$K_e = \frac{\$0.63}{\$10.00} + 0.05 = 0.113 = 11.3 \text{ percent.}$$

Note that by year 1, dividends are expected to have grown to 63 cents per share.

b. If government-bond rates were 12 percent, a K_e of 11.3 percent would be too low. K_e should include a risk premium over and above the government-bond rate. A likely possibility is that the current market price of $10 is based on higher expected growth than was the past growth of dividends. For example, assume growth is expected to be 12 percent. We can calculate K_e as follows:

$$K_e = \frac{D_1}{P_0} + g = \frac{\$0.60(1 + 0.12)}{\$10.00} = 0.12$$

$$= 0.187.$$

This 18.7 percent figure is higher than the 12 percent rate on bonds.

5. Because the firm intends to maintain its current capital structure, the weights ascribed to its various forms of financing are as follows:

Bank debt:
$$\frac{\$8,000}{\$52,000} = 0.154.$$

Long-term debt:
$$\frac{\$7,000}{\$52,000} = 0.135.$$

Preferred stock:
$$\frac{\$4,000}{\$52,000} = 0.077.$$

Common equity:
$$\frac{\$8,000 + \$25,000}{\$52,000} = 0.635.$$

Note that accounts payable and accruals are excluded, because they are short-term non-interest-bearing forms of financing. Using the after-tax required rate of return for each

Table S–33

Source of Funds		Pretax RRR (percent)	After-tax RRR (percent)	Weight	Weighted Required Rate of Return (percent)
$ 8,000	Bank debt, K_1	12.0	6.48 ×	0.154	= 1.00
$ 7,000	Long-term debt, K_d	10.7	5.78 ×	0.135	= 0.78
$ 4,000	Preferred stock, K_p	11.5	11.5 ×	0.077	= 0.89
$33,000	Common equity, K_e	16.4	16.4 ×	0.635	= 10.41
$52,000				Weighted-Average Required Return = K_w = 13.08	

component, the weighted-average required return is shown in Table S–33.

7. If the $52,000 invested earns a 20 percent rate of return, the return to debt and preferred stockholders is fixed, but the return on the $33,000 contributed by common equity is 27.3 percent, well above their *RRR* of 16.4 percent. If investments returns exceed the *RRR*, more investors will be attracted to the firm and the stock price will increase.

$10,000.00	0.2($52,000)
− 518.40	Bank interest
− 404.50	Long-term debt interest
− 460.00	Preferred dividends
$ 9,017.10	Available for common

$$\frac{\$9,017.10}{\$33,000} = 27.3 \text{ percent on common-equity funds}.$$

If investments earn less than the *WARR*, the common-equity funds will earn less than the *RRR*, and if continued, the stock price will fall as investors run to more competitive returns. An investment return of 7 percent on $52,000 provides $3,640 for all sources of funds. The debt interest is fixed and contractual and must be paid. The preferred dividends are also fixed at 11.5 percent, if the board of directors declares the distribution. Assuming they are paid, the return to common is only 6.8 percent, well below the *RRR* of 16.4 percent.

$3,640.00	0.07($52,000)
− 518.40	Bank interest
− 404.50	Long-term debt interest
− 460.00	Preferred dividends
$2,257.10	Available for common

$$\frac{\$2,257.10}{\$33,000} = 6.8 \text{ percent return on common-equity funds}$$

Chapter 13

1. After the fifth year, cash flows are the same under the two alternatives, so the decision needs to be analyzed only over

five years. Since the two-step alternative involves a fixed-price contract, the second outlay of $350,000 is subject to little uncertainty (assuming only that the contractor remains in business). Maintenance and utilities are also subject to little uncertainty. Therefore, a case can be made for discounting all cash flows at the risk-free rate, 10 percent. The problem is to pick the low-cost alternative. Because the hospital is not taxed, depreciation is not a factor. Cash flows for the first five years and their present values are shown (in thousands of dollars) in Table S–34. Note that plan B, which delays construction of half the facility, is the less expensive of the two alternatives, but the costs are quite close in present-value terms.

Table S–34

Year	Cash Flows	
	Alternative A	Alternative B
0	(500)	(300)
1	(10)	(5)
2	(10)	(5)
3	(10)	(5)
4	(10)	(5)
5	(10)	(355)
Present value at 10 percent =	(537.91)	(536.28)

3. The following equation is used to solve this problem: $K_j = R_f + (K_m - R_f)$ (project-risk ratio). Return targets are calculated as follows:

K(cost reduction) = 10 + 7.2(0.40) = 12.88 percent.

K(expansion) = 10 + 7.2(1.00) = 17.20 percent.

K(new-existing) = 10 + 7.2(1.75) = 22.60 percent.

K(new-new) = 10 + 7.2(3.00) = 31.60 percent.

5. The following equation is used to solve this problem: $K_j = R_f + (K_m - R_f)$ (project-risk ratio). See Table S–35 for return targets for each division, assuming a government-bond rate of 11 percent.

Table S–35

	Return Targets (percent)		
Category	Electric Motors Division	Electrical Components Division	Microelectronics Division
Cost reduction	14.60	13.16	16.76
Expansion	18.20	18.20	21.80
New products	25.40	21.80	36.20

7. To solve this problem, the following calculations must be made:

Present value of $115/year in years 1–10 at 13 percent

$$= 5.426(\$115) = \$623.99 .$$

Present value of $1,000/year in year 10 at 18 percent

$$= 0.191(\$1,000) = \$191.00$$

Present value sum = $623.99 + $191.00 = $814.99

Net present value = $814,990 − $1,000,000

$$= -\$185,010 .$$

Atlantic should not undertake the project.

Chapter 15

1. a. The expected earnings per share (EPS) and return on equity (ROE) are reflected in the first column of Table S–36.
   b. The firm's pretax operating return on assets ($440,000 × $2,000,000 = 22 percent) exceeds the interest rate on debt (14 percent). Therefore, an increase in leverage will increase expected EPS and ROE.
   c. The expected EPS and ROE for 25 percent and 50 percent debt ratios are calculated in Table S–37.
   d. Table S–37 shows the expected EPS and ROE at low and high EBIT levels for debt ratios of 0 percent, 25 percent, and 50 percent. Table S–38 summarizes the results in terms of impact on EPS and ROE.
   e. The use of increased debt financing produces greater variability of returns and increased financial risk. The choice depends upon the extent of operating risk associated with the commercial strategy and the risk attitudes of shareholders.
3. a. See Table S–39 for calculation of earnings per share based on debt financing. Note that total debt interest = 0.10($5,000,000) + 0.08($6,000,000) = $980,000, and shares outstanding = 400,000. See Table S–40 for calculation of earnings per share based on equity financing. Note that, in this case, interest equals 0.08($5,000,000) =

Table S–36

	Thousands of Dollars		
	No Leverage	25% Debt	50% Debt
Assets	2,000	2,000	2,000
Debt	0	500	1,000
Equity	2,000	1,500	1,000
EBIT	440	440	440
Interest at 14 percent	0	70	140
Profit before tax	440	370	300
Tax at 50 percent	220	185	185
Profit after tax	220	185	150
Shares	100	75	50
EPS (dollars)	**2.20**	2.47	3.0
ROE (percent)	**11.0**	12.33	15.0

$480,000, and shares outstanding equal $5,000,000/ $20 + 400,000 = 650,000.
   b. The answer here depends on the expected level of earnings before interest and taxes (EBIT) and its variance. Above EBIT of $1.78 million, debt produces higher earnings per share (EPS). Below $1.78 million, equity gives higher EPS. The EBIT/EPS analysis makes explicit the risk/return trade-off, but does not identify the superior plan.

Chapter 16

1. For debt financing, the earnings-before-interest-and-taxes/ earnings-per-share (EBIT/EPS) calculations are:

$$\text{Total debt interest} = 0.10(\$5,000,000)$$
$$+ 0.08(\$6,000,000)$$
$$= \$980,000$$

Shares outstanding = 400,000

At EPS = 0,   EBIT = $980,000 .

At EBIT = $2,000,000,

$$EPS = \frac{(1 - 0.48)(\$2,000,000 - \$980,000)}{400,000} = \$1.33 .$$

For equity financing, the EBIT/EPS calculations are:

$$\text{Total debt interest} = 0.08(\$600,000) = \$480,000$$

$$\text{Shares outstanding} = \frac{\$5,000,000}{\$20} + 400,000 = 650,000 .$$

At EPS = 0, EBIT = $480,000. At EBIT = $2,000,000,

$$EPS = \frac{(1 - 0.48)(\$2,000,000 - \$480,000)}{650,000} = \$1.22 .$$

The recommended financing alternative depends on the expected level of EBIT and its variance. Figure S–5 shows, in

Table S–37

	Debt Ratio of 0 Percent		Debt Ratio of 25 Percent		Debt Ratio of 50 Percent	
	Bad Year	*Good Year*	*Bad Year*	*Good Year*	*Bad Year*	*Good Year*
EBIT	100	750	100	750	100	750
Interest at 14 percent	0	0	70	70	140	140
PBT	100	750	30	680	(40)	610
Tax at 50 percent	50	375	15	340	(20)	305
PAT	50	375	15	340	(20)	305
Shares	100	100	75	75	50	50
EPS (dollars)	0.50	3.75	0.20	4.53	(.40)	6.10
ROE (percent)	2.5	18.75	1.0	22.67	(2.00)	30.5

Table S–38

	Dollar Results: EPS			Percentage Results: ROE		
	Bad Year	*Expected Year*	*Good Year*	*Bad Year*	*Expected Year*	*Good Year*
No leverage	$0.50	$2.20	$3.75	2.5	11.0	18.75
25 percent debt	0.20	2.47	4.53	1.0	12.33	22.67
50 percent debt	(0.40)	3.00	6.10	(2.0)	15.0	30.5

Table S–39

Earnings before interest and taxes	$1,000,000	$2,000,000	$3,000,000	$ 4,000,000
less Interest	− 980,000	− 980,000	− 980,000	− 980,000
equals Profit before taxes	$ 20,000	$1,020,000	$2,020,000	$ 3,020,000
less Tax at 48 percent	− 9,600	− 489,600	− 969,600	−1,449,600
equals Profit after taxes	$ 10,400	$ 530,400	$1,050,400	$ 1,570,400
Earnings per share	$0.03	$1.33	$2.63	$3.93

Table S–40

EBIT	$1,000,000	$2,000,000	$ 3,000,000	$ 4,000,000
less Interest	− 480,000	− 480,000	− 480,000	− 480,000
equals Profit before taxes	$ 520,000	$1,520,000	$ 2,520,000	$ 3,520,000
less Tax at 48 percent	− 249,600	− 729,600	−1,209,600	−1,689,600
equals Profit after taxes	$ 270,400	$ 790,400	$ 1,310,400	$ 1,830,400
Earnings per share	$0.42	$1.22	$2.02	$2.82

Figure S–5

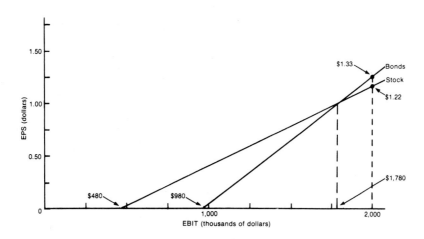

terms of expected EPS, that debt is better above the point of intersection, whereas equity is better below that point. The point of intersection is at EBIT = $1,780,000, calculated algebraically in problem (2).

3. a. We can calculate the key figures under the stock (S) and bond (B) plans and then calculate the break-even (BE) level of EBIT as follows:

$$N_s = \frac{\$7,200,000}{\$4} + \frac{\$7,500,000}{\$6.25} = 3,000,000 \text{ shares}.$$

$$I_s = 0.08(\$10,000,000) = \$800,000.$$

$$N_B = \frac{\$7,200,000}{\$4} = 1,800,000 \text{ shares}$$

$$I_B = 0.08(\$10,000,000) + 0.13(\$7,500,000)$$

$$= \$1,775,000.$$

$$\text{EBIT}_{BE}$$

$$= \frac{[3,000,000(\$1,775,000)] - [(1,800,000)(\$800,000)]}{3,000,000 - 1,800,000}$$

$$= \$3,237,500.$$

   b. Following the format of Table 16–2 for an expected EBIT level of $1,930,500(0.033 × $58,500,000), Table S–41 shows that the inclusion of a sinking-fund payment under the bond plan results in a lower coverage ratio.

With the new contract, EBIT will be below the break-even point ($3,237,500). The firm can barely cover the interest payments if the bond plan is used and cannot cover the sinking-fund payments. The stock plan is the only reasonable alternative.

The use of debt lowers the coverage ratios of Rafferty Corp. relative to the stock plan. If loan principal payments associated with the debt plan were considered, the coverage ratios would be lower.

5. a. With all payments converted to a pretax basis, the earnings before interest and taxes (EBIT) required to cover interest and dividend payments are reflected in Table S–42.

Table S–42

Bond Plan:	
Interest on existing debt	$155,000[a]
Interest on new debt	360,000[b]
Debt retirement	
Old, pretax basis	240,385[c]
Common stock dividends, pretax	192,308
Required EBIT	$947,693
Stock Plan:	
Interest on existing debt	$155,000
Debt retirement, pretax	240,385
Common stock dividends, pretax	346,154
Required EBIT	$741,539

$$^a\left(\$2,000,000 - \frac{\$125,000}{2}\right)(0.08) = \$155,000$$

$$^b(\$4,000,000)(0.09) = 360,000$$

$$^c\frac{125,000}{0.52} = \$240,385 \quad \text{(Principal payments are made with after-tax funds.)}$$

Table S–41

Coverage	Times Interest Earned
Interest (bond plan)	1.09
Interest (stock plan)	2.41

b. Earnings-per-share (EPS) break-even points for the bond plan compared with the stock plan for year 1 are calculated as follows:

$$Stock = Bond$$

$$\frac{(EBIT - 155)(0.52)}{360} = \frac{(EBIT - 506)(0.52)}{200}$$

$$104 \text{ EBIT} - 16{,}120 = 187.2 \text{ EBIT} - 94{,}723.2$$

$$83.2 \text{ EBIT} = 78{,}603.2$$

$$\text{EBIT} = 944.75 \text{ thousand}$$

$$= \$944{,}750 \, .$$

c. The expected earnings before interest and taxes (EBIT) are not much higher than the earnings-per-share (EPS) break-even point, suggesting that the stock plan may be preferred. Assuming that EBIT is distributed normally, a 68 percent probability corresponds to one standard deviation about the mean of the distribution. Standardizing the distance between the expected EBIT level and the break-even level (assuming a standard deviation of 200 thousand):

$$\frac{1{,}033 - 945}{200} = 0.44 \, .$$

Using a normal distribution table, this corresponds to approximately a 33 percent probability that the actual EBIT will be below $944,750, again suggesting that the stock plan may be preferred. (That is, there is a 33 percent chance EBIT will be more than 0.44 standard deviations below its expected level.)

Divide the after-tax amount by $(1 - 0.48)$ to compute the pretax EBIT needed to generate $125,000 after tax. If principal payments were required with the new debt, the minimum level of EBIT would increase.

Chapter 17

1. a. The declaration date is April 16, the record date is May 18, the ex-dividend date is May 12, and the payment date is June 18.
   b. (1) The dividend increase from $4.00 to $5.00 must have been perceived by the market as a favorable sign, because the stock price rises around the announcement date (April 17). Note that the stock price rises on the meeting date of April 16, indicating some information leakage prior to the announcement in the *Wall Street Journal* on April 17. (2) The stock price drops on May 12 by slightly less than the magnitude of the $5.00 dividend. This occurs because those purchasing the stock on or after May 12 would not be entitled to the $5.00 dividend, so the value of the claim is less than it was prior to May 12. The stock price does not fall by the full amount of the dividend, probably due in part to changes in general market conditions. (3) Theoretically, no stock-price changes related to the dividend are expected in June, because all reac-

tion took place around the announcement date and the record date. Therefore, the decline in price in the middle of June is most likely related to factors external to the dividend payment.

3. This problem considers the effects of dividend policy on external financing requirements and the trade-offs between alternative dividend financing policies.
   a. The dividend paid equals $2.50/share $\times$ 4,000,000 shares = $10,000,000. This result implies a payout ratio of:

$$\frac{\$10{,}000{,}000}{\$25{,}000{,}000} = 40 \text{ percent} \, .$$

Table S–43 is helpful in answering parts (b) and (c) of this question.

Table S–43

		Policies (thousands of dollars)	
			No External Equity
	No Residual	Debt/Equity Residual	Dividend Residual
Before external financing			
Debt	14,000	14,000	14,000
Equity	40,000	40,000	40,000
Investment opportunities	30,000	30,000	30,000
Earnings	25,000	25,000	25,000
Payout ratio (percent)	0.4	0.4	0.12
Dividends	10,000	10,000	3,000
Earnings retained	15,000	15,000	22,000
External financing	15,000	15,000	8,000
Debt	8,000	15,000	8,000
Equity	7,000	0	0
After external financing			
Debt	22,000	29,000	22,000
Equity	62,000	55,000	62,000
Debt/equity (percent)	0.35	0.53	0.35

b. To maintain the dividend-payout ratio of 40 percent and undertake the new investment, $15 million in external financing will be required. To maintain the target debt/equity ratio of 35 percent, $7 million in new equity is required. The number of new shares required is calculated as follows:

$$\frac{\$7{,}000{,}000}{\$40/\text{share}} = 175{,}000 \text{ shares} \, .$$

The dollar dividend per share can then be determined.

Before new issue: $\dfrac{\$10,000,000}{4,000,000 \text{ shares}} = \$2.50/\text{share}$.

After new issue: $\dfrac{\$10,000,000}{4,175,000 \text{ shares}} = \$2.40/\text{share}$.

c. There are two alternative policies available. One policy would be to maintain the dividend-payout ratio and to raise the $15 million through new debt. This action would increase Troxler's debt/equity ratio to 53 percent. The other alternative is to raise $8 million in new debt and the balance through retained earnings by reducing the dividend-payout ratio to 12 percent.

The principal advantage of the policy to use no new external equity financing is that it allows Troxler to maintain its dividend policy. To the extent that a stable dividend policy carries informational effects, this may be important to Troxler. There are two major disadvantages to this policy: (1) It increases the riskiness of the firm to shareholders and may have an adverse effect on the market's valuation of the stock; and (2) it reduces Troxler's future flexibility. These two disadvantages may be especially important as the firm enters a new, higher-risk area of operation.

Reducing the dividend-payout ratio alters what has been a stable dividend policy. Without a careful explanation to the market by management of the reason this change in policy is necessary, the market may react adversely to it. The new investment opportunities for Troxler may signal increased earnings growth, justifying a change in current dividend policy.

*5. a. The results of a 10 percent stock dividend appear in Table S–44. The number of shares outstanding increased by 10 percent, or 200,000, which increases common stock by 200,000 × $2 = $400,000. Retained earnings are reduced by the number of new shares multiplied by the current market value of $45 per share: 200,000 × $45 = $9,000,000. The differences between the reduction in retained earnings and the increase in common stock appears as an increase in paid-in surplus of $9,000,000 − $400,000 = $8,600,000.

b. Results of a 20 percent stock dividend appear in Table S–44.

c. Results of a two-for-one stock split appear in Table S–44.

d. Stock dividends and stock splits have no effect on net worth; they merely restructure the net-worth section of the balance sheet. Likewise, they have no positive effect on shareholder wealth.

Chapter 18

1. a. $3.50 January option
$4.875 February option
$7.875 April option
The longer the time, the greater the probability of increased stock prices.

b. $118.00 closing price

c. If an April option at a strike price of $110 were purchased for $12.50, the stock price would have to move up to $122.50, the sum of the strike price of $110 and $12.50 cost of the option.

Table S–44

10 Percent Stock Dividend

Common stock (4,000,000 shares at $1 par value)	$ 4,000,000
Paid-in surplus	16,000,000
Retained earnings	28,000,000
	$48,000,000

20 Percent Stock Dividend

Common stock (2,400,000 shares at $2 par value)	$ 4,800,000
Paid-in surplus	33,200,000
Retained earnings	10,000,000
	$48,000,000

Two-for-One Split

Common stock (2,200,000 shares at $2 par value)	$ 4,400,000
Paid-in surplus	24,600,000
Retained earnings	19,000,000
	$48,000,000

d. The value of the option would move up (down) as the underlying security value moved up (down). The option investor could sell the option prior to the maturity date or exercise if the investor wanted to hold the stock.

3.

Zip Products Call-Option Payoff

Price of Stock at Maturity	Exercise Price	Payoff
20	9	$1,100
16	9	700
12	9	300
8	Don't exercise	0
4	Don't exercise	0
2	Don't exercise	0

$1,100/100 = $11.00-per-share payout subtracted from the stock price of $20.00, equals $9.00. The other payoffs are calculated by subtracting the EP from the market price times 100.

5.

Price of Stock at Maturity	Exercise Price	Payoff
29	Don't exercise	0
25	Don't exercise	0
21	23	0
18	23	300
15	23	600
10	23	1,100

The break-even cost is $2,100 ($21 × 100) plus the $200 option cost, or $2,300. The $2,300/100 = $23.00 exercise price.

*7. a. The bond value is $859.75.

$$V_B = \sum_{t=1}^{20} \frac{110}{(1.13)^t} + \frac{\$1,000}{(1.13)^{20}}$$

$$= (\$110 \times 7.025) + (\$1,000 \times 0.087)$$

$$= \$859.75 .$$

b. The conversion of the bonds is calculated as:

$$\$22 \times 50 = \$1,100 .$$

c. Following the format of Table 18A-1, we obtain Table S-45. Expected EPS decreases $0.23 per share as a result of the conversion.

Table S-45

	Thousands of Dollars	
	Before Conversion	After Conversion
Expected EBIT	8,000	8,000
Interest	1,100	—
PBT	6,900	8,000
Tax @ 46%	3,174	3,680
PAT	3,726	4,320
Shares	1,700	2,200
Expected EPS (dollars)	2.19	1.96

Chapter 19

1. a. $350,000—no tax impact.
   b. $60,000(1 − 0.34) = $39,600 after-tax cost per year—leasing expenses are deductible expenses.
   c. $24,000(0.34) = $8,160 loss of depreciation tax shield or $8,160 more taxes paid if leased versus borrowed (owned).
   d. $500(1 − 0.34) = $330 *benefit* to leasing. If paid by lessee, this deductible cost would have an after-tax cost of

$330 with $500(0.34) = $170 saved in taxes (because it is deductible). If paid by lessee it would be a $330 *cost* of leasing.
   e. $20,000 cost of leasing net of taxes (tax loss) on any difference between sale value and ending book value.

3. We follow the format of Table 19-2 to develop Table S-46. By leasing, the firm avoids the initial outlay of $85,000, which becomes an inflow in period 0. The depreciation forgone is $85,000/10 = $8,500 per year, which results in a tax shield forgone of $8,500(0.45) = $3,825 per year. The lease payment net of taxes is $11,000(1 − 0.45) = $6,050 per year. Finally, the $5,000 residual value will result in an ordinary gain in year 10 of $5,000 and a tax liability of 0.45($5,000) = $2,250, for an adjusted residual value of $5,000 − $2,250 = $2,750. Using present-value (PV) tables, at a rate of 5 percent,

$$\$9,875(7.108) + \$12,625(0.614) = \$77,943.25 .$$

At 3 percent,

$$\$9,875(7.786) + \$12,625(0.744) = \$86,279.75 .$$

The equivalent interest cost (EIC) is slightly over 3 percent and can be found through interpolation as follows:

$$\frac{\text{Change in } PV}{\text{Change in } i} = \frac{\$77,943.25 - \$86,279.75}{5 - 3} = -\$4,168.25 .$$

Thus, change in PV = $4,168.25 for a 1 percent change in interest rate (i):

$$\text{EIC} = 3 + \frac{\$86,279.75 - \$85,000}{\$4,168.25} = 3.31 \text{ percent} .$$

After-tax equivalent rate for debt = 10(1 − 0.45) = 5.5 percent. Thus, it is cheaper to lease.

5. a. This problem involves a complicated lease/purchase decision. The firm has three options: purchase initially, lease for five years and then purchase, or lease for ten years. Following the format of Table 19-2, the lease and lease/purchase options are analyzed over ten years using the purchase option as a benchmark in Table S-47. The present-value (PV) tables at the end of the textbook are useful in calculating the following net present values (NPV):

$$NPV \text{ for lease option at } 12\% = -\$2,344 .$$

$$NPV \text{ for lease option at } 13\% = \$1,873 .$$

$$NPV \text{ for lease/purchase option at } 11\% = -\$2,793 .$$

$$NPV \text{ for lease/purchase option at } 12\% = \$723 .$$

Table S-46

Year	Acquisition Cost	After-Tax Lease Payment	Depreciation Tax Shield	After-Tax Residual Value	Total Cash Flow
0	$85,000				$85,000
1–9		$(6,050)	$(3,825)		(9,875)
10		(6,050)	(3,825)	$(2,750)	(12,625)

Table S–47

Year	Acquisition Cost	After-Tax Lease Payment	Depreciation Tax Shield	After-Tax Maintenance	After-Tax Residual Value	Total Cash Flow
Lease Decision						
0	$112,500	—	—	—	—	$112,500
1–5	—	($19,440)	(15,750)	$2,700	—	($22,490)
6–9	—	($12,960)	($5,750)	12,700	—	($16,010)
10	—	($12,960)	($5,750)	$2,700	($3,240)	($19,250)
Lease/Purchase Decision						
0	$112,500	—	—	—	—	$112,500
1–4	—	($19,440)	($5,750)	$2,700	—	($22,490)
5	($50,000)	($19,440)	($5,750)	$2,700	—	($72,490)
6–10	—	—	($1,150)[a]	—	—	($1,150)

[a]Depreciation during years 6–10 under the lease/purchase option is 50,000 ÷ 5 = $10,000. The tax shield is $4,600. The incremental tax shield compared to purchase option (at year 0) then is 5,750 − 4,600 = $1,150 outflow.

The firm's after-tax cost of debt is 6.48 percent. Hence, both the lease and the lease/purchase options are more expensive. Lease/purchase is slightly less expensive than leasing for the full ten years, indicating that, if the firm enters into the lease (for other than economic reasons), it should not renew at the end of year 5, but should exercise the purchase option at that point. This point can be seen more clearly if the renewal option is analyzed in isolation. If the firm renews at year 5, it avoids the $50,000 outlay, obligates itself for lease payments in years 6–10, gives up the tax shield and residual, and saves the maintenance expense. The analysis is shown in Table S–48.

b. Rapidly changing technology increases the risk of purchasing the machine and may make leasing more attractive. If the risk of owning the machine increases, however, the lessor would be expected to require greater compensation for the use of the machine to compensate for bearing those risks. The relatively high equivalent interest costs (EIC) in this case are indicative of just such a situation.

Chapter 20

1. Step One: Determine the annual cash flows. See table on top of page S–26.
   The call price of the new bonds, Dave's salary, and next year's estimated rates are irrelevant.

3. Follow the format of Table 20–1 in the text to develop Table S–49. For an initial outlay of $6,712,000, the firm can obtain cash flows of $868,600 per year for 15 years. The after-tax cost of new debt is 0.12(1 − 0.46) = 0.065, which is used as the discount rate.

$$NPV = -\$6,712,000 + \sum_{t=1}^{15} \frac{\$868,600}{(1 + 0.065)^t}$$

The average of the present-value annuity factors for 6 percent and 7 percent can be used as an approximation, so that $NPV = -\$6,712,000 + \$868,600(9.4) = \$1,452,840$. Since the *NPV* is positive, the firm should undertake the refunding.

Table S–48

Year	Acquisition Cost	After-Tax Lease Payment	Depreciation Tax Shield	After-Tax Maintenance	After-Tax Residual Value	Total Cash Flow
5	$50,000					$50,000
6–9		($12,960)	($4,600)	$2,700		($14,860)
10		($12,960)	($4,600)	$2,700	($3,240)	($18,100)

Net present value at 16 percent = −$193
Net present value at 17 percent = $985

Initial Outlay	*Cash Flows*
Cost of calling old bonds (18,000 bonds at $1140)	−$20,520,000
Receipts from new bonds	+$18,000,000
a. Net outlay	−$ 2,520,000
b. Flotation cost—new bonds	−$ 200,000
c. Tax savings: unamortized flotation cost of old bonds = (20 yrs. remaining/25-yr. maturity)	($150,000)(0.34) = +40,800
Net cash outlay	−$ 2,679,200
Annual Cash Flows for 20 years	
d. After-tax interest cost—new bonds $18 million (10.5%)(1 − 0.34)	−$ 1,247,400
e. After-tax interest savings from retiring old bonds = $18 million (14%)(1 − 0.34)	+$ 1,663,200
f. Net after-tax interest savings (d + e)	+$ 415,800
g. Loss of tax shield on amortization of flotation costs of old bonds ($150,000/25)(0.34) =	−$ 2,040
h. Tax shield on amortization of flotation costs on new bonds ($200,000/20)(0.34) =	+$ 3,400
i. Net savings (g + h)	+$ 1,360
Total annual cash flows (f + i)	$ 417,160

Table S–49

Initial Outlay

Cost of calling old bonds (40,000 bonds at $1,160)	−$46,400,000
Receipts from new bond issue	40,000,000
(1) Net outlay	−$ 6,400,000
Expenses	
(2) Flotation costs on new bonds	− 450,000
	−$ 6,850,000
Tax savings	
(3) Unamortized flotation cost on old bonds 0.46(300,000)	+ 138,000
Net cash flows	−$ 6,712,000

Annual Cash Flows (15 years)

(4) After-tax interest *expense* on new bonds (0.12)(1 − 0.46)($40,000,000)	−$ 2,592,000
(5) After-tax interest *savings* on retired bonds (0.16)(1 − 0.46)($40,000,000)	+ 3,456,000
(6) Net after-tax savings	+$ 864,000
Tax effects on flotation costs	
(7) Loss of tax shield on amortization of old bonds 0.46($20,000)	− 9,200
(8) Tax shield on amortization of flotation costs on new bond 0.46($30,000)	+ 13,800
Total annual cash flow	$ 868,600

5. a. EPS = 4,320,000/1,125,000 = $3.84.
   EPS falls to $3.84 from $4.32.
   b. The P/E ratio before rights issue is:

$$P/E = 100/4.32 = 23.15.$$

The P/E ratio after rights issue is:

$$P/E = 97.78/3.84 = 25.46.$$

The P/E ratio increases to 25.46. This increase reflects the fact that total earnings have not increased despite the new capital, so EPS has fallen more than we would expect.
   c. Working backward, to yield earnings per share (EPS) of $4.32, the firm must have after-tax earnings of $4.32(1,125,000) = $4,860,000. This requires pretax earnings of:

$$\frac{\$4,860,000}{(1 − T)} = \$9,000,000.$$

Add back interest expense of $2,000,000. Total earnings must be $11,000,000, or an increase of $1,000,000.

Chapter 21

1. Note that the dollar value of the invoice (P) is not required in these calculations, since it shows up in both the numerator and denominator and thus cancels out of the equations.

a. $\dfrac{0.02P}{0.98P} \times \dfrac{365}{30} = 0.2483 = 24.8$ percent.

b. $\dfrac{0.03P}{0.97P} \times \dfrac{365}{20} = 0.5644 = 56.4$ percent.

c. $\dfrac{0.01P}{0.99P} \times \dfrac{365}{25} = 0.1475 = 14.8$ percent.

d. $\dfrac{0.02P}{0.98P} \times \dfrac{365}{30} = 0.2483 = 24.8$ percent.

3. a. The firm would effectively be borrowing money for 40 days (from day 15 to day 55). As a result, the effective annual interest cost is

$$\dfrac{0.02P}{0.98P} \times \dfrac{365}{40} = 0.186 = 18.6 \text{ percent}.$$

b. If paid on time, the firm would only have a 30-day loan. The effective annual interest cost is

$$\dfrac{0.02P}{0.98P} \times \dfrac{365}{30} = 0.248 = 24.8 \text{ percent}.$$

Note that the effective annual interest rate is lower in part (a) (18.6 percent versus 24.8 percent) because of the extra ten days by which the firm delayed payment.

5. a. To obtain the use of $10,000, the firm must borrow

$$\dfrac{\$10,000}{(1 - 0.1)} = \$11,111.11.$$

This loan would cost $0.15(\$11,111.11) = \$1,666.67$.

$$\text{Effective annual rate} = \dfrac{\$1,666.67}{\$10,000} = 16.67 \text{ percent}.$$

b. To obtain the use of $250,000, the firm must borrow

$$\dfrac{\$250,000}{(1 - 0.15)} = \$294,117.65.$$

This loan would cost $0.16(\$294,117.65) = \$47,058.82$.

$$\text{Effective annual rate} = \dfrac{\$47,058.82}{\$250,000} = 18.82 \text{ percent}.$$

7. a. In this case, MSM is only using the credit for 10 days, since it is paying 20 days after delivery. The effective annual rate is

$$\dfrac{0.01P}{0.99P} \times \dfrac{365}{10} = 36.87 \text{ percent}.$$

b. If MSM is to forgo the discount, then they should postpone payment until the 45th day, which would result in an effective annual rate of

$$\dfrac{0.01P}{0.99} \times \dfrac{365}{35} = 10.53 \text{ percent}.$$

Thus, MSM's optimal strategy is to forgo the discount and not pay until the 45th day, since the interest rate on the bank loan exceeds the cost of not taking the discount.

9. In order to choose between the two loan arrangements, it is necessary to compare the effective interest rate of each. To increase funds by $2,000,000 with a 16 percent discount loan (Loan A), $2,380,952 must be borrowed, as can be seen in the following calculation:

$$\text{Loan} - 0.16(\text{Loan}) = \$2,000,000$$

$$0.84(\text{Loan}) = \$2,000,000$$

$$\text{Loan} = (\$2,000,000)/0.84$$

$$= \$2,380,952.38.$$

The effective interest rate for loan A is calculated as follows:

$$\dfrac{\text{Discount}}{\text{Proceeds}} = \dfrac{\$2,380,952.38 - \$2,000,000}{\$2,000,000}$$

$$= \dfrac{\$380,952.38}{\$2,000,000}$$

$$= 19.05 \text{ percent}.$$

To increase funds by $2,000,000 with a 10 percent compensating balance (Loan B), $2,222,222 must be borrowed, as shown in the following calculation:

$$\text{Loan} - 0.10(\text{Loan}) = \$2,000,000$$

$$\text{Loan} = \$2,222,222.$$

Interest paid is 16 percent of $2,222,222, or $355,555.52. The effective interest rate for Loan B is therefore

$$\dfrac{\text{Interest}}{\text{Proceeds}} = \dfrac{\$355,555.52}{\$2,000,000}$$

$$= 17.78 \text{ percent}.$$

Loan B offers the lower effective interest rate and is the preferred loan arrangement.

Chapter 22

1. Reduction in funds tied up in accounts receivable = $8,000 × 1 day = $8,000. Annual savings = $0.12(\$8,000) = \$960$.

3. Purchases of $3 million per year = $8,219.18 per day. Payment five days later increases accounts payable by $8,219.18 × 5 = $41,096, which, at 11 percent per year, gives annual savings of $4,520.55.

5. a. Total float = $300,000(5 days) = $1,500,000. Cost = $0.12(\$1,500,000) = \$180,000/\text{year}$.

b. Reduced expense of float = $0.12(2.5 \text{ days})(\$300,000) = \$90,000$. Total reduced costs = $90,000 + $30,000 = $120,000.

$$\text{Maximum acceptable compensating balances} = \dfrac{\$120,000}{0.12}$$

$$= \$1,000,000.$$

7. a. The cost of the current system is calculated as follows:

$$\$20,000 + 0.05\dfrac{\$50,000,000}{\$1,000} = \$22,500.$$

The savings under the lockbox system are calculated as follows:

Savings from float reduction

= (Average daily collections) (Reduction float days)
(Opportunity cost of short-term funds)

$$= \left(\frac{\$50,000,000}{250}\right)(2)(0.11)$$

$$= \$44,000 .$$

Savings from reduced check-clearing costs

= (Average number of checks/year) (Savings per check)

$$= \frac{\$50,000,000}{\$1,000}(0.02)$$

$$= \$1,000 .$$

The bank's offer of lockboxes is acceptable as a cost-savings measure.

Opportunity cost of compensating balances

$$= (\$300,000)(0.11)$$

$$= \$33,000 .$$

Net savings = $44,000 + 1,000 − 33,000 = $12,000.

b. The break-even compensating balance is determined as follows:

$$\text{Net savings} = 0 .$$

$44,000 + 1,000 − 0.11(Compensating balance) = 0.

Break-even compensating balance = $409,090.91.

Flyer would accept compensating balances for the lock-box system no greater than $409,090.91.

Chapter 23

1. This problem considers the trade-offs between inventory-carrying costs and lost sales. It brings up the issues of the use of accounting ratios as performance measures and the potential for conflicting policies among departments within a firm. An analysis is shown in tabular form (in thousands of dollars) in Table S–50. The expected return exceeds the 15 percent required rate of return through Policy B, indicating that the firm should aim for an inventory turnover of 6 with an inventory level of $64,667.

3. Policy A provides the following expected incremental dollar return:

(Pretax profit margin) × (Change in sales) ×
$$(1 − \text{tax rate}) =$$
$$0.20(\$4,350,000)0.5 = \$435,000 .$$

The required incremental dollar investment includes the additional investment in accounts receivable from incremental sales, plus the effect of the change in average collection period (ACP) on original sales:

[(1 − pretax profit margin) × (New sales per day) ×
(ACP)] + [(Change in ACP) × (Original sales per day)]

$$= 0.8(\$4,350,000/365)45 + 15(\$20,000,000/365)$$

$$= \$429,041.10 + \$821,917.81$$

$$= \$1,250,958.91 .$$

The cost of the incremental investment is K × (Incremental investment) = 0.16($1,250,958.91) = $200,153.43. The net profit from Policy A, therefore, is $435,000.00 − $200,153.43 = $234,846.57.

Policy B provides the following expected reduction in dollar return:

$$0.20(\$2,570,000)0.5 = \$257,000 .$$

The reduction in required dollar investment is as follows:

0.8($2,750,000/365) (22) +

$$(8)(\$20,000,000/365) = \$132,602.74 + \$438,356.16$$

$$= \$570,958.90 .$$

The savings from carrying the reduced investment is 0.16($570,958.90) = $91,353.42. Because the reduced

Table S–50

Policy	Turnover	Inventory Level	Sales	Cost of Goods Sold	Contribution	Carrying Cost	Incremental Operating Profit Before Tax	After Tax	Incremental Investment	E(R) Incremental Investment (percent)
Current	10	32.50	$450	$325	$125	$1.625	—	—	—	—
A	8	45.00	$500	$360	$140	$2.25	$14.375	$7.763	$12.50	62.10
B	6	64.67	$540	$388	$152	$3.233	$11.020	$5.951	$19.67	30.25
C	4	101.38	$565	$405.50	$159.50	$5.069	$ 5.664	$3.058	$36.71	8.33

profit from Policy B exceeds the savings from reduced investment, Policy B is unacceptable. Policy A generates incremental dollar returns that exceed the cost of the incremental investment and, therefore, should be adopted.

5. The required return remains the same while the expected return declines. For risk class 3, bad-debt expense = $0.04 \times$ ($500,000) = $20,000. Expected dollar return = ($100,000 − $20,000 − $5,000)(0.50) = $75,000(0.50) = $37,500. On the basis of these results, risk class 3 is still accepted.

The expected dollar return is equal to the pretax profit—based on a 0.20 profit margin and $500,000 of new sales, $0.20 \times \$500,000 = \$100,000$—adjusted downward to reflect bad-debt expense ($20,000) and credit-department expense ($5,000). All of this is then converted to an after-tax figure by multiplying by (1 − tax rate): 1 − 0.5 = 0.50.

For risk class 4, bad-debt expense = 0.07($400,000) = $28,000. Expected dollar return = ($80,000 − $28,000 − $5,000)(0.50) = $47,000(0.50) = $23,500. Risk class 4 is still accepted.

For risk class 5, bad-debt expense = 0.12($300,000) = $36,000. Expected dollar return = ($60,000 − $36,000 − $5,000)(0.50) = $19,000(0.50) = $9,500. Risk class 5 is still accepted.

For risk class 6, bad-debt expense = 0.20($200,000) = $40,000. Expected dollar return = ($40,000 − $40,000 − $5,000)(0.50) = −$5,000(0.50) = −$2,500. Risk class 6 is rejected.

7. a. The increased annual profit to Delta is shown in Table S–51. Investment by Delta is illustrated in Table S–52. Annual expected return is $675/$850 = 79.41 percent (before tax).

   b. The expected return of 79 percent exceeds the minimum return of 30 percent and is likely to extend credit to Bill's.

Table S–51

Sales	$ 5,000
Cost of goods sold (83 percent)	−4,150
Gross profit	$ 850
Sales commission (2 percent)	− 100
Warehousing (1.5 percent)	− 75
Profit before tax	$ 675

Table S–52

Goods delivered	$ 1,000
Less profit (17 percent)	− 170
Cost of goods sold	$ 830
Sales commission (2 percent)	− 20
Investment	$ 850

9. a. The economic order quantity (EOQ) can be calculated as:

$$EOQ = \sqrt{\frac{2RO}{C}} = \sqrt{\frac{2(10,000)(\$100)}{\$50}} = 200 \text{ units}.$$

   b. Total inventory costs can be determined as follows:

$$\text{Number of orders/years} = \frac{10,000}{200} = 50$$

$$\text{Total ordering cost} = 50(\$100) = \$5,000$$

$$\text{Average inventory} = \frac{200}{2} = 100 \text{ units}$$

$$\text{Total carrying costs} = \$50(100) = \$5,000$$

$$\text{Total annual inventory costs} = \$5,000 + \$5,000$$

$$= \$10,000.$$

11. a.
$$EOQ = \sqrt{\frac{2RO}{C}}$$

$$= \sqrt{\frac{2(280,000)(150)}{(0.30)(7.50)}}$$

$$= 6110.10; \quad 6,200 \text{ would be ordered}.$$

   b. Number of orders (assuming 6,200 units ordered) per year = 280,000/6,200 = 45.16.

   c. Daily usage rate = 280,000/365 = 767.12 units per day.

$$\text{Reorder point} = (\text{Safety stock}) + [(\text{Usage per day})$$
$$\times (\text{Days til delivery})]$$
$$= 35,000 + (767.12)(10)$$
$$= 42,671.2.$$

Therefore, reorder at 42,672 units.

Chapter 24

1. a. The 180-day French franc is priced at a premium relative to the U.S. dollar.

   b. $\dfrac{F - S}{S} \times \dfrac{12}{6} \times \dfrac{100}{1} = \dfrac{0.1777 - 0.1768}{0.1768} \times \dfrac{12}{6} \times \dfrac{100}{1}$

$$= 1.02 \text{ percent}.$$

   c. Inflation rates and interest rates are higher in the United States than in France. The sign of the solution indicates the U.S. rate relative to another country's rate. If positive (premium), U.S. rates are higher. If negative (discount), U.S. rates are below that of the country in question.

3. The U.S. importer must exchange U.S. dollars to pay Canadian dollars in 90 days and thus bears the foreign-exchange risk. The U.S. importer could have (a) negotiated payment in U.S. dollars; (b) purchased 90-day Canadian in the forward market; (c) purchased a Canadian-dollar futures contract or a call option on Canadian futures at the Chicago Mercantile Exchange; (d) purchased a spot hedge; or (e) obtained a parallel loan. Forward exchange rates represent expected spot rates. See Table 24–2 for the forward rates.

5. C$/US$ = 1.3114.
    US$/G = 0.5325.
    C$/US$ × US$/G = C$/G.
    1.3114 × 0.5325 = C$/G = 0.6983.
    0.6983 × 150,000 guilder = 104,748 Canadian dollars.

7. 2,383,500,000 yen = $9,998,783 at $0.004195/yen.

    476,700,000 yen = $1,999,757 at $0.004195/yen.

The present value (PV) of $19,997,572 for 10 years at 15 per-
cent = $19,997,572 × 5.019 = $10,036,778. The positive
NPV of $37,995 indicates the project is worthwhile, but the
financial manager must evaluate the riskiness of the project.

On 12/4/87 the dollar had depreciated against the yen to
$0.007561/yen.

    2,383,500,000 yen = $18,021,644 at $.007561/yen.

    476,700,000 yen = $3,604,329 at $.007561/yen.

The PV of $3,604,329 for 10 years at 15 percent =
$3,604,329 × 5.019 = $18,090,127. The positive NPV of
$68,483 indicates the project is worthwhile. The higher U.S.
cost of the investment, due to the falling U.S. dollar, has
been offset by the higher yen return converted to dollars.
The appreciation or depreciation during the term of the investment (not assumed in this problem) can have a major impact when planning capital projects and when actual NPVs of
projects are later reviewed.

9. US$ 1(1 + 0.076/2)

                        = $1.038/dollar invested.

SwFr 1.3590(1 + 0.035/2)(0.7508)

                        = $1.0382/dollar invested.

Marks 1.6655(1 + 0.038/2)(0.6127)

                        = $1.0398/dollar invested.

The rates on all three currencies are very similar due to
foreign-exchange-market arbitrage activities.

Chapter 25

1. a. We must look at price/earnings (P/E) ratios to answer
      this question.

                    P/E of XYZ = $50/$1.00 = 50

                    P/E of ABC = $25/$2.50 = 10.

      XYZ's expected earnings
                          = $1 × 1,000,000 = $1,000,000

      ABC's expected earnings
                          = $2.50 × 1,000,000 =   2,500,000
      Expected earnings of merged firm = $3,500,000

A rule of thumb says the firm with the high price/earnings
ratio should acquire the firm with the low P/E.
      If, in a perfect world, XYZ can acquire ABC for
stock in an exchange based on market value, it should offer 1 share of XYZ for every 2 shares of ABC. Thus, the

offer would require 1,000,000/2 = 500,000 new shares
of XYZ, making its total shares outstanding 1,500,000.
      With expected earnings of $3,500,000 and 1,500,000
shares, the earnings per share (EPS) for the merged firm
is expected to be $2.33, a nice increase for XYZ's pre-
merger EPS of $1.00.
      Checking this by working the problem with ABC
doing the acquiring in the same perfect world results
in a postmerger EPS for ABC of $1.17 ($3,500,000/
3,000,000), quite a decrease from the $2.50 EPS.

   b. Paying a 20 percent premium is equivalent to treating the
      $25.00 market price as if it were $30. Thus, instead of
      giving ABC's shareholders 1 share for every 2 shares, we
      now must give them $60/$50 = 1.2 shares for every
      2 shares (a 20 percent increase). Or we could have calcu-
      lated $30/$50 = 0.6, 0.6 of a share of XYZ for each
      share of ABC. The total number of shares XYZ must now
      give becomes 0.6 × 1,000,000 = 600,000, a 20 percent
      or 100,000 share increase over that in part (a).

   c. Using the assumptions in part (b), the merged firm would
      have 1,000,000 + 600,000 = 1,600,000 shares with ex-
      pected earnings of 3,500,000. Thus, expected earnings
      per share (EPS) would be $2.1875.

   d. No, XYZ's earnings per share (EPS) would not remain at
      their current level. Even though EPS rises initially, share
      price may not increase, and may actually fall, because
      experience has shown that mergers often reduce the ex-
      pected long-term growth rate of EPS.

   e. As we saw in part (b), if ABC offered a 20 percent pre-
      mium for XYZ, it would be treating XYZ's stock as if it
      were worth $50 × 1.2 = $60/share. Thus, it would re-
      quire $60/25 = 2.4 shares of ABC stock for each share
      of XYZ. ABC would have to give 2.4 × 1,000,000 =
      2,400,000 shares to XYZ's stockholders. Its new total
      shares outstanding would be 3,400,000. With expected
      earnings of $3,500,000, new EPS would be $1.03.

   f. The calculations alone indicate that XYZ should acquire
      ABC because its EPS increases significantly. However, a
      merger decision should not be based solely on EPS con-
      siderations. Many other factors will determine whether a
      merger is appropriate and, if so, who should purchase
      whom.

3. a. The Slam-Dunk postmerger balance sheet reflecting pool-
      ing of interest is shown in Table S–53.

Table S–53

Current assets	$270	Current liabilities	$220
Fixed assets	480	Long-term debt	100
Total	$750	Equity	430
		Total	$750

   b. The Slam-Dunk postmerger balance sheet based on pur-
      chase of assets is illustrated in Table S–54. Here the dif-
      ference in the value of Dunkirk's assets ($150) and the
      value of Statistical Lab's offer ($180) is $30 and is treated
      as goodwill and added to equity.

Table S-54

Current assets	$270	Current liabilities	$220
Fixed assets	480	Long-term debt	100
Goodwill	30	Equity	460
Total	$780	Total	$780

   c. The purchase method would have no effect on cash flow in this example, but it would affect profits, depending on the period over which the goodwill was amortized. For example, if goodwill of $30 were amortized over 30 years, operating profits each year would be reduced by $1 million.

5. a. If Franklin's stock is valued at $20, it will have to offer 1.5 shares of its stock for each share of Stove in order to produce the $30-per-share purchase price. Since Stove has 4,000,000 shares of stock, Franklin will have to give 6,000,000 shares of its stock to complete the merger.

   b. The new company will now have 10 + 6 million = 16 million shares and expected earnings per share as shown in Table S-55.

   c. In the same problem, Franklin had a 1988 price/earnings ratio (P/E) of 15 and Stove had a P/E of 8. Franklin's offer of $30 per share for Stove was an effective P/E of 12 ($30/2.5 = 12).

     The P/E of Franklin is now 10, which is still higher than the Franklin market P/E of 8. However, the actual P/E of this offer is 12, which is higher than Franklin's P/E of 10. Thus, the earnings Franklin is buying are no longer as cheap as they were in the sample problem, and it does not get the short-term increase in earnings per share (EPS). In fact, postmerger EPS drops below the premerger EPS level of $2.00 immediately.

Table S-55

Year	Profit after Tax	Number of shares (millions)	Earnings per Share	Sample Problem Merger Earnings per Share
1988	$30	16	$1.875	$2.14
1989	$38	16	$2.375	$2.71
1990	$48.2	16	$3.013	$3.44
1991	$61.18	16	$3.824	$4.37

Name Index

Subject Index

Finance in Practice

Essays Included in Each Chapter Which Describe Current Practice